The SAGE Handbook of
Personality and Individual Differences

EDITORIAL BOARD

Robert A. Ackerman, PhD, University of Texas at Dallas
Jonathan M. Adler, PhD, Olin College of Engineering
Mathias Allemand, PhD, Universität Zürich
Jack J. Bauer, PhD, University of Dayton
Peter Borkenau, PhD, Martin-Luther-Universität Halle-Wittenberg
Bradley J. Brummel, PhD, University of Tulsa
Amy B. Brunell, PhD, The Ohio State University at Mansfield
Susan T. Charles, PhD, University of California at Irvine
A. Timothy Church, PhD, Washington State University
C. Randall Colvin, PhD, Northeastern University
Anthony D. Hermann, PhD, Bradley University
Jan Hofer, PhD, Universität Osnabrück
Christopher J. Holden, PhD, Appalachian State University
Chris J. Jackson, PhD, University of New South Wales Sydney
John A. Johnson, PhD, Pennsylvania State University
Kevin Lanning, PhD, Florida Atlantic University
Christopher T. Leone, PhD, University of North Florida
Shanhong Luo, PhD, University of North Carolina Wilmington
Charlotte N. Markey, PhD, Rutgers University
Matthew J. W. McLarnon, PhD, Oakland University
Kate C. McLean, PhD, Western Washington University
Fred L. Oswald, PhD, Rice University
Peter J. Rentfrow, PhD, University of Cambridge
Willibald Ruch, PhD, Universität Zürich
William G. Shadel, PhD, RAND Corporation
Jefferson A. Singer, PhD, Connecticut College
Ashton C. Southard, PhD, Oakland University
Steven J. Stanton, PhD, Oakland University
Howard Tennen, PhD, University of Connecticut Health Center
Todd M. Thrash, PhD, College of William and Mary
Viviana A. Weekes-Shackelford, PhD, Oakland University
Dustin Wood, PhD, Wake Forest University

The SAGE Handbook of Personality and Individual Differences

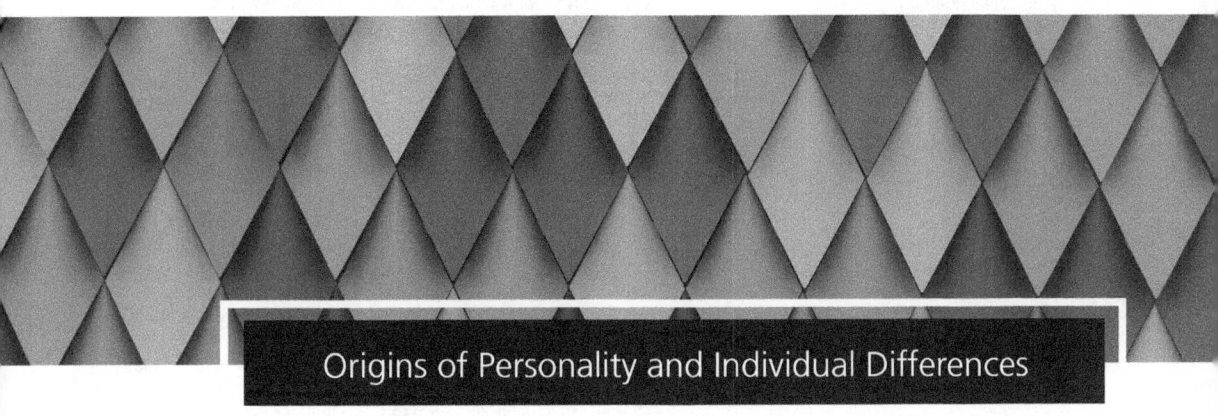

Origins of Personality and Individual Differences

Edited by
Virgil Zeigler-Hill and
Todd K. Shackelford

$SAGE reference

Los Angeles | London | New Delhi
Singapore | Washington DC | Melbourne

SAGE Publications Ltd
1 Oliver's Yard
55 City Road
London EC1Y 1SP

SAGE Publications Inc.
2455 Teller Road
Thousand Oaks, California 91320

SAGE Publications India Pvt Ltd
B 1/I 1 Mohan Cooperative Industrial Area
Mathura Road
New Delhi 110 044

SAGE Publications Asia-Pacific Pte Ltd
3 Church Street
#10-04 Samsung Hub
Singapore 049483

Editor: Becky Taylor
Editorial Assistant: Umeeka Raichura
Production Editor: Rudrani Mukherjee
Copyeditor: Sunrise Setting
Proofreader: Sunrise Setting
Indexer: Sunrise Setting
Marketing Manager: Emma Turner
Cover Design: Wendy Scott
Typeset by: Cenveo Publisher Services
Printed in the UK

At SAGE we take sustainability seriously. Most of our products are printed in the UK using responsibly sourced papers and boards. When we print overseas we ensure sustainable papers are used as measured by the PREPS grading system. We undertake an annual audit to monitor our sustainability.

Chapter 1 © Jennifer Guinn Sellers and Thanh Thanh L. Nguyen 2018
Chapter 2 © Kostas A. Papageorgiou and Vijeinika Vipulananthan 2018
Chapter 3 © John T. Manning and Bernhard Fink 2018
Chapter 4 © James Marvel-Coen, Coltan Scrivner and Dario Maestripieri 2018
Chapter 5 © Turhan Canli 2018
Chapter 6 © Theodore E. A. Waters and Christin Köber 2018
Chapter 7 © Marie-Hélène Cigna, Jean-Pierre Guay and Nathalie M. G. Fontaine 2018
Chapter 8 © Eunike Wetzel, M. Brent Donnellan, Richard W. Robins and Kali H. Trzesniewski 2018
Chapter 9 © Ugo Pace and Alessia Passanisi 2018
Chapter 10 © Julia Zimmermann and Anne K. Reitz 2018
Chapter 11 © Theo A. Klimstra, Jeroen Borghuis and Wiebke Bleidorn 2018
Chapter 12 © P. Douglas Sellers II, Karin Machluf and David F. Bjorklund 2018
Chapter 13 © Marc A. Fournier and D. S. Moskowitz 2018
Chapter 14 © Odilia M. Laceulle and Marcel A. G. van Aken 2018
Chapter 15 © Marcus Mund, Julia Zimmermann and Franz J. Neyer 2018
Chapter 16 © Erik G. Helzer, Eranda Jayawickreme and R. Michael Furr 2018
Chapter 17 © Jüri Allik and Anu Realo 2018
Chapter 18 © Iris M. Wang, Nicholas M. Michalak and Joshua M. Ackerman 2018
Chapter 19 © Daniel J. Kruger 2018
Chapter 20 © Takeshi Hamamura, Karim Bettache and Yi Xu 2018
Chapter 21 © Siobhan Kennedy-Costantini and Mark Nielsen 2018
Chapter 22 © Brent A. Mattingly, Kevin P. McIntyre and Dylan Faulkner Selterman 2018
Chapter 23 © Jennifer L. Petersen 2018
Chapter 24 © Eranda Jayawickreme and Corinne E. Zachry 2018
Chapter 25 © Jocelyn J. Bélanger, Birga M. Schumpe, Bhavna Menon, Joanna Conde Ng and Noëmie Nociti 2018

Apart from any fair dealing for the purposes of research or private study, or criticism or review, as permitted under the Copyright, Designs and Patents Act, 1988, this publication may be reproduced, stored or transmitted in any form, or by any means, only with the prior permission in writing of the publishers, or in the case of reprographic reproduction, in accordance with the terms of licences issued by the Copyright Licensing Agency. Enquiries concerning reproduction outside those terms should be sent to the publishers.

Library of Congress Control Number: 2017955554

British Library Cataloguing in Publication data

A catalogue record for this book is available from the British Library

ISBN 978-1-5264-4518-6

Contents

List of Figures	viii
List of Tables	ix
Notes on the Editors and Contributors	x

PART I BIOLOGICAL ORIGINS OF PERSONALITY AND INDIVIDUAL DIFFERENCES — 1

1 Hormonal Influences on Personality and Individual Differences — 3
   Jennifer Guinn Sellers and Thanh Thanh L. Nguyen

2 Molecular Genetic Studies of Human Temperament — 20
   Kostas A. Papageorgiou and Vijeinika Vipulananthan

3 Digit Ratio and Personality and Individual Differences — 40
   John T. Manning and Bernhard Fink

4 Morningness–Eveningness and Sociosexuality from a Life History Perspective — 51
   James Marvel-Coen, Coltan Scrivner and Dario Maestripieri

5 Toward the Molecular Basis of Personality — 67
   Turhan Canli

PART II DEVELOPMENTAL ORIGINS OF PERSONALITY AND INDIVIDUAL DIFFERENCES — 93

6 Individual Differences in Personal Narrative: Coherence, Autobiographical Reasoning and Meaning Making — 95
   Theodore E. A. Waters and Christin Köber

7 Developmental Profiles of Individuals with Psychopathic Traits: The Good, the Bad and the Snake — 112
   Marie-Hélène Cigna, Jean-Pierre Guay and Nathalie M. G. Fontaine

8 Generational Changes in Self-Esteem and Narcissism — 132
   Eunike Wetzel, M. Brent Donnellan, Richard W. Robins and Kali H. Trzesniewski

9 The Role of the Family in Personality Development — 146
   Ugo Pace and Alessia Passanisi

10	The Role of Peers in Personality Development *Julia Zimmermann and Anne K. Reitz*	164
11	Personality Development in Adolescence and Young Adulthood *Theo A. Klimstra, Jeroen Borghuis and Wiebke Bleidorn*	181
12	The Development of Evolutionarily Adaptive Individual Differences: Children as Active Participants in Their Current and Future Survival *P. Douglas Sellers II, Karin Machluf and David F. Bjorklund*	203
13	Cross-Situational Consistency, Variability and the Behavioral Signature *Marc A. Fournier and D. S. Moskowitz*	218
14	Transactions of Personality and the Social Environment During Development *Odilia M. Laceulle and Marcel A. G. van Aken*	241
15	Personality Development in Adulthood *Marcus Mund, Julia Zimmermann and Franz J. Neyer*	260
16	Moral Character: Current Insights and Future Directions *Erik G. Helzer, Eranda Jayawickreme and R. Michael Furr*	278
PART III	**ENVIRONMENTAL ORIGINS OF PERSONALITY AND INDIVIDUAL DIFFERENCES**	**301**
17	Cross-Cultural Perspectives on Personality and Individual Differences *Jüri Allik and Anu Realo*	303
18	Threat of Infectious Disease *Iris M. Wang, Nicholas M. Michalak and Joshua M. Ackerman*	321
19	Sex Ratio Influences on Personality and Individual Differences *Daniel J. Kruger*	346
20	Individualism and Collectivism *Takeshi Hamamura, Karim Bettache and Yi Xu*	365
21	Exploring Potential Causes of Individual Differences in the Expression of Neonatal Imitation *Siobhan Kennedy-Costantini and Mark Nielsen*	383
22	Individual Differences and Romantic Relationships: Bidirectional Influences on Self and Relational Processes *Brent A. Mattingly, Kevin P. McIntyre and Dylan Faulkner Selterman*	402
23	The Gender Similarities Hypothesis *Jennifer L. Petersen*	431

24	Positive Personality Change Following Adversity *Eranda Jayawickreme and Corinne E. Zachry*	450
25	Self-Sacrifice for a Cause: A Review and an Integrative Model *Jocelyn J. Bélanger, Birga M. Schumpe, Bhavna Menon,* *Joanna Conde Ng and Noëmie Nociti*	465

Index 486

List of Figures

1.1	The hypothalamus–pituitary–gonadal axis	5
1.2	The hypothalamus–pituitary–adrenal axis	10
1.3	Testosterone metabolism	12
11.1	Graphical representation of the magnitude of individual differences in boys' personality trait change in conscientiousness	186
12.1	Belsky et al. (1991) identified pathways of developmental individual differences that lead to different reproductive strategies in humans	209
12.2	Boyce et al. (1998) reported differential susceptibility to injury of monkeys when confined to a new environment based upon their inhibitory abilities	210
14.1	Graphical representations of social selection, social influence, and reciprocal effects	245
14.2	Associations between number of idiosyncratic stressful experiences and adolescent temperament change	246
14.3	Example of a longitudinal mediation model of how person-characteristics can predict life outcomes via their effects on the social environment	251
15.1	Hypothetical development of six individuals and sample mean	262
15.2	Hypothetical development of six individuals and sample mean	264
17.1	Multidimensional scaling plot of 75 samples representing 62 countries/cultures	311
21.1	The four social and non-social gestures, as modeled by experimenter	388
22.1	Bidirectional association of individual differences and relational processes	403
22.2	Two-dimensional model of relationship-induced self-concept change	417

List of Tables

2.1	Brief description of frequently used terms in genetic research on temperament	22
2.2	Candidate genes that have been associated with temperament across development	24
7.1	The Good, the Bad and the Snake: proposed characteristics distinguishing profiles of individuals with psychopathic traits	121
8.1	Illustration of developmental changes and cohort differences in a cohort-sequential longitudinal design	133
8.2	Research on generational differences in narcissism and related constructs	138
21.1	Infant behavior as a function of gesture modeled	389
21.2	Mean and standard deviations of maternal responses to BF-SF items	391
21.3	Intercorrelations between matching frequency and individual items	391
21.4	Intercorrelations between matching frequency and reasons for modeling	392
21.5	Infant behavior as a function of gesture modeled	395
21.6	Intercorrelations between matching frequency and individual items	396

Notes on the Editors and Contributors

THE EDITORS

Virgil Zeigler-Hill is a Professor and the Director of Graduate Training for the Department of Psychology at Oakland University in Rochester, Michigan. He earned his PhD in Social-personality from the University of Oklahoma in 2004 under the guidance of Dr Carolin J. Showers. His primary research interests are in three interrelated areas: (1) dark personality features (e.g., narcissism, spitefulness), (2) self-esteem, and (3) interpersonal relationships. He is the author of more than 180 publications including edited volumes such as *The Dark Side of Personality*, *Self-Esteem, Evolutionary Perspectives on Social Psychology*, and *The Evolution of Psychopathology*. He is currently an associate editor for the *Journal of Personality*, *Journal of Personality Assessment*, and *Self and Identity* as well as serving as a co-editor for the *Encyclopedia of Personality and Individual Differences*.

Todd K. Shackelford received his PhD in Evolutionary Psychology in 1997 from the University of Texas at Austin. Since 2010, he has been Professor and Chair of the Department of Psychology at Oakland University in Rochester, Michigan, where he is Co-Director of the Evolutionary Psychology Lab. In 2016, he was appointed Distinguished Professor by the Oakland University Board of Trustees. Shackelford has published around 250 journal articles and his work has been cited about 15,000 times. Much of Shackelford's research addresses sexual conflict between men and women, with a special focus on testing hypotheses derived from sperm-competition theory. Since 2006, Shackelford has served as editor of the journal *Evolutionary Psychology*, and in 2014 he founded the journal *Evolutionary Psychological Science* as Editor-in-Chief.

THE CONTRIBUTORS

Joshua M. Ackerman is Associate Professor of Psychology at the University of Michigan and is affiliated with the Ross School of Business at UM. He received his PhD from Arizona State University in 2007. His research focuses on how adaptive mental mechanisms drive perception, decision-making, and behavior, often in non-conscious ways, with particular attention to the management of fundamental, ecological threats such as infectious disease, mating-related problems, and intergroup conflict. Much of this work is viewed through the lens of life history theory as a means of understanding person-environment fit. He also has programs of research investigating sensorimotor processing, vicarious experience, and related aspects of consumer behavior.

Marcel A. G. van Aken studied Developmental Psychology and in 1991 defended his PhD thesis at the Radboud University Nijmegen, the Netherlands on a longitudinal study on the development of competence. Since 2003, he has been a full professor at the Department of Developmental Psychology at Utrecht University. His research focuses on personality development in children, adolescents, and young adults, more particularly the way that transactional relations between personality characteristics and elements of the social relationships with parents and peers may result in either competence, maladaptation, or personality pathology. This research often involves studying children and adolescents in longitudinal designs but sometimes also using experimental paradigms. The subjects in this research are often typically developing children and adolescents but sometimes also involve clinical samples. For the latter, he holds an affiliation with the Center of Adolescent Psychiatry in Den Bosch, the Netherlands, where he conducts research specifically aimed at personality pathology in adolescents.

Jüri Allik (University of Tartu, Estonia) received his first PhD from the Moscow University and the second from the University of Tampere, Finland. His primary field of research is visual psychophysics, especially perception of visual motion and numerosity. His recent research is more focused on personality, emotions, intelligence, and cross-cultural psychology. According to the Essential Science Indicators he belongs to the top 1% of the most cited scientists in the category psychiatry/psychology. He is a member of the Estonian Academy of Sciences, Academia Europaea, and the Finnish Academy of Science and Letters.

Jocelyn J. Bélanger is Professor of Psychology at New York University Abu Dhabi. He earned his doctorate from the University of Maryland, College Park. He has conducted several large-scale projects with the National Consortium for Study of Terrorism and Responses to Terrorism (START) to examine the motivational underpinnings of radicalization and deradicalization among terrorists located in the Middle East and South-East Asia. In 2015, he was appointed by the City of Montréal to create the first deradicalization centre in North America to tackle home-grown terrorism (the CPRLV). Dr Bélanger is the recipient of several awards such as the APA Dissertation Research Award and the Guy-Bégin Award for Best Research Paper in Social Psychology. He is the author of numerous scientific articles published in top-tier journals and his research is funded by the Social Sciences and Humanities Research Council of Canada, the US Department of Homeland Security, and Public Safety Canada.

Karim Bettache acquired his PhD in Psychology at the Chinese University of Hong Kong and his BSc and MSc in Psychology at the University of Groningen, the Netherlands. Because of a strong interest in social psychological processes related to intergroup relations and cross-cultural phenomena, after acquiring his MSc in his native country the Netherlands, Dr Bettache decided to spend several years of his academic career in Hong Kong. Besides acquiring his PhD degree, he also worked there as a lecturer for the Education University of Hong Kong, a managing editor for the *Asian Journal of Social Psychology*, and as a Postdoctoral Fellow at the Chinese University of Hong Kong. He is currently based in Kuala Lumpur, Malaysia, where he works on one of the international campuses of Monash University (Melbourne, Australia). He is strongly interested in the following research areas: intergroup relations, cultural psychology, and political psychology with a focus on dogmatism and conservatism.

David F. Bjorklund is Professor of Psychology at Florida Atlantic University. He received a BA in Psychology from the University of Massachusetts, an MA degree in Psychology from the University of Dayton, and a PhD degree in Developmental Psychology from the University of North Carolina at Chapel Hill. He is the author of *Children's Thinking: Cognitive Development and Individual Differences*, now in its sixth edition (with Kayla Causey), and *Why Youth is Not Wasted on the Young*, as well as the co-author of *Looking at Children: An Introduction to Child Development*, and *Parents Book of Discipline* (both with Barbara Bjorklund), *Applied Child Study* and *The Origins of Human Nature: Evolutionary Developmental Psychology* (both with Anthony Pellegrini), *Child and Adolescent Development: An Integrative Approach* (with Carlos Hernández Blasi), and *General Psychology*, eighth edition (with Peter Gray). He is the editor of *Children's Strategies: Contemporary Views of Cognitive Development*; *False-Memory Creation in Children and Adults: Theory, Research, and Implications*; and *Origins of the Social Mind: Evolutionary Psychology and Child Development* (with Bruce Ellis). He served as Associate Editor of *Child Development* (1997–2001) and the *Journal of Experimental Child Psychology* (2005–7), and is currently serving as Editor of the *Journal of Experimental Child Psychology*.

Wiebke Bleidorn is Associate Professor of Psychology at the University of California, Davis. She earned her PhD in Personality and Assessment from Bielefeld University, Germany in 2010 under the guidance of Dr Rainer Riemann. Professor Bleidorn examines the conditions, mechanisms, and consequences of personality change. Her current research involves questions about the cultural and social conditions under which people change, the genetic and environmental mechanisms that account for change, and the consequences of these changes for psychological functioning and important life outcomes. She currently serves as an associate editor of *Social Psychological and Personality Science* and *Collabra* and as consulting editor for the *Journal of Personality and Social Psychology*, the *European Journal of Personality*, and *Personality and Social Psychology Bulletin*.

Jeroen Borghuis obtained a Master's degree in Sociology and a Research Master's degree in Social and Behavioral sciences. Under the supervision of Jaap Denissen, Wiebke Bleidorn, and Klaas Sijtsma, he is working on his PhD project about personality trait development. In his PhD projects, he mainly focuses on the period of adolescence. He studies rank-order and mean-level stability and change in the Big Five and predictors of individual differences in change, such as the personality trait trajectories of best friends and siblings, everyday pleasant and unpleasant emotional and social experiences, and social status in classrooms (i.e., likability and perceived popularity).

Turhan Canli is Professor of Psychology and Psychiatry at Stony Brook University, New York. He is the Founder and Director of the SCAN (Social, Cognitive, and Affective Neuroscience) Center (2008) and Founder and Director of the Mind/Brain Center on War and Humanity (2016), a global network of scientists, clinicians, healers, and policy experts devoted to the human condition in times of war and that is active in refugee camps in the Middle East and Africa. Turhan Canli holds an undergraduate degree (BA, *summa cum laude, summo cum honore in thesi*) from Tufts University, a PhD in Biopsychology from Yale University, and a Certificate in Trauma Recovery from Harvard's Program in Refugee Trauma. His work on the biology of emotion, personality, and depression has been featured in the *New York Times*, *Huffington Post*, NPR, CNN, and many international newspapers and TV programs. His TEDxStony Brook talk on his theory of depression as an infectious disease has been viewed 160,000 times on YouTube. He advises the National Science Foundation, National Institutes of Health, and the national science-funding bodies of Austria, Germany, Iceland, Israel, and the Netherlands. In 2010, he was elected Fellow of the Association for Psychological Science.

Marie-Hélène Cigna is a PhD student in the School of Criminology at the University of Montreal, Canada. She earned her MSc under the guidance of Dr Jean-Pierre Guay, Professor in the School of Criminology at the University of Montreal. Her primary research interests revolve around psychopathic personality and its different manifestations, emotional intelligence (e.g., facial affect recognition, political skills, empathy), and success (such as in the business field). She received the 2013 award for the best Master's Thesis, School of Criminology, University of Montreal, for her thesis on psychopathic personality. Throughout her graduate studies, she received several grants from the Canadian government to pursue her research.

Joanna Conde Ng is a recent Psychology graduate from the University of British Columbia, Vancouver. An advocate for positive psychology, Joanna's primary research interests lie in the influence of diet on self-esteem, and subsequently the influence of self-esteem on motivation, life satisfaction, and self-actualization. Throughout her undergraduate studies, Joanna was a Research Assistant in Dr Steven Heine's Culture and Self Lab at the University of British Columbia and presented her study on *the underlying mechanisms of awe fostering a sense of meaning using virtual reality* at the UBC Psychology Undergraduate Research Conference. With a keen interest in Cultural and Positive Psychology, Joanna hopes to pursue a career in Industrial-Organizational Psychology.

M. Brent Donnellan is Professor in the Department of Psychology at Michigan State University. He earned his PhD from the University of California, Davis in 2001. His primary research interests are at the intersections of personality psychology, personality assessment, and developmental psychology. He is the author or co-author of more than 150 publications and is currently the senior associate editor for the *Journal of Research in Personality* and a senior editor at *Collabra: Psychology*.

Bernhard Fink is a Heisenberg Fellow of the German Science Foundation (DFG) at the University of Göttingen. He earned his PhD in Anthropology from the University of Vienna in 2003. His research interest focuses on human adaptations to social perception and mating behavior. He is the author of more than 130 publications, including work on digit ratio (2D:4D), facial attractiveness, and the perception of human body movement. Recent research activities extend this work to cross-cultural studies in Africa and Russia. He is currently an associated editor of *Evolutionary Psychology* and *Personality and Individual Differences*.

Nathalie M. G. Fontaine is Associate Professor in the School of Criminology at the University of Montreal, Canada, and a researcher at the Research Unit of Children's Psychosocial Maladjustment. In 2015, she obtained a career award from the Fonds de recherche du Québec – Santé (Junior 1 research scholar award). Her research focuses on the development of antisocial behavior in youth, as well as related risk factors (e.g., callous-unemotional traits) and outcomes (e.g., mental health problems). She is currently working on a project that aims to examine the association between facial emotion processing and callous-unemotional traits in a sample of adolescent females.

Marc A. Fournier is Associate Professor in the Department of Psychology at the University of Toronto Scarborough. His research interests are focused on personality integration, person × situation interactions, and interpersonal processes and dynamics. He is principally interested in the integrative processes through which people develop and act from a unified sense of self, and the interpersonal transaction patterns that support these integrative processes. He employs a range of methodologies as part of this research, including the intensive repeated measurement of individuals in their naturalistic settings. Professor Fournier is a past president of the Society for Interpersonal Theory and Research.

R. Michael Furr is Professor of Psychology at Wake Forest University, Winston-Salem, North Carolina. His research interests include personality processes, people's interpersonal perceptions (particularly with regard to morality), personality pathology, and psychological measurement. His research has appeared in journals such as *Psychological Science*, *Journal of Personality and Social Psychology*, and *Psychological Methods*. In addition, he has authored two books on psychological measurement, including *Psychometrics: An Introduction*, which has been translated into Russian. He is a fellow of the Society for Personality and Social Psychology, a fellow of the Association for Psychological Science, a fellow of both Division 5 (Quantitative and Qualitative Methods) and Division 8 (Social and Personality Psychology) of the American Psychological Association, and a recipient of WFU's Award for Excellence in Research. He earned a BA from the College of William and Mary, Williamsburg, Virginia, a MS from Villanova University, Radnor Township, Philadelphia, and a PhD from the University of California at Riverside.

Jean-Pierre Guay is Professor in the School of Criminology at the University of Montreal, Canada, and a senior researcher at the International Centre for Comparative Criminology and at the Centre de recherche de l'Institut Philippe-Pinel de Montréal. His research focuses on measuring criminal phenomena, including risk factors associated with re-offending such as psychopathic traits as well as predatory processes. He has been teaching evaluative research, statistics, and risk assessment at the University of Montreal in the School of Criminology since 1999. He is currently working on a project relying on virtual reality to increase the understanding of the processes associated with predatory behavior and victim selection.

Takeshi Hamamura was born and raised in Japan. In high school, he made a decision to continue his study in the United States. He earned his BA in Psychology and Philosophy from the University of Minnesota. He obtained his PhD in Psychology in 2008 from the University of British Columbia under the guidance of Dr Steve Heine. He moved to Hong Kong for his first academic job and taught Social Psychology and Cultural Psychology at the Chinese University of Hong Kong. In 2014, he decided to continue his cross-cultural journey and moved to Australia to take up a position at the School of Psychology and Speech Pathology at Curtin University.

Erik G. Helzer is Assistant Professor of Management and Organization at the Johns Hopkins Carey Business School. His research focuses on moral character, personal control and agency, and self- and social-assessment. He earned his PhD in Social and Personality Psychology from Cornell University in 2012 and his BA from Oregon State University in 2005. His work has been published in outlets such as *Psychological Science*, *Journal of Personality and Social Psychology*, and *Personality and Social Psychology Bulletin*, and has received funding from the Johns Hopkins University Berman Institute for Bioethics and the Templeton Religion Trust.

Eranda Jayawickreme is Assistant Professor of Psychology at Wake Forest University, Winston-Salem, North Carolina. He received his PhD from the University of Pennsylvania in 2010. He is currently the Project Co-Leader of the Pathways to Character Project, a $3.4 million initiative funded by the John Templeton Foundation examining the possibilities for the strengthening of character following adversity, challenge, or failure. His research focuses on well-being, moral psychology, growth following adversity, wisdom, and integrative theories of personality, and he has worked with populations in Rwanda, Sri Lanka, and the United States. His awards include the 2015 Rising Star award from the Association for Psychological Science, Wake Forest University's Award for Excellence in Research, a Mellon Refugee Initiative Fund Fellowship, and grants from the John Templeton Foundation, the Templeton Religion Trust, and the Asia Foundation/USAID.

Siobhan Kennedy-Costantini is a Research Fellow at the Auckland Bioengineering Institute and School of Psychology at the University of Auckland. She earned her PhD at the University of Queensland in Developmental Psychology in 2017 under the guidance of Associate Professor Mark Nielsen and Professor Virginia Slaughter. Her primary research interests lie broadly in the field of developmental psychology, with a particular focus on the parent–infant relationship and early social development. Her current research focuses on modeling infants' interactive behavior, social learning, and characterizing the microdynamics of early social interactions between parents and their infants. Using these models she hopes to test how discrete changes in infants' behavior, such as variations in social responsiveness, shape the nature of ongoing interactions with their caregiver.

Theo A. Klimstra is Associate Professor at the Department of Developmental Psychology at Tilburg University, the Netherlands. He earned his PhD from Utrecht University in 2010 under the guidance of Dr Wim Meeus. After being a postdoctoral researcher at KU Leuven, Belgium, he joined Tilburg University in 2012. His primary research interests are personality development and identity formation in adolescence and young adulthood. He employs typological and trait (e.g., Big Five and Dark Triad) approaches to the study of personality, combines quantitative dimensional approaches with a narrative approach to study identity, and examines how identity processes and personality traits mutually affect each other.

Christin Köber is Postdoctoral Associate in NYUAD. She earned her doctorate in Developmental Psychology at Goethe University, Frankfurt under the guidance of Professor Tilmann Habermas in 2015. Throughout her PhD years, she served as junior lecturer in the American University Paris (AUP) and in the YMCA University of Applied Sciences, Kassel. In September 2016, she joined NYUAD to work with Professor Theodore E. A. Waters on the development of autobiographical memory and the life story, contributing to well-being, the sense of self-sameness, and identity. Currently, her research focuses on the stability of the self and narrative identity as well as the interchange of identity and social context.

Daniel J. Kruger is Research Assistant Professor at the University of Michigan's Institute for Social Research. He applies evolutionary principles to advance the understanding of a wide range of human psychology and behavior. Much of his work is founded on Life History Theory, which provides a powerful framework for understanding individual variation. He pursues both basic research to advance theory as well as applied projects that directly benefit the communities of study. Much of his current work leverages evolutionary theory, the most powerful theoretical framework in the life sciences, to address real-world challenges in order to promote human well-being and sustainability.

Odilia M. Laceulle is Assistant Professor at the Department of Developmental Psychology at Utrecht University. After studying Psychology at Utrecht University, she obtained her PhD thesis at University Medical Center Groningen (completed September 2013, with honor). Both in her dissertation and in her work as a postdoctoral researcher (UMC Groningen and Utrecht University), she focused on how adversity affects adolescent development. Currently, she studies the complex interplay between individuals and their environments in the prediction of psychopathology. Specifically, she aims at disentangling longitudinal associations between person characteristics (e.g., personality, temperament) and environmental factors (e.g., stress, trauma, social relationships) in the prediction of adolescent mental health (general psychopathology and personality pathology specifically).

Karin Machluf is Assistant Professor of Psychology at Pennsylvania State University. She received a BA in Psychology from Florida Atlantic University, and a MA and PhD in Experimental Psychology from Florida Atlantic University. She is the co-founder of the CODES lab (Cognitions of Developmental and Evolutionary Science) at PSU and the author of numerous chapters and articles on evolutionary developmental psychology. She is a section editor for the *Encyclopaedia of Evolutionary Psychological Science* and serves as a reviewer for the *Journal of Experimental Child Psychology*, *Evolutionary Psychology*, and *Psychological Reports*. Additionally, she serves on the council of the Southern Society for Philosophy and Psychology (SSPP). Her research interests include evolutionary developmental psychology, specifically the impact of neoteny on adult behavior and cognitions.

Dario Maestripieri is Professor of Comparative Human Development and Evolutionary Biology at the University of Chicago. He earned his PhD in Biopsychology from the University of Rome La Sapienza in 1992. His primary research interests are the evolution of human behavior and the relationship between science and literature. He has published more than 200 articles and five books. He is the Editor-in-Chief of the journal *Adaptive Human Behavior and Physiology*. He is a Fellow of the American Association for the Advancement of Science and of the Association for Psychological Science.

John T. Manning is an Honorary Research Fellow at Swansea University. His PhD was from Liverpool University and focused on theoretical aspects of the maintenance of sexual reproduction and behavioral implications of sexual selection. He has published on sexually selected behavioral traits in crustaceans, insects, birds (peafowl), non-human primates (cradling behavior), and humans (fluctuating asymmetry). Since 1998, his work has focused on sex-dependent behavioral aspects of digit ratio (2D:4D), including the biological basis of gender, occupational preferences, and gender inequality across nations.

James Marvel-Coen received his BA in Biology and English from Williams College in 2015 and his MA in Comparative Human Development from the University of Chicago in 2017. His master's research examined the relationship between morningness-eveningness and a range of physiological, self-report, psychological, and behavioral measures, in the context of how variation in morningness-eveningness might constitute a part of broader differences in life history strategy between individuals. Currently, his research focuses on circulating extracellular microRNAs in blood plasma in human patients. Apart from humans, he has also worked in crickets and *E. coli*. James' research interests include evolution, development, genetics, and behavior.

Brent A. Mattingly is Associate Professor of Psychology at Ursinus College in Collegeville, Pennsylvania. He earned his PhD in Social Psychology from Saint Louis University in 2008. His research focuses on the intersection of romantic relationships and the self, and is strongly rooted in the self-expansion model of motivation, which posits that individuals are motivated to broaden their sense of self by acquiring new and enhancing existing identities, perspectives, capabilities, and resources. Dr Mattingly has published original research in numerous outlets, including *Social Psychological and Personality Science*, the *Journal of Social and Personal Relationships*, *Personal Relationships*, *Self and Identity*, and *Personality and Individual Differences*. He is currently an Associate Editor for the *Journal of Social and Personal Relationships*.

Kevin P. McIntyre is Associate Professor in the Department of Psychology at Trinity University in San Antonio, Texas. He received his PhD from Saint Louis University in 2007. His research examines how romantic relationships affect individuals' self-concepts. In particular, he studies how romantic relationships lead to self-concept improvement and degradation, as well as the consequences of these types of self-concept change on relationship functioning. He has published his research in outlets such as the *Journal of Social and Personal Relationships, Personal Relationships,* and *Self and Identity.* He is also the creator of OpenStatslab.com, a website that provides free resources for the teaching of statistics.

Bhavna Menon graduated from New York University Abu Dhabi with a Bachelor's degree in Psychology. She spent her final year doing research on hostile and benevolent sexism in a village in South India. Her research interests include sexism, the structure of gender roles in various cultures, and the nature of sexual discrimination in different cultures. She plans to pursue a PhD in Social Psychology.

Nicholas M. Michalak is a third-year PhD candidate in Social Psychology working with Joshua M. Ackerman at the University of Michigan. Broadly, he uses advanced methods and statistics to study how both modern and evolutionarily-relevant threats affect how people perceive themselves and others. In his current work, he focuses on three main questions: (1) How do people mentally represent threatening persons? (2) How do people use emotional expressions in their trait judgements? and (3) What are the effects of negative stereotypes changing over time?

D. S. Moskowitz is Professor in the Department of Psychology at McGill University in Montreal. Her main line of research is focused on personality and situational factors that influence interpersonal behavior in daily social interactions. This line of research has led her to be interested in the influence of both personal relationships and work relationships on interpersonal behavior. She is an expert on event-contingent recording measures in daily life, a form of intensive repeated measurement in naturalistic settings. She has developed indices for measuring the extent of within-person variability in interpersonal behavior, referred to as flux, pulse, and spin. Professor Moskowitz is a fellow of the Society for Personality and Social Psychology and the American Psychological Association Division on Evaluation, Measurement, and Statistics and is a past president of the Society for Interpersonal Theory and Research.

Marcus Mund is Postdoctoral Researcher at the Department of Personality, Psychology, and Psychological Assessment at the Friedrich-Schiller-Universität Jena, Germany. He earned his PhD in 2015 under the supervision of Franz J. Neyer. His research focuses primarily on (a) the conditions and consequences of personality development, (b) the interpersonal consequences of personality development, (c) partner relationships, (d) loneliness, and (e) dynamic personality–relationship transactions.

Franz J. Neyer is Full Professor at and chair of the Department of Personality, Psychology, and Psychological Assessment at the Friedrich-Schiller-Universität Jena, Germany. He received his PhD at the Ludwigs-Maximilians-Universität Munich in 1994 and received his venia legendi for Psychology in 2002. His research interests span topics such as personality development, dynamic personality–relationship transactions, partner relationships, friendships, and regional identity. Franz J. Neyer has authored more than 100 publications and serves as reviewer for more than 30 international scientific journals as well as advisor for leading international research councils.

Thanh Thanh L. Nguyen graduated from Green Mountain College, Poultney, Vermont in 2017 with a BA in Biopsychology and minor in Chemistry. She started her PhD training in 2017 at the Mayo Clinic Graduate School of Biomedical Sciences, Rochester, MN, with a focus on Molecular Pharmacology and Experimental Therapeutics. Her work focuses on basic and translational research that allows a better understanding of the etiology of psychiatric disorders, and hence better treatment targets towards individualized medicine. Topics include the pharmacogenomics of antidepressants, biological mechanisms underlying sex differences in psychiatric diseases, and the philosophical and psychological implications of applying clinical neuroscience and technology in the management of psychiatric therapies.

Mark Nielsen is Associate Professor in the School of Psychology at the University of Queensland, where he has been since 2002, after completing his PhD at La Trobe University. He has studied a range of interrelated aspects of socio-cognitive development in young human children and non-human primates, with his research primarily focused on charting the origins and development of the human cultural mind. He is also interested in how culture shapes the way children develop, and he has set up field sites in remote indigenous communities in the Northern Territory, Southern Africa, and Vanuatu. He has published over 70 articles and is an associate editor of the *Journal of Experimental Child Psychology*.

Noëmie Nociti is a graduate student at the Université of Québec à Montréal in collaboration with the New York University, Abu Dhabi. She has served as a consultant to number of national and international agencies including the United Nations and the US Department of Homeland Security. Her research interests lie in the psychology of terrorism, the notion of identity fusion and defusion in relation to extremism, and the effectiveness of diverse psychological interventions toward a path of deradicalization. Having already contributed to several scientific publications, she wishes to use her sphere of knowledge to advance the general understanding of psychological mechanisms posing a threat to public safety in different part of the world.

Ugo Pace, PsyD, is Professor of Developmental Psychology and Director of the School of Psychology at UKE – Kore University of Enna, Sicily. Since 2009, he has been the Director of the Clinic Psychology MA Degree at UKE, where he teaches Psychology of Adolescence and Developmental Risk and Protective Factors. His research interests are concerned with the psychological health of adolescents, focusing primarily on the development of identity and autonomy and the relative level of adjustment (behaviors, addictions, moods). He is Associate Editor of the *Journal of Educational and Training Studies* and an editorial-board member of the journals *Child Indicators Research* and *Journal of Child and Family Studies*. He is currently research fellow at Universitat Autonoma de Barcelona, Spain.

Kostas A. Papageorgiou is Lecturer in Developmental Psychopathology at Queen's University Belfast and an Associate Professor in Personality Psychology at Tomsk State University in Russia. Kostas lectures on MSc courses in the School of Psychology at Queen's and supervises BSc, MSc, and PhD students' research. He is also the convener of the course Interdisciplinary Study of Development I in the International MSc in Human Development: Genetics, Neuroscience and Psychology at Tomsk State University. Kostas is the Director of the InteRRaCt Lab and an International Associate Member of InLab at Goldsmiths and the Russian–British Behavioural Genetics Laboratory at the Psychological Institute of the Russian Academy of Education. He is also a member of the committee of the Special Interest Group in Paediatric Psychology of the Psychological Society of Ireland and a member of the International Society for Intelligence Research.

Alessia Passanisi is Professor of General Psychology for the School of Psychology at Kore University of Enna, Sicily. She earned her PhD from the University of Catania in 2009. Her primary research interests are in the following areas: personality traits leading to dysfunctional behaviors (e.g., gambling and problematic internet use), and concepts and categorization, including the way in which people understand the world by classifying objects, people, events, or situations. She has published often in prestigious journals such as *Personality and Individual Differences*, *Journal of Memory and Language,* and *Child Psychiatry and Human Development*. She is currently research fellow at City University, London.

Jennifer L. Petersen is Associate Professor in the Department of Educational Foundations at the University of Wisconsin, Whitewater. She earned her PhD from the University of Wisconsin, Madison where she worked with Dr Janet Hyde and earned her Bachelor's degree from the University of Georgia. Jennifer teaches courses in the College of Education including child development, introduction to human development, and development of the young child. Her research interests generally fall in one of two areas: (1) gender differences and similarities in academic motivation and performance and (2) gender differences in student social engagement, such as peer sexual harassment, and the effects on adolescent development.

Anu Realo (University of Warwick, UK and University of Tartu, Estonia) is interested in personality and cross-cultural psychology and has conducted research on cultural and individual variation in personality traits, emotional experience, values, and subjective well-being. She has been a visiting professor and scholar at several universities in Belgium, Finland, Iceland, the Netherlands, Russia, Sweden, and Switzerland. Her current research also tackles complex relationships among personality, health, and subjective well-being, as well as the genetics of personality traits. She is the author of more than 130 articles in internationally renowned scientific journals and books. In 2010, she was awarded the National Science Award of the Republic of Estonia in social sciences for her studies on personality and stereotypes in a cross-cultural perspective. She is the principal investigator for the World Values Survey in Estonia and a member of the Scientific Advisory Board of the European Social Survey ERIC.

Anne K. Reitz is Assistant Professor at the Department of Developmental Psychology at Tilburg University, the Netherlands. She earned her PhD in Personality Psychology at Humboldt University Berlin under the guidance of Professor Jens Asendorpf in 2013. She is an alumna of the International Max Planck Research School LIFE and completed her postdoctoral training at Columbia University and New York University. Her main research interests are the dynamic short- and long-term processes between the individual and the environment that underlie personality development with a focus on social relations, life transitions, sociocultural contexts, and daily life experiences.

Richard W. Robins is Professor in the Department of Psychology at the University of California, Davis. He earned his PhD in Personality Psychology from the University of California at Berkeley. His research focuses on the nature and development of personality and its consequences for important life outcomes, self-esteem processes and development, and the regulation and expression of self-conscious emotions. His publications have appeared in *Science, American Psychologist, American Scientist, Psychological Review, Psychological Science*, and numerous other prominent journals. He co-edited the *Handbook of Personality* and the *Handbook of Research Methods in Personality Psychology*; served as Associate Editor of the *Journal of Personality and Social Psychology*; and is incoming Associate Editor of *Personality and Social Psychology Review*. He received the Distinguished Scientific Award for Early Career Contribution from the American Psychological Association, and the Theoretical Innovation Prize and the Diener Award for Outstanding Mid-Career Contributions from the Society for Personality and Social Psychology.

Birga M. Schumpe is Postdoctoral Researcher at New York University Abu Dhabi. She earned her PhD in Social Psychology from the University of the Federal Armed Forces in Hamburg. Her main research interest lies in the science of persuasion and motivation, which she applies to various topics. Over the last years, she studied why individuals engage in extreme behaviors and how to counteract these tendencies. Building on her expertise as a clinical psychologist, she successfully developed and tested several interventions to decrease violence. Providing insights on the rehabilitation and reintegration of violent extremist offenders, Dr Schumpe also served as a consultant to the United Nations and trained prison personnel.

Coltan Scrivner is a PhD student in the Department of Comparative Human Development at the University of Chicago and a Fellow at the Institute for Mind and Biology. He holds a BA in Anthropology and an MS in Forensic Biology. His research is interdisciplinary and includes theoretical models and empirical methods from biology, psychology, cognitive science, and anthropology. His research interests include the evolution of human behavior, violence, emotions, and stress physiology. Recently, his work has focused on using eye tracking and focus interviews to better understand how people make meaning from violence, including how this varies according to personality and individual differences.

Jennifer Guinn Sellers is Associate Professor of Psychology at Green Mountain College in Poultney, Vermont. She received her PhD from the University of Texas, Austin, under the guidance of Robert A. Josephs and a BS in Psychology with a minor in Anthropology from the University of Washington, Seattle. Her research is focused broadly in the domain of status. She is interested in the role that contributors to our personality, such as testosterone, play in motivating individuals to seek out positions of power. She is also interested in how socially conferred status differences impact educational performance and attainment, especially in the realm of higher education.

P. Douglas Sellers II is Assistant Professor of Psychology at Pennsylvania State University. He received his BS in Psychology from Furman University in Greenville, South Carolina and a MA and PhD in Experimental Psychology from Florida Atlantic University. He is the co-founder of the CODES lab (Cognitions of Developmental and Evolutionary Science) at PSU and is the author of numerous chapters and articles on evolutionary developmental psychology, memory, and memory development. He is a section editor for the *Encyclopaedia of Evolutionary Psychological Science* and the *Encyclopaedia of Animal Cognition and Behavior* and serves as a reviewer for the *Journal of Experimental Child Psychology*, *Evolutionary Psychology*, and *Psychological Reports*. His research interests include evolutionary developmental psychology and the functional study of memory adaptations, specifically memory for animacy.

Dylan Faulkner Selterman is Lecturer in the Psychology Department at the University of Maryland, College Park. He received his PhD in Psychology from Stony Brook University, New York in 2011. Dr Selterman has research interests including romantic attraction and interpersonal relationships, dreaming, and morality/ethics. Dr Selterman has published original research in *Social Psychological and Personality Science, the Journal of Social and Personal Relationships, Attachment and Human Development, Motivation and Emotion*, and *Dreaming*. He contributes to *Science of Relationships* and *In-Mind* magazine, and is an active member of the International Association for Relationships Research. He currently serves on the editorial board for the *Journal of Social and Personal Relationships* and *Personal Relationships*.

Kali H. Trzesniewski is a Specialist in Cooperative Extension and Associate Director of Research for the Statewide 4-H Youth Development Program at the University of California (UC), Davis, and UC Agriculture and Natural Resources. She received her PhD in 2003 from UC Davis. She studies the development of self-views across the lifespan with extra focus on childhood and adolescence. This work is conducted in the lab, schools, and at afterschool programs, using experimental and longitudinal designs in addition to conducting and evaluating interventions. Her research has been published in leading psychological journals including *Psychological Science* and *Child Development*.

Vijeinika Vipulananthan completed her undergraduate degree in Psychology with a First-Class Degree and has been working in mental-health trusts in London facilitating research trials as well as delivering evidence-based treatment, gaining a profound understanding of a wide range of severe mental-health disorders. Currently she is a Trainee Psychological Wellbeing Practitioner completing her training at University College London in Low Intensity Cognitive Behavioral Therapy with a special interest in perinatal psychology and long-term health conditions. Her current research interests include genetics in neurodevelopmental disorders and the efficacy of therapeutic interventions.

Iris M. Wang is a third year PhD student at the University of Michigan mentored by Joshua M. Ackerman and Oscar Ybarra. Her research broadly applies evolutionary perspectives in explaining self-identity, social relationships, and culture. Specifically, she examines how contagious disease threats impact people's decisions in group situations, as well as people's bodily awareness. In a second line, she examines how life history strategies predict the stability of people's personality across different relationship contexts. Finally, she is interested in explaining cultural phenomena as influenced by the ecologies that people inhabit. Specifically, she is interested in whether cultural level differences can be explained by variation in ecological factors such as pathogen prevalence, genetic relatedness, and harshness.

Theodore E. A. Waters is Assistant Professor of Psychology at New York University Abu Dhabi and a Global Network Assistant Professor of Psychology in the Steinhardt School of Culture, Education, and Human Development at New York University. He received his PhD from Emory University in 2013. His research focuses on the developmental and cognitive mechanisms that account for the enduring effects of early experience across the lifespan. He integrates traditional narrative, developmental, and cognitive methodologies to advance our knowledge of how representations of early experience form, develop, and interact with the social environment to influence critical developmental processes. Currently his lab's work focuses on the development, organization, and impact of attachment representations and representations of self/identity across the lifespan.

Eunike Wetzel is Assistant Professor of Psychological Assessment with a focus on test theory in the Department of Psychology at the University of Mannheim, Germany. She earned her PhD in 2013 from the Otto-Friedrich-University, Bamberg. Her research interests include item response theory, response biases, test construction, and the Dark Triad of personality. Her publications have appeared in journals such as *Psychological Science*, *Educational and Psychological Measurement*, *Assessment*, and *Psychological Assessment*. She currently serves as associate editor for the *European Journal of Psychological Assessment*.

Yi Xu is a researcher at the USC-SJTU Institute of Cultural and Creative Industry in Shanghai Jiao Tong University in Shanghai, China. She received her BA in Electronic Engineering from Fudan University in China, an MA in psychology from Columbia University and earned her PhD in Social Psychology from the Chinese University of Hong Kong in 2015 under the guidance of Dr Takeshi Hamamura. Her research explores the adjustment of multicultural environments; cultural change, in particular Chinese cultural change; cultural differences of online social behavior. She is currently working on project focusing on how trust influences people such as economic behavior, health, as well as prosocial behaviors in consideration of Chinese culture influence.

Corinne E. Zachry is currently a graduate student in Psychology at Wake Forest University. Her graduate research focuses on examining intellectual humility as a component of wisdom. She is particularly interested in predictors of the manifestation of intellectual humility in daily life, as well as the positive outcomes associated with being wise in the context of challenge and adversity. Her recent projects include a series of studies aimed at developing interventions to promote intellectual humility among individuals who have experienced adversity and examining the extent to which change in intellectual humility predicts other positive outcomes, such as tolerance and well-being.

Julia Zimmermann is a Postdoctoral Researcher at the Department of Educational Psychology at the FernUniversität in Hagen (Germany). She earned her PhD in 2012 from Friedrich-Schiller-Universität Jena (Germany) under the guidance of Professor Dr Franz J. Neyer. Her main research interests include the development of personality and social relationships in adolescence and young adulthood, the (social) mechanisms of personality development, and the psychological conditions and consequences of geographical mobility. In particular, her research focuses on education-related international mobility experiences, such as participation in student exchange programs or degree mobility, and the personal, social, and academic development of adolescents and young adults.

PART I

Biological Origins of Personality and Individual Differences

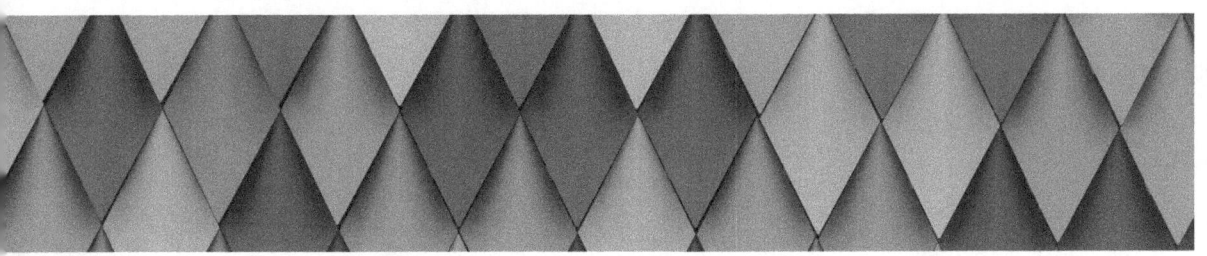

Hormonal Influences on Personality and Individual Differences

Jennifer Guinn Sellers and Thanh Thanh L. Nguyen

I became a huffer, a grunter, a screamer. Anyone who frequents gyms knows those guys who make ungodly noises while hurling weights around. I'd always found their displays childish and tended to look away, as I would from a toddler having a tantrum in a supermarket. So imagine my surprise to find myself bellowing, shrieking, groaning. A silverback gorilla's mating ritual: I wanted everyone to know I was the biggest [expletive] in the place.
Craig Davidson

THIS IS WHAT HAPPENS TO YOU ON STEROIDS, ESQUIRE

Craig Davidson is a writer, and like many writers, he prefers to draw from his experiences when he is developing characters. So when he began to develop a story about a fighter, one who would do anything necessary to win his battles, he decided to embark on a month long journey of injecting himself with steroids. He thought the synthetic form of testosterone he plunged into his muscles would allow him to gain the strength and power fighters need; his research had indicated that was many fighters' motivation at least. What Davidson did not anticipate, however, was that the synthetic hormone he was injecting into his bloodstream did more than just allow him to gain muscle mass more easily. He also began feeling about, acting in, and perceiving his environment differently. As the above quote illustrates, he was acting in a way that just a month prior, he would have thought were the behaviors of a completely different person. He had changed. The hormones had altered his personality.

Hormones, it turns out, are important contributors to our personality. Many hormones exert an influence on our motivations, moods, and relationships with other people, to list a few of their contributions, in addition to their major known biological function, such as carbohydrate metabolism and tissue development. Of course, normally, hormones are allowed to respond to our internal and external environments, something that Davidson's experience with hormone injection inevitably cannot portray. Thus, our understanding of the role of hormones on personality is far more nuanced than anecdotal influences of steroid abusers could suggest. In this chapter, we will discuss what hormones are and how they are assessed; as well as point out ways this approach to assessing personality differs from more traditional personality assessment techniques. Although using hormones to predict behavior – especially when these hormones can be experimentally manipulated – provides many exciting opportunities, they also pose unique challenges. We will then give a synopsis of the current state of our understanding of the influences of commonly studied hormones on personality. For the purposes of this chapter, however, we will limit our discussion of the literature to studies that focus on human participants. Although we are able to learn many things about human personality through comparative research (Gosling, 2001), inclusion of this literature is beyond the scope of what we are able to discuss. Additionally, we will limit our discussion of hormones to those found outside the central nervous system and to their peripheral effects. Most research conducted with humans does not test for hormones in the central nervous system as the method of assessment involves the use of a spinal tap to withdraw cerebrospinal fluid, a highly invasive procedure. Researchers wishing to learn more about the influence of a specific hormone on personality or effects within the central nervous system should also look to studies with non-human animals as much of our mechanistic understanding, in addition to the primary basis for early work with humans, builds off this literature.

HORMONES AND HOW THEY ARE MEASURED

Broadly speaking, hormones are chemicals produced in one part of the body that have to travel to a target receptor site in a location separate from where they are produced. Although research into the role of hormones on personality is relatively recent, it is not a new proposition that a biological agent moving throughout the body affects our personality. Greek physicians such as Hippocrates and Galen proposed that our health and personality are dependent on the balance of four bodily fluids (i.e., yellow bile, black bile, blood, and phlegm), and Freud theorized that personality develops from libidinal energy that navigates through the body to target locations. Although the specifics of these approaches have been largely abandoned, the focus on finding a biological basis to personality has not. In recent years, researchers have added to our understanding of personality by integrating findings from affective neuroscience and neurobiology (e.g., Canli, 2006). And, just as functional magnetic resonance imaging (fMRI) technologies have allowed researchers the opportunity to peer inside the working brain, the emergence of non-invasive hormone sampling techniques has allowed researchers to incorporate hormones in their studies with human participants.

Hormones are generally produced in the Golgi cells of glands and travel through the circulatory system to specific target receptors. They differ from the other most common class of chemical messengers in the body, neurotransmitters, in that the effects that they produce take much longer to occur because of the time it takes for them to travel. This time can take anywhere from seconds to hours as opposed to the milliseconds it takes neurotransmitters to cross a synapse. Whereas neurotransmitters are released in the space between neurons, and exert an effect on pre-established pathways by making the activation of neural circuits more or less likely, hormones have to travel through the bloodstream to exert an effect (although it should be noted that some hormones, such as norepinephrine, share commonalities with neurotransmitters; Nelson, 2005).

Just as with the humors, there are four main classes of hormones: steroids (e.g., cortisol, testosterone), peptides and proteins (e.g., vasopressin, oxytocin), amines (e.g., epinephrine, norepinephrine), and lipid-based hormones (e.g., prostaglandins). Of this list, steroid hormones are the most accessible hormone for personality researchers to study as they are able to cross from the bloodstream into saliva where they can be measured by a single salivary sample in addition to more invasive methods such as blood draws. Steroid hormones that can be assayed from saliva include cortisol, estradiol, progesterone, and testosterone. These hormones are regulated by the hypothalamus and pituitary gland through the release of precursor hormones (see Figure 1.1). As these hormones are regulated by the hypothalamus and pituitary gland, however, there are certain biological constraints that researchers need to be aware of before incorporating them into research (Nelson, 2005).

ASSESSMENT CHALLENGES: CIRCADIAN VARIANCE

Steroid hormones have their own rhythms. When the circadian rhythms of steroid hormones such as cortisol, estradiol, and testosterone are not taken into account, it can decrease the power of detecting between-subject differences (Schultheiss and Stanton, 2009). For instance, it has been well established that cortisol has a strong circadian rhythm (Dickerson and Kemeny, 2004). Cortisol levels normally increase by 50–100% to peak levels 30 minutes after waking. Levels then begin to decline steadily until a second secretory episode near the middle of the day, and then further decrease throughout the day until they are minimally detectable around midnight (Kirschbaum and Hellhammer, 2000). Researchers who sample without taking this curve into account will find that time of sampling dwarfs any individual differences. Moreover, individuals also differ in respect to the magnitude of

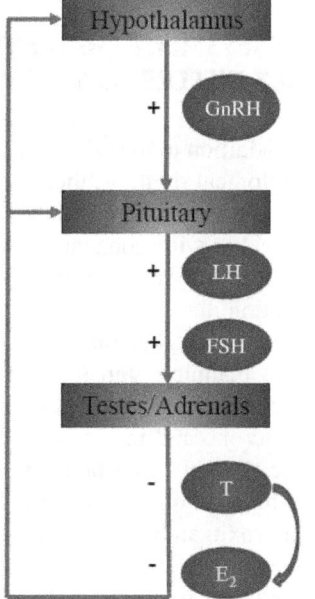

Abbreviation:
GnRH = Gonadotropin releasing hormone
LH = Luteinizing hormone
FSH = Follicle-stimulating hormone
T = Testosterone
E_2 = Estradiol

Figure 1.1 The hypothalamus–pituitary–gonadal axis

their circadian fluctuations. Although between-subject differences in the diurnal cycle of salivary free cortisol have been found among healthy individuals, 10–15% of those sampled demonstrate a flattened circadian rhythm (Stone et al., 2001). Thus, the magnitude of the circadian rhythm itself is a possible individual difference.

Testosterone also shows a circadian rhythm, with levels highest in the morning followed by decreasing levels throughout the day. The likelihood of detecting effects depends on the time of day testosterone is sampled as well as the nature of the outcome variable testosterone is posited to influence (Wirth and Schultheiss, 2007, but see Liening et al., 2010). Additionally, seasonal variations of testosterone have been observed in men, with testosterone levels higher in the fall and lower in the spring (Harris, 1999). As research studies are typically conducted over the course of a single season, however, this variation is seldom addressed in the literature.

The appropriate methods used to measure cortisol and other steroid hormones that follow circadian rhythms partly depend on the research question. There are three major approaches to measuring cortisol: basal cortisol levels throughout the day (area-under-the-curve, AUC approach), diurnal variation (rhythm profile approach), and cortisol response to acute stress (Nicolson, 2008). Aspects to be considered in the collection process include the time of the day samples are collected, the number of samples to be collected, and whether assessment is single-day or multiple-day. It has been shown that free cortisol after waking is more reliable than single assessments at a fixed time and is not dependent on sleep duration, time of waking, and alcohol consumption, provided that it is measured repeatedly at 10- or 15-minute intervals for a strict 30- to 60-minute timeframe after waking (Pruessner et al., 1997). Additionally, single-day assessment is weaker than multiple-day assessment due to its inability to rule out day-to-day variations. For a one-day cortisol measurement protocol, researchers agree that four measurements at time points one, four, nine, and 11 hours after waking provide good coverage for AUC. Collections over three to four days provide reliable assessment of 'trait' daily concentration, and collections over six to nine days provide reliable assessment of 'trait' rhythm (Stewart and Seeman, 2000).

Although the methods described above provide good reliability, it is often not feasible for researchers to collect the number of samples that these protocols dictate because of constraints due to cost, experimental design, and participant compliance. Because of this, many personality researchers collect single salivary samples at a single time of day or between the hours of 1 pm and 4 pm when the decline in these hormones begins to plateau and levels are most stable. Single measurements of testosterone collected within this time constraint demonstrate good test–retest reliability across days and weeks in both sexes, enough that it satisfies the basic reliability necessities of a personality variable (Sellers et al., 2007).

ASSESSMENT CHALLENGES: SEX DIFFERENCES

In addition to the within-person variability of biological rhythms, there are also known sex differences among many hormones. When working with gonadal, or sex, hormones for instance, it is important to take into consideration the sex-dependent variations when designing protocols, recruiting participants, and planning statistical analyses. Although the primary gonadal hormone in men is testosterone and in women it is estrogen, both are present in all humans. The normal concentration of salivary testosterone in men is approximately seven times greater than that in women (Sellers et al., 2007). Consequently, methods used to evaluate testosterone in women have to be sensitive enough to yield meaningful data. For example, in healthy women, it is recommended that conventional radioimmunoassay is unreliable, whereas immunoassay after extraction and chromatography or liquid chromatography/tandem mass spectrometry (LC/MS-MS) is more reliable (Rosner et al., 2007). In addition to the mean differences between sexes, there are also monthly variations of hormones in women. As such, there are two major considerations when female participants are used in an investigation: (1) it has been recommended that women taking oral contraceptives should be excluded from studies involving gonadal hormone because the medication suppresses gonadal hormone production and (2) women with a spontaneous menstrual cycle tend to have an increased plasma testosterone level during mid-cycle, even though this rise is brief and not systematically apparent (Harris, 1999). Moreover, when modeling testosterone-behavior relationships in children, sex appears to moderate the developmental context as studies have shown that these variables predict significantly more systematic variance in boys' testosterone level than in girls. Thus, cross-gender analysis of testosterone-behavior effects is not recommended (Granger et al., 2004).

There are two types of circulating testosterone in the human body. 'Free' testosterone is not bound to sex-hormone binding globulin, and is free to bind to receptors. As such, free testosterone is the psychologically 'active' fraction of total testosterone. 'Total' testosterone is a measure of both bound and unbound testosterone. Measures of testosterone in saliva only capture free testosterone (Granger et al., 1999). Studies examining the relationship between testosterone and behavior look almost exclusively at free testosterone as measured in saliva because of both the ease of collection and assay procedure. Another issue regarding gender differences in measuring testosterone is that, regardless of assay method, salivary testosterone is correlated with plasma testosterone in males but not always in females, whereas blood spot assays are highly correlated with free and total serum testosterone in both sexes. Furthermore, the observed association between testosterone and behavior when substituting plasma assay with salivary assay was found to be more profoundly underestimated in females than in males (Shirtcliff et al., 2002). Along these same lines, the validity of salivary assays for estradiol has been questioned in males (Shirtcliff et al., 2000). When designing or evaluating studies involving gonadal hormones, researchers should take these factors into account, especially when interpreting null findings and sex differences.

In an attempt to circumvent hormonal variations and complications unique to each sex, many studies have included only one sex in their sample that they deem to be in accordance with the hormone they are examining (e.g., testosterone was initially studied almost exclusively in males, whereas oxytocin was more commonly studied in females). Even though this approach is methodologically convenient, it is important to keep in mind that such exclusion of a sex can sacrifice important findings and have implications for subsequent research. For example, in their seminal review of the fight-or-flight response literature, Taylor et al. (2000) pointed out that the majority of studies linking the fight-or-flight response to stress, epinephrine and norepinephrine, were conducted exclusively in males. They argued that, while the flight-or-fight response had been well established as the primary physiological response to stress in both sexes, a different model more accurately reflected the stress response in women. Dubbed the tend-or-befriend response, this behavioral mechanism is predominantly demonstrated in females and intimately related to the hormone oxytocin and other female reproductive hormones. Importantly, the exclusion of females in earlier biobehavioral stress studies led to untested assumptions that took decades for researchers to correct. Because of this, it is recommended that analyses be conducted within sex to account for the mean differences in hormone levels between men and women, but not for researchers to focus exclusively on one sex when conducting their studies. Such myopic participant selection can mask potentially important findings. With these important methodological considerations addressed, we are now ready to review what we know about the influence of specific hormones on our personality.

TESTOSTERONE AND THE QUEST FOR DOMINANCE

Recall the opening quote by Craig Davidson. He described a need for everyone in the weight room to know that he was the most dominant person in the room. The major biological action of testosterone is to regulate the secondary sexual characteristics of males. The primary psychological action is the motivation for people to seek out positions of power over others. Testosterone is one of the most studied hormones in personality research, partly because it is measurable through non-invasive salivary immunoassay, has high test–retest reliability, and has good convergent as well as divergent validity (Sellers et al., 2007). It is a steroid hormone derived from cholesterol and is secreted by the adrenals in women and the testes in men. Numerous studies have discovered that testosterone predicts behaviors associated with acquiring and maintaining dominance – both within the laboratory (e.g., Grant and France, 2001; van Honk et al., 1999, 2001) and outside of the laboratory (e.g., prison; Dabbs et al., 1995; Dabbs and Hargrove, 1997). High levels of baseline testosterone have been linked to dominance displays among female roommates (Cashdan, 1995) as well as more extreme behaviors such as rule-breaking (Dabbs et al., 1987), and getting into fights (Dabbs et al., 1995) as means of demonstrating dominance in prison. When status is 'up for grabs', testosterone consistently predicts behavior. Importantly, when status is not up for grabs, testosterone does not appear to influence behavior. Given this evidence, and good psychometric qualities, researchers have compiled evidence that testosterone serves as a biological marker of dominance strivings.

Although a great deal of research is focused on the dominance strivings of those high in testosterone, these strivings are not limited to them. In research on the '*mismatch effect*' (e.g., Josephs et al., 2006), it has been shown that, whereas people high in testosterone are motivated to achieve high status, those low in testosterone appear motivated to maintain *low status*. When experimentally placed into a high status position, low testosterone individuals showed evidence of discomfort (i.e., an increase in emotional arousal and heart rate, cognitive distraction, and an implicit attention to status). Importantly, baseline testosterone predicted these effects *only* when status was threatened. Testosterone does not predict behavior in the absence of competition or status threats.

Coupled with a motivation to achieve dominance, testosterone has also been scrutinized as an inhibiting factor in empathy. Empathy is the ability to recognize and experience the emotional state of another person (Davis, 1983). Women with high levels of endogenous testosterone, as well as those receiving sublingual testosterone administrations, demonstrate reduced ability to infer mental states (van Honk et al., 2011). Exogenous testosterone administration has also been shown to dampen facial mimicry (Hermans et al., 2006) and reduce the ability to consciously detect angry faces among women (van Honk and Schutter, 2007). Therefore, it appears that one of the ways in which testosterone allows individuals to pursue dominance is by inhibiting their likelihood of noticing or vicariously experiencing the emotional state of another person. Although it is unknown what influence this dampened empathy has on one's potential leadership style, it nonetheless makes some sense that being overly aware of the emotional states of others might interfere with an individual's pursuit of power.

For example, people who are motivated to ensure a high level of group status are less likely to concern themselves with the welfare of low status groups (Pratto et al., 1994), presumably as a means to enhance their groups' status.

Perhaps related to both the lack of empathy and need for dominance, testosterone has been shown to be correlated with narcissism (Pfattheicher, 2016). It has also been found to be correlated with novelty seeking and reward dependence (Määttänen et al., 2013) in addition to attachment-related avoidance, dominance, disconnectedness, and loneliness (Turan et al., 2014). All of these studies limited participation to men only.

HORMONES PREDICT BEHAVIOR, BUT ALSO RESPOND TO SITUATIONS

Although testosterone satisfies the necessary psychometric property of stability, levels of this and other hormones also change in response to situations. In addition to predicting dominance strivings, changing levels of testosterone have been associated with winning and losing. In their reciprocal model, Mazur and Booth (1998) argue that as status increases, so do testosterone levels. According to the model, testosterone levels rise after a successful dominance confrontation as a signal to continue maintaining or enhancing status. Indeed, after a contest such as chess or tennis, testosterone levels are higher in winners than they are in the losers (e.g., Booth et al., 1989; Mazur et al., 1992; Mazur and Lamb, 1980). Additionally, both testosterone and mood increased from pre-game baseline after a win among female soccer players, while the reverse was true among those on the losing team (Oliveira et al., 2009). Vicarious competitions can also produce similar findings. Testosterone levels increased among fans of the winning team in one World Cup soccer tournament (Bernhardt et al., 1998) as well as in people from the states that supported the winning candidates of the US presidential election (Markey and Markey, 2010), while the reverse was true among people on the losing sides in all the studies. Acquiring status symbols can likewise have similar effects. Men who had the chance to drive fancy and expensive cars showed a subsequent increase in testosterone (Saad and Vongas, 2009), presumably because the car was a newly acquired means of asserting dominance over others. Importantly, all of these changes from baseline are transitory and last an average of one to two hours. Additionally, participants must view the victories as relevant in order for testosterone to be affected. For participants who view a win as unimportant, testosterone levels remain stable or show only the expected diurnal decline (see Archer, 2006 or Carre et al., 2011 for reviews). Additionally, increases in testosterone following a victory have been shown to occur only in participants with a strong desire to win (Schultheiss et al., 1999; Suay et al., 1999). Thus, hormones – and their effects – are intimately tied to the cognitive, motivational, and social aspects of personality.

CORTISOL AND THE DUAL-HORMONE HYPOTHESIS

So far, we have only been discussing the role of a single hormone on personality, but interactions among hormones are a fruitful line of research as well. The dual-hormone hypothesis is one such inquiry which makes predictions about how testosterone and cortisol interact to predict social behavior. Before discussing this interactionist model, we will first turn our attention to cortisol. Commonly called 'the stress hormone', cortisol is a glucocorticoid hormone regulated by the hypothalamic–pituitary–adrenal (HPA) axis (see Figure 1.2). Under normal conditions, cortisol is responsible for regulating metabolic activities. Under threat, however,

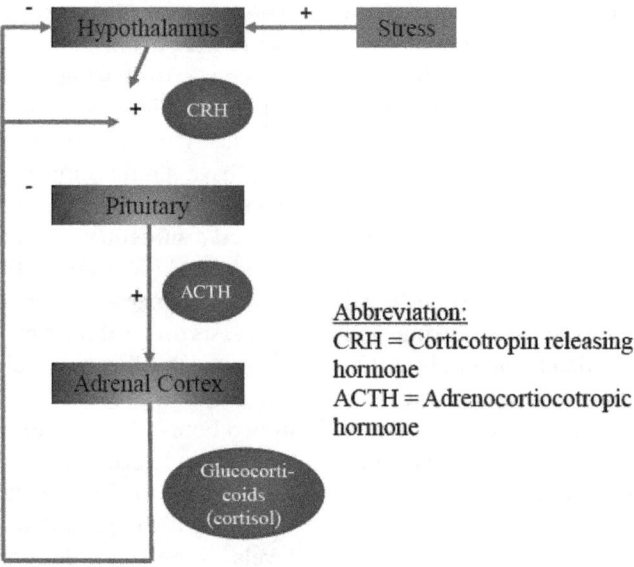

Figure 1.2 The hypothalamus–pituitary–adrenal axis

cortisol plays a significant role in the stress response by mobilizing energy. Stress is the resulting state of physiological imbalance, and the goal of the stress response is to provide the resources necessary (e.g., increased blood pressure, oxygen-rich blood, increased blood glucose) to sustain the organism under threat (Sapolsky, 2005). Cortisol is also related to the stress associated with status. For example, individuals low in socio-economic status (SES) – a marker of relative standing – are more vulnerable than those high in SES to stress-related illnesses such as cardiovascular diseases (Smith and Hart, 2002).

Basal cortisol has been shown to be negatively correlated with novelty seeking in men (Tyrka et al., 2006), even after controlling for age and testosterone (Rosenblitt et al., 2001). It is also positively associated with self-esteem, hardiness, affective stability (Zorrilla et al., 1995), and narcissism in men (Pfattheicher, 2016), whereas it is negatively correlated with trait shyness and social anxiety in both sexes (Beaton et al., 2006). Although trait levels of cortisol appear to predict facets of extraversion, the magnitude of the cortisol response to acute stress paints a slightly different picture. For example, attachment anxiety is positively correlated with the cortisol response to acute stress in women (Quirin et al., 2008). Additionally, higher scores in narcissism predicted a higher cortisol response to acute stress and increased negative affect in men but not women (Edelstein, Yim et al., 2010). Switching to studies that look at the cortisol awakening response, attachment anxiety appears to be negatively related with the awakening response in women (Quirin et al., 2008) but positively correlated with hopelessness (van Santen et al., 2011), extraversion, and positive affect (Miller et al., 2016).

The Dual Hormone Hypothesis

Although the bulk of research on testosterone and cortisol has investigated each hormone independently, a recent set of studies provides evidence that cortisol may antagonize the relationship between testosterone and behavior. In their study on how these hormones work together to influence perceptions of leadership, Mehta and Josephs (2010) found that judges rated participants' leadership style as being dominant only when those targets had high testosterone and low cortisol levels. In a follow-up study utilizing an entirely male sample, the researchers wanted to see if perceptions translated into dominant behaviors. Consistent with their hypothesis, it was found that only individuals high in testosterone but low in cortisol were willing to compete in multiple dominance contests. The authors argue that high levels of cortisol block the relationship between testosterone and behavior, effectively canceling out the status-seeking influence of testosterone entirely. The interaction between these hormones has important implications for how individuals interact with others in non-competitive domains as well. People who are high in basal testosterone but low in basal cortisol have been found to be rated as more popular and socially connected than their low testosterone, high cortisol counterparts (Ponzi et al., 2016). High testosterone levels have also been linked with the likelihood of maintaining friendships, but interestingly, these high testosterone individuals were less likely to create friendships. High levels of cortisol, on the other hand, predicted the opposite pattern. People high in cortisol were found to be less likely to maintain friendships and more likely to create friendships (Kornienko et al., 2015).

GENDER DIFFERENCES IN THE EFFECTS OF HORMONES

Without question, a non-negligible percentage of studies on hormones and personality use a single-sex sample. In the case of testosterone, many of these studies have been conducted only with men. Although the association between both baseline and fluctuating testosterone levels and dominance-related behaviors in males is well-documented, finding a similar relationship among females has been less consistent. Whereas female athletes consistently show a rise in testosterone after victory and a decline after defeat (e.g., Edwards et al., 2006; Oliveira et al., 2009), similar findings have not been replicated in more controlled lab settings. This has led some researchers to argue that estradiol may be a more fruitful line of investigation towards understanding the physiological correlates of dominance among women (e.g., Stanton and Edelstein, 2009; Stanton and Schultheiss, 2007, 2009).

A closer look at the types of studies cited as support for this argument, however, leads one to remain dubious of this assertion. For example, in a study conducted by Schultheiss et al. (2004), participants watched movies intended to activate an implicit need for power. The researchers expected that this unconscious measure of dominance strivings would likewise be correlated with increases in testosterone. As expected, they found that men high in testosterone showed a subsequent increase in testosterone after the movie. Women high in testosterone, on the other hand, showed a decline. The authors took this as evidence that testosterone is unrelated to dominance striving in women. However, the movie participants watched was *The Godfather*, a film filled with violent imagery. An alternative hypothesis is that *The Godfather* is indicative of a paternalistic social structure and instead reminded female participants that being female does not have the same level of inherent status as being male (cf. Glick and Fiske, 2001). Given this alternative hypothesis, one would expect that women concerned with status would show a subsequent decline when reminded of their lower social status. Similar studies failing to find a relationship in women have utilized paradigms such as video games as proxies for dominance contests (see Mazur and Booth, 1998). However, if women do not view video games as routes to status, we would likewise expect to see this null effect.

As previously stated, the vast majority of research with testosterone has been conducted on men. As such, a great deal more research utilizing female samples needs to be conducted before any definitive statements on the predictive utility of testosterone in women ought to be made. The same is also true of estradiol, which has only recently gained the attention of researchers.

THE ROLE OF ESTRADIOL IN PREDICTING BEHAVIOR

Testosterone is aromatized into estradiol after losing an OH bond (see Figure 1.3). Both men and women have estradiol, only women have greater amounts as their 'free' testosterone is aromatized into estradiol much more rapidly. The major biological action of estradiol is female tissue development. Returning to our opening example, Davidson and other 'dopers' tend to have firsthand experience with this biological action as breast tissue swelling is a common side-effect of steroid use as excess testosterone is rapidly aromatized into estradiol.

As with testosterone, the findings regarding estradiol and dominance behaviors are likewise mixed. Utilizing a diary study, Cashdan (2003) found no relationship in a female sample between estradiol and either seeking out competitive situations or displays of aggressive behavior. This is in contrast to research by Stanton and Schultheiss (2007) which found a correlation between implicit power motivation and baseline estradiol in a female sample. In this research, it was also found that female participants high in implicit power motive showed a subsequent increase in estradiol after winning a rigged competition. Although there are few studies, one unfortunate pattern is emerging. Just as early studies on testosterone utilized a predominantly male sample; it appears that early investigations into estradiol are following the same lead with an exclusively female sample.

There are some studies that looked simultaneously at both men and women and the relationship between estradiol and attachment. In their mixed-sex sample, Edelstein, Stanton et al. (2010) found that estradiol is associated with low attachment avoidance and high implicit intimacy. In other words, people high in estradiol appear motivated to form close attachments to other people. This association appears to have a reciprocal relationship, in a similar manner to that which has been documented with testosterone and dominance. Experiences of emotional intimacy have been shown to cause an increase

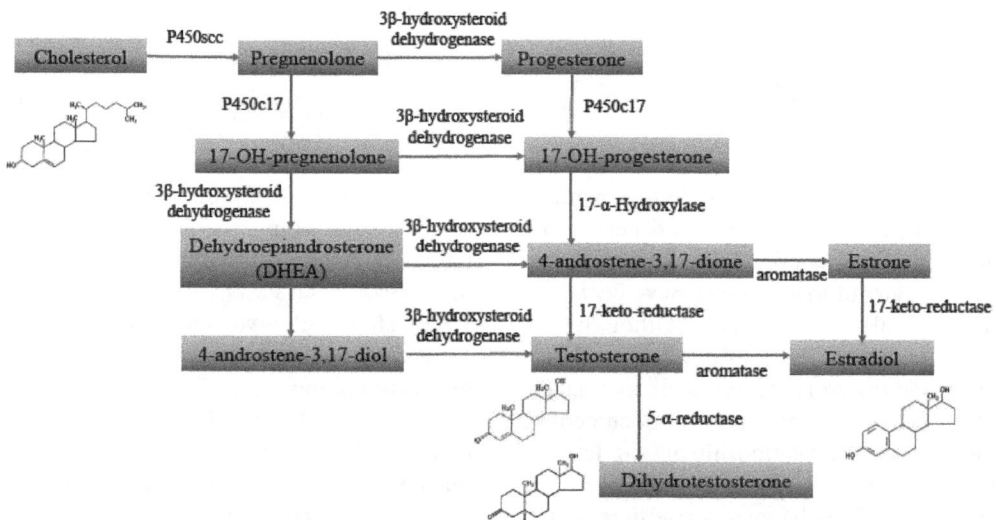

Figure 1.3 Testosterone metabolism

in estradiol level, with the effect being moderated by gender and attachment style. Specifically, women with a highly avoidant attachment style showed smaller increases in estradiol after being exposed to an emotionally intimate clip than did women high in this attachment style (Edelstein et al., 2012). These findings point to how testosterone and estradiol may be eliciting distinct, yet complementary, behaviors. Recall that estradiol is aromatized from testosterone. It is possible that following a competitive interaction individuals might then be motivated to focus on maintaining relationships. Changes in testosterone – which serve as signals to change in status – may be precursors to changes in estradiol; a signal that individuals must now work on maintaining their relationships. Estradiol also appears to be associated with the traits of temperamental activity and endurance and negatively correlated with emotional reactivity (Ziomkiewicz et al., 2012).

In addition to investigating a possible interaction between estradiol and testosterone, there are indications that estradiol may interact with the steroid hormone progesterone. Progesterone is produced in the corpus lutea and placenta, with its major biological actions related to the development and maintenance of pregnancy. One study found that during cyclical hormone changes, among women high in Borderline Personality Disorder features, estradiol deviation was negatively associated with borderline features only when progesterone was higher than usual (Eisenlohr-Moul et al., 2015). As this is only one study, however, caution should be taken before extrapolating these findings too broadly.

OXYTOCIN

A considerable amount of literature has shown that oxytocin affects a multitude of social behaviors. Oxytocin is a neuropeptide hormone, released by the posterior pituitary and centrally involved in maternal onset of behaviors such as milk letdown and uterine contractions during birth (Nelson, 2005). Oxytocin is typically assayed through blood, as there are still reliability questions about newly emerging salivary assessment techniques. There are also clear sex-differences in oxytocin, although the hormone and its receptors are present in both sexes. Concerns for researchers include the recognition that estrogen, of which women have more than men, upregulates the effects of oxytocin. Additionally, there is some concern that the molecularly similar hormone arginine vasopressin can bind to oxytocin receptors, and this hormone has been shown to elicit different social behaviors among women and men. Finally, studies that experimentally manipulate oxytocin tend to rely on men because of the concern that excess levels could cause uterine contractions in women (Campbell, 2010). Thus, the landscape surrounding oxytocin research is difficult to navigate at the outset.

Despite the difficulties of conducting oxytocin research utilizing human samples, popular media has picked up on a simple story. Although often called 'the love hormone' by the press, oxytocin does not indiscriminately induce social bonding. The influence of oxytocin is far more nuanced. It does appear to increase trusting behavior when it involves empathizing with a social partner (Kosfeld et al., 2005). A review of the research on the influence of oxytocin on social memory, however, left Campbell (2010; but see also Bartz et al., 2011; Theodoridou et al., 2011) to conclude that the association was 'inconclusive to say the least' (p. 286). Studies have also linked oxytocin to in-group conformity and preference (De Dreu et al., 2011; Stallen et al., 2012), empathy and generosity (Zak et al., 2007), and perspective taking (Domes et al., 2007). Oxytocin is also thought to play a critical role in the tend-and-befriend biobehavioral responses to stress in females (Taylor et al., 2000). The effects of oxytocin on the promotion of social support and the reduction of stress and anxiety have also received good support, and oxytocin is being evaluated for its efficacy in treating certain psychiatric disorders (Bakermans-Kranenburg and van IJzendoorn, 2013; Heinrichs et al., 2003).

Even though there are an ever-increasing number of studies that examine the causal effect of oxytocin on behavior, comparatively fewer studies have attempted to link oxytocin to personality traits. Some studies have looked into the role of oxytocin in women's attachment, affiliation, and aggression (see Campbell, 2008, for a review). A recent study showed that, in healthy women, plasma oxytocin levels were negatively correlated with novelty seeking scores and positively with both harm avoidance and attachment (Nigro et al., 2016). Interestingly, basal salivary oxytocin was shown to predict certain intra-personal dimensions of emotional intelligence in women (Koven and Max, 2014).

Another angle that researchers have considered in studies of oxytocin and individual differences are the moderating or mediating effects of personality traits on the social effects of oxytocin. Literature has shown an inconsistent pattern of oxytocin in promoting prosocial behavior, which prompted the development of an interactionist model where the effects of oxytocin on social behavior might be dependent on certain features of the social environment (Bartz et al., 2011; Olff et al., 2013). Building off of this interactionist approach, the social salience hypothesis of oxytocin proposes that oxytocin regulates the salience of social cues by interacting with the dopaminergic system, and the salience is itself dependent on 'baseline individual differences such as gender, personality traits' (Shamay-Tsoory and Abu-Akel, 2015, p. 194). Another study looked into the interaction of oxytocin and the dopaminergic system and its association with neuroticism. Specifically, the study found that the correlation between striatal dopamine availability and oxytocin plasma level is dependent upon the genetic variants of oxytocin receptor polymorphism rs53576, and this interaction is significantly correlated with neuroticism scores among individuals with this allelic variant (Chang et al., 2014).

Perhaps in the case of oxytocin more so than any of the other hormones discussed thus far, it is clear that much of our understanding of the influence of this hormone is derived from animal studies. This is in many ways a result of the interest surrounding the effects of this hormone within the central nervous system. The research on basal levels and changes in plasma concentrations are still difficult to interpret without delving into the animal literature, of which others have already raised concerns as to the appropriateness of some of the animal models commonly used in these investigations (e.g., Campbell, 2010).

FUTURE DIRECTIONS

The emergence of techniques that have allowed researchers to incorporate hormones into their studies on personality in humans has led to a rapid expansion of our understanding of these chemical messengers in a short period of time. Although correlational designs proved especially informative in the beginning, more recent studies have begun to incorporate endogenous administration into their designs in the hopes of making more definitive statements about causality. However, as we have shown through examples throughout this chapter, nothing is ever simple with hormones. Hormones change molecular structure and can bind to other receptors. When conducting studies on humans, it can be difficult to assess whether or not these pitfalls are occurring. Nonetheless, experimental manipulation provides a degree of explanation that more traditional self-report theorists are unable to include in their work.

As for the future directions of this field, research seems to be headed in an interactionist direction. There are many variables in addition to a specific hormone of interest that can be included in a research design. Studies continue to include multiple hormones, genotypes, situations, and more traditional personality variables. Care should be taken to ensure that these advances include equal attention to both men and women in their models.

REFERENCES

Archer, J. (2006). Testosterone and human aggression: An evaluation of the challenge hypothesis. *Neuroscience and Biobehavioral Reviews*, *30*, 319–345.

Bakermans-Kranenburg, M. J., & van IJzendoorn, M. H. (2013). Sniffing around oxytocin: Review and meta-analyses of trials in healthy and clinical groups with implications for pharmacotherapy. *Translational Psychiatry*, *3*, e258.

Bartz, J. A., Zaki, J., Bolger, N., & Ochsner, K. N. (2011). Social effects of oxytocin in humans: Context and person matter. *Trends in Cognitive Sciences*, *15*, 301–309.

Beaton, E. A., Schmidt, L. A., Ashbaugh, A. R., Santesso, D. L., Antony, M. M., McCabe, R. E., & Schulkin, J. (2006). Low salivary cortisol levels among socially anxious young adults: Preliminary evidence from a selected and a non-selected sample. *Personality and Individual Differences*, *41*, 1217–1228.

Bernhardt, P. C., Dabbs, J. M., Jr., Fielden, J. A., & Lutter, C. D. (1998). Testosterone changes during vicarious experiences of winning and losing among fans at sporting events. *Physiology & Behavior*, *65*, 59–62.

Booth, A., Shelley, G., Mazur, A., Tharp, G., & Kittok, R. (1989). Testosterone, winning and losing in human competition. *Hormones and Behavior*, *23*, 556–571.

Campbell, A. (2008). Attachment, aggression and affiliation: The role of oxytocin in female social behavior. *Biological Psychology*, *77*, 1–10.

Campbell, A. (2010). Oxytocin and human social behavior. *Personality and Social Psychology Review*, *14*, 281–295.

Canli, T. (Ed.). (2006). *Biology of Personality and Individual Differences*. New York: Guilford Press.

Carre, J. M., McCormick, C. M., & Hariri, A. R. (2011). The social neuroendocrinology of human aggression. *Psychoneuroendocrinology*, *36*, 935–944.

Cashdan, E. (1995). Hormones, sex, and status in women. *Hormones and Behavior*, *29*, 354–366.

Cashdan, E. (2003). Hormones and competitive aggression in women. *Aggressive Behavior*, *29*, 107–115.

Chang, W. H., Lee, I. H., Chen, K. C., Chi, M. H., Chiu, N. T., Yao, W. J., & Chen, P. S. (2014). Oxytocin receptor gene rs53576 polymorphism modulates oxytocin-dopamine interaction and neuroticism traits – A SPECT study. *Psychoneuroendocrinology*, *47*, 212–220.

Dabbs, J. M., Frady, R. L., Carr, T. S., & Besch, N. F. (1987). Saliva testosterone and criminal violence in young adult prison inmates. *Psychosomatic Medicine*, *49*, 174–182.

Dabbs, J. M., Jr., Carr, T. S., & Frady, R. L. (1995). Testosterone, crime, and misbehavior among 692 male prison inmates. *Personality and Individual Differences*, *18*, 627–633.

Dabbs, J. M., Jr., & Hargrove, M. F. (1997). Age, testosterone, and behavior among female prison inmates. *Psychosomatic Medicine*, *59*, 477–480.

Davis, M. (1983). The effects of dispositional empathy on emotional reactions and helping: A multidimensional approach. *Journal of Personality*, *70*, 713–726.

De Dreu, C. K. W., Greer, L. L., Van Kleef, G. A., Shalvi, S., & Handgraaf, M. J. J. (2011). Oxytocin promotes human ethnocentrism. *Proceedings of the National Academy of Sciences of the United States of America*, *108*, 1262–1266.

Dickerson, S. S., & Kemeny, M. E. (2004). Acute stressors and cortisol responses: A theoretical integration and synthesis of laboratory research. *Psychological Bulletin*, *130*, 355–391.

Domes, G., Heinrichs, M., Michel, A., Berger, C., & Herpertz, S. C. (2007). Oxytocin improves 'mind-reading' in humans. *Biological Psychiatry*, *61*, 731–733.

Edelstein, R. S., Kean, E. L., & Chopik, W. J. (2012). Women with an avoidant attachment style show attenuated estradiol responses to emotionally intimate stimuli. *Hormones and Behavior*, *61*, 167–175.

Edelstein, R. S., Stanton, S. J., Henderson, M. M., & Sanders, M. R. (2010). Endogenous estradiol levels are associated with attachment avoidance and implicit intimacy motivation. *Hormones and Behavior*, *57*, 230–236.

Edelstein, R. S., Yim, I. S., & Quas, J. A. (2010). Narcissism predicts heightened cortisol reactivity to a psychosocial stressor in men. *Journal of Research in Personality*, *44*, 565–572.

Edwards, D. A., Wetzel, K., & Wyner, D. R. (2006). Intercollegiate soccer: Saliva cortisol and testosterone are elevated during competition, and testosterone is related to status and social connectedness with teammates. *Physiology and Behavior*, *87*, 135–143.

Eisenlohr-Moul, T. A., DeWall, C. N., Girdler, S. S., & Segerstrom, S. C. (2015). Ovarian hormones and borderline personality disorder features: Preliminary evidence for interactive effects of estradiol and progesterone. *Biological Psychology*, *109*, 37–52.

Glick, P., & Fiske, S. T. (2001). An ambivalent alliance: Hostile and benevolent sexism as complementary justifications for gender inequality. *American Psychologist*, *56*(2), 109–118.

Gosling, S. D. (2001). From mice to men: What can we learn about personality from animal research? *Psychological Bulletin*, *127*, 45–86.

Granger, D. A., Schwartz, E. B., Booth, A., & Arentz, M. (1999). Salivary testosterone determination in studies of child health and development. *Hormones and Behavior*, *35*, 18–27.

Granger, D. A., Shirtcliff, E. A., Booth, A., Kivlighan, K. T., & Schwartz, E. B. (2004). The 'trouble' with salivary testosterone. *Psychoneuroendocrinology*, *29*, 1229–1240.

Grant, V. J., & France, J. T. (2001). Dominance and testosterone in women. *Biological Psychology*, *58*, 41–47.

Harris, J. A. (1999). Review and methodological considerations in research on testosterone and aggression. *Aggression and Violent Behavior*, *4*, 273–291.

Heinrichs, M., Baumgartner, T., Kirschbaum, C., & Ehlert, U. (2003). Social support and oxytocin interact to suppress cortisol and subjective responses to psychosocial stress. *Biological Psychiatry*, *54*, 1389–1398.

Hermans, E. J., Putman, P., & van Honk, J. (2006). Testosterone administration reduces empathic behavior: A facial mimicry study. *Psychoneuroendocrinology*, *31*, 859–866.

Josephs, R. A., Sellers, J. G., Newman, M. L., & Mehta, P. H. (2006). The mismatch effect: When testosterone and status are at odds. *Journal of Personality and Social Psychology*, *90*, 993–1013.

Kirschbaum, C., & Hellhammer, D. H. (2000). Salivary cortisol. *Encyclopedia of Stress*, *3*, 379–383.

Kornienko, O., Schaefer, D., Weren, S., Hill, G., & Granger, D. (2015). Cortisol and testosterone associations with social network dynamics. *Psychoneuroendocrinology*, *61*, 75.

Kosfeld, M., Heinrichs, M., Zak, P. J., Fischbacher, U., & Fehr, E. (2005). Oxytocin increases trust in humans. *Nature*, *435*, 673–677.

Koven, N. S., & Max, L. K. (2014). Basal salivary oxytocin level predicts extra- but not intra-personal dimensions of emotional intelligence. *Psychoneuroendocrinology*, *44*, 20–29.

Liening, S. H., Stanton, S. J., Saini, E. K., & Schultheiss, O. C. (2010). Salivary testosterone, cortisol, and progesterone: Two-week stability, interhormone correlations, and effects of time of day, menstrual cycle, and oral contraceptive use on steroid hormone levels. *Physiology and Behavior*, *99*, 8–16.

Määttänen, I., Jokela, M., Hintsa, T., Firtser, S., Kähönen, M., Jula, A., ... & Keltikangas-Järvinen, L. (2013). Testosterone and temperament traits in men: Longitudinal analysis. *Psychoneuroendocrinology*, *38*(10), 2243–2248.

Markey, P. M., & Markey, C. N. (2010). Changes in pornography-seeking behaviors following political elections: An examination of the challenge hypothesis. *Evolution and Human Behavior*, *31*, 442–446.

Mazur, A., & Booth, A. (1998). Testosterone and dominance in men. *Behavioral and Brain Sciences*, *21*, 353–397.

Mazur, A., Booth, A., & Dabbs, J. M., Jr. (1992). Testosterone and chess competition. *Social Psychology Quarterly*, *55*, 70–77.

Mazur, A., & Lamb, T. (1980). Testosterone, status, and mood in human males. *Hormones and Behavior*, *14*, 236–246.

Mehta, P. H. & Josephs, R. A. (2010). Testosterone and cortisol jointly regulate dominance:

Evidence for a dual-hormone hypothesis. *Hormones and Behavior*, *58*, 898–906.

Miller, K. G., Wright, A. G. C., Peterson, L. M., Kamarck, T. W., Anderson, B. A., Kirschbaum, C., & Manuck, S. B. (2016). Trait positive and negative emotionality differentially associate with diurnal cortisol activity. *Psychoneuroendocrinology*, *68*, 177–185.

Nelson, R. J. (2005). *An Introduction to Behavioral Endocrinology* (4th ed.). Sunderland, MA: Sinauer Associates.

Nicolson, N. A. (2008). Measurement of cortisol. In L. J. Luecken & L. C. Gallo (Eds.), *Handbook of Physiological Research Methods in Health Psychology* (pp. 37–74). New York, NY: Sage.

Nigro, M., Monteleone, A. M., Steardo, L., Patriciello, G., Di Maso, V., Cimino, M., & Monteleone, P. (2016). Oxytocin secretion in anorexia nervosa and bulimia nervosa: Investigation of its relationships to temperament personality dimensions. *European Psychiatry*, *33*, S161–S162.

Olff, M., Frijling, J. L., Kubzansky, L. D., Bradley, B., Ellenbogen, M. A., Cardoso, C., & van Zuiden, M. (2013). The role of oxytocin in social bonding, stress regulation and mental health: An update on the moderating effects of context and interindividual differences. *Psychoneuroendocrinology*, *38*(9), 1883–1894.

Oliveira, T., Gouveia, M. J., & Oliveira, R. F. (2009). Testosterone responsiveness to winning and losing experiences in female soccer players. *Psychoneuroendocrinology*, *34*, 1056–1064.

Pfattheicher, S. (2016). Testosterone, cortisol, and the Dark Triad: Narcissism (but not Machiavellianism or psychopathy) is positively related to basal testosterone and cortisol. *Personality and Individual Differences*, *97*, 115–119.

Ponzi, D., Zilioli, S., Mehta, P., Maslov, A., & Watson, N. V. (2016). Social network centrality and hormones: The interaction of testosterone and cortisol. *Psychoneuroendocrinology*, *68*, 6–13.

Pratto, F., Sidanius, J., Stallworth, L. M., & Malle, B. F. (1994). Social dominance orientation: A personality variable predicting social and political attitudes. *Journal of Social and Personality Psychology*, *67*, 741–763.

Pruessner, J. C., Wolf, O. T., Hellhammer, D. H., Buske-Kirschbaum, A., Von Auer, K., Jobst, S., & Kirschbaum, C. (1997). Free cortisol levels after awakening: A reliable biological marker for the assessment of adrenocortical activity. *Life Sciences*, *61*, 2539–2549.

Quirin, M., Pruessner, J. C., & Kuhl, J. (2008). HPA system regulation and adult attachment anxiety: Individual differences in reactive and awakening cortisol. *Psychoneuroendocrinology*, *33*, 581–590.

Rosenblitt, J. C., Soler, H., Johnson, S. E., & Quadagno, D. M. (2001). Sensation seeking and hormones in men and women: Exploring the link. *Hormones and Behavior*, *40*, 396–402.

Rosner, W., Auchus, R. J., Azziz, R., Sluss, P. M., & Raff, H. (2007). Utility, limitations, and pitfalls in measuring testosterone: An endocrine society position statement. *Journal of Clinical Endocrinology and Metabolism*, *92*, 405–413.

Saad, G., & Vongas, J. G. (2009). The effect of conspicuous consumption on men's testosterone levels. *Organizational Behavior and Human Decision Processes*, *110*, 80–92.

Sapolsky, R. M. (2005). The influence of social hierarchy on primate health. *Science*, *308*(5722), 648–652.

Schultheiss, O. C., Campbell, K. L., & McClelland, D. C. (1999). Implicit power motivation moderates men's testosterone responses to imagined and real dominance successes. *Hormones and Behavior*, *36*, 234–241.

Schultheiss, O. C., & Stanton, S. J. (2009). Assessment of salivary hormones. In E. Harmon-Jones & J. S. Beer (Eds.), *Methods in the Neurobiology of Social and Personality Psychology* (pp. 17–44). New York, NY: Guilford.

Schultheiss, O. C., Wirth, M. M., & Stanton, S. J. (2004). Effects of affiliation and power motivation arousal on salivary progesterone and testosterone. *Hormones & Behavior*, *46*, 592–599.

Sellers, J. G., Mehl, M., & Josephs, R. A. (2007). Hormones and personality: Testosterone as a marker of individual differences. *Journal of Research in Personality*, *41*, 126–138.

Shamay-Tsoory, S. G., & Abu-Akel, A. (2015). The social salience hypothesis of oxytocin. *Biological Psychiatry*, *79*, 194–202.

Shirtcliff, E., Granger, D., & Likos, A. (2002). Gender differences in the validity of testosterone measured in saliva by immunoassay. *Hormones and Behavior*, 42, 62–69.

Shirtcliff, E. A., Granger, D. A., Schwartz, E. B., Curran, M. J., Booth, A., & Overman, W. H. (2000). Assessing estradiol in biobehavioral studies using saliva and blood spots: Simple radioimmunoassay protocols, reliability, and comparative validity. *Hormones and Behavior*, 38, 137–147.

Smith, G. D., & Hart, C. (2002). Life-course socioeconomic and behavioral influences on cardiovascular disease mortality: The collaborative study. *American Journal of Public Health*, 92, 1295–1298.

Stallen, M., De Dreu, C. K. W., Shalvi, S., Smidts, A., & Sanfey, A. G. (2012). The herding hormone: Oxytocin stimulates in-group conformity. *Psychological Science*, 23, 1288–1292.

Stanton, S. J., & Edelstein, R. S. (2009). The physiology of women's power motive: Implicit power motivation is positively associated with estradiol levels in women. *Journal of Research in Personality*, 43, 1109–1113.

Stanton, S. J., & Schultheiss, O. C. (2007). Basal and dynamic associations between implicit power motivation and estradiol in women. *Hormones and Behavior*, 52, 571–580.

Stanton, S. J., & Schultheiss, O. C. (2009). The hormonal correlates of implicit power motivation. *Journal of Research in Personality*, 43, 942–949.

Stewart, J., & Seeman, T. (2000). *Salivary Cortisol Measurement*. MacArthur Research Network on SES & Health, Allostatic Load Notebook.

Stone, A. A., Schwartz, J. E., Smyth, J., Kirschbaum, C., Cohen, S., Hellhammer, D., & Grossman, S. (2001). Individual differences in the diurnal cycle of salivary free cortisol: A replication of flattened cycles for some individuals. *Psychoneuroendocrinology*, 26, 295–306.

Suay, F., Salvador, A., González-Bono, E., Sanchis, C., Martinez, M., & Martinez-Sanchis, S. (1999). Effects of competition and its outcome on serum testosterone, cortisol and prolactin. *Psychoneuroendocrinology*, 24, 551–566.

Taylor, S. E., Klein, L. C., Lewis, B. P., Gruenewald, T. L., Gurung, R. A., & Updegraff, J. A. (2000). Biobehavioral responses to stress in females: Tend-and-befriend, not fight-or-flight. *Psychological Review*, 107, 411–429.

Theodoridou, A., Rowe, A. C., Rogers, P. J., & Penton-Voak, I. S. (2011). Oxytocin administration leads to a preference for masculinized male faces. *Psychoneuroendocrinology*, 36, 1257–1260.

Turan, B., Guo, J., Boggiano, M. M., & Bedgood, D. (2014). Dominant, cold, avoidant, and lonely: Basal testosterone as a biological marker for an interpersonal style. *Journal of Research in Personality*, 50, 84–89.

Tyrka, A. R., Mello, A. F., Mello, M. F., Gagne, G. G., Grover, K. E., Anderson, G. M., ... & Carpenter, L. L. (2006). Temperament and hypothalamic–pituitary–adrenal axis function in healthy adults. *Psychoneuroendocrinology*, 31, 1036–1045.

van Honk, J., & Schutter, D. J. (2007). Testosterone reduces conscious detection of signals serving social correction: Implications for antisocial behavior. *Psychological Science*, 18, 663–667.

van Honk, J., Schutter, D. J., Bos, P. A., Kruijt, A., Lentjes, E. G., & Baron-Cohen, S. (2011). Testosterone administration impairs cognitive empathy in women depending on second-to-fourth digit ratio. *Proceedings of the National Academy of Science*, 108, 3448–3452.

van Honk, J., Tuiten, A., Hermans, E., Putnam, P., Koppeschaar, H., Thijssen, J., ... & van Doornen, L. (2001). A single administration of testosterone induces cardiac accelerative responses to angry faces in healthy young women. *Behavioral Neuroscience*, 115, 238–242.

van Honk, J., Tuiten, A., & Verbaten, R. (1999). Correlations among salivary testosterone, mood, and selective attention to threat in humans. *Hormones and Behavior*, 36, 17–24.

van Santen, A., Vreeburg, S. A., Van der Does, A. J. W., Spinhoven, P., Zitman, F. G., & Penninx, B. W. J. H. (2011). Psychological traits and the cortisol awakening response: Results from the Netherlands Study of Depression and Anxiety. *Psychoneuroendocrinology*, 36, 240–248.

Wirth, M. M., & Schultheiss, O. C. (2007). Basal testosterone moderates responses to anger faces in humans. *Physiology and Behavior*, 90, 496–505.

Zak, P. J., Stanton, A. A., & Ahmadi, S. (2007). Oxytocin increases generosity in humans. *PLoS ONE*, *2*, 1–6.

Ziomkiewicz, A., Wichary, S., Bochenek, D., Pawlowski, B., & Jasienska, G. (2012). Temperament and ovarian reproductive hormones in women: Evidence from a study during the entire menstrual cycle. *Hormones and Behavior*, *61*, 535–540.

Zorrilla, E. P., DeRubeis, R. J., & Redei, E. (1995). High self-esteem, hardiness and affective stability are associated with higher basal pituitary–adrenal hormone levels. *Psychoneuroendocrinology*, *20*, 591–601.

Molecular Genetic Studies of Human Temperament

Kostas A. Papageorgiou and
Vijeinika Vipulananthan

In the eighteenth-century book titled *Anthropology from a Pragmatic Point of View*, Immanuel Kant referred to temperament as 'what nature makes of the human being' and character as 'what the person makes of himself' (Kant, 1789/2006, p. 192). As such, Kant perceived temperament as a human trait that has primarily a biological basis. He put forward a typology of temperament that consisted of the dimensions of activity–passivity and emotionality (Kant, 1789/2006; Rothbart, 2012). Since the second half of the twentieth century (if not earlier), a major shift in the study of temperament has occurred, such that research has focused primarily on exploring temperament dimensions rather than postulating typologies (Rothbart, 2012).

This shift toward exploring dimensions of individual differences in temperament raised the question of *'why do individuals differ in temperament?'*. Quantitative genetics research attempted to answer this question by showing that genetic influences account for 20 to 60% of the observed variance in temperament (Saudino and Wang, 2012). Recent advances in the area of molecular genetics allowed the search for the biological underpinnings of variation in dimensions of human temperament; that is, molecular genetics research attempted to identify specific genetic variants that contribute to individual variation in temperament. Taken together, these three distinct but intertwined areas of research aimed to *define* and *accurately measure* dimensions of temperament; to study *why* individuals differ in their temperament; and to *uncover the causes* of individual differences in temperament.

The interested reader is encouraged to consult Zentner and Shiner (2012) for a comprehensive presentation of the most popular definitions of temperament (see, in particular, part 1 of Zentner and Shiner, 2012); methods to assess temperament across development (see, in particular, part 2 of Zentner and Shiner, 2012); and studies on the genetic and environmental contributions to individual variation in temperament (see, in particular, part 3 of Zentner and Shiner, 2012).

This chapter reviews and discusses molecular genetics research that aimed to identify genes influencing temperament across development (birth to 18 years). Exploring the genetic factors that influence temperament is of paramount importance for the field of personality psychology. This is because temperament traits emerge early on in development, forming the building blocks that underlie individual differences in personality traits later in adulthood. As such, investigating the genetic causes of individual variation in temperament pre-adulthood can shed light on uncovering the mechanisms that underlie individual variation in personality traits in adulthood.

Table 2.1 provides a brief description of terms that the reader will find throughout this chapter. It is advised that the reader become familiar with these terms before proceeding to the following sections. The interested reader is encouraged to consult Plomin et al. (2008) and Plomin et al. (2013) for more detailed information regarding these terms.

MOLECULAR GENETICS RESEARCH ON TEMPERAMENT

This section reviews molecular genetics research on temperament. The majority of studies have explored the association between variation in the Dopamine Receptor D4 (DRD4) gene and the Serotonin Transporter Polymorphism (5-HTTLPR) gene with individual variation in temperament. Genes that are involved in the synthesis of dopamine and serotonin have been studied extensively in relation to psychological outcomes. This is because empirical data have demonstrated that the dopaminergic system strongly influences the frontal lobe and basal ganglia and acts as a strong regulator of several aspects of cognition and behavior (Nieoullon, 2002). Furthermore, serotoninergic neurons in mammals form the most extensive axonal arborizations of all neuronal systems and their innervations appear early in development. Converging evidence supports the hypothesis that serotonin is a neurotransmitter that plays a major role in cognition and behavior (Turlejski, 1996).

The studies that explored the association between variation in the DRD4 and 5-HTTLPR genes are presented together in this chapter, followed by studies that explored variation in other genes (other than DRD4 and 5-HTTLPR) with individual differences in temperament. Studies that explored the association between DRD4 and 5-HTTLPR in infancy are presented first, followed by presentation of the studies that investigated the association between DRD4 and 5-HTTLPR in childhood and adolescence. These sections are followed by the presentation of studies that explored the association between other genes and temperament in infancy, childhood, and adolescence, respectively. The studies are presented in chronological order (oldest to newest) within each section. The presentation of the review of the molecular genetics research on infants' temperament only is based on Papageorgiou and Ronald (2013) and Papageorgiou and Ronald (in press). As such, the interested reader is encouraged to also consult Papageorgiou and Ronald (2013, in press) for a review specifically on the genetics of infants' temperament.

All studies – but one – have used the candidate gene design. These studies usually involve typing 5–50 single nucleotide polymorphisms (SNPs) within a gene. The gene can be either a positional candidate that results from a prior linkage study or a functional candidate that is based, for example, on homology with a gene of known function in a model species (Balding, 2006). The candidate gene design involves using regression models to search for an association between a phenotype of interest (outcome variable) and a known candidate gene (the predictor). The gene might be chosen because of its genomic position or because it codes for the synthesis

Table 2.1 Brief description of frequently used terms in genetic research on temperament

Term	Definition	Reference
Allele	'An alternative form of a gene at a locus, for example, A_1 versus A_2'. (p. 411)	Plomin et al., 2008
Candidate gene	'A gene whose function suggests that it might be associated with a trait. For example, dopamine genes are considered as candidate genes for hyperactivity because the drug most commonly used to treat hyperactivity, methylphenidate, acts on the dopamine system'. (p. 412)	Plomin et al., 2008
Chromosome	'A structure that is composed mainly of chromatin, which contains DNA, and resides in the nucleus of cells. Latin for "colored body" because chromosomes stain differently from the rest of the cell'. (p. 412)	Plomin et al., 2008
Dizygotic	'Fraternal, or nonidentical, twins; literally, "two zygotes"'. (p. 413)	Plomin et al., 2008
Gene	'The basic unit of inheritance. A sequence of DNA bases that codes for a particular product. Includes DNA sequences that regulate transcription…'. (p. 414)	Plomin et al., 2008
Gene expression	'Transcription of DNA into mRNA'. (p. 414)	Plomin et al., 2008
Genome-wide association (GWAS)	'An association study that assesses DNA variation throughout the genome'. (p. 415)	Plomin et al., 2008
Genotype	'The genetic constitution of an individual, or the combination of alleles at a particular locus'. (p. 415)	Plomin et al., 2008
Genotype–environment interaction (G × E)	'Genetic sensitivity or susceptibility to environments. In quantitative genetics, genotype–environment interaction is usually limited to statistical interactions, such as genetic effects that differ in different environments'. (p. 415)	Plomin et al., 2008
Heritability	'The proportion of phenotypic differences among individuals that can be attributed to genetic differences in a particular population'. (p. 416)	Plomin et al., 2008
Monozygotic	'Identical twins; literally, "one zygote"'. (p. 418)	Plomin et al., 2008
Nonshared environment	'Environmental influences that do not contribute to resemblance between family members'. (p. 418)	Plomin et al., 2008
Polymorphism	'A locus with two or more alleles. Greek for "multiple forms"'. (p. 418)	Plomin et al., 2008
Shared environment	'Environmental factors responsible for resemblance between family members'.	Plomin et al., 2008
Single nucleotide polymorphism(s) (SNP(s))	'The most common type of DNA polymorphism which involves a mutation in a single nucleotide. SNPs (pronounced "snips") can produce a change in an amino acid sequence…'. (p. 420)	Plomin et al., 2008
Twin study	'Comparing the resemblance of identical and fraternal twins to estimate genetic and environmental components of variance'. (p. 421)	Plomin et al., 2008
Variable number tandem repeats (VNTR)	'A tandem repeat from a single genetic locus in which the number of repeated DNA segments varies from individual to individual and is used for identification purposes (as in DNA fingerprinting)'.	'VNTR'. (n.d.) Merriam-Webster's online dictionary. Retrieved from http://www.merriam-webster.com/medical/VNTR

Note: Please refer to Plomin and colleagues (2013) and Plomin and colleagues (2008) for more detailed information about these terms.

of a protein, which is hypothesized to contribute to the phenotype's causal pathway (Balding, 2006). Only one study has explored the expression (transcription of DNA into mRNA) of candidate genes and whether individual differences in gene expression predict individual variation in temperament traits.

Table 2.2 presents the candidate genes that have been assessed in genetic research on temperament across development. The table includes information on the name of the genes and their location, as well as a brief summary of the function of these genes.

DRD4, 5-HTTLPR, and Infants' Temperament

Ebstein and colleagues (1998) reported that two-week-old infants with the long alleles of the dopamine receptor D4 gene (L-DRD4) variant had higher scores on orientation, motor organization, range, and regulation of state in comparison to infants with the short DRD4 variant (S-DRD4; Ebstein et al., 1998). Moreover, they found that infants homozygous for the short variant (s/s) of the serotonin transporter (5-HTTLPR) gene exhibited significantly lower orientation. No direct effect of the 5-HTTLPR was found on any of the temperamental clusters (Ebstein et al., 1998). The same infants were followed up at two-months of age and carriers of the L-DRD4 variant were reported by their mothers to exhibit lower distress to limitations and to display less negative emotionality in comparison to those with the S-DRD4 variant. Infants who were carrying the s/s 5-HTTLPR variant exhibited the highest scores on distress to limitations and negative emotionality in comparison to both l/s and l/l variants. Infants with the s/s 5-HTTLPR genotype, who were also lacking the L-DRD4, were reported to display higher negative emotionality and to exhibit poorer responses to frustration (Auerbach et al., 1999). A third follow-up of the infant sample described above (Auerbach et al., 1999; Ebstein et al., 1998), reported that infants with the L-DRD4 variant showed less negative emotionality and higher activity level scores at 12-months of age (Auerbach et al., 2001b). Infants with the s/s 5-HTTLPR genotype showed lower scores on the fearful distress composite and significantly longer latency to the first fear expression, but they scored lower on a positive emotionality composite (Auerbach et al., 2001b).

A sample was assessed longitudinally from 4–8 months to 15–16 years (please see section on DRD4, 5-HTTLPR, and temperament in childhood and adolescence for details) on the temperamental parameter of approach-withdrawal, from 3–4 to 15–16 years on anxiety, and from 11–12 years to 15–16 years on depression. No significant associations were reported between the 5-HTTLPR and all of the infants' temperament domains that were assessed in this study (Jorm et al., 2000).

The effect of the L-DRD4 on infants' temperament reported by Auerbach et al. (2001b) has been replicated by a longitudinal study, which found that one-month-olds with the L-DRD4 variant showed significantly lower adaptability in comparison to infants lacking the L-DRD4 variant. This study failed to replicate the results in the same sample at five-months of age (De Luca et al., 2001).

A longitudinal study assessed temperamental characteristics and regulatory problems based on observations of infant behavior and structured parent interview data at age three months. The results showed that individuals with the L-DRD4 variant and classified as having regulatory problems at three-months of age had a higher risk of developing Attention Deficit Hyperactivity Disorder (ADHD) symptoms in childhood. Individuals with either the L-DRD4 variant or with a history of regulatory problems in infancy were not at elevated risk for ADHD (Becker et al., 2010). Finally, a study tested the effect of the DRD4 and 5-HTTLPR on infants' temperament. They found that 12-month-old infants who carried the L-DRD4 variant and the s/s 5-HTTLPR genotype exhibited higher

Table 2.2 Candidate genes that have been associated with temperament across development

Gene and location	Official full name of the gene	Quick look summary of the gene's function
APOE 19 (19q13.32)	Apolipoprotein E	'The protein encoded by this gene is a major apoprotein of the chylomicron… This gene maps to chromosome 19 in a cluster with the related apolipoprotein C1 and C2 genes. Mutations in this gene result in familial dysbetalipoproteinemia, or type III hyperlipoproteinemia (HLP III), in which increased plasma cholesterol and triglycerides are the consequence of impaired clearance of chylomicron and VLDL remnants'. NCBI's article on APOE gene, retrieved from https://www.ncbi.nlm.nih.gov/gene/348
BDNF 11 (11p14.1)	Brain-derived neurotrophic factor	'This gene encodes a member of the nerve growth factor family of proteins. Alternative splicing results in multiple transcript variants, at least one of which encodes a preproprotein that is proteolytically processed to generate the mature protein. Binding of this protein to its cognate receptor promotes neuronal survival in the adult brain. Expression of this gene is reduced in Alzheimer's, Parkinson's, and Huntington's disease patients. This gene may play a role in the regulation of the stress response and in the biology of mood disorders'. NCBI's article on BDNF gene, retrieved from https://www.ncbi.nlm.nih.gov/gene/627
CHRNA4 20 (20q13.2–20q13.3)	Cholinergic receptor, nicotinic alpha 4	'This gene encodes a nicotinic acetylcholine receptor, which belongs to a superfamily of ligand-gated ion channels that play a role in fast signal transmission at synapses…. Mutations in this gene cause nocturnal frontal lobe epilepsy type 1…'. NCBI's article on CHRNA4 gene, retrieved from http://www.ncbi.nlm.nih.gov/sites/entrez?db=gene&cmd=Retrieve&dopt=full_report&list_uids=1137
COMT 22 (22q11.21-q11.23)	Catechol-O-methyltransferase	'Catechol-O-methyltransferase catalyzes the transfer of a methyl group from S-adenosylmethionine to catecholamines, including the neurotransmitters dopamine, epinephrine, and norepinephrine. This O-methylation results in one of the major degradative pathways of the catecholamine transmitters…'. NCBI OMT gene, retrieved from http://www.ncbi.nlm.nih.gov/gene/1312's article on C
CRH 8 (8q13.1)	Corticotropin releasing hormone	'This gene encodes a member of the corticotropin-releasing factor family. The encoded preproprotein is proteolytically processed to generate the mature neuropeptide hormone… Marked reduction in this protein has been observed in association with Alzheimer's disease… In the placenta it is a marker that determines the length of gestation and the timing of parturition and delivery…'. NCBI's article on CRH gene, retrieved from https://www.ncbi.nlm.nih.gov/gene/1392
DAT1 (also known as SLC6A3) 5 (5p15.3)	Dopamine transporter, also known as solute carrier family 6, member 3	'This gene encodes a dopamine transporter which is a member of the sodium- and chloride-dependent neurotransmitter transporter family. The 3' UTR of this gene contains a 40 bp tandem repeat…. Variation in the number of repeats is associated with idiopathic epilepsy, attention-deficit hyperactivity disorder, dependence on alcohol and cocaine, susceptibility to Parkinson disease and protection against nicotine dependence'. NCBI's article on DAT1 gene, retrieved from http://www.ncbi.nlm.nih.gov/sites/entrez?db=gene&cmd=Retrieve&dopt=full_report&list_uids=6531

(Continued)

Table 2.2 Candidate genes that have been associated with temperament across development (continued)

Gene and location	Official full name of the gene	Quick look summary of the gene's function
DRD2 11 (11q22-q23)	Dopamine receptor D2	'This gene encodes the D2 subtype of the dopamine receptor... A missense mutation in this gene causes myoclonus dystonia; other mutations have been associated with schizophrenia...'. NCBI's article on DRD2 gene, retrieved from http://www.ncbi.nlm.nih.gov/sites/entrez?db=gene&cmd=Retrieve&dopt=full_report&list_uids=1813
DRD4 11 (11p15.5)	Dopamine receptor D4	'This gene encodes the D4 subtype of the dopamine receptor. The D4 subtype is a G-protein coupled receptor which inhibits adenylyl cyclase...'. NCBI's article on DRD4 gene, retrieved from http://www.ncbi.nlm.nih.gov/sites/entrez?db=gene&cmd=Retrieve&dopt=full_report&list_uids=1815
5-HTR2C X (Xq23)	Serotonin transporter linked polymorphic region, also known as solute carrier family 6, member 4	'This gene encodes an integral membrane protein that transports the neurotransmitter serotonin from synaptic spaces into presynaptic neurons.... A repeat length polymorphism in the promoter of this gene has been shown to affect the rate of serotonin uptake and may play a role in sudden infant death syndrome, aggressive behavior in Alzheimer disease patients, and depression-susceptibility in people experiencing emotional trauma'. NCBI's article on 5-HTTLPR gene, retrieved from http://www.ncbi.nlm.nih.gov/sites/entrez?db=gene&cmd=Retrieve&dopt=full_report&list_uids=6532
5-HTTLPR (also known as SLC6A4) 17 (17q11.2)	5-Hydroxytryptamine receptor 2C	'This gene encodes a seven-transmembrane G-protein-coupled receptor. The encoded protein responds to signaling through the neurotransmitter serotonin... Abnormalities in RNA editing of this gene have been detected in victims of suicide that suffer from depression. In addition, naturally-occurring variation in the promoter and 5' non-coding and coding regions of this gene may show statistically-significant association with mental illness and behavioral disorders...'. NCBI's article on 5-HTR2C gene, retrieved from https://www.ncbi.nlm.nih.gov/gene/3358
MAOA X (Xp11.4 – p11.3)	Monoamine oxidase A	'This gene encodes monoamine oxidase A, an enzyme that degrades amine neurotransmitters, such as dopamine, norepinephrine, and serotonin.... The gene is adjacent to a related gene on the opposite strand of chromosome X. Mutation in this gene results in monoamine oxidase deficiency, or Brunner syndrome'. NCBI's article on MAOA gene, retrieved from http://www.ncbi.nlm.nih.gov/sites/entrez?db=gene&cmd=Retrieve&dopt=full_report&list_uids=4128
MT-ATP6 Chromosome MT - NC_012920.1 (location is the same for all MT genes below)	Mitochondrially encoded ATP synthase 6	'The MT-ATP6 gene provides information for making a protein that is essential for normal mitochondrial function. Mitochondria are structures within cells that convert the energy from food into a form that cells can use. These cellular structures produce energy through a process called oxidative phosphorylation, which uses oxygen and simple sugars to create adenosine triphosphate (ATP), the cell's main energy source...'. US National Library of Medicine article on MT-ATP6 gene, retrieved from https://ghr.nlm.nih.gov/gene/MT-ATP6#location
MT-ATP8	Mitochondrially encoded ATP synthase 8	Please see section on MT-ATP6 above

(Continued)

Table 2.2 Candidate genes that have been associated with temperament across development (continued)

Gene and location	Official full name of the gene	Quick look summary of the gene's function
MT-CO1	Mitochondrially encoded cytochrome c oxidase I	'Cytochrome c oxidase is the component of the respiratory chain that catalyzes the reduction of oxygen to water. Subunits 1-3 form the functional core of the enzyme complex…'. US National Library of Medicine article on MT-CO1 gene, retrieved from https://ghr.nlm.nih.gov/gene/MT-CO1
MT-CO2	Mitochondrially encoded cytochrome c oxidase II	'Cytochrome c oxidase is the component of the respiratory chain that catalyzes the reduction of oxygen to water. Subunits 1-3 form the functional core of the enzyme complex. Subunit 2 transfers the electrons from cytochrome c via its binuclear copper A center to the bimetallic center of the catalytic subunit 1'. US National Library of Medicine article on MT-CO2 gene, retrieved from https://ghr.nlm.nih.gov/gene/MT-CO2
MT-CO3	Mitochondrially encoded cytochrome c oxidase III	'Subunits I, II and III form the functional core of the enzyme complex' (please also see section on MT-CO1 and MT-CO2 above). US National Library of Medicine article on MT-CO3 gene, retrieved from https://ghr.nlm.nih.gov/gene/MT-CO3
MT-CYB	Mitochondrially encoded cytochrome b	'The MT-CYB gene provides instructions for making a protein called cytochrome b. This protein plays a key role in structures called mitochondria, which convert the energy from food into a form that cells can use. Cytochrome b is one of 11 components of a group of proteins called complex III… Although most DNA is packaged in chromosomes within the nucleus (nuclear DNA), mitochondria also have a small amount of their own DNA, called mitochondrial DNA (mtDNA). This type of DNA contains many genes essential for normal mitochondrial function…'. US National Library of Medicine article on MT-CYB gene, retrieved from https://ghr.nlm.nih.gov/gene/MT-CYB
MT-ND1	Mitochondrially encoded NADH dehydrogenase 1	'The MT-ND1 gene provides instructions for making a protein called NADH dehydrogenase 1. This protein is part of a large enzyme complex known as complex I, which is active in mitochondria…'. US National Library of Medicine article on MT-ND1 gene, retrieved from https://ghr.nlm.nih.gov/gene/MT-ND1
MT-ND2	Mitochondrially encoded NADH dehydrogenase 2	'Core subunit of the mitochondrial membrane respiratory chain NADH dehydrogenase (Complex I) that is believed to belong to the minimal assembly required for catalysis. Complex I functions in the transfer of electrons from NADH to the respiratory chain. The immediate electron acceptor for the enzyme is believed to be ubiquinone'. US National Library of Medicine article on MT-ND2 gene, retrieved from https://ghr.nlm.nih.gov/gene/MT-ND2
MT-ND3	Mitochondrially encoded NADH dehydrogenase 3	'Core subunit of the mitochondrial membrane respiratory chain NADH dehydrogenase (Complex I) that is believed to belong to the minimal assembly required for catalysis. Complex I functions in the transfer of electrons from NADH to the respiratory chain. The immediate electron acceptor for the enzyme is believed to be ubiquinone'. US National Library of Medicine article on MT-ND3 gene, retrieved from https://ghr.nlm.nih.gov/gene/MT-ND3

(Continued)

Table 2.2 Candidate genes that have been associated with temperament across development (continued)

Gene and location	Official full name of the gene	Quick look summary of the gene's function
MT-ND4	Mitochondrially encoded NADH dehydrogenase 4	'The MT-ND4 gene provides instructions for making a protein called NADH dehydrogenase 4. This protein is part of a large enzyme complex known as complex I, which is active in mitochondria...'. US National Library of Medicine article on MT-ND4 gene, retrieved from https://ghr.nlm.nih.gov/gene/MT-ND4
MT-ND4L	Mitochondrially encoded NADH 4L dehydrogenase	'The MT-ND4L gene provides instructions for making a protein called NADH dehydrogenase 4L. This protein is part of a large enzyme complex known as complex I, which is active in mitochondria... Complex I is responsible for the first step in the electron transport process, the transfer of electrons from a molecule called NADH to another molecule called ubiquinone...'. US National Library of Medicine article on MT-ND4L gene, retrieved from https://ghr.nlm.nih.gov/gene/MT-ND4L
MT-ND5	Mitochondrially encoded NADH dehydrogenase 5	'The MT-ND5 gene provides instructions for making a protein called NADH dehydrogenase 5. This protein is part of a large enzyme complex known as complex I, which is active in mitochondria...' (See also sections on MT-ND4 and 4L). US National Library of Medicine article on MT-ND5 gene, retrieved from https://ghr.nlm.nih.gov/gene/MT-ND5
MT-ND6	Mitochondrially encoded NADH dehydrogenase 6	'The MT-ND6 gene provides instructions for making a protein called NADH dehydrogenase 6. This protein is part of a large enzyme complex known as complex I, which is active in mitochondria...' (See also sections on MT-ND4 and 4L). US National Library of Medicine article on MT-ND6 gene, retrieved from https://ghr.nlm.nih.gov/gene/MT-ND6
RGS2 1 (1q31.2)	Regulator of G-protein signaling 2	'Regulator of G protein signaling (RGS) family members are regulatory molecules that act as GTPase activating proteins (GAPs) for G alpha subunits of heterotrimeric G proteins... The protein acts as a mediator of myeloid differentiation and may play a role in leukemogenesis'. NCBI's article on RGS2 gene, retrieved from https://www.ncbi.nlm.nih.gov/gene/5997
SNAP25 20 (20p12–20p11.2)	Synaptosomal-associated protein, 25 KDa	'Synaptic vesicle membrane docking and fusion is mediated by SNAREs (soluble N-ethylmaleimide-sensitive factor attachment protein receptors) located on the vesicle membrane (v-SNAREs) and the target membrane (t-SNAREs).... this gene product is a presynaptic plasma membrane protein involved in the regulation of neurotransmitter release...'. NCBI's article on SNAP25 gene, retrieved from http://www.ncbi.nlm.nih.gov/sites/entrez?db=gene&cmd=Retrieve&dopt=full_report&list_uids=6616

anxiety and were uninterested in interacting with a stranger in the Ainsworth's Strange Situation procedure (Ainsworth et al., 1978). Participants who carried the L-DRD4 variant and the l/l 5-HTTLPR genotype were calmer and interacted smoothly with an unfamiliar person (Lakatos et al., 2003).

Ivorra and colleagues (2010) conducted a systematic review on the molecular genetics of child temperament and analyzed infants' temperament (at eight weeks and 32 weeks after birth) as a function of the interaction between infants' genetic variation in 5-HTTLPR, DRD4 and the Monoamine Oxidase A (MAOA) genes and mothers' emotional state. L-DRD4 and the H- and L-MAOA variable number tandem repeat (VNTR) alleles did not associate with any of the outcome variables. The short alleles of the 5-HTTLPR were associated with irritability in eight- and 32-week-old infants. Infants' irritability was also associated positively at both times with mother's anxiety. A G × E interaction was also found: infants who were carriers of the short alleles of the 5-HTTLPR exhibited irritability that correlated linearly with their mothers' anxiety at eight and 32 weeks. Infants who were carriers of the long alleles of the 5-HTTLPR exhibited lower irritability than infants who were carriers of the short alleles; this effect was independent of their mothers' anxiety (Ivorra et al., 2010). Considering these findings and a review of the previous literature, the authors suggested that carrying the short alleles of the 5-HTTLPR gene is associated with higher scores on several negative temperament traits, such as irritability and shyness (Ivorra et al., 2010).

Another longitudinal study found that the L-DRD4 variant was consistently associated with higher levels of negative affect in four- and nine-month-old infants (Holmboe et al., 2011). In addition, participants carrying both the L-DRD4 variant and the highest expressing l/l 5-HTTLPR genotype displayed the highest level of negative affect (Holmboe et al., 2011).

Finally, Pluess and colleagues (2011) reported that six-month-old infants with the s/s 5-HTTLPR genotype had higher negative emotionality scores (in comparison to those carrying the l/l 5-HTTLPR), but only under the condition that their mothers had reported high anxiety levels during pregnancy (Pluess et al., 2011).

DRD4, 5-HTTLPR, and Temperament in Childhood and Adolescence

Noble and colleagues (1998) explored the association between variation in the DRD4 and DRD2 genes (see section on other genetic variants and temperament in childhood and adolescence for details on the association between DRD2 and temperament) with novelty seeking, harm avoidance, and reward dependence in 12-year-old males. The results showed that males with the L-DRD4 genotype scored higher on novelty seeking in comparison to those without this genotype. The L-DRD4 did not associate significantly with either harm avoidance or reward dependence (Noble et al., 1998).

Jorm and colleagues (2000) assessed longitudinally a sample of 660 individuals from 4–8 months to 15–16 years on the temperamental parameter of approach-withdrawal, from 3–4 to 15–16 years on anxiety, and from 11–12 years to 15–16 years on depression. No significant associations at all ages were reported between the 5-HTTLPR and all of the temperamental domains measured in that study. However, at 13–14 years and 15–16 years, the l/l variant of the 5-HTTLPR was associated with higher anxiety (Jorm et al., 2000).

A study assessed the associations between variation in the DRD4, the 5-HTTLPR, and the serotonin 2C receptor (5-HT2C) genes with four-year-old children's shyness and aggression (Schmidt et al., 2002). Children with the L-DRD4 were reported by their mothers to have significantly higher aggression levels in comparison to children with the S-DRD4. However, no significant difference was observed between L-DRD4 carriers and S-DRD4 carriers on observed behavioral measures of aggression. No significant associations were found between variations in the serotonin genes and any of the temperament traits assessed in this study (Schmidt et al., 2002).

De Luca and colleagues (2003) examined the association between three-year-old children's temperament and the L-DRD4 in an attempt to extend previous research on the association between DRD4 and infants' adaptability (see De Luca et al., 2001). The authors reported that L-DRD4 carriers showed worse response to new stimuli when compared to S-DRD4 carriers. As such, this study failed to replicate the previous association between the L-DRD4 genotype and adaptability (reported in an infants' sample) in children (De Luca et al., 2003).

A study investigated whether variation in the DRD4, 5-HTTLPR, catechol-*O*-methyltransferase (COMT), and MAOA (please refer to the section on other genes and temperament traits in childhood and adolescence for details on the association between COMT and MAOA genes and shyness) explain individual differences in the trait of shyness in seven- to eight-year-old children. No significant association between the L-DRD4 and shyness was found. However, s/s 5-HTTLPR carriers scored significantly lower on shyness as compared to l/l 5-HTTLPR carriers (Arbelle et al., 2003).

Lee and colleagues (2003) explored the role of the L-DRD4 and the -521 C/T genotype – which is a genetic variant in the upstream regulatory region of the DRD4 – in explaining variation in temperament in Korean female adolescents (14-year-old). The study did not find a direct association between both genetic variants and temperament. However, they reported an epistatic effect (the effect of the interaction between two or more genes on a phenotype): participants who had the L-DRD4 and -521 C/T SNP had the highest scores on novelty seeking and persistence in adolescence (Lee et al., 2003).

Battaglia et al. (2005) tested the association between genetic variants and the temperament trait of shyness. The authors explored whether variants in the 5-HTTLPR gene predict variation in children's (nine-year-old) shyness. They also investigated whether Event-Related Potential (ERP) responses (latencies and amplitudes of the N400 waveform) are altered in response to happy, neutral, and angry expressions, as a factor of participants' levels of shyness and their genotype. The results showed that s/s 5-HTTLPR participants had the highest level of shyness in comparison to l/l 5-HTTLPR carriers. Furthermore, carriers of the s/s or s/l 5-HTTLPR genotype exhibited smaller N400 amplitude in response to hostile and neutral facial expressions. The authors suggested that smaller N400 amplitude indicates diminished cortical involvement and emotional processing (Battaglia et al., 2005).

A G × E interaction study tested whether children's 5-HTTLPR genotype interacts with maternal reports of social support to predict inhibited behavior with unfamiliar peers in childhood. Behavioral inhibition and social support were assessed longitudinally at 14 and 84 months. Carriers of the s/s 5-HTTLPR genotype who received low support were at an increased risk for behavioral inhibition at seven-years of age (Fox et al., 2005).

Hayden et al. (2007) also explored the role of the 5-HTTLPR genotype on fearfulness in three- to four-year-old children. This study used a multi-method assessment approach using both maternal report and standardized laboratory observations of children's temperament. The results indicated that l/l or l/s 5-HTTLPR carriers were rated as significantly more nervous during standardized laboratory tasks in comparison to s/s 5-HTTLPR carriers. Furthermore, s/s 5-HTTLPR carriers scored higher on the temperament trait of shyness (Hayden et al., 2007). The results of this study are consistent with the findings reported by Battaglia and colleagues (2005) but they contradict the findings reported by Arbelle and colleagues (2003), adding more mixed findings in genetic research on temperament.

Sheese et al. (2007) investigated the interaction between L-DRD4 genotype and caregiver quality in influencing variation in 18- to 21-month-old children's temperament. L-DRD4 carriers who had received lower quality parenting exhibited higher levels of sensation seeking. The G × E interaction did not influence participants' effortful control. Children without the L-DRD4 were unaffected by quality of parenting. The authors suggested that L-DRD4 increases children's sensitivity to environmental factors; as such, studying the interaction between this genotype and the environment may facilitate the factors that contribute to variation in normal development and psychopathology (Sheese et al., 2007). In a follow-up assessment, the authors reported that parenting quality interacted with the L-DRD4 genotype to predict effortful control in three- to four-year-old children. These results indicate that the executive attention system may play a more important role later in later childhood as compared to its role in infancy and early childhood (Sheese et al., 2009).

Hayden and colleagues (2010c) investigated whether variants in the 5-HTTLPR gene were associated with three-year-old children's negative emotionality and whether this relationship is moderated by positive emotionality. No direct associations between the 5-HTTLPR genotype were found for negative emotionality or positive emotionality. Low positive emotionality moderated the association between the 5-HTTLPR s/s genotype and negative emotionality. Specifically, carriers of the s/l or s/s genotype who exhibited low positive emotionality had the highest levels of negative emotionality. Carriers of the s/l or s/s genotype who exhibited high positive emotionality had the lowest levels of negative emotionality. In contrast, for children homozygous for the L allele, positive emotionality and negative emotionality were not associated with each other (Hayden et al., 2010c).

A longitudinal G × E interaction study investigated the degree to which children's early child-care experiences – quantity, quality, and type – were associated with attention and inhibitory control in four- to five-year-old children. They further explored whether these relations were conditional on the DRD4 genotype (Berry et al., 2013). In line with previous research, the main effects of genotype on attention and inhibition were inconsistent and were influenced by the task used and the age of the sample. Across most outcome measures, L-DRD4 carriers spending fewer hours in child care exhibited more effective attention and inhibitory control. For S-DRD4 carriers, such associations were typically not significant. The results for child-care quality and type indicated no interactions with genotype (Berry et al., 2013).

More recently a G × E longitudinal study investigated whether average sleep duration between 6- and 36-months of age interact with polymorphisms in the 5-HTTLPR gene to predict negative emotionality in three-year-old children (Bouvette-Turcot et al., 2015). The results indicated that for 5-HTTLPR s/s and s/l carriers shorter sleep duration was associated with higher ratings of negative emotionality. The findings suggest that the short allele of the 5-HTTLPR represents a marker of increased environmental sensitivity in relation to emotional development (Bouvette-Turcot et al., 2015).

Other Genetic Variants and Infants' Temperament

Jorm and colleagues (2001; please see section on DRD4, 5-HTTLPR, and infants' temperament for details) tested for an association between the dopamine transporter gene (DAT1) and temperament traits (from 4–8 months to 15–16 years), as well as behavior problems (from 3–4 years to 15–16 years), but failed to report significant associations (Jorm et al., 2001).

Rueda and colleagues (2005) combined assessment of temperament in childhood (four- to six-year-old) and ERPs and examined their association with variants in the DAT1 gene. The long allele (L group) group of children had lower surgency (extraversion) scores and higher effortful control as compared to children carrying the long/short alleles (L/S group). Furthermore the L group of children showed more negative amplitude for incongruent trials (N2 effect in the expected direction) at prefrontal leads in an attentional task, whereas the L/S group showed the reverse pattern of activation (Rueda et al., 2005). This was one of the few studies that linked genes and temperament at both the behavioral level (parental report measures of temperament) and the cognitive level (ERP data). As such, the study stresses the importance of bringing together data from different levels of description (e.g., genetic level, cognitive level, behavioral level) in order to understand the mechanisms that influence individual differences in temperament.

A study explored the interactive effect of TaqIA (A1+, A1−) DRD2 genotype and prenatal tobacco exposure on attention, reactivity, and regulatory behaviors in four-week-old infants (Wiebe et al., 2009). Prenatal tobacco exposure had been assessed during pregnancy, including biochemical verification of self-reported smoking. The results showed that infants with the A1+ DRD2 genotype who had not been exposed to tobacco prenatally were more attentive to stimuli and less irritable in comparison to infants with the A1− DRD2 genotype who had not been exposed to tobacco prenatally. The attention factor and irritability scores were comparable in A1+ and A1− participants among the group of infants who had been exposed to tobacco prenatally. There were neither main nor interactive effects on infants' regulatory behavior.

Sheese et al. (2009) measured temperament longitudinally on the same sample of infants at six- to seven-months and 18-months and tested for associations with the COMT, the cholinergic receptor, nicotinic alpha 4 (CHRNA4), and the synaptosomal-associated protein, 25KDa (SNAP25) genes. They found that infants with the G/A COMT genotype exhibited higher levels of positive affect at six- to seven-months-old, in comparison to infants with the G/G or A/A COMT genotype. No equivalent associations were found at age 18-months. Finally, six-month-old infants with one or two copies of the SNAP25 C allele exhibited lower negative affect as compared to those that were homozygous for the T allele; the same effect was also present at age 18-months.

Ivorra and colleagues (2010) conducted a systematic review on the molecular genetics of child temperament and analyzed infants' temperament (at eight weeks and 32 weeks after birth) as a function of the interaction between infants' genetic variation in 5-HTTLPR, DRD4 and MAOA genes and mothers' emotional state. The H- and L-MAOA VNTR alleles did not associate with any of the outcome variables (for more details please see section on DRD4, 5-HTTLPR, and infants' temperament).

Zhang and colleagues (2011) tested for an association between the MAOA gene and six-month-old infants' self-regulatory behavior. The authors reported that the more active 4/4 genotype was associated with better regulatory behavior, but this effect was present only in girls (Zhang et al., 2011).

A longitudinal genotype–environment (G × E) interaction study examined whether genetic variation in the MAOA gene interacts with environmental factors during pregnancy to predict negative emotionality in a sample of 209 five-week-old infants (Hill et al., 2013). The results revealed that there was a threefold increase in the likelihood of infants to react with fussing or crying if they were carrying the low activity MAOA-LPR and if their mothers were reporting four or more stressful life events during pregnancy. On the contrary, infants with the MAOA-LPR high activity variant and with mothers who were reporting four or more life events during pregnancy were either unaffected or they were exhibiting less negative emotionality (Hill et al., 2013).

Finally, a longitudinal G × E interaction study explored the main effect of MAOA genotype and interactions with maternal sensitivity on infant temperament (Pickles et al., 2013). There were no significant associations between MAOA status and infant temperament at 29 weeks or at 14-months of age. There was a significant interaction between MAOA status and maternal sensitivity at 29-weeks of age. Participants carrying the low expression genotype (MAOA-L carriers versus MAOA-H carriers) and with mothers who were exhibiting low sensitivity showed the highest scores on proneness to anger at 14 months of age (Pickles et al., 2013).

Associations between the COMT gene and seven-month-old infants' temperament have also been tested (Markant et al., 2014). The results indicated that COMT-Val carriers received higher scores on the temperament trait of approach to novelty and behavioral regulation (Markant et al., 2014).

More recently, a novel study explored the expression of 13 protein-coding genes [mitochondrially encoded NADH dehydrogenase 1 (MT-ND1); mitochondrially encoded NADH dehydrogenase 2 (MT-ND2); mitochondrially encoded cytochrome c oxidase I (MT-CO1); mitochondrially encoded cytochrome c oxidase II (MT-CO2); mitochondrially encoded ATP synthase 8 (MT-ATP8); mitochondrially encoded ATP synthase 6 (MT-ATP6); mitochondrially encoded cytochrome c oxidase III (MT-CO3); mitochondrially encoded NADH dehydrogenase 3 (MT-ND3); mitochondrially encoded NADH 4L dehydrogenase (MT-ND4L); mitochondrially encoded NADH dehydrogenase 4 (MT-ND4); mitochondrially encoded NADH dehydrogenase 5 (MT-ND5); mitochondrially encoded NADH dehydrogenase 6 (MT-ND6); mitochondrially encoded cytochrome b (MT-CYB)] encoded by the mitochondria in relation to maternal psychosocial stress in pregnancy and infant temperament (Lambertini et al., 2015). Expression of the MT-ND2, MTND6, and MT-CO2 genes was associated positively with indices of maternal psychosocial stress in pregnancy, such as perceived stress and anxiety during pregnancy. MT-ND2 expression was also associated negatively with the temperament traits of activity and smile and laughter in infancy. These findings indicate that mitochondria-related genes play a significant role in maternal psychosocial stress in pregnancy as well as infant temperament development. This study moved forward from reporting associations between genetic polymorphisms and traits to providing evidence of the mechanisms that underlie individual variation in human temperament (Lambertini et al., 2015).

Other Genetic Variants and Temperament in Childhood and Adolescence

A longitudinal study tested the association between apolipoprotein E (APOE) polymorphism with temperament in a sample of 1,577 children, adolescents, and young adults during a follow-up period of nine years (Keltikangas-Järvinen et al., 1993). APOE has six possible genotypes: E2/2, E3/2, E4/2, E3/3, E4/3, and E4/4.

The study found that APOE genotypes were significantly associated with motor activity at three-, six-, and nine-years. The association between motor activity and APOE was the most evident. Specifically, activity increased as one moved on the APOE classification from E2/2, E3/2, E4/2, E3/3, E4/3, to E4/4. Extreme activity was found in individuals in the APOE genotype groups of E3/4 and E4/4 (Keltikangas-Järvinen et al., 1993). No significant associations were reported between APOE and motor activity at 12-, 15-, and 18-years. No associations between the APOE genotypes and motor activity in childhood were reported in a three-year follow-up study; however, APOE genotypes were significantly associated with sociability, responsivity, and positive emotionality. Furthermore, mental vitality increased with the APOE genotypes in the order of E3/2, E4/2, E3/3, E4/3, E4/4, at 15-, 18-, and 21-years (Keltikangas-Jarvinen et al., 1993). APOE genotypes were significantly associated with aggression–competitiveness (direction of association as reported above) at 18-, 21-, and 24-years in a six-year follow-up study. Finally, APOE genotypes were significantly associated with aggression (direction of association as reported above) at 21-, 24-, and 27-years in a nine-year follow-up study (Keltikangas-Järvinen et al., 1993).

Noble and colleagues (1998) explored the association between variation in the DRD4 (see section above for details) and DRD2 with novelty seeking, harm avoidance, and reward dependence in 12-year-old males. Novelty seeking score was significantly higher in males having, in common, all three minor (A1, B1, and Intron 6) alleles of the DRD2 compared to males without any of these alleles. The greatest difference in novelty seeking was found when males having all three minor DRD2 alleles and the L-DRD4 were contrasted to those without any of these alleles. Neither the DRD2 nor the DRD4 polymorphisms differentiated harm avoidance score. Males having all three minor DRD2 alleles had a significantly higher reward dependence score than subjects without any of these alleles. The authors suggested that, while DRD2 and DRD4 polymorphisms individually associated with novelty seeking behavior, the interaction of DRD2 and DRD4 polymorphisms contributed more strongly (than when these two gene polymorphisms were individually considered) to novelty seeking in male children (Noble et al., 1998).

Jorm and colleagues (2003) attempted to replicate the findings reported by Keltikangas-Järvinen and colleagues (1993) in a sample of 683 Australian children who had participated in a longitudinal study of childhood temperament from four- to eight-months up to 17 to 18 years. Associations were examined between APOE genotype and a range of measures of activity and hyperactivity. The study reported only one significant association (at age 13 to 14 years) out of 29 examined between APOE genotype and a range of activity and hyperactivity measures taken from infancy to adolescence. This number is not more than what it is expected by chance and, as such, this study did not replicate the findings reported by Keltikangas-Järvinen et al. (1993). The authors discussed the possibility of previous findings being a Type-1 error and stressed the importance of replication in genetic research on temperament.

Arbelle et al. (2003) investigated whether variation in the DRD4, 5-HTTLPR, COMT, and MAOA (please refer to the section on DRD4, 5-HTTLPR and temperament traits in childhood and adolescence for further information on the results of this study) genes explain individual differences in the trait of shyness in seven- to eight-year-old children. The study failed to report significant associations between variation in the COMT and MAOA genes and shyness in childhood (Arbelle et al., 2003).

Smoller and colleagues (2005) tested whether genetic variation in the Corticotropin-Releasing Hormone gene (CRH) associates with behavioral inhibition in children at risk for panic disorder. The children were assessed at 21 months, four years, or six years. Three (rs6999100, rs6159, and rs1870393) of the eight SNPs tested were individually associated with behavioral inhibition in childhood. The authors suggested that variation in the CRH gene influences inhibited temperament, a risk factor for panic and phobic anxiety disorders (Smoller et al., 2005).

Smoller et al. (2008) tested whether variation in the gene encoding regulator of G protein signaling 2 (Rgs2) was associated with behavioral inhibition in the same sample of children described above (see Smoller et al., 2005) and with personality and brain function in undergraduate adult students (for detailed description of the findings on adult samples, please see Smoller et al., 2008). Nine of the 15 SNPs tested were associated with behavioral inhibition in children but only three SNPs (rs10801152, rs4606, and rs1819741) returned p-values that were significant after Bonferroni correction. The findings indicated that Rgs2 is associated with anxiety-related temperament traits (behavioral inhibition) as well as adult personality traits and brain function.

Wiebe and colleagues (2009; see also section above on other genes and infants' temperament) also tested the interactive effect of the *Taq1*A polymorphism, related to the DRD2 gene, with prenatal exposure to tobacco on preschool children's executive functions. Similar to the results reported in this study for the infants' sample, children with both the A1+ genotype and a history of prenatal tobacco exposure displayed significantly poorer executive control in comparison to all other groups (Wiebe et al., 2009).

A study examined the association between the DRD2 gene and early-emerging symptoms of depression and anxiety in a sample of preschool children. They also explored whether the A1 allele of the DRD4 gene was associated with child emotional behavior during parent–child interactions and whether this allele was associated with either decreased positive parenting or increased negative parenting (Hayden et al., 2010b). The findings indicated that the DRD2 A1 allele was associated with children's depressive and anxious symptoms, measured using both maternal report and interview methods. Furthermore, child DRD2 genotype was associated with parenting behavior exhibited during laboratory tasks. This finding indicates the possibility of a gene on environment correlation, whereby exposure to environmental conditions is influenced by one's genotype (Hayden et al., 2010b).

Hayden and colleagues (2010a) also tested whether the SNP producing a valine-to-methionine substitution at codon 66 (val66met) of the brain-derived neurotrophic factor (BDNF) gene was associated with preschool children's negative emotionality. Parental depression was also assessed to test for possible gene on environment interactions. The results showed that children homozygous for the val allele exhibited similar and intermediate levels of negative emotionality irrespectively of whether parental depression was present. G × E interactions were observed: children with the met/met or val/met genotype and a depressed parent exhibited the highest levels of negative emotionality, whereas those with nondepressed parents had particularly low levels of negative emotionality (Hayden et al., 2010a).

DISCUSSION AND CONCLUSION

Temperament is a complex trait that emerges early on in development, forming the building blocks that underlie individual differences in personality traits later in life. As such, studying the causes of individual differences in temperament across development could facilitate the identification of some of the factors that contribute to individual differences in personality traits in adulthood. A large number of quantitative genetics studies have shown that 20 to 60% of the variation in temperament is due to genetic factors. These genetic factors (that influence temperament) may vary across age, measures, and situations (Saudino and Wang, 2012). In this chapter, we have reviewed studies that investigated the genetic factors that contribute to individual differences in temperament across development.

It has been almost 25 years since the first study (see Keltikangas-Järvinen et al., 1993) explored specific genetic polymorphisms and their association with temperament. Since that time, more than 35 studies (we identified and reviewed 37 studies in this chapter) have attempted to link genes with temperament traits in infancy, childhood, and adolescence. Some studies used a longitudinal design and/or have explored G × E and G × G interactions in relation to temperament. Despite that, little is currently known regarding the possible association between genes and temperament traits. This is mainly due to the lack of replication in genetic research on temperament. For example, some studies failed to replicate the associations between candidate genes and temperament traits in the same sample assessed longitudinally (for example, see De Luca et al., 2001). Other studies have failed to replicate previously reported associations between the same genetic variants and temperament traits assessed in independent samples (for example, see Arbelle et al., 2003 and Hayden et al., 2007.

Lack of replication in genetic research is not specific to research on temperament. For example, in a review of 600 reported associations with common medical diseases, only six had been consistently replicated (Hirschhorn et al., 2002). The main reason behind these failures to replicate was that the studies were underpowered to detect associations of small effects between genetic variants and traits (Plomin et al., 2013).

Another reason – which is more specific to research on temperament – for these failures to replicate is the lack of a general consensus regarding the definition of temperament and its measures (see Zentner and Shiner, 2012). Indeed, the genetic studies that were reviewed in this chapter have used different models of temperament and, subsequently, different methods to assess temperament traits. As such, lack of replication could be because different measures are tapping into different constructs of temperament.

Considerable progress will need to be made to understand the factors that underlie variation in temperament across development. Future studies could use larger samples to achieve adequate statistical power to detect small effect associations. Newer genetic methods, such as Genome-Wide Association, DNA sequencing and polygenic scores (see Plomin et al., 2013) could also be used to explore the genetics of temperament. Along with increasing the sample size, future studies could attempt to replicate associations between genes and temperament using the same temperament measures and homogeneous (in terms of age) samples. Finally, it was shown that a considerable amount of variation in temperament is due to the environment (Saudino and Wang, 2012). Research on the environmental factors that influence temperament and on their interaction with genetic factors could have considerable theoretical and applied implications in terms of promoting positive temperament traits, the building blocks of adults' personality traits.

REFERENCES

Ainsworth, M., Blehar, M., Wall, S., & Waters, E. (1978). *Patterns of attachment: A psychological study of the strange situation*. Hillsdale, NJ: Lawrence Erlbaum Associates.

Arbelle, S., Benjamin, J., Golin, M., Kremer, I., Belmaker, R. H., & Ebstein, R. P. (2003). Relation of shyness in grade school children to the genotype for the long form of the serotonin transporter promoter region polymorphism. *American Journal of Psychiatry, 160*, 671–676.

Auerbach, J., Geller, V., Lezer, S., Shinwell, E., Belmaker, R. H., Levine, J., & Ebstein, R. (1999). Dopamine D4 receptor (D4DR) and serotonin transporter promoter (5-HTTLPR) polymorphisms in the determination of temperament in 2-month-old infants. *Molecular Psychiatry, 4*, 369–373.

Auerbach, J. G., Faroy, M., Ebstein, R., Kahana, M., & Levine, J. (2001b). The association of the dopamine D4 receptor gene (DRD4) and the serotonin transporter promoter gene (5-HTTLPR) with temperament in 12-month-old infants. *Journal of Child Psychology and Psychiatry, 42*, 777–783.

Balding, D. J. (2006). A tutorial on statistical methods for population association studies. *Nature Reviews Genetics, 7*, 781–791.

Battaglia, M., Ogliari, A., Zanoni, A., Citterio, A., Pozzoli, U., Giorda, R., ... Marino, C. (2005). Influence of the serotonin transporter promoter gene and shyness on children's cerebral responses to facial expressions. *Archives of General Psychiatry, 62*, 85–94.

Becker, K., Blomeyer, D., El-Faddach, M., Esser, G., Schmidt, M. H., Banaschewski, T., & Laucht, M. (2010). From regulatory problems in infancy to attention-deficit/hyperactivity disorder in childhood: A moderating role for the dopamine D4 receptor gene? *Journal of Pediatrics, 156*, 798–803.

Berry, D., McCartney, K., Petrill, S., Deater-Deckard, K., & Blair, C. (2013). Gene–environment interaction between DRD4 7-repeat VNTR and early child-care experiences predicts self-regulation abilities in prekindergarten. *Developmental Psychobiology, 56*, 373–391.

Bouvette-Turcot, A. A., Pluess, M., Bernier, A., Pennestri, M. H., Levitan, R., Sokolowski, M. B., ... Gaudreau, H. (2015). Effects of genotype and sleep on temperament. *Pediatrics, 136,* e914–e921.

De Luca, A., Rizzardi, M., Buccino, A., Alessandroni, R., Salvioli, G. P., Filograsso, N., ... Dallapiccola, B. (2003). Association of dopamine D4 receptor (DRD4) exon III repeat polymorphism with temperament in 3-year-old infants. *Neurogenetics, 4,* 207–212.

De Luca, A., Rizzardi, M., Torrente, I., Alessandroni, R., Salvioli, G. P., Filograsso, N., ... Novelli, G. (2001). Dopamine D4 receptor (DRD4) polymorphism and adaptability trait during infancy: A longitudinal study in 1- to 5-month-old neonates. *Neurogenetics, 3,* 79–82.

Ebstein, R. P., Levine, J., Geller, V., Auerbach, J., Gritsenko, I., & Belmaker, R. H. (1998). Dopamine D4 receptor and serotonin transporter promoter in the determination of neonatal temperament. *Molecular Psychiatry, 3,* 238–246.

Fox, N. A., Nichols, K. E., Henderson, H. A., Rubin, K., Schmidt, L., Hamer, D., ... Pine, D. S. (2005). Evidence for a gene–environment interaction in predicting behavioral inhibition in middle childhood. *Psychological Science, 16,* 921–926.

Hayden, E. P., Dougherty, L. R., Maloney, B., Durbin, C. E., Olino, T. M., Nurnberger, Jr, J. I., ... Klein, D. N. (2007). Temperamental fearfulness in childhood and the serotonin transporter promoter region polymorphism: A multimethod association study. *Psychiatric Genetics, 17,* 135–142.

Hayden, E. P., Klein, D. N., Dougherty, L. R., Olino, T. M., Dyson, M. W., Durbin, C. E., ... Singh, S. M. (2010a). The role of brain-derived neurotrophic factor genotype, parental depression, and relationship discord in predicting early-emerging negative emotionality. *Psychological Science, 21,* 1678–1685.

Hayden, E. P., Klein, D. N., Dougherty, L. R., Olino, T. M., Laptook, R. S., Dyson, M. W., ... Singh, S.M. (2010b). The dopamine D2 receptor gene and depressive and anxious symptoms in childhood: Associations and evidence for gene–environment correlation and gene–environment interaction. *Psychiatric Genetics, 20,* 304–310.

Hayden, E. P., Klein, D. N., Sheikh, H. I., Olino, T. M., Dougherty, L. R., Dyson, M. W., ... Singh, S. M. (2010c). The serotonin transporter promoter polymorphism and childhood positive and negative emotionality. *Emotion, 10,* 696–702.

Hill, J., Breen, G., Quinn, J., Tibu, F., Sharp, H., & Pickles, A. (2013). Evidence for interplay between genes and maternal stress in utero: Monoamine Oxidase A polymorphism moderates effects of life events during pregnancy on infant negative emotionality at 5 weeks. *Genes, Brain and Behavior, 12,* 388–396.

Hirschhorn, J. N., Lohmueller, K., Byrne, E., & Hirschhorn, K. (2002). A comprehensive review of genetic association studies. *Genetics in Medicine, 4,* 45–61.

Holmboe, K., Nemoda, Z., Fearon, R. M., Sasvari-Szekely, M., & Johnson, M. H. (2011). Dopamine D4 receptor and serotonin transporter gene effects on the longitudinal development of infant temperament. *Genes Brain and Behavior, 10,* 513–522.

Ivorra, J. L., Sanjuan, J., Jover, M., Carot, J. M., de Frutos, R., & Molto, M. D. (2010). Gene–environment interaction of child temperament. *Journal of Developmental and Behavioral Pediatrics, 31,* 545–554.

Jorm, A. F., Prior, M., Sanson, A., Smart, D., Zhang, Y., & Easteal, S. (2000). Association of a functional polymorphism of the serotonin transporter gene with anxiety-related temperament and behavior problems in children: A longitudinal study from infancy to the mid-teens. *Molecular Psychiatry, 5,* 542–547.

Jorm, A. F., Prior, M., Sanson, A., Smart, D., Zhang, Y., & Easteal, S. (2001), Association of a polymorphism of the dopamine transporter gene with externalizing behavior problems and associated temperament traits: A longitudinal study from infancy to the mid-teens. *American Journal of Medical Genetics, 105,* 346–350.

Jorm, A., Prior, M., Sanson, A., Smart, D., Zhang, Y., & Easteal, S. (2003). Apolipoprotein E genotype and temperament: A longitudinal study from infancy to the late teens. *Psychosomatic Medicine, 65,* 662–664.

Kant, I. (2006). *Kant: Anthropology from a pragmatic point of view.* Cambridge: Cambridge University Press.

Keltikangas-Järvinen, L., Räikkönen, K., & Lehtimäki, T. (1993). Dependence between apolipoprotein E phenotypes and temperament in children, adolescents, and young adults. *Psychosomatic Medicine, 55,* 155–163.

Lakatos, K., Nemoda, Z., Birkas, E., Ronai, Z., Kovacs, E., Ney, K., ... Gervai, J. (2003). Association of D4 dopamine receptor gene and serotonin transporter promoter polymorphisms with infants' response to novelty. *Molecular Psychiatry, 8,* 90–97.

Lambertini, L., Chen, J., & Nomura, Y. (2015). Mitochondrial gene expression profiles are associated with maternal psychosocial stress in pregnancy and infant temperament. *PLOS ONE, 10,* e0138929.

Lee, H. J., Lee, H. S., Kim, Y. K., Kim, S. H., Kim, L., Lee, M. S., ... Kim, S. (2003). Allelic variants interaction of dopamine receptor D4 polymorphism correlate with personality traits in young Korean female population. *American Journal of Medical Genetics, 118B,* 76–80.

Markant, J., Cicchetti, D., Hetzel, S., & Thomas, K. M. (2014). Relating dopaminergic and cholinergic polymorphisms to spatial attention during infancy. *Developmental Psychology, 50,* 360–369.

NCBI. Pubmed, US Library of Medicine. Retrieved from http://www.ncbi.nlm.nih.gov/pubmed/

NCBI. (2016, October 6). *APOE apolipoprotein E* [Homo sapiens]. Retrieved from https://www.ncbi.nlm.nih.gov/gene/348

NCBI. (2016, October 6). *BDNF brain derived neurotrophic factor* [Homo sapiens]. Retrieved from https://www.ncbi.nlm.nih.gov/gene/627

NCBI. (2012, March 10). *CHRNA4 cholinergic receptor, nicotinic, alpha 4* [Homo sapiens]. Retrieved from http://www.ncbi.nlm.nih.gov/sites/entrez?db=gene&cmd=Retrieve&dopt=full_report&list_uids=1137

NCBI. (2012, March 10). *COMT catechol-O-methyltransferase* [Homo sapiens]. Retrieved from http://www.ncbi.nlm.nih.gov/gene/1312

NCBI. (2016, October 6). *CRH coritcotropin releasing hormone* [Homo sapiens]. Retrieved from https://www.ncbi.nlm.nih.gov/gene/1392

NCBI. (2012, March 10). *DAT1 dopamine transporter* [Homo sapiens]. Retrieved from http://www.ncbi.nlm.nih.gov/sites/entrez?db=gene&cmd=Retrieve&dopt=full_report&list_uids=6531

NCBI. (2012, March 10). *DRD2 dopamine receptor D2* [Homo sapiens]. Retrieved from http://www.ncbi.nlm.nih.gov/sites/entrez?db=gene&cmd=Retrieve&dopt=full_report&list_uids=1813

NCBI. (2012, March 10). *DRD4 dopamine receptor D4* [Homo sapiens]. Retrieved from http://www.ncbi.nlm.nih.gov/sites/entrez?db=gene&cmd=Retrieve&dopt=full_report&list_uids=1815

NCBI. (2016, October 9). *HTR2C 5-hydroxytryptamine receptor 2C* [Homo sapiens]. Retrieved from https://www.ncbi.nlm.nih.gov/gene/3358

NCBI. (2012, March 10). *5-HTTLPR serotonin-transporter-linked polymorphic region* [Homo sapiens]. Retrieved from http://www.ncbi.nlm.nih.gov/sites/entrez?db=gene&cmd=Retrieve&dopt=full_report&list_uids=6532

NCBI. (2012, March 10). *MAOA monoamine oxidase A* [Homo sapiens]. Retrieved from http://www.ncbi.nlm.nih.gov/sites/entrez?db=gene&cmd=Retrieve&dopt=full_report&list_uids=4128

NCBI. (2016, October 6). *RGS2* [Homo sapiens]. Retrieved from https://www.ncbi.nlm.nih.gov/gene/5997

NCBI. (2012, March 10). *SNAP25 synaptosomal-associated protein, 25 kDa* [Homo sapiens]. Retrieved from http://www.ncbi.nlm.nih.gov/sites/entrez?db=gene&cmd=Retrieve&dopt=full_report&list_uids=6616

Nieoullon, A. (2002). Dopamine and the regulation of cognition and attention. *Progress in Neurobiology, 67,* 53–83.

Noble, E. P., Ozkaragoz, T. Z., Ritchie, T. L., Zhang, X., Belin, T. R., & Sparkes, R. S. (1998). D2 and D4 dopamine receptor polymorphisms and personality. *American Journal of Medical Genetics, 81,* 257–267.

Papageorgiou, K. A., & Ronald, A. (2013). 'He who sees things grow from the beginning will have the finest view of them': A systematic review of genetic studies on psychological traits in infancy. *Neuroscience and Biobehavioral Reviews, 37,* 1500–1517.

Papageorgiou, K. A., & Ronald, A. (in press). *The handbook of developmental psychopathology*. Hoboken, NJ: Wiley-Blackwell.

Pickles, A., Hill, J., Breen, G., Quinn, J., Abbott, K., Jones, H., & Sharp, H. (2013). Evidence for interplay between genes and parenting on infant temperament in the first year of life: Monoamine oxidase A polymorphism moderates effects of maternal sensitivity on infant anger proneness. *Journal of Child Psychology and Psychiatry, 54,* 1308–1317.

Plomin, R., DeFries, J. C., Knopik, V. S., & Neiderheiser, J. (2013). *Behavioral genetics.* London: Palgrave Macmillan.

Plomin, R., DeFries, J. C., McClearn, G. E., & McGuffin, P. (2008). *Behavioral genetics* (5th ed.). New York, NY: Worth.

Pluess, M., Velders, F. P., Belsky, J., van IJzendoorn, M. H., Bakermans-Kranenburg, M. J., Jaddoe, V. W., ... Tiemeier, H. W. (2011). Serotonin transporter polymorphism moderates effects of prenatal maternal anxiety on infant negative emotionality. *Biological Psychiatry, 69,* 520–525.

Rothbart, M. K. (2012). Advances in temperament: History, concepts, and measures. In M. Zentner & R. L. Shiner (Eds.), *Handbook of temperament* (pp. 3–20). New York, NY: Guilford Publications.

Rueda, M. R., Rothbart, M. K., McCandliss, B. D., Saccomanno, L., & Posner, M. I. (2005). From the cover: Training, maturation, and genetic influences on the development of executive attention. *Proceedings of the National Academy Of Sciences, 102,* 14931–14936.

Saudino, K. J., & Wang, M. (2012). Quantitative and molecular genetic studies of temperament. In M. Zentner & R. L. Shiner (Eds.), *Handbook of temperament* (pp. 315–346). New York, NY: Guilford Publications.

Schmidt, L. A., Fox, N. A., Rubin, K. H., Hu, S., & Hamer, D. H. (2002). Molecular genetics of shyness and aggression in preschoolers. *Personality and Individual Differences, 33,* 227–238.

Sheese, B. E., Voelker, P., Posner, M. I., & Rothbart, M. K. (2009). Genetic variation influences on the early development of reactive emotions and their regulation by attention. *Cognitive Neuropsychiatry, 14,* 332–355.

Sheese, B. E., Voelker, P., Rothbart, M. K., & Posner, M. I. (2007). Parenting quality interacts with genetic variation in dopamine receptor D4 to influence temperament in early childhood. *Developmental Psychopathololgy, 19,* 1039–1046.

Smoller, J. W., Paulus, M. P., Fagerness, J. A., Purcell, S., Yamaki, L. H., Hirshfeld-Becker, D., ... Stein, M. B. (2008). Influence of RGS2 on anxiety-related temperament, personality, and brain function. *Archives of General Psychiatry, 65,* 298–308.

Smoller, J. W., Yamaki, L. H., Fagerness, J. A., Biederman, J., Racette, S., Laird, N. M., ... Sklar, P. B. (2005). The corticotropin-releasing hormone gene and behavioral inhibition in children at risk for panic disorder. *Biological Psychiatry, 57,* 1485–1492.

Turlejski, K. (1996). Evolutionary ancient roles of serotonin: Long-lasting regulation of activity and development. *Acta neurobiologiae experimentalis, 56,* 619–636.

US National Library of Medicine. (2016, October 18). *MT-ATP6 gene mitochondrially encoded ATP synthase 6.* Retrieved from https://ghr.nlm.nih.gov/gene/MT-ATP6#location

US National Library of Medicine. (2016, October 18). *MT-CO1 gene mitochondrially encoded cytochrome c oxidase I.* Retrieved from https://ghr.nlm.nih.gov/gene/MT-CO1

US National Library of Medicine. (2016, October 18). *MT-CO2 gene mitochondrially encoded cytochrome c oxidase II.* Retrieved from https://ghr.nlm.nih.gov/gene/MT-CO2#

US National Library of Medicine. (2016, October 18). *MT-CO3 gene mitochondrially encoded cytochrome c oxidase III.* Retrieved from https://ghr.nlm.nih.gov/gene/MT-CO3

US National Library of Medicine. (2016, October 18). *MT-CYB gene mitochondrially encoded cytochrome b.* Retrieved from https://ghr.nlm.nih.gov/gene/MT-CYB

US National Library of Medicine. (2016, October 18). *MT-ND1 gene mitochondrially encoded NADH: Ubiquinone oxidoreductase core subunit 1.* Retrieved from https://ghr.nlm.nih.gov/gene/MT-ND1

US National Library of Medicine. (2016, October 18). *MT-ND2 gene mitochondrially encoded NADH dehydrogenase 2.* Retrieved from https://ghr.nlm.nih.gov/gene/MT-ND2

US National Library of Medicine. (2016, October 18). *MT-ND3 gene mitochondrially encoded NADH dehydrogenase 3.* Retrieved from https://ghr.nlm.nih.gov/gene/MT-ND3

US National Library of Medicine. (2016, October 18). *MT-ND4 gene mitochondrially encoded NADH: Ubiquinone oxireductase core subunit 4.* Retrieved from https://ghr.nlm.nih.gov/gene/MT-ND4

US National Library of Medicine. (2016, October 18). *MT-ND4L gene mitochondrially encoded NADH: Ubiquinone oxioreductase core subunit 4L*. Retrieved from https://ghr.nlm.nih.gov/gene/MT-ND4L

US National Library of Medicine. (2016, October 18). *MT-ND5 gene mitochondrially encoded NADH: Ubiquinone oxioreductase core subunit 5*. Retrieved from https://ghr.nlm.nih.gov/gene/MT-ND5

US National Library of Medicine. (2016, October 18). *MT-ND6 gene mitochondrially encoded NADH: Ubiquinone oxioreductase core subunit 6*. Retrieved from https://ghr.nlm.nih.gov/gene/MT-ND6

'VNTR'. (n.d.). *Merriam-Webster's online dictionary*. Retrieved from http://www.merriam-webster.com/medical/VNTR

Wiebe, S. A., Espy, K. A., Stopp, C., Respass, J., Stewart, P., Jameson, T. R., … Huggenvik, J. I. (2009). Gene–environment interactions across development: Exploring DRD2 genotype and prenatal smoking effects on self-regulation. *Developmental Psychology*, *45*, 31–44.

Zentner, M., & Shiner, R. L. (Eds.). (2012). *Handbook of temperament*. New York, NY: Guilford Publications.

Zhang, M., Chen, X., Way, N., Yoshikawa, H., Deng, H., Ke, X., Ye, W., Chen, P., He, C., Chi, X., & Lu, Z. (2011). The association between infants' self-regulatory behavior and MAOA gene polymorphism. *Developmental Science*, *14*, 1059–1065.

Digit Ratio and Personality and Individual Differences

John T. Manning and Bernhard Fink

The current interest in 2D:4D began with Manning et al. (1998) who suggested that 2D:4D was negatively correlated with prenatal testosterone (PT) and positively correlated with prenatal estrogen (PE). In support of this, they reported that 2D:4D was sexually dimorphic (2D:4D males < females), the dimorphism was stable across age groups two years to 25 years and was not affected by puberty, and low 2D:4D (particularly right 2D:4D) was associated with high sperm number. Subsequently, it has become apparent that the sex difference in 2D:4D is determined by the end of the first trimester (Galis et al., 2010; Malas et al., 2006). Digit ratio is, in general, stable in postnatal growth but with a tendency to increase, with right 2D:4D showing the greatest stability (McIntyre et al., 2005; Trivers et al., 2006). Much of the sex difference in 2D:4D resides in the bones of the fingers, giving stability to the trait (Robertson et al., 2008). Sexually dimorphic soft-tissue traits, such as anogenital distance (AGD), are not stable and do not reliably retain the imprint of PT and PE in adults. Thus, postnatal application of sex steroids in neonate mice leaves 2D:4D unchanged but modifies AGD (Zheng and Cohn, 2011; and for sex steroid changes in AGD in adult rats, see Mitchell et al., 2015).

With regard to links between 2D:4D and PT, there is evidence that (1) PT levels correlate negatively with postnatal 2D:4D, (2) there is no strong relationship between 2D:4D and 'baseline' adult sex hormone levels (Hönekopp et al., 2007; Muller et al., 2011), and (3) as a result of the organizational influences of PT, adults with low 2D:4D are sensitive to testosterone (T) and produce high levels of T in aggressive-challenge situations. We now consider the evidence for (1) and (3) in more detail.

2D:4D AND ORGANIZATIONAL EFFECTS OF PT

In humans, children with congenital adrenal hyperplasia (CAH; a syndrome associated with high PT) have lower 2D:4D than controls (Brown et al., 2002; Ciumas et al., 2009; Okten et al., 2002; but see Buck et al., 2003; and for meta-analysis Hönekopp and Watson, 2010), and Klinefelter's men (with XXY sex chromosomes) have low PT and higher 2D:4D than population norms (Chang et al., 2015; Manning et al., 2013; Savic, 2014). In addition, insensitivity to T has been linked to high 2D:4D in adults while variation in 2D:4D is retained – a finding that is consistent with an effect of both PT and PE on 2D:4D (Berenbaum et al., 2009). More directly, PT from amniocentesis is negatively correlated with 2D:4D (Lutchmaya et al., 2004; Ventura et al., 2013), low 2D:4D is associated with high functioning of T-producing prenatal Leydig cells (Mitsui et al., 2015), and maternal T is correlated with fetal 2D:4D (Barona et al., 2015; Ventura et al., 2013).

In rodents, exogenous PT or the blocking of estrogen receptors lowers 2D:4D, whereas administration of PT or blocking androgen receptors increases 2D:4D (Auger et al., 2013; Talarovicová et al., 2009; Zheng and Cohn, 2011). These findings confirm that 2D:4D is fixed in a narrow prenatal window and is linked to the activation of 'skeletogenic' genes by sex steroids. The genes (some 20 in number) have multiple functions, which include the morphogenesis of the skeleton, reproductive organs, and the brain (Zheng and Cohn, 2011).

2D:4D AND ADULT T: PRODUCTION AND SENSITIVITY TO T IN CHALLENGE SITUATIONS

Sensitivity to T, as measured from the CAG repeat region of the androgen receptor gene, has been linked to low 2D:4D in some published studies. However, the number of CAG repeats (CAGn) has no, weak, or inconsistent effects on 2D:4D (see Hönekopp, 2013, for a meta-analysis; and Voracek, 2014, for an alternative view). Furthermore, there are many genetic modifiers of androgen receptor function other than CAGn (Mailhos et al., 2016), and there is evidence for a T feedback, such that high insensitivity (high CAGn) is linked to increased T production (Knickmeyer et al., 2011).

A more direct and reliable method of considering sensitivity to T is to administer the hormone and note whether 2D:4D modulates the behavioral response. It has been reported that 2D:4D powerfully modulates the behavioral effect of exogenous T application on empathy, moral judgments, cooperation, and trust (Buskens et al., 2016; Carré et al., 2015; Chen et al., 2016; Montoya et al., 2013; van Honk et al., 2011, 2012). In addition, T acts together with cortisol (C) to modulate behaviors such as risk taking and aggression, and 2D:4D modulates the effect of C on aggressive behavior (Portnoy et al., 2015).

The link between 2D:4D and sensitivity to T may be further amplified by associations between low 2D:4D and production of T in competition-induced circumstances. Thus, men with low 2D:4D and low right–left 2D:4D produce higher levels of T and higher T:C ratios when challenged with intense exercise and/or aggressive stimuli (Crewther et al., 2015; Kilduff et al., 2013a, 2013b).

So, there is evidence that 2D:4D is a marker for prenatal sex steroids (PT and PE) and for certain consequences and patterns of adult sex steroids (sensitivity to T and production of T under challenge). We use this knowledge to inform our interpretation of the associations between 2D:4D and personality and individual differences.

DIGIT RATIO, AGGRESSION, AND DOMINANCE

Levels of T and T:C and behaviors such as aggression and rule-breaking are sexually dimorphic, with males showing higher concentrations of T and T:C and higher frequency and intensity of externalizing behavior (Liu et al., 2012; Portnoy et al., 2015).

Accordingly, the associations between 2D:4D and externalizing behavior also show sex differences, such that larger effect sizes are found among males than females (e.g., Hönekopp and Watson, 2011). There is evidence that T and C influence such behaviors, with greater intensity of expression associated with high T and low C (Portnoy et al., 2015). It is to be expected that 2D:4D is related to aggression, risky or criminal behavior, and dominance because 2D:4D modulates the action of both T (Buskens et al., 2016; Carré et al., 2015; Chen et al., 2016; Montoya et al., 2013; van Honk et al., 2011, 2012) and C (Portnoy et al., 2015). For example, low C is associated with externalizing behavior but only in low 2D:4D individuals. As expected, this effect is present in males but not females (Portnoy et al., 2015).

AGGRESSION

There are reliable negative relationships between 2D:4D and sports performance, and many of these sports involve aggressive, competitive interactions (Hönekopp and Schuster, 2010; Manning and Taylor, 2001). Therefore, it would seem reasonable to assume that 2D:4D and aggression are reliably negatively associated. However, the effect size of the 2D:4D and aggression relationship has proved difficult to quantify. The first study to report correlations between 2D:4D and aggression found no significant link (Austin et al., 2002). This was followed by others which reported a mix of non-significant and significant correlations, with the latter often found in one sex and not the other. A meta-analysis reported no significant relationship for women ($n = 19$ studies) and a small but significant negative relationship for men ($n = 18$ studies, $r = -.06$; Hönekopp and Watson, 2011). Subsequent large-sample studies have reported male effect sizes of about $r = -.10$ (Butovskaya et al., 2013; Hönekopp, 2011).

Correlations of male 2D:4D associations with aggression are small ($r = -.06$ to $-.10$) and baseline differences in T also do not correlate strongly with between-individual variation in aggression. Rather, it is variation in competition-induced spikes in T characteristic of aggressive-challenge situations that relate strongly to levels of aggression (Carré and Olmstead, 2015). Low 2D:4D (particularly low right–left 2D:4D) individuals tend to (1) produce marked spikes of T on challenge with aggressive stimuli and/or intense exercise (Crewther et al., 2015; Kilduff et al., 2013a, 2013b), (2) be sensitive to high concentrations of T and modulate T-dependent behavior (Buskens et al., 2016; Carré et al., 2015; Montoya et al., 2013; van Honk et al., 2011, 2012), and (3) show significant negative correlations between 2D:4D and aggression in aggressive-challenge conditions but not in non-challenge situations (Kilduff et al., 2013b; Millet and Dewitte, 2007). Therefore, it has been suggested that the 2D:4D and aggression correlation is significant in males when in aggressive-challenge conditions associated with T-spikes (e.g., contact sports; Mailhos et al., 2016) but is weak in contexts other than aggressive challenges (Kilduff et al., 2013b; Manning et al., 2014; Millet and Dewitte, 2007).

RISKY AND CRIMINAL BEHAVIOR

The relationships between 2D:4D and risky/criminal behavior show higher effect sizes than those found for the 2D:4D and aggression relationship. For example, Hoskin and Ellis (2015) reported mean correlations of about $r = -.40$ between 2D:4D and criminality. Schwerdtfeger et al. (2010) reported a correlation of $r = -.36$ between 2D:4D and traffic violations. The relatively high effect sizes do not appear to be the result of small sample size. For example, there were 445 participants in the Hoskin and Ellis (2015) study. In addition, large internet samples of 2D:4D enable us to consider risk avoidance among nations rather than individuals. In the BBC internet data set ($n > 200,000$), Manning and Fink (2011) reported significant correlations for mean male 2D:4D per nation and national values of uncertainty avoidance. It is not clear why risky and criminal behavior shows stronger links to 2D:4D than does aggression. However, it may be possible that large effect sizes for 2D:4D and risky/criminal behavior arise because such behaviors are usually associated with large short-term spikes of T.

DOMINANCE

Patterns of relationships between 2D:4D and dominance are similar to those of 2D:4D and aggression. Low 2D:4D is related to high dominance in some studies (Manning and Fink, 2008) but not in others (Putz et al., 2004). Context again seems to be important as van der Meij et al. (2012) reported that 2D:4D is related to aggressive dominance but not to sociable dominance. Thus, Ryckmans et al. (2015) showed that 2D:4D is negatively related to dominance in men when they had an interaction with a male with dominant facial features. The correlation between 2D:4D was not obtained when the interaction was with a male with submissive or neutral facial characteristics. This pattern again points to a link with short-term T levels.

DIGIT RATIO AND SPATIAL ABILITY

Spatial ability shows one of the most robust sex differences, with men outperforming women. Studies investigating the relationship between 2D:4D and visuospatial ability have produced mixed results. Manning and Taylor (2001) found a negative relationship of 2D:4D with mental rotation ability (MRT) in a sample of 125 men. However, Coolican and Peters (2003) did not find significant relationships of 2D:4D and MRT in a sample of 237 men and 399 women. Poulin et al. (2003) investigated picture recall abilities and spatial ability in a sample of 86 men and 132 women. Women outperformed men in a picture recall task, and higher scoring women had higher 2D:4D, whereas no such relationship was found in men. Sanders et al. (2005) reported three independent studies (total 115 men, 119 women) from Sweden, Hungary, and the UK. Men performed better in the MRT than women, and men's (but not women's) 2D:4D ratio was significantly negatively correlated with MRT in each of the three studies.

Falter et al. (2006) investigated a series of cognitive measures, including mental rotation, targeting, figure disembedding, and perceptual discrimination (34 men and 34 women). Circulating T was measured in addition to 2D:4D. Men outperformed women in MRT, and this difference in performance was not influenced by circulating T. Participants' sex was the exclusive predictor of MRT, whereas 2D:4D predicted targeting and figure disembedding. Chai and Jacobs (2012) tested spatial ability by constructing a computerized (3D) virtual reality (VR) environment. Participants (41 men, 41 women) had to complete a navigation task in two conditions, using directional and positional cues, and MRT was measured. Men outperformed women in MRT. In the virtual navigation task, men exhibited higher accuracy than women in the directional cue conditions, but not in the positional cue conditions, and 2D:4D had a significant effect on performance. Women who were more accurate in their sense of direction had lower 2D:4D, whereas this effect was not found in men. In addition, no significant relationship was found for MRT performance and 2D:4D. The authors concluded that women with low 2D:4D have better orientation abilities in conditions that typically favor men (i.e., when only directional cues are available in a given environment).

Considering the results of these studies together, there is evidence for a negative relationship of 2D:4D with MRT performance.

This relationship is primarily found in men. The impression is one of significant but weak relationships, and some studies were underpowered. In a meta-analysis, Puts et al. (2008) reported a mean effect size of −.068 for males and .0005 for females. However, a limitation of this report was that right 2D:4D only was examined.

The BBC Internet Study is the largest investigation ($n > 250,000$) of associations between self-reported 2D:4D, MRT, and visuospatial performance in a line angle and position test (JLAP-15). Peters et al. (2007) reported MRT data. Men outperformed women and right and left 2D:4D were negatively correlated with performance in both men and women. Collaer et al. (2007) reported JLAP-15 data. Men outperformed women, and in both sexes, better visuospatial performance was associated with lower 2D:4D. These large-sample studies constitute the strongest evidence in support of the hypothesis that 2D:4D shows negative relationships with MRT and JLAP-15 in both men and women, albeit with small effect size.

Little is known of the relationship between 2D:4D, navigation, and MRT when T levels undergo short-lived spikes. However, there is one study (Pintzka et al., 2016) that examined changes in spatial cognition in relation to 2D:4D when a single dose of exogenous T was administered to women (21 participants, 21 controls). The T group had increased activity within the temporal lobe during navigation, improved MRT scores, and their parahippocampal activity interacted significantly with 2D:4D. We need further studies on effect sizes for 2D:4D and spatial ability when conditions favor T-spikes.

DIGIT RATIO AND SYSTEMIZING/ EMPATHIZING

According to the extreme male brain (EMB) theory, PT exposure contributes to sex differences in cognitive styles, such that high levels of PT lead to male-typical cognition and behavior, whereas low levels of PT lead to female-typical cognition and behavior (Baron-Cohen and Hammer, 1997). Thus, PT has an organizing effect on brain development, accounting for part of the variation observed between-sex and within-sex. The EMB theory posits that autism spectrum disorder (ASD) is an extreme form of male-typical cognitive development, with individuals showing high systemizing ability but low empathizing ability. Boys are more likely to be diagnosed with ASD than girls, and amniotic fluid studies suggest that PT contributes to this sex bias. Manning et al. (2001) investigated whether 2D:4D ratio was different in ASD (autism or Asperger Syndrome [AS]) children of 95 families, as compared to sex- and age-matched controls. Children with autism had significantly lower 2D:4D ratios than control children, and lower 2D:4D than children with AS. Moreover, siblings, fathers, and mothers of autistic children showed lower 2D:4D ratios compared to controls. The authors concluded that families with low 2D:4D ratios are at increased risk of autism, possibly because of high levels of PT that amplify the tendency toward developing autism.

A number of studies have been conducted in recent years to examine the relationships between 2D:4D, ASD, and systemizing/empathizing ability (measured by the empathy quotient, EQ, and the systemizing quotient, SQ; Baron-Cohen and Wheelwright, 2004). With regard to SQ and EQ, some studies have reported significant positive correlations between 2D:4D and EQ and/or significant negative correlations with SQ in males and/or females (e.g., Manning et al., 2010), whereas others have reported unsuccessful replications (e.g., Hönekopp, 2012). These mixed findings have stimulated two meta-analytic reviews (Hönekopp, 2012; Teatero and Netley, 2013). Both reviews found substantial relationships between low 2D:4D and ASD, but much weaker support for correlations with systemizing and empathizing. More recently, Barona et al. (2015)

reported that low 2D:4D is correlated with social communication and emotion difficulties in a large community sample of children. However, this relationship was confined to boys with the lowest 10% of 2D:4D ratios. It may be that high PT does represent a risk factor for ASD but that this only applies as a result of a threshold effect.

Future work should explore the relationships between 2D:4D, ASD, and T-spikes. Importantly, the questions that need to be addressed include: do high ASD scores link to low 2D:4D and high T-spikes? Is there a threshold effect for these associations and are they strongly sex-linked?

DIGIT RATIO AND PERSONALITY DIMENSIONS

In a preliminary investigation, Austin et al. (2002) examined relationships between digit ratio and personality. A series of personality measures was collected in two studies. Study one (79 men, 86 women) detected significant negative correlations of right-hand 2D:4D with disinhibition and sensation-seeking in women (but not men). Study two (49 men, 51 women) found a significant positive correlation of left-hand 2D:4D and neuroticism and a negative correlation with psychoticism in the total sample (men and women combined). Fink et al. (2004) measured 2D:4D from 50 men and 70 women and administered the NEO-FFI to test for relationships of 2D:4D with the Big Five Inventory (BFI). Like Austin et al. (2002), they obtained a significant positive correlation of 2D:4D with neuroticism in the total sample, and in women. Sindermann et al. (2016) replicated the positive correlation between 2D:4D and neuroticism in women in samples from China (n = 78) and Germany (n = 370). Luxen and Buunk (2005) reported that right-hand 2D:4D correlated significantly positively with agreeableness in a sample of 44 men and 37 women – a finding in contrast with that of Fink et al. (2004). In expanding previous reports of 2D:4D and sensation-seeking, Fink et al. (2006) reported a significant negative correlation of right- and left-hand 2D:4D with boredom susceptibility and sensation-seeking in men.

The largest study on the BFI in relation to 2D:4D was reported by Lippa (2006). Of the initial sample (n > 2,000 men and women), correlations of 2D:4D with the BFI scores were investigated in heterosexuals (351 men, 707 women). There were significant associations of 2D:4D (mean of left and right hand) with extraversion (negative) and with openness (positive), but no significant sex and personality interaction effects on 2D:4D. In addition, a negative association was detected for agreeableness. It was suggested that, because of the weak associations, studies concerning relationships between 2D:4D and personality should include large samples of men and women to maintain the statistical power required for detecting small effects. Manning and Fink (2011) reported data from the BBC Internet Study on 2D:4D and aggregate personality across nations by considering self-measured 2D and 4D lengths together with previously reported measures of neuroticism and uncertainty avoidance of 23 nations. Significant positive correlations were detected for (national) mean 2D:4D with uncertainty avoidance in men and women, and with neuroticism in men. It was concluded that the positive associations of 2D:4D with neuroticism and uncertainty avoidance may also be found at the individual level.

Shaw (2013) used the HEXACO personality model to examine relationships between 2D:4D and personality (204 men and 201 women). A significant positive relationship was reported for 2D:4D and emotionality which was no longer significant when controlling for the effect of sex. The other HEXACO traits did not show significant relationships with either the right- or left-hand 2D:4D ratio. Finally, Moskowitz et al. (2015) investigated 2D:4D and social behavior (78 men, 77 women) in naturalistic settings by employing the Circumplex Model of interpersonal behavior. Men were found to be more agreeable toward women, and this was especially so for men with low 2D:4D. These men were also less quarrelsome toward women than toward other men. No such effects were detected in women.

Thus, the available studies on 2D:4D and personality dimensions indicate mixed and often weak results. However, there does appear to be a positive relationship between 2D:4D and neuroticism. This may be one personality construct that is influenced by T-spikes. If this is so, we predict that high T-spikes would reduce neuroticism scores and this may then link to low 2D:4D.

CONCLUSIONS

In comparison to sports-related behaviors, the relationships of 2D:4D with personality and individual differences are generally weak. However, it is important to consider the context when studying relationships of 2D:4D and behavior. Relationships of 2D:4D and aggression, for example, have produced mixed results, and meta-analyses have reported significant, but low (negative), correlations of 2D:4D and aggression in men. Meta-analyses may underestimate the relationship of 2D:4D and behavior when they do not take into account the context of the included studies.

With regard to the context, many studies have not considered special circumstances when assessing effect sizes. Most studies assume that individual differences across situations are stable. However, recent findings on 2D:4D relationships with aggression suggest that 2D:4D modulates the action of, and sensitivity to, both T and T:C. It has been suggested that the 2D:4D relationship with aggression is particularly evident in men who are challenged (e.g., in aggressive male–male encounters) because these challenge conditions are associated with short-term peaks of T and T:C, which are not observed in control conditions. Such peaks are sexually dimorphic (males > females). This adds to differences in effect sizes reported for male and female 2D:4D relationships with target traits. Thus, the absence of the specific context in which 2D:4D and aggression relationships have been studied might be one of the reasons for ambiguous findings.

The problem of investigating 2D:4D relationships with behavior is not limited to the study of aggression, but extends to many more traits. Short-term peaks in T, C, and T:C can be stimulated by aggressive stimuli and/or strenuous exercise which mimics male–male conflict, and characteristically these events are more intense in men than women (Crewther et al., 2015; Kilduff et al., 2013a, 2013b; Manning et al., 2014; Millet and Dewitte, 2007). Exposure to such stimuli may change the effect sizes associated with 2D:4D and traits such as aggression, criminality, dominance, visuospatial perception, empathy, and systemizing. Other traits, such as the Big Five personality constructs, may be more resistant to the effects of T-spikes (but show lower effect sizes). However, in general, any behavioral trait that shows sexual dimorphism may be influenced by acute changes in T, C, and T:C and may be linked to 2D:4D.

Finally, we encourage the use of an experimental approach as distinct from an approach that relies on correlations and requires large numbers of participants. Manipulating variables and predicting their effects through, for example, the administration of exogenous T or challenging participants with aggressive stimuli is a powerful approach to understanding 2D:4D relationships. Recent research has revealed that such paradigms are especially important in the investigation of 2D:4D and behavioral measures, as effects become more evident (Kilduff et al., 2013a, 2013b; Manning et al., 2014). Part of the problem with mixed results from previous 2D:4D studies results from the absence of such experimental conditions. Therefore, we recommend that future investigations into 2D:4D and its relationships with behavior emphasize the specificity of the context in order to provide meaningful conclusions about possible organizational effects of T and E on personality and individual differences.

REFERENCES

Auger, J., Le Denmat, D., Berges, R., Doridot, L., Salmon, B., Canivenc-Lavier, M. C., & Eustache, F. (2013). Environmental levels of oestrogenic and antiandrogenic compounds feminize digit ratios in male rats and their unexposed male progeny. *Proceedings of the Royal Society of London, Series B*, *280*, 20131532.

Austin, E. J., Manning, J. T., McInroy, K., & Mathews, E. (2002). A preliminary investigation of the associations between personality, cognitive ability and digit ratio. *Personality and Individual Differences*, *33*, 1115–1124.

Baron-Cohen, S., & Hammer, J. (1997). Parents of children with Asperger syndrome: what is the cognitive phenotype? *Journal of Cognitive Neuroscience*, *9*, 548–554.

Baron-Cohen, S., & Wheelwright, S. (2004). The Empathy Quotient: an investigation of adults with Asperger syndrome or high functioning autism, and normal sex differences. *Journal of Autism and Developmental Disorders*, *34*, 163–175.

Barona, M., Kothari, R., Skuse, D., & Micali, N. (2015). Social communication and emotion difficulties and second to fourth digit ratio in a large community-based sample. *Molecular Autism*, *6*, 68.

Berenbaum, S. A., Bryk, K. K., Nowak, N., Quigley, C. A., & Moffat, S. (2009). Fingers as a marker of prenatal androgen exposure. *Endocrinology*, *150*, 5119–5124.

Brown, W. M., Hines, M., Fane, B. A., & Breedlove, S. M. (2002). Masculinized finger length patterns in human males and females with congenital adrenal hyperplasia. *Hormones and Behavior*, *42*, 380–386.

Buck, J. J., Williams, R. M., Hughes, I. A., & Acerini, C. L. (2003). In-utero androgen exposure and 2nd to 4th digit length ratio-comparisons between healthy controls and females with classical congenital adrenal hyperplasia. *Human Reproduction*, *18*, 976–979.

Buskens, V., Raub, W., van Miltenburg, N., Montoya, E. R., & van Honk, J. (2016). Testosterone administration moderates effect of social environment on trust in women depending on second-to-fourth digit ratio. *Scientific Reports*, *6*, 27655.

Butovskaya, M., Fedenok, J., Burkova, V., & Manning, J. (2013). Sex differences in 2D:4D and aggression in children and adolescents from five regions of Russia. *American Journal of Physical Anthropology*, *152*, 130–139.

Carré, J. M., & Olmstead, N. A. (2015). Social neuroendocrinology of human aggression: examining the role of competition-induced testosterone dynamics. *Neuroscience*, *286*, 171–186.

Carré, J. M., Ortiz, T. L., Labine, B., Moreau, B. J., Viding, E., Neumann, C. S., & Goldfarb, B. (2015). Digit ratio (2D:4D) and psychopathic traits moderate the effect of exogenous testosterone on socio-cognitive processes in men. *Psychoneuroendocrinology*, *62*, 319–326.

Chai, X. J., & Jacobs, L. F. (2012). Digit ratio predicts sense of direction in women. *PLOS ONE*, *7*, e32816.

Chang, S., Skakkebæk, A., Trolle, C., Bojesen, A., Hertz, J. M., Cohen, A., Hougaard, D. M., Wallentin, M., Pedersen. A. D., Østergaard, J. R., & Gravholt, C. H. (2015). Anthropometry in Klinefelter syndrome – multifactorial influences due to CAG length, testosterone treatment and possible intrauterine hypogonadism. *Journal of Clinical Endocrinology & Metabolism*, *100*, E508–E517.

Chen, C., Decety, J., Huang, P. C., Chen, C. Y., & Cheng, Y. (2016). Testosterone administration in females modulates moral judgement and patterns of brain activation and functional connectivity. *Human Brain Mapping*, *37*, 3417–3430.

Ciumas, C., Linden Hirschberg, A., & Savic, I. (2009). High fetal testosterone and sexually dimorphic cerebral networks in females. *Cerebral Cortex*, *19*, 1167–1174.

Collaer, M. C., Reimers, S., & Manning, J. T. (2007). Visuospatial performance on an internet line judgement task and potential hormonal markers: sex, sexual orientation, and 2D:4D. *Archives of Sexual Behavior*, *36*, 177–192.

Coolican, J., & Peters, M. (2003). Sexual dimorphism in the 2D/4D ratio and its relation to mental rotation performance. *Evolution and Human Behavior*, *24*, 179–183.

Crewther, B., Cook, C., Kilduff, L., & Manning, J. (2015). Digit ratio (2D:4D) and salivary testosterone, oestradiol and cortisol levels under challenge: evidence for prenatal effects on adult endocrine responses. *Early Human Development*, *91*, 451–456.

Falter, C., Arroyo, M., & Davis, G. (2006). Testosterone: activation or organization of spatial cognition? *Biological Psychology*, *73*, 132–140.

Fink, B., Manning, J. T., & Neave, N. (2004). Second to fourth digit ratio and the 'big five' personality factors. *Personality and Individual Differences*, *37*, 495–503.

Fink, B., Neave, N., Laughton, K., & Manning J. T. (2006). Second to fourth digit ratio and sensation seeking. *Personality and Individual Differences*, *41*, 1253–1262.

Galis, F., Ten Broek, C. M., Van Dongen, S., & Wijnaendts, L. C. (2010). Sexual dimorphism in the prenatal digit ratio (2D:4D). *Archives of Sexual Behavior*, *39*, 57–62.

Hönekopp, J. (2011). Relationships between digit ratio 2D:4D and self-reported aggression and risk taking in an online study. *Personality and Individual Differences*, *51*, 77–80.

Hönekopp, J. (2012). Digit ratio 2D:4D in relation to autism spectrum disorders, empathizing, and systemizing: a quantitative review. *Autism Research*, *5*, 221–230.

Hönekopp, J. (2013). No evidence that 2D:4D is related to the number of CAG repeats in the androgen receptor gene. *Frontiers in Endocrinology*, *4*, 185.

Hönekopp, J., Bartholdt, L., Beier, L., & Liebert, A. (2007). Second to fourth digit length ratio (2D:4D) and adult sex hormone levels: new data and a meta-analytic review. *Psychoneuroendocrinology*, *32*, 313–321.

Hönekopp, J., & Schuster, M. (2010). A meta-analysis on 2D:4D and athletic prowess: substantial relationships but neither hand out-predicts the other. *Personality and Individual Differences*, *48*, 4–10.

Hönekopp, J., & Watson, S. (2010). Meta-analysis of digit ratio 2D:4D shows greater sex difference in the right hand. *American Journal of Human Biology*, *22*, 619–630.

Hönekopp, J., & Watson S. (2011). Meta-analysis of the relationship between digit ratio 2D:4D and aggression. *Personality and Individual Differences*, *51*, 381–386.

Hoskin, A. W., & Ellis, L. (2015). Fetal testosterone and criminality: test of evolutionary neuroandrogenic theory. *Criminology*, *53*, 54–73.

Kilduff, L., Cook, C. J., Bennett, M., Crewther, B., Bracken, R. M., & Manning, J. (2013a). Right-left digit ratio (2D:4D) predicts free testosterone levels associated with a physical challenge. *Journal of Sports Sciences*, *31*, 677–683.

Kilduff, L. P., Hopp, R. N., Cook, C. J., Crewther, B. T., & Manning, J. T. (2013b). Digit ratio (2D:4D), aggression, and testosterone in men exposed to an aggressive visual stimulus. *Evolutionary Psychology*, *11*, 953–964.

Knickmeyer, R. C., Woolson, S., Hamer, R. M., Konneker, T., & Gilmore, J. H. (2011). 2D:4D ratios in the first 2 years of life: stability and relation to testosterone exposure and sensitivity. *Hormones and Behavior*, *60*, 256–263.

Lippa, R. A. (2006). Finger lengths, 2D:4D ratios, and their relation to gender-related personality traits and the Big Five. *Biological Psychology*, *71*, 116–121.

Liu, J., Portnoy, J., & Raine, A. (2012). Association between a marker for prenatal testosterone exposure and externalizing behavior problems in children. *Development and Psychopathology*, *24*, 771–782.

Lutchmaya, S., Baron-Cohen, S., Raggatt, P., Knickmeyer, R., & Manning, J. T. (2004). 2nd to 4th digit ratios, fetal testosterone and estradiol. *Early Human Development*, *77*, 23–28.

Luxen, M. F., & Buunk, B. P. (2005). Second-to-fourth digit ratio related to verbal and numerical intelligence and the big five. *Personality and Individual Differences*, *39*, 959–966.

Mailhos, A., Buunk, A. P., Arca, D. D., & Tutte, V. (2016) Soccer players awarded one or more red cards exhibit lower 2D:4D ratios. *Aggressive Behavior*, *42*, 417–426.

Malas, M. A., Dogan, S., Evcil, E. H., & Desdicioglu, K. (2006) Fetal development of the hand, digits and digit ratio (2D:4D). *Early Human Development*, *82*, 469–475.

Manning, J. T., Baron-Cohen, S., Wheelwright, S., & Fink, B. (2010). Is digit ratio (2D:4D) related to systemizing and empathizing? Evidence from direct finger measurements reported in the BBC Internet Survey. *Personality and Individual Differences*, *48*, 767–771.

Manning, J. T., Baron-Cohen, S., Wheelwright, S., & Sanders, G. (2001). The 2nd to 4th digit ratio and autism. *Developmental Medicine & Child Neurology*, 43, 160–164.

Manning, J. T., & Fink, B. (2008). Digit ratio (2D:4D), dominance, reproductive success, asymmetry, and sociosexuality in the BBC Internet Study. *American Journal of Human Biology*, 20, 451–461.

Manning, J. T., & Fink, B. (2011). Digit ratio (2D:4D) and aggregate personality scores across nations: data from the BBC Internet Study. *Personality and Individual Differences*, 51, 387–391.

Manning, J., Kilduff, L., Cook, C., Crewther, B., & Fink, B. (2014). Digit ratio (2D:4D): a biomarker for prenatal sex steroids and adult sex steroids in challenge situations. *Frontiers in Endocrinology*, 5, 9.

Manning, J. T., Kilduff, L. P., & Trivers, R. (2013). Digit ratio (2D:4D) in Klinefelter's syndrome. *Andrology*, 1, 94–99.

Manning, J. T., Scutt, D., Wilson, J., & Lewis-Jones, D. I. (1998). The ratio of 2nd to 4th digit length: a predictor of sperm numbers and concentrations of testosterone, luteinizing hormone and oestrogen. *Human Reproduction*, 13, 3000–3004.

Manning, J. T., & Taylor, R. P. (2001). Second to fourth digit ratio and male ability in sport: implications for sexual selection in humans. *Evolution and Human Behavior*, 22, 61–69.

McIntyre, M. H., Ellison, P. T., Lieberman, D. E., Demerath, E., & Towne, B. (2005). The development of sex differences in digital formula from infancy in the Fels Longitudinal Study. *Proceedings of the Royal Society of London, Series B*, 272, 1473–1479.

Millet, K., & Dewitte, S. (2007). Digit ratio (2D:4D) moderates the impact of an aggressive music video on aggression. *Personality and Individual Differences*, 43, 289–294.

Mitchell, R. T., Mungall, W., McKinell, C., Sharpe, R. M., Cruickshanks, L., Milne, L., & Smith, L. B. (2015). Anogenital distance plasticity in adulthood: implications for its use as a biomarker of fetal androgen action. *Endocrinology*, 156, 24–31.

Mitsui, T., Araki, A., Imai, A., Sato, S., Miyashita, C., Ito, S., Sasaki, S., Kitta, T., Moriya, K., Cho, K., Morioka, K., Kishi, R., & Nonmura, K. (2015). Effects of prenatal Leydig cell function on the ratio of the second to fourth digit lengths in school-aged children. *PLOS ONE*, 10, e0120636.

Montoya, E. R., Terburg, D., Bos, P. A., Will, G. J., Buskens, V., Raub, W., & van Honk, J. (2013). Testosterone administration modulates moral judgements depending on second-to-fourth digit ratio. *Psychoneuroendocrinology*, 38, 1362–1369.

Moskowitz, D. S., Sutton, R., Zuroff, D. C., & Young, S. N. (2015). Fetal exposure to androgens, as indicated by digit ratios (2D:4D), increases men's agreeableness with women. *Personality and Individual Differences*, 75, 97–101.

Muller, D. C., Giles, G. G., Bassett, J., Morris, H. A., Manning, J. T., Hopper, J. L., English, D. R., & Severi, G. (2011). Second to fourth digit ratio (2D:4D) and concentrations of circulating sex hormones in adulthood. *Reproductive Biology and Endocrinology*, 9, 57.

Okten, A., Kalyoncu, M., & Yaris, N. (2002). The ratio of second- and fourth-digit lengths and congenital adrenal hyperplasia due to 21-hydroxylase deficiency. *Early Human Development*, 70, 47–54.

Peters, M., Manning, J. T., & Reimers, S. (2007). The effects of sex, sexual orientation, and digit ratio (2D:4D) on mental rotation performance. *Archives of Sexual Behavior*, 36, 251–260.

Pintzka, C. W. S., Evensmoen, H. R., Lehn, H., & Haberg, A. K. (2016). Changes in spatial cognition and brain activity after a single dose of testosterone in healthy women. *Behavioral Brain Research*, 298, 78–90.

Portnoy, J., Raine, A., Glenn, A. L., Chen, F. R., Choy, O., & Granger, D. A. (2015). Digit ratio (2D:4D) moderates the relationship between cortisol reactivity and self-reported externalizing behaviour in young adolescent males. *Biological Psychology*, 112, 94–106.

Poulin, M., O'Connell, R., & Freeman, L. M. (2003). Picture recall skills correlate with 2D:4D ratio in women but not men. *Evolution and Human Behavior*, 25, 174–181.

Puts, D. A., McDaniel, M. A., Jordan, C. L., & Breedlove, S. M. (2008). Spatial ability and prenatal androgens: meta-analyses of congenital adrenal hyperplasia and digit ratio (2D:4D) studies. *Archives of Sexual Behavior*, 37, 100–111.

Putz, D. A., Gaulin, S. J., Sporter, R. J., & McBurney, D. H. (2004). Sex hormones and finger length: what does 2D:4D indicate? *Evolution and Human Behavior, 25*, 182–199.

Robertson, J., Zhang, W., Liu, J. J., Muir, K. R., Maciewicz, R. A., & Doherty, M. (2008). Radiographic assessment of the index to ring finger ratio (2D:4D) in adults. *Journal of Anatomy, 212*, 42–48.

Ryckmans, J., Millet, K., & Warlop, L. (2015). The influence of facial characteristics on the relation between male 2D:4D and dominance. *PLOS ONE, 10*, e0143307.

Sanders, G., Bereczkei, T., Csathó, A., & Manning, J. T. (2005). The ratio of the 2nd to 4th finger length predicts spatial ability in men but not women. *Cortex, 41*, 789–795.

Savic, I. (2014). Asymmetry of cerebral gray and white matter and structural volumes in relation to sex hormones and chromosomes. *Frontiers in Neuroscience, 8*, 329.

Schwerdtfeger, A., Heims, R., & Heer, J. (2010). Digit ratio (2D:4D) is associated with traffic violations for male frequent car drivers. *Accident Analysis and Prevention, 42*, 269–274.

Shaw, Z. A. (2013). The effect of prenatal androgen exposure on the development of neural reactivity systems: a study of the HEXACO Personality Inventory. *Personality and Individual Differences, 55*, 19–23.

Sindermann, C., Li, M., Saryska, R., Lachmann, B., Duke, E., Cooper, A., Warneck, L., & Montag, C. (2016). The 2D:4D-ratio and neuroticism revisited: empirical evidence from Germany and China. *Frontiers in Psychology, 7*, 811.

Talarovicová, A., Krsková, L., & Blazeková, J. (2009). Testosterone enhancement during pregnancy influences the 2D:4D ratio and open field motor activity of rat siblings in adulthood. *Hormones and Behavior, 55*, 235–239.

Teatero, M. L., & Netley, C. (2013). A critical review of the research on the extreme male brain theory and digit ratio (2D:4D). *Journal of Autism and Developmental Disorders, 43*, 2664–2676.

Trivers, R., Manning, J. T., & Jacobson, A. (2006). A longitudinal study of digit ratio (2D:4D) and other finger ratios in Jamaican children. *Hormones and Behavior, 49*, 150–156.

van der Meij, L., Almela, M., Buunk, A. P., Dubbs, S., & Salvador, A. (2012). 2D:4D in men is related to aggressive dominance but not to sociable dominance. *Aggressive Behavior, 38*, 208–212.

van Honk, J., Montoya, E. R., Bos, P. A., van Vugt, M., & Terburg, D. (2012). New evidence on testosterone and cooperation. *Nature, 485*, E4–E5.

van Honk, J., Schutter, D. J., Bos, P. A., Kruijt, A-W., Lentjes, E. G., & Baron-Cohen, S. (2011). Testosterone administration impairs cognitive empathy in women depending on second-to-fourth digit ratio. *Proceedings of the National Academy of Sciences of the United States of America, 108*, 3448–3452.

Ventura, T., Gomes, M. C., Pita, A., Neto, M. T., & Taylor, A. (2013). Digit ratio (2D:4D) in newborns: influences of prenatal testosterone and maternal environment. *Early Human Development, 89*, 107–112.

Voracek, M. (2014). No effects of androgen receptor gene CAG and GGC repeat polymorphisms or digit ratio (2D:4D): a comprehensive meta-analysis and critical evaluation of research. *Evolution and Human Behavior, 35*, 430–437.

Zheng, Z., & Cohn, M. J. (2011). Developmental basis of sexually dimorphic digit ratios. *Proceedings of the National Academy of Sciences of the United States of America, 108*, 16289–16294.

Morningness–Eveningness and Sociosexuality from a Life History Perspective

James Marvel-Coen, Coltan Scrivner and Dario Maestripieri

MORNINGNESS–EVENINGNESS

Basic Aspects of Morningness–Eveningness

Many human biological processes are regulated by circadian rhythms, sometimes referred to as 'internal clocks'. These circadian rhythms apply to hormone concentrations, brain activity, heart rate, and body temperature. In humans and many other animals, a 'master clock' is attuned to a 24-hour cycle, and corresponds to sleep and wakefulness. The master clock in humans operates through the action of the suprachiasmatic nucleus (SCN) in the hypothalamus (Herzog et al., 1998). Although our circadian rhythms have been selected based on a general pattern of light and dark, environmental factors can influence circadian rhythms, and rhythms can vary between people.

Morningness–eveningness – or chronotype – refers to the notion that individuals vary from one another in preferences for the timing of waking up and falling asleep, as well as for diurnal peaks in activity and performance, such that some individuals tend to be more active, both cognitively and physiologically, in the morning, whereas others tend to be more active in the evening (Randler et al., 2016). Variation in morningness–eveningness tends to occur along a continuum, and the individuals at the two extremes of this continuum are often denoted as morning-types and evening-types, or 'early birds' and 'night owls'. Research has shown that approximately 40% of individuals are either morning- or evening-types, with the other 60% falling into a more neutral category (Adan et al., 2012). Propensities for being a morning- or an evening-type are significantly heritable (e.g., Hur, 2007; Hur et al., 1998; Vink et al., 2001) but age, sex, and environment are important as well.

Children are typically morning-oriented but evening orientation tends to increase in both males and females throughout adolescence (Randler, 2011; Roenneberg et al., 2004). Sex differences in morningness–eveninness also begin to appear in adolescence, with more males being represented in the evening-type category than females (Randler, 2007). However, these sex differences disappear after women reach menopause, suggesting that they may be functionally linked to reproduction and be regulated by reproductive physiology, at least in women (Adan et al., 2012). Early experience and environment can influence variation in morningness–eveningness. For example, individuals who spend their first few months of life in a short photoperiod (i.e., autumn and winter) tend to be morning-types, whereas those who spend their first few months in a long photoperiod (i.e., spring and summer) tend to be evening-types (Mongrain et al., 2006; Natale and Di Milia, 2011). Latitude has also been shown to have a strong effect on chronotype, with people at northern latitudes having significantly later midpoints of sleep (Natale et al., 2009). This effect is moderated by residency type, however, with larger towns being less affected by latitude (Borisenkov et al., 2012). Thus, it is probable that sunlight, and potentially artificial light as well, plays a role in the development and shaping of chronotype. However, this effect is not entirely clear, as evening-types tend to have been exposed to more sunlight post-birth, but less during life.

Measuring Morningness–Eveningness

Measurement methods for chronotype were first developed in the late 1970s. These methods include the Morningness–Eveningness Questionnaire (MEQ; Horne and Östberg, 1976), the Circadian Type Questionnaire (CTQ; Folkard et al., 1979), and the Diurnal Type Scale (DTS; Torsvall and Åkerstedt, 1980). The MEQ remains the most cited and most used technique today for assessing chronotype. It is a fairly reliable technique, with ~0.8 reliability coefficient across countries and ~0.9 across time for an individual (Adan et al., 2012). The MEQ uses 19 multiple-choice questions to generate a composite number that falls on a spectrum of eveningness (low) to morningness (high). However, the MEQ is somewhat lengthy, and some items provide little discriminatory power. This led to the creation of the reduced MEQ (rMEQ; Adan and Almirall, 1991), which contains only five items.

One of the newest measures of chronotype is the Munich Chronotype Questionnaire (MCTQ; Roenneberg et al., 2003). The MCTQ determines chronotype by midpoint of sleep calculated on days off. It has been validated by the use of sleep logs, physiological parameters, and correlation with MEQ results (Roenneberg et al., 2003). The focus on midpoint of sleep and sleep on days off sets the MCTQ apart from its predecessors by collecting supplementary information in the questionnaire that may be useful for future comparisons.

Many biological markers, including temperature, cortisol, melatonin, and certain genetic variants, are associated with chronotype and are often used to assess measurement technique reliability. Morning-types have been shown to have a body temperature circadian phase that occurs about two hours earlier than the evening-types (Baehr et al., 2000; Kerkhof and Van Dongen, 1996). Morning-types also show stronger cortisol awakening responses (CAR) than evening-types (Griefahn and Robens, 2008; Randler and Schaal, 2010). Correspondingly, melatonin rhythms in morning-types occur about three hours earlier than in evening-types (Gibertini et al., 1999; Griefahn et al., 2002; Mongrain et al., 2004). Furthermore, it has been suggested that melatonin is the best marker for the circadian master clock (Arendt, 2006). In addition to circadian rhythms of temperature, cortisol, and melatonin, some genetic variants are associated with chronotype. Polymorphisms in certain genes, including CLOCK, PER1, and PER3, have been shown to correlate with chronotype (Adan et al., 2012) but these associations are not well understood.

Psychological and Behavioral Correlates of Morningness–Eveningness

Associations between morningness–eveningness and personality traits have been documented by a number of studies. Early studies used the Eysenck Personality Questionnaire (e.g., Matthews, 1988), whereas the Big Five Model has been used in more recent studies concerning chronotype (e.g., Tonetti et al., 2009). This model recognizes five main dimensions of personality: agreeableness, extraversion, conscientiousness, neuroticism, and openness (Costa and McCrae, 1992). Several other personality models have also been used to assess the relationship between chronotype and personality, including the Alternative Five-Factor Model, Temperament and Character Inventory, and the Milton Index of Personality Styles.

In general, it has been found that morning-types are more conscientious (Tsaousis, 2010), agreeable (DeYoung et al., 2007; Hogben et al., 2007; Randler, 2008), proactive (Randler, 2009), optimistic, and resilient (Antúnez et al., 2015). Evening-types tend to be more unconventional (Vollmer and Randler, 2012); more impulsive (Adan et al., 2010; Selvi et al., 2011); more into sensation-seeking (Muro et al., 2011), novelty-seeking (Adan et al., 2010; Caci et al., 2004; Randler and Saliger, 2011), and risk-taking (Killgore, 2007; Maestripieri, 2014; Ponzi et al., 2014; Wang and Chartrand, 2015); display greater openness to experience, extraversion, lower agreeableness, lower conscientiousness (Randler, 2008; Randler et al., 2014; Tsaousis, 2010), and lower self-control (Digdon and Howell, 2008); are more emotionally unstable and prone to depression (Hidalgo et al., 2009; Randler, 2008; Selvi et al., 2011), and have higher levels of Dark Triad traits (i.e., narcissism, Machiavellianism, and psychopathy; Jonason et al., 2013).

It has been suggested that evening-types suffer from 'social jetlag', in that they frequently experience a mismatch between their preferred timing of diurnal activity and the demands of their environment (e.g., having to get up early for school or work; Wittmann et al., 2006). Social jetlag in evening-types may be associated with drowsiness, headaches, and difficulty in concentration, as well as low HDL cholesterol, greater insulin resistance, and greater adiposity (Wong et al., 2015). These side effects may be due in part to – or are exacerbated by – attempts at coping with social jetlag, such as increased intake of sugary and caffeinated drinks (Foster, 2013). Morning-types may have an advantage in school due to social demands lining up with their chronotype. For example, if exams are taken in the morning, then morning-types may perform better than evening-types (Randler and Frech, 2006; see also Borisenkov et al., 2010). Indeed, there is evidence that eveningness is generally associated with overall worse performance in school (see Tonetti et al., 2015, for a review). However, several lines of evidence indicate that eveningness is associated with higher performance on a number of different cognitive tasks. Roberts and Kyllonen (1999) showed that evening-types have greater working memory than morning-types, even when the tasks were performed in the morning. Although the effect size was small ($r = 0.08$), Preckel et al. (2011) found in a meta-analysis that evening-types had significantly higher cognitive abilities than morning-types. Moreover, Piffer et al. (2014) found that evening-types had significantly greater GMAT scores (an admission test for Business Schools) than morning-types in both male and female business graduate students. Kanazawa and Perina (2009) have also shown that evening-types tend to have greater verbal intelligence than morning-types. In all of these studies, the effects are not due to differences in hours of sleep (this variable is usually controlled for in the analyses) but to chronotype itself. The reason why evening-types exhibit greater cognitive function remains unclear but Preckel et al. (2011) have suggested that evening-types may have developed greater problem-solving skills as a result of living in a social world that is out of sync with their chronotype.

In addition to differences in personality profiles and cognitive function, there are a host of behavioral differences between morning- and evening-types. In general, evening-types engage in unhealthy or addictive behavior more often than morning-types, including increased smoking, drinking, and physical inactivity (Schaal et al., 2010; Urbán et al., 2011; Wittmann et al., 2010). Other differences in behavior are associated with evening-types' tendencies to engage in novelty-seeking, sensation-seeking, or risk-taking. In general, evening-types are generally found to be more unconventional whereas morning-types tend to be more traditional and conservative.

Until recently (Kanazawa and Perina, 2009; Piffer, 2010), investigations of the psychological, cognitive, and behavioral correlates of morningness and eveningness did not include any functional considerations concerning the possible adaptive value of these traits. New information about differences in sociosexuality associated with morningness and eveningness, however, has led to the formulation of specific functional hypotheses concerning these traits, as well as to some speculation about their possible evolutionary history. In this chapter, we argue that the functional/evolutionary significance of variation in chronotype is best understood if this trait is framed within evolutionary life history theory (LHT) and in relation to differences in sociosexuality between slow and fast life history individuals. In the next sections of this chapter, we illustrate some fundamental concepts in LHT, examine how LHT predicts interindividual variation in sociosexuality, and then review and discuss recent studies of morningness–eveningness and sociosexuality from an evolutionary perspective.

LIFE HISTORY THEORY AND SOCIOSEXUALITY

Fundamental Concepts of Life History Theory

LHT provides an evolutionary framework that examines how organisms allocate resources to activities that are relevant to their growth, survival, and reproduction in ways that maximize their fitness and based on their own characteristics and those of their environment (Del Giudice et al., 2015; Roff, 2002). One fundamental assumption of LHT is that organisms cannot capture and expend unlimited resources; therefore, investments of time and energy into one process or activity mean that investment into other processes must be reduced. Organisms that allocate resources in ways that maximize their fitness will out-compete those who allocate resources less optimally.

Individuals have two main paths to increasing fitness: investing in traits that improve survivorship and investing in traits that improve reproduction. Traits that enhance some aspects of fitness typically also have costs for other aspects of fitness, so that many traits have opposite effects on survival and reproduction, on present and future reproduction or survival, or on personal survival and reproduction and that of related individuals. However, a trade-off between two traits does not necessarily imply they must be negatively correlated because individuals with better genes or more resources can invest more in both processes than those with worse genes or fewer resources (Reznick et al., 2000). These trade-offs appear at all life stages and are relevant to a wide range of traits. The main fundamental life history trade-offs are those between growth/survival and reproduction, between current and future reproduction, between mating and parenting, and between quantity and quality of offspring (Del Giudice et al., 2015; Roff, 2002).

Allocation decisions made in relation to different trade-offs can be collectively referred to as life history strategies. Life history strategies are composed of combinations of co-adapted morphological, physiological, and behavioral traits (Flatt and Heyland, 2011). Demographic traits are also important, particularly age at maturity, age-specific fertility, and age-specific survival (Roff, 2002). Variation in life history strategies can occur at the level of species as well as at the level of individuals of the same species. In both cases, life history strategies may be broadly grouped on a fast–slow continuum. Models of *r*–K selection divided species into those with early maturation, early reproduction, fast growth, short lifespan, high fertility, high quantity of offspring, and little investment in offspring quality (*r*-selected, or fast life history) and those with slow growth, late maturation, low fertility, and an emphasis on offspring quality rather than quantity (K-selected, or slow life history; Pianka, 1970).

Life history strategies vary as a function of age-specific rates of extrinsic mortality or extrinsic morbidity–mortality, including unavoidable causes of disability and decay that limit reproductive capacity (Del Giudice et al., 2015; Ellis et al., 2009). The degree of unpredictable environmental variation and the overall availability of resources are also relevant variables for determining optimal allocation trade-offs. For example, high extrinsic mortality in adulthood selects for typically fast life history traits, particularly early maturation, reproduction, and senescence, and concentration of reproductive effort in a short window of time, whereas high extrinsic mortality in juveniles also selects for early maturation but spreads reproductive effort over a longer window of time (Kirkwood and Rose, 1991). Similarly, variability in rates of adult mortality select for quick maturation and a concentration of reproductive effort, whereas stable adult mortality conditions but unstable pre-reproductive conditions select for iteroparity (Murphy, 1968). More generally, high extrinsic mortality in juveniles and adults reduces the relative payoff of investment in embodied capital (Kaplan, 1996).

Sexual selection may alter the fundamental life history trade-offs experienced by males and females. As a result of these differences, males and females may pursue divergent life history strategies (Kruger and Nesse, 2006; Magwere et al., 2004). Patterns of sexual selection within a species may have profound effects on differences between sexes in vital demographic traits, including time of maturation, timing of reproductive effort, and senescence. Characteristics of the environment can account for variation in life history strategies both between and within sexes. Populations in highly variable environments may evolve a generalist strategy that performs adequately in a wide range of circumstances, or generate stochastic variation in life history strategy among offspring to increase phenotypic diversity and the likelihood that at least some offspring have optimal strategies for the environment (Ellis et al., 2009; Starrfelt and Kokko, 2012). In situations where the environment provides predictive cues, there may be selection for plasticity in life history traits, such that perception of specific cues triggers changes in traits relevant to life history (Stearns and Koella, 1986). These processes may thus produce variation in life history strategy at the individual level as well as at the population level (Belsky et al., 1991). Individual variation may also arise through genotypic factors, whether through variation in average level of a trait or degree of plasticity (Del Giudice et al., 2015).

Life History Theory and Interindividual Variation in Sociosexuality

In human research, sociosexuality refers to an individual's willingness to engage in sexual relations without closeness or commitment (Gangestad and Simpson, 1990; Jackson and Kirkpatrick, 2007). Interindividual variation in sociosexuality is typically measured in terms of restricted or unrestricted sociosexual behavior or attitudes (and, in some cases, also desires). Restricted sociosexuality typically includes monogamous sexual and relationship orientation, low number of sexual partners, and low levels of sexual activity, whereas unrestricted sociosexuality includes promiscuous sexual relationships, high number of sexual partners, and high levels of sexual activity (Gangestad and Simpson, 1990; Jackson and Kirkpatrick, 2007). Such variation in sociosexuality is relevant to differences in mating strategies; more unrestricted sociosexuality would be beneficial for a more short-term mating strategy that emphasizes many uncommitted matings and limited parental investment (Gangestad and Simpson, 2000).

Although uncommitted and committed mating strategies have been conceptualized as opposite ends of a continuum (Gangestad and Simpson, 1990; Simpson and Gangestad, 1991), research suggests that individuals are flexible enough to simultaneously pursue short- and long-term strategies to different degrees (Buss and Schmitt, 1993; Fisher, 1998; Havlicek et al., 2005; Jackson and Kirkpatrick, 2007; Webster and Bryan, 2007). Furthermore, the relationship between sociosexual preferences and behavior is often confounded by environmental differences in opportunities for short- or long-term mating (Bailey et al., 1994). Therefore, it makes sense to consider committed and uncommitted sociosexuality, and sociosexual preferences and behaviors, on different scales (Jackson and Kirkpatrick, 2007). Jackson and Kirkpatrick (2007) propose three subscales of sociosexuality: long-term mating, short-term mating, and previous sexual behavior.

LHT provides a powerful tool for considering the adaptive value of variation in sociosexuality (Belsky et al., 1991; Del Giudice, 2009). As sociosexuality measures preferences and behaviors related to short- and long-term mating strategies, it is inherently linked to life history trade-offs between mating and parenting activity. Thus, it is possible to use LHT to make predictions about connections between sociosexuality and life history traits. Sociosexuality might also be relevant to divergence in life history strategy between sexes, as there are different costs and benefits to short-term and long-term mating strategies for males and females. Finally, sociosexuality appears to be connected to the concept of embodied capital; self-perceived mate value, which is connected to physical condition, is related to psychological and behavioral orientation toward short-term mating among men and to previous sexual behavior among women (Jackson and Kirkpatrick, 2007).

Physical traits relevant to life history (e.g., birth weight) are also linked with sociosexuality. For example, lower birth weight typically corresponds to traits typical of faster life history strategies such that individuals with lower birth weight have a greater propensity toward short-term mating on average (Frederick, 2012). Sociosexuality also appears to be linked to endocrine function, as cortisol and testosterone concentrations and reactivity may mediate links between individuals' stable characteristics, their environment, and their sociosexuality (Puts et al., 2015; Wilson et al., 2015). In fact, the endocrine system provides a means of coordinating responses to the environment across a wide range of systems, from psychology to immunity to reproduction (Del Giudice et al., 2015). Finally, a number of personality traits are linked to sociosexuality across diverse cultures (Holtzman and Strube, 2013; Schmitt, 2008). In the rest of this chapter, we present and illustrate the hypothesis that differences in sociosexuality between morning- and evening-types may represent the expression of slow and fast life history strategies, respectively (Ponzi et al., 2015a). We begin by illustrating some possible scenarios for the evolution of morningness–eveningness in the human lineage.

MORNINGNESS–EVENINGNESS, LIFE HISTORY, AND SOCIOSEXUALITY

The Evolution of Eveningness as a Sexually Selected Trait

Since humans evolved from diurnal primate ancestors, morningness was probably the ancestral evolutionary condition for our species. Thus, hypotheses concerning the evolution of chronotype should mainly address the evolution of eveningness, under the assumption that this trait evolved relatively recently in the human lineage. Piffer (2010) was the first to propose a hypothetical scenario for the evolution of eveningness in which this trait is specifically linked to sociosexuality and mating-related fitness benefits (see Kanazawa and Perina, 2009, for a different evolutionary hypothesis, focusing on eveningness-related intelligence). In this scenario, increased safety from predation and other ecological dangers during early human evolution may have increased opportunities to engage in social and mating activities in the late evening hours, when adults are less burdened by work or child-rearing. Individuals – both male and female – with a new genetic predisposition for eveningness presumably benefited more from these new social and mating opportunities, particularly if these individuals were not permanently pair-bonded, or if they were pair-bonded but engaged in extra-pair mating. In this scenario, evening-type males had a higher reproductive success than morning-type males, thus a genetic predisposition for eveningness gradually became more and more prevalent in the male population (morning-type males, however, continued to reproduce successfully, e.g., in the context of long-term pair-bonds with faithful morning-type females). Finally, since eveningness increased the fitness of men more than the fitness of women, eveningness became a sexually dimorphic trait, being more prevalent in men than in women (see Maestripieri, 2014; Putilov, 2014, for further elaboration of this hypothesis).

Piffer (2010) also speculated that eveningness may be a sexually selected indicator of genotypic and phenotypic quality, which includes good sleep and good health (see also Putilov, 2014; Randler et al., 2012b). The basis for this speculation lies in the fact that evening-types are at odds with the social schedule, and thus experience energetically negative effects. It has also been suggested that eveningness is an honest signal since mating and social activities often occur in the evening, when evening-types are at their peak performance. Of course, it is also possible that it is a mixture of a handicap and honest signal. In either case, it seems likely that eveningness evolved somewhat recently in response to more modern social schedules (Jankowski et al., 2014a).

Based on his hypotheses, Piffer (2010) predicted that evening-type men would report a higher number of mating partners than morning-type men. Consistent with these predictions, Piffer et al. (2011) reported that evening-type Italian men had significantly more sexual partners than morning-type men. Gunawardane et al. (2011) then analyzed chronotype and number of sexual partners in Sri Lanka and Italy and found that, in both instances, evening-type men reported significantly more sexual partners than morning-type men. In a follow-up study, Randler et al. (2012b) found that, in male German students, eveningness was associated with higher mating success (defined as a greater number of sexual partners in the lifespan, sexual partners mated with others, and extra-pair sexual partners during committed relationships), even when controlling for age, extraversion, and propensity for staying out late.

Morningness and Eveningness as Life History Traits

Piffer's (2010) evolutionary hypothesis was later re-framed in terms of LHT by Ponzi et al. (2015a). In this view, the behavioral and personality differences between morning- and evening-types are expressions of different life history strategies: slow life history strategies for morning-types and fast life history strategies for evening-types. Consistent with this hypothesis, morningness–eveningness assessed with the rMEQ was found to be correlated with a composite measure of life history, the mini-K (Figueredo et al., 2005), so that morning-types tended to show a slower life history than evening-types (Ponzi et al., 2015a). Furthermore, in the same study, evening-types scored higher on the present fatalism subscale of the Zimbardo

Time Perspective Inventory (ZTPI), whereas morning-types scored higher on the future orientation subscale of the ZTPI. Therefore, consistent with a life history perspective, evening-types are more present-oriented whereas morning-types are more future-oriented. In another study involving Polish students, morningness was positively correlated with the past-negative and present-fatalisms subscores of the ZTPI, whereas eveningness was positively correlated with the past-positive dimension (Stolarski et al., 2013). It has also been reported that morning-types scored lower on the Deviation from Balanced Time Perspective (DBTP) scale, so that they tended to have a more balanced, or closer to 'optimal', time perspective across scales (Stolarski et al., 2011, 2013). Associations between chronotype and ZTPI subscales, as well as between chronotype and the Delayed Gratification Inventory (DGI), were also found in samples of New Zealand students and Germans of various ages (Milfont and Schwarzenthal, 2014). The effects of morningness–eveningness on future orientation and DGI were mediated by self-control, as morning-types have greater self-control and impulse inhibition than evening-types (Milfont and Schwarzenthal, 2014). Further support for links between chronotype and time perspective comes from samples with larger age ranges (Díaz-Morales et al., 2008; Nowack and van der Meer, 2013). However, there is some evidence that relationships between time perspective and chronotype may shift with age and interact with sex. In a sample of Germans of various ages, morningness was associated with future time perspective among men of all ages and women under 30, but there was no such relationship among women over 30 (Nowack and van der Meer, 2013). Since present- verus future-orientation is a key difference between fast and slow life history strategies, the reported associations between time perspective and chronotype are consistent with the hypothesis that variation in chronotype reflects variation in life history.

Morningness–Eveningness and Sociosexuality

The most important prediction of the hypothesis that morningness and eveningness are life history traits is that they should be associated with differences in sociosexuality that are characteristic of slow and fast life history strategies, respectively. Therefore, morning- and evening-types should exhibit restricted and unrestricted sociosexuality, respectively.

Some recent studies have provided evidence in support of this hypothesis. Jankowski et al. (2014b) examined the relationship between morningness–eveningness and three aspects of sociosexuality (sexual behavior, attitude, and desire) in male and female Polish adults. They reported that, when age was controlled for, greater eveningness was related to less restricted sociosexuality, particularly to greater acceptance of casual sex (attitude). Analysis of partial correlations done separately for females and males showed, however, that greater eveningness was related to less restricted orientation and its three facets only in females, whereas in males no relationship was found between eveningness and sociosexuality. In a related paper, Jankowski et al. (2014a) reported that chronotype had some influence on the timing for desire for sex, such that while all males and females desired sex in the evening, morning-type women were more similar to men in desiring sex also in the morning, while all evening-types desired sex later in the evening than morning-types. In a follow-up study with German students, Randler et al. (2016) reported that eveningness was associated with more unrestricted sociosexuality (both attitudes and desire, but not behavior) in both men and women.

Ponzi et al. (2015a) investigated sociosexuality in US male college students and hypothesized that time perspective may be the psychological mechanism underlying the link between chronotype and sociosexuality. Specifically, they predicted that morning-types are more long-term mating-oriented and more sociosexually restricted because they are more future-oriented, whereas evening-types are more short-term mating-oriented and less sociosexually restricted because they are more present-oriented. Ponzi et al. (2015a) reported that rMEQ scores were negatively correlated with short-term mating orientation, indicating that evening-types are oriented toward short-term mating. A mediation analysis revealed that time perspective was a significant mediator of the association between chronotype and sociosexuality: the future orientation of morning-types was associated with their long-term mating orientation and relatively low sexual experience, whereas the present orientation of evening-types was associated with their short-term mating orientation and greater sexual experience. The finding that morning-types tend to be future-oriented whereas evening-types are more present-oriented was also replicated by Marvel-Coen et al. (in press). Finally, Ponzi et al. (2015b) reported that evening-type men are more competitive with other men in the context of mate competition than morning-type men are.

Although the best evidence that evening-types, especially males, pursue fast life history strategies is provided by measures of their unrestricted sociosexuality or mating competitiveness, evidence that morning-types follow slow life history strategies can be provided by aspects of their social behavior that are not necessarily linked to their sexuality or mating strategies. This evidence indicates that morning-types are more relationship-oriented, more cooperative, and better team players than evening-types. For example, Maestripieri (2014) reported that morning-types, both male and female, were significantly more likely to be in a stable relationship than single when compared to evening-types. Furthermore, Marvel-Coen et al. (in press) showed that rMEQ scores were significantly negatively correlated with subjective social status, as measured by the MacArthur scale, such that morning-types, on average, considered themselves to have lower social status. In the same study, the cooperative tendencies of morning- and evening-types were examined in two experimental economic games, the Prisoner's Dilemma and the Ultimatum game. In the Prisoner's Dilemma, morning-type men were more likely to cooperate in the task than evening-type men, whereas the opposite was true for women. In the Ultimatum Game, morning-types, both men and women, tended to require a larger offer from their partner in order to accept, whereas evening-types were, on average, willing to accept smaller offers. The cooperative and competitive tendencies of morning- and evening-types need to be investigated more systematically before any firm conclusions can be drawn. Nevertheless, the existing evidence suggests that differences in cooperativeness and competitiveness between morning- and evening-types are consistent with their slow and fast life history profiles.

Mechanisms

In addition to time perspective, there may be other psychological and physiological mechanisms mediating the association between chronotype, sociosexuality, and other aspects of social preferences or social behavior. These other mechanisms include personality traits, the brain dopaminergic system, and hormones such as testosterone and cortisol.

Although Randler et al. (2012b) found that eveningness in males is associated with a higher number of sexual partners independent of extraversion, extraversion and other personality traits characteristic of evening-types probably contribute to their sociosexuality. In addition to extraversion – which is known to be associated with short-term mating orientation and greater sexual experience (Simpson and Gangestad, 1991; Wilson et al., 2015; Wright and Reise, 1997) – other behavioral and psychological traits that have been associated with eveningness, such as Machiavellianism, impulsiveness, risk-taking, and sensation-seeking, are also associated with unrestricted sociosexuality and short-term mating orientation (e.g., Caci et al., 2004; Digdon and Howell, 2008; Jonason et al., 2013).

Work on this is sparse but there have been some studies that have examined genetic factors at play in behavioral dispositions associated with eveningness and unrestricted sociosexuality. In particular, the dopamine receptor D4 (DRD4) and dopamine receptor D2 (DRD2) gene polymorphisms have been investigated as possible mediators of behavioral characteristics associated with chronotype. These studies have not linked chronotype directly with allelic variants, but have done so indirectly through linking them with behaviors that have independently been linked with eveningness. For example, Eisenberg et al. (2007b) found that individuals with the DRD2 A1 allele and the DRD4 long allele (7+ repeats) have increased impulsivity. A possible biological explanation for this is that individuals with DRD2 A1 have a greater sensitivity to reward, whereas those with the long allele of DRD4 exhibit decreased inhibition (Eisenberg et al., 2007b). Thus, individuals with both of these variants would display far greater impulsivity than individuals with only one or neither. Consistent with these findings, Dreber et al. (2009) found that men with the DRD4 long allele were significantly more likely to be risk-takers, particularly in a financial situation. Dreber et al. (2009) suggest that the biological explanation for this lies in the fact that the long allele is associated with decreased binding, thus individuals with this allele require more dopamine for a 'normal' response. This is particularly interesting considering the role dopaminergic pathways play in reward anticipation and motivation (Kelley, 2004; Kelley et al., 2005; Wise, 2002). Supplementing the connection between DRD4, sociosexuality, and chronotype, Eisenberg et al. (2007a) showed that young adults with the DRD4 long allele were also more likely to have had sex and reproduced earlier in life. These results corroborate findings from Zion et al. (2006) demonstrating that allelic variations of DRD4 are associated with sexual desire, arousal, and function.

Testosterone and cortisol can play potentially important roles as physiological mechanisms underlying life history-relevant psychological and behavioral traits, including perhaps also morningness–eveningness. Randler et al. (2012a) reported that basal salivary testosterone was higher in evening-type men than in morning-type men and suggested that higher testosterone may be a proximate factor regulating the fast life history traits in evening-types. Other studies, however, failed to detect any significant differences in basal testosterone between morning- and evening-types, men or women (Marvel-Coen et al., in press; Ponzi et al., 2015a).

Randler and Schaal (2010) reported that morning-types had higher cortisol levels immediately after awakening than evening-types, whereas Maestripieri (2014) reported that afternoon cortisol concentrations were higher in evening- than in morning-types. Maestripieri (2014) also reported that basal cortisol was a significant predictor of risk-taking in both men and women, and that the association between eveningness and higher risk-taking in women was mediated by cortisol; the cortisol profiles and risk-taking tendencies of evening-type females were more similar to those of males than to those of morning-type females. Other studies, however, did not report any significant differences in basal cortisol between morning- and evening-types, men or women (Marvel-Coen et al., in press; Ponzi et al., 2015a). Recently, Marvel-Coen et al. (in press) showed that morning-types had a greater increase in salivary cortisol in response to psychosocial stress than evening-types. In other work from the same lab, greater cortisol responses to psychosocial stress were associated with sociosexuality profiles characteristic of slow life histories, such as low sexual experience, low number of sexual partners, and low frequency of sexual behavior (Ponzi et al., 2016; Wilson et al., 2015). Taken together, these findings suggest that the variation in the activity of the brain dopaminergic system and of the hypothalamic–pituitary–adrenal (HPA) and hypothalamic–pituitary–gonadal (HPG) axes may explain some of the life history-related differences in sociosexuality and other behavioral propensities between morning- and evening-types.

CONCLUSIONS

The functional significance of psychological, physiological, and behavioral differences between morning- and evening-types may be crucially linked to variation in sociosexuality associated with chronotype. Morning- and evening-types have a constellation of traits that are commonly associated with slow and fast life histories. The findings that variation in chronotype is significantly heritable, that sex differences in chronotype exist, and are most apparent in the time period between puberty and the onset of menopause in women, also strongly suggest that examining the mating strategies of morning- and evening-types can enhance our understanding of the evolution of morningness–eveningness and its functional significance. Further research on morningness–eveningness should test additional predictions of LHT, for example, with regard to the growth rates, timing of sexual maturation, and patterns of mating and parenting effort of morning- and evening-types, as well as further investigate the genetic, physiological, neurobiological, cognitive, emotional, and temperamental mechanisms underlying variation in morningness–eveningness both between the sexes and among individuals of the same sex.

REFERENCES

Adan, A., & Almirall, H. (1991). Horne and Östberg morningness–eveningness questionnaire: A reduced scale. *Personality and Individual Differences, 12*, 241–253.

Adan, A., Archer, S. N., Hidalgo, M. P., Di Milia, L., Natale, V., & Randler, C. (2012). Circadian typology: A comprehensive review. *Chronobiology International, 29*, 1153–1175.

Adan, A., Natale, V., Caci, H., & Prat, G. (2010). Relationship between circadian typology and functional and dysfunctional impulsivity. *Chronobiology International, 27*, 606–619.

Antúnez, J. M., Navarro, J. F., & Adan, A. (2015). Circadian typology is related to resilience and optimism in healthy adults. *Chronobiology International, 32*, 524–530.

Arendt, J. (2006). Melatonin and human rhythms. *Chronobiology International, 23*, 21–37.

Baehr, E. K., Revelle, W., & Eastman, C. I. (2000). Individual differences in the phase and amplitude of the human circadian temperature rhythm: With an emphasis on morningness–eveningness. *Journal of Sleep Research, 9*, 117–127.

Bailey, J. M., Gaulin, S., Agyei, Y., & Gladue, B. A. (1994). Effects of gender and sexual orientation on evolutionarily relevant aspects of human mating psychology. *Journal of Personality and Social Psychology, 66*, 1081–1093.

Belsky, J., Steinberg, L., & Draper, P. (1991). Childhood experience, interpersonal development, and reproductive strategy: An evolutionary theory of socialization. *Child Development, 62*, 647–670.

Borisenkov, M. F., Kosova, A. L., & Kasyanova, O. N. (2012). Impact of perinatal photoperiod on the chronotype of 11- to 18-year-olds in northern European Russia. *Chronobiology International, 29*, 305–310.

Borisenkov, M. F., Perminova, E. V., & Kosova, A. L. (2010). Chronotype, sleep length, and school achievement of 11- to 23-year-old students in northern European Russia. *Chronobiology International, 27*, 1259–1270.

Buss, D. M., & Schmitt, D. P. (1993). Sexual Strategies Theory: An evolutionary perspective on human mating. *Psychological Review, 100*, 204–232.

Caci, H., Robert, P., & Boyer, P. (2004). Novelty seekers and impulsive subjects are low in morningness. *European Psychiatry, 19*, 79–84.

Costa, P. T., & McCrae, R. R. (1992). Normal personality assessment in clinical practice: The NEO Personality Inventory. *Psychological Assessment, 4*, 5–13.

Del Giudice, M. (2009). Sex, attachment, and the development of reproductive strategies. *Behavioral and Brain Sciences, 32*, 1–21.

Del Giudice, M., Gangestad, S. W., & Kaplan, H. S. (2015). Life history theory and evolutionary psychology. In D. M. Buss (Ed.), *The handbook of evolutionary psychology – Vol 1: Foundations* (2nd ed., pp. 88–114). New York, NY: Wiley.

DeYoung, C. G., Hasher, L., Djikic, M., Criger, B., & Peterson, J. B. (2007). Morning people are stable people: Circadian rhythm and the higher-order factors of the Big Five. *Personality and Individual Differences, 43*, 267–276.

Díaz-Morales, J. F., Ferrari, J. R., & Cohen, J. R. (2008). Indecision and avoidant procrastination: The role of morningness–eveningness and time perspective in chronic delay lifestyles. *The Journal of General Psychology, 135*, 228–240.

Digdon, N. L., & Howell, A. J. (2008). College students who have an eveningness preference report lower self-control and greater procrastination. *Chronobiology International, 25*, 1029–1046.

Dreber, A., Apicella, C. L., Eisenberg, D. T., Garcia, J. R., Zamore, R. S., Lum, J. K., & Campbell, B. (2009). The 7R polymorphism in the dopamine receptor D 4 gene (DRD4) is associated with financial risk taking in men. *Evolution and Human Behavior, 30*, 85–92.

Eisenberg, D. T., Campbell, B., MacKillop, J., Modi, M., Dang, D., Lum, J. K., & Wilson, D. S. (2007a). Polymorphisms in the dopamine D4 and D2 receptor genes and reproductive and sexual behaviors. *Evolutionary Psychology, 5*, 696–715.

Eisenberg, D. T., MacKillop, J., Modi, M., Beauchemin, J., Dang, D., Lisman, S. A., Lum, J. K., & Wilson, D. S. (2007b). Examining impulsivity as an endophenotype using a behavioral approach: A DRD2 TaqI A and DRD4 48-bp VNTR association study. *Behavioral and Brain Functions, 3*, 2.

Ellis, B. J., Figueredo, A. J., Brumbach, B. H., & Schlomer, G. L. (2009). Fundamental dimensions of environmental risk: The impact of harsh versus unpredictable environments on the evolution and development of life history strategies. *Human Nature, 20*, 204–268.

Figueredo, A. J., Vasquez, G., Brumbach, B. H., Sefcek, J. A., Kirsner, B. R., & Jacobs, W. J. (2005). The K-factor: Individual differences in life history strategies. *Personality and Individual Differences, 39*, 1349–1360.

Fisher, H. E. (1998). Lust, attraction, and attachment in mammalian reproduction. *Human Nature, 9*, 23–52.

Flatt, T., & Heyland, A. (2011). *Mechanisms of life history evolution. The genetics and physiology of life history traits and trade-offs*. Oxford: Oxford University Press.

Folkard, S., Monk, T. H., & Lobuan, M. C. (1979). Towards a predictive test of adjustment to shift work. *Ergonomics, 22*, 79–91.

Foster, R. G. (2013, April 20). Why teenagers really do need an extra hour in bed. *New Scientist, 2913*.

Frederick, M. J. (2012). Birth weight predicts scores on the ADHD self-report scale and attitudes towards casual sex in college men: A short-term life history strategy? *Evolutionary Psychology, 10*, 342–351.

Gangestad, S. W., & Simpson, A. (1990). Toward an evolutionary history of female sociosexual variation. *Journal of Personality, 51*, 69–96.

Gangestad, S. W., & Simpson, J. A. (2000). The evolution of human mating: Trade-offs and strategic pluralism. *Behavioral and Brain Sciences, 23*, 573–587.

Gibertini, M., Graham, C., & Cook, M. R. (1999). Self-report of circadian type reflects the phase of the melatonin rhythm. *Biological Psychology, 50*, 19–33.

Griefahn, B., Künemund, C., Golka, K., Thier, R., & Degen, G. (2002). Melatonin synthesis: A possible indicator of intolerance to shiftwork. *American Journal of Industrial Medicine, 42*, 427–436.

Griefahn, B., & Robens, S. (2008). The cortisol awakening response: A pilot study on the effects of shift work, morningness and sleep duration. *Psychoneuroendocrinology, 33*, 981–988.

Gunawardane, K. G. C., Piffer, D., & Custance, D. M. (2011). Evidence of sexual selection for evening orientation in human males: A cross-cultural study in Italy and Sri Lanka. *Interdisciplinary Bio Central, 3*, 1–8.

Havlicek, J., Roberts, S. C., & Flegr, J. (2005). Women's preference for dominant male odour: Effects of menstrual cycle and relationship status. *Biology Letters, 1*, 256–259.

Herzog, E. D., Takahashi, J. S., & Block, G. D. (1998). Clock controls circadian period in isolated suprachiasmatic nucleus neurons. *Nature Neuroscience, 1*, 708–713.

Hidalgo, M. P., Caumo, W., Posser, M., Coccaro, S. B., Camozzato, A. L., & Chaves, M. L. F. (2009). Relationship between depressive mood and chronotype in healthy subjects. *Psychiatry and Clinical Neurosciences, 63*, 283–290.

Hogben, A. L., Ellis, J., Archer, S. N., & von Schantz, M. (2007). Conscientiousness is a predictor of diurnal preference. *Chronobiology International, 24*, 1249–1254.

Holtzman, N. S., & Strube, M. J. (2013). Above and beyond short-term mating, long-term mating is uniquely tied to human personality. *Evolutionary Psychology, 11*, 1101–1129.

Horne, J. A., & Östberg, O. (1976). A self-assessment questionnaire to determine morningness–eveningness in human circadian rhythms. *International Journal of Chronobiology, 4*, 97–110.

Hur, Y.-M. (2007). Stability of genetic influence on morningness–eveningness: A cross-sectional examination of South Korean twins from preadolescence to young adulthood. *Journal of Sleep Research, 16*, 17–23.

Hur, Y. M., Bouchard, T. J., & Lykken, D. T. (1998). Genetic and environmental influence on morningness–eveningness. *Personality and Individual Differences, 25*, 917–925.

Jackson, J. J., & Kirkpatrick, L. A. (2007). The structure and measurement of human mating strategies: Toward a multidimensional model of sociosexuality. *Evolution and Human Behavior, 28*, 382–391.

Jankowski, K. S., Díaz-Morales, J. F., & Randler, C. (2014a). Chronotype, gender, and time for sex. *Chronobiology International, 31*, 911–916.

Jankowski, K. S., Díaz-Morales, J. F., Vollmer, C., & Randler, C. (2014b). Morningness eveningness and sociosexuality: Evening females are less restricted than morning ones. *Personality and Individual Differences, 68*, 13–17.

Jonason, P. K., Jones, A., & Lyons, M. (2013). Creatures of the night: Chronotypes and the Dark Triad traits. *Personality and Individual Differences, 55*, 538–541.

Kanazawa, S., & Perina, K. (2009). Why night owls are more intelligent. *Personality and Individual Differences, 47*, 685–690.

Kaplan, H. S. (1996). A theory of fertility and parental investment in traditional and modern human societies. *Yearbook of Physical Anthropology, 39*, 91–135.

Kelley, A. (2004). Ventral striatal control of appetitive motivation: Role in ingestive behavior and reward-related learning. *Neuroscience and Biobehavioral Reviews, 27*, 765–776.

Kelley, A. E., Schiltz, C. A., & Landry, C. F. (2005). Neural systems recruited by drug- and food-related cues: Studies of gene activation in corticolimbic regions. *Physiology and Behavior, 86*, 11–14.

Kerkhof, G. A., & Van Dongen, H. P. (1996). Morning-type and evening-type individuals differ in the phase position of their endogenous circadian oscillator. *Neuroscience Letters, 218*, 153–156.

Killgore, W. D. S. (2007). Effects of sleep-deprivation and morningness–eveningness traits on risk-taking. *Psychological Reports, 100*, 613–626.

Kirkwood, A. T. B. L., & Rose, M. R. (1991). Evolution of senescence: Late survival sacrificed for reproduction. *Philosophical Transactions: Biological Sciences, 332*, 15–24.

Kruger, D. J., & Nesse, R. M. (2006). An evolutionary life-history framework for understanding sex differences in human mortality rates. *Human Nature, 17*, 74–97.

Maestripieri, D. (2014). Night owl women are similar to men in their relationship orientation, risk-taking propensities, and cortisol levels: Implications for the adaptive significance and evolution of eveningness. *Evolutionary Psychology, 12*, 130–147.

Magwere, T., Chapman, T., & Partridge, L. (2004). Sex differences in the effect of dietary restriction on life span and mortality rates in female and male *Drosophila melanogaster*. *Journal of Gerontology: Biological Sciences, 59*, 3–9.

Marvel-Coen, J. Nickels, N., & Maestripieri, D. (in press). The relationship between morningness–eveningness, psychosocial variables, and cortisol reactivity to stress from a life history perspective. *Evolutionary Behavioral Sciences*.

Matthews, G. (1988). Morningness–eveningness as a dimension of personality: Trait, state and psychophysiological correlates. *European Journal of Personality, 2*, 277–293.

Milfont, T. L., & Schwarzenthal, M. (2014). Explaining why larks are future-oriented and owls are present-oriented: Self-control mediates the chronotype–time perspective relationships. *Chronobiology International*, 2, 581–588.

Mongrain, V., Lavoie, S., Selmaoui, B., Paquet, J., & Dumont, M. (2004). Phase relationships between sleep-wake cycle and underlying circadian rhythms in morningness eveningness. *Journal of Biological Rhythms*, 19, 248–257.

Mongrain, V., Paquet, J., & Dumont, M. (2006). Contribution of the photoperiod at birth to the association between season of birth and diurnal preference. *Neuroscience Letters*, 406, 113–116.

Muro, A., Gomà-i-Freixanet, M., Adan, A., & Cladellas, R. (2011). Circadian typology, age, and the alternative five-factor personality model in an adult women sample. *Chronobiology International*, 28, 690–696.

Murphy, G. I. (1968). Pattern in life history and the environment. *American Naturalist*, 102, 391–403.

Natale, V., Adan, A., & Fabbri, M. (2009). Season of birth, gender, and social-cultural effects on sleep timing preferences in humans. *Sleep*, 32, 423–426.

Natale, V., & Di Milia, L. (2011). Season of birth and morningness: Comparison between the northern and southern hemispheres. *Chronobiology International*, 28, 727–730.

Nowack, K., & van der Meer, E. (2013). Are larks future-oriented and owls present-oriented? Age- and sex-related shifts in chronotype–time perspective associations. *Chronobiology International*, 30, 1240–1250.

Pianka, E. (1970). On r- and K-Selection. *American Naturalist*, 104, 592–597.

Piffer, D. (2010). Sleep patterns and sexual selection: An evolutionary approach. *Mankind Quarterly*, 50, 361–375.

Piffer, D., Gunawardane, K. G. C., & Custance, D. M. (2011). Evidence of sexual selection for evening orientation in human males: A cross-cultural study in Italy and Sri Lanka. *Interdisciplinary Bio Central Journal*, 3, 1–8.

Piffer, D., Ponzi, D., Sapienza, P., Zingales, L., & Maestripieri, D. (2014). Morningness–eveningness and intelligence among high-achieving US students: Night owls have higher GMAT scores than early morning types in a top-ranked MBA program. *Intelligence*, 47, 107–112.

Ponzi, D., Henry, A., Kubicki, K., Nickels, N., Wilson, M. C., & Maestripieri, D. (2015a). The slow and fast life histories of early birds and night owls : Their future- or present-orientation accounts for their sexually monogamous or promiscuous tendencies. *Evolution and Human Behavior*, 36, 117–122.

Ponzi, D., Henry, A., Kubicki, K., Nickels, N., Wilson, M. C., & Maestripieri, D. (2015b). Morningness–eveningness and intrasexual competition in men. *Personality and Individual Differences*, 76, 228–231.

Ponzi, D., Henry, A., Kubicki, K., Nickels, N., Wilson, M. C., & Maestripieri, D. (2016). Autistic-like traits, socio-sexuality, and hormonal responses to socially stressful and sexually arousing stimuli in male students. *Adaptive Human Behavior and Physiology*, 2, 150–165.

Ponzi, D., Wilson, M. C., & Maestripieri, D. (2014). Eveningness is associated with higher risk-taking, independent of sex and personality. *Psychological Reports*, 115, 932–947.

Preckel, F., Lipnevich, A. A., Schneider, S., & Roberts, R. D. (2011). Chronotype, cognitive abilities, and academic achievement: A meta-analytic investigation. *Learning and Individual Differences*, 21, 483–492.

Putilov, A. A. (2014). What were 'owls' doing in our ancestral photoperiodic environment? Chronobiological account for the evolutionary advantage of nocturnal lifestyle. *Biological Rhythm Research*, 45, 759–787.

Puts, D. A., Pope, L. E., Hill, A. K., Cárdenas, R. A., Welling, L. L. M., Wheatley, J. R., & Breedlove, S. M. (2015). Hormones and behavior fulfilling desire: Evidence for negative feedback between men's testosterone, sociosexual psychology, and sexual partner number. *Hormones and Behavior*, 70, 14–21.

Randler, C. (2007). Gender differences in morningness–eveningness assessed by self-report questionnaires: A meta-analysis. *Personality and Individual Differences*, 43, 1667–1675.

Randler, C. (2008). Morningness–eveningness, sleep-wake variables and big five personality factors. *Personality and Individual Differences, 45*, 191–196.

Randler, C. (2009). Proactive people are morning people. *Journal of Applied Social Psychology, 39*, 2787–2797.

Randler, C. (2011). Age and gender differences in morningness–eveningness during adolescence. *Journal of Genetic Psychology, 172*, 302–308.

Randler, C., Baumann, V. P., & Horzum, M. B. (2014). Morningness–eveningness, Big Five and the BIS/BAS inventory. *Personality and Individual Differences, 66*, 64–67.

Randler, C., Ebenhöh, N., Fischer, A., Höchel, S., Schroff, C., Stoll, J. C., & Vollmer, C. (2012a). Chronotype but not sleep length is related to salivary testosterone in young adult men. *Psychoneuroendocrinology, 37*, 1740–1744.

Randler, C., Ebenhöh, N., Fischer, A., Höchel, S., Schroff, C., Stoll, J. C., Vollmer, C., & Piffer, D. (2012b). Eveningness is related to men's mating success. *Personality and Individual Differences, 53*, 263–267.

Randler, C., & Frech, D. (2006). Correlation between morningness–eveningness and final school leaving exams. *Biological Rhythm Research, 37*, 233–239.

Randler, C., Jankowski, K. S., Rahafar, A., & Diaz-Morales, J. F. (2016). Sociosexuality, morningness–eveningness, and sleep duration. *SAGE Open, 6*, 1–8.

Randler, C., & Saliger, L. (2011). Relationship between morningness–eveningness and temperament and character dimensions in adolescents. *Personality and Individual Differences, 50*, 148–152.

Randler, C., & Schaal, S. (2010). Morningness–eveningness, habitual sleep-wake variables and cortisol level. *Biological Psychology, 85*, 14–18.

Reznick, D., Nunney, L., & Tessier, A. (2000). Big houses, big cars, superfleas and the costs of reproduction. *Trends in Ecology and Evolution, 15*, 421–425.

Roberts, R. D., & Kyllonen, P. C. (1999). Morningness–eveningness and intelligence: Early to bed, early to rise will likely make you anything but wise! *Personality and Individual Differences, 27*, 1123–1133.

Roenneberg, T., Kuehnle, T., Pramstaller, P. P., Ricken, J., Havel, M., Guth, A., & Merrow, M. (2004). A marker for the end of adolescence. *Current Biology, 14*, R1038–R1039.

Roenneberg, T., Wirz-Justice, A., & Merrow, M. (2003). Life between clocks: Daily temporal patterns of human chronotypes. *Journal of Biological Rhythms, 18*, 80–90.

Roff, D. A. (2002). *Life history evolution*. Sunderland, MA: Sinauer.

Schaal, S., Peter, M., & Randler, C. (2010). Morningness–eveningness and physical activity in adolescents. *International Journal of Sport and Exercise Psychology, 8*, 147–159.

Schmitt, D. P. (2008). Big five traits related to short-term mating: From personality to promiscuity across 46 nations. *Evolutionary Psychology, 6*, 246–282.

Selvi, Y., Aydin, A., Atli, A., Boysan, M., Selvi, F., & Besiroglu, L. (2011). Chronotype differences in suicidal behavior and impulsivity among suicide attempters. *Chronobiology International, 28*, 170–175.

Simpson, J. A, & Gangestad, S. W. (1991). Individual differences in sociosexuality: Evidence for convergent and discriminant validity. *Journal of Personality and Social Psychology, 60*, 870–883.

Starrfelt, J., & Kokko, H. (2012). Bet-hedging: A triple trade-off between means, variances and correlations. *Biological Reviews, 87*, 742–755.

Stearns, S. C., & Koella, J. C. (1986). The evolution of phenotypic plasticity in life-history traits: Predictions of reaction norms for age and size at maturity. *Evolution, 40*, 893–913.

Stolarski, M., Bitner, J., & Zimbardo, P. G. (2011). Time perspective, emotional intelligence and discounting of delayed awards. *Time and Society, 20*, 346–363.

Stolarski, M., Ledzińska, M., & Matthews, G. (2013). Morning is tomorrow, evening is today: Relationships between chronotype and time perspective. *Biological Rhythm Research, 44*, 181–196.

Tonetti, L., Fabbri, M., & Natale, V. (2009). Relationship between circadian typology and big five personality domains. *Chronobiology International, 26*, 337–347.

Tonetti, L., Natale, V., & Randler, C. (2015). Association between circadian preference and academic achievement: A systematic review and meta-analysis. *Chronobiology International*, *32*, 792–801.

Torsvall, L., & Åkerstedt, T. (1980). A diurnal type scale: Construction, consistency and validation in shift work. *Scandinavian Journal of Work, Environment & Health*, *6*, 283–290.

Tsaousis, I. (2010). Circadian preferences and personality traits: A meta-analysis. *European Journal of Personality*, *24*, 356–373.

Urbán, R., Magyaródi, T., & Rigó, A. (2011). Morningness–eveningness, chronotypes and health-impairing behaviors in adolescents. *Chronobiology International*, *28*, 238–247.

Vink, J. M., Groot, A. S., Kerhof, G. A., & Boomsma, D. I. (2001). Genetic analysis of morningness and eveningness. *Chronobiology International*, *18*, 809–822.

Vollmer, C., & Randler, C. (2012). Circadian preferences and personality values: Morning types prefer social values, evening types prefer individual values. *Personality and Individual Differences*, *52*, 738–743.

Wang, L., & Chartrand, T. L. (2015). Morningness–eveningness and risk taking. *Journal of Psychology*, *149*, 394–411.

Webster, G. D., & Bryan, A. (2007). Sociosexual attitudes and behaviors: Why two factors are better than one. *Journal of Research in Personality*, *41*, 917–922.

Wilson, M. C., Zilioli, S., Ponzi, D., Henry, A., Kubicki, K., Nickels, N., & Maestripieri, D. (2015). Cortisol reactivity to psychosocial stress mediates the relationship between extraversion and unrestricted sociosexuality. *Personality and Individual Differences*, *86*, 427–431.

Wise, R. A. (2002). Brain reward circuitry: Insights from unsensed incentives. *Neuron*, *36*, 229–240.

Wittmann, M., Dinich, J., Merrow, M., & Roenneberg, T. (2006). Social jetlag: Misalignment of biological and social time. *Chronobiology International*, *23*, 497–509.

Wittmann, M., Paulus, M., & Roenneberg, T. (2010). Decreased psychological well-being in late 'chronotypes' is mediated by smoking and alcohol consumption. *Substance Use and Misuse*, *45*, 15–30.

Wong, P. M., Hasler, B. P., Kamarck, T. W., Muldoon, M. F., & Manuck, S. B. (2015). Social jetlag, chronotype, and cardiometabolic risk. *Journal of Clinical Endocrinology and Metabolism*, *100*, 4612–4620.

Wright, T. M., & Reise, S. P. (1997). Personality and unrestricted sexual behavior: Correlations of sociosexuality in Caucasian and Asian college students. *Journal of Research in Personality*, *31*, 166–192.

Zion, I. B., Tessler, R., Cohen, L., Lerer, E., Raz, Y., Bachner-Melman, R., & Benjamin, J. (2006). Polymorphisms in the dopamine D4 receptor gene (DRD4) contribute to individual differences in human sexual behavior: Desire, arousal and sexual function. *Molecular Psychiatry*, *11*, 782–786.

Toward the Molecular Basis of Personality

Turhan Canli

Many of us are fascinated by other people – the way they look or dress, their attractiveness, accomplishments or foibles, their life stories – especially if these stories are etched in their faces; we seem to be attracted to expressions of *individuality*. We are particularly fascinated when we encounter a challenge to this individuality in identical twins. The physical similarity notwithstanding, how similar are they, *really*? What would it be like to have a genetic duplicate of oneself to speak to? Would the vicissitudes of life make them more or less alike with time?

Twin studies have been a mainstay of personality psychology for many decades, addressing these kinds of questions with increasing methodological rigor and driving discoveries about genetic and environmental contributions to traits. In the past two decades, new technologies have begun to reveal underlying molecular markers and processes. The molecular results are coming in fast and furious, but they do not fit the established genetic narrative all that well. It turns out that traits, although heritable, do not easily reveal their underlying molecular genetic architecture, creating a mystery known as 'missing heritability' (Maher, 2008; Manolio et al., 2009). In this chapter, I draw an arc from behavior genetics, to candidate gene studies, to genome-wide association studies (GWAS). I will then consider plausible explanations for missing heritability, suggest solutions that apply molecular approaches within the context of systems biology, and support a convergence of reductionist and systems biology approaches in future molecular psychology studies of personality.

BEHAVIOR GENETICS

Efforts to catalogue heritable behaviors have been ongoing for many decades, revealing genetic contributions to such activities as hours spent watching television, attending church, or doing crossword puzzles (see Kendler, 2013), which led Turkheimer to suggest that the first law of behavior genetics is that all human behavioral traits are heritable (Turkheimer, 2001). This does not mean that there is a gene (or many genes) 'for' television-watching, church-attendance, or crossword-puzzle-playing. Rather, it highlights that all behavior is generated by the brain, which itself has a genetic blueprint for its fundamental design and processing circuits (Kendler, 2013). Indeed, twin studies suggest that the heritability of human brain volume is as high as 90–95% in the frontal lobe and 40–69% in other regions such as the hippocampus (Peper et al., 2007). Beyond their interrelation with the genetics of the brain, what else do, and do not, heritability estimates tell us about the genetics of behavioral traits?

This question was addressed by Johnson and colleagues (2011) who discussed the limitations of heritability estimates in the context of molecular genetic approaches to the study of behavioral traits. They remind their readers that heritability estimates are simply based on measures of variance, and can therefore produce surprising results, when they state that 'for traits completely genetically determined, such as the presence of two eyes in humans, heritability is nonexistent because there is no variance' (p. 258). Moreover, variance may be contributed by both genetic and environmental factors in unequal amounts, which can affect heritability estimates. Johnson and colleagues note:

> As a ratio of genetic to total (genetic plus environmental) variance, heritability is dependent on the magnitudes of both the genetic and the environmental variances. With the same magnitude of genetic variance, heritability can be high because environmental variance is relatively low, or low because environmental variance is relatively high. This again points to the importance of the environment in what is measured in heritability. Where relevant environmental circumstances are tightly constrained, heritability will be high even if there is little genetic variance. And where relevant environmental circumstances vary widely, heritability will be low even with substantial genetic variance. (p. 258)

The relation between heritability estimates and environmental variance is particularly important for twin studies, in which the phenotypic similarity of identical (monozygotic, MZ) twins is compared to that of fraternal (dizygotic, DZ) twins. These studies rest on the assumption that the rearing environmental factors that could influence a given trait are similar for MZ and DZ twins. A violation of this *Equal Environment Assumption* (EEA; Kendler et al., 1993) would be problematic because it would inflate heritability estimates: the greater phenotypic similarity of MZ twins would be attributable not only to greater genetic similarity, relative to DZ twins, but also to greater rearing environment similarity. In other words, prior estimates of genetic contributions to observed traits would be contaminated by environmental factors. Tests of the EEA have been conducted across a number of phenotypes. For example, rearing environment similarity was not a significant moderator of the observed phenotypic correlations for MZ and DZ twins for childhood externalizing disorders, consistent with the EEA (LoParo and Waldman, 2014). Other studies found support for the EEA for phenotypes such as emotional and behavioral problems in female twins (Cronk et al., 2002), aggression and spatial ability (Derks et al., 2006), and eating attitudes (Klump et al., 2000). A clever study by Conley and colleagues examined misclassified twins – twins that experienced their environment as MZ or DZ but genetically belonged to the opposite group (Conley et al., 2013). Their analysis of three large datasets (Add Health, the Minnesota Twin Family Study, and the Child and Adolescent Twin Study in Sweden) also supported the EEA.

On the other hand, a recent re-analysis of 11 twin studies, totaling a dataset of over 9,000 twin pairs, examined the relation between five categories of childhood social adversity (i.e., bullying, sexual abuse, physical maltreatment, emotional neglect and abuse, and general trauma) and schizophrenia and found significantly higher correlations in environmental exposure in each of these categories for MZ relative to DZ twins

(Fosse et al., 2015). Other critics of supportive EEA studies point to methodological weaknesses, such as inadequate measurements of the environment or limited outcome measures (Pam et al., 1996; Richardson and Norgate, 2005).

Felson addressed critics of the EEA by conducting a re-analysis of prior EEA tests with better environmental measures and adding a dataset with a comprehensive set of outcome measures (Felson, 2014). He concluded that 'it is likely that the EEA is not strictly valid for most outcomes, but the resulting bias is likely modest' (p. 184).

Environment and Heritability

Johnson and colleagues discuss another central assumption regarding the role of the environment in heritability estimates: that genetic and environmental influences are independent; that is, that genes and the environment both have causal effects on behavior that can be separated from each other. This assumption would be violated if there is evidence for gene–environment correlations (rGEs) or gene–environment interactions (GxEs). rGEs represent genetic influences on environmental exposure. These correlations can present in three forms: as *passive* rGEs when the genes and environment that an individual inherits from his or her parents reinforce each other (e.g., the child of depressed parents receives susceptibility genes for depression and also is emotionally neglected); as *active* rGEs when the individual seeks out environments that reinforce her genetic predispositions (e.g., an extraverted child participates in many social extracurricular activities she finds enjoyable); or as *evocative* rGEs when the individual evokes particular responses from his environment because of his genetic predisposition (e.g., a child genetically predisposed to aggression is difficult to parent, which provokes parental aggression). If genes can influence the environmental exposure of an individual, then these environments themselves may attain heritability (Kendler and Eaves, 1986; Plomin et al., 1977). Evidence in support of rGEs comes from behavior genetic studies that find heritability for some environments, such as marital quality or social support. Kendler and Baker conducted a comprehensive review of psychology or psychiatry studies that examined the heritability of measures of environments and found that negative life events that are not under the control of the individual (such as death of a loved one) are less heritable than negative life events that are, at least to some extent, under the control of an individual (such as divorce; Kendler and Baker, 2007). Jaffee and Price (2012) commented:

> The significance of this research in quantitative behavioral genetics has been to call into question the assumption that putative environments have causal effects on behavior. This work raises the alternative possibility that such environments arise because of heritable characteristics of the person or that the association between exposures and outcomes is confounded by genotype. (p. 1254)

GxEs are another challenge to the assumption that genetic and environmental influences are independent. GxEs are present when genetic factors moderate the influence of the environment on the observed phenotype or vice versa. For example, genetic factors contribute to physical health, but the degree to which this is the case is moderated by income (Johnson and Krueger, 2005), such that lower-income individuals show stronger genetic associations with poor health (e.g., for chronic illness, the associated genetic variance was .55 versus .33 for individuals who ranked 1 SD below versus 1 SD above the income mean), perhaps due to higher levels of socio-economic-related stressors that activate genetic vulnerabilities to illness.

However, de Moor and Boomsma (2011) disagree with the notion that rGEs and GxEs play an important role in explaining heritability estimates, based on the results of advanced analytic techniques and study designs (de Moor and Boomsma, 2011). They point out that causal mechanisms of traits, such as mediation of genetic influences on traits by other traits, can be examined with analytic approaches (direction-of-causality modeling), children-of-twin study designs, and the co-twin control method. De Moor and Boomsma argue that, based on extended twin family designs, in which data from parents and first- and second-degree relatives are added, there is no evidence for passive rGEs and a negligible impact of shared environment on heritability estimates.

Taken together, although there is evidence that genetic and environmental factors do correlate and interact with each other (a point I will revisit in the section on 'Missing Heritability'), rather than have a causal influence on phenotypic expression independently of each other, the extent to which this interaction biases heritability estimates remains a matter of debate. As Johnson and colleagues (2011) put it:

> Estimating heritability provides a rough and ready way of cutting the processes involved into genetic and environmental pieces, and the persistent observation that the genetic piece is not small has real meaning. But heritability alone does not help us identify and understand the processes that generate patterns of behaviour nor what can or cannot be done about them. (p. 255)

Application to Personality Traits

The heritability of personality traits has been studied for many decades and was recently reviewed in a comprehensive meta-analysis by Vukasovic and Bratko (2015) who examined the behavioral genetics literature on personality traits between 1951 and 2011. The meta-analysis was designed to capture studies that were based on any one of four influential personality models. Cattel's (1943) model was a taxonomy of sixteen primary personality traits. Eysenck's (1970) model reduced the number of independent primary traits to three (i.e., neuroticism, extraversion, and psychoticism). Tellegen et al.'s (1988) model conceptualized personality as three higher-order factors of negative emotionality, positive emotionality, and constraint, which together organized 11 primary personality scales. Lastly, studies based on the five-factor models of Goldberg (1990; emotional stability, extraversion, agreeableness, conscientiousness, and intellect) and Costa and McCrae (1992; neuroticism, extraversion, agreeableness, conscientiousness, and openness) were included. Of these, none of the first-pass eligible studies using Cattel's model passed exclusion criteria. The final set of meta-analyzed publications was comprised of 39 primary published and six unpublished studies, producing a total of 62 independent effect sizes, obtained from a total sample size of over 100,000 participants.

Across all studies, genetic factors accounted for 40% of the variance. Furthermore, the type of personality model was not a significant moderator: each of the three personality trait models (Eysenck's, Tellegen's, and the five-factor models) produced similar heritability estimates, particularly with respect to extraversion and neuroticism, consistent with earlier analyses (Loehlin, 1978, 1982, 2012; Turkheimer et al., 2014).

A key finding from the meta-analysis by Vukasovic and Bratko (2015) was that a significant moderator of the heritability estimate was whether the study design was based on the analysis of families and adoptions, or of twins. It turns out that family and adoption studies estimated genetic contributions to personality trait variance at 22%, whereas twin studies estimated genetic contributions to personality trait variance at 47%. Plomin and colleagues (1998) had earlier noted this puzzling pattern of discrepant heritability estimates in personality trait studies and offered this conclusion: that the higher personality trait heritability estimates of twin studies most likely reveal the influence of *non-additive* genetic influences, which cannot be detected in family and adoption studies.

Additive genetic effects simply reflect the *sum* of all genetic variations (alleles) of genes that affect a trait; they can be detected in both family/adoption and in twin studies.

Non-additive genetic effects, on the other hand, reflect *interactions* between alleles. One example of a non-additive effect discussed by Plomin and colleagues (1998) is *Dominance*, in which the presence of one (dominant) allele may obscure the phenotypic expression of the other (recessive) allele *of the same gene*. Another example of a non-additive effect discussed by Plomin and colleagues is *Epistasis* (gene–gene interactions), in which *alleles from different genes* interact with each other. Only identical (MZ) twins, by virtue of their identical genomes, will share *all* additive and non-additive (dominance and epistatic) effects, and it is the comparison of the phenotypic trait resemblance of MZ versus fraternal (DZ) twins that allows such non-additive effects to be revealed.

Plomin and colleagues (1998) noted that twin studies indeed suggest the presence of non-additive effects, because several studies reported correlations for MZ twins that were more than twice the correlations for DZ twins (if genetic effects were exclusively additive, correlations for MZ twins should be twice that of DZ twins). The possibility of non-additive, particularly epistatic, genetic effects contributing to heritability estimates in twin studies is highly relevant with regard to the likelihood of molecular genetic studies discovering specific genes associated with personality. Plomin and colleagues put it this way:

> If epistasis is important for self-reported personality, it would have grave consequences for attempts to identify specific genes responsible for genetic influence. Genetic studies have moved beyond single-gene traits, in which a single gene is necessary and sufficient to cause a trait, to complex quantitative traits influenced by multiple genes of varying effect size, which is the provenance of personality and most other psychological traits (Plomin, Owen, & McGuffin, 1994). However, these new strategies assume additive or dominance effects of genes. If genetic effects involve interactions among a large number of genes, it may be very difficult to identify individual genes in such complex systems. If there are 30,000 genes expressed in the brain, two- and three-way interactions alone could yield millions of possible interactions. (pp. 217–218)

With this thought in mind, I next discuss the molecular genetics of personality, tracing the historical development from candidate genes to current GWAS and the issue of 'missing heritability'.

CANDIDATE GENE STUDIES

As reviewed elsewhere (Canli, 2008a, 2015), the history of 'molecular psychology' – which uses the tools of molecular biology to study behavior and its associated underlying neural structure and function – can be traced to 1996, when three studies reported significant associations between personality traits and specific common gene variants ('polymorphisms'). Lesch and colleagues (1996) reported an association between neuroticism and a polymorphism in the serotonin transporter gene (*SLC6A4*), referred to as the serotonin (5-HT) transporter-linked polymorphic region, 5-HTTLPR, such that presence of the short allele was associated with higher neuroticism scores. Benjamin and colleagues (1996) and Ebstein and colleagues (1996) reported an association between novelty seeking and a repeat sequence in the dopamine D receptor gene, such that presence of the 7-repeat allele was associated with higher novelty seeking scores. The association with novelty seeking was later disconfirmed and instead probably reflects an association with attention deficit hyperactivity disorder. These first studies inspired the field of so-called 'candidate gene' studies, in which individual genes with known biological functions were selected a priori to examine associations between DNA variations within these genes and behavioral phenotypes. A comprehensive review of this literature is beyond the scope of this chapter, but these sorts of reviews have been published elsewhere (Bertolino et al., 2006; Buckholtz and Meyer-Lindenberg, 2008; Canli, 2008a, 2008b, 2015; Canli et al., 2009; Canli and Lesch, 2007; Congdon and Canli, 2005, 2008a, 2008b; Ebstein et al., 2015; Hariri et al., 2006;

Hariri and Holmes, 2006; Meyer-Lindenberg et al., 2006a, 2006b). Here, I will focus on the 5-HTTLPR, for which there is a large literature of replications and extension studies that has also grown to include studies of additive and epistatic gene effects, GxEs, and epigenetic mechanisms. Thus, work on the 5-HTTLPR serves as an illustration of how flexibly the candidate gene approach can be applied to examine the role of individual gene variants across topic areas in molecular psychology.

The association between the 5-HTTLPR polymorphism and neuroticism has been subjected to extensive replication efforts and inspired 75 meta-analyses (PubMed, September 2016). Early meta-analyses focused on examining the link to neuroticism, which have been largely confirmatory although the selection of the measurement instrument assessing neuroticism may be an important moderator (Munafo et al., 2005, 2009b; Schinka et al., 2004; Sen et al., 2004). Some of the later extensions focused on behavioral phenotypes and physiological endophenotypes, which were confirmed by meta-analyses on behaviors, traits, and endophenotypes, including antisocial behavior (Ficks and Waldman, 2014), biased attention for emotional stimuli (Pergamin-Hight et al., 2012), cortisol stress reactivity (Miller et al., 2013), and amygdala activity (Murphy et al., 2013). These analyses also noted potential caveats, such as evidence for oversampling of statistically significant effect sizes (Ficks and Waldman, 2014), the small number of available studies (Pergamin-Hight et al., 2012), and excess statistical significance among published studies and underpowered samples (Murphy et al., 2013). A large number of extension studies examined possible associations with psychopathology, some of which were confirmed by meta-analyses, such as suicide or suicide attempts (Clayden et al., 2012; de Medeiros Alves et al., 2015), geriatric depression (Gao et al., 2014), post-stroke depression (Mak et al., 2013), and bipolar disorder (Jiang et al., 2013). Some meta-analyses specifically addressed the question of GxEs, to which I will return in a later section. The literature on substance and drug-use has produced meta-analyses examining substance use disorder, with one meta-analysis confirming significant associations between 5-HTTLPR and alcohol, heroin, cocaine, and methamphetamine dependence and abuse (Cao et al., 2013), but another failing to find a significant association for alcohol dependence (Villalba et al., 2015). Meta-analyses on smoking found a significant association with smoking rate (Ohmoto et al., 2013), but not with smoking initiation or with smoking cessation or persistence (Li et al., 2015; Ohmoto et al., 2013).

The discovery of the link between the 5-HTTLPR and neuroticism, as well as other emotion-related behavioral phenotypes, serves as a springboard for the discussion of studies of additive and interactive effects with other genes, the environment, and epigenetic mechanisms.

Additive and Epistatic Genetic Effects

As discussed above, Plomin and colleagues noted the plausible presence of epistatic effects in twin studies of personality (Plomin et al., 1998). Molecular genetic candidate gene studies affirm such relationships. Earlier work by Lesch and colleagues, and by my group in collaboration with Lesch, had identified additive effects of the 5-HTTLPR and a polymorphism (rs4570625, SNP G-703T) within the tryptophan hydroxylase-2 gene (*TPH2*), a gene that is a critical element in the pathway of 5-HT synthesis: based on event-related potentials (Herrmann et al., 2007) or fMRI (Canli et al., 2008), we found that individuals who carried both genes' risk alleles for increased emotional responses (5-HTTLPR S allele + *TPH2* T allele) exhibited the highest degree of response to emotionally arousing scenes, faces, or Stroop-task words. In contrast, individuals who carried neither of these genes' risk alleles exhibited the least amount of activation. More recently, Lehto and colleagues (2015) conducted a study of the five-factor model (FFM) in an Estonian birth cohort, the Children Personality Behaviour and Health Study at ages 15 ($n = 742$) and 18 ($n = 834$). In addition to main effects, they reported on a gene × gene effect on Conscientiousness, such that *TPH2* T/T carriers scored significantly higher on Conscientiousness, but only in the presence of the 5-HTTLPR short allele.

In collaboration with Klein and colleagues, we studied hypothalamic–pituitary–adrenal (HPA) axis reactivity to stress as a function of the 5-HTTLPR and *BDNF* Val66Met polymorphisms in a sample of 144 preschool-aged children (Dougherty et al., 2010). We found that homozygous carriers of the 5-HTTLPR short allele exhibited significantly lower baseline levels of salivary cortisol, followed by a positive increase in cortisol in response to laboratory stressors, which was moderated by presence of the Met-*BDNF* allele. In contrast, presence of the Val-*BDNF* allele was associated with a greater decline in salivary cortisol in response to the laboratory stressors. These data suggest that the *BDNF* gene moderates the association between 5-HTTLPR and children's biological stress responses.

Most of these studies used relatively small samples (Gauderman, 2002), and did not include replication samples, as is now common for GWAS (discussed later in this chapter), and were not independently replicated. Thus, one should remain cautious in weighing these results. Nonetheless, they illustrate that candidate gene studies are well-suited to examine specific gene pairs with plausible biological interactions for epistatic effects. This approach therefore can illuminate specific biological interactions that behavior genetic studies can only infer.

Gene–Environment Interactions (GxEs)

Molecular GxEs were first reported by Caspi and colleagues (2002) from a longitudinal cohort of 442 males for the Monoamine Oxidase A gene (*MAOA*, an X-linked gene), variants of which were reported to moderate the association between childhood maltreatment and adult antisocial behavior. This work was followed up in about 30 replication studies and confirmed in meta-analyses (Byrd and Manuck, 2014; Taylor and Kim-Cohen, 2007).

In the following year, Caspi and colleagues (2003) reported a GxE for 5-HTTLPR from the same cohort (847 individuals of both sexes): they found that presence of the 5-HTTLPR short allele moderated the association between stressful life events and depressive symptoms, and this interaction did not reflect a gene–environment correlation. Replication studies by other groups identified additional moderating factors such as social support (Kaufman et al., 2004) and sex (Eley et al., 2004), but also produced non-replications (Gillespie et al., 2005; Surtees et al., 2005).

Several meta-analyses reported conflicting conclusions about the role of 5-HTTLPR in moderating environmental effects on depression. Two of these disconfirmed a significant association (Munafo et al., 2009a; Risch et al., 2009). A rebuttal argued that these meta-analyses were based on a biased selection of included studies (Kaufman et al., 2010), and a more expansive meta-analysis confirmed a GxE, noting that the degree of statistical robustness depended on the type of stressor (Karg et al., 2011). Others remain skeptical of any GxE claims in light of the heterogeneity of mental disorders (Flint and Kendler, 2014) and the possibility of publication bias and false positive results in underpowered studies (Duncan and Keller, 2011; Munafo et al., 2014).

Other studies have evaluated GxEs for 5-HTTLPR measuring endophenotypes. For example, Alexander and colleagues (2009) used a public speaking task and showed that high levels of Stressful Life Events (SLEs) were associated with differential cortisol responses as a function of 5-HTTLPR genotype. A similar finding was reported by Mueller and colleagues (2011), although the interaction was only observed in a cohort of young adults (not children or older adults) and only for SLEs that occurred in the first five years of life. We have reported differential amygdala activation to emotional word stimuli and during resting conditions as a function of 5-HTTLPR genotype and SLEs (Canli et al., 2006), which was also observed in one study of emotional face processing (Alexander et al., 2012), but not in another (Walsh et al., 2012). These studies differed in their composition of sexes and age distributions, and in their assessment of SLEs, making it difficult to determine how genotype, SLEs, and other variables interact with one another.

Going forward, several recommendations have been made to increase confidence in GxE results. Dick and colleagues (2015) argued for the need to carefully assess polymorphisms and to integrate candidate gene information with data from large-scale genetic screens or other model organisms. They recommended that measures of environmental factors should be treated according to their hypothesized role in underlying biological mechanism and phenotypic outcome measures, which would differentiate predictions for, say, chronic stress conditions from acute stressful life events. Furthermore, they highlighted a number of statistical considerations, such as the use of scale, which affects the interaction term; selection of risk-difference versus risk-ratio approaches, which spell different meanings for the interaction term; use of cross-product terms, particularly in nonlinear G-E-Outcome relations or in tri-allelic categorical genotypes; use of covariates in G and E interaction terms; statistical power; and the need to measure and control for rGEs.

Epigenetics

Following a demonstration in rats that early life experience can alter gene methylation at so-called 'CpG islands' (regions of the DNA in which the frequency of the nucleotides cytosine-followed-by-guanine is higher than average, which are preferred sites for gene methylation to occur) and affect gene expression within the stress response system (Weaver et al., 2004) and subsequent replication in human postmortem tissue (McGowan et al., 2009), there was great interest in studying gene methylation of *SLC6A4*. Some studies addressed the relation between SLEs and *SLC6A4* methylation: for example, a history of child abuse was associated with overall *SLC6A4* hyper-methylation in 96 females (but not 96 males) from the Iowa Adoption Study (IAS; Beach et al., 2010). This observation was replicated in a second sample of 155 IAS females who had experienced sexual abuse, and extended to show that methylation was associated with antisocial personality disorder (Beach et al., 2011).

Other studies reported differential *SLC6A4* methylation as a function of 5-HTTLPR genotype. Philibert and colleagues (2007) examined *SLC6A4* mRNA expression in 49 lymphoblast cell lines obtained from IAS participants. They identified one CpG island, in which 5-HTTLPR short allele carriers exhibited hyper-methylation that was associated with decreased mRNA expression. In another study of 200 individuals, cortisol response during the Trier Social Stress Test (TSST) was moderated by 5-HTTLPR genotype (Alexander et al., 2014). In a TSST study of 105 individuals, we identified a *SLC6A4* gene region, in which carriers of the 5-HTTLPR short allele exhibited increased methylation, compared to homozygous long allele carriers, as function of early life stress (Duman and Canli, 2015).

Taken together, these early studies of gene methylation, SLEs, and gene variants illustrate the utility in integrating across different levels of genetic, epigenetic, and environmental measures. Such efforts can contribute to elucidating the underlying molecular mechanisms of GxEs.

GENOME-WIDE ASSOCIATION STUDIES (GWAS)

Whereas the candidate gene approach focused on one or two genes at a time, GWAS used new technology that made it possible to assess genetic variation, mostly single nucleotide polymorphisms, across the entire set of an estimated 20,000 protein-coding human genes. Given that known candidate genes only account for a small proportion of the genetic variance, there was hope that GWAS would soon discover the remaining genes associated with personality traits.

The first GWAS of personality focused on neuroticism (Shifman et al., 2008). Shifman and colleagues selected approximately 3,600 extreme scorers (based on the neuroticism scale of the revised Eysenck Personality Questionnaire, EPQ) out of a community cohort of over 88,000 individuals. The sample was divided into a discovery cohort of over 2,000 concordant or discordant siblings and a replication sample of over 1,500 unrelated individuals. At a time when genome-wide SNP assessment was expensive, cost was reduced by pooling samples of DNA by sex and degree of extreme score ('high' or 'low' categories were 1–1.5 standard deviations above or below the mean, respectively; 'very high' or 'very low' were more than 1.5 standard deviations above or below the mean). SNPs were identified using a gene array (Affymetrix 100k and 500k) that contained approximately 450,000 probes that were tested for association with neuroticism, based on frequency differences between high and low neuroticism pools. In this study, one SNP (rs702543) – which was located within the phosphodiesterase 4D gene (*PDE4D*) – survived statistical significance testing in both samples. Shifman and colleagues then tested for differential frequencies of rs702543 by neuroticism score in three additional samples (*N*s of 761, 1,022, and 417), which did not replicate the initial association, although a later study by another group did produce a replication (Calboli et al., 2010). The authors noted that there was no evidence for any gene locus to account for more than 1% of variance, suggesting that the genetic basis of trait neuroticism may be in a large number of SNPs with small effects, requiring much larger sample sizes than anticipated.

Another GWAS of neuroticism was published in the same year by van den Oord and colleagues (van den Oord et al., 2008). Their approach was different by not using extreme scorers and not pooling DNA. The discovery sample consisted of more than 1,200 healthy individuals who completed the 12-item short version of the Eysenck Personality Questionnaire Neuroticism Scale46 (EPQR-N) and who were genotyped using the same SNP-array (Affymetrix 500k) used by Shifman and colleagues. The most significant SNPs associated with neuroticism were then genotyped in an independent replication sample of almost 1,900 individuals. Based on a false-discovery-rate threshold of 10% false positives, only four SNPs, all belonging to one gene (*MAMDC1*, also known as *MDGA2*; MAM-Meprin/A5-protein/PTPmu-domain containing glycosylphosphatidylinositol anchor 2) were found to be significant and replicable. Yet, later replication studies, including one by the same group of researchers, failed to confirm this association (Calboli et al., 2010; Hettema et al., 2009). A GWAS of neuroticism and antisocial personality disorder that was conducted based on about 2,700 subjects found no SNPs that reached statistical significance at the genome-wide level (Aragam et al., 2013). However, another replication study using a small cohort of approximately 200 depressed patients versus more than 500 controls replicated the association between neuroticism and *MAMDC1* (Heck et al., 2011).

GWAS continued to increase in size. A study by Terracciano and colleagues (2010), examining all Big Five traits, had a total sample of approximately 6,000 individuals (a discovery cohort of over 3,900 and two replication cohorts of over 900 and 1,100), in which only one SNP (rs 6832769, located within the *CLOCK* gene), associated with Agreeableness, replicated across cohorts.

One approach to increasing GWAS sample sizes is to conduct a meta-analysis. A 2012 study used a meta-analysis approach to analyze GWAS neuroticism data from over 6,200 subjects and a replication sample of another

6,000 individuals (Luciano et al., 2012). This study reported SNPs within two genes (Lectin, Mannose Binding 1 Like, *LMAN1L*, and Secretory Carrier Membrane Protein 2, *SCAMP2*) that replicated across all groups. Yet, a larger meta-analysis based on data from more than 17,000 individuals failed to replicate *any* associations with neuroticism (de Moor et al., 2012).

Although the aggregation of study cohorts increases GWAS samples, it comes at a cost if the personality trait of interest was assessed using different instruments across these cohorts, as is often the case. That is because the same term, say 'neuroticism', may not be conceptually synonymous across instruments and may therefore have different underlying genetic structures. Pace and Brannick (2010) conducted a meta-analysis of 79 personality studies to examine the degree to which different personality inventories were commensurate for the same construct. They found that convergent validity, the correlations among all personality measure instruments (five-factor-models (FFM) and non-FFM), were low for Agreeableness (0.31–0.54), Conscientiousness (0.27–0.51), Openness to Experience (0.26–0.51), Extraversion (0.37–0.66), and for Emotional Stability (0.32–0.66). When their meta-analysis was limited to studies based on the FFM, correlations improved to ranges from 0.48 (Openness) to 0.68 (Emotional Stability). Given the low convergent validity across instruments, it is plausible that genetic loadings onto similarly labeled scales across these instruments may also vary. Indeed, as mentioned earlier, meta-analyses from the domain of candidate genes suggest that the choice of measurement instrument moderates the link between the 5-HTTLPR and neuroticism.

Investigators of the Genetics of Personality Consortium (GPC) addressed the problem of multiple personality measurement instruments across GWAS by developing a technique to 'harmonize' data using Item–Response Theory (IRT; van den Berg et al., 2014). The study applied this harmonizing technique to neuroticism and extraversion data collected from 23 study cohorts, totaling more than 160,000 subjects, who were assessed with nine different personality inventories. Using this method, investigators confirmed that IRT-based neuroticism and extraversion scores showed heritability estimates of 48 and 49%, respectively, which were largely due to non-additive genetic factors.

A follow-up study by the GPC applied these principles in a meta-analysis of GWAS for neuroticism and MDD (Genetics of Personality et al., 2015). The study was based on harmonized neuroticism data across 29 discovery cohorts, totaling over 63,000 individuals, and a replication cohort of almost 10,000 individuals. The study reported one genome-wide significant SNP (rs35855737, located in the Membrane Associated Guanylate Kinase, WW and PDZ Domain Containing 1 gene, *MAGI1*) that was associated with neuroticism from the discovery cohort, although it did not replicate. The effect size of this SNP was low, with a regression coefficient of −0.04, and all SNPs together accounted for approximately 15% of the variance in neuroticism (compared to heritability estimates of 40% from twin studies, as discussed above). These results underscore the highly polygenic nature of personality traits like neuroticism.

A similar analysis using the same cohorts was conducted by the GPC for extraversion (van den Berg et al., 2016). This study found no genome-wide significant SNPs, but did find one site (LOC101928162) for a long non-coding RNA that was significant at the gene level. Furthermore, SNP-based heritability estimates for extraversion were low (5% for the Netherland Twin Registry) to absent (Queensland Institute of Medical Research cohort). These results suggest non-additive genetic effects, such as dominance or epistasis, and/or the involvement of rare variants with larger effect sizes.

In 2016, GWAS studies exceeding 100,000 individuals were published. Smith and colleagues (2016) conducted a meta-analysis of neuroticism GWAS based on a sample of 106,000 individuals. The sample was comprised of three study cohorts: the UK Biobank cohort (N = 91,370), the Generation Scotland: Scottish Family Health Study (GS:SFHS; N = 6,659), and the Queensland Institute of Medical Research (QIMR) cohort (N = 8,687). Unlike other meta-analyses of GWAS, all participants were assessed with the same instrument (Eysenck Personality Questionnaire-Revised [EPQ-R-S] Short Form's Neuroticism scale). As in the previous neuroticism study by the GPC (Genetics of Personality et al., 2015), SNPs accounted for 15% of heritability. The combined dataset identified nine regions that were associated with neuroticism, including one that contains at least 36 genes, although *MAGI1* (the SNP previously identified by the GPC) was not among them (it reached a significance of p = 0.07). When data were analyzed by cohort, however, the authors noted that:

> ...most of the associated alleles identified from the UK Biobank GWAS were not independently replicated within the GS:SFHS and QIMR cohorts, nor within the large Genetics of Personality Consortium meta-analysis. Of the eight loci that were genome-wide significant in the UK Biobank data set, only five were significant within the meta-analysis. With the exception of the locus on chromosome 17, none of these were replicated across the GS:SFHS and QIMR samples, and the most significantly associated locus, that on chromosome 8, is not significant in either sample. (p. 755)

Okbay and colleagues (2016) conducted the largest-to-date GWAS on subjective well-being, depressive symptoms, and neuroticism from 59 cohorts, totaling almost 300,000 individuals. The neuroticism sample was comprised of pooled data from the previously discussed GPC meta-analysis of more than 63,000 individuals (Genetics of Personality et al., 2015), plus new analyses from the UK Biobank cohort of more than 107,000 individuals. This study discovered 11 SNPs that were associated with neuroticism, including six SNPs that were located within an inversion polymorphism on chromosome 8, similar to what was reported earlier by Smith and colleagues (Smith et al., 2016), whose GWAS was based in part on a subset of the UK Biobank data used by Okbay and colleagues (a reminder that samples within various large-scale GWAS meta-analyses are rarely independent, and that the same datasets tend to reappear in later publications as their sample sizes grow and are recombined with other study cohorts). These 11 neuroticism-related SNPs were then compared against an ongoing large-scale depression GWAS (n = 368,890) 23andMe cohort, which showed that four SNPs were significantly associated with depression. The large sample size of this study comes at the cost of using heterogeneous neuroticism measures, which (for reasons discussed earlier) may reflect different underlying genetic factors. Indeed, despite the large sample, this study produced low SNP-based heritability estimates of 0.9% for neuroticism. Bayesian calculations for true explanatory power (corrected for winner's curse) were 0.011% for the top neuroticism-related SNP – suggesting that hundreds, if not thousands, of additional SNPs would need to be identified to account for only 9% of heritability. The data suggest that even larger GWAS will be required in the future, as the statistical power to detect even the lead SNP was only 13%.

MISSING HERITABILITY

The low success rate of GWAS to discover (and replicate) gene variants that add up to expected trait heritability estimates has been coined 'missing heritability' (Maher, 2008; Manolio et al., 2009). Several explanations have been put forward to account for this missing heritability.

Rare Variants

GWAS to date are usually based on data obtained from genotyping arrays that contain pre-selected probes to cover selected genomic regions containing SNPs. Earlier arrays contained probes for which the minor allele frequency (MAF) in the population was about 5%

of the population (Manolio et al., 2009), with today's arrays reaching MAFs of 1%, as used in the 1000 Genome Project (http://www.1000genomes.org/). That means that rarer SNPs would not have been captured in the collected datasets. It is possible that the genetic architecture of heritable traits rests on rare genetic variants with large effect sizes. Trumbetta and Gottesman (2011) have speculated that rare variants associated with different genes may have large effects on different endophenotypes (e.g., structural or functional features of the brain), but these different endophenotypes may all produce the same behavioral phenotype (e.g., trait neuroticism) in a process named 'equifinality'. Studies based on measures of endophenotypes (Gottesman and Gould, 2003), such as imaging genetics (for reviews, see Bigos and Weinberger, 2010; Canli, 2004; Casey et al., 2010; Congdon and Canli, 2005; Domschke and Dannlowski, 2010; Durston, 2010; Hariri et al., 2006; Hariri and Weinberger, 2003; Martin et al., 2009; Mattay and Goldberg, 2004; Meyer-Lindenberg, 2010; Meyer-Lindenberg and Weinberger, 2006; Meyer-Lindenberg and Zink, 2007; Potkin et al., 2009; Scharinger et al., 2010; Tost et al., 2012; Wiers, 2012) are well-placed to dissociate different genetic factors to equifinality. However, such work would require GWAS-like sample sizes, as are currently being aggregated in consortia such as ENIGMA (Thompson et al., 2014), but would also require genomic technologies that can capture rare variants, such as next-generation sequencing (Ezewudo and Zwick, 2013; Li et al., 2013; Matullo et al., 2013). The use of so-called 'next-gen' methods would also address another concern, that older probe arrays covered SNPs but not more complex genetic variations.

Structural Variants

Most GWAS are based on array technology that only captures SNPs. Yet, many polymorphisms of interest have different or more complex structures. For example, the 5-HTTLPR has a variable repeat polymorphic structure that is not captured by these arrays. Vinkhuyzen and colleagues (2011) worked around this limitation by genotyping a sample of 2,823 individuals for the 5-HTTLPR and merging the data from several genome-wide SNP array platforms. They found no individual SNPs that were in high linkage disequilibrium (LD) with the 5-HTTLPR, but did identify two-SNP haplotypes can be used as proxies for the 5-HTTLPR in GWAS, correlating with the polymorphism at $r^2 = 0.775$. Haenisch and colleagues (2013) conducted a haplotype analysis to test for an association with Major Depressive Disorder (MDD), based on GWAS data from 1,505 cases and 2,168 controls. This analysis confirmed a significant association between the haplotype that tags the 5-HTTLPR S-allele and MDD. However, the authors acknowledged that the haplotype approach has limitations, as it does not fully capture the polymorphic structure of 5-HTTLPR. This is an inherent limitation of array-based technologies, which contain only selected SNP-based probes. Next-generation sequencing will offer the potential to capture all of the genomic structure to overcome this limitation.

Sample Size, Additive and Non-Additive Gene Effects

Perhaps the most common explanation for missing heritability has been that current sample sizes are too small to capture the small genetic contributions of a large number of individual SNPs. This explanation rests, at least in part, on the assumption that trait-related genes can be sufficiently modeled by including only additive genetic effects. Reynolds and Finkel (2015) tested this assumption explicitly in a meta-analysis of heritability of cognitive aging: based on 27 studies, they found declining heritability for some cognitive functions with age. They then conducted a second meta-analysis to address the differing heritability estimates for cognitive functions obtained from SNP-based versus twin-based GWAS and found that non-additive genetic variance may increase with age, such that the lower heritability estimates obtained from SNP-based studies may reflect influences such as Dominance, Epistasis, or rGEs.

Others have likewise argued that genetic models based only on additive effects are not biologically realistic and should include epistatic models, for which statistical methods and tools have recently been reviewed by Wei and colleagues (Wei et al., 2014). An empirical study by this group (Hemani et al., 2014) tested for epistasis in a discovery sample of 846 individuals and a replication sample from three cohorts of 2,270 individuals, based on 7,339 gene expression levels measured in peripheral blood. There was evidence for epistasis: in the discovery set, there were 501 significant pairwise interactions from 238 genes, of which 30 replicated. However, the effects were small: whereas additive effects accounted for 2.16% of expression levels of 7,339 genes, epistatic variance only accounted for 0.22%. In their review of the larger literature of both GWAS and candidate gene studies, Wei and colleagues (2014) conclude:

> The emerging trend is that there are hints of epistasis being uncovered through exhaustive searches for epistasis between pairs of SNPs underlying complex traits, but as yet there is rather little evidence that this approach detects epistatic interactions that are easily interpreted and statistically replicated in comparison to additive effects. It is reasonable to conclude at this stage that large epistatic effects (that have thus far eluded detection) are unlikely to exist. (p. 729)

Jaffee and Price (2007) reviewed the evidence for rGEs in the behavioral and in the molecular genetic literature as a possible explanation for missing heritability. In the behavioral genetic literature, they point to reports of heritability of environmental measures as evidence for rGEs. For example, they point to heritable environmental measures such as parental negativity or social support, which can be accounted for by genetic contributions to individual differences in personality.

A particularly important example is the reporting of life events, because many studies of GxEs rest on the assumption that negative life events are independent from genetic variables. Yet, controllable life events (i.e., events that are under the individual's control) are heritable, whereas uncontrollable life events are not (Mcgue et al., 1991; Plomin et al., 1990). This observation suggests that some life events are heritable because they are under the control of some attributes of the individual, which are (partially) under genetic control. Saudino and colleagues (1997) tested the hypothesis that personality traits may be a suitable mediator between genetic influences and life events, based on a sample of 320 twin pairs. They tested the effect of neuroticism, extraversion, and openness to experience on 25 measures of life events. For women, genetic variance for these three traits explained all of the genetic variance for controllable, desirable, and undesirable life events. Surprisingly, men showed no genetic influence on life events. The authors speculated that, rather than reflecting sex differences in the heritability of personality per se, the results may reflect sex differences in the heritability of attributional processes related to the perception or interpretation of life events. This is an intriguing hypothesis that awaits future examination.

In a twin study of over 1,100 pairs of adolescents, McAdams and colleagues (2013) reported heritability of about 40% for negative life events, without any sex differences. The heritability of negative life events could be accounted for by other traits, with which they shared high genetic correlations, specifically Oppositionality (0.94), Delinquency (0.99), Physical Aggression (0.68), and Depression (0.57).

Power and colleagues (Power et al., 2013) tested for heritability of reporting SLEs based on GWAS data from 2,578 individuals. They found that SNPs accounted for 30% of the variance in SLEs. Furthermore, they found that this heritability estimate was associated with individual differences in Neuroticism and Psychoticism. Thus, both twin and GWAS converge on confirming an intermediate role for personality in the heritability of life event reporting. Future GxE studies should therefore be designed to be able to account for potential rGE confounds.

SOLUTIONS AND FUTURE DIRECTIONS

The literature reviewed above traces an arc of discovery from behavior genetic studies, to candidate gene studies, to GWAS. These are often presented as competing approaches (Wilkening et al., 2009). Yet, they complement each other in important ways. With the heritability of personality traits well-established, behavior genetic studies now turn their attention to more complex study designs, longitudinal datasets, and innovations in causal modeling to reveal common genetic factors between behaviors that were previously believed to be causally related (de Moor and Boomsma, 2011). Meanwhile, candidate gene studies and GWAS represent different approaches to link phenotypes to molecular gene targets. Candidate gene studies are hypothesis-driven and thus dependent on prior biological data; they focus on one (or few) gene(s) at a time; they tend to be obtained from single-laboratory, small-scale samples, but with the benefit of (or opportunity for) detailed phenotyping. GWAS are hypothesis-free and thus maximize the opportunity for discovery; they focus on the genome; they are increasingly based on consortia compiling large-scale samples, at a cost of limited phenotyping. Yet, candidate gene studies have only identified a small set of genes that account for only a small amount of genetic variance, and GWAS have failed to detect sufficient genetic variance to account for much of the known heritability of complex traits. Past solutions have been ever-larger samples and improvements in genomic coverage. In this final section, I discuss future solutions for discovering missing heritability and gaining a deeper understanding of the biological molecular mechanisms that link genes to personality.

From Genes to Gene Networks

One reason for the low yield of significant results from traditional GWAS analyses is that genes are treated as single statistical observations that need to exceed a genome-wide correction threshold based on single-marker association tests. Yet, a gene does not function in isolation from other biological processes (Schadt, 2009), but rather belongs to a larger family of genes, with which it shares homology and/or biological functions. Thus, one potentially promising solution is pathway analysis, in which sets of genes are analyzed that share particular biological functions within common molecular pathways. For example, the Gene Ontology (GO) Consortium (http://geneontology.org/) classifies gene sets by molecular function ('What are the molecular activities carried out by gene products?'), cellular component ('Where in the cell are gene products active?'), and biological process ('Which signaling pathways or complex processes associate with gene products?'). Statistical analysis tools such as Ingenuity Pathway Analysis, IPA (www.ingenuity.com), or gene set enrichment analysis, GSEA (Subramanian et al., 2005, 2007) (http://software.broadinstitute.org/gsea/index.jsp), have been developed to capture these functional and structural relationships. Wang and colleagues (2007, 2010) developed the application of pathway-based analyses to GWAS, and others developed online tools for the analysis of SNP datasets using pathway analysis (e.g., Zhang et al., 2010, 2015).

Verweij and colleagues (2010) conducted a GWAS of association with Cloninger's temperament scales in a sample of 5,117 individuals, but failed to find any significant SNPs at genome-level corrected significance thresholds. IPA pathway analysis also failed to detect any significantly enriched pathways. A follow-up analysis was conducted on a sample of over 11,000 individuals from four cohorts, which again failed to find any genome-wide significant SNPs or enriched pathways at corrected levels (Service et al., 2012).

Kim and colleagues (2015) applied pathway analysis to GWAS of Big Five personality traits. In a discovery sample of 1,089 and replication sample of 1,490 women, they tested for trait associations with 1,042 pathways (comprising 8,297 genes) selected from the molecular signature database (MSigDB, http://software.broadinstitute.org/gsea/msigdb/index.jsp). This analysis generated 14 pathways that were significantly associated (nominal P-value < .01) with all traits except Openness. For example, they found that Neuroticism was associated with gene sets involved in axon guidance, which play a critical role during development but also play a role in synaptic plasticity. This is an intriguing finding, given reports that early life stress moderates the association of Neuroticism or Neuroticism-associated gene variants with mood disorders (Caspi et al., 2003).

Another study applied pathway analysis to GWAS of fluid and crystallized intelligence (Christoforou et al., 2014). Christoforou and colleagues used a discovery sample of 670 and a replication sample of 3,511 men and women, and tested for associations of general fluid intelligence (gF) and general crystallized intelligence (gC) with gene pathways. Their analysis proceeded in two steps. In the first step, they conducted SNP-based and gene-based association analyses to generate a list of genes. Genes that showed a significant association (nominal P-value < 0.05) in both the discovery and replication samples were then subjected to Ingenuity Pathway Analysis (IPA) in a second step. IPA then compares the submitted gene list to its knowledge base of gene function annotations to identify genes that aggregate for a particular function at greater-than-chance levels (Fisher's Exact Test P < 0.05). Using this approach, Christoforou and colleagues found that gC was enriched for genes involved in synaptic depression and long-term depression, which play a central role in synaptic plasticity, learning, and memory. (This association was robust enough to meet statistical correction at a false-discovery rate of 0.05.) In contrast, gF was enriched for genes regulating long-term potentiation and functions related to neuronal quantity, morphology, and integrity. Thus, gC and gF could be dissociated at the molecular genetic level by the functional properties of gene sets, rather than individual gene SNPs.

Taken together, these pathway studies illustrate how available GWAS data can be exploited to map complex traits onto networks of genes that may further illuminate the underlying biological mechanisms and guide future gene-association or experimental studies. However, molecular signaling pathways are only incompletely characterized at the level of DNA, as epigenetic regulators can alter its transcription to mRNA and other modifiers can affect translation to proteins. Indeed, the correlation between mRNA and protein expression in the human cerebellum, for example, is only 0.29 (Ostlund and Sonnhammer, 2012). Thus, other levels of gene expression and regulation are likely to improve our understanding of gene networks. This perspective characterizes the 'systems biology' approach.

Systems Biology

Systems biology emphasizes the integration of biological data across levels of analysis. The field can be traced back to visionaries in physiology, cybernetics, and thermodynamics (Saks et al., 2009) and maintains a multi-disciplinary identity that is shaped by multiple branches of biology, as well as mathematics, computer science, philosophy, physics, and the social sciences (Werner, 2013; for historical perspectives on systems biology, see Chuang et al., 2010; Ideker et al., 2001a;

Kitano, 2002; Noble, 2008; Peitsch and de Graaf, 2014; Saks et al., 2009; Werner, 2013). Kitano (Kitano, 2002) characterized systems biology this way:

> System-level understanding, the approach advocated in systems biology (2), requires a shift in our notion of 'what to look for' in biology. While an understanding of genes and proteins continues to be important, the focus is on understanding a system's structure and dynamics. Because a system is not just an assembly of genes and proteins, its properties cannot be fully understood merely by drawing diagrams of their interconnections. Although such a diagram represents an important first step, it is analogous to a static roadmap, whereas what we really seek to know are the traffic patterns, why such traffic patterns emerge, and how we can control them. (p. 1662)

Thus, systems biology emphasizes both the structure of, and dynamic changes within, networks. Ideker and colleagues (2001b) characterize the dynamic approach by perturbing biological systems to measure the system's response to the perturbation at the gene, protein, or pathway level, and then building mathematical models to describe the system and its dynamics. They applied this approach to develop a model of a cellular metabolic network (Ideker et al., 2001b). Contemporary systems biology has expanded into translational emerging applications that include pathway-based biomarkers, global genetic interaction maps, and systems approaches to identify genes for complex diseases (Chuang et al., 2010) and that aim to integrate different levels of genome-wide measures (the 'omics': genome, epigenome, transcriptome, proteome, metabolome) and environmental exposures that can perturb them (Li, 2013; Sun and Hu, 2016).

The systems biology approach has been applied in some personality and trait studies. Chen and colleagues (Chen et al., 2011) examined the role of dopaminergic pathways and environmental stressors in the Highly Sensitive Person (HSP) trait. Four-hundred-and-eighty individuals completed measures of HSP and two environmental variables, stressful life events (SLEs) and parental warmth, and were genotyped for 98 dopaminergic genes. The study identified 10 polymorphisms, primarily associated with modulation and receptor subsystems, which accounted for 15% of HSP variance, with recent SLEs contributing an additional 2% of variance.

Zhao and colleagues (2014) applied a systems biology approach to the genetic pathways of intelligence. They identified 158 IQ-associated genes based on a literature search and applied online analysis tools and databases to search for enrichment in function and pathways. This analysis identified seven regions of chromosome 7 and the X chromosome that were enriched in IQ-associated genes, which were functionally enriched in seven transcription factors and 16 microRNAs. Pathway analysis then identified dopamine and norepinephrine systems in IQ-related biological processes.

We have recently conducted a pathway analysis of gene expression profiles in postmortem nucleus accumbens tissue from 26 donors with known levels of loneliness (Canli et al., 2017). Loneliness is a stable, heritable trait (Boomsma et al., 2005) and the nucleus accumbens a brain region implicated in reduced processing of positive social stimuli among lonely individuals (Cacioppo et al., 2008). Furthermore, loneliness is associated with a host of apparently unrelated mental and physical illnesses. We identified almost 1,600 genes that were differentially expressed as a function of loneliness in the nucleus accumbens. Pathway analysis identified gene sets associated with a range of psychological and neurological disorders, cancer, and other illnesses. Furthermore, we identified upstream RNA regulators that could account for pleiotropic effects across gene sets. This initial study was limited by the small sample size and reliance on a gene expression array. We addressed these limitations in a follow-up study (Canli et al., 2018) by studying the gene expression profiles of more than 180 donors, based on a form of next-generation sequencing called RNA-Seq. In this follow-up study, we investigated gene expression in the dorsolateral prefrontal cortex, using gene set enrichment analysis, and discovered 337 up-regulated and 43 down-regulated gene sets, which were statistically significant at a false-discovery rate of < 0.05. Similar to our results from the nucleus accumbens, significant gene sets includes those previously associated with Alzheimer's disease, psychiatric illness, immune dysfunction, and cancer, all of which are exacerbated by loneliness. We suggest that these gene sets may contain novel candidates for socially regulated genes (i.e., genes whose expression levels may be regulated by social environmental variables such as loneliness) across a wide range of neurodegenerative, psychiatric, and somatic illnesses.

Convergence

Williams and Auwerx (2015) argue for a convergence of reductionist and systems biology approaches in the study of complex traits. They characterize the reductionist approach as one that favors 'forward genetics', in which variations in phenotypes in humans (or crops) are sought to be linked to causal genes, using tools such as GWAS; although capable of generating large amounts of data from large human cohorts, they note that this approach is hampered by the missing heritability issue. They characterize the systems biology approach as one that favors 'reverse genetics', in which genes of interest are manipulated to perform gain- or loss-of-function (G/LOF) studies in model populations such as mice, fruit flies (*Drosophila*), worms, yeast, or plants (*Arabidopsis*); although this approach can examine functional variants, epistatic, and GxE effects in some model populations, it may not generalize to humans. The convergent application of both approaches can facilitate scientific discovery. For example, model organisms such as yeast, worms, or flies can serve as screens to evaluate hundreds of genes, which can then be tested against human GWAS data. This approach was used by Yamamoto and colleagues (Yamamoto et al., 2014) to screen in *Drosophila* for genes involved in the development, function, and maintenance of the nervous system; it generated 165 gene candidates which were then merged with a human dataset of 1,929 human exomes from families with unsolved Mendelian disease. This process produced the discovery of disease-associated mutations in six families. As Williams and Auwerx point out, convergence can be surprising: a comparison of human genome sequences with that of the plant *Arabidopsis thaliana* revealed that 71% of genes associated with neurological diseases have orthologs in *Arabidopsis* (Xu and Moller, 2011).

It will be exciting to see applications of this convergent thinking in the molecular psychology of personality. Indeed, we apply this convergent thinking in a study of trait anxiety, in which we integrate study approaches based on gene expression analysis in postmortem tissue, array and RNA-Seq in healthy and patient cohorts, and in vivo gene-manipulations in rodent behavioral studies. Studies of the social regulation of gene expression in fish (Korzan et al., 2014), or the genomics of social insects like honeybees (Honeybee Genome Sequencing et al., 2006; Kapheim et al., 2015) or ants (Gadau et al., 2012), can be informative for translation to human personality studies. We may discover that watching bugs can be as illuminating as watching people.

ACKNOWLEDGMENTS

The work presented here was supported by funding from NIA R01 AG034578-01, NSF BCS-0843346, BCS-0224221, OIA #0722874, and by Stony Brook GCRC#*M01RR10710*.

REFERENCES

Alexander, N., Klucken, T., Koppe, G., Osinsky, R., Walter, B., Vaitl, D., ... Hennig, J. (2012).

Interaction of the serotonin transporter-linked polymorphic region and environmental adversity: Increased amygdala–hypothalamus connectivity as a potential mechanism linking neural and endocrine hyperreactivity. *Biological Psychiatry*, *72*, 49–56.

Alexander, N., Kuepper, Y., Schmitz, A., Osinsky, R., Kozyra, E., & Hennig, J. (2009). Gene–environment interactions predict cortisol responses after acute stress: Implications for the etiology of depression. *Psychoneuroendocrinology*, *34*, 1294–1303.

Alexander, N., Wankerl, M., Hennig, J., Miller, R., Zankert, S., Steudte-Schmiedgen, S., ... Kirschbaum, C. (2014). DNA methylation profiles within the serotonin transporter gene moderate the association of 5-HTTLPR and cortisol stress reactivity. *Translational Psychiatry*, *4*, e443.

Aragam, N., Wang, K.-S., Anderson, J. L., & Liu, X. (2013). TMPRSS9 and GRIN2B are associated with neuroticism: A genome-wide association study in a European sample. *Journal of Molecular Neuroscience*, *50*, 250–256.

Beach, S. R., Brody, G. H., Todorov, A. A., Gunter, T. D., & Philibert, R. A. (2010). Methylation at SLC6A4 is linked to family history of child abuse: An examination of the Iowa Adoptee sample. *American Journal of Medical Genetics Part B: Neuropsychiatric Genetics*, *153B*, 710–713.

Beach, S. R., Brody, G. H., Todorov, A. A., Gunter, T. D., & Philibert, R. A. (2011). Methylation at 5HTT mediates the impact of child sex abuse on women's antisocial behavior: An examination of the Iowa adoptee sample. *Psychosomatic Medicine*, *73*, 83–87.

Benjamin, J., Li, L., Patterson, C., Greenberg, B. D., Murphy, D. L., & Hamer, D. H. (1996). Population and familial association between the D4 dopamine receptor gene and measures of Novelty Seeking. *Nature Genetics*, *12*, 81–84.

Bertolino, A., Rubino, V., Sambataro, F., Blasi, G., Latorre, V., Fazio, L., ... Scarabino, T. (2006). Prefrontal–hippocampal coupling during memory processing is modulated by comt val158met genotype. *Biological Psychiatry*, *60*, 1250–1258.

Bigos, K. L., & Weinberger, D. R. (2010). Imaging genetics: Days of future past. *Neuroimage*, *53*, 804–809.

Boomsma, D. I., Willemsen, G., Dolan, C. V., Hawkley, L. C., & Cacioppo, J. T. (2005). Genetic and environmental contributions to loneliness in adults: The Netherlands twin register study. *Behavior Genetics*, *35*, 745–752.

Buckholtz, J. W., & Meyer-Lindenberg, A. (2008). MAOA and the neurogenetic architecture of human aggression. *Trends in Neuroscience*, *31*, 120–129.

Byrd, A. L., & Manuck, S. B. (2014). MAOA, childhood maltreatment, and antisocial behavior: Meta-analysis of a gene–environment interaction. *Biological Psychiatry*, *75*, 9–17.

Cacioppo, J. T., Norris, C. J., Decety, J., Monteleone, G., & Nusbaum, H. (2008). In the eye of the beholder: Individual differences in perceived social isolation predict regional brain activation to social stimuli. *Journal of Cognitive Neuroscience*, *21*, 83–92.

Calboli, F. C., Tozzi, F., Galwey, N. W., Antoniades, A., Mooser, V., Preisig, M., ... Balding, D. J. (2010). A genome-wide association study of neuroticism in a population-based sample. *PLoS One*, *5*, e11504.

Canli, T. (2004). Functional brain mapping of extraversion and neuroticism: Learning from individual differences in emotion processing. *Journal of Personality*, *72*, 1105–1132.

Canli, T. (2008a). Toward a 'molecular psychology' of personality. In O. John, R. W. Robbins, & L. A. Pervin (Eds.), *Handbook of personality: Theory and research* (3rd ed., pp. 311–327). New York, NY: Guilford Press.

Canli, T. (2008b). Toward a neurogenetic theory of neuroticism. *Annals of the New York Academy of Sciences*, *1129*, 153–174.

Canli, T. (2015). Molecular psychology: A brief history and introduction. In T. Canli (Ed.), *The Oxford handbook of molecular psychology* (pp. 3–15). New York, NY: Oxford University Press.

Canli, T., Congdon, E., Constable, T. R., & Lesch, K. P. (2008). Additive effects of serotonin transporter and tryptophan hydroxylase-2 gene variation on neural correlates of affective processing. *Biological Psychology*, *79*, 118–125.

Canli, T., Ferri, J., & Duman, E. A. (2009). Genetics of emotion regulation. *Neuroscience*, *164*, 43–54.

Canli, T., & Lesch, K.-P. (2007). Long story short: The serotonin transporter in emotion regulation and social cognition. *Nature Neuroscience, 10*, 1103–1109.

Canli, T., Qiu, M., Omura, K., Congdon, E., Haas, B. W., Amin, Z., ... Lesch, K. P. (2006). Neural correlates of epigenesis. *Proceedings of the National Academy of Sciences of the United States of America, 103*, 16033–16038.

Canli, T., Wen, R., Wang, X., Mikhailik, A., Yu, L., Fleischman, D., ... Bennett, D. A. (2017). Differential transcriptome expression in human nucleus accumbens as a function of loneliness. *Molecular Psychiatry, 22*, 1069–1078.

Canli, T., Yu, L., Yu, X., Zhao, H., Fleischman, D., Wilson, R. S., ... Bennett, D. A. (2018). Loneliness five years ante-mortem is associated with disease-related differential gene expression in postmortem dorsolateral prefrontal cortex. *Translational Psychiatry, 8*, 2–9.

Cao, J., Hudziak, J. J., & Li, D. (2013). Multicultural association of the serotonin transporter gene (SLC6A4) with substance use disorder. *Neuropsychopharmacology, 38*, 1737–1747.

Casey, B. J., Soliman, F., Bath, K. G., & Glatt, C. E. (2010). Imaging genetics and development: Challenges and promises. *Human Brain Mapping, 31*, 838–851.

Caspi, A., McClay, J., Moffitt, T. E., Mill, J., Martin, J., Craig, I. W., ... Poulton, R. (2002). Role of genotype in the cycle of violence in maltreated children. *Science, 297*, 851–854.

Caspi, A., Sugden, K., Moffitt, T. E., Taylor, A., Craig, I. W., Harrington, H., ... Poulton, R. (2003). Influence of life stress on depression: Moderation by a polymorphism in the 5-HTT gene. *Science, 301*, 386–389.

Cattell, R. B. (1943). The description of personality: Basic traits resolved into clusters. *Journal of Abnormal and Social Psychology, 38*, 476–506. http://dx.doi.org/10.1037/h0054116

Chen, C. H., Chen, C. S., Moyzis, R., Stern, H., He, Q. H., Li, H., ... Dong, Q. (2011). Contributions of dopamine-related genes and environmental factors to highly sensitive personality: A multi-step neuronal system-level approach. *PLoS One, 6*, e21636.

Christoforou, A., Espeseth, T., Davies, G., Fernandes, C. P. D., Giddaluru, S., Mattheisen, M., ... Le Hellard, S. (2014). GWAS-based pathway analysis differentiates between fluid and crystallized intelligence. *Genes, Brain and Behavior, 13*, 663–674.

Chuang, H.-Y., Hofree, M., & Ideker, T. (2010). A decade of systems biology. *Annual Review of Cell and Developmental Biology, 26*, 721–744.

Clayden, R. C., Zaruk, A., Meyre, D., Thabane, L., & Samaan, Z. (2012). The association of attempted suicide with genetic variants in the SLC6A4 and TPH genes depends on the definition of suicidal behavior: A systematic review and meta-analysis. *Translational Psychiatry, 2*, e166.

Congdon, E., & Canli, T. (2005). The endophenotype of impulsivity: Reaching consilience through behavioral, genetic, and neuroimaging approaches. *Behavioral and Cognitive Neuroscience Reviews, 4*, 262–281.

Congdon, E., & Canli, T. (2008a). Genomic imaging of personality: Towards a molecular neurobiology of impulsivity. In G. Boyle, G. Matthews, & D. Saklowsky (Eds.), *The SAGE handbook of personality theory and assessment: Personality measurement and testing* (Vol. 2, pp. 334–351). Thousand Oaks, CA: Sage.

Congdon, E., & Canli, T. (2008b). A neurogenetic approach to impulsivity. *Journal of Personality, 76*, 1447–1484.

Conley, D., Rauscher, E., Dawes, C., Magnusson, P. K., & Siegal, M. L. (2013). Heritability and the equal environments assumption: Evidence from multiple samples of misclassified twins. *Behavior Genetics, 43*, 415–426.

Costa, P. T., & McCrae, R. R. (1992). *Revised NEO Personality Inventory (NEO-PI-R) and NEO Five-Factor Inventory (NEOFFI). Professional Manual*. Odessa, FL: Psychological Assessment Resources, Inc.

Cronk, N. J., Slutske, W. S., Madden, P. A., Bucholz, K. K., Reich, W., & Heath, A. C. (2002). Emotional and behavioral problems among female twins: An evaluation of the equal environments assumption. *Journal of the American Academy of Child and Adolescent Psychiatry, 41*, 829–837.

de Medeiros Alves, V., Bezerra, D. G., de Andrade, T. G., de Melo Neto, V. L., & Nardi, A. E. (2015). Genetic polymorphisms might predict suicide attempts in mental disorder patients: A systematic review and meta-analysis. *CNS and Neurological Disorders: Drug Targets, 14*, 820–827.

de Moor, M. H., & Boomsma, D. (2011). Understanding heritability by explaining heritability: Recent developments in behaviour genetics tell us more. *European Journal of Personality*, 25, 267–286.

de Moor, M. H. M., Costa, P. T., Terracciano, A., Krueger, R. F., de Geus, E. J., Toshiko, T., ... Boomsma, D. I. (2012). Meta-analysis of genome-wide association studies for personality. *Molecular Psychiatry*, 17, 337–349.

Derks, E. M., Dolan, C. V., & Boomsma, D. I. (2006). A test of the equal environment assumption (EEA) in multivariate twin studies. *Twin Research and Human Genetics*, 9, 403–411.

Dick, D. M., Agrawal, A., Keller, M. C., Adkins, A., Aliev, F., Monroe, S., ... Sher, K. J. (2015). Candidate gene–environment interaction research: Reflections and recommendations. *Perspectives on Psychological Science*, 10, 37–59.

Domschke, K., & Dannlowski, U. (2010). Imaging genetics of anxiety disorders. *Neuroimage*, 53, 822–831.

Dougherty, L. R., Klein, D. N., Congdon, E., Canli, T., & Hayden, E. P. (2010). Interaction between 5-HTTLPR and BDNF Val66Met polymorphisms on HPA axis reactivity in preschoolers. *Biological Psychology*, 83, 93–100.

Duman, E. A., & Canli, T. (2015). Influence of life stress, 5-HTTLPR genotype, and SLC6A4 methylation on gene expression and stress response in healthy Caucasian males. *Biology of Mood and Anxiety Disorders*, 5, 2.

Duncan, L. E., & Keller, M. C. (2011). A critical review of the first 10 years of candidate gene-by-environment interaction research in psychiatry. *American Journal of Psychiatry*, 168, 1041–1049.

Durston, S. (2010). Imaging genetics in ADHD. *Neuroimage*, 53, 832–838.

Ebstein, R. P., Novick, O., Umansky, R., Priel, B., Osher, Y., Blaine, D., ... Belmaker, R. H. (1996). Dopamine D4 receptor (D4DR) exon III polymorphism associated with the human personality trait of Novelty Seeking. *Nature Genetics*, 12, 78–80.

Ebstein, R. P., Zhong, S., Chark, R., San Lai, P., & Chew, S. H. (2015). Modeling the genetics of social cognition in the laboratory. In T. Canli (Ed.), *The Oxford handbook of molecular psychology* (pp. 167–209). New York, NY: Oxford University Press.

Eley, T. C., Sugden, K., Corsico, A., Gregory, A. M., Sham, P., McGuffin, P., ... Craig, I. W. (2004). Gene–environment interaction analysis of serotonin system markers with adolescent depression. *Molecular Psychiatry*, 9, 908–915.

Eysenck, H. J. (1970). *The structure of human personality* (3rd ed.). London, England: Methuen.

Ezewudo, M., & Zwick, M. E. (2013). Evaluating rare variants in complex disorders using next-generation sequencing. *Current Psychiatry Reports*, 15, 349.

Felson, J. (2014). What can we learn from twin studies? A comprehensive evaluation of the equal environments assumption. *Social Science Research*, 43, 184–199.

Ficks, C. A., & Waldman, I. D. (2014). Candidate genes for aggression and antisocial behavior: A meta-analysis of association studies of the 5HTTLPR and MAOA-uVNTR. *Behavior Genetics*, 44, 427–444.

Flint, J., & Kendler, K. S. (2014). The genetics of major depression. *Neuron*, 81, 484–503.

Fosse, R., Joseph, J., & Richardson, K. (2015). A critical assessment of the equal-environment assumption of the twin method for schizophrenia. *Frontiers in Psychiatry*, 6, 62.

Gadau, J., Helmkampf, M., Nygaard, S., Roux, J., Simola, D. F., Smith, C. R., ... Smith, C. D. (2012). The genomic impact of 100 million years of social evolution in seven ant species. *Trends in Genetics*, 28, 14–21.

Gao, Z., Yuan, H., Sun, M., Wang, Z., He, Y., & Liu, D. (2014). The association of serotonin transporter gene polymorphism and geriatric depression: A meta-analysis. *Neuroscience Letters*, 578, 148–152.

Gauderman, W. J. (2002). Sample size requirements for association studies of gene–gene interaction. *American Journal of Epidemiology*, 155, 478–484.

Genetics of Personality Consortium, de Moor, M. H., van den Berg, S. M., Verweij, K. J., Krueger, R. F., Luciano, M., ... Boomsma, D. I. (2015). Meta-analysis of genome-wide association studies for neuroticism, and the polygenic association with major depressive disorder. *JAMA Psychiatry*, 72, 642–650.

Gillespie, N. A., Whitfield, J. B., Williams, B., Heath, A. C., & Martin, N. G. (2005). The relationship between stressful life events, the serotonin transporter (5-HTTLPR) genotype and major depression. *Psychological Medicine, 35*, 101–111.

Goldberg, L. R. (1990). An alternative 'description of personality': The Big-Five factor structure. *Journal of Personality and Social Psychology, 59*, 1216–1229. http://dx.doi.org/10.1037/0022-3514.59.6.1216

Gottesman, I. I., & Gould, T. D. (2003). The endophenotype concept in psychiatry: Etymology and strategic intentions. *American Journal of Psychiatry, 160*, 636–645.

Haenisch, B., Herms, S., Mattheisen, M., Steffens, M., Breuer, R., Strohmaier, J., ... Cichon, S. (2013). Genome-wide association data provide further support for an association between 5-HTTLPR and major depressive disorder. *Journal of Affective Disorders, 146*, 438–440.

Hariri, A. R., Drabant, E. M., & Weinberger, D. R. (2006). Imaging genetics: Perspectives from studies of genetically driven variation in serotonin function and corticolimbic affective processing. *Biological Psychiatry, 59*, 888–897.

Hariri, A. R., & Holmes, A. (2006). Genetics of emotional regulation: The role of the serotonin transporter in neural function. *Trends in Cognitive Science, 10*, 182–191.

Hariri, A. R., & Weinberger, D. R. (2003). Imaging genomics. *British Medical Bulletin, 65*, 259–270.

Heck, A., Pfister, H., Czamara, D., Muller-Myhsok, B., Putz, B., Lucae, S., ... Ising, M. (2011). Evidence for associations between MDGA2 polymorphisms and harm avoidance: Replication and extension of a genome-wide association finding. *Psychiatric Genetics, 21*, 257–260.

Hemani, G., Shakhbazov, K., Westra, H.-J., Esko, T., Henders, A. K., McRae, A. F., ... Powell, J. E. (2014). Detection and replication of epistasis influencing transcription in humans. *Nature, 508*, 249–253.

Herrmann, M. J., Huter, T., Muller, F., Muhlberger, A., Pauli, P., Reif, A., ... Lesch, K.-P. (2007). Additive effects of serotonin transporter and tryptophan hydroxylase-2 gene variation on emotional processing. *Cerebral Cortex, 17*, 1160–1163.

Hettema, J. M., van den Oord, E. J., An, S. S., Kendler, K. S., & Chen, X. (2009). Follow-up association study of novel neuroticism gene MAMDC1. *Psychiatric Genetics, 19*, 213–214.

Honeybee Genome Sequencing Consortium, Weinstock, G. M., Robinson, G. E., Gibbs, R. A., Weinstock, G. M., Robinson, G. E., ... Wright, R. (2006). Insights into social insects from the genome of the honeybee *Apis mellifera*. *Nature, 443*, 931–949.

Ideker, T., Galitski, T., & Hood, L. (2001a). A new approach to decoding life: Systems biology. *Annual Review of Genomics and Human Genetics, 2*, 343–372.

Ideker, T., Thorsson, V., Ranish, J. A., Christmas, R., Buhler, J., Eng, J. K., ... Hood, L. (2001b). Integrated genomic and proteomic analyses of a systematically perturbed metabolic network. *Science, 292*, 929–934.

Jaffee, S. R., & Price, T. S. (2007). Gene–environment correlations: A review of the evidence and implications for prevention of mental illness. *Molecular Psychiatry, 12*, 432–442.

Jaffee, S. R., & Price, T. S. (2012). The implications of genotype–environment correlation for establishing causal processes in psychopathology. *Developmental Psychopathology, 24*, 1253–1264.

Jiang, H.-Y., Qiao, F., Xu, X.-F., Yang, Y., Bai, Y., & Jiang, L.-L. (2013). Meta-analysis confirms a functional polymorphism (5-HTTLPR) in the serotonin transporter gene conferring risk of bipolar disorder in European populations. *Neuroscience Letters, 549*, 191–196.

Johnson, W., & Krueger, R. F. (2005). Genetic effects on physical health: Lower at higher income levels. *Behavior Genetics, 35*, 579–590.

Johnson, W., Penke, L., & Spinath, F. M. (2011). Heritability in the era of molecular genetics: Some thoughts for understanding genetic influences on behavioural traits. *European Journal of Personality, 25*, 254–266.

Kapheim, K. M., Pan, H., Li, C., Salzberg, S. L., Puiu, D., Magoc, T., ... Zhang, G. (2015). Social evolution: Genomic signatures of evolutionary transitions from solitary to group living. *Science, 348*, 1139–1143.

Karg, K., Burmeister, M., Shedden, K., & Sen, S. (2011). The serotonin transporter promoter variant (5-HTTLPR), stress, and depression meta-analysis revisited: Evidence of genetic moderation. *Archives of General Psychiatry, 68*, 444–454.

Kaufman, J., Gelernter, J., Kaffman, A., Caspi, A., & Moffitt, T. (2010). Arguable assumptions, debatable conclusions. *Biological Psychiatry, 67*, e19–e20.

Kaufman, J., Yang, B. Z., Douglas-Palumberi, H., Houshyar, S., Lipschitz, D., Krystal, J. H., & Gelernter, J. (2004). Social supports and serotonin transporter gene moderate depression in maltreated children. *Proceedings of the National Academy of Sciences of the United States of America, 101*, 17316–17321.

Kendler, K. S. (2013). What psychiatric genetics has taught us about the nature of psychiatric illness and what is left to learn. *Molecular Psychiatry, 18*, 1058–1066.

Kendler, K. S., & Baker, J. H. (2007). Genetic influences on measures of the environment: A systematic review. *Psychological Medicine, 37*, 615–626.

Kendler, K. S., & Eaves, L. J. (1986). Models for the joint effect of genotype and environment on liability to psychiatric illness. *American Journal of Psychiatry, 143*, 279–289.

Kendler, K. S., Neale, M. C., Kessler, R. C., Heath, A. C., & Eaves, L. J. (1993). A test of the equal-environment assumption in twin studies of psychiatric illness. *Behavior Genetics, 23*, 21–27.

Kim, H. N., Kim, B. H., Cho, J., Ryu, S., Shin, H., Sung, J., ... Kim, H.-L. (2015). Pathway analysis of genome-wide association datasets of personality traits. *Genes, Brain and Behavior, 14*, 345–356.

Kitano, H. (2002). Systems biology: A brief overview. *Science, 295*, 1662–1664.

Klump, K. L., Holly, A., Iacono, W. G., McGue, M., & Willson, L. E. (2000). Physical similarity and twin resemblance for eating attitudes and behaviors: A test of the equal environments assumption. *Behavior Genetics, 30*, 51–58.

Korzan, W. J., Grone, B. P., & Fernald, R. D. (2014). Social regulation of cortisol receptor gene expression. *Journal of Experimental Biology, 217*, 3221–3228.

Lehto, K., Vaht, M., Maestu, J., Veidebaum, T., & Harro, J. (2015). Effect of tryptophan hydroxylase-2 gene polymorphism G-703 T on personality in a population representative sample. *Progress in Neuro-Psychopharmacology and Biological Psychiatry, 57*, 31–35.

Lesch, K. P., Bengel, D., Heils, A., Sabol, S. Z., Greenberg, B. D., Petri, S., ... Murphy, D. L. (1996). Association of anxiety-related traits with a polymorphism in the serotonin transporter gene regulatory region. *Science, 274*, 1527–1531.

Li, B., Liu, D. J., & Leal, S. M. (2013). Identifying rare variants associated with complex traits via sequencing. *Current Protocols in Human Genetics, 78*, 1.26:1.26.1–1.26.22.

Li, H. (2013). Systems genetics in '-omics' era: Current and future development. *Theory in Biosciences, 132*, 1–16.

Li, H., Li, S., Wang, Q., Pan, L., Jiang, F., Yang, X., ... Jia, C. (2015). Association of 5-HTTLPR polymorphism with smoking behaviors: A meta-analysis. *Physiology and Behavior, 152*, 32–40.

Loehlin, J. C. (1978). Are CPI scales differently heritable: How good is the evidence? *Behavior Genetics, 8*, 381–382.

Loehlin, J. C. (1982). Are personality traits differentially heritable? *Behavior Genetics, 12*, 417–428.

Loehlin, J. C. (2012). The differential heritability of personality item clusters. *Behavior Genetics, 42*, 500–507.

LoParo, D., & Waldman, I. (2014). Twins' rearing environment similarity and childhood externalizing disorders: A test of the equal environments assumption. *Behavior Genetics, 44*, 606–613.

Luciano, M., Huffman, J. E., Arias-Vásquez, A., Vinkhuyzen, A. A. E., Middeldorp, C. M., Giegling, I., ... Deary, I. J. (2012). Genome-wide association uncovers shared genetic effects among personality traits and mood states. *American Journal of Medical Genetics Part B: Neuropsychiatric Genetics, 159B*, 684–695.

Maher, B. (2008). Personal genomes: The case of the missing heritability. *Nature, 456*, 18–21.

Mak, K. K., Kong, W. Y., Mak, A., Sharma, V. K., & Ho, R. C. M. (2013). Polymorphisms of the serotonin transporter gene and post-stroke depression: A meta-analysis. *Journal of Neurology, Neurosurgery, and Psychiatry, 84*, 322–328.

Manolio, T. A., Collins, F. S., Cox, N. J., Goldstein, D. B., Hindorff, L. A., Hunter, D. J., ... Visscher, P. M. (2009). Finding the missing heritability of complex diseases. *Nature, 461*, 747–753.

Martin, E. I., Ressler, K. J., Binder, E., & Nemeroff, C. B. (2009). The neurobiology of anxiety disorders: Brain imaging, genetics, and psychoneuroendocrinology. *Psychiatric Clinics of North America, 32*, 549–575.

Mattay, V. S., & Goldberg, T. E. (2004). Imaging genetic influences in human brain function. *Current Opinions in Neurobiology, 14*, 239–247.

Matullo, G., Di Gaetano, C., & Guarrera, S. (2013). Next generation sequencing and rare genetic variants: From human population studies to medical genetics. *Environmental and Molecular Mutagenesis, 54*, 518–532.

McAdams, T. A., Gregory, A. M., & Eley, T. C. (2013). Genes of experience: Explaining the heritability of putative environmental variables through their association with behavioural and emotional traits. *Behavior Genetics, 43*, 314–328.

McGowan, P. O., Sasaki, A., D'Alessio, A. C., Dymov, S., Labonté, B., Szyf, M., ... Meaney, M. J. (2009). Epigenetic regulation of the glucocorticoid receptor in human brain associates with childhood abuse. *Nature Neuroscience, 12*, 342–348.

Mcgue, M., Bouchard, T. J., Lykken, D. T., & Finkel, D. (1991). On genes, environment and experience. *Behavioral and Brain Sciences, 14*, 400–401.

Meyer-Lindenberg, A. (2010). Imaging genetics of schizophrenia. *Dialogues in Clinical Neuroscience, 12*, 449–456.

Meyer-Lindenberg, A., Buckholtz, J. W., Kolachana, B., Hariri, A, R., Pezawas, L., Blasi, G., ... Weinberger, D. R. (2006a). Neural mechanisms of genetic risk for impulsivity and violence in humans. *Proceedings of the National Academy of Sciences of the United States of America, 103*, 6269–6274.

Meyer-Lindenberg, A., Nichols, T., Callicott, J. H., Ding, J., Kolachana, B., Buckholtz, J., ... Weinberger, D. R. (2006b). COMT haplotype variation affects human prefrontal function. *Molecular Psychiatry, 11*, 797.

Meyer-Lindenberg, A., & Weinberger, D. R. (2006). Intermediate phenotypes and genetic mechanisms of psychiatric disorders. *Nature Reviews Neuroscience, 7*, 818–827.

Meyer-Lindenberg, A., & Zink, C. F. (2007). Imaging genetics for neuropsychiatric disorders. *Child and Adolescent Psychiatric Clinics of North America, 16*, 581–597.

Miller, R., Wankerl, M., Stalder, T., Kirschbaum, C., & Alexander, N. (2013). The serotonin transporter gene-linked polymorphic region (5-HTTLPR) and cortisol stress reactivity: A meta-analysis. *Molecular Psychiatry, 18*, 1018–1024.

Mueller, A., Armbruster, D., Moser, D. A., Canli, T., Lesch, K.-P., Brocke, B., & Kirschbaum, C. (2011). Interaction of serotonin transporter gene-linked polymorphic region and stressful life events predicts cortisol stress response. *Neuropsychopharmacology, 36*, 1332–1339.

Munafo, M. R., Clark, T. G., & Flint, J. (2005). Does measurement instrument moderate the association between the serotonin transporter gene and anxiety-related personality traits? A meta-analysis. *Molecular Psychiatry, 10*, 415–419.

Munafo, M. R., Durrant, C., Lewis, G., & Flint, J. (2009a). Gene X environment interactions at the serotonin transporter locus. *Biological Psychiatry, 65*, 211–219.

Munafo, M. R., Freimer, N. B., Ng, W., Ophoff, R., Veijola, J., Miettunen, J., ... Flint, J. (2009b). 5-HTTLPR genotype and anxiety-related personality traits: A meta-analysis and new data. *American Journal of Medical Genetics Part B: Neuropsychiatric Genetics, 150B*, 271–281.

Munafo, M. R., Zammit, S., & Flint, J. (2014). Practitioner review: A critical perspective on gene–environment interaction models – what impact should they have on clinical perceptions and practice? *Journal of Child Psychology and Psychiatry, and Allied Disciplines, 55*, 1092–1101.

Murphy, S. E., Norbury, R., Godlewska, B. R., Cowen, P. J., Mannie, Z. M., Harmer, C. J., & Munafo, M. R. (2013). The effect of the serotonin transporter polymorphism (5-HTTLPR) on amygdala function: A meta-analysis. *Molecular Psychiatry, 18*, 512–520.

Noble, D. (2008). Claude Bernard, the first systems biologist, and the future of physiology. *Experimental Physiology, 93*, 16–26.

Ohmoto, M., Hirakoshi, M., & Mitsumoto, Y. (2013). Effects of moderating factors including serotonin transporter polymorphisms on smoking behavior: A systematic review and meta-analysis update. *Nicotine and Tobacco Research, 15*, 572–582.

Okbay, A., Baselmans, B. M., De Neve, J. E., Turley, P., Nivard, M. G., Fontana, M. A., ... Cesarini, D. (2016). Genetic variants associated with subjective well-being, depressive symptoms, and neuroticism identified through genome-wide analyses. *Nature Genetics, 48*, 624–633.

Ostlund, G., & Sonnhammer, E. L. (2012). Quality criteria for finding genes with high mRNA-protein expression correlation and coexpression correlation. *Gene, 497*, 228–236.

Pace, V. L., & Brannick, M. T. (2010). How similar are personality scales of the 'same' construct? A meta-analytic investigation. *Personality and Individual Differences, 49*, 669–676.

Pam, A., Kemker, S. S., Ross, C. A., & Golden, R. (1996). The 'equal environments assumption' in MZ-DZ twin comparisons: An untenable premise of psychiatric genetics? *Acta Geneticae Medicae et Gemellologiae, 45*, 349–360.

Peitsch, M. C., & de Graaf, D. (2014). A decade of systems biology: Where are we and where are we going to? *Drug Discovery Today, 19*, 105–107.

Peper, J. S., Brouwer, R. M., Boomsma, D. I., Kahn, R. S., & Hulshoff Pol, H. E. (2007). Genetic influences on human brain structure: A review of brain imaging studies in twins. *Human Brain Mapping, 28*, 464–473.

Pergamin-Hight, L., Bakermans-Kranenburg, M. J., van IJzendoorn, M. H., & Bar-Haim, Y. (2012). Variations in the promoter region of the serotonin transporter gene and biased attention for emotional information: A meta-analysis. *Biological Psychiatry, 71*, 373–379.

Philibert, R., Madan, A., Andersen, A., Cadoret, R., Packer, H., & Sandhu, H. (2007). Serotonin transporter mRNA levels are associated with the methylation of an upstream CpG island. *American Journal of Medical Genetics Part B: Neuropsychiatric Genetics, 144*, 101–105.

Plomin, R., Corley, R., Caspi, A., Fulker, D. W., & DeFries, J. (1998). Adoption results for self-reported personality: Evidence for non-additive genetic effects? *Journal of Personality and Social Psychology, 75*, 211–218.

Plomin, R., DeFries, J. C., & Loehlin, J. C. (1977). Genotype–environment interaction and correlation in the analysis of human behavior. *Psychological Bulletin, 84*, 309–322.

Plomin, R., Pedersen, N. L., Lichtenstein, P., McClearn, G. E., & Nesselroade, J. R. (1990). Genetic influence on life events during the last half of the life-span. *Psychology and Aging, 5*, 25–30.

Potkin, S. G., Turner, J. A., Fallon, J. A., Lakatos, A., Keator, D. B., Guffanti, G., & Macciardi, F. (2009). Gene discovery through imaging genetics: Identification of two novel genes associated with schizophrenia. *Molecular Psychiatry, 14*, 416–428.

Power, R. A., Wingenbach, T., Cohen-Woods, S., Uher, R., Ng, M. Y., Butler, A. W., ... McGuffin, P. (2013). Estimating the heritability of reporting stressful life events captured by common genetic variants. *Psychological Medicine, 43*, 1965–1971.

Reynolds, C. A., & Finkel, D. (2015). A meta-analysis of heritability of cognitive aging: Minding the 'missing heritability' gap. *Neuropsychology Review, 25*, 97–112.

Richardson, K., & Norgate, S. (2005). The equal environments assumption of classical twin studies may not hold. *British Journal of Educational Psychology, 75*, 339–350.

Risch, N., Herrell, R., Lehner, T., Liang, K. Y., Eaves, L., Hoh, J., ... Merikangas, K. R. (2009). Interaction between the serotonin transporter gene (5-HTTLPR), stressful life events, and risk of depression: A meta-analysis. *JAMA, 301*, 2462–2471.

Saks, V., Monge, C., & Guzun, R. (2009). Philosophical basis and some historical aspects of systems biology: From Hegel to Noble – applications for bioenergetic research. *International Journal of Molecular Sciences, 10*, 1161–1192.

Saudino, K. J., Pedersen, N. L., Lichtenstein, P., McClearn, G. E., & Plomin, R. (1997). Can personality explain genetic influences on life events? *Journal of Personality and Social Psychology, 72*, 196–206.

Schadt, E. E. (2009). Molecular networks as sensors and drivers of common human diseases. *Nature, 461*, 218–223.

Scharinger, C., Rabl, U., Sitte, H. H., & Pezawas, L. (2010). Imaging genetics of mood disorders. *Neuroimage, 53*, 810–821.

Schinka, J. A., Busch, R. M., & Robichaux-Keene, N. (2004). A meta-analysis of the association between the serotonin transporter gene polymorphism (5-HTTLPR) and trait anxiety. *Molecular Psychiatry, 9,* 197–202.

Sen, S., Burmeister, M., & Ghosh, D. (2004). Meta-analysis of the association between a serotonin transporter promoter polymorphism (5-HTTLPR) and anxiety-related personality traits. *American Journal of Medical Genetics, 127B,* 85–89.

Service, S. K., Verweij, K. J. H., Lahti, J., Congdon, E., Ekelund, J., Hintsanen, M., ... Freimer, N. B. (2012). A genome-wide meta-analysis of association studies of Cloninger's Temperament Scales. *Translational Psychiatry, 2,* e116.

Shifman, S., Bhomra, A., Smiley, S., Wray, N. R., James, M. R., Martin, N. G., ... Flint, J. (2008). A whole genome association study of neuroticism using DNA pooling. *Molecular Psychiatry, 13,* 302–312.

Smith, D. J., Escott-Price, V., Davies, G., Bailey, M. E., Colodro-Conde, L., Ward, J., ... O'Donovan, M. C. (2016). Genome-wide analysis of over 106,000 individuals identifies 9 neuroticism-associated loci. *Molecular Psychiatry, 21,* 749–757.

Subramanian, A., Kuehn, H., Gould, J., Tamayo, P., & Mesirov, J. P. (2007). GSEA-P: A desktop application for Gene Set Enrichment Analysis. *Bioinformatics, 23,* 3251–3253.

Subramanian, A., Tamayo, P., Mootha, V. K., Mukherjee, S., Ebert, B. L., Gillette, M. A., ... Mesirov, J. P. (2005). Gene set enrichment analysis: A knowledge-based approach for interpreting genome-wide expression profiles. *Proceedings of the National Academy of Sciences of the United States of America, 102,* 15545–15550.

Sun, Y. V., & Hu, Y.-J. (2016). Integrative analysis of multi-omics data for discovery and functional studies of complex human diseases. *Advances in Genetics, 93,* 147–190.

Surtees, P. G., Wainwright, N. W., Willis-Owen, S. A., Luben, R., Day, N. E., & Flint, J. (2005). Social adversity, the serotonin transporter (5-HTTLPR) polymorphism and major depressive disorder. *Biological Psychiatry, 59,* 224–229.

Taylor, A., & Kim-Cohen, J. (2007). Meta-analysis of gene–environment interactions in developmental psychopathology. *Developmental Psychopathology, 19,* 1029–1037.

Tellegen, A., Lykken, D. T., Bouchard, T. J., Jr., Wilcox, K. J., Segal, N. L., & Rich, S. (1988). Personality similarity in twins reared apart and together. *Journal of Personality and Social Psychology, 54,* 1031–1039. http://dx.doi.org/10.1037/0022-3514.54.6.1031

Terracciano, A., Sanna, S., Uda, M., Deiana, B., Usala, G., Busonero, F., ... Costa, P. T., Jr. (2010). Genome-wide association scan for five major dimensions of personality. *Molecular Psychiatry, 15,* 647–656.

Thompson, P. M., Stein, J. L., Medland, S. E., Hibar, D. P., Vasquez, A. A., Renteria, M. E., ... Drevets, W. (2014). The ENIGMA Consortium: Large-scale collaborative analyses of neuroimaging and genetic data. *Brain Imaging and Behavior, 2,* 153–182.

Tost, H., Bilek, E., & Meyer-Lindenberg, A. (2012). Brain connectivity in psychiatric imaging genetics. *Neuroimage, 62,* 2250–2260.

Trumbetta, S. L., & Gottesman, I. I. (2011). Equifinality and endophenotypes enrich personality research. *European Journal of Personality, 25,* 284–285.

Turkheimer, E. (2001). Three Laws of Behavior Genetics and what they mean. *Current Directions in Psychological Science, 9,* 160–164.

Turkheimer, E., Pettersson, E., & Horn, E. E. (2014). A phenotypic null hypothesis for the genetics of personality. *Annual Review of Psychology, 65,* 515–540.

van den Berg, S. M., de Moor, M. H., McGue, M., Pettersson, E., Terracciano, A., Verweij, K. J., ... Boomsma, D. I. (2014). Harmonization of neuroticism and extraversion phenotypes across inventories and cohorts in the Genetics of Personality Consortium: An application of Item Response Theory. *Behavior Genetics, 44,* 295–313.

van den Berg, S. M., de Moor, M. H. M., Verweij, K. J. H., Krueger, R. F., Luciano, M., Arias Vasquez, A., ... Boomsma, D. I. (2016). Meta-analysis of genome-wide association studies for extraversion: Findings from the Genetics of Personality Consortium. *Behavior Genetics, 46,* 170–182.

van den Oord, E. J. C. G., Kuo, P.-H., Hartmann, A. M., Webb, B. T., Moller, H.-J., Hettema, J. M., ... Rujescu, D. (2008). Genomewide association analysis followed by a replication study implicates a novel candidate gene for neuroticism. *Archives of General Psychiatry, 65,* 1062–1071.

Verweij, K. J. H., Zietsch, B. P., Medland, S. E., Gordon, S. D., Benyamin, B., Nyholt, D. R., ... Wray, N. R. (2010). A genome-wide association study of Cloninger's temperament scales: Implications for the evolutionary genetics of personality. *Biological Psychology*, *85*, 306–317.

Villalba, K., Attonito, J., Mendy, A., Devieux, J. G., Gasana, J., & Dorak, T. M. (2015). A meta-analysis of the associations between the SLC6A4 promoter polymorphism (5HTTLPR) and the risk for alcohol dependence. *Psychiatric Genetics*, *25*, 47–58.

Vinkhuyzen, A. A. E., Dumenil, T., Ryan, L., Gordon, S. D., Henders, A. K., Madden, P. A. F., ... Wray, N. R. (2011). Identification of tag haplotypes for 5HTTLPR for different genome-wide SNP platforms. *Molecular Psychiatry*, *16*, 1073–1075.

Vukasovic, T., & Bratko, D. (2015). Heritability of personality: A meta-analysis of behavior genetic studies. *Psychologial Bulletin*, *141*, 769–785.

Walsh, N. D., Dalgleish, T., Dunn, V. J., Abbott, R., St Clair, M. C., Owens, M., ... Goodyer, I. M. (2012). 5-HTTLPR-environment interplay and its effects on neural reactivity in adolescents. *Neuroimage*, *63*, 1670–1680.

Wang, K., Li, M. Y., & Bucan, M. (2007). Pathway-based approaches for analysis of genomewide association studies. *American Journal of Human Genetics*, *81*, 1278–1283.

Wang, K., Li, M. Y., & Hakonarson, H. (2010). Analysing biological pathways in genome-wide association studies. *Nature Reviews Genetics*, *11*, 843–854.

Weaver, I. C., Cervoni, N., Champagne, F. A., D'Alessio, A. C., Sharma, S., Seckl, J. R., ... Meaney, M. J. (2004). Epigenetic programming by maternal behavior. *Nature Neuroscience*, *7*, 847–854.

Wei, W.-H., Hemani, G., & Haley, C. S. (2014). Detecting epistasis in human complex traits. *Nature Reviews Genetics*, *15*, 722–733.

Werner, E. (2013). History of the seminar on the conceptual foundations of systems biology. *Progress in Biophysics and Molecular Biology*, *111*, 57–58.

Wiers, C. E. (2012). Methylation and the human brain: Towards a new discipline of imaging epigenetics. *European Archives of Psychiatry and Clinical Neuroscience*, *262*, 271–273.

Wilkening, S., Chen, B. W., Bermejo, J. L., & Canzian, F. (2009). Is there still a need for candidate gene approaches in the era of genome-wide association studies? *Genomics*, *93*, 415–419.

Williams, E. G., & Auwerx, J. (2015). The convergence of systems and reductionist approaches in complex trait analysis. *Cell*, *162*, 23–32.

Xu, X. M., & Moller, S. G. (2011). The value of *Arabidopsis* research in understanding human disease states. *Current Opinion in Biotechnology*, *22*, 300–307.

Yamamoto, S., Jaiswal, M., Charng, W.-L., Gambin, T., Karaca, E., Mirzaa, G., ... Bellen, H. J. (2014). A *Drosophila* genetic resource of mutants to study mechanisms underlying human genetic diseases. *Cell*, *159*, 200–214.

Zhang, K. L., Chang, S. H., Guo, L. Y., & Wang, J. (2015). I-GSEA4GWAS v2: A web server for functional analysis of SNPs in trait-associated pathways identified from genome-wide association study. *Protein and Cell*, *6*, 221–224.

Zhang, K. L., Cui, S. J., Chang, S. H., Zhang, L. Y., & Wang, J. (2010). I-GSEA4GWAS: A web server for identification of pathways/gene sets associated with traits by applying an improved gene set enrichment analysis to genome-wide association study. *Nucleic Acids Research*, *38*, W90–W95.

Zhao, M., Kong, L., & Qu, H. (2014). A systems biology approach to identify intelligence quotient score-related genomic regions, and pathways relevant to potential therapeutic treatments. *Science Reports*, *4*, 4176.

PART II

Developmental Origins of Personality and Individual Differences

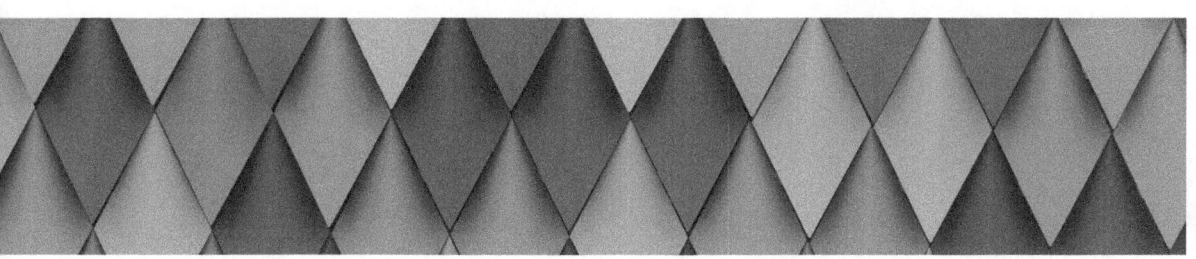

Individual Differences in Personal Narrative: Coherence, Autobiographical Reasoning and Meaning Making

Theodore E. A. Waters and Christin Köber

Sharing our personal experiences through narrative is a nearly ubiquitous human behavior. The construction and sharing of personal narratives helps us to understand ourselves, establish a sense of continuity and purpose, strengthen and maintain our social bonds, guide future behavior, and cope with stressful life events (e.g., Bluck et al., 2005; Fivush and Waters, 2013; Waters, 2014). As universal as personal narrative might be, the ways in which individuals narrate, integrate, and make meaning from their personal experiences exhibits tremendous variability. Further, this variability can have significant implications for mental health and psychological well-being (Adler et al., 2016).

The study of individual differences in personal narrative typically focuses on coherence, autobiographical reasoning, meaning making, explicit/implicit motives, narrative themes, and emotional expression. To date, these features of personal narrative have been studied in respect to their development (e.g., Habermas and Reese, 2015; Haden et al., 1997; Köber et al., 2015; McLean and Pasupathi, 2010), socialization (e.g., Fivush et al., 2006; Fivush and Zaman, 2015), association with personality traits (e.g., Lilgendahl and McAdams, 2011; Lodi-Smith et al., 2009; McAdams et al., 2004; Raggatt, 2006; Thomsen et al., 2014), and links to psychopathology (e.g., Allé et al., 2015, 2016; Habermas, 2015; Raffard et al., 2010). Since it is beyond the scope of this chapter to provide an exhaustive review of this literature, we instead focus on what we consider to be the predominant constructs of interest and those which pertain to the broadest research audience. Accordingly, we begin this chapter focusing on the developmental, sociocultural, and clinical factors associated with (a) narrative coherence, (b) autobiographical reasoning, and (c) meaning making. Next, we discuss the potential role of schemas in the construction of personal narrative and conclude with a discussion of potential future directions and pressing issues in the field.

FACTORS ACCOUNTING FOR INDIVIDUAL DIFFERENCES IN NARRATIVE COHERENCE

Individual differences in personal narratives are examined at two levels of analysis, the single event narrative and life narrative. Single event narratives tell the story of a specific event (e.g., a wedding, car accident, trip to the zoo) and are shared frequently in our daily lives. Single events provide insights into both mundane and biographically salient memories which can help explain who the narrator is today and give insight into their subjective perspective (McAdams, 1993; Singer and Salovey, 1993; Waters et al., 2014). Life narratives, in contrast, include numerous single events and cover the significant events from the entire lifespan – from narrators' beginnings to their present. An individual's ability to construct coherent narratives of single events or the entire life is considered a hallmark of healthy adjustment (Baerger and McAdams, 1999; Waters and Fivush, 2015). Coherence in both single event and life narratives is defined in terms of temporal, causal-motivational, and thematic dimensions (Habermas and Bluck, 2000; Reese et al., 2011). Whereas temporal coherence is achieved through clear description of the sequence of events or actions in the narrative, causal-motivational coherence stems from the provision of insight into causes, motivations, and consequences of past events and actions. Conversely, thematic coherence is achieved by staying on topic and often includes a climax, resolution, and the presence of affective and evaluative information (Reese et al., 2011).

In practice, coding of these dimensions differs somewhat. For example, in life narratives, thematic coherence refers to the connections between the different events from the life narrative with the narrator's personality. Thematic coherence in this context represents the dominant themes of the narrator's life story (e.g., the life story continuously revolves around friendships, motives of intimacy or power; or is thematically summarized: '…and you see, my life is very much organized around my occupation'; Köber et al., 2015). In contrast, in the context of single event narratives, thematic coherence represents the narrator's ability to stay on topic, develop, and resolve the central theme of the narrative. Each of the three dimensions of coherence has been investigated in single event narratives (Chen et al., 2012; Reese et al., 2011) and in life narratives (Köber et al., 2015) and produced parallel results. We review these results below.

The coherence measurable within single event narratives is referred to as narrative coherence at a *local level* (Habermas and Reese, 2015). Several measures have been developed to assess individual differences in local level narrative coherence. The Narrative Coherence Coding Scheme (NaCCs), proposed by Reese et al. (2011), rates the coherence of single event narratives along three dimensions: chronology, context, and theme. Chronology designates the temporal ordering of the narrative, whereas the context dimension rates the clarity and specificity of time and place information. Conversely, thematic coherence ratings measure the extent to which a clear topic is elaborated, developed, resolved, and finally connected to other autobiographical experiences or to self-concept. Therefore, thematic coherence is conceptually overlapping with both causal-motivational and thematic ratings of global coherence. The ability to narrate coherent single events develops with age. As early as age five, children start to competently present the temporal order of actions and events within their narratives. In addition to chronological order, children at this age begin to provide contextual information which helps orient the listener, which moves the mere listing of actions toward an actual narrative or story of what happened. Importantly, studies show that children's ability to organize temporal-causal actions and provide contextual details in narrative improves incrementally until early/mid adolescence (Berman, 2004; Peterson and

McCabe, 1983; Reese et al., 2011). Thematic coherence, in contrast, develops more slowly and remains relatively limited until early adolescence, but becomes considerably refined during the teenage years before leveling-out throughout adulthood (Chen et al., 2012; Reese et al., 2011). Altogether, the three aspects of local narrative coherence for single events develop gradually: with chronological coherence developing first, but followed closely by contextual coherence. Finally, thematic coherence begins to show substantial improvements across the adolescent and young adult period and potentially continues to increase moderately throughout the lifespan.

The operationalization of narrative coherence in life narratives is referred to as *global* coherence (Habermas and Reese, 2015) because, when telling an entire life story, narrators are challenged to create coherence with event narratives but also to connect and integrate different events of their lives into a coherent whole. This leads to a complex nested structure, with single and recurring events being organized into chapters or periods (e.g., when I lived in New York City or my *first* marriage; Chen et al., 2013; Thomsen, 2009, 2015). Consequently, due to its complexity, the ability to structure and tell a coherent life narrative with respect to temporal, causal-motivational, and thematic aspects, takes longer to develop than narratives of single events. Temporal coherence constitutes the most basic aspect of global coherence and is acquired throughout late childhood and early adolescence, as children above the age of 10 start to relate more than one event chronologically and to efficiently use temporal indicators (Bohn and Berntsen, 2008, 2013; Köber et al., 2015; Köber and Habermas, 2017a). Causal-motivational coherence that describes the extent to which the individual articulates their personality development across the life story develops during adolescence and continues to increase moderately until early adulthood (Köber et al., 2015). Thematic coherence is thought to be the most advanced aspect of global coherence, as it requires not only a fully formed life narrative, but also the recognition of similarities between various life events and the abstraction of common themes. Accordingly, thematic coherence is limited in personal narratives before emerging adulthood and increases until midlife (Köber et al., 2015). To summarize, longitudinal and cross-sectional data suggest that (1) temporal coherence is the first to develop, becoming well-established in early adolescence; (2) causal-motivational coherence follows, increasing steeply from adolescence to early adulthood; and (3) thematic coherence develops last, emerging in late adolescence and improving steadily until middle adulthood.

Temporal, causal-motivational, and thematic coherence develop in both kinds of personal narratives in a parallel manner, with each aspect being earlier established in narratives of single events than in life narratives. In a comparison of the differential developmental pathways of life versus single event narratives, Bohn and Berntsen (2008) found that, while global temporal coherence increased steeply across early adolescence (age 9–15), only a moderate increase emerged for the temporal (local) coherence of single event narratives. Thus, local temporal coherence of single event narratives may develop earlier than the global temporal coherence of life narratives and both seem to develop independently of one another. To our knowledge, research has not yet addressed the development of causal-motivational and thematic coherence in both single event and life narratives in this way. Therefore, deconstructing the various dimensions of coherence (i.e., local causal-motivational and thematic coherence) from their global counterparts remains an important direction for future research.

Notably, parental reminiscing with their young children appears to be a critical factor in the development of personal narratives. Even before babies can speak, their primary caregivers begin reminiscing about past events they have shared. As children's language ability develops they become more and more involved in reminiscing and sharing past events with their primary caregivers (Fivush et al., 2006; Nelson and Fivush, 2004; Reese, 2014). These reminiscing interactions are an important context for the development of autobiographical memory and narrative ability. Most critical to the development of these abilities is the elaborative style of the primary caregiver during reminiscing. Caregivers who are low on elaborative reminiscing style do not talk regularly about the past, and when they do, they tend to ask yes/no questions and redundant questions which do not prompt the child to produce new information or their own subjective perspective. In contrast, parents high on elaborative style engage frequently in joint reminiscing and ask open-ended questions that require the child to provide new information, greater detail, and their perspective on the event (e.g., 'what was your favorite part of the trip to the zoo?'; Nelson and Fivush, 2004). Children and adolescents whose mothers reminisce with a more elaborative style and with more emotional information have earlier (Bauer and Larkina, 2014; Jack et al., 2009) and more detailed (Farrant and Reese, 2000; Harley and Reese, 1999; Newcombe and Reese, 2004; Reese et al., 1993) autobiographical memories/narratives. Further on, the provision of parental narrative devices such as orientations, evaluations, and emotional information help preschool children to contextualize their personal narratives in terms of space and time as well as personal significance (Haden et al., 1997). By the end of preschool, children of more elaborative mothers tell more detailed and more coherent narratives of their personal experiences with both their mother and unfamiliar adults (Fivush, 2007; Fivush et al., 1995, 1996; Haden et al., 1997; Reese, 2002; Tessler and Nelson, 1994). As children grow older and become more equipped to participate fully in joint reminiscing, mothers adapt their elaboration and narrative scaffolding to the children's age and increasing narrative skills, leading to bidirectional co-constructed narratives about the past (Fivush et al., 1996; Reese et al., 1993). Similarly, adapted maternal support was also found in a cross-sectional study with participants aged 8, 12, 16, and 20 in which mothers scaffolded the narration of their children's entire lives (Habermas et al., 2010). Whereas mothers of the children and early adolescents focused more on supporting temporal coherence, the mothers of the adolescent and young adult participants helped to find the personal meaning of the events by commenting on their children's personality, thus facilitating the creation of causal-motivational and thematic coherence.

Gender differences have also been identified in predicting narrative style across development. For example, parents tend to be more elaborative and emotionally expressive when reminiscing with their daughters than with their sons (Reese et al., 1993, 1996). Fivush and colleagues argued that differential elaborative style with daughters during early childhood leads to the development of more detailed and emotional personal narratives in adolescence and adulthood for females compared to males (Fivush et al., 2012; see Grysman and Hudson, 2013, for a review).

In addition to age-related changes, reminiscing with parents, and gender differences, data suggest that personality traits also contribute to personal narratives. For example, when senior college students were asked to narrate personality change, Lodi-Smith and colleagues (2009) found that the Big Five personality traits measured in the first year of college predicted narrative and linguistic structure of the stories of personality change assessed four years later. Conscientiousness predicted more coherence in narratives, whereas openness and extraversion predicted greater exploration of one's life experiences as well as more elaboration of the perceived personality change. These results coincide with the claim that personality traits shape self-narratives (Lilgendahl, 2015; McAdams, 2013) and may therefore account for further, yet unstudied, differences in the coherence of narrative identity.

Psychopathology has also been identified as a contributing factor in narrative coherence for both single event and life narratives. For instance, adults reporting higher rates of depression were found to construct less coherent narratives with respect to the organization, conveyed affect, and expression of personal meaning (Baerger and McAdams, 1999; see also Waters and Fivush, 2015). Similarly, individuals diagnosed with Borderline Personality Disorder (BPD) show decreased quality of narrative coherence, which was thought to be precipitated by deficiencies concerning the orientation of information, unintelligible temporal ordering, insufficient expression of the personal meaning, and lacking integration into the wider life story (Adler et al., 2012). Throughout therapy, however, narrative coherence of patients has been found to improve (Hermans, 2006; Neimeyer et al., 2006; Singer and Bonalume, 2010). Notably, ego development, otherwise defined as the level of sophistication with which patients make sense of their experiences (Loevinger, 1976), is significantly associated with the coherence of personal narratives of their experiences with psychotherapy (Adler, 2012; Adler et al., 2007). Those patients who showed higher levels of ego development and well-being after therapy narrated their therapeutic endeavors more coherently and integrated their experiences into the broader scope of their lives (Adler et al., 2007, 2008). These results indicate that psychological well-being is significantly related to an individual's ability to create and maintain an integrated and coherent personal narrative.

Given that significant disturbances in self-understanding and identity are symptoms of schizophrenia, researchers have also started to examine the coherence of personal narratives in patients diagnosed with this illness (e.g., Lysaker and Lysaker, 2010). For instance, narratives of single events (i.e., self-defining memories) of participants with schizophrenia were less coherent with regard to temporal, causal-motivational, and thematic aspects than those of a control group (Raffard et al., 2010). This is consistent with the finding that schizophrenia is related to difficulties reflecting on one's self and to convey meaningful personal narratives to others (Lysaker et al., 2005). Accordingly, patients in a post-acute phase of schizophrenia enrolled in outpatient treatment were found to produce rather incoherent narratives with respect to (1) specific events in their lives, and (2) living with and the understanding of their mental illness (Lysaker et al., 2008).

Schizophrenia patients' difficulties developing coherent narratives regarding their personal experiences also extends to their life narratives. Compared to a control group, each aspect of global coherence (i.e., temporal, causal-motivational, and thematic coherence) was impaired in the life narratives of patients with schizophrenia (Allé et al., 2015). More precisely, the schizophrenia patients had an especially difficult time explaining the development of their personality, affecting global causal-motivational coherence, and integrating different life events along thematic lines, affecting global thematic coherence (Allé et al., 2015).

FACTORS ACCOUNTING FOR INDIVIDUAL DIFFERENCES IN AUTOBIOGRAPHICAL REASONING

When individuals gain new knowledge about the self through experience or introspection – or change in perspective – this information needs to be coherently integrated into the individual's broader life story. This process of integration is termed autobiographical reasoning (Habermas, 2011). More specifically, autobiographical reasoning is the narrative process by which we link personal experiences to other parts of our life, or to our identity, by employing autobiographical arguments and self-event connections that explain both change and stability in personality and life (Habermas, 2011; Habermas and Köber, 2015a;

Pasupathi et al., 2007). Thus, autobiographical reasoning primarily serves to create a sense of personal continuity across change (Habermas and Köber, 2015b; Pasupathi, 2015). This is especially useful in times of biographical change and upheaval. In terms of content, autobiographical arguments and self-event connections may concern individual dispositions, outlooks into one's attitudes about the self or the world in general, one's values and moral principles, and personal growth that emphasizes one's maturing after mostly critical life events (Lilgendahl and McAdams, 2011; Mansfield et al., 2010; McLean and Fournier, 2008).

Autobiographical reasoning ability emerges during middle childhood and improves rapidly until early adulthood (Köber et al., 2015; Pasupathi and Mansour, 2006). Besides age-related differences in autobiographical reasoning, some autobiographical arguments also seem to be differentially utilized during various periods across the lifespan. Whereas self-event connections which point to *changes* in personality are used more frequently in emerging adulthood, middle-aged and older adults employ more self-event connections to emphasize the *stable* aspects of their personality (McLean, 2008). On the other hand, both kinds of self-event connections, namely, those engendering change and those emphasizing stability, develop in parallel throughout adulthood (Köber et al., 2015), presumably in response to the ongoing challenge of counterbalancing change/growth and stability in adult identity.

Much like local and global coherence, the development of autobiographical reasoning seems to be supported by reminiscing with caregivers about the past. For example, young adolescents who experience more elaborative reminiscing with their mothers about specific memories in early childhood show greater personal insight into their self-reported life events (Reese et al., 2010). This suggests that differences in parental reminiscing style impacts later autobiographical reasoning in personal narrative.

Importantly, however, it is not necessarily the *amount* of autobiographical reasoning that determines whether individuals derive meaning from their experiences. Indeed, longitudinal data examining the frequency of autobiographical arguments and self-events connections at the level of propositions (coded for presence or absence in every main or subordinate clause) suggest that autobiographical reasoning constitutes less than three percent of the transcript (Köber et al., 2015). Pasupathi (2015) extended this perspective by proposing that, although people tell personal experiences all the time (McLean et al., 2007; Pasupathi et al., 2009; Rimé et al., 1998), they employ autobiographical reasoning only rarely. Therefore, it is unlikely that the mere frequency of autobiographical reasoning leads to the meaning associated with a personal narrative, but rather its content and valence.

Negatively-valenced events (e.g., transgressions) are shared less often (Pasupathi et al., 2009), but if people decide to disclose these events they can be rich in meaning and connection to self. For example, individuals who believe that positive personality change is possible are more likely to narrate their transgressions in terms of self-event connections that emphasize personal growth (Lilgendahl et al., 2013). Whether people tell their negative events in terms of positive meaning and growth or negative meaning and degradation seems to also depend on their personality traits. Though coming to a positive self-view and a sense of personal growth after a traumatic experience is generally difficult to achieve (Banks and Salmon, 2013; Boals and Schuettler, 2011; Waters et al., 2013a), it appears to be easier for those people who score low on neuroticism (i.e., who are more emotionally stable) and who believe that positive personality change is possible (Lilgendahl et al., 2013). Autobiographical reasoning in terms of positive change was also found to differ in narratives of abstinent alcoholics. Those participants that reflected about themselves with autobiographical arguments of positive change in the wake of their drinking problem showed higher levels of self-esteem and mental health than those that made autobiographical connections that reflected stability (Dunlop and Tracy, 2013a).

FACTORS ACCOUNTING FOR INDIVIDUAL DIFFERENCES IN OTHER KINDS OF MEANING MAKING

Meaning making is a broad psychological concept, and autobiographical reasoning is only one process thought to contribute to the integration of meaning and event memories into the life story. Other psychological processes implicated in meaning making include closure, redemption and contamination, and agency and communion (Adler et al., 2016). Though closure is a structural feature of narrative, referring to the construction of a coherent and complete story with a clear evaluative point (Pals, 2006), redemption and contamination are affective themes, which capture shifts in the emotional tone, either from a negative-affect to positive (redemption) or positive-affect to negative (contamination; McAdams et al., 2001). Conversely, agency and communion are motivational themes. Agency refers to the ability to exert some influence on the life course, whereas communion reflects the need for relatedness (Adler et al., 2015).

Although little is known about how these narrative constructs/devices are related to age, reminiscing, and gender, the ways in which these relate to personality, psychopathology, and well-being are better understood. For example, one study on closure in self-narratives points to a connection with personality traits (Pals, 2006). Women who scored higher on openness were more likely to narrate their most difficult and identity-challenging experiences with a sense of closure (Pals, 2006). Redemption and contamination also show links to personality, specifically generativity, which captures a concern for future generations (McAdams et al., 1997; McAdams et al., 2001). For example, late adolescents who scored higher on generativity and optimism were more likely to narrate turning points in their identity/lives in terms of redemption than adolescents scoring low on these personality dimensions (McLean and Pratt, 2006). Interestingly, a similar trend was observed throughout adulthood (McAdams et al., 2001). Conversely, evidence supports an inverse association between generativity and contamination in adults (McAdams et al., 1997, 2001). Furthermore, redemption and contamination seem to remain somewhat stable narrative themes in individuals across time. One study of emerging adults investigating the stability of redemption and contamination sequences averaged across ten narratives of key events found both to exhibit moderate stability after two years ($r = .50$, $r = .28$, respectively; McAdams et al., 2006). In middle-aged adults, only redemption, but not contamination, averaged across three narratives of key events, exhibited modest stability ($r = .31$) after three years (Dunlop et al., 2016).

In terms of psychological well-being, the inclusion of redemption in narratives about critical life events has been associated with greater psychological well-being (Adler and Poulin, 2009; Benish-Weisman, 2009; Leonard and Burns, 2006; McAdams et al., 2001; McLean and Breen, 2009), whereas contamination is associated with impaired psychological functioning (Adler and Poulin, 2009; McAdams, 2006; Singer et al., 2013). This might be especially relevant when it comes to patients suffering from certain psychopathologies. For example, Waters et al. (2013a) found that greater levels of contamination in narratives of highly traumatic events were associated with higher levels of post-traumatic stress. On the other hand, Dunlop and Tracy (2013b) found that recovering alcoholics who provided narratives of redemption (i.e., bouncing back from a setback) were more likely to maintain sobriety over time, compared to those who did not include redemptive themes in their narratives. Also, participants diagnosed with schizophrenia have been found to incorporate greater redemption when telling a self-defining memory that is related to their illness compared to other self-defining memories, presumably in order to lower the negative impact of the illness-related crisis and to rebuild self-esteem (Berna et al., 2011).

Much like redemption and contamination, agency and communion capture thematic elements of personal narrative, rather than structural ones as in the case of coherence. Whereas agency is concerned with the individual's autonomy, achievement, mastery, and ability to influence the course of life, communion is concerned with the individual's motivation for attachment, affiliation, love, friendship, and nurturance (McAdams et al., 1996). Like redemption and contamination, there is limited research investigating the relations that agency and communion have with age, reminiscing style, or gender. However, there is some evidence that personality traits and psychopathology account for some individual differences in these motivational themes.

One study investigating narrative themes and their relation to personality traits found that more conscientious and less neurotic undergraduate students expressed a greater number of agency themes in their narratives compared to those lower on conscientiousness and higher on neuroticisms. Further, more extraverted and agreeable students tend to emphasize communal themes in personal narratives to a greater extent than introverted less agreeable students (McAdams et al., 2004). Interestingly the stability of communion themes in the life story is relatively low, whereas agency remains relatively stable across a three-year period (McAdams et al., 2006).

Other factors thought to influence agency and communion include life circumstances and concurrent psychopathology. Not surprisingly, re-incarcerated individuals show a reduced sense of agency in both their reflection and their narratives about themselves compared to previously incarcerated individuals who had not been re-incarcerated (Liem and Richardson, 2014). Individuals diagnosed with BPD show similarly diminished themes of agency in their narratives (but not communion; Adler et al., 2012). Adult children of alcoholics were also found to exhibit lower levels of agency in their self-narratives compared with adults without alcoholic parents (McCoy and Dunlop, 2017). Further, their themes of agency were positively associated with psychological well-being. Having engaged in psychotherapy has also been linked with increases in themes of agency, communion, and well-being (Adler, 2012; Adler et al., 2015). Further, increased agency in narratives of psychotherapy has been linked with the maintenance of treatment gains following the conclusion of therapy (Adler, 2013).

Taken together, this literature on meaning making suggests that personality and psychopathological characteristics are related to the content of our narratives. Presumably, both personality traits and psychopathology influence identity development, which in turn shapes narrative patterns (McAdams, 2013). However, little work has been done to fully establish the direction of these effects. Thus, future research is needed to elucidate any causal connections between personality traits, psychopathology, and narrative meaning making. In addition, research into additional factors associated with meaning making is needed, as the roles of developmental period, parental reminiscing style, and gender are largely unknown.

MEMORY RECONSTRUCTION AND THE ROLE OF SCHEMATA IN PERSONAL NARRATIVE

We now turn to a discussion of what we consider to be a largely understudied area in personal narrative research: cognitive schemas and scripts (Bartlett, 1932; Schank and Abelson, 1977). Schemas and scripts are abstract generalized memory structures that detail the central or most commonly occurring features of a class or event type. Although there is a rich research tradition examining these constructs in terms of their impacts on basic memory processes (e.g., retrieval, memory intrusions), this research generally falls short of connecting these findings to personal narrative. Instead, cognitive and developmental research on schemas and scripts predominantly focuses on representations that are commonly held, or culturally normative, rather than the source or product of individual differences (e.g., script for going to the dentist, schema for what belongs in an office, schemas about gender norms). However, over the last two decades, there has been increasing interest in individual differences in schemas and scripts across a diverse set of research areas. Individual differences in maladaptive schemas about self and the world (e.g., that one is defective, unworthy of love, or superior) have become the focus of clinical assessments and interventions (e.g., Young et al., 2003), whereas individual differences in relationship schemas and scripts have become increasingly influential in developmental, cognitive, and clinical work on parent–child and romantic partner attachment (Bosmans and Kerns, 2015; De Winter et al., 2016; Dujardin et al., 2014; Waters et al., 2013a, 2015). We argue, here, that differences in these abstract representations of self and relationships have implications beyond behavior and functioning and likely influence and constrain personal narrative.

Brewer and Nakamura (1984) propose several ways in which schemas and scripts may influence memory processes. Below, we focus on the two most relevant for the construction of personal narrative; namely (1) integrating with incoming information, and (2) guiding retrieval. We briefly review these processes and highlight the potential connections between the influence of schemas and scripts on memory processes and individual differences in personal narrative.

Integration with New Information

Most research examining the effects of schemas and scripts on memory for new information shows that subsequent recall is often affected by existing schemas (Brewer and Nakamura, 1984). To varying degrees, recall of newly acquired information is blended or integrated with existing schemas and scripts. Sulin and Dooling (1974) found that subjects who were told that a passage they heard was about a famous person (e.g., Helen Keller) were more likely to falsely recognize sentences after a week delay if those sentences matched an existing schema for the character (e.g., that the character was blind or had a book written about her) compared to those who heard the same passage but did not know who it was about. Similar effects have been found for non-verbal materials as well (Jenkins et al., 1978; Loftus et al., 1978). For example, Brewer and Treyens (1981) brought subjects into an office for a brief period and later quizzed them about the contents of that office. Participants produced numerous schema-consistent errors in both recall and recognition tasks (e.g., recalling a typewriter that was not present in the room). Several studies have examined this type of integration effect over longer delays and found the strength of the effect typically increases over time (Brewer and Dupree, 1983), suggesting that, as forgetting progresses, the influence of schemas increases.

Scripts show similar integration effects on memory, with research generally showing that memory discrimination for scripted or typical actions is extremely poor, whereas memory discrimination for atypical actions is significantly better. Graesser et al., (1979) asked participants to listen to script-based stories with varying amounts of typical (scripted), related, and unrelated actions and provide recognition ratings for statements about the actions in the story after a delay. Participants displayed significantly better discrimination for items that were atypical compared to items that were typical of – or related to – the underlying script. These findings suggest that, as individuals encode new information, their existing knowledge about the world is integrated with or linked to the newly formed memory (Graesser et al., 1979). As a result of this integration, individuals are less able to discriminate actions of newly formed memories from those in their representation of the relevant underlying script. Much like schemas, the magnitude of the integration effects shown by scripts increases over time. Greenberg et al., (1998) examined participants' recognition memory for a scripted robbery scenario. Results showed that, as delay increased from five minutes to one week, participants' false alarms for omitted details central to the script significantly increased (Greenberg et al., 1998).

The cognitive literature on schemas' and scripts' impact on memory suggests that our autobiographical memories, and thus our personal narratives, integrate with our existing knowledge structures and produce predictable and systematic errors or intrusions of schematic/scripted information. For example, research shows that individuals have difficulties discriminating between what happened in a specific instance and what typically happens, with this effect increasing with a delay. In terms of personal narrative, it is plausible that our personal narratives come to increasingly reflect what *generally* happens rather than what *actually* happened. Given that this effect is contingent on schemas and scripts held by the remeniberer, individual differences in those representations should manifest in personal narrative. For example, individuals who have more or less trust in the supportiveness of their partner may produce personal narratives of conflict that, over time, come to show more schema-consistent themes, independent of how that partner actually responded. Simpson et al. (2010) found support for this argument, observing that attachment schemas predicted memory distortions of reports of the romantic interactions that took place in the laboratory one week prior (see also De Winter et al., 2016).

Retrieval

Schemas and scripts have also been shown to bias retrieval of episodic and autobiographical information. Anderson and Pichert (1978) provided a classic demonstration of the effect that schemas have on memory retrieval. The experimenters asked undergraduates to read a story about two children skipping school and hanging out at home from the perspective of either a burglar or a real-estate agent. Following this reading, the participants wrote down all they could remember from the story. Depending on what schema the participants were assigned (i.e., burglar or real-estate agent), they recalled more information relevant to their assigned schema compared to the other. Following a distraction task, participants were asked to recall the story again, this time from the alternative perspective. Results from the second recall showed again that participants recalled more information related to the newly assigned schema. Participants also showed a drop in the amount of information they recalled related to the original schema they were assigned.

Again, scripts demonstrate parallel effects. Graesser et al. (1980) compared the effects of scripts on memory in both recognition tasks as well as a recall task. Participants listened to stories involving scripted actions that included both typical and atypical information. Following the story, participants were either asked to recall as much of the story as they could or were given a recognition task that included both statements that appeared in the story and statements that did not. Participants were given one of these two tasks after a delay interval of either a half hour or one week. Results indicated that recall memory was better for atypical than typical actions from the story after the short delay, but recall was significantly better for typical actions after the week delay (Graesser et al., 1980). This effect was paralleled in the recognition task. The results from this experiment suggest that scripts become increasingly important retrieval cues as time from encoding increases and memory traces become weaker (Graesser et al., 1980).

In terms of personal narrative, the research on biases in memory retrieval suggests that the schemas and scripts impact which events and which details we choose to include in our personal narratives. They may also impact the coherence and organization of those personal narratives. For example, Waters et al. (2017) found that individual differences in scripted representations of parental support during distress (i.e., secure base script knowledge) predicted the level of detail, elaboration, and internal consistency in personal narratives of early experiences with caregivers. Waters et al. (2017) argued that this was, in part, due to the effect of scripted representations on memory retrieval and reconstruction.

The literature documenting effects of schemas and scripts on memory is extensive and provides several fruitful avenues for determining additional sources of influence on personal narrative. We chose to highlight the role of schemas and scripts in personal narrative as we believe this to be an exciting research domain with broad implication across psychology, including developmental, personality, and clinical research.

CONCLUSIONS AND FUTURE DIRECTIONS

Personal narratives help define who we are as individuals, helping us to understand and make meaning from our relationships and the world around us. They provide a framework for sharing and revising our subjective perspective. Personal narratives are believed to contribute to and reflect development and adaptation. As such, we have argued for four key domains by which psychological science has examined and operationalized individual differences in personal narrative (i.e., coherence, autobiographical reasoning, meaning making, and schemas/scripts). Each of these domains has their own unique developmental trajectory and consequences for the narratives we construct about our lives. Further, each of these domains may uniquely contribute to psychological adjustment or maladaptation (e.g., Waters et al., 2013a). Each of the domains we reviewed likely interacts with the others. For example, autobiographical reasoning is critical in the formation of meaning and the coherent organization of personal narrative. We argue that meaning making is not an arbitrary process, but rather something that relies on the ability to reason about autobiographical events, abstract common themes, and connect those abstractions with existing schemas or scripts. Thus, meaning may be constrained or imbued by the schemas or scripts we hold. Our approach to examining individual differences in personal narratives had the goal of presenting a diverse set of perspectives and research findings in an effort to highlight current understanding and potential points of growth. However, these diverse perspectives are by no means operating in isolation, and the development of an integrative model of the contributing factors to individual differences in personal narrative will be a critical next step for research.

An integrative model of personal narrative should not only cover the sources of individual differences but also their nature. Specifically, how stable are the features of a single event narrative across multiple tellings, how stable is an individual's narrative style across the telling of multiple different event narratives, and what is the base rate/frequency of the constructs highlighted in this chapter (e.g., self-event connections)? To date, we know very little regarding the stability of narrative variables across multiple tellings of the same event (but see Köber and Habermas, 2017b; McAdams et al., 2006). The limited data on this issue suggest only moderate stability across tellings of the life story, but these studies did not specifically ask that individuals narrate the exact same events across the repeated measures. As a result, the estimates currently available may significantly underestimate the actual stability of repeated narration of a specific event. Further, we know little regarding the stability of these constructs in personal narrative across events. Does an individual tell all their stories in the same way? Stability information of this kind is critical in evaluating arguments that individual differences in personal narrative represent meaningful facets of personality and assumptions regarding the presence of a trait-like narrative style. Finally, it is unclear what base rates should be predicted from the existing theories of individual differences in personal narrative, and there has yet to be a comprehensive examination of this issue. From our own experience, many of these variables appear quite rare. This is especially true in the case of self-event connections and other meaning-related variables (see Merrill et al., 2016). It is unclear how meaningful our personal narratives actually are, how many different meanings they should contain, and how much meaning we really need.

With these future directions in mind, the study of individual differences in personal narrative has made tremendous strides forward over the last several decades. It has seen the integration of developmental, personality, and clinical perspectives and has identified numerous distinct and consequential constructs. There is still much to learn regarding how these individual differences develop, their stability across time and telling, and their frequency, but narrative researchers are well positioned to address these issues in the coming years.

REFERENCES

Adler, J. M. (2012). Living into the story: Agency and coherence in a longitudinal study of narrative identity development and mental health over the course of psychotherapy. *Journal of Personality and Social Psychology*, *102*, 367–389.

Adler, J. M. (2013). Clients' and therapists' stories about psychotherapy. *Journal of Personality*, *81*, 595–605.

Adler, J. M., Chin, E. D., Kolisetty, A. P., & Oltmanns, T. F. (2012). The distinguishing characteristics of narrative identity in adults with features of borderline personality disorder: An empirical investigation. *Journal of Personality Disorders*, *26*, 498–512.

Adler, J. M., Lodi-Smith, J., Philippe, F. L., & Houle, I. (2016). The incremental validity of narrative identity in predicting well-being: A review of the field and recommendations for the future. *Personality and Social Psychology Review*, *20*, 142–175.

Adler, J. M., & Poulin, M. J. (2009). The political is personal: Narrating 9/11 and psychological well-being. *Journal of Personality*, *77*, 903–932.

Adler, J. M., Skalina, L. M., & McAdams, D. P. (2008). The narrative reconstruction of psychotherapy and psychological health. *Psychotherapy Research*, *18*, 719–734.

Adler, J. M., Turner, A. F., Brookshier, K. M., Monahan, C., Walder-Biesanz, I., Harmeling, L. H., … Oltmanns, T. F. (2015). Variation in narrative identity is associated with trajectories of mental health over several years. *Journal of Personality and Social Psychology*, *108*, 476–496.

Adler, J. M., Wagner, J. W., & McAdams, D. P. (2007). Personality and the coherence of psychotherapy narratives. *Journal of Research in Personality*, *41*, 1179–1198.

Allé, M. C., Gandolphe, M.-C., Doba, K., Köber, C., Potheegadoo, J., Coutelle, R., … Berna, F. (2016). Grasping the mechanisms of narratives' incoherence in schizophrenia: An analysis of the temporal structure of patients' life story. *Comprehensive Psychiatry*, *69*, 20–29.

Allé, M. C., Potheegadoo, J., Köber, C., Schneider, P., Coutelle, R., Habermas, T., … Berna, F. (2015). Impaired coherence of life narratives of patients with schizophrenia. *Scientific Reports*, *5*, 12934.

Anderson, R. C., & Pichert, J. W. (1978). Recall of previously unrecallable information following a shift in perspective. *Journal of Verbal Learning and Verbal Behavior*, *17*, 1–12.

Baerger, D. R., & McAdams, D. P. (1999). Life story coherence and its relation to psychological well-being. *Narrative Inquiry*, *9*, 69–96.

Banks, M. V., & Salmon, K. (2013). Reasoning about the self in positive and negative ways: Relationship to psychological functioning in young adulthood. *Memory*, *21*, 10–26.

Bartlett, F. C. (1932). *Remembering: A study in experimental and social psychology.* Cambridge, UK: Cambridge University Press.

Bauer, P. J., & Larkina, M. (2014). The onset of childhood amnesia in childhood: A prospective investigation of the course and determinants of forgetting of early-life events. *Memory, 22,* 907–924.

Benish-Weisman, M. (2009). Between trauma and redemption: Story form differences in immigrant narratives of successful and non-successful immigration. *Journal of Cross-Cultural Psychology, 40,* 953–968.

Berman, R. A. (2004). How children begin to tell a story. In K. E. Nelson, A. Aksu-Koç, & C. E. Johnson (Eds.), *Children's language. Vol.10: Developing narrative and discourse competence* (pp. 1–27). New York, NY: Taylor & Francis.

Berna, F., Bennouna-Greene, M., Potheegadoo, J., Verry, P., Conway, M. A., & Danion, J.-M. (2011). Self-defining memories related to illness and their integration into the self in patients with schizophrenia. *Psychiatry Research, 189,* 49–54.

Bluck, S., Alea, N., Habermas, T., & Rubin, D. C. (2005). A tale of three functions: The self-reported uses of autobiographical memory. *Social Cognition, 23,* 91–117.

Boals, A., & Schuettler, D. (2011). A double-edged sword: Event centrality, PTSD and posttraumatic growth. *Applied Cognitive Psychology, 25,* 817–822.

Bohn, A., & Berntsen, D. (2008). Life story development in childhood: The development of life story abilities and the acquisition of cultural life scripts from late middle childhood to adolescence. *Developmental Psychology, 44,* 1135–1147.

Bohn, A., & Berntsen, D. (2013). The future is bright and predictable: The development of prospective life stories across childhood and adolescence. *Developmental Psychology, 49,* 1232–1241.

Bosmans, G., & Kerns, K. A. (2015). Attachment in middle childhood: Progress and prospects. *New Directions for Child and Adolescent Development, 148,* 1–14.

Brewer, W. F., & Dupree, D. A. (1983). Use of plan schemata in the recall and recognition of goal-directed actions. *Journal of Experimental Psychology: Learning, Memory, and Cognition, 9,* 117–129.

Brewer, W. F., & Nakamura, G. V. (1984). The nature and functions of schemas. In R. S. Wyer Jr & T. K. Srull (Eds.), *Handbook of social cognition* (Vol. 1, pp. 119–160). Hillsdale, NJ: Erlbaum.

Brewer, W. F., & Treyens, J. C. (1981). Role of schemata in memory for places. *Cognitive Psychology, 13,* 207–230.

Chen, Y., McAnally, H. M., & Reese, E. (2013). Development in the organization of episodic memories in middle childhood and adolescence. *Frontiers in Behavioral Neuroscience, 7,* 84.

Chen, Y., McAnally, H. M., Wang, Q., & Reese, E. (2012). The coherence of critical event narratives and adolescents' psychological functioning. *Memory, 20,* 667–681.

De Winter, S., Vandevivere, E., Waters, T. E. A., Braet, C., & Bosmans, G. (2016). Lack of trust in maternal support is associated with negative interpretations of ambiguous maternal behavior. *Journal of Child and Family Studies, 25,* 146–151.

Dujardin, A., Bosmans, G., Braet, C., & Goossens, L. (2014). Attachment-related expectations and mother-referent memory bias in middle childhood. *Scandinavian Journal of Psychology, 55,* 296–302.

Dunlop, W. L., Guo, J., & McAdams, D. P. (2016). The autobiographical author through time: Examining the degree of stability and change in redemptive and contaminated personal narratives. *Social Psychological and Personality Science, 7,* 428–436.

Dunlop, W. L., & Tracy, J. L. (2013a). Sobering stories: Narratives of self-redemption predict behavioral change and improved health among recovering alcoholics. *Journal of Personality and Social Psychology, 104,* 576–590.

Dunlop, W. L., & Tracy, J. L. (2013b). The autobiography of addiction: Autobiographical reasoning and psychological adjustment in abstinent alcoholics. *Memory, 21,* 64–78.

Farrant, K., & Reese, E. (2000). Maternal style and children's participation in reminiscing: Stepping stones in children's autobiographical memory development. *Journal of Cognition and Development, 1,* 193–225.

Fivush, R. (2007). Maternal reminiscing style and children's developing understanding of self and emotion. *Clinical Social Work Journal, 35,* 37–46.

Fivush, R., Bohanek, J. G., Zaman, W., & Grapin, S. (2012). Gender differences in adolescents' autobiographical narratives. *Journal of Cognition and Development*, *13*, 295–319.

Fivush, R., Haden, C. A., & Adam, S. (1995). Structure and coherence of preschoolers' personal narratives over time: Implications for childhood amnesia. *Journal of Experimental Child Psychology*, *60*, 32–56.

Fivush, R., Haden, C., & Reese, E. (1996). Remembering, recounting, and reminiscing: The development of autobiographical memory in social context. In D. Rubin (Ed.), *Reconstructing our past: An overview of autobiographical memory* (pp. 341–359). New York: Cambridge University Press.

Fivush, R., Haden, C. A., & Reese, E. (2006). Elaborating on elaborations: Role of maternal reminiscing style in cognitive and socioemotional development. *Child Development*, *77*, 1568–1588.

Fivush, R. & Waters, T. E. A. (2013). Sociocultural and functional approaches to autobiographical memory. In T. J. Perfect & D. S. Lindsay (Eds.), *The handbook of applied memory* (pp. 221–238). London: Sage.

Fivush, R., & Zaman, W. (2015). Gendered narrative voices. In K. C. McLean & M. Syed (Eds.), *The Oxford handbook of identity development* (pp. 33–52). Oxford: Oxford University Press.

Graesser, A. C., Gordon, S. E., & Sawyer, J. D. (1979). Recognition memory for typical and atypical actions in scripted activities: Tests of a script pointer + tag hypothesis. *Journal of Verbal Learning and Verbal Behavior*, *18*, 319–332.

Graesser, A. C., Woll, S. B., Kowalski, D. J., & Smith, D. A. (1980). Memory for typical and atypical actions in scripted activities. *Journal of Experimental Psychology: Human Learning & Memory*, *6*, 503–515.

Greenberg, M. S., Westcott, D. R., & Bailey, S. E. (1998). When believing is seeing: The effect of scripts on eyewitness memory. *Law and Human Behavior*, *22*, 685–694.

Grysman, A., & Hudson, J. A. (2013). Gender differences in autobiographical memory: Developmental and methodological considerations. *Developmental Review*, *33*, 239–272.

Habermas, T. (2011). Autobiographical reasoning: Arguing and narrating from a biographical perspective. *New Directions for Child and Adolescent Development*, *131*, 1–17.

Habermas, T. (2015). A model of psychopathological distortions of autobiographical memory narratives: An emotion narrative view. In L. A. Watson & D. Berntsen (Eds.), *Clinical perspectives on autobiographical memory* (pp. 267–290). Cambridge, UK: Cambridge University Press.

Habermas, T., & Bluck, S. (2000). Getting a life: The emergence of the life story in adolescence. *Psychological Bulletin*, *126*, 748–769.

Habermas, T., & Köber, C. (2015a). Autobiographical reasoning in life narratives buffers the effect of biographical disruptions on the sense of self-continuity. *Memory*, *23*, 664–674.

Habermas, T., & Köber, C. (2015b). Autobiographical reasoning is constitutive for narrative identity. In K. C. McLean & M. Syed (Eds.), *The Oxford handbook of identity development* (pp. 149–165). Oxford, UK: Oxford University Press.

Habermas, T., Negele, A., & Mayer, F. B. (2010). 'Honey, you're jumping about' – Mothers' scaffolding of their children's and adolescents' life narration. *Cognitive Development*, *25*, 339–351.

Habermas, T., & Reese, E. (2015). Getting a life takes time: The development of the life story in adolescence, its precursors and consequences. *Human Development*, *58*, 172–201.

Haden, C. A., Haine, R. A., & Fivush, R. (1997). Developing narrative structure in parent–child reminiscing across the preschool years. *Developmental Psychology*, *33*, 295–307.

Harley, K., & Reese, E. (1999). Origins of autobiographical memory. *Developmental Psychology*, *35*, 1338–1348.

Hermans, H. J. M. (2006). The self as a theater of voices: Disorganization and reorganization of a position repertoire. *Journal of Constructivist Psychology*, *19*, 147–169.

Jack, F., MacDonald, S., Reese, E., & Hayne, H. (2009). Maternal reminiscing style during early childhood predicts the age of adolescents' earliest memories. *Child Development*, *80*, 496–505.

Jenkins, J. J., Wald, J., & Pittenger, J. B. (1978). Apprehending pictorial events: An instance of psychological cohesion. In *Minnesota studies in the philosophy of science. Vol. 9.*

(pp. 129–163). Minneapolis, MN: University of Minnesota Press.

Köber, C., & Habermas, T. (2017a). Development of temporal macrostructure in life narratives across the lifespan. *Discourse Processes*, *54*, 143–162.

Köber, C., & Habermas, T. (2017b). How stable is the personal past? Stability of most important autobiographical memories and life narratives across eight years in a lifespan sample. *Journal of Personality and Social Psychology*, *113*, 608–626.

Köber, C., Schmiedek, F., & Habermas, T. (2015). Characterizing lifespan development of three aspects of coherence in life narratives: A cohort-sequential study. *Developmental Psychology*, *51*, 260–275.

Leonard, R., & Burns, A. (2006). Turning points in the lives of midlife and older women: Five-year follow-up. *Australian Psychologist*, *41*, 28–36.

Liem, M., & Richardson, N. J. (2014). The role of transformation narratives in desistance among released lifers. *Criminal Justice and Behavior*, *41*, 692–712.

Lilgendahl, J. P. (2015). The dynamic role of identity processes in personality development. In K. C. McLean & M. Syed (Eds.), *The Oxford handbook of identity development* (pp. 490–507). Oxford, UK: Oxford University Press.

Lilgendahl, J. P., & McAdams, D. P. (2011). Constructing stories of self-growth: How individual differences in patterns of autobiographical reasoning relate to well-being in midlife. *Journal of Personality*, *79*, 391–428.

Lilgendahl, J. P., McLean, K. C., & Mansfield, C. D. (2013). When is meaning making unhealthy for the self? The roles of neuroticism, implicit theories, and memory telling in trauma and transgression memories. *Memory*, *21*, 79–96.

Lodi-Smith, J., Geise, A. C., Roberts, B. W., & Robins, R. W. (2009). Narrating personality change. *Journal of Personality and Social Psychology*, *96*, 679–689.

Loevinger, J. (1976). *Ego development: Conceptions and theories*. San Francisco, CA: Jossey-Bass.

Loftus, E. F., Miller, D. G., & Burns, H. J. (1978). Semantic integration of verbal information into a visual memory. *Journal of Experimental Psychology: Human Learning & Memory*, *4*, 19–31.

Lysaker, P. H., Davis, L. W., Eckert, G. J., Strasburger, A. M., Hunter, N. L., & Buck, K. D. (2005). Changes in narrative structure and content in schizophrenia in long term individual psychotherapy: A single case study. *Clinical Psychology & Psychotherapy*, *12*, 406–416.

Lysaker, P. H., & Lysaker, J. T. (2010). Schizophrenia and alterations in self-experience: A comparison of 6 perspectives. *Schizophrenia Bulletin*, *36*, 331–340.

Lysaker, P. H., Tsai, J., Maulucci, A. M., & Stanghellini, G. (2008). Narrative accounts of illness in schizophrenia: Association of different forms of awareness with neurocognition and social function over time. *Consciousness and Cognition*, *17*, 1143–1151.

Mansfield, C. D., McLean, K. C., & Lilgendahl, J. P. (2010). Narrating traumas and transgressions: Links between narrative processing, wisdom, and well-being. *Narrative Inquiry*, *20*, 246–273.

McAdams, D. P. (1993). *The stories we live by: Personal myths and the making of the self*. New York, NY: Guilford Press.

McAdams, D. P. (2006). *The redemptive self: Stories Americans live by*. New York, NY: Oxford University Press.

McAdams, D. P. (2013). The psychological self as actor, agent, and author. *Perspectives on Psychological Science*, *8*, 272–295.

McAdams, D. P., Anyidoho, N. A., Brown, C., Huang, Y. T., Kaplan, B., & Machado, M. A. (2004). Traits and stories: Links between dispositional and narrative features of personality. *Journal of Personality*, *72*, 761–784.

McAdams, D. P., Bauer, J. J., Sakaeda, A. R., Anyidoho, N. A., Machado, M. A., Magrino-Failla, K., … Pals, J. L. (2006). Continuity and change in the life story: A longitudinal study of autobiographical memories in emerging adulthood. *Journal of Personality*, *74*, 1371–1400.

McAdams, D. P., Diamond, A., de St. Aubin, E., & Mansfield, E. D. (1997). Stories of commitment: The psychosocial construction of generative lives. *Journal of Personality and Social Psychology*, *72*, 678–694.

McAdams, D. P., Hoffman, B. J., Mansfield, E. D., & Day, R. (1996). Themes of agency and communion in significant autobiographical scenes. *Journal of Personality, 64*, 339–377.

McAdams, D. P., Reynolds, J., Lewis, M., Patten, A. H., & Bowman, P. J. (2001). When bad things turn good and good things turn bad: Sequences of redemption and contamination in life narrative and their relation to psychosocial adaptation in midlife adults and in students. *Personality and Social Psychology Bulletin, 27*, 474–485.

McCoy, T. P., & Dunlop, W. L. (2017). Down on the upside: Redemption, contamination, and agency in the lives of adult children of alcoholics. *Memory, 25*, 586–594.

McLean, K. C. (2008). Stories of the young and the old: Personal continuity and narrative identity. *Developmental Psychology, 44*, 254–264.

McLean, K. C., & Breen, A. V. (2009). Processes and content of narrative identity development in adolescence: Gender and well-being. *Developmental Psychology, 45*, 702–710.

McLean, K. C., & Fournier, M. A. (2008). The content and processes of autobiographical reasoning in narrative identity. *Journal of Research in Personality, 42*, 527–545.

McLean, K. C., & Pasupathi, M. (2010). *Narrative development in adolescence: Creating the storied self*. New York, NY: Springer.

McLean, K. C., Pasupathi, M., & Pals, J. L. (2007). Selves creating stories creating selves: A process model of self-development. *Personality and Social Psychology Review, 11*, 262–278.

McLean, K. C., & Pratt, M. W. (2006). Life's little (and big) lessons: Identity statuses and meaning-making in the turning point narratives of emerging adults. *Developmental Psychology, 42*, 714–722.

Merrill, N., Waters, T. E. A., & Fivush, R. (2016). Connecting the self to traumatic and positive events: Links to identity and well-being. *Memory, 24*, 1321–1328.

Neimeyer, R. A., Herrero, O., & Botella, L. (2006). Chaos to coherence: Psychotherapeutic integration of traumatic loss. *Journal of Constructivist Psychology, 19*, 127–145.

Nelson, K., & Fivush, R. (2004). The emergence of autobiographical memory: A social cultural developmental theory. *Psychological Review, 111*, 486–511.

Newcombe, R., & Reese, E. (2004). Evaluations and orientations in mother–child narratives as a function of attachment security: A longitudinal investigation. *International Journal of Behavioral Development, 28*, 230–245.

Pals, J. L. (2006). Narrative identity processing of difficult life experiences: Pathways of personality development and positive self-transformation in adulthood. *Journal of Personality, 74*, 1079–1109.

Pasupathi, M. (2015). Autobiographical reasoning and my discontent. In K. C. McLean & M. Syed (Eds.), *The Oxford handbook of identity development* (pp. 166–181). Oxford, UK: Oxford University Press.

Pasupathi, M., & Mansour, E. (2006). Adult age differences in autobiographical reasoning in narratives. *Developmental Psychology, 42*, 798–808.

Pasupathi, M., Mansour, E., & Brubaker, J. R. (2007). Developing a life story: Constructing relations between self and experience in autobiographical narratives. *Human Development, 50*, 85–110.

Pasupathi, M., McLean, K. C., & Weeks, T. L. (2009). To tell or not to tell: Disclosure and the narrative self. *Journal of Personality, 77*, 89–123.

Peterson, C., & McCabe, A. (1983). *Developmental psycholinguistics: 3 ways of looking at child's narrative*. New York, NY: Plenum Press.

Raffard, S., D'Argembeau, A., Lardi, C., Bayard, S., Boulenger, J.-P., & Van der Linden, M. (2010). Narrative identity in schizophrenia. *Consciousness and Cognition, 19*, 328–340.

Raggatt, P. (2006). Putting the five-factor model into context: Evidence linking big five traits to narrative identity. *Journal of Personality, 74*, 1321–1348.

Reese, E. (2002). A model of the origins of autobiographical memory. In J. W. Fagen & H. Hayne (Eds.), *Progress in infancy research* (Vol. 2, pp. 215–260). Mahwah, NJ: Erlbaum.

Reese, E. (2014). Taking the long way: Longitudinal approaches to autobiographical memory development. In P. J. Bauer & R. Fivush (Eds.), *The Wiley-Blackwell handbook on the development of children's memory* (pp. 972–995). Chichester, UK: John Wiley & Sons.

Reese, E., Haden, C. A., Baker-Ward, L., Bauer, P. J., Fivush, R., & Ornstein, P. A. (2011). Coherence of personal narratives across the lifespan: A multidimensional model and coding method. *Journal of Cognition and Development, 12,* 424–462.

Reese, E., Haden, C. A., & Fivush, R. (1993). Mother–child conversations about the past: Relationships of style and memory over time. *Cognitive Development, 8,* 403–430.

Reese, E., Haden, C. A., & Fivush, R. (1996). Mothers, fathers, daughters, sons: Gender differences in autobiographical reminiscing. *Research on Language & Social Interaction, 29,* 27–56.

Reese, E., Jack, F., & White, N. (2010). Origins of adolescents' autobiographical memories. *Cognitive Development, 25,* 352–367.

Rimé, B., Finkenauer, C., Luminet, O., Zech, E., & Philippot, P. (1998). Social sharing of emotion: New evidence and new questions. *European Review of Social Psychology, 9,* 145–189.

Schank, R. C., & Abelson, R. (1977). *Scripts, goals, plans, and understanding.* Hillsdale, NJ: Erlbaum.

Simpson, J. A., Rholes, W. S., & Winterheld, H. A. (2010). Attachment working models twist memories of relationship events. *Psychological Science, 21,* 252–259.

Singer, J. A., Blagov, P. S., Berry, M., & Oost, K. M. (2013). Self-defining memories, scripts, and the life story: Narrative identity in personality and psychotherapy. *Journal of Personality, 81,* 569–582.

Singer, J. A., & Bonalume, L. (2010). Autobiographical memory narratives in psychotherapy: A coding system applied to the case of Cynthia. *Pragmatic Case Studies in Psychotherapy, 6,* 134–188.

Singer, J. A., & Salovey, P. (1993). *The remembered self.* New York, NY: Free Press.

Sulin, R. A., & Dooling, D. J. (1974). Intrusion of a thematic idea in retention of prose. *Journal of Experimental Psychology, 103,* 255–262.

Tessler, M., & Nelson, K. (1994). Making memories: The influence of joint encoding on later recall by young children. *Consciousness and Cognition, 3,* 307–326.

Thomsen, D. K. (2009). There is more to life stories than memories. *Memory, 17,* 445–457.

Thomsen, D. K. (2015). Autobiographical periods: A review and central components of a theory. *Review of General Psychology, 19,* 294–310.

Thomsen, D. K., Olesen, M. H., Schnieber, A., & Tønnesvang, J. (2014). The emotional content of life stories: Positivity bias and relation to personality. *Cognition & Emotion, 28,* 260–277.

Waters, T. E. A. (2014). Relations between the functions of autobiographical memory and psychological well-being. *Memory, 22,* 265–275.

Waters, T. E. A., Bauer, P. J., & Fivush, R. (2014). Autobiographical memory functions served by multiple event types. *Applied Cognitive Psychology, 28,* 185–195.

Waters, T. E. A., Bosmans, G., Vandevivere, E., Dujardin, A., & Waters, H. S. (2015). Secure base representations in middle childhood across two Western cultures: Associations with parental attachment representations and maternal reports of behavior problems. *Developmental Psychology, 51,* 1013–1025.

Waters, T. E. A., Brockmeyer, S. L., & Crowell, J. A. (2013b). AAI coherence predicts caregiving and care seeking behavior: Secure base script knowledge helps explain why. *Attachment & Human Development, 15,* 316–331.

Waters, T. E. A., & Fivush, R. (2015). Relations between narrative coherence, identity, and psychological well-being in emerging adulthood. *Journal of Personality, 83,* 441–451.

Waters, T. E. A., Ruiz, S. K., & Roisman, G. I. (2017). Origins of secure base script knowledge and the developmental construction of attachment representations. *Child Development, 88,* 198–209.

Waters, T. E. A., Shallcross, J. F., & Fivush, R. (2013a). The many facets of meaning making: Comparing multiple measures of meaning making and their relations to psychological distress. *Memory, 21,* 111–124.

Young, J. E., Klosko, J. S., & Weishaar, M. E. (2003). *Schema therapy: A practitioner's guide.* New York, NY: Guilford Press.

Developmental Profiles of Individuals with Psychopathic Traits: The Good, the Bad and the Snake

Marie-Hélène Cigna, Jean-Pierre Guay and Nathalie M. G. Fontaine

Antisocial behavior is associated with significant social and economic costs and, therefore, should be an important global concern. It can be defined as acts that break social norms or rules, threaten or intimidate others, and may cause harm to others or damage to their property (Frick and Viding, 2009). Such acts may be either premeditated or reactive/impulsive. Examples include physical aggression, conduct problems, and bullying, as well as delinquent and criminal activity.

Research in developmental psychopathology has shown that individuals who engage in antisocial behavior form a heterogeneous group. Several subgroups of children and youth with antisocial behavior have been proposed (Frick and Viding, 2009). For example, a distinction has been made in the *Diagnostic and Statistical Manual of Mental Disorders – 5th edition* (*DSM-5*; American Psychiatric Association, 2013) between oppositional/defiant behaviors (Oppositional Defiant Disorder) and aggressive/deceitful behaviors (Conduct Disorder). Other subgroups have also been proposed based on different trajectories of antisocial behavior over time (e.g., high and stable, increasing, low) and based on different types of behaviors, such as overt behaviors (confrontational acts such as fighting) versus covert behaviors (concealing acts such as lying) and reactive behaviors (e.g., in response to real or perceived provocation) versus proactive behaviors (e.g., premeditated or for instrumental gain; see Frick and Viding, 2009).

Recently, a new distinction has been made in the *DSM-5* (American Psychiatric Association, 2013) with respect to the diagnosis of Conduct Disorder. Recent evidence for a subgroup of children and youth with antisocial behavior distinguished by their high levels of callous–unemotional (CU) traits led to the inclusion of these traits as a specifier (labeled 'limited prosocial emotions') to Conduct Disorder. CU traits – which include characteristics such as lack of empathy, lack of guilt, and shallow or deficient affect – have been identified as a temperamental risk factor associated with severe and persistent antisocial behavior in children and in youth (Fontaine et al., 2011; Frick et al., 2003). Moreover, CU traits have been identified as a precursor to adult psychopathy (Lynam et al., 2007) and are considered the hallmark characteristics of this syndrome (Cleckley, 1976; Hare, 2003).

Psychopathy is described as a constellation of maladaptive behaviors and personality traits, which are often divided into two main factors, as indexed by the Psychopathy Checklist-Revised (PCL-R; Hare and Neumann, 2006). Factor 1 includes items in the interpersonal (e.g., superficial, grandiose, deceitful) and the affective (e.g., CU traits) domains and Factor 2 includes items in the lifestyle (e.g., impulsivity, stimulation seeking) and antisocial (e.g., early behavior problems, criminal versatility) domains. Psychopathic offenders are more likely than non-psychopathic offenders to be involved in a wider range and higher rate of violent behaviors, including instrumental and stranger-directed violence (Hart and Dempster, 1997; Patrick et al., 1997). Research has highlighted the asymmetric relationship between psychopathic traits and antisocial/criminal behavior. Individuals with psychopathic traits are highly likely to be involved in antisocial/criminal behavior; by contrast, only a small proportion of the individuals involved in antisocial/criminal behavior also have high levels of psychopathic traits (Hart and Hare, 1997). This asymmetric relationship has also been noted between CU traits and conduct problems in children (Fontaine et al., 2011). In addition, findings from longitudinal studies suggest that CU/psychopathic traits are moderately stable throughout age periods (e.g., from childhood to adolescence and from adolescence to adulthood; Neumann et al., 2011; Obradović et al., 2007). Nevertheless, it should be noted that individual variability and change over time have been reported in CU/psychopathic traits, suggesting that these traits can be malleable in some individuals (e.g., Bloningen et al., 2006; Fontaine et al., 2010).

Theoretically and empirically, CU/psychopathic traits have been traditionally conceptualized as symptoms of psychopathology. However, other theoretical frameworks describe CU/psychopathic traits as an adaptation rather than as a form of psychopathology (Glenn et al., 2011). These theoretical models postulate that CU/psychopathic traits may be adaptive in certain contexts. For instance, CU traits may be associated with resilience to stress when handling social rejection, criticism, or other challenging situations (e.g., laying off workers or saving someone's life; Del Giudice et al., 2012). These two conceptualizations of CU/psychopathic traits (i.e., psychopathology versus adaptation) may occur concurrently. This suggests that certain individuals may be characterized by a constellation of traits and behaviors that lead to adaptive behavioral patterns and positive life outcomes, whereas others may be characterized by a constellation of traits and behaviors that lead to antisocial/criminal acts and negative life outcomes.

In this chapter, we review research on the development of antisocial behavior with a focus on the influence of CU and psychopathic traits. We aim to shed light on potential profiles of youth with antisocial behavior combined with CU traits as well as their resulting characteristics in adulthood. We propose that different profiles, characterized by distinct constellations of traits and behaviors, may lead to either positive or negative outcomes. First, we present an overview of possible profiles of youth with CU traits. Second, we discuss theoretical explanations of potential developmental pathways to psychopathic traits in adulthood. Finally, we present three profiles of adults with psychopathic traits, which differ in terms of their traits, behaviors, and outcomes: the Good, the Bad, and the Snake.

OVERVIEW OF POSSIBLE PROFILES OF YOUTH WITH CU TRAITS

Longitudinal research suggests that youths who show antisocial behavior with CU/psychopathic traits have a more severe behavioral profile and more long-term adjustment problems than youths who show antisocial behavior with lower levels of CU/psychopathic traits (Fontaine et al., 2011; Frick and Viding, 2009). Moreover, youths with combined antisocial behavior and CU traits have been found to be resistant to some forms of traditional interventions recommended for antisocial behavior, such as time-out disciplinary strategies (Hawes and Dadds, 2005). They also seem to be emotionally under-reactive, particularly to others' distress, whereas youths who have antisocial behavior without CU traits appear to be emotionally over-reactive, especially to perceived threat (Jones et al., 2009; Marsh et al., 2008; Sebastian et al., 2012; Viding et al., 2012). Theoretical explanations suggest that socialization processes are disturbed in youths who have antisocial behavior combined with CU traits. It is hypothesized that these youths, characterized by a fearless temperament, do not form adequate associations between their wrongdoings and their consequences, and do not find others' distress aversive, which could lead to problems developing empathy (Blair et al., 2006; Frick and Viding, 2009). This affective profile is therefore different than the one that often describes youths who have antisocial behavior without CU traits: these youths are often hypervigilant to threat-related emotions and they may not have problems developing empathy (Frick and Viding, 2009; Jones et al., 2010; Schwenck et al., 2012; Viding et al., 2012). In addition, there is evidence suggesting that youths with CU traits may be genetically vulnerable to antisocial behavior, whereas the etiology of antisocial behavior in youths without elevated levels of CU traits may be mainly driven by environmental factors (Fontaine et al., in press).

Moreover, there is growing empirical evidence suggesting that youths with CU traits do not form a homogeneous group. Building upon the literature on primary and secondary psychopathy (Karpman, 1941; Poythress and Skeem, 2006; also see the section on this topic below), researchers have proposed the presence of two subtypes of youths with CU traits, namely primary CU traits and secondary CU traits. Primary CU traits are hypothesized to be driven by an inherent deficit that is expressed by an absence of conscience, lack of guilt, and no feeling or regard for others, whereas secondary CU traits could emerge as a result of childhood maltreatment, inconsistent and harsh discipline, family conflicts, and rejection. Recent studies have provided evidence for the distinction between primary and secondary CU traits in youth samples on the basis of anxiety, trauma, and other psychological difficulties (e.g., Fanti et al., 2013; Kahn et al., 2013).

Although the majority of studies to date have focused on CU traits in the presence of antisocial behavior, there is also evidence suggesting that some youths can have high levels of CU traits even in the absence of significant antisocial behavior (Frick et al., 2014). Elevated levels of CU traits may be rare in large representative population-based samples (Fontaine et al., 2011) but this presentation may be more prevalent in samples of youths who have been exposed to trauma and deprivation (Kumsta et al., 2012). Still, youths from population-based samples who are high on CU traits without antisocial behavior may be at risk for future adjustment problems, including antisocial behavior and anxiety symptoms (Rowe et al., 2010). However, not all youths with high levels of CU traits appear to engage in disturbed functioning patterns. More research is needed on youths with high levels of CU traits without concurrent antisocial behavior and, more specifically, on the mechanisms that are more likely to lead to future adaptive versus maladaptive behavioral patterns.

POTENTIAL DEVELOPMENTAL PATHWAYS TO PSYCHOPATHIC TRAITS IN ADULTHOOD

The following section aims to present different pathways to psychopathic traits that may be undertaken by youths with CU traits as they transition into adulthood. We briefly introduce adult psychopathy and present various etiological explanations. In order to present different profiles of psychopathy, we challenge the traditional approach to psychopathy and consider potential functional and dysfunctional forms. We first present studies on two different manifestations of psychopathy; more specifically, the primary and secondary subtypes. Second, we discuss other studies that focused on successful (or functional) and unsuccessful psychopathy. Building on these notions, we propose three main profiles of individuals with psychopathic traits: the Good, the Bad, and the Snake.

ETIOLOGICAL PATHWAYS TO AGGRESSION AND PSYCHOPATHY IN ADULTHOOD

Psychopathy is defined as a blend of interpersonal, affective, and behavioral traits (Blair et al., 2005; Cleckley, 1976). The affective traits (i.e., CU traits) are often considered to be the hallmark characteristics that make this syndrome distinct from more common forms of antisocial behavior (Glenn and Raine, 2014). For several years, the prevailing theoretical perspective on psychopathy has been that it is a unitary syndrome, which emerges from a core underlying pathology or deficit (Patrick et al., 2012). One proposed mechanism is that psychopathy is the result of brain disturbances. There is evidence suggesting that dysfunctions in certain brain regions, mainly the prefrontal cortex (more specifically the orbitofrontal cortex) and the amygdala, are associated with psychopathy (for a review see Glenn and Raine, 2014; Weber et al., 2008). However, frontal impairment – found to be associated with problems in domains such as information processing, decision-making, and behavioral inhibition – appears to be more specifically related to reactive aggression than proactive aggression, often considered as the type of aggression primarily used by individuals high on Factor 1 of psychopathy (Blair et al., 2005). Dysfunctions in the frontal region therefore appear to be more strongly associated with impulsivity and lack of self-control (i.e., Factor 2 of psychopathy) than with interpersonal and affective deficits (i.e., Factor 1 of psychopathy; Glenn and Raine, 2014; Yang and Raine, 2009).

There is also evidence suggesting that psychopathy is associated with an atypical pattern of emotion processing, including reduced emotional reactivity when processing negative emotions, such as fear or sadness (e.g., Blair et al., 2005; Lykken, 1995). Blair (2005) proposed that this atypical pattern of emotion processing arises from dysfunction in the amygdala, a brain structure involved in the treatment of emotional stimuli (Adolphs, 2008). Based on this model, genetic factors would lead to this emotional dysfunction (Blair, 2006). It is also postulated that disturbance in emotion processing interferes with socialization processes and, in turn, leads to difficulty in inhibiting antisocial behavior (Blair, 2005, 2006; Frick and Marsee, 2006).

Although a genetic contribution to impairment in emotion processing puts the individual at risk for the development of the full syndrome of psychopathy, other factors, such as social or environmental factors (e.g., birth trauma, abuse), may also have an influence (Blair, 2006). Indeed, environmental factors need to be taken into consideration in order to understand how psychopathic traits develop, notably because biological risk factors (e.g., genetic factors) may be triggered by aversive psychosocial variables (see Glenn and Raine, 2014, for a review). Birth trauma, environmental stressors, and family variables (e.g., abuse) could affect the structure and the functioning of biological systems responsible for the regulation of the basic threat system. This could increase the risk for engaging in reactive aggression (i.e., aggressive behavior in response to real or perceived provocation; see Blair et al., 2005, or Glenn and Raine, 2014, for reviews) and other behaviors related to Factor 2 of psychopathy (e.g., impulsive behavior).

More research on the social and environmental influences associated with adult psychopathy is needed, including research focusing on Factor 1 and Factor 2 of psychopathy separately, given that they seem to be differentially sensitive to social and environmental influences (e.g., Blair et al., 2005; Farrington, 2006; Glenn and Raine, 2014).

COMPETING CONCEPTUALIZATIONS OF PSYCHOPATHY

It is often thought that psychopathic traits and antisocial behavior are inextricably tied to one another given their strong association (Babiak and Hare, 2006). However, not all psychopathic individuals are involved in antisocial behavior. In fact, several researchers have suggested that a certain number of psychopathic individuals live and thrive within specific contexts and professions (Dutton, 2013; Hare, 1999; Lilienfeld et al., 2015; Lykken, 1995). Cleckley (1976) – who is often regarded as making tremendous contributions to the contemporary conceptualization of psychopathy – documented cases of non-criminalized psychopaths who were able to function quite well and with a certain level of success in society. In line with this idea, the inclusion of impulsive and antisocial behavior as essential criteria for psychopathy has been questioned (see Dutton, 2013; Gao and Raine, 2010; Poythress and Hall, 2011). The stereotypical vision of psychopathy needs to be revisited. To this end, we must look at research on the various manifestations of psychopathy.

Instead of viewing psychopathy as a unitary condition emanating from a common underlying pathology, some researchers have focused their attention on the distinct variants of psychopathic personality. Each variant could be tied to different neurobiological and developmental processes. The distinct variants of psychopathic personality could be differentiated based on three main aspects: their etiology, their constellation of personality traits, and their expression of antisocial behavior (see Poythress and Skeem, 2006, for a review). Psychopathic individuals appear to form a heterogeneous group, composed of various profiles, but all characterized by similar traits related to emotional detachment (Murphy and Vess, 2003; Skeem et al., 2007). Not only can this distinction between the different profiles of individuals with psychopathic traits be useful at the theoretical level, it can also help to explain conflicting findings observed with respect to the etiology of psychopathy. Indeed, the notion of psychopathy as a unitary condition is being challenged by research findings, which suggest that the core components of psychopathy have different correlates. For instance, Factor 2 of psychopathy has been found to be positively associated with measures of anxiety, negative emotionality, impulsivity, and reactive aggression, whereas Factor 1 of psychopathy has been found to be correlated with low anxiety, low empathy, and instrumental aggression (Hicks et al., 2004; Patrick et al., 2012; for a review, see Poythress and Skeem, 2006). These findings are consistent with two proposed variants of psychopathy, namely primary and secondary psychopathy.

Primary and Secondary Psychopathy

Primary and secondary psychopathy (also referred to as emotionally stable and aggressive psychopaths, Hicks et al., 2004; or low anxious and high anxious psychopaths, Kosson and Newman, 1995) have been proposed as two possible variants of psychopathy. These variants are rooted in Karpman's work (1941), which introduced the concept of primary and secondary psychopathy. The primary variant has been theoretically conceptualized as a constitutional affective deficit that is manifested by a lack of conscience, shallow affect, lack of anxiety, and incapacity to feel empathy or other forms of social emotions (Hicks et al., 2004; Lykken, 1995). In contrast, the secondary variant has been postulated as an affective disturbance that develops through exposure to aversive environmental factors, such as parental abuse, rejection, and other traumatic experiences (Karpman, 1941; Mealey, 1995; Wiebe, 2004). Individuals with secondary psychopathy are expected to have high levels of anxiety, anger, and impulsivity compared to the blunted affect manifested by individuals with primary psychopathy (Hicks et al., 2004; Lykken, 1995). The two variants are not only expected to be distinct in terms of etiological factors and affective disturbances, they are also expected to differ with respect to the expression of aggression. Individuals with the primary variant may be more prone to act intentionally in order to attain their goals (proactive aggression), whereas individuals with the secondary variant may be more inclined to act in reaction to specific circumstances (reactive aggression; for a review, see Poythress and Skeem, 2006).

For Lykken (1995), primary and secondary variants of psychopathy are associated with different neurologically-based systems and temperamental characteristics. Fearless temperament, specifically a lessened capacity to feel fear or anxiety, would influence the development of primary psychopathy. On the other hand, secondary psychopathy would be attributable to an over-reactive temperament linked to problems in aversive conditioning and impulsivity. Unlike Karpman's (1941) conceptualization, Lykken proposed that secondary psychopathy is associated with neurologically-based factors rather than environmental factors.

Successful and Unsuccessful Psychopathy

It has been proposed that the different components of psychopathic traits are associated with distinct patterns of social and personal adaptation. For instance, there is evidence suggesting that Factor 1 of psychopathy is associated with success to some extent, especially in the professional area (e.g., income, holding leadership positions, job performance), whereas Factor 2 of psychopathy is associated with maladaptive behaviors inconsistent with organizational performance (e.g., counterproductive and unethical work behavior, passive leadership; Howe et al., 2014; Lilienfeld et al., 2012; Neo et al., 2017). More precisely, the interpersonal characteristics of Factor 1 (e.g., superficial, grandiose, deceitful) could contribute to success (e.g., interpersonal skills could override negative performance reviews; see Babiak et al., 2010). High levels of traits on Factor 2 (e.g., impulsivity, irresponsibility) could be associated with work failure, whereas moderate levels could be rather adaptive and perhaps be less of an obstacle to success (Dutton, 2013). This is consistent with the leadership and work behavior literature concerning the 'bright side' of dark personality traits, which has shown that moderate levels of dark traits may actually be advantageous in certain situations (Judge et al., 2009).

Research suggests that successful and unsuccessful psychopathy may be linked to separate underlying mechanisms (Gao and Raine, 2010; Glenn and Raine, 2014; Ishikawa et al., 2001; Yang et al., 2005, 2010). Successful psychopathy is expected to be associated with high levels of Factor 1 traits coupled with moderate levels of Factor 2 traits, whereas unsuccessful psychopathy is expected to be associated with high levels of Factor 2 traits (Hall and Benning, 2006). Unsuccessful psychopathy would be associated with a number of structural and functional brain abnormalities, especially with respect to the amygdala and orbitofrontal cortex. These abnormalities would lead to cognitive impairment, predisposing unsuccessful psychopathic individuals to severe aggressive and uninhibited antisocial behavior (Glenn and Raine, 2014). On the other hand, successful psychopathy may not be associated with brain abnormalities to the same extent as unsuccessful psychopathy. Intact or even enhanced neurobiological features, including normative volumes of the prefrontal cortex and normative brain functioning, could be observed in some of the individuals considered as 'successful psychopaths'.

Conceptual and Methdological Issues

Following the idea of a certain constellation of psychopathic traits being linked to success, some researchers have focused on the study of successful psychopathy (also known as subclinical, noncriminal, noninstitutional, or adaptive psychopathy). It must be emphasized that findings have been found to be inconsistent and colored by conceptual and methodological issues in the relatively scarce empirical research done on this topic. Although there is no consensual definition (Lilienfeld et al., 2015), successful psychopathy is often illustrated by individuals who manifest the core symptoms of psychopathic traits (e.g., they are manipulative) but who are able to function in society and do not get into trouble with the law (Gao and Raine, 2010; Hall and Benning, 2006; Stevens et al., 2012).

Successful psychopathy has often been studied in individuals with high levels of psychopathic traits who were not incarcerated at the time of the study or who had never been convicted of a crime (Glenn and Raine, 2014). In that sense, success relies mostly on the ability to avoid contact with the criminal justice system, especially being convicted of a crime. Another approach is to study psychopathic individuals who are successful from a societal standpoint, specifically via their ability to prosper in organizational settings (Babiak and Hare, 2006; Lilienfeld et al., 2012; Lykken, 1995; Stevens et al., 2012). Some investigations explored noninstitutional psychopathy by recruiting psychopathic individuals in the community without relying on specific criteria to evaluate success (e.g., Gao and Raine, 2010). In addition, some of the study participants could not be considered as truly prosperous in terms of social status (e.g., low socioeconomic status; Widom, 1978) or in terms of their ability to avoid contact with the criminal justice system (i.e., a high proportion of noninstitutionalized individuals with psychopathic traits have a criminal history; Belmore and Quinsey, 1994).

Defining 'success' is challenging. Focusing solely on being, or not, convicted of a crime may not be sufficient to assess success, especially when considering that someone could be designated as 'successful' up to when he or she gets arrested or convicted of a crime. This individual, previously considered as 'successful', would then be perceived as 'unsuccessful', while still likely displaying the same personality traits (e.g., impulsivity) and neurobiological characteristics, unless, for instance, exposed to a major adverse event, such as a brain injury. In sum, conceptual and methodological issues in past studies limit the examination of 'high-functioning psychopaths', as depicted by Cleckley (1976), and even lead us to challenge the usefulness of designating individuals as 'successful psychopaths'.

Triarchic Conceptualization of Psychopathy

Patrick et al. (2009) have recently offered a triarchic conceptualization of psychopathy (Triarchic Psychopathy Measure; TriPM), which helps to explain the different manifestations of psychopathy, including successful and unsuccessful psychopathy. The authors formulated this model in an effort to reconcile and integrate various conceptualizations of psychopathy. In recent years, it has received empirical support from a growing number of studies (Patrick and Drislane, 2015). According to this model, psychopathy encompasses three distinct constructs: boldness, meanness, and disinhibition (Patrick, 2010).

Boldness is described as the adaptive component of psychopathy highlighted in Cleckley's (1976) work, but also inspired by Lykken's work (Lykken, 1995; Patrick et al., 2013). It indexes fearlessness in three domains: social efficacy, emotional stability, and venturesomeness. It is defined by social dominance, low levels of anxiousness, resiliency, tolerance for uncertainty, and a taste for adventure (Patrick, 2010). The meanness component captures callousness, exploitativeness, low levels of empathy, low levels of anxiety, and instrumental aggression (Patrick, 2010; Stanley et al., 2013). Disinhibition is consistent with the concept of secondary psychopathy, as it reflects a propensity toward externalizing problems (Patrick et al., 2012). It entails characteristics such as irresponsibility, problematic impulsivity, poor planning skills, impaired affect regulation, and impulse control problems (Patrick, 2010; Patrick and Drislane, 2015). Although disinhibition and meanness tend to reflect the maladaptive features of psychopathy, boldness is not purely adaptive (Drislane et al., 2014a). Notably, all three components have been found to contribute separately to the antisocial domain of psychopathy as indexed by the PCL-R (Patrick, 2010). Drislane et al. (2014a) noted that the maladaptive features of boldness may particularly arise when boldness is accompanied by high levels of meanness or disinhibition.

From the TriPM standpoint, psychopathy could emerge when disinhibitory tendencies are coupled with boldness and/or meanness (Patrick et al., 2012). More specifically, successful psychopathy could emerge as a combination of both high levels of boldness and low levels of disinhibition coexisting with emotional coldness (Lilienfeld et al., 2015). The TriPM has been found useful to identify distinct subtypes of psychopathic individuals. For instance, Drislane and colleagues (2014b) reported evidence for two distinct subtypes of high overall TriPM scorers: a classically low-neurotic, high-bold ('primary') subtype and a high-neurotic, high-disinhibited ('secondary') subtype. Additional empirical research on the TriPM constructs is needed in order to clarify the different configurations of psychopathic components associated with adaptive (e.g., work performance) and maladaptive outcomes (e.g., violent behavior) as well as the different subtypes of individuals with psychopathic traits.

The TriPM model proposes that the full syndrome of psychopathy would stem from two distinct mechanisms: neurobiologically-based deficits in emotional reactivity and cognitive-attentional processing (Patrick et al., 2012). The disinhibition component would indicate a dysfunction in anterior brain systems, specifically in the prefrontal cortex and anterior cingulate cortex. Reduced sensitivity of lower brain structures – including the amygdala and affiliated structures linked to the brain's defensive motivational system – is hypothesized to be more relevant to the affective-interpersonal features of psychopathy (Patrick, 2010; Patrick et al., 2012; Patrick and Drislane, 2015). Both boldness and meanness are hypothesized to arise from an underlying fearless disposition. However, while boldness is conceptualized as adaptive to some extent, meanness is associated with a pathological expression of a fearless temperament (Patrick, 2010). Different environmental factors could influence these two components. One main hypothesis is that meanness arises from factors that affect the process related to the formation of empathy and that contribute to interpersonal detachment (e.g., punitive parenting, abuse, neglect; Patrick, 2010; Patrick et al., 2009, 2012). Important research questions need further investigation, such as how the phenotypic components of the TriPM (i.e., boldness, meanness, and disinhibition) may be expressed in children and how such characteristics may lead to the different configurations of psychopathy in adulthood. For instance, such research could help to clarify if CU tendencies – which are particularly related to the construct of meanness – are effectively the more prototypic expression of core affective-interpersonal traits early in life and if assessment of precursors of psychopathy should also include other characteristics reflecting boldness, such as social efficacy, stress resiliency, and venturesomeness (Drislane et al., 2014a).

PROFILES OF INDIVIDUALS WITH PSYCHOPATHIC TRAITS: THE GOOD, THE BAD, AND THE SNAKE

Although it is still unclear what constellations of behavior (e.g., impulsive and antisocial behavior) and traits (e.g., CU traits) early in life may lead to the different manifestations of psychopathy in adulthood, it appears that different profiles of adults with psychopathic traits can be identified. These profiles may differ in terms of developmental factors, emotional and behavioral characteristics, and levels of functioning in society. Based on extant research (including the work by Patrick and colleagues, 2009, and Lykken, 1995), we propose three profiles of individuals with psychopathic traits in adulthood: the Good, the Bad, and the Snake. We hypothesized that different childhood characteristics, with a focus on the different variants of CU traits (i.e., primary versus secondary CU traits), could lead to distinct profiles of psychopathic traits in adulthood. The profiles are divided into two categories, namely unsuccessful and successful psychopathy. The Bad profile is associated with unsuccessful manifestations of psychopathy. Successful manifestations of psychopathy are considered in the view of society (i.e. the Good profile) and in view of the individuals (e.g., the Snake profile). These profiles are presented as a theoretical framework (see Table 7.1). Empirical research examining the validity of these profiles is needed.

Unsuccessful Psychopathy: The Bad

This profile represents the most unsuccessful manifestations of psychopathy. It resembles the secondary psychopath variant or the high-disinhibited subtype proposed by Patrick and colleagues (Drislane et al., 2014b; Poythress and Skeem, 2006). Individuals with this profile are expected to have low or moderate levels of Factor 1 traits as well as high levels of Factor 2 traits (Glenn and Raine, 2014; Lykken, 1995). Adults with this profile are likely to have been youths with secondary CU traits. Individuals with this profile could be more prone to negative affect (e.g., depression, irritability, anxiety), feelings of guilt, shame and personal inadequacy (Del Gaizo and Falkenbach, 2008; Lykken, 1995; Patrick et al., 2009; Poythress and Skeem, 2006). There is evidence suggesting that individuals with this profile may have low affective empathy (e.g., the ability to respond with an appropriate emotion to others' mental states; e.g., Mullins-Nelson et al., 2006; Wai and Tilipoulos, 2012). However, findings from recent studies based on the TriPM suggest that deficits in affective empathy may be more related to the meanness component of psychopathy than the disinhibition component (Sellbom and Phillips, 2013; Stanley et al., 2013). Therefore, it may be important to consider the different configurations of the TriPM constructs in order to clarify empathic response in psychopathic individuals (e.g., deficits may be observed when disinhibition is combined with high levels of meanness).

In addition, individuals with this profile are expected to have high emotional reactivity, potentially due to a dysfunction in the prefrontal cortex (Patrick, 2010). This dysfunction could be the result of various aversive environmental and social factors (e.g., birth trauma, abuse, and neglect). Such factors could influence the basic threat circuitry and, in turn, the risk for engaging in reactive aggression (Blair et al., 2005). Emotional and behavioral characteristics of the individuals with this profile are likely to reduce chances of success (e.g., by increasing the risks for getting into trouble with the law and for having poor work performance).

Successful Psychopathy

We identified two profiles of successful psychopathy: the Good and the Snake. From an evolutionary perspective, even traits deemed undesirable could be considered adaptive as

Table 7.1 The Good, the Bad and the Snake: proposed characteristics distinguishing profiles of individuals with psychopathic traits

	Successful psychopath		Unsuccessful psychopath
Youth profile	Primary callous–unemotional (CU) traits		Secondary CU traits
Adult profile	Good	Snake	Bad
Sources	Cleckley (e.g., businessman)	Babiak and Hare's work	Secondary psychopath
	Lykken's primary psychopath	Karpman's primary psychopath	Patrick's disinhibition component
	Patrick's boldness component	Patrick's meanness component	
Neurobiological factors	Reduced activity in the amygdala and affiliated structures		Anterior brain systems dysfunction (i.e., prefrontal cortex)
Environmental factors	Adequate socialization and parenting methods, positive opportunities	Factors affecting social connectedness and the formation of empathy (e.g., poor parenting, abuse)	Birth trauma, stressors, and family variables leading to dysfunction in systems responsible for the regulation of the basic threat response
Temperament	Fearless temperament		Impulsivity, negative affect and emotional distress (e.g., anxiety, anger, depression)
Emotional and empathic profile	Certain deficits in emotional capacity (reduced responsiveness to fear and anxiety) Ability to feel genuine emotion and empathy	General deficit in emotional capacity (CU tendencies) Inability to feel emotions and lack of empathy	Acquired affective disturbance (high emotional reactivity) May have the ability to feel social emotions (e.g., guilt, inadequacy) but seem to lack empathy
Behaviors	Adaptive attributes in everyday life (e.g., heroism) Adaptive workplace behaviors	Proactive aggression Maladaptive workplace behaviors	Reactive aggression Maladaptive workplace behaviors
Success	Can truly prosper, especially within professions where an attenuated emotional experience is beneficial (e.g., law enforcement, business)	Success is more of an illusion, attributed to good impression management skills and obtained at the expense of others	Lower chance of success in achieving goals, because of emotional and behavioral characteristics

long as they help individuals maximize their benefits and solve problems fostering their survival (da Silva et al., 2015). Hence, the Snake can be seen as successful if success is defined in individual terms, without taking into account possible consequences for others. However, from the standpoint of the TriPM constructs, only the Good would be seen as adaptive, whereas the Snake would reflect maladaptive tendencies. A number of authors (e.g., Babiak, 1995; Lykken, 1995) have suggested that high levels of Factor 1 traits and low or moderate levels of Factor 2 traits characterize successful psychopathic individuals. We postulate that adults in these profiles are likely to have been youths with primary CU traits. Brain functioning impairments (e.g., dysfunction in the amygdala) associated with reduced emotional responsiveness and fearless temperament could be at the origin of these two forms of psychopathic manifestations. However, youth with a fearless temperament could follow different trajectories through adulthood.

Notably, it is hypothesized that exposure to different environmental factors (e.g., positive versus negative parenting) could lead to either the Good profile or the Snake profile. More precisely, interaction between individual and environmental factors could lead to a more or less successful phenotypic expression. For the Good profile, emotional detachment would translate as boldness, whereas for the Snake profile, emotional detachment would emerge as meanness.

The Snake

The Snake is perhaps the most popular illustration of primary psychopathy, especially in business settings. It is mainly inspired by the work of Babiak and Hare (e.g., Babiak, 1995; Babiak and Hare, 2006; Babiak et al., 2010). It also takes inspiration in recent studies led on the negative consequences of psychopathy in the workplace (Boddy, 2011; Mathieu and Babiak, 2016; Mathieu et al., 2014). This profile resembles Karpman's (1941) description of primary psychopathy and embodies the meanness component proposed by Patrick and colleagues (2009). It refers mainly to manipulative and deceitful psychopathic individuals who thrive at the expense of others thanks to their deviant, sneaky, and indirect behaviors.

Theoretically, interpersonal skills – revolving around superficial charm and pathological lying – would be the Snake's biggest advantage. These would allow the individuals with this profile to adapt to social situations and to influence others. By doing so, they would be able to manipulate people who are useful to them in order to reach their goals, while keeping up a good impression on others (Babiak, 1995; Babiak and Hare, 2006). This idea is consistent with research on political skills and influential tactics, which are important to consider when studying professional success (e.g., Ferris et al., 2007; Harris et al., 2007; Treadway et al., 2013). Indeed, Babiak and colleagues (2010) found out that psychopathic individuals were identified as high potential candidates in various businesses because of their interpersonal style, although they received negative performance appraisal ratings. The Snake's success appears to be an illusion and would therefore rely mainly upon his or her interpersonal capacities rather than actual skills.

Individuals with this profile are expected to be characterized by an inability to feel emotions and by a profound lack of social connectedness (Patrick, 2010). Various factors contributing to interpersonal detachment, such as inadequate socialization or aversive experiences (e.g., punitive parenting, abuse; Patrick, 2010), could lead to desensitization to the suffering of others (Farrington, 2006; Glenn and Raine, 2014), hindering the development of empathy but fostering the emergence of meanness. In line with this idea, Craig et al. (2013) recently observed that poor parental bonding (e.g., lack of affection and compassion) was positively correlated with meanness but negatively correlated with boldness.

According to an evolutionary perspective, behaviors from individuals with this profile could reflect a cheating strategy based on exploitation of conspecifics for their own advantage (Glenn and Raine, 2009; Walsh and Wu, 2008). Lack of guilt and empathy would therefore promote antisocial strategies (Wiebe, 2012). Indeed, the reduced capacity to feel emotions could be a competitive advantage for the individuals with this profile. Although some of their behaviors lead to negative consequences, they are still likely to engage in deviant behaviors and exploit others to attain their goals (Walsh and Wu, 2008). The strong association between Factor 1 of psychopathy and instrumental aggression (e.g., Declercq et al., 2012) may be particularly driven by individuals with this profile.

Similarly, counterproductive workplace behaviors and other negative behaviors in the workplace (e.g., bullying, abusive supervision) may be observed more particularly in individuals in the Snake profile. Findings from a meta-analysis revealed that psychopathy may not be as strongly related to deviant behaviors in the workplace as expected (O'Boyle et al., 2012). This may be due to methodological limitations (Smith and Lilienfeld, 2013), including the failure to take into account the presence of different profiles of individuals with psychopathic traits. For instance, while both the Snake and the Good profiles may be associated with prosperity in the workplace, only the former may also be associated with negative workplace behaviors. There is evidence suggesting that specific psychopathic components are differentially related to workplace behaviors. For instance, meanness has been found to be associated with maladaptive workplace behaviors (e.g., unethical decision-making, hard tactics of influence), whereas boldness has been found to be associated with the use of adaptive behaviors, including adaptive leadership and team play (Neo et al., 2017). Future investigations should take into consideration the different psychopathic configurations as well as the different profiles of individuals with psychopathic traits (e.g., the Snake and the Good).

Extant studies (e.g., Babiak et al., 2010; Boddy, 2011; Wilson and McCarthy, 2011) also provide evidence that the corporate world (i.e., the realms of business, finance, commerce), where success is contingent upon emotionally distancing oneself from competitors (Hassall et al., 2015), is the type of environment in which individuals with the Snake profile may be particularly active. It is well recognized that psychopathic individuals, driven by the need for prestige and power, are more often found in businesses that allow them to have power and accumulate wealth (Babiak and Hare, 2006). Moreover, data suggest that primary psychopathic traits can be associated with holding leadership and management positions (Howe et al., 2014; Lilienfeld et al., 2014; Smith et al., 2014). Although this might seem surprising at first, the psychopathic individual embodies, for many businesses, the essence of the ideal leader (Babiak and Hare, 2006). For instance, ambition and need of power are also traits found in leaders (Parker and Chusmir, 1991; Winsborough and Sambath, 2013); grandiosity and superficial charm are linked to self-worth and charismatic leadership; interpersonal skills would mark the ability to make persuasive arguments and to ease interaction with others; emotional detachment would equate with a capacity to remain calm under pressure, make ruthless decisions, and be less vulnerable to the judgement of others (Babiak and Hare, 2006; Crossley et al., 2016; Dutton, 2013; Howe et al., 2014). Furthermore, moderate levels of Factor 2 of psychopathy – which have been associated with the Snake profile – appear relevant to successful psychopathy given that impulsivity may also be associated with the capacity to react rapidly, seize opportunities, and take calculated risks (Jones and Paulhus, 2011; Poythress and Hall, 2011). All in all, it seems that many psychopathic characteristics can be useful in leadership positions that revolve around the notions of ambition, charm, and power. Extant data suggest that individuals with the Snake profile are quite present in the corporate world, but it is hypothesized that individuals with the Good profile could also be active in this field. For individuals with the Good profile, their rise to success would rely on their skills, whereas for individuals with the Snake profile, their rise to success would rather fall within the dark side of leadership (Hogan and Kaiser, 2005). Future research on psychopathy in the workplace should include an appropriate assessment of boldness, which is particularly associated with the Good profile (Neo et al., 2017).

The Good

This profile is hypothesized to be the one with the optimal constellation of psychopathic traits. It is inspired by Patrick and colleagues' boldness construct (Patrick et al., 2009) and by the idea of a 'socialized' form of primary psychopathy (Lykken, 1995). Echoing Cleckley's (1976) idea that some psychopathic individuals could be successful in their legitimate endeavors (e.g., the businessman), several authors have argued that psychopathy could be linked to adaptive attributes in everyday life, profiting the individuals themselves but also the community at large (Dutton, 2013; Lilienfeld et al., 2014; Lykken, 1995). Lykken (1995) mentioned that heroes and psychopathic individuals could be twigs on the same genetic branch, as heroic acts and leadership are similar to psychopathy with respect to fearlessness and bravery. Similarly, Dutton (2013) associated successful psychopaths to special force soldiers, bomb-disposal operatives, and surgeons. A few empirical studies have explored this idea and focused on the characteristic traits of heroes, namely individuals who engage in high-risk professions, such as law enforcement, military forces, and emergency medicine. Findings suggest that individuals engaged in high-risk, prosocial occupations could have higher scores on affective-interpersonal traits compared to incarcerated offenders (Falkenbach and Tsoukalas, 2011). Similarly, there is evidence suggesting that heroism is associated with fearless dominance (Lilienfeld et al., 2014; Smith et al., 2013).

Similar to the Snake profile, the fearless temperament observed in individuals in the Good profile may be due to atypical brain functioning (e.g., amygdala dysfunction). However, fearless temperament in these individuals would not lead to the full syndrome of psychopathy, although it would still put them at risk for developing antisocial behavior. Whether they engage in antisocial behavior would depend on their social environment and learning history (Blair et al., 2005). Adequate socialization (i.e., responding consistently and contingently to the child's behavior; Glenn and Raine, 2014), positive educational opportunities, as well as parental influences that promote competence, mastery, or innate talent could enable these individuals to achieve success through licit (rather than illicit) means (Hall and Benning, 2006; Lykken, 1995; Patrick, 2010).

Individuals in the Good profile may have the ability to feel emotions. Indeed, they may have an attenuated experience not of all emotional states, but of anxiety and fear more specifically (Lykken, 1995). Their reduced emotional response to aversive stimuli would play a crucial role in their success. Low-stress responsiveness and high levels of boldness would allow these individuals to be more resilient, remain composed, recover quickly from stressful or threatening situations, and tolerate risks and uncertainty. Moreover, their skills would allow them to respond to environmental pressures with a detached, focused, and impassive attitude (da Silva et al., 2015; Dutton, 2013; Lykken, 1995; Patrick et al., 2009). A certain level of emotional detachment could also act as a shield to protect the individual against unpleasant emotions, which are typical of harsh environments (e.g., stress, competition, conflict, criticism; da Silva et al., 2015). Dutton (2013) gave the example of stock traders who must be able to deal with pressure at work. He suggested that these individuals may have a certain ability to compartmentalize so that they can focus on the job at hand. Further, these individuals may be able to just walk away when the job is finished and forget it even happened. Such skills could be beneficial for several of us when it is time to deal with daily situations; individuals in the Good profile would find themselves advantaged by their innate abilities. Hence, unlike the individuals in the Snake profile, who give the appearance of success, the individuals in the Good profile could truly prosper and blossom, notably within high-risk professions (e.g., law enforcement, military, medicine), where feelings may be bad for business (Dutton, 2013). In sum, individuals in the Good profile could be seen as having the ability to regulate their emotions when necessary or to experience emotions with low intensity.

DISCUSSION

In this chapter, we reviewed profiles of individuals with CU/psychopathic traits as well as their potential developmental pathways in adulthood. The current data led us to propose three profiles of adults with psychopathic traits – the Good, the Bad, and the Snake – characterized by distinct constellations of traits leading to adaptive or maladaptive outcomes. In this section, we summarize the key points presented in the chapter, highlight directions for future research, and discuss potential implications for prevention and intervention strategies.

Evidence suggests that psychopathic individuals form a heterogeneous group. Building upon the literature on primary and secondary psychopathy, researchers have proposed distinct variants or profiles of CU/psychopathic traits in both youths and adults, differing in terms of developmental factors, emotional and behavioral patterns, and social and personal adaptation. It is deemed important to distinguish between these various profiles because their respective constellations of traits may lead to different developmental pathways, with some being associated with greater risk of engaging in persistent antisocial behavior.

Individuals with high levels of CU/psychopathic traits may not engage in significant antisocial behavior and may even achieve success from a societal standpoint. Building upon these ideas, we suggested that opposing conceptualizations of psychopathy (i.e., psychopathology versus adaptation) may both occur concurrently. Namely, specific constellations of psychopathic components may lead to adaptive tendencies, whereas other constellations may lead to maladaptive tendencies (antisocial/criminal acts).

FUTURE DIRECTIONS

The triarchic conceptualization of psychopathy (Patrick and Drislane, 2015) is a promising framework to facilitate the understanding of the different psychopathic manifestations, including successful psychopathy, by deconstructing psychopathy into phenotypic components and clarifying the mechanisms underlying these distinguishable components. However, despite significant advances in this area, several questions remain. First, research is needed in order to clarify how the different configurations of the TriPM constructs develop and lead to adaptive or maladaptive outcomes, and potentially to different profiles, such as the ones we proposed in this chapter (i.e., the Good, the Bad, and the Snake). In line with this, an important issue in studying adaptive manifestations of psychopathy concerns the use of tools assessing relevant constructs such as boldness, which has been, so far, under-studied, especially in the workplace. Similarly, there is also a need for a better assessment of the precursors of psychopathy during childhood (Drislane et al., 2014a). So far, the focus has been on the hallmark characteristic of the development of psychopathic traits (i.e., CU traits); however, other characteristics, such as social efficacy, stress resiliency, venturesomeness, may also be considered. Continuing research in this area would provide a better understanding of the developmental factors of psychopathy, including potential protective factors leading to adaptive behavioral patterns.

IMPLICATIONS FOR TREATMENT AND PREVENTION: SPECIFIC INTERVENTIONS FOR DISTINCT PSYCHOPATHIC COMPONENTS

Considering the substantial social costs related to psychopathy, it is critical to continue studying the etiology of CU/psychopathic traits as well as the mechanisms that lead to socially adaptive or maladaptive outcomes. Such research may not only be useful at the theoretical and etiological levels, it may also be helpful to identify, refine, or develop the most adequate treatment and prevention methods (Patrick et al., 2012). Since each psychopathic component may be linked to different underlying mechanisms, different intervention approaches may be needed.

Although psychopathic traits are influenced by genetic factors, it is important to bear in mind that genetic vulnerability does not signify immutability (Fontaine et al., in press). For instance, there is evidence suggesting that CU traits can be malleable during childhood (Fontaine et al., 2011) and that CU traits in youth can decrease in response to interventions focusing on rewarding good behavior (e.g., Hawes and Dadds, 2005). Future investigations are needed to shed light on the environmental factors that could lead to positive effects on CU traits in youth as well as adaptive outcomes.

In addition, the development of new neurobiological techniques appears promising. Such techniques could affect the functioning of specific brain regions, and in turn, could have positive effects on psychopathic traits and related maladaptive outcomes (Glenn and Raine, 2014). Patrick and colleagues (2012) discussed two broad classes of intervention: feedback-based response modification as well as cognitive and attentional bias retraining. Because it can be used to modify brain reactivity, feedback-based response modification may be especially useful to address affective deficits underlying boldness and meanness constructs. For instance, biofeedback (e.g., using the functional magnetic resonance imaging (fMRI) technique while viewing aversive stimuli) could promote emotional resonance by enhancing amygdala reactivity. Difficulty recognizing and processing distress cues, which has been observed in youths and adults with CU/psychopathic traits, could also be improved using attentional retraining procedures directed at establishing attentional biases toward threatening or aversive stimuli. Further research is needed in order to evaluate the effectiveness of these novel approaches. New longitudinal and experimental studies following individuals across time should shed light on the developmental mechanisms and the intervention strategies that are optimal to address the specific strengths and vulnerabilities associated with each profile of individuals with CU/psychopathic traits.

REFERENCES

Adolphs, R. (2008). Fear, faces, and the human amygdala. *Neurobiology, 18*, 166–172.

American Psychiatric Association. (2013). *Diagnostic and statistical manual of mental disorders* (5th ed.). Washington, DC: American Psychiatric Association.

Babiak, P. (1995). When psychopaths go to work: A case study of an industrial psychopath. *Applied Psychology, 44*, 171–188.

Babiak, P., & Hare, R. D. (2006). *Snakes in suits: When psychopaths go to work*. New York, NY: Regan Books/Harper Collins Publishers.

Babiak, P., Neumann, C. S., & Hare, R. D. (2010). Corporate psychopathy: Talking the walk. *Behavioral Sciences & the Law, 28*, 174–193.

Belmore, M. F., & Quinsey, V. L. (1994). Correlates of psychopathy in a noninstitutional sample. *Journal of Interpersonal Violence, 9*, 339–349.

Blair, J., Mitchell, D., & Blair, K. (2005). *The psychopath: Emotion and the brain*. Hoboken, NJ: Blackwell Publishing.

Blair, R. J. R. (2005). Applying a cognitive neuroscience perspective to the disorder of psychopathy. *Development and Psychopathology, 17*, 865–891.

Blair, R. J. R. (2006). Subcortical brain systems in psychopathy: The amygdala and associated structures. In C. J. Patrick (Ed.), *Handbook of psychopathy* (pp. 296–312). New York, NY: Guilford Press.

Blair, R. J. R., Peschardt, K. S., Budhani, S., Mitchell, D. G. V., & Pine, D. S. (2006). The development of psychopathy. *Journal of Child Psychology and Psychiatry, 47*, 262–275.

Blonigen, D. M., Hicks, B. M., Krueger, R. F., Patrick, C. J., & Iacono, W. G. (2006). Continuity and change in psychopathic traits as measured via normal-range personality: A longitudinal biometric study. *Journal of Abnormal Psychology, 115*, 85–95.

Boddy, C. (2011). *Corporate psychopaths: Organizational destroyers*. New York, NY: Palgrave Macmillan.

Cleckley, H. (1976). *The mask of sanity: An attempt to clarify some issues about the so-called psychopathic personality* (5th ed.). St. Louis, MO: Mosby.

Craig, R. L., Gray, N. S., & Snowden, R. J. (2013). Recalled parental bonding, current attachment, and the triarchic conceptualisation of psychopathy. *Personality and Individual Differences, 55*, 345–350.

Crossley, L., Woodworth, M., Black, P. J., & Hare, R. (2016). The dark side of negotiation: Examining the outcomes of face-to-face and computer-mediated negotiations among dark personalities. *Personality and Individual Differences, 91*, 47–51.

da Silva, D. R., Rijo, D., & Salekin, R. T. (2015). The evolutionary roots of psychopathy. *Aggression and Violent Behavior, 21*, 85–96.

Declercq, F., Willemsen, J., Audenaert, K., & Verhaeghe, P. (2012). Psychopathy and predatory violence in homicide, violent, and sexual offences: Factor and facet relations. *Legal and Criminological Psychology, 17*, 59–74.

Del Gaizo, A. L., & Falkenbach, D. M. (2008). Primary and secondary psychopathic-traits and their relationship to perception and experience of emotion. *Personality and Individual Differences, 45*, 206–212.

Del Giudice, M., Hinnant, J. B., Ellis, B. J., & El-Sheikh, M. (2012). Adaptive patterns of stress responsivity: A preliminary investigation. *Developmental Psychology, 48*, 775–790.

Drislane, L. E., Patrick, C. J., & Arsal, G. (2014a). Clarifying the content coverage of differing psychopathy inventories through reference to the Triarchic Psychopathy Measure. *Psychological Assessment, 26*, 350–362.

Drislane, L. E., Patrick, C. J., Sourander, A., Sillanmäki, L., Aggen, S. H., Elonheimo, H., Parkkola, K., Multimaki, P., & Kendler, K. S. (2014b). Distinct variants of extreme psychopathic individuals in society at large: Evidence from a population-based sample. *Personality Disorders: Theory, Research, and Treatment, 5*, 154–163.

Dutton, K. (2013). *The wisdom of psychopaths: What saints, spies, and serial killers can teach us about success*. Canada: Anchor Canada.

Falkenbach, D., & Tsoukalas, M. (2011, May). *Can adaptive traits be observed in hero populations?* Poster session presented at biennial meeting of the Society for the Scientific Study of Psychopathy. Montreal, Canada.

Fanti, K. A., Demetriou, C. A., & Kimonis, E. R. (2013). Variants of callous–unemotional conduct problems in a community sample of adolescents. *Journal of Youth and Adolescence, 42*, 964–979.

Farrington, D. P. (2006). Family background and psychopathy. In C. J. Patrick (Ed.), *Handbook of psychopathy* (pp. 229–250). New York, NY: Guilford Press.

Ferris, G. R., Zinko, R., Brouer, R. L., Buckley, M. R., & Harvey, M. G. (2007). Strategic bullying as a supplementary, balanced perspective on destructive leadership. *The Leadership Quarterly, 18*, 195–206.

Fontaine, N. M. G., McCrory, E. J. P., Boivin, M., Moffitt, T. E., & Viding, E. (2011). Predictors and outcomes of joint trajectories of callous–unemotional traits and conduct problems in childhood. *Journal of Abnormal Psychology, 120*, 730–742.

Fontaine, N. M. G., McCrory, E. J., & Viding, E. (in press). Genetic contributions to the development of psychopathic traits and antisocial behavior in youths. In A. R. Beech, A. J. Carter, R. E. Mann, & P. Rotshtein (Eds.), *The Wiley Blackwell handbook of forensic neuroscience*. Oxford, UK: Wiley Blackwell.

Fontaine, N. M. G., Rijsdijk, F. V., McCrory, E. J. P., & Viding, E. (2010). Etiology of different developmental trajectories of callous–unemotional traits. *Journal of the American Academy of Child and Adolescent Psychiatry, 49*, 656–664.

Frick, P. J., Cornell, A. H., Bodin, S. D., Dane, H. E., Barry, C. T., & Loney, B. R. (2003). Callous–unemotional traits and developmental pathways to severe conduct problems. *Developmental Psychology, 39*, 246–260.

Frick, P. J., & Marsee, M. A. (2006). Psychopathy and developmental pathways to antisocial behavior in youth. In C. J. Patrick (Ed.), *Handbook of psychopathy* (pp. 353–374). New York, NY: Guilford Press.

Frick, P. J., Ray, J. V., Thornton, L. C., & Kahn, R. E. (2014). Can callous–unemotional traits enhance the understanding, diagnosis, and treatment of serious conduct problems in children and adolescents? A comprehensive review. *Psychological Bulletin, 140*, 1–57.

Frick, P. J., & Viding, E. (2009). Antisocial behavior from a developmental psychopathology perspective. *Development and Psychopathology, 21*, 1111–1131.

Gao, Y., & Raine, A. (2010). Successful and unsuccessful psychopaths: A neurobiological model. *Behavioral Sciences & the Law, 28*, 194–210.

Glenn, A. L., Kurrzban, R., & Raine, A. (2011). Evolutionary theory of psychopathy. *Aggression and Violent Behavior, 16*, 371–380.

Glenn, A. L., & Raine, A. (2009). Psychopathy and instrumental aggression: Evolutionary, neurobiological, and legal perspectives. *International Journal of Law and Psychiatry, 32*, 253–258.

Glenn, A. L., & Raine, A. (2014). *Psychopathy: An introduction to biological findings and their implications*. New York, NY: New York University Press.

Hall, J. R., & Benning, S. D. (2006). The successful psychopath: Adaptive and subclinical manifestations of psychopathy in the general population. In C. J. Patrick (Ed.), *Handbook of psychopathy* (pp. 459–478). New York, NY: The Guilford Press.

Hare, R. D. (1999). *Without conscience: The disturbing world of the psychopaths among us*. New York, NY: Guilford Press.

Hare, R. D. (2003). *The Hare Psychopathy Checklist-Revised* (2nd ed.). Toronto, ON: Multi-Health Systems.

Hare, R. D., & Neumann, C. S. (2006). The PCL-R assessment of psychopathy: Development, structural properties, and new direction. In C. J. Patrick (Ed.), *Handbook of psychopathy* (pp. 58–88). New York, NY: Guilford Press.

Harris, K. J., Kacmar, K. M., Zivnuska, S., & Shaw, J. D. (2007). The impact of political skill on impression management effectiveness. *Journal of Applied Psychology, 92*, 278–285.

Hart, S. D., & Dempster, R. J. (1997). Impulsivity and psychopathy. In C. D. Webster and M. A. Jackson (Eds.), *Impulsivity: Theory, assessment, and treatment* (pp. 212–232). New York, NY: Guilford Press.

Hart, S. D., & Hare, R. D. (1997). Psychopathy: Assessment and association with criminal conduct. In D. M. Stoff, J. Breiling, & J. D. Maser (Eds.), *Handbook of antisocial behavior* (pp. 22–35). Hoboken, NJ: Wiley.

Hassall, J., Boduszek, D., & Dhingra, K. (2015). Psychopathic traits of business and psychology students and their relationship to academic success. *Personality and Individual Differences, 82*, 227–231.

Hawes, D. J., & Dadds, M. R. (2005). The treatment of conduct problems in children with callous–unemotional traits. *Journal of Consulting and Clinical Psychology, 73*, 737–741.

Hicks, B. M., Markon, K. E., Patrick, C. J., Krueger, R. F., & Newman, J. P. (2004). Identifying psychopathy subtypes on the basis of personality structure. *Psychological Assessment, 16*, 276–288.

Hogan, R., & Kaiser, R. B. (2005). What we know about leadership. *Review of General Psychology, 9*, 169–180.

Howe, J., Falkenbach, D., & Massey, C. (2014). The relationship among psychopathy, emotional intelligence, and professional success in finance. *International Journal of Forensic Mental Health, 13*, 337–347.

Ishikawa, S. S., Raine, A., Lencz, T., Bihrle, S., & Lacasse, L. (2001). Autonomic stress reactivity and executive functions in successful and unsuccessful criminal psychopaths from the community. *Journal of Abnormal Psychology, 110*, 423–432.

Jones, A. P., Happé, F. G., Gilbert, F., Burnett, S., & Viding, E. (2010). Feeling, caring, knowing: Different types of empathy deficit in boys with psychopathic tendencies and autism spectrum disorder. *Journal of Child Psychology and Psychiatry, 51*, 1188–1197.

Jones, A. P., Laurens, K. R., Herba, C. M., Barker, G. J., & Viding, E. (2009). Amygdala hypoactivity to fearful faces in boys with conduct problems and callous–unemotional traits. *American Journal of Psychiatry, 166*, 95–102.

Jones, D. N., & Paulhus, D. L. (2011). The role of impulsivity in the Dark Triad of personality. *Personality and Individual Differences, 51*, 679–682.

Judge, T. A., Piccolo, R. F., & Kosalka, T. (2009). The bright and dark sides of leader traits: A review and theoretical extension of the leader trait paradigm. *The Leadership Quarterly, 20*, 855–875.

Kahn, R. E., Frick, P. J., Youngstrom, E. A., Youngstrom, J. K., Feeny, N. C., & Findling, R. L. (2013). Distinguishing primary and secondary variants of callous–unemotional traits among adolescents in a clinic-referred sample. *Psychological Assessment, 25*, 966–978.

Karpman, B. (1941). On the need of separating psychopathy into two distinct clinical types: the symptomatic and the idiopathic. *Journal of Criminal Psychopathology, 3*, 112–137.

Kosson, D. S., & Newman, J. P. (1995). An evaluation of Mealey's hypotheses based on psychopathy checklist: Identified groups. *Behavioral and Brain Sciences, 18*, 562–563.

Kumsta, R., Sonuga-Barke, E., & Rutter, M. (2012). Adolescent callous–unemotional traits and conduct disorder in adoptees exposed to severe early deprivation. *British Journal of Psychiatry, 200*, 197–201.

Lilienfeld, S. O., Latzman, R. D., Watts, A. L., Smith, S. F., & Dutton, K. (2014). Correlates of psychopathic personality traits in everyday life: Results from a large community survey. *Frontiers in Psychology, 5*, 740.

Lilienfeld, S. O., Waldman, I. D., Landfield, K., Watts, A. L., Rubenzer, S., & Faschingbauer, T. R. (2012). Fearless dominance and the US presidency: Implications of psychopathic personality traits for successful and unsuccessful political leadership. *Journal of Personality and Social Psychology, 103*, 489–505.

Lilienfeld, S. O., Watts, A. L., & Smith, S. F. (2015). Successful psychopathy: A scientific status report. *Current Directions in Psychological Science, 24*, 298–303.

Lykken, D. T. (1995). *The antisocial personalities*. Hillsdale, NJ: Erlbaum.

Lynam, D. R., Caspi, A., Moffitt, T. E., Loeber, R., & Stouthamer-Loeber, M. (2007). Longitudinal evidence that psychopathy scores in early adolescence predict psychopathy. *Journal of Abnormal Psychology, 116*, 155–165.

Marsh, A. A., Finger, E. C., Mitchell, D. G., Reid, M. E., Sims, C., Kosson, D. S., Towbin, K. E., Leibenluft, E., Pine, D. S., & Blair, R. J. (2008). Reduced amygdala response to fearful expressions in children and adolescents with callous–unemotional traits and disruptive behavior disorders. *American Journal of Psychiatry, 165*, 712–720.

Mathieu, C., & Babiak, P. (2016). Corporate psychopathy and abusive supervision: Their influence on employees' job satisfaction and turnover intentions. *Personality and Individual Differences, 91*, 102–106.

Mathieu, C., Neumann, C. S., Hare, R. D., & Babiak, P. (2014). A dark side of leadership: Corporate psychopathy and its influence on employee well-being and job satisfaction. *Personality and Individual Differences, 59*, 83–88.

Mealey, L. (1995). The sociobiology of sociopathy: An integrated evolutionary model. *Behavioral and Brain Sciences, 18*, 523–541.

Mullins-Nelson, J. L., Salekin, R. T., & Leistico, A. R. (2006). Psychopathy, empathy, and perspective-taking ability in a community sample: Implications for the successful psychopathy concept. *International Journal of Forensic Mental Health, 5*, 133–149.

Murphy, C., & Vess, J. (2003). Subtypes of psychopathy: Proposed differences between narcissistic, borderline, sadistic, and antisocial psychopaths. *Psychiatric Quarterly, 74*, 11–29.

Neo, B., Sellbom, M., Smith, S. F., & Lilienfeld, S. O. (2017). Of boldness and badness: Insights into workplace malfeasance from a Triarchic Psychopathy Model perspective. *Journal of Business Ethics*. Advance online publication. doi: 10.1007/s10551-016-3108-8

Neumann, C., Wampler, M., Taylor, J., Blonigen, D. M., & Iacono, W. G. (2011). Stability and invariance of psychopathic traits from late adolescence to young adulthood. *Journal of Research in Personality, 45*, 145–152.

O'Boyle, E. H., Forsyth, D. R., Banks, G. C., & McDaniel, M. A. (2012). A meta-analysis of the dark triad and work behavior: A social exchange perspective. *Journal of Applied Psychology, 97*, 557–579.

Obradović, J., Pardini, D. A., Long, J. D., & Loeber, R. (2007). Measuring interpersonal callousness in boys from childhood to adolescence. An examination of longitudinal invariance and temporal stability. *Journal of Clinical Child and Adolescent Psychology, 36*, 276–292.

Parker, B., & Chusmir, L. H. (1991). Motivation needs and their relationship to life success. *Human Relations, 44*, 1301–1312.

Patrick, C. J. (2010). *Operationalizing the triarchic conceptualization of psychopathy: Preliminary description of brief scales for assessment of boldness, meanness, and disinhibition*. Unpublished test manual, Florida State University, Tallahassee, FL.

Patrick, C. J., & Drislane, L. E. (2015). Triarchic model of psychopathy: Origins, operationalizations, and observed linkages with personality and general psychopathology. *Journal of Personality, 83*, 627–643.

Patrick, C., Drislane, L. E., & Strickland, C. (2012). Conceptualizing psychopathy in triarchic terms: Implications for treatment. *International Journal of Forensic Mental Health, 11*, 253–266.

Patrick, C. J., Fowles, D. C., & Krueger, R. F. (2009). Triarchic conceptualization of psychopathy: Developmental origins of disinhibition, boldness, and meanness. *Development and Psychopathology*, *21*, 913–938.

Patrick, C. J., Venables, N. C., & Drislane, L. E. (2013). The role of fearless dominance in differentiating psychopathy from antisocial personality disorder: Comment on Marcus, Fulton, and Edens. *Personality Disorders: Theory, Research, and Treatment*, *4*, 80–82.

Patrick, C. J., Zempolich, K. A., & Levenston, G. K. (1997). Emotionality and violent behavior in psychopaths: A biosocial analysis. In A. Raine, P. A. Brennan, D. P. Farrington, & S. A. Mednick (Eds.), *Biosocial bases of violence* (pp. 145–161). New York, NY: Plenum Press.

Poythress, N. G., & Hall, J. R. (2011). Psychopathy and impulsivity reconsidered. *Aggression and Violent Behavior*, *16*, 120–134.

Poythress, N. G., & Skeem, J. L. (2006). Disaggregating psychopathy: Where and how to look for subtypes. In C. J. Patrick (Ed.), *Handbook of psychopathy* (pp. 172–192). New York, NY: Guilford Press.

Rowe, R., Maughan, B., Moran, P., Ford, T., Briskman, J., & Goodman, R. (2010). The role of callous and unemotional traits in the diagnosis of conduct disorder. *Journal of Child Psychology and Psychiatry*, *51*, 688–695.

Schwenck, C., Mergenthaler, J., Keller, K., Zech, J., Salehi, S., Taurines, R., ... & Freitag, C. M. (2012). Empathy in children with autism and conduct disorder: Group-specific profiles and developmental aspects. *Journal of Child Psychology and Psychiatry*, *53*, 651–659.

Sebastian, C. L., McCrory, E. J. P., Cecil, C. A. M., Lockwood, P. L., De Brito, S. A., Fontaine, N. M. G., & Viding, E. (2012). Neural responses to affective and cognitive Theory of Mind in children with conduct problems and varying levels of callous–unemotional traits. *Archives of General Psychiatry*, *69*, 814–822.

Sellbom, M., & Phillips, T. R. (2013). An examination of the triarchic conceptualization of psychopathy in incarcerated and nonincarcerated samples. *Journal of Abnormal Psychology*, *122*, 208–214.

Skeem, J. L., Johansson, P., Andershed, H., Kerr, M., & Eno Louden, J. (2007). Two subtypes of psychopathic violent offenders that parallel primary and secondary variants. *Journal of Abnormal Psychology*, *116*, 395–409.

Smith, S. F., & Lilienfeld, S. O. (2013). Psychopathy in the workplace: The knowns and unknowns. *Aggression and Violent Behavior*, *18*, 204–218.

Smith, S. F., Lilienfeld, S. O., Coffey, K., & Dabbs, J. M. (2013). Are psychopaths and heroes twigs off the same branch? Evidence from college, community, and presidential samples. *Journal of Research in Personality*, *47*, 634–646.

Smith, S. F., Watts, A., & Lilienfeld, S. (2014). On the trail of the elusive successful psychopath. *Psychological Assessment*, *15*, 340–350.

Stanley, J. H., Wygant, D. B., & Sellbom, M. (2013). Elaborating on the construct validity of the Triarchic Psychopathy Measure in a criminal offender sample. *Journal of Personality Assessment*, *95*, 343–350.

Stevens, G. W., Deuling, J. K., & Armenakis, A. A. (2012). Successful psychopaths: Are they unethical decision-makers and why? *Journal of Business Ethics*, *105*, 139–149.

Treadway, D. C., Shaughnessy, B. A., Breland, J. W., Yang, J., & Reeves, M. (2013). Political skill and the job performance of bullies. *Journal of Managerial Psychology*, *28*, 273–289.

Viding, E., Sebastian, C. L., Dadds, M. R., Lockwood, P. L., Cecil, C. A. M., DeBrito, S., & McCrory, E. J. (2012) Amygdala response to pre-attentive masked fear is associated with callous–unemotional traits in children with conduct problems. *American Journal of Psychiatry, 169,* 1109–1116.

Wai, M., & Tillpoulos, N. (2012). The affective and cognitive empathic nature of the dark triad of personality. *Personality and Individual Differences*, *52*, 794–799.

Walsh, A., & Wu, H. H. (2008). Differentiating antisocial personality disorder, psychopathy, and sociopathy: Evolutionary, genetic, neurological, and sociological considerations. *Criminal Justice Studies*, *21*, 135–152.

Weber, S., Habel, U., Amunts, K., & Schneider, F. (2008). Structural brain abnormalities in psychopaths: A review. *Behavioral Sciences & the Law*, *26*, 7–28.

Widom, C. S. (1978). A methodology for studying non-institutionalized psychopaths.

In R. D. Hare & D. Schalling (Eds.), *Psychopathic behavior: Approaches to research* (pp. 71–84). Toronto: Wiley.

Wiebe, R. P. (2004). Psychopathy and sexual coercion: A Darwinian analysis. *Counseling and Clinical Psychology Journal, 1*, 24–41.

Wiebe, R. P. (2012). Integrating criminology through adaptive strategy and life history theory. *Journal of Contemporary Criminal Justice, 28*, 346–365.

Wilson, M. S., & McCarthy, K. (2011). Greed is good? Student disciplinary choice and self-reported psychopathy. *Personality and Individual Differences, 51*, 873–876.

Winsborough, D. L., & Sambath, V. (2013). Not like us: An investigation into the personalities of New Zealand CEOs. *Consulting Psychology Journal: Practice and Research, 65*, 87–107.

Yang, Y., & Raine, A. (2009). Prefrontal structural and functional brain imaging findings in antisocial, violent, and psychopathic individuals: A meta-analysis. *Psychiatry Research: Neuroimaging, 174*, 81–88.

Yang, Y., Raine, A., Colletti, P., Toga, A. W., & Narr, K. L. (2010). Morphological alterations in the prefrontal cortex and the amygdala in unsuccessful psychopaths. *Journal of Abnormal Psychology, 119*, 546–554.

Yang, Y., Raine, A., Lencz, T., Bihrle, S., LaCasse, L., & Colletti, P. (2005). Volume reduction in prefrontal gray matter in unsuccessful criminal psychopaths. *Biological Psychiatry, 57*, 1103–1108.

Generational Changes in Self-Esteem and Narcissism

Eunike Wetzel, M. Brent Donnellan,
Richard W. Robins and Kali H. Trzesniewski

History and popular culture provide vivid examples of individuals brimming with confidence, enthusiasm, and a willingness to extol their own virtues. Muhammad Ali proclaimed 'I am the greatest'; John Lennon boasted that his band was more popular than Jesus; and Donald Trump vowed to be the 'greatest jobs president God ever created'. These larger-than-life individuals are hardly representative of all people, everywhere; however, these examples raise interesting questions about the origins of narcissism and self-worth, especially in light of concerns about the impact of contemporary culture on the characteristics of individuals (e.g., Lasch, 1979).

It is worth noting that personality traits are influenced by many factors. Most of the variability in personality can be explained by genetic differences and 'non-shared' environmental factors, such as idiosyncratic experiences that make siblings different from each other (e.g., Polderman et al., 2015; Vukasovic and Bratko, 2015). Likewise, there is usually considerable variance within a particular group or cohort of people. It is often easy to lose sight of this fact when talking in broad terms about generations. Nonetheless, people entering adulthood in the 1960s to 1970s (Baby Boomers) were exposed to a different environment in terms of the political, historical, and economic zeitgeist than people entering adulthood today (Millennials).

According to popular opinion, Millennials are more narcissistic than their Baby Boomer parents. It is easy to think of examples to support this claim (e.g., Paris Hilton vs. Richard Hilton) but it is also easy to think of examples that counter this claim (e.g., Ivanka Trump vs. Donald Trump). The sociocultural environment changes over time and this might play a role in shaping people's personality and help explain why people are different from one another. For example, Twenge (2000) found increases in anxiety and neuroticism between 1952 and 1993 for student and child samples from the United States. Smits et al. (2011) reported small increases in extraversion, agreeableness, and conscientiousness, no change in openness to experience, and a small decrease in neuroticism for Dutch students between 1982 and 2007.

In an effort to extend work examining generational differences in personality traits, this chapter reviews research on generational changes in self-esteem and narcissism. We focus on these traits because they are among the most widely studied variables in social/personality psychology and have been frequently tied to generational influences (e.g., Trzesniewski et al., 2008b; Wetzel et al., 2017). First, we clarify terms and distinguish different types of changes associated with generation and age. Second, we describe study designs and methods for the investigation of generational changes. Third, we summarize research on generational changes in self-esteem and narcissism. Finally, we discuss limitations of the extant literature on generational changes and highlight some directions for future research.

TERMINOLOGY AND TYPES OF CHANGE

A *generation* consists of people born in a range of years that share a certain sociocultural environment. The way that different birth years are combined to form different generations is typically post hoc and the boundaries are fuzzy. A common convention is to refer to people who went through early adulthood from the early 1960s to the 1980s as the Baby Boomer generation, whereas people who went through early adulthood in the mid-1980s to late-1990s are Generation X (named after a fictional book by Douglas Copeland). Young adults today (early 2000s to late 2010s) are referred to as Generation Y or Millennials. Given that the definition of generations is somewhat imprecise, though, since there are no clear cut-offs for the birth years of a generation, researchers use the term *cohort*, which is defined as people born in the same year or the same range of years (e.g., 2000–2009).

It is important to distinguish developmental changes from cohort differences. Developmental changes (or age-related changes) refer to changes that accompany maturation and growing older, and thus can only be studied by following individuals over time and assessing change as a function of age. This is illustrated in Table 8.1 with the grey-shaded cells. For example, on average people may show decreases in narcissism as they age from 20 to 30 to 40 (e.g., Wilson and Sibley, 2011) due to changes in social roles and the demands of adulthood (see Roberts et al., 2010). Cohort differences refer to comparisons between people from different birth cohorts assessed when they are the same age (or age range). This is illustrated in Table 8.1 with the cells in bold. For example, we could compare 40-year olds born in 1960 with those born in 1970 and 1980 to determine whether

Table 8.1 Illustration of developmental changes and cohort differences in a cohort-sequential longitudinal design

Year of Measurement	Age of Participant		
2000	20	30	**40**
2010	30	**40**	50
2020	**40**	50	60
	1980	1970	1960
	Birth year (i.e., Cohort)		

Note: The grey-shaded cells indicate a design for investigating developmental changes and the cells in bold indicate a design for investigating cohort differences.

growing up in the 1960s, 1970s, and 1980s has an effect on narcissism and self-esteem. When differences between birth cohorts are investigated, the assumption is not that cohorts differ because they were born in different years. Rather, the assumption is that because birth cohorts share a sociocultural environment and the sociocultural environment changes over time, cohort differences allow inferences about the influence of the sociocultural environment on traits. That is, birth cohort is considered a proxy for the sociocultural environment (Twenge, 2002).

METHODS FOR INVESTIGATING GENERATIONAL DIFFERENCES

To investigate generational differences, studies with a cross-sectional design are not suitable because they confound developmental and cohort effects (Nesselroade and Baltes, 1974; Schaie, 1965). For instance, mean differences in narcissism found in a cross-sectional study between 20-year olds, 30-year olds, and 40-year olds assessed in 2000 could be due to cohort differences (higher or lower narcissism for people born in 1980, 1970, or 1960) and/or due to developmental changes (increasing or decreasing narcissism from age 20 to 40). Instead, *time-lag studies* are needed in which different cohorts are assessed at the same age (or age range) at different points in time. For example, to investigate cohort differences in narcissism, one could analyze data from 40-year olds collected in 2000, 2010, and 2020 (see Table 8.1). In this case, developmental changes cannot affect the results because participants were the same age during data collection. The time-lag method can be combined with a longitudinal study design, resulting in the cohort-sequential design, which allows the investigation of developmental changes and generational differences simultaneously (Schaie, 1965). For example, the Americans' Changing Lives study is a national panel survey that assessed participants of different ages (between 25 and 104) at four time points (1986, 1989, 1994, and 2002; House, 1986). These data have, for example, been analyzed to investigate cohort differences and developmental changes in self-esteem (Orth et al., 2010; for another example of a cohort-sequential design see Table 8.1).

When data from a time-lag study are available, an essential, but often omitted, first step is to check the measurement invariance of the scale across cohorts. *Measurement invariance* refers to whether the scale functions equivalently for participants from different cohorts. Put simply, this means that the same latent trait is being measured in the same way across cohorts. This allows researchers to meaningfully interpret mean differences across cohorts. Comparisons using non-invariant scales risk comparing not just apples and oranges but 'apples and spark plugs', to use the language of Vandenberg and Lance (2000; p. 9). Non-invariance can occur, for example, when the meaning of an item shifts with time. One of the items on the Narcissistic Personality Inventory (NPI) has the phrase 'If I ruled the world it would be a much better place' and the interpretation of this may shift across time with accompanying changes in the qualities of leaders. During some time periods, agreeing to this item could reflect narcissistic tendencies, but during other time periods, it might not differentiate between people high and low in narcissism. It might instead reflect individual differences in engagement in politics. In this case, the item would be non-invariant across cohorts, and ignoring this non-invariance might lead to possibly erroneous conclusions regarding differences in narcissism between cohorts.

Measurement invariance can be checked using multiple-group confirmatory factor analysis (CFA), as well as using item response theory methods. In the CFA procedure, models imposing different equality constraints from least restrictive to most restrictive are tested against each other (Meredith, 1993;

Widaman and Reise, 1997). Starting with a model that imposes the same factor structure for all cohorts, but allows all parameters to be estimated independently within cohorts, *configural invariance* is tested. If this model fits well, this indicates that the same factor structure holds for all cohorts. Second, *metric invariance* is tested by constraining factor loadings to be equal across cohorts. If this model does not fit significantly worse than the configural invariance model, it can be inferred that the relationship between the items and the latent traits is the same across cohorts. In other words, each item contributes to the overall scale to the same extent across cohorts. Third, *scalar invariance* is tested by additionally constraining item intercepts (i.e., means) to be equal across cohorts. If this restriction is justified, it implies that participants from different cohorts – but with the same latent trait levels – have the same observed means on the items. Scalar invariance has to hold to correctly interpret observed mean differences on the traits as representing true mean differences on the underlying latent traits. Lastly, *strict invariance* can additionally be tested by constraining residual variances to equality across cohorts. Strict invariance implies that the amount of variance in the items not accounted for by the latent trait is equal across cohorts. This level of invariance is not required for examining mean differences across cohorts. For methods of testing measurement invariance in an item response theory framework see, for example, Penfield and Camilli (2007).

Studies of generational differences in personality rarely test for the measurement invariance of the scale across cohorts before analyzing and making inferences about mean differences between cohorts.[1] There is one notable exception: Smits et al. (2011) investigated cohort changes in the Big Five from 1982 to 2007. In their measurement invariance analyses, several items on conscientiousness and neuroticism showed non-invariance between cohorts. When it is known which items are non-invariant, this can be taken into account and mean differences can be analyzed using partial invariance models where non-invariant items are freely estimated for each cohort, whereas invariant items are constrained to equality across cohorts (Byrne et al., 1989). The resulting estimates of mean differences will be unbiased as long as there are enough invariant items to establish a common metric across groups (Guenole and Brown, 2014; Reise et al., 1993).

Besides using estimates of latent mean differences from full or partial invariance models, other methods have been applied to quantify generational changes. One simple method is to compute the correlation between the year of data collection and the individual responses (Donnellan and Trzesniewski, 2009). This method makes sense especially when data from many consecutive years are available (e.g., annually from 1995 to 2015). When data from only a few years are available (e.g., 1995, 2005, 2015), testing for cohort mean differences is more adequate. Another approach is to compare important correlates of a construct across cohorts. For example, if the correlation between self-esteem and education level were similar across different cohorts, this would indicate that cohorts do not differ on self-esteem whereas differences in correlates across cohorts would point to cohort differences. When samples from multiple sources are available, cross-temporal meta-analysis (Twenge, 2000) can be applied. Cross-temporal meta-analysis analyzes data from samples with the same age range collected at different points in time and – in most cases – by different research groups. The general principle of cross-temporal meta-analysis is to regress the mean score on year of data collection (with mean score and year weighted by sample size or with means weighted by the inverse of the variance). To obtain an individual-level effect size similar to Cohen's *d* (Cohen, 1988), the unstandardized regression coefficient is multiplied with the number of years and divided by the average standard deviation of the individual samples. This method can also be applied when only means at each year are available as opposed to raw data (e.g., when means are taken from published research). However, in this case, it is not possible to test for measurement invariance and there is a reduction in variance within year of data collection that can lead to other issues (see Trzesniewski and Donnellan, 2010).

Sampling issues also need to be considered when investigating generational differences. Aggregating convenience samples from different sources can yield valuable information but large, nationally representative surveys that have administered the same instruments for long periods of time are more appropriate for analyzing cohort effects. For example, Monitoring the Future (MTF; Johnston et al., 2003) is a large, ongoing national study of high school seniors across the United States drawn with a multi-stage random sampling procedure. MTF started in 1975 with annual assessments of self-esteem and a wide range of other constructs. A number of studies have analyzed these data to investigate generational differences (see below).

GENERATIONAL DIFFERENCES IN SELF-ESTEEM

Self-esteem can be defined as an individual's subjective evaluation of her or his worth as a person (Donnellan et al., 2011). Self-esteem predicts important life outcomes such as depression, occupational success, relationship satisfaction, and physical health (e.g., Orth et al., 2012). The life-span trajectory of self-esteem shows a decrease in adolescence, a gradual increase during adulthood, and another decrease in old age (Orth et al., 2010; Robins et al., 2002).

Several studies have investigated generational differences in self-esteem. O'Malley and Bachman (1979) analyzed data from male high school seniors in the classes of 1969 and 1977 and found that the correlation between self-esteem and several educational variables, such as grades and parental education, was similar between the two cohorts, indicating that no change in self-esteem had taken place (e.g., $r = .08$ between parental education and self-esteem for both cohorts). Twenge and Campbell (2001) confirmed the result that no generational changes had occurred for high school students for the period from 1965 to 1994 ($r = .05$ between year of data collection and self-esteem scores). In contrast, they found a positive correlation of $r = .48$ between scores on the Rosenberg Self-Esteem Scale (RSE; Rosenberg, 1965; Rosenberg, 1979) and year of data collection (1969–1994) for college undergraduates aged 18 to 22. For children, a curvilinear effect was found with decreasing scores on the Coopersmith Self-Esteem Inventory (Coopersmith, 1975) from 1967 to 1979 ($d = 1.09$) and increasing scores from 1980 to 1993 ($d = 0.55$).

Trzesniewski et al. (2008b) analyzed MTF data on self-esteem (based on a modified and abridged version of the RSE) and found a null correlation between year of data collection (1976–2006) and self-esteem (see also Trzesniewski and Donnellan, 2010). Gentile et al. (2010) conducted a cross-temporal meta-analysis with data from middle schoolers, high schoolers, and college students. They found increases in RSE scores in all three age groups between 1988 and 2008 ($d = 0.78$ for middle school, $d = 0.39$ for high school, and $d = 0.30$ for college students), although for college students the result was only significant when the RSE was administered with a four-point scale and not when it was administered with a five-point scale. Orth et al. (2009) investigated reciprocal relations between self-esteem and depressive symptoms for samples from the United States and Germany. In both samples, the finding that self-esteem predicted depressive symptoms longitudinally (but not vice versa) held across cohorts (age groups of 18–29, 30–39, ..., 70 and older). Finally, Orth et al. (2010) analyzed data from the Americans' Changing Lives study, a cohort-sequential longitudinal study with four waves (1986, 1989, 1994, and 2002) assessing participants between the ages of 25 and 104. They divided the participants into six age groups (25–34, 35–44, ..., 75 and above) and tested whether the lifespan trajectory of self-esteem (assessed with an abbreviated version of the RSE) differed significantly across these cohorts. This was not the case, indicating that no generational changes had occurred for self-esteem between 1986 and 2002.

In sum, data from large panel surveys using probability samples indicate that self-esteem scores have stayed stable across cohorts from the 1970s to the 2000s. However, a caveat concerning these results is that the measurement invariance of the instruments (in most cases the RSE) between cohorts has not been checked. It is possible that taking measurement invariance into account would confirm this finding, but it is also possible that cohort differences in either direction would be found.

GENERATIONAL DIFFERENCES IN NARCISSISM

Narcissism is characterized by inflated and grandiose self-views. In contrast to self-esteem, which involves liking and accepting oneself, narcissism involves feeling superior to others and a sense of entitlement. Narcissism is a multi-faceted trait encompassing diverse characteristics. Some features of narcissism, including a sense of grandiosity and vanity, have been linked to positive outcomes, such as high self-esteem and emotional stability as well as low depression and loneliness (Rhodewalt and Morf, 1995; Sedikides et al., 2004; Trzesniewski et al., 2008b). Other features of narcissism, including exploitativeness and feelings of entitlement, have been linked to negative outcomes, in particular in the interpersonal domain, such as dysfunctional interpersonal relationships, aggression, and counterproductive work behaviors (Bushman and Baumeister, 1998; Campbell and Foster, 2002; Campbell et al., 2002; Penney and Spector, 2002). Longitudinal research on narcissism has mostly found stability in narcissism scores over time, though mean-level changes have also been reported. For example, a study of young adults found that narcissism was stable over a period of 18 months (Orth and Luciano, 2015). Two studies investigating the development of narcissism in childhood and adolescence also found moderate stability over a period of 18 months with children aged seven to 11 at time 1 (Brummelman et al., 2015) as well as over a period of two years with adolescents aged 14 at time 1 (Wetzel and Robins, 2016). Carlson and Gjerde (2009) reported a mean-level increase of $d = 0.58$ in narcissism scores for adolescents from age 14 to age 18. Furthermore, Edelstein et al. (2012) reported substantial stability of three narcissistic traits (hypersensitivity, autonomy, and willfulness) in women from age 43 to 53 (correlations between .40 and .68). They also discovered mean-level decreases in hypersensitivity ($d = -0.96$) and autonomy ($d = -0.81$), but increases in willfulness ($d = 0.46$).

There has been a controversy regarding generational changes in narcissism, with some researchers finding that narcissism has increased in the past decades and others finding no changes or even a slight decline. Table 8.2 briefly summarizes the results of studies concerning generational changes in narcissism. For example, Twenge et al. (2008) reported an increase of one third standard deviation on scores from the NPI (Raskin and Hall, 1979; Raskin and Terry, 1988) between 1982 and 2006. However, using the same data and two additional samples as well as the same method, Roberts et al. (2010) found no changes in NPI scores between 1982 and 2009. Donnellan et al. (2009) analyzed changes in NPI scores for undergraduates from 1996 to 2008 separately for ethnic groups due to concerns that ethnicity might affect findings, in particular at

Table 8.2 Research on generational differences in narcissism and related constructs

Study authors	Construct(s)	Years	Sample(s)	Results
Barry and Lee-Rowland (2015)	Narcissism	2005–2014	Age 16–19, N = 2,696	$r = -.15$ ($p = .65$) between mean narcissism scores and year of data collection
Donnellan et al. (2009)	Narcissism	1996–2008	Age 18–24, N = 30,073	$r = .024$ ($p < .01$) between individual narcissism scores and year of data collection
Grijalva et al. (2015)	Narcissism	1990–2013	Undergraduates, meta-analysis of 75 samples	Regression of d for gender difference on year of data collection: $\beta = -.06, p > .05$
Roberts et al. (2010)	Narcissism	1982–2009	Samples from Twenge et al. (2008) and Donnellan et al. (2009), additionally N = 234 undergraduates	No changes
Stewart and Bernhardt (2010)	Narcissism	pre-1990 and 2004–2008	Age 18–25, N = 588	Partial eta-square = .12 for F-test between pre-1990 and 2004–2008 undergraduates
Trzesniewski et al. (2008a)	Narcissism	1979–2007	Age 18–24 for samples from 2002–2007, N = 26,867	$d = -0.06$
Trzesniewski and Donnellan (2010)	Egotism, self-enhancement, individualism, and others	1976–2006	High school seniors, N = 477,380	For example: $d = 0.05$ for egotism, $d = -0.07$ for self-enhancement, $d = 0.16$ for individualism
Twenge et al. (2008)	Narcissism	1979–2006	Undergraduates, meta-analysis of 85 samples	$d = 0.33$
Twenge and Campbell (2008)	Self-satisfaction, self-liking	1975–2006	High school students, Ns between 5,441 and 9,582	$d = 0.12$ for self-satisfaction, ds between 0.06 and 0.16 for items assessing self-liking
Twenge et al. (2012)	Agentic self-evaluations (academic ability, leadership ability, public speaking ability, and others)	1966–2009	Undergraduates, N = 6.5 million	For example: $d = 0.17$ for academic ability, $d = 0.39$ for leadership ability, $d = 0.31$ for public speaking ability
Twenge and Foster (2010) (study 2)	Narcissism	1994–2009	Undergraduates, N = 4,152	$d = 0.37$
Wetzel et al. (2017)	Narcissism	1992–2015	18–24, N = 60,225	$d = -0.27$

Note: If no exact age range was given in the study, but participants were described as undergraduates, column 4 says 'undergraduates'. Samples with age ranges of 18 to 24 or 18 to 25 also consist of undergraduates.

University of California campuses (Twenge and Foster, 2008). The correlation between year of data collection and NPI overall scores was .02 for Caucasians and .04 for both African Americans and Asian Americans, which according to Cohen's (1988) guidelines, are less than small effects (< .10). All correlations at the NPI subscale level were also below .10.

Concerning constructs related to narcissism, Twenge et al. (2012) reported an increase in agentic self-evaluations pertaining, for example, to academic ability ($d = 0.17$), leadership ability ($d = 0.39$), and public speaking ability ($d = 0.31$) in college students between 1966 and 2009. On the other hand, Trzesniewski and Donnellan (2010) analyzed MTF data from 1976 to 2006 and did not find evidence of more than negligible cohort differences on constructs such as egotism ($d = 0.05$), self-enhancement ($d = -0.07$), and individualism ($d = 0.16$).

A recent meta-analysis by Grijalva et al. (2015) on gender differences in narcissism also investigated whether there were cohort effects in the gender difference of men scoring consistently higher than women (overall $d = 0.26$). For data from 75 samples of undergraduates, no change in the gender difference on narcissism scores from 1990 to 2013 was found ($\beta = -.06, p > .05$ for the regression of d for the gender difference on year of data collection), indicating also that scores overall have been stable.

None of the previous studies checked the measurement invariance of the NPI across cohorts. Wetzel et al. (2017) investigated this for cohorts of undergraduates from the 1990s, the 2000s, and the 2010s (total $N = 60,225$), both at the level of overall narcissism and at the level of three NPI facets, namely leadership, vanity, and entitlement. They found that invariance of factor loadings and item intercepts was violated for several items. For example, the intercept of the vanity item 'When people compliment me I sometimes get embarrassed – I know that I am good because everybody keeps telling me so'[2] was non-invariant across all cohorts, indicating that endorsement levels differed across cohorts when conditioning on the trait level. The reason for this might be that people from different cohorts interpret this item differently. When controlling for non-invariant items in partial invariance models, Wetzel et al. (2017) found a small decrease on latent estimates of overall narcissism ($d = -0.27$) between the 1990s and the 2010s. At the facet level, leadership ($d = -0.20$), vanity ($d = -0.16$), and entitlement ($d = -0.28$) all showed small decreases. Thus, when accounting for the measurement (non-)invariance of the NPI, decreases rather than increases or no changes are found across cohorts.

Taken together, recent studies do not provide strong support for a so-called epidemic of narcissism sweeping college campuses (e.g., Twenge and Campbell, 2009). Several factors may account for inconsistencies in the results of studies investigating generational changes in narcissism. One important factor appears to be the ethnic composition of the sample. For example, Wetzel et al. (2017) found a small increase in vanity for Asians between the 1990s and the 2010s, but a small decline for non-Asians. Thus, different proportions of Asians, African Americans, and Caucasians in the sample can affect whether increases, decreases, or no changes are found. In addition, results may differ depending on the particular construct investigated. Since narcissism is a multidimensional construct, cohort differences can vary across facets. A related issue is that some studies did not assess narcissism directly, but rather related traits such as self-enhancement or egotism. Finally, previous studies have used a variety of methodological approaches, which can influence results. When modern psychometric techniques are used to evaluate measurement invariance, the evidence seems to point toward similarities, rather than differences, across generations. To be sure, there are members of any generation who are exceptionally narcissistic as well as those who are exceptionally modest and humble.

Nonetheless, there are reasons to be skeptical of claims of dramatic generational differences in narcissism.

DISCUSSION AND FUTURE DIRECTIONS

Despite mixed findings, the picture that emerges is that there are no substantial generational differences for self-esteem and narcissism. Young adults today, on average, appear to possess similar levels of self-esteem and narcissism as young adults since the 1960s. Thus, the sociocultural environment appears to play a minor role in influencing people's personality, at least in terms of self-esteem and narcissism. Developmental changes appear to be more important for personality development. Moreover, persistent age-related differences in traits could be one reason why older adults perceive young adults today as more self-focused and narcissistic than young adults in the past (Roberts et al., 2010; Trzesniewski and Donnellan, 2014). Today's young people appear narcissistic because they are young, not necessarily because they were exceptionally coddled or over-valued by their parents during their development (Brummelman et al., 2015).

Studies on generational differences in narcissism have almost exclusively relied on undergraduate samples, though panel survey data have been analyzed to gain insight into changes in constructs related to narcissism. Studies on generational changes in self-esteem have used more diverse samples, both with respect to age (children, adolescents, young adults) and with respect to sampling methods (convenience samples, probability samples). Thus, future research on cohort effects in narcissism could conduct studies on other age groups as well as young adults from more diverse backgrounds and utilize probability samples.

All studies on generational differences in narcissism so far have used the NPI and – in most cases – only the total score. This is problematic because the majority of the items in the NPI assess leadership (19 out of 40 in Wetzel et al., 2016), which is often not considered to be the defining core of narcissism (see Ackerman et al., 2017; Brown et al., 2009; Brown and Tamborski, 2011). Only 12 items assess vanity and 4 items capture entitlement (Wetzel et al., 2016). Several researchers have come to the conclusion that the NPI does not capture the construct of narcissism well, but rather contains predominantly adaptive content (Ackerman et al., 2011; Rosenthal and Hooley, 2010; Wetzel et al., 2016).[3] Thus, even if there were an increase in NPI scores – which does not appear to be the case – this would not necessarily indicate problematic levels of narcissism. It would therefore be important to investigate generational differences in narcissism in instruments that better balance agentic and antagonistic aspects of narcissism, such as the Narcissistic Admiration and Rivalry Questionnaire (Back et al., 2013), and instruments that address pathological aspects of narcissism, such as the Pathological Narcissism Inventory (Pincus et al., 2009).

So far, there are no studies that address generational differences in pathological narcissism, for example, investigating the prevalence of Narcissistic Personality Disorder (NPD; American Psychiatric Association, 2013) across cohorts. Trull et al. (2010) estimated a prevalence rate of 1.0 for NPD. Future research could investigate whether the prevalence of NPD in the general population has changed across generations.

More cross-cultural research on generational changes is needed. Cross-sectional research indicates that there might be differences in narcissism and self-esteem scores across cultures (Schmitt and Allik, 2005; but see Chen, 2008, for concerns about measurement invariance with self-esteem). For example, Foster et al. (2003) found the highest narcissism scores in US participants, followed by Europeans, Canadians, and participants from Asia and the Middle East.

Note, however, that these results should be interpreted cautiously because cross-cultural differences in responding to rating scale items might bias findings (Johnson et al., 2005). Thus, considering cross-cultural differences in traits and the sociocultural environment (e.g., differences in the cultural dimensions of individualism-collectivism or power distance; Hofstede, 2001), it would be interesting to investigate generational differences in self-esteem and narcissism in other cultures besides the United States (e.g., Cai et al., 2012).

Even within cultures, differences between ethnic groups may also exist. For example, African Americans tend to score higher than Caucasians on self-esteem, though Caucasians tend to score higher than Hispanics, Asians, and American Indians (Gray-Little and Hafdahl, 2000; Twenge and Crocker, 2002). Ethnic differences have also been found for narcissism, with African Americans and Hispanics scoring higher than Caucasians and Asian Americans (Foster et al., 2003; Zeigler-Hill and Wallace, 2011) and Caucasians scoring higher than Asian Americans (Twenge and Foster, 2008). With respect to generational differences, this means that findings can differ across ethnic groups. Wetzel et al. (2017) analyzed cohort differences separately for Asians and non-Asians, while taking into account the measurement invariance of the NPI items, and found no change in overall narcissism for Asians from the 1990s to the 2010s, but a small to moderate decline for non-Asians ($d = -0.36$).

Research on generational changes should routinely check the measurement invariance of the applied instruments before drawing conclusions about mean differences across cohorts. The discrepancies in findings for narcissism between studies that took measurement invariance into account and studies that did not show that this can impact the results. Future research on generational changes in self-esteem should therefore check the measurement invariance of the RSE (or other self-esteem measures) across cohorts prior to analyzing mean differences. In addition, research could take advantage of more sophisticated modeling techniques with latent variables as opposed to relying on observed scores to investigate generational differences (see Wetzel et al., 2017, for an example). Research on generational differences should also use other methods of data collection than just self-reports, for example peer-reports, psychologist reports, and naturalistic observation (for examples for studying narcissism, see Carlson et al., 2011; Holtzman et al., 2010; John and Robins, 1994).

CONCLUSION

Self-esteem and narcissism appear to be relatively stable across generations. Thus, even though prominent examples of narcissistic children with less narcissistic parents or vice versa stand out, on average, generations do not appear to differ on these traits. Nevertheless, there are still a number of open questions with respect to cross-cultural and cross-ethnic differences in generational changes.

Notes

1 Note that if only mean differences between cohorts are of interest, the longitudinal invariance of the instrument is not relevant. In contrast, when both cohort differences and developmental changes are of interest, as in the context of a cohort-sequential design, both types of invariance (across cohorts and over time) need to be checked. In particular, longitudinal invariance needs to be established prior to investigating cohort differences in developmental trajectories.
2 In the NPI, a forced-choice format consisting of pairwise comparisons is used. That is, two response options (one narcissistic, one non-narcissistic) are presented to participants simultaneously, and they have to select the one that is closest to their feelings and beliefs.
3 In addition, all studies, with the exception of Wetzel et al. (2017), analyzed the NPI data without taking the forced-choice nature of the items

into account. According to Wetzel et al. (2016), this does not appear to bias criterion-related validities, but it is unclear whether it might affect the analysis of mean differences across cohorts.

REFERENCES

Ackerman, R. A., Hands, A. J., Donnellan, M. B., Hopwood, C. J., & Witt, E. A. (2017). Experts' views regarding the conceptualization of narcissism. *Journal of Personality Disorders, 31*, 346–361.

Ackerman, R. A., Witt, E. A., Donnellan, M. B., Trzesniewski, K. H., Robins, R. W., & Kashy, D. A. (2011). What does the Narcissistic Personality Inventory really measure? *Assessment, 18*, 67–87.

American Psychiatric Association. (2013). *Diagnostic and statistical manual of mental disorders* (5th ed.). Washington, DC: Author.

Back, M. D., Küfner, A. C., Dufner, M., Gerlach, T. M., Rauthmann, J. F., & Denissen, J. J. (2013). Narcissistic admiration and rivalry: Disentangling the bright and dark sides of narcissism. *Journal of Personality and Social Psychology, 105*, 1013–1037.

Barry, C. T., & Lee-Rowland, L. M. (2015). Has there been a recent increase in adolescent narcissism? Evidence from a sample of at-risk adolescents (2005–2014). *Personality and Individual Differences, 87*, 153–157.

Brown, R. P., Budzek, K., & Tamborski, M. (2009). On the meaning and measure of narcissism. *Personality and Social Psychology Bulletin, 35*, 951–964.

Brown, R. P., & Tamborski, M. (2011). Of tails and their dogs: A critical view of the measurement of trait narcissism in social-personality research. In W. K. Campbell & J. D. Miller (Eds.), *The handbook of narcissism and narcissistic personality disorder* (pp. 141–145). Hoboken, NJ: John Wiley & Sons.

Brummelman, E., Thomaes, S., Nelemans, S. A., Orobio de Castro, B., Overbeek, G., & Bushman, B. J. (2015). Origins of narcissism in children. *Proceedings of the National Academy of Sciences of the United States of America, 112*, 3659–3662.

Bushman, B. J., & Baumeister, R. F. (1998). Threatened egotism, narcissism, self-esteem, and direct and displaced aggression: Does self-love or self-hate lead to violence? *Journal of Personality and Social Psychology, 75*, 219–229.

Byrne, B. M., Shavelson, R. J., & Muthen, B. (1989). Testing for the equivalence of factor covariance and mean structures: The issue of partial measurement invariance. *Psychological Bulletin, 105*, 456–466.

Cai, H. J., Kwan, V. S. Y., & Sedikides, C. (2012). A sociocultural approach to narcissism: The case of modern China. *European Journal of Personality, 26*, 529–535.

Campbell, W. K., & Foster, C. A. (2002). Narcissism and commitment in romantic relationships: An investment model analysis. *Personality and Social Psychology Bulletin, 28*, 484–495.

Campbell, W. K., Foster, C. A., & Finkel, E. J. (2002). Does self-love lead to love for others? A story of narcissistic game playing. *Journal of Personality and Social Psychology, 83*, 340–354.

Carlson, E. N., Vazire, S., & Oltmanns, T. F. (2011). You probably think this paper's about you: Narcissists' perceptions of their personality and reputation. *Journal of Personality and Social Psychology, 101*, 185–201.

Carlson, K. S., & Gjerde, P. F. (2009). Preschool personality antecedents of narcissism in adolescence and emergent adulthood: A 20-year longitudinal study. *Journal of Research in Personality, 43*, 570–578.

Chen, F. F. (2008). What happens if we compare chopsticks with forks? The impact of making inappropriate comparisons in cross-cultural research. *Journal of Personality and Social Psychology, 95*, 1005–1018.

Cohen, J. (1988). *Statistical power analysis for the behavioral sciences*. New York, NY: Erlbaum.

Coopersmith, S. (1975). *Coopersmith Self-Esteem Inventory, technical manual*. Palo Alto, CA: Consulting Psychologists Press.

Donnellan, M. B., & Trzesniewski, K. H. (2009). How should we study generational 'changes' – Or should we? A critical examination of the evidence for 'generation me'. *Social and Personality Psychology Compass, 3*, 775–784.

Donnellan, M. B., Trzesniewski, K. H., & Robins, R. W. (2009). An emerging epidemic of narcissism or much ado about nothing? *Journal of Research in Personality, 43*, 498–501.

Donnellan, M. B., Trzesniewski, K. H., & Robins, R. W. (2011). Self-esteem: Enduring issues and controversies. In T. Chamorro-Premuzic, S. von Stumm, & A. Furnham (Eds.), *The Wiley-Blackwell handbook of individual differences* (pp. 718–746). Chichester, England: Wiley-Blackwell.

Edelstein, R. S., Newton, N. J., & Stewart, A. J. (2012). Narcissism in midlife: Longitudinal changes in and correlates of women's narcissistic personality traits. *Journal of Personality*, 80, 1179–1204.

Foster, J. D., Campbell, W. K., & Twenge, J. M. (2003). Individual differences in narcissism: Inflated self-views across the lifespan and around the world. *Journal of Research in Personality*, 37, 469–486.

Gentile, B., Twenge, J. M., & Campbell, W. K. (2010). Birth cohort differences in self-esteem, 1988–2008: A cross-temporal meta-analysis. *Review of General Psychology*, 14, 261–268.

Gray-Little, B., & Hafdahl, A. R. (2000). Factors influencing racial comparisons of self-esteem: A quantitative review. *Psychological Bulletin*, 126, 26–54.

Grijalva, E., Newman, D. A., Tay, L., Donnellan, M. B., Harms, P. D., Robins, R. W., & Yan, T. (2015). Gender differences in narcissism: A meta-analytic review. *Psychological Bulletin*, 141, 261–310.

Guenole, N., & Brown, A. (2014). The consequences of ignoring measurement invariance for path coefficients in structural equation models. *Frontiers in Psychology*, 5, 980.

Hofstede, G. (2001). *Culture's consequences*. Thousand Oaks, CA: Sage.

Holtzman, N. S., Vazire, S., & Mehl, M. R. (2010). Sounds like a narcissist: Behavioral manifestations of narcissism in everyday life. *Journal of Research in Personality*, 44, 478–484.

House, J. S. (1986). *Americans' changing lives: Waves I and II, 1986 and 1989* [Dat file]. Ann Arbor, MI: University of Michigan, Survey Research Center.

John, O. P., & Robins, R. W. (1994). Accuracy and bias in self-perception: Individual differences in self-enhancement and the role of narcissism. *Journal of Personality and Social Psychology*, 66, 206–219.

Johnson, T., Kulesa, P., Cho, Y. I., & Shavitt, S. (2005). The relation between culture and response styles – Evidence from 19 countries. *Journal of Cross-Cultural Psychology*, 36, 264–277.

Johnston, L. D., Bachman, J. G., & O'Malley, P. M. (2003). *Monitoring the future: A continuing study of the lifestyles and values of youth*. Ann Arbor, MI: Inter-university Consortium for Political and Social Research.

Lasch, C. (1979). *The culture of narcissism: American life in an age of diminishing expectations*. New York, NY: Norton.

Meredith, W. (1993). Measurement invariance, factor-analysis and factorial invariance. *Psychometrika*, 58, 525–543.

Nesselroade, J. R., & Baltes, P. B. (1974). Adolescent personality development and historical change: 1970–1972. *Monographs of the Society for Research in Child Development*, 39, 1–80.

O'Malley, P. M., & Bachman, J. G. (1979). Self-esteem and education: Sex and cohort comparisons among high-school seniors. *Journal of Personality and Social Psychology*, 37, 1153–1159.

Orth, U., & Luciano, E. C. (2015). Self-esteem, narcissism, and stressful life events: Testing for selection and socialization. *Journal of Personality and Social Psychology*, 109, 707–721.

Orth, U., Robins, R. W., Trzesniewski, K. H., Maes, J., & Schmitt, M. (2009). Low self-esteem is a risk factor for depressive symptoms from young adulthood to old age. *Journal of Abnormal Psychology*, 118, 472–478.

Orth, U., Robins, R. W., & Widaman, K. F. (2012). Life-span development of self-esteem and its effects on important life outcomes. *Journal of Personality and Social Psychology*, 102, 1271–1288.

Orth, U., Trzesniewski, K. H., & Robins, R. W. (2010). Self-esteem development from young adulthood to old age: A cohort-sequential longitudinal study. *Journal of Personality and Social Psychology*, 98, 645–658.

Penfield, R. D., & Camilli, G. (2007). Differential item functioning and item bias. In C. R. Rao & S. Sinharay (Eds.), *Handbook of statistics: Vol. 26. Psychometrics* (pp. 125–167). Amsterdam, The Netherlands: Elsevier.

Penney, L. M., & Spector, P. E. (2002). Narcissism and counterproductive work behavior: Do bigger egos mean bigger problems?

International Journal of Selection and Assessment, 10, 126–134.

Pincus, A. L., Ansell, E. B., Pimentel, C. A., Cain, N. M., Wright, A. G., & Levy, K. N. (2009). Initial construction and validation of the Pathological Narcissism Inventory. Psychological Assessment, 21, 365–379.

Polderman, T. J., Benyamin, B., de Leeuw, C. A., Sullivan, P. F., van Bochoven, A., Visscher, P. M., & Posthuma, D. (2015). Meta-analysis of the heritability of human traits based on fifty years of twin studies. Nature Genetics, 47, 702–709.

Raskin, R. N., & Hall, C. S. (1979). Narcissistic Personality Inventory. Psychological Reports, 45, 590–590.

Raskin, R. N., & Terry, H. (1988). A principal-components analysis of the Narcissistic Personality Inventory and further evidence of its construct validity. Journal of Personality and Social Psychology, 54, 890–902.

Reise, S. P., Widaman, K. F., & Pugh, R. H. (1993). Confirmatory factor analysis and item response theory: Two approaches for exploring measurement invariance. Psychological Bulletin, 114, 552–566.

Rhodewalt, F., & Morf, C. C. (1995). Self and interpersonal correlates of the Narcissistic Personality Inventory – A review and new findings. Journal of Research in Personality, 29, 1–23.

Roberts, B. W., Edmonds, G., & Grijalva, E. (2010). It is developmental me, not generation me: Developmental changes are more important than generational changes in narcissism – Commentary on Trzesniewski & Donnellan (2010). Perspectives on Psychological Science, 5, 97–102.

Robins, R. W., Trzesniewski, K. H., Tracy, J. L., Gosling, S. D., & Potter, J. (2002). Global self-esteem across the life span. Psychology and Aging, 17, 423–434.

Rosenberg, M. (1965). Society and the adolescent self-image. Princeton, NJ: Princeton University Press.

Rosenberg, M. (1979). Conceiving the self. New York, NY: Basic Books.

Rosenthal, S. A., & Hooley, J. M. (2010). Narcissism assessment in social-personality research: Does the association between narcissism and psychological health result from a confound with self-esteem? Journal of Research in Personality, 44, 453–465.

Schaie, K. W. (1965). A general model for the study of developmental problems. Psychological Bulletin, 64, 92–107.

Schmitt, D. P., & Allik, J. (2005). Simultaneous administration of the Rosenberg Self-Esteem Scale in 53 nations: Exploring the universal and culture-specific features of global self-esteem. Journal of Personality and Social Psychology, 89, 623–642.

Sedikides, C., Rudich, E. A., Gregg, A. P., Kumashiro, M., & Rusbult, C. (2004). Are normal narcissists psychologically healthy? Self-esteem matters. Journal of Personality and Social Psychology, 87, 400–416.

Smits, I. A. M., Dolan, C. V., Vorst, H. C. M., Wicherts, J. M., & Timmerman, M. E. (2011). Cohort differences in Big Five personality factors over a period of 25 years. Journal of Personality and Social Psychology, 100, 1124–1138.

Stewart, K. D., & Bernhardt, P. C. (2010). Comparing Millennials to pre-1987 students and with one another. North American Journal of Psychology, 12, 579–602.

Trull, T. J., Jahng, S., Tomko, R. L., Wood, P. K., & Sher, K. J. (2010). Revised NESARC personality disorder diagnoses: Gender, prevalence, and comorbidity with substance dependence disorders. Journal of Personality Disorders, 24, 412–426.

Trzesniewski, K. H., & Donnellan, M. B. (2010). Rethinking 'Generation Me': A study of cohort effects from 1976–2006. Perspectives on Psychological Science, 5, 58–75.

Trzesniewski, K. H., & Donnellan, B. M. (2014). 'Young people these days'. Evidence for negative perceptions of emerging adults. Emerging Adulthood, 2, 211–226.

Trzesniewski, K. H., Donnellan, M. B., & Robins, R. W. (2008a). Do today's young people really think they are so extraordinary? An examination of secular trends in narcissism and self-enhancement. Psychological Science, 19, 181–188.

Trzesniewski, K. H., Donnellan, M. B., & Robins, R. W. (2008b). Is 'Generation Me' really more narcissistic than previous generations? Journal of Personality, 76, 903–918.

Twenge, J. M. (2000). The age of anxiety? Birth cohort change in anxiety and neuroticism, 1952–1993. Journal of Personality and Social Psychology, 79, 1007–1021.

Twenge, J. M. (2002). Birth cohort, social change, and personality: The interplay of dysphoria and individualism in the 20th century. In D. Cervone & W. Mischel (Eds.), *Advances in personality science* (pp. 196–218). New York, NY: Guilford.

Twenge, J. M., & Campbell, W. K. (2001). Age and birth cohort differences in self-esteem: A cross-temporal meta-analysis. *Personality and Social Psychology Review, 5*, 321–344.

Twenge, J. M., & Campbell, W. K. (2008). Increases in positive self-views among high school students: Birth-cohort changes in anticipated performance, self-satisfaction, self-liking, and self-competence. *Psychological Science, 19*, 1082–1086.

Twenge, J. M., & Campbell, W. K. (2009). *The narcissism epidemic: Living in the age of entitlement*. New York: Atria Paperback.

Twenge, J. M., Campbell, W. K., & Gentile, B. (2012). Generational increases in agentic self-evaluations among American college students, 1966–2009. *Self and Identity, 11*, 409–427.

Twenge, J. M., & Crocker, J. (2002). Race and self-esteem: Meta-analyses comparing whites, blacks, Hispanics, Asians, and American Indians and comment on Gray-Little and Hafdahl (2000). *Psychological Bulletin, 128*, 371–408.

Twenge, J. M., & Foster, J. D. (2008). Mapping the scale of the narcissism epidemic: Increases in narcissism 2002–2007 within ethnic groups. *Journal of Research in Personality, 42*, 1619–1622.

Twenge, J. M., & Foster, J. D. (2010). Birth cohort increases in narcissistic personality traits among American college students, 1982–2009. *Social Psychological and Personality Science, 1*, 99–106.

Twenge, J. M., Konrath, S., Foster, J. D., Campbell, W. K., & Bushman, B. J. (2008). Egos inflating over time: A cross-temporal meta-analysis of the Narcissistic Personality Inventory. *Journal of Personality, 76*, 875–902.

Vandenberg, R. J., & Lance, C. E. (2000). A review and synthesis of the measurement invariance literature: Suggestions, practices, and recommendations for organizational research. *Organizational Research Methods, 3*, 4–70.

Vukasovic, T., & Bratko, D. (2015). Heritability of personality: A meta-analysis of behavior genetic studies. *Psychological Bulletin, 141*, 769–785.

Wetzel, E., Brown, A., Hill, P. L., Chung, J. M., Robins, R. W., & Roberts, B. W. (2017). The narcissism epidemic is dead; long live the narcissism epidemic. *Psychological Science, 28*, 1833–1847. Advance online publication. doi: 10.1177/0956797617724208.

Wetzel, E., Roberts, B. W., Fraley, R. C., & Brown, A. (2016). Equivalence of Narcissistic Personality Inventory constructs and correlates across scoring approaches and response formats. *Journal of Research in Personality, 61*, 87–98.

Wetzel, E., & Robins, R. W. (2016). The influence of parenting practices on the development of narcissism: Findings from a longitudinal study of Mexican-origin youth. *Journal of Research in Personality, 63*, 84–94.

Widaman, K. F., & Reise, S. P. (1997). Exploring the measurement invariance of psychological instruments: Applications in the substance use domain. In K. J. Bryant & M. Windle (Eds.), *The science of prevention: Methodological advances from alcohol and substance abuse research* (pp. 281–324). Washington, DC: American Psychological Association.

Wilson, M. S., & Sibley, C. G. (2011). 'Narcissism creep?': Evidence for age-related differences in narcissism in the New Zealand general population. *New Zealand Journal of Psychology, 40*, 89–95.

Zeigler-Hill, V., & Wallace, M. T. (2011). Racial differences in narcissistic tendencies. *Journal of Research in Personality, 45*, 456–467.

The Role of the Family in Personality Development

Ugo Pace and Alessia Passanisi

Environment occupies a significant place among factors that affect the development of personality. Many researchers believe that environment shapes one's personality. On the other hand, other researchers argue that personality is pre-determined at the time of birth, which means it is hereditary. However, it appears that both environmental and hereditary factors act as important determinants of personality. The relationship between these factors is one of the most ancient and fascinating issues that humans face. The nature-versus-nurture debate is one of the most enduring in the field of psychology; to what extent are human behaviors, ideas, and feelings innate, and to what extent are they learned? Almost 400 years ago, Descartes set out the view that individual human beings hold certain ideas that are inherent and that strengthen our approach to the world.

Conversely, and somewhat contemporarily, Hobbes stressed the importance of the role of experience in behavioral development. Both maturation and learning factors have been key issues when studying personality development. In the last two decades, studies in behavioral genetics have afforded significant insight into the hereditary and ecological sources of stability and change in personality variations over time. They have shown that both factors are the driving forces of both continuity and change (Bleidorn et al., 2014). Genetic and environmental variables do not separately affect personality development; rather, the interaction of these factors and their involvement in stability, change, and personality differentiation vary across different age groups. This has significant theoretical repercussions for personality development (Specht et al., 2014).

From birth to old age, genetic factors play the most important role in determining continuity in personality differentiation, whereas hereditary and ecological variables contribute to individual differences in personality (Spengler et al., 2012). Studies concerning the interplay of different factors have emphasized the involvement of hereditary features in rank-order differences, which decrease with age, signifying a declining genome-based plasticity (Baltes, 1997). Ecological sources of rank-order stability (i.e., environmental setting and changes such as grade change or the birth of a new sibling), on the other hand, tend to increase from the beginning of puberty to late adolescence (Kandler, 2012). Hereditary factors achieve their stability at the beginning of middle adulthood, which is consistent with the fact that personality differences in heritably induced maturation could be considered minor beyond the third decade of life (McCrae and Costa, 2008). Conversely, environmental variables seem to gradually stabilize personality differences throughout adulthood (Bleidorn et al., 2009). The reason for this is linked to the many social situations in which individuals are involved in relationship experiences that tend to stabilize during middle adulthood. That is, the social roles that individuals occupy within different situations may be relatively constant during middle adulthood, which may heighten the environmental continuity of individual differences (Roberts and Wood, 2006).

Psychological theories, in recent years, have proposed a profound paradigm shift in which personality is no longer defined as a set of inherited structures that mature within a social environment but is defined using transactional models in which the same internal structures are derived from an interpersonal field (e.g., Lynch and Cicchetti, 1998). This relational model of personality structures tries to overcome the dichotomy of nature and culture, conceiving individual development as an integration of traits deriving from constitutional and relational interaction (i.e., elements that constantly influence each other in a reciprocal manner throughout life). The fundamental theoretical crux of this position – which emphasizes the relational nature of human experience – is the need for intense and long-lasting relations. This view is based primarily on Bowlby's (1973) attachment theory, which offers an understanding of the personality characteristics that exist within the interpersonal context. The same self-development reflects the needs, thoughts, and self-understanding of others.

Within this perspective, the study of the influence of family interactions on the development of personality can be considered one of the most critical issues. This chapter will highlight those studies and the theoretical models derived from them, in which basic themes of the psychology of family relationships have been linked to the development of personality. In particular, the following themes will be covered: the role of parental personality and the birth order of the child; the relationship between emotion regulation, attachment bonds, and personality; and, finally, the role of family in the development of personality disorders.

PARENTAL PERSONALITY

Belsky and Kelly (1994) proposed that parents' personalities would influence parenting and children's behavior. They emphasized the role of family systems, which are considered as determinants of the ability to organize interactive models that begin during pregnancy and are rearranged later, as a factor influencing the development of personality/psychopathology of the child. Recent studies have pointed out that the presence of psychopathic traits in the parents constitutes a risk factor that can affect the development of an adaptive personality in children and adolescents (Van Loon et al., 2014). From an epidemiological perspective, it has been shown that disorders in parents double the chance of maladaptive personality development (Maybery and Reupert, 2006). These parents often tend to establish a struggle for power and control through highly aggressive, intrusive, and punitive behaviors. Also, they tend to reverse the parent–child relationship and to force their children's relational mode, characterized by aggression, hostility, control, and intrusiveness. Despite this, it is not correct to affirm that a deterministic relationship between psychiatric disease of parents and development of maladaptive personality in children exists. The parenting process is not reducible to a mechanical one-to-one relationship because it is necessary to take into account contextual variables (e.g., the presence/absence of support networks), the psychological variables of the actors (e.g., the experiences and the child's representations about the mental illness of a parent), and incidental variables (e.g., age of onset of the disease in the child's life).

Patterson et al. (2002) stressed that the influence of parental personality/psychopathology on children's adaptation is mediated by its disturbing impact on parenting practice. With the same goal, Schofield et al. (2012) studied the role played by parents' positive personality features in predicting comparable adolescent personality characteristics over time. The authors highlighted that consistent levels of parental agreeableness, conscientiousness, and emotional stability were associated with higher levels of the same traits in adolescents. These findings suggest that parents' personality may play an important role in personality development during adolescence (Schofield et al., 2012). Even though parental personality can be considered a fundamental part of a child's developmental context, surprisingly few studies have linked parents' personality traits with parenting styles in determining a child's personality. Moreover, studies in behavioral genetics show that some parenting behaviors are heritable (Plomin, 1994; Spinath and O'Connor, 2003). Genetic influence on the environment is explained by the fact that the genes affect the personality of the individual and, consequently, the individual's ability to respond to environmental stimuli. For example, genes can affect unacceptable behavior; conversely, experiences of antisocial behavior can influence the distribution of these genes in the population (e.g., Rhee and Waldman, 2002; Robins, 1978). Men and women will mate on the basis of their similarity in social behavior, and it often happens that couples in which both partners exhibit antisocial behavior tend to have more children than the norm (Farrington et al., 2001; Krueger et al., 1998). This means that, from generation to generation, the genes that are relevant to that particular phenotype present with a higher frequency in these families than they would if the couplings between individuals were completely random (Krueger et al., 1998). According to this position, maternal neuroticism has been linked to externalizing behaviors during childhood and, more generally, to delinquency during adolescence (Bates et al., 1991). In turn, these children – probably as a result of the high levels of stress in their parents – will display externalizing problematic behaviors. Thus, parents with scarce capacity for emotional stability could experience a failure in parenting effectiveness, resulting in further escalation of problem behaviors. Parents who are emotionally stable would be expected to provide the consistency and monitoring often lacking in the homes of antisocial children (Patterson et al., 1992). As a result, children might also develop personality traits that may lead to high levels of externalizing problem behaviors. Thus, personality development is often associated with the development of externalizing problem behaviors.

According to research findings, parents with a low level of conscientiousness would also present maladaptive traits such as low self-discipline and the tendency to act before thinking: their children may inherit a tendency toward low inhibitory control and may therefore exhibit rising levels of externalizing behaviors (Costa and McCrae, 1992). Even research that uses the five-factor model of personality has shown how parental personality might relate to parenting, pointing mainly to parenting as playing a mediating role between the personalities of the parents and those of their children. These studies have underlined that parents with high levels of extraversion, agreeableness, conscientiousness, emotional stability (or low neuroticism), and openness showed more supportive and responsive parenting and less negative, controlling parenting (Belsky and Barends, 2002; Verhoeven et al., 2010). Conversely, parents characterized by high negative emotionality and disagreeableness would have more harmful effects and would exhibit less nurturing parenting, whereas neuroticism was found to be associated with less sensitive, less affective, and less stimulating parenting (Belsky et al., 1995). Thus, parent personality would often play a crucial role on both positive and negative personality development in children.

In sum, personality development is complex. In fact, it can be considered the result of both biological and social components. At birth, a child is not a *tabula rasa*. Heredity and environment are inseparable in human development. From birth, personality is bio-psycho-social. The evolution of personality includes the child–parent relationship, school experiences, relationships with peers, and the ability to assess oneself in a balanced way (Küçük et al., 2012).

The family's emotional climate is essential for the positive and functional development of a child. If a relationship of love and esteem exists between the parents and the child, then the child's personality is likely to develop in a positive way. In contrast, if dysfunctional conflict is frequent, then the child may experience a state of anxiety and emotional insecurity. The balanced development of the child's personality from a psychological and social perspective assumes that the child lives in an atmosphere of affective security, which is why children tend to demand exclusive affection from parents. The biological organism dynamically interacts with the environment during the life cycle. Recognizing that biology and experience influence each other poses new questions: to what extent are organisms born with behavioral skills already established? To what extent are such capabilities influenced by the family in shaping a child's personality? Environmental influences tend to make children raised in the same family more different than similar (Lo Cascio et al., 2013). These influences are called 'non-shared environment' (Neiderhiser et al., 2007). The main aspects of the environment are not shared due to birth order, distance in age, the quality of a child's relationship with parents, and the different subjective perceptions or personal interpretations that the individual can develop in relation to the same situations.

BIRTH ORDER

Does birth order establish the features of personality? Popular ways of thinking, including those regarding the personalities of siblings from the same family, propose simple and undemanding explanations of what we observe, but these are not always based on scientific data.

Determining the influence that birth order has on personality is a controversial subject, and the majority of studies have concluded that birth order does not shape personality (Beer and Horn, 2000). Some studies, however, have credited almost 35% of the variance in personality to birth order (Borkenau et al., 2001; Eaves et al., 1989). Others have highlighted that birth order affects behaviors and individual achievement and therefore has an impact on personality (Somit et al., 1996).

The study of birth order began in 1874 with Francis Galton, the eclectic scientist and cousin of Charles Darwin. Galton, the youngest of nine children, studied a sample of almost 200 British scientists and found that the majority were firstborn. According to Galton, this was because the firstborn child enjoys more consideration from his or her parents, which has a positive impact on intellectual capacity. Following in the same footsteps, Alfred Adler extended Galton's speculations on personality traits. According to Adler (1964), the firstborn, the last sibling, and the middle sibling have entirely different social experiences and thus develop correspondingly different types of personalities. Adler noted that the firstborn occupies the center of the parents' attention until he or she is supplanted by a younger sibling. Consequently, according to Adler, the firstborn can develop an attitude of insecurity and hostility toward others. He said that criminals, neurotics, and alcoholics are often individuals of this type. The second child, in turn, tends to be highly ambitious, rebellious, and jealous, and continually attempts to overcome the older sibling. As for the youngest child, Adler considered those children to be the most damaged of all and the most likely to develop problematic behaviors both as children and as adults. Adler never provided any empirical support for his hypothesis, and his ideas remain deeply rooted in popular psychology despite decades of inconclusive studies.

More recently, Sulloway (1995) proposed family niche theory, which states that birth order affects the personalities of children who share the same family environment and who adapt to it by decreasing conflict and increasing collaboration. According to Sulloway, siblings are similar to Darwin's famous finches in that they rival other organisms for limited resources and adapt to survive. The firstborn is, during childhood, necessarily more physically imposing, which favors the development of supremacy. Younger siblings, in contrast, are free to choose any position in the family, and this helps the personality to develop imagination, extraversion, and sociability. Despite the enthusiasm generated by Sulloway's (1995) idea – especially in the field of non-academic psychology – most research has failed to confirm the author's hypothesis. For a long time, in fact, the author's ideas remained confined to a mere hypothesis refuted by empirical experience. Empirical studies on birth order and the development of personality have shown only a weak association between personality and birth order (e.g., Dixon et al., 2008). Moreover, various researchers (Healey and Ellis, 2007; Paulhus et al., 1999) have recently stressed the relevance of the relationship between birth order and personality traits among children in the same family. As reported by Sulloway (2010) in a meta-analytic study, when adults are asked to compare themselves to their children in terms of different personality traits, firstborns are evaluated as achieving more and as careful, whereas late-born children are judged as more rebellious and open. Thus, according to Sulloway (1995), a high level of extraversion in late-born children is an attempt to attract parental consideration. The firstborn's self-descriptive characteristics, which differ from those of the lastborn, are evidence that some traits with which individuals define themselves are the result of a special relationship, in which every parent engages differently with each child as a function of his or her birth order. Healey and Ellis (2007) found moderate correlations between birth order and personality traits such as conscientiousness and openness in two separate samples. Paulhus et al. (1999) reported a weak-to-moderate influence of birth order on conscientiousness and rebelliousness in four separate samples. Furthermore, studies conducted with brothers underlined weak-to-moderate effects of birth order on personality (Damian and Roberts, 2015; Rohrer et al., 2015). To account for the birth order effects seen with parent ratings, Ernst and Angst (1983) suggested that 'first- and late-borns have specific parent-related behaviors because the attitude acquired toward them is different, without their personality being profoundly affected' (p. 171). In other words, differentiation in personality traits linked to birth order is only relevant within the family context due to parents' differential behaviors, but these differences may not be applicable in all other environments in which the individual develops his own personality. In like manner, birth order effects might be seen when studies gather the evaluations of relatives; however, they may not be seen when studies gather appraisals from contexts outside the family.

EMOTION REGULATION AND PERSONALITY

The fundamental roles performed by the family are social control and individual psychological development. Relatives arrange commitments to and confinements of individual flexibility with the aim of guaranteeing support and care. Family bonds play a fundamental role in shaping emotional systems, which manage the understanding and expression of emotional representations. According to Gross (1998), emotion regulation refers to how we try to influence which emotions we have, when we have them, and how we experience and express these emotions. For other scholars, emotion regulation represents the capability to emotionally answer environmental demands that arise throughout the course of one's life in a socially acceptable manner and in a manner that is plastic enough to permit spontaneous reactions (e.g., Cole et al., 1994; Di Maggio et al., 2016). Moreover, according to the authors, emotion regulation should allow individuals to manage these reactions. Individual differences in emotion regulation patterns reflect personality characteristics. Achievement of adaptive emotion regulation can be seen as a greatly important child development aim. This attainment seems, in fact, to play an important role in the process of personality building, affecting both social and emotional ability with emotion regulation being one of the most important protective factors against the development of psychiatric illness, which is most often associated with the dysregulation of early problems (e.g., Schore, 2003). The possibility for the child to have experiences of a positive emotional match with a caregiver first and with family members later, or to change negative affect into positive affect, is a primary process for the development of an adaptive personality.

According to Tronick (2005) and Emde (1999), emotion regulation allows the child to build a representation of the self; each one within the mother–child interaction tries to increase the coherence of the meaning attributed to the self and to what the mother and child do together. When the interaction is well adjusted on the dyadic level, it creates the sense of a more coherent and complex world. According to Tronick (2005), this is the basis of human personality. The state of consciousness (SOC) is defined by Tronick as a state of psychobiological organization with a particular set of implicit and explicit meanings, intentions, and procedures. Dyadic states of consciousness (DSC) are realized when creating new meanings that are incorporated into both parties' states of consciousness. When mothers promote an emotional exchange with their children, the latter tend to acquire more expertise in decoding emotional experiences. Later on, the length of states of mind suggests that they are an integral part of personality traits, and research has supported this hypothesis (Emde, 1999). People who frequently feel positive emotions and rarely feel negative emotions are, in all likelihood, extraverted and sociable. Instead, those who frequently feel anger, revulsion, and contempt probably have a hostile and aggressive personality.

According to Emde (1999), healthy personality development depends on the proper development of cognitive, affective, and social interactions of the child with the external environment. The analysis of affectivity has been particularly influenced by individuals' psychic experiences, which are placed along a pleasure–displeasure axis. Based on the length, persistence, and mode of onset of affective states, they can be divided into feelings, emotions, and moods. Some empirical studies have confirmed the link between personality and emotion regulation. Eisenberg et al. (2010) underlined that both temperament and personality are intertwined with the development of emotion regulation processes; moreover, this interaction, they argued, is the most important factor affecting the quality of social functioning. Santucci et al. (2008) studied the relation among indices of vagal tone and temperament as predictors of emotion regulation strategies in children with negative experiences of parenting, such as the parenting characteristics of a depressed mother. The data highlighted that a low-level vagal upturn and higher negative affectivity in temperament were associated with maladaptive emotion regulation in response to a feeling of frustration. These findings suggest that vagal tone and temperament are indicators of individual differences in emotion regulation (Passanisi and Di Nuovo, 2015). Nader-Grosbois et al., (2012) argued that personality traits such as agreeableness, emotional stability, and extraversion are associated with emotion regulation. The authors emphasized that the more a child is agreeable, emotionally stable, and extraverted, the better the child will be able to regulate his or her emotions. If the child is less agreeable, less emotionally stable, and less extraverted, he or she will have more difficulty in regulating his or her emotional experiences. Extraversion was positively linked with scores of emotion regulation and negatively associated with emotion dysregulation. The regression analyses showed that agreeableness, emotional stability, and level of intellectual efficiency explained 49% of the variance of the composite score in emotion regulation; agreeableness and extraversion explained 34.8% of the variance of score in emotion regulation; and emotional stability, extraversion, and agreeableness explained 61.3% of the variance of score in emotion dysregulation.

ATTACHMENT AND INDIVIDUAL DIFFERENCES

Every child has an active role in building and shaping relationships since birth (Ainsworth and Bowlby, 1991; Bowlby, 1973). In a significant relationship, there is a continuous and interactive exchange with a caregiver providing the child with opportunities for self-regulation through a feedback system. Bowlby's (1973) studies have shown that early relationships between children and their caregivers are linked to an instinctive need in children to get in touch with components of their own species. Attachment behavior is behavior where the child becomes attached to a significant adult considered able to face the world appropriately (Van IJzendoorn and Kroonenberg, 1988). This behavior becomes fundamental, as every time children are scared, tired, sick, or relieved, they receive comfort and care. If the external goal of the attachment system is to ensure proximity to the caregiver, the internal one is to motivate the child to reach an adaptive level of internal security. The biological and psychosocial task of caregivers is to provide a secure base for the child, where the child can look out into the outside world and return knowing that he or she will be welcomed, nurtured, reassured, and comforted. In this sense, the role of the caregiver is to be available and responsive when called into action. The internal working model (IWM) is a core assumption that argues that children build representations of the self with respect to an attachment figure. The IWM includes a representation of the self and the caregiver in attachment relationships, organizes thoughts and memories, and guides future behavior of attachment. Attachment experiences during childhood influence personality and style relationships in adulthood concerning adaptation to environments and people. The experience of attachment is a significant part of an individual's life and constitutes the psychosocial background on the base of which develops personality. Internal working models are not passive filters, but contribute to the continuous and active re-creation of individual patterns of development. In other words, the attachment strategies that children develop in the early stages of life consolidate and give structure over time to the organization of personal experiences and emotional and cognitive systems as adaptive behaviors. Conversely, the experience of insecure attachment is a risk factor for the construction of a solid ground of personality, as unmet basic needs are relegated to the background.

According to Ainsworth and Bowlby (1991), interactions between children and caregivers shape behavioral patterns that are reflected in later relationships. A clear example of development of personality, as a result of these bonds, can be seen in securely attached infants. As a result of sensitivity and responsiveness on the part of the caregiver, an infant may develop a 'secure' attachment style (Main et al., 1985; Rothbard and Shaver, 1994). Infants who develop 'secure' personality styles feel confident in their relations with others. They learn how to take turns, how to lead and follow, and how to express and receive. Studies on the topic of the relation between attachment and personality focus their topics on aspects of emotion regulations and social behavior that draw from the qualities of observed behavior assumed to belong to differing attachment patterns. Adults with a secure attachment style tend to evaluate their relationships and their attachment experiences consistently, both when they give a positive or a negative assessment to others. They consider these to be important experiences for the formation of their own personality (Pace and Zappulla, 2011; Pace et al., 2016). Shaver and Brennan (1992) have underlined that a personality quality relevant to attachment styles is extraversion. Individuals with secure attachments not only feel comfortable around others, but are actively drawn to them. Conversely, those with avoidant attachments should be intrinsically less likely to be drawn to involvement with others. Children who experience a rejecting primary caregiver (i.e., mother) who does not respond with openness, energy, and warmth to requests for help and comfort develop a defined pattern of attachment as adults and are 'anxious-ambivalent'. These people do not develop a personality that rests confidently on a secure base and do not have emotional security. This follows a mental model of the self as a person unworthy of being loved who has to rely on himself or herself and a mental model of the primary caregiver as a bad person who does not expect anything good. This is an unconscious process that affects the development of personality. Finally, disorganized attachment leads to the development of aggressive behavior in children and conduct disorders, factors that could then contribute to the development of antisocial personality. Moreover, disorganized attachment style, as well as any other style of attachment, can have an intergenerational transmission. Parents who grew up in violent and abusive families send their fears and their unresolved conflicts to children through abuse or emotional deprivation. In this way, children live in a real paradox: on the one hand, the proximity to the parent increases the child's fears, and on the other, it soothes fears (Lyons-Ruth, 1996; Schimmenti et al., 2014). Longitudinal data suggest that early attachment relationships may affect personality traits later in adulthood (Hagekull and Bohlin, 2003). Some research has stressed that heritability estimates for the individual personality traits related to negative affect and impulsivity range from 40 to 50%, and it has been suggested that a considerable part of the residual variance in personality traits could be explained by attachment patterns (Fransson et al., 2013; Jang et al., 1998). Several studies have related adult attachment style to different personality traits, such as interpersonal behaviors, social competencies, emotional functioning (Fraley and Shaver, 1999), and social self-efficacy (Wright and Perrone, 2010). Studies investigating the relationship between adult attachment style and the five-factor model (FFM; Digman, 1990) personality traits support positive correlations between secure attachment, extraversion, and agreeableness, and there is a negative association of this attachment style with neuroticism (Bäckström and Holmes, 2001; Picardi et al., 2005). Similarly, research on the relationships between attachment and FFM personality traits during childhood has underlined that attachment is a significant predictor of personality traits, particularly extraversion, openness, and neuroticism (Hagekull and Bohlin, 2003). Attachment experiences during childhood influence the personality styles and relationships in adulthood concerning the adaptation to the environment and to people. The IWM filters the incoming information, processes the outgoing information, and triggers processes of selective attention, selective perception, and selective memory, all of which occur unconsciously for the individual. This happens due to a need for consistency by the individual, who selects the information consistent with his or her expectations. Furthermore, this is a system to prevent and defensively exclude information that could reactivate the attachment system.

THE IMPACT OF ATTACHMENT STYLES ON PERSONALITY TRAITS

Studies that have analyzed the direct relationship between attachment styles and personality traits have shown interesting results. These results are often consistent with each other and often relate internal working models to both regulatory personality traits and personality disorders, a topic that will be discussed in more detail in the next paragraph (Weinfield et al., 2008). Besides positive caregiver behaviors, a constructive view of self and others makes adaptive all the aspects of social skills, first of all cooperation and reciprocity, which are core constituents of agreeableness (Fransson et al., 2013).

Results derived from studies on the relation between attachment and personality traits indicate that avoidant attachment is inversely related to extraversion, whereas secure attachment was related positively to extraversion and agreeableness, but also significantly negatively correlated to neuroticism (Shiota et al., 2006). Individuals with a high level of neuroticism are typically reliant in nature, often having relationships that are important, and they depend on people, especially on partners. Need for approval and a sensation of being embarrassed and insecure when talking with others (Feeney et al., 1994) are significantly negatively correlated to extraversion. Extraversion is characterized by assertiveness, dominance, lack of reflection, impulsivity, risk-taking behavior, and other similar behaviors. Preoccupation, worry over relationships, and feelings of disappointment are significantly positively correlated to neuroticism (Jenkins-Guarnieri et al., 2012). Noftle and Shaver (2006) found similar results, such that avoidant attachment – which is found in people who are comfortable without close emotional relationships and who often deny needing close relationships – was significantly negatively related to extraversion. In contrast, attachment anxiety is significantly negatively correlated with extraversion and significantly positively correlated with neuroticism (Nakash-Eisikovits et al., 2002). People belonging to the anxious attachment style agree that they want to be completely emotionally intimate with others, but often find that others are reluctant to get as close as they would like. Individuals with this style of attachment look for elevated amounts of closeness, endorsement, and responsiveness from their accomplices. In this sense, it might explain the negative relationship with extraversion. They tend to focus on only one relationship, being greatly clingy in it and not blending with other individuals. They can value closeness to the point that they turn out to be excessively reliant on their caregivers (Bartholomew and Horowitz, 1991). Nakash-Eisikovits et al. (2002) found that secure attachment was negatively correlated with personality pathology. Confidence is a characteristic of a secure attachment style that signifies feelings of worthiness, confidence, and ease in getting close to a person (Hazan and Shaver, 1987); hence, it is negatively correlated with psychoticism and neuroticism, which predispose individuals to pathology. According to Bowlby (1973), the child has confidence in the availability of his or her attachment figure, so he or she feels free to explore the world. The child feels a lack of closeness with the primary caregiver when they are apart, protesting vigorously, and when the primary caregiver returns, he or she calms down and seeks closeness. This type of attachment is due to a tangible form of the child's signals, as the caregiver is helpful and ready to give support and comfort when the child requires it.

Experiences regarding first relationships with attachment figures serve as the foundation for the achievement of potential skills, such as emotion regulation and exploratory behaviors (e.g., Sroufe et al., 2005; Weinfield et al., 2008), strictly linked to personality development. Hence, sensitivity and understanding on the part of caregivers will lead to a secure attachment and introjection of positive working models of self and others (Bretherton, 1985). When the communication efforts of a small child have success in stimulating care and comfort by adults, they begin the development of good social effectiveness (Schneider et al., 2001; Tronick, 2005): a positive view of self and others who facilitates aspects of social skills, such as cooperation and reciprocity, which are core constituents of agreeableness (Bohlin et al., 2000). Moreover, when an individual feels secure (or *sine cura*, without any concern), he or she is also able to explore and to be autonomous: a social correspondent of this feeling is a high openness to experience. If the child feels safe and reassured by the primary caregiver, he or she activates exploration patterns of behaviors, but if the primary caregiver transmits warning signs or is absent, then the child ceases to explore. A balanced and competent primary caregiver is then able to gradually encourage exploration and, consequently, the autonomy of the child, without exposing him or her to dangers or, in any case, with an acceptable safety margin. On the contrary, an absent or apprehensive primary caregiver does not favor the development of a motivational and behavioral exploration system and the consequent construction of autonomy of the child. Children who have experienced a secure attachment will be able to implement a physical separation from the caregiver without problems, for example, at the time of schooling, and progressively develop a balanced personality and a flexible attitude toward themselves and toward external reality. In this case, the primary caregiver would accept the requests for proximity and would encourage exploration, according to the following epistemological criteria: I trust him/he trusts me – I am worth/he is worth. In contrast, when a child was characterized by anxious-resistant attachment, he or she would show problems at the time of schooling, showing a phobic attitude characterized by difficulty in exploring and socializing. Also, even if conscientiousness in part might be a higher-order cognitive ability, secure attachment has been associated with a higher level of postponement of fulfillment, decision-making ability, and plasticity of thought (Jacobsen et al., 1997; Main, 2000; Passanisi and Pace, 2017). Attachment patterns are considered to be associated with regulation strategies; these strategies fulfill the function of simultaneously assessing the environment, the state of the organism, the availability of attachment figures, and the eventual success of the attachment behavior in maintaining a sense of internal security. From birth, building an affective regulation system between primary caregiver and child allows a continuous oscillation between successful and erroneous communications (Hagekull and Bohlin, 2003; Roisman et al., 2007). From the beginning, primary caregivers play a transformative function in the emotions of a child, especially negative ones. Failure in transformative and regulative processes might lead to prolonged use of forms of self-regulation that may negatively affect the child's social skills

(Tronick, 2005), which represents one of the most frequent characteristics of a personality characterized by neuroticism.

FAMILY AND PERSONALITY DISORDERS

The American Psychiatric Association (2013) defines a personality disorder as a pattern of internal experiences and behaviors that diverge considerably from the expectations of an individual's culture. These patterns produce important emotional pain and/or life impairment. Individuals who suffer from personality disorders may express a broad variety of emotions and behaviors that can be considered damaging for adaptive relationships. The transition from personality traits to personality disorders does not occur often with traumatic modes; in other words, such transitions rarely happen instantaneously, but rather happen slowly over a series of exposures and reactions. Thus, individuals can slightly assume maladaptive patterns and models of thinking, behaviors, or attitudes, thus passing from a personality style to a personality disorder. Among potential causes of personality disorders are genetic factors, a family history of disorders and upbringing, and failures in family relationships. Dysfunctional family interactions during early childhood and adolescence can develop into personality disorders during adulthood (e.g., Stepp et al., 2011; Verhoeven et al., 2010).

An important part of the psychological literature involves studies linking personality disorders to abuse propagated by family members during childhood (i.e., physical, sexual, or emotional abuse; witnessing violence) as well as to genetic influences relating to the temperamental characteristics of affected individuals. A great deal of research has studied the relationship between family relationships and the development of personality disorders. Data have shown that relatives of individuals suffering from personality disorders have had, in turn, family experiences characterized by uncaring, conflict, invalidation and criticism, less nurturing, emotional withholding, hostility, or, conversely, over-protection (e.g., Wilson and Durbin, 2010; Winsper et al., 2012). People who suffer from personality disorders have intense difficulties in processing adaptation and are characterized by particular styles of thought and behavior that remain rigid over time and in different contexts (Riso, 2013). Several studies have suggested possible communication difficulties from parental rigidity in adult roles in relation to their children. For example, Cohen et al., (2005) highlighted that the presence of personality disorders in caregivers leads to critical parenting and risk to the developmental trajectories of children. Other studies have shown that personality disorders are associated with a variety of maladaptive parenting behaviors, particularly harsh punishments, disciplinary incoherence (Ehrensaft et al., 2003), poor supervision, poor sensitivity, and behavior that is rarely affectionate (Eiden et al., 2014; Finger et al., 2010). Research has also shown that certain clusters of personality disorders are more strongly linked to dysfunctional parenting than others (e.g., Walsh and Wu, 2008). Particularly, parents with dramatic, emotional, or erratic disorders, such as personality disorders belonging to Cluster B (antisocial, borderline, histrionic, and narcissistic personality disorder), are more likely have children with maladaptive development in comparison to parents with disorders belonging to other clusters. Walsh and Wu (2008) found, for example, that mothers with a diagnosis of antisocial personality disorders tend to establish problematic relationships with their children, who are six times more at risk of being victims of abuse. Moreover, recently, Wilson and Durbin (2010) showed that mothers with higher levels of Cluster B personality disorders demonstrated lower levels of sensitivity to children, providing good evidence that mothers with this kind of personality disorder showed disturbances of affective communication with their children, especially communications characterized by frightened and disoriented behavior (American Psychiatric Association, 2013). Moreover, they underline difficulties with the perception of identity, also showing incapability in the perceiving of human gradation, categorizing people only through strict modes. Finally, other common symptoms of the disorder are feelings of isolation, difficulty feeling empathy for others, anxiety, worry, depression, and self-destructive and dangerous behaviors, including suicide. Several empirical studies offer insight into borderline personality disorder (BPD) individuals' bonds with their mothers. Mothers who are the subject of these studies showed egocentric and ego-gratifying needs and lower levels of caring (Johnson et al., 2001). Adults with BPD have described their parents as invalidating, emotionally over- or under-involved, and indifferent (Gunderson and Lyoo, 1997). These individuals also describe relationships with caregivers and the ambience in their households as conflictual and inconsistent (Winsper et al., 2012). Several studies have outlined parental psychopathology as antecedent of BPD (e.g., Gunderson and Lyoo, 1997; Stepp et al., 2011). BPD, antisocial personality disorder, substance abuse, depression, and anxiety have been found to be over-represented in parents of children with BPD.

Trull et al. (2003) emphasized not only the relevance of traumatic and adverse life events in the development of BPD, but also the importance of a broader family context in which the traumatic events take place. Winsper et al. (2012) emphasized that traumatic experiences in childhood and adolescence of people with BPD often occur in a context of an extensive family dysfunction where parents with significant psychopathology fail to establish a secure and predictable family context by not protecting children against trauma, or by being themselves the perpetrators. Borderline patients can be seen as people who continually relive early childhood crises in which fear is linked to every separation from the mother, meaning she has disappeared. For this reason, they are therefore unable to tolerate periods of loneliness and are constantly afraid of being abandoned by others. Gunderson and Hoffman (2016) emphasize how patients with BPD usually consider their relationship with their detached mother as oppositional and avoidant. Moreover, in borderline families, the lack of fatherly presence is an even stronger determinant than the relationship with the mother. Results show that a unique dysfunctional family background was associated with dependent personality disorder. The distinguishing features of this family environment were low expressiveness and high control in the families of the dependent personality group (Head et al., 1991).

CONCLUSION

In the present chapter, we sought to examine the studies and the theoretical models in which the psychology of family relationships has been related to the development of personality. In particular, we highlighted the role of parental personality, the birth order of children, and the link between emotion regulation, attachment bonds, and the development of certain personality traits, and we placed a final focus on the role of the family in personality disorders.

In conclusion, personality development is a critical issue that may be considered the result of both biological and social factors as inseparable components of human development. The evolution of personality is based on the child–parent relationship, relationships with peers and educators, and the capacity to assess the self in an equilibrated way. We have seen that differences in personality traits related to birth order only make sense within the family context as a result of parents' differential behaviors.

Moreover, we focused on studies that have explored the relationship between personality and emotion regulation. According to Eisenberg et al. (2010), both temperament and personality are fundamental for the development of emotion regulation processes. Further, family bonds play a crucial role in shaping emotional systems as well as in giving the child a self-regulation system through the feedback exchanged with the primary caregiver. According to massive research, secure attachment is positively associated with the development of functional personality traits and negatively related to dysfunctional personality traits (i.e., neuroticism).

Finally, this chapter focused on the potential causes of personality disorders as genetic factors, family history of disorders and upbringing, and failure in family relationships. Research showed that dysfunctional family interactions during early childhood and adolescence can develop into personality disorders during adulthood.

Considering all these aspects, we see that the solidity of an individual's personality is very important and that family is largely responsible for 'creating' a healthy individual, as the child inherits his/her temperamental traits from the parents and the development of his/her personality is affected by the experience he/she lives in the environment. Unfortunately, the importance of family in development has often been overlooked, despite research demonstrating that young people are likely to have positive outcomes if their lives are characterized by the presence of caring and continuous relationships with healthy significant others. Therefore, it is essential to take into account the family, both as context and inheritance, as it is responsible for the development of functional personality traits.

REFERENCES

Adler, A. (1964). *Problems of neurosis*. New York, NY: Harper and Row.

Ainsworth, M. D. S., & Bowlby, J. (1991). An ethological approach to personality development. *American Psychologist, 46,* 331–341.

American Psychiatric Association. (2013). *Diagnostic and statistical manual of mental disorders* (5th ed.). Washington, DC: Author.

Bäckström, M., & Holmes, B. M. (2001). Measuring adult attachment: A construct validation of two self-report instruments. *Scandinavian Journal of Psychology, 42,* 79–86.

Baltes, P. B. (1997). On the incomplete architecture of human ontogeny: Selection, optimization, and compensation as foundation of developmental theory. *American Psychologist, 52,* 366–380.

Bartholomew, K., & Horowitz, L. M. (1991). Attachment styles among young adults. A test of a four category model. *Journal of Personality and Social Psychology, 61,* 226–244.

Bates, J. E., Bayles, K., Bennett, D. S., Ridge, B., & Brown, M. (1991). Origins of externalizing behavior problems at eight years of age. In D. J. Pepler & K. H. Rubin (Eds.), *The development and treatment of childhood aggression* (pp. 93–120). Hillsdale, NJ: Erlbaum.

Beer, J. M., & Horn, J. M. (2000). The influence of rearing order on personality development within two adoption cohorts. *Journal of Personality, 68,* 789–819.

Belsky, J., & Barends, N. (2002). Personality and parenting. In M. H. Bornstein (Ed.), *Handbook of parenting* (2nd ed., pp. 415–438). Mahwah, NJ: Lawrence Erlbaum.

Belsky, J., Crnic, K., & Woodworth, S. (1995). Personality and parenting: Exploring the mediating role of transient mood and daily hassles. *Journal of Personality, 63,* 905–929.

Belsky, J., & Kelly, J. (1994). *The transition to parenthood: How a first child changes a marriage*. London: Vermilion.

Bleidorn, W., Kandler, C., & Caspi, A. (2014). The behavioural genetics of personality development in adulthood: Classic, contemporary, and future trends. *European Journal of Personality, 28,* 244–255.

Bleidorn, W., Kandler, C., Riemann, R., Angleitner, A., & Spinath, F. M. (2009). Patterns and sources of adult personality development: Growth curve analyses of the NEO PI-R scales in a longitudinal twin study. *Journal of Personality and Social Psychology, 97,* 142–155.

Bohlin, G., Hagekull, B., & Rydell, A.-M. (2000). Attachment and social functioning: A longitudinal study from infancy to middle childhood. *Social Development, 9,* 24–39.

Borkenau, P., Riemann, R., Angleitner, A., & Spinath, F. M. (2001). Genetic and environmental influences on observed personality: Evidence from the German observational study of adult twins. *Journal of Personality and Social Psychology, 80,* 655–668.

Bowlby, J. (1973). *Attachment and loss, Vol. 2: Separation.* New York, NY: Basic Books.

Bretherton, I. (1985). Attachment theory: Retrospect and prospect. In I. Bretherton & E. Waters (Eds.), *Growing points of attachment theory and research: Monographs of the Society for Research in Child Development, 50* (1–2, Serial No. 209, pp. 3–35).

Cohen, P., Crawford, T. N., Johnson, J. G., & Kasen, S. (2005). The children in the community study of developmental course of personality disorder. *Journal of Personality Disorders, 19,* 466–486.

Cole, P. M., Michel, M., & Teti, L. (1994). The development of emotion regulation and dysregulation: A clinical perspective. In Nathan Fox (Ed.), *The development of emotion regulation: Biological and behavioral considerations: Monographs of the Society for Research in Child Development, 59* (Serial no. 240, Nos. 2–3).

Costa, P. T., Jr., & McCrae, R. R. (1992). *Revised NEO Personality Inventory (NEO-PI-R) and NEO Five-Factor Inventory (NEO-FFI) professional manual.* Odessa, FL: Psychological Assessment Resources.

Damian, R. I., & Roberts, B. (2015). The associations of birth order with personality and intelligence in a representative sample of US high school students. *Journal of Research in Personality, 58,* 96–105.

Di Maggio, R., Zappulla, C., & Pace, U. (2016). The relationship between emotion knowledge, emotion regulation and adjustment in preschoolers: A mediation model. *Journal of Child and Family Studies, 25,* 2626–2635.

Digman, J. M. (1990). Personality structure: Emergence of the five-factor model. *Annual Review of Psychology, 41,* 417–440.

Dixon, M. M., Reyes, C. J., Leppert, M. F., & Pappas, L. M. (2008). Personality and birth order in large families. *Personality and Individual Differences, 44,* 953–959.

Eaves, L. J., Eysenck, H. J., & Martin, N. G. (1989). *Genes, culture and personality: An empirical approach.* London: Academic Press.

Ehrensaft, M. K., Cohen, P., Brown, J., Smailes, E., Chen, H., & Johnson, J. G. (2003). Intergenerational transmission of partner violence: A 20-year prospective study. *Journal of Consulting and Clinical Psychology, 71,* 741–753.

Eiden, R. D., Godleski, S., Colder, C. R., & Schuetze, P. (2014). Prenatal cocaine exposure: The role of cumulative environmental risk and maternal harshness in the development of child internalizing behavior problems in kindergarten. *Neurotoxicology and Teratology, 44,* 1–10.

Eisenberg, N., Spinrad, T. L., & Eggum, N. D. (2010). Emotion-related self-regulation and its relation to children's maladjustment. *Annual Review of Clinical Psychology, 6,* 495–525.

Emde, R. N. (1999). Moving head: Integrative influences of affective processes for development and for psychoanalysis. *International Journal of Psychoanalysis, 80,* 317–339.

Ernst, C., & Angst, J. (1983). *Birth order: Its influence on personality.* Berlin: Springer-Verlag.

Farrington, D. P., Jolliffe, D., Loeber, R., Stouthamer-Loeber, M., & Kalb, L. (2001). The concentration of offenders in families, and family criminality in the prediction of boys' delinquency. *Journal of Adolescence, 24,* 579–596.

Feeney, J. A., Noller, P., & Hanrahan, M. (1994). Assessing adult attachment. In M. B. Sperling & W. H. Berman (Eds.), *Attachment in adults: Clinical and developmental perspectives* (pp. 122–158). New York, NY: Guilford.

Finger, B., Kachadourian, L. K., Molnar, D. S., Eiden, R. D., Edwards, E. P., & Leonard, K. E. (2010). Alcoholism, associated risk factors, and harsh parenting among fathers: Examining the role of marital aggression. *Addictive Behaviors, 35,* 541–548.

Fraley, R. C., & Shaver, P. R. (1999). Loss and bereavement: Attachment theory and recent controversies concerning 'grief work' and the nature of detachment. In J. Cassidy & P. R. Shaver (Eds.), *Handbook of attachment: Theory, research, and clinical applications* (pp. 735–759). New York, NY: Guilford.

Fransson, M., Granqvist, P., Bohlin, G., & Hagekull, B. (2013). Interlinkages between attachment and the Five-Factor Model of personality in middle childhood and young adulthood: A longitudinal approach. *Attachment and Human Development, 15,* 219–239.

Gross, J. J. (1998). The emerging field of emotion regulation: An integrative review. *Review of General Psychology, 2,* 271–299.

Gunderson, J. G., & Hoffman, P. D. (2016). *Beyond borderline: True stories of recovery from borderline personality disorder.* Oakland, CA: New Harbinger Publications.

Gunderson, J., & Lyoo, I. (1997). Family problems and relationships for adults with borderline personality disorder. *Harvard Review of Psychiatry, 4,* 272–278.

Hagekull, B., & Bohlin, G. (2003). Early temperament and attachment as predictors of the Five Factor Model of Personality. *Attachment and Human Development, 5,* 2–18.

Hazan, C., & Shaver, P. (1987) Romantic love conceptualized as an attachment process. *Journal of Personality and Social Psychology, 52,* 511–524.

Head, S. B., Baker, J. D., & Williamson, D. A. (1991). Family environment characteristics and dependent personality disorders. *Journal of Personality Disorders, 5,* 256–263.

Healey, M. D., & Ellis, B. J. (2007). Birth order, conscientiousness, and openness to experience – tests of the family-niche model of personality using a within family methodology. *Evolution and Human Behavior, 28,* 55–59.

Jacobsen, T., Huss, M., Fendrich, M., Kruesi, M. J. P., & Ziegenhain, U. (1997). Children's ability to delay gratification: Longitudinal relations to mother–child attachment. *Journal of Genetic Psychology, 158,* 411–426.

Jang, K. L., McCrae, R. R., Angleitner, A., Riemann, R., & Livesley, W. J. (1998). Heritability of facet-level traits in a cross-cultural twin sample: Support for a hierarchical model of personality. *Journal of Personality and Social Psychology, 74,* 1556–1565.

Jenkins-Guarnieri, M. A., Wright, S. L., & Hudiburgh, L. M. (2012). The relationships among attachment style, personality traits, interpersonal competency, and Facebook use. *Journal of Applied Developmental Psychology, 33,* 294–301.

Johnson, J. G., Cohen, P., Smailes, E., Skodol, A., Brown, J., & Oldham, J. (2001). Childhood verbal abuse and risk for personality disorders during adolescence and early adulthood. *Comprehensive Psychiatry, 42,* 16–23.

Kandler, C. (2012). Nature and nurture in personality development: The case of neuroticism and extraversion. *Current Directions in Psychological Science, 21,* 290–296.

Krueger, R. F., Moffitt, T. E., Caspi, A., & Bleske, A. (1998). Assortative mating for antisocial behavior: Developmental and methodological implications. *Behavior Genetics, 28,* 173–186.

Küçük, S., Habaci, M., Göktürk, T., Ürker, A., & Adiguzelli, F. (2012). Role of family, environment and education on the personality development. *Middle-East Journal of Scientific Research, 12,* 1078–1084.

Lo Cascio, V., Guzzo, G., Pace, F., & Pace, U. (2013). Anxiety and self-esteem as mediators of the relation between family communication and indecisiveness in adolescence. *International Journal for Educational and Vocational Guidance, 13,* 135–149.

Lynch, M., & Cicchetti, D. (1998). An ecological-transactional analysis of children and contexts: The longitudinal interplay among child maltreatment, community violence, and children's symptomatology. *Development and Psychopathology, 10,* 235–257.

Lyons-Ruth, K. (1996). Attachment relationships among children with aggressive behavior problems: The role of disorganized early attachment patterns. *Journal of Consulting and Clinical Psychology, 64,* 64–73.

Main, M. (2000). The organized categories of infant, child, and adult attachment: Flexible vs. inflexible attention under attachment related stress. *Journal of the American Psychoanalytic Association, 48,* 1055–1096.

Main, M., Kaplan, N., & Cassidy, J. (1985). Security in infancy, childhood and adulthood. A move to the level of representation. In I. Bretherton & E. Waters (Eds.), *Growing points in attachment theory and research:*

Monographs of the Society for Research in Child Development, 50, (1–2, Serial No. 209, pp. 66–104).

Maybery, D., & Reupert, A. (2006). Workforce capacity to respond to children whose parents have a mental illness. Australian and New Zealand Journal of Psychiatry, 40, 657–664.

McCrae, R. R., & Costa, P. T., Jr. (2008). Empirical and theoretical status of the Five-Factor Model of personality traits. In G. Boyle, G. Matthews & D. Saklofske (Eds.), Sage handbook of personality theory and assessment (Vol. 1, pp. 273–294). Los Angeles, CA: Sage.

Nader-Grosbois, N., Baurain, C., & Mazzone, S. (2012). Emotion regulation, social cognition and social adjustment: Specificities in children with autism spectrum disorder. In C. E. Richardson & R. A. Wood (Eds.), Autism spectrum disorders: New research (pp. 1–39). Hauppauge, NY: Nova Science Publishers.

Nakash-Eisikovits, O., Dutra, L., & Westen, D. (2002). Relationship between attachment patterns and personality pathology in adolescents. Journal of the American Academy of Child and Adolescent Psychiatry, 41, 1111–1123.

Neiderhiser, J. M., Reiss, D., & Hetherington, E. M. (2007). The Nonshared Environment in Adolescent Development (NEAD) project: A longitudinal family study of twins and siblings from adolescence to young adulthood. Twin Research and Human Genetics, 10, 74–83.

Noftle, E. E., & Shaver, P. R. (2006). Attachment dimensions and the big five personality traits: Associations and comparative ability to predict relationship quality. Journal of Research in Personality, 40, 179–208.

Pace, U., & Zappulla, C. (2011). Problem behaviors in adolescence: The opposite role played by insecure attachment and commitment strength. Journal of Child and Family Studies, 20, 854–862.

Pace, U., Zappulla, C., & Di Maggio, R. (2016). The mediating role of perceived peer support in the relation between quality of attachment and internalizing problems in adolescence: A longitudinal perspective. Attachment and Human Development, 18, 508–524.

Passanisi, A., & Di Nuovo, S. (2015). Social and pragmatic impairments in individuals with Autism Spectrum Disorder: A lack of Theory of Mind? Life Span and Disability, 18, 75–99.

Passanisi, A., & Pace, U. (2017). The unique and common contributions of impulsivity and decision-making strategies among young adult Italian regular gamblers. Personality and Individual Differences, 105, 24–29.

Patterson, G.R., Reid, J.B., & Dishion, T.J. (1992). Antisocial Boys. Eugene, OR: Castalia.

Patterson, C. J., Fulcher, M., & Wainright, J. (2002). Children of lesbian and gay parents: Research, law, and policy. In B. L. Bottoms, M. B. Korvera, & B. D. McAuliff (Eds.), Children and the law: Social science and policy (pp. 176–199). New York, NY: Cambridge University Press.

Paulhus, D. L., Trapnell, P. D., & Chen, D. (1999). Birth order effects on personality and achievement within families. Psychological Science, 10, 482–488.

Picardi, A., Caroppo, E., Toni, A., Bitetti, D., & Di Maria, G. (2005). Stability of attachment-related anxiety and avoidance and their relationships with the five-factor model and the psychobiological model of personality. Psychology and Psychotherapy, 78, 327–345.

Plomin, R. (1994). Genetics and experience: The interplay between nature and nurture. Newbury Park, CA: Sage.

Rhee, S. H., & Waldman, I. D. (2002). Genetic and environmental influences on antisocial behavior: A meta-analysis of twin and adoption studies. Psychological Bulletin, 128, 490–529.

Riso, P. (2013). Psicopatologia e Genitorialità (Psychopathology and Parenting). Cognitivismo Clinico, 10, 23–44.

Roberts, D. W., & Wood, D. (2006). Personality development in the context of the Neo-Socioanalytic Model of personality. In D. Mroczek & T. Little (Eds.), Handbook of personality development (pp. 11–39). Mahwah, NJ: Erlbaum.

Robins, L. N. (1978). Sturdy childhood predictors of antisocial behaviour: Replications from longitudinal studies. Psychological Medicine, 8, 611–622.

Rohrer, J. M., Egloff, B., & Schmukle, S. C. (2015). Examining the effects of birth order on personality. Proceedings of the National Academy of Sciences, 112, 14224–14229.

Roisman, G. I., Holland, A., Fortuna, K., Fraley, R. C., Clausell, E., & Clarke, A. (2007). The Adult Attachment Interview and self-reports of attachment style: An empirical rapprochement. *Journal of Personality and Social Psychology*, 92, 678–697.

Rothbard, J. C., & Shaver, P. R. (1994). Continuity of attachment across the life span. In M. B. Sperling & W. H. Berman (Eds.), *Attachment in adults: Clinical and developmental perspectives* (pp. 31–71). New York, NY: Guilford Press.

Santucci, A. K., Silk, J. S., Shaw, D. S., Gentzler, A., Fox, N. A., & Kovacs, M. (2008). Vagal tone and temperament as predictors of emotion regulation strategies in young children. *Developmental Psychobiology*, 50, 205–216.

Schimmenti, A., Passanisi, A., Pace, U., Manzella, S., Di Carlo, G., & Caretti, V. (2014). The relationship between attachment and psychopathy: A study with a sample of violent offenders. *Current Psychology*, 33, 256–270.

Schneider, B. H., Atkinson, L., & Tardif, C. (2001). Child–parent attachment and children's peer relations. A quantitative review. *Developmental Psychology*, 37, 86–100.

Schofield, T. J., Conger, R. D., Donnellan, M. B., & Jochem, R. (2012). Parent personality and positive parenting as predictors of positive adolescent personality development over time. *Merrill-Palmer Quarterly*, 58, 255–283.

Schore, A. (2003). *Affect dysregulation and disorders of the self*. New York, NY: Norton.

Shaver, P. R., & Brennan, K. A. (1992). Attachment style and the big five personality traits: Their connection with romantic relationship outcomes. *Personality and Social Psychology Bulletin*, 18, 536–545.

Shiota, M. N., Keltner, D., & John, O. P. (2006). Positive emotion dispositions differentially associated with Big Five personality and attachment style. *Journal of Positive Psychology*, 1, 61–71.

Somit, A., Arwine, A., & Peterson, S. A. (1996). *Birth order and political behavior*. New York, NY: University Press of America.

Specht, J., Bleidorn, W., Denissen, J. J., Hennecke, M., Hutteman, R., Kandler, C., … & Zimmermann, J. (2014). What drives adult personality development? A comparison of theoretical perspectives and empirical evidence. *European Journal of Personality*, 28, 216–230.

Spengler, M., Gottschling, J., & Spinath, F. M. (2012). Personality in childhood: A longitudinal behavior genetic approach. *Personality and Individual Differences*, 53, 411–416.

Spinath, F. M., & O'Connor, T. G. (2003). A behavioral genetic study of the overlap between personality and parenting. *Journal of Personality*, 71, 785–808.

Sroufe, L. A., Egeland, B., Carlson, E., & Collins W. A. (2005). The place of early attachment experiences in developmental context. In K. E. Grossmann, K. Grossmann, & E. Waters (Eds.), *The power of longitudinal attachment research: From infancy and childhood to adulthood* (pp. 48–70). New York, NY: Guilford.

Stepp, S. D., Whalen, D. J., Pilkonis, P. A., Hipwell, A. E., & Levine, M. D. (2011). Children of mothers with borderline personality disorder: Identifying parenting behaviors as potential targets for intervention. *Personal Disorders*, 3, 76–91.

Sulloway, F. J. (1995). Birth order and evolutionary psychology: A meta-analytic overview. *Psychological Inquiry*, 6, 75–80.

Sulloway, F. J. (2010). Why siblings are like Darwin's finches: Birth order, sibling competition, and adaptive divergence within the family. In D. M. Buss & P. H. Hawley (Eds.), *The evolution of personality and individual differences* (pp. 86–119). Oxford: Oxford University Press.

Tronick, E. Z. (2005). La cronicità della depressione (chronicity of depression). *Infanzia e Adolescenza*, 4, 1–17.

Trull, T. J., Stepp, S. D., & Durrett, C. A. (2003). Research on borderline personality disorder: An update. *Current Opinion in Psychiatry*, 16, 77–82.

Van IJzendoorn, M. H., & Kroonenberg, P. M. (1988). Cross-cultural patterns of attachment: A meta-analysis of the strange situation. *Child Development*, 59, 147–156.

Van Loon, L. M., Van de Ven, M. O., Van Doesum, K. T., Witteman, C. L., & Hosman, C. M. (2014). The relation between parental mental illness and adolescent mental health: The role of family factors. *Journal of Child and Family Studies*, 23, 1201–1214.

Verhoeven, M., Junger, M., Van Aken, C., Dekovic, M., & Van Aken, M. A. G. (2010). Parenting and children's externalizing behavior: Bidirectionality during toddlerhood. *Journal of Applied Developmental Psychology, 31*, 93–105.

Walsh, A., & Wu, H. (2008). Differentiating antisocial personality disorder, psychopathy, and sociopathy: Evolutionary, genetic, neurological, and sociological considerations. *Criminal Justice Studies, 21*, 135–152.

Weinfield, N. S., Sroufe, L. A., Egeland, B., & Carlson, E. A. (2008). Individual differences in infant–caregiver attachment: Conceptual and empirical aspects of security. In J. Cassidy & P. R. Shaver (Eds.), *Handbook of attachment* (2nd ed., pp. 78–101). New York, NY: Guilford Press.

Wilson, S., & Durbin, C. E. (2010). Effects of paternal depression on fathers' parenting behaviors: A meta-analytic review. *Clinical Psychology Review, 30*, 167–180.

Winsper, C., Zanarini, M., & Wolke, D. (2012). Prospective study of family adversity and maladaptive parenting in childhood and borderline personality disorder symptoms in a non-clinical population at 11 years. *Psychological Medicine, 42*, 2405–2420.

Wright, S. L., & Perrone, K. M. (2010). An examination of the role of attachment and efficacy in life satisfaction. *The Counseling Psychologist, 38*, 796–823.

The Role of Peers in Personality Development

Julia Zimmermann and Anne K. Reitz

The dynamic interplay between individuals and their social environments is considered a central determinant of personality development (Fraley and Roberts, 2005; Sameroff, 1983). Research on the role of different social relationship types for the development of personality – such as parent–child relationships or romantic relationships – is accumulating. Peer relationships, in contrast, have less often been the focus of research for personality development. This is surprising given that peers play an important role across the entire lifespan (Reitz et al., 2014). Peers are part of many social contexts for individuals: peer groups, such as groups of classmates or coworkers, and dyadic peer relationships, such as close friends. We thus contend that the consideration of peers is essential to the understanding of lifespan personality development.

As compared to other relationship categories, the definition of peers is less clear-cut. The present chapter thus begins with a description of the characteristics of peers at individual and relationship levels and the consideration of their function and meaning in different life phases. Next, we address different types of peer effects on personality development. In particular, we suggest that it is important to disentangle peer effects that occur in the context of groups versus dyadic relationships to better understand similarities and differences in personality development that occur both *between* and *within* peer groups.

As a main task in the current field of personality research is to identify mechanisms that account for personality development, we finally compare theoretical approaches discussed in the peer literature with respect to the developmental mechanisms they suggest and evaluate them with regard to empirical findings from recent studies. We conclude by delineating implications for understanding the role of peers in personality development and provide suggestions for future research.

CHARACTERISTICS AND FUNCTIONS OF PEERS ACROSS THE LIFESPAN

Most people share a general understanding of what peers are: classmates, fellow students, colleagues, work-out buddies, or members of the same association or community. Identifying the essence of what they have in common is, in contrast, more challenging. In the scientific literature, there is also no clear-cut definition of the relationship type 'peers'. One challenge is that different disciplines highlight different characteristics of peers. A limitation of previous work that has to be overcome is that most research on peers focuses on children and adolescents, which limits the range of peer types as this research focuses mostly on classmates. This is important because peers play an important role across the entire lifespan (Reitz et al., 2014). A more general definition of peers is thus necessary that applies across different life phases. Following the notion that social relationships can be studied on the individual and the relationship level (Back and Kenny, 2010), we delineate characteristics and functions of peers at both the individual and dyadic level across the lifespan in the following.

Characteristics of Peers

Individual peer characteristics

Relationship partners or members of a group are often alike in various individual characteristics, such as gender, race, ethnicity, age, educational attainment, attitudes, or social class – a phenomenon that is termed *homophily* (e.g., McPherson et al., 2001). Children and early adolescents in particular tend to segregate into groups of their own gender and age (Maccoby, 2002; Martin and Fabes, 2001), socioeconomic status (Louch, 2000), and ethnicity (Titzmann and Silbereisen, 2009). Evidence suggests that peer homophily decreases from middle adolescence on as the stratification by social institutions such as schools decreases (Feld, 1982; Lempers and Clark-Lempers, 1993). A general preference for homogeneous peers, however, seems to hold across the entire lifespan (Smith et al., 2014). In adulthood, homophily was found to shift from demographic characteristics such as age and gender (Marsden, 1987) to attitudes and behavior (Urberg et al., 1997), such as homogeneous Twitter networks (Himelboim et al., 2013).

Two mechanisms seem to contribute to this phenomenon. First, similar people have a higher chance to meet. For instance, children of the same social class or ethnicity (which often cluster in neighborhoods) are likely to attend the same schools, where they are stratified in grades based on age (Denrell and Le Mens, 2007). Second, individuals with similar attitudes (Byrne, 1971), personality (Buss, 1984), and physical characteristics (Berscheid and Walster, 1974) are more likely to maintain their peer relations ('similarity breeds liking').

In sum, homophily of individual characteristics is a commonality of different types of peers. The general importance of homophily and the specific individual characteristics change over the lifespan, which is why individual characteristics are not ideal defining criteria.

Peer relationship characteristics

Social relationships are not simply the sum of two individuals but involve relatively stable interaction patterns between those individuals (Hinde, 1979). The characteristics of these interaction patterns in peer relationships have not yet been clearly specified. We posit that a common characteristic of peer relationships is that interactions between peers are reciprocal with respect to giving and receiving affection and support (Clark and Mills, 1979; Cosmides and Tooby, 1992; Laursen and Hartup, 2002). Peer relationships are characterized by equivalent resource-based exchanges, which defines *equality matching,* one of four of Fiske's (1992) fundamental social relationship types. Equality matching also implies equal status between members of a (peer) group and thus distinguishes peer relationships from less balanced and less egalitarian relationship types, such as parent–child relationships or teacher–pupil relationships (Bugental, 2000). If peer relationships are unbalanced, they are at risk to be terminated, as imbalance in reciprocity and social exchange are powerful risk factors for relationship satisfaction (Laursen and Bukowski, 1997; Neyer et al., 2011). This may be one explanation for why peer relationships tend to be more temporary than other relationship types (Laursen and Bukowski, 1997).

Equality matching applies across the entire lifespan (Hartup and Stevens, 1997). No matter whether at the playground, at college, in the office, or at the nursing home – peer relationships are formed and maintained based on equality and exchange at all stages of life. Equality matching is thus better suited as the common denominator of peer relationships than individual peer characteristics that are less specific and change across the lifespan.

In addition, equality matching is a useful criterion of peer relationships because it applies to both dyadic peer relationships and peer groups. In dyadic peer relationships, equality matching is reflected in social exchange between peers at the same level, such as two colleagues who support each other in work tasks. In peer groups, equality matching regulates contributions and benefits. For instance, members of a work team who are all assigned the same tasks may work in synchrony by aligning the allotted tasks or by taking turns (Fiske, 1992).

Beyond the common characteristic of equality matching, peer relationships also differ from each other, particularly in terms of their closeness (Aron and Fraley, 1999). Peer relationships range from rather weak ties (e.g., acquainted fellow students) to very close ties (e.g., a fellow student who is a close friend; Trinke and Bartholomew, 1997). A useful way to distinguish close from less close peer relationships is to think of them as core versus peripheral relationships. Building on social convoy theory (Antonucci et al., 2010), close peer relationships are rather stable across the lifespan (e.g., best friends remain in the network), whereas peripheral peer relationships fluctuate more (e.g., losing touch with acquainted fellows when leaving college). Particularly in late adulthood, peripheral peer relationships wane more than core relationships (Lang et al., 1998; Wrzus et al., 2013).

In sum, peers are a distinct relationship category. Peers can be described in terms of individual and relationship characteristics. Individual characteristics, which pertain to homophily among peer characteristics, change across the lifespan. Relationship characteristics, which pertain to equality matching in terms of equal social exchange, are a useful common denominator of all kinds of peer relationships across the entire lifespan.

Functions of Peers

Peer relationships are not fixed entities. The predominant roles and functions of peers change across the lifespan. To date, research has mostly focused on the role of peers in childhood and adolescence. In the following, we provide an overview of evidence showing that peers also play important, yet different, roles in young, middle, and old adulthood.

Childhood to adolescence

Peers become a central social influence on individuals' development from childhood to adolescence (Harter, 2012). Whereas children focus more on parent–child relationships, adolescents spend increasing amounts of time with their peers as they spend increasing time at school (Brown, 2011; Richards et al., 1998). The size of the friendship network increases during puberty (Wrzus et al., 2013). Adolescents become increasingly susceptible to social feedback from peers due to the growing desire for companionship, which plays a major role for their self-esteem (Greene and Way, 2005; Reitz et al., 2016). Dyadic relationships remain an important influence on adolescents' development, but in contrast to childhood, they are marked by increased attachment and closeness (McCormick et al., 2011).

Young adulthood

Research suggests that peer relationships in late adolescence and emerging adulthood are a developmental precursor and serve a model function for romantic relationships in young adulthood and later life phases (cf. Fraley and Davis, 1997). Secure attachment styles in childhood predicted secure attachment styles with peers in adolescence, which in turn predicted positive relationship quality of romantic relationships in adulthood (Simpson et al., 2007). The bridging function of peers is also indicated by a study showing that attachment styles with peers resembled those with parents and partners, whereas those with parents were less similar to those with partners (Furman et al., 2002).

Peer relationships are also relevant for the adjustment to life events in young adulthood. For example, it was shown that international relationship gains were important mediators in the explanation of international mobility effects on personality development (Zimmermann and Neyer, 2013). Life transitions also change the network composition. For example, meta-analytic findings revealed that entering the job market increased the network through the inclusion of coworkers and new friends (Wrzus et al., 2013).

Middle to old adulthood

Not much is known about the role of peers in personality development beyond young adulthood. There is evidence that the number of peer relationships decreases across adulthood, which is predominantly due to a decrease of peripheral relationships (Lang and Carstensen, 1994). Socioemotional selectivity theory proposes that this decline is due to the decreasing role of information acquisition goals and the increasing role of emotion regulation goals (Carstensen, 1995). Older adults seem to focus their energy increasingly on a smaller number of friends with whom the relationship quality increases (Birditt et al., 2009) instead of their larger peer network. One contributing factor to the shrinking networks in old adulthood may also be beyond the choice of individuals as peers die. Another factor may be the sudden increase of relocation rates from about 80 years of age onwards (Zimmermann and Neyer, 2017), which hampers maintenance of peer relationships (Wrzus et al., 2013).

Despite the decrease in network sizes, peers fulfill important roles in middle to old adulthood. Peers may have important compensating potential when faced with role losses such as widowhood or retirement as well as age-related decreases in cognitive functions, health, and openness to experience (Reitz and Staudinger, 2016). For instance, in old adulthood, when loneliness is prevalent and harmful for adjustment (Dykstra et al., 2005), peers are likely to play important protective roles.

In sum, peers play important yet changing roles across the lifespan. Peer relationships are therefore likely to be a powerful influence on personality development across the lifespan, which we will discuss in the following.

PEER GROUP AND PEER RELATIONSHIP EFFECTS ON PERSONALITY DEVELOPMENT

The next section delineates the different social contexts for personality development that peers provide. A reason why peers are a pervasive aspect of individuals' daily lives is that they surround us on different levels: peers are important partners in dyadic relationships, such as a close friend in whom one confides, a colleague one regularly collaborates with, or a sports teammate who supports one's training efforts. In addition, individuals are part of several peer groups, such as cliques of classmates, groups of colleagues, or sports teams. We contend that both types of peer contexts influence individual development. The conjoint analysis of peer effects at both levels – peer groups and dyadic peer relationships – provides valuable complementary perspectives to understand lifespan personality development.

In the following sections, we will first address the importance of peer group effects on individual development. We then turn to research on effects of peer relationships before we provide an integration of both kinds of peer effects for the study of personality development.

Peer Group Effects on Personality Development

One of the few approaches that explicitly considered the role of peer groups in individual development is group socialization theory (Harris, 1995). According to this theory, outside-the-home socialization in peer groups is an essential factor in children's development that becomes increasingly important with age. The theory posits that peer groups affect children by providing group norms that guide attitudes and behavior and make group members more similar over time, while differences between different peer groups increase. Hence, personality differences between siblings who grow up in the same family are not only attributed to genetic differences or non-shared environmental experiences within the family, but also to their belonging to different peer groups (Bleske-Rechek and Kelley, 2014; Harris, 2000).

Likewise, peer group effects may also help explain how certain life experiences that provide distinct peer contexts affect personality development. Examples involve research concerning different educational paths (Lüdtke et al., 2011), graduation (Bleidorn, 2012), entering university (Leikas and Salmela-Aro, 2015), living arrangements (Jonkmann et al., 2014), military service (Jackson et al., 2012), occupations (Denissen et al., 2014), acculturation (Reitz et al., 2014), and international mobility experiences (Greischel et al., 2016; Hutteman et al., 2015; Zimmermann and Neyer, 2013). All of these diverse life experiences have in common that they involve social experiences in different peer groups such as fellow students, classmates, flatmates, comrades, colleagues, or (international) fellows which can be assumed to play a crucial role for personality development (Neyer et al., 2014).

In sum, the investigation of distinct peer group contexts may contribute to the understanding of developmental differences *between* peer groups. However, there is also evidence for personality differences between individuals who share the same peer (group) experiences (e.g., Bleidorn, 2012; Hutteman et al., 2015; Jonkmann et al., 2014). Group socialization theory does not consider interindividual differences in the development of individuals *within* the same peer groups. Although differences in group status and social comparisons are expected to explain some variance of developmental trajectories of peer group members, it has not yet been specified how such differentiation processes might operate. We contend that such within-group differences can be explained, at least in part, by experiences that individuals have in specific dyadic peer relationships.

Peer Relationship Effects on Personality Development

A comprehensive theoretical framework that is suited to help explain the generic processes that account for peer relationship effects on individual development is the PERSOC framework (Back et al., 2011). PERSOC integrates a number of earlier models such as the social relations model (Back and Kenny, 2010; Kenny, 1994) and the neo-socioanalytic theory (Hogan and Roberts, 2004). Similar to its precursors, the PERSOC framework emphasizes the componential nature of interpersonal behavior and perceptions by specifying the processes of dyadic personality–relationship interactions. According to this framework, relationship dispositions and individual dispositions influence each other in so-called social interaction units that are determined by characteristics of the actor, the interaction partner, and their relationship. Individual dispositions are specific to a person and relationship dispositions characterize individuals in relation to a specific relationship partner. Relationship dispositions are unique to a specific dyadic relationship, such as the relationship with a close friend, and they include explicit and implicit mental representations of this relationship (e.g., feelings toward the friend and cognitions that describe the specific relationship). When relationship dispositions are continuously experienced, these accumulating experiences can become individual dispositions – hence, specific to a person – and thus influence personality development.

Relationship dispositions result from the experience of interactions between relationship partners that are based on bidirectional interpersonal behaviors and perceptions. Interpersonal behaviors encompass all actions of an interaction partner that are potentially perceivable by the other person. Interpersonal perceptions include inferences about the interaction partner or one's own feelings, cognitions, and motivations toward the partner as well as meta-perceptions. As illustrated by these broad definitions of interpersonal behaviors and perceptions, the PERSOC framework provides generic perspectives on micro-level interpersonal processes of dyadic interactions that account for the development of relationship dispositions and their effects on individual development. As such, PERSOC provides theoretical arguments for the claim that the consideration of *dyadic* peer relationships is essential for the understanding of personality development. However, PERSOC does not specify the content of such exchanges or their concrete implications for different psychological functions relevant for personality (e.g., changes in individuals' behavior, thoughts, and feelings).

INTEGRATING PEER GROUP AND PEER RELATIONSHIP EFFECTS ON PERSONALITY DEVELOPMENT

Having outlined two different theoretical approaches and empirical evidence that corroborate the importance of both peer groups and peer relationships in personality development we contend that the integration of these different levels of peer effects (i.e., peer group-level and peer relationship-level) helps to better understand developmental differences both between and within peer groups. To date, empirical evidence on the distinct effects of peer group contexts and dyadic peer relationships is limited. To the best of our knowledge, there are no empirical studies on personality development that have addressed both kinds of effects in a comprehensive design. There is, however, some evidence concerning the distinct impact of peer groups and peer relationships on affective and behavioral outcomes that underline their incremental effects. For example, a study by Larson and Ham (1993) showed that the experience of conflicts with a group of friends versus with the best friend has distinct (incremental) effects on adolescents' dysphoric affect.

More recently, Balbo and Barban (2014) investigated peer effects on young adults' fertility behavior. They distinguished between the effects of shared peer group contexts and specific effects of close peer relationships. To this end, they estimated the effects of fertility behavior of (a) the former school network and (b) former schoolmates who were considered as 'friends' on individuals' likelihood to become parents. Indeed, the results showed distinct effects for both predictors. Although both a friend becoming a parent and the fertility of the peer group increased the individuals' likelihood of having a child, the effect of the peer group was smaller than the effect of the friends. This finding corroborates differences in the role of peer contexts and effects of close peer relationships on individual behavior. Further research that specifically addresses the impact of both kinds of peer effects on measures of personality is needed, however. Such research should focus on development in different contexts and life phases (see Reitz et al., 2014).

To summarize, we presented theoretical perspectives and empirical evidence that highlight the importance of both peer groups and peer relationships for the understanding of lifespan personality development. We contend that their conjoint consideration is a fruitful approach for further research on personality development as previous studies pointed to incremental peer group and peer relationship effects on behavioral and affective measures. Further research on personality effects that takes the dynamic interplay between peer effects at both levels of analysis and across different life contexts and life phases into account is needed. Furthermore, the specific mechanisms through which peer groups and peer relationships impact personality development have not yet been thoroughly considered. This also concerns the question about which psychological functions (e.g., cognitions, feelings, and behaviors) are primarily involved in dyadic interaction units and during experiences in peer group contexts. In the following sections, we will provide a short overview on the theoretical approaches that have most frequently appeared in the literature to explain the mechanisms of peer effects. We highlight the communalities and differences between the psychological mechanisms that these theories suggest and relate them to relevant empirical findings.

UNDERLYING MECHANISMS OF PEER EFFECTS ON PERSONALITY DEVELOPMENT

Many theoretical approaches discussed in the peer literature do not explicitly link peer influences to the development of personality traits but rather provide suggestions on how peers affect changes in specific aspects of individual behavior, thoughts, and cognitions. As the sociogenomic model of personality (Roberts and Jackson, 2008) suggests, the environment is generally not assumed to affect personality traits directly, except for some dramatic physiological changes such as cortical lesions. Instead, environmental effects are expected to be mediated by bottom-up processes that are reflected in accumulating state changes (i.e., the way the environment makes people behave, feel, or think in different situations). Hence, all theoretical models and empirical findings that explain peer effects on (state) changes in any of these psychological functions are valuable resources for understanding the mechanisms that link peer experiences to personality development. Theoretical approaches, however, differ with respect to the psychological functions they focus on (e.g., behaviors, feelings, and cognitions). As a result, they differ with respect to the specific mediating mechanisms they assume (e.g., some propose behavior regulation versus others propose affective relationship experiences).

Group Socialization and Self-categorization Theory

As mentioned before, group socialization theory (Harris, 1995) is a prominent theoretical approach that states that peer groups affect individual development. To explain these effects, Harris refers to the mechanisms that have been suggested in the context of social group research, such as self-categorization theory (Turner et al., 1987). According to this theory, individuals who identify with a group, that is, who categorize themselves as members of the group and attach emotional significance to their membership (Tajfel, 1978), adopt the group's norms about appropriate attitudes and behaviors. Hence, group identification is assumed to promote within-group assimilation. That is, group members become more similar to each other over time by their adherence to norm-compliant attitudes and behaviors. For example, the peer group norms on how to behave toward members of an outgroup have been shown to affect children's intergroup attitudes (McGuire et al., 2015). Because there is frequently a strong motivation to maintain a positive image in the eyes of one's peers, peer group norms can be assumed to be very relevant to behavior regulation. Furthermore, the principle of equality matching implies equal status of peer group members. Feelings of being *one among equals* may further increase adherence to the groups' norms as group members may obey the group norms to fit in and to maintain their group identity.

The Social Investment Framework

Social investment theory (Roberts et al., 2005) proposes complementary mechanisms of social influence on personality development via behavior regulation. Caspi and Roberts (2001) suggested four mechanisms to initiate behavioral changes that account for personality development: (1) responding to explicit and implicit behavioral contingencies in social roles, (2) watching oneself and reflecting upon one's own actions, (3) watching others and using them as role models for one's own behavior, and (4) listening to others and incorporating their feedback into future behavioral strategies. All four strategies refer to behavioral changes.

The social investment framework does not explicitly circumscribe the specific relationship contexts to which these strategies relate (i.e., the nature of the role relationships and whether groups or dyadic relationships are considered). Applying them to the peer context may help those generic mechanisms to take some more shape. The principle of equality matching in peer relationships involves the impression of 'being two of the same kind' in terms of the same hierarchical level, which may promote horizontal norm transmission. For instance, peers are likely to provide respective contingencies for behavior change by rewarding behaviors that are in line with role expectations (e.g., classmates sitting next to each other may reward each other for helping each other out with assignments; and A may stop helping B after B told the teacher on A, which is a behavior that is incompatible with equality matching). Peers are also strong role models, sources of feedback, and comparison standards for the reflection of one's own behaviors. In a work team, one can, for instance, imagine that colleagues adjust their 'office behavior' (e.g., dress code, work hours, level of dedication) on one another through continuously modeling each other's behavior. Likewise, students, who are all on the same level working toward the same goal, may adjust their work habits to each other, which may have an impact on their conscientiousness development.

In line with the notions of group socialization theory and social investment theory, previous research provided rich evidence for the effects of peers on individual behavior. In particular, many studies considered the role of peer groups and peer relationships in dysfunctional behaviors, such as substance abuse (e.g., Damphousse and Kaplan, 1998; Soloski et al., 2016; Taylor, 2006; Windle, 2000), antisocial behaviors and conduct problems (e.g., Bacchini et al., 2013; Berger and Rodkin, 2012; Cheung and Cheung, 2008), or dysfunctional health behaviors (e.g., Hasking et al., 2013; Klump et al., 2002). Less is known about the positive effects of peers on (normative) functional behaviors. However, some of the studies that are available point to positive peer effects on adaptive behaviors such as individual training efforts (Spink et al., 2013), engagement in novel academic behaviors (Masland and Lease, 2013), or personal future planning (Zhang and Zhang, 2008).

This summary of current research findings is by no means exhaustive, but it provides substantial evidence for peer effects on individual behavior and its development over time. Hence, as suggested by the sociogenomic model of personality (Roberts and Jackson, 2008), studies that investigate peer-induced behavioral changes may provide a promising avenue to explore the mechanisms by which peers affect personality development.

Attachment theory

Another theoretical approach that helps understand the mechanisms by which peers affect individual development is attachment theory (Bowlby, 1969; Hazan and Shaver, 1987). In contrast to the theoretical models discussed above, attachment theory is more concerned with the affective experiences of individuals in dyadic relationships. According to attachment theory, adult attachment relationships are similar to childhood attachment relationships as they are characterized by (1) active proximity maintenance as the company of the attachment partner is enjoyed and separations are responded to with negative emotions, (2) the use of the other as a safe haven to provide reassurance and feelings of safety in distressing situations, and (3) the use of the other as a secure base from which to explore the environment. In contrast to childhood attachment relationships, adult attachment relationships are not primarily reflected in external, observable behaviors but characterized by internally represented beliefs and expectations. For example, adults may derive comfort and positive feelings from the mere knowledge that their attachment figures could be contacted in situations of need (Hazan and Shaver, 1994).

Several researchers emphasized that specific peer relationships, such as close friends, may serve important attachment functions (Nickerson and Nagle, 2005; Trinke and Bartholomew, 1997). Evidence suggests that peer attachment relationships contribute relationship-specific effects on individuals' well-being and psychological functioning (Caron et al., 2012). In particular, young adults who are in a transitional life stage shift attachment-related functions from parents to peers by first relying on peers for safe haven and later for secure base functions (Hazan and Zeifman, 1994).

Studies on peer attachment effects revealed that attachment experiences in friendships during childhood and adolescence shape later attachments, e.g., to a romantic partner, which underlines their long-lasting effects on cognitive representations such as inner working models (Fraley et al., 2013). Furthermore, several studies provided evidence for the positive effects of peer attachment on measures of well-being and psychological functioning (Greenberg et al., 1983; Lu et al., 2015; Wilkinson, 2010). Likewise, peer attachment was shown to impede aggressive and deviant behaviors (Burton et al., 2013; Laible et al., 2000).

Apart from attachment, there are several studies that focused on other related relationship qualities, such as experiences of insecurity and closeness in peer relationships. For example, Neyer and Lehnart (2007) found that experiences of insecurity in peer relationships were associated with higher levels of neuroticism and shyness and lower levels of extraversion and self-esteem in young adults. Higher levels of peer relationship closeness were associated with higher levels of extraversion, agreeableness, and self-esteem and with lower levels of neuroticism and shyness. Similar associations were reported by Mund and Neyer (2014). Their study revealed that peer closeness was positively correlated with extraversion and agreeableness, whereas peer insecurity was negatively correlated with extraversion, agreeableness, and conscientiousness, but positively correlated with neuroticism. From a longitudinal perspective, several studies corroborated positive correlations between changes in peer insecurity and neuroticism (Mund and Neyer, 2014; Neyer and Lehnart, 2007; Parker et al., 2012). Taken together, all of the reported findings make a strong case for the argument that experiences of attachment and related affective experiences in peer relationships are relevant to personality development.

Sociometer theory

Not all of the studies reported above match the original idea of attachment as a relationship-specific experience between two relationship partners but also investigated unspecific attachments toward (groups of) peers in general, such as cliques of friends. This may not reflect the initial understanding of attachment as referring to specific relationship bonds, but is in line with the basic ideas of sociometer theory (Baumeister and Leary, 1995; Leary and Baumeister, 2000). According to Baumeister and Leary (1995), the need to belong is an innate human need reflected in the tendency to experience affective distress in situations of social deprivation and a boost in positive affect and self-esteem from social relatedness. In contrast to the attachment framework, this perspective assumes that relationships can substitute each other so that new relationship partners can replace lost partners.

Furthermore, it is proposed that the need to belong can also be satisfied in social contexts other than specific relationships, such as large social groups or abstract social entities (Baumeister and Leary, 1995). Hence, larger peer groups, with or without direct interpersonal contact between group members, play a role for individuals' affective experiences in their social worlds, which in turn, will determine their development (Leary, 2005; Leary and Baumeister, 2000). Indeed, perceived peer group acceptance was found to predict higher levels of self-esteem in adolescents (Sarkova et al., 2014) and young adults (Chen et al., 2012). This was shown to hold for both subjective and objective measures of peer approval (Gruenenfelder-Steiger et al., 2016). This finding was replicated in an experimental study that showed that peer group rejection predicted a decrease in children's self-esteem and increase in anxiety (Nesdale and Pelyhe, 2009). A recent longitudinal study by Reitz et al. (2016) provided first insights into an internal, conscious mechanism that accounts for these effects: students' sociometric popularity among classmates predicted their self-esteem development via their self-perceived popularity.

To conclude, we provided an overview of different theoretical perspectives on the mechanisms that may mediate peer effects on personality development. The selection of theories is not exhaustive but represents the current theoretical bandwidth of theories that can be applied to peer effects on personality development. All theories suggest psychological mechanisms through which peers affect feelings, thoughts, and behaviors, which thus may contribute to personality development. They differ, however, in the psychological functions they focus on (feelings, thoughts, and behaviors), the level of peer effects they take into account (i.e., peer group versus peer relationship effects), and thus, the specific mechanisms they suggest. In simplified terms, one set of popular theories in the peer literature focuses on the mechanisms by which peers promote behavior changes that may, in turn, result in long-term personality development (group socialization theory, social investment theory). Other approaches are more concerned with the (affective) experiences of individuals in the contexts of their peer relationships (attachment theory) and peer groups (sociometer theory) and their resulting implications for individual development.

The empirical findings presented provide initial evidence for some of the proposed mechanisms. However, few studies incorporated differentiated measures concerning peer variables, mediators, and developmental outcomes in a comprehensive (longitudinal) design. Hence, future research is needed to draw conclusions about the validity of the discussed approaches and the (relative) importance of different mediating mechanisms for the explanation of peer group and peer relationships effects.

CONCLUSION AND FUTURE RESEARCH

Several conclusions on peers and their role in personality development can be drawn. First, peers are a pervasive aspect of human lives and are important across the entire lifespan. Due to their changing functions in different life phases, it is difficult to derive individual characteristics that consistently characterize peers in all life phases. At the level of relationships and groups, peers are best described by the principle of equality matching, which involves equivalent resource-based exchanges that apply to peers across different life phases. Equality matching allows differentiation between peers and other relationship types such as kin relationships and romantic partners (Bugental, 2000; Hartup and Stevens, 1997; Neyer et al., 2011). Research on the characteristics and functions of peers beyond young adulthood is still limited. Considering the changes and challenges that come along with a rapidly aging population and the dissolution of established family structures, it is important to consider peers and their role in individual development and well-being in older age groups to a larger degree.

Second, peers affect personality development through peer relationship and peer group effects. The investigation of peer group effects is particularly useful in order to understand developmental differences *between* individuals in different peer group contexts. The consideration of peer relationship effects, in contrast, can add to the understanding of differences between individuals *within* the same peer group. Unfortunately, research including both kinds of effects in a comprehensive design is rare. In particular, little is known about the (relative) importance of peer group and peer relationship effects in different life phases as well as their longitudinal interplay over time. Furthermore, several characteristics at the individual, relationship, and group level (e.g., group identification, group status, relationship closeness, group cohesion) may moderate the effects of peer groups and peer relationships on individual development. Their simultaneous consideration in longitudinal designs is another promising avenue for future research.

Third, the current literature suggests that peers affect personality development by different mechanisms. For example, group socialization theory suggests that group norms regulate the behavior of peer group members, whereas the social investment framework emphasizes the importance of peer feedback on role-appropriate behavior. Hence, both perspectives focus on the question how peers affect individual behavior and thus suggest accumulating behavioral changes as a mechanism that explains peer effects on personality development. Manifold studies provided evidence for peer effects on – mostly dysfunctional – behaviors. Other studies illustrated the effect of accumulating behavior changes, such as achievement behavior, on the development of personality traits (Bleidorn, 2012).

To date, we are not aware of any studies that used a comprehensive design including all factors of the proposed mediating mechanism (i.e., information on peer norms or feedback, individual behaviors, and trait measures) in a longitudinal design. Behavior changes in response to group norms or feedback also require individual capacities in order to perform the required behaviors (Hennecke et al., 2014). Hence, future research might also benefit from taking the moderating role of individual motivation and self-regulation into account when investigating the impact of peers on behavior and development. Furthermore, it may be promising to more thoroughly consider the implications of the equality matching principle. As noted above, peers should be motivated to maintain equality in social exchange and behaviors. As a result, they may be particularly keen to obey peer group norms or to consider the feedback of their equal status relationship partners, which may increase the potential of peers (as compared to other relationship types) to affect personality development.

Other theoretical approaches, such as attachment theory (Bowlby, 1969; Hazan and Shaver, 1987) and sociometer theory (Leary and Baumeister, 2000), emphasize the role of (affective) experiences individuals make in peer groups and peer relationships for individual development. Several studies found support for a link between peer attachment as well as related relationship qualities and adaptive developmental outcomes. It may be an interesting question for future research to examine whether peer relationships that are characterized by more equal exchange (e.g., in the form of mutual social support) are more likely to affect individuals' development than experiences in less balanced relationship types. One argument to support this idea is that balanced relationships may provide more positive affective experiences than unbalanced ones. One could, for instance, imagine that a student's self-esteem is more susceptible to social feedback from his or her neighbor in class, with whom there is balanced social exchange, as it leads to stronger emotional responses (e.g., feelings of acceptance).

It is, however, not yet clear whether the described mechanisms are exclusive to certain peer contexts. The differentiated consideration of core and peripheral relationships may help to gain new insights. For example, one might assume that close peer relationships or peer groups with high levels of group cohesion (e.g., a clique) are more likely to provide individuals with pervasive (affective) experiences. By contrast, more peripheral peer relationship context (e.g., a loose network of coworkers) might affect individual development by providing norms, reference standards, and direct or indirect feedback on individual behavior. Similarly, different mediating mechanisms might be particularly relevant for the explanation of changes in particular trait domains. These assumptions have not been thoroughly investigated and are promising avenues for future peer research.

There are some general issues in the field of peer research that call for consideration. First, previous studies placed great emphasis on negative developmental implications of peer group contexts, as illustrated by accumulating research that reported on the role of peers in the explanation of detrimental behaviors such as substance abuse, conduct problems, and negative health behaviors in adolescence and young adulthood. As peers are pervasive social relationship partners who can influence individuals in many ways, it seems worthwhile to devote more attention to their potential to also foster positive behaviors, such as positive adaptation processes via social support, secure attachment, or positive role behaviors. The potential positive impact of peers on positive development is likely to play a role not just in adolescence and young adulthood, but across the entire lifespan.

Second, most peer research is restricted to self-report measures that only reflect individual perspectives. In order to gain a more encompassing understanding of peer contexts, the combination of individual, dyadic, and group-level data that reflect different perspectives (self- and other-reports) on peer contexts (e.g., group norms, attachment, social relationship characteristics) is essential.

Finally, in view of the growing cultural diversity in many societies and, in particular, in important peer contexts such as educational institutions and work environments, there is a need to incorporate intergroup and cross-cultural perspectives on the role of peer effects on individual development. A recent longitudinal study concerning adolescents found that peer group effects are moderated by adolescents' group status (Reitz et al., 2016). That is, the popularity of peers only affected adolescents' self-esteem when they shared the same socially relevant group membership (i.e., being an immigrant versus not). Another longitudinal study complements this finding by showing that immigrant adolescents' popularity of peers from the mainstream culture but neither from the own nor other immigrant groups resulted in perceptions of personal discrimination (Reitz et al., 2015). These findings highlight the need to consider the intergroup contexts of peers as they can shape the specific effects peer groups have on personality.

Furthermore, a recent study suggested that, contrary to self-control theory and many previous studies based on Western samples, self-control fails to predict delinquency when social variables such as peer delinquency are controlled among Chinese adolescents (Cheung and Cheung, 2008). The effects of social factors on delinquency, however, remained significant beyond the effect of self-control, which suggests that the combination of self-control and social factors in the prediction of delinquency might vary across cultures. Hence, the consideration of cross-cultural similarities and differences in the role of peers for development may provide some valuable insights as to the cultural generalizability of psychological theories and assumptions in general.

In sum, our aim for the present chapter was to point to the important functions of peers for personality development across the lifespan. We contend that a thorough examination of peer group and peer relationship effects, as well as their dynamic interplay over time, will help to advance the understanding of personality development. Furthermore, peer contexts provide a valuable resource for the investigation of the mechanisms that mediate social effects on personality development, as several moderators, such as different relationship and group characteristics, can be considered. Future research that places a stronger emphasis on peer effects and their underlying mediating mechanisms will thus advance the understanding of lifespan personality development.

REFERENCES

Antonucci, T. C., Fiori, K. L., Birditt, K., & Jackey, L. H. (2010). Convoys of social relations: Integrating life-span and life-course perspectives. In M. E. Lamb, A. M. Freund, & R. M. Lerner (Eds.), *The handbook of lifespan development, Vol 2: Social and Emotional Development* (pp. 434–473). Hoboken, NJ: John Wiley & Sons Inc.

Aron, A., & Fraley, B. (1999). Relationship closeness as including other in the self: Cognitive underpinnings and measures. *Social Cognition, 17*, 140–160.

Bacchini, D., Affuso, G., & De Angelis, G. (2013). Moral vs. non-moral attribution in adolescence: Environmental and behavioural correlates. *European Journal of Developmental Psychology, 10*, 221–238.

Back, M. D., Baumert, A., Denissen, J. A., Hartung, F., Penke, L., Schmukle, S. C., ... Wrzus, C. (2011). PERSOC: A unified framework for understanding the dynamic interplay of personality and social relationships. *European Journal of Personality, 25*, 90–107.

Back, M. D., & Kenny, D. A. (2010). The social relations model: How to understand dyadic processes. *Social and Personality Psychology Compass, 4*, 855–870.

Balbo, N., & Barban, N. (2014). Does fertility behavior spread among friends? *American Sociological Review, 79*, 412–431.

Baumeister, R. F., & Leary, M. R. (1995). The need to belong: Desire for interpersonal attachments as a fundamental human motivation. *Psychological Bulletin, 117*, 497–529.

Berger, C., & Rodkin, P. C. (2012). Group influences on individual aggression and prosociality: Early adolescents who change peer affiliations. *Social Development, 21*, 396–413.

Berscheid, E., & Walster, E. (1974). Physical attractiveness. *Advances in Experimental Social Psychology, 7*, 157–215.

Birditt, K. S., Jackey, L. H., & Antonucci, T. C. (2009). Longitudinal patterns of negative relationship quality across adulthood. *Journals of Gerontology Series B: Psychological Sciences and Social Sciences, 64B*, 55–64.

Bleidorn, W. (2012). Hitting the road to adulthood: Short-term personality development during a major life transition. *Personality and Social Psychology Bulletin, 38*, 1594–1608.

Bleske-Rechek, A., & Kelley, J. A. (2014). Birth order and personality: A within-family test using independent self-reports from both firstborn and laterborn siblings. *Personality and Individual Differences, 56*, 15–18.

Bowlby, J. (1969). *Attachment and loss: Vol. 1. Attachment*. New York, NY: Basic Books.

Brown, B. B. (2011). Popularity in peer group perspective: The role of status in adolescent peer systems. In A. H. N. Cillessen, D. Schwartz, & L. Mayeux (Eds.), *Popularity in the peer system* (pp. 165–192). New York, NY: Guilford Press.

Bugental, D. (2000). Acquisition of the algorithms of social life: A domain-based approach. *Psychological Bulletin, 126*, 187–219.

Burton, K. A., Florell, D., & Wygant, D. B. (2013). The role of peer attachment and normative beliefs about aggression on traditional bullying and cyberbullying. *Psychology in the Schools, 50*, 103–115.

Buss, D. M. (1984). Marital assortment for personality dispositions: Assessment with three different data sources. *Behavior Genetics, 14*, 111–123.

Byrne, D. (1971). *The attraction paradigm*. New York, NY: Academic Press.

Caron, A., Lafontaine, M., Bureau, J., Levesque, C., & Johnson, S. M. (2012). Comparisons of close relationships: An evaluation of relationship quality and patterns of attachment to parents, friends, and romantic partners in young adults. *Canadian Journal of Behavioural Science, 44*, 245–256.

Carstensen, L. L. (1995). Evidence for a lifespan theory of socioemotional selectivity. *Current Directions in Psychological Science, 4*, 151–156.

Caspi, A., & Roberts, B. W. (2001). Target article: Personality development across the life course: The argument for change and continuity. *Psychological Inquiry, 12*, 49–66.

Chen, W., Chen, C., Lin, Y., & Chen, T. (2012). Sport participation and self-esteem as mediated by perceived peer acceptance and sport self-concept in Taiwanese college students. *Social Behavior and Personality, 40*, 699–704.

Cheung, N. T., & Cheung, Y. W. (2008). Self-control, social factors, and delinquency: A test of the general theory of crime among adolescents in Hong Kong. *Journal of Youth and Adolescence, 37*, 412–430.

Clark, M. S., & Mills, J. (1979). Interpersonal attraction in exchange and communal relationships. *Journal of Personality and Social Psychology, 37*, 12–24.

Cosmides, L., & Tooby, J. (1992). Cognitive adaptations for social exchange. In J. H. Barkow, L. Cosmides, & J. Tooby (Eds.), *The adapted mind: Evolutionary psychology and the generation of culture* (pp. 163–228). New York, NY: Oxford University Press.

Damphousse, K. R., & Kaplan, H. B. (1998). Intervening processes between adolescent drug use and psychological distress: An examination of the self-medication hypothesis. *Social Behavior and Personality, 26*, 115–130.

Denissen, J. A., Ulferts, H., Lüdtke, O., Muck, P. M., & Gerstorf, D. (2014). Longitudinal transactions between personality and occupational roles: A large and heterogeneous study of job beginners, stayers, and changers. *Developmental Psychology, 50*, 1931–1942.

Denrell, J., & Le Mens, G. (2007). Interdependent sampling and social influence. *Psychological Review, 114*, 398–422.

Dykstra, P. A., van Tilburg, T. G., & de Jong Gierveld, J. (2005). Changes in older adult loneliness: Results from a seven-year longitudinal study. *Research on Aging, 27*, 725–747.

Feld, S. L. (1982). Social structural determinants of similarity among associates. *American Sociological Review, 47*, 797–801.

Fiske, A. P. (1992). The four elementary forms of sociality: Framework for a unified theory of social relations. *Psychological Review, 99*, 689–723.

Fraley, R., & Davis, K. E. (1997). Attachment formation and transfer in young adults' close friendships and romantic relationships. *Personal Relationships, 4*, 131–144.

Fraley, R. C., & Roberts, B. W. (2005). Patterns of continuity: A dynamic model for conceptualizing the stability of individual differences in psychological constructs across the life course. *Psychological Review, 112*, 60–74.

Fraley, R. C., Roisman, G. I., Booth-LaForce, C., Owen, M. T., & Holland, A. S. (2013). Interpersonal and genetic origins of adult attachment styles: A longitudinal study from infancy to early adulthood. *Journal of Personality and Social Psychology, 104*, 817–838.

Furman, W., Simon, V. A., Shaffer, L., & Bouchey, H. A. (2002). Adolescents' working models and styles for relationships with parents, friends, and romantic partners. *Child Development, 73*, 241–255.

Greenberg, M. T., Siegel, J. M., & Leitch, C. J. (1983). The nature and importance of attachment relationships to parents and peers during adolescence. *Journal of Youth and Adolescence, 12*, 373–386.

Greene, M. L., & Way, N. (2005). Self-esteem trajectories among ethnic minority adolescents: A growth curve analysis of the patterns and predictors of change. *Journal of Research on Adolescence, 15*, 151–178.

Greischel, H., Noack, P., & Neyer, F. J. (2016). Sailing uncharted waters: Adolescent personality development and social relationship experiences during a year abroad. *Journal of Youth and Adolescence, 45*, 2307–2320.

Gruenenfelder-Steiger, A. E., Harris, M. A., & Fend, H. A. (2016). Subjective and objective peer approval evaluations and self-esteem development: A test of reciprocal, prospective, and long-term effects. *Developmental Psychology, 52*, 1563–1577.

Harris, J. (1995). Where is the child's environment? A group socialization theory of development. *Psychological Review, 102*, 458–489.

Harris, J. (2000). Socialization, personality development, and the child's environments: Comment on Vandell (2000). *Developmental Psychology, 36*, 711–723.

Harter, S. (2012). *The construction of the self: Developmental and sociocultural foundations* (2nd ed.). New York, NY: Guilford Press.

Hartup, W. W., & Stevens, N. (1997). Friendships and adaptation in the life course. *Psychological Bulletin, 121*, 355–370.

Hasking, P., Andrews, T., & Martin, G. (2013). The role of exposure to self-injury among peers in predicting later self-injury. *Journal of Youth and Adolescence, 42*, 1543–1556.

Hazan, C., & Shaver, P. (1987). Romantic love conceptualized as an attachment process. *Journal of Personality and Social Psychology, 52*, 511–524.

Hazan, C. & Shaver, P. (1994). Attachment as an organizational framework for research on close relationships. *Psychological Inquiry, 5*, 1–22.

Hazan, C., & Zeifman, D. (1994). Sex and the psychological tether. In K. Bartholomew & D. Perlman (Eds.), *Advances in personal relationships. Vol. 5. Attachment processes in adulthood* (pp. 151–171). London: Jessica Kingsley.

Hennecke, M., Bleidorn, W., Denissen, J. A., & Wood, D. (2014). A three-part framework for self-regulated personality development across adulthood. *European Journal of Personality, 28*, 289–299.

Himelboim, I., McCreery, S., & Smith, M. (2013). Birds of a feather tweet together: Integrating network and content analyses to examine cross-ideology exposure on Twitter. *Journal of Computer-Mediated Communication, 18*, 40–60.

Hinde, R. A. (1979). *Towards understanding relationships* (Vol. 18). London: Academic Press.

Hogan, R., & Roberts, B. W. (2004). A socioanalytic model of maturity. *Journal of Career Assessment, 12*, 207–217.

Hutteman, R., Nestler, S., Wagner, J., Egloff, B., & Back, M. D. (2015). Wherever I may roam: Processes of self-esteem development from adolescence to emerging adulthood in the context of international student exchange. *Journal of Personality and Social Psychology, 108*, 767–783.

Jackson, J. J., Thoemmes, F., Jonkmann, K., Lüdtke, O., & Trautwein, U. (2012). Military training and personality trait development: Does the military make the man, or does the man make the military? *Psychological Science, 23*, 270–277.

Jonkmann, K., Thoemmes, F., Luedke, O., & Trautwein, U. (2014). Personality traits and living arrangements in young adulthood: Selection and socialization. *Developmental Psychology, 50*, 683–698.

Kenny, D. A. (1994). *Interpersonal perception: A social relations analysis*. New York, NY: Guilford Press.

Klump, K. L., Wonderlich, S., Lehoux, P., Lilenfeld, L. R., & Bulik, C. M. (2002). Does environment matter? A review of nonshared environment and eating disorders. *International Journal of Eating Disorders, 31*, 118–135.

Laible, D. J., Carlo, G., & Raffaelli, M. (2000). The differential relations of parent and peer attachment to adolescent adjustment. *Journal of Youth and Adolescence, 29*, 45–59.

Lang, F. R., & Carstensen, L. L. (1994). Close emotional relationships in late life: Further support for proactive aging in the social domain. *Psychology and Aging, 9*, 315–324.

Lang, F. R., Staudinger, U. M., & Carstensen, L. L. (1998). Perspectives on socioemotional selectivity in late life: How personality and social context do (and do not) make a difference. *Journals of Gerontology: Series B: Psychological Sciences and Social Sciences, 53B*, 21–30.

Larson, R., & Ham, M. (1993). Stress and 'storm and stress' in early adolescence: The relationship of negative events with dysphoric affect. *Developmental Psychology, 29*, 130–140.

Laursen, B., & Bukowski, W. M. (1997). A developmental guide to the organisation of close relationships. *International Journal of Behavioral Development, 21*, 747–770.

Laursen, B., & Hartup, W. W. (2002). The origins of reciprocity and social exchange in friendships. In B. Laursen & W. G. Graziano (Eds.), *Social exchange in development: New directions for child and adolescent development* (pp. 27–40). San Francisco, CA: Jossey-Bass.

Leary, M. R. (2005). Sociometer theory and the pursuit of relational value: Getting to the root of self-esteem. *European Review of Social Psychology, 16*, 75–111.

Leary, M. R., & Baumeister, R. F. (2000). The nature and function of self-esteem: Sociometer theory. In M. P. Zanna (Ed.), *Advances in experimental social psychology*, Vol. 32 (pp. 1–62). San Diego, CA: Academic Press.

Leikas, S., & Salmela-Aro, K. (2015). Personality trait changes among young Finns: The role of life events and transitions. *Journal of Personality, 83*, 117–126.

Lempers, J. D., & Clark-Lempers, D. S. (1993). A functional comparison of same-sex and opposite sex friendships during adolescence. *Journal of Adolescent Research, 8*, 89–108.

Louch, H. (2000). Personal network integration: Transitivity and homophily in strong-tie relations. *Social Networks, 22*, 45–64.

Lu, A., Tian, H., Yu, Y., Feng, Y., Hong, X., & Yu, Z. (2015). Peer attachment and social anxiety: Gender as a moderator across deaf and hearing adolescents. *Social Behavior and Personality, 43*, 231–240.

Lüdtke, O., Roberts, B. W., Trautwein, U., & Nagy, G. (2011). A random walk down university avenue: Life paths, life events, and personality trait change at the transition to university life. *Journal of Personality and Social Psychology, 101*, 620–637.

Maccoby, E. E. (2002). Gender and group process: A developmental perspective. *Current Directions in Psychological Science, 11*, 54–58.

Marsden, P. V. (1987). Core discussion networks of Americans. *American Sociological Review, 52*, 122–131.

Martin, C. L., & Fabes, R. A. (2001). The stability and consequences of young children's same-sex peer interactions. *Developmental Psychology, 37*, 431–446.

Masland, L. C., & Lease, A. M. (2013). Effects of achievement motivation, social identity, and peer group norms on academic conformity. *Social Psychology of Education, 16*, 661–681.

McCormick, C. M., Kuo, S. I.-C., & Masten, A. S. (2011). Developmental tasks across the lifespan. In K. F. Fingerman, J. Smith, & T. C. Antonucci (Eds.), *Handbook of lifespan development* (pp. 117–140). New York, NY: Springer.

McGuire, L., Rutland, A., & Nesdale, D. (2015). Peer group norms and accountability moderate the effect of school norms on children's intergroup attitudes. *Child Development, 86*, 1290–1297.

McPherson, M., Smith-Lovin, L., & Cook, J. M. (2001). Birds of a feather: Homophily in social networks. *Annual Review of Sociology, 27*, 415–444.

Mund, M., & Neyer, F. J. (2014). Treating personality–relationship transactions with respect: Narrow facets, advanced models, and extended time frames. *Journal of Personality and Social Psychology, 107*, 352–368.

Nesdale, D., & Pelyhe, H. (2009). Effects of experimentally induced peer-group rejection and out-group ethnicity on children's anxiety, self-esteem, and in-group and out-group attitudes. *European Journal of Developmental Psychology, 6*, 294–317.

Neyer, F. J., & Lehnart, J. (2007). Relationships matter in personality development: Evidence from an 8-year longitudinal study across young adulthood. *Journal of Personality, 75*, 535–568.

Neyer, F. J., Mund, M., Zimmermann, J., & Wrzus, C. (2014). Personality–relationship transactions revisited. *Journal of Personality, 82*, 539–550.

Neyer, F. J., Wrzus, C., Wagner, J., & Lang, F. R. (2011). Principles of relationship differentiation. *European Psychologist, 16*, 267–277.

Nickerson, A. B., & Nagle, R. J. (2005). Parent and peer attachment in late childhood and early adolescence. *Journal of Early Adolescence, 25*, 223–249.

Parker, P. D., Lüdtke, O., Trautwein, U., & Roberts, B. W. (2012). Personality and relationship quality during the transition from high school to early adulthood. *Journal of Personality, 80*, 1061–1089.

Reitz, A. K., Asendorpf, J. B., & Motti-Stefanidi, F. (2015). When do immigrant adolescents feel personally discriminated against? Longitudinal effects of peer preference. *International Journal of Behavioral Development, 39*, 197–209.

Reitz, A. K., Motti-Stefanidi, F., & Asendorpf, J. B. (2014). Mastering developmental transitions in immigrant adolescents: The longitudinal interplay of family functioning, developmental and acculturative tasks. *Developmental Psychology, 50*(3), 754–765.

Reitz, A. K., Motti-Stefanidi, F., & Asendorpf, J. B. (2016). Me, us, and them: Testing sociometer theory in a socially diverse real-life context. *Journal of Personality and Social Psychology, 110*, 908–920.

Reitz, A. K. & Staudinger, U. M. (2016). Getting older, getting better? Towards understanding positive personality development across adulthood. In J. Specht (Ed.), *Personality development across the lifespan* (pp. 219–242). Amsterdam: Elsevier.

Reitz, A. K., Zimmermann, J., Hutteman, R., Specht, J., & Neyer, F. J. (2014). How peers make a difference: The role of peer groups and peer relationships in personality development. *European Journal of Personality, 28,* 279–288.

Richards, M. H., Crowe, P. A., Larson, R., & Swarr, A. (1998). Developmental patterns and gender differences in the experience of peer companionship during adolescence. *Child Development, 69,* 154–163.

Roberts, B. W., & Jackson, J. J. (2008). Sociogenomic personality psychology. *Journal of Personality, 76,* 1523–1544.

Roberts, B. W., Wood, D., & Smith, J. L. (2005). Evaluating Five Factor Theory and social investment perspectives on personality trait development. *Journal of Research in Personality, 39,* 166–184.

Sameroff, A. J. (1983). Developmental systems: Contexts and evolution. In W. Kessen (Ed.), *Handbook of child psychology. History, theory, and methods* (4th ed., Vol. 1, pp. 237–294). New York, NY: Wiley.

Sarkova, M., Bacikova-Sleskova, M., Geckova, A. M., Katreniakova, Z., van den Heuvel, W., & van Dijk, J. P. (2014). Adolescents' psychological well-being and self-esteem in the context of relationships at school. *Educational Research, 56,* 367–378.

Simpson, J. A., Collins, W., Tran, S., & Haydon, K. C. (2007). Attachment and the experience and expression of emotions in romantic relationships: A developmental perspective. *Journal of Personality and Social Psychology, 92,* 355–367.

Smith, J. A., McPherson, M., & Smith-Lovin, L. (2014). Social distance in the United States: Sex, race, religion, age, and education homophily among confidants, 1985 to 2004. *American Sociological Review, 79,* 432–456.

Soloski, K. L., Monk, J. K., & Durtschi, J. A. (2016). Trajectories of early binge drinking: A function of family cohesion and peer use. *Journal of Marital and Family Therapy, 42,* 76–90.

Spink, K. S., Crozier, A. J., & Robinson, B. (2013). Examining the relationship between descriptive norms and perceived effort in adolescent athletes: Effects of different reference groups. *Psychology of Sport and Exercise, 14,* 813–818.

Tajfel, H. (1978). *Differentiation between social groups: Studies in the social psychology of intergroup relations.* Oxford, England: Academic Press.

Taylor, J. (2006). Life events and peer substance use and their relation to substance use problems in college students. *Journal of Drug Education, 36,* 179–191.

Titzmann, P. F., & Silbereisen, R. K. (2009). Friendship homophily among ethnic German immigrants: A longitudinal comparison between recent and more experienced immigrant adolescents. *Journal of Family Psychology, 23,* 301–310.

Trinke, S. J., & Bartholomew, K. (1997). Hierarchies of attachment relationships in young adulthood. *Journal of Social and Personal Relationships, 14,* 603–625.

Turner, J. C., Hogg, M. A., Oakes, P. J., Reicher, S. D., & Wetherell, M. S. (1987). *Rediscovering the social group: A self-categorization theory.* Cambridge, MA: Basil Blackwell.

Urberg, K. A., Değirmencioğlu, S. M., & Pilgrim, C. (1997). Close friend and group influence on adolescent cigarette smoking and alcohol use. *Developmental Psychology, 33,* 834–844.

Wilkinson, R. B. (2010). Best friend attachment versus peer attachment in the prediction of adolescent psychological adjustment. *Journal of Adolescence, 33,* 709–717.

Windle, M. (2000). Parental, sibling, and peer influences on adolescent substance use and alcohol problems. *Applied Developmental Science, 4,* 98–110.

Wrzus, C., Hänel, M., Wagner, J., & Neyer, F. J. (2013). Social network changes and life events across the life span: A meta-analysis. *Psychological Bulletin, 139,* 53–80.

Zhang, L., & Zhang, W. (2008). Personal future planning in middle and late adolescence and its relation to adolescents' communication with parents and friends. *Acta Psychologica Sinica, 40,* 583–592.

Zimmermann, J., & Neyer, F. J. (2013). Do we become a different person when hitting the road? Personality development of sojourners. *Journal of Personality and Social Psychology, 105,* 515–530.

Zimmermann, J. & Neyer, F. J. (2017). Entwicklung und Mobilität im jungen Erwachsenenalter. In B. Kracke und P. Noack (Eds.), *Handbuch Entwicklungs- und Erziehungspsychologie.* Berlin: Springer.

Personality Development in Adolescence and Young Adulthood

Theo A. Klimstra, Jeroen Borghuis and Wiebke Bleidorn

The phrase 'personality development' would have looked like a *contradictio in terminis* to many researchers until approximately 30 years ago, as personality was widely believed to be a stable construct. In contrast, it is now widely acknowledged that there is much change in personality throughout the lifespan, with the most pronounced changes occurring during adolescence and young adulthood. This chapter focuses on these key periods of personality development, roughly spanning ages 12 to 40 years.

Personality is a broad concept and was originally defined as 'the dynamic organization within the individual of those psychophysical systems that determine his unique adjustments to his environment' (Allport, 1937, p. 48). This definition emphasized that personality is not static and thus may change, and therefore already pointed to the importance of studying personality *development*. In addition, the definition refers to personality as a configuration of attributes within a particular individual, and therefore points to the importance of studying how multiple characteristics develop together and how their configuration within an individual may change. Therefore, in this chapter, we will refer to changes in both single personality traits and in personality profiles.

A further consideration in studying personality is that there are different kinds of traits representing different levels and different functions in a broader personality system. Within such a system, dispositions encompassing a wide range of behaviors and cognitions, such as the Big Five personality traits, are usually considered the core of personality (e.g., Asendorpf and van Aken, 2003; McAdams and Olson, 2010; McCrae and Costa, 2008). However, personality also encompasses more process-like constructs like attitudes, goals, motives, and self-related constructs (e.g., narrative identity, self-esteem). In addition, Big Five trait domains are defined by more specific traits referred to as facets. For example, the trait domain neuroticism can be divided into facets of anxiety, angry hostility, depression, self-consciousness, impulsiveness, and vulnerability (McCrae et al., 2005). In the present chapter, the main focus will be on core characteristics, typically summarized in the Big Five personality trait domains, but we will briefly touch upon facet traits.

Our chapter is divided into four sections. In the first section, we will discuss developmental trends in personality traits by referring to findings regarding structural stability, rank-order stability, mean-level change, and individual-level change. The second section is focused on the correlates of personality development. We will distinguish broad mechanisms and narrow mechanisms in this section. The third section summarizes findings obtained with person-centered approaches (i.e., approaches focused on profile stability and typological approaches). Finally, the fourth section summarizes the states of research on adolescent and young adult development and provides potential future directions for this field of research.

DEVELOPMENTAL TRENDS IN PERSONALITY TRAITS FROM ADOLESCENCE THROUGH YOUNG ADULTHOOD

Structural Stability

A key consideration before studying developmental trends in any construct is whether the construct itself is relevant and valid for individuals of all ages included in your design. Much like it is useful to study crawling in infants, but not in adolescents, psychological constructs may lose or gain relevance. Constructs that lose direct relevance are definitely not meaningless for predicting future behavior, as certain characteristics may just change in the way they manifest themselves. To stick with the crawling example, individual differences in this behavior may predict individual differences in other abilities related to gross motor skills, such as running. Thus, there may be *heterotypic continuity*, in the sense that the same underlying asset (i.e., gross motor skills) may manifest itself differently.

This heterotypic continuity is also an issue in the study of personality traits from childhood through adolescence into adulthood, in the sense that stable individual differences are typically examined along temperamental dimensions in childhood and along personality traits in adulthood. This raises the question when one should stop studying temperament and start studying personality traits, and thus whether studying personality traits in adolescence is appropriate. Based on previous work in which the overlap between temperament and personality dimensions was examined (e.g., Caspi and Shiner, 2006; De Pauw et al., 2009), Soto and John (2014) developed an integrative model called the Little Six. This model adds an activity factor to the Big Five to provide a more encompassing view on important individual differences from childhood to late adolescence, thereby breaking the trend to only consider Big Five traits when studying personality trait development.

Soto and John (2014) also show that the meaning of traits may change with age. For example, they showed that conscientiousness was increasingly defined by socially responsible versus deceitful behavior. This finding points out that it is crucial to formally test for such shifts in meaning in the study of adolescent and young adult personality trait development. Such tests, referred to as measurement invariance tests, are increasingly often conducted (e.g., Lucas and Donnellan, 2011), but are still not common practice. Given that such tests were usually not conducted in studies that were summarized in influential meta-analyses (e.g., Roberts et al., 2006), much of what we appear to 'know' about personality trait development might not be entirely accurate. That is, what appear to be changes in levels of an entire trait domain might actually be due to changes in the mean-level scores of only some parts (i.e., items or facets) of that trait domain. The mean levels of other parts of that trait might remain the same or even decrease. Thus, we argue that testing for measurement invariance is crucial, especially in research on personality trait change focusing on developmental periods characterized by rapid changes in cognitive capacity and social skills. Such tests should feature prominently, and not be buried away in one sentence in the method section with results being 'available from the first author upon request' (e.g., Klimstra, Hale et al., 2012).

Rank-Order Stability

Rank-order stability refers to the maintenance of individuals' relative standing on a trait dimension within a population over time. Rank-order stability is commonly assessed by means of a test–retest correlation or a stability coefficient in a path or structural equation model. Previous research clearly shows that not all people change to the same extent and in the same direction. Therefore, rank-order stability of personality trait dimensions is by no means perfect. Although rank-order stability tends to decrease as intervals between assessments increase, there is even substantial rank-order stability over decades (Fraley and Roberts, 2005). This suggests that some portion of the between-person variance in personality traits is truly stable. Indeed, research has shown that some personality or temperament traits in childhood show small, positive correlations with personality traits in adulthood (Asendorpf et al., 2008; Block, 1993; Kagan and Moss, 1962; Shiner et al., 2003). In addition, research on lifespan personality trait development shows that 6-year rank-order stability of personality or temperament traits is moderately high in preschool years ($r \approx .50$), increases until middle adulthood ($r \approx .70$), and then plateaus (Anusic and Schimmack, 2016; Bazana and Stelmack, 2004; Briley and Tucker-Drob, 2014; Roberts and DelVecchio, 2000). The robust finding that trait stability increases from childhood through middle adulthood has been referred to as the cumulative continuity principle of personality development (Roberts and Mroczek, 2008).

However, the stability and change of personality traits varies across adolescence and young adulthood. Existing meta-analyses have aggregated rank-order stability findings across relatively broad age categories (e.g., ages 12 to 18), and therefore less is known about differences in rank-order stability across narrower age categories. Two studies that attempted to address this gap found different results with respect to stability and change in the one-year rank-order stability of Big Five traits in adolescence and young adulthood. One study found that rank-order stability increased throughout adolescence (Klimstra et al., 2009). However, another study found that rank-order stability only increased from early through middle adolescence, and remained stable in late adolescence and early adulthood (Borghuis et al., 2017).

A handful of studies have also examined rank-order stability in facets. A study using parent reports found that in early adolescence, rank-order stability was similar for facets and domains (De Fruyt et al., 2006). This result was more or less confirmed in more recent work, which found high rank-order stability of facets in mother-reports on children and adolescents, but did not compare these coefficients to those for domains (de Haan et al., 2017). One study examining a sample that was heterogeneous in terms of age, but also included young adults, found that rank-order stability was only slightly lower for facets than for trait domains (Bleidorn et al., 2009). A study specifically focused on young adult college students confirmed in two samples that rank-order stability of facets is indeed as high as rank-order stability of trait domains (Klimstra et al., 2016). In general, individual differences in personality facets seem to be about as stable as individual differences in personality trait domains.

Mechanisms Explaining Change in Rank-Order Stability

Relatively little is known about the exact mechanisms that drive age-graded increases in the rank-order stability of personality traits. Nevertheless, meta-analytic research has provided important hints about the nature of these mechanisms. First, Briley and Tucker-Drob (2014) conducted a meta-analysis of genetically informed longitudinal (mostly twin) studies to illuminate the environmental and genetic contributions to personality continuity across the lifespan. They found that both genetic and environmental influences on personality increase in stability with age. However, because the relative influence of genetic effects on personality traits has been found to decrease with age, the environmental contributions to stability were found to increase with age. Therefore, increasing rank-order stability of personality with age is largely accounted for by the increasingly stable environmental effects, rather than by the increasingly stable genetic effects (see also Bleidorn et al., 2014).

Second, a meta-analysis by Anusic and Schimmack (2016) focused on the extent to which personality traits, across the lifespan, are influenced by stable effects (i.e., all influences on personality traits that never change) and by changing effects (i.e., all influences on personality traits that change over time). Examples of the former are permanent internal biological influences and environmental experiences with permanent effects; examples of the latter are temporary effects of genes and social role transitions. Importantly, they found that the increase in the rank-order stability of personality traits was attributable to an increase in the relative influence of stable factors on personality, rather than to an increase in the stability of change factors. Taken together, these two meta-analyses suggest that the increasing stability of personality traits is driven by increasingly stable environmental influences on personality traits.

One mechanism that may drive increasing personality stability with age is increasing commitment to, and thus maintenance of, an identity (Roberts and Caspi, 2003; Roberts et al., 2008). Identity maintenance has been argued to stimulate personality stability because an identity provides clear reference points for making life decisions (Caspi et al., 2005), facilitates 'strategic' information selection and processing, resulting in the maintenance of consistent self-perceptions (Roberts and Caspi, 2003), and results in consistent role demands and social expectations (Roberts et al., 2008). This reasoning is consistent with identity theory, as defined by Erikson (1950, 1968) and Marcia (1966). However, despite a growing number of studies examining linkages between personality traits or types on the one hand and identity formation processes on the other hand (e.g., Hatano et al., 2017; Luyckx et al., 2014), the role of identity formation in predicting the *stability* of personality still awaits empirical scrutiny.

Mean-Level Change

Mean-level change refers to the change in the average trait levels of a population over time. Mean-level change is conceptually independent from rank-order change because rank orders can be perfectly maintained in groups that change on average and rank orders might be completely reordered in groups that do not change in their average trait level (Roberts et al., 2006).

Previous research has provided a clear picture of how mean levels of broad personality traits change. A meta-analysis found that, in young adulthood, individuals show significant mean-level increases in the Big Five traits agreeableness, emotional stability, and conscientiousness (Roberts et al., 2006). These mean-level increases have been referred to as the maturity principle of personality development (Roberts and Mroczek, 2008). That is because being agreeable, conscientious, and emotionally stable corresponds closely to definitions of maturity that emphasize functioning in society and social relationships, such as being liked, respected, and admired (Roberts and Mroczek, 2008; Roberts et al., 2008).

In contrast with the period of young adulthood, there is convincing evidence that, in adolescence, the mean levels of most Big Five trait domains tend to first decrease and then increase (i.e., U-shaped change). Specifically, both a recent meta-analysis (Denissen et al., 2013) and a large-scale cross-sectional study (Soto et al., 2011) found evidence for temporary mean-level decreases in conscientiousness, openness, extraversion, and emotional stability (among girls) in early adolescence, whereas they found evidence for mean-level increases in conscientiousness, emotional stability, and openness in late adolescence and early adulthood. In addition, though contrary to Denissen et al. (2013), Soto et al. (2011) also found evidence for U-shaped change in agreeableness.

These mean-level trends at the trait-domain level do not necessarily directly translate into findings at the facet level. That is, De Fruyt et al. (2006) showed that in early adolescence mean-level changes in facets belonging to the same domain (e.g., the self-confidence and anxiety facets of the neuroticism domain) did not always correspond. For example, mean levels of self-confidence did not change significantly whereas anxiety decreased. De Haan et al. (2017) showed that differences in mean-level changes between facets belonging to the same trait domain are typically not that large, but do seem to become larger as individuals grow older (i.e., enter middle adolescence). A large-scale cross-sectional study (Soto et al., 2011) had similar findings but, within the neuroticism domain, they did show that mean levels of anxiety in late adolescent females remained relatively stable whereas their mean levels of depression dropped. Thus, in adolescence there is only some evidence for different mean-level trends for facets belonging to the same domain.

Several studies on young adults examined mean-level age trends in cross-sectional studies (Jackson et al., 2009; McCrae et al., 2004; Soto et al., 2011). This research provided more evidence for diverging mean-level trends for facets belonging to the same domain. The most consistent patterns were found for extraversion and conscientiousness. Specifically, across different extraversion facets, the mean-level change was more pronounced for the facets of excitement seeking and positive emotions than for facets like activity and assertiveness. For conscientiousness, mean levels of dutifulness and self-discipline facets increased more than mean levels of orderliness-related facets. Longitudinal studies distinguishing facets in early adult samples (Klimstra et al., 2016; Soto and John, 2012) yielded relatively similar findings. Notably, Klimstra et al. (2016) included college samples from the US and Belgium and found subtle differences between those samples. In particular, students in the US changed toward a more laid-back and intellectually curious profile whereas Belgian students changed toward a more anxious profile. These findings may well be attributable to contextual differences in how competitive selection procedures are and how much value a particular college degree has for finding a job. Overall, the pattern of findings across studies suggests that considering facets in addition to broad trait domains may provide a few nuances that would be overlooked if only the domain level of personality were to be considered.

Individual-Level Change

Perhaps even more important is to note that the aforementioned research on personality trait change has been concerned more with describing mean-level trends of personality traits than with accounting for individual differences in development. This holds especially for the period of adolescence. Mean-level change coefficients summarize the average development in a population and can therefore not be used to make inferences about development at the individual level. Considering the individual

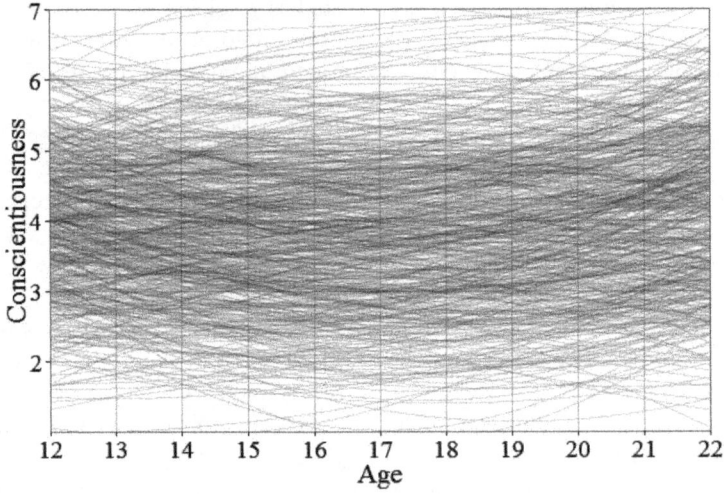

Figure 11.1 Graphical representation of the magnitude of individual differences in boys' personality trait change in conscientiousness; the regression curves represent development of individuals across age. Regression curves (N = 500) were drawn from a simulated multivariate normal distribution based on the parameter estimates of a latent growth curve model (N = 2,230).

Source: adapted from Borghuis et al. (2017)

level is important, as adolescents and young adults differ substantially with respect to their personality trajectories. As Figure 11.1 (adapted from Borghuis et al., 2017) illustrates with respect to boys' conscientiousness, some adolescents increase, some decrease, and others remain stable in their personality trait level. This suggests that mean-level trajectories do not always provide accurate descriptions for individuals' personality change. A deeper understanding of personality development requires moving beyond stability and change at the population level in order to understand and account for individual variation in developmental trajectories (Asendorpf, 1992; Lönnqvist et al., 2008; Roberts and Mroczek, 2008).

CORRELATES OF PERSONALITY TRAIT DEVELOPMENT

In examining predictors and correlates of individual differences in change, both broad and narrow mechanisms can be distinguished (cf. Klimstra et al., 2013a). We will first discuss and define these broad mechanisms, and then move to the more specific mechanisms.

Broad Mechanisms

Attempts at identifying broad predictors of personality change in adolescence and young adulthood have been guided by several theories and principles (for reviews, see Bleidorn, 2015; Specht et al., 2014). Two of these are particularly prominent, and these are five-factor theory (FFT, McCrae and Costa, 2008) and the social investment principle (Roberts et al., 2005). FFT posits that personality traits are mainly influenced by evolved, genetically controlled biological processes, and that life experiences play only a negligible role (unless these alter gene expression). The Social Investment Principle holds that social role transitions (e.g., marriage, becoming a parent, getting a 'real' job) do play a significant role in personality maturation, especially if one psychologically commits to a new social role.

In order to examine whether personality trait development is driven by broad mechanisms driving change in multiple traits or narrow mechanisms driving change in specific traits, several studies have addressed correlated change among personality traits (for a review, see Allemand and Martin, 2016). Research on this phenomenon covering adolescence and young adulthood (Klimstra et al., 2013a) found that there is indeed evidence for correlated change among specific pairs of Big Five traits. Specific pairs of traits that have been hypothesized to be affected by the same neurobiological system (i.e., the serotonergic or dopaminergic system) or same developmental principle (i.e., the social investment principle) produced the highest correlated change estimates. Especially, changes in extraversion and openness, which are the two traits that have been associated with the dopaminergic system (DeYoung et al., 2002), were strongly correlated with each other. Thus, there was some evidence for broad mechanisms affecting personality trait development. However, this approach may contribute to uncovering whether or not broad mechanisms are involved and may also provide hints regarding what these mechanisms are, but it does not actually *test* mechanisms triggering personality trait development.

One method that explicitly tests concrete broad mechanisms, especially those related to FFT, is longitudinal behavioral genetic research. Such studies can help to quantify the proportion of individual differences that are due to genetic and environmental influences. Reviews suggest that the relative influence of genetic influences on personality traits (i.e., heritability) decreases from childhood to old adulthood. By implication, this suggests that environmental influences on individual differences in personality traits increase with age (Bleidorn et al., 2014; Briley and Tucker-Drob, 2014). Yet, it remains a mostly unanswered question which genes and environmental factors matter (Turkheimer and Waldron, 2000; Vinkhuyzen et al., 2012). Despite this, Briley and Tucker-Drob (2014) have drawn the encouraging conclusion that a substantial amount of environmental variance is not attributable to random measurement error and is stable across time, and should therefore, in principle, be measurable.

Somewhat consistent with the propositions of FFT, several cross-cultural studies have found relatively similar mean-level personality changes across different cultures with different societal structures, different political systems, and different historical backgrounds (Bleidorn et al., 2013; McCrae and Terracciano, 2005). However, Bleidorn et al. (2013) also found substantial cultural differences in the timing and magnitude of mean-level age trends in the Big Five. Providing some evidence for the relevance of environmental influences, these cultural differences in personality change were related to cultural differences in the timing of social role transitions (e.g., graduation from school, marriage, parenthood). Thus, there appears to be evidence for both genetic effects and environmental effects on age-related differences in personality trait development (for a review, also see Bleidorn, 2015).

Although FFT and the social investment principle have also been used to explain mean-level changes in adolescent personality traits, little is known about the mechanisms that drive these changes. Soto and Tackett (2015) speculated that the temporal dips in personality maturity (as defined by conscientiousness, agreeableness, and emotional stability) during early adolescence are related to the rapid and significant biological, psychological, and social changes that characterize this period. Other possible reasons for the U-shaped mean-level changes are that adolescents temporarily adhere to less mature peer norms (Moffitt, 1993) and that they experience initial difficulties in adjusting to increasingly mature expectations (Denissen et al., 2013).

Narrow Mechanisms: Correlates Within the Broader Personality Trait System

Instead of broad mechanisms that are hypothesized to affect multiple traits, narrow mechanisms are supposed to affect single traits. Moreover, narrower mechanisms do not refer to broad biological or sociological processes, but rather to specific variables such as relationship satisfaction, self-esteem, or anxiety symptoms. When examining narrow mechanisms of personality trait change, one direction is to consider other variables within the broader personality system. Several theories emphasize the importance of this. For example, the social investment principle, which is often interpreted as predicting that it is 'just' transitions into social roles of adult life that trigger personality trait change, emphasizes the importance of committing to these social roles. The commitment processes referred to for the social investment principle are identical to the commitment processes that feature in Erikson's (1950, 1968) developmental theory (Lodi-Smith and Roberts, 2007). Hence, such processes feature in models of identity formation (e.g., Crocetti et al., 2008; Luyckx et al., 2008). These models also emphasize the importance of exploration processes. The social investment principle would predict that the aforementioned identity processes, but especially commitment, would predict changes in personality traits.

FFT (McCrae and Costa, 2008) and the core versus surface trait model (Asendorpf and van Aken, 2003) emphasize a distinction between basic tendencies (i.e., Big Five personality traits) and more specific 'characteristic' adaptations such as identity formation processes. This model would predict that Big Five traits and identity processes are associated, and that the effects of Big Five traits on identity processes are larger than those in the inverse direction.

McAdams' multilayered model (e.g., McAdams and Olson, 2010) presents a sort of compromise between the previous standpoint regarding directionality of effects between identity processes and personality traits. That is, infant and child behavior is thought to be largely driven by basic tendencies (i.e., personality traits). In late childhood, motivations and goals are added to the equation, and behavior becomes more goal-directed. From late adolescence onwards, individuals start behaving in a way that is in line with the way they perceive themselves. Thus, their (narrative) identity starts to play an important role in their behavior. At first, these self-views are largely built upon the way individuals typically behaved up to that point, making traits as well as goals and motivations better predictors of identity at that point. Once identities become solidified, they also start to affect traits. Typically, this should happen from young adulthood onwards. Hence, McAdams would predict that personality traits are good predictors of identity processes throughout development, whereas identity processes only become better predictors of personality traits in young adulthood.

Longitudinal research on the linkages of identity formation processes with personality traits is rather scarce. Overall, these studies suggest that personality traits are often better predictors of identity processes than the other way around (e.g., Luyckx et al., 2014). In adolescence, identity processes rarely predict changes in personality traits (Luyckx et al., 2014), but this is more common in young adults (Luyckx et al., 2006), confirming McAdams' theorizing. However, recent research on Japanese early and middle adolescents questions this conclusion by demonstrating bidirectional identity–personality trait linkages from early adolescence onwards (Hatano et al., 2017). This latter study also considered personality facets underlying broader trait domains and showed that facets belonging to the same trait domain were often differentially associated with identity processes.

Other studies provided more specificity on the identity side by considering life-domain-specific identity processes. These studies also found few effects of these processes on personality traits, but the few effects of identity on personality that were found tended to be in line with the social investment principle. That is, educational and relational commitment predicted relative increases in emotional stability and conscientiousness, respectively (Klimstra, Luyckx et al., 2012; Kimstra et al., 2013b).

Overall, these studies show that linkages between identity processes and personality traits are complex. There appears to be some evidence for each of the theoretical perspectives on these linkages, but none of the evidence is overwhelming. Yet, the development of identity processes seems to be associated with the development of adolescent and young adult personality traits.

Another variable in the self-system that has been associated with personality trait development is self-esteem. Self-esteem reflects an overall evaluation of one's worth and positive versus negative feelings about the self (e.g., Orth et al., 2008). Large-scale cross-sectional studies research in young adults (e.g., Erdle et al., 2009; Robins et al., 2001b, 2001c) and adolescents (e.g., Mlacic et al., 2007; Vaszonyi et al., 2015) generally found strong negative associations of self-esteem with extraversion and conscientiousness, and strong negative associations with neuroticism. In addition to self-esteem levels, self-esteem stability is also associated with Big Five personality trait domains in young adulthood. Especially high emotional stability, agreeableness, and conscientiousness are associated with high self-esteem stability (Zeigler-Hill et al., 2015). In fact, young adults who had a high level of self-esteem and who were also stable had the most optimal personality profile, characterized by high emotional stability, agreeableness, and conscientiousness. Individuals with stable low self-esteem had low levels of openness. This suggests that considering aspects of self-esteem beyond the level (e.g., also considering stability of self-esteem) can produce further insights into its relation with personality trait domains. In addition, longitudinal research can also provide additional insight in the personality trait–self-esteem link.

There are few longitudinal studies examining linkages between personality traits and self-esteem. A study on adolescents showed that neuroticism mattered in how much not meeting expectancies regarding peer acceptance affected self-esteem development (Poorthuis et al., 2014). That is, adolescents who were neurotic and saw their expectancies regarding peer acceptance not being met experienced a decrease in self-esteem. Furthermore, the importance of adolescent personality development was underscored, as a more favorable personality profile in adolescence was predictive of higher self-esteem later in adulthood (Blatný et al., 2015).

Research on young adults (Klimstra et al., 2016; Lönnqvist et al., 2009; Wagner et al., 2013) provides some evidence for high levels of favorable personality traits (especially emotional stability) predicting high levels of, or even increases in, self-esteem. However, another study (Erol and Orth, 2011) found that Big Five traits were related to self-esteem concurrently but did not predict change in self-esteem. Thus, the predictive role of personality traits for the development of self-esteem is still somewhat unclear. Furthermore, a recent study showed that self-esteem can also affect the development of personality traits (Klimstra et al., 2016), as high self-esteem predicted decreases in facets of neuroticism in two independent samples.

These studies show that the development of self-related processes and core personality trait domains are closely intertwined. However, the development of personality domains is obviously also linked to the development of variables that are less directly related to the self.

Narrow Mechanisms: Correlates Outside of the Personality System

Adolescent and young adult personality development affects, and is affected by, changes in a wide range of other phenomena. Especially, interpersonal relationships, psychopathology symptoms, and academic experiences have received the attention of various researchers.

Studies that consider interpersonal relationships in adolescence examined associations with parenting. In a study covering childhood and adolescence, parenting had few effects on the child's personality (van den Akker et al., 2014). The child's personality did have more of an effect on parenting, with agreeableness and openness eliciting positive parenting, whereas extraversion seemed a mixed blessing. That is, extraversion triggered warm parenting, but also more overreactivity from parents, possibly because extraverted children are charming yet expressive. Their expressiveness may cause more conflicts with parents. Most convincing was the evidence for parallel development between parenting and personality, with increases in agreeableness, conscientiousness, and openness running parallel with increased positive parenting. Thus, it is somewhat unclear what the directionality between parenting and personality is, but it is clear that the two are intertwined.

The quality of adolescent relationships with their family members has been somewhat more extensively studied in association with personality. An extensive study examining entire families across time showed that, especially, agreeableness was of major importance in this regard. That is, more agreeable individuals perceived more support from others, and others also perceived more support from them (Branje et al., 2004). However, the development of other Big Five personality traits was also somewhat associated with changes in support. A study that focused on the relative contributions of adolescents' and parents' personalities to the quality of their mutual relationship showed that the older the adolescents got, the more the quality of the relationship was determined by their personality instead of the parents' (Denissen et al., 2009). A study examining peer support in addition to parental support suggested that conscientiousness was the only trait domain that prospectively predicted support from both the father and the mother (Asendorpf and van Aken, 2003). However, conscientiousness did not predict peer support (but see Jensen-Campbell and Malcolm, 2007). For that, especially, extraversion and agreeableness seemed important trait domains (Asendorpf and van Aken, 2003; Jensen-Campbell et al., 2002).

Toward late adolescence and into young adulthood, romantic relationships become more important and more common. Personality traits are known to predict relationship development (e.g., Ahmetoglu et al., 2010; Lehnart and Neyer, 2006), including who is more likely to get into a relationship in the first place (e.g., Neyer and Lehnart, 2007). That is, more emotionally stable, extraverted, and conscientiousness young adults seemed more likely to end up in a relationship. Once in a relationship, emotional stability, agreeableness, and conscientiousness are associated with better relationship quality. Romantic relationships – especially the more serious and enduring ones – also have an effect on personality development (e.g., Lehnart et al., 2010; Neyer and Asendorpf, 2001; Robins et al., 2002). That is, entering a relationship has been most clearly associated with increases in emotional stability and conscientiousness. Thus, personality traits affect relationships, but relationship experiences also have a considerable effect on personality trait development (Mund and Neyer, 2014).

Another potential major influence on personality development is experiences related to psychopathology. The linkages between personality traits and psychopathology are complex and can take many shapes (Durbin and Hicks, 2014), but there certainly are strong associations. Research on adolescents has suggested that psychopathology symptoms have an effect on, and are affected by, personality trait development (Klimstra et al., 2010a). However, these associations may be due to psychopathology symptoms being manifestations of very high, or very low, scores on particular personality traits (De Bolle et al., 2012). In this regard, especially, emotional stability and extraversion are consistently associated with internalizing symptoms (e.g., depressive and anxiety symptoms), whereas emotional stability and agreeableness are the most consistently associated with adolescent externalizing symptoms (e.g., aggression, delinquency, substance abuse). In young adulthood, the pattern of associations is pretty much the same (Mezquita et al., 2015). However, it should be noted that these linkages may be slightly different depending on the particular kind of type of psychopathology that is examined within the broader internalizing and externalizing domains (Klimstra et al., 2014). In sum, it remains a question whether personality and psychopathology should be seen as separate constructs, but the development of the two is clearly interconnected.

Academic experiences are also strongly associated with personality trait development. A study by Bleidorn (2012) suggested that personality trait development is triggered by nearing the transition from high school to college, probably mostly due to students preparing for their high school exams. That is, mean levels of conscientiousness clearly increased in the final year of high school, whereas no such changes were found in the year before that. Moreover, these increases in conscientiousness were associated with increases in academic achievement behavior. Somewhat related to this are findings suggesting that education commitment predicts increases in emotional stability (Klimstra, Luyckx et al., 2012). However, it should be noted that there were many more effects of personality traits on changes in educational commitment. Finally, adjustment to one's educational institution also seems to matter for personality maturation, as a recent study (Klimstra et al., 2016) found that academic and social adjustment to college predicted relative increases in several personality trait domains and facets. Academic adjustment predicted increases in emotional stability, agreeableness, and conscientiousness, whereas social adjustment predicted increases in extraversion and conscientiousness. Thus, attitudes and affective experience toward education may trigger personality maturation.

Actual academic performance (e.g., Grade Point Average; GPA) has rarely been considered as a predictor of personality development. We are aware of only one study examining such an effect. This study showed that GPA had no effect on the differential stability of personality traits in adolescence (Pullmann et al., 2006). More research is needed to confirm whether or not academic performance can affect personality trait development.

TRUE PERSONALITY DEVELOPMENT: TAKING A PERSON-CENTERED APPROACH

The aforementioned research on personality development focused on trait domains, or on the facets underlying these domains. However, personality refers to a dynamic organization of traits within an individual (cf. Allport, 1937). The study of personality development should therefore also focus on changes in the configuration of traits, also referred to as profiles. To examine development at the profile-level, one can examine profile stability or examine change from a typological perspective on personality. In both approaches, the configuration of variables within an individual is the study object, which is why these are referred to as person-centered approaches.

Profile Stability

Profile stability provides information on the stability of a constellation of traits for every single person in a research sample. To assess profile stability, one computes the within-individual consistency of the mean scores on personality traits. It is possible, for example, that a person is more conscientious than agreeable, more agreeable than open to experience, more open to experience than emotionally stable, and more emotionally stable than extraverted. The extent to which this pattern of trait scores of this person remains the same across time indicates that person's profile stability (e.g., Furr, 2008). Thus, profile stability is about the extent to which, for example, the tidy, adventurous, and friendly person is still like that at a later point in time.

The calculation of profile stability for every person within a research sample is done by correlating the individual's set of personality trait scores at one time point with that same person's set of personality trait scores at the next time point. Every individual gets a stability score. Therefore, this profile stability score has a sample mean. Using this approach, relatively high profile stability has been demonstrated in early adolescents (De Fruyt et al., 2006). Using data on multiple measurement occasions (i.e., five), and therefore multiple time lags (i.e., four), Klimstra et al. (2009) were able to demonstrate that personality profile stability increased substantially from early to late adolescence. Other studies (Donnellan et al., 2007; Roberts et al., 2001; Robins et al., 2001a) have shown that profile stability remains high in young adulthood.

High profile stability has been linked to more desirable personality traits and well-being in several studies (e.g., Donnellan et al., 2007; Lönnqvist et al., 2008; Roberts et al., 2001), and it should therefore be indicative of positive adjustment. However, profile stability coefficients suffer from conceptual and statistical problems arising from the confounding effect of profile normativeness. That is, profile stability might not only arise from people's tendency to retain their idiosyncratic, distinctive qualities over time, but could also arise from their tendency to consistently resemble the normative personality profile (e.g., Furr, 2008). When these two different sources of consistency are disentangled from each other, it turns out that it is not the stability of the distinctive qualities of one's profile that drives the association with adjustment, but mainly the similarity of one's profile to the norm (i.e., average) in a sample (Klimstra et al., 2010c). Thus, individuals with a stable profile are not necessarily the better-adjusted ones. Instead, the individuals who are more similar to the average person in the sample appear to be better adjusted.

Profile stability is one way to approach personality development from a person-centered perspective, but it has its limitations. The main limitation is that it remains unclear what exactly remains stable and what changes in an individual's profile (cf. Bleidorn et al., 2012). To obtain greater insight into what changes about personality profiles, and to answer questions about whether the general direction of development is favorable or not, typological approaches are needed.

Typological Approaches

The study of personality types can be more or less traced back to ancient Greece and China, but the most relevant to the contemporary view on personality types is inspired by the work that Block and Block started in the 1970s (Block, 1971; Block and Block, 1980). Block (1971) initially identified separate typologies for men and women using a Q-sorting procedure. These typologies were actually development trajectories, as data on multiple measurement occasions were used. From the early 1980s onwards, the focus shifted to three replicable types that were derived on one measurement occasion and were distinguished on the temperamental traits of ego-control (comparable to impulse control) and ego-resiliency (the ability to adapt one's level of ego-control to fit the environmental demands). Specifically, Block and Block (1980) distinguished Resilients (high ego-resiliency, flexible levels of ego-control), Undercontrollers (low ego-resiliency, low ego-control), and Overcontrollers (low ego-resiliency, high ego-control). These types have distinguishable Big Five profiles (e.g., Asendorpf and van Aken, 1999; Robins et al., 1996). Resilients have high levels of all Big Five traits if emotional stability is considered instead of its counterpart neuroticism. Undercontrollers are mostly distinguishable by their particularly low levels of agreeableness and conscientiousness, coupled with high extraversion. Overcontrollers do have high levels of agreeableness and conscientiousness, but are low on extraversion and emotional stability.

Several studies used these types to examine personality development in adolescence. Somewhat older studies (van Aken and Dubas, 2004; Akse et al., 2007) found moderate stability of type membership, with about 50% of adolescents remaining in the same personality type across time. This is partly due to the analysis technique (i.e., cluster analysis) used in these studies. Cluster analysis does not account for measurement error or classification inaccuracy. This classification inaccuracy is an important issue, since personality types should not be viewed as a fully categorical variable, such as sex. Instead, they are best viewed as 'fuzzy' categories with somewhat unclear boundaries, or zones of classification uncertainty (Asendorpf et al., 2001). That is, some individuals fall almost perfectly in between being, for example, a Resilient or an Overcontroller. With contemporary techniques to create types, such as latent profile analysis, there are several options to account for this classification inaccuracy (e.g., Vermunt, 2010). Hence, studies using these techniques find much higher stability of personality type membership, with over 70% being classified in the same type across time (Meeus et al., 2011). If adolescents do change from one type to another, they tend to change from the Over- or Undercontroller types to the Resilient type. Specht et al. (2014) mainly found evidence for stability in personality type membership in young adulthood. Only one transition from one type to another occurred more often than would be expected by chance: the transition from Undercontroller to Resilient. This transition pattern and the transition patterns found in other person-centered studies are thus in line with the maturity principle, which suggests that individuals, on average, become more agreeable, conscientious, and emotionally stable (e.g., Klimstra et al., 2009; Roberts et al., 2001).

Studying transitions between types is only one way to approach personality development from a typological perspective. Another way is to use clustering techniques that take development into account when assigning individuals to a certain class. This technique was used in Block's (1971) groundbreaking study on personality development. He distinguished developmental trajectories of personality from junior high school into adulthood. Five male and six female trajectories were distinguished. These were described along a large number of attributes obtained by using a q-sort procedure, and a description of these types would therefore be too much for the purpose of this chapter. The key message obtained from the Block (1971) study is that individuals not only differ remarkably in their personality in junior high school, but also in their developmental trajectory thereafter. To give one example, the belated adjusters Block (1971) identified ended up being (almost) as adjusted as the ego resilients, even though they experienced much more turbulence in adolescence. This provides evidence for a developmental phenomenon referred to as equifinality (i.e., ending up in the same way from a different starting point; Cicchetti and Rogosch, 1996). More recently, Morizot and Le Blanc (2005) used a similar technique (i.e., longitudinal cluster analysis) to distinguish developmental trajectories from middle adolescence into adulthood. A key finding of this study was that large individual differences in extraversion may come into existence as individuals (i.e., men) enter young adulthood, providing evidence for multifinality (starting at approximately the same point but ending up at different points; Cicchetti and Rogosch, 1996).

This shows the potential of longitudinal clustering techniques to capture important developmental phenomena.

More recent studies use techniques like Latent Class Growth analysis and General Mixture Modeling (e.g., Nagin, 2005) to provide a more advanced spin on Block's (1971) classification procedure. Using such procedures, Resilients, Undercontrollers, and Overcontrollers have been replicated as developmental trajectories of personality from childhood into adolescence (de Haan et al., 2013), from early to middle adolescence (Klimstra et al., 2010b), from middle to late adolescence (Luyckx et al., 2014), and from early to late adolescence (Branje et al., 2010). Across studies, these three types remained distinguishable from each other across time but, especially in the study by de Haan et al. (2013), between-type differences on particular traits became larger (for conscientiousness) or smaller (especially for agreeableness). Overall, these studies clearly show the potential for using techniques to classify individuals based on developmental trends in multiple traits simultaneously. Such procedures are more in line with the way personality was originally defined than studies distinguishing different developmental trajectories on single personality traits (e.g., Durbin et al., 2016; Johnson et al., 2007). However, the latter studies are useful for visualizing and quantifying hetereogeneity in development.

SUMMARY AND FUTURE DIRECTIONS

In this chapter, we reviewed research on personality development in adolescence and young adulthood. A large number of cross-sectional and longitudinal studies have provided convincing evidence that personality traits undergo important changes during the period of adolescence and early adulthood. We know now that rank-order stability increases as individuals grow older, that mean levels of personality traits typically increase, and that individuals grow toward a more mature personality profile. Yet, there are important individual differences in the amount of change and stability of personality. We still know little about the conditions, correlates, and consequences of these individual differences. Below, we provide some suggestions regarding future directions that could help to fill this relative gap of knowledge.

A first suggestion is to study personality development in an even more detailed manner. We already reviewed some literature on personality facets underlying broader trait domains, with, for example, depression and anxiety underlying the domain neuroticism. Recently, evidence has been found for the validity of traits that are even more specific than facets. These traits are called nuances (Mõttus et al., 2017). Usually measured with few or single items, nuances represent one of the lowest levels in personality and are much closer to actual behavior than trait domains are. Examples of such nuances are liking parties with many people, making a detailed plan before going on holiday, or liking loud music. The idea that personality traits are hierarchically ordered, and that traits further down than the facet level in the trait hierarchy are also important, is not new (e.g., Eysenck, 1990). Yet, research on personality development tends to overlook the nuance level. It could be that changes at the trait-domain level can be traced back to changes (much) lower in the trait hierarchy. Future research considering changes in all levels of the trait hierarchy simultaneously may eventually teach us much about how personality trait development actually comes about.

A second suggestion concerns implementing measurements at various timescales. There is growing consideration of the state level in contemporary models of personality (Fleeson and Jayawickreme, 2015). Such personality states refer to patterns of thinking, feeling, and behaving at a particular moment. Therefore, these states can be measured several times a week or even several times a day. Due to the widespread availability of smartphones, researchers can now ask participants to report either actively (by prompting individuals to report on their behavior, feelings, or thoughts) or passively (by recording their behavior) on their personality states (Wilson et al., 2017). Considering traits and states in one longitudinal design will eventually allow us to trace back the origins of personality development to changing patterns of daily activity.

A third, broader, point is that much of the research that claims to examine personality development is actually examining personality *trait* development. Studying traits in isolation can be useful, but to gain a better understanding of true personality development, the configuration of traits within particular individuals and changes herein need to be studied over time. Studies examining changes in personality trait profiles across time are by far outnumbered by studies examining change in a trait-by-trait fashion (for exceptions, see for example, Meeus et al., 2011 and Specht et al., 2014). Moreover, research examining longitudinal associations of changes in trait profiles with changes in other variables is scarce. Thus, little is known about the antecedents, correlates, and effects of changes in personality types.

Among the reasons why personality types are underexamined are concerns regarding their replicability and their predictive power (Costa et al., 2002). Regarding replicability, it should be noted that the literature suggests that there are usually at least three types that appear (i.e., Resilients, Undercontrollers, and Overcontrollers) but that sometimes other types are found too (cf., Chapman and Goldberg, 2011). Note that this is partly inherent to the techniques that are used nowadays to identify types. Such techniques (e.g., Latent Profile Analysis) are exploratory in nature and (perhaps therefore) sensitive to the peculiarities of each sample. Thus, different types can be found for several reasons, including method effects (e.g., using self-reports instead of peer-reports, or the other way around), examining a particular part of the population (e.g., only including the higher end of the distribution on conscientiousness as a result of focusing on the higher educated), or using a measure that operationalizes Big Five trait domains in a slightly different manner when compared to the measures that were used in other studies that did find Resilients, Undercontrollers, and Overcontrollers. One way to proceed would be to use latent profile analysis and not get too hung up on replicating the exact three types (and only these types) all the time. Latent profile analysis comes with an additional advantage, as the results of these analyses no longer have to be used in a fully categorical manner. Individuals get relative class assignment, which means that they can, for example, be classified as having a 40% chance of being Resilient and a 60% chance of being an Overcontroller. These chances can be taken into account in follow-up analyses (e.g., Vermunt, 2010), thereby accounting for the fact that types may be fuzzy instead of truly categorical (Asendorpf et al., 2001). Moreover, this approach potentially addresses the issue of the limited predictive power that is inherent to fully categorical approaches when compared to continuous traits (cf. Asendorpf and Denissen, 2006). Specifically, a recent study using Latent Profile Analysis found clear evidence for an increase in explained variance in outcome variables if relative classification (i.e., classification probabilities) instead of absolute classification (i.e., using a classic categorical distinction) was used (Hadiwijaya et al., 2015). Thus, new data-analytical advancements have opened the door for the possible resurrection of psychological types, such as personality types.

Fourth, much of the work that has been done concerning personality development has relied on quantitative data. To attain a better understanding on the actual processes and experiences that go along with personality development, it would be useful to complement this quantitative data more often with qualitative data. So far, the narrative identity research tradition has done the best job in supplementing quantitative data on personality trait development with qualitative data (for an illustration, see Pals, 2006). However, there appears to be no published research yet on adolescents or young adults that includes multiple measurement occasions of narrative accounts and personality traits. Such research likely provides important insights into how personality development comes about and should therefore be prioritized.

We only provided four possible future directions for the study of adolescent and young adult personality development, but there obviously are many more possible directions. Overall, this chapter shows that our knowledge of personality development has rapidly expanded over the past 15 to 20 years. We know much more about the direction of personality development and individual differences around the general patterns, while our insight into the possible mechanisms, predictors, and consequences of personality development is also growing. Together with the many available possible future directions, this suggests that research on adolescent and young adult personality development is thriving and will continue to thrive.

REFERENCES

Ahmetoglu, G., Swami, V., & Chamorro-Premuzic, T. (2010). The relationship between dimensions of love, personality, and relationship length. *Archives of Sexual Behavior, 39*, 1181–1190.

Akse, J., Hale, W. W., III, Engels, R. C. M. E., Raaijmakers, Q. A. W., & Meeus, W. H. J. (2007). Stability and change in personality type membership and anxiety in adolescence. *Journal of Adolescence, 30*, 813–834.

Allemand, M., & Martin, M. (2016). On correlated change in personality. *European Psychologist, 21*, 237–253.

Allport, G. W. (1937). *Personality: A psychological interpretation*. New York, NY: Holt, Rinehart, & Winston.

Anusic, I., & Schimmack, U. (2016). Stability and change of personality traits, self-esteem, and well-being: Introducing the meta-analytic stability and change model of retest correlations. *Journal of Personality and Social Psychology, 110*, 766–781.

Asendorpf, J. B. (1992). Beyond stability: Predicting inter-individual differences in intra-individual change. *European Journal of Personality, 6*, 103–117.

Asendorpf, J. B., Borkenau, P., Ostendorf, F., & van Aken, M. A. G. (2001). Carving personality description at its joints: Confirmation of three replicable personality prototypes for both children and adults. *European Journal of Personality, 15*, 169–198.

Asendorpf, J. B., & Denissen, J. J. A. (2006). Predictive validity of personality types versus personality dimensions from early childhood to adulthood: Implications for the distinction between core and surface traits. *Merrill-Palmer Quarterly, 52*, 486–513.

Asendorpf, J. B., Denissen, J. J. A., & van Aken, M. A. G. (2008). Inhibited and aggressive preschool children at 23 years of age: Personality and social transitions into adulthood. *Developmental Psychology, 44*, 997–1011.

Asendorpf, J. B., & van Aken, M. A. G. (1999). Resilient, overcontrolled and undercontrolled personality prototypes in childhood: Replicability, predictive power, and the trait-type issue. *Journal of Personality and Social Psychology, 77*, 815–832.

Asendorpf, J. B., & van Aken, M. A. G. (2003). Personality–relationship transaction in adolescence: Core versus surface personality characteristics. *Journal of Personality, 71*, 629–666.

Bazana, P. G., & Stelmack, R. M. (2004). Stability of personality across the life span: A meta-analysis. In R. M. Stelmack (Ed.), *On the psychobiology of personality* (pp. 113–144). New York, NY: Elsevier.

Blatný, M., Millová, K., Jelínek, M., & Osecká, T. (2015). Personality predictors of succesful development: Toddler temperament and adolescent personality traits predict well-being and career stability in middle adulthood. *PLoS ONE, 10*, e0126032.

Bleidorn, W. (2012). Hitting the road to adulthood: Short-term personality development during a major life transition. *Personality and Social Psychology Bulletin, 38*, 1594–1608.

Bleidorn, W. (2015). What accounts for personality maturation in early adulthood? *Current Directions in Psychological Science, 24,* 245–252.

Bleidorn, W., Kandler, C., & Caspi, A. (2014). The behavioural genetics of personality development in adulthood: Classic, contemporary, and future trends. *European Journal of Personality, 28,* 244–255.

Bleidorn, W., Kandler, C., Riemann, R., Angleitner, A., & Spinath, F. M. (2009). Patterns and sources of adult personality development: Growth curve analyses of the NEO-PI-R scales in a longitudinal twin study. *Journal of Personality and Social Psychology, 97,* 142–155.

Bleidorn, W., Kandler, C., Riemann, R., Angleitner, A., & Spinath, F. M. (2012). Genetic and environmental influences on personality profile stability: Unraveling the normativeness problem. *Journal of Personality, 80,* 1029–1060.

Bleidorn, W., Klimstra, T. A., Denissen, J. J. A., Rentfrow, P. J., Potter, J., & Gosling, S. D. (2013). Personality maturation around the world: A cross-cultural examination of social-investment theory. *Psychological Science, 24,* 2530–2540.

Block, J. (1971). *Lives through time.* Berkeley, CA: Bancroft Books.

Block, J. (1993). Studying personality the long way. In D. C. Funder, R. D. Parke, C. Tomlinson-Keasey, & K. Widaman (Eds.), *Studying lives through time: Personality and development* (pp. 9–41). Washington, DC: American Psychological Association.

Block, J. H., & Block, J. (1980). The role of ego-control and ego-resiliency in the organization of behavior. In W. A. Collins (Ed.), *Development of cognition, affect, and social relations* (Vol. 13, pp. 39–101). Hillsdale, NJ: Erlbaum.

Borghuis, J., Denissen, J. J. A., Oberski, D., Sijtsma, K., Meeus, W. H. J., Branje, S. J. T., ... Bleidorn, W. (2017). Big Five personality stability, change, and codevelopment across adolescence and early adulthood. *Journal of Personality and Social Psychology, 113,* 641–657.

Branje, S. J. T., Hale, W. W. H., III, Frijns, T., & Meeus, W. H. J. (2010). Longitudinal associations between perceived parent–child relationship quality and depressive symptoms in adolescence. *Journal of Abnormal Child Psychology, 38,* 751–763.

Branje, S. J. T., van Lieshout, C. F. M., & van Aken, M. A. G. (2004). Relations between Big Five personality characteristics and perceived support in adolescents' families. *Journal of Personality and Social Psychology, 86,* 615–628.

Briley, D. A., & Tucker-Drob, E. M. (2014). Genetic and environmental continuity in personality development: A meta-analysis. *Psychological Bulletin, 140,* 1303–1331.

Caspi, A., Roberts, B. W., & Shiner, R. L. (2005). Personality development: Stability and change. *Annual Review of Psychology, 56,* 453–484.

Caspi, A., & Shiner, R. L. (2006). Personality development. In W. Damon, R. Lerner, & N. Eisenberg (Eds.), *Handbook of child psychology: Vol. 3. Social, emotional, and personality development* (6th ed., pp. 300–364). New York, NY: Wiley.

Chapman, B. P., & Goldberg, L. R. (2011). Replicability and 40-year predictive power of childhood ARC types. *Journal of Personality and Social Psychology, 101,* 593–606.

Cicchetti, D., & Rogosch, F. A. (1996). Equifinality and multifinality in developmental psychopathology. *Development and Psychopathology, 8,* 597–600.

Costa, P. T., Jr., Herbst, J. H., McCrae, R. R., Samuels, J., & Ozer, D. J. (2002). The replicability and utility of three personality types. *European Journal of Personality, 16,* S73–S87.

Crocetti, E., Rubini, M., & Meeus, W. H. J. (2008). Capturing the dynamics of identity formation in various ethnic groups: Development and validation of a three-dimensional model. *Journal of Adolescence, 31,* 207–222.

De Bolle, M., Beyers, W., De Clercq, B., & De Fruyt, F. (2012). General personality and psychopathology in referred and nonreferred children and adolescents: An investigation of continuity, pathoplasty, and complication models. *Journal of Abnormal Psychology, 121,* 958–970.

De Fruyt, F., Bartels, M., Van Leeuwen, K. G., De Clercq, B., Decuyper, M., & Mervielde, I. (2006). Five types of personality continuity in childhood and adolescence. *Journal of Personality and Social Psychology, 91,* 538–552.

de Haan, A. D., Deković, M., van den Akker, A. L., Stoltz, S. E. M. J., & Prinzie, P. (2013). Developmental personality types from childhood to adolescence: Associations with

parenting and adjustment. *Child Development*, *84*, 2015–2030.
de Haan, A. D., De Pauw, S. S. W., van den Akker, A. L., & Prinzie, P. (2017). Long-term developmental changes in children's lower-order Big Five personality facets. *Journal of Personality*, *85*, 616–631.
De Pauw, S. W., Mervielde, I., & Van Leeuwen, K. G. (2009). How are traits related to problem behavior in preschoolers? Similarities and contrasts between temperament and personality. *Journal of Abnormal Child Psychology*, *37*, 309–325.
Denissen, J. J. A., van Aken, M. A. G., & Dubas, J. S. (2009). It takes two to tango: How parents' and adolescents' personalities link to the quality of their mutual relationship. *Developmental Psychology*, *45*, 928–941.
Denissen, J. J. A., van Aken, M. A. G., Penke, L., & Wood, D. (2013). Self-regulation underlies temperament and personality: An integrative developmental framework. *Child Development Perspectives*, *7*, 255–260.
DeYoung, C. G., Peterson, J. B., & Higgins, D. M. (2002). Higher-order factors of the Big Five predict conformity: Are there neuroses of health? *Personality and Individual Differences*, *33*, 533–552.
Donnellan, M. B., Conger, R. D., & Burzette, R. G. (2007). Personality development from late adolescence to young adulthood: Differential stability, normative maturity, and evidence for the maturity-stability hypothesis. *Journal of Personality*, *75*, 237–263.
Durbin, C. E., & Hicks, B. M. (2014). Personality and psychopathology: A stagnant field in need of development. *European Journal of Personality*, *28*, 362–386.
Durbin, C. E., Hicks, B. M., Blonigen, D. M., Johnson, W., Iacono, W. G., & McGue, M. (2016). Personality trait change across late childhood to young adulthood: Evidence for nonlinearity and sex differences in change. *European Journal of Personality*, *30*, 31–44.
Erdle, S., Gosling, S. D., & Potter, J. (2009). Does self-esteem account for the higher-order factors of the Big Five? *Journal of Research in Personality*, *43*, 921–922.
Erikson, E. H. (1950). *Childhood and society*. New York, NY: Norton.
Erikson, E. H. (1968). *Identity: Youth and crisis*. New York, NY: Norton.
Erol, R. Y., & Orth, U. (2011). Self-esteem development from age 14 to 30 years: A longitudinal study. *Journal of Personality and Social Psychology*, *101*, 607–619.
Eysenck, H. J. (1990). Biological dimensions of personality. In L. A. Pervin (Ed.), *Handbook of personality: Theory and research* (pp. 244–276). New York, NY: Guilford.
Fleeson, W., & Jayawickreme, E. (2015). Whole trait theory. *Journal of Research in Personality*, *56*, 82–92.
Fraley, R. C., & Roberts, B. W. (2005). Patterns of continuity: A dynamic model for conceptualizing the stability of individual differences in psychological constructs across the life course. *Psychological Review*, *112*, 60–74.
Furr, R. M. (2008). A framework for profile similarity: Integrating similarity, normativeness, and distinctiveness. *Journal of Personality*, *76*, 1267–1316.
Hadiwijaya, H., Klimstra, T. A., Vermunt, J. K., Branje, S. J. T., & Meeus, W. H. J. (2015). Parent–adolescent relationships: An adjusted person-centred approach. *European Journal of Developmental Psychology*, *12*, 728–739.
Hatano, K., Sugimura, K., & Klimstra, T. A. (2017). Which came first, personality traits or identity processes during early and middle adolescence? *Journal of Research in Personality*, *67*, 120–131.
Jackson, J. J., Bogg, T., Walton, K. E., Wood, D., Harms, P. D., Lodi-Smith, J., … Roberts, B. W. (2009). Not all conscientiousness scales change alike: A multimethod, multisample study of age differences in the facets of conscientiousness. *Journal of Personality and Social Psychology*, *96*, 446–459.
Jensen-Campbell, L. A., Adams, R., Perry, D. G., Workman, K. A., Furdella, J. Q., & Egan, S. K. (2002). Agreeableness, extraversion, and peer relations in early adolescence: Winning friends and deflecting aggression. *Journal of Research in Personality*, *36*, 224–251.
Jensen-Campbell, L. A., & Malcolm, K. T. (2007). The importance of conscientiousness in adolescent interpersonal relationships. *Personality and Social Psychology Bulletin*, *33*, 368–383.
Johnson, W., Hicks, B. M., McGue, M., & Iacono, W. G. (2007). Most of the girls are alright, but some aren't: Personality trajectory groups from ages 14 to 24 and some

associations with outcomes. *Journal of Personality and Social Psychology, 93,* 266–284.

Kagan, J., & Moss, H. A. (1962). *Birth to maturity: A study in psychological development.* Hoboken, NY: John Wiley & Sons.

Klimstra, T. A., Akse, J., Hale, W. W., Raaijmakers, Q. A. W., & Meeus, W. H. J. (2010a). Longitudinal associations between Big Five personality traits and problem behavior in adolescence. *Journal of Research in Personality, 44,* 273–284.

Klimstra, T. A., Bleidorn, W., Asendorpf, J. B., van Aken, M. A. G., & Denissen, J. J. A. (2013a). Correlated change of big five personality traits across the lifespan: A search for determinants. *Journal of Research in Personality, 47,* 768–777.

Klimstra, T. A., Hale, W. W., Raaijmakers, A. W., Branje, S. J. T., & Meeus, W. H. J. (2009). Maturation of personality in adolescence. *Journal of Personality and Social Psychology, 96,* 898–912.

Klimstra, T. A., Hale, W. W., Raaijmakers, Q. A., Branje, S. J., & Meeus, W. H. (2010b). A developmental typology of adolescent personality. *European Journal of Personality, 24,* 309–323.

Klimstra, T. A., Hale, W. W., Raaijmakers, Q. A. W., & Meeus, W. H. J. (2012). Hypermaturity and immaturity of personality profiles in adolescents. *European Journal of Personality, 26,* 203–211.

Klimstra, T. A., Luyckx, K., Branje, S. J. T., Teppers, E., Goossens, L., & Meeus, W. H. J. (2013b). Personality traits, interpersonal identity, and relationship stability: Longitudinal linkages in late adolescence and young adulthood. *Journal of Youth and Adolescence, 42,* 1661–1673.

Klimstra, T. A., Luyckx, K., Germeijs, V., Meeus, W. H. J., & Goossens, L. (2012). Personality traits and educational identity formation in late adolescents: Longitudinal associations and academic progress. *Journal of Youth and Adolescence, 41,* 346–361.

Klimstra, T. A., Luyckx, K., Hale, W. W., & Goossens, L. (2014). Personality and externalizing behavior in the transition to young adulthood: The additive value of personality facets. *Social Psychiatry and Psychiatric Epidemiology, 49,* 1319–1333.

Klimstra, T. A., Luyckx, K., Hale, W. W., Goossens, L., & Meeus, W. H. J. (2010c). Longitudinal associations between personality profile stability and adjustment in college students: Distinguishing among overall stability, distinctive stability, and within-time normativeness. *Journal of Personality, 78,* 1163–1184.

Klimstra, T. A., Noftle, E. E., Luyckx, K., Goossens, L., & Robins, R. W. (2016). *Personality facets and adjustment in college students from Belgium and the US.* Manuscript submitted for publication.

Lehnart, J., & Neyer, F. J. (2006). Should I stay or should I go? Attachment and personality in stable and instable romantic relationships. *European Journal of Personality, 20,* 475–495.

Lehnart, J., Neyer, F. J., & Eccles, J. (2010). Long-term effects of social investment: The case of partnering in young adulthood. *Journal of Personality, 78,* 639–670.

Lodi-Smith, J., & Roberts, B. W. (2007). Social investment and personality: A meta-analysis of the relationship of personality traits to investment in work, family, religion, and volunteerism. *Personality and Social Psychology Review, 11,* 68–86.

Lönnqvist, J. E., Mäkinen, S., Paunonen, S. V., Henriksson, M., & Verkasalo, M. (2008). Psychosocial functioning in young men predicts their personality stability over 15 years. *Journal of Research in Personality, 42,* 599–621.

Lönnqvist, J. E., Verkasalo, M., Mäkinen, S., & Henriksson, M. (2009). High neuroticism at age 20 predicts history of mental disorders and low self-esteem at age 35. *Journal of Clinical Psychology, 65,* 781–790.

Lucas, R. E., & Donnellan, B. (2011). Personality development across the lifespan: Longitudinal analyses with a national sample from Germany. *Journal of Personality and Social Psychology, 101,* 847–861.

Luyckx, K., Schwartz, S. J., Berzonsky, M. D., Soenens, B., Vansteenkiste, M., Smits, I., & Goossens, L. (2008). Capturing ruminative exploration: Extending the four-dimensional model of identity formation in late adolescence. *Journal of Research in Personality, 42,* 58–82.

Luyckx, K., Soenens, B., & Goossens, L. (2006). The personality-identity interplay in emerging adult women: Convergent findings from complementary analyses. *European Journal of Personality, 20,* 195–215.

Luyckx, K., Teppers, E., Klimstra, T. A., & Rassart, J. (2014). Identity processes and personality traits and types in adolescence:

Directionality of effects and developmental trajectories. *Developmental Psychology, 50,* 2144–2153.

Marcia, J. E. (1966). Development and validation of ego-identity status. *Journal of Personality and Social Psychology, 3,* 551–558.

McAdams, D. P., & Olson, B. D. (2010). Personality development: Continuity and change over the life course. *Annual Review of Psychology, 61,* 517–542.

McCrae, R. R., & Costa, P. T., Jr. (2008). The five-factor theory of personality. In O. P. John, R. W. Robins, & L. A. Pervin (Eds.), *Handbook of personality: Theory and research* (3rd ed., pp. 159–181). New York, NY: Guilford.

McCrae, R. R., Costa, P. T., Jr., Hrebickova, M., Urbanek, T., Martin, T. A., Oryol, V. E., ... Senin, I. G. (2004). Age differences in personality traits across cultures: Self-report and observer perspectives. *European Journal of Personality, 18,* 143–157.

McCrae, R. R., Costa, P. T., Jr., & Martin, T. A. (2005). The NEO PI-3: A more readable revised NEO Personality Inventory. *Journal of Personality Assessment, 84,* 261–270.

McCrae, R. R., & Terracciano, A. (2005). Universal features of personality traits from the observer's perspective: Data from 50 cultures. *Journal of Personality and Social Psychology, 88,* 547–561.

Meeus, W., Van de Schoot, R., Klimstra, T., & Branje, S. (2011). Personality types in adolescence: Change and stability and links with adjustment and relationships: A five-wave longitudinal study. *Developmental Psychology, 47,* 1181–1195.

Mezquita, L., Ibáñez, M. I., Villa, H., Fañanás, L., Moya-Higueras, J., & Ortet, G. (2015). Five-factor model and internalizing and externalizing syndromes: A 5-year prospective study. *Personality and Individual Differences, 79,* 98–103.

Mlacic, B., Milas, G., & Kratohvil, A. (2007). Adolescent personality and self-esteem: An analysis of self-reports and parent-ratings. *Drustvena Istrazivanja, 16,* 213–236.

Moffitt, T. E. (1993). Adolescence-limited and life-course-persistent antisocial behavior: A developmental taxonomy. *Psychological Review, 100,* 674–701.

Morizot, J., & Le Blanc, M. (2005). Searching for a developmental typology of personality and its relations to antisocial behavior: A longitudinal study of a representative sample of men. *Journal of Personality, 73,* 139–182.

Mõttus, R., Kandler, C., Bleidorn, W., Riemann, R., & McCrae, R. R. (2017). Personality traits below facets: The consensual validity, longitudinal stability, heritability, and utility of personality nuances. *Journal of Personality and Social Psychology, 112,* 474–490.

Mund, M., & Neyer, F. J. (2014). Treating personality–relationship transactions with respect: Narrow facets, advanced models, and extended time frames. *Journal of Personality and Social Psychology, 107,* 352–368.

Nagin, D. S. (2005). *Group-based modeling of development.* Cambridge, MA: Harvard University Press.

Neyer, F. J., & Asendorpf, J. B. (2001). Personality–relationship transaction in young adulthood. *Journal of Personality and Social Psychology, 81,* 1190–1204.

Neyer, F. J., & Lehnart, J. (2007). Relationships matter in personality development: Evidence from an 8-year longitudinal study across young adulthood. *Journal of Personality, 75,* 535–568.

Orth, U., Robins, R. W., & Roberts, B. W. (2008). Low self-esteem prospectively predicts depression in adolescence and young adulthood. *Journal of Personality and Social Psychology, 95,* 695–708.

Pals, J. L. (2006). Narrative identity processing of difficult life experiences: Pathways of personality development and positive self-transformation in adulthood. *Journal of Personality, 74,* 1079–1110.

Poorthuis, A. M. G., Thomaes, S., van Aken, M. A. G., Denissen, J. J. A., & Orobio de Castro, B. (2014). Dashed hopes, dashed selves? A sociometer perspective on self-esteem change across the transition to secondary school. *Social Development, 23,* 770–783.

Pullmann, H., Raudsepp, L., & Allik, J. (2006). Stability and change in adolescents' personality: A longitudinal study. *European Journal of Personality, 20,* 447–459.

Roberts, B. W., & Caspi, A. (2003). The cumulative continuity model of personality development: Striking a balance between continuity and change in personality traits across the life course. In U. Staudinger & U. Lindenberger (Eds.), *Understanding human development* (pp. 183–214). Dordrecht, The Netherlands: Kluwer.

Roberts, B. W., Caspi, A., & Moffitt, T. E. (2001). The kids are alright: Growth and stability in personality development from adolescence to adulthood. *Journal of Personality and Social Psychology*, 81, 670–683.

Roberts, B. W., & DelVecchio, W. F. (2000). The rank-order consistency of personality traits from childhood to old age: A quantitative review of longitudinal studies. *Psychological Bulletin*, 126, 3–25.

Roberts, B. W., & Mroczek, D. (2008). Personality trait change in adulthood. *Current Directions in Psychological Science*, 17, 31–35.

Roberts, B. W., Walton, K. E., & Viechtbauer, W. (2006). Patterns of mean-level change in personality traits across the life-course: A meta-analysis of longitudinal studies. *Psychological Bulletin*, 132, 1–25.

Roberts, B. W., Wood, D., & Caspi, A. (2008). The development of personality traits in adulthood. In O. P. John, R. W. Robins, & L. A. Pervin (Eds.), *Handbook of personality: Theory and research* (3rd ed., pp. 375–398). New York, NY: Guilford.

Roberts, B. W., Wood, D., & Smith, J. L. (2005). Evaluating Five Factor Theory and social investment perspectives on personality trait development. *Journal of Research in Personality*, 39, 166–184.

Robins, R. W., Caspi, A., & Moffitt, T. E. (2002). It's not just who you're with, it's who you are: Personality and relationship experiences across multiple relationships. *Journal of Personality*, 70, 925–964.

Robins, R. W., Fraley, R. C., Roberts, B. W., & Trzesniewski, K. H. (2001a). A longitudinal study of personality change in young adulthood. *Journal of Personality*, 69, 617–640.

Robins, R. W., Hendin, H. M., & Trzesniewski, K. H. (2001b). Measuring global self-esteem: Construct validation of a single-item measure and the Rosenberg Self-Esteem Scale. *Personality and Social Psychology Bulletin*, 27, 151–161.

Robins, R. W., John, O. P., Caspi, A., Moffitt, T. E., & Stouthamer-Loeber, M. (1996). Resilient, overcontrolled, and undercontrolled boys: Three replicable personality types. *Journal of Personality and Social Psychology*, 70, 157–171.

Robins, R. W., Tracy, J. L., Trzesniewski, K., Potter, J., & Gosling, S. D. (2001c). Personality correlates of self-esteem. *Journal of Research in Personality*, 35, 463–482.

Shiner, R. L., Masten, A. S., & Roberts, J. M. (2003). Childhood personality foreshadows adult personality and life outcomes two decades later. *Journal of Personality*, 71, 1145–1170.

Soto, C. J., & John, O. P. (2012). Development of Big-Five domains and facets in adulthood: Mean-level age trends and broadly versus narrowly acting mechanisms. *Journal of Personality*, 80, 881–914.

Soto, C. J., & John, O. P. (2014). Traits in transition: The structure of parent-reported personality traits from early childhood to early adulthood. *Journal of Personality*, 82, 182–199.

Soto, C. J., John, O. P., Gosling, S. D., & Potter, J. (2011). Age differences in personality traits from 10 to 65: Big Five domains and facets in a large cross-sectional sample. *Journal of Personality and Social Psychology*, 100, 330–348.

Soto, C. J., & Tackett, J. L. (2015). Personality traits in childhood and adolescence: Structure, development, and outcomes. *Current Directions in Psychological Science*, 24, 358–362.

Specht, J., Luhmann, M., & Geiser, C. (2014). On the consistency of personality types across adulthood: Latent profile analyses in two large-scale panel studies. *Journal of Personality and Social Psychology*, 107, 540–556.

Turkheimer, E., & Waldron, M. (2000). Nonshared environment: A theoretical, methodological, and quantitative review. *Psychological Bulletin*, 126, 78–108.

van Aken, M. A. G., & Dubas, J. S. (2004). Personality type, social relationships, and problem behaviour in adolescence. *European Journal of Developmental Psychology*, 1, 331–348.

van den Akker, A. L., Deković, M., Asscher, J., & Prinzie, P. (2014). Mean-level personality development across childhood and adolescence: A temporary defiance of the maturity principle and bidirectional associations with parenting. *Journal of Personality and Social Psychology*, 107, 736–750.

Vaszonyi, A. T., Ksinan, A., Mikušba, J., & Jiskrova, G. (2015). The big five and adolescent adjustment: An empirical test across six cultures. *Personality and Individual Differences, 83*, 234–244.

Vermunt, J. K. (2010). Latent class modeling with covariates: Two improved three-step approaches. *Political Analysis, 18*, 450–469.

Vinkhuyzen, A., Pedersen, N. L., Yang, J., Lee, S. H., Magnusson, P. K. E., Iacono, W. G., … Wray, N. R. (2012). Common SNPs explain some of the variation in the personality dimensions of neuroticism and extraversion. *Translational Psychiatry, 2*, e102.

Wagner, J., Lüdtke, O., Jonkmann, K., & Trautwein, U. (2013). Cherish yourself: Longitudinal patterns and conditions of self-esteem change in the transition to young adulthood. *Journal of Personality and Social Psychology, 104*, 148–163.

Wilson, R. E., Thompson, R. J., & Vazire, S. (2017). Are fluctuations in personality states more than just fluctuations in affect? *Journal of Research in Personality, 69*, 110–123.

Zeigler-Hill, V., Holden, C. J., Enjaian, B., Southard, A. C., Besser, A., Li, H., & Zhang, Q. (2015). Self-esteem instability and personality: The connection between feelings of self-worth and the big five dimensions of personality. *Personality and Social Psychology Bulletin, 41*, 183–198.

The Development of Evolutionarily Adaptive Individual Differences: Children as Active Participants in Their Current and Future Survival

P. Douglas Sellers II, Karin Machluf and David F. Bjorklund

Individual differences are the fodder of evolution and natural selection, the stuff upon which it feeds and uses to produce outcomes. Without variability in traits and behavior between the members of a given population, change is slow, impossible, or dependent upon dramatic shifts in the environment to force these differences. As such, studying the sources and outcomes of individual differences is critical to an understanding of evolution itself and the specific species under consideration.

Of course, species-typical traits are equally valuable to science and the study of evolution. For example, recognizing the commonalities in human brain size, structure, and connectivity allows us to understand much about hominin evolution and what makes *Homo sapiens* different from other apes. But let us not forget that the origins of what are now species-typical behaviors in humans could be found in atypical individual apes 5 to 10 million years ago. Indeed, weird apes gave rise to typical humans.

Especially for humans, a serious discussion of individual differences requires a developmental perspective. Genes, environments, and their bidirectional interactions work together to produce adaptive and evolutionarily relevant behaviors. It is apparent that these interactions work together over an evolutionary timescale, phylogeny; however, what might be less obvious is that they also exert an influence in changes on the scale of an individual lifespan, ontogeny. Humans are special in the animal kingdom for the impact that development and time exert on individuals. In many ways, we are the most immature of animals, depending upon a long and slow development before getting to the business of reproduction. To understand how and why individual differences are relevant to human evolution and functioning we must first know how those individual differences come to be and the impact of this prolonged immaturity; that process is development.

WHY DOES DEVELOPMENT MATTER FOR EVOLUTION?

Typically, application of an evolutionary perspective to the study of an organism results in a focus on adult behaviors. Mating, coalitions, and resource acquisition are most important once physical and sexual maturity are reached. However, the journey to adulthood begins many years earlier, in fact at conception, and before organisms can engage in the all-important behaviors of adulthood, they must survive the prenatal period, infancy, and the juvenile period. Moreover, in many instances, success in adulthood will be dependent on achievements made during earlier stages of life. If one cannot survive childhood or prepare adequately for adulthood, then how can success in adulthood be achieved?

Proponents of *evolutionary developmental psychology* (Bjorklund, 2015; Bjorklund and Ellis, 2014; Bjorklund et al., 2016; Bjorklund and Pellegrini, 2000, 2002; Burgess and MacDonald, 2004; Del Giudice and Ellis, 2016; Ellis and Bjorklund, 2005; Geary and Bjorklund, 2000) argue that natural selection operates at all phases of the lifespan. In fact, selection is likely to have its greatest effects during early stages of development, as the length of human development (and its inherent dangers) serves as a bottleneck for survival. For example, although 95% of children born in the modern developed world can expect to live to adolescence, the rate is closer to 50% in traditional cultures. Mortality was likely as high, or higher, for our hunter-gatherer ancestors, making infancy and childhood the crucible of natural selection for *Homo sapiens* (Volk and Atkinson, 2013). Any benefits that foster development through these early stages will be favored, even if they have deleterious effects later in life. Time's arrow only moves in one direction and cannot skip ahead, forcing the hand of natural selection often to play its best cards first. As such, we concur with Konner (2010), who boldly stated that 'life *is* development' (p. 741) and, modifying Theodosius Dobzhansky's famous line, 'nothing in childhood makes sense except in the light of evolution' (p. 749).

Humans spend a profoundly long proportion of their lives developing. Typically, consistent reproductive ability is not achieved until the late teen years, meaning that humans spend more time alive and unable to reproduce than the entire lifespan of many mammalian species. Given such metabolic cost and risk of death over this timeframe, there must be substantial selection pressures that molded the human lifespan and subsequent payoffs for the effort of human development. Contemporary theories often emphasize that the complexity of human social interactions necessitates that children have time in order to learn the ways of their community. The *social-brain hypothesis* holds that humans evolved superior intelligence not so much to engage with predators, prey, or their physical environment, but in order to cooperate and compete with conspecifics (e.g., Alexander, 1989; Dunbar, 2003, 2010; Kappeler and Silk, 2010), and that humans' advanced form of social cognition was the result of the confluence of an extended juvenile period, a large brain, and increased social complexity (e.g., Bjorklund and Bering, 2003; Bjorklund et al., 2005). Consistent with this, the length of the juvenile period across 27 primate species positively correlates with group size and size of the nonvisual neocortex (Joffe, 1997). That is, among primates, the size of neocortical brain tissue not associated with the visual system was positively related to both the length of the juvenile period and the size of the social group.

Adaptations necessary for surviving human childhood were likely major driving forces behind the traits and abilities of modern human adults, making our phylogenetic children the fathers and mothers of modern humans. In particular, a large, slow-developing brain affords *plasticity*, the ability to modify behavior as a function of experience. For a long-lived species that inhabits a wide range of environments, developmental plasticity would seem to be especially important. Individuals could assess aspects of their early environment and alter their behavior/cognition in accordance with environmental conditions on the assumption that contexts of adulthood will be similar to contexts of childhood (Boyce and Ellis, 2005; Ellis et al., 2006). We argue that plasticity, rather than being merely a by-product of slow development, was selected in human phylogeny; children's sensitivities to conditions in their early environments, coupled with a high degree of plasticity, enables them to modify their behaviors, cognitions, and aspects of their personalities to best adapt to local ecologies, creating evolutionarily relevant individual differences in traits and behavior.

EVOLUTIONARY DEVELOPMENTAL PSYCHOLOGY AND DEVELOPMENTAL SYSTEMS

The emphasis on the role of developmental plasticity in human ontogeny stems from evolutionary developmental psychology's adoption of *developmental systems theory*. Developmental systems theory (Gottlieb, 1992, 2007; Witherington and Lickliter, 2016) is a multi-level interactive framework of development that acknowledges the importance of the interactions between genes, the nervous system, the individual, and the environment for producing both developmental and adult outcomes. For developmental systems theorists, nothing is preformed. Rather, structure and organization emerge via the bidirectional transaction of components at all levels of organization, from DNA through culture.

At its core, developmental systems theory champions the importance of plasticity for both an organism's individual development and long-term evolutionary changes. However, if there is so much plasticity in development, as proposed by developmental systems theorists, why is it that members of a species, be they bobwhite quail, rhesus monkeys, or humans, are so similar to one another?

The simple answer is that organisms inherit not only a species-typical genome but also a structured species-typical environment. Each generation does not recreate their environment from scratch, so environmental selection pressures stay relatively constant across time. Yet, normal variation in early experience exists and can produce individual differences in developmental outcomes, as young organisms adjust their developmental trajectory conditional on early experience. Similarly, *life-history theory*, the study of how organisms differentially allocate metabolic and behavioral resources both within and between species, can help explain many evolutionarily relevant variations in both ontogeny and phylogeny (see further discussion to follow).

Conceptualizing these adaptations in terms of individual differences upon which natural selection can act is perhaps somewhat novel in humans, but an example from the comparative literatures can help elucidate this reframing. Bluehead wrasse – a colorful coral fish found in tropical and subtropical waters – are sensitive to the social dynamics of sex in their surrounding community. When developing in an area with substantially more females than males, some of the females will transition to male reproduction. Thus, male phenotypes can be determined by the ontogenetic timing of environmental sex ratios, an environmentally sensitive evolutionary-developmental strategy to maximize reproduction (Munday et al., 2006). It is our contention that humans are also sensitive to environmental variables that can lead to substantial behavioral and/or physical changes that are relevant for meeting evolutionary ends, however not quite as dramatically as a fish switching its sex.

Having established the rationale behind plasticity and individual differences, a clarification is needed regarding developmental systems. There is actually no single developmental systems theory. Rather, there is variation among developmental systems theorists, although all seem to agree that structure and function in ontogeny emerge as the result of the transaction of components at all levels of organization. Genes are a necessary, but not sufficient, part of developmental systems and are always expressed within a context. Some philosophers and developmental psychologists have proposed two versions of developmental systems theory, a 'soft' version and a 'hard' version, with vastly different implications for developmental science (Bjorklund and Ellis, 2014; Del Giudice and Ellis, 2016; Frankenhuis et al., 2013; Pradeu, 2010; Robert et al., 2001). In the soft version, although continuous bidirectional interaction between the organism and the environment is recognized, the organism is the focus of natural selection, as in mainstream biology. In contrast, in the hard version of developmental systems theory, the entire organism–environment whole of replicable developmental systems is the focus of natural selection. This removes the organism as the focus of natural selection, and natural selection can only operate at the population level (see Overton, 2015; Witherington and Lickliter, 2016). The hard form of developmental systems theory is incompatible with an adaptationist perspective, and it is the soft form of developmental systems theory that evolutionary developmental psychologists advocate (see Bjorklund, 2016).

Developmental Adaptations

Critical to evolutionary developmental psychological theory is the existence of *developmental adaptations*, traits or behaviors that are specific to times of development that serve an adaptive purpose. Without such adaptations, the argument for childhood as the crucible of evolution falls flat. The entirety of the lifespan, not simply adulthood, should be rife with demonstrably adaptive behaviors and physical features. Indeed, when investigating development with a critical adaptationist eye, one can clearly see the fingerprints of natural selection. Some are obvious, such as the umbilical cord during gestation or neonatal reflexes, both of which are clearly only useful when the individual is immature. Other adaptations require an extended timeline for recognizing their utility, such as early variables that impact mating strategies or epigenetic change across generations. These two sets of examples represent two major classes of developmental adaptations: ontogenetic and deferred adaptations.

Ontogenetic adaptations are those that are present in childhood and whose utility is realized in childhood, not adulthood (Bjorklund, 1997; Oppenheim, 1981). Like the umbilical cord, these adaptations are exclusively of and for childhood. As such, they are typically crucial to the survival of children and have a limited timeframe of existence. Instead of paying dividends in adult mating or survival behaviors, these adaptations serve to adapt children to their immediate and current surroundings. Many ontogenetic adaptations take on forms that are temporarily expedient and may seem counter-intuitive if viewed through the lens of adaptations needed in adulthood. Indeed, childhood is a vastly different physiological, psychological, and social landscape that presents sometimes dramatically different selection pressures than adulthood.

Many cognitive or behavioral characteristics have been considered as candidates for ontogenetic adaptations. For example, young infants' limited perceptual abilities might protect them from overstimulation and competition between developing senses (Turkewitz and Kenny, 1982) and newborns' tendency to imitate the facial gestures of adults (e.g., Meltzoff and Moore, 1977; Nagy and Molnar, 2004) might serve to enhance social interaction between an infant and its mother (e.g., Bjorklund, 1987; Byrne, 2005; Legerstee, 1991). Sellers and Bjorklund (2014) suggest that children's 'I did it' errors in source monitoring, what they term *promiscuous selfsourcing*, may lead to more rich elaborations of memory and thus serve an adaptive function to bolster memory at a time when cognitive functions are somewhat limited.

Although individual differences and plasticity may be seen in ontogenetic adaptations (e.g., Heimann, 1989), individual differences and plasticity play a more significant role in *deferred adaptations,* which occur in childhood but whose payoff is in adulthood (Hernández Blasi and Bjorklund, 2003). Deferred adaptations are most likely to be selected when ecological conditions remain consistent over time, allowing for high fidelity in the prediction of conditions across the lifespan. This may be especially true in the social realm as children learn to navigate complex human social environments. Unlike most other social species, human social groups vary considerably in their roles and rules for social engagement, and this requires a plastic brain, flexible cognitions, and a variety of behaviors for children to master the peculiarities of their culture. It also requires an extended period of time.

Forms of deferred adaptations that are especially relevant for this chapter are *facultative* or *conditional adaptations* (Boyce and Ellis, 2005; Konner, 2010). Konner (2010) defines facultative adaptations as 'reproductive advantages gained through different evolved developmental paths in different external conditions detected in early life' (p. 746). Similarly, Boyce and Ellis (2005) defined conditional adaptations as:

> evolved mechanisms that detect and respond to specific features of childhood environments – features that have proven reliable over evolutionary time in predicting the nature of the social and physical world into which children will mature – and entrain developmental pathways that reliably matched those features during a species' natural selective history. Conditional adaptations ... underpin development of contingent survival and reproductive strategies and thus enable individuals to function competently in a variety of different environments. (p. 290)

The concept of conditional adaptations hinges on a high degree of developmental plasticity, necessitating that the young of a species be able to adjust their pathway of development dependent upon current environmental circumstances. A central tenet of such flexible adaptations is that one's current environment is often the best predictor of later environments. Children are sensitive to particular conditions at specific times in ontogeny and modify their development accordingly to maximize fitness in anticipation of what environmental conditions will be like in the future.

Although most of our discussion will be related to children's sensitivity to early rearing environments, sensitivity to early environmental conditions as cues to later environments can also be found in prenatal development. For example, somewhat counter-intuitively, pregnant women with poor nutrition give birth to lighter infants who then as children are more likely to be overweight. Such children are said to have 'thrifty phenotypes', producing higher levels of the appetite-regulating hormone leptin and storing greater amounts of fat than children with more nutritious prenatal diets (Breier et al., 2001). This response to poor fetal nutrition would likely have been adaptive to our hominin ancestors when early malnutrition closely predicted a future scarcity of calories. In the modern world, however, complete with readily available high fat and sugar foods, such an adaptation may lead to obesity (Gluckman and Hanson, 2005).

Other research has shown that fetuses are sensitive to maternal stress that signals possible unpredictable and harsh postnatal environments. For instance, human fetuses exposed to heightened levels of maternal stress show subsequent increased cortisol levels and poorer health as children (e.g., Flinn, 2006) and often display increased levels of impulsivity, risk-taking, anxiety, fearfulness, basal activity, and responsivity of the HPA axis in childhood, as well as reduced levels of attention and executive function (e.g., Glover, 2011; Pluess and Belsky, 2011; see also Sandman et al., 2013 for fetuses' adaptive response to maternal depression). That prenatal experience – rather than genetic inheritance – is responsible for these effects was demonstrated in a study in which pregnant women were either genetically related or unrelated to their child as a result of in vitro fertilization (IVF; Rice et al., 2010). The researchers reported that children's antisocial behavior between 4 and 10 years of age was related to the stress experienced by their birth mothers, independent of genetic relationship. Prenatal exposure to the stress of their birth mothers appears to be preparing infants for anticipated harsh and unpredictable environments. Gluckman and Hanson (2005) refer to such potentially adaptive changes in fetuses' developmental trajectory as *predictive adaptive responses*.

Conditional Adaptations

One of the earliest studies examining the role of plasticity in individual differences in behavior from an evolutionary perspective was by Belsky et al. (1991) who investigated how early rearing environment affected pubertal timing of girls and their future mating strategies as adults. Given that children's early environments are reliable predictors of later environments, Belsky et al. (1991) proposed an evolutionary theory of socialization, specifically examining individual differences of children raised in two substantially different environments. Belsky and his colleagues write that:

> a principal evolutionary function of early experience – the first 5–7 years of life – is to induce in the child an understanding of the availability and predictability of resources (broadly defined) in the environment, of the trustworthiness of others, and of the enduringness of close interpersonal relationships, all of which will affect how the developing person apportions reproductive effort. (p. 650)

Belsky et al. (1991) reported that children growing up in high-stress, low-resource, and unpredictable environments were likely to reach puberty, become sexually active, and procreate earlier than children reared in low-stress, high-resource, and predictable environments (Figure 12.1).

Although the theorizing of Belsky and his colleagues (1991) received little initial attention among developmentalists, this was soon to change. More than a decade after the publication of Belsky et al.'s paper, Boyce and Ellis (2005; Ellis and Boyce, 2008) examined individual differences in response to early environments from an evolutionary developmental perspective. They proposed a theory of *biological sensitivity to context*, which attempted to explain the adaptive relationship between early life experience and stress reactivity. The theory posits that early environments prime future stress reactivity, and that early experience with stress interacts with individual differences in children's genetic predispositions to produce adaptive long-term outcomes. Individual differences in children's phenotypic plasticity enable some children to match their biological and behavioral systems to the parameters of their early developmental environments. Those who are sensitive to early environments are impacted by their environment both 'for better and for worse' relative to those who are less sensitive. These less sensitive children are termed 'low-reactive', and they are sometimes referred to as dandelions owing to their analogous resiliency and ability to thrive in both negative and positive environments, whereas children who are highly sensitive to environments are termed 'high-reactive' and are equated to orchids, whose outcomes and survival are highly conditional upon specific environmental settings.

Such *differential sensitivity to context* is illustrated in two studies by Boyce and his colleagues. In one study (Boyce et al., 1998), Rhesus macaques (*Macaca mulatta*) were assessed for levels of reactivity to novel experiences. High-reactive animals showed elevated levels of cortisol to novel experiences, compared to other animals. When these animals were living in a low-stress environment, a 5-acre wooded habitat, rates of injuries (usually through aggressive interactions with other monkeys) were generally low, but slightly higher for the low-reactive than the high-reactive monkeys. This pattern changed significantly, however, when the monkeys were moved to a high-stress environment, a 1,000-square foot building for

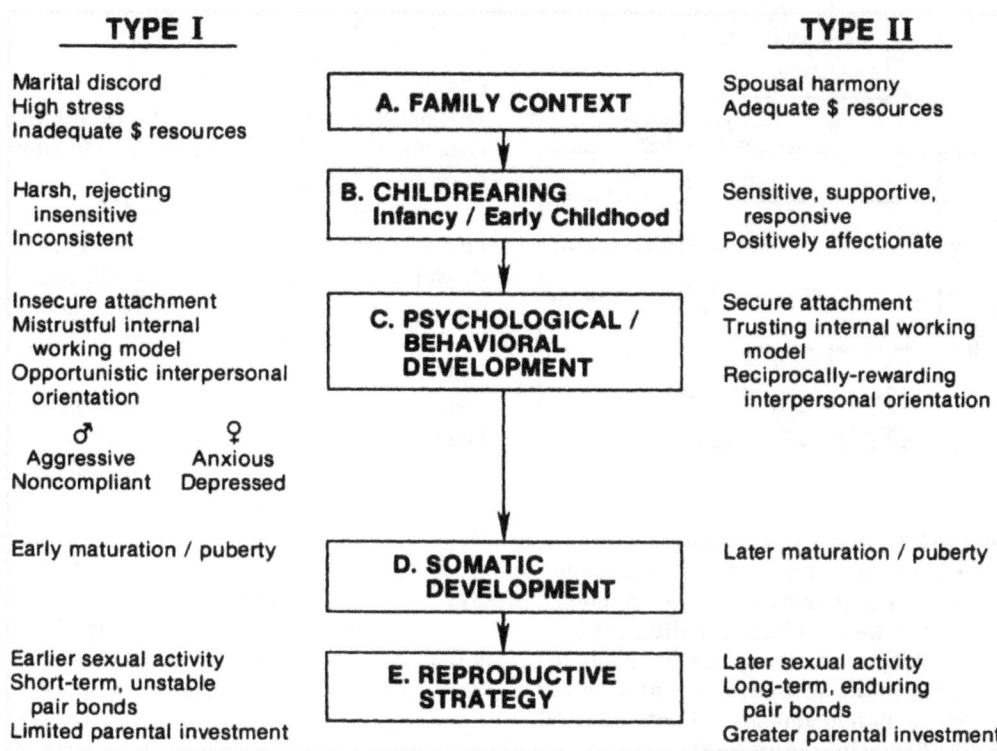

Figure 12.1 Belsky et al. (1991) identified pathways of developmental individual differences that lead to different reproductive strategies in humans. Type 1 is characterized by a stressful early environment and leads to a reproductive strategy of early mating, short-term mating, increased number of offspring, and limited parental investment. Type 2 is characterized by a supportive and less stressful early environment, leading to a reproductive strategy of fewer delayed sexual activity, long-term pair bonding, fewer offspring, and greater parental investment. One should not be thought of as better than the other in an evolutionary sense, as they represent different, but still successful, life-history strategies.

a period of six months. The rate of injuries between the high- and low-stress environments did not vary significantly for the monkeys classified as low in biological reactivity (see Figure 12.2). However, as can be seen in the figure, rates of injuries skyrocketed for the high-reactive monkeys in the stressful environment. Whereas these monkeys had the lowest rate of injuries in the low-stress environment, they had the highest rate in the high-stress environment.

In an analogous study with human children, Boyce et al. (1995) examined the occurrence of respiratory infection in three- to five-year-old children classified as either low- or high-reactive. They found that incidence of respiratory infection did not vary with the stress levels of the homes for low-reactive children. However, for high-reactive children, incidences of respiratory infection were higher for children from high-stress homes and *lowest* for those from low-stress homes.

In related work, researchers classified five- and six-year-old children as having high or low neurobiological stress reactivity based on their respiratory sinus arrhythmia (RSA), a measure of heart rate variability with

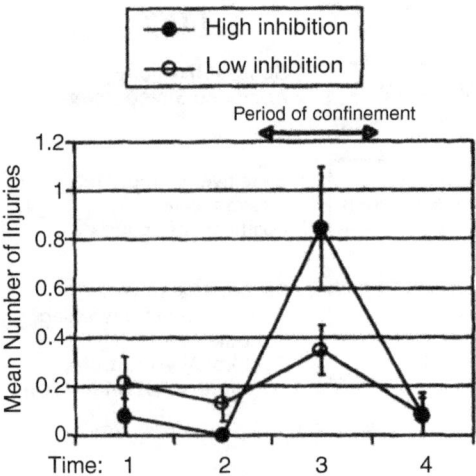

Figure 12.2 Boyce et al. (1998) reported differential susceptibility to injury of monkeys when confined to a new environment based upon their inhibitory abilities. The high inhibition animals were more likely to be injured in the new environment, whereas the low inhibition animals are not impacted by the change in environment.

respiration, which can be used as a measure of the nervous system's response to stress and a measure of children's ability to regulate reactions to environmental stimuli (Obradović et al., 2010). Highly reactive children from high-stressed homes (low socioeconomic status (SES), harsh parenting, maternal depression) showed poor psychological adjustment (e.g., decreased prosocial behavior, poor school performance, increased externalizing behavior) relative to highly reactive children from low-stress homes. That is, these orchid children flourished when early life conditions were positive but suffered when they were negative. In contrast, the less-sensitive dandelion children showed little change for most measures as a function of level of adversity.

Research has also shown that highly fearful and anxious children are more affected by parental behavior (e.g., maternal style of discipline) than less-anxious or 'average' children (Gilissen et al., 2008; Kochanska, 1993), as are infants with difficult temperaments (Stright et al., 2008; see Belsky, 2005, for an extended discussion). According to Belsky (2000, 2005; Belsky et al., 2007), children who are highly responsive to parental influence are easily able to adapt to a wide range of contexts, which is beneficial when environments are unpredictable and less-than-optimal (e.g., father absence). They will also do well in enriched environments. Other children who are more stable are less influenced by extreme environments, as well as by their parents. These children will do particularly well in 'average' environments. Parents can hedge their bets, so to speak, by producing both types of children, some who will be receptive to change and others who will thrive in the 'expected' environment.

This pattern has recently been confirmed by a meta-analysis, examining children's sensitivity to harsh versus supportive parenting as a function of their temperament (Slagt et al., 2016). Slagt and her colleagues examined 84 longitudinal studies with a total of 105 samples and reported that children with difficult temperaments (orchid children) showed generally good adjustment in terms of internalizing and externalizing behavior and social and cognitive competence when they experienced positive, supportive parenting, but were more vulnerable in terms of psychological adjustment when they experienced negative, harsh parenting. Children with easy temperaments (dandelion children) were less affected by differences in quality of parenting.

Behavioral genetic research has identified a gene associated with susceptibility to parental influence (Bakermans-Kranenburg et al., 2008). In this study, one- to three-year-old children with high levels of externalizing behavior participated in a 'positive parenting' program. One year after completing the program, children who had one version of an allele associated with a dopamine receptor showed significant reductions in externalizing behavior, relative to children in a control group who did not participate in the positive-parenting program. In contrast, children with a different allele displayed no change in externalizing behavior. Thus, a substantial history of findings exists confirming individual differences in how children respond to their environments, particularly in reference to reproductive and social factors.

This differential susceptibility perspective should not be taken for granted. Until recently, the diathesis-stress model (also called the mental-health model) was the dominant scientific paradigm for explaining the relationship between detrimental, high-risk environments and subsequent outcomes. The diathesis-stress paradigm posits that early environments predict the differential development of psychopathological conditions and disturbances across development. According to this model, positive and supportive environments will produce 'good' developmental outcomes, such as secure attachment, good mental health, and academic success. In contrast, adverse early environments will produce 'bad' outcomes, such as insecure attachment, psychopathology, and early sexual activity. This model only highlights the costs of children's responses to their local environments, ignoring the potential adaptive benefits. The differential susceptibility approach outlined above is an evolutionary developmental perspective which emphasizes that humans have evolved to respond to different early environmental contexts by detecting and responding to the fitness-relevant costs and benefits provided by those environments. It states that development is not so much disturbed when exposed to negative early environments, as it is *directed* or *regulated* toward attaining adaptive strategies to function in these stressful environments (see Del Giudice and Ellis, 2016; Ellis et al., 2012). For example, as discussed earlier, it is *adaptive* for girls who experience adverse early environments to reach reproductive age earlier than girls who experience positive early environments. It is important to beware of making the naturalistic fallacy; although these adaptations evolved to help the organism in its evolutionary goals, they may be seen as harmful in modern societal terms. In the example above, having sex and reproducing early is seen as maladaptive from a societal perspective but, given the ecological conditions in which such strategies develop, may be adaptive when viewed through the lens of evolutionary psychology. (For elaboration on the naturalistic fallacy, see Teehan and diCarlo, 2004.)

LIFE-HISTORY THEORY AND DIFFERENTIAL SUSCEPTIBILITY

The findings and subsequent theories discussed earlier were arguably the beginning of the new subfield of evolutionary developmental psychology, with roots in the then-emerging life-history theory (e.g., Del Giudice et al., 2016; Ellis et al., 2012; Hill and Kaplan, 1999; Stearns, 1992). Life-history theory – which is rooted in evolutionary biology – explains differences in how organisms allocate their time and resources by studying the variations both across and within species. Its main premise is that, given that organisms cannot simultaneously maximize all aspects of fitness, they are forced to make trade-offs between reproductive efforts and somatic efforts. For example, reproductive efforts include attracting mates, gestation (for females), and parental investment in offspring. Somatic efforts include physical growth, maintenance, and brain development. Natural selection should favor organisms that can successfully manage these trade-offs. Across the lifespan, an organism must make many choices that relate to these life-history factors, and the accumulation of these resource-allocation decisions makes up that organism's life-history strategy. These strategies can essentially be summed up as the trade-offs between current or future reproduction and the quality or quantity of offspring (see Ellis et al., 2009).

Although life-history strategies are species-typical adaptations to past ecological contexts, there are individual differences within a given species due to variation in the developmental contexts that alter the potential costs and benefits of the trade-offs. One key influence on the variation of life-history strategies is extrinsic morbidity–mortality (sometimes termed environmental harshness; Ellis et al., 2009), which describes the mortality rate and rates of nonlethal injuries, pathogen loads and diseases, and other forms of stress in the local environment. Life-history theory states that it is adaptive to mate early, reproduce early, and have low parental investment in offspring when extrinsic morbidity–mortality is high, at the cost of growth or development. Similarly, it predicts that when morbidity–mortality is low, mating and reproduction will be postponed, high parental investment will be afforded once reproduction occurs, and the organism will take more time to develop physically and psychologically (Ellis et al., 2009). When put on a single continuum, these life-history strategies are anchored by r-selected (i.e., fast life-history) and K-selected (i.e., slow life-history) strategies, respectively. In addition to extrinsic morbidity–mortality, unpredictability in the environment also influences the development of either fast or slow life-history strategies (Ellis et al., 2009). In environments that vary unpredictably, persisting in a slow life-history strategy is not adaptive because mating and reproduction opportunities are not guaranteed. Life-history theory predicts that an organism will be sensitive to predictability throughout development and will respond to signals of unpredictability by adopting a faster life-history strategy.

The findings of Belsky et al. (1991) and Boyce and Ellis (2005) that early developmental environment can regulate and predict later reproductive strategies were in line with this life-history perspective. These findings can be explained by experiences in early childhood that affect children's somatic and behavioral development, which subsequently influence pubertal timing and reproductive strategies that serve to match an adaptive life-history strategy to the local ecology. Consistent with life-history theory and the influence of early stress, strategies can be said to fall on a slow–fast continuum, ranging from higher stress (e.g., high marital discord, unstable employment, low SES) to lower stress (e.g., low marital discord, stable employment, higher SES).

Another example – and one of the most thoroughly researched examples of phenotypic plasticity (and one which has been documented in numerous species) – is the effect of rat maternal stress on parenting behavior and how this ultimately impacts the stress responses (as well as other behaviors) of offspring (e.g., Cameron et al., 2005; Champagne and Curley, 2008; Meaney, 2001; Weaver et al., 2004). Individual differences in hypothalamic–pituitary–adrenal (HPA) and behavioral responses to stress in offspring have been shown to be associated with maternal licking/grooming behavior. Specifically, offspring who receive high amounts of maternal grooming as infants display less fear of novelty and show more modest HPA responses to stress than do offspring that receive lower amounts of maternal grooming. Moreover, when infants of mothers with low levels of grooming are fostered by mothers with high levels of grooming, they show the behavioral responses consistent with the foster mothers (e.g., Francis et al., 1999). These effects have been shown to persist for at least two generations, with the foster offspring of high-grooming mothers displaying high levels of grooming themselves and having offspring who show low levels of stress in novel situations, irrespective of their genetic background (Francis et al., 1999).

Meaney (2001) provided a model for how maternal anxiety and care can influence neural development in her offspring, which in turn, affects gene expression related to chemicals involved in stress responses and production of neurotransmitters and hormones such as dopamine and oxytocin, which are involved in emotional expression and regulation. This pattern would influence the behavior of female animals when they become mothers, affecting the neural development and behavior of their offspring. According to Meaney (2001), 'Individual differences in behavioral and neuroendocrine responses to stress in rats are, in part, derived from naturally occurring variations in maternal care. Such effects might serve as a possible mechanism by which selected traits are transmitted from one generation to another' (pp. 1170–1171).

It is important to note that increased sensitivity to stress is, to a point, not necessarily maladaptive: during the first few weeks of life, a rat pup's experience of the environment consists almost exclusively of its littermates and its mother. A stressed mother is the product of a stressful and/or unstable environment, which, ordinarily, her pups can expect to inherit. Thus, the mother acts as a sort of 'translator' for information from the environment. And so, it is advantageous for the pups to be sensitive to their mother's behavior, as this is a fairly good predictor of the manner of behavior that will prove most adaptive for their future environment (Cameron et al, 2005; Meaney, 2001).

The amalgamation of the findings discussed here developed into the cornerstone for understanding what is now called *differential susceptibility*. Belsky and colleagues (e.g., Belsky, 2005; Belsky et al., 2007) proposed that some children are more sensitive (or differentially susceptible) to environmental influences. In other words, there is a high degree of phenotypic plasticity. According to this perspective, when environments are unpredictable, children who are highly responsive to differences in the environment will be able to adjust to negative environments and will also do particularly well in positive environments. Conversely, other children are less susceptible to environmental cues and are more stable in their responsiveness. These children tend to thrive in a species-typical 'expected' environment.

In terms of life-history theory, children growing up in harsh and unpredictable environments tend to follow a fast life-history strategy, growing up to engage in more risk-taking and aggressive behavior, forming unstable pair bonds, investing less in offspring, with girls attaining menarche and engaging in sex earlier than children growing up in less harsh and more predictable environments, who tend to follow a slow life-history strategy (e.g., Ellis, 2004; Ellis et al., 2009; Nettle, 2010; Nettle and Cockerill, 2010; Placek and Quinlan, 2012). For example, in one study, children who spent their first five years living in unpredictable environments (e.g., parental job changes, changes in residences, different adult males living in the household) had more sexual partners, had an earlier sexual debut, and engaged in higher levels of delinquent and risk-taking behavior at age 23 than children growing up in more predictable homes (Simpson et al., 2012). In another study, adults who had grown up in unpredictable environments performed worse on cognitive inhibition tasks but better on tasks requiring cognitive flexibility – a likely valuable skill in unpredictable environments – especially when tested in uncertain contexts (Mittal et al., 2015).

It is easy to view the actions of children who follow a fast life-history strategy as a result of early aversive environments as maladaptive, which from a societal perspective, they clearly are (i.e., teen pregnancy). Yet, from an evolutionary developmental perspective, this pattern reflects young children's neural plasticity to adjust their cognitions and behavior in anticipation of equally aversive adult environments (Ellis et al., 2009, 2012). Surviving in harsh and unpredictable environments likely requires prioritizing short-term success over what is best in the long term, allowing for the selection of these adaptations.

We view evolutionary developmental psychology as a powerful subfield that integrates two traditionally biological theories (life-history theory and adaptation) under an interactive framework (developmental systems) for its application to human development and psychology. This framework does not simply tack on functional or evolutionary explanations to developmental findings.

Rather, it reconceptualizes how developmental psychology approaches the process of development itself. The ultimate purpose of behaviors and traits in childhood is to promote survival and to produce an individual capable of reproductive success in adulthood (adaptation). However, due to the complex nature of the human species and the selection pressures it has faced, there is substantial flexibility and variability in the behaviors and traits that might constitute success (life-history theory). This ability to adapt to environmental conditions with changes in behavioral and somatic traits has consequences not simply for the individual but for evolution of the species (developmental systems). Such connections have been clear in the field of biology, but have been largely uninvestigated or, at best, implicit in developmental psychology. Evolutionary developmental psychology strives to make explicit these connections between development and evolution in hope that it can elucidate previously unanswered questions, shed light on new hypotheses, and discover new areas of inquiry.

CONCLUSION

Survival and adaptation are not passive processes; individuals actively participate in their own survival through behaviors and traits directly related to reproduction and resource acquisition. Throughout this chapter, we have demonstrated that this active participation is not confined to the behaviors of adults; children use development to tune their strategies for current and future success. Individual differences across development serve to powerfully dictate the fitness of adults and exert influence well beyond the cessation of these early selection pressures as they serve as predictors of one's future environment. One could even claim that children are the fathers of men and the mothers of women and that, as evolutionary psychology searches for ultimate causation, the process of development itself may be the ultimate of causes.

REFERENCES

Alexander, R. D. (1989). Evolution of the human psyche. In P. Mellers & C. Stringer (Eds.), *The human revolution: Behavioural and biological perspectives on the origins of modern humans* (pp. 455–513). Princeton, NJ: Princeton University Press.

Bakermans-Kranenburg, M. J., van IJzendoorn, M. H., Pijlman, F. T., Mesman, J., & Juffer, F. (2008). Experimental evidence for differential susceptibility: Dopamine D4 receptor polymorphism (DRD4 VNTR) moderates intervention effects on toddlers' externalizing behavior in a randomized controlled trial. *Developmental Psychology, 44*, 293–300.

Belsky, J. (2000). Conditional and alternative reproductive strategies: Individual differences in susceptibility to rearing experiences. In J. L. Rodgers, D. C. Rowe, & W. B. Miller (Eds.), *Genetic influences on human fertility and sexuality* (pp. 127–146). New York, NY: Springer.

Belsky, J. (2005). Differential susceptibility to rearing influence. In B. J. Ellis & D. F. Bjorklund, (Eds.), *Origins of the social mind: Evolutionary psychology and child development* (pp. 139–163). New York, NY: Guilford.

Belsky, J., Steinberg, L., & Draper, P. (1991). Childhood experience, interpersonal development, and reproductive strategy: An evolutionary theory of socialization. *Child Development, 62*, 647–670.

Belsky, J., Steinberg, L. D., Houts, R. M., Friedman, S. L., DeHart, G., Cauffman, E., ... & Susman, E. (2007). Family rearing antecedents of pubertal timing. *Child Development, 78*, 1302–1321.

Bjorklund, D. F. (1987). A note on neonatal imitation. *Developmental Review, 7*, 86–92.

Bjorklund, D. F. (1997). The role of immaturity in human development. *Psychological Bulletin, 122*, 153–169.

Bjorklund, D. F. (2015). Developing adaptations. *Developmental Review, 38*, 13–35.

Bjorklund, D. F. (2016). Prepared is not preformed: Comment on Witherington and Lickliter. *Human Development, 59*, 235–241.

Bjorklund, D. F., & Bering, J. M. (2003). Big brains, slow development, and social complexity: The developmental and evolutionary origins of social cognition. In M. Brüne, H. Ribbert, & W. Schiefenhövel (Eds.), *The social brain: Evolutionary aspects of development and pathology* (pp. 133–151). New York, NY: Wiley.

Bjorklund, D. F., Cormier, C., & Rosenberg, J. S. (2005). The evolution of theory of mind: Big brains, social complexity, and inhibition. In W. Schnieder, R. Schumann-Hengsteler, & B. Sodian (Eds.), *Young children's cognitive development: Interrelationships among executive functioning, working memory, verbal ability and theory of mind* (pp. 147–174). New York, NY: Psychology Press.

Bjorklund, D. F., & Ellis, B. J. (2014). Children, childhood, and development in evolutionary perspective. *Developmental Review, 34*, 225–264.

Bjorklund, D. F., Hernández Blasi, C., & Ellis, B. J. (2016). Evolutionary developmental psychology. In D. M. Buss (Ed.), *Evolutionary psychology handbook* (2nd ed., Vol. 2, pp. 904–925). New York, NY: Wiley.

Bjorklund, D. F., & Pellegrini, A. D. (2000). Child development and evolutionary psychology. *Child Development, 71*, 1687–1798.

Bjorklund, D. F., & Pellegrini, A. D. (2002). *The origins of human nature: Evolutionary developmental psychology*. Washington, DC: American Psychological Association.

Boyce, W. T., Chesney, M., Alkon, A., Tschann, J. M., Adams, S., Chesterman, B., ... & Wara, D. (1995). Psychobiologic reactivity to stress and childhood respiratory illnesses: Results of two prospective studies. *Psychosomatic Medicine, 57*, 411–422.

Boyce, W. T., & Ellis, B. J. (2005). Biological sensitivity to context: I. An evolutionary-developmental theory of the origins and functions of stress reactivity. *Development and Psychopathology, 17*, 271–301.

Boyce, W. T., O'Neill-Wagner, P., Price, C. S., Haines, M., & Suomi, S. J. (1998). Crowding stress and violent injuries among behaviorally inhibited rhesus macaques. *Health Psychology, 17*, 285–289.

Breier, B. H., Vickers, M. H., Ikenasio, B. A., Chan, K. Y., & Wong, W. P. S. (2001). Fetal programming of appetite and obesity. *Molecular and Cellular Endocrinology, 185*, 73–79.

Burgess, R. L., & MacDonald, K. (Eds.). (2004). *Evolutionary perspectives on human development*. New York, NY: Sage.

Byrne, R. W. (2005). Social cognition: Imitation, imitation, imitation. *Current Biology, 15*, R489–R500.

Cameron, N. M., Champagne, F. A., Parent, C., Fish, E. W., Ozaki-Kuroda, K., & Meaney, M. J. (2005). The programming of individual differences in defensive responses and reproductive strategies in the rat through variations in maternal care. *Neuroscience and Biobehavioral Reviews, 29*, 843–865.

Champagne, F. A., & Curley, J. P. (2008). Maternal regulation of estrogen receptor α methylation. *Current Opinion in Pharmacology, 8*, 735–739.

Del Giudice, M., & Ellis, E. J. (2016). Evolutionary foundations of developmental psychopathology. In D. Cicchetti (Ed.), *Developmental psychopathology, Vol. 2: Developmental neuroscience* (3rd ed., pp. 1–58). New York, NY: Wiley.

Del Giudice, M., Gangestad, S. W., & Kaplan, H. S. (2016). Life history theory and evolutionary psychology. In D. Buss (Ed.), *Evolutionary psychology handbook* (Vol. 2, pp. 88–114). New York, NY: Wiley.

Dunbar, R. I. M. (2003). The social brain: Mind, language, and society in evolutionary perspective. *Annual Review of Anthropology, 32*, 163–181.

Dunbar, R. (2010). *How many friends does one person need? Dunbar's number and other evolutionary quirks*. London: Faber & Faber.

Ellis, B. J. (2004). Timing of pubertal maturation in girls: An integrated life history approach. *Psychological Bulletin, 130*, 920–958.

Ellis, B. J., & Bjorklund, D. F. (Eds.). (2005). *Origins of the social mind: Evolutionary psychology and child development*. New York, NY: Guilford.

Ellis, B. J., & Boyce, W. T. (2008). Biological sensitivity to context. *Current Directions in Psychological Science, 17*, 183–187.

Ellis, B. J., Del Giudice, M., Dishion, T. J., Figueredo, A. J., Gray, P., Griskevicius, V., ... &

Wilson, D. S. (2012). The evolutionary basis of risky adolescent behavior: Implications for science, policy, and practice. *Developmental Psychology, 48*, 598–623.

Ellis, B. J., Figueredo, A. J., Brumbach, B. H., & Schlomer, G. L. (2009). Fundamental dimensions of environmental risk: The impact of harsh versus unpredictable environments on the evolution and development of life history strategies. *Human Nature, 20*, 204–268.

Ellis, B. J., Jackson, J. J., & Boyce, W. T. (2006). The stress response systems: Universality and adaptive individual differences. *Developmental Review, 26*, 175–212.

Flinn, M. V. (2006). Evolution and ontogeny of stress response to social change in the human child. *Child Development, 26*, 138–174.

Francis, D., Diorio, J., Liu, D., & Meaney, M. J. (1999). Nongenomic transmission across generations of maternal behavior and stress responses in the rat. *Science, 286*, 1155–1158.

Frankenhuis, W. E., Panchanathan, K., & Barrett, H. C. (2013). Bridging developmental systems theory and evolutionary psychology using dynamic optimization. *Developmental Science, 16*, 584–598.

Geary, D. C., & Bjorklund, D. F. (2000). Evolutionary developmental psychology. *Child Development, 71*, 57–65.

Gilissen, R., Bakermans-Kranenburg, M. J., van IJzendoorn, M. H., & Linting, M. (2008). Electrodermal reactivity during the Trier Social Stress Test for children: Interaction between the serotonin transporter polymorphism and children's attachment representation. *Developmental Psychobiology, 50*, 615–625.

Glover, V. (2011). Prenatal stress and the origins of psychopathology: An evolutionary perspective. *Journal of Child Psychology and Psychiatry, 52*, 356–367.

Gluckman, P., & Hanson, M. (2005). *The fetal matrix: Evolution, development, and disease*. Cambridge, UK: Cambridge University Press.

Gottlieb, G. (1992). *Individual development and evolution: The genesis of novel behavior*. New York, NY: Oxford University Press.

Gottlieb, G. (2007). Probabilistic epigenesis. *Developmental Science, 10*, 1–11.

Heimann, M. (1989). Neonatal imitation gaze aversion and mother–infant interaction. *Infant Behavior and Development, 12*, 495–505.

Hernández Blasi, C., & Bjorklund, D. F. (2003). Evolutionary developmental psychology: A new tool for better understanding human ontogeny. *Human Development, 46*, 259–281.

Hill, K., & Kaplan, H. (1999). Life history traits in humans: Theory and empirical studies. *Annual Review of Anthropology, 28*, 397–430.

Joffe, T. H. (1997). Social pressures have selected for an extended juvenile period in primates. *Journal of Human Evolution, 32*, 593–605.

Kappeler, P. M., & Silk, J. B. (Eds.). (2010). *Mind the gap*. New York, NY: Springer.

Kochanska, G. (1993). Toward a synthesis of parental socialization and child temperament in early development of conscience. *Child Development, 64*, 325–347.

Konner, M. (2010). *The evolution of childhood: Relationships, emotions, mind*. Cambridge, MA: Belknap Press.

Legerstee, M. (1991). The role of person and object in eliciting early imitation. *Journal of Experimental Child Psychology, 51*, 423–433.

Meaney, M. J. (2001). Maternal care, gene expression, and the transmission of individual differences in stress reactivity across generations. *Annual Review of Neuroscience, 24*, 1161–1192.

Meltzoff, A. N., & Moore, M. K. (1977). Imitation of facial and manual gestures by human neonates. *Science, 198*, 75–78.

Mittal, C., Griskevicius, V., Simpson, J. A., Sung, S., & Young, E. S. (2015). Cognitive adaptations to stressful environments: When childhood adversity enhances adult executive function. *Journal of Personality and Social Psychology, 109*, 604–621.

Munday, P. L., White, J. W., & Warner, R. R. (2006). A social basis for the development of primary males in a sex-changing fish. *Proceedings of the Royal Society of London B: Biological Sciences, 273*, 2845–2851.

Nagy, E., & Molnar, P. (2004). Homo imitans or homo provocans? Human imprinting model of neonatal imitation. *Infant Behavior and Development, 27*, 54–63.

Nettle, D. (2010). Dying young and living fast: Variation in life history across English neighborhoods. *Behavioral Ecology, 21*, 387–395.

Nettle, D., & Cockerill, M. (2010). Development of social variation in reproductive schedules:

A study of an English urban area. *PLoS ONE*, 5, e12690.

Obradović, J., Bush, N. R., Stamperdahl, J., Adler, N. E., & Boyce, W. T. (2010). Biological sensitivity to context: The interactive effects of stress reactivity and family adversity on socioemotional behavior and school readiness. *Child Development*, *81*, 270–289.

Oppenheim, R. W. (1981). Ontogenetic adaptations and retrogressive processes in the development of the nervous system and behavior. In K. J. Connolly & H. F. R. Prechtl (Eds.), *Maturation and development: Biological and psychological perspectives* (pp. 73–108). Philadelphia, PA: International Medical Publications.

Overton, W. F. (2015). Processes, relations, and relational-developmental-systems. In W. F. Overton & P. C. M. Molenaar (Eds.), *Handbook of child psychology and developmental science. Vol. 1: Theory & method* (7th ed., pp. 9–62). Hoboken, NJ: Wiley.

Placek, C. D., & Quinlan, R. J. (2012). Adolescent fertility and risky environments: A population-level perspective across the lifespan. *Proceedings of the Royal Society B*, *279*, 4003–4008.

Pluess, M., & Belsky, J. (2011). Prenatal programming of postnatal plasticity? *Development and Psychopathology*, *23*, 29–38.

Pradeu, T. (2010). The organism in developmental systems theory. *Biological Theory*, *5*, 216–222.

Rice, F., Harold, G. T., Boivin, J., van den Bree, M., Hay, D. F., & Thapar, A. (2010). The links between prenatal stress and offspring development and psychopathology: Disentangling environmental and inherited influences. *Psychological Medicine*, *40*, 335–345.

Robert, J. S., Hall, B. K., & Olson, W. M. (2001). Bridging the gap between developmental systems theory and evolutionary developmental biology. *BioEssays*, *23*, 954–962.

Sandman, C. A., Davis, E. P., & Glynn, L. M. (2013). Prescient human fetuses thrive. *Psychological Science*, *23*, 93–100.

Sellers, P. D., II, & Bjorklund, D. F. (2014). The development of adaptive memory. In B. L. Schwartz, M. L. Howe, M. P. Toglia, & H. Otgaar (Eds.), *What's adaptive about adaptive memory?* (pp. 286–307). New York, NY: Oxford University Press.

Simpson, J. A., Griskevicius, V., Kuo, S., Sung, S., & Collins, W. A. (2012). Evolution, stress, and sensitive periods: The influence of unpredictability in early versus late childhood on sex and risky behavior. *Developmental Psychology*, *48*, 674–686.

Slagt, M., Dubas, J. S., Deković, M., & van Aken, M. A. G. (2016). Differences insensitivity to parenting depending on child temperament: A meta-analysis. *Psychological Bulletin*, *142*, 865–907.

Stearns, S. (1992). *The evolution of life histories*. Oxford: Oxford University Press.

Stright, A. D., Gallagher, K. C., & Kelley, K. (2008). Infant temperament moderates relations between maternal parenting in early childhood and children's adjustment in first grade. *Child Development*, *79*, 186–200.

Teehan, J. & diCarlo, C. (2004). On the naturalistic fallacy: A conceptual basis for evolutionary ethics. *Evolutionary Psychology*, *2*, 32–46.

Turkewitz, G., & Kenny, P. (1982). Limitations on input as a basis for neural organization and perceptual development: A preliminary theoretical statement. *Developmental Psychobiology*, *15*, 357–368.

Volk, A. A., & Atkinson, J. A. (2013). Infant and child death in the human environment of evolutionary adaptation. *Evolution and Human Behavior*, *34*, 182–192.

Weaver, I. C., Cervoni, N., Champagne, F. A., D'Alessio, A. C., Sharma, S., Seckl, J. R., ... & Meaney, M. J. (2004). Epigenetic programming by maternal behavior. *Nature Neuroscience*, *7*, 847–854.

Witherington, D. C., & Lickliter, R. (2016). Integrating development and evolution in psychological science: Evolutionary developmental psychology, developmental systems, and explanatory pluralism. *Human Development*, *59*, 200–234.

13

Cross-Situational Consistency, Variability and the Behavioral Signature

Marc A. Fournier and D. S. Moskowitz

Questions concerning the extent and nature of cross-situational consistency in behavior have been at the heart of personality since the inception of the field. In this chapter, we review the sources of influence on cross-situational consistency and variability in behavior. In the context of this review, we use the term *behavior* to refer to any discernable change in the psychological state of the individual. We organize our review around the *person* as a source of consistency, the *situation* as a source of variability, and the *person × situation interaction* as a source of consistency in the patterning of variability, known at the level of the individual as the *behavioral signature*. We consider these influences in relation to the framework of the multilevel model, and then examine both historical and contemporary approaches to their classification and the conceptualization of their causative factors.

CONSISTENCY AND VARIABILITY IN MULTILEVEL PERSPECTIVE

The study of consistency and variability in people's behavior necessarily requires researchers to obtain repeated measurements of individuals. Over the last several decades, the proliferation of tools and methods for the intensive repeated measurement of individuals in their naturalistic settings (IRM-NS; Moskowitz et al., 2009), including interval-contingent (e.g., daily diary), signal-contingent (e.g., experience sampling), and event-contingent (e.g., social interaction) recording procedures, alongside the increasingly widespread availability of data-analytic software with which to model the dependencies commonly found in such data (e.g., de Leeuw and Meijer, 2008), have afforded researchers with unprecedented opportunities to assess the extent and nature of people's consistencies. Although *in vivo* data collection methods have been available to researchers for more than a generation (e.g., Csikszentmihalyi et al., 1977), it was not until the statistical tools for modeling multilevel phenomena became more accessible over the last two decades that researchers began to more fully appreciate the richness and complexity of such multilevel data.

Within the multilevel framework, we begin with the observation that every person generates a stream of behavior over the course of time. When multiple people generate multiple streams of behavior, two forms of variation occur. First, each person's behavior over time differs from their own central tendency, reflecting within-person variation. Second, each person's central tendency in behavior differs from the central tendencies in others' behavior, reflecting between-person variation. Taken together, the within-person and between-person variation comprise the total variation in behavior.

From the simplest multilevel model, called the unconditional means model, the extent to which people are consistent in their behavior can be estimated. By dividing the between-person variation in behavior by the total variation in behavior, called the intraclass correlation (ICC), we can estimate the extent to which any two samples of behavior obtained from the same person would be expected to correlate; in other words, the extent to which people serve as a source of consistency in the organization of their behavior. The person has long been conceptualized to be a source of consistency. Indeed, the *doctrine of traits* postulates that people's behavior varies as a function of the internal dispositions that render it coherent, stable, and predictable (Kihlstrom, 2013). Although there is more to understanding people than understanding their traits (e.g., McAdams, 1995), traits can be useful for summarizing the consistencies that people demonstrate across occasions and situations. Therefore, in the first part of our review, we consider the trait as a source of consistency in the organization of behavior.

A variety of factors can cause people's behavior to depart from their respective central tendencies (e.g., the linear and cyclical effects of time). By adding these factors to the prediction of behavior, we can estimate the extent to which variation in each factor accounts for the within-person variation in behavior; in other words, the extent to which that factor serves as a source of variability in the organization of behavior. The situation has long been conceptualized to be a source of variability. Indeed, the *doctrine of situationism* postulates that people's behavior varies as a function of the external environment that communicates incentives, expectations, or demands (Kihlstrom, 2013). Although situation research continues to confront a number of pressing challenges, including whether to define situations in objective or subjective terms and what level of analysis to focus on (e.g., Rauthmann, 2015), researchers have begun to make progress in classifying and measuring situation characteristics. Therefore, in the next part of our review, we consider the situation as a source of variability in the organization of behavior.

Importantly, situations can have both normative and distinctive effects, such that the effect of a given situation can vary from one individual to the next. To the extent that there are meaningful individual differences in the effect of a given situation, we can conclude that the person and the situation interact in the organization and determination of behavior. Over the last 30 years, a growing literature has identified the idiographic patterns of situation–behavior relationships that people demonstrate around the nomothetic influences of situations. Although the nomenclature has changed from conditional dispositions (e.g., Wright and Mischel, 1987) to behavioral signatures (e.g., Mischel and Shoda, 1995) to situation-based contingencies (e.g., Fleeson, 2007), the message has remained the same: people are consistent in the extent and nature of their behavioral variability. However, although there is widespread acceptance of the *doctrine of interactionism* (Kihlstrom, 2013), the details of interactionism have yet to be fully articulated. Therefore, in the last part of our review, we confront the problem of person × situation interactionism and consider the idiographic signature of personality as a source of dynamic consistency (or stable variability) in the organization of behavior.

THE PERSON: A SOURCE OF CONSISTENCY

A critical issue concerns the range of observations over which consistency should be evident. In this section, we consider historically significant approaches to conceptualizing traits and specifying the relevant forms of consistency. We then summarize current ideas regarding the nature of personality traits, including their hierarchical organization, their predictive validity, and the trade-offs that invariably occur in prediction between bandwidth and fidelity. We conclude by reviewing two contemporary explanatory accounts of the origin and operation of traits.

Important Contributions to the Conceptualization of Traits

Allport (1937) suggested that traits were characteristics of the person consisting of a set of equivalent responses that were consistently displayed within a delimited set of situations. He proposed: 'it is the repeated occurrence of actions having the *same significance* (equivalence of response), following upon a definable range of stimuli having the same personal significance (equivalence of stimuli) that makes necessary the postulation of traits' (Allport, 1937, p. 340, italics in original). Consistency, then, would be expected for some traits across some limited set of situations. Allport (1937) acknowledged that perfect consistency 'will never be found and must not be expected' (p. 330) but that some degree of consistency should be observed across situations. Allport (1937) provided three explanations for the absence of trait consistency. First, inconsistency could result from momentary fluctuations in behavior or error variance. In this case, it would be reasonable to presume that better trait measures would reveal better evidence of consistency. Second, inconsistency could result from incorrectly conceptualizing the trait. In this case, it would be reasonable to presume that a better understanding of the trait would reveal better evidence of consistency. Finally, different situations could be responsible for activating different traits. In this case, repeated instances of the same situation could be a source of consistency across time.

Subsequent personality research focused on prediction. Cattell (1965) advocated a focus on the prediction of behavior in specific situations. He proposed combining traits weighted with respect to the focal situation to predict situation-specific behavior. His work distinguished between source traits that operate 'as an underlying source of observed behaviour' (p. 67) and surface traits that have multiple sources of influence. Consistency in behavior conceptually originated from the trait, such that when one part of a trait was 'present in a certain degree, we can infer that a person will show the other parts in a certain degree' (Cattell, 1965, p. 375). Traits were to be discovered by identifying the shared variance in many measurements of personality, including life history interviews, self-report questionnaires, and objective measures obtained from standardized situations. Cattell (1965) emphasized that many measurements should be obtained from many participants to inform the factor analyses that reveal traits, but he did not explicitly address how to sample person and situation factors to obtain 'some concept of the totality of human behaviour... the *personality sphere*' (p. 60, italics in original). Traits were taken as a principal source of consistency to the extent that the weighted value of traits to predict behavior in one situation was similar to the weighted value of traits to predict behavior in another situation.

The quest to demonstrate consistency led to a sense of crisis, as reviews of the empirical literature led personality researchers to doubt whether measures of traits could accurately predict measures of behavior, or whether measures of behavior in one situation could accurately predict measures of behavior in another (e.g., Mischel, 1968). In response to these concerns, Epstein (1979) sought to demonstrate the power of aggregation to reveal the consistency in people's behavior. As single instances of behavior are likely to contain a sizable amount of error variance, the process of aggregating across repeated occasions and situations should help to separate the signal in such measures from the noise, and in turn, reveal greater evidence of consistency. Using self-reports, informant reports, and objective measures (e.g., counts), Epstein (1979) aggregated measures of behavior across days to demonstrate sizable increases in temporal consistency. Epstein did not explicitly examine cross-situational consistency, but instead relied on the situation sampling that naturally and spontaneously occurred when people were measured on different occasions.

The power of aggregation was further demonstrated by Moskowitz (1982, 1988, 1994), who provided evidence for the beneficial effects of aggregating across occasions, situations, and behavioral referents (or trait indicators). In an early investigation, Moskowitz (1982) collected observational records of young children's dominance and dependency across multiple referents and within multiple situations in a naturalistic setting. She found that temporal stability increased as a function of the number of weeks that were sampled, coherence increased as a function of the number of behavioral referents that were sampled, and generality increased as a function of the number of situations that were sampled. Similar results were obtained with university students, whose behavior was observed in the laboratory across six standardized situations (Moskowitz, 1988). She then took this research question from the lab out into the field and conducted an event-contingent recording study to obtain multiple self-reports of behavior from community adults across multiple occasions in multiple situations (Moskowitz, 1994). She found modest to moderate levels of cross-situational consistency in people's behavior across sets of situations varying in social status and acquaintanceship. Thus, using multiple age groups and multiple methods, Moskowitz (1982, 1988, 1994) demonstrated that there are different ways to define consistency (across occasions, situations, and referents) and that each kind of consistency increases as a function of aggregation.

Fleeson (2001; Fleeson and Gallagher, 2009) subsequently developed a method for the assessment of momentary personality states corresponding to the five-factor model or 'Big Five' (i.e., extraversion, agreeableness, conscientiousness, neuroticism, and openness/intellect; Digman, 1990; Goldberg, 1993). In a series of experience-sampling studies, participants recorded their personality states throughout the day over several days (Fleeson, 2001; Fleeson and Gallagher, 2009). Each participant's states in turn were summarized by a density distribution with its own characteristic location (i.e., central tendency), size (i.e., standard deviation), and shape (i.e., skew and kurtosis). In a set of analyses that combined the data from 15 previous experience-sampling studies (Fleeson and Gallagher, 2009), ICCs ranged from 22% (extraversion) to 51% (openness/intellect), indicating that the person serves as a source of consistency in the manifestation of momentary personality states. However, virtually all of the density distribution parameters evinced significant levels of temporal stability (Fleeson, 2001), suggesting that we should not equate personality traits with people's average personality states, but rather with the entire distribution of such states that people manifest over time. Comparable results were obtained when participants' behavior was observed in a standardized set of laboratory situations (Fleeson and Law, 2015), suggesting that people are consistent because of who they are rather than because of the consistency in the situations that people naturally encounter in their everyday lives.

The Search for a Theory of Traits

Although there is no universally accepted theory of personality traits, contemporary trait researchers, for the most part, appear to have the following beliefs in common: first, personality traits reflect the operation of underlying 'neurogenic structures' (Allport, 1937) instantiated in the brain and nervous system (DeYoung and Gray, 2009); second, personality traits have become encoded into the language and everyday words that people use to differentiate the behavior of one individual from that of another (Goldberg, 1993); and third, personality traits varying in their conceptual breadth and depth can be reconciled within an integrative hierarchy, where a small number of broad factors at the top of the hierarchy serves to organize a much larger number of narrow facets underneath (Cattell, 1957; McCrae and Costa, 2008). Indeed, it can be shown that varying factor solutions of the trait domain, ranging from two-factor to five-factor solutions, can be reconciled within a hierarchy of such factor solutions (Markon et al., 2005).

The question for trait researchers may thus be less a matter of which factor solution is correct, and more a matter of which factor solution yields trait constructs at a level of conceptual breadth suitable for the criteria to be predicted. A comprehensive comparison of commonly used personality measures found that most instruments demonstrate comparable levels of validity in the prediction of behavioral acts, informant reports, and clinical indicators of psychopathology (Grucza and Goldberg, 2007). Moreover, a compelling literature has accumulated attesting to the power of personality traits to predict life's consequential outcomes. Ozer and Benet-Martínez (2006) concluded from their narrative review of the literature that each of the five-factor traits is associated with a broad range of consequential life outcomes across individual, interpersonal, and institutional life domains. Roberts et al. (2007) concluded from their meta-analytic review of the literature that traits predict consequential life outcomes (i.e., mortality, divorce, occupational attainment) over and above the established effects of socioeconomic status and intelligence. Although the broad traits at the top of the personality trait hierarchy are capable of predicting a broad array of significant life outcomes, there is a growing recognition that the narrower traits underneath can often provide useful incremental information. Facets, for instance, have demonstrated incremental validity over and above broad traits in the prediction of a range of criteria, from indices of personality disorder (Reynolds and Clark, 2001) to everyday behaviors (Paunonen and Ashton, 2001). Below facets in the hierarchy are personality nuances (corresponding approximately with single items), highly contextualized behavioral tendencies that have also demonstrated incremental predictive validity (Mõttus et al., 2017).

A shared understanding of the trait construct, however, has not translated into a shared definition of consistency. Fleeson and Noftle (2008) sought to organize the various definitions of consistency into a systematic order that would serve to specify and clarify their relationships. They organized the consistency concepts around what they called the basic consistency question (p. 1364): 'Does the enactment of behavior by the same person remain similar across variations in competing determinants of behavior?' The consistency question contains three components, the specifications to which permit comparisons and contrasts between differing definitions of consistency. First, consistency concepts differ in terms of the competing determinant of behavior across which consistency is expected. The competing determinant of behavior is the alternative to personality that might be responsible for a person's behavior;

if a person's behavior does not change despite a change in the competing determinant, then the person is likely the cause of that behavior. Variations in time, situation content, and behavior content have all been considered as potentially competing determinants. Second, consistency concepts differ in terms of how similarity has been defined. Similarity has been defined in terms of the degree to which the person's behavior remains: in the same absolute position (absolute similarity), the same relative to others' behavior (relative similarity), and the same relative to their other behaviors (ipsative similarity). Third, consistency concepts differ in terms of how the enactment of behavior has been defined: single enactment, aggregated enactment, contingent enactment, and patterned enactment. Taken together, these three components generate a 3 × 3 × 4 supermatrix of 36 consistency concepts. Each different specification of the three components yields a different type of consistency.

Although Fleeson and Noftle (2008) recognize that some kind of consistency in behavior must be demonstrated to infer the existence of personality (Allport, 1937), they maintain that no particular type of consistency is necessarily privileged. Rather, the degree to which various types of consistency are evident should inform researchers about how to conceptualize the underlying nature of personality. Indeed, as some kinds of consistency are unlikely to ever be demonstrated (e.g., ipsative similarity in the patterned enactment of behavior), researchers cannot expect that every personality construct will demonstrate every kind of consistency. On the contrary, Fleeson and Noftle (2008) argue that demonstrating even one kind of consistency would be sufficient for establishing the scientific value of a personality construct. Nevertheless, other researchers have argued that some types of consistency are privileged in the study of personality. Reflecting on the field's longstanding preoccupation with demonstrating cross-situational consistency, Roberts (2009) has advanced the more radical position that temporal consistency is paramount. Noting that cross-situational inconsistencies in behavior have long been taken as signs that traits are questionable constructs (Mischel, 1968), Roberts (2009) has countered by noting that 'the issue of cross-situational consistency was never germane to the definition of personality trait' (p. 139) and that cross-situational variation is in fact critical to most trait conceptualizations. Traits, he has argued, are inherently contextualized, and consequently we should expect people's behavior to vary from one situation to another. For Roberts (2009), what matters is the configural consistency of behavior across functionally equivalent situations and time.

Given the extent to which the content of personality traits overlaps with the content of the behavior that trait variables are often tasked to predict, it is reasonable to question whether personality traits provide noncircular explanations for behavior or whether they merely stand in as summary descriptions. Although personality researchers have made considerable progress in taxonomizing traits, their work has yet to explain 'where traits come from, how they operate, and how they produce differences in behavior' (Fleeson and Jayawickreme, 2015, p. 83). What traits need is a theory that specifies the mechanisms through which personality traits manifest in personality states and trait-relevant behavior.

The Sociogenomic Model of Personality (Roberts and Jackson, 2008) is intended to provide a contemporary account of how biological and environmental factors interact to determine a person's personality traits. In contrast to the traditional assumption that biological factors are immutable, the authors delineate how genetic effects depend upon the environment for their activation and maintenance. The model consists of four constructs: (a) biological factors, (b) the environment, (c) personality states, and (d) personality traits. Both biological factors and the environment are posited to have bidirectional paths linking them to personality states; personality states, in turn, are posited to have a bidirectional path linking them to personality traits. Biological factors can affect personality traits directly, but can only affect the environment through the indirect effects that they have on personality states and personality traits. Crucially, the environment can affect biological factors directly (such as accidents that directly cause biological traumas or insults) as well as indirectly through the effects they have on the person's momentary personality states (such as socialization effects that indirectly and incrementally influence enduring personality traits through their direct and more immediate influence on momentary personality states). The model developed by Roberts and Jackson (2008) thus represents how environments interact with genes to produce the biology behind behavior and how personality traits reciprocally and indirectly influence biology through the effects that personality traits have on states and behavior.

Whole Trait Theory (Fleeson and Jayawickreme, 2015) is intended to integrate the trait and social-cognitive approaches to personality, by advocating that a full account of traits would include both descriptive and explanatory sides, and that the trait and social-cognitive approaches each provide one part of a 'whole theory' of traits. On the descriptive side, the theory suggests that we think of traits as density distributions of states, summarizing how frequently a person manifests a given trait at every possible level of that trait. Fleeson has shown that people's density distributions are stable over time, although different distributional parameters (i.e., location, size, shape) are stable to different degrees (Fleeson, 2001; Fleeson and Gallagher, 2009). On the explanatory side, the theory suggests that we identify the social-cognitive processes responsible for these density distributions, including interpretative processes (e.g., appraisals of situations), motivational processes (e.g., hoped-for or feared-for end-states), and stability-inducing processes (e.g., homeostatic forces). Consistent with Whole Trait Theory, Fleeson has demonstrated that variation in goal pursuit predicts within- and between-person variation in trait enactment, such that the same person will momentarily enact different traits because he or she is momentarily pursuing different goals, and different people will consistently enact different traits because they consistently pursue different goals (McCabe and Fleeson, 2016). Social-cognitive mechanisms thus serve to explain within-person variation in personality states as well as between-person variation in the parameters of the resulting density distributions.

In summary, personality theorists and researchers have identified multiple ways to conceptualize the consistency of a personality characteristic. Of paramount importance is deciding which consistency coefficients are most relevant to a personality characteristic, given how it has been defined. Indeed, the systematic examination of which forms of consistency a personality characteristic manifests, and which forms of consistency it does not, should provide a better understanding of that personality characteristic (e.g., Fleeson and Noftle, 2008; Moskowitz, 1982). Although evidence of temporal consistency is often a reasonable requirement to make for a personality characteristic, it is not a necessary requirement for all personality characteristics, such as personality states. Furthermore, researchers will still need to determine the length of time over which the temporal consistency of a personality characteristic should be demonstrated. Nevertheless, the most complex decisions concern how to assess cross-situational consistency, given the lack of agreement among researchers as to how situations should be defined. We subsequently consider the situation as a source of variability in behavior.

THE SITUATION: A SOURCE OF VARIABILITY

A critical issue concerns how to incorporate the situation into our understanding of consistency and variability. In this section, we consider historically significant approaches to conceptualizing the situation. We then summarize the fundamental problems currently confronting the study of situations, including whether to focus on objective or subjective features of situations, how to decide on the level of resolution, and the need for a comprehensive taxonomy. We conclude by reviewing contemporary research involving promising systems for the classification of situation characteristics.

Important Contributions to the Conceptualization of Situations

Murray's (1938) early ideas concerning the press of situations continue to be cited in contemporary situation research. Murray (1938) classified aspects of the situation, which he referred to as *press*, in regard to the benefits and harms that a given situation exerts in relation to a particular need. For example, the press of affiliation could occur in the presence of others, whereas the press of rejection could occur in their absence. Importantly, Murray (1938) distinguished between alpha press, which he identified with the objective reality as it might be judged by trained observers, and beta press, which he identified with the subjective reality of the person *in situ*. Murray (1938) suggested that it was the person's subjective experience that was the primary determinant of their behavior. Thus, early on, there was recognition of the importance of both distinguishing between objective and subjective features of the situation and classifying need-press units or *thema* (i.e., patterns of press and need that coalesce around specific interactions), although no systematic empirical research on situations was to follow until much later.

Rotter (1954, 1955, 1981) was the first to attempt a comprehensive analysis of the psychological situation as part of his social learning theory of personality. For Rotter (1954), 'the unit of investigation for the study of personality is the interaction of the individual and his meaningful environment' (p. 85), with the term *meaningful environment* referring to the acquired significance or meaning that the environment has for the individual. All variables in social learning theory are thus situationally bound. Rotter (1954) defined the psychological situation as the complex set of interacting cues that are perceived by the individual over a designated period of time. He suggested that these cues determine for the individual the expectancies for behavior–reinforcement sequences and the reinforcement value of the situation. Cues can become grouped or classified through shared learning experiences, such that shared cultural experiences can produce shared expectancies for groups of individuals who respond similarly to situational cues. Rotter (1954) argued that, although the psychological situation is, in a sense, an aspect of the individual, the subjective situation does not exist independently of the objective situation; furthermore, objective descriptions of the situation are necessary to examine both the differences in people's behavior in reaction to a specific situation and the consistencies in people's behavior in reaction to classes of similar situations. For Rotter (1955), situations could be identified on the basis of their objective characteristics and then studied in terms of their psychological significance or meaning to the individual.

Pervin (1978) reviewed issues relevant to the definition, measurement, and classification of stimuli, situations, and environments. He noted that such terms were frequently used without adequate definition, oftentimes interchangeably and other times haphazardly. He suggested that the distinctions between them appear to concern the scale of analysis, from molecular variables in the case of stimuli to molar variables in the case of environments (with situations in between), and cautioned that such distinctions may be of importance if different relationships to behavior are observed depending on the scale of analysis. Situations, he noted, concern the organism's engagement with an array of objects and actions over a designated period of time, and as such, a situation can be defined by who was present, what took place, and both where and when the situation occurred. He acknowledged that researchers differed in their tendencies to focus upon the objective situation or the perceived situation and indicated that studying how the two relate would be a valuable endeavor. Finally, he noted that the study of situations had been hampered by the lack of standardized units and structure, stressing the importance of taxonomic classification for advancing a cumulative psychological science of situations.

Magnusson (1981) distinguished between two different kinds of situational effects on behavior: general effects (in which the rank order of individuals stays the same across situations) and differential effects (in which the rank order of individuals changes across situations). He noted the distinction that others had made between actual and perceived situations and that the units of analysis in regard to perceived situations could be organized in figure-ground terms, such that the (molar) environmental units form the ground for the perception and interpretation of the (molecular) situational stimuli. Magnusson (1981) brought attention to the issue of how to demarcate situations as a unit of measurement when the temporal boundaries between situations are often ambiguous. Finally, although he recognized that the field at the time was far from a definitive taxonomy of situation characteristics, Magnusson (1981) noted a number of situation characteristics that could serve as the starting point for such a taxonomy, including the structural characteristics of situations that he viewed in quantitative terms, such as complexity, clarity, strength, and promotion versus restriction, as well as the content characteristics of situations that he viewed in qualitative terms, such as tasks, rules, roles, physical settings, and the other person.

Block and Block (1981) distinguished between three different levels of situational analysis reflecting the 'successive stages of the interpretation of the situation by the experiencing individual' (p. 86). First, there is the physico-biological situation, which they defined as 'the infinitely detailable, perceptually unfiltered and uninterpreted, sensorily available intakes by the individual' (p. 86) that reflect the most objective and observable features of the situation. Next, there is the canonical situation, which they defined as 'the consensually defined, consensually structured, or consensually accepted situation' (p. 87). Finally, there is the functional situation, which they defined as 'the psychological demand-qualities and structure of the immediately pressing situation as it effectively registers on or is construed by the particular individual at the particular moment under scrutiny' (p. 87). For Block and Block (1981), individuals respond only to the functional situation. Any differences between the canonical situation and the individual's functional situation are attributable to the operation of the individual's personality structure. However, as the functional situation represents a potential tautology (i.e., where the functional situation is inferred from the person's behavior, and the person's behavior is explained by their functional situation), Block and Block (1981) proposed that the interactionist approach would require researchers to formulate 'a psychologically nontrivial set of situational parameters' (p. 88) to characterize the entire range of canonical situations that people encounter.

The Search for a Taxonomy of Situations

A number of issues and controversies have thus hindered situation research, such as deciding whether to define situations in objective or subjective terms, determining what level of analysis to focus on, establishing a comprehensive taxonomy of situation characteristics, and validating measures of situation dimensions. Because no situation taxonomy has yet to achieve widespread acceptance, most researchers have relied on non-validated, in-house measures. Several research strategies for generating or sampling situational information have emerged. Descriptive lists of situation variables can be compiled from the social psychological literature; however, as Rotter (1981) noted, no such list or catalogue is likely to be exhaustive or complete. Alternative strategies vary in whether they use bottom-up or top-down approaches and whether they are restrictive or inclusive in focus. First, situational variables can be generated ad hoc by the researchers themselves for their specific research purposes (researcher-derived situations). Second, situational variables can be generated by laypersons by having them recall previous situations, speculate on hypothetical situations, or track the situations they encounter over time (layperson-derived situations). Third, situational variables can be generated through scientific theorizing (theory-derived situations). Fourth, situational variables can be generated through systematic examination of natural language (lexicon-derived situations). We consider each of these four strategies in turn.

First, situational variables can be generated ad hoc by the researchers themselves. Fleeson (2007), for instance, examined whether situational variation could explain the extent to which people manifest various traits in their behavior. The goal was to determine which situation characteristics would elicit changes in personality states related to four of the five-factor personality traits (i.e., extraversion, agreeableness, conscientiousness, and emotional stability). The exploratory strategy he adopted for selecting situation characteristics 'was to identify situations that seemed to differ in the kind of behavior that is evident in them and then to speculate what characteristics in those situations was [sic] responsible for the behavioral differences' (p. 830). Over a period of several weeks, participants were asked to report several times per day on their personality states and to concurrently rate characteristics of the situation. Eleven potentially important situational variables were measured, including the number of other people that were present and the extent to which the situation was structured. Fleeson (2007) found that people's momentary states were contingent upon the momentary characteristics of the situation and that these situation-based contingencies played a part in explaining the within-person variation in people's states.

Second, situational variables can be generated by laypersons. A series of field studies conducted through the 1980s and 1990s at Wediko Children's Services, a residential summer camp for children characterized by significant behavioral difficulties (Wright and Mischel, 1987, 1988; Shoda et al., 1989, 1994), distinguished between nominal situations that have limited generalizability (e.g., 'cabin meeting') and the active psychological ingredients or features of situations that are potentially generalizable to other situations (e.g., 'being teased'). The research included assessments of situations with 'distinct sets of salient psychological features that are relevant, important, and consensually encoded by people in the population sampled' (Shoda et al., 1994, p. 677). As part of this project, camp counselors were asked to provide personality descriptions of the children to determine the extent to which conditional 'hedges' were spontaneously incorporated into their personality descriptions (i.e., 'If the child is in situation X, then he or she will display behavior Y'). Both children and adults were found to use hedges in their personality descriptions, reflecting their understanding of the variability in behavior. Content analyses of these conditional statements were later used to identify the most salient and observable psychological features of children's situations, namely the valence of the interaction (positive vs. negative) and the type of interaction partner (adult counselor vs. child peer). Using behavioral ratings obtained from hourly observations of the children over a six-week period, the researchers found that the similarity and differences across psychological situations helped to explain the variability in the children's behavior. For most behavioral dimensions, children showed significant levels of consistency within the same psychological situation, and their levels of consistency across psychological situations increased with the number of the situational features that were shared (Shoda et al., 1994).

Third, situational variables can be generated on the basis of theory. One theory that has made important contributions to the study of cross-situational consistency and variability is Social Role Theory (e.g., Stryker, 2007). A social role refers to 'a set of behavioral expectations attached to a position in an organized set of social relationships' (Stryker, 2007, p. 1083). Roberts (2007) suggested that social roles have a number of features making them well suited for personality research. First, social roles are a common way that people understand themselves, as evinced in their spontaneous responses to the question, 'Who am I?' (Grossack, 1960). Second, social roles are conceptualized at a level of breadth similar to that of personality traits. Third, social roles can be organized around the interpersonal dimensions of affiliation and power, allowing nominal role variables (e.g., supervisor, coworker, supervisee) to be reconceptualized as ordinal role variables (e.g., higher-status, equal-status, lower-status) with their attendant statistical advantages. For instance, using event-contingent recordings of working adults' behavior collected over a 20-day period, Moskowitz et al. (1994) demonstrated that work roles varying in their levels of social status (or power) influenced people's levels of dominance and submissiveness, such that people behaved more dominantly in higher-status situations (i.e., the role of supervisor) and more submissively in lower-status situations (i.e., the role of supervisee).

Fourth, situational variables can be generated by systematically examining the lexicon. In much the same way that research has examined how traits are encoded into the natural language (e.g., Allport and Odbert, 1936; Goldberg, 1993), so has research begun to examine how situations are linguistically encoded. As prior lexical studies of situations were limited by their focus upon frequently used descriptors, Parrigon and colleagues conducted a series of studies using a diverse array of methodological and sampling strategies to identify the largest number of descriptors to date for capturing the characteristics of the psychological situation (Parrigon et al., 2017). Beginning with a database with more than 10,000 adjectives representing natural language use, an initial set of situation characteristics containing 851 adjectives (535 non-redundant adjectives) were identified. Seven dimensions of situations emerged through a diverse array of derivation strategies including (a) qualitative analysis, (b) factor analyses of large-scale *in situ* ratings of situations, and (c) the use of lexical-vector representations from neural-network-based models (derived from millions of sources of natural-language usage with a total of 146.7 billion words): Complexity, Adversity, Positive Valence, Typicality, Importance, humOr, and Negative Valence. Measures of the CAPTION dimensions have demonstrated good psychometric properties and early evidence of predictive validity, even when pitted against other taxonomic frameworks (such as the Situational Eight DIAMONDS, discussed below). However, as the CAPTION model is so new, no studies have examined the extent to which variation in these situation dimensions is responsible for the variation in behavior that is observed when people are measured intensively in their naturalistic settings.

Critically, these strategies have been unsuccessful insofar as they have led neither to a comprehensive taxonomy of situation characteristics nor to a reliable and valid measure with which to assess the underlying situation dimensions. To fill this void, Funder, Nave, Rauthmann, Sherman, and colleagues have been developing a framework for organizing and measuring the psychologically important meanings of situation characteristics (Rauthmann et al., 2014; Rauthmann et al., 2015). Their instrument, the Riverside Situational Q-Sort (RSQ; Wagerman and Funder, 2009) was not based on any explicit theory; rather, its items were developed from the 100-item California Adult Q-Sort (CAQ; Block, 1961). The items were originally written to describe situations in which the personality characteristics described by CAQ items might be expected to emerge. The original version consisted of exactly 100 items (one per CAQ item; Wagerman and Funder, 2009); subsequent versions eliminated or reworded items that were deemed unclear or redundant or that produced little to no variance (Sherman et al., 2010). A 32-item version (RSQ-8; Rauthmann et al., 2014) and a 24-item version (S8; Rauthmann and Sherman, 2016a) have since been developed to measure what they now call the Situational Eight DIAMONDS: Duty, Intellect, Adversity, Mating, pOsitivity, Negativity, Deception, and Sociality.

Across its various incarnations, the RSQ has produced a number of insights. ICCs on the RSQ range from .17 to .36 ($M = .26$; Sherman et al., 2015), indicating that situations described by the same person tend to be more similar than situations described by different people. Indeed, the temporal stability of people's situational experiences is comparable to the temporal stability of their personality states (Rauthmann et al., 2016). Some people report more situational similarity than others, and people's levels of situational similarity predict their levels of behavioral consistency (Sherman et al., 2010). However, as behavior is more consistent than the situations that people experience (Sherman et al., 2015), something more than situations must be responsible for their behavioral consistency (i.e., personality). Still, people's situational experiences significantly predict their behavior both within and between persons, such that people's momentary situational experiences predict their momentary behavior and people's overall situational experiences predict their overall behavior (Sherman et al., 2015). Finally, although the dimensions of the RSQ were empirically rather than theoretically derived, the RSQ can assess the situation characteristics that are relevant to particular psychological theories through template-matching procedures, whereby experts use the RSQ to describe the prototype for a situation relevant to a particular theory and their ratings are averaged together to form a template. Participants' responses on the RSQ are then correlated with the situational template to index the extent to which each participant's RSQ profile matched the profile of the situational template (called template match scores). To date, template-matching procedures have been used to assess the extent to which situations fulfill people's basic psychological needs for autonomy, competence, and relatedness, as posited by Self-Determination Theory (Deci and Ryan, 1987, 2000; Sherman et al., 2012), and the extent to which situations relate to evolutionarily relevant motives (self-protection, disease avoidance, affiliation, kin care, mate seeking, mate retention, and status seeking), as posited by Fundamental Motives Theory (Kenrick et al., 2010a, 2010b; Morse et al., 2015).

In summary, theory and research into the conceptualization, measurement, and taxonomization of situations have been hindered by a number of issues and controversies, including whether to define situations in objective or subjective terms and what level of analysis to focus on. In the absence of a comprehensive and consensually accepted taxonomy of situation characteristics, researchers have used a number of strategies to generate or sample situation information, including relying on themselves to specify the situational variables (researcher-derived situations), turning to participants (laypeople) to specify the situational variables (layperson-derived situations), relying on established theories to specify the situational variables (theory-derived situations), or turning to natural languages to specify the situational variables (lexicon-derived situations). Although there is no widely accepted theory about the nature of situations, scholars have been attempting to outline the core principles that will be needed to guide future situation research (Rauthmann et al., 2015), such as the importance of obtaining multiple perspectives on the situation, the importance of specifying the distinct levels of reality at which situations can be said to exist, and the importance of understanding the subjective, psychological situation of the individual (i.e., the situation as it has been psychologically processed and ascribed meaning).

THE PERSON × SITUATION INTERACTION

People differ in their ways of encoding, understanding, and responding to the characteristics of the situation. Consequently, persons and situations do not exist in isolation; rather, their characteristics have the potential to combine and interact in the organization and determination of behavior. In this section, we consider three different programs of research that have been aimed at understanding individual differences in situation–behavior relationships, from the early studies of children's behavioral signatures (Shoda et al., 1994), to the study of adults' behavioral signatures in the interpersonal domain (Fournier et al., 2008) and the domain of athletic competition (Smith et al., 2009), to the identification of situation-based contingencies in the manifestation of trait-relevant behavior (Fleeson, 2007) and vulnerability to stress (Shoda et al., 2013).

The study of situation–behavior relationships began with a field research program conducted at Wediko Children's Services, a residential summer camp for children characterized by significant behavioral difficulties (Mischel and Shoda, 1995; Shoda et al., 1989, 1994; Wright and Mischel, 1987, 1988). As part of this research, hourly observations of the children were collected by the camp counselors over a six-week period. An early goal of this research was to demonstrate that the fundamental unit for studying behavioral dispositions is not the overall frequency of behavior, but rather the conditional probability of behavior relevant to that disposition in circumscribed situations. From this perspective, consistency arises from if–then propositions that characterize contingencies between categories of situations and categories of behavior rather than generalized response tendencies. Wright and Mischel (1987) found that children judged to be aggressive or withdrawn varied in their dispositionally relevant behavior across situations, diverging into relatively predictable levels of aggressive and withdrawn behavior in situations that taxed the children's limited social, self-regulatory, and cognitive competencies.

A follow-up study sought to test the stability of the children's discriminating patterns of situation–behavior relationships, to which the researchers now referred as behavioral signatures (Shoda et al., 1994). Counselors recorded the category of situation that each child encountered (e.g., peer approach, peer tease) and whether the child responded with any of the categories of behavior (e.g., compliance, prosocial talk). To test the stability of children's situation–behavior profiles, Shoda et al. (1994) randomly divided the data for each child from each situation in half, thereby yielding two situation–behavior profiles for each child from non-overlapping samples of occasions. Stability of the situation–behavior profiles was indexed by within-person correlations, which estimated the degree of resemblance between the two profiles for each child. Mean levels of profile stability ranged from .28 to .47, leading Shoda and colleagues (1994) to conclude that the typical child at the summer camp could be characterized by idiographic signatures, or stable within-person patterns of variability across salient psychological situations.

Mischel and Shoda (1995) subsequently proposed a meta-theoretical framework, the cognitive-affective processing system (CAPS), to conceptualize the within-person processes responsible for behavioral variability. According to the CAPS framework, individuals encode the subjective psychological features of the situation through a complex configuration of within-person variables (or cognitive-affective units), including self-regulatory systems and plans (i.e., subjective goals and standards), competencies (i.e., subjective beliefs about one's skills and abilities), expectancies (i.e., subjective beliefs about behavior–outcome probabilities), and values (i.e., subjective values for reinforcements). What individuals do in a given situation is thus modeled dynamically within CAPS as a function of what they want, what behaviors they believe themselves able to perform, what outcomes they expect follow from those behaviors, and what values they assign to those outcomes. Individuals differ with respect to the accessibility or availability of cognitive-affective units and with respect to the organization of relations between cognitive-affective units. This complex system of interrelated variables gives rise to stable but conditional if–then dispositions, such that each individual demonstrates stable levels of behavior within situations and stable patterns of behavior (i.e., behavioral signatures) across situations. The CAPS framework thus provides one account of how individuals encode the psychological features of the situation and, in turn, how the psychological features of the situation activate the within-person processes responsible for the manifest variability in behavior.

Fournier and colleagues (2008) sought to determine whether the behavior of adults could also be characterized by stable behavioral signatures. This research focused on the interpersonal domain, and relied on the dimensions of agency (dominance–submissiveness) and communion (agreeableness–quarrelsomeness) to characterize both the domains of situations and the domains of behavior. Participants recruited from the community were asked to complete event-contingent records of their social interactions over a 20-day period. Participants recorded their own social behavior (dominant, agreeable, submissive, quarrelsome) in four situations defined by the perceived social behavior of their primary interaction partners (agreeable–dominant, agreeable–submissive, quarrelsome–submissive, quarrelsome–dominant). Each participant's data from each situation were randomly divided in half, thereby yielding two situation–behavior profiles for each participant from non-overlapping samples of occasions. Following Shoda and colleagues (1994), stability of the situation–behavior profiles was indexed by within-person correlations, which estimated the degree of resemblance between the two profiles for each participant. Mean levels of profile stability ranged from .24 to .52, leading Fournier and colleagues (2008) to conclude that the typical adult displays stable behavioral signatures in the interpersonal domain.

Despite widespread focus on the psychological situation, a potential limitation of this research is its reliance on the participants to rate both their own behavior and the situation. To examine behavioral signatures using independent ratings of behavior in situations whose salient psychological features could be objectively coded, researchers turned to athletic competitions in which situations (i.e., wins, losses, ties) can be clearly identified. Youth baseball coaches were unobtrusively observed *in vivo* across a variety of game situations, and their situation–behavior contingencies were related to athletes' attitudes toward the coaches (Smith et al., 2009). Most coaches exhibited stable and idiographically distinctive situation–behavior contingencies in both their supportive and instructional behaviors across the three salient psychological situations of (a) winning, (b) losing, and (c) tied or close half-innings. Although the coaches' overall rates of behavior accounted for little variance in the extent to which their athletes expressed liking them, specific situation–behavior contingencies (e.g., if the team is winning, then be supportive; if the team is losing, then be punitive) were significantly related to children's attitudes toward their coaches. Coaches' contextualized behaviors were stable and more highly correlated with being liked than were their aggregated, decontextualized behaviors.

The traditional if–then situation–behavior profile has thus portrayed how continuous ratings of behavior change across discontinuous categories of situations; these profiles, in turn, can be characterized in terms of their elevation (i.e., the average or central tendency of an individual's behavior across situations), scatter (i.e., the spread or dispersion of an individual's behavior across situations), and shape (i.e., the organization or patterning of an individual's behavior across situations). However, to the extent that nominal categories of situations can be arranged into an ordinal or interval scale, the shape or pattern of each profile should reduce to a pattern approximating that of a straight line, characterized by an intercept (corresponding to the elevation of the profile) and a slope (corresponding to the scatter or spread of the profile). As researchers have moved away from thinking about situations in terms of discrete or dichotomous categories to thinking about situations in terms of characteristics or features that are more appropriately described dimensionally, the study of situation–behavior relationships has moved away from the idea of profiles and toward the idea of slopes, reflecting the extent to which continuous variation in an individual's behavior is contingent upon the continuous variation in the occurrence of some situation characteristic.

Fleeson (2007) adopted such an approach in an effort to demonstrate that the within-person variation in people's behavior arises, at least in part, from the within-person variation in the situation characteristics that they report experiencing. Over the course of several weeks, participants were asked several times each day to report on their personality states as well as on the characteristics of the concurrent situation. Participants demonstrated sizable within-person variation in their manifestation of each trait.

Within-person variation was meaningful, insofar as it was partly predictable from the characteristics of the situation. For example, people showed higher state levels of extraversion when they were in the presence of others with whom they were well acquainted and higher state levels of conscientiousness when the situation presented an obligation, imposition, or impending deadline. People's situation–behavior contingencies explained a significant portion of the sizable within-person variation that was demonstrated in their behavior. People, however, differed reliably from each other in their situation–behavior contingencies, indicating that people differed not only in terms of how likely they were to manifest various personality states but also in terms of the conditions under which those personality states were most likely to manifest (i.e., their behavioral signatures).

Shoda and colleagues (2013) extended this dimensional approach to the study of stress vulnerability. Web-based daily-diary assessment data were collected over a two-month period, during which participants reported on the characteristics of situations as well as their cognitions, affects, and coping behaviors in response to varying levels of daily life stress. Participants' stress levels were regressed onto each of several situation characteristics, allowing each participant to be described by their own stress-vulnerability signature, with each point on the stress-vulnerability profile corresponding to the regression slope reflecting the relationship between a situation characteristic and the level of stress experienced. Plotting the regression slopes in this way, the distinctive high and low points of a participant's profile suggest the specific situation characteristics to which the participant is particularly vulnerable or resilient. They subsequently asked whether participants differed meaningfully in their profiles. Multilevel modeling was used to test the null hypothesis that the effects of situations are the same across individuals, with rejection of the null hypothesis suggesting individual differences in the effects of situations (i.e., a person × situation interaction). Shoda and colleagues (2013) did find that participants differed significantly in the patterning of their stress-vulnerability signatures.

It is of interest to note that researchers attempting to simulate the dynamics underlying stable behavioral dispositions like those summarized by the Big Five found that their simulations were also capable of generating person × situation interactions and if–then contingencies. Read et al. (2010) presented neural network simulations in which specific evolutionarily relevant motivational systems (e.g., social bonding, dominance) were organized underneath two basic motivational systems (i.e., approach, avoidance) that were in turn moderated by an overarching constraint system. Several important within-person mechanisms were modeled: the chronic activation of motives, differences in the sensitivities of specific motives and the motivational systems to inputs, and inhibitory processes. Traits were modeled as: (a) individual differences in the baseline levels of activation for each of the specific motives; (b) individual differences in the overall sensitivities of the approach and avoidance systems; and (c) individual differences in the general constraint system, which moderated the activity level of the entire system and provided focus to the underlying motivational systems. Hidden layers were introduced to enhance computational power and enable the models to learn complex configurations and links between situational features and goals. The resulting models successfully learned complex relationships between different situations and the behaviors appropriate to those situations, in which each situation was associated with multiple behaviors and each behavior was associated with multiple situations. Although simulated variation in the relative sensitivities of these systems produced recognizable patterns of behavioral consistency, these simulations also demonstrated the capacity to capture dynamic person × situation interactions and idiographic situation–behavior contingencies.

Having established that individuals can be characterized by stable but idiographically distinct patterns of situation–behavior relations (or signatures), the most pressing question for person × situation interaction researchers concerns what to do with these idiographic patterns. Vansteelandt and Van Mechelen (2004) have suggested that model-based cluster analyses (specifically, discrete mixture distribution linear logistic test models) can be used to identify the multidimensional individual differences underlying the variation in situation–behavior profiles. To illustrate, Vansteelandt and Van Mechelen (2004) collected vignette data where participants rated the extent to which they would display five anger-out responses (e.g., 'I lose my temper') and five anger-in responses (e.g., 'I boil inside') in three hypothetical situations varying in their level of frustration. Vansteelandt and Van Mechelen's (2004) analyses of these 30 situation–response combinations revealed three interpretable types, suggesting that individual differences in situation–response profiles for the expression of anger could not be captured by a single dimension. Nevertheless, although this data-analytic strategy permits researchers to explore the multidimensional structure of situation–behavior profiles without requiring researchers to have clear a priori knowledge about which external factors are most relevant or predictive, the study of situation–behavior profiles still has yet to identify a replicable taxonomy of person × situation interaction patterns.

In summary, there is a growing literature attesting to the claim that individuals differ in how they encode, understand, and respond to a given situation. Children at camp differ in how they respond to being praised and teased (Shoda et al., 1994); youth sports coaches differ in how they respond to wins and losses (Smith et al., 2009). Adults differ in how they respond to others' dominance and warmth (Fournier et al., 2008) and in the stress they experience in response to a range of upsetting situations (Shoda et al., 2013). However, a limiting factor of this literature is its failure to date to produce a replicable and generalizable system for classifying and organizing the range of situation–behavior patterns that people manifest. Personality is often conceptualized as a complex and self-organizing system (e.g., Mischel and Shoda, 1995); self-organizing systems consist of parameters that are not entirely free to vary and that tend as a consequence to 'snap in' to one of a limited number of coherent configurations that can satisfy the system's constraints (Cervone and Shoda, 1999). To the extent that 'a complex system of social-cognitive mediating processes does not result in an infinite number of configurations or freely variable parameters' (Cervone and Shoda, 1999, p. 19), we would expect that behavioral signature variation would reduce to a limited number of underlying personality configurations or personality types.

REFLECTIONS AND FUTURE DIRECTIONS

Before concluding, we note what we believe to be the most challenging problems at the level of the person, the situation, the person × situation interaction, the outcome variable of interest, and the multilevel framework itself in researchers' ongoing efforts to understand the cross-situational consistency and variability in people's behavior. We discuss each of these problems in turn.

The Person

One longstanding challenge that trait researchers have faced is establishing that traits can serve as explanatory or causal constructs rather than mere summary descriptions. In trait theories, the latent trait variable is taken as more fundamental than the item responses; indeed, the item responses are thought to vary as a function of the latent variable. However, the problem with latent traits as explanatory variables is that they cannot operate as explanations at the level of the individual. A necessary condition to establish causation is covariation; if there is no covariation, then there cannot be causation. Consequently, a person's latent variable value can never be said to cause their item responses, as a person's position on the latent variable is conceptualized as a constant, and a constant cannot be a cause. In this sense, traits as constants cannot be causative at the level of individuals (Borsboom et al., 2003). One potential approach to solving this problem is Fleeson and Jayawickreme's (2015) Whole Trait Theory, which equates (a) the descriptive aspect of a person's trait with the entire density distribution of states relevant to that trait that the person manifests over time, and (b) the explanatory aspect of a person's trait with the social-cognitive processes that are responsible for producing that density distribution.

The Situation

One longstanding challenge that situation researchers have faced is deciding how to reconcile the objective situation with the normative and distinctive ways in which the objective situation is subjectively construed. Following the Thomas Theorem, which holds that any situation perceived to be real will be real in its consequences (Thomas and Thomas, 1928), researchers have returned time and again to the psychological situation as the proximal cause of people's behavior. However, while it may be that any situation that is perceived to be real will have real consequences for how people behave, it does not follow that any situation of consequence for a person's behavior was necessarily first perceived by that person. For instance, exposure to bright light has been found to affect people's social behavior, such that they become more agreeable and less quarrelsome (aan het Rot et al., 2008), most likely by increasing people's levels of serotonergic functioning; however, it is not obvious that light would need to be psychologically processed, either implicitly or explicitly, to affect people's behavior. Consequently, while it may be difficult for researchers to underestimate the profound importance of the psychological situation, it may be solipsistic for researchers to presume that all situations must be psychologically processed for them to affect our behavior.

The Person × Situation Interaction

Since Cronbach (1975), scholars have warned that the study of person × situation interactions would be like entering 'a hall of mirrors that extends to infinity' (p. 119), with an ever-increasing number of higher-order interactions that would inevitably lead to a combinatorial explosion. Shoda and colleagues (Shoda et al., 2014) have suggested that psychologists should follow the example set by the biologists, who 'do not study differences among species by examining *N*-way interactions between characteristics of species and their environmental challenges' (p. 493), but rather study one species at a time. With an understanding that generalizability should be the goal of science, and not a requirement of each and every study, Shoda and colleagues (2014) have argued for a cumulative science that proceeds from individual studies that examine the processing dynamics of a specific group of individuals, to later culling the 'local' knowledge that such studies contain through 'integrative, discovery-oriented, theory building literature reviews' that ultimately lead to 'discoveries about the commonalities and differences across all individuals' (p. 492). Tools for identifying subgroups of individuals with similar situation–behavior dynamics are available (e.g., Vansteelandt and Van Mechelen, 2004), but researchers are still far from developing a usable and broadly applicable taxonomy of interaction concepts relative to the advances that have been made in the taxonomization of traits and even the taxonomization of situations.

The Psychological Outcome Variable

There is a growing consensus among researchers that personality functioning can be described at three distinct levels (McAdams, 2013): *personality traits*, which capture how people dispositionally think, feel, and behave (i.e., the person as *actor*); *characteristic adaptations*, which capture what people want and value (i.e., the person as *agent*); and *integrative life stories*, which capture how people self-reflect (i.e., the person as *author*). Each level of personality is thought to offer unique information or insights that cannot be interpolated from the other levels (McAdams et al., 2004; Roberts and Robins, 2000). However, researchers have only begun to examine the issue of cross-situational consistency at the motivational and autobiographical levels of personality (Dunlop, 2015). One study found that indices of cross-situational consistency were largely independent across the three levels of personality; furthermore, indices of cross-situational consistency were differentially associated with psychological adjustment across levels of personality (Dunlop et al., 2013). Extending the study of cross-situational consistency and variability to the motivational and autobiographical levels of personality thus represents a promising direction for future research.

The Multilevel Framework

We have relied on the general principles of the multilevel framework to scaffold our understanding of how person and situation factors contribute – both independently and in combination – to the consistency and variability in behavior. Although the multilevel framework provides a plausible representation of how person and situation factors mechanistically interact, this is not the only way to conceptualize the nature of their interaction. Person and situation factors also reciprocally interact (e.g., Bandura, 1978; Lewin, 1935), giving rise to transactional processes through which the characteristics of persons and the characteristics of situations become interrelated (Buss, 1987; Caspi and Roberts, 2001; Rauthmann and Sherman, 2016b; Scarr and McCartney, 1983). One promising next step would thus be to model situation–behavior covariation with dynamic factor analysis (Molenaar, 1985; Ram et al., 2013) to represent both the within-person bidirectional causal relationships between situations and behavior and the between-person similarities and differences in these relationships.

CONCLUSIONS

In this chapter, we examined three sources of cross-situational consistency and variability in behavior: the person, the situation, and the person × situation interaction. In regard to each, we reviewed how researchers' conceptualizations of the relevant constructs have developed and we considered the current state of the science. Trait research has progressed from the development of reliable and valid trait measures (e.g., Grucza and Goldberg, 2007), to the development of taxonomies that are widely shared and used (e.g., Goldberg, 1993), to the development of theories with which to account for the origins (e.g., Roberts and Jackson, 2008) and operations (e.g., Fleeson and Jayawickreme, 2015) of traits. Although much work still needs to be done to clarify the organization of constructs at the lower trait levels (i.e., facets and nuances), there is nevertheless considerable evidence to suggest that different factor solutions of the trait domain reflect different levels of the trait hierarchy (Markon et al., 2005). Situation research has progressed from a wide array of disparate situation measures to a set of taxonomies that converge on seven or eight broad situation dimensions (e.g., Parrigon et al., 2017; Rauthmann et al., 2014). Although principles for how to study situations have been proposed (Rauthmann et al., 2015), there is to date no widely accepted theory of situations or their dimensions. Interaction research is still in a formative stage, having focused mostly to date on the tasks of measuring and documenting the significant variation in how different people respond to different situations (e.g., Fleeson, 2007; Fournier et al., 2008). There is no consensus on whether the variation in people's idiographic signatures can be reduced to a nomothetic taxonomy of interaction types, but the statistical procedures to address this issue are becoming increasingly accessible (e.g., Muthén and Muthén, 1998–2012). Given the growing consensus among researchers that people's states and behavior can be reduced to five or six different content dimensions, and that people's experiences of situations can be reduced to seven or eight different content dimensions, perhaps interaction research will soon be ready to confront the challenges of conceptualizing and classifying the patterns in people's situation–behavior dynamics.

REFERENCES

aan het Rot, M., Moskowitz, D. S., & Young, S. N. (2008). Exposure to bright light is associated with positive social interaction and good mood over short time periods: A naturalistic study in mildly seasonal people. *Journal of Psychiatric Research*, 42, 311–319.

Allport, G. W. (1937). *Personality: A psychological interpretation*. New York, NY: Henry Holt.

Allport, G. W., & Odbert, H. S. (1936). *Trait-names: A psycho-lexical study*. Princeton, NJ: Psychological Review Company.

Bandura, A. (1978). The self system in reciprocal determinism. *American Psychologist, 33,* 344–358.

Block, J. (1961). *The Q-sort method in personality assessment and psychiatric research.* Springfield, IL: Charles C. Thomas (reprinted in 1978 by Consulting Psychologists Press, Palo Alto, CA).

Block, J., & Block, J. H. (1981). Studying situational dimensions: A grand perspective and some limited empiricism. In D. Magnusson (Ed.), *Toward a psychology of situations: An interactional perspective* (pp. 85–103). Hillsdale, NJ: Lawrence Erlbaum Associates.

Borsboom, D., Mellenbergh, G. J., & van Heerden, J. (2003). The theoretical status of latent variables. *Psychological Review, 110,* 203–219.

Buss, D. M. (1987). Selection, evocation, and manipulation. *Journal of Personality and Social Psychology, 53,* 1214–1221.

Caspi, A., & Roberts, B. W. (2001). Personality development across the life course: The argument for change and continuity. *Psychological Inquiry, 12,* 49–66.

Cattell, R. B. (1957). *Personality and motivation structure and measurement.* New York, NY: World Book.

Cattell, R. B. (1965). *The scientific analysis of personality.* Baltimore, MD: Penguin Books.

Cervone, D., & Shoda, Y. (1999). Social-cognitive theories and the coherence of personality. In D. Cervone & Y. Shoda (Eds.), *The coherence of personality: Social-cognitive bases of consistency, variability, and organization* (pp. 3–33). New York, NY: Guilford Press.

Cronbach, L. J. (1975). Beyond the two disciplines of scientific psychology. *American Psychologist, 30,* 116–127.

Csikszentmihalyi, M., Larson, R., & Prescott, S. (1977). The ecology of adolescent activity and experience. *Journal of Youth and Adolescence, 6,* 281–294.

Deci, E. L., & Ryan, R. M. (1987). The support of autonomy and the control of behavior. *Journal of Personality and Social Psychology, 53,* 1024–1037.

Deci, E. L., & Ryan, R. M. (2000). The 'what' and 'why' of goal pursuits: Human needs and the self-determination of behavior. *Psychological Inquiry, 11,* 227–268.

de Leeuw, J., & Meijer, E. (Eds.). (2008). *Handbook of multilevel analysis.* New York, NY: Springer.

DeYoung, C. G., & Gray, J. R. (2009). Personality neuroscience: Explaining individual differences in affect, behavior, and cognition. In P. J. Corr & G. Matthews (Eds.), *The Cambridge handbook of personality* (pp. 323–346). New York, NY: Cambridge University Press.

Digman, J. (1990). Personality structure: Emergence of the five-factor model. *Annual Review of Psychology, 41,* 417–440.

Dunlop, W. L. (2015). Contextualized personality, beyond traits. *European Journal of Personality, 29,* 310–325.

Dunlop, W. L., Walker, L. J., & Wiens, T. K. (2013). What do we know when we know a person across contexts? Examining self-concept differentiation at the three levels of personality. *Journal of Personality, 81,* 376–389.

Epstein, S. (1979). The stability of behavior: I. On predicting most of the people much of the time. *Journal of Personality and Social Psychology, 37,* 1097–1126.

Fleeson, W. (2001). Toward a structure- and process-integrated view of personality: Traits as density distributions of states. *Journal of Personality and Social Psychology, 80,* 1011–1027.

Fleeson, W. (2007). Situation-based contingencies underlying trait-content manifestation in behavior. *Journal of Personality, 75,* 825–861.

Fleeson, W., & Gallagher, P. (2009). The implications of Big Five standing for the distribution of trait manifestation in behavior: Fifteen experience-sampling studies and a meta-analysis. *Journal of Personality and Social Psychology, 97,* 1097–1114.

Fleeson, W., & Jayawickreme, E. (2015). Whole trait theory. *Journal of Research in Personality, 56,* 82–92.

Fleeson, W., & Law, M. K. (2015). Trait enactments as density distributions: The role of actors, situations, and observers in explaining stability and variability. *Journal of Personality and Social Psychology, 109,* 1090–1104.

Fleeson, W., & Noftle, E. E. (2008). Where does personality have its influence? A supermatrix of consistency concepts. *Journal of Personality, 76,* 1355–1386.

Fournier, M. A., Moskowitz, D. S., & Zuroff, D. C. (2008). Integrating dispositions, signatures, and the interpersonal domain. *Journal of Personality and Social Psychology, 94*, 531–545.

Goldberg, L. R. (1993). The structure of phenotypic personality traits. *American Psychologist, 48*, 26–34.

Grossack, M. M. (1960). The 'Who am I' test. *Journal of Social Psychology, 51*, 399–402.

Grucza, R. A., & Goldberg, L. R. (2007). The comparative validity of 11 modern personality inventories: Predictions of behavioral acts, informant reports, and clinical indicators. *Journal of Personality Assessment, 89*, 167–187.

Kenrick, D. T., Griskevicius, V., Neuberg, S. L., & Schaller, M. (2010a). Renovating the pyramid of needs: Contemporary extensions built upon ancient foundations. *Perspectives on Psychological Science, 5*, 292–314.

Kenrick, D., Neuberg, S., Griskevicius, V., Becker, D., & Schaller, M. (2010b). Goal-driven cognition and functional behavior: The fundamental-motives framework. *Current Directions in Psychological Science, 19*, 63–67.

Kihlstrom, J. F. (2013). The person–situation interaction. In D. Carlston (Ed.), *The Oxford handbook of social cognition* (pp. 786–805). Oxford: Oxford University Press.

Lewin, K. (1935). *A dynamic theory of personality*. New York, NY: McGraw-Hill.

Magnusson, D. (1981). Wanted: A psychology of situations. In D. Magnusson (Ed.), *Toward a psychology of situations: An interactional perspective* (pp. 9–36). Hillsdale, NJ: Lawrence Erlbaum Associates.

Markon, K. E., Krueger, R. F., & Watson, D. (2005). Delineating the structure of normal and abnormal personality: An integrative hierarchical approach. *Journal of Personality and Social Psychology, 88*, 139–157.

McAdams, D. P. (1995). What do we know when we know a person? *Journal of Personality, 63*, 365–396.

McAdams, D. P. (2013). The psychological self as actor, agent, and author. *Perspectives on Psychological Science, 8*, 272–295.

McAdams, D. P., Anyidoho, N. A., Brown, C., Huang, Y. T., Kaplan, B., & Machado, M. A. (2004). Traits and stories: Links between dispositional and narrative features of personality. *Journal of Personality, 72*, 761–784.

McCabe, K. O., & Fleeson, W. (2016). Are traits useful? Explaining trait manifestations as tools in the pursuit of goals. *Journal of Personality and Social Psychology, 110*, 287–301.

McCrae, R. R., & Costa, P. T., Jr. (2008). The five-factor theory of personality. In O. P. John, R. W. Robins, & L. A. Pervin (Eds.), *Handbook of personality: Theory and research* (3rd ed., pp. 159–181). New York, NY: Guilford Press.

Mischel, W. (1968). *Personality and assessment*. New York, NY: Wiley.

Mischel, W., & Shoda, Y. (1995). A cognitive-affective system theory of personality: Reconceptualizing situations, dispositions, dynamics, and invariance in personality structure. *Psychological Review, 102*, 246–268.

Molenaar, P. C. M. (1985). A dynamic factor model for the analysis of multivariate time series. *Psychometrika, 50*, 181–202.

Morse, P. J., Neel, R., Todd, E., & Funder, D. (2015). Renovating situation taxonomies: Exploring the construction and content of fundamental motive situation types. *Journal of Personality, 83*, 389–403.

Moskowitz, D. S. (1982). Coherence and cross-situational generality in personality: A new analysis of old problems. *Journal of Personality and Social Psychology, 43*, 754–768.

Moskowitz, D. S. (1988). Cross-situational generality in the laboratory: Dominance and friendliness. *Journal of Personality and Social Psychology, 54*, 829–839.

Moskowitz, D. S. (1994). Cross-situational generality and the interpersonal circumplex. *Journal of Personality and Social Psychology, 66*, 921–933.

Moskowitz, D. S., Russell, J. J., Sadikaj, G., & Sutton, R. (2009). Measuring people intensively. *Canadian Psychology/Psychologie Canadienne, 50*, 131–140.

Moskowitz, D. S., Suh, E. J., & Desaulniers, J. (1994). Situational influences on gender differences in agency and communion. *Journal of Personality and Social Psychology, 66*, 753–761.

Mõttus, R., Kandler, C., Bleidorn, W., Riemann, R., & McCrae, R. R. (2017). Personality traits below facets: The consensual validity, longitudinal stability, heritability, and utility of personality nuances. *Journal of Personality and Social Psychology*, *112*, 474–490.

Murray, H. A. (1938). *Explorations in personality: A clinical and experimental study of fifty men of college age*. New York, NY: Oxford University Press.

Muthén, L. K., & Muthén, B. O. (1998–2012). *Mplus user's guide* (7th ed.). Los Angeles, CA: Muthén & Muthén.

Ozer, D. J., & Benet-Martínez, V. (2006). Personality and the prediction of consequential outcomes. *Annual Review of Psychology*, *57*, 401–421.

Parrigon, S., Woo, S. E., Tay, L., & Wang, T. (2017). CAPTION-ing the situation: A lexically-derived taxonomy of psychological situation characteristics. *Journal of Personality and Social Psychology*, *112*, 642–681.

Paunonen, S. V., & Ashton, M. C. (2001). Big five factors and facets and the prediction of behavior. *Journal of Personality and Social Psychology*, *81*, 524–539.

Pervin, L. (1978). Definitions, measurements, and classifications of stimuli, situations, and environments. *Human Ecology*, *6*, 71–105.

Ram, N., Brose, A., & Molenaar, P. C. M. (2013). Dynamic factor analysis: Modeling person-specific process. In T. D. Little (Ed.), *The Oxford handbook of quantitative methods in psychology: Vol. 2: Statistical analysis* (pp. 451–457). Oxford: Oxford University Press.

Rauthmann, J. F. (2015). Structuring situational information: A road map of the multiple pathways to different situational taxonomies. *European Psychologist*, *20*, 176–189.

Rauthmann, J. F., Gallardo-Pujol, D., Guillaume, E. M., & Todd, E. (2014). The situational eight DIAMONDS: A taxonomy of major dimensions of situation characteristics. *Journal of Personality and Social Psychology*, *107*, 677–718.

Rauthmann, J. F., Jones, A. B., & Sherman, R. A. (2016). Directionality of person–situation transactions: Are there spillovers among and between situation experiences and personality states? *Personality and Social Psychology Bulletin*, *42*, 893–909.

Rauthmann, J. F., & Sherman, R. A. (2016a). Measuring the situational eight DIAMONDS characteristics of situations: An optimization of the RSQ-8 to the S8. *European Journal of Psychological Assessment*, *32*, 155–164.

Rauthmann, J. F., & Sherman, R. A. (2016b). Situation change: Stability and change of situation variables between and within persons. *Frontiers in Psychology*, *6*, 1938.

Rauthmann, J. F., Sherman, R. A., & Funder, D. C. (2015). Principles of situation research: Towards a better understanding of psychological situations. *European Journal of Personality*, *29*, 363–381.

Read, S. J., Monroe, B. M., Brownstein, A. L., Yang, Y., Chopra, G., & Miller, L. C. (2010). A neural network model of the structure and dynamics of human personality. *Psychological Review*, *117*, 61–92.

Reynolds, S. K., & Clark, L. A. (2001). Predicting dimensions of personality disorder from domains and facets of the five-factor model. *Journal of Personality*, *69*, 199–222.

Roberts, B. W. (2007). Contextualizing personality psychology. *Journal of Personality*, *75*, 1071–1082.

Roberts, B. W. (2009). Back to the future: Personality and assessment and personality development. *Journal of Research in Personality*, *43*, 137–145.

Roberts, B. W., & Jackson, J. J. (2008). Sociogenomic personality psychology. *Journal of Personality*, *76*, 1523–1544.

Roberts, B. W., Kuncel, N. R., Shiner, R., Caspi, A., & Goldberg, L. R. (2007). The power of personality: The comparative validity of personality traits, socioeconomic status, and cognitive ability for predicting important life outcomes. *Perspectives on Psychological Science*, *2*, 313–345.

Roberts, B. W., & Robins, R. W. (2000). Broad dispositions, broad aspirations: The intersection of personality traits and major life goals. *Personality and Social Psychology Bulletin*, *26*, 1284–1296.

Rotter, J. B. (1954). *Social learning and clinical psychology*. New York, NY: Prentice Hall.

Rotter, J. B. (1955). The role of the psychological situation in determining the direction of human behavior. In M. R. Jones (Ed.), *Nebraska symposium on motivation* (pp. 245–269). Lincoln, NE: University of Nebraska Press.

Rotter, J. B. (1981). The psychological situation in social learning theory. In D. Magnusson

(Ed.), *Toward a psychology of situations: An interactional perspective* (pp. 169–178). Hillsdale, NJ: Lawrence Erlbaum Associates.

Scarr, S., & McCartney, K. (1983). How people make their own environments: A theory of genotype greater than environment effects. *Child Development*, *54*, 424–435.

Sherman, R. A., Nave, C. S., & Funder, D. C. (2010). Situational similarity and personality predict behavioral consistency. *Journal of Personality and Social Psychology*, *99*, 330–343.

Sherman, R. A., Nave, C. S., & Funder, D. C. (2012). Properties of persons and situations related to overall and distinctive personality–behavior congruence. *Journal of Research in Personality*, *46*, 87–101.

Sherman, R. A., Rauthmann, J. F., Brown, N. A., Serfass, D. G., & Jones, A. B. (2015). The independent effects of personality and situations on real-time expressions of behavior and emotion. *Journal of Personality and Social Psychology*, *109*, 872–888.

Shoda, Y., Mischel, W., & Wright, J. C. (1989). Intuitive interactionism in person perception: Effects of situation–behavior relations on dispositional judgments. *Journal of Personality and Social Psychology*, *56*, 41–53.

Shoda, Y., Mischel, W., & Wright, J. C. (1994). Intraindividual stability in the organization and patterning of behavior: Incorporating psychological situations into the idiographic analysis of personality. *Journal of Personality and Social Psychology*, *67*, 674–687.

Shoda, Y., Wilson, N. L., Chen, J., Gilmore, A. K., & Smith, R. E. (2013). Cognitive-affective processing system analysis of intra-individual dynamics in collaborative therapeutic assessment: Translating basic theory and research into clinical applications. *Journal of Personality*, *81*, 554–568.

Shoda, Y., Wilson, N. L., Whitsett, D. D., Lee-Dussud, J., & Zayas, V. (2014). The person as a cognitive-affective processing system: From quantitative idiography to cumulative science. In M. L. Cooper & R. J. Larsen (Eds.), *Handbook of personality processes and individual differences* (pp. 491–513). Washington, DC: American Psychological Association.

Smith, R. E., Shoda, Y., Cumming, S. P., & Smoll, F. L. (2009). Behavioral signatures at the ballpark: Intraindividual consistency of adults' situation–behavior patterns and their interpersonal consequences. *Journal of Research in Personality*, *43*, 187–195.

Stryker, S. (2007). Identity theory and personality theory: Mutual relevance. *Journal of Personality*, *75*, 1083–1102.

Thomas, W. I., & Thomas, D. S. T. (1928). *The child in America: Behavior problems and programs.* New York, NY: A. A. Knopf.

Vansteelandt, K., & Van Mechelen, I. (2004). The personality triad in balance: Multidimensional individual differences in situation–behavior profiles. *Journal of Research in Personality*, *38*, 367–393.

Wagerman, S. A., & Funder, D. C. (2009). Personality psychology of situations. In P. J. Corr & G. Matthews (Eds.), *Cambridge handbook of personality* (pp. 27–42). Cambridge, NY: Cambridge University Press.

Wright, J. C., & Mischel, W. (1987). A conditional approach to dispositional constructs: The local predictability of social behavior. *Journal of Personality and Social Psychology*, *53*, 1159–1177.

Wright, J. C., & Mischel, W. (1988). Conditional hedges and the intuitive psychology of traits. *Journal of Personality and Social Psychology*, *55*, 454–469.

Transactions of Personality and the Social Environment During Development

Odilia M. Laceulle and Marcel A. G. van Aken

Personality is conceptualized as relatively enduring patterns of thoughts, feelings, and behaviors that distinguish individuals from one another. Personality is often broken into components and operationalized as broad personality *traits*, such as the Big Five, which are openness to experience, conscientiousness, extraversion, agreeableness, and neuroticism (or negative emotionality; e.g., Goldberg, 1981; John and Srivastava, 1999). However, other typologies have also been used, including typologies allowing the assessment of more narrow facets (e.g., as used in the NEO-PI; Costa and McCrae, 1992) and personality profiles (i.e., as used with the person-centered approach; Asendorpf et al., 2001). In addition, we also consider temperament as part of personality, defined as any traits that relate to the 'three A's of personality': affect, arousal, and attention (Rothbart, 2011; Shiner, 2014). In the current chapter, we refer to personality traits in this broader interpretation when using the term personality.

Regardless of the typology, personality is inherently related to how an individual deals with his or her environment. Over the last few decades, researchers have undertaken repeated efforts to understand this link between personality and the (social) environment. Since the 1960s, it has been suggested that people seek out situations that are compatible with their personality traits (Allport, 1961). In subsequent decades, the notion that people actively select, choose, and create their social environments according to their personality has increasingly been acknowledged (e.g., Buss, 1987; Caspi et al., 2005; Denissen and Penke, 2008; Neyer et al., 2014; Roberts et al., 2005).

The notion of personality, based on which people create their environment, implies at least a certain level of stability (Costa and McCrae, 1994). However, over the last 20 years, cross-sectional and longitudinal studies of personality-trait change in adolescence and adulthood have forced a reevaluation of this stability assumption (Mroczek and Spiro, 2003; Roberts et al., 2006; Srivastava et al., 2003). Although, indeed, personality is relatively stable over time, small changes have been found in both mean level and rank order. This is the case for all personality traits and across all ages. For example, from adolescence until later adulthood, people generally show small personality changes towards a more 'adaptive' personality profile (e.g., lower levels of neuroticism, higher levels of conscientiousness). Moreover, behavioral genetic studies on personality stability and change have provided evidence for a 'change component' in addition to substantial stability (Kandler et al., 2010; Viken et al., 1994).

Both personality stability and change are related to the interplay between individuals and their (social) environment. As mentioned above, personality can have social consequences. But, in addition to this, the social environment may also affect personality, either in terms of further reinforcing and stabilizing people's already existing position on certain personality characteristics or in terms of contributing to small changes in one or more traits (e.g., experiencing a major social stressful event may result in a temporary increase in neuroticism). Thus, personality may both affect and be affected by the social environment. In the quest to understand how people affect and are affected by their social environment, researchers and psychologists have often used the term *person–environment transactions*. In general, person–environment transactions refer to the way personality and the social environment mutually reinforce each other. Researchers, however, have used a range of terms and distinctions with regard to person–environment transactions. We will now review this literature in more detail.

MODELS OF PERSON–ENVIRONMENT TRANSACTIONS

Over the years, a number of models have been proposed that may explain the association between personality and characteristics of the social environment. These models tend to focus on (a) the way people create their social environments based on their personality, (b) the role of the environment in personality stability, and (c) change and transactional (e.g., bidirectional) processes. We will discuss the most prominent of these models in turn.

Active, Reactive, and Evocative Transactions

A distinction has sometimes been made between active, reactive, and evocative transactions (e.g., Caspi and Roberts, 2001). *Active person–environment transactions* occur when individuals select specific environments that are consistent with their already existing personality characteristics. Adventurous and impulsive people are more likely to spend their leisure time bungee jumping or karting than people with a more thoughtful, anxiety-prone personality. *Reactive person–environment transactions* occur when personality characteristics affect the way individuals react differently to a certain situation. For example, whereas outgoing, extraverted people enjoy big parties with many new people to socialize with, more introverted people might feel highly uncomfortable and react by being more reserved and self-conscious. Finally, *evocative person–environment transactions* occur when personality characteristics affect the way an individual triggers certain responses from his or her social environment. A tendency to approach peers with empathy and affection most likely results in different reactions than a tendency to approach peers in a way that is more cold, arrogant, or selfish.

The ASTMA Model

Another central differentiation made within the concept of person–environment transactions is the distinction between mechanisms that are likely to (1) reinforce an individual's already existing personality and, as such, lead to personality stability and (2) alter an individual's personality characteristics and, as such, lead to personality change (Roberts, 2006; Roberts et al., 2008). Specifically, as part of the ASTMA model, Roberts (2006) identified *attraction, selection, transformation, manipulation,* and *attrition* as the most important processes contributing to personality stability and change. Specifically, the first four processes refer to the way by which individuals sort themselves into certain life paths in a non-random fashion: people may be attracted to social gatherings because of their extraversion; employers may select conscientious individuals because of their reliability and sense of duty; youngsters who have difficulties with responsibilities, commitment, or (self-)discipline may be more likely to drop out of high school (attrition); and agreeable people will find (manipulate) ways to get along well with others and avoid social conflicts. As such, attraction, selection, manipulation, and attrition may predominantly confirm someone's personality characteristics and enhance personality stability. In contrast, transformation mainly refers to the effects of environmental characteristics on personality. Specifically, based on the assumption and recent empirical findings that personality is not perfectly stable but shows small changes with age and time, it seems plausible that major environmental influences (e.g., stressful social events) have the ability to transform an individual's personality traits (e.g., emotional stability), resulting in personality change.

The Corresponsive Principle

Attraction, selection, manipulation, and attrition all reflect how matching occurs between an individual's personality characteristics and his or her social environment. It is likely that this matching stabilizes, or even reinforces, the already existing personality traits. A model explicitly taking into account this personality stabilization is the *corresponsive principle*. The corresponsive principle was initially developed based on the dynamic interactionism paradigm. This paradigm, which has become the main paradigm for personality research since the early 1960s of the twentieth century (Allport, 1961), states that individuals develop through dynamic, continuous, and reciprocal transactions with their environment (Caspi, 1998; Magnusson, 1990; Sameroff, 1983). The corresponsive principle further specified dynamic interactionism with regard to interactions between personality and the social environment across development (Caspi et al., 2005; Fraley and Roberts, 2005), in that it hypothesizes that personality stability and change is the result of mutually reinforcing person–environment transactions, including the processes described above: (1) social selection (people select social environments that fit their personality) and (2) social influence (these environments produce experiences that stabilize personality (Caspi et al., 2005; Roberts and Caspi, 2003)). Specifically, the corresponsive principle assumes that selection and socialization effects are not necessarily independent of each other, as life experiences do not always arise randomly but are at least partly predictable by characteristics of the individual person, which are, in turn, further shaped by those social experiences. Moreover, selection and influence effects may predominantly contribute to cumulative continuity (i.e., stabilization and reinforcement of already existing traits), whereas only small changes in personality (often in the context of non-normative negative life experiences) can be expected.

Socialization and Social Investment Models

Whereas the models above emphasize the stabilizing effects the social environment may have on personality characteristics, other models have a stronger focus on the link between environmental characteristics and personality change. Overall, small changes in personality often occur in relation to developmental transitions (Lodi-Smith and Roberts, 2007; Roberts and DelVecchio, 2000;

Roberts et al., 2006). Such developmental transitions often involve age-graded normative tasks (i.e., developmental tasks) based on societal expectations about the developmental milestones in terms of work, family, and social relationships that should be reached in specific life phases (McCormick et al., 2011). Two theoretical models emphasizing developmental transition as a driving force underlying personality change are the *socialization hypothesis* (Harris, 1995) and the *social investment model* (Roberts et al., 2005; Roberts and Wood, 2006). In line with the socialization hypothesis, it has been suggested that individuals tend to develop a more socially desirable personality profile which fits social expectations and developmental tasks (Back et al., 2011; Hill et al., 2014; Hutteman et al., 2014; Neyer et al., 2014). Similarly, and consistent with the *social investment theory*, personality change may be the result from investment in social institutions, including age-graded normative tasks, because these transitions stimulate individuals to invest in new social roles (i.e., getting a job or becoming a parent). These social roles especially apply to young adulthood and are typically associated with behavioral expectations to act in a more mature way (i.e., more emotionally stable, agreeable, and conscientious), which can lead to long-term changes in personality traits (Bleidorn, 2015; Hennecke et al., 2014; Roberts and Jackson, 2008).

Idiosyncratic Social Experiences and Personality Change

In addition to these social influences on normative personality change, *idiosyncratic social experiences* are likely to create opportunities for individual differences in personality development. Studies investigating these effects suggest that non-normative changes (i.e., increases) in neuroticism often have their origins in major interpersonal events, such as loss of a loved one (Costa, Jr. et al., 2000; Jeronimus et al., 2013; Laceulle et al., 2015a; Löckenhoff et al., 2009; Mroczek and Spiro, 2003). Such links can be interpreted in the light of the scar model, which argues that, analogous to the scar tissue that will never become like normal skin again, people who have experienced an adverse event (i.e., death of a friend), will never be the same as before (Zeiss and Lewinsohn, 1988). Originally, the scar model was developed to explain the association between adverse events and depression, but it may also provide a theoretical base for the association between adverse idiosyncratic social experiences and personality change.

Figure 14.1 shows conceptual representations of social selection (i.e., personality predicts levels of, and change in, social environmental characteristics), social influence (i.e., social environmental characteristics predict levels of, and change in, personality) and bidirectional effects (i.e., social environmental characteristics and personality mutually predict each other).

EVIDENCE FOR PERSON–ENVIRONMENT TRANSACTIONS

Although the above-mentioned models, principles, and hypotheses can help us to grasp the various ways by which personality and the social environment are intertwined, disentangling them empirically can be difficult. However, there is consistent scientific evidence for person–environment transactions with regard to the social consequences of personality and also evidence with regard to environmental effects leading to personality change, and evidence for bidirectional effects has been increasing steadily. Evidence for transactional patterns was found both across development stages and in a range of social contexts (Kandler et al., 2012; Kendler and Baker, 2007). We will now discuss some of the main findings for social selection,

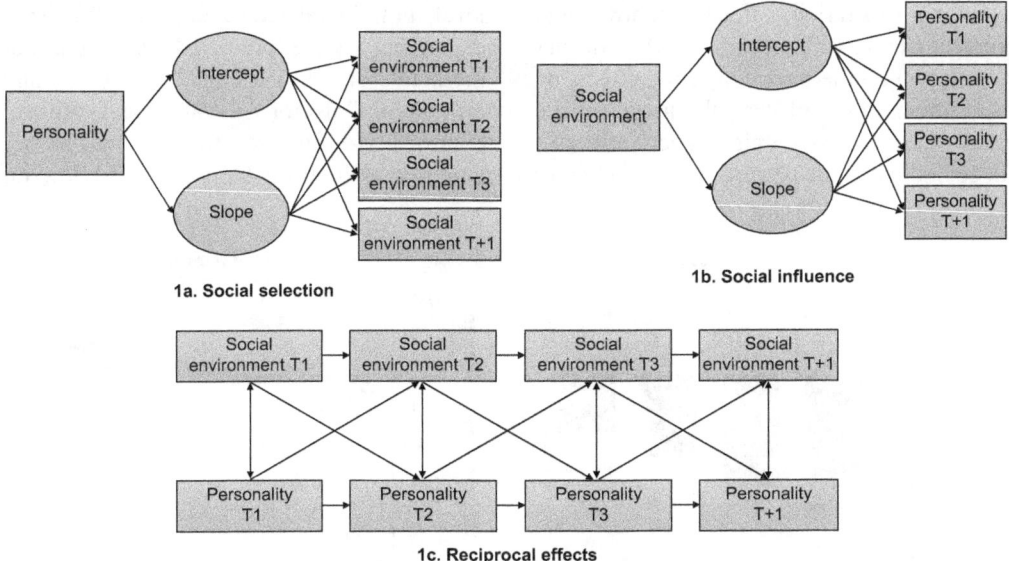

Figure 14.1 Graphical representations of social selection, social influence, and reciprocal effects; whereas selection and influence predict change (slope) in social environmental factors and personality, respectively, reciprocal effects primarily show bidirectional links.

social influence, and bidirectional effects on both childhood temperament and Big Five personality traits.

Childhood temperament

Differences in how individuals select or evoke social experiences are already present early in life. Research in infants showed that children may evoke certain behaviors of their parents based on their temperament. Several studies found evidence that infants and toddlers high on negative affect, irritability, or difficult temperament in general experience more negative parenting, such as less responsiveness, involvement, social interactions, and more conflict and inconsistent discipline (in a review; Kiff et al., 2011). For example, children high in negative affect can easily become over-aroused and difficult to sooth, which in turn, increases parental attempts to control the children's affect and behavior in more negative and adverse ways. However, early temperament may not only elicit parenting behaviors, the opposite has also been found. For example, more harsh parenting styles contribute to the negative emotionality of toddlers (Scaramella et al., 2008). Although not all studies examining both parenting effects on temperament and temperamental effects on parenting found reciprocal associations (Kiff et al., 2011), most empirical findings point to the direction of negative and escalating cycles of mutual influence between toddlers' early social environment and temperament traits.

Similar patterns were found in studies on adolescent temperament traits and negative social experiences (Laceulle et al., 2012; Laceulle et al., 2015a, 2015b). In particular, those adolescents who were easily frustrated and low on effortful control tended to experience social conflicts with their peers and parents. Adolescents exposed to idiosyncratic negative experiences showed less maturation in a range of traits over a four-year period, including frustration, effortful control, and fear (see Figure 14.2). However, when further zooming in on the direction of the effects by using more waves of data, the nature of the effects varied across traits. Whereas stressful social experiences were related to higher levels in traits related to fear, stressful social experiences were predicted by – but not predictive of – traits related to shyness and affiliation. Only for frustration and effortful control was a fully reciprocal model found: adolescents high on frustration and low on

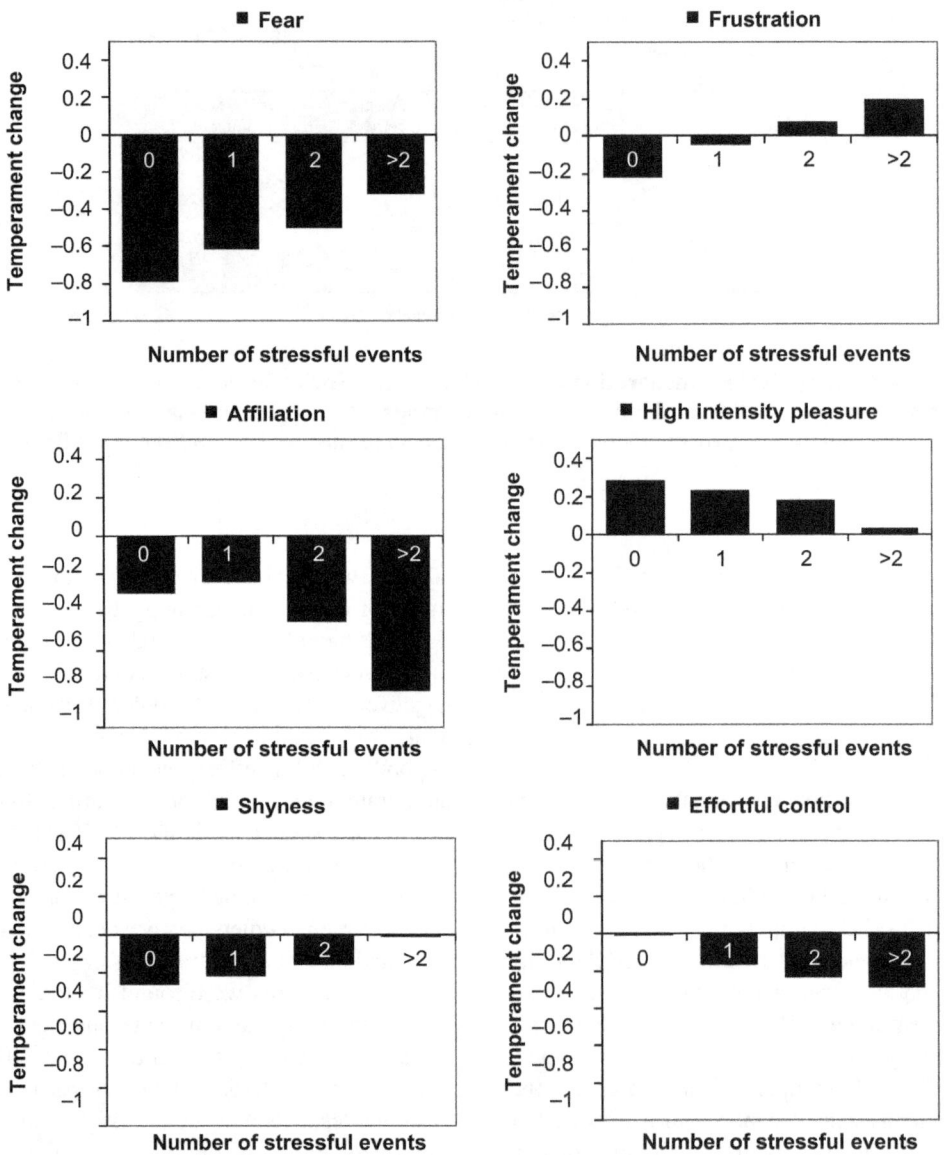

Figure 14.2 Associations between number of idiosyncratic stressful experiences and adolescent temperament change

Source: adapted from Laceulle et al. (2012)

effortful control at age 11 reported more social stressful events between age 11 and 16, and experiencing more social stressful events between age 11 and 16 were related to higher levels of frustration and lower levels of effortful control at age 19.

BIG FIVE PERSONALITY TRAITS

Most of the work done on social consequences of personality operationalized personality in terms of the Big Five personality characteristics and focused on adolescent and young adult samples. However, in their study on individuals aged 14–82, Wrzus and Mehl (2015) demonstrated that the active role of personality in shaping one's social environment is largely invariant across the lifespan. As such, the research findings make a strong case that personality traits contribute to shaping the social environment across development and in a variety of relevant social domains. We will subsequently review examples of findings so far for each of the Big Five traits.

Extraversion

Studies showed that adolescents and young adults high on extraversion reported a larger number of friends and more time spent with them (Mehl et al., 2006; Selfhout et al., 2010; Wrzus et al., 2016; Zimmermann and Neyer, 2013). Also, extraverted adolescents tend to participate in more leisure activities and experience more positive social life events, such as the start of a new romantic relationship (Barnett, 2006; Lüdtke et al., 2011), than their less extraverted peers. Some studies examined the bidirectional links between extraversion and the social environment and found unidirectional (i.e., selection or influence) effects as well as bidirectional (i.e., selection and influence) effects. Neyer and Asendorpf (2001) found

evidence that individual differences in personality, particularly traits related to extraversion (i.e., extraversion, shyness), predicted social relationships much better (selection) than vice versa (influence). An elaborate study on social selection and influence in adult personality development was presented by Specht et al. (2011), where the authors demonstrated once again that certain personality traits predicted the occurrence of several objective major life experiences (selection effects), whereas others were found to change in reaction to these events (influence effects). When life experiences were clustered, both selection and influence were found for extraversion: extraverted individuals reported more positive experiences but declined in extraversion after experiencing the events. Finally, and supporting the correspondence principle and the social investment model, Roberts et al. (2003) provided another example of stabilization by showing that the personality trait of dominance (related to extraversion) selected people into jobs that involved power, and employment in such jobs further increased their levels of dominance.

Conscientiousness

Highly conscientious adolescents reported less time spent with friends and colleagues than those low on conscientiousness (Barnett, 2006; Fleeson, 2007; Mehl et al., 2006; Wrzus et al., 2016). However, when participating in social interactions, they also experience less negative and more positive social events than their less conscientious peers (Laceulle et al., 2015b; Lüdtke et al., 2011). In addition to these selection effects, the social environment has also been found to have socialization effects on conscientiousness. For example, research in elderly people showed that older adults who perceived greater social support at baseline were more likely to gain in conscientiousness over a seven-month period

(Hill et al., 2014). Similar evidence for an effect of the environment on personality was reported by Specht and colleagues (2011), who found that individuals who separated from their partner became more conscientious. In the same study, both selection and influence effects were found for the link between conscientiousness and starting a first job: those starting a first job were less conscientious before they started than a reference group who did not start a first job, but afterwards increased in conscientiousness to a considerable extent (and more than those who did not start working).

Neuroticism

Social conflicts within the family are common during early adolescence, but the number and intensity of these conflicts tend to decrease when adolescents get older. In contrast to peers low on neuroticism, however, adolescents high on neuroticism showed only small declines (Neyer and Asendorpf, 2001). Similarly, neurotic individuals experience more conflicts with romantic partners compared to less neurotic individuals (Caspi et al., 1989; Jeronimus et al., 2013; Robins et al., 2002). Finally, they experience less family support (Windle, 1992) and more negative social life events in general (Lüdtke et al., 2011). With regard to socialization effects, research on sojourners in young adulthood demonstrated that time abroad may drive personality maturation, i.e., decreased neuroticism (Zimmermann and Neyer, 2013). Almost all studies examining links between idiosyncratic social experiences and personality change focused on adverse life events and neuroticism only, and the few studies including multiple personality characteristics found the largest effects on neuroticism, rather than on other traits such as extraversion and conscientiousness (Löckenhoff et al., 2009). Finally, several studies have investigated the bidirectional links between neuroticism and the social environment. An early example is a two-wave study by Magnus and colleagues examining the causal pathways between stressful life experiences and neuroticism (Magnus et al., 1993). High neuroticism predisposed people to more stressful experiences (selection), whereas the experiences were not found to predict later personality (influence). As such, no evidence was found for fully recursive associations. Similarly, in their study on adult personality development, Specht and colleagues (2011) found that highly neurotic women (but not men) were more likely to get married in the next years than their less neurotic counterparts (selection), which is in line with earlier findings by Neyer and Lehnart (2007). Possibly, high neurotic women may be more concerned with, and alert about, (starting) relationships (Neyer and Lehnart, 2007). Other studies, however, did find some evidence for neuroticism both affecting and being affected by the social environment. In their three-wave prospective twin study, for example, Middeldorp and colleagues (2008) found that individuals high on neuroticism experienced more subsequent life experiences and vice versa.

Openness

Like individuals high on conscientiousness, young people high on openness spent less time with others than their peers low on openness (Wrzus et al., 2016). Other studies found that individuals high on openness reported both more positive and more negative social events (Lüdtke et al., 2011). When zooming in on the content of the events, individuals high on openness were found to prefer cultural leisure activities (Morris et al., 2005). With regard to socialization effects, Specht and colleagues (2011) found that individuals got less open to experience after getting married. Zimmerman and Neyer (2013) found direct empirical support for the assumption of the corresponsive principle that selection and influence processes contribute to personality stability. In their sample of German university students, it was demonstrated that the expression of openness predisposes people for certain life transitions (i.e., going abroad), and that it was this particular trait that, in turn, became accentuated. Finally, although most of the research on idiosyncratic events was done on neuroticism, it has been demonstrated that individuals who experienced an extremely stressful event showed decreases in openness to experience two years later (Löckenhoff et al., 2009).

Agreeableness

Individuals high on agreeableness reported more positive social events in general (Lüdtke et al., 2011). More specifically, agreeable people spent more time with friends than their less agreeable peers (Wrzus et al., 2016) and experienced fewer social conflicts (Suls et al., 1998). Like most other traits, agreeableness was found to increase (mature) in young solo travelers (Zimmermann and Neyer, 2013). Some evidence was also found for effects of idiosyncratic events on changes in agreeableness. Specifically, individuals who experienced an extremely stressful event showed decreases in the compliance facet of agreeableness two years later (Löckenhoff et al., 2009). However, in a study on the bidirectional associations between agreeableness and the social environment, Neyer and Asendorpf (2001) found that individual differences in agreeableness predicted social relationships much better than vice versa (selection). The opposite was found in the longitudinal study by Specht and colleagues (2011); individuals who separated from their partner became more agreeable (influence), whereas no effects of agreeableness on separation (selection) were found.

CONSEQUENCES OF TRANSACTIONS BETWEEN PERSONALITY AND THE SOCIAL ENVIRONMENT

It is now well established that personality traits have long-lasting consequences for mental health outcomes, including psychopathology (Kotov et al., 2010), but also well-being, self-perceived health status, adaptive personality development, and even longevity (Ozer and Benet-Martínez, 2006; Roberts et al., 2007). Though the effect sizes of the links between personality and mental health may be small, they can accumulate over time and, as such, may not only impair individual lives but also strain healthcare systems. It is therefore crucial to gain insight into mechanisms underlying the link between personality and health outcomes. We believe that the social environment is the key factor here and that person–(social) environment transactions are an inevitable part of human existence and can have important consequences for all aspects of human health and well-being. Indeed, contemporary theories for the etiology of psychopathology emphasize the combined effects of individual differences in personality and the environment on life outcomes (Masten and Cicchetti, 2010; Shanahan et al., 2014b). Specifically, environmental characteristics may both enhance and buffer (moderate) the effects of personality on subsequent mental health and explain part of the associations (mediation).

MODELS OF PERSON–ENVIRONMENT TRANSACTIONS AND LIFE OUTCOMES

Cumulative Effects of Personality and the Social Environment on Life Outcomes

Social environmental characteristics may interact with personality and, as such, *moderate* the association between personality and life outcomes if they exacerbate the effect of certain personality characteristics on future outcomes. This would be in line with the *stress-vulnerability* and *diathesis-stress* models, proposing that person-characteristics and environmental risk factors interact and, as such, result in an increased risk of later adverse outcomes. This would, for example, mean that adolescents who are bullied will be especially likely to develop psychological problems if they are easily emotionally aroused or upset (because emotionally unstable individuals are more vulnerable to environmental influences; Belsky and Pluess, 2009; Monroe and Simons, 1991). This model was adapted and extended with the *differential susceptibility hypothesis* (Belsky and Pluess, 2009) and the notion of *biological sensitivity to context* (Boyce and Ellis, 2005). According to these models, individuals do not simply vary in the degree to which they are vulnerable to the negative effects of adverse (social) experience but, more generally, in their developmental plasticity (i.e., their responsiveness to both negative and positive influences). Last, an alternative model explaining combined effects of person and environmental characteristics on life outcomes is the *resource substitution hypothesis*. According to this model, individuals may particularly benefit from 'adaptive' personality traits (e.g., low neuroticism, high conscientiousness) if they have fewer social resources (e.g., social disadvantage, low socioeconomic status; Shanahan et al., 2014a).

Sequences of Personality, Social Environment, and Life Outcomes

Social environmental characteristics may *mediate* the link between the association between personality and life outcomes if the social environment represents an intervening variable (i.e., mechanism) via which personality characteristics increase the risk for adverse life outcomes (Kim et al., 2001).

For example, a child may elicit harsh parenting practices because of his or her difficult temperament-driven behaviors (e.g., excessive crying). These parenting practices, in turn, may contribute to the development of psychological problems. But also, later in life, personality traits may set in motion sequences of traits, social environmental factors, and (mal)adaption. For example, individuals who have problems regulating their emotions, cognitions, and behaviors may be more likely to get caught in a negative spiral of low regulation, social conflicts both at home and in the work environment, and problems with regard to (mental) health, social outcomes, and school/academic attainment.

Modern psychologists have increasingly focused on more complex models, allowing examination of the bi- or tridirectional, long-term links between multiple variables. Such models better serve the complexity of human development and functioning than the traditional models of moderation and mediation. For example, long-term developmental sequences are well captured by the developmental cascade models (Masten and Cicchetti, 2010). These models refer to the general notion that developmental effects in one ecological domain may spill over to influence multiple domains later in development and have been studied in a range of psychological domains including, but not limited to, personality and social environment. Such cascades can be disentangled using structural equation modeling and longitudinal mediation models specifically (Selig and Preacher, 2009; see Figure 14.3).

EVIDENCE FOR PERSON–ENVIRONMENT TRANSACTIONS AND LIFE OUTCOMES

Among personality, social, developmental, clinical, and health psychologists there seems to be a common agreement that person–environment transactions are the key in

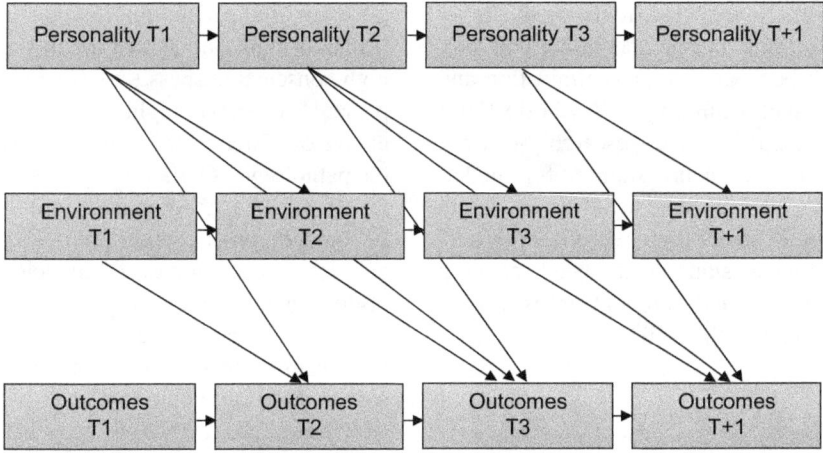

Figure 14.3 Example of a longitudinal mediation model of how person-characteristics can predict life outcomes via their effects on the social environment

long-term life outcomes. However, empirical support for the joined effects of person and environmental characteristics on why some people seem protected from disease, do better with regard to social and career outcomes, and even live longer is only slowly increasing. With regard to the social environment, the focus of research has often been on – but not limited to – stress, interpersonal trauma, daily hassles, social relationships, parenting, etc. With regard to person-characteristics, the scope has been even broader, including not only personality and temperament but also other factors related to risk and resilience, including coping, control and self-efficacy, emotions and stress management (Rutter, 1985). We will review the literature on neuroticism and conscientiousness, as they seem the main trait dispositions in the context of person–environment transactions and life outcomes, but also briefly mention some work on other traits, self-regulation, and coping.

Neuroticism–Environment Transactions and Life Outcomes

The majority of the literature on person–environment transactions and life outcomes has been done in the field of clinical and health psychology. In particular, transactions between neuroticism, social stress, and depression are now well established. Specifically, individuals with neurotic tendencies may be more prone to relatively high negative appraisals of threat during interpersonal stress, have more difficulty in coping adaptively with the experience and, as such, may be more likely to develop depression and health problems more generally (Deković et al., 2008). Indeed, across samples (age, sex, clinical vs. population cohorts) the impact of neuroticism on the risk for depression is greater at high than at low levels of social stress (Kendler et al., 2004). Similarly, the effect of daily social stress on negative affect has been found to be stronger in individuals high on neuroticism as compared to those low on the trait (Mroczek and Almeida, 2004). In addition to a cumulative (moderation) effect, social stress may explain (mediate) part of the link between neuroticism and depression. That is, individuals high on neuroticism have been suggested to experience (or at least report) more interpersonal problems that, in turn, contribute to depression and affiliated psychological problems. Some support for such sequences was found in research on sexual victimization.

That is, neuroticism (but none of the other personality traits) was found to mediate part of the link between sexual victimization and general psychopathology (Gallardo-Pujol and Pereda, 2013). Other research, however, did not find convincing support for mediational models but underscores the complexity of the association between neuroticism, social stress, and depression and the need for more dynamic person–environment transactional models (Ormel et al., 2001).

Conscientiousness–Environment Transactions and Life Outcomes

Paralleling the impact of neuroticism, conscientiousness may be another key factor in person–environment transactions and health outcomes. This might be unsurprising given that conscientiousness includes constructs that are indicative of deliberative, self-controlled, and goal-directed behaviors, including impulse control, planning, the delay of gratification, orderliness, and the propensity to follow social norms and rules (Roberts et al., 2014; Shanahan et al., 2014b). Such dispositions may help in health-promoting behaviors, prevention of, and coping with, interpersonal stress and environmental demands. However, and again similar to neuroticism, the pathways via which conscientiousness and the social environment are intertwined and related to the development of health issues are poorly understood. Both moderation and mediational processes may play a role. Recently, Shanahan and colleagues (2014b) proposed a comprehensive model, comprising a series of hypotheses capturing mediational chains and individual differences in conscientiousness, the (social) context, and health. So far, however, this life course of personality model has barely been empirically tested, although support has been found for some of the specific hypotheses that were proposed. For example, conscientiousness (and extraversion) was found to compensate for social disadvantage to some extent, although this did not lead to a full 'catch-up' effect (Damian et al., 2015). In addition, a study by Gallardo-Pujol and Pereda demonstrated that high conscientiousness (but none of the other personality traits) might buffer the harmful effects of sexual victimization on general psychopathology (Gallardo-Pujol and Pereda, 2013). Whereas these studies provide support for moderation effects, in line with mediation and developmental cascade models, individuals low on conscientiousness are more likely to make bad decisions, get into arguments, and behave irresponsibly. This, in turn, has been suggested to contribute to higher divorce rates (Roberts et al., 2009) but may also lead to problems in getting or keeping a job, criminal behavior and incarceration, having financial problems, and substance abuse. Effects of conscientiousness–environment transactions can be even more extreme: people high on conscientiousness have been found to live longer (Deary et al., 2010), which can probably mainly be explained by their tendency to avoid unhealthy behaviors (e.g., substance abuse, unsafe driving) but may also be related to their interactions with the social environment (e.g., sexual risk taking, interpersonal violence; Bogg and Roberts, 2013).

Self-regulation–Environment Transactions and Life Outcomes

Conceptually related to the traits of both neuroticism and conscientiousness, self-regulation can be defined as the capacity to inhibit behaviors, cognitions, and emotions. No surprise, evidence has been found for self-regulation–environment transactions and life outcomes. Children with low self-regulation were found to experience more negative social interactions which, in turn, contributed to more mental health problems one year later (Kim and Cicchetti, 2010). Similarly, Laceulle and colleagues found that adolescents who had problems regulating emotions and behaviors reported more internalizing and externalizing psychological problems, and that this effect could partly be explained through the effect of self-regulation on negative social interactions (Laceulle et al., 2017). Importantly, in addition to actual self-regulation and control, subjective perceptions of control may also positively affect the (social) environment and contribute to better health and well-being. For example, people characterized by high feelings of control (i.e., high self-efficacy) experience less social stress and better interpersonal relations, which are associated with better health (O'Leary, 1985).

Coping–Environment Transactions and Life Outcomes

Clearly, how individuals cope with the social environment can also have a significant impact on life outcomes (Billings and Moos, 1981; Herman-Stabl et al., 1995). Particularly in the short term, emotion-focused coping (i.e., regulating emotions that come with stress) can be a successful way to reduce the effects of stress on well-being. In the long term, however, problem-focused coping (i.e., actively addressing the stressor) is the key in person–environment transactions and life outcomes. Specifically, problem-focused coping is likely to have positive effects on the social environment (under the condition that the social environment or event is to some extent controllable), which in turn, contributes to better life outcomes (better social relations, less (mental) health problems, higher academic and career success).

CURRENT AND FUTURE DIRECTIONS

In their quest to better understand transactions of personality and the social environment during development, researchers in the fields of social, personality, developmental, and clinical psychology have focused on a range of traits and environmental characteristics, studied associations in numerous samples and at various ages, and used increasingly sophisticated statistical techniques. With the increasing empirical evidence and the parallel development of theoretical models, several promising directions have emerged which may allow researchers to further disentangle the complex transactional processes under study. These current and future directions include both conceptual and methodological developments. We will briefly discuss some of them below.

First, although the number of studies examining fully transactional models is limited, evidence now clearly suggests the dynamic interplay of personality and the social environment. As such, integrated frameworks are needed to capture the full complexity of person-characteristics, (social) environmental factors, and their transactions. Some of the theoretical frameworks mentioned in this chapter provide important specific insights regarding this interplay. Empirical work, however, has traditionally focused on the social consequences of personality (e.g., attraction, selection, manipulation, attrition as defined by the ASTMA model; Roberts, 2006) rather than on social influence (e.g., transformation as defined by the ASTMA models) or fully transactional processes. Further development of theoretical and methodological models which allow the examination of long-term growth and development is needed. This may enable researchers to better understand how multiple variables affect, reinforce, or attenuate over time and, as such, how individuals get caught in adaptive (or maladaptive) spirals of person-characteristics, environmental factors, and life outcomes.

Second, is the ongoing question how transactions between personality and the social environment can best be measured. Although an elaborate overview of the methodological challenges is beyond the scope of this chapter, some of them need to be mentioned. Central, of course, are the measures of personality and of the social environment (Luhmann et al., 2014). Dependent on the research questions under study, broad traits (e.g., Big Five) or more narrow facets of personality (e.g., as proposed with the NEO-PI) may be more or less valuable. Consideration may also be given to the difference between core and surface traits (Asendorpf and Van Aken, 2003). Core characteristics are relatively stable traits and, as such, more likely to affect the social environment than to change as a function of the environmental influences. In contrast, surface traits may fluctuate over time and, as such, may be more likely to be affected by the social environment. Also relevant, and maybe even harder to operationalize in an adequate manner, is the measurement of the social environment. Although researchers have repeatedly mentioned the need for better measurements of the environment (Wrzus et al., 2016; Wrzus and Mehl, 2015), translating this call to feasible research methods has been proven difficult. Nonetheless, increasing attempts have been made, including the development of a theoretical framework, the situational construal model (SCM), and an assessment tool, the riverside situational Q-sort (RSQ; Funder, 2016), allowing a better understanding and measurement of transactions between persons and (social) situations.

Third, parallel to the development of theoretical models on person–environment transactions, there has been an increasing need, and search, for research methods to disentangle complex transactional models. These include, but are not limited to, cross-lagged models, longitudinal mediation models, and (developmental) cascade models (e.g., Selig and Preacher, 2009). Moving even beyond these quite sophisticated models, Voelkle and Oud (2013) recently introduced continuous time modeling allowing for individually varying time intervals. Specifically, based on the conclusion that different time intervals between assessment waves and between individuals are more rule than exception in practice, this model explicitly deals with irregularly spaced assessment waves. Methodological developments like these are crucial to keep (or catch) up with the conceptual developments in the field of person–environment transactions.

CONCLUSION

In the current chapter we aimed at providing an overview of basic associations between personality and characteristics of the social environment, as well as a review of evidence for later outcomes of transactions of personality and the social environment. The following key points can be formulated:

- Multiple, not mutually exclusive, models have been proposed regarding personality–environment transactions.
- Strongest empirical support was found for the link between social experiences (both positive and negative) and extraversion, particularly in terms of social selection.
- Social experiences (both age-graded events and idiosyncratic life events) can also result in small changes in personality.
- Evidence for bidirectional effects is largely limited to traits related to conscientiousness.
- Findings underscore that the nature of the associations varies across traits and social experiences.
- Person–environment transactions are assumed to be crucial for later life outcomes.
- Some cumulative (moderation) effects were found for traits related to self-regulation and social stress in the prediction of social, psychological, academic/career, and health outcomes.
- Person-characteristics were found to affect features of the social environment, which in turn, contribute to life outcomes (mediation).

Together, findings provide convincing evidence for the social consequences of personality and increasing support for the effect of the environment on personality and person–environment transactions. At the same time, further development of theoretical models and research methods is needed to allow further developments in the field. These include, but are not limited to, more integrative frameworks taking time explicitly into account to fully capture the longitudinal nature of transactional processes, full consideration of the measurement of both person and environmental factors, and further development of statistics methods to enable robust tests of transactional models. Such developments could direct future research, contribute to a further understanding of transactions between person-characteristics and the social environment during development, and ultimately, guide clinicians and policy makers in breaking maladaptive spirals and enhancing positive person–environment transactions.

REFERENCES

Allport, G. W. (1961). *Pattern and growth in personality*. New York, NY: Holt, Rinehart & Watson.

Asendorpf, J. B., Borkenau, P., Ostendorf, F., & van Aken, M. A. G. (2001). Carving personality description at its joints: Confirmation of three replicable personality prototypes for both children and adults. *European Journal of Personality*, *15*, 169–198.

Asendorpf, J. B., & Van Aken, M. A. G. (2003). Personality–relationship transaction in adolescence: Core versus surface personality characteristics. *Journal of Personality*, *71*, 629–666.

Asendorpf, J. B., & Wilpers, S. (1998). Personality effects on social relationships. *Journal of Personality and Social Psychology*, *74*, 1531–1544.

Back, M. D., Baumert, A., Denissen, J. J., Hartung, F., Penke, L., Schmukle, S. C., ... Wagner, J. (2011). PERSOC: A unified framework for understanding the dynamic interplay of personality and social relationships. *European Journal of Personality*, *25*, 90–107.

Barnett, L. A. (2006). Accounting for leisure preferences from within: The relative contributions of gender, race or ethnicity, personality, affective style, and motivational orientation. *Journal of Leisure Research*, *38*, 445–474.

Belsky, J., & Pluess, M. (2009). Beyond diathesis stress: Differential susceptibility to environmental influences. *Psychological Bulletin*, *135*, 885–908.

Billings, A. G., & Moos, R. H. (1981). The role of coping responses and social resources in attenuating the stress of life events. *Journal of Behavioral Medicine*, *4*, 139–157.

Bleidorn, W. (2015). What accounts for personality maturation in early adulthood? *Current Directions in Psychological Science*, *24*, 245–252.

Bogg, T., & Roberts, B. W. (2013). The case for conscientiousness: Evidence and implications for a personality trait marker of health and longevity. *Annals of Behavioral Medicine*, *45*, 278–288.

Boyce, W. T., & Ellis, B. J. (2005). Biological sensitivity to context: I. an evolutionary-developmental theory of the origins and functions of stress reactivity. *Development and Psychopathology*, *17*, 271–301.

Buss, D. M. (1987). Selection, evocation, and manipulation. *Journal of Personality and Social Psychology*, *53*, 1214–1221.

Caspi, A. (1998). Personality development across the life course. In W. Damon (Series Ed.) & N. Eisenberg (Vol. Ed.), *Handbook of child psychology. Volume 3: Social, emotional, and personality development* (5th ed., pp. 311–388). New York, NY: Wiley.

Caspi, A., Bem, D. J., & Elder, G. H. (1989). Continuities and consequences of interactional styles across the life course. *Journal of Personality*, *57*, 375–406.

Caspi, A., & Roberts, B. W. (2001). Personality development across the life course: The argument for change and continuity. *Psychological Inquiry*, *12*, 49–66.

Caspi, A., Roberts, B. W., & Shiner, R. L. (2005). Personality development: Stability and change. *Annual Review of Psychology*, *56*, 453–484.

Costa, P. T., Jr., Herbst, J. H., McCrae, R. R., & Siegler, I. C. (2000). Personality at midlife: Stability, intrinsic maturation, and responses to life events. *Assessment*, *7*, 365–378.

Costa, P. T., Jr., & McCrae, R. R. (1992). *Revised NEO Personality Inventory (NEO-PI-R) and the Five Factor Inventory (NEO-FFI): Professional Manual*. Odessa, FL: Psychological Assessment Resources, Inc.

Costa, P. T., Jr., & McCrae, R. R. (1994). Set like plaster? Evidence for the stability of adult personality. In T. F. Heatherton & J. L. Weinberger (Eds.), *Can personality change?*

(pp. 21–40). Washington, DC: American Psychological Association.

Damian, R. I., Su, R., Shanahan, M., Trautwein, U., & Roberts, B. W. (2015). Can personality traits and intelligence compensate for background disadvantage? Predicting status attainment in adulthood. *Journal of Personality and Social Psychology*, *109*, 473–489.

Deary, I. J., Weiss, A., & Batty, G. D. (2010). Intelligence and personality as predictors of illness and death: How researchers in differential psychology and chronic disease epidemiology are collaborating to understand and address health inequalities. *Psychological Science in the Public Interest: A Journal of the American Psychological Society*, *11*, 53–79.

Deković, M., Koning, I. M., Jan Stams, G., & Buist, K. L. (2008). Factors associated with traumatic symptoms and internalizing problems among adolescents who experienced a traumatic event. *Anxiety, Stress, and Coping*, *21*, 377–386.

Denissen, J. J., & Penke, L. (2008). Neuroticism predicts reactions to cues of social inclusion. *European Journal of Personality*, *22*, 497–517.

Fleeson, W. (2007). Situation-based contingencies underlying trait-content manifestation in behavior. *Journal of Personality*, *75*, 825–862.

Fraley, R. C., & Roberts, B. W. (2005). Patterns of continuity: A dynamic model for conceptualizing the stability of individual differences in psychological constructs across the life course. *Psychological Review*, *112*, 60–74.

Funder, D. (2016). Taking situations seriously: The situation construal model and the riverside situational Q-sort. *Current Directions in Psychological Science*, *25*, 203–208.

Gallardo-Pujol, D., & Pereda, N. (2013). Person–environment transactions: Personality traits moderate and mediate the effects of child sexual victimization on psychopathology. *Personality and Mental Health*, *7*, 102–113.

Goldberg, L. R. (1981). Language and individual differences: The search for universals in personality lexicons. *Review of Personality and Social Psychology*, *2*, 141–165.

Harris, J. R. (1995). Where is the child's environment? A group socialization theory of development. *Psychological Review*, *102*, 458–489.

Hennecke, M., Bleidorn, W., Denissen, J. J., & Wood, D. (2014). A three-part framework for self-regulated personality development across adulthood. *European Journal of Personality*, *28*, 289–299.

Herman-Stabl, M. A., Stemmler, M., & Petersen, A. C. (1995). Approach and avoidant coping: Implications for adolescent mental health. *Journal of Youth and Adolescence*, *24*, 649–665.

Hill, P. L., Payne, B. R., Jackson, J. J., Stine-Morrow, E. A., & Roberts, B. W. (2014). Perceived social support predicts increased conscientiousness during older adulthood. *The Journals of Gerontology, Series B: Psychological Sciences and Social Sciences*, *69*, 543–547.

Hutteman, R., Hennecke, M., Orth, U., Reitz, A. K., & Specht, J. (2014). Developmental tasks as a framework to study personality development in adulthood and old age. *European Journal of Personality*, *28*, 267–278.

Jeronimus, B., Ormel, J., Aleman, A., Penninx, B., & Riese, H. (2013). Negative and positive life events are associated with small but lasting change in neuroticism. *Psychological Medicine*, *43*, 2403–2415.

John, O. P., & Srivastava, S. (1999). The Big Five trait taxonomy: History, measurement, and theoretical perspectives. In L. A. Pervin & O. P. John (Eds.), *Handbook of personality: Theory and research* (2nd ed., pp. 102–138). New York, NY: Guilford Press.

Kandler, C., Bleidorn, W., Riemann, R., Angleitner, A., & Spinath, F. M. (2012). Life events as environmental states and genetic traits and the role of personality: A longitudinal twin study. *Behavior Genetics*, *42*, 57–72.

Kandler, C., Bleidorn, W., Riemann, R., Spinath, F. M., Thiel, W., & Angleitner, A. (2010). Sources of cumulative continuity in personality: A longitudinal multiple-rater twin study. *Journal of Personality and Social Psychology*, *98*, 995–1008.

Kendler, K. S., & Baker, J. H. (2007). Genetic influences on measures of the environment: A systematic review. *Psychological Medicine*, *37*, 615–626.

Kendler, K. S., Kuhn, J., & Prescott, C. A. (2004). The interrelationship of neuroticism, sex, and stressful life events in the prediction of episodes of major depression. *American Journal of Psychiatry*, *161*, 631–636.

Kiff, C. J., Lengua, L. J., & Zalewski, M. (2011). Nature and nurturing: Parenting in the context of child temperament. *Clinical Child and Family Psychology Review, 14*, 251–301.

Kim, J., & Cicchetti, D. (2010). Longitudinal pathways linking child maltreatment, emotion regulation, peer relations, and psychopathology. *Journal of Child Psychology and Psychiatry, 51*, 706–716.

Kim, J., Kaye, J., & Wright, L. K. (2001). Moderating and mediating effects in causal models. *Issues in Mental Health Nursing, 22*, 63–75.

Kotov, R., Gamez, W., Schmidt, F., & Watson, D. (2010). Linking 'big' personality traits to anxiety, depressive, and substance use disorders: A meta-analysis. *Psychological Bulletin, 136*, 768–821.

Laceulle, O. M., Jeronimus, B. F., van Aken, M. A. G., & Ormel, J. (2015b). Why not everybody gets their fair share of stress: Adolescent's perceived relationship affection mediates associations between temperament and subsequent stressful social events. *European Journal of Personality, 29*, 125–137.

Laceulle, O. M., Nederhof, E., Karreman, A., Ormel, J., & Van Aken, M. A. G. (2012). Stressful events and temperament change during early and middle adolescence: The TRAILS study. *European Journal of Personality, 26*, 276–284.

Laceulle, O. M., van Aken, M. A. G., Ormel, J., & Nederhof, E. (2015a). Stress-sensitivity and reciprocal associations between stressful events and adolescent temperament. *Personality and Individual Differences, 81*, 71–83.

Laceulle, O. M., Veenstra, R., Vollebergh, W. A., & Ormel, J. (2017). Sequences of maladaptation: Preadolescent self-regulation, adolescent negative social interactions, and young adult psychopathology. *Development and Psychopathology, 12*, 1–14.

Löckenhoff, C. E., Terracciano, A., Patriciu, N. S., Eaton, W. W., & Costa, P. T. (2009). Self-reported extremely adverse life events and longitudinal changes in five-factor model personality traits in an urban sample. *Journal of Traumatic Stress, 22*, 53–59.

Lodi-Smith, J., & Roberts, B. W. (2007). Social investment and personality: A meta-analysis of the relationship of personality traits to investment in work, family, religion, and volunteerism. *Personality and Social Psychology Review, 11*, 68–86.

Lüdtke, O., Roberts, B. W., Trautwein, U., & Nagy, G. (2011). A random walk down university avenue: Life paths, life events, and personality trait change at the transition to university life. *Journal of Personality and Social Psychology, 101*, 620–637.

Luhmann, M., Orth, U., Specht, J., Kandler, C., & Lucas, R. E. (2014). Studying changes in life circumstances and personality: It's about time. *European Journal of Personality, 28*, 256–266.

Magnus, K., Diener, E., Fujita, F., & Pavot, W. (1993). Extraversion and neuroticism as predictors of objective life events: A longitudinal analysis. *Journal of Personality and Social Psychology, 65*, 1046–1053.

Magnusson, D. (1990). *Personality development from an interactional perspective*. New York, NY: Guilford Press.

Masten, A. S., & Cicchetti, D. (2010). Developmental cascades. *Development and Psychopathology, 22*, 491–495.

McCormick, C. M., Kuo, S. I.-C., & Masten, A. S. (2011). Developmental tasks across the lifespan. In K. L. Fingerman, C. A. Berg, J. Smith, & T. C. Antonucci (Eds.), *Handbook of lifespan development* (pp. 117–140). New York, NY: Springer.

Mehl, M. R., Gosling, S. D., & Pennebaker, J. W. (2006). Personality in its natural habitat: Manifestations and implicit folk theories of personality in daily life. *Journal of Personality and Social Psychology, 90*, 862–877.

Middeldorp, C., Cath, D., Beem, A., Willemsen, G., & Boomsma, D. (2008). Life events, anxious depression and personality: A prospective and genetic study. *Psychological Medicine, 38*, 1557–1565.

Monroe, S. M., & Simons, A. D. (1991). Diathesis-stress theories in the context of life stress research: Implications for the depressive disorders. *Psychological Bulletin, 110*, 406–425.

Morris, B. A., Shakespeare-Finch, J., Rieck, M., & Newbery, J. (2005). Multidimensional nature of posttraumatic growth in an Australian population. *Journal of Traumatic Stress, 18*, 575–585.

Mroczek, D. K., & Almeida, D. M. (2004). The effect of daily stress, personality, and age on daily negative affect. *Journal of Personality, 72*, 355–378.

Mroczek, D. K., & Spiro, A. (2003). Modeling intraindividual change in personality traits:

Findings from the normative aging study. *The Journals of Gerontology, Series B: Psychological Sciences and Social Sciences, 58*, 153–165.

Neyer, F. J., & Asendorpf, J. B. (2001). Personality–relationship transaction in young adulthood. *Journal of Personality and Social Psychology, 81*, 1190–1204.

Neyer, F. J., & Lehnart, J. (2007). Relationships matter in personality development: Evidence from an 8-year longitudinal study across young adulthood. *Journal of Personality, 75*, 535–568.

Neyer, F. J., Mund, M., Zimmermann, J., & Wrzus, C. (2014). Personality–relationship transactions revisited. *Journal of Personality, 82*, 539–550.

O'Leary, A. (1985). Self-efficacy and health. *Behaviour Research and Therapy, 23*, 437–451.

Ormel, J., Oldehinkel, A. J., & Brilman, E. I. (2001). The interplay and etiological continuity of neuroticism, difficulties, and life events in the etiology of major and subsyndromal, first and recurrent depressive episodes in later life. *American Journal of Psychiatry, 158*, 885–891.

Ozer, D. J., & Benet-Martínez, V. (2006). Personality and the prediction of consequential outcomes. *Annual Review of Psychology, 57*, 401–421.

Roberts, B. W. (2006). Personality development and organizational behavior. *Research in Organizational Behavior, 27*, 1–40.

Roberts, B. W., & Caspi, A. (2003). The cumulative continuity model of personality development: Striking a balance between continuity and change in personality traits across the life course. In U. M. Staudinger & U. Lindenberger (Eds.), *Understanding human development: Dialogues with lifespan psychology* (pp. 183–214). Dordrecht, the Netherlands: Kluwer Academic Publishers.

Roberts, B. W., Caspi, A., & Moffitt, T. E. (2003). Work experiences and personality development in young adulthood. *Journal of Personality and Social Psychology, 84*, 582–593. DOI: 10.1037/0022-3514.84.3.582

Roberts, B. W., & DelVecchio, W. F. (2000). The rank-order consistency of personality traits from childhood to old age: A quantitative review of longitudinal studies. *Psychological Bulletin, 126*, 3–25.

Roberts, B. W., & Jackson, J. J. (2008). Sociogenomic personality psychology. *Journal of Personality, 76*, 1523–1544.

Roberts, B. W., Jackson, J. J., Burger, J., & Trautwein, U. (2009). Conscientiousness and externalizing psychopathology: Overlap, developmental patterns, and etiology of two related constructs. *Development and Psychopathology, 21*, 871–888.

Roberts, B. W., Kuncel, N. R., Shiner, R., Caspi, A., & Goldberg, L. R. (2007). The power of personality: The comparative validity of personality traits, socioeconomic status, and cognitive ability for predicting important life outcomes. *Perspectives on Psychological Science, 2*, 313–345.

Roberts, B. W., Lejuez, C., Krueger, R. F., Richards, J. M., & Hill, P. L. (2014). What is conscientiousness and how can it be assessed? *Developmental Psychology, 50*, 1315–1330.

Roberts, B. W., Walton, K. E., & Viechtbauer, W. (2006). Patterns of mean-level change in personality traits across the life course: A meta-analysis of longitudinal studies. *Psychological Bulletin, 132*, 1–25.

Roberts, B. W., & Wood, D. (2006). Personality development in the context of the neo-socioanalytic model of personality. In D. K. Mroczek and T. D. Little (Eds.), *Handbook of personality development* (pp. 11–39). Mahwah, NJ: Lawrence Erlbaum.

Roberts, B. W., Wood, D., & Caspi, A. (2008). The development of personality traits in adulthood. *Handbook of Personality: Theory and Research, 3*, 375–398.

Roberts, B. W., Wood, D., & Smith, J. L. (2005). Evaluating five factor theory and social investment perspectives on personality trait development. *Journal of Research in Personality, 39*, 166–184.

Robins, R. W., Caspi, A., & Moffitt, T. E. (2002). It's not just who you're with, it's who you are: Personality and relationship experiences across multiple relationships. *Journal of Personality, 70*, 925–964.

Rothbart, M. K. (2011). *Becoming who we are: Temperament and personality in development*. New York, NY: Guilford Press.

Rutter, M. (1985). Resilience in the face of adversity: Protective factors and resistance to psychiatric disorder. *British Journal of Psychiatry, 147*, 598–611.

Sameroff, A. J. (1983). Developmental systems: Contexts and evolution. In W. Kessen (Ed.), *Handbook of child psychology: Vol.1. History, theory, and methods* (pp. 237–294). New York, NY: Wiley.

Scaramella, L. V., Sohr-Preston, S. L., Mirabile, S. P., Robison, S. D., & Callahan, K. L. (2008). Parenting and children's distress reactivity during toddlerhood: An examination of direction of effects. *Social Development, 17*, 578–595.

Selfhout, M., Burk, W., Branje, S., Denissen, J., Van Aken, M., & Meeus, W. (2010). Emerging late adolescent friendship networks and big five personality traits: A social network approach. *Journal of Personality, 78*, 509–538.

Selig, J. P., & Preacher, K. J. (2009). Mediation models for longitudinal data in developmental research. *Research in Human Development, 6*, 144–164.

Shanahan, M. J., Bauldry, S., Roberts, B. W., Macmillan, R., & Russo, R. (2014a). Personality and the reproduction of social class. *Social Forces, 93*, 209–240.

Shanahan, M. J., Hill, P. L., Roberts, B. W., Eccles, J., & Friedman, H. S. (2014b). Conscientiousness, health, and aging: The life course of personality model. *Developmental Psychology, 50*, 1407–1425.

Shiner, R. L. (2014). The development of temperament and personality traits in childhood and adolescence. In M. Mikulincer, P. Shaver, M. L. Cooper, & R. Larsen (Eds.), *APA handbook of personality and social psychology: Vol. 3. Personality processes and individual differences* (pp. 85–105). Washington, DC: American Psychological Association.

Specht, J., Egloff, B., & Schmukle, S. C. (2011). Stability and change of personality across the life course: The impact of age and major life events on mean-level and rank-order stability of the big five. *Journal of Personality and Social Psychology, 101*, 862–882.

Srivastava, S., John, O. P., Gosling, S. D., & Potter, J. (2003). Development of personality in early and middle adulthood: Set like plaster or persistent change? *Journal of Personality and Social Psychology, 84*, 1041–1053.

Suls, J., Martin, R., & David, J. P. (1998). Person–environment fit and its limits: Agreeableness, neuroticism, and emotional reactivity to interpersonal conflict. *Personality and Social Psychology Bulletin, 24*, 88–98.

Viken, R. J., Rose, R. J., Kaprio, J., & Koskenvuo, M. (1994). A developmental genetic analysis of adult personality: Extraversion and neuroticism from 18 to 59 years of age. *Journal of Personality and Social Psychology, 66*, 722–730.

Voelkle, M. C., & Oud, J. H. (2013). Continuous time modelling with individually varying time intervals for oscillating and non-oscilating processes. *British Journal of Mathematical and Statistical Psychology, 66*, 103–126.

Windle, M. (1992). A longitudinal study of stress buffering for adolescent problem behaviors. *Developmental Psychology, 28*(3), 522–530.

Wrzus, C., & Mehl, M. R. (2015). Lab and/or field? Measuring personality processes and their social consequences. *European Journal of Personality, 29*, 250–271.

Wrzus, C., Wagner, G. G., & Riediger, M. (2016). Personality–situation transactions from adolescence to old age. *Journal of Personality and Social Psychology, 110*, 782–799.

Zeiss, A. M., & Lewinsohn, P. M. (1988). Enduring deficits after remissions of depression: A test of the scar hypothesis. *Behaviour Research and Therapy, 26*, 151–158.

Zimmermann, J., & Neyer, F. J. (2013). Do we become a different person when hitting the road? Personality development of sojourners. *Journal of Personality and Social Psychology, 105*, 515–530.

Personality Development in Adulthood

Marcus Mund, Julia Zimmermann and Franz J. Neyer

Over the last two decades, ample evidence for the plasticity of personality has accumulated (Denissen et al., 2011; Roberts et al., 2008). As the number of studies on personality development has increased, so has the complexity of the analyses and the age ranges covered. Consequently, many of the questions the pioneers were examining – Can personality change at all? Does plasticity end at some point in time? What influences personality development? – have been covered, although not answered exhaustively. Building on this large body of literature, in this chapter we will (a) discuss different forms of stability and change, (b) review the most recent findings on personality development, (c) introduce current theoretical accounts to explain personality development, and (d) outline research desiderata and future directions that might advance the field.

Two things should be noted beforehand: first, personality development is not only about change but about change *and* stability. Thus, along with questions on how personality changes, questions concerning the *if*, *how*, and *why* inter-individual differences stabilize across the lifespan are of genuine interest to personality development. Second, personality is an iridescent construct which has been defined differently by different authors. We will thus begin with a brief discussion of what we mean by referring to personality and personality development.

CONCEPTIONS OF PERSONALITY

Generally, personality is considered by many authors as an individual's relatively stable disposition to feel, think, and behave in a certain manner across a wide variety of situations (Barenbaum and Winter, 2008; McAdams, 1995; McAdams and Pals, 2006; McCrae and Costa, 2008; Winter et al., 1998). These cross-situational consistencies have mainly been conceived of as pertaining to the individual way of doing things and were thus often termed stylistic or expressive traits (Barenbaum and Winter, 2008; Winter et al., 1998). Dynamic traits, in contrast, have been thought of as being more volatile across situations and to change over time. Motives, values, and goals are examples of such dynamic traits that are thought to guide behavior and lead to the endorsement of specific personality traits (Barenbaum and Winter, 2008; Winter et al., 1998). The distinction between stylistic and dynamic traits can be traced back to the pioneers of the field of personality psychology – Allport, Cattell, Murray – and thus inspired other frameworks that partially build on these ideas but, at the same time, further subdivide personality into three layers (McAdams, 1995; McAdams and Pals, 2006; McCrae and Costa, 2008): First, basic tendencies – sometimes also termed core traits – are thought to be stable, broad, and recognizable dispositions. Second, characteristic adaptations are thought to be context-dependent and to change as individuals' environments change. Finally, narrative identity, sometimes also referred to as self-concept, describes individual differences in how individuals talk about their experiences and life stories. Irrespective of whether one prefers to think of personality in terms of stylistic and dynamic traits or in terms of basic tendencies, characteristic adaptations, and self-concept, it should be noted that the lines between these concepts are gradual (Kandler et al., 2014; for an in-depth discussion and comparison of different concepts, see Winter et al., 1998).

Most previous chapters on personality development have focused on the development of the Big Five traits of neuroticism, extraversion, openness, agreeableness, and conscientiousness; in the present chapter, we will extend this focus whenever possible by discussing the development of the Big Five along with findings for self-esteem – an individual's consideration of him- or herself as a person of worth (Donnellan et al., 2011) – and also consider typical dynamic traits guiding individual behavior: goals and values (Austin and Vancouver, 1996; Schwartz, 1992).

FORMS OF PERSONALITY DEVELOPMENT AND EMPIRICAL FINDINGS

Out of the forms of stability and change that can be differentiated (Caspi, 1998; Roberts et al., 2008), we will pick those that have garnered the most attention in prior research or – in our view – are the most promising to further examine personality development: stability and change concerning individual scores, mean levels, and the rank order of individuals as well as inter-individual differences in intra-individual change.

Individual Stability and Change

Individual development is the prerequisite for all other forms of development to occur (see Figure 15.1). Individual stability and change are typically examined by modeling difference scores, capturing changes in the scores on a given characteristic between at least two time points for each individual (McArdle, 2009). As no construct in psychology can be measured without error, differences in individuals' scale scores over time might simply occur due to random measurement error. One method that is particularly suited to examine reliable changes in individuals over time is the reliable change index (RCI; Jacobson and Truax, 1991).

The RCI examines whether observed changes extend beyond any deviations that have to be expected given the unreliability of the measurement instrument. When applied in its conventional form, an individual's score on a given characteristic needs to have changed 1.96 standard deviations to be considered a reliable change – a huge effect in terms of effect sizes (Cohen, 1992). This strict assumption has been criticized by some authors (Roberts et al., 2008), but even studies applying somewhat more liberal criteria (Steunenberg et al., 2005) found a consistent pattern: most individuals do not change on any given dimension. Of those

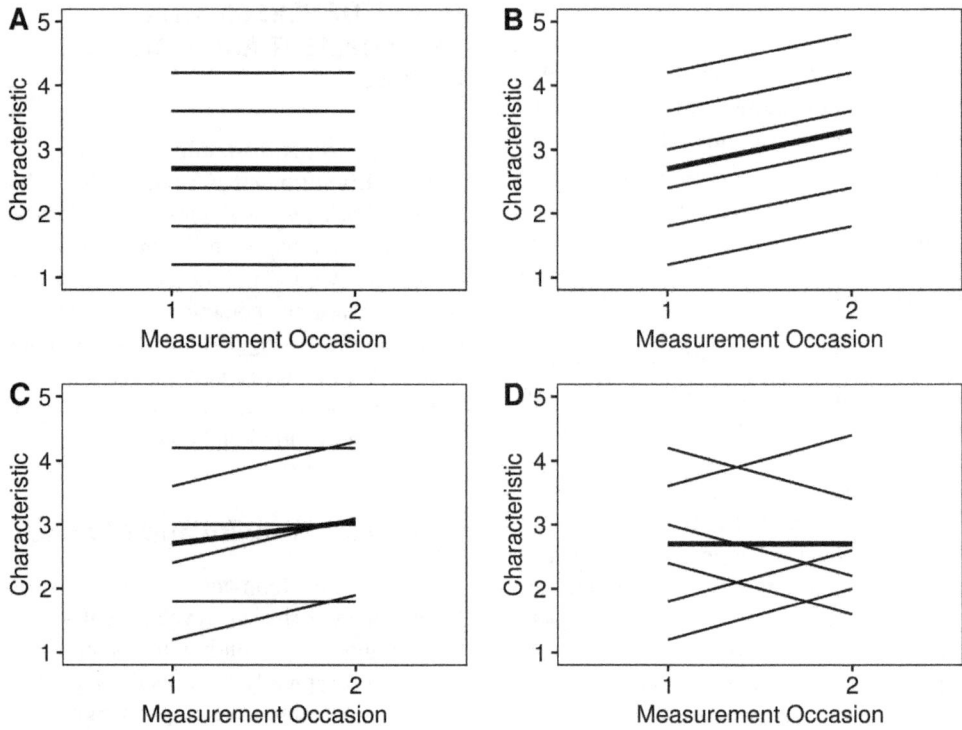

Figure 15.1 Hypothetical development of six individuals and sample mean

who change, half change in a direction that is typically considered less socially desirable, that is, for example, they become more neurotic, less agreeable, or less conscientious (Branje et al., 2004; Donnellan et al., 2007; Letzring et al., 2014; Roberts et al., 2001; Robins et al., 2001; Steunenberg et al., 2005; Vaidya et al., 2002; van Aken et al., 2006). The above figures apply to the Big Five traits but are similar with respect to goals (Lüdtke et al., 2009); we are not aware, however, of studies examining individual change via the RCI in self-esteem or values.

As most studies on personality development are more concerned with population-based indices such as stability and change in the mean levels and rank orders (Denissen et al., 2011; Roberts et al., 2008), individual change is as yet understudied although it might have implications for the understanding of and research on personality development, as we will discuss later in this chapter.

Mean-Level Stability and Change

Since mean-level changes represent the average amount of all individual changes in a given sample, they provide information on changes of a given personality characteristic across age for an average person in that sample (see Figure 15.1). Such changes have sometimes been termed normative developmental trends or trends toward or away from maturity. However, these labels appear too strong given that findings concerning individual change indicate that the scores of most individuals on a given personality characteristic remain stable. If developmental trends were to be normative, a majority of individuals could be expected to follow such trends. Instead, individuals appear to follow distinct developmental trajectories over time (Bleidorn, 2015; Johnson et al., 2007; Morin et al., 2013; Mund and Neyer, 2016).

Apostrophizing mean-level changes as reflecting trends toward or away from maturity might be critical because the term maturation implies that development would have an endpoint, thereby contradicting the widely adopted notion of development as a life-long process (Baltes et al., 2006; Caspi, 1998). At the same time, it is unclear what is expected to happen after an individual has reached this endpoint (i.e., maturity). Instead of referring to normative development or personality maturation, we suggest referring to mean-level trends as reflecting the tendency of personality characteristics to become – on average – more socially desirable, which takes into account that both social norms and attitudes of what is considered desirable can change (Hogan and Roberts, 2004; Neyer et al., 2014). Mean-level changes are often correlated with age and thus of genuine interest to developmental psychology. They become, however, increasingly interesting to personality psychologists as soon as they co-occur with any form of differential development, as we will discuss later in this chapter.

A large number of studies have demonstrated that the mean scores of the Big Five traits on average indeed tend toward higher social desirability from adolescence to old age. This trend is evidenced by decreases in neuroticism and increases in both agreeableness and conscientiousness (Roberts et al., 2006). Extraversion and openness seem to follow curvilinear patterns with increases up until midlife and decreases thereafter (Roberts et al., 2006), a trend that has been observed for self-esteem as well (Orth et al., 2012, 2015).

Unlike research on the Big Five and self-esteem, research on values and goals is much more disparate concerning the level of abstraction (e.g., major life goals vs. short-term goals) and specificity (e.g., higher-order values vs. specific values). Nevertheless, mean-level changes have also been found for both values (Gouveia et al., 2015; Milfont et al., 2016; Sheldon, 2005; Vecchione et al., 2016) and goals (Corker et al., 2013; Dunlop et al., 2017; Lüdtke et al., 2009; Roberts et al., 2004; Salmela-Aro et al., 2000, 2007). Concerning the four higher-order values (self-transcendence, conservation, self-enhancement, and openness to change) established by Schwartz (1992), for instance, it has been found that the endorsement of all value dimensions decreases over time. These decreases are particularly pronounced for older age groups (age 70 and above) with respect to conservation and self-enhancement values and for both younger (age 25 to 40) and older age groups with respect to openness to change and self-transcendence values. Cross-sectionally, it has been found that the endorsement of conservation and self-transcendence values increases with age, whereas openness to change and, particularly, self-enhancement values remain fairly stable across all age groups (Milfont et al., 2016). As a side note, these findings concerning the development of values illustrate how longitudinal and cross-sectional findings might diverge. In cross-sectional studies, age and cohort effects are inextricably confounded and can only be unraveled in longitudinal studies, which are thus more conclusive when it comes to issues of development.

Research concerning the development of goals has shown that major life goals such as health-related (being a physically healthy person), wealth-related (being a wealthy person), and relationship-related (having committed and intimate relationships) goals decrease (Lüdtke et al., 2009; Roberts et al., 2004) or remain stable (Dunlop et al., 2017) between ages 18 and 25 and in middle adulthood. In the time between ages 25 and 40, however, increases in work-related, family-related, and health-related goals have been reported (Salmela-Aro et al., 2007). Furthermore, it should be noted that goals lose their motivational power as soon as they are achieved. Thus, changes in goals can be found surrounding typically aspired life events such as becoming a parent (Heckhausen et al., 2001; Salmela-Aro et al., 2000).

It has often been claimed that the time of emerging adulthood – the time between ages 18 and 25 (Arnett, 2000) – would evince particularly strong mean-level changes (Corker et al., 2013; Donnellan et al., 2007; Lüdtke et al., 2009, 2011; Roberts et al., 2001, 2004; Robins et al., 2001; Salmela-Aro et al., 2007; Sheldon, 2005; Wagner et al., 2013b). However, although weaker than in emerging adulthood, mean-level changes in the Big Five, self-esteem, values, and goals have likewise been found in young adulthood (between ages 25 and 40; Branje et al., 2004; Lehnart et al., 2010; Milfont et al., 2016; Mund and Neyer, 2014; Neyer and Asendorpf, 2001; Salmela-Aro et al., 2000; Vecchione et al., 2016), middle adulthood (between ages 40 and 60; Letzring et al., 2014; Stephan et al., 2015; van Aken et al., 2006), old age (between ages 60 and 80; Kandler et al., 2015; Steunenberg et al., 2005; but see Mõttus et al., 2012), and oldest old age (age 80 and above; Lucas and Donnellan, 2011; Mõttus et al., 2012; Wagner et al., 2013a, 2016; Wortman et al., 2012). Recently, the age periods of old age and oldest old age have garnered increased attention. Research conducted so far has shown that mean-level changes in these age periods deviate from those found in other periods: neuroticism has been found to increase in older age (Kandler et al., 2015; Wagner et al., 2016), whereas the mean level of self-esteem seems to remain stable (Wagner et al., 2013a) and thus not to continue the decreasing trend that other studies have reported to begin in midlife (Orth et al., 2012, 2015).

Not all individuals change alike (Bleidorn, 2015; Johnson et al., 2007; Morin et al., 2013; Mund and Neyer, 2016): Some might change faster than others and again others might remain stable (see Figures 15.1C, 15.1D, and 15.2). These differences in personality development lead to the phenomena of differential change. Differential change can be examined by investigating the rank order of individuals or by directly addressing inter-individual differences in intra-individual change.

Rank-Order Stability and Change

The rank order indicates how individuals in a sample stand relative to each other (e.g., who is most extraverted, who is least neurotic). Rank-order stability is typically measured by correlating the scores of two measurement occasions and provides valuable information

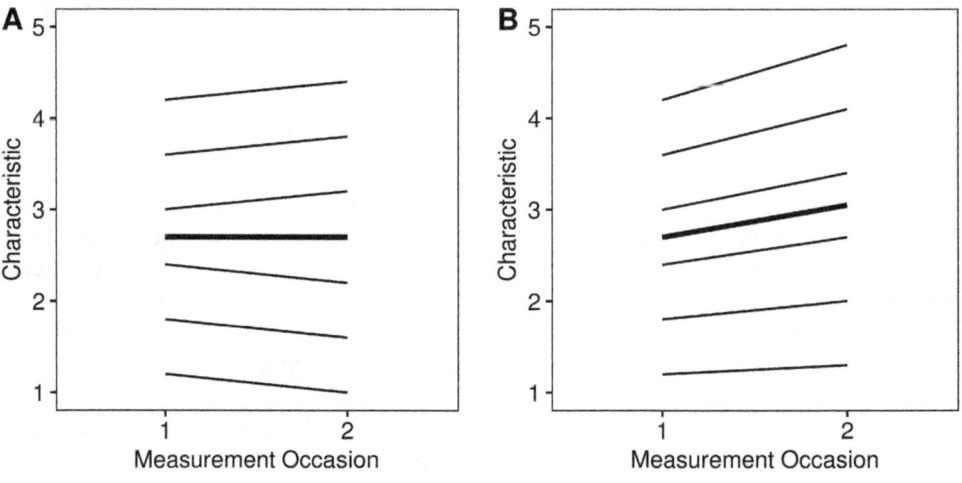

Figure 15.2 **Hypothetical development of six individuals and sample mean**

about personality development. For instance, a perfect rank order ($r = 1.0$) would indicate a perfect stability of inter-individual differences on a given characteristic as all individuals would retain their relative rank (e.g., the most extraverted person would remain the most extraverted; see Figures 15.1A, 15.1B, and 15.2). However, in almost all research scenarios, even over short time periods of several weeks (Anusic et al., 2012; Chmielewski and Watson, 2009), rank-order stability is lower than 1.0, which indicates that at least some individuals change their position on a given characteristic relative to the other individuals in the sample (Figure 15.1C). Changes in the rank order of individuals thus imply that individuals differ in their development.

Empirical findings suggest that the rank-order stability for both the Big Five traits and self-esteem increases up until midlife and decreases thereafter (Kuster and Orth, 2013; Roberts and DelVecchio, 2000; Trzesniewski et al., 2003). Values, in contrast, evince constant rank-order stability across the lifespan. Depending on the specific value under examination, these stabilities range from below to above the stability of the Big Five traits and self-esteem (Milfont et al., 2016; Vecchione et al., 2016). Inter-individual differences in goals exhibit generally less stability in young adulthood than the Big Five, self-esteem, and values (Corker et al., 2013; Dunlop et al., 2017; Lüdtke et al., 2009; Roberts et al., 2004). However, the stability of inter-individual differences in goals appears to increase across adulthood (Dunlop et al., 2017).

The rank-order stability generally decreases as measurement intervals increase (Kuster and Orth, 2013; Roberts and DelVecchio, 2000; Trzesniewski et al., 2003). However, contrary to earlier notions proposing a rapid decline of the stability of inter-individual differences down to zero (Conley, 1984), the rank-order stability is approaching a non-zero asymptote. Thus, even over long time periods, inter-individual differences in personality are preserved to some degree. Fraley and Roberts (2005) have shown that this non-zero asymptote of the rank-order stability is best explained by developmental constancy factors such as an individual's genetic makeup or environmental consistency (see Denissen et al., 2011; Fraley and Roberts, 2005 for extended discussions).

As a final note on rank-order stability and change, it should be stressed that it is independent of mean-level development. Thus, differential development in the form of shifts in the rank order can occur in the absence of mean-level changes (Figure 15.1D).

Inter-Individual Differences in Intra-Individual Change

Although changes in the rank order of individuals necessarily imply inter-individual differences in intra-individual change, inter-individual differences in intra-individual change might – but not necessarily do – affect shifts in the rank ordering of individuals over time (see Figure 15.2).

Although inter-individual differences in intra-individual change have frequently been reported in studies concerning personality development, their substantive meaning is still understudied. More thoroughly investigating these differences could help shed light on the processes underlying personality development and thus help to understand which individuals change and why they change. In studies focusing on this form of development, it has been shown, for instance, that inter-individual differences in intra-individual change in self-esteem can be attributed to four latent classes of individuals following different developmental pathways (Morin et al., 2013; Mund and Neyer, 2016). Individuals in these latent classes were found to differ with respect to their average level of self-esteem, their development over time, and their state-like variability of self-esteem. Similarly, inter-individual differences in intra-individual change in the Big Five traits have been shown to be attributable to four or five latent classes of individuals, depending on the exact trait examined (Johnson et al., 2007). These latent trajectory classes are uniquely related to a broad range of intrapersonal (e.g., satisfaction with life), interpersonal (e.g., conflict frequency), and objective (e.g., academic achievement) correlates and thus are psychologically relevant (Johnson et al., 2007; Morin et al., 2013; Mund and Neyer, 2016).

Approaching personality development by focusing on inter-individual differences in intra-individual change affords a more precise description of groups of individuals experiencing changes in personality characteristics and examination of factors distinguishing individuals experiencing change from those who do not change, for instance, regarding the (changing) quality of their social relationships or life transitions (Mund and Neyer, 2016). In addition to examining inter-individual differences in intra-individual change via latent trajectory classes, both natural experiments (Rutter, 2007) and prospective control group designs have proven useful. In both research scenarios, a group of individuals experiencing a life event that cannot be assigned randomly (e.g., entering a partnership, going abroad for a while) are compared to a group not experiencing this event (for exemplary studies, see Greischel et al., 2016; Lehnart et al., 2010; Neyer and Lehnart, 2007; Zimmermann and Neyer, 2013). Comparing both groups with regard to their development might point to mechanisms underlying inter-individual differences in intra-individual change.

It should be noted that mean-level and rank-order stability and change, as well as inter-individual differences in intra-individual change, are conceptually distinct – albeit empirically related – phenomena that can occur independent of each other (Denissen et al., 2011; Roberts and DelVecchio, 2000; Roberts et al., 2006, 2008). It is thus possible that personality is both stable (in terms of inter-individual differences) and changing (in terms of mean levels; Figure 15.1B) – or vice versa (Figure 15.1D) – at the same time or that inter-individual differences in intra-individual change exist under mean-level and rank-order stability (Figure 15.2). Thus, it is crucially important for researchers to clearly differentiate between the forms of development considered when referring to personality conveying either plasticity or stability, as both might be associated with distinct mechanisms (Geukes et al., 2017b; Neyer et al., 2014; Roberts et al., 2008).

THEORETICAL ACCOUNTS OF PERSONALITY DEVELOPMENT

The growing body of empirical findings concerning personality development gained from diverse samples from almost all around the world has stimulated the development of theoretical accounts dedicated to explaining these findings. Meta-theoretical accounts such as dynamic transactionism (Magnusson, 1990, 2001) or developmental systems approaches (Lerner, 1996) suggest that personality development is set in motion by the interaction of two or more complex dynamic systems such as an individual's personality and this individual's environment. However, these approaches are too broad to derive concrete hypotheses about specific processes underlying personality development. In the following, we briefly introduce three recent theoretical approaches that are devised to understand personality development in terms of the Big Five and related constructs and thus to relatively broad personality characteristics (for an introduction to other theoretical accounts, see Specht et al., 2014).

Social Investment Principle

The social investment principle (SIP) argues that personality development is mainly driven by psychological investments in age-graded social roles, such as being a partner, being a parent, or being a person in the labor force (Lodi-Smith and Roberts, 2007; Roberts et al., 2005, 2008; Vandewater et al., 1997). These social roles are thought to be equipped with a multitude of societal expectations regarding the appropriate behavior in the respective role. These expectations can be explicit or implicit, but they are widely agreed upon in a society. If an individual takes over a certain role, he or she will be – implicitly or explicitly – rewarded for endorsing role-appropriate behavior (e.g., adhering to deadlines) and – implicitly or explicitly – punished for inappropriate behavior, such as stealing at work. SIP has long been the principal framework for explaining personality development and its assumptions have been supported regarding the occupational context (Denissen et al., 2014; Hudson et al., 2012; Hudson and Roberts, 2016; Lodi-Smith and Roberts, 2007) and concerning partner relationships (Lehnart et al., 2010; Luciano and Orth, 2017; Neyer and Asendorpf, 2001; Wagner et al., 2013b, 2015). Concerning parenthood, however, empirical results for the SIP are mixed with studies reporting differences in the Big Five traits between parents and non-parents and others reporting no differences (Dijkstra and Barelds, 2009; Jokela et al., 2009, 2011; Specht et al., 2011; van Scheppingen et al., 2016). Thus, the psychological investment in age-graded social roles seems to be but one mechanism driving personality development.

Functional Approaches to Personality

According to a functional perspective, personality trait conceptions such as the Big Five merely describe inter-individual differences in individuals' habitual styles of thinking, feeling, and behaving – thus their stylistic way of acting in the world – but remain silent about the intrapsychic dynamics of individuals' motives, values, and goals (Cramer et al., 2012; Denissen and Penke, 2008; Denissen et al., 2013; Fleeson and Jayawickreme, 2015; Wood et al., 2015). Indeed, contrary to the notion that basic personality traits such as the Big Five influence all other characteristics (McCrae and Costa, 2008), the Big Five seem to be likewise influenced by other, less basic characteristics (Kandler et al., 2014). Specifically, the endorsement of personality traits has been shown to vary depending on (a) current situational demands (Fleeson, 2001; Fleeson and Law, 2015), (b) individual motivational states (Denissen and Penke, 2008), and (c) goals that individuals currently pursue (McCabe and Fleeson, 2012, 2016). The self-regulation framework by Denissen et al. (2013) explains how these findings might relate to personality development in the long run.

According to Denissen et al. (2013), the main mechanism underlying personality development is the increasing capacity of individuals to regulate behaviors in order to achieve their goals. Concretely, if an individual is motivated to be seen as a charming partner, a loyal employee, a caring parent, or a trustworthy friend, it might be necessary to adapt his or her behavior to meet these standards. In the long run, these processes of adaptation should lead to increases in socially desirable characteristics such as agreeableness, conscientiousness, and emotional stability (Denissen et al., 2013) – a pattern found in a variety of studies (Roberts et al., 2006).

TESSERA Framework

The focus of the TESSERA framework is to illuminate the mechanisms through which life events such as entering a partnership translate into short-term changes that accumulate over time to manifest in longer-term personality development (Wrzus and Roberts, 2017). It is assumed that specific situations trigger (T) – internal or assumed external – expectations (E) about appropriate behavior or behavior that is most suitable to achieve one's goals. Out of the possible pool of personality states, the one most appropriate in the given situation is chosen and expressed in overt behavioral states (SSE), finally provoking a reaction (Ra) by either oneself (e.g., positive emotions) or the environment (e.g., reinforcement). Change in personality characteristics is assumed to occur when the behavioral states (SSE) deviate from an individual's habitual level of this characteristic and/or if the reaction to an expressed personality state is incongruent with an individual's personality (Wrzus and Roberts, 2017).

To illustrate, taking up one's first job might confront the employee with strict deadlines (T) that he or she wants to adhere to in order to be seen as reliable (E). This goal might lead the employee to work more efficiently and thoroughly than ever before (SSE). The good and punctual work is lauded by the employer (Ra), who subsequently confronts the employee with other deadlines, starting a new sequence of TESSERA. In the long run, repeated sequences of TESSERA might lead to changes in, or the stabilization of, personality characteristics (Wrzus and Roberts, 2017).

New frameworks such as the self-regulation framework (Denissen et al., 2013) or TESSERA (Wrzus and Roberts, 2017) highlight gaps in previous research and point to new directions that should be pursued in future research on personality development. In the following section, we will discuss some of these future directions.

OPEN QUESTIONS AND FUTURE DIRECTIONS

Functional Perspectives on Personality Development

Research on personality development in adulthood has primarily been concerned with the Big Five personality traits. This is not surprising as this taxonomy has emerged as the most widely adopted conceptualization of core traits (John et al., 2008; McCrae and Costa, 2008). This line of research has brought valuable insights into personality as it has shown that even core traits are malleable (Roberts and DelVecchio, 2000; Roberts et al., 2006) and that environmental factors such as life events and social relationships play an important role in this regard (Neyer et al., 2014; Reis et al., 2000; Reitz et al., 2014). However, although the Big Five traits are of utmost importance for describing inter-individual differences in affect, cognition, and behavior, they are less powerful in explaining why these differences occur (Fleeson and Jayawickreme, 2015). This is due to the Big Five traits being conceptualized as broad and general dispositions that do not represent specific psychological functions but instead subsume many of these functions in an inextricable fashion (Denissen and Penke, 2008; Pytlik Zillig et al., 2002; Wilt and Revelle, 2015). To better understand the mechanisms underlying personality development, it might thus be worthwhile to complement and enrich research concerning the Big Five traits with more concrete, functionally defined constructs (Cramer et al., 2012; Wood et al., 2015). Such a broadened research focus might also help to get closer to the classic conception of personality containing dynamic and stylistic traits.

Another way to address this issue could be the wider adoption of more specific facets of traits. Several studies have shown that such facets (e.g., negative affect as a facet of neuroticism; goal-striving as a facet of conscientiousness; McCrae and Costa, 2008) exhibit discriminant validity (Ashton, 1998; Paunonen and Ashton, 2001) and, even more importantly, differ in terms of their developmental course both from each other and their respective overarching trait (Jackson et al., 2009; Mund and Neyer, 2014; Soto and John, 2012). More widely examining personality facets could thus deepen the understanding of what factors stimulate personality development and whether these factors act narrowly on single or few facets or broadly on the global trait (Klimstra et al., 2013; Soto and John, 2012). Going one step further, personality nuances might provide an even more detailed picture. Personality nuances describe specific aspects of a facet (McCrae, 2015; Mõttus et al., 2017) and can be investigated by analyzing personality inventories item-wise.

Zeroing in on Life Events

Life events are one of the most widely assessed factors influencing personality development. Among the events found to stimulate personality development are first partnership experiences (Lehnart et al., 2010; Luciano and Orth, 2017; Neyer and Asendorpf, 2001; Wagner et al., 2013b, 2015), entrance into the labor force (Denissen et al., 2014; Hudson and Roberts, 2016; Hudson et al., 2012; Roberts et al., 2003), and temporal international mobility (Greischel et al., 2016; Hutteman et al., 2015; Zimmermann and Neyer, 2013). Most of these studies have compared a group of individuals who have experienced the life event in question with another group of individuals who have not experienced this event. In typical studies of this kind, the measurement occasions for each of these two groups are several months, or even years, apart and thus do not allow examination of specific trajectories of personality development surrounding a specific event. The next step in understanding how life events might influence personality characteristics should thus be to incorporate time in a more nuanced way, allowing researchers to investigate trajectories of personality characteristics shortly before and after the actual event has occurred (Bleidorn, 2015; Luhmann et al., 2014). In this way, exact trajectories of personality development could be mapped against events, which would yield information on whether life events evoke rapid mean-level changes that stabilize in the long run or whether life events need time – and how much time – to exert influence on personality characteristics (for examples, see Bleidorn et al., 2016; Salmela-Aro et al., 2000). Such an approach would particularly allow for the examination of assumptions underlying the TESSERA framework (Wrzus and Roberts, 2017).

Most studies investigating personality development associated with life events strongly focus on the changes in personality characteristics that are initiated by these events. To capture the full meaning of personality development – change and stability – it might likewise be worthwhile to extend the focus in future research to investigate how life events contribute to the stabilization of inter-individual differences.

By combining these strategies with the consideration of functionally defined personality characteristics, facets, or nuances, it might also be possible to examine whether life events are specific in their effects. For instance, it would be possible to examine whether life events predominantly confronting individuals with behavioral constraints (e.g., entering the labor force) influence behavioral personality characteristics (e.g., industriousness) more strongly than affective (e.g., depressiveness) or cognitive aspects (e.g., beliefs about the world; Neyer et al., 2015). Furthermore, it will be important to extract the ingredients of life events – specific situations, demands, or episodes within a life event – that foster personality development (Wrzus and Roberts, 2017). This could be achieved by complementing longitudinal research with intermediate experience sampling phases to assess micro-level processes of development (Mund et al., 2016; Wrzus and Mehl, 2015).

Focusing on the Person from Different Perspectives

The majority of studies on personality development have been concerned with the description of patterns of both mean-level and rank-order development, which are variable-centered indices (Denissen et al., 2011; Roberts et al., 2008). However, as stated earlier in this chapter, several empirical findings imply that large proportions of typical samples do not follow universal trends. Complementing variable-centered with person-centered perspectives in future research would allow researchers to identify and examine such idiographic developmental trajectories (for examples, see Johnson et al., 2007; Morin et al., 2013; Mund and Neyer, 2016). Furthermore, by taking into account the idiographic nature of personality and combining it with classical variable-centered approaches (Asendorpf, in press), future research might be able to investigate intra-individual variability of personality characteristics and to assess its association with development. For instance, a greater variability of self-esteem has been found to relate to less favorable psycho-social outcomes such as depression and dissatisfying relationships (Kernis, 2005; Mund and Neyer, 2016; Sowislo et al., 2014; Zeigler-Hill and Wallace, 2012). However, as of yet it is unclear what factors influence the intra-individual variability of personality characteristics (for a pioneering approach, see Geukes et al., 2017a) and whether this variability promotes personality development – because, for instance, individuals more easily adapt to a wider range of situations – or hinders it – because, for example, the individual's self-concept is weak.

Although it is a widely accepted notion that personality development does not occur in a social vacuum (Neyer et al., 2014; Reis et al., 2000; Reitz et al., 2014), the majority of research on personality development still exclusively relies on self-reports. The notable exceptions to this rule (Branje et al., 2007; Luan et al., 2017; Watson and Humrichouse, 2006), however, have demonstrated that subjective evaluations of personality development do not always match with other-ratings by romantic partners or family members. It will thus be challenging for future research to substantiate that personality development translates into changes in overt behavior and is perceivable by others instead of being merely a subjective experience or an artifact of individuals' self-enhancement tendencies (O'Brien and Kardas, 2016).

CONCLUSION

Research on personality development is dedicated to the questions of whether, how, and why different personality characteristics – Big Five traits, self-esteem, values, goals, and many others – change across the lifespan in both individuals and populations. When referring to personality development, it is important to clearly communicate the aspect of interest, as personality can be stable and changing at the same time, depending on the indicator of change under investigation. In this chapter, we have discussed the concepts of stability and change in individual scores, mean levels, and rank orders as well as inter-individual differences in intra-individual change. These aspects of personality development are conceptually independent but empirically interrelated and tap into different aspects of development that can all be observed in typical samples. However, the majority of studies have focused on the analysis of mean-level changes and rank-order stability and their findings suggest that (a) mean levels of personality characteristics are changing across the lifespan and (b) individuals differ in the extent to which they follow these mean-level trends. Mean-level changes and differential stability in personality are the starting point for current theoretical accounts dedicated to explaining these patterns of personality development. As of yet, none of these theoretical approaches is able to explain all empirical findings, but tailoring research designs to test specific parts of these models might help to uncover the strong and the weak points of each framework. To achieve this, future research on personality development should become both more specific and more differential. Greater specificity concerning the personality characteristics that are assessed should be encouraged. Given the criticism raised against the broad Big Five traits, it might be useful to additionally consider (a) functionally defined personality characteristics, (b) more specific facets of the Big Five traits, and/or (c) personality nuances. Also, future research needs to become more specific concerning the mechanisms underlying personality development. To this end, the effects of life events should be investigated in a way that incorporates time to or since the event as an additional variable and to extract specific situations that might foster personality development within certain events. Finally, research concerning personality development needs to become more differential in the sense that intra-individual variability of personality characteristics, as well as inter-individual differences therein, should be more widely investigated to examine their associations with personality development and, ultimately, to help answer the question of who changes when and why.

REFERENCES

Anusic, I., Lucas, R. E., & Donnellan, M. B. (2012). Dependability of personality, life satisfaction, and affect in short-term longitudinal data. *Journal of Personality, 80,* 33–58.

Arnett, J. J. (2000). Emerging adulthood: A theory of development from the late teens through the twenties. *American Psychologist, 55,* 469–480.

Asendorpf, J. B. (2014). Person-centered approaches to personality. In M. L. Cooper & R. J. Larsen (Eds.), *Handbook of personality and social psychology* (Vol. 4, pp. 403–424). Washington, DC: American Psychological Association.

Ashton, M. C. (1998). Personality and job performance: The importance of narrow traits. *Journal of Organizational Behavior, 19,* 289–303.

Austin, J. T., & Vancouver, J. B. (1996). Goal constructs in psychology: Structure, process, and content. *Psychological Bulletin, 120,* 338–375.

Baltes, P. B., Lindenberger, U., & Staudinger, U. M. (2006). Life-span theory in developmental psychology. In W. Damon & R. M. Lerner (Eds.), *Handbook of child psychology* (Vol. 1, pp. 1029–1143). New York, NY: Wiley.

Barenbaum, N. B., & Winter, D. G. (2008). History of modern personality theory and research. In O. P. John, R. W. Robins, & L. A. Pervin (Eds.), *Handbook of personality: Theory and research* (3rd ed.; pp. 3–26). New York, NY: Guilford Press.

Bleidorn, W. (2015). What accounts for personality maturation in early adulthood? *Current Directions in Psychological Science, 24,* 245–252.

Bleidorn, W., Buyukcan-Tetik, A., Schwaba, T., van Scheppingen, M. A., Denissen, J. J. A., & Finkenauer, C. (2016). Stability and change in self-esteem during the transition to parenthood. *Social Psychological and Personality Science, 7,* 560–569.

Branje, S. J. T., van Lieshout, C. F. M., & Gerris, J. R. M. (2007). Big Five personality development in adolescence and adulthood. *European Journal of Personality, 21,* 45–62.

Branje, S. J. T., van Lieshout, C. F. M., & van Aken, M. A. G. (2004). Relations between Big Five personality characteristics and perceived support in adolescents' families. *Journal of Personality and Social Psychology, 86,* 615–628.

Caspi, A. (1998). Personality development across the life course. In W. Damon & N. Eisenberg (Eds.), *Handbook of child psychology: Social, emotional, and personality development* (5th ed., Vol. 3, pp. 311–388). Hoboken, NJ: Wiley.

Chmielewski, M., & Watson, D. (2009). What is being assessed and why it matters: The impact of transient error on trait research. *Journal of Personality and Social Psychology, 97,* 186–202.

Cohen, J. (1992). A power primer. *Psychological Bulletin, 112,* 155–159.

Conley, J. J. (1984). The hierarchy of consistency: A review and model of longitudinal findings on adult individual differences in intelligence, personality and self-opinion. *Personality and Individual Differences, 5,* 11–25.

Corker, K. S., Donnellan, M. B., & Bowles, R. P. (2013). The development of achievement goals throughout college: Modeling stability and change. *Personality and Social Psychology Bulletin, 39*, 1404–1417.

Cramer, A. O. J., van der Sluis, S., Noordhof, A., Wichers, M., Geschwind, N., Aggen, S. H., ... Borsboom, D. (2012). Dimensions of normal personality as networks in search of equilibrium: You can't like parties if you don't like people. *European Journal of Personality, 26*, 414–431.

Denissen, J. J. A., & Penke, L. (2008). Motivational individual reaction norms underlying the Five-Factor model of Personality: First steps towards a theory-based conceptual framework. *Journal of Research in Personality, 43*, 1285–1302.

Denissen, J. J. A., Ulferts, H., Lüdtke, O., Muck, P. M., & Gerstorf, D. (2014). Longitudinal transactions between personality and occupational roles: A large and heterogeneous study of job beginners, stayers, and changers. *Developmental Psychology, 50*, 1931–1942.

Denissen, J. J. A., van Aken, M. A. G., Penke, L., & Wood, D. (2013). Self-regulation underlies temperament and personality: An integrative developmental framework. *Child Development Perspectives, 7*, 255–260.

Denissen, J. J. A., van Aken, M. A. G., & Roberts, B. W. (2011). Personality development across the life span. In T. Chamorro-Premuzic, S. von Stumm, & A. Furnham (Eds.), *The Wiley-Blackwell handbook of individual differences* (pp. 77–100). Chichester: Blackwell.

Dijkstra, P., & Barelds, D. P. H. (2009). Women's well-being: The role of individual differences. *Scandinavian Journal of Psychology, 50*, 309–315.

Donnellan, M. B., Conger, R. D., & Burzette, R. G. (2007). Personality development from late adolescence to young adulthood: Differential stability, normative maturity, and evidence for the maturity-stability hypothesis. *Journal of Personality, 75*, 237–263.

Donnellan, M. B., Trzesniewski, K. H., & Robins, R. W. (2011). Self-esteem: Enduring issues and controversies. In T. Chamorro-Premuzic, S. von Stumm, & A. Furnham (Eds.), *The Wiley-Blackwell handbook of individual differences* (pp. 718–746). Chichester: Blackwell.

Dunlop, W. L., Bannon, B. L., & McAdams, D. P. (2017). Studying the motivated agent through time: Personal goal development during the adult life span. *Journal of Personality, 85*, 207–219.

Fleeson, W. (2001). Toward a structure- and process-integrated view of personality: Traits as density distributions of states. *Journal of Personality and Social Psychology, 80*, 1011–1027.

Fleeson, W., & Jayawickreme, E. (2015). Whole Trait Theory. *Journal of Research in Personality, 56*, 82–92.

Fleeson, W., & Law, M. K. (2015). Trait enactments as density distributions: The role of actors, situations, and observers in explaining stability and variability. *Journal of Personality and Social Psychology, 109*, 1090–1104.

Fraley, R. C., & Roberts, B. W. (2005). Patterns of continuity: A dynamic model for conceptualizing the stability of individual differences in psychological constructs across the life course. *Psychological Review, 112*, 60–74.

Geukes, K., Nestler, S., Hutteman, R., Küfner, A. C. P., & Back, M. D. (2017a). Trait personality and state variability: Predicting individual differences in within- and cross-context fluctuations in affect, self-evaluations, and behavior in everyday life. *Journal of Research in Personality, 69*, 124–138.

Geukes, K., van Zalk, M. H. W., & Back, M. D. (2017b). Analyzing processes in personality development. In J. Specht (Ed.), *Personality development across the lifespan* (pp. 455–472). San Diego, CA: Elsevier.

Gouveia, V. V., Vione, K. C., Milfont, T. L., & Fischer, R. (2015). Patterns of value change during the life span: Some evidence from a functional approach to values. *Personality and Social Psychology Bulletin, 41*, 1276–1290.

Greischel, H., Noack, P., & Neyer, F. J. (2016). Sailing uncharted waters: Adolescent personality development and social relationship experiences during a year abroad. *Journal of Youth and Adolescence, 45*, 2307–2320.

Heckhausen, J., Wrosch, C., & Fleeson, W. (2001). Developmental regulation before and after a developmental deadline: The sample case of 'biological clock' for childbearing. *Psychology and Aging, 16*, 400–413.

Hogan, R., & Roberts, B. W. (2004). A socioanalytic model of maturity. *Journal of Career Assessment, 12,* 207–217.

Hudson, N. W., & Roberts, B. W. (2016). Social investment in work reliably predicts change in conscientiousness and agreeableness: A direct replication and extension of Hudson, Roberts, and Lodi-Smith (2012). *Journal of Research in Personality, 60,* 12–23.

Hudson, N. W., Roberts, B. W., & Lodi-Smith, J. (2012). Personality trait development and social investment in work. *Journal of Research in Personality, 46,* 334–344.

Hutteman, R., Nestler, S., Wagner, J., Egloff, B., & Back, M. D. (2015). Wherever I may roam: Processes of self-esteem development from adolescence to emerging adulthood in the context of international student exchange. *Journal of Personality and Social Psychology, 108,* 767–783.

Jackson, J. J., Bogg, T., Walton, K. E., Wood, D., Harms, P. D., Lodi-Smith, J., ... Roberts, B. W. (2009). Not all conscientiousness scales change alike: A multimethod, multisample study of age differences in the facets of conscientiousness. *Journal of Personality and Social Psychology, 96,* 446–459.

Jacobson, N. S., & Truax, P. (1991). Clinical significance: A statistical approach to defining meaningful change in psychotherapy research. *Journal of Consulting and Clinical Psychology, 59,* 12–19.

John, O. P., Naumann, L. P., & Soto, C. J. (2008). Paradigm shift to the integrative Big Five trait taxonomy: History, measurement, and conceptual issues. In O. P. John, R. W. Robins, & L. A. Pervin (Eds.), *Handbook of personality* (3rd ed., pp. 114–158). New York, NY: Guilford Press.

Johnson, W., Hicks, B. M., McGue, M., & Iacono, W. G. (2007). Most of the girls are alright, but some aren't: Personality trajectory groups from ages 14 to 24 and some associations with outcomes. *Journal of Personality and Social Psychology, 93,* 266–284.

Jokela, M., Alvergne, A., Pollet, T. V., & Lummaa, V. (2011). Reproductive behavior and personality traits of the five factor model. *European Journal of Personality, 25,* 487–500.

Jokela, M., Kivimäki, M., Elovainio, M., & Keltikangas-Järvinen, L. (2009). Personality and having children: A two-way relationship. *Journal of Personality and Social Psychology, 96,* 218–230.

Kandler, C., Kornadt, A. E., Hagemeyer, B., & Neyer, F. J. (2015). Patterns and sources of personality development in old age. *Journal of Personality and Social Psychology, 109,* 175–191.

Kandler, C., Zimmermann, J., & McAdams, D. P. (2014). Core and surface characteristics for the description and theory of personality differences and development. *European Journal of Personality, 28,* 231–243.

Kernis, M. H. (2005). Measuring self-esteem in context: The importance of stability of self-esteem in psychological functioning. *Journal of Personality, 73,* 1569–1605.

Klimstra, T. A., Bleidorn, W., Asendorpf, J. B., van Aken, M. A. G., & Denissen, J. J. A. (2013). Correlated change of Big Five personality traits across the lifespan: A search for determinants. *Journal of Research in Personality, 47,* 768–777.

Kuster, F., & Orth, U. (2013). The long-term stability of self-esteem: Its time-dependent decay and nonzero asymptote. *Personality and Social Psychology Bulletin, 39,* 677–690.

Lehnart, J., Neyer, F. J., & Eccles, J. (2010). Long-term effects of social investment: The case of partnering in young adulthood. *Journal of Personality, 78,* 639–670.

Lerner, R. M. (1996). Relative plasticity, integration, temporality, and diversity in human development: A developmental contextual perspective about theory, process, and method. *Developmental Psychology, 32,* 781–786.

Letzring, T. D., Edmonds, G. W., & Hampson, S. E. (2014). Personality change at mid-life is associated with changes in self-rated health: Evidence from the Hawaii personality and health cohort. *Personality and Individual Differences, 58,* 60–64.

Lodi-Smith, J., & Roberts, B. W. (2007). Social investment and personality: A meta-analysis of the relationship of personality traits to investment in work, family, religion, and volunteerism. *Personality and Social Psychology Review, 11,* 68–86.

Luan, Z., Hutteman, R., Denissen, J. J. A., Asendorpf, J. B., & van Aken, M. A. G. (2017). Do you see my growth? Two longitudinal studies on personality development from childhood to young adulthood from multiple perspectives. *Journal of Research in Personality*, *67*, 44–60.

Lucas, R. E., & Donnellan, M. B. (2011). Personality development across the life span: Longitudinal analyses with a national sample from Germany. *Journal of Personality and Social Psychology*, *101*, 847–861.

Luciano, E. C., & Orth, U. (2017). Transitions in romantic relationships and development of self-esteem. *Journal of Personality and Social Psychology*, 112, 307–328.

Lüdtke, O., Roberts, B. W., Trautwein, U., & Nagy, G. (2011). A random walk down university avenue: Life paths, life events, and personality trait change at the transition to university life. *Journal of Personality and Social Psychology*, *101*, 620–637.

Lüdtke, O., Trautwein, U., & Husemann, N. (2009). Goal and personality trait development in a transitional period: Assessing change and stability in personality development. *Personality and Social Psychology Bulletin*, *35*, 428–441.

Luhmann, M., Orth, U., Specht, J., Kandler, C., & Lucas, R. E. (2014). Studying changes in life circumstances and personality: It's about time. *European Journal of Personality*, *28*, 256–266.

Magnusson, D. (1990). Personality development from an interactional perspective. In L. Pervin (Ed.), *Handbook of personality: Theory and research* (pp. 193–222). New York, NY: Guilford Press.

Magnusson, D. (2001). The holistic-interactionistic paradigm: Some directions for empirical developmental research. *European Psychologist*, *6*, 153–162.

McAdams, D. P. (1995). What do we know when we know a person? *Journal of Personality*, *63*, 365–396.

McAdams, D. P., & Pals, J. L. (2006). A new Big Five: Fundamental principles for an integrative science of personality. *American Psychologist*, *61*, 204–217.

McArdle, J. J. (2009). Latent variable modeling of differences and changes with longitudinal data. *Annual Review of Psychology*, *60*, 577–605.

McCabe, K. O., & Fleeson, W. (2012). What is extraversion for? Integrating trait and motivational perspectives and identifying the purpose of extraversion. *Psychological Science*, *23*, 1498–1505.

McCabe, K. O., & Fleeson, W. (2016). Are traits useful? Explaining trait manifestations as tools in the pursuit of goals. *Journal of Personality and Social Psychology*, *110*, 287–301.

McCrae, R. R. (2015). A more nuanced view of reliability: Specificity in the trait hierarchy. *Personality and Social Psychology Review*, *19*, 97–112.

McCrae, R. R., & Costa, P. T. (2008). The Five-Factor Theory of personality. In O. P. John, R. W. Robins, & L. A. Pervin (Eds.), *Handbook of personality: Theory and research* (3rd ed., pp. 159–181). New York, NY: Guilford Press.

Milfont, T. L., Milojev, P., & Sibley, C. G. (2016). Values stability and change in adulthood: A 3-year longitudinal study of rank-order stability and mean-level differences. *Personality and Social Psychology Bulletin*, *42*, 572–588.

Morin, A. J. S., Maïano, C., Marsh, H. W., Nagengast, B., & Janosz, M. (2013). School life and adolescents' self-esteem trajectories. *Child Development*, *84*, 1967–1988.

Mõttus, R., Johnson, W., & Deary, I. J. (2012). Personality traits in old age: Measurement and rank-order stability and some mean-level change. *Psychology and Aging*, *27*, 243–249.

Mõttus, R., Kandler, C., Bleidorn, W., Riemann, R., & McCrae, R. R. (2017). Personality traits below facets: The consensual validity, longitudinal stability, heritability, and utility of personality nuances. *Journal of Personality and Social Psychology*, *112*, 474–490.

Mund, M., Finn, C., Hagemeyer, B., & Neyer, F. J. (2016). Understanding dynamic transactions between personality traits and partner relationships. *Current Directions in Psychological Science*, *25*, 411–416.

Mund, M., & Neyer, F. J. (2014). Treating personality–relationship transactions with respect: Narrow facets, advanced models, and extended time frames. *Journal of Personality and Social Psychology*, *107*, 352–368.

Mund, M., & Neyer, F. J. (2016). Rising high or falling deep? Pathways of self-esteem in a representative German sample. *European Journal of Personality*, *30*, 341–357.

Neyer, F. J., & Asendorpf, J. B. (2001). Personality–relationship transaction in young adulthood. *Journal of Personality and Social Psychology*, *81*, 1190–1204.

Neyer, F. J., & Lehnart, J. (2007). Relationships matter in personality development: Evidence from an 8-year longitudinal study across young adulthood. *Journal of Personality*, *75*, 535–568.

Neyer, F. J., Mund, M., & Zimmermann, J. (2015). The person makes the situation matter. *European Journal of Personality*, *29*, 403–404.

Neyer, F. J., Mund, M., Zimmermann, J., & Wrzus, C. (2014). Personality–relationship transactions revisited. *Journal of Personality*, *82*, 539–550.

O'Brien, E., & Kardas, M. (2016). The implicit meaning of (my) change. *Journal of Personality and Social Psychology*, *111*, 882–894.

Orth, U., Maes, J., & Schmitt, M. (2015). Self-esteem development across the life span: A longitudinal study with a large sample from Germany. *Developmental Psychology*, *51*, 248–259.

Orth, U., Robins, R. W., & Widaman, K. F. (2012). Life-span development of self-esteem and its effects on important life outcomes. *Journal of Personality and Social Psychology*, *102*, 1271–1288.

Paunonen, S. V., & Ashton, M. C. (2001). Big Five factors and facets and the prediction of behavior. *Journal of Personality and Social Psychology*, *81*, 524–539.

Pytlik Zillig, L. M., Hemenover, S. H., & Dienstbier, R. A. (2002). What do we assess when we assess a Big 5 trait? A content analysis of the affective, behavioral, and cognitive processes represented in Big 5 personality inventories. *Personality and Social Psychology Bulletin*, *28*, 847–858.

Reis, H. T., Collins, W. A., & Berscheid, E. (2000). The relationship context of human behavior and development. *Psychological Bulletin*, *126*, 844–872.

Reitz, A. K., Zimmermann, J., Hutteman, R., Specht, J., & Neyer, F. J. (2014). How peers make a difference: The role of peer groups and peer relationships in personality development. *European Journal of Personality*, *28*, 279–288.

Roberts, B. W., Caspi, A., & Moffitt, T. E. (2001). The kids are alright: Growth and stability in personality development from adolescence to adulthood. *Journal of Personality and Social Psychology*, *81*, 670–683.

Roberts, B. W., Caspi, A., & Moffitt, T. E. (2003). Work experience and personality development in young adulthood. *Journal of Personality and Social Psychology*, *84*, 582–593.

Roberts, B. W., & DelVecchio, W. F. (2000). The rank-order consistency of personality traits from childhood to old age: A quantitative review of longitudinal studies. *Psychological Bulletin*, *126*, 3–25.

Roberts, B. W., O'Donnell, M., & Robins, R. W. (2004). Goal and personality trait development in emerging adulthood. *Journal of Personality and Social Psychology*, *87*, 541–550.

Roberts, B. W., Walton, K. E., & Viechtbauer, W. (2006). Patterns of mean-level change in personality traits across the life course: A meta-analysis of longitudinal studies. *Psychological Bulletin*, *132*, 1–25.

Roberts, B. W., Wood, D., & Caspi, A. (2008). The development of personality traits in adulthood. In O. P. John, R. W. Robins, & L. A. Pervin (Eds.), *Handbook of personality: Theory and research* (3rd ed., pp. 375–398). New York, NY: Guilford Press.

Roberts, B. W., Wood, D., & Smith, J. L. (2005). Evaluating Five Factor Theory and social investment perspectives on personality trait development. *Journal of Research in Personality*, *39*, 166–184.

Robins, R. W., Fraley, R. C., Roberts, B. W., & Trzesniewski, K. H. (2001). A longitudinal study of personality change in young adulthood. *Journal of Personality*, *69*, 617–640.

Rutter, M. (2007). Proceeding from observed correlation to causal inference: The use of natural experiments. *Perspectives on Psychological Science*, *2*, 377–395.

Salmela-Aro, K., Aunola, K., & Nurmi, J.-E. (2007). Personal goals during emerging adulthood: A 10-year follow up. *Journal of Adolescent Research*, *22*, 690–715.

Salmela-Aro, K., Nurmi, J.-E., Saisto, T., & Halmesmäki, E. (2000). Women's and men's personal goals during the transition to parenthood. *Journal of Family Psychology*, *14*, 171–186.

Schwartz, S. H. (1992). Universals in the content and structure of values: Theoretical advances and empirical tests in 20 countries. In M. P. Zanna (Ed.), *Advances in experimental social psychology* (pp. 1–65). London: Academic Press.

Sheldon, K. M. (2005). Positive value change during college: Normative trends and individual differences. *Journal of Research in Personality, 39*, 209–223.

Soto, C. J., & John, O. P. (2012). Development of Big Five domains and facets in adulthood: Mean-level age trends and broadly versus narrowly acting mechanisms. *Journal of Personality, 80*, 881–914.

Sowislo, J. F., Orth, U., & Meier, L. L. (2014). What constitutes vulnerable self-esteem? Comparing the prospective effects of low, unstable, and contingent self-esteem on depressive symptoms. *Journal of Abnormal Psychology, 123*, 737–753.

Specht, J., Bleidorn, W., Denissen, J. J. A., Hennecke, M., Hutteman, R., Kandler, C., ... Zimmermann, J. (2014). What drives adult personality development? A comparison of theoretical perspectives and empirical evidence. *European Journal of Personality, 28*, 216–230.

Specht, J., Egloff, B., & Schmukle, S. C. (2011). Stability and change of personality across the life course: The impact of age and major life events on mean-level and rank-order stability of the Big Five. *Journal of Personality and Social Psychology, 101*, 862–882.

Stephan, Y., Sutin, A. R., & Terracciano, A. (2015). Subjective age and personality development: A 10-year study. *Journal of Personality, 83*, 142–154.

Steunenberg, B., Twisk, J. W. R., Beekman, A. T. F., Deeg, D. J. H., & Kerkhof, A. J. F. M. (2005). Stability and change of neuroticism in aging. *The Journals of Gerontology Series B: Psychological Sciences and Social Sciences, 60*, P27–P33.

Trzesniewski, K. H., Donnellan, M. B., & Robins, R. W. (2003). Stability of self-esteem across the life span. *Journal of Personality and Social Psychology, 84*, 205–220.

Vaidya, J. G., Gray, E. K., Haig, J., & Watson, D. (2002). On the temporal stability of personality: Evidence for differential stability and the role of life experiences. *Journal of Personality and Social Psychology, 83*, 1469–1484.

van Aken, M. A. G., Denissen, J. J. A., Branje, S. J. T., Dubas, J. S., & Goossens, L. (2006). Midlife concerns and short-term personality change in middle adulthood. *European Journal of Personality, 20*, 497–513.

van Scheppingen, M. A., Jackson, J. J., Specht, J., Hutteman, R., Denissen, J. J. A., & Bleidorn, W. (2016). Personality trait development during the transition to parenthood. A test of social investment theory. *Social Psychological and Personality Science, 7*, 452–462.

Vandewater, E. A., Ostrove, J. M., & Stewart, A. J. (1997). Predicting women's well-being in midlife: The importance of personality development and social role investments. *Journal of Personality and Social Psychology, 72*, 1147–1160.

Vecchione, M., Schwartz, S., Alessandri, G., Döring, A. K., Castellani, V., & Caprara, M. G. (2016). Stability and change of basic personal values in early adulthood: An 8-year longitudinal study. *Journal of Research in Personality, 63*, 111–122.

Wagner, J., Becker, M., Lüdtke, O., & Trautwein, U. (2015). The first partnership experience and personality development: A propensity score matching study in young adulthood. *Social Psychological and Personality Science, 6*, 455–463.

Wagner, J., Gerstorf, D., Hoppmann, C., & Luszcz, M. A. (2013a). The nature and correlates of self-esteem trajectories in late life. *Journal of Personality and Social Psychology, 105*, 139–153.

Wagner, J., Lüdtke, O., Jonkmann, K., & Trautwein, U. (2013b). Cherish yourself: Longitudinal patterns and conditions of self-esteem change in the transition to young adulthood. *Journal of Personality and Social Psychology, 104*, 148–163.

Wagner, J., Ram, N., Smith, J., & Gerstorf, D. (2016). Personality trait development at the end of life: Antecedents and correlates of mean-level trajectories. *Journal of Personality and Social Psychology, 111*, 411–429.

Watson, D., & Humrichouse, J. (2006). Personality development in emerging adulthood: Integrating evidence from self-ratings and spouse ratings. *Journal of Personality and Social Psychology, 91*, 959–974.

Wilt, J., & Revelle, W. (2015). Affect, behaviour, cognition and desire in the Big Five: An analysis of item content and structure. *European Journal of Personality*, *29*, 478–497.

Winter, D. G., John, O. P., Stewart, A. J., Klohnen, E. C., & Duncan, L. E. (1998). Traits and motives: Toward an integration of two traditions in personality research. *Psychological Review*, *105*, 230–250.

Wood, D., Gardner, M. H., & Harms, P. D. (2015). How functionalist and process approaches to behavior can explain trait covariation. *Psychological Review*, *122*, 84–111.

Wortman, J., Lucas, R. E., & Donnellan, M. B. (2012). Stability and change in the Big Five personality domains: Evidence from a longitudinal study of Australians. *Psychology and Aging*, *27*, 867–874.

Wrzus, C., & Mehl, M. R. (2015). Lab and/or field? Measuring personality processes and their social consequences. *European Journal of Personality*, *29*, 250–271.

Wrzus, C., & Roberts, B. W. (2017). Processes of personality development in adulthood: The TESSERA framework. *Personality and Social Psychology Review*, *21*, 253–277.

Zeigler-Hill, V., & Wallace, M. T. (2012). Self-esteem instability and psychological adjustment. *Self and Identity*, *11*, 317–342.

Zimmermann, J., & Neyer, F. J. (2013). Do we become a different person when hitting the road? Personality development of Sojourners. *Journal of Personality and Social Psychology*, *105*, 515–530.

Moral Character: Current Insights and Future Directions

Erik G. Helzer, Eranda Jayawickreme and R. Michael Furr

The study of moral character has enjoyed a renaissance in recent years, thanks in large part to a renewed interest in the scientific study of morality, recent discoveries about the nature of moral thought and behavior, and advances in the study of personality. In this chapter, we review the fruits of contemporary moral character research and argue that this body of work puts the study of moral character on firm empirical ground: there is cross-situational and temporal stability in thoughts and behaviors related to traditional virtues such as honesty, fairness, and compassion. Further, these dispositions are outwardly visible and carry real consequences in social life. We go on to describe theoretical and empirical work that aims to deepen our understanding of character by asking about the nature of these moral dispositions and how they relate to standard personality constructs (e.g., Big Five traits). We also draw attention to a line of research centered around moral exceptionalism (i.e., individuals who exude moral virtues to a notable degree), which takes an exemplar approach to understanding what differentiates the morally exceptional from the rest of us. We then attempt to integrate across these diverse methodological approaches to understanding the nature of character. We close by reviewing recent research on positive character change and the potential for character improvement through intentional effort. Throughout our discussion of each of these topics, we intersperse reflections that might serve as direction for future research.

The study of moral character is important for many reasons, not least of which is the potential for scholarship to lead the way toward improving moral education and developing moral leaders and citizens. Such a goal is lofty and contingent upon moral psychologists arriving at an accurate understanding of the mechanisms that give rise to individual differences in moral thought and behavior. It also requires that those mechanisms turn out to be, at least to some degree, open to intentional environmental shaping.

A second reason it is crucial to understand the nature of moral character is its prevalence in folk theories of moral behavior and person perception, as well as its impact on social relationships. At the most basic level, morality arguably constitutes one of three distinct dimensions – along with warmth and competence – of person perception (Goodwin et al., 2014; Wojciszke et al., 1998). Morality is not only a unique and fundamental input into these processes, it guides judgments of liking and respect (Hartley et al., 2016) and affiliation (Goodwin et al., 2014) even more than the other two dimensions. In short, people are attuned to understanding others' moral traits and their evaluations of morality guide their desire for interaction with social partners.

Contrast this prominence with the historical academic debate waged over much of the twentieth century, which has focused on understanding whether moral character even exists in the first place. Although there is no evidence that this debate did much to lessen lay beliefs about the existence or importance of character, claims coming from skeptics in philosophy and psychology were, to some degree, attempts to put to rest naïve beliefs about the existence of character. If such critiques were accepted, the aforementioned importance of moral character to ordinary person perception would be misguided. Fortunately, scientific inquiry into the existence and nature of moral character has persisted in spite of, and perhaps because of, these critiques and, in our view, has justified the premium that everyday people place on understanding others' character.

MORAL CHARACTER DEFINED AND DEFENDED

The debate within philosophy and psychology over the existence of moral character begins with a hypothesis about the psychological roots of moral behavior, namely that 'much of morality and ethical behavior [is] based on long-standing psychological characteristics that exist within individual persons and on which individuals differ' (Fleeson et al., 2014, p. 178). Different researchers may look to different behaviors when defining *morality* and *ethical behavior* (see Fleeson et al., 2014 for a discussion of this issue), but typically behaviors related to traditional virtues, such as caring for others (compassion), playing by the rules (fairness), or telling the truth (honesty) are top candidates for study. Similarly, researchers often differ in their understanding of the kinds of psychological characteristics that produce moral or ethical behavior. In the end, though, the viability of the hypothesis rests on the degree to which there exist stable individual differences in moral/ethical thought and behavior, meaning that differences between people in compassionate behavior or honest behavior, for example, are consistent across time and situations and maintained by 'machinery' within the person.

In the last 100 years, most scholars familiar with extant empirical evidence have argued against the character hypothesis on the basis of two prominent classes of social-psychological evidence (see Batson et al., 1983; Doris, 2002; Harman, 2003; see Miller, 2013, 2014 for a review). The first concerns studies demonstrating that people, on average, act differently in different situations, such as displaying an increased tendency for people to aid a person in need when alone than with a large group of onlookers (bystander nonintervention). The second class of evidence comes from studies that suggest that when people engage in seemingly moral behavior they often do so for amoral reasons, such as when a person helps another person merely to relieve their own distress at seeing that person suffer (Batson et al., 1983). Collectively, hundreds of studies belonging to these two classes have been taken as evidence that moral behavior is largely determined by the situation and that the internal mediators of moral behavior (the psychological 'machinery') are rooted in self-interest, rather than moral concerns per se. Based on this view, any talk of moral character, moral dispositions, virtues, or any other construct that situates the causes of moral behavior within the person is swiftly rejected, both because moral behavior is portrayed as inconsistent across time and situations (lacking character; Hartshorne and May, 1928/1975; Mischel, 1968) and because people seem to be improperly motivated (lacking morality; Doris, 2002).

More recently, however, researchers have become reinvigorated by the moral character hypothesis stated above, and innovative research methods have provided a different perspective on character; one that reveals supportive evidence in favor of robust individual differences. Evidence in favor of the moral character hypothesis comes in two varieties. The first type, which is less direct, is that different observers tend to agree with one another and with the self in their perceptions of a target's moral character. The second type employs longitudinal approaches to examine the stability of people's moral behavior, revealing that, particularly in the long-run, differences between people in moral behavior are robust across time and situations.

INDIRECT EVIDENCE: INDIVIDUAL DIFFERENCES IN MORALITY ARE VISIBLE AND AGREED UPON

A first piece of evidence in favor of moral character comes from agreement studies, in which different judges (including the self) are asked to evaluate a person's moral character. As one example, Cohen and colleagues (2012) asked 'target' people to evaluate their own standing on moral character traits such as honesty and guilt proneness, and then asked one of each target's peers to evaluate the target on the same dimensions. Their results showed that the way a target person rated himself or herself was highly correlated with the way that person was evaluated by his or her peers on both dimensions (see also Ashton and Lee, 2010; Lee et al., 2009). Helzer et al. (2014) conducted a similar set of studies, but with multiple peers per target, a different set of character traits (in addition to honesty, they evaluated compassion, fairness, and temperance), and two different samples (students and community members). Their results indicated that targets and peers significantly agreed with one another about targets' character and that peers agreed with each other about the target's character traits, bolstering and extending evidence for agreement.

Why does agreement bear on the question of character? First, agreement signifies that moral character traits are manifested in outward behavior. Agreement, whether between self and other(s) or only between others, suggests that there is more to character than a person's private beliefs, concerns, or biases. Although character may start from introspective contents, those internal states manifest into behaviors that people other than the self can see and ultimately agree upon. The second conclusion supported by studies of agreement is that moral behaviors are cross-situationally stable. To the degree that observers from different contexts in a person's life nonetheless agree with one another about that person's character, it suggests that the person acts in roughly the same way with different people in different situations. To illustrate, consider what it would take for informants to agree with one another about the amount of fairness that Joe, a hypothetical research participant, manifests in day-to-day life. Informants include Joe's wife, Joe's friend from college, and Joe's coworker. Even though each of them knows Joe in a different context, results from existing studies suggest that their ratings of Joe's fairness will correlate positively with one another and with ratings furnished by Joe himself. This means that the amount of fairness Joe shows with his wife is roughly on par with the level of fairness Joe shows with his friend and at work. Although there are alternative interpretations of what such findings mean (for a discussion, see Helzer et al., 2014), the most parsimonious is that there is something stable in Joe that serves as the basis for agreement on his fairness; namely, an actual moral disposition.

DIRECT EVIDENCE: MORAL THOUGHT AND ACTION ARE RELATIVELY STABLE ACROSS SITUATIONS AND ACROSS TIME

The second kind of evidence directly examines the degree to which individual differences in moral behavior are consistent across time and/or situations. In a recent review, Jayawickreme et al. (2014) argued, in contrast to situationist claims, that situational influences on moral behavior are less damning to the moral character hypothesis than they are often taken to be. They argued that the viability of moral character does not rest upon whether people's behavior is responsive to situations as much as it does whether differences between people in moral behavior are stable in the long-run across situations and time (see also Fleeson and Furr, in press).

Suppose that, over the course of one week, John helps others more often than Mark. What does it mean to say that John is (dispositionally) more helpful than Mark? Jayawickreme and colleagues (2014) argue that the key data point is whether week in and week out John tends to remain more helpful than Mark. Any informed view of character has to allow that there will be situations in which John does not help and Mark does; however, such cases are not damning evidence for lack of character – the critical piece of evidence is whether John is *consistently*, though not perfectly, more helpful than Mark. If behavioral differences between people are fairly consistent across situations and time, then it is reasonable to conclude that those behavioral differences arise from personality characteristics that are themselves consistent across situations and time. In the context of moral behavior, those personality characteristics may well be moral dispositions such as compassion, honesty, and fairness. Thus, if John is consistently more helpful than Mark, we would likely conclude that John and Mark differ on the disposition to be compassionate. Jayawickreme and his colleagues argue that this type of finding would be evidence for the existence of moral character.

Novel methodologies have brought forth evidence of just this kind of consistency. In one example, Meindl et al. (2015) tracked college students for nine days in an experience sampling study. Employing a novel methodology that reduced socially desirable responding, they found that differences between people in honesty, compassion, and fairness were consistent at multiple levels of analysis. Knowing how moral a person was, relative to others, at one point in the day was indicative of how moral they would be at other points in the day (correlations ranged from .35 to .64 across the different moral domains). Correlations of this size indicate some degree of stability in behavior, but particularly on the low end, these same correlation coefficients might just as readily be taken as evidence of the variability in people's moment-to-moment behavior. More stunning was the consistency revealed through aggregation: a person's moral behavior during one half of the study was a strong indicator of their moral behavior for the other half of the study (with correlations ranging from .66 up to .97, depending on the metric). That is, the degree to which a person was more or less compassionate (or honest or fair) than other people during the first half of the study was strongly consistent with the degree to which he or she was more or less compassionate (or honest or fair) during the second half of the study. These results were replicated in a community sample, suggesting that consistency is generalizable across different age groups and life situations (see also Bleidorn and Denissen, 2015).

Motivated by the same basic research questions, Bollich et al. (2016) used a similar longitudinal design but substituted more direct measures of people's moral behavior. Participants wore a device that recorded their speech for several hours interspersed over the course of one to two weekends. Blind coders then listened to these recordings and scored them for the presence of a variety of moral behaviors, such as showing empathy, expressing gratitude, blaming others, and acting condescendingly. Whether looking at the consistency of moment-to-moment behavior or the consistency of behavior from one week to another, results indicated that moral behavior was quite stable: individual differences in empathy or condescension at one point in the study were significantly consistent with individual differences at other points in the study, at remarkable levels ($rs > .47$), especially considering the sparse information and context conveyed by 30–50 second clips of conversation. An obvious advantage to this approach is that it does not rely upon participants' own judgments of their moral behaviors and thus rules out concerns about socially desirable responding, systematic response bias tendencies between people, and other common pitfalls of self-report. It is thus promising that results using recorded behavior mimicked those from studies that have relied upon self-reports to measure the consistency of moral behavior (e.g., Bleidorn and Denissen, 2015; Meindl et al., 2015).

In yet another set of studies, Helzer et al. (2017) examined the consistency of moral cognition. Participants were asked to make a series of moral judgments about right and wrong using moral dilemmas that tapped a similar underlying moral dimension (benefiting the greater good), but differed in their specifics in two ways. First, the scenarios differed from one another in terms of experimental manipulations known to evoke different moral intuitions about what is 'right' in each case; second, they differed in terms of non-essential details, such as the time or place of the scenario. The researchers tested for two forms of consistency: whether the judgments a person made one day were predictive of the judgments they made a week later, and whether the judgments people made in one experimental condition were predictive of the judgments made in the other experimental conditions. Across all studies, results indicated a strong degree of consistency: individuals' underlying concern for the greater good was reflected in their judgments across time and experimental conditions, and this consistency was evident both at the level of individual and aggregated judgments. For example, knowing a person's judgments on two randomly selected dilemmas predicted their judgments on any other two randomly selected dilemmas anywhere from $r = .57$ to .71.

Taken together, the research reviewed above reveals a degree of stability in moral thought and behavior that was assumed to be absent by those who based their conclusions about character on classic social-psychological studies of morality. The reason for the assumed absence may have much to do with differing methodologies. The standard 30-minute, two-condition, between-subjects social-psychological study provides no insight into people's long-range behavioral tendencies, nor the degree to which the same person would act differently in different situations. Such studies are excellent for carefully examining the social-psychological mechanisms that give rise to particular instances of behavior, but ill-suited for shedding light on mechanisms that produce stability (of individual differences) in long-run patterns of behavior (Fleeson and Furr, in press). Recent technological advancements (of the sort that make experience sampling studies possible) and statistical innovations (of the sort that can model complex relationships among dynamic variables) have provided the vantage point from which to examine the possibility of behavioral stability and have yielded positive results in favor of moral character.

UNDERSTANDING VARIABILITY IN LIGHT OF CHARACTER TRAITS

Of course, a skeptic could easily point to correlations that fall far below 1.0 (such as the typical correlations for moment-to-moment behavior) and ask what defenders of character have to say about such departures. Indeed, one characteristic of the stalemate that marked much of the person–situation debate was a fight about which was more important to conclusions about character: the variance that was explained or the variance left unexplained by personality measures (Furr and Funder, in press). Challenges like these encourage researchers to determine whether there is anything systematic about the way in which people change their behavior from situation to situation; in effect, whether variability is predictable between people, and if so, whether it can be incorporated into an overarching model of moral character.

Attempts to do just this are nascent, even in the study of standard personality traits, such as those that compose the Big Five. Nonetheless, some initial research findings suggest that intra-individual variability in moral thought and behavior may not be entirely random nor reflect the unmediated effect of situational forces on behavior. Indeed, the way in which individuals act differently in different situations may itself be a stable feature of persons.

In one study, Bleidorn and Denissen (2015) examined the consistency of parents' moral behavior across ten days of their lives. Participants reported moral behaviors 'over the last hour' six times each day across two important contexts: at work and at home. The authors hypothesized that the demands associated with the social roles of *parent* and *professional* were sufficiently different and powerful that participants were likely to act differently in these two situations and, indeed, they did. Although participants' moral behavior was highly stable from one half of the study to the other (split-half correlations were above $r = .90$ across different virtues), they nonetheless acted in predictably different ways in different situations. People manifested more wisdom and courage in their professional lives than in their parenting lives; and showed more temperance and humanity when acting as parents than as professionals. In other words, the average person acted differently in different situations, but nonetheless differences between people on any particular moral behavior were highly stable across time (see Funder and Colvin, 1991 for a similar demonstration across a wide variety of behaviors).

Such findings are consistent with the idea that both person-level and situation-level factors give rise to moral behavior. A more interactionist approach (relying upon more speculative data) asks whether some people's moral behavior is more cross-situationally stable than others. That is, are some people reliably more consistent than others in the moral behavior they bring to different situations? Bleidorn and Denissen's (2015) data speak to this in two ways. First, people who showed greater variability in moral behavior during one half of their study (relative to those who showed less variability) tended to show greater variability during the other half of the study, $rs > .77$ (see also Fleeson and Law, 2015). Second, people differed systematically from one another in terms of how impactful the situation was on their behavior. For some people, the degree of wisdom or temperance they exhibited in their behavior was strongly dependent on the role they assumed (parent vs. professional). For other people, their wisdom and temperance were more stable, regardless of the role they assumed. This sensitivity to situations was stable across the study: those whose behavior was most (or least) sensitive to situations remained so throughout the ten-day period (see also Bleidorn, 2015). Thus, it appears that at least some degree of variability in people's moral behavior can be explained as a feature of their personality. There exist individual differences in how variable people's moral behavior is across different situations, and those individual differences appear just as stable across time as are differences in the actual content of people's behavior.

There is still much to be learned before the study of systematic variability can be deeply incorporated into theories of moral character. Recently, personality psychologists have made empirical advancements on this front with respect to the Big Five personality traits (Fleeson, 2007; McCabe and Fleeson, 2012, 2016), and this integration has proven fruitful (Fleeson and Jayawickreme, 2015). Understanding individual differences in the (in)consistency of *moral* behavior may be of additional conceptual interest owing to people's intuitive notions of *strong character*. The abstract notion of strong character (as well as particular virtues, like integrity) depend on two semi-independent characteristics of behavior: the frequency of a person's moral behavior and the lack of variability in behavior from one situation or context to another. We say that a person has strong character, for example, if the person is honest or kind, relative to their peers, and if they are consistently so. Thus, consistency may be an independent dimension of character, and existing evidence suggests that consistency itself is consistent.

A NEW DAWN FOR CHARACTER

Although no one study or one single class of evidence (e.g., agreement, temporal stability, cross-situational stability) can convincingly tip the scales in favor of the moral character hypothesis, it would certainly be difficult to account for the breadth and totality of these findings without granting the hypothesis that, when it comes to moral character, there really is something 'there'. Thus, contemporary moral character research is on firm empirical ground, having garnered a large amount of convergent evidence in favor of character to justify exploration of additional questions, such as the nature of these traits, their relationship with other personality constructs (especially the Big Five personality traits), as well as the development and improvement of character traits.

WHAT IS THE NATURE OF MORAL CHARACTER?

If the preceding review suggests that there is something there with regard to character, the next question is what is it? What are the constituent characteristics that together comprise a person's moral character? Below, we review two different approaches to answering this question, which operate on different levels of analysis. The first approach attempts to accommodate moral character within the structure of broad personality traits (i.e., the Big Five). The second approach is more functionalist and focuses on the specific capabilities or components that are required for moral thought and action and on identifying the corresponding dispositions that give rise to those capabilities. We then discuss research on the morally exceptional, which can be used to unify both perspectives by implicating both broad traits and specific capabilities in its understanding of those with noteworthy character.

Moral Character at the Level of Broad Traits

Prior to the recent renaissance in the study of moral character, a prominent personality account of moral behavior was to situate individual differences in moral thought and action within existing personality constructs; namely, the broad traits composing the Big Five. In this approach, researchers operate under the assumption that character traits are components of broad personality traits. To some degree, this approach is premised on the theoretical view that the Big Five is an umbrella term for the totality of personality and that moral personality should be no exception. However, various empirical projects have attempted to map out the actual relationships between specific Big Five constructs and aspects of morality to understand just how well moral behavior can be fit to Big Five personality structure.

The major empirical question for this approach concerns the degree to which individual differences in moral thought and behavior can be explained by individual differences in Big Five traits, either directly or through interactions among the traits and/or their facets. Certainly, many broad traits are correlated with the dispositions that are commonly associated with character. Individual differences in empathy are correlated with trait agreeableness (Habashi et al., 2016; Mooradian et al., 2011), as well as trait extraversion, conscientiousness, and openness to experience (del Barrio et al., 2004). Similarly, helping behavior has been shown to correlate with four out of five broad traits: neuroticism (Tobin et al., 2000), extraversion (Carlo et al., 2005), conscientiousness (Jensen-Campbell et al., 2002), and agreeableness (Graziano and Habashi, 2010; Habashi et al., 2016). The fact that moral behavior cuts across so many different broad traits certainly suggests that the Big Five offer clues for understanding moral character.

However, the key to evaluating the viability of this approach is not so much whether there is a non-zero correlation between the Big Five traits and moral thought and behavior, but rather, the amount of overlap between morality and the Big Five traits. In other words, how much can individual differences in moral thought and behavior be accounted for by invoking the Big Five? In one line of work, Noftle and colleagues (Noftle and Fleeson, 2010; Noftle et al., 2011) examined this question by attempting to map a wide array of virtues measured by Peterson and Seligman's (2004) Values in Action Scale (including equity/fairness, prudence, integrity/honesty/authenticity, and others) to Big Five personality traits and their facets. In this work, most virtues correlated with one or more personality dimensions; however, correlations averaged around $r = .30$. When the entire Big Five was invoked to explain moral behavior, it rarely accounted for more than 30% of the variance, suggesting that the lion's share of what makes some people more moral than others was unexplained by the Big Five.

More recently, personality psychologists have attempted to accommodate moral behavior within broad traits by cordoning off all or much of moral character within its own personality construct. The HEXACO model of personality is a dominant example of this, wherein standard personality traits have been reconfigured so as to cluster fairness, greed avoidance, humility, and sincerity (i.e., character) under the umbrella of Honesty–Humility (H; Lee and Ashton, 2004). According to this view, many dispositions that give rise to moral behavior have been unified under a single broad trait rather than distributed across various facets of openness, conscientiousness, extraversion, agreeableness, and emotional stability. From this perspective, character is largely represented and summarized by the H factor of HEXACO personality.

The development of the HEXACO model has been extremely helpful in reinvigorating the study of moral behavior as a topic in personality psychology. H is by far the most successful of the six broad traits for predicting moral behavior: it is negatively correlated with the 'dark triad' of personality characteristics (i.e., Narcissism, Psychopathy, and Machiavellianism; Lee and Ashton, 2004), vengefulness (Lee and Ashton, 2012), cheating (Hershfeld et al., 2012), adultery (Bourdage et al., 2007), and counterproductive workplace behavior (Cohen and Morse, 2014), and positively correlated with integrity and ethical decision-making (Lee et al., 2008).

The success of the H factor notwithstanding, it should be clear that it alone cannot account for the totality of moral character. First, H may be suited toward certain kinds of moral behavior (e.g., standing up against injustice) but not other kinds (e.g., offering sympathy to a person who is suffering). Second, other traits – or facets of those traits – may contribute to the moral behaviors not exhausted by H. Of course, one could then take the approach of invoking all six traits (or their 24 facets) to account for individual differences in morality, but doing so is likely to yield the same explanatory holes as are evident in past attempts to do the same thing using the Big Five. Thus, H should continue to take a central role in the study and conceptualization of moral character, writ large, but might best be viewed as one component of a broader array of dispositions that comprise moral character or an aggregate of more fundamental aspects of morality.

The broad trait approach to understanding character offers the opportunity to view moral thought and behavior through the lens of established personality constructs and models; however, a number of questions about the nature of character remain unanswered by invoking this approach alone. First, the overlapping correlations between many of the broad traits and particular moral behaviors (like helping or empathy) lend little clarity to the nature of these moral dispositions. What should one conclude about the nature of empathy, for example, based on the fact that it is correlated with almost all of the Big Five traits? Second, the broad trait approach only hints at the specific mental capacities that produce individual differences in moral behavior – a question that is at the heart of virtue ethics and moral education. Indeed, many who have studied the morally exceptional rely upon life narrative methods (Matsuba and Walker, 2005; Walker and Frimer, 2007) precisely because they find the standard broad trait-level analysis ill-equipped to account for the breadth and depth of these individuals. At the least, this approach seems to leave a lot of important residual variance unexplained; at worst, it does not fully capture where the action 'really is' with regard to character: embedded within more specific and differentiated belief, value, and identity constructs.

These outstanding questions point to specific issues that moral character researchers have had to wrestle with in an attempt to offer a satisfying account of moral personality. Some of the considerations listed below point to the need for additional theoretical assumptions that are not currently a part of models based on broad traits. The first consideration is how to incorporate a broader array of psychological constructs into a theory of moral character. To the degree that moral character is composed of a suite of cognitive and meta-cognitive beliefs, personal narratives, attributional styles, and motivations that predispose people in various degrees to do morally good things and avoid morally bad things in different situations, our theory of character must accommodate a range of social-cognitive constructs that are often not accounted for in broad trait theories.

Second, according to almost all virtue theorists, doing a seemingly moral thing is not enough to prove the existence of an underlying disposition. A minimum requirement is that one must have engaged in the seemingly moral action for the morally correct reasons (i.e., the reasons a virtuous person would have for engaging in the act). It is not enough for the virtue theorist that John gives to charity every holiday season – such actions might reflect an underlying moral disposition or they might not. If John gives because he knows his boss keeps track of who gives and who does not and smiles upon the former, he would not qualify as generous. Only if John's actions are motivated by the right reasons (say, a genuine concern for the recipients of the charitable gift or a concern for fairness) might he qualify as a generous person. Thus, moral character relies on a tighter coupling of motives and actions than is typical of broad trait frameworks. Certainly, we are not arguing that motives do not matter to such frameworks (a person who visits art museums and acts unconventionally merely to curry favor with art students probably would not rightly qualify as being open to experience), only that existing frameworks seem not to put as much emphasis on this motive–behavior link as moral theorists would require (but see Emmons, 1986 and Emmons and McCullough, 2003).

Finally, moral character researchers should attend to underlying psychometric assumptions and perhaps adjust them in their study of the virtues and character. Virtually all broad trait frameworks of personality in use by the scientific community adopt the view that a given trait is normally distributed across a population and that trait-standing is a continuous phenomenon: a person is not extraverted or introverted, but rather has behavior that, on average, places them somewhere on a continuum from low to high extraversion (Fleeson, 2001). Moral character may be different, or at least researchers should consider the possibility that it is. For example, many moral philosophers stipulate that the possession of a certain virtue, say honesty, requires the absence of its complementary vice (in this case, dishonesty). Thus, it would be a contradiction to say that an honest person sometimes lies – a person who sometimes lies would lack the virtue of honesty (see, for example, Miller, 2013). It is unclear how this consideration would be accommodated under a framework that assumes that the moral thoughts and behaviors corresponding to any particular moral character trait are continuously and normally distributed (see Jayawickreme and Fleeson, 2017 for further discussion).

This is not just a matter of philosophical interest because a weaker version of this idea is consistent with intuition. Suppose, in the first case, that John tells the truth 90% of the time and lies 10% of the time. Now suppose, in a second case, that John is talkative in groups 90% of the time but quiet in groups 10% of the time. Recent data collected by one of us (Helzer) suggest that people have a harder time labeling John honest in the first case than labeling John extraverted in the second case. Put another way, people see behavior that is 'out of character' as more disqualifying in the moral domain than in other domains of person perception. If these perceptions reveal something true about the nature of moral character traits, researchers will need to think carefully about the expected distribution of moral character traits within a given population, as well as assumptions about the continuous nature of (at least some) moral dispositions.

Some of these considerations can be addressed by supplementing a broad trait framework with a functionalist approach. The functionalist approach can shed light on the range of social-psychological mechanisms that give rise to moral thought and behavior, including motivational components, which are less well defined by the broad trait approach. These mechanisms, then, may be tied back to broad trait constructs in an attempt to provide an integrated understanding of moral character. For example, if it turns out that self-regulatory ability is part of the nature of character, it helps to explain the role that the broad trait of conscientiousness plays in character. Other considerations – such as the expected distribution of moral character traits – are challenges for either perspective as they pertain to basic psychometric assumptions about the nature of moral character traits.

A Functionalist Approach to Understanding Moral Character

A functionalist approach to understanding the nature of moral character starts by defining the different capacities that are required for a person to think and behave in moral ways, and then identifies the psychological dispositions that promote each capacity. As such, this approach is more domain-specific than the broad trait approach; although some of the mechanisms it points to are no doubt domain-general, others will be particular to morality or even specific domains of morality.

Researchers taking this approach have identified a number of capacities that are proposed to lie at the heart of individual differences in moral character. Recently, Cohen and Morse (2014) offered a three-component conceptual model of moral character, which offers a means of unifying across different research programs. Their model suggests that consistent, stable individual differences in moral thought and action are traceable to three latent dispositions: moral identity, concern for others, and the capacity for self-regulation. Although their theory is premised on research conducted on the moral character of adults, similar themes emerge from the study of character development in children (see Boerger and Hoffman, 2015, for a review). Below, we review and expand on Cohen and Morse's taxonomy for classifying these three components of character.

Moral identity. A first component to moral character concerns the degree to which people desire to be moral and to be seen by themselves and others as moral. For some people, morality is a central aspect of who they are or want to be: they desire and maximize opportunities to do good and regularly reflect upon their success at living up to moral ideals. For others, morality is less central: for these individuals, the important thing might be to simply pass a threshold of 'good enough', or to pursue morality alongside other goals that are of equal (or at least competing) importance. The identity component of character includes psychological dispositions reflective of the degree to which morality is integrated into one's sense of self.

The study of Moral Identity Centrality (MIC; Aquino and Reed, 2002) attempts to measure and understand individual differences on this dimension, as well as to document the situational factors that might temporarily 'push' morality to a more central position in one's identity (see Shao et al., 2008 for a review). Knowing a person's chronic (or trait-level) MIC has proven to be a reliable indicator and predictor of ethical leadership (Mayer et al., 2012; Zhu et al., 2016) as well as increased prosocial behavior (Aquino and Reed, 2002; Reed and Aquino, 2003; Reynolds and Ceranic, 2007). Similarly, when moral identity is temporarily activated by situational cues, individuals are more likely to engage in charitable behavior and less likely to engage in deceptive behavior (Aquino et al., 2009).

In their initial theorizing, Cohen and Morse (2014) focused on MIC as the central feature of the identity component of character. One limitation of this is that the MIC measure, which assesses the degree to which being a generally moral person is important to respondents, represents only a small part of what might rightly be thought of as *moral identity*. The measure itself taps the importance of being moral, but does not reveal which aspects of morality are valued by different people – in other words, it is silent with regard to the content of a person's identity. We imagine that a fully formed account of moral identity will need to take into account the broad swath of values, beliefs, and ideologies that shape thoughts and behavior, and account for individual differences in the particular virtues or moral identities to which different people aspire.

Existing research offers little guidance with regard to understanding such contents. Although many personality scales assess a person's standing on particular traits by asking about the degree to which they endorse an assortment of beliefs and values, a rich literature on beliefs and values per se is missing from our most prominent theories. Thus, one goal for moral character researchers should be to develop measures of a richer set of identity constructs with which to understand moral identity, broadly construed.

With respect to values, Moral Foundations Theory (MFT; Graham et al., 2013; Haidt and Graham, 2007) provides a starting point for understanding differences in the range of moral concerns that people might hold, as well as how such basic concerns map onto broader ideologies (Inbar et al., 2009). To be sure, knowing the degree to which one prioritizes fairness, harm, authority, loyalty, and purity in determining right and wrong is one way of understanding the values that compose moral identity, but like the broad trait approach, it is possible that MFT is overly general in its attempt to map broad foundations onto specific moral beliefs and concerns.

With respect to beliefs, we encourage researchers to attend to the literature on moral conviction as a way of thinking about the importance of specific beliefs (or belief systems) as a component of moral identity. Moral attitudes held with strong conviction, versus those held with lesser conviction, evoke stronger moral emotions, are experienced more as objective truths, and act as motivators of autonomous action (Skitka, 2010). For example, moral conviction about candidates and issues in the 2000 and 2004 elections predicted voting behavior over and above education, strength of party affiliation, and preference for the candidates (Skitka and Bauman, 2008). If conviction is evidence that a particular belief is deeply intertwined with a sense of self, existing measures of conviction might be used to identify the beliefs that are most central to a person's moral identity.

Concern for others. A second component of Cohen and Morse's (2014) model is 'consideration of others' wants and needs, and how one's actions affect other people' (p. 49). Moral behavior requires people to move beyond their own narrow self-interest and perspective, and the model points to several dispositions that might serve this function.

The moral emotions of shame, guilt, gratitude, and empathic concern are other-oriented emotions that have been theorized and empirically demonstrated to motivate moral judgment and behavior (Blasi, 1999; Caprara et al., 2010; Cohen, 2010; Eisenberg, 2010; Tangney et al., 2007). Although much of this work has been conducted through a situationist lens (*when people are feeling X, they are more likely to Y*), individual differences in the experience of certain types of moral emotions are strong candidates for this component of character because they represent a basic 'tuning' to the concerns and reactions of others. As one example, Cohen et al. (2012) have introduced the construct of guilt proneness, which refers to individual differences in the tendency to experience guilty feelings about one's own public and private wrongdoing. Those who experience guilt more readily (i.e., those high in guilt proneness) may engage in moral behaviors or refrain from immoral behaviors due to a motivation to avoid guilty feelings in the future. In line with this, Cohen and colleagues have found that individuals high versus low in guilt proneness are less likely to engage in unscrupulous business decision-making, lie for money, engage in dishonest negotiations, or perform counterproductive workplace behaviors, such as stealing small items from work or being rude to coworkers (Cohen et al., 2011, 2012; see also Cohen et al., 2014).

In addition, one might look to general cognitive capacities that bolster a person's concern for others. Individual differences in perspective-taking (Cohen, 2010) or mind perception (Gray et al., 2012) are likely important insofar as they allow a person to anticipate others' reactions and to move beyond one's narrow egocentric perspective to an understanding of the experiences of others. Individuals who find it more difficult to take others' perspectives are unlikely to understand their impact on others, which may lead them to take actions that unwittingly affect others in a negative manner.

Self-regulation. A third component of character concerns individual differences in the capacity to regulate one's thoughts and behaviors in the service of moral action. According to most common views of moral character, it would be insufficient for a person to desire to be moral and to feel concern for others; the person must also be able to turn those intentions into actions via self-regulation. Lacking this capacity is what effectively paves the road to hell with good intentions.

Importantly, self-regulatory capacity involves both the ability to pursue moral action and inhibit immoral action. The personality trait of conscientiousness may, broadly, reflect individual differences in success at self-regulation across a number of domains, as well as other capacities (Roberts et al., 2009). And, in fact, conscientiousness regularly emerges as one of the best predictors of workplace citizenship behaviors; it is associated with a decreased likelihood of absenteeism, theft, and sabotage (Bolton et al., 2010).

Although much of the variance in moral self-regulation can be captured by conscientiousness, research suggests that self-regulatory ability may vary by domain (Duckworth and Tsukayama, 2015; Tsukayama et al., 2013). Individuals may display more self-regulation in some areas (work and finance) than others (interpersonal domains). Moreover, these domain-specific contingencies are stable across time: the domains in which one excels at self-control at any particular time are likely to continue to be that way at other time points. Note that, on this view of self-control, character may well be manifested differently in different domains and thus appears less of a global disposition toward moral action. This view helps clarify why Eliot Spitzer or Anthony Weiner can show exemplary self-control in some areas (diet and exercise) but not in others (sexual monogamy). In so doing, it allows for greater specificity in understanding the nature of the self-regulatory component of character by cautioning that good self-control in one area may or may not reflect strong moral character.

Taken together, the picture of a person with good moral character emerging from this particular perspective is one who has a strong internal commitment to being a moral person, is attuned to others and concerned with her impact on them, and has the ability to resist temptation and to follow through on moral intentions. Additional research will help to flesh out this framework and tackle additional questions, such as 'What specific moral commitments do those with strong moral identity possess?'; 'What is the proper balance between being attuned to others, on the one hand, and able to act against social norms when necessary?'; 'What explains a person's ability to exert good self-control in one, non-moral domain, but not in the moral domain?'

MORAL EXCEPTIONALISM AS A BLUEPRINT FOR UNDERSTANDING THE NATURE OF CHARACTER

Traditional approaches to studying moral character, represented in much of the work reviewed above, typically focus on the thoughts and behavior of the average person drawn from a convenience sample; as a result, our understanding of character is built from observations of normal variation around a population mean. There are many reasons to like this approach – the most prominent being that it will capture much of the variance in everyday moral behavior, informing us about how moral character works within ordinary people.

On the other hand, one might argue that the study of moral character is best conducted as an investigation of human potential: rather than study how moral character typically manifests itself in the lives of ordinary people, the argument goes, it may be more informative to try to understand the nature of moral character when it is at its best. Just as one might come to understand the nature of intelligence through studying those who are intellectually gifted, a richer understanding of the nature of fairness, compassion, or overall morality might be gained by understanding those who most exude these characteristics.

Ideally, both approaches (examining the nature of moral character through the study of the average person and through the study of exemplars) will turn up overlapping conclusions about what character is. We can look to the morally exceptional – individuals who embody character traits to a degree that distinguishes them from their peers – to see whether existing theoretical models of character derived from the broad trait and functionalist approaches reviewed above are reflected in those who exemplify character most fully. Where conclusions reached from the study of the morally exceptional and the study of the average person overlap, we can feel more confident that researchers have hit upon a necessary component of moral character. When conclusions do not overlap, we can ask whether the divergence reflects something fundamental that distinguishes the morally exceptional from the average person.

Beyond this, the scientific study of the morally exceptional advances the study of moral character in at least two other ways. The research employs both quantitative and qualitative methods, which bring together both 'outside' (statistical) and 'inside' (experiential) perspectives on these individuals. It also opens our eyes to what is possible for human morality. Although the subjects of study are, indeed, exceptional, they are not hidden away or 'freaks of nature': they are people who live among us and use their time and talents to improve the lives of others. Understanding what makes them different from the rest of us with respect to morality may provide guidance for shaping moral development and education. It is, in fact, a cornerstone of classical virtue ethics (Hursthouse, 1999).

The first step in the study of the morally exceptional is to identify these individuals. Researchers have typically focused on those who have received public recognition for their moral actions, including winners of national awards, influential leaders, or those nominated by a peer group for their consistent good deeds. Once identified, researchers conduct in-depth interviews with these individuals, in addition to administering batteries of personality measures. In many cases, researchers rely upon extensive life narrative techniques to better understand the landmark events in their lives, their attributions for success and failure, and their values and beliefs. Data from the morally exceptional are then compared against a control group of average individuals (matched on key demographic variables, such as age and gender) in order to identify the 'markers' that differentiate the morally exceptional from their peers. From this research, the morally exceptional are distinguished by several characteristics.

First, confirming theorizing from Cohen and Morse (2014), the morally exceptional show strong moral identity. These individuals do not simply *do* moral things; they are committed to becoming moral people and engage in moral behavior because they feel it is important to be moral. A concern for doing what is right tends to be a central organizing principle for how these individuals structure their lives (Colby and Damon, 1993; Matsuba and Walker, 2005; Monroe, 2012; Walker and Frimer, 2007, 2009), and they prioritize moral goals and values (Frimer et al., 2012; Walker and Frimer, 2007). Morally exceptional individuals also tend to hold their beliefs with certainty and conviction (Colby and Damon, 1993), perhaps validating the proposal above that moral conviction serves as a crucial ingredient in moral identity. It is interesting to contrast this with the implications of many social-psychological experiments, which highlight how mindlessly people can act when it comes to moral action (as evidenced by the ease with which behavior can be swayed). It may well be that developing a strong moral identity provides a buffer against the pushes and pulls of the situation by ensuring that one's superordinate moral goals remain accessible even in environments that may distract.

Second – also a point of convergence with conclusions reached by Cohen and Morse (2014) – the morally exceptional are less self-focused than the average person. Their self-concepts are more interdependent (McFarland et al., 2013) and they perceive more overlap between their own identity and humanity as a whole (McFarland et al., 2012; Monroe, 2002). Their life narratives reflect an earlier awareness of others' suffering, as well as an awareness of how their own advantages were gained through help from other people (Matsuba and Walker, 2005; Walker and Frimer, 2007). Another marker of the morally exceptional is the way they balance needs for agency (the need to *get ahead*, or to achieve power and status) and communion (the need to *get along*, or to affiliate with others). The morally exceptional embody 'enlightened self-interest': pursuing agentic goals in the service of communion (Frimer et al., 2011, 2012). When these individuals pursue or exert power or influence, it is typically in the service of community goals, rather than individual ones.

Third, the morally exceptional are distinguished by a general sense of optimism and positivity about the world, which contributes to psychological resilience and adjustment. More than the average person, they interpret negative life events as having turned out 'for the best', either because such events promoted growth and learning or because they conferred benefit to someone else (Matsuba and Walker, 2005; Walker and Frimer, 2007). They report more positive childhood attachments (Walker and Frimer, 2009), have greater faith (Colby and Damon, 1993; Matsuba and Walker, 2004), do not struggle with themselves, work in isolation, or live grim, joyless lives (Colby and Damon, 1993). Relative to the average person, many morally exceptional individuals are relatively high in traits like agreeableness, agency, communion, social responsibility, nurturance, generativity, and affiliation (Matsuba and Walker, 2005; Walker and Frimer, 2007), which taken together, promote resilience as well as awareness of, and connection to, others.

It is also instructive to look to places where the two literatures diverge from one another. For example, Cohen et al. (2014) emphasize self-regulatory ability as a crucial component of moral character; however, research on the morally exceptional identifies no central role for self-control in the etiology of these individuals. Studies that have compared conscientiousness of the morally exceptional against that of the average person, for example, have yielded mixed conclusions regarding between-group differences on the broad trait that is most closely tied to self-regulation (Matsuba and Walker, 2004; Walker et al., 2010). What does it mean that self-regulation is not a bigger part of the story of the morally exceptional when it features so prominently in models of moral character describing character of the average person? One possibility is the morally exceptional have less to regulate in the first place. That is, they have more good impulses and fewer bad ones, and this motivational purity obviates the need for self-control. Another possibility is that moral self-regulation has become automated in the psychology of the morally exceptional, in much the same way that experts in other domains show advanced automaticity for the cognitions and behaviors that help them excel. A third possibility is that strong moral identity and conviction – combined with a heightened awareness of others – is sufficiently motivating of moral thought and behavior. Just as one would not have to will oneself not to step off a cliff if one were committed to staying alive, sure that the fall would kill them and bothered by the thought of their own death, the morally exceptional may find less need to self-regulate because less moral courses of action cannot compete in attractiveness with moral courses of action.

In sum, we see tremendous potential for integration across two bodies of research that take distinct, but complementary, approaches to understanding moral character. A cursory attempt (of the sort just developed) yields useful insights into both the nature of moral character and, perhaps, its developmental trajectory.

CHARACTER CHANGE AND IMPROVEMENT IN ADULTHOOD

Across a number of research programs, clear evidence emerges that the average person desires to improve their standing on a range of morally relevant personality (and character) traits (Hudson and Roberts, 2014; Noftle, 2015; Robinson et al., 2015). For this reason, and others, a central question for virtue theorists and moral psychologists interested in moral education concerns how effective these attempts are likely to be. We should note here that the study of character change has focused primarily on Big Five personality characteristics, due largely to the well-developed state of knowledge about these traits. For our purposes, we will focus on two traits that have been most often linked to moral character, agreeableness and conscientiousness, supplementing with more specific character traits when available. We should also note that we will focus only on character growth in adulthood; for a discussion of character development in children, please see Boerger and Hoffman, 2015.

We will first discuss normative personality change, which refers to changes that happen for the average person over time. Early adulthood is a time of noteworthy personality change (Roberts et al., 2006). Meta-analyses looking across culture suggest that, during these years, young adults show positive changes in agreeableness and conscientiousness (Bleidorn et al., 2009). Recent research has expanded these findings by examining the degree to which moral character changes over students' college experience (Robinson et al., 2015). At least two noteworthy findings emerged. First, across a range of virtues, character traits, and moral self-views, the researchers found moderate to high levels of stability over a two-year period, indicating that the individuals who were most honest, fair, or empathic coming into college tended to maintain their relative position two years later. Second, in addition to consistency of individual differences, researchers saw evidence for normative changes across the same time period. On average, students grew significantly more empathic and tolerant as they progressed through college.

Normative changes in moral character are encouraging; however, the mechanisms underlying such changes are opaque – such changes may result in full or in part from volitional acts (the desire to be a 'better person') but they may also result from impersonal developmental forces that have little to do with a person's desires. The question of whether people can bring about intentional character change in themselves is one that has received less empirical attention but is central to the study of moral character, where development and improvement are often cited as justifications for understanding the nature of character traits.

Two notable longitudinal studies offer mixed evidence on the possibility for successful attempts at intentional character change, suggesting that changing one's moral character requires concentrated effort and intervention. This research also points toward the sorts of interventions that might be most promising for a person set on changing his or her character.

First, the bad news. In one recent study, Robinson and colleagues (2015) tracked young adults' success at intentionally improving their agreeableness and conscientiousness (as well as the other three Big Five traits) over a 12-month time period. Participants were drawn from global samples, including China, the UK, and Iran. Participants' personality traits were measured at the beginning of each study, as were their goals for personality change (ranging from a desire to be less agreeable or conscientious to a desire to be more so) on each trait. Not surprisingly, the less agreeable and conscientious participants were at the beginning of the study, the more they endeavored to improve on their traits over time. However, these goals proved ineffective: change goals were negatively correlated with changes in conscientiousness and unrelated to changes in agreeableness at Time 2. In other words, the desire to change one's character had either no effect or perhaps even a negative effect on actual personality change.

Another set of studies provides a more optimistic view. In a conceptually similar study design, Hudson and Fraley (2015) tracked college students over the course of a 16-week period (roughly one third as long as Robinson and colleagues). In two studies, students' change goals for agreeableness and conscientiousness (as well as other traits) were positively correlated with change over the four-month period. Those who had the strongest goals to change their personality changed their personality the most, and in the direction of their goals. Moreover, personality change was most effective when students were trained to form implementation intentions (Gollwitzer, 1999), which are concrete *if–then* action plans for how students plan to respond to situations that might interfere with their change goals (e.g., *if I am tempted to shop online at work rather than complete a project, then I will turn off my wifi and plan to shop during lunch*).

Despite similar methodologies and sample characteristics, these two rigorous research programs point to opposite conclusions about the possibility for intentional character change. One obvious difference is the length of time assessed in each study – it may be meaningful that positive evidence for character change was obtained over a four-month period, whereas negative evidence emerged when looking across a longer timeframe. Recently, Hennecke et al. (2014) theorized that success at intentional personality change requires three conditions: the person must value and want to change; the person must see it as possible to change; and the person must enact these changes through concrete, habitual behaviors. As with any self-improvement goal (e.g., dieting, exercising), these three preconditions for change may be easier to muster up in the short term (over four months) than the long-run (a year or longer). A person may lose weight over four to six months because he is motivated, optimistic, and committed to getting to the gym three times a week. Beyond that, though, he may see diminished returns for the effort, which lower his motivation and allow the old habits to creep back in, eventually returning him to his starting weight. The same may be true of attempts to be kinder or more responsible.

Of course, none of this theorizing suggests that intentional character change is impossible, just hard and perhaps elusive to the average person living day-to-day life. However, just as there are those who remain fit throughout their lives through concerted and continued effort, the same is likely true of moral character. It would be interesting to tailor the study of the morally exceptional to those who are exceptional due to prolonged changes in their moral character, perhaps in an effort to understand what leads to long-term self-directed character development.

DO MORAL PEOPLE TRANSMIT THEIR MORALITY TO OTHERS?

Another route to character change, which lies somewhere on a continuum from passive to intentional change, is social influence. Moral theorists have long held that character is shaped through socialization – that people 'pick up' their morality from early influences from caregivers as well as daily interactions with coworkers, family members, and friends. Although a full treatment of the research supporting these ideas is beyond the scope of this chapter, we wish to mention one recent example that bears directly on the question of character change in adulthood vis-à-vis social influence.

Recently, Zhu et al. (2016) studied organizational leaders and their employees in Chinese businesses. Supervisors and employees reported their own moral identity (described earlier) and moral awareness (attentiveness to the ethical issues present in various decisions) at different time points across a three-week period. In addition, employees reported the degree to which they felt their supervisor exhibited ethical leadership. The researchers asked whether these reports offered any indication that supervisors 'transmit' their morality to those who work for them and found evidence that they did. Employees' reports of their own morality (identity and awareness), furnished at the end of the study, were positively correlated with supervisors' reports of their own morality, furnished at the beginning of the study. Moreover, this correlation between supervisor morality and employee morality was explained by employees' perceptions of ethical leadership. These findings are consistent with the idea that more ethical leaders create a more ethical climate that then influences and improves the moral character of their employees. Thus, leaders with good character may 'transmit' their values and actions to those with whom they work and supervise – a promising conclusion for the possibility of virtue education.

CONCLUSIONS

The rapid growth of moral character research over the last ten or more years has yielded many important findings that have revamped the prominence of character in moral psychology. Although there is still much to be learned, we feel confident in drawing the following conclusions about the state of knowledge about moral character:

- Moral character traits are central to person perception, and these perceptions are not held in isolation. Different observers, including the self, tend to agree with one another on targets' moral standing relative to others.
- Moral cognition and behavior are consistent across time and across situations. Although situational forces are undoubtedly important to shaping moment-to-moment behavior, in the long-run, individual differences in moral thought and action are highly stable.
- Consequently, moral character exists and affects behavior.

We also point to exciting developments in understanding the nature of moral dispositions. These conclusions are drawn from recent research and are thus more tenuous; however, we see them as promising first steps toward understanding what moral character traits are and how they work:

- Individual differences in moral thought and behavior are correlated with many broad personality traits, such as agreeableness and conscientiousness, but invoking broad traits alone to understand the nature of character leaves many questions unanswered. Researchers should also focus on the rich constellation of values, motivations, and beliefs that seem critical to a full picture of moral character.
- Functionalist accounts of moral character point to three components: identity, concern for others, and self-regulation, as essential constituents of character. Research on the morally exceptional underscores the importance of these first two components, in particular, in the psychology of the most moral among us. Further development of identity constructs is needed in order for theories to fully capture the contents of individuals' moral identities and to explain individual differences in identity.
- There is consistency of individual differences in how situationally contingent behavior is, suggesting that variability may itself be a feature of moral character that is maintained by personality mechanisms. The mechanisms that give rise to individual differences in situational-contingent behavior are not yet understood.
- Moral character changes across the lifetime in predictable, and positive, ways. However, to date, there is mixed evidence for the efficacy of intentional personality change. Additional research, perhaps informed by successful interventions for other kinds of intentional personality change (for example, in clinical psychology), may illuminate how moral character can be changed according to one's volition, or why it cannot be.
- Studying the morally exceptional has the potential to significantly expand our understanding of morality and to facilitate future efforts dedicated to character improvement.

The methods, conceptual models, and populations of study that are currently available to researchers make this an exciting time to work in the field of moral character. In combination with the well-developed social-psychological literature on moral behavior, a person-centered approach will continue to highlight important insights that are unavailable to the former field of study. Questions like 'Why are some people more moral than others?', 'Why do different people respond in different ways to the same moral situation?', and 'How can people make long-term changes to their own character?' are uniquely answered by a personality approach to moral behavior. In our view, moral character researchers are well-poised to answer these and other questions in the years to come.

REFERENCES

Aquino, K., Freeman, D., Reed, A., II, Lim, V. K., & Felps, W. (2009). Testing a social-cognitive model of moral behavior: The interactive influence of situations and moral identity centrality. *Journal of Personality and Social Psychology*, 97, 123–141.

Aquino, K., & Reed, A. (2002). The self-importance of moral identity. *Journal of Personality and Social Psychology*, 83, 1423–1440.

Ashton, M. C., & Lee, K. (2010). Trait and source factors in HEXACO-PI-R self- and observer reports. *European Journal of Personality*, 24, 278–289.

Batson, C. D., O'Quin, K., Fultz, J., Vanderplas, M., & Isen, A. M. (1983). Influence of self-reported distress and empathy on egoistic versus altruistic motivation to help. *Journal of Personality and Social Psychology*, 45, 706–718.

Blasi, A. (1999). Emotions and moral motivation. *Journal for the Theory of Social Behaviour*, 29, 1–19.

Bleidorn, W. (2015). What accounts for personality maturation in early adulthood? *Current Directions in Psychological Science*, 24, 245–252.

Bleidorn, W., & Denissen, J. J. A. (2015). Virtues in action – The new look of character traits. *British Journal of Psychology*, 106, 700–723.

Bleidorn, W., Kandler, C., Riemann, R., Angleitner, A., & Spinath, F. M. (2009). Patterns and sources of adult personality development: Growth curve analyses of the NEO PI-R scales in a longitudinal twin study. *Journal of Personality and Social Psychology*, 97, 142–155.

Boerger, E. A., & Hoffman, A. J. (2015). Character development in the school years: Relations among theory of mind, moral identity, and positive and negative behavior toward peers. In C.B. Miller, R. M. Furr, A. Knobel, & W. Fleeson (Eds.), *Character: New directions from philosophy, psychology, and theology* (pp. 467–489). New York, NY: Oxford University Press.

Bollich, K. L., Doris, J. M., Vazire, S., Raison, C. L., Jackson, J. J., & Mehl, M. R. (2016). Eavesdropping on character: Assessing everyday moral behaviors. *Journal of Research in Personality*, 61, 15–21.

Bolton, L. R., Becker, L. K., & Barber, L. K. (2010). Big Five trait predictors of differential counterproductive work behavior dimensions. *Personality and Individual Differences*, 49, 537–541.

Bourdage, J. S., Lee, K., Ashton, M. C., & Perry, A. (2007). Big Five and HEXACO model personality correlates of sexuality. *Personality and Individual Differences*, 43, 1506–1516.

Caprara, G. V., Alessandri, G., Giunta, L. D., Panerai, L., & Eisenberg, N. (2010). The contribution of agreeableness and self-efficacy beliefs to prosociality. *European Journal of Personality*, 24, 36–55.

Carlo, G., Okun, M. A., Knight, G. P., & de Guzman, M. R. T. (2005). The interplay of traits and motives on volunteering: Agreeableness, extraversion and prosocial value motivation. *Personality and Individual Differences*, 38, 1293–1305.

Cohen, T. R. (2010). Moral emotions and unethical bargaining: The differential effects of empathy and perspective taking in deterring deceitful negotiation. *Journal of Business Ethics*, 94, 569–579.

Cohen, T. R., & Morse, L. (2014). Moral character: What it is and what it does. *Research in Organizational Behavior*, 34, 43–61.

Cohen, T. R., Panter, A. T., & Turan, N. (2012). Guilt proneness and moral character. *Current Directions in Psychological Science*, 21, 355–359.

Cohen, T. R., Panter, A. T., Turan, N., Morse, L., & Kim, Y. (2014). Moral character in the workplace. *Journal of Personality and Social Psychology*, 107, 943–963.

Cohen, T. R., Wolf, S. T., Panter, A. T., & Insko, C. A. (2011). Introducing the GASP scale: A new measure of guilt and shame proneness. *Journal of Personality and Social Psychology, 100*, 947–966.

Colby, A., & Damon, W. (1993). The uniting of self and morality in the development of extraordinary moral commitment. In G. G. Noam, T. E. Wren, G. Nunner-Winkler, & W. Edelstein (Eds.), *The moral self* (pp. 149–174). Cambridge, MA: The MIT Press.

del Barrio, V., Aluja, A., & Garcia, L. (2004). Relationship between empathy and the Big Five personality traits in a sample of Spanish adolescents. *Social Behavior and Personality, 32*, 677–682.

Doris, J. M. (2002). *Lack of character: Personality and moral behavior*. Cambridge: Cambridge University Press.

Duckworth, A. L., & Tsukayama, E. (2015). Domain-specificity in self-control. In C. Miller, R. M. Furr, A. Knobel, and W. Fleeson (Eds.), *Character: New directions from philosophy, psychology, and theology* (pp. 393–411). New York, NY: Oxford University Press.

Eisenberg, N. (2010). Empathy-related responding: Links with self-regulation, moral judgment, and moral behavior. In M. Mikulincer & P. R. Shaver (Eds.), *Prosocial motives, emotions, and behavior: The better angels of our nature* (pp. 129–148). Washington, DC: American Psychological Association.

Emmons, R. A. (1986). Personal strivings: An approach to personality and subjective well-being. *Journal of Personality and Social Psychology, 51*, 1058–1068.

Emmons, R. A., & McCullough, M. E. (2003). Counting blessings versus burdens: An experimental investigation of gratitude and subjective well-being in daily life. *Journal of Personality and Social Psychology, 84*, 377–389.

Fleeson, W. (2001). Toward a structure- and process-integrated view of personality: Traits as density distributions of states. *Journal of Personality and Social Psychology, 80*, 1011–1027.

Fleeson, W. (2007). Situation-based contingencies underlying trait-content manifestation in behavior. *Journal of Personality, 75*, 825–862.

Fleeson, W., & Furr, R. M. (in press). Do broad character traits exist? Repeated assessments of individuals, not group summaries from classic experiments, provide the relevant evidence. In I. Fileva (Ed.), *Character: Interdisciplinary perspectives* (pp. 231–248). Oxford: Oxford University Press.

Fleeson, W., Furr, R. M., Jayawickreme, E., Meindl, P., & Helzer, E. G. (2014). Character: The prospects for a personality-based perspective on morality. *Social and Personality Psychology Compass, 8*, 178–191.

Fleeson, W., & Jayawickreme, E. (2015). Whole trait theory. *Journal of Research in Personality, 56*, 82–92.

Fleeson, W., & Law, M. K. (2015). Trait enactments as density distributions: The role of actors, situations, and observers in explaining stability and variability. *Journal of Personality and Social Psychology, 109*, 1090–1104.

Frimer, J. A., Walker, L. J., Dunlop, W. L., Lee, B. H., & Riches, A. (2011). The integration of agency and communion in moral personality: Evidence of enlightened self-interest. *Journal of Personality and Social Psychology, 101*, 149–163.

Frimer, J. A., Walker, L. J., Lee, B. H., Riches, A., & Dunlop, W. L. (2012). Hierarchical integration of agency and communion: A study of influential moral figures. *Journal of Personality, 80*, 1117–1145.

Funder, D. C., & Colvin, C. R. (1991). Explorations in behavioral consistency: Properties of persons, situations, and behaviors. *Journal of Personality and Social Psychology, 52*, 773–794.

Furr, R. M., & Funder, D. C. (in press). Persons, situations, and person–situation interactions. In O. John & R. Robins (Eds.), *Handbook of personality: Theory and research* (4th ed.). New York, NY: Guilford Press.

Gollwitzer, P. M. (1999). Implementation intentions: Strong effects of simple plans. *American Psychologist, 54*, 493–503.

Goodwin, G. P., Piazza, J., & Rozin, P. (2014). Moral character predominates in person perception and evaluation. *Journal of Personality and Social Psychology, 106*, 148–168.

Graham, J., Haidt, J., Koleva, S., Motyl, M., Iyer, R., Wojcik, S. P., & Ditto, P. H. (2013). Moral foundations theory: The pragmatic validity of moral pluralism. In P. Devine & A. Plant (Eds.), *Advances in experimental social psychology* (pp. 55–130). New York, NY: Elsevier.

Gray, K., Young, L., & Waytz, A. (2012). Mind perception is the essence of morality. *Psychological Inquiry*, 23, 101–124.

Graziano, W. G., & Habashi, M. M. (2010). Motivational processes underlying both prejudice and helping. *Personality and Social Psychology Review*, 14, 313–331.

Habashi, M. M., Graziano, W. G., & Hoover, A. E. (2016). Searching for the prosocial personality: A Big Five approach to linking personality and prosocial behavior. *Personality and Social Psychology Bulletin*, 42, 1177–1192.

Haidt, J., & Graham, J. (2007). When morality opposes justice: Conservatives have moral intuitions that liberals may not recognize. *Social Justice Research*, 20, 98–116.

Harman, G. (2003). No character or personality. *Business Ethics Quarterly*, 13, 87–94.

Hartley, A. G., Furr, R. M., Helzer, E. G., Jayawickreme, E., Velasquez, K., & Fleeson, W. (2016). Morality's centrality to liking, respecting, and understanding others. *Social Psychological and Personality Science*, 7, 648–657.

Hartshorne, H., & May, M. (1928/1975). *Studies in the nature of character: Studies in deceit*. New York, NY: Ayer.

Helzer, E. G., Fleeson, W., Furr, R. M., Meindl, P., & Barranti, M. (2017). Once a utilitarian, consistently a utilitarian? Examining principledness in moral judgment via the robustness of individual differences. *Journal of Personality*, 85, 505–517.

Helzer, E. G., Furr, R. M., Hawkins, A., Barranti, M., Blackie, L. E. R., & Fleeson, W. (2014). Agreement on the perception of moral character. *Personality and Social Psychology Bulletin*, 40, 1698–1710.

Hennecke, M., Bleidorn, W., Denissen, J. J. A., & Wood, D. (2014). A three-part framework for self-regulated personality development across adulthood. *European Journal of Personality*, 28, 289–299.

Hershfeld, H., Cohen, T., & Thompson, L. (2012). Short horizons and tempting situations: Lack of continuity to our future selves leads to unethical decision making and behavior. *Organizational Behavior and Human Decision Processes*, 117, 298–310.

Hudson, N. W., & Fraley, R. C. (2015). Volitional personality trait change: Can people choose to change their personality traits? *Journal of Personality and Social Psychology*, 109, 490–507.

Hudson, N. W., & Roberts, B. W. (2014). Goals to change personality traits: Concurrent links between personality traits, daily behavior, and goals to change oneself. *Journal of Research in Personality*, 53, 68–83.

Hursthouse, R. (1999). *On virtue ethics*. New York, NY: Oxford University Press.

Inbar, Y., Pizarro, D. A., & Bloom, P. (2009). Conservatives are more easily disgusted than liberals. *Cognition and Emotion*, 23, 714–725.

Jayawickreme, E., & Fleeson, W. (2017). Does whole trait theory work for the virtues. *Moral Psychology*, 5, 75–103.

Jayawickreme, E., Meindl, P., Helzer, E. G., Furr, R. M., & Fleeson, W. (2014). Virtuous states and virtuous traits: How the empirical evidence regarding the existence of broad traits saves virtue ethics from the situationist critique. *Theory and Research in Education*, 12, 283–308.

Jensen-Campbell, L. A., Rosselli, M., Workman, K. A., Santisi, M., Rios, J. D., & Bojan, D. (2002). Agreeableness, conscientiousness, and effortful control processes. *Journal of Research in Personality*, 36, 476–489.

Lee, K., & Ashton, M. C. (2004). Psychometric properties of the HEXACO personality inventory. *Multivariate Behavioral Research*, 39, 329–358.

Lee, K., & Ashton, M. C. (2012). Getting mad and getting even: Agreeableness and Honesty–Humility as predictors of revenge intentions. *Personality and Individual Differences*, 52, 596–600.

Lee, K., Ashton, M. C., Morrison, D. L., Cordery, J., & Dunlop, P. D. (2008). Predicting integrity with the HEXACO personality model: Use of self- and observer reports. *Journal of Occupational and Organizational Psychology*, 81, 147–167.

Lee, K., Ashton, M. C., Pozzebon, J. A., Visser, B. A., Bourdage, J. S., & Ogunfowora, B. (2009). Similarity and assumed similarity in personality reports of well-acquainted persons. *Journal of Personality and Social Psychology*, 96, 460–472.

Matsuba, M. K., & Walker, L. J. (2004). Extraordinary moral commitment: Young adults involved in social organizations. *Journal of Personality*, 72, 413–436.

Matsuba, M. K., & Walker, L. J. (2005). Young adult moral exemplars: The making of self through stories. *Journal of Research on Adolescence, 15*, 275–297.

Mayer, D. M., Aquino, K., Greenbaum, R. L., & Kuenzi, M. (2012). Who displays ethical leadership, and why does it matter? An examination of antecedents and consequences of ethical leadership. *Academy of Management Journal, 55*, 151–171.

McCabe, K. O., & Fleeson, W. (2012). What is extraversion for? Integrating trait and motivational perspectives and identifying the purpose of extraversion. *Psychological Science, 23*, 1498–1505.

McCabe, K. O., & Fleeson, W. (2016). Are traits useful? Explaining trait manifestations as tools in the pursuit of goals. *Journal of Personality and Social Psychology, 110*, 287–301.

McFarland, S., Brown, D., & Webb, M. (2013). Identification with all humanity as a moral concept and psychological construct. *Current Directions in Psychological Science, 22*, 194–198.

McFarland, S., Webb, M., & Brown, D. (2012). All humanity is my ingroup: A measure and studies of identification with all humanity. *Journal of Personality and Social Psychology, 103*, 830–853.

Meindl, P., Jayawickreme, E., Furr, R. M., & Fleeson, W. (2015). A foundation beam for studying morality from a personological point of view: Are individual differences in moral behaviors and thoughts consistent? *Journal of Research in Personality, 59*, 81–92.

Miller, C. B. (2013). *Moral character: An empirical theory*. New York, NY: Oxford University Press.

Miller, C. B. (2014). *Character and moral psychology*. New York, NY: Oxford University Press.

Mischel, W. (1968). *Personality and assessment*. Mahwah, NJ: Lawrence Erlbaum Associates.

Monroe, K. R. (2002). Explicating altruism. In S. G. Post, L. G. Underwood, J. P. Schloss, & W. B. Hurlbut (Eds.), *Altruism and altruistic love: Science, philosophy, and religion in dialogue* (pp. 106–122). New York, NY: Oxford University Press.

Monroe, K. R. (2012). *Ethics in an age of terror and genocide: Identity and moral choice*. Princeton, NJ: Princeton University Press. Retrieved from http://www.jstor.org/stable/j.ctt7rtff

Mooradian, T. A., Davis, M., & Matzler, K. (2011). Dispositional empathy and the hierarchical structure of personality. *American Journal of Psychology, 124*, 99–109.

Noftle, E. E. (2015). Character across early emerging adulthood: Character traits, character strivings, and moral self-attributes. In C.B. Miller, R. M. Furr, A. Knobel, & W. Fleeson (Eds.), *Character: New directions from philosophy, psychology, and theology* (pp. 490–521). New York, NY: Oxford University Press.

Noftle, E. E., & Fleeson, W. (2010). Age differences in Big Five behavior averages and variabilities across the adult life span: Moving beyond retrospective, global summary accounts of personality. *Psychology and Aging, 25*, 95–07.

Noftle, E. E., Schnitker, S. A., & Robins, R. W. (2011). Character and personality: Connections between positive psychology and personality psychology. In K. M. Sheldon, T. B. Kashdan, & M. F. Steger (Eds.), *Designing the future of positive psychology: Taking stock and moving forward* (pp. 207–227). New York, NY: Oxford University Press.

Peterson, C., & Seligman, M. E. P. (2004). *Character strengths and virtues: A classification and handbook*. New York: Oxford University Press.

Reed II, A., & Aquino, K. F. (2003). Moral identity and the expanding circle of moral regard toward out-groups. *Journal of Personality and Social Psychology, 84*, 1270–1286.

Reynolds, S. J., & Ceranic, T. L. (2007). The effects of moral judgment and moral identity on moral behavior: An empirical examination of the moral individual. *Journal of Applied Psychology, 92*, 1610–1624.

Roberts, B. W., Jackson, J. J., Fayard, J. V., Edmonds, G., & Meints, J. (2009). Conscientiousness. In M. Leary & R. Hoyle (Eds.), *Handbook of individual differences in social behavior* (pp. 369–381). New York, NY: Guilford.

Roberts, B. W., Walton, K. E., & Viechtbauer, W. (2006). Patterns of mean-level change in personality traits across the life course: A meta-analysis of longitudinal studies. *Psychological Bulletin, 132*, 1–25.

Robinson, O. C., Noftle, E. E., Guo, J., Asadi, S., & Zhang, X. (2015). Goals and plans for Big

Five personality trait change in young adults. *Journal of Research in Personality*, 59, 31–43.

Shao, R., Aquino, K., & Freeman, D. (2008). Beyond moral reasoning: A review of moral identity research and its implications for business ethics. *Business Ethics Quarterly*, 18, 513–540.

Skitka, L. J. (2010). The psychology of moral conviction. *Social and Personality Psychology Compass*, 4, 267–281.

Skitka, L. J., & Bauman, C. W. (2008). Moral conviction and political engagement. *Political Psychology*, 29, 29–54.

Tangney, J. P., Stuewig, J., & Mashek, D. J. (2007). Moral emotions and moral behavior. *Annual Review of Psychology*, 58, 345–372.

Tobin, R. M., Graziano, W. G., Vanman, E. J., & Tassinary, L. G. (2000). Personality, emotional experience, and efforts to control emotions. *Journal of Personality and Social Psychology*, 79, 656–669.

Tsukayama, E., Duckworth, A. L., & Kim, B. (2013). Domain-specific impulsivity in school-age children. *Developmental Science*, 16, 879–893.

Walker, L. J., & Frimer, J. A. (2007). Moral personality of brave and caring exemplars. *Journal of Personality and Social Psychology*, 93, 845–860.

Walker, L. J., & Frimer, J. A. (2009). Moral personality exemplified. In D. Narvaez & D. K. Lapsley, (Eds.) *Personality, identity, and character: Explorations in moral psychology* (pp. 232–255). New York, NY: Cambridge University Press.

Walker, L. J., Frimer, J. A., & Dunlop, W. L. (2010). Varieties of moral personality: Beyond the banality of heroism. *Journal of Personality*, 78, 907–942.

Wojciszke, B., Bazinska, R., & Jaworski, M. (1998). On the dominance of moral categories in impression formation. *Personality and Social Psychology Bulletin*, 24, 1251–1263.

Zhu, W., Treviño, L. K., & Zheng, X. (2016). Ethical leaders and their followers: The transmission of moral identity and moral attentiveness. *Business Ethics Quarterly*, 26, 95–115.

PART III

Environmental Origins of Personality and Individual Differences

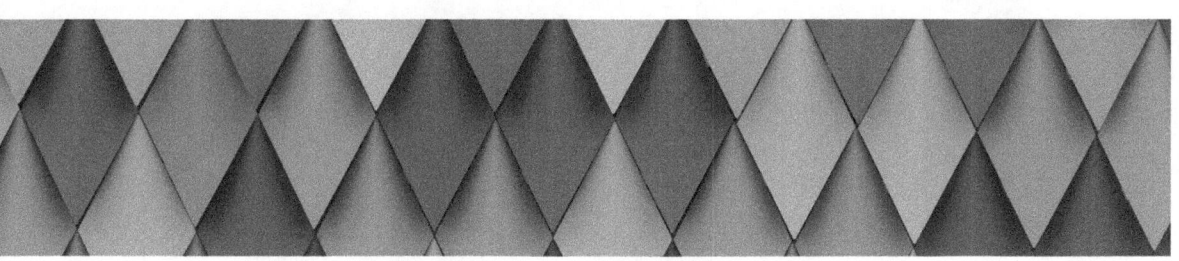

Cross-Cultural Perspectives on Personality and Individual Differences

Jüri Allik and Anu Realo

Although Immanuel Kant (Kant, 2006/1798) made the ancient theory of four temperaments – choleric, melancholic, phlegmatic, and sanguine – popular, not only for his contemporaries but also for the following generations, nobody cared about measuring these and other individual differences for a long time. Except perhaps for Friedrich Bessel (1784–1846), the astronomer at the Königsberg Observatory, who proposed that errors of astronomical observation may be due to individual differences of the observers but that these could be compensated for by constructing 'personal equations' which characterize constant individual differences in the mean reaction times between two observers (Boring, 1929/1957). Prior to Axel Oehrn's doctoral dissertation (Oehrn, 1889), which was done under the supervision of Emil Kraepelin at the Universität Dorpat (now known as the University of Tartu), there were only a few published studies on individual differences. For example, Cattell (1890) proposed to measure an almost random collection of attributes – he called them 'mental tests' – including dynamometric pressure, bisection of a 50 cm line, and judgment of 10 seconds of time. Francis Galton (1890) who commented on Cattell's paper in the same issue of *Mind*, pointed out the need to learn which of these eclectic measures were most instructive for measuring mental faculties. Galton, in his comments, made no secret of what kind of criteria he had in mind: his mental tests were supposed to determine to what extent somebody is 'mobile, eager, energetic; well shaped; successful at games requiring good eye and hand; sensitive; good at music and drawing' (Galton, 1890, p. 380). It took researchers a few more years to realize that being successful at games does not automatically imply that an individual is also good at music or drawing, to say nothing about the bisection of a 50 cm line. Binet and Henri (1895) were among the first to realize this simple truth and, consequently, were successful in identifying tests that measured intelligence by excluding other measures of individual differences, including temperament or character. This, as we know well, led Spearman (1904) to formulate the concept of general intelligence.

DIMENSIONS OF CULTURE AND PERSONALITY

All cross-cultural studies struggle with two apparently contradicting tendencies. Although the declaration 'all men are created equal' served, and serves, as one of the guiding principles of comparative research, there also seem to be too many opportunities for making exceptions based on religion, education, race, or even climate, as Baron de Montesquieu and some modern authors seem to think (e.g., de Montesquieu, 2011/1748; Pennebaker et al., 1996; Van de Vliert, 2013). As a result, psychology, like anthropology, has been striving in seemingly two opposite directions. The postulate of 'the psychic unity of mankind', which states that all human beings, regardless of their culture or race, share the same basic psychological and cognitive make-up, excludes a possibility that people in one culture have abilities or psychological mechanisms that are totally different or absent in some other cultures. In its extreme form (universalism), the relevance of cross-cultural variation will be completely denied. At the same time, there is an endless variety of material artifacts, social practices, habits, and customs both within and across cultures. This variety creates an impression that everything around us is created by culture, which penetrates even the deepest layers of how people feel, think, and behave, and as a result, culture and psyche are mutually formed and inseparable. It is entirely understandable that researchers are interested in describing, cataloguing, and systemizing this complex world of cultural and social differences.

Although books can be written about various definitions of culture (e.g., Kroeber and Kluckhohn, 1952), a short and sweet definition of culture is this: the way of organizing and storing information that is passed from one generation to another that is not entirely managed by biological mechanisms.[1] For example, variations in the behavioral repertoires suggest that there is significant cultural variation among different groups of chimpanzees (*Pan troglodytes*) across Africa which is maintained entirely by social learning and imitation (Whiten et al., 1999). Similar variation in human behavioral repertoires, to say nothing about endless artifacts, suggests that even close neighbors try to create their own distinctive culture. Nevertheless, George Peter Murdock (1897–1985) believed that almost an endless variation of human cultures could be reduced to a small set of underlying dimensions by systematically collecting data from many different cultures and by applying statistically verifiable hypotheses on this dataset. In 1957, he published his first cross-cultural dataset, the *World Ethnographic Sample*, consisting of 565 cultures which were characterized by 30 basic economic, ecological, social, and political variables (Murdock, 1957). These 30 variables were designed, as he formulated it, to be as representative as possible of the entire known range of cultural variation. He rated nearly all ethnographic materials himself and, in general, these ratings were reliable. Sawyer and LeVine (1966) applied a factor analysis to Murdock's data and found nine dimensions that summarized the original 30 characteristics. These dimensions primarily characterized the means of subsistence (e.g., agriculture, fishery) and the dominant family structures (e.g., patrilinearity, matrilinearity) of these cultures. Later, Sawyer (1967) applied the same approach to 82 modern nations that had been described by 236 social, economic, political, and other characteristics back in 1955, and found three dimensions – size, wealth, and politics – that accounted for 40% of the total variance in cultural differences across nations.

However, these three dimensions were not informative for most cross-cultural researchers. The fact that Iceland is smaller in size than China tells us something (e.g., Iceland likely being a more homogeneous culture than China) but not too much about their cultures. Fortunately, it was realized quite soon that there is another way to describe and account for cultural differences apart from analyzing all basic economic, ecological, social, and political variables, and that is via basic values. In cross-cultural psychology, values are seen as a central axis around which shared beliefs, symbols, and norms are grouped and that shape and justify people's beliefs, goals, habits, and actions (Schwartz, 1994).

In his pioneering work, Hofstede (1980) analyzed survey data of 171,100 IBM employees from 40 largest subsidiaries in 64 countries. Although the survey focused only on work-related values, Hofstede was able to derive dimensions characterizing the culture as a whole. Indeed, for several decades, researchers exploited Hofstede's (1980, 2001) dimensions – power distance, individualism–collectivism, masculinity–femininity, and uncertainty avoidance – as the main, if not the only possible, typology of cultures. Particularly, individualism and collectivism became a hot topic because, usually, they explained the largest proportion of variance in almost any cross-cultural comparison. Although Hofstede's dimensions describe a large portion of variance in cross-cultural differences in almost every study, there may still be some meaningful information beyond individualism and collectivism or the other three dimensions. Hofstede himself extended the list of his dimensions by adding long-term versus short-term orientation (Hofstede and Bond, 1988) and indulgence versus restraint (Hofstede, Hofstede, and Minkov, 2010) but, over the years, several other dimensions of cultural variation have been proposed by different researchers (e.g., Inglehart and Baker, 2000; Schwartz, 1994; Welzel, 2013). For example, it was proposed that tightness and looseness is an additional dimension, which provides extra explanation power to already explored ones (Gelfand et al., 2011; Mandel and Realo, 2015). Some researchers also believe that what they call social axioms – what is believed to be true about the world – provide some added value to how we understand human culture (Bond et al., 2004; Stankov and Saucier, 2015). In all cases, however, it was believed that a relatively small number of dimensions are sufficient to describe a large amount of cross-cultural differences. Researchers are still disputing which dimensions deserve a place on this short list (de Mooij, 2013; Minkov et al., 2015).

Personality is usually understood as enduring dispositions to feel, think, and act in a characteristic way in similar situations. Although the two disciplines – anthropology and psychology – developed separately, there are many similarities in their history. Both had a vocal group of researchers who were primarily fascinated about the richness and variety of their research topic. For example, organic chemistry, too, tries to catalogue millions of different compounds, all made from the simple elements of carbon, oxygen, hydrogen, and nitrogen (McCrae, 2009). When Allport and Odbert (1936) scanned through Webster's dictionary of English, they were able to identify approximately 18,000 unique terms used to describe personality or behavior out of about a half million words. It seems that Allport had little hope of understanding this 'incredible complexity' because 30 years later he wrote:

> Since traits, like all intervening variables, are never directly observed but only inferred, we must expect difficulties and errors in the process of discovering their nature. The incredible complexity of the structure we seek to understand is enough to discourage the realist, and to tempt him to play some form of positivistic gamesmanship. (Allport, 1966, p. 3)

Nevertheless, only a few years later, personality researchers came to a consensus that five independent dimensions are enough to describe the whole richness of personality traits, not only in English but supposedly in many other spoken languages as well (John et al., 1988, 2008).

Although personality researchers still debate about the exact number and the content of personality dimensions (Block, 1995; Eysenck, 1991; Thalmayer and Saucier, 2014), they generally agree that there are a limited number of independent themes around which all personality traits can be organized (Allik and McCrae, 2002; Goldberg, 1993; McCrae and Costa, 1999). These personality traits are not an accident of evolution, as some researchers tried to portray them (Tooby and Cosmides, 1990). It is more realistic to perceive personality traits as a genotypic reaction to different environmental demands (Penke et al., 2007). Thus, even though the origins and the exact meaning of personality traits are still debated, it is obvious that personality researchers have finally found a common language, which helps to make sense of the cacophony of literally thousands of personality tests and traits they are supposed to measure.

LINKING DIMENSIONS OF PERSONALITY AND CULTURE

For many researchers, it is meaningless to talk about the link between culture and personality because personality is a product of social construction and, consequently, a cultural phenomenon in the first place. If culture is understood as socially shared information that is coded in symbols, then practically the only tools for the study of personality – questionnaires – are the most distinctive feature of human culture, that is, language (Toomela, 2003). Specifically, it was proposed that a coherent Big Five personality structure emerges only for those who have moved from one dominant structure of word meaning of thinking in 'everyday concepts' (concrete categories) to another level of thinking in 'scientific concepts' (abstract categories) (Toomela, 2003). However, a reanalysis of the reported data found no evidence of structural differences between adults classified as concrete or abstract thinkers (Allik and McCrae, 2004a). More abstractly, the use of cultural tools such as language does not automatically mean that the object of description – personality traits – is affected by what we usually call culture. Nevertheless, the standard theory was, and still is, that personality is a product of social or interpersonal processes.

As said above, the Five Factor Model (FFM) is a symbol of a consensus that five broad personality dimensions are generally enough to characterize the largest amount of variance in all sorts of personality data (Goldberg, 1993; John et al., 2008; McCrae and Costa, 2008; McCrae and John, 1992). The Five Factor Theory (FFT), however, first formulated by McCrae and Costa (1996, 1999) was a completely different story. The FFT was perceived as a dissident theory that challenged all established theories and doctrines. The FFT originated in efforts to understand the extraordinary stability of personality traits across periods of many years because longitudinal research had shown that decades of life experience appear to have little, if any, systematic impact on basic personality traits (McCrae and Costa, 2003). Combined with findings from behavior genetic studies that had shown a powerful effect of genes and a vanishingly small effect of the shared environment, these observations led to the proposal that traits are endogenous dispositions, relatively untouched by life experience (including culture). That theory certainly explains the findings of longitudinal stability and heritability together with an immunity to cultural influences (Allik and McCrae, 2002).

The authors of the FFT did not believe that their main postulate – that culture never has any effect whatsoever on traits – was literally true. But they did believe that it is a parsimonious first approximation to the truth (Allik and McCrae, 2002). Usually, it is believed that the effects of culture on personality are overwhelming, but there is only limited evidence to support the claim that culture indeed shapes personality traits according to a certain template. Among the evidence, there are two effects that are particularly informative about the FFT: the cohort effects of secular trends and the effects of acculturation on personality traits (Allik and McCrae, 2002). When these questions were visited again more than ten years later, there was only meager support for the unquestionable effect of culture on personality (Allik and Realo, 2017a). For example, recent evidence supports that acculturation of personality takes place – personality becomes more similar to the people of the host/adopted country and less similar to those in the country of origin (Güngör et al., 2013; Söldner, 2013; Zimmermann and Neyer, 2013). However, these studies also showed that a more sophisticated methodology is needed to study acculturation. To make firm conclusions about acculturation, it is necessary to determine personality traits before sojourning into a new cultural environment. It was shown that many acculturation effects can be explained by self-selection: open and extraverted people are more likely to contact new cultures in which they become even more open and experience more positive emotions (Allik and Realo, 2017a).

However, independently developed taxonomies of personality traits and cultural values created a new possibility to explore the link between these two domains. There is a highly unusual paper by Hofstede and McCrae (2004) which examines these possible links. This influential paper advances two apparently incompatible explanations, which are supported only by one of the two authors. Hofstede (the first author) believes that culture, as the collective programmer of the mind, affects the process of socialization, and as a result, people's minds and personalities are shaped by culture. For example, higher levels of masculinity and uncertainty avoidance produce higher numbers of people who are prone to neurotic tendencies. In contrast, McCrae (the second author) supports a radically different interpretation of these associations between personality and culture. His reverse causation hypothesis implies that there are innate temperamental differences between various populations that give rise to cultural differences.

To support the reverse causation hypothesis, it is important to understand the mechanism that could produce changes in the frequency of gene variants. For instance, it was noticed relatively long ago that new nations like Australia, Canada, and the United States, whose populations are almost entirely made up of relatively recent emigrants, tend to have higher extraversion scores than those European countries from which the emigrants largely came (Lynn, 1981). Indeed, extraverts are more susceptible to boredom than introverts and have greater enjoyment of novelty, excitement, and risk, such as would seem to be involved in emigration to new places (Camperio Ciani and Capiluppi, 2010; Camperio Ciani et al., 2007). Individuals who are extraverted and open to new experiences are among those who are ready to explore new territories. Consequently, this could lead to gene drift, changes in the frequency of allele variants: explorers carry genes for extraversion and openness. Having different personality dispositions could lead, in turn, to the adoption of different social and cultural practices. As a possible scenario, consider a population that has a relatively high concentration of neurotic and not-so-agreeable people. They will, in general, be tense, irritable, and conflict-prone, and interpersonal interactions will be difficult. Each new decision will be a potential source of distressing conflict. Such people may find that they can coexist only if they adopt a rigid set of rules and screen out new situations that would require new decisions. In other words, they would develop the values and institutions that typify high uncertainty avoidance countries (Hofstede and McCrae, 2004).

However, the choice between two alternative explanations is even more difficult because the direct and reverse causation hypotheses are not mutually exclusive. It is possible, in principle at least, that certain personality traits dispose people to adopt certain social and cultural practices. At the same time, cultural norms can suppress and/or express personality dispositions that provide a better match to a particular culture.

RELATIVISTS AND UNIVERSALISTS

Strictly speaking, universal means that something is characteristic of all members of a class, without any limits or exceptions (Allik et al., 2013). In fact, little in nature meets this absolute criterion, but many characteristics appear to be relatively invariant, suggesting that they could be near or semi-universal. However, both programs – universalist and relativist – seem to have certain limitations. Because universalism requires verifiability – enumeration of all members of a class – its claims are tentative. The relativistic program, on the other hand, is also ambiguous because observed deviations from a general pattern may be caused by measurement errors or by a wrong conceptualization of the general pattern itself. In any case, because absolute universality is rare, the main task is to establish a degree, not merely the presence or absence of universality.

In the past, cross-cultural research projects or even expeditions were initiated equally by universalists and relativists. For example, Charles Darwin suspected that people's facial expressions of emotions are identical, irrespective of their cultural background (Darwin, 1998/1872). In 1867, he circulated a leaflet 'Queries about expression' among acquaintances (often missionaries in South Africa, India, and other places) who were in touch with 'primitive' peoples, or 'savages', all around the world in order to study how emotions are recognized and expressed in different cultures. The answers to these queries formed one basis of his book, where, on pages 26 and 27, he even gave the names of the 29 correspondents who had kindly replied to his query (cf., Freeman, 1977). However, it took almost 100 years to bring actual photographs of different facial expressions to people who had never encountered Western culture. The ability of preliterate cultures to recognize facial expressions obviously refuted a dominant theory that facial displays of emotions are socially learned and therefore culturally determined (Ekman et al., 1969).

Claude Lévi-Strauss, perhaps the best-known cultural anthropologist of the twentieth century, once said that anthropology found its Galileo in W. H. R. Rivers (Lévi-Strauss, 1963). Indeed, Rivers was one of the organizers and members of the 1898 Torres Straits Expedition (Rouse and Herle, 1998). It is obvious that Rivers and his colleagues, including William McDougall, had certain expectations. For example, not many years earlier, an eminent British politician named William Ewart Gladstone, still ten years away from becoming the prime minister, published a monumental book about Homeric poetry (cf., Deutscher, 2010). Observing how color words were used in *Iliad* and *Odyssey*, Gladstone concluded that ancient Greeks had no refined color vision and were effectively colorblind. The idea that the perception of colors improves with practice and these acquired improvements can be passed on to the offspring captivated the minds of many of his contemporaries. It is not surprising that various color vision tests were carried out during the Torres Straits Expedition. The results, however, were surprising. Studied 'savages' not only had absolutely normal color vision, they also did not have color defects that impact a sizable fraction of (mainly male) Europeans (Rivers et al., 1901).

One of the most important results of Rivers' Torres Straits work was his conclusion that the human mind is everywhere fundamentally the same, and that the development of culture is not dependent on mental abilities or disabilities. Various experiments, such as estimation of the length of a line, bisection of lines, division of lines into three or more equal parts, estimation of the length of vertical or horizontal lines, the Müller-Lyer and other visual illusions demonstrated that the savages were not far behind their European brothers in perceptual capacities (Rivers et al., 1901).

Important events in the history of psychology happened during the exhibition, which was organized to commemorate the centenary of the Louisiana Purchase in St. Louis in 1904. One of the main attractions was a large ethnologic display. Exotic ethnic groups from all over the world were brought to St. Louis and exhibited in separate 'villages' arranged according to their alleged degree of cultural evolution (Deutscher, 2010).[2] Robert Woodworth, one of the most eminent American psychologists, had been inspired by Rivers' fieldwork, which led him to test hundreds of 'exhibits' at St. Louis, not just for elementary sensory processes but also for higher mental processes. In the report of his studies, published in *Science*, Woodworth (1910) concluded: 'We are probably justified in inferring from the results cited that the sensory and motor processes, and the elementary brain activities, though differing in degree from one individual to another, are about the same from one race to another' (p. 179). He also regretted that there was no good test for intelligence, not to mention tests for personality, which leaves the question about 'higher' mental functions open.

The Torres Straits Expedition inspired not only Americans but also Marxist psychologists who later tried to demonstrate how social environment shapes or molds the human mind. Aleksander Luria, under the guidance of his mentor Lev Vygotsky, organized two expeditions to Central Asia in 1931 and 1932. Unfortunately, a detailed report of these two expeditions was not published immediately after 1932, but only some 40 years later (Luria, 1976). Like Woodworth, Luria published only a short resume of his main findings in *Science* (Luria, 1932). During the first expedition in 1931, Luria was eager to find proof that socio-cultural practices shape almost every aspect of the human mind. After finding that illiterate Uzbeks did not see the Müller-Lyer illusion, he sent a triumphant cable to Vygotsky: 'Uzbeks do not have illusions!'[3] Only when Kurt Koffka – one of the founders of the Gestalt psychology – joined the expedition in 1932, were Uzbeks' visual illusions 'rediscovered' (Luria, 1932).[4] However, unlike Rivers and Woodworth, Luria tested not only simple perceptual functions but also thinking and self-awareness. As it turned out, participants who did not have school education and were illiterate had difficulties describing their interior world and intrinsic qualities (Luria, 1976). Typically, concrete forms of external behavior replaced intrinsic qualities and the collective 'we' replaced the individual 'I'.

Mainstream psychology seems to accept, implicitly at least, the universalist position. As was noticed by several observers, psychologists and other behavioral scientists routinely publish broad claims about human psychology and behavior in the world's top journals based on samples drawn entirely from Western, Educated, Industrialized, Rich, and Democratic (WEIRD) societies (Henrich et al., 2010c). It is certainly alarming that, in the top psychological journals, 96% of all research participants typically come from Western industrialized countries (Arnett, 2008; Henrich et al., 2010a, 2010b; Jones, 2010). Even in the flagship of all 'non-weird' people – *Journal of Cross-Cultural Psychology* – a majority of empirical studies involved a comparison of only two different ethnic, racial, or cultural groups, one of which usually belonged to the 'weird' category (Allik, 2013). Of course, this is a result of convenience rather than a deep theoretical insight.

GEOGRAPHY OF INDIVIDUAL DIFFERENCES

If we compare two individuals who have different cultural backgrounds, it is difficult to decide whether the observed differences between these two individuals are caused by culture or by any other factors. Even siblings may have different personalities, although less likely than any random pair of individuals. The same story repeats with samples. If we have two groups of people, then the differences in mean scores can be caused by differences in their cultural background but also by any other differences that may exist between these two samples (e.g., climatic, economic). For this reason, if we only have data from three or four cultures, it is almost impossible to determine what differences (or similarities) are culture-specific and what transcend culture, not only in personality but in the human mind in general. Nevertheless, a recent study in largely illiterate, Tsimane forager-horticulturalist men and women of Bolivia ($N = 632$) was a sensation. Tsimanes completed a translation of the 44-item Big Five Inventory (Gurven et al., 2013). Because the authors found that Tsimanes have only two personality factors instead of the five that are common in all 56 cultures that had been tested earlier (Schmitt et al., 2007), they concluded that the FFM is not universal but dependent upon socio-cultural environment. However, before we have a satisfactory explanation for the deviance of the Tsimane data, it is important to note that evidence from a limited number of cultures may leave room for all sorts of errors. Purely statistical considerations will determine that we need data from at least 20 cultures to say something reliable about their true ranking (Allik and Realo, 2017b). However, collection of data from many countries is expensive and time-consuming. For example, it usually takes years to properly adapt a personality questionnaire to other languages and cultures and to collect data in many countries. The Eysenck Personality Questionnaire and the NEO-PI-R/3 are good examples of this relatively slow and complicated method of collecting data (Allik et al., 2017; van Hemert et al., 2002).

Understandably, the most effective method to recruit participants from various countries is through the Internet. One recent example is a study of self-esteem that managed to collect responses from nearly three million participants who came from 101 different countries (Gebauer et al., 2015). In a similar study, relationships of Openness – one of the Big Five personality dimensions – with religiosity were studied among 1.1 million participants who came from 66 different countries (Gebauer et al., 2014).

Because culture is not an easy target to measure, many researchers prefer to study a less ambiguous parameter, which often serves as a good proxy for culture. This is geography. In general, every group of people tends to be slightly different from its neighbors. For example, based on genetic similarity alone, it is possible to reconstruct the map of Europe with amazing precision (Nelis et al., 2009; Novembre et al., 2008). However, it is unlikely that any psychological trait would 'remember' geography so well. Nevertheless, the distribution of many psychological characteristics contains at least certain geographical regularities. For example, researchers of intellectual abilities were the first to notice that the distribution of IQ has a distinctive geographic pattern (Lynn and Vanhanen, 2006; Rindermann, 2008). Because personality data are trickier to collect than IQ data, it took some time before the first world maps of personality traits were published (Allik and McCrae, 2004b). The most distinctive property of these personality maps is that geographical neighbors tend to have similar personality profiles. Since then, the geography of personality traits has become a rapidly progressing field (Gelade, 2013; Jokela et al., 2015; Oishi et al., 2015; Rentfrow, 2010; Rentfrow et al., 2009). It is fascinating to see the detailed maps of how different attributes (e.g., income, happiness, savings) are distributed around the world.

The Revised NEO Personality Inventory, the NEO PI-R, and its latest version, the NEO PI-3, were designed to measure 30 distinctive personality facets, which are grouped into the higher-order dimensions

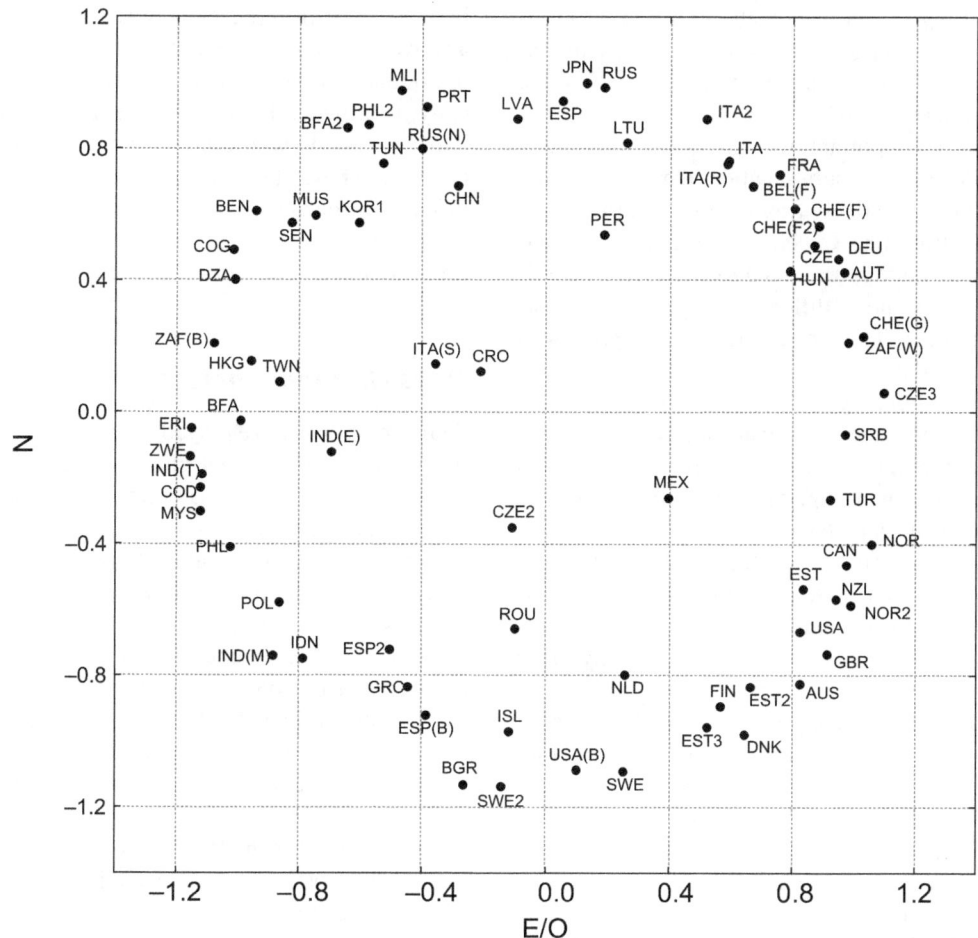

Figure 17.1 Multidimensional scaling plot of 75 samples representing 62 countries/cultures (Allik et al., 2017); N = Neuroticism; E/O = Extraversion/Openness. Labels for the countries are according to three-letter country codes (ISO 3166-1) with suffixes if it is necessary to differentiate various versions or languages.

of Neuroticism, Extraversion, Openness, Agreeableness, and Conscientiousness, with six facets per dimension (Costa and McCrae, 1992; McCrae et al., 2005). More than 20 years later, NEO PI-R/3 was translated into 37 languages and applied in 62 different countries or territories (Allik et al., 2017). Based on similarity of personality profiles across 30 subscales, we came to a two-dimensional pattern, which resembles the original map published in 2004 (Allik and McCrae, 2004b).

It is important to remember that the similarities and differences shown in Figure 17.1 are computed based on the distinctive profiles. They show how much the mean of each sample is above or below the average score of all 75 samples on each trait. In addition to the contrast between European and African-Asian countries/cultures, it is also possible to notice some smaller groupings. For example, all English-speaking countries such as Australia, Canada, Great Britain, and New Zealand are located in the lower-right (low N and high E) corner of the plot. Their neighbors are Scandinavian countries – Denmark, Finland, Iceland, Norway, and Sweden (Allik et al., 2017).

It is important to notice that, despite a relatively robust replication, the details of the map are relatively fragile. For example, many countries like Czechia, Estonia, Spain, and Sweden are represented by different NEO PI versions and/or different samples and/or testing times. These replications are supposed to be similar to the original data from 2004 but, quite often, the position of different samples from the same country are significantly apart. Even relatively small details such as new samples, wording, or age cohorts can alter the position on the map.

An obvious reason for this fragility is the size of cross-cultural differences. One possibility for estimating the size of cross-cultural differences in personality (or any other attribute) is to compare the standard deviation of the country means with the standard deviation of individual-level scores within countries (Allik, 2005). For example, the NEO PI-R/3 data showed that the mean differences in personality traits across countries and cultures were about 8.5 times smaller than differences between any two individuals randomly selected from these samples (Allik et al., 2017). It could be argued that within-country differences are larger for most psychological traits when compared to mean scores that were aggregated across countries or cultures. This is, however, not entirely true because there are substantial differences in the mean scores of at least some psychological characteristics. For instance, during the *World Value Survey* (WVS 2005–2008), a question of 'How important is God in your life?' was asked of 82,992 participants in 57 different countries (World Values Survey Association, 2014). Differences between countries were only slightly smaller than the typical interindividual variance within each sample. The ratio of country-level variance in the perception of God importance to the mean within-country variance was only 1.28. This indicates that differences between means of any two randomly selected countries in the importance of God in people's life is practically as large as the difference between any two individuals who are living in the same country. Thus, there could be substantial differences between countries on some constructs or characteristics – but personality traits are not among them (Allik et al., 2017).

Does National Character Exist?

Anthropologists have played a dominant role in the study of national character (Inkeles, 1997). Decades were characterized by their views that enduring personality characteristics of an individual are almost entirely determined by culture, in general, and by early socialization process, in particular (LeVine, 2001). Because of the assumed plasticity of personality characteristics, cultural anthropologists from a school of thought later known as the 'Culture and Personality' era often talked about distinctive personality types for each culture. *Patterns of Culture* by Ruth Benedict became one of the most popular bestsellers, promoting an idea that the personality of entire cultures could be characterized by a single dominant trait (Benedict, 1959/1934). For example, the Dobuans of Melanesia were suspicious and paranoid, the Kwakiutl were autocrats and despots, and the Pueblos of New Mexico were typically unemotional and passive (Benedict, 1959/1934). Later, an anthropologist named Cora Du Bois (1944) introduced the concept of modal personality. There are many different personality types in each culture but one, which is the most frequent or dominant ('modal'), is believed to represent the whole nation or culture.

However, people also believe that the representatives of different nations/cultures possess a distinctive set of psychological and physical characteristics. For instance, Germans are often seen as humorless, Finns are silent, and Italians are known for being somewhat disorderly. People have these and other similar beliefs not because they have seen or met many Germans, Finns, or Italians in order to make an accurate statistical summary but rather these are generalizations that may or not be true. Such beliefs are classified as stereotypes – opinions about groups or categories that exaggerate some of the salient characteristics of this group or category (Allport, 1978/1954, p. 191). For example, Katz and Braly (1933) asked 100 college students about their opinions concerning various racial or ethnic groups: Jews were characterized as shrewd and mercenary, Blacks as lazy and superstitious, and Turks as cruel and religious. Many of these stereotypes resisted time and were replicated, at least in part, many years later (Devine and Elliot, 1995; Gilbert, 1951; Karlins et al., 1969; Madon et al., 2001). If stereotypes are exaggerated beliefs, as Allport defined them, then we need to find some objective measures for the traits in question, such as greed, laziness, and cruelty. One obvious option is to determine national mean scores on these traits. For example, if we are interested in stereotypes of intelligence, then we need to compare answers to words such as 'intelligent', 'brilliant', 'witty', 'stupid', and 'ignorant' – words that Katz and Braly included as a measure of mental abilities – with the objective measure of intelligence for the same racial or ethnic groups. Analogously, if we want to establish a kernel of truth in a stereotype about humorless Germans, we need a scale for measuring the sense of humor (e.g., Martin and Lefcourt, 1984; Ruch, 1996). Furthermore, we also need a sufficiently large number of nations or ethnic groups to answer these questionnaires. If Germans indeed score lower than most other nations on the sense of humor scale, then we have some evidence that the perception of the comical side of life is not one of the strengths of the German character. Indeed, compared with Italians, Germans seem to have a lower appreciation of at least some kinds of humor (Ruch and Forabosco, 1996).[5]

Thus, for making judgments about the accuracy of a stereotype, we need, in addition to a belief itself, an objective measure of that group or category on that trait. For example, one of the most comprehensive of the Big Five personality questionnaires is the NEO PI-R or NEO PI-3, which has been translated from the original English into 36 different languages and was administered in 62 different countries or cultures (Allik et al., 2017). Besides self-rating, however, it is possible to ask respondents to describe the personality traits of a typical representative of a country, a nation, or an ethnic group using exactly the same set of personality items. It was a surprise when national character ratings of 3,989 people from 49 cultures did not converge with the average personality scores assessed by observer ratings and self-reports (Terracciano et al., 2005). Thus, there was little support for the view that perceptions of national character profiles are accurate in any culture. Probably because national character stereotypes look authentic, several commentators questioned the meaning of these results (Krueger and Wright, 2006; Perugini and Richetin, 2007). One plausible explanation is the reference group explanation (Heine et al., 2002). It was Leon Festinger (1954) who maintained that people usually base their understanding of themselves on how they compare with others around them. For example, there is no universal consensus on what the objective threshold is for being considered tall – rather, being tall depends on comparisons with appropriate targets, typically those of similar age, sex, and nationality. The same height – for example, 5 feet 9 inches – is seen as tall in some contexts (e.g., among elementary school children or Japanese women) and short in others (e.g., among professional basketball players or Dutch men) (Heine et al., 2002). As an example closer to personality, people's perception of their own conscientiousness – one of the Big Five personality traits – is probably mediated through the perception of how methodical, determined, and purposeful his or her 'average countryman' typically is (Heine et al., 2008). Although deceptively simple, this explanation was seriously questioned because participants do not use comparison when they are asked to evaluate their own conscientiousness (Mõttus et al., 2012a, 2012b).

Studies that followed the initial high-profile publication in *Science* (Terracciano et al., 2005) slightly modified the original thesis that the averaged traits and stereotypes are not related (Hřebíčková and Graf, 2014; McCrae et al., 2007, 2013; Realo et al., 2009). For example, national character reflects mean personality traits slightly more accurately when both are measured by the same instrument (Allik et al., 2010). However, even a moderate resemblance that could be occasionally observed between stereotypes and directly measured personality traits cannot obscure the truth that there are special mechanisms for how national stereotypes are formed. For example, countries that have a dominant neighbor are inclined to form their own national stereotype by mirror imaging of the dominant neighbor's national stereotype. Americans are typically perceived as neurotic, dominant, not friendly, but laborious. Canadians, in contrast, are perceived as an inverted copy of Americans – emotionally stable, submissive, agreeable, and more relaxed (Terracciano et al., 2005). Analogously, the neighboring countries of Russia have designed their national character stereotypes based not on observing their own traits but by doctoring a shared stereotype they have about Russians. According to a dominant view, Russians are perceived to their neighbors as hostile, dominant, extraverted, and not particularly keen on a Protestant work ethic (Allik et al., 2011; Boster and Maltseva, 2006; Realo et al., 2009). Compared to noisy, intrusive, and dominating Russians, all their neighbors – but particularly Estonians, Finns, and Latvians – tend to conceptualize themselves as extremely introverted, disciplined, and hardworking (Realo et al., 2009).

The mechanism of polarization appears to operate not only between neighboring countries but between different regions within countries or similar ethnic groups. For example, North Italians are perceived as polar opposites of archetypical Italians who, by generally shared opinion, live in the South. Nevertheless, neither of these two stereotypes reflect actual personality traits that are the same regardless of whether the personality ratings are completed by Italians who live in either the South or North of Italy (McCrae et al., 2007). As another example, the mean self-reported personality traits of participants were mostly identical for two Finno-Ugric ethnic groups known as the Erzians and the Mokshans who live, together with Russians, in the Republic of Mordovia in the Russian Federation (Allik et al., 2015). Nevertheless, Erzians' personality stereotypes about a typical Mokshan and, in turn, Mokshans' stereotypes about a typical Erzian were socially less favorable compared with the way in which both ethnic groups perceived a typical Russian and, especially, a representative of their own ethnic group (Allik et al., 2015). Thus, two stereotypes could be different, or even opposite, even if there are no differences in the average personality scores.

Allport (1978/1954) was certainly right when he claimed that some stereotypes are totally unsupported by facts, whereas others develop from sharpening and overgeneralizing certain facts. Objectively measured, there was no difference in personality between Americans and Canadians or between Souther and Northern Italians (McCrae et al., 2007). Nevertheless, they have polarized stereotypes of the national character, which are shared by both contrasted parties. Thus, perceptions of national character appear to be (mainly) unfounded stereotypes that may serve the function of maintaining a national identity or rationalize conduct in relation to that category (Allport, 1978/1954; McCrae et al., 2013; Terracciano et al., 2005).

Notes

1. Perhaps not completely original, this was how Juri Lotman, one of the most original thinkers who lived and worked in Tartu, usually defined culture (Lotman, 1970).
2. An outraging story of the Igorrotes, a group of 'headhunting, dog eating' tribespeople, who were also exhibited in St. Louis and were brought to America from the Philippines by the opportunistic showman Truman K. Hunt, was recently told (Prentice, 2014).
3. Since the message came through the cable, it was a reasonable fear to think that its true meaning is that Uzbeks have no illusion on collectivization. A legend tells that Vygotsky's comment was 'Luria has no brains!' (Yasnitsky, 2013).
4. The perception of the Müller-Lyer illusion was back on the pages of *Science* some years later celebrating an apparent victory of the relativist viewpoint. Data from 15 cultures showed that, in different cultures, it was perceived differently (Segall et al., 1963), meaning that all people see the illusion but those who are living in a more 'carpeted world' are more susceptible to optical illusions. However, any of these results are inconclusive because it was shown that observers could shift their psychometric functions without losing sensitivity (Morgan et al., 2012), meaning that perception is not separable from response strategies.
5. Readers can also entertain themselves by reading Durrell's 'Ludwig' (Durrell, 1992).

REFERENCES

Allik, J. (2005). Personality dimensions across cultures. *Journal of Personality Disorders, 19*, 212–232.

Allik, J. (2013). Bibliometric analysis of the *Journal of Cross-Cultural Psychology* during the first ten years of the new millennium. *Journal of Cross-Cultural Psychology, 44*, 657–667.

Allik, J., Alyamkina, E., & Meshcheryakov, B. (2015). The personality stereotypes of three cohabiting ethnic groups: Erzians, Mokshans, and Russians. *Cross-Cultural Research, 49*, 111–134.

Allik, J., Church, A. T., Ortiz, F. A., Rossier, J., Hřebíčková, M., de Fruyt, F., Realo, A., & McCrae, R. R. (2017). Mean profiles of the NEO Personality Inventory. *Journal of Cross-Cultural Psychology, 48*, 402–420.

Allik, J., & McCrae, R. R. (2002). A Five-Factor Theory perspective. In R. R. McCrae & J. Allik (Eds.), *The Five Factor Model of personality across cultures* (pp. 303–322). New York, NY: Kluwer Academic/Plenum Publishers.

Allik, J., & McCrae, R. R. (2004a). Escapable conclusions: Toomela (2003) and the universality of trait structure. *Journal of Personality and Social Psychology, 87*, 261–265.

Allik, J., & McCrae, R. R. (2004b). Toward a geography of personality traits: Patterns of profiles across 36 cultures. *Journal of Cross-Cultural Psychology, 35*, 13–28.

Allik, J., Mõttus, R., & Realo, A. (2010). Does national character reflect mean personality traits when both are measured by the same instrument? *Journal of Research in Personality, 44*, 62–69.

Allik, J., & Realo, A. (2017a). Universal and specific in the Five-Factor Model of Personality. In T. A. Widiger (Ed.), *The Oxford handbook of the Five Factor Model of personality* (pp. 173–190). Oxford: Oxford University Press.

Allik, J., & Realo, A. (2017b). How valid are culture-level mean personality scores? In A. T. Church (Ed.), *The Praeger handbook of personality across cultures, Vol 1: Trait psychology across cultures* (pp. 193–224). Santa Barbara, CA: Praeger & ABC-Clio.

Allik, J., Realo, A., & McCrae, R. R. (2013). Universality of the Five-Factor Model of personality. In P. T. Costa, Jr. & T. Widiger (Eds.), *Personality disorders and the Five Factor Model of personality* (pp. 61–74). Washington, DC: American Psychological Association.

Allik, J., Realo, A., Mõttus, R., Pullmann, H., Trifonova, A., McCrae, R. R., . . . Korneeva, E. E. (2011). Personality profiles and the 'Russian soul': Literary and scholarly views evaluated. *Journal of Cross-Cultural Psychology, 42*, 372–389.

Allport, G. W. (1966). Traits revisited. *American Psychologist, 21*, 1–10.

Allport, G. W. (1978/1954). *The nature of prejudice*. New York, NY: Basic Books.

Allport, G. W., & Odbert, H. S. (1936). Trait-names: A psycho-lexical study. *Psychological Monographs, 47*, No. 211.

Arnett, J. J. (2008). The neglected 95%: Why American psychology needs to become less American. *American Psychologist, 63*, 602–614.

Benedict, R. (1959/1934). *Patterns of culture*. Boston, MA: Houghton Mifflin.

Binet, A., & Henri, V. (1895). La psychologie individuelle. *L'année psychologique, 2*, 411–465.

Boring, E. G. (1929/1957). *A history of experimental psychology* (2nd ed.). New York: Appleton-Century-Crofts.

Block, J. (1995). A contrarian view of the five-factor approach to personality description. *Psychological Bulletin, 117*, 187–215.

Bond, M. H., Leung, K., Au, A., Tong, K.-K., de Carrasquel, S. R., Murakami, F., . . . Lewis, J. R. (2004). Culture-level dimensions of social axioms and their correlates across 41 cultures. *Journal of Cross-Cultural Psychology, 35*, 548–570.

Boster, J. S., & Maltseva, K. (2006). A crystal seen from each of its vertices: European views of European national characters. *Cross-Cultural Research, 40*, 47–64.

Camperio Ciani, A., & Capiluppi, C. (2010). Gene flow by selective emigration as a possible cause for personality differences between small islands and mainland populations. *European Journal of Personality, 24*, 53–64.

Camperio Ciani, A., Capiluppi, C., Veronese, A., & Sartori, G. (2007). The adaptive value of personality differences revealed by small island population dynamics. *European Journal of Personality, 21*, 3–22.

Cattell, J. M. (1890). Mental tests and measurements. *Mind, 15*, 373–381.

Costa, P. T., Jr., & McCrae, R. R. (1992). *Revised NEO Personality Inventory (NEO PI-R) and NEO Five-Factor Inventory (NEO-FFI) professional manual*. Odessa, FL: Psychological Assessment Resources.

Darwin, C. (1998/1872). *The expression of the emotions in man and animals*. London: HarperCollins.

de Montesquieu, B. (2011/1748). *The spirit of laws*. Holmes Beach, FL: Gaunt, Inc.

de Mooij, M. (2013). On the misuse and misinterpretation of dimensions of national culture. *International Marketing Review, 30*, 253–261.

Deutscher, G. (2010). *Through the language glass: Why the world looks different in other languages*. London: Arrow Books.

Devine, P. G., & Elliot, A. J. (1995). Are racial stereotypes really fading: The Princeton trilogy revisited. *Personality and Social Psychology Bulletin, 21*, 1139–1150.

Digman, J. M. (1990). Personality structure: Emergence of the Five-Factor Model. *Annual Review of Psychology, 41*, 417–440.

Du Bois, C. A. (1944). *The people of Alor: A social-psychological study of an East Indian island*. Minneapolis, MN: University of Minnesota Press.

Durrell, G. (1992). *Marrying off mother and other stories*. New York, NY: Arcade.

Ekman, P., Sorenson, E. R., & Friesen, W. V. (1969). Pan-cultural elements in facial displays of emotions. *Science, 164*, 86–88.

Eysenck, H. J. (1991). Dimensions of personality – 16, 5 or 3: Criteria for a taxonomic paradigm. *Personality and Individual Differences, 12*, 773–790.

Festinger, L. (1954). A theory of social comparison processes. *Human Relations, 7*, 117–140.

Freeman, R. B. (1977). *The works of Charles Darwin: An annotated bibliographical handlist* (2nd ed.). Folkestone, UK: Dawson.

Galton, F. (1890). Remarks. *Mind, 15*, 380–381.

Gebauer, J. E., Bleidorn, W., Gosling, S. D., Rentfrow, P. J., Lamb, M. E., & Potter, J. (2014). Cross-cultural variations in Big Five relationships with religiosity: A sociocultural motives perspective. *Journal of Personality and Social Psychology, 107*, 1064–1091.

Gebauer, J. E., Sedikides, C., Wagner, J., Bleidorn, W., Rentfrow, P. J., Potter, J., & Gosling, S. D. (2015). Cultural norm fulfillment, interpersonal belonging, or getting ahead? A large-scale cross-cultural test of three perspectives on the function of self-esteem. *Journal of Personality and Social Psychology, 109*, 526–548.

Gelade, G. A. (2013). Personality and place. *British Journal of Psychology, 104*, 69–82.

Gelfand, M. J., Raver, J. L., Nishii, L., Leslie, L. M., Lun, J., Lim, B. C., . . . Yamaguchi, S. (2011). Differences between tight and loose cultures: A 33-nation study. *Science, 332*, 1100–1104.

Gilbert, G. M. (1951). Stereotype persistence and change among college students. *Journal of Abnormal and Social Psychology, 46*, 245–254.

Goldberg, L. R. (1993). The structure of phenotypic personality traits. *American Psychologist, 48*, 26–34.

Güngör, D., Bornstein, M. H., De Leersnyder, J., Cote, L., Ceulemans, E., & Mesquita, B. (2013). Acculturation of personality: A three-culture study of Japanese, Japanese Americans, and European Americans. *Journal of Cross-Cultural Psychology, 44*, 701–718.

Gurven, M., von Rueden, C., Massenkoff, M., Kaplan, H., & Lero Vie, M. (2013). How universal is the Big Five? Testing the Five-Factor Model of personality variation among forager-farmers in the Bolivian Amazon. *Journal of Personality and Social Psychology, 104*, 354–370.

Heine, S. J., Buchtel, E. E., & Norenzayan, A. (2008). What do cross-national comparisons of personality traits tell us? The case of conscientiousness. *Psychological Science, 19*, 309–313.

Heine, S. J., Lehman, D. R., Peng, K., & Greenholtz, J. (2002). What's wrong with cross-cultural comparisons of subjective Likert scales: The reference-group problem. *Journal of Personality and Social Psychology, 82*, 903–918.

Henrich, J., Heine, S. J., & Norenzayan, A. (2010a). Beyond WEIRD: Towards a broad-based behavioral science. *Behavioral and Brain Sciences, 33*, 111–135.

Henrich, J., Heine, S. J., & Norenzayan, A. (2010b). Most people are not WEIRD. *Nature, 466*, 29.

Henrich, J., Heine, S. J., & Norenzayan, A. (2010c). The weirdest people in the world? *Behavioral and Brain Sciences, 33*, 1–75.

Hofstede, G. (1980). *Culture's consequences: International differences in work-related values*. Beverly Hills, CA: Sage.

Hofstede, G. (2001). *Culture's consequences: Comparing values, behaviors, institutions and organizations across nations* (2nd ed.). Beverly Hills, CA: Sage.

Hofstede, G., Hofstede, G. J., & Minkov, M. (2010). *Cultures and organizations: Software of the mind* (3rd ed.). New York, NY: McGraw-Hill.

Hofstede, G., & McCrae, R. R. (2004). Personality and culture revisited: Linking traits and dimensions of culture. *Cross-Cultural Research, 38*, 52–88.

Hřebíčková, M., & Graf, S. (2014). Accuracy of national stereotypes in Central Europe: Outgroups are not better than ingroup in considering personality traits of real people. *European Journal of Personality, 28*, 60–72.

Inglehart, R., & Baker, W. E. (2000). Modernization, cultural change, and the persistence of traditional values. *American Sociological Review, 65*, 19–51.

Inkeles, A. (1997). *National character: A psycho-social perspective*. New Brunswick, NJ: Transaction Publishers.

John, O. P., Angleitner, A., & Ostendorf, F. (1988). The lexical approach to personality: A historical review of trait taxonomic research. *European Journal of Personality, 2*, 171–203.

John, O. P., Naumann, L. P., & Soto, C. J. (2008). Paradigm shift to the integrative Big Five trait taxonomy: History, measurement, and conceptual issues. In O. P. John, R. W. Robins, & L. A. Pervin (Eds.), *Handbook of personality: Theory and research* (3rd ed., pp. 114–158). New York, NY: Guilford Press.

Jokela, M., Bleidorn, W., Lamb, M. E., Gosling, S. D., & Rentfrow, P. J. (2015). Geographically varying associations between personality and life satisfaction in the London metropolitan area. *Proceedings of the National Academy of Sciences, 112*, 725–730.

Jones, D. (2010). A WEIRD view of human nature skews psychologists' studies. *Science, 328*, 1627–1627.

Kant, I. (2006/1798). *Anthropology from a pragmatic point of view*. Cambridge, UK: Cambridge University Press.

Karlins, M., Coffman, T. L., & Walters, G. (1969). On the fading of social stereotypes: Studies in three generations of college students. *Journal of Personality and Social Psychology, 13*, 1–16.

Katz, D., & Braly, K. (1933). Racial stereotypes of one hundred college students. *Journal of Abnormal and Social Psychology, 28*, 280–290.

Kroeber, A. L., & Kluckhohn, C. (1952). *Culture; a critical review of concepts and definitions*. Cambridge, MA: Museum.

Krueger, J. I., & Wright, J. C. (2006). How to measure national stereotypes? *Science, 311*, 776–779.

Lévi-Strauss, C. (1963). *Structural anthroplogy*. New York, NY: Basic Books.

LeVine, R. A. (2001). Culture and personality studies, 1918–1960: Myth and history. *Journal of Personality, 69*, 803–818.

Lotman, J. (1970). *Lectures on typology of culture*. Tartu: Tartu Riiklik Ülikool.

Luria, A. R. (1932). The second psychological expedition to Central Asia. *Science, 78*, 191–192.

Luria, A. R. (1976). *Cognitive development: Its cultural and social foundations*. Cambridge, MA: Harvard University Press.

Lynn, R. (1981). Cross-cultural differences in neuroticism, extraversion and psychoticism. In R. Lynn (Ed.), *Dimensions of personality. Papers in honour of H. J. Eysenck* (pp. 263–286). Oxford: Pergamon Press.

Lynn, R., & Vanhanen, T. (2006). *IQ and global inequality*. Augusta, GA: Washington Summit Publishers.

Madon, S., Guyll, M., Aboufadel, K., Montiel, E., Smith, A., Palumbo, P., & Jussim, L. (2001). Ethnic and national stereotypes: The Princeton trilogy revisited and revised. *Personality and Social Psychology Bulletin, 27*, 996–1010.

Mandel, A., & Realo, A. (2015). Across-time change and variation in cultural tightness-looseness. *PLoS ONE, 10*(12), e0145213.

Martin, R. A., & Lefcourt, H. M. (1984). Situational Humor Response Questionnaire: Quantitative measure of sense of humor. *Journal of Personality and Social Psychology, 47*, 145–155.

McCrae, R. R. (2009). The physics and chemistry of personality. *Theory and Psychology, 19*, 670–687.

McCrae, R. R., & Allik, J. (2002). *The Five-Factor Model of personality across cultures*. New York, NY: Kluwer Academic/Plenum Publishers.

McCrae, R. R., Chan, W., Jussim, L., De Fruyt, F., Löckenhoff, C. E., De Bolle, M., . . . Terracciano, A. (2013). The inaccuracy of national character stereotypes. *Journal of Research in Personality, 47*, 831–842.

McCrae, R. R., & Costa, P. T., Jr. (1996). Towards a new generation of personality theories: Theoretical context for the Five-Factor Theory. In J. S. Wiggins (Ed.), *The Five-Factor Model of personality: Theoretical perspectives* (pp. 51–87). New York: Guilford Press.

McCrae, R. R., & Costa, P. T., Jr. (1999). A Five-Factor Theory of personality. In L. A. Pervin & O. P. John (Eds.), *Handbook of personality: Theory and research* (Vol. 2, pp. 139–153). New York, NY: Guilford Press.

McCrae, R. R., & Costa, P. T., Jr. (2003). *Personality in adulthood: A Five-Factor Theory perspective*. New York, NY: Guilford.

McCrae, R. R., & Costa, P. T., Jr. (2008). Empirical and theoretical status of the five-factor model of personality traits. In G. Boyle, G. Matthews, & D. Saklofske (Eds.), *Sage handbook of personality theory and assessment* (Vol. 1, pp. 273–294). Los Angeles, CA: Sage.

McCrae, R. R., Costa, P. T., Jr., & Martin, T. A. (2005). The NEO-PI-3: A more readable revised Neo Personality Inventory. *Journal of Personality Assessment, 84*, 261–270.

McCrae, R. R., & John, O. P. (1992). An introduction to the five-factor model and its applications. *Journal of Personality, 60*, 175–215.

McCrae, R. R., Terracciano, A., Realo, A., & Allik, J. (2007). Climatic warmth and national wealth: Some culture-level determinants of national character stereotypes. *European Journal of Personality, 21*, 953–976.

Minkov, M., Bond, M. H., & Blagoev, V. (2015). Do different national samples yield similar dimensions of national culture? *Cross Cultural Management – An International Journal, 22*, 259–277.

Morgan, M. J., Dillenburger, B., Raphael, S., & Solomon, J. A. (2012). Observers can voluntarily shift their psychometric functions without losing sensitivity. *Attention Perception & Psychophysics, 74*, 185–193.

Mõttus, R., Allik, J., Realo, A., Pullmann, H., Rossier, J., Zecca, G., . . . Tseung, C. N. (2012a). Comparability of self-reported conscientiousness across 21 countries. *European Journal of Personality, 26*, 303–317.

Mõttus, R., Allik, J., Realo, A., Rossier, J., Zecca, G., Ah-Kion, J., . . . Johnson, W. (2012b). The effect of response style on self-reported conscientiousness across 20 countries. *Personality and Social Psychology Bulletin, 38*, 1423–1436.

Murdock, G. P. (1957). World ethnographic sample. *American Anthropologist, 59*, 664–687.

Nelis, M., Esko, T., Mägi, R., Zimprich, F., Zimprich, A., Toncheva, D., . . . Metspalu, A. (2009). Genetic structure of Europeans: A view from the north-east. *PLoS ONE, 4*(5), e5472.

Novembre, J., Johnson, T., Bryc, K., Kutalik, Z., Boyko, A. R., Auton, A., . . . Bustamante, C. D. (2008). Genes mirror geography within Europe. *Nature, 456*, 98–101.

Oehrn, A. (1889). *Experimentelle studien zur individual psychologie*. Dorpat: Laakmann.

Oishi, S., Talhelm, T., & Lee, M. (2015). Personality and geography: Introverts prefer mountains. *Journal of Research in Personality, 58*, 55–68.

Penke, L., Denissen, J. J. A., & Miller, G. F. (2007). The evolutionary genetics of personality. *European Journal of Personality, 21*, 549–587.

Pennebaker, J. W., Rime, B., & Blankenship, V. E. (1996). Stereotypes of emotional expressiveness of northerners and southerners: A cross-cultural test of Montesquieu's hypotheses. *Journal of Personality and Social Psychology, 70*, 372–380.

Perugini, M., & Richetin, J. (2007). In the land of the blind, the one-eyed man is king. *European Journal of Personality, 21*, 977–981.

Prentice, C. (2014). *The lost tribe of Coney Island: Headhunters, Luna Park, and the man who pulled off the spectacle of the century*. Boston, MA: New Harvest.

Realo, A., Allik, J., Verkasalo, M., Lönnqvist, J. E., Kwiatkowska, A., Kööts, L., . . . Renge, V. (2009). Mechanisms of the national character stereotype: How people in six neighboring countries of Russia describe themselves and the typical Russian. *European Journal of Personality, 23*, 229–249.

Rentfrow, P. J. (2010). Statewide differences in personality toward a psychological geography of the United States. *American Psychologist, 65*, 548–558.

Rentfrow, P. J., Mellander, C., & Florida, R. (2009). Happy States of America: A state-level analysis of psychological, economic, and social well-being. *Journal of Research in Personality, 43*, 1073–1082.

Rindermann, H. (2008). Relevance of education and intelligence for the political development of nations: Democracy, rule of law and political liberty. *Intelligence, 36*, 306–322.

Rivers, W. H. R., Seligman, C. G., Myers, C. S., McDougall, W., Ray, S. H., Wilkin, A., & Haddon, A. C. (1901). *Reports of the Cambridge anthropological expedition to Torres Straits*. Cambridge: The University Press.

Rouse, S., & Herle, A. (1998). *Cambridge and the Torres Strait: Centenary essays on the 1898 anthropological expedition*. Cambridge: Cambridge University Press.

Ruch, W. (1996). Measurement approaches to the sense of humor: Introduction and overview. *Humor: International Journal of Humor Research, 9*, 239–250.

Ruch, W., & Forabosco, G. (1996). A cross-cultural study of humor appreciation: Italy and Germany. *Humor: International Journal of Humor Research, 9*, 1–18.

Sawyer, J. (1967). Dimensions of nations: Size, wealth and politics. *American Journal of Sociology, 72*, 145–172.

Sawyer, J., & LeVine, R. A. (1966). Cultural dimensions: A factor analysis of the World Ethnographic Sample. *American Anthropologist, 68*, 708–731.

Schmitt, D. P., Allik, J., McCrae, R. R., Benet-Martinez, V., Alcalay, L., Ault, L., . . . Zupancic, A. (2007). The geographic distribution of big five personality traits: Patterns and profiles of human self-description across 56 nations. *Journal of Cross-Cultural Psychology, 38*, 173–212.

Schwartz, S. H. (1994). Beyond individualism/collectivism: New cultural dimensions of values. In U. Kim, H. C. Triandis, Ç. Kagitçibasi, S. C. Choi, & G. Yoon (Eds.), *Individualism and collectivism: Theory, method, and applications* (pp. 85–119). Thousand Oaks, CA: Sage.

Segall, M. H., Campbell, D. T., & Herskovits, M. J. (1963). Cultural differences in the perception of geometric illusions. *Science, 139*, 769–771.

Söldner, T. M. L. (2013). *Personality, values, and cultural perception in the sojourner context: A new perspective on acculturation in Germany, Japan, and the US*. Berlin: Humboldt-Universität zu Berlin.

Spearman, C. (1904). 'General intelligence', Objectively determined and measured. *The American Journal of Psychology, 15*, 201–292.

Stankov, L., & Saucier, G. (2015). Social axioms in 33 countries: Good replicability at the individual but less so at the country level. *Journal of Cross-Cultural Psychology, 46*, 296–315.

Terracciano, A., Abdel-Khalek, A. M., Adam, N., Adamovova, L., Ahn, C., Ahn, H. N., . . . McCrae, R. R. (2005). National character does not reflect mean personality trait levels in 49 cultures. *Science, 310*, 96–100.

Thalmayer, A. G., & Saucier, G. (2014). The Questionnaire Big Six in 26 Nations: Developing cross-culturally applicable Big Six, Big Five and Big Two Inventories. *European Journal of Personality, 28*, 482–496.

Tooby, J., & Cosmides, L. (1990). On the universality of human nature and the uniqueness of the individual: The role of genetics and adaptation. *Journal of Personality, 58*, 17–68.

Toomela, A. (2003). Relationships between personality structure, structure of word meaning, and cognitive ability: A study of cultural mechanisms of personality. *Journal of Personality and Social Psychology, 85*, 723–735.

Van de Vliert, E. (2013). Climato-economic habitats support patterns of human needs, stresses, and freedoms. *Behavioral and Brain Sciences, 36*, 465–480.

van Hemert, D. A., van de Vijver, F. J. R., Poortinga, Y. H., & Georgas, J. (2002). Structural and functional equivalence of the Eysenck Personality Questionnaire within and between countries. *Personality and Individual Differences, 33*, 1229–1249.

Welzel, C. (2013). *Freedom rising: Human empowerment and the quest for emancipation*. Cambridge, UK: Cambridge University Press.

Whiten, A., Goodall, J., McGrew, W. C., Nishida, T., Reynolds, V., Sugiyama, Y., . . . Boesch, C. (1999). Cultures in chimpanzees. *Nature, 399*, 682–685.

Woodworth, R. S. (1910). Racial differences in mental traits. *Science, 31*, 171–186.

World Values Survey Association. (2014). World Values Survey Wave 5 2005–2008 Official Aggregate v.20140429. Aggregate File Producer. Madrid: Asep/JDS.

Yasnitsky, A. (2013). Kurt Koffka: Uzbeks do have illusions! Discussion in absentia between Luria and Koffka. *Dubna Psychological Journal, 3*, 1–25.

Zimmermann, J., & Neyer, F. J. (2013). Do we become a different person when hitting the road? Personality development of sojourners. *Journal of Personality and Social Psychology, 105*, 515–530.

Threat of Infectious Disease

Iris M. Wang, Nicholas M. Michalak and Joshua M. Ackerman

Management of infectious disease represents one of the most fundamental selection pressures humans have confronted over their evolutionary history (Ackerman et al., 2012). To our ancestors, parasites and pathogens were ever-present and significant dangers (Gangestad and Buss, 1993; Low, 1990), with the impact of these infectious agents extending beyond hominids, potentially to the origins of sexual reproduction itself (Brockhurst, 2011). Even in contemporary society, contracting infectious disease is an everyday possibility. Colds and flus are some of the leading causes of workplace absenteeism (and general discomfort) in the United States (Japsen, 2012). Pathogenic agents infect hundreds of millions of people and cause approximately 9,500,000 deaths (over 16% of all deaths) worldwide per year (World Health Organization, 2008). And the annual mortality rate from infectious diseases outpaces the annual mortality rate from all twentieth-century wars combined (Pirages, 2005). Clearly, this is a big problem for human fitness.

Perhaps the best-known defense against invading parasites and germs is the physiological immune system. This complex system is often highly effective, allowing us to overcome both novel and familiar threats. However, engagement of the physiological immune system is also energetically costly and imperfect in that it must continually adapt to the co-evolution of germs themselves (Lochmiller and Deerenberg, 2000). Further, it fights only those germs that have already entered the body. As a complement to this system, researchers have proposed that humans also possess a behavioral immune system (BIS) through which activation of certain psychological responses reduces the probability of initial infection (Neuberg et al., 2011; Schaller, 2015; Schaller et al., 2015). These responses aid individuals in both the detection and avoidance of infection threats by attuning people to cues associated with disease and by motivating evasive or intervening responses against these cues. For example, many illnesses produce external symptoms such as sores and lesions (Kurzban and Leary, 2001) and, accordingly, perceivers' reactions to these features are often strongly negative (e.g., Park et al., 2003). Moreover, the BIS uses liberal criteria when identifying potential threats in order to minimize the probability of contracting disease, even though this liberal bias increases the rate of false alarms to non-existent threats (Haselton and Nettle, 2006; Nesse, 2005). Thus, just as a smoke detector will sound an alarm in response to benign cues such as cooking fumes, a number of non-contagious physical and mental features are treated as cues to the presence of pathogens in other people. Such features include disfigurements (Ackerman et al., 2009; Miller and Maner, 2011), disabilities (Park et al., 2003), obesity (Lund and Miller, 2014; Park et al., 2007), elderly appearance (Duncan and Schaller, 2009; Miller and Maner, 2012), mental illness (Lund and Boggero, 2014), and outgroup association or membership (Faulkner et al., 2004; Huang et al., 2011; Navarrete et al., 2007).

Much like the physiological immune system, the BIS includes a complex set of processes that meet the end goal of infection avoidance through a variety of means. Research indicates that the BIS draws on psychological mechanisms, including interpersonal attention (Ackerman et al., 2009), social categorization (Miller and Maner, 2012), preferences for mates and leaders (Lee and Zietsch, 2011; Murray et al., 2013; White et al., 2013), prejudicial attitudes (Faulkner et al., 2004; Huang et al., 2011), and behavioral activation (Mortensen et al., 2010). This system also interfaces with the physiological immune system in a functionally flexible manner, such that people or contexts conveying heightened vulnerability (or perceived vulnerability) to infection trigger stronger BIS responses (Schaller et al., 2015). For instance, situational factors indicating weakened physiological immunity – as occurs subsequent to fighting an actual infection (van der Sluijs et al., 2004) – can exaggerate BIS responses as a means of compensating for this increased vulnerability (Miller and Maner, 2011). Activation of the BIS in healthy people may even kick-start aspects of the physiological immune system in preparation for possible infection (Schaller et al., 2010; Stevenson et al., 2011).

Thus, not only would an infectious disease tracking and avoidance system be functionally useful in theory, evidence indicates that we have likely evolved such a system. In the current chapter, we consider whether individual differences might play an important role in this system's operation, and perhaps more critically, the implications such a system has for shaping human personality. To do so, we first highlight the theoretical reasons to expect variation in pathogen management mechanisms and the psychological models relevant to these mechanisms (e.g., BIS, disgust). Next, we review research on the direct impact of pathogen threats on specific personality attributes. Subsequently, we place relevant individual differences within a motivational structure in order to organize specific content domains of personality linked to pathogen threats. Finally, we propose some unanswered questions for the field that may be promising directions for future research.

WHY EXPECT INDIVIDUAL DIFFERENCES?

Individual differences reflect invariances or consistencies in behavior, cognition, affect, and so on. These are generally presumed to stem from some combination of genes and environment, often with early-life environments playing an especially important role (Simpson et al., 2011). We suggest that factors indexing potential exposure to pathogens and vulnerability to infection will predict the expression of individual differences in BIS-relevant sensitivities.

Consider variation in the environments that humans inhabit. Since early hominid migrations out of Africa, people have occupied a wide range of ecological niches. Some of these ecologies are more amenable than others to propagation and transmission of disease-causing agents. Climates that are warm and wet – such as those found near the equator – help to facilitate pathogen prevalence (Guernier et al., 2004) and threaten both subsistence cultures and industrialized nations. In such places, continual exposure (or threat of exposure) to infection may have acted as a selection pressure on the mental and cultural evolution of behaviors and practices that function to cope with disease hazards. Societies that inhabit more temperate, drier locations face less pressure to respond to pathogen threats in order to thrive. Indeed, as we review later, ecological pathogen prevalence is a key predictor of a range of individual and cultural differences (e.g., Gangestad et al., 2006). Thus, environmental variance may set the stage for the development of individual differences in BIS activity.

Variation between people can also play an important role in the management of infectious diseases. For instance, physiological immunity to germs is heavily influenced by personal factors such as genes, gut microbiota, fatigue, and psychological distress (e.g., Beck et al., 1999; Hickie et al., 1999; Round and Mazmanian, 2009). Relatedly, a life history perspective suggests that people reared in resource-limited and unpredictable childhood environments may suffer deficits in the growth and maintenance of their physiological immune systems (McDade, 2005), leaving people vulnerable to external pathogen threats. Such dysregulation can also result in hyperactive immune activity, as seen in allergic and autoimmune disorders. Therefore, people with dysregulated systems may compensate through relatively stronger or more frequent use of the BIS.

Individual differences in the BIS may present in one of two ways. First, people may express different chronic degrees of BIS activity, much as one person could be high in agreeableness and another low in agreeableness. Second, people may vary in responsivity to contextual information indicating the presence of potential germ threats. This sensitivity to context forms the basis of the 'functional flexibility principle', the proposition that the physical and cognitive costs of motivational activation led to the evolution of mechanisms that track when a cue (such as vulnerability to infection) is present or not (Schaller et al., 2015; Schaller and Neuberg, 2012). Thus, people may exhibit their given level of BIS response only when pathogens are especially prevalent or when personal susceptibility is relatively high (e.g., from fatigue). It is important to note that, because the BIS is psychological in nature, the types of individual differences being discussed here include personality characteristics that facilitate disease avoidance in addition to basic behaviors.

EMOTIONAL MARKERS OF THE BIS: DISGUST

Thus far, we have considered the role of disease avoidance from a primarily cognitive perspective, the BIS. A related perspective emphasizes the role of affective responses like disgust in promoting aversion to, and expulsion of, toxic and disease-causing substances. By many theoretical accounts, disgust emerged as an adaptation to the selection pressures posed by pathogens (e.g., Tybur et al., 2013). Evidence does suggest that disgust initiates behaviors that reduce the likelihood of pathogen exposure. Across cultures, people react with disgust to feces, rotting food, and body fluids, all of which reliably house pathogens. Simply seeing or imagining, as well as actually touching, such items can elicit a cross-culturally recognizable facial expression, increased salivation, vomiting, lowered blood pressure, increased galvanic skin response, active serotonin pathways, increased activation in the parasympathetic branch of the autonomic nervous system, increased immune response, reported nausea, and, ultimately, avoidance and/or withdrawal behavior (Curtis et al., 2011; Olatunji et al., 2012; Rozin and Haidt, 2013). Experiencing disgust also motivates decisions intended to reduce pathogen transmission risk (Tybur et al., 2011).

Yet, the story of disgust is not entirely straightforward. Many carriers of pathogens do not evoke this emotion. For instance, the thought of maggot-ridden meat may gross you out, but the thought of peanut butter laced with *Salmonella* likely will not produce the same response. Conversely, people often feel (or at least report feeling) disgusted by pathogen-free items, such as hotdogs threaded with pasta (think about it). Human behaviors that seem entirely irrelevant to pathogen transmission, such as learning that a colleague stole money from a children's charity or cheated on a romantic partner, can also elicit feelings of disgust. Existing models of disgust reflect a similar variation in which antecedents and functions of disgust are represented. For instance, Rozin et al. (2000) argue that, although disgust first evolved as a food rejection system, it was later re-purposed for motivating the cleansing, avoiding, and expelling of a broad array of contaminants. They claim that not only does disgust motivate pathogen avoidance, it also functions to help individuals avoid reminders of humans' animal (thus mortal) nature and to protect sacred values and objects. Kelly (2011) also makes use of disgust re-purposing; he argues that disgust evolved first to motivate pathogen avoidance and then to motivate moral judgments and intergroup attitudes. Curtis et al. (2011) argue that group-level hygienic behaviors supplement an imperfect disgust system through cultural rules about purity and pollution, which are responsible for social divisions (e.g., social class). Finally, Tybur et al. (2013) distinguish three motivational domains of disgust – pathogen, sexual, and moral. Their model posits that sexual disgust discourages engaging in low-value mating opportunities and that expressions of moral disgust signal to nearby conspecifics that certain actions deserve condemnation.

Despite the differences among these models, it is not obvious from existing data that disgust ever betrays its historical roots: pathogen avoidance. More often than not, disgust is associated with targets that pose some pathogen threat, real or perceived. Disgust undoubtedly plays an important role in more social domains, but it seems that it does so largely in service to a pathogen avoidance system (Inbar and Olatunji 2014). Because of this, the experience of disgust, and its consequences, can be integrated with the BIS system model to explain aspects of personality and individual differences. We consider several such examples next.

DIRECT IMPACTS OF PATHOGEN THREAT ON INDIVIDUAL DIFFERENCES

Perceived Vulnerability to Disease

As an individual difference, perceived vulnerability to disease represents chronic sensitivities involving detection and aversion of infectious disease cues as well as beliefs about the relevancy of these cues to the individual. A commonly used measure in the behavioral immune literature, the Perceived Vulnerability to Disease (PVD) scale, was developed by Duncan et al. (2009) to assess two types of sensitivities – Germ Aversion (GA), which refers to 'discomfort in situations that connote an increased likelihood for the transmission of pathogens' (p. 545), and includes items such as, 'I do not like to write with a pencil someone else has obviously chewed on', and Perceived Infectability (PI), which refers to 'beliefs pertaining to their susceptibility to infectious diseases' (p. 545), and includes items such as, 'In general, I am very susceptible to colds, flu, and other infectious diseases'. Duncan and colleagues (2009) characterize GA as a set of aversive affective responses geared specifically toward pathogen-relevant contexts, whereas they characterize PI as a set of cognitions about one's immune functioning and likelihood of being infected in the future.

The PVD scale is associated with, yet distinct from, other indices of health threat. For example, classic measures of hypochondria and beliefs about health (i.e., the Health Anxiety Inventory, Whitely Index, and Illness Attitude Scale) correlate positively with the PVD scale, particularly with the PI subscale (Duncan et al., 2009). The Disgust Sensitivity scale (Haidt et al., 1994) correlates most strongly with GA, as disgust is an emotion motivating avoidance or expulsion rather than an indicator of one's own vulnerability. Despite these associations, PVD is different from instruments designed to gauge health anxiety or hypochondria, which measure health concerns in general and may include health problems that are non-contagious (e.g., cancer, heart disease), as well as from disgust sensitivity, which assesses reactions to non-disease-relevant stimuli and situations.

PVD is also tied to traits and attitudes with more indirect relevance to pathogen transmission but which reflect the potential for exposure to, or changes in, infection susceptibility. As we expand upon in later sections, these constructs are tied to specific motivations associated with BIS activation, such as self-protection motives, as well as a preference for fixed norms. Indeed, GA positively correlates with Social Dominance Orientation (SDO), Belief in a Dangerous World (BDW), Need for Structure, Affect Intensity, and Faith in Intuition (Duncan et al., 2009). Here, social dominance aligns with self-protection motives, as higher scores on SDO reflect aggression toward outgroups (that may carry foreign germs). The connection with self-protection is also found in the (relatively weak) association with BDW, a measure of individual differences in perception of interpersonal hostility and danger. The relationship between GA and Need for Structure likely reflects a desire to follow traditions and norms, which serve to protect people from disease risks associated with deviating from established norms (e.g., hygiene, food preparation). Correlations between GA and Affect Intensity and Faith in Intuition are consistent with the affect-based (disgust) nature of the GA subscale.

The PVD scale is also tied to social judgments and inferences. Specifically, GA predicts anti-fat attitudes (Park et al., 2007), anti-immigrant attitudes (Faulkner et al., 2004), and Implicit Association Test (IAT) scores indicating a tendency to implicitly associate negative words with the physically disabled, whereas PI predicts negative implicit attitudes toward the elderly. Finally, both PVD subscales are negatively correlated with people's self-reported number of friends with disabilities (Park et al., 2003) and with Sociosexual Orientation Inventory scores, such that higher levels of either GA or PI are associated with weaker preferences for low-investment, short-term relationships.

Given the theoretical distinctions between GA and PI, one might expect that GA scores predict relatively stronger reactions to external cues in the environment and PI scores predict relatively stronger reactions to internal cues. If so, this could account for the greater association between GA and negative attitudes toward obese individuals, immigrants, and physically disabled individuals, but the link between PI and anti-elderly attitudes is surprising. It may be that seeing elderly people evokes a self-reflective sense of internal vulnerability associated with aging.

PVD represents a useful measure for testing the principle discussed earlier involving 'functional flexibility' – responsivity to infectious disease cues depends, in part, on people's chronic sensitivity to such cues, which often reflects susceptibility to, or concern about, infection (Schaller et al., 2015).

Indeed, some studies find that pathogen threat cues affect people differently as a function of their perceived vulnerability, usually showing that responses are strongest for those scoring highly on PVD factors (e.g., Huang et al., 2011; Mortensen et al., 2010). Yet, PVD does not always interact with situational disease threats (e.g., Ackerman et al., 2009; Murray and Schaller, 2012). It may be that, when the cues to pathogen threat are strong, people exhibit classic BIS responses regardless of their chronic sensitivities, real or perceived. In weaker or more ambiguous contexts, interaction effects may dominate, such that the effect of the prime depends only on GA or PI (e.g., Ackerman et al., 2017; Fessler et al., 2005). The contexts in which one subscale plays more of a significant role than the other have been inconsistent. Why and when such effects occur therefore remain important questions for future research (see Tybur et al., 2014).

Disgust Sensitivity

As discussed earlier, disgust plays an important role in managing infectious disease threats. Although many objects, people, concepts, and situations can evoke disgust in the moment, people vary in the extent to which they feel disgust; that is, disgust responses can reflect individual differences. Tybur et al. (2009) extended work on disgust by proposing that this emotion is comprised of three functionally specialized domains. The first is pathogen disgust, which motivates pathogen avoidance. Sexual disgust, the second domain, discourages sexual behavior with sexual partners who may threaten long-term reproductive success. Finally, moral disgust discourages interactions and behaviors that are socially costly to an individual or his/her group. In order to capture individual differences in these distinct disgust domains, they developed a self-report scale: The Three Domains of Disgust Scale (TDDS). These researchers predicted that each of the disgust-based motivations should share variability with other individual differences in domain-specific ways. Consistent with the prediction that chronic concern about pathogens should motivate avoidance, the Pathogen Disgust subscale correlated with relevant measures of Big Five personality traits (e.g., positively with neuroticism, negatively with openness to experience) and, unsurprisingly, correlated positively with PVD. In contrast, sexual disgust – which should impede sexual motivations and, ultimately, contact with low-quality mates – positively correlated with conscientiousness and agreeableness. Finally, moral disgust negatively correlated with psychopathy, a fundamentally antisocial aspect of personality. Armed with predictions that disgust should motivate domain-specific attitudes and behaviors, researchers in later articles describe a variety of confirmatory correlations. For example, pathogen disgust is positively associated with women's facial masculinity preferences, contamination fear, obsessive–compulsive tendencies, depression, anti-fat attitudes, behavioral avoidance, moral purity (moral disgust is instead correlated with Harm/Care and Ingroup Loyalty on the Moral Foundations Questionnaire), and increased galvanic skin response to pathogen cues (DeBruine et al., 2010; Lieberman et al., 2012; Olatunji et al., 2012; Tybur and de Vries, 2013).

Extreme responses, such as the contamination fears and washing behaviors that characterize Obsessive–Compulsive Disorder (OCD), also likely reflect trait variation in pathogen threat concerns. Researchers have observed positive correlations between individual differences in disgust – as measured by Pathogen Disgust from the TDDS and most subscales of the Disgust Sensitivity scale and its revised version (Haidt et al., 1994; Olatunji et al., 2007) – and self-reported washing and checking symptoms of OCD in clinical and non-clinical samples (Olatunji et al., 2012; Woody and Tolin, 2002). Moreover, in a series of studies, non-clinical participants reporting high contamination obsessions reported greater disgust in response to aversive videos (Woody and Tolin, 2002). High-contamination participants were also less willing to touch (or even approach) a variety of disgusting objects in a series of behavioral avoidance tasks. Thus, to the extent that OCD symptomology represents an individual difference, pathogen threat appears to elevate its manifestation.

Five-Factor Model of Personality

Although it may sometimes be beneficial for individuals to form social relationships and experience novel situations, engaging in these behaviors increases their risk for infection. To the extent that personality motivates behavior, the BIS model predicts that heightened pathogen risk should dampen personality traits associated with risky behavior. A variety of disease threat indicators have been linked to weakened expression of specific (Big Five) personality factors. One such indicator is ecological pathogen prevalence, which indexes the degree to which an individual is likely to become infected by pathogenic agents. As would be expected from a BIS perspective, greater pathogen prevalence appears negatively correlated with extraversion and openness to experience (as measured by the NEO-PI-R; Schaller and Murray, 2008). In other words, as the likelihood of contact with pathogens increases, people report less willingness to interact with others and less openness to novel experiences. These effects hold even controlling for GDP, life expectancy, and climate, and they are stronger with measures of historical as compared to current pathogen prevalence, suggesting that high levels of extraversion and openness may have been genetically selected against in pathogen-rich environments. In this particular study, the other three personality traits of the Big Five – neuroticism, agreeableness, and conscientiousness – did not have a consistent relationship with pathogen prevalence.

Expanding on Schaller and Murray's analysis (2008), Thornhill et al. (2010) separated types of parasites in a region (parasite richness) into zoonotic (i.e., parasites that only infect animals), human-specific, and multi-host (i.e., parasites that infect both animals and humans) parasites. Distinguishing among parasites in this way affords a stricter test of the infection hypothesis: people should be sensitive primarily to those diseases that are transmittable to humans. Indeed, Thornhill and colleagues (2010) found that only human-specific and multi-host parasite-richness were negatively correlated with extraversion and openness. Parasite severity, the number of cases of infections per person, yielded a similar negative correlation with these traits.

At an individual level, chronic concerns about infection are associated with a broader range of personality traits. The GA subscale of the PVD correlates negatively with extraversion, agreeableness, and openness, and it correlates positively with neuroticism (Duncan et al., 2009). The PI subscale correlates negatively with agreeableness and conscientiousness, and it correlates positively with neuroticism. The findings with extraversion and openness here are consistent with the ecological data presented earlier. Correlations for the remaining traits are less consistent with findings from the ecological data. There have also been subsequent analyses attempting to link the TDDS with various instantiations of Big Five personality factors (Tybur and de Vries, 2013). These have yielded somewhat inconsistent results compared to the more consistent associations found between PVD and the Big Five. Controlling for sex and age, the pathogen disgust subscale of the TDDS correlates positively with extraversion, neuroticism, and orderliness on the Five-Dimension Personality Test (5DT). Controlling for sex and age again, the pathogen disgust subscale correlates positively with emotionality and conscientiousness, and negatively with agreeableness and openness to experience on the HEXACO model of personality. Together, it seems the pathogen disgust subscale consistently correlates with neuroticism and orderliness/conscientiousness. However, there are some divergent findings between the PVD and TDDS (e.g., differences in correlations with extraversion) suggesting that different personality scales may be tapping different behaviors or tendencies associated with each trait. These scales also may have different psychometric properties (e.g., the 5DT is measured using yes or no questions, the HEXACO uses five-point Likert-type scales), which could contribute to fluctuations in findings across studies.

Although personality traits can be stable within individuals, nonrandom fluctuations in how people judge their own personality traits can occur across time (Funder, 2006). One study investigated changes in personality dimensions as a result of situational disease cues (Mortensen et al., 2010). Following a slideshow designed to trigger pathogen threat concerns or a pathogen-irrelevant slideshow, participants completed both the Big Five Inventory (John and Srivastava, 1999) and the PVD scale. The pathogen threat prime led to overall lower levels of extraversion, similar to the pattern demonstrated in the chronic and ecological studies above. Additionally, interactions between situational cues and PVD emerged for agreeableness and openness, with highly disease-sensitive people reporting less agreeableness and less openness. No published experiments have tested whether the TDDS, or other measures of disgust sensitivity, moderate the relationship between immediate disease cues and the Big Five. Overall, the ecological, correlational, and experimental evidence does point to a connection between environmental pathogen cues and decreased extraversion and openness. In more specific terms, chronic and incidental concerns about disease lead people to adopt strategies of reducing social contact and avoiding novel experiences.

FUNDAMENTAL MOTIVES AS A FRAMEWORK FOR UNDERSTANDING THE INFLUENCE OF PATHOGEN THREAT ON INDIVIDUAL DIFFERENCES

Central to our discussion in the following section is the notion that individual differences (e.g., personality traits) can represent attunement to, predisposition to adopt, and chronic pursuit of goals (e.g., Dweck and Leggett, 1988; Funder, 2006). For example, a person high in threat sensitivity may pay more attention to stimuli perceived to indicate the presence of danger and be more likely to engage in protective actions. From this point of view, certain individual differences can reflect underlying motives to pursue and complete specific, often fundamental, goals (Neel et al., 2015).

A fundamental motives framework provides a comprehensive, theory-driven approach that has been successful in organizing situation-level phenomena and in generating new predictions about situational factors. This approach builds from the assumption that human cognition and behavior consists of many mental processes adapted to solve important, recurrent problems over the course of human evolution. These processes draw on inputs from local ecologies and cultures to motivate actions that are relevant to problem domains that include self-protection, affiliation, mating, management of status hierarchies, and parenting (e.g., Ackerman et al., 2012; Ackerman and Kenrick, 2008; Kenrick et al., 2003, 2010). In addition to advancing our understanding of situational forces, this framework can help to organize individual differences according to (1) domains likely to be influenced by infectious disease threats, and (2) response mechanisms to these threats, including the BIS. This organization is distinct from personality models like the Big Five, although it does help to identify types of content and action relevant to these models (see Neel et al., 2015, for an extended discussion of the similarities and differences in fundamental motives and traditional personality approaches). Next, we detail several motive domains in which pathogens and pathogen threat appear to have played a substantive role in shaping the psychology of individual differences.

Self-protection

Perhaps no fundamental motive is more closely tied to the management of infectious disease threats than that of self-protection. Survival is clearly important from both a personal perspective and an evolutionary perspective (in the service of differential reproduction). Physiological harm also saps energetic resources that could be used in the pursuit of other goals. Individual differences within the domain of self-protection are myriad, one of which – emotional (disgust) sensitivity – we have described earlier. Here, we focus on two major categories of action that afford possible injury to the self: food consumption and intergroup interaction. Both involve key vectors of infectious disease, and both can be represented through individual differences such as food preferences and stereotypic attitudes, respectively. Thus, behavioral immune responses should be specially tailored to manage such threats. Important for the following discussion, recall that pathogen management systems like the BIS use liberal detection criteria for potential threats. The costs of missing a real pathogen threat are likely greater than the costs of false alarming to a nonexistent threat (Haselton and Nettle, 2006; Nesse, 2005), and thus the selection pressures created by these differential costs have led to inherent bias in behavioral immune mechanisms.

Food choices

Not eating is difficult. People may struggle with individual diets, but avoiding food altogether does not make for a long or happy life. Yet, consumption of the wrong foods (e.g., those containing dangerous pathogens) can, in mild cases, cause digestive distress and, in severe cases, death. Food is unique in that we allow it to bypass our body's first line of physiological immune defense – our skin – and so people should prioritize psychological mechanisms that help us to choose the 'right' foods. Research does indicate we are particularly sensitive to food cues that connote the possibility of germ contamination, such as signs of spoilage. Not only do we readily detect such cues (even over-perceiving them), our chronic food preferences support avoidance of them. Given its association with bodily expulsion, disgust plays an important role in these preferences. Physiological disgust is a common reaction to the experience of eating contaminated or spoiled foods, even foods that only have the appearance of contamination (Rozin et al., 2000). Our preferences also reflect the fact that some foods are more pathogenically dangerous than others. Tybur and Lieberman (2016) found that pairing pathogen cues with images of meats led to less willingness to eat those meats, whereas pathogen cues paired with images of plants did not produce aversion. Over the course of our cultural evolutionary history, human groups have discovered means of inhibiting pathogen growth in foods, and the preferences of people in pathogen-rich ecologies reflect these discoveries. For instance, spices such as garlic, onion, and chili contain antimicrobial properties. People in climates that cultivate pathogens and parasites tend to use more spices in their recipes (Sherman and Billing, 1999), and the cultural normalization of these recipes becomes part of what it means to be an individual within those cultures.

Beyond clear indicators of contamination such as spoilage, individuals also differ in their preferences for novel or strange foods. This may be because novel food (particularly if the novelty is geographic or cultural in origin) is more likely to harbor germs to which one's body has not adapted immune defenses compared to commonly eaten food.

Indeed, food neophobia (i.e., the avoidance of unfamiliar foods) is predicted by pathogen stress (Thornhill and Fincher, 2014a). For instance, women who score highly on pathogen disgust tend to distrust novel foods (Al-Shawaf et al., 2015). People with high levels of GA also tend to hold more distrustful and negative attitudes toward genetically modified foods (Prokop et al., 2013). More generally, disease concern is associated with reduced openness to experience (Duncan et al., 2009), which is itself associated with reduced risk taking and increased preference for familiarity. This could account for the specific patterns of food preferences reviewed here, and it could also help explain broader aversions to novel stimuli (e.g., people), as we discuss next.

Stereotyping and prejudice

Just as unfamiliar foods may contain pathogens to which we have not been previously exposed, so might unfamiliar people. Our adaptive immune defenses are quite effective in developing targeted reactions (e.g., antibodies) to infection-causing germs, providing we survive the initial infection. Unfortunately, history shows that a lack of early exposure to pathogens (often due to differences in the ecologies societies inhabit) can result in extreme harm once those pathogens are introduced to naïve populations. Consider the epidemics that can result when societies first come into contact (e.g., smallpox and measles in the Americas; Diamond, 1997). Such diseases are often spread from person to person. Given such dangers, a BIS that is already tuned to overgeneralize the cues signaling threat (Schaller and Park, 2011) is liable to produce chronic suspicion and dislike of unfamiliar people, particularly those who harbor cues that have reliably indicated infection. Heuristically however, infection risk may be signaled by any deviation from typical morphology and behavior (e.g., facial disfigurement, rashes, convulsions) as well as foreign or outgroup markers (e.g., race, sexual orientation, cultural differences).

From this perspective, a degree of the stereotypic attitudes and prejudices expressed toward others – and the corresponding pull toward a homogeneous ingroup – may stem from the threat of infectious disease.

Some existing evidence supports this conclusion. Fincher and Thornhill (2012) have demonstrated that philopatry (i.e., persistently residing in a familiar environment), ingroup favoritism, and outgroup dislike may have all emerged as beliefs, behaviors, and cultural practices serving to reduce the threat of local pathogens. Societal structures that serve to fraction people into groups, such as religions, appear more common in areas of high pathogen stress (Fincher and Thornhill, 2008). Chronic levels of pathogen concern also are associated with negative attitudes toward individuals bearing a variety of outgroup and non-normative features. For instance, people with strong GA and pathogen disgust report greater anti-fat prejudice, particularly after viewing images of obese people (Park et al., 2007). In one study, disgust-sensitive and disease-concerned people responding to postings on psychology and political websites expressed greater ethnocentrism, ingroup attraction, and outgroup negativity (Navarrete and Fessler, 2006). People with such concerns also report fewer numbers of family members and friends with disabilities (Park et al., 2003), suggesting that these prejudicial attitudes spill over into behavior. These reactions may be explicit, but they also can involve implicit reactions held as well. Studies show that people with greater PVD hold more implicit negative attitudes toward unfamiliar, foreign groups and people with disabilities, and they implicitly associate such groups with danger (Faulkner et al., 2004). In some contexts, implicit stereotypes emerge for chronically concerned people only when cued by situational pathogen threats, highlighting the functional flexibility principle of the BIS (e.g., participants reporting greater PI to disease showed stronger implicit associations between elderly adults and disease; Duncan and Schaller, 2009).

Finally, individual differences in disease vulnerability may also change according to the state of the perceiver. For example, American women in their first trimester of pregnancy – a period of increased risk for infection – revealed greater ingroup attraction and outgroup negativity (Navarrete et al., 2007). These women liked an American-born, pro-American author more and a foreign-born, anti-American author less. People also become more vulnerable to infection after having been sick recently. For these people, enhanced BIS reactions may protect from additional infection. Consistent with this idea, recently ill people show faster avoidant behaviors toward disfigured others (Miller and Maner, 2011).

Affiliation

People everywhere desire to form social groups (Baumeister and Leary, 1995; Caporael, 1997). Relationships with group members afford a number of benefits – safety, romance, direction in uncertain situations – and thus people attempt to manage those social connections using a variety of rules, incentives, and cognitive biases, from empathy to reciprocity. Behaviors such as cooperation and mutual provisioning of assistance would clearly be valuable in the context of infectious diseases where effective prevention and treatment of illnesses often require interpersonal care. Yet, active infection concerns can also lead to down-regulation of affiliative desires, at least with unspecified others (Sacco et al., 2014).

The establishment of social relationships typically involves separating people into 'good' and 'bad' coalitional partners, or ingroups and outgroups. Therefore, an affiliation motive draws on group formation processes and mechanisms that track conformity to, and violation of, group rules. In this section, we discuss several types of affiliation-relevant individual differences that have been linked to behavioral immune activity: individualism/collectivism, political orientation, and morality.

Individualism and collectivism

Individualism/collectivism represents one of the most widely researched psychological distinctions between cultures (see Hofstede, 2001, or Triandis, 1995, for reviews). A collectivistic culture is one in which the boundary between ingroup and outgroup is strong, whereas an individualistic culture is one in which the boundary between these is relatively weak. Collectivism is associated with relatively more social tightness – a strong emphasis on conformity and adherence to norms – compared to individualism, which is characterized by greater tolerance of norm violations (Gelfand et al., 2006; Murray et al., 2011). These cultural-level differences in group structures also extend to the individual, in turn affecting their self-concepts, personalities, chronic motivations, chronic experiences of emotions, and chronic ways of interpreting and reasoning about the world (Markus and Kitayama, 1991; Nisbett et al., 2001). For example, collectivists tend to form stronger ties with their ingroups than individualists. This means that the self-concepts of collectivists tend to include their group memberships, whereas the self-concepts of individualists do not. Thus, individualism/collectivism can be represented as both an individual difference as well as a cultural difference.

Several reasons have been proposed to explain why higher levels of pathogen prevalence predict greater levels of collectivism within individuals and cultures (Thornhill and Fincher, 2014b). As discussed in the section on stereotyping and prejudice, in the presence of pathogens, people are motivated to avoid outgroup members who display cues to novelty and may carry novel pathogens, leading people to more readily draw distinctions between ingroup and outgroup members. Second, the greater nepotism and ingroup altruism found in collectivistic groups help ensure that those ingroup members who fall ill are given care. Finally, stronger observance of certain ingroup norms (i.e., food preparation, cleaning, and hygiene practices) can serve as protective qualities against disease transmission.

These ideas have typically been examined at the level of culture, although a conceptual equivalency exists with individual cognition. Fincher and colleagues (2008) conducted one test using four separate multi-national surveys of individualism and collectivism (Gelfand et al., 2004; Hofstede, 2001; Kashima and Kashima, 1998; Suh et al., 1998) that included direct survey measurement of individuals and secondary examination of language-use within nations. Across cultures, pathogen severity (i.e., the number of cases of individuals with infectious diseases) was strongly negatively correlated with individualism and strongly positively correlated with collectivism. This was most prominently the case for measures of historical pathogen prevalence (i.e., incidence rates dating before the 1990s) rather than for contemporary prevalence (i.e., rates from June–August of 2007). This may be because of the slow rate of cultural change or the relatively slow action of natural selection in creating large-scale genetic shifts. Importantly, however, this helps to clarify any causal claims, as the ecological factor of prevalence preceded the cultural expression of collectivism. This link between historical pathogen prevalence and collectivism held even when controlling for alternative influences such as GDP, the GINI index (i.e., an index of income disparity), population density, and residual life expectancy (i.e., life expectancy variance not accounted for by pathogen prevalence).

An analysis was also performed separating human-host, multi-host, and zoonotic parasites (i.e., parasites that only infect animals), revealing that the collectivism effect is driven solely by the levels of human and multi-host parasites, but not zoonotic ones (Thornhill et al., 2010). This again helps to rule out alternative explanations, including ones tying collectivism and its consequents to increased levels of human–animal interaction (e.g., farming and fishing; Uskul et al., 2008). In another cultural-level analysis, Fincher and Thornhill (2012) looked at the strength of family ties as measured by five items in the World Values Survey (e.g., importance of family, respecting parents regardless of faults or qualities). Higher pathogen prevalence was positively related to the strength of family ties, even controlling for various economic indices and civil liberties. Within the United States, tests of association between broader measures of collectivism and family ties mirrored the cross-national data, particularly for analyses of human-host/mixed-host pathogens (Fincher and Thornhill, 2012).

As mentioned earlier, collectivistic cultures are typically tighter than individualistic cultures in their emphasis on conformity and adherence to norms (Gelfand et al., 2006). One might expect that, in areas where pathogen prevalence is high, deviations from norms that are designed to offer protection from pathogens could be costly. Murray and colleagues (2011) examined this link between pathogen prevalence and cross-national differences in conformity pressure, using four country-level measures. These included the number of left-handed people, personality variability, attitudes toward obedience as measured in the World Values Survey, and a meta-analysis of dozens of behavioral conformity experiments performed globally (Bond and Smith, 1996). Again, historical pathogen prevalence was a strong predictor of conformity pressure at both regional and national levels, such that greater levels of pathogens were associated with lower levels of left-handed people and less personality variability, as well as more positive attitudes toward obedience and greater behavioral conformity. The predictive power of historical pathogen prevalence held even when entering collectivism into the regression, suggesting that this is not a by-product of this cultural structure.

Cultural-level differences in conformity should be reflected in the products that cultures generate, as well as in their individual phenotypes. In fact, some evidence indicates that pathogen prevalence predicts lower levels of innovation, as indexed by the number of Nobel Prize Laureates per capita, the Global Innovation Index, the Technology Achievement Index, innovative capacity, and number of patent applications (Murray, 2014). Although these are national-level metrics, we can speculate that conformity pressures stemming from chronic ecological cues could lead to a decrease in individual creativity or a decreased willingness to express novel ideas. This possibility is supported by data that both replicate the negative relationship between patent applications and pathogen prevalence in US state data and show experimentally that pathogen threat reduces openness to innovation (Huang et al., 2016).

Finally, at the individual level, in a study by Murray and Schaller (2012), people who scored highly on the GA subscale of the PVD measure tended to also score highly on conformist attitudes (e.g., 'Breaking social norms can have harmful, unintended consequences'). People high in PVD-GA also expressed greater liking for people with conformist traits and were more likely to value obedience in their children. Together, these findings highlight how an affiliation motive can produce different types of cognitive and behavioral responses, dependent on the existing degree of pathogen concern.

Political orientation

By 2013, at least 24 studies had tested whether chronic motivations to avoid pathogens are related to factors underlying political orientation, in particular social conservatism and religiosity (Terrizzi et al., 2013). One prominent hypothesis is that socially conservative beliefs – which promote adherence to tradition, ingroup cohesion, and wariness of outgroup members – reflect a strategy that reduces the risk of pathogen exposure associated with foreign and unfamiliar people. Aggregating across these studies, Terrizzi et al. (2013) estimated a moderate relationship between political conservatism and BIS strength ($rs = .23–.31$).

Tybur et al. (2015) tested this connection with several large US samples and found no direct relation between multiple measures of pathogen disgust and social conservatism. However, they found that sexual disgust and sociosexuality – an index of openness toward uncommitted sex – mediated the association between pathogen disgust and social conservatism, suggesting that people who are chronically concerned with pathogen threat tend to follow a monogamous sexual strategy, and these same people tend to hold socially conservative political ideologies.

The lack of a direct connection between conservatism and pathogen disgust seems to conflict with evidence implying that intergroup attitudes can function to reduce the pathogen exposure risk associated with novel outgroup members. Fincher and Thornhill (2012) have demonstrated that philopatry (i.e., staying put in a familiar environment), ingroup favoritism, and outgroup dislike may have all emerged as beliefs, behaviors, and cultural practices serving to reduce the threat of local pathogens. Their results are consistent with those presented by Schaller and Murray (2008), who find that historical levels of pathogen prevalence negatively correlate with more promiscuous sexual strategies, openness to experience, and extraversion. Why then does social conservatism in the United States fail to correlate with chronic concerns about infectious disease?

The tendency toward social exclusivity and outgroup avoidance characteristic of conservatism in the United States might serve as a pathogen avoidance strategy, but emergence of associations between conservatism and pathogen threat may depend on the existence and salience of those threats. For instance, the United States is only slightly above average in non-zoonotic pathogen prevalence according to Thornhill and Fincher's (2014) data on pathogen prevalence in 147 countries. Moreover, even if infectious pathogens are prevalent, this fact may escape notice. For example, both young and White Americans (who comprise most psychology samples) are the least likely to agree (23% and 27%, respectively) that the widely reported Zika virus was a major health threat in the United States (Rainie and Funk, 2016). However, some evidence suggests that salient pathogen threats can strengthen traits associated with US conservatism. One study found that, when cued with pathogen threat, the chronic concern germ concerns of US undergraduates negatively correlated with agreeableness and openness (Mortensen et al., 2010), personality traits which negatively correlate with political orientation and party identification (Hirsh et al., 2010). Additional studies on Canadian and US participants have found that disease salience leads to greater conformist attitudes and avoidance tendencies (Mortensen et al., 2010; Murray and Schaller, 2012). Finally, when participants felt protected from infectious disease, they reported lower levels of prejudice (Huang et al., 2011). Taken together, these data suggest that the link between chronic pathogen concern and traits comprising US political conservatism (i.e., social exclusivity, outgroup avoidance) may depend on salient infectious disease cues.

Morality

Lay thinking has often connected aspects of moral thinking to disease. Empirically, recent research in the domain of situated cognition uses the embodied experience of dirtiness/cleanliness as a bridge between morality and pathogen threat (e.g., Lee and Schwarz, 2011). For example, committing (or recalling) immoral acts makes the act of cleaning more mentally accessible and desirable (Zhong and Liljenquist, 2006), whereas exposure to physical dirtiness heightens the desire to punish immoral others (Schnall et al., 2008b). This connection is quite specific to actions that mitigate infection risk. Lee and Schwarz (2010) found that immoral acts committed verbally heighten preference for mouthwash, but immoral acts committed with the hands heighten preference for hand sanitizer. Engaging in physical cleaning behavior also interrupts the typical downstream consequences for moral perception, as would be expected given a conceptual overlap. Thus, hand washing leads people to feel less guilty about past transgressions (Zhong and Liljenquist, 2006) and can reduce condemnation toward immoral others (Schnall et al., 2008a). Such experimental findings make the case for mental associations between morality and pathogen threat.

However, a recent meta-analysis of the effect of disgust inductions on moral judgments (Landy and Goodwin, 2015), coupled with certain replication problems (e.g., Johnson et al., 2016), raise doubts about a clear path from disgust to moral judgments. As suggested earlier, disgust is grounded in the service of pathogen avoidance, and so its influence may be specific to pathogen-related moral content. Inbar and Pizarro (2014) also argue that the relationship between disgust and morality can be explained by a motivation to avoid pathogens: if objects, acts, and/or concepts are judged both immoral and disgusting, it is because they are heuristically associated with pathogens.

This connection is perhaps best observed with moral questions in two domains – sexual acts and food. Studies commonly find that people perceive immorality in behaviors such as having sex with relatives (e.g., Lieberman et al., 2003) and eating dog or human meat (Haidt et al., 1993; Russell and Giner-Sorolla, 2011). Disgust is also positively correlated with religious attitudes about sex and negatively correlated with attitudes toward groups that threaten traditional sexual morality (Crawford et al., 2014; Tybur et al., 2015). Despite such findings, research examining the influence of disgust on pathogen-specific moral issues is relatively rare. This leaves open the question of whether disgust is associated with moral thinking in a domain-general fashion, or whether this association relates primarily to pathogen threat management.

Mating

From the perspective of evolutionary biology, no set of problems is as central to human existence as those involved in mating (Maner and Ackerman, 2015). It is clear why – differential reproduction represents the primary end of the evolutionary game. A mating motive relates to a number of specific goals, from selecting to attracting to retaining romantic partners. Information about pathogen threats is relevant to each of these goals, and should influence the criteria people use to evaluate potential mates as well as the style of romantic relationships people attempt to form. Indeed, sexual reproduction owes its existence to the co-evolutionary interplay between organisms and pathogens (Brockhurst, 2011; Hamilton, 1980; Hamilton et al., 1990; Morran et al., 2011). In the following sections, we detail these influences on individual differences in romantic selectivity and sociosexuality.

Selectivity

Sexual recombination is only one piece of the mating puzzle. In the evasion of infection, not only is the ability to create novel combinations important, but so too are individual differences in sexual selectivity. In ecologies where infection is prevalent, organisms should prefer mates that have strong pathogen resistance. How do organisms solve the problem of identifying cues that reliably signal pathogen resistance? The parasite theory of sexual selection posits that animals indicate inherent pathogen resistance through sexual signaling and costly displays (Hamilton and Zuk, 1982; Jacobs and Zuk, 2010). Supporting this proposal, Hamilton and Zuk (1982) found that high regional incidence of disease was positively associated with brightness of feathers and complexity of male vocals across 109 species of birds. In a separate study, Møller (2002) found that male barn swallows with longer tails were less likely to be infested with mites. A male swallow's reproductive success was also positively associated with the length of his tail, and his offspring were more likely to be resistant to mites. This was true even when relocating the chicks to other nests to be parented by other swallows, ruling out the possibility females were trying to avoid the spread of mites from the male to the offspring. These studies provide support for the idea that sexual signaling is a proxy for information about a mate's 'good genes', or their resistance to parasites, and that this resistance is indeed heritable. Such studies further suggest that organisms should be particularly swayed by costly or sexual signals in areas that are high in pathogen prevalence.

The same is true for people as well. High levels of pathogens in the ecology should evoke increased sensitivity to traits that confer high mate value. For example, people may become more selective about who they are willing to mate with and qualities of those people, such as physical attractiveness (Sugiyama, 2005). To test these predictions, Gangestad and Buss (1993) analyzed data from 37 societies on the importance conferred to physical attractiveness in mates during the selection process. They found a strong positive relationship between pathogen prevalence and importance of attractiveness ratings across countries. In a reanalysis of the same dataset, these effects were replicated even when controlling for gender inequality (Gangestad et al., 2006). For both men and women, pathogen prevalence was positively correlated with a preference for attractive mates, as well as a preference for health and good genes. For men, pathogen prevalence was negatively correlated with age of mate, indicating a preference for younger mates, where youth likely signals health. For women, pathogen prevalence was positively correlated with a preference for status and intelligence, traits which are also often associated with genetic fitness

(Miller, 2001). Similarly, women's preferences for masculine faces were also greater in nations and states with higher levels of pathogen stress (DeBruine et al., 2012). Such findings indicate that mate seekers use more selective criteria in areas marked by greater dangers of infectious disease.

Patterns of influence on costly and sexual signals are also found at an individual level of analysis. High scores on trait pathogen disgust predict women's preferences for more masculine faces, voices, and bodies (Jones et al., 2013a) and men's preferences for more feminine shapes in women's faces (Jones et al., 2013b). Similarly, pathogen disgust predicts men's preferences for low waist-to-hip female ratios and women's preferences for high shoulder-to-hip male ratios (Lee et al., 2015). Perhaps even more directly indexing behavioral immune influences on selectivity, GA (as measured with the subscale of the PVD scale) positively correlates with preference for facial symmetry (Young et al., 2011).

Pathogen threat appears to play a role not only on general selectivity, but also on individual differences in trade-offs relevant to mate selectivity. As the threat of infection increases, women should value genetic quality over and above other investments from mates, leading to a stronger preference for mate attractiveness compared to other features commonly associated with female romantic preference, such as a mate's resources. In essence, females should trade-off male parental investment for male genetic fitness, or proxies of fitness such as attractiveness (Gangestad and Simpson, 2000). To study this trade-off, Lee and Zietsch (2011) randomly assigned female participants to complete either a questionnaire related to resource scarcity, a questionnaire containing the PVD scale, or an unrelated questionnaire as the control. Then, people were given a limited amount of 'mate dollars' which they could allocate to a set of five 'good-genes' or five 'good-parent' traits. Intelligence, creativity, muscularity, social level, and confidence were the traits reflective of good genes, whereas earning potential, commitment, warmth, kindness, and a nurturing personality were traits reflective of good parenting. When participants were cued by disease, they tended to value the traits that signaled good genes over those that signaled good parenting. In contrast, participants cued with resource scarcity showed the opposite pattern, presumably because good parenting involves resource provisioning. Thus, pathogen threat appears to be tied to increased selectivity for genetic quality more than other types of mate qualities.

Sociosexuality

Romantic selectivity is commonly studied in terms of the traits or resources a potential mate brings to the table, but it is also reflected in the romantic behaviors of individuals. Sociosexuality (and its corresponding trait measure, the Sociosexual Orientation Inventory [SOI]; Simpson and Gangestad, 1991) refers to selectivity in the willingness to engage in sexual and romantic commitment behaviors. An unrestricted sexual strategy, as indicated by high scores on the SOI, reflects a preference for short-term, uncommitted, and novel sexual relationships. A restricted sexual strategy indicates a preference for long-term romantic relationships in which commitment is required for sex to occur. These strategies are chronic in nature and thus signify individual differences. Pathogen threat plays an important role in expressions of sociosexuality such that greater pathogen prevalence is associated with more sexual restrictedness in populations (i.e., a decrease in willingness to pursue short-term relationships of low-commitment; Schaller and Murray, 2008; Thornhill et al., 2010).

Specifically, Schaller and Murray (2008) analyzed SOI scores from 48 regions around the world and found that higher levels of pathogens predicted lower SOI values, indicating greater sexual restrictedness. This pattern was primarily found in females. This sex difference may have emerged because women face relatively higher obligatory parental investment costs than do men, and women are commonly more risk-averse in general (Byrnes et al., 1999), thus they may be more sensitive to cues that signal increased costs associated with unrestricted sexual behavior, in this case, pathogen transmission. These data were later reanalyzed after breaking down pathogen prevalence by type (i.e., zoonotic, multi-host, and human-specific; Thornhill et al., 2010). In 45 of the 48 regions, the same pattern for sociosexuality was found, with levels of multi-host or human-specific pathogens predicting sexual restrictedness. However, no such relationship was found for zoonotic pathogens (e.g., parasites that infect animals). Thus, it appears that only parasites that infect humans elicit threats that impact sexual strategies.

For chronic measures of pathogen threat sensitivity, both subscales of the perceived vulnerability to disease scale (GA and PI) have been shown to correlate negatively with SOI scores (Duncan et al., 2009). In one study, people who scored high on trait-level aversion to germs also scored lower on unrestricted sexuality and reported wanting fewer future sexual partners, and this effect was strongest when situational indicators of disease threat were present (Murray et al., 2013). This effect was strongest among women, again suggesting that women have more to lose in employing a sexually unrestricted strategy (Schmitt, 2005). Examining affective measures, Al-Shawaf et al. (2015) found that SOI correlated negatively with scores on the sexual disgust subscale of the TDDS, but not with the moral disgust or the pathogen disgust subscales. This failure to find a connection between SOI and pathogen disgust may be due to how the pathogen disgust subscale was constructed. That is, the original authors of the TDDS wanted to measure orthogonal constructs so the pathogen disgust subscale contains almost no content related to mating, perhaps isolating sociosexuality from this measure. Nevertheless, across a variety of studies and countries, individual differences in mating preferences (here, as reflected by sexual restrictedness) appear to serve as functional solutions to the dangers associated with infectious disease threats.

FUTURE DIRECTIONS

The three fundamental motives just discussed – self-protection, affiliation, and mating – are central to most of the extant BIS research. There are also two other domains included within the fundamental motives framework (Kenrick et al., 2010) which may help categorize reactions to infectious disease threats but have not as yet received much empirical attention. Next, we describe several predictions associated with each of these motives. Following these, we identify additional unanswered questions about the issue of psychological defenses against disease, which we hope might stimulate additional research.

Status

The drive for power and prestige within social groups is a hallmark of all societies, and in fact, all group-living primates (Barkow, 1989; Brown, 1991; Fiske, 2010). Indeed, one of the primary dimensions on which people categorize ingroup members is dominant–submissive (Wiggins and Broughton, 1985). Virtually no research has examined the role of pathogen threat on mental processes involved in status perception and seeking behavior, although some suggestive cross-national work ties political structures to ecological pathogen exposure. As discussed in the section on political orientation, pathogen prevalence is correlated with the tendency for societies to employ authoritarian governments (Murray et al.,

2013; Thornhill et al., 2009). This suggests that people exposed to pathogen threats might prefer hierarchical systems where high status is held by a subset of group members rather than egalitarian social systems. If so, what kind of hierarchy might people prefer?

There are two pathways toward status (see Cheng and Tracy, 2014, for a review) – dominance and prestige. Dominance involves the procurement of status and rank through force, coercion, and intimidation. Dominant individuals essentially use fear to their advantage by threatening to withhold resources or physically harm someone else. This form of status is said to have evolved in response to conflict over resources or mates. In contrast, prestige is freely conferred deference or status granted to someone who is knowledgeable, skillful, or successful. Prestige relies on social learning, where there is a pressure to recognize and copy people who have skills and knowledge.

In attempting to link infectious disease threat responses to a status motive, prestige appears to be a promising pathway. If it is costly to acquire knowledge through direct experience (e.g., individual exploration and experimentation), then people should rely on cultural learning (e.g., the experiences of fellow group members; Henrich and McElreath, 2003). Prestige is a central cue to which people attend when seeking a person from which to learn (Henrich, 2015). Thus, in harsh ecologics characterized by high pathogen levels, people should be more likely to heed advice and copy behaviors of prestigious individuals in their groups. This suggests that skillful, successful, and knowledgeable people are more likely to gain status in pathogenic environments, and people should be particularly more willing to grant status to people in these environments by way of the prestige pathway. Alternately, dominance may be relatively more effective for certain pathogen-mitigating behaviors such as enforcing social norms and preventing contact with outgroup members.

Parenting

The study of how pathogen threats impact parenting will likely be a rich avenue for future research. From direct influences on child mortality, to social influences on decisions around vaccination, to quite indirect influences on the extent to which people invest in attachment relationships with children, pathogens have the potential to affect a wide range of behaviors. The existing work in this area focuses primarily on the role of ecological disease cues. As mentioned in the Individualism and Collectivism section of the chapter, such ecological cues are associated with stronger family ties. For example, in their cross-national analysis, Fincher and Thornhill (2012b) examined the link between parasite stress and familial beliefs, as measured in the World Values Survey (e.g., items concerning beliefs about the importance of family, parental love and connection, sacrifice for children, familial living situation). Pathogen stress correlated positively with family ties. That is, pathogen stress predicted the endorsement of unconditional love and respect for parents and of parents' duty to do their best for their children, as well as the importance of family, cohabitation with parents, and goals of making parents proud. These findings suggest that pathogen prevalence influences parents' investment in their children, but also children's investment in, and respect of, their parents. It is not clear whether this investment is characterized best by a supportive style of parenting or by an authoritative style, given that children are expressing unconditional respect.

In contrast to this positive association between pathogen prevalence and stronger family ties, the predictions made from a life history perspective seem, at first glance, to suggest different patterns of behavior. After all, life history theory predicts that ecological cues of mortality danger lead to the adoption of fast strategies, categorized partially by a decreased investment in parenting in favor of continued reproduction (Kaplan and

Gangestad, 2005). An explanation for this seeming inconsistency may lie in the intrinsic or extrinsic nature of disease threats. When the prevalence and severity of pathogens in an environment is high enough such that the threat becomes extrinsic (i.e., contact is unavoidable) and will likely produce serious consequences, a close family structure may yield few benefits. For example, a parent who invests copious time and energy into rearing a single child with a low chance of survival might garner a bigger genetic benefit from diverting that time and energy into further reproductive opportunities. Therefore, low investment in family members and offspring may become a better strategy in the face of extrinsic pathogen threat. Some evidence for this pattern exists. Quinlan (2007) analyzed a sample of 186 pre-industrial societies and found that, as pathogen stress increased, the time a mother spent nursing also increased. However, as pathogen stress became extreme, nursing duration decreased. Similarly, Thornhill and Fincher (2014a) found that an inverse curvilinear pattern provided the best fit for the relationship between pathogen stress and collectivism, such that, at extreme pathogen stress, nation-level scores on collectivism start to decrease. These findings suggest that, under extreme levels of pathogen threat, parenting styles may resemble those consistent with a fast life history strategy, with parents offering relatively little support and behaving in an insecurely attached manner with their children. As with our status motive discussion, these hypotheses are speculative and would benefit from further empirical investigation.

therefore shaped not only our bodies, but also our cultures, our behaviors, and the personalities we exhibit as individuals. Perhaps the most common, lay understanding of this influence involves experiences and individual differences related to disgust and anxiety, but research on psychological constructs such as the BIS demonstrate the complex and widespread means by which the mind responds to pathogen-related threats. Many of the personality traits we consider foundational, from extraversion to openness, owe aspects of their exhibition and action to our history of managing infectious disease. Looking ahead, the relative infancy of the literature on comprehensive approaches to pathogen management, such as the BIS, ensures that much more research remains to be done. For instance, virtually all of the empirical work on psychological responses to pathogen threat has focused on externally oriented behavior and cognitions. Yet, might perceptions of the self and other inwardly directed responses also be susceptible to infectious disease cues? Additionally, as methodological and analytical techniques advance, integration of psychological with physiological activity likely represents one of the most needed next steps in furthering our understanding of how and when pathogen management systems function. We expect that empirical and theoretical attention to these issues will represent a large part of future research on the consequences of pathogen threat. We also hope that the current discussion has provided a window into the vast psychological landscape originating from our interactions with organisms as minute as germs.

CONCLUSION

As one of the most significant dangers confronting humans over our history as a species, infectious disease has played a critical role as an evolutionary selection pressure. Adaptations that address this danger have

REFERENCES

Ackerman, J. M., Becker, D. V., Mortensen, C. R., Sasaki, T., Neuberg, S. L., & Kenrick, D. T. (2009). A pox on the mind: Disjunction of attention and memory in the processing of physical disfigurement. *Journal of Experimental Social Psychology, 45*, 478–485.

Ackerman, J. M., Huang, J. Y., & Bargh, J. A. (2012). Evolutionary perspectives on social cognition. In S. T. Fiske & C. N. Macrae (Eds.), *The SAGE handbook of social cognition* (pp. 451–473). Thousand Oaks, CA: Sage.

Ackerman, J. M., & Kenrick, D. T. (2008). The costs of benefits: Help-refusals highlight key trade-offs of social life. *Personality and Social Psychology Review, 12*, 118–140.

Ackerman, J. M., Tybur, J. M., & Mortensen, C. R. (2017). Infectious disease and imperfections of self-image. *Psychological Science.* Advance online publication. doi: 10.1177/0956797617733829.

Al-Shawaf, L., Lewis, D. M., & Buss, D. M. (2015). Disgust and mating strategy. *Evolution and Human Behavior, 36*, 199–205.

Barkow, J. H. (1989). The elastic between genes and culture. *Ethology and Sociobiology, 10*, 111–129.

Baumeister, R. F., & Leary, M. R. (1995). The need to belong: Desire for interpersonal attachments as a fundamental human motivation. *Psychological Bulletin, 117*, 497–529.

Beck, S., Geraghty, D., Inoko, H., & Rowen, L. (1999). Complete sequence and gene map of a human major histocompatibility complex. *Nature, 401*, 921–923.

Bond, R., & Smith, P. B. (1996). Culture and conformity: A meta-analysis of studies using Asch's (1952b, 1956) line judgment task. *Psychological Bulletin, 119*, 111–137.

Brockhurst, M. A. (2011). Sex, death, and the Red Queen. *Science, 333*, 166–167.

Brown, D. E. (1991). *Human universals* (p. 118). New York, NY: McGraw-Hill.

Byrnes, J. P., Miller, D. C., & Schafer, W. D. (1999). Gender differences in risk taking: A meta-analysis. *Psychological Bulletin, 125*, 367–383.

Caporael, L. R. (1997). The evolution of truly social cognition: The core configurations model. *Personality and Social Psychology Review, 1*, 276–298.

Cheng, J. T., & Tracy, J. L. (2014). Toward a unified science of hierarchy: Dominance and prestige are two fundamental pathways to human social rank. In J. T. Cheng, J. L. Tracy, & C. Anderson (Eds.), *The psychology of social status* (pp. 3–27). New York, NY: Springer.

Crawford, J. T., Inbar, Y., & Maloney, V. (2014). Disgust sensitivity selectively predicts attitudes toward groups that threaten (or uphold) traditional sexual morality. *Personality and Individual Differences, 70*, 218–223.

Curtis, V., de Barra, M., & Aunger, R. (2011). Disgust as an adaptive system for disease avoidance behaviour. *Philosophical Transactions of the Royal Society of London B: Biological Sciences, 366*, 389–401.

DeBruine, L. M., Jones, B. C., Tybur, J. M., Lieberman, D., & Griskevicius, V. (2010). Women's preferences for masculinity in male faces are predicted by pathogen disgust, but not by moral or sexual disgust. *Evolution and Human Behavior, 31*, 69–74.

DeBruine, L. M., Little, A. C., & Jones, B. C. (2012). Extending parasite-stress theory to variation in human mate preferences. *Behavioral and Brain Sciences, 35*, 86–87.

Diamond, J. (1997). *Guns, germs, and steel: The fates of human societies.* New York, NY: Norton.

Duncan, L. A., & Schaller, M. (2009). Prejudicial attitudes toward older adults may be exaggerated when people feel vulnerable to infectious disease: Evidence and implications. *Analyses of Social Issues and Public Policy, 9*, 97–115.

Duncan, L. A., Schaller, M., & Park, J. H. (2009). Perceived vulnerability to disease: Development and validation of a 15-item self-report instrument. *Personality and Individual Differences, 47*, 541–546.

Dweck, C. S., & Leggett, E. L. (1988). A social-cognitive approach to motivation and personality. *Psychological Review, 95*, 256–273.

Faulkner, J., Schaller, M., Park, J. H., & Duncan, L. A. (2004). Evolved disease-avoidance mechanisms and contemporary xenophobic attitudes. *Group Processes & Intergroup Relations, 7*, 333–353.

Fessler, D. M., Eng, S. J., & Navarrete, C. D. (2005). Elevated disgust sensitivity in the first trimester of pregnancy: Evidence supporting the compensatory prophylaxis hypothesis. *Evolution and Human Behavior, 26*, 344–351.

Fincher, C. L., & Thornhill, R. (2008). Assortative sociality, limited dispersal, infectious disease and the genesis of the global pattern of religion diversity. *Proceedings of the Royal*

Society of London B: Biological Sciences, 275, 2587–2594.

Fincher, C. L., & Thornhill, R. (2012a). Parasite-stress promotes in-group assortative sociality: The cases of strong family ties and heightened religiosity. Behavioral and Brain Sciences, 35, 61–79.

Fincher, C. L., & Thornhill, R. (2012b). The parasite-stress theory may be a general theory of culture and sociality. Behavioral and Brain Sciences, 35, 99–119.

Fincher, C. L., Thornhill, R., Murray, D. R., & Schaller, M. (2008). Pathogen prevalence predicts human cross-cultural variability in individualism/collectivism. Proceedings of the Royal Society of London B: Biological Sciences, 275, 1279–1285.

Fiske, S. T. (2010). Interpersonal stratification: Status, power, and subordination. In S. T. Fiske, D. T. Gilbert, & G. Lindzey (Eds.), Handbook of social psychology (pp. 941–982). Hoboken, NJ: Wiley.

Funder, D. C. (2006). Towards a resolution of the personality triad: Persons, situations, and behaviors. Journal of Research in Personality, 40, 21–34.

Gangestad, S. W., & Buss, D. M. (1993). Pathogen prevalence and human mate preferences. Ethology and Sociobiology, 14, 89–96.

Gangestad, S. W., Haselton, M. G., & Buss, D. M. (2006). Evolutionary foundations of cultural variation: Evoked culture and mate preferences. Psychological Inquiry, 17, 75–95.

Gangestad, S. W., & Simpson, J. A. (2000). The evolution of human mating: Trade-offs and strategic pluralism. Behavioral and Brain Sciences, 23, 573–587.

Gelfand, M. J., Bhawuk, D. P. S., Nishii, L. H., & Bechtold, D. J. (2004). Individualism and collectivism. In R. J. House, P. J. Hanges, M. Javidan, P. W. Dorfman, & V. Gupta (Eds.), Culture, leadership, and organizations: The GLOBE study of 62 societies (pp. 437–512). Thousand Oaks, CA: Sage.

Gelfand, M. J., Nishii, L. H., & Raver, J. L. (2006). On the nature and importance of cultural tightness-looseness. Journal of Applied Psychology, 91, 1225–1244.

Guernier, V., Hochberg, M. E., & Guégan, J. F. (2004). Ecology drives the worldwide distribution of human diseases. PLoS Biol, 2, e141.

Haidt, J., Koller, S. H., & Dias, M. G. (1993). Affect, culture, and morality, or is it wrong to eat your dog? Journal of Personality and Social Psychology, 65, 613–628.

Haidt, J., McCauley, C., & Rozin, P. (1994). Individual differences in sensitivity to disgust: A scale sampling seven domains of disgust elicitors. Personality and Individual Differences, 16, 701–713.

Hamilton, W. D. (1980). Sex versus non-sex versus parasite. Oikos, 35, 282–290.

Hamilton, W. D., Axelrod, R., & Tanese, R. (1990). Sexual reproduction as an adaptation to resist parasites (a review). Proceedings of the National Academy of Sciences, 87, 3566–3573.

Hamilton, W. D., & Zuk, M. (1982). Heritable true fitness and bright birds: A role for parasites? Science, 218, 384–387.

Haselton, M. G., & Nettle, D. (2006). The paranoid optimist: An integrative evolutionary model of cognitive biases. Personality and Social Psychology Review, 10, 47–66.

Henrich, J. (2015). Culture and social behavior. Current Opinion in Behavioral Sciences, 3, 84–89.

Henrich, J., & McElreath, R. (2003). The evolution of cultural evolution. Evolutionary Anthropology: Issues, News, and Reviews, 12, 123–135.

Hickie, I., Bennett, B., Lloyd, A., Heath, A., & Martin, N. (1999). Complex genetic and environmental relationships between psychological distress, fatigue and immune functioning: A twin study. Psychological Medicine, 29, 269–277.

Hirsh, J. B., DeYoung, C. G., Xu, X., & Peterson, J. B. (2010). Compassionate liberals and polite conservatives: Associations of agreeableness with political ideology and moral values. Personality and Social Psychology Bulletin, 36, 655–664.

Hofstede, G. H. (2001). Culture's consequences: Comparing values, behaviors, institutions, and organizations across nations. Atlanta, GA: Sage.

Huang, J. Y., Sedlovskaya, A., Ackerman, J. M., & Bargh, J. A. (2011). Immunizing against prejudice effects of disease protection on attitudes toward out-groups. Psychological Science, 22, 1550–1556.

Huang, J. Y., Williams, L. E., & Ackerman, J. A. (2016). Pathogen threat and openness to product innovation. Unpublished manuscript.

Inbar, Y., & Pizarro, D. (2014). Disgust, politics, and responses to threat. *Behavioral and Brain Sciences, 37*, 315–316.

Jacobs, A. & Zuk, M. (2010). Parasites and sexual selection. In M. D. Breed & J. Moore (Eds.), *Encyclopedia of animal behavior* (pp. 636–641). Oxford: Academic Press.

Japsen, B. (2012). *U.S. Workforce Illness Costs $576B Annually From Sick Days To Workers Compensation*. Retrieved from http://www.forbes.com/sites/brucejapsen/2012/09/12/u-s-workforce-illness-costs-576b-annually-from-sick-days-to-workers-compensation/ (accessed 27 March 2017).

John, O. P., & Srivastava, S. (1999). The big five trait taxonomy: History, measurement, and theoretical perspectives. In L. A. Pervin & O. P. John (Eds.), *Handbook of personality: Theory and research* (2nd ed., pp. 102–138). New York, NY: Guilford Press.

Johnson, D. J., Wortman, J., Cheung, F., Hein, M., Lucas, R. E., Donnellan, M. B., ... Narr, R. K. (2016). The effects of disgust on moral judgments testing moderators. *Social Psychological and Personality Science, 7*, 640–647.

Jones, B. C., Feinberg, D. R., Watkins, C. D., Fincher, C. L., Little, A. C., & DeBruine, L. M. (2013a). Pathogen disgust predicts women's preferences for masculinity in men's voices, faces, and bodies. *Behavioral Ecology, 24*, 373–379.

Jones, B. C., Fincher, C. L., Welling, L. L., Little, A. C., Feinberg, D. R., Watkins, C. D., ... DeBruine, L. M. (2013b). Salivary cortisol and pathogen disgust predict men's preferences for feminine shape cues in women's faces. *Biological Psychology, 92*, 233–240.

Kaplan, H. S., & Gangestad, S. W. (2005). Life history theory and evolutionary psychology. In D. M. Buss (Ed.), *The handbook of evolutionary psychology* (pp. 69–95). Hoboken, NJ: Wiley.

Kashima, E. S., & Kashima, Y. (1998). Culture and language: The case of cultural dimensions and personal pronoun use. *Journal of Cross-Cultural Psychology, 29*, 461–486.

Kelly, D. (2011). *Yuck! The nature and moral significance of disgust*. Cambridge, MA: MIT Press.

Kenrick, D. T., Li, N. P., & Butner, J. (2003). Dynamical evolutionary psychology: Individual decision rules and emergent social norms. *Psychological Review, 110*, 3–28.

Kenrick, D. T., Neuberg, S. L., Griskevicius, V., Becker, D. V., & Schaller, M. (2010). Goal-driven cognition and functional behavior: The fundamental-motives framework. *Current Directions in Psychological Science, 19*, 63–67.

Kurzban, R., & Leary, M. R. (2001). Evolutionary origins of stigmatization: The functions of social exclusion. *Psychological Bulletin, 127*, 187–208.

Landy, J. F., & Goodwin, G. P. (2015). Does incidental disgust amplify moral judgment? A meta-analytic review of experimental evidence. *Perspectives on Psychological Science, 10*, 518–536.

Lee, A. J., Brooks, R. C., Potter, K. J., & Zietsch, B. P. (2015). Pathogen disgust sensitivity and resource scarcity are associated with mate preference for different waist-to-hip ratios, shoulder-to-hip ratios, and body mass index. *Evolution and Human Behavior, 36*, 480–488.

Lee, A. J., & Zietsch, B. P. (2011). Experimental evidence that women's mate preferences are directly influenced by cues of pathogen prevalence and resource scarcity. *Biology Letters, 7*, 892–895.

Lee, S. W., & Schwarz, N. (2010). Dirty hands and dirty mouths: Embodiment of the moral-purity metaphor is specific to the motor modality involved in moral transgression. *Psychological Science, 21*, 1423–1425.

Lee, S. W., & Schwarz, N. (2011). Wiping the slate clean: Psychological consequences of physical cleansing. *Current Directions in Psychological Science, 20*, 307–311.

Lieberman, D., Tooby, J., & Cosmides, L. (2003). Does morality have a biological basis? An empirical test of the factors governing moral sentiments relating to incest. *Proceedings of the Royal Society of London B: Biological Sciences, 270*, 819–826.

Lieberman, D. L., Tybur, J. M., & Latner, J. D. (2012). Disgust sensitivity, obesity stigma, and gender: Contamination psychology predicts weight bias for women, not men. *Obesity, 20*, 1803–1814.

Lochmiller, R. L., & Deerenberg, C. (2000). Trade-offs in evolutionary immunology: Just what is the cost of immunity? *Oikos, 88*, 87–98.

Low, B. S. (1990). Marriage systems and pathogen stress in human societies. *American Zoologist, 30*, 325–340.

Lund, E. M., & Boggero, I. A. (2014). Sick in the head? Pathogen concerns bias implicit perceptions of mental illness. *Evolutionary Psychology, 12*, 706–718.

Lund, E. M., & Miller, S. L. (2014). Is obesity un-American? Disease concerns bias implicit perceptions of national identity. *Evolution and Human Behavior, 35*, 336–340.

Maner, J. K., & Ackerman, J. M. (2015). Sexually selective cognition. *Current Opinion in Psychology, 1*, 52–56.

Markus, H. R., & Kitayama, S. (1991). Culture and the self: Implications for cognition, emotion, and motivation. *Psychological Review, 98*, 224–253.

McDade, T. W. (2005). The ecologies of human immune function. *Annual Review of Anthropology, 34*, 495–521.

Miller, G. (2001). *The mating mind: How sexual choice shaped the evolution of human nature*. New York, NY: Anchor Books.

Miller, S. L., & Maner, J. K. (2011). Sick body, vigilant mind: The biological immune system activates the behavioral immune system. *Psychological Science, 22*, 1467–1471.

Miller, S. L., & Maner, J. K. (2012). Overperceiving disease cues: The basic cognition of the behavioral immune system. *Journal of Personality and Social Psychology, 102*, 1198–1213.

Møller, A. P. (2002). Temporal change in mite abundance and its effect on barn swallow reproduction and sexual selection. *Journal of Evolutionary Biology, 15*, 495–504.

Morran, L. T., Schmidt, O. G., Gelarden, I. A., Parrish, R. C., & Lively, C. M. (2011). Running with the Red Queen: Host-parasite coevolution selects for biparental sex. *Science, 333*, 216–218.

Mortensen, C. R., Becker, D. V., Ackerman, J. M., Neuberg, S. L., & Kenrick, D. T. (2010). Infection breeds reticence: The effects of disease salience on self-perceptions of personality and behavioral avoidance tendencies. *Psychological Science, 21*, 440–447.

Murray, D. R. (2014). Direct and indirect implications of pathogen prevalence for scientific and technological innovation. *Journal of Cross-Cultural Psychology, 45*, 971–985.

Murray, D. R., Jones, D. N., & Schaller, M. (2013). Perceived threat of infectious disease and its implications for sexual attitudes. *Personality and Individual Differences, 54*, 103–108.

Murray, D. R., & Schaller, M. (2012). Threat(s) and conformity deconstructed: Perceived threat of infectious disease and its implications for conformist attitudes and behavior. *European Journal of Social Psychology, 42*, 180–188.

Murray, D. R., Trudeau, R., & Schaller, M. (2011). On the origins of cultural differences in conformity: Four tests of the pathogen prevalence hypothesis. *Personality and Social Psychology Bulletin, 37*, 318–329.

Navarrete, C. D., & Fessler, D. M. (2006). Disease avoidance and ethnocentrism: The effects of disease vulnerability and disgust sensitivity on intergroup attitudes. *Evolution and Human Behavior, 27*, 270–282.

Navarrete, C. D., Fessler, D. M., & Eng, S. J. (2007). Elevated ethnocentrism in the first trimester of pregnancy. *Evolution and Human Behavior, 28*, 60–65.

Neel, R., Kenrick, D. T., White, A. E., & Neuberg, S. L. (2015). Individual differences in fundamental social motives. *Journal of Personality and Social Psychology, 110*, 887–907.

Nesse, R. M. (2005). Natural selection and the regulation of defenses: A signal detection analysis of the smoke detector principle. *Evolution and Human Behavior, 26*, 88–105.

Neuberg, S. L., Kenrick, D. T., & Schaller, M. (2011). Human threat management systems: Self-protection and disease avoidance. *Neuroscience & Biobehavioral Reviews, 35*, 1042–1051.

Nisbett, R. E., Peng, K., Choi, I., & Norenzayan, A. (2001). Culture and systems of thought: Holistic versus analytic cognition. *Psychological Review, 108*, 291–310.

Olatunji, B. O., Adams, T., Ciesielski, B., David, B., Sarawgi, S., & Broman-Fulks, J. (2012). The three domains of disgust scale factor structure, psychometric properties, and conceptual limitations. *Assessment, 19*, 205–225.

Olatunji, B. O., Lohr, J. M., Sawchuk, C. N., & Tolin, D. F. (2007). Multimodal assessment of disgust in contamination-related obsessive-compulsive disorder. *Behaviour Research and Therapy, 45*, 263–276.

Park, J. H., Faulkner, J., & Schaller, M. (2003). Evolved disease-avoidance processes and contemporary anti-social behavior: Prejudicial attitudes and avoidance of people with physical disabilities. *Journal of Nonverbal Behavior, 27*, 65–87.

Park, J. H., Schaller, M., & Crandall, C. S. (2007). Pathogen-avoidance mechanisms and the stigmatization of obese people. *Evolution and Human Behavior, 28*, 410–414.

Pirages, D. (2005). Containing infectious diseases. In Linda Starke (Ed.), *State of the World 2005: Redefining Global Security* (pp. 42–59). Washington DC: Worldwatch Institute, WRI.

Prokop, P., Ozel, M., Usak, M., & Senay, I. (2013). Disease-threat model explains acceptance of genetically modified products. *Psihologija, 46*, 229–243.

Quinlan, R. J. (2007). Human parental effort and environmental risk. *Proceedings of the Royal Society of London, Series B: Biological Sciences, 274*, 121–125.

Rainie, L., & Funk, C. (2016). Half of Americans say threats from infectious diseases are growing. *Pew Research Center*. Retrieved from http://assets.pewresearch.org/wp-content/uploads/sites/14/2016/07/PS_2016.07.07_Zika_FINAL.pdf (accessed 27 March 2017).

Round, J. L., & Mazmanian, S. K. (2009). The gut microbiota shapes intestinal immune responses during health and disease. *Nature Reviews Immunology, 9*, 313–323.

Rozin, P., & Haidt, J. (2013). The domains of disgust and their origins: Contrasting biological and cultural evolutionary accounts. *Trends in Cognitive Sciences, 17*, 367–368.

Rozin, P., Haidt, J., & McCauley, C. R. (2000). Disgust. In M. Lewis & J. M. Haviland-Jones (Eds.), *Handbook of emotions* (2nd ed., pp. 637–653). New York, NY: Guilford Press.

Russell, P. S., & Giner-Sorolla, R. (2011). Moral anger, but not moral disgust, responds to intentionality. *Emotion, 11*, 233–240.

Sacco, D. F., Young, S. G., & Hugenberg, K. (2014). Balancing competing motives: Adaptive trade-offs are necessary to satisfy disease avoidance and interpersonal affiliation goals. *Personality and Social Psychology Bulletin, 40*, 1611–1623.

Schaller, M. (2015). The behavioral immune system. In D. M. Buss (Ed.), *The handbook of evolutionary psychology* (2nd ed., pp. 206–224). Hoboken, NY: Wiley.

Schaller, M., Miller, G. E., Gervais, W. M., Yager, S., & Chen, E. (2010). Mere visual perception of other people's disease symptoms facilitates a more aggressive immune response. *Psychological Science, 21*, 649–652.

Schaller, M., & Murray, D. R. (2008). Pathogens, personality, and culture: Disease prevalence predicts worldwide variability in sociosexuality, extraversion, and openness to experience. *Journal of Personality and Social Psychology, 95*, 212–221.

Schaller, M., Murray, D. R., & Bangerter, A. (2015). Implications of the behavioural immune system for social behaviour and human health in the modern world. *Philosophical Transactions of the Royal Society B: Biological Sciences, 370*, 20140105.

Schaller, M., & Neuberg, S. L. (2012). Danger, disease, and the nature of prejudice(s). *Advances in Experimental Social Psychology, 46*, 1–54.

Schaller, M., & Park, J. H. (2011). The behavioral immune system (and why it matters). *Current Directions in Psychological Science, 20*, 99–103.

Schmitt, D. P. (2005). Sociosexuality from Argentina to Zimbabwe: A 48-nation study of sex, culture, and strategies of human mating. *Behavioral and Brain Sciences, 28*, 247–275.

Schnall, S., Benton, J., & Harvey, S. (2008a). With a clean conscience: Cleanliness reduces the severity of moral judgments. *Psychological Science, 19*, 1219–1222.

Schnall, S., Haidt, J., Clore, G. L., & Jordan, A. H. (2008b). Disgust as embodied moral judgment. *Personality and Social Psychology Bulletin, 34*, 1096–1109.

Sherman, P. W., & Billing, J. (1999). Darwinian gastronomy: Why we use spices: Spices taste good because they are good for us. *BioScience, 49*, 453–463.

Simpson, J. A., & Gangestad, S. W. (1991). Individual differences in sociosexuality: Evidence for convergent and discriminant validity. *Journal of Personality and Social Psychology, 60*, 870–883.

Simpson, J. A., Griskevicius, V., & Kim, J. S. (2011). Evolution, life history theory, and personality. In L. M. Horowitz & S. Strack (Eds.), *Handbook of interpersonal psychology: Theory,* research, assessment, and therapeutic interventions (pp. 75–89). New York, NY: Wiley.

Stevenson, R. J., Hodgson, D., Oaten, M. J., Barouei, J., & Case, T. I. (2011). The effect of disgust on oral immune function. *Psychophysiology, 48*, 900–907.

Sugiyama, L. S. (2005). Physical attractiveness in adaptationist perspective. In D. M. Buss (Ed.), *The handbook of evolutionary psychology* (pp. 292–343). New York: Wiley.

Suh, E., Diener, E., Oishi, S., & Triandis, H. C. (1998). The shifting basis of life satisfaction judgments across cultures: Emotions versus norms. *Journal of Personality and Social Psychology, 74*, 482–493.

Terrizzi, J. A., Shook, N. J., & McDaniel, M. A. (2013). The behavioral immune system and social conservatism: A meta-analysis. *Evolution and Human Behavior, 34*, 99–108.

Thornhill, R., & Fincher, C. L. (2014a). The parasite-stress theory of sociality, the behavioral immune system, and human social and cognitive uniqueness. *Evolutionary Behavioral Sciences, 8*, 257–264.

Thornhill, R., & Fincher, C. L. (2014b). *The parasite-stress theory of values and sociality: Infectious disease, history and human values worldwide*. New York, NY: Springer.

Thornhill, R., Fincher, C. L., & Aran, D. (2009). Parasites, democratization, and the liberalization of values across contemporary countries. *Biological Reviews, 84*, 113–131.

Thornhill, R., Fincher, C. L., Murray, D. R., & Schaller, M. (2010). Zoonotic and non-zoonotic diseases in relation to human personality and societal values: Support for the parasite-stress model. *Evolutionary Psychology, 8*, 151–169.

Triandis, H. C. (1995). *Individualism and collectivism*. Boulder, CO: Westview Press.

Tybur, J. M., Bryan, A. D., Magnan, R. E., & Hooper, A. E. C. (2011). Smells like safe sex: Olfactory pathogen primes increase intentions to use condoms. *Psychological Science, 22*, 478–480.

Tybur, J. M., & de Vries, R. E. (2013). Disgust sensitivity and the HEXACO model of personality. *Personality and Individual Differences, 55*, 660–665.

Tybur, J. M., Frankenhuis, W. E., & Pollet, T. V. (2014). Behavioral immune system methods: Surveying the present to shape the future. *Evolutionary Behavioral Sciences, 8*, 274–283.

Tybur, J. M., Inbar, Y., Güler, E., & Molho, C. (2015). Is the relationship between pathogen avoidance and ideological conservatism explained by sexual strategies? *Evolution and Human Behavior, 36*, 489–497.

Tybur, J. M., & Lieberman, D. (2016). Human pathogen avoidance adaptations. *Current Opinion in Psychology, 7*, 6–11.

Tybur, J. M., Lieberman, D., & Griskevicius, V. (2009). Microbes, mating, and morality: Individual differences in three functional domains of disgust. *Journal of Personality and Social Psychology, 97*, 103–122.

Tybur, J. M., Lieberman, D., Kurzban, R., & DeScioli, P. (2013). Disgust: Evolved function and structure. *Psychological Review, 120*, 65–84.

Uskul, A. K., Kitayama, S., & Nisbett, R. E. (2008). Ecocultural basis of cognition: Farmers and fishermen are more holistic than herders. *Proceedings of the National Academy of Sciences, 105*, 8552–8556.

van der Sluijs, K. F., van Elden, L. J. R., Nijhuis, M., Schuurman, R., Pater, J. M., Florquin, S., ... van der Poll, T. (2004). IL-10 is an important mediator of the enhanced susceptibility to pneumococcal pneumonia after influenza infection. *Journal of Immunology, 172*, 7603–7609.

White, A. E., Kenrick, D. T., & Neuberg, S. L. (2013). Beauty at the ballot box: Disease threats predict preferences for physically attractive leaders. *Psychological Science, 24*, 2429–2436.

Wiggins, J. S., & Broughton, R. (1985). The interpersonal circle: A structural model for the integration of personality research. *Perspectives in Personality, 1*, 1–47.

Woody, S. R., & Tolin, D. F. (2002). The relationship between disgust sensitivity and avoidant behavior: Studies of clinical and nonclinical samples. *Journal of Anxiety Disorders, 16*, 543–559.

Young, S. G., Sacco, D. F., & Hugenberg, K. (2011). Vulnerability to disease is associated with a domain-specific preference for symmetrical faces relative to symmetrical nonface stimuli. *European Journal of Social Psychology, 41*, 558–563.

Zhong, C. B., & Liljenquist, K. (2006). Washing away your sins: Threatened morality and physical cleansing. *Science, 313*, 1451–1452.

Sex Ratio Influences on Personality and Individual Differences

Daniel J. Kruger

Recognition of the importance of the sex ratio dates back at least to Darwin (1871), who deduced that a species' sex ratio was usually nearly balanced between males and females. Because each offspring has one mother and one father, on average males and females in a population will have equivalent reproductive success. If there are more females in a population than males, the daughters' average reproductive success will be lower, and selection will favor the production of sons. A stable equilibrium is generated on an evolutionary timescale through the advantageous production of the scarcer sex. Darwin's (1871) description of influential factors would later appear as components in the formal mathematical models of Düsing (1884) and Fisher (1930).

The numerical equilibrium of males and females occurs on an evolutionary timescale, so some human populations will exhibit imbalanced sex ratios (Darwin, 1871). Following the economic patterns of supply and demand, the rare sex is more valuable in the mating market (Fisher, 1930). Because females and males have somewhat divergent reproductive strategies, imbalances in the sex ratio have differential effects consistent with the strategies of each sex. Females are the limiting factor in reproduction in most animal and all mammalian species because they provide almost all of the physiological resources required for offspring production. Because of the larger necessary investment required for females, females have much lower potential reproductive capacities than males. Thus, females are more discriminating in selecting mates and males expend comparatively more effort in acquiring and retaining mates in most animal, and all mammalian, species (Trivers, 1972).

Emlen and Oring (1977) originally defined the Operational Sex Ratio (OSR) as the number of sexually active males per 100 sexually receptive females in a population. An OSR of 100 represents a sex ratio with balanced proportions of males and females. An OSR below 100 is considered a low sex ratio, representing a female-biased population (i.e., more available females than males). An OSR above 100 is considered a high sex ratio, representing a male-biased population (i.e., more available males than females). Researchers have operationally defined the human OSR in terms of raw population counts (e.g., Barber, 2000) and as the ratio of unmarried adult men to unmarried adult women (e.g., Kruger et al., 2010).

SEX RATIOS DRIVE INDIVIDUAL DIFFERENCES ACROSS THE ANIMAL KINGDOM

Understanding patterns of behavior across species helps inform our understanding of behavioral patterns in our own species (Tinbergen, 1963). Humans are part of the natural world and, despite our complex cultures and technological capacities, we share an evolutionary heritage with our distant relatives. The sex ratio influences individual differences in reproductive behaviors and behaviors related to reproduction across species from insects to mammals, including katydids, pipefish, frogs, squirrels, macaques, chimpanzees, and humans (Berglund, 1994; Elmberg, 1990; Emlen and Oring, 1977; Gwynne, 1990; Kvarnemo and Ahnesjö, 1996; Michener and McLean, 1996; Mitani et al., 1996; Symington, 1987; Takahashi, 2001; Valero et al., 2006). The common theme is greater leverage for the rare sex when the sex ratio is substantially imbalanced. Both observational and experimental research demonstrate higher male–male competition when the sex ratio is more male-biased and higher female–female competition when the sex ratio is more female-biased (e.g., Gwynne, 1991; Mills and Reynolds, 2003).

Experiments with katydids (bush crickets) demonstrate that sex ratio imbalances make both males and females more selective in choosing mating partners when their own sex is scarce. Females are more likely to reject potential male mates when there are fewer sexually active females in the local environment, and males are more likely to reject potential female mates when there are fewer sexually active males nearby (Gwynne and Simmons, 1990). The coreid bug is a monogamous insect species in which females glue their eggs to the backs of conspecifics, as insect eggs are vulnerable to predation and the resulting mobility and passive guarding reduces the risk of predation. Ordinarily, females are not selective of the individuals hosting their eggs; however, when researchers induced a male-biased sex ratio, females were more likely to glue their eggs to the backs of their mates who actually fertilized the eggs (Kaitala and Miettinen, 1997). Carrying such eggs represents a form of paternal investment and may also interfere with male attempts to pursue extra-pair mates.

The two-spotted goby is a small fish living in the brackish waters of the eastern Atlantic Ocean. During the summer mating season, males become territorial and create nests under stones in the sand on the seafloor. After attracting a female and fertilizing her eggs, the male guards the eggs until they hatch. The sex ratio gradually transitions from female-biased to male-biased across the summer mating season, with increasing male–male competition and decreasing female–female competition (Forsgren et al., 2004). Snapping shrimp are also socially monogamous and territorial; however, male and female pairs establish a common habitat and defend it together. When experimenters induced a heavily female-biased local sex ratio, males were more likely to abandon their female mates and their commonly established territories (Mathews, 2002). Female-biased sex ratios are also detrimental to monogamous behavior in other aquatic animals, such as the Kentish plover (Székely et al., 1999) and rainbow cichlid (Keenleyside, 1983).

Male *Panorpa* scorpionflies have two distinct mating strategies: attracting female mating partners by offering a dead insect as a nutritional gift and coercive copulation where males hold the wings of females and do not provide any gift. Nutritional gifts are a form of paternal investment that helps ensure the production of viable offspring; however, prey insects are limited and hunting exposes males to the threat of predation themselves. Thus, each strategy has costs and benefits for males. When the sex ratio is more male-biased, male–male competition is intensified and prey insects are more difficult to acquire. In these male-biased environments, males are more likely to use the forced-copulation strategy (Thornhill, 1980).

The Syngnathidae family of pipefish, seahorses, and seadragons are remarkable for their post-gametic reversal of sexual roles. Males have brood pouches that receive the eggs of female mates and fertilize them internally, carrying them for several weeks until they hatch and are born swimming freely. In these and a few other animal species, males make a greater parental contribution than females, females have greater intrasexual competition for partners than do males and also have brighter coloration (Berglund and Rosenqvist, 2003). Although the local pipefish sex ratio is often female-biased for most of the mating season, pipefish males predominantly engage in monogamous behavior. Unmated pipefish females often attempt to poach male partners from mated females, and though the males are not necessarily unreceptive, mated females are vigilant of mate-poaching attempts and will disrupt them (Matsumoto and Yanagisawa, 2001).

Sex ratios are also associated with patterns of reproductive dynamics in non-human primates. As sex ratios become increasingly male-biased, males compete more intensely for fewer females. Both male body size and sexual size dimorphism increase; being larger and stronger enhances competitive abilities, consistent with greater levels of conflict among males (Mitani et al., 1996). Spider monkeys generally have a strongly female-biased population (Chapman et al., 1989; Symington, 1987; Valero et al., 2006); however, the OSR for one wild spider monkey population in the Yucatan increased from 58.8 in 2000 to 100 in 2002 (mostly due to females becoming pregnant). This dramatic shift from a strongly female-biased OSR to a balanced one led to a decrease in male selective power. This was associated with increased male competition for preferred mates, including the first documented incidence of intragroup coalitional aggression leading to a fatality (Valero et al., 2006).

Across primate societies, high-ranking males have the most opportunities to mate with highly fecund females. However, when the sex ratio is female-biased, lower-ranking males have greater mating opportunities than they would if the sex ratio is balanced or male-biased. In rhesus macaques, for example, dominant males are able to control females and ward off competitors when females are scarce or the sex ratio is balanced, but when females outnumber males, it becomes more difficult for the dominant males to monitor all of the fecund females (Berard et al., 1993). When females are plentiful, it is easier for them to elude the dominant male and mate surreptitiously with other males, decreasing the impact that a male's social rank will have on his reproductive success (Berard et al., 1993).

Many Rhesus macaques join troops. Troop membership enhances a male macaque's reproductive potential when the OSR is equal or male-biased, as troop males are better able to protect their reproductively viable females from non-troop males (Takahashi, 2001). However, when the OSR becomes female-biased, non-troop males are able to infiltrate troops and mate with females because there are too many reproductively capable females for troop males to simultaneously guard (Takahashi, 2001).

The availability of fertile females over time in a specific environment will also influence male intrasexual competition and sexual size dimorphism, as non-human female primates can only reproduce while in estrous (Ims, 1988; Mitani et al., 1996). If the females in an environment enter estrous at different times, there are fewer females to mate with at one time – increasing the sex ratio of the spatial distribution of primates – but, ultimately, there will be more mating opportunities for males over time (when some females' estrous cycles end, other females' estrous cycles are beginning) – decreasing the sex ratio of the temporal distribution of reproductively viable primates and allowing continuous mating opportunities for males (Ims, 1988).

The length of birth intervals also influences the effective OSR. As the amount of time increases between births, fewer fecund females are available at any one time, shifting the OSR toward male bias. A population OSR of 50 will have differential effects on male intrasexual competition in baboons and gorillas because gorillas have a longer birth interval (Clutton-Brock et al., 1977). Baboon females reproduce once every two years and female gorillas reproduce once every three to four years (Mitani et al., 1996). The effective OSR increases with the length of birth intervals, leading to greater competition among males for fertile females.

The duration of maternal care can have a similar influence on the OSR as the expenditure of time and resources decreases the mother's time for reproduction. Chimpanzee infants do not travel out of their mothers' sight until the age of five to six years (Lawick-Goodall, 1967). During this time, the mother cares for her offspring. If a female chimpanzee's infant dies, she does not wait nearly as long to reproduce again than if her offspring survives (Nishida et al., 1990), so higher infant mortality rates will contribute to creating and maintaining a female-biased OSR.

SEX RATIO AND INDIVIDUAL DIFFERENCES IN HUMANS

Preferences that men and women express when evaluating potential partners for romantic relationships reflect the differential roles and contributions made by men and women in successful reproduction (Buss, 1989).

When the sex ratio is imbalanced in a human population, the less numerous sex has increased leverage in intersexual relationship dynamics. Because men and women have somewhat divergent reproductive strategies, there will be contrasting consequences for male-biased and female-biased human sex ratios. Women and men actively seek the resources related to reproductive value which men and women provide in reproductive relationships (Kruger, 2008). The attributes of what each sex offers as enticements and requires of partners for relationships will shift based on the leverage conferred by numerical scarcity.

Both women and men share preferences for partner characteristics such as kindness, understanding, and intelligence (Buss, 1989; Kenrick and Simpson, 1997); however, male and female preferences also show divergence following reproductively relevant attributes. Women provide physiological investment and men typically provide substantial material resource investment. Men seek women with cues of fecundity, the physiological potential for bearing offspring, whereas women prefer men with the ability and willingness to commit to long-term relationships and provide substantial paternal investment (Buss, 1989). Although the parental investment provided by women is typically higher than that provided by men, male parental investment is still much larger in humans than in other primates (Buss and Schmitt, 1993; Geary and Flinn, 2001). Children in families without a father present suffer higher mortality rates (Hill and Hurtado, 1996), and the level of paternal investment in offspring may enhance the offspring's reproductive success (Geary, 2005). Men with higher social status and greater resource control have higher reproductive success across a wide variety of societies (Hopcroft, 2006).

Women attract partners through signals of fecundity and suggestions of sexual access. Men attract partners through signals of potential commitment to long-term relationships and resource provisioning. The economics of numerical supply and demand influence the levels of attributes each sex offers in order to attract partners, as well as what individuals can demand (*ceteris paribus*) from prospective mates. Because the reproductive strategies of men and women are somewhat divergent, imbalances in the sex ratio exhibit directional effects consistent with the strategies of each sex. These patterns have been demonstrated in pre-industrial human populations (Lummaa et al., 1998).

Female-Biased Sex Ratios Increase Female Intrasexual Competition

In female-biased populations, women need to compete more intensely for male partners. The forms of competition reflect attributes related to female mate value that men seek in partners: fecundity and sexual availability (Cunningham, 1986; Tesser and Martin, 1996). Sexuality and fecundity are emphasized in fashion trends for revealing clothing, such as shorter skirt lengths (Barber, 1999; Time Out New York, 2007). Women are more self-conscious about their physical appearance and the appearance of other women. Women wear revealing clothing, derogate other women who are wearing revealing clothing, and may even derogate other women for wearing the same fashions that they display themselves (Guttentag and Secord, 1983; Time Out New York, 2007).

Female-Biased Sex Ratios Destabilize Male Commitment Investment

When women are more numerous than men, men have less incentive to provide relationship commitment and paternal investment (Pedersen, 1991). Female-biased sex ratios are associated with a destabilization and devaluation of marriage, as indicated by higher divorce rates, more out-of-wedlock births and single mother households, and lower paternal investment (Guttentag and Secord, 1983; Trent and South, 1989). Across nations, greater proportions of females are associated with more promiscuous mating strategies (Schmitt, 2005). In the nation of Colombia, areas with high male mortality rates result in a relative abundance of women, lower marital rates, and a greater proportion of men with multiple concurrent partners (Jones and Ferguson, 2006). In the post-World War II German state of Bavaria, variation in the magnitude of war-induced scarcity of men predicted rates of out-of-wedlock fertility. Both areas with fewer resident men and areas with lower expected future levels of men had higher non-marital fertility (Bethmann and Kvasnicka, 2013). Areas with greater proportions of men missing because they were prisoners of war, rather than casualties and thus possible to return, had lower rates of out-of-wedlock fertility, indicating that women may have considered their future mating prospects in their reproductive decision making.

In early adulthood, men in modern female-biased populations have less incentive to shift effort toward committed relationships due to ample mating opportunities (Gangestad and Simpson, 2000). Male reproductive success will benefit from multiple partnerships because even a brief sexual affair may increase the number of a man's descendants. Young men in low sex ratio populations are less likely to be married than their peers in less female-biased populations (Kruger and Schlemmer, 2009). Women have less selective power and exhibit lower thresholds for male commitment in order to have sexual relations, as indicated by higher rates of teenage pregnancies (Barber, 2000). Sociologists note that it is more difficult for women to get married when there is a relative shortage of men (Lichter et al., 1992). Women tend to marry at significantly later ages in female-biased metropolitan areas (Kruger et al., 2010). Women are also more likely to marry men of low socio-economic status (SES) in female-biased populations (Lichter et al., 1995).

Life History Theory (LHT) can be used to help clarify relationships between the sex ratio and behavioral and physiological patterns. LHT models life cycles and life history traits in an ecological context (Chisholm, 1999), integrating evolutionary, ecological, and socio-developmental perspectives in the study of sex differences in developmental patterns (Geary, 2002). LHT illustrates how organisms must make trade-offs in the allocation of resources between somatic effort and reproductive effort, mating effort and parenting effort, and offspring quantity versus quality (for more detailed discussion, see Roff, 1992; Stearns, 1992). LHT can also be used to predict and illustrate how the optimal degree of a trade-off varies based on social and ecological conditions.

Female-biased sex ratios are associated with higher birth rates among young women in the poorest areas, yet higher birth rates among older women in the richest areas. Adverse conditions of high female–female competition may induce disadvantaged women to adopt a riskier fast life history strategy and give birth early, whereas women with greater resource access may delay reproduction in a slower, high-investment strategy (Chipman and Morrison, 2013). Rates of infant prematurity and low birth weight are higher in female-biased populations, even when accounting for socio-demographic factors known to predict birth outcomes such as race, income, and educational attainment (Kruger et al., 2013). The proportion of single mother-headed households, a demographic indicator of paternal investment, partially mediates these relationships (Kruger et al., 2013).

Males in technologically advanced societies shift their resource allocation from mating effort to paternal effort across adulthood. Indicators of this life history pattern include declines in androgen levels (Baker and Hudson, 1983), fertility levels (Tuljapurkar et al., 2007), and mortality rates from risky behaviors (Kruger and Nesse, 2006), beginning in the third decade of life. The shift in male life history effort may occur as a response to diminishing returns from mating effort. Also in the third decade of life, there is an increasing tendency for men to use their market scarcity for establishing marital relationships (Kruger and Schlemmer, 2009).

The returns from a high mating effort strategy may decline with male age because of the observable physiological correlates of senescence. When male commitment and resource investment are unreliable, the reproductive benefits of sexual relationships for women may be genes that promote health and attractiveness to the opposite sex in the developmental environment. Female preferences for phenotypic signals of genetic quality are especially strong when selecting partners for short-term relationships (Kruger, 2006; Kruger et al., 2003), and these signals may be especially important when the likelihood of paternal investment is relatively low (Gangestad and Simpson, 2000). Male ability to signal genetic quality through phenotypic features declines with age. As adult men age, they increasingly shift from short-term mating to long-term mating, and with this shift, different characteristics become more salient. Masculinity and physical prowess become more trivial while fidelity, potential care for offspring, and SES become more important (Buss, 1989; Pollet and Nettle, 2007). Younger men were usually the fathers of offspring from extra-pair sexual affairs among Ache foragers, whereas older men tended to produce most of their offspring within long-term relationships (Hill and Hurtado, 1996).

Male-Biased Sex Ratios Increase Male Intrasexual Competition

Men compete for female partners through resource acquisition and signals of willingness to commit to long-term relationships and provide resources for offspring. When women are scarce, there will be more competition among men with regards to signals of relationship commitment and paternal investment

(Pedersen, 1991). Men who have lower social status and less abundant resources will have an especially difficult time getting married (Pollet and Nettle, 2007).

Men compete directly for reproductive partners, as well as for the social status and resource control that enable them to better attract and retain partners. Men who succeed in these competitions will have more offspring, and this will select for traits that enhance reproductive success (Daly and Wilson, 1978). Male physiological and behavioral strategies are both riskier than those of females on average (Kruger and Nesse, 2006). Because these strategies have historically produced sufficient reproductive benefits for some proportion of men, they have been maintained in the population even if they produce largely adverse effects for many individuals (Wilson and Daly, 1997). Across cultures, men have higher mortality rates than women from behavioral and most (often behaviorally mediated) internal causes of death (Kruger and Nesse, 2004, 2006).

Interpersonal violence, including lethal aggression, is one component of human male mating competition. This includes both conflicts among individual and allied males within groups and conflicts between the men of two or more groups (Chagnon, 1992). Violence may be part of competition over access to and control of resources, as well as attempts to advance or maintain position in the status hierarchy (Buss and Shackelford, 1997). Although violence is seen as an adverse issue for public health in modern societies, men have successfully used violence across many cultures to elevate their social status and gain respect from others (Campbell, 1993; Chagnon, 1992; Hill and Hurtado, 1996). Higher male mortality rates also arise from greater non-violent risk taking, leading to higher numbers of accidents, especially in young adulthood when males are entering into mating competition (Kruger and Nesse, 2004, 2006). Because of the greater degree of male mating competition in male-biased populations, the sex differences in contemporary mortality rates are larger than in more balanced or female-biased metropolitan areas across the United States, following from the intensification of risky strategies (Kruger and Nesse, 2009). The local sex ratio at sexual maturity was also associated with mortality patterns among 1957 high school graduates across the state of Wisconsin, such that the proportion of males in a high school class was directly associated with mortality risk for men but had no relationship to mortality risk for women (Jin et al., 2010). The state-level sex ratio for men and women of typical marriage ages (18–27 and 15–24, respectively) at sexual maturity was associated with increased mortality risk for the 12.7 million American men enrolled in Medicare from 1993 to 2001 (Jin et al., 2010).

Male-Biased Sex Ratios Increase Paternal Investment

The economics of numerical supply and demand influences what individuals can demand from prospective mates. As the sex ratio becomes increasingly male-biased, males compete more intensely for fewer females. The enhanced power of female choice raises the quality of valued male attributes necessary for securing female partners. Women will expect husbands to be of relatively higher social status, be kind, loving, and generous, and share the responsibilities of parental care (Guttentag and Secord, 1983). There is more competition among men in signals of relationship commitment and paternal investment (Pedersen, 1991). In high sex ratio populations, men will tend to offer more in a relationship, invest more time to wooing, be more romantic in dyadic interactions, and attempt to demonstrate more investment potential (Guttentag and Secord, 1983). When women are scarce, they are able to secure male commitment earlier and tend to marry at younger ages (Kruger et al., 2010). Many men also marry younger as they have more motivation to secure a prospective partner before another male retains her. However, many other men need to acquire greater social status and resources to be considered marriageable. Men with lower social status and fewer resources have an especially difficult time getting married (Pollet and Nettle, 2007). Thus, the variance in male marital age increases as the population becomes increasingly male-biased (Kruger et al., 2010).

Women in high sex ratio societies can make sexual access a scarce commodity and thus enhance their value in the marriage market (Guttentag and Secord, 1983). Although the sexual revolution has changed sexual dynamics in modern Western nations, men have historically preferred chastity in a potential spouse across many cultures, presumably because this assures men that their paternal investment will be supporting their own offspring (Barber, 2000). Both men and women report being less willing to engage in uncommitted sexual relationships in areas where women are scarce (Kandrik et al., 2015).

Male-Biased Sex Ratios Increase Constraints on Women's Sexuality

As women are the primary physiological engines of reproduction, they perform a vital role, which is valued by both their families and prospective male partners. The economics of supply and demand still give greater leverage and bargaining power to women when they are scarce; however, men will also use their social power to constrain female advantages, especially in societies where greater male social power is legally enshrined. The tendencies of families to treat women as a valuable resource and enforce practices to guard their virginity and reproductive output are intensified when women are scarce in the population compared to men. The stresses on sexual morality will be especially directed toward women (Guttentag and Secord, 1983). Some cultural practices in male-biased societies are quite extreme, such as sequestering women in their homes (for high-caste women in India) and surgical infibulations to physically prevent them from having sex (in the Sudan and other parts of Africa; Daly and Wilson, 1978).

Men in male-biased populations may also increase enforcement of social norms that favor stability in existing relationships, creating constraints through male social power, devaluing promiscuity in women so as to reduce the perceived alternatives for their female partners. Women will be loved, respected, protected, admired, and cherished, but only within a narrowly defined traditional role that limits their ability to take advantage of their market scarcity (Guttentag and Secord, 1983). Male-biased sex ratios result in emphasis on traditional sex roles, but women will experience more power and control when they can choose their own marriage partners (Guttentag and Secord, 1983).

Polygyny and the Effective Population Sex Ratio

Most mammalian species are polygynyous, where one male has several female mates and male reproductive success is more highly skewed. This is likely due to the high degree of female parental investment, including breastfeeding, and male specialization in mating effort (Low, 2003, 2007; Reichard and Boesch, 2003). In highly polygynous species, a few males will have many offspring while many others will have none, creating powerful selection pressure for traits that lead to success in mating competition at the expense of longevity (Plavcan, 2000).

Humans are far less polygynous than most other primates, but the variation in male reproductive success is still substantially higher than that for females, and thus male mating competition has been a potent selection force (Betzig, 1986). Polygyny occurs in the vast majority of cultures (84%) documented by anthropologists, and the degree of polygyny corresponds with factors such as high male mortality in war and high pathogen stress (Ember et al., 2007).

The greater the extent to which elite males are able to retain multiple female partners, the higher the effective sex ratio will be. A population with a numerical balance of reproductive aged men and women may have an effectively male-biased sex ratio if some men are able to monopolize multiple female partners (Hendrix, 1996). For every woman who is polygynously mated, there is one less woman available to other men. The degree of polygyny influences the intensity of male mating competition, and the degree to which male mortality rates are elevated above those for females directly follows from the degree of polygyny across societies (Kruger, 2010). The degree of polygyny will constrain the effects of relative female surplus, as well as accentuate male competition in balanced or male-biased populations.

Sex Ratios in the Laboratory

Although laboratory-based priming studies should be interpreted with caution, there have been several reported findings relevant to risk taking and reproductive strategies. In these studies, participants were shown contrived articles reporting trends for male-biased or female-biased college campuses, or were shown arrays of facial profiles with high or low sex ratios. Presenting cues of male-biased sex ratios was associated with greater male intentions to save less money, take on debt to obtain immediate resources (Griskevicius et al., 2012), and concentrate investment in high-risk/high-return options rather than diversify allocations (Ackerman et al., 2016). When women were presented cues of female-biased sex ratios, they had lower expectations of finding a suitable mate and reported stronger intentions to pursue a career path rather than raise a family (Durante et al., 2012). Both female and male participants viewing a series of facial images would exert more effort in a keyboard task to view attractive opposite-sex faces when an unfavorable sex ratio suggested higher competition for mates (Hahn et al., 2014).

SEX RATIOS IN HUMAN HISTORY

Guttentag and Secord (1983) extensively documented social phenomena associated with imbalanced sex ratios throughout history. Guttentag was initially inspired by the shift in personalities of male characters in the American popular media during the mid twentieth century. From the 1930s to the 1950s, male protagonists spoke about making life-long commitments and considerable investments in their partners. Prior to the Second World War, the OSR in the United States was always higher than 100, due to the greater immigration of males. The sex ratio declined from 1910 to 1970, passing equity in the early 1940s. The male characters of the 1960s and 1970s – a period characterized by female-biased sex ratios – expressed 'love 'em and leave 'em' attitudes, in contrast to their pop culture predecessors (Guttentag and Secord, 1983).

Guttentag and Secord (1983) actively avoided attributing behavioral and social patterns to ultimate or evolutionary causes, yet their descriptions are remarkably consistent with an evolutionary explanatory framework. Because of the post Second World War 'baby boom' in the United States, the population bulge created sex ratio imbalances due to sex differences in average marital age, coinciding with increasing divorce rates and other changes in the socio-political climate that lasted until the 1980s (Pedersen, 1991). Guttentag and Secord (1983) believed that female-biased sex ratios result in powerless women who are treated as sex objects and predicted that the proportion of father-absent, female-headed households would rise dramatically in these female-biased populations. Under these conditions, men could more easily achieve serial, or even simultaneous, polygyny. Interest in feminism and women's rights may increase, as women attempt to change the balance of power between the sexes and establish their independence.

Pre-literate societies with high sex ratios allowed husbands to beat or kill their wives for infidelity. Male power was related to physical strength and prowess as a warrior, women were unable to use their market scarcity to their advantage and were instead treated as chattel. The British colonizers had suppressed the traditional social structures of the Bakweri in Cameroon, West Africa. The Bakweri had a high sex ratio in the 1950s because of the constant migration of men from other areas for plantation labor. The British protectorate created a British-style justice system and effective state government, destroying the old order of male power (Ardener et al., 1960). Bakweri society was characterized by unstable marriages where women divorced men for insufficient support. Men made substantial bride wealth payments; some women sought new male partners with greater wealth who could buy out their previous bride wealth, and some paid off the bride wealth themselves to be rid of their husbands. Women could generate substantial incomes in exchange for casual sex (Ardener et al., 1960).

High Sex Ratios Followed the Fall of the Western Roman Empire

The collapse of the Western Roman Empire corresponded with a reduction in the European population and the abandonment of cities due to the frequent invasions of Germanic tribes (Herlihy, 1973). Coleman (1976) documents this historical period with many relevant details. As people fled into the countryside, society became almost completely rural and most people engaged in subsistence agriculture. Parents had a strong preference for sons because of the need for agricultural labor, and daughters were considered to be a liability. Preferential treatment of sons (e.g., breastfeeding males for twice as long as females) resulted in a high sex ratio. The larger the household was, the larger the proportion of males in the family. However, women who survived to childbearing ages were highly valued (Herlihy, 1973). These male-biased populations fostered notions of 'Courtly love', where men emphasized devotion to their partners, restraint, tenderness, and avoidance of pleasure for pleasure's sake. Men who were not able to secure a partner would instead be rewarded only the unconsummated approval of an already married woman (Guttentag and Secord, 1983).

Low Sex Ratios in the Late Middle Age Western Europe

Herlihy (1976) describes conditions in the late Middle Ages, when the Western European sex ratio became female-biased because of the loss of men to Crusades, monasteries, and plagues of infectious diseases. The population as a whole expanded and the redevelopment of urban areas was beneficial to the longevity of women, as it freed them from the hard physical labor of agriculture. Marriage payments gradually shifted from bride prices, when the man's family provides financial incentives, to dowries provided by the woman's family.

In the fourteenth century, Dante noted the inflation of dowry amounts and lamented for earlier times when 'the birth of a daughter did not strike terror into her father's heart' (Guttentag and Secord, 1983, p. 59). Many women were unable to find husbands, not only because of the relative scarcity of men, but also because of the reluctance of these males to marry. St. Bernadine of Siena estimated that there were 20,000 women in the city of Milan alone who could not find husbands, which he chiefly blamed on males' avoidance of marriage (Herlihy, 1975). Sexually libertarian male bachelors proliferated in this environment with relatively lower female selective power (Herlihy, 1978).

Women increasingly questioned their traditional roles in society (Guttentag and Secord, 1983). Many single women joined religious orders, and these became so numerous that it was difficult for the church hierarchy to monitor them effectively. The Vatican officials refused to recognize new orders and placed restrictions on existing ones. Heretical groups that strongly questioned traditional marriage and procreation flourished by raising and educating girls abandoned by their parents (Herlihy, 1973). Beguine communities – which resembled quasi-secular communes – also flourished (Bolton, 1976). The Beguines believed that women could commune directly with God, without the intervention of a male priest. The Beguines produced feminist literature that was remarkably radical for the time, although they found little support among the general female population, who were largely illiterate and uneducated. These events were repeated in the experiences of nineteenth-century American Suffragettes (Guttentag and Secord, 1983).

Low Sex Ratios in Colonial New England

Colonial New England's initially high sex ratio dropped off quickly, falling below 100 from the eighteenth century onwards. From the Colonial period through the eighteenth century, economic production was largely within the household. By 1835, the New England economy had a mercantile and commercial base. Because so many unmarried females engaged in yarn production for outside income, the meaning of the term 'spinster' shifted from female spinner to unmarried woman (Cott, 1977). Many women worked in textile mills and later factories. By the mid nineteenth century, industrialization greatly reduced the need for manual labor and improved living conditions sufficiently for women to return to their homes (Bloch, 1978).

Men married respectable women and supported their households and family members. However, many men also maintained relationships with one or more women who, because they were sexually active, were not considered respectable. New England was the source of many of the varied feminist movements that emerged in the nineteenth century (Gordon, 1976). Near the end of the nineteenth century, several different feminist groups argued that motherhood should be voluntary and advocated for greater independence for women. So called 'free love' groups, which were often led by men, argued against the institution of marriage on the grounds that marital constraints stifled 'real love'. These groups remained small and were never popular, though they shared beliefs with Suffragettes and other social reformers that women should have access to birth control – which included coitus interruptus, abortion, infanticide, and restriction of sex, even with husbands (Gordon, 1976).

Guttentag and Secord (1983) indicated striking parallels between cultural conditions in the late European Middle Ages and the similarly low sex ratio United States of the 1960s and 1970s. In 1970, there were only about two potential husbands for every three women. Books and magazines marketed toward women focused on enhancing physical attractiveness and serving the needs of men. In contrast to earlier feminist movements, those in the twentieth century connected with an audience of women who were literate and often college educated, leading to greater successes in advancing women's rights and status than in previous eras.

High Sex Ratios in the American South

In contrast to the female-biased British colonies in New England, the importation of white male indentured servants in the central Atlantic states created a high sex ratio. Georgia recruited families, rather than single women, because the colonial administrators feared that single women might take husbands from military garrisons and increase the threat of invasion by the Spanish colonists to the south (Spruill, 1938). The Governor of Virginia made a prohibition against women committing themselves to more than one man at a time (Calhoun, 1945). The extremely high sex ratios in the Southern colonies attenuated rapidly at first, then gradually declined toward a slight male bias just before the Civil War. The Southern Belle was an archetypal character of the antebellum South. Although of high social standing, she was expected to love, honor, and obey her husband and raise his children. These high status women were thought to be physically weak and dependent on men for protection, but intuitive and adept at understanding people (Scott, 1970). The reality of this role was likely more complex, as plantation owners would often sleep with female slaves rather than conform to the fidelity expected of their wives.

Near the end of the colonial period, censuses showed that the sex ratio became increasingly more male-biased the closer to the Western frontier (US Bureau of the Census, 1976). The proportion of unmarried men increased, but the proportion of women who were married increased and the proportion of (female) widows decreased. The proportion of women married depended on the sex ratio, as men married at a fairly constant rate. Compared to the more established areas in the East, women in the West married at a younger age and had higher fertility rates (Wells, 1975). Sex ratios in the American Far West were astronomical, even compared to the Midwest. The phrase 'Hell on wheels' was invented to describe the stores, saloons, gambling houses, and brothels that filled railroad cars and moved along with the construction of the railroad and the railroad construction workers (Sprague, 1940).

Female-Biased Sex Ratios in the Northeastern United States

Because of the migration of women from more rural areas to larger cities for white-collar employment opportunities, large cities in the Northeastern United States tend to have low (female-biased) sex ratios (Gwin, 2007). Men have disproportionally moved to cities and surrounding areas in the Western United States for technology-oriented careers and agricultural labor, with resulting male-biased sex ratios (Gwin, 2007). The abundance of single women in the New York metropolitan area has been a reoccurring topic in New York City area entertainment magazines. One article contained interviews of 50 non-married women of various ages and socio-economic levels who report experiences remarkably consistent with the expected intersexual dynamics in female-biased populations (Time Out New York, 2007). These women consistently tell of their troubles with finding a stable and reliable partner, as single men are scarce, and the men who are available are not seen as good partners because they are not interested in long-term relationships.

Many men are described as simultaneously polygynous or just looking for short-term sexual relationships. Men are seen as emotionally unavailable or unsuitable for a partnership because they are in another relationship and just interested in a sexual affair. There are some reports of men cheating on their partners, then forming a new partnership with the other woman and even cheating on her as well. Some women even explicitly mentioned the availability of potentially promiscuous women who reduce incentives for male commitment because of easy sexual access. Others suggest that men may be prone to multiple simultaneous relationships and a fear of commitment because they do not have father figures themselves (Time Out New York, 2007).

Women express a preference for a settle-down partner, but often end up settling for less (Time Out New York, 2007). They find it difficult to stay with one person, partially because the men they are dating are not interested in marriage. Relationships are often 'fast and casual', even when the women are middle aged, and women find themselves becoming accepting of this fact. Some women remarked that they were puzzled why many of their friends, who are intelligent, have good careers, and interesting personalities, are still unmarried. Some women advise other women to take advantage of their situation and 'have fun' with the opportunities they are presented. Several women report ending up single with children. One woman reported that she was 'single not by choice, but because my baby's father cheated on me'. Other women become accepting of being single for the long term. They see themselves as independent – someone who does not need a man to take care of them or support them.

Sex Ratios Among Immigrants to the United States

During the late-nineteenth-century creation of transcontinental railroads across the United States, Chinese laborers were recruited to build railroads in the American West. Few Chinese women immigrated in comparison and, in some groups, there were as many as 200 men for every woman. The male Chinese immigrants also imported fraternal associations, some of which were secret societies, and other social structures based on village affiliation or kinship that suppressed female social power. Many of the Chinese women ended up working as prostitutes in brothels or married to wealthy Chinese-American males who sheltered and protected them to the point of being virtual prisoners (Lyman, 1974). Immigrants to the United States predominantly married within their own ethnic group, creating a naturalistic experiment of high sex ratio effects on the second generation. As a consequence of these high sex ratios, second-generation immigrant women were more likely to be married and less likely to be in the labor force (Angrist, 2001). Higher sex ratios were associated with greater male earnings and higher incomes for parents with young children, consistent with the increased intensity of male resource competition. Second-generation immigrant men were also more likely to be married as an increasing function of immigrant sex ratios, demonstrating the value of securing scarce female partners.

Viking Raids as a Product of an Effectively High Sex Ratio

Raffield et al. (2016) have recently argued that Viking raids in Medieval Europe were a product of an effectively high sex ratio created by the practices of polygyny and concubinage. These features were associated with increasing social inequality in Late Iron Age Scandinavia. The payment of a brideprice to a woman's family was a prerequisite for marriage, and thus a large pool of unmarried men competed to secure sufficient wealth and status. The elevated risk in male strategies may have culminated in raiding expeditions, both to kidnap foreign women and plunder resources to exchange for wives at home. Historians have attributed the end of the Viking age to the Christianization of Scandinavia, though the role of the promotion of monogamy may be under-recognized.

Sex Ratios in China

As the country with the largest national population, China is particularly notable for the possible impact of demographic trends. Mainland China has a considerable male bias resulting from historical population control programs. Following the implementation of China's single-child law in 1979, sex-specific abortions have resulted in a surplus of men, especially in rural areas (Ding and

Hesketh, 2006; Zhu and Hesketh, 2009). Census data from 2005 indicated an overall OSR of 119, and some areas are reporting an OSR as high as 130. There is considerable documentation of the impact of this highly imbalanced sex ratio on individual differences, as well as patterns consistent with the extent of male bias. In areas where the surplus of men is greater, men spend more money on courting female partners (Xu and Ren, 2014). In areas where women are more prevalent than men, women have more difficulties in finding a suitable partner and are more likely to choose careers over starting families (Xu and Ren, 2014). Higher sex ratios are associated with lower levels of employment, professional employment, wage, and income for women, and more extensive education for men relative to women (Edlund et al., 2013). The influence of the sex ratio can be specific, even within a metropolitan area based on a localized population. At an engineering university in Wuhan with more than twice as many men as women, men spend more on courtship than men at a neighboring female-biased university training elementary and secondary school teachers (Kim, 2013). Women at the Chinese normal university (training teachers) report more difficulties in finding romantic partners than women at the engineering university (Kim, 2013).

The high and rising household savings rate in China is not consistent with traditional economic models; however, it is consistent with the sex ratio, which explains a stunning 50% of the variance (Wei and Zhang, 2011a). Parents with sons have to increase their savings competitively in order to improve their son's relative attractiveness for marriage. As the sex ratio rises, the household savings rate increases, and nearly doubled from 1990 to 2007 (Wei and Zhang, 2011a). Chinese parents with sons were also more likely to engage in risky jobs and set up businesses when they lived in areas with more highly male-biased sex ratios (Wei and Zhang, 2011b). Successful entrepreneurs could earn considerably more than comparably successful salaried workers, but entrepreneurs also exhibit higher variance in outcomes. Following the Chinese civil war, more than 500,000 Nationalist solders retreated to Taiwan in 1949. The military marriage ban was lifted in 1959, suddenly creating a shortage of marriageable women. Men exposed to high sex ratios as a result of the removal of the marriage ban were more likely to become entrepreneurs, pursuing a higher risk/higher reward strategy compared to obtaining higher education (Changa and Zhang, 2015).

The male-biased sex ratio in China intensified the commercialization of sexuality and marriage markets, with an increased prevalence of commercial sexual services, bride kidnapping, mail-order brides from neighboring countries, compensated dating, and marriages arranged through a financial transaction for brideprice (Greenhalgh, 2012). Sex ratios account for one-seventh of the rise in arrests for property and violent crimes per capita among those aged 16 to 25, a pattern attributed to adverse conditions for men in the marriage market (Edlund et al., 2013).

Overall, mortality rates in China have decreased considerably due to the rapidly modernizing health infrastructure and other advances. However, the gains in survival for women are twice as large as the gains for men. The increase in differences of mortality rates between Chinese men and women was most prevalent in late adolescence and young adulthood, the ages when male mating competition is most intense (Kruger and Polanski, 2011). In contrast, males saw more survival gains than women did in infancy and early childhood, consistent with preferential treatment of male offspring.

CONCLUSION

The sex ratio is a powerful influence on individual differences across a broad range of domains in humans, as well as reproductive dynamics in other species. These effects are a product of the market pressures of supply and demand, combined with the divergence in male and female reproductive strategies. These patterns are best understood in an evolutionary framework, where ultimate explanations are the foundation for understanding patterns in psychological processes, behavioral patterns, and other proximate mechanisms. It should be readily apparent that the sex ratio is an important factor in maintaining a stable and healthy society. Substantial imbalances in the sex ratio are associated with the severity of problematic psychological and social issues.

REFERENCES

Ackerman, J. M., Maner, J. K., & Carpenter, S. M. (2016). *Psychological Science*, *27*, 799–809.

Angrist, J. (2001). *How do sex ratios affect marriage and labor markets? Evidence from America's second generation*. IZA Discussion Paper No 368. Bonn, Germany: Institute for the Study of Labor (IZA).

Ardener, E., Ardener, S., & Warmington, W. A. (1960). *Plantation and village in the Cameroons: Some economic and social studies*. London: Oxford University Press.

Baker, H. W. G., & Hudson, B. (1983). Changes in the pituitary–testicular axis with age. In D. M. de Kretser, H. G. Burger, and B. Hudson (Eds.), *Monographs in endocrinology: The pituitary and testes, clinical and experimental studies Volume 25*, (pp. 71–83). Berlin: Springer Verlag.

Barber, N. (1999). Women's dress fashions as a function of reproductive strategy. *Sex Roles*, *40*, 459–471.

Barber, N. (2000). On the relationship between country sex ratios and teen pregnancy rates: A replication. *Cross-Cultural Research*, *34*, 26–37.

Berard, J. D., Nürnberg, P., Epplen, J. T., & Schmidtke, J. (1993). Male rank, reproductive behavior, and reproductive success in free-ranging rhesus macaques. *Primates*, *4*, 481–489.

Berglund, A. (1994). The operational sex ratio influences choosiness in a pipefish. *Behavioral Ecology*, *5*, 254–258.

Berglund, A., & Rosenqvist, G. (2003). Sex role reversal in pipefish. *Advances in the Study of Behavior*, *32*, 131–167.

Bethmann, D., & Kvasnicka, M. (2013). World War II, missing men and out of wedlock childbearing. *The Economic Journal*, *123*, 162–194.

Betzig, L. (1986). *Despotism and differential reproduction: A Darwinian view of history*. Hawthorne, NY: Aldine de Gruyter.

Bloch, R. H. (1978). Untangling the roots of modern sex roles: A survey of four centuries of change. *Signs: Journal of Women in Culture and Society*, *4*, 237–252.

Bolton, B. M. (1976). Mulieres Sanctae. In S. M. Stuard (Ed.), *Women in medieval society* (pp. 141–156). Philadelphia: University of Pennsylvania Press.

Buss, D. M. (1989). Sex difference in human mate preferences: Evolutionary hypotheses tested in 37 cultures. *Behavioral and Brain Sciences*, *12*, 1–49.

Buss, D. M., & Schmitt, D. P. (1993). Sexual strategies theory: An evolutionary perspective on human mating. *Psychological Review*, *100*, 204–232.

Buss, D. M., & Shackelford, T. K. (1997). Human aggression in evolutionary psychology perspective. *Clinical Psychology Review*, *17*, 605–619.

Calhoun, A. W. (1945). *A social history of the American family from Colonial times to the present, Vol. 1*. New York, NY: Barnes & Noble.

Campbell, A. (1993). *Men, women, and aggression*. New York, NY: Basic Books.

Chagnon, N. A. (1992). *Yanomamo* (4th ed.). New York, NY: Harcourt Brace.

Changa, S., & Zhang, X. (2015). Mating competition and entrepreneurship. *Journal of Economic Behavior & Organization*, *116*, 292–309.

Chapman, C. A., Fedigan, L. M., Fedigan, L., & Chapman, L. J. (1989). Post-weaning resource competition and sex ratios in spider monkeys. *Oikos*, *54*, 315–319.

Chipman, A., & Morrison, E. (2013). The impact of sex ratio and economic status on local birth rates. *Biology Letters*, *9*, 20130027.

Chisholm, J. S. (1999). *Death, hope and sex: Steps to an evolutionary ecology of mind and morality.* Cambridge, England: Cambridge University Press.

Clutton-Brock, T., Harvey, P., & Rudder, B. (1977). Sexual dimorphism, socionomic sex ratio, and body weight in primates. *Nature, 269,* 797–800.

Coleman, E. (1976). Infanticide in the early Middle Ages. In S. M. Stuard (Ed.), *Women in medieval society* (pp. 47–70). Philadelphia, PA: University of Pennsylvania Press.

Cott, N. F. (1977). *The bonds of womanhood: 'Woman's sphere' in New England, 1780–1835.* New Haven, CT: Yale University Press.

Cunningham, M. (1986). Measuring the physical in physical attractiveness: Quasi-experiments on the sociobiology of female facial beauty. *Journal of Personality and Social Psychology, 50,* 925–935.

Daly, M., & Wilson, M. (1978). *Sex, evolution, and behavior: Adaptations for reproduction.* North Scituate, MA: Duxbury Press.

Darwin, C. (1871). *The descent of man, and selection in relation to sex.* London: John Murray.

Ding, Q. J., & Hesketh, T. (2006). Family size, fertility preferences, and sex ratio in China in the era of the one child family policy: Results from national family planning and reproductive health survey. *British Medical Journal, 333,* 371–373.

Durante, K. M., Griskevicius, V., Simpson, J. A., Cantu, S. M., & Tybur, J. M. (2012). Sex ratio and women's career choice: Does a scarcity of men lead women to choose briefcase over baby? *Journal of Personality and Social Psychology, 103,* 121–134.

Düsing, C. (1884). On the regulation of the sex-ratio. *Theoretical Population Biology, 58,* 255–257.

Edlund, L., Li, H., Yi, J., & Zhang, J. (2013). Sex ratios and crime: Evidence from China. *The Review of Economics and Statistics, 95,* 1520–1534.

Elmberg, J. (1990). Long-term survival, length of breeding season, and operational sex ratio in a boreal population of common frogs, *Rana temporaria* L. *Canadian Journal of Zoology, 68,* 121–127.

Ember, M., Ember, C. R., & Low, B. S. (2007). Comparing explanations of polygyny. *Cross-Cultural Research, 41,* 428–440.

Emlen, S. T., & Oring, L. W. (1977). Ecology, sexual selection and the evolution of mating systems. *Science, 197,* 215–223.

Fisher, R. A. (1930). *The genetical theory of natural selection.* Oxford: Oxford University Press.

Forsgren, E., Amundsen, T., Borg, A. A., & Bjelvenmark, J. (2004). Unusually dynamic sex roles in a fish. *Nature, 429,* 551–554.

Gangestad, S. W., & Simpson, J. A. (2000). The evolution of human mating: Trade-offs and strategic pluralism. *Behavioral and Brain Sciences, 23,* 573–644.

Geary, D. C. (2002). Sexual selection and human life history. In R. Kail (Ed.), *Advances in child development and behavior* (pp. 41–101). San Diego, CA: Academic Press.

Geary, D. C. (2005). Evolution of paternal investment. In D. Buss (Ed.), *The handbook of evolutionary psychology* (pp. 483–505). Hoboken, NJ: John Wiley & Sons.

Geary, D. C., & Flinn, M. V. (2001). Evolution of human parental behavior and the human family. *Parenting: Science and Practice, 1,* 5–61.

Gordon, L. (1976). *Woman's body, woman's right: A social history of birth control in America.* New York, NY: Viking Press.

Greenhalgh, S. (2012). Patriarchal demographics? China's sex ratio reconsidered. *Population and Development Review, 38,* S130–S149.

Griskevicius, V., Tybur, J. M., Ackerman, J. M., Delton, A. W., Robertson, T. E., & White, A. E. (2012). The financial consequences of too many men: Sex ratio effects on saving, borrowing, and spending. *Journal of Personality and Social Psychology, 102,* 69–80.

Guttentag, M. & Secord, P. F. (1983). *Too many women? The sex ratio question.* Beverly Hills, CA: Sage.

Gwin, P. (2007). Geography: Singles. *National Geographic, 211,* 22.

Gwynne, D. T. (1990). Testing parental investment and the control of sexual selection in katydids: The operational sex ratio. *The American Naturalist, 136,* 474–484.

Gwynne, D. T. (1991). Sexual competition among females: What causes courtship-role reversal? *Trends in Ecology and Evolution, 6,* 118–121.

Gwynne, D. T., & Simmons, L. W. (1990). Experimental reversal of courtship roles in an insect. *Nature, 346,* 172–174.

Hahn, A. C., Fisher, C. I., DeBruine, L. M., & Jones, B. C. (2014). Sex ratio influences the motivational salience of facial attractiveness. *Biology Letters*, *10*, 20140148.

Hendrix, L. (1996). *Illegitimacy and social structures: Cross-cultural perspectives on non-marital birth*. Westport, CT: Greenwood.

Herlihy, D. (1973). Alienation in medieval culture and society. In *The social history of Italy and Western Europe 700–1500* (pp. 125–140). London, UK: Variorum.

Herlihy, D. (1975). Life expectancies for women in medieval society. In R. T. Morewedge (Ed.), *The role of women in the Middle Ages* (pp. 1–2). Albany, NY: State University of New York Press.

Herlihy, D. (1976). Land, family, and women in Continental Europe, 701–1200. In S. M. Stuard (Ed.), *Women in medieval society* (pp. 13–46). Philadelphia, PA: University of Pennsylvania Press.

Herlihy, D. (1978). The medieval marriage market. In *The social history of Italy and Western Europe 700–1500* (pp. 3–27). London, UK: Variorum.

Hill, K. & Hurtado, A. M. (1996). *Ache life history: The ecology and demography of a foraging people*. Hawthorne, NY: Aldine de Gruyter.

Hopcroft, R. L. (2006). Sex, status, and reproductive success in the contemporary United States. *Evolution and Human Behavior*, *27*, 104–120.

Ims, R. A. (1988). The potential for sexual selection in males: Effect of sex ratio and spatiotemporal distribution of receptive females. *Evolutionary Ecology*, *2*, 338–352.

Jin, L., Elwert, F., Freese, J., & Christakis, N. A. (2010). Preliminary evidence regarding the hypothesis that the sex ratio at sexual maturity may affect longevity in men. *Demography*, *47*, 579–586.

Jones, J. H., & Ferguson, B. D. (2006). Excess male death leads to a severe marriage squeeze in Colombia, 1973–2005. *Social Biology*, *54*, 140–151.

Kaitala, A., & Miettinen, M. (1997). Female egg dumping and the effect of sex ratio on male egg carrying in a coreid bug. *Behavioral Ecology*, *8*, 429–432.

Kandrik, M., Jones, B. C., & DeBruine, L. M. (2015). Scarcity of female mates predicts regional variation in men's and women's sociosexual orientation across US states. *Evolution and Human Behavior*, *36*, 206–210.

Keenleyside, M. H. (1983). Mate desertion in relation to adult sex ratio in the biparental cichlid fish *Herotilapia multispinosa*. *Animal Behaviour*, *31*, 683–688.

Kenrick, D. T., & Simpson, J. A. (1997). Why social psychology and evolutionary psychology need one another. In J. Simpson & D. Kenrick (Eds.), *Evolutionary social psychology* (pp. 1–20). Mahwah, NJ: Lawrence Erlbaum Associates.

Kim, J. S. (2013). *The influence of local sex ratio on romantic relationship maintenance processes* (Doctoral dissertation, University of Minnesota). Retrieved from http://hdl.handle.net/11299/158564 (accessed on 20 April, 2017).

Kruger, D. J. (2006). Male facial masculinity influences attributions of personality and reproductive strategy. *Personal Relationships*, *13*, 451–463.

Kruger, D. J. (2008). Young adults attempt exchanges in reproductively relevant currencies. *Evolutionary Psychology*, *6*, 204–212.

Kruger, D. J. (2010). Socio-demographic factors intensifying male mating competition exacerbate male mortality rates. *Evolutionary Psychology*, *8*, 194–204.

Kruger, D. J., Clark, J., & Vanas, S. (2013). Male scarcity is associated with higher prevalence of premature gestation and low birth weight births across the USA. *American Journal of Human Biology*, *25*, 225–227.

Kruger, D. J., Fisher, M., & Jobling, I. (2003). Proper and dark heroes as dads and cads: Alternative mating strategies in British Romantic literature. *Human Nature*, *14*, 305–317.

Kruger, D. J., Fitzgerald, C. J., & Peterson, T. (2010). Female scarcity reduces women's marital ages and increases variance in men's marital ages. *Evolutionary Psychology*, *8*, 420–431.

Kruger, D. J., & Nesse, R. M. (2004). Sexual selection and the Male:Female Mortality Ratio. *Evolutionary Psychology*, *2*, 66–77.

Kruger, D. J., & Nesse, R. M. (2006). An evolutionary life-history framework for understanding sex differences in human mortality rates. *Human Nature*, *17*, 74–97.

Kruger, D. J., & Nesse, R. M. (2009, September). *Understanding sex differences in mortality* rates with an evolutionary life history framework. Oral presentation given at the International Union for the Scientific Study of Population's XXVI International Population Conference, Marrakech, Morocco.

Kruger, D. J., & Polanski, S. P. (2011). Sex differences in mortality rates have increased in China following the single-child law. *Letters on Evolutionary Behavioral Science, 2*, 1–4.

Kruger, D. J., & Schlemmer, E. (2009). Male scarcity is differentially related to male marital likelihood across the life course. *Evolutionary Psychology, 7*, 280–287.

Kvarnemo, C., & Ahnesjö, I. (1996). The dynamics of operational sex ratios and competition for mates. *Trends of Ecology and Evolution, 11*, 404–408.

Lawick-Goodall, J. (1967). Mother–offspring relationships in free-ranging chimpanzees. In D. Morris (Ed.), *Primate ethology*, (pp. 287–346). Chicago, IL: Aldine.

Lichter, D. T., Anderson, R. N., & Hayward, M. D. (1995). Marriage markets and marital choice. *Journal of Family Issues, 16*, 412–431.

Lichter, D. T., Kephart, G., McLaughlin, D. K., & Landry, D. J. (1992). Race and the retreat from marriage: A shortage of marriageable men. *American Sociological Review, 57*, 781–799.

Low, B. (2003). Ecological and social complexities in monogamy. In U. Reichard & C. Boesch (Eds.), *Monogamy: Mating strategies and partnerships in birds, humans, and other mammals* (pp. 161–176). Cambridge, UK: Cambridge University Press.

Low, B. (2007). Ecological and socio-cultural impacts on mating and marriage systems. In R. Dunbar & L. Barrett (Eds.), *The Oxford handbook of evolutionary psychology* (pp. 449–462). Oxford, UK: Oxford University Press.

Lummaa, V., Merila, J., & Kause, A. (1998). Adaptive sex ratio variation in pre-industrial human (*Homo sapiens*) populations? *Proceedings of the Royal Society of London, Series B, 265*, 563–568.

Lyman, S. (1974). *Chinese Americans*. New York, NY: Random House.

Mathews, L. M. (2002). Tests of the mate-guarding hypothesis for social monogamy: Does population density, sex ratio, or female synchrony affect behavior of male snapping shrimp (*Alpheus angulatus*)? *Behavioral Ecology and Sociobiology, 51*, 426–432.

Matsumoto, K., & Yanagisawa, Y. (2001). Monogamy and sex role reversal in the pipefish *Corythoichthys haematopterus*. *Animal Behaviour, 61*, 163–170.

Michener, G. R., & McLean, I. G. (1996). Reproductive behavior and operational sex ratio in Richardson's ground squirrels. *Animal Behavior, 52*, 743–758.

Mills, S. C., & Reynolds, J. D. (2003). Operational sex ratio and alternative reproductive behaviours in the European bitterling, *Rhodeus sericeus*. *Behavioral Ecology and Sociobiology, 54*, 98–104.

Mitani, J. C., Gros-Louis, J., & Richards, A. F. (1996). Sexual dimorphism, the operational sex ratio, and the intensity of male competition in polygynous primates. *The American Naturalist, 147*, 966–980.

Nishida, T., Takasaki, H., & Takahata, Y. (1990). Demography and reproductive profiles. In T. Nishida (Ed.), *The chimpanzees of the Mahale Mountains* (pp. 63–97). Tokyo: University of Tokyo Press.

Pedersen, F. A. (1991). Secular trends in human sex ratios: Their influence on individual and family behavior. *Human Nature, 2*, 271–291.

Plavcan, J. M. (2000). Inferring social behavior from sexual dimorphism in the fossil record. *Journal of Human Evolution, 39*, 327–344.

Pollet, T. V., & Nettle, D. (2007). Driving a hard bargain: Sex ratio and male marriage success in a historical US population. *Biology Letters, 4*, 31–33.

Raffield, B., Price, N., & Collard, M. (2016). Male-biased operational sex ratios and the Viking phenomenon: An evolutionary anthropological perspective on Late Iron Age Scandinavian raiding. *Evolution and Human Behavior, 38*, 315–324.

Reichard, U., & Boesch, C. (Eds.). (2003). *Monogamy: Mating strategies and partnerships in birds, humans, and other mammals*. Cambridge, UK: Cambridge University Press.

Roff, D. A. (1992). *The evolution of life histories: Theory and analysis*. New York, NY: University of Chicago Press.

Schmitt, D. P. (2005). Sociosexuality from Argentina to Zimbabwe: A 48-nation study of sex, culture, and strategies of human mating. *Behavioral and Brain Sciences, 28,* 247–311.

Scott, A. F. (1970). *The southern lady: From pedestal to politics, 1830–1930.* Chicago, IL: University of Chicago Press.

Sprague, W. F. (1940). *Women and the West: A short social history.* Boston, MA: Christopher.

Spruill, J. C. (1938). *Women's life and work in the Southern colonies.* Chapel Hill, NC: University of North Carolina Press.

Stearns, S. C. (1992). *The evolution of life histories.* Oxford: Oxford University Press.

Symington, M. M. (1987). Sex ratio and maternal rank in wild spider monkeys: When daughters disperse. *Behavioral Ecology and Sociobiology, 20,* 421–425.

Székely, T., Cuthill, I. C., & Kis, J. (1999). Brood desertion in Kentish plover: Sex differences in remating opportunities. *Behavioral Ecology, 10,* 185–190.

Takahashi, H. (2001). Influence of fluctuation in the operational sex ratio to mating of troop and non-troop male Japanese macaques for four years on Kinkazan Island, Japan. *Primates, 42,* 183–191.

Tesser, A., & Martin, L. (1996). The psychology of evaluation. In E. Higgins and A. Kruglanski (Eds.), *Social psychology: Handbook of basic principles* (pp. 400–432). New York, NY: Guilford Press.

Thornhill, R. (1980). Rape in *Panorpa* scorpionflies and a general rape hypothesis. *Animal Behavior, 28,* 52–59.

Time Out New York. (2007, June 28). Single women: Single minded. *Time Out New York, 613,* 28–34.

Tinbergen, N. (1963). On aims and methods in ethology. *Zeitschrift für Tierpsychologie, 20,* 410–433.

Trent, K., & South, S. J. (1989). Structural determinants of the divorce rate: A cross-societal analysis. *Journal of Marriage and the Family, 51,* 391–404.

Trivers, R. (1972). Parental investment and sexual selection. In B. Campbell (Ed.), *Sexual selection and the descent of man* (pp. 136–179). Chicago, IL: Aldine-Atherton.

Tuljapurkar, S. D., Puleston, C. O., & Gurven, M. D. (2007). Why men matter: Mating patterns drive evolution of human lifespan. *PLOS One, 2,* e785.

US Bureau of the Census. (1976). *Historical statistics of the United States: Colonial times to 1970.* Washington, DC: US Government Printing Office.

Valero, A., Schaffner, C. M., Vick, L. G., Aureli, F., & Ramos-Fernandez, G. (2006). Intragroup lethal aggression in wild spider monkeys. *American Journal of Primatology, 68,* 732–737.

Wei, S.-J., & Zhang, X. (2011a). The competitive saving motive: Evidence from rising sex ratios and savings rates in China. *Journal of Political Economy, 119,* 511–564.

Wei, S.-J., & Zhang, X. (2011b). Sex ratios, entrepreneurship and economic growth in the People's Republic of China. *NBER Working Paper 16800.* Retrieved from http://www.nber.org/papers/w16800 (accessed on 15 July, 2016).

Wells, R. W. (1975). *The population of the British colonies in America before 1776.* Princeton, NJ: Princeton University Press.

Wilson, M. & Daly, M. (1997). Life expectancy, economic inequality, homicide, and reproductive timing in Chicago neighbourhoods. *British Medical Journal, 314,* 1271–1274.

Xu, J., & Ren, X. (2014). The effect of imbalance sex ratio on consumer behavior of mating. *Advances in Psychology, 4,* 271–278.

Zhu, W. X., & Hesketh, T. (2009). China's excess males, sex selective abortion, and one child policy: Analysis of data from 2005 national intercensus survey. *British Medical Journal, 338,* b1211.

Individualism and Collectivism

Takeshi Hamamura, Karim Bettache and Yi Xu

People's participation in local culture shapes their psyches, which in turn creates their cultural environment. In this sense, culture and mind are mutually reinforcing. Therefore, a satisfactory understanding of human psychology requires investigations of cultural influence (Henrich et al., 2010). Individualism–collectivism is the most frequently used conceptual tool by researchers examining this issue. This chapter provides a current overview of research concerning individualism–collectivism.

DEFINITION

Triandis (1995) described individualism–collectivism as follows:

> *Collectivism* may be initially defined as a social pattern consisting of closely linked individuals who see themselves as parts of one or more collectives (family, co-workers, tribe, nation); are primarily motivated by the norms of, and duties imposed by, those collectives; are willing to give priority to the goals of these collectives over their own personal goals; and emphasize their connectedness to members of these collectives. A preliminary definition of *individualism* is a social pattern that consists of loosely linked individuals who view themselves as independent of collectives; are primarily motivated by their own preferences, needs, rights, and contracts they establish with others; give priority to their personal goals over the goals of others; and emphasize rational analysis of the advantages and disadvantages to associating with others. (p. 2)

Contemporary individualism–collectivism research reflects earlier works in social sciences, such as the distinction between Gemeinschaft (community) and Gesellschaft (society) by Tönnies in the 1800s. One of the influential works in recent decades is Hofstede's work to extract dimensions of culture from a large international survey (Hofstede, 1980). Among the large number of societies surveyed by Hofstede in the

1970s, Western societies such as the United States were found to be individualistic and non-Western societies were found to be collectivistic. Students of cross-cultural psychology are often interested in whether these differences are static and how cultures have come to differ on the individualism–collectivism dimension. There are several views on this issue in the literature. The first section of this chapter provides a review of these different viewpoints, which raises questions regarding sources of cultural differences in individualism–collectivism. Following this review, the chapter provides an overview of many psychological processes associated with individualism–collectivism differences, focusing on self-concept, emotion, motivation, cognition, and group processes. This discussion also touches on the limitations of the individualism–collectivism dimension, raising questions such as whether individualism and collectivism represent a single bipolar dimension or are comprised of multiple sub-dimensions (Brewer and Chen, 2007; Vignoles et al., 2016). For this part of the discussion, our focus is on the recent developments with the goal of adding to the existing reviews that are more comprehensive (Heine, 2008; Kitayama and Cohen, 2010; Markus and Kitayama, 1991; Miyamoto, 2013).

WHY DO CULTURES DIFFER ON INDIVIDUALISM–COLLECTIVISM?

One influential approach to addressing why cultures differ on individualism–collectivism is to associate cultural differences in individualism–collectivism with differences in social ecology that are linked with economic prosperity. This approach has a long tradition. Inkeles (1975) argued that social and economic institutions of industrialized societies, such as factories for mass production, advanced education, mass media, and urbanization, have fostered modernism characterized by a set of attributes such as personal efficacy, openness to new experience, gender equality, achievement motivation, civic participation, greater social relationships beyond kin, distancing from tradition and religion as a source of authority, and acceptance of social mobility. The contemporary approach differs in its explicit focus on individualism–collectivism as defined above.

One influential theory in recent research argues that a society transitions from collectivism to individualism as its social ecology shifts toward being more urban, affluent, and technologically advanced (Greenfield, 2009, 2013). A variety of evidence is available for this theory. First, in cross-national comparison studies, indices of economic prosperity, such as per capita GDP, are strongly correlated with indices of individualism (Hofstede, 1980; Inglehart and Baker, 2000). This pattern extends to analyses conducted within a society – regional differences in economic development predict indices of individualism in a number of countries, including China (Takemura et al., 2016), Japan (Yamawaki, 2012), and the United States (Vandello and Cohen, 1999).

Research on socioeconomic status reports a similar pattern. Earlier research on this topic suggested that individuals from a high socioeconomic background are likely more individualistic because they are more exposed to institutions of a modern economy that are urban and foster the sense of independence from traditional sources of social influences (Inkeles, 1975). Many findings in support of this idea have been reported in the United States. A range of measures is used to assess individualistic psychology, reflecting a variety of ways in which individualism–collectivism is examined in research (as detailed later). Compared to Americans from a working-class background, those of middle-class background have been found to show greater preferences for choices that express uniqueness (Snibbe and Markus, 2005), more inflated sense of self-worth

(Piff, 2014), and patterns of social attribution that place greater focus on individual actors and internal factors (Kraus et al., 2009). The association between socioeconomic status and individualism has been reported in other countries as well (Grossmann and Varnum, 2010; Hamamura et al., 2013; Inkeles, 1975; Ma and Schoeneman, 1997; Takemura et al., 2016).

The proposed association between individualism and economic prosperity has also been examined across time. Particularly influential work comes from Greenfield (2009, 2015), who longitudinally observed Mayan communities and their weaving practices. Greenfield observed a shift in their production methods, away from adherence to the traditional style of weaving and toward a style that favors individual innovation. In turn, this shift was driven by a change in the economic foundation of communities from a subsistence economy to a market economy. According to Greenfield, these changes led to corresponding shifts in beliefs, values, and habits toward individualism.

Greenfield (2015) has maintained that shifts toward individualism have been a global trend. Research evidence on this point is clear for American culture, where increasing individualism has been identified in a number of studies incorporating a variety of measures and methods, including temporal meta-analyses of commonly assessed psychological constructs such as self-esteem (Gentile et al., 2010; Twenge and Campbell, 2001; Twenge et al., 2012a) and narcissism (Twenge et al., 2008). A similar pattern has been found in studies that examine cultural artifacts such as names given to newborn babies (Twenge et al., 2010) and usage of words associated with individualism in digitalized book archives (Greenfield, 2013; Twenge et al., 2012b). One recent study analyzed the temporal association between economic growth and individualism in the United States using multiple indices of individualism and indices of factors other than economic prosperity that could possibly explain rising individualism (Grossmann and Varnum, 2015). Their analysis found the rise of individualism across all indices and that change in socioeconomic structure (i.e., percentage of labor force working in white collar jobs) was more robustly associated with changes in individualism than other factors examined.

Greenfield's theory further postulates that although there is a trend for cultures to move toward becoming more urban, affluent, and technologically advanced – which contributes to rising levels of individualism – the opposing trend toward collectivism is also feasible. One recent study demonstrated this in the context of changes in American culture before and after the Great Recession (Park et al., 2014). This study found that, compared to the pre-recession period (2004–2006), in the recession years (2008–2010), high school students' concerns for community increased. Bianchi (2016) also reported a temporal fluctuation of individualism that tracked economic growth using multiple indices of individualism.

In spite of these findings that provide support for Greenfield's theory, there are several lines of findings that appear inconsistent with the theory. First, many temporal analyses conducted in the United States indicated a pattern that suggests rising individualism, but there are also findings that are inconsistent with this pattern, for example, increasing external locus of control (Twenge et al., 2004). Second, some of the temporal changes observed in the United States have not been found in other societies during periods of economic growth. In particular, data from Denmark (Torpe, 2003) and Japan (Hamamura, 2011a; Inoguchi, 2000) suggest that generalized trust has not declined as it has in the United States (Putnam, 2001), and data from Australia (Hamamura and Septarini, 2017), China (Liu and Xin, 2015), and Japan (Ogihara et al., 2015; Oshio et al., 2014) suggest that self-esteem has not increased in these societies as it has in the United States (Twenge and Campbell, 2001).

Third, the idea that individualism is caused by economic prosperity does not account for the pervasive collectivism observed in affluent East Asian societies. Examining this issue in Japan, Hamamura (2012) found the rise of individualism in Japan in a subset of indices and a pattern of continuing collectivism in another subset. For example, valuing of social harmony, obligation, and communal orientation was relatively unchanged among Japanese survey respondents over time. Finally, as detailed below, there are factors other than economic prosperity that have been proposed as causing cultural differences in individualism–collectivism.

Historical Migration to Frontiers

Kitayama and colleagues (Kitayama et al., 2006a) have proposed that some cultures are individualistic today due to their history as a frontier settled by many independently minded individuals. For example, the Western frontier in the United States during the eighteenth to nineteenth centuries attracted settlers for the prospects of wealth and freedom. Inhabited by these individuals with an independent and goal-oriented mindset, a culture of individualism emerged in these frontiers. Consequently, these frontiers socialized those individualistic beliefs, values, and customs to newcomers. Interestingly, this theory posits that individualistic culture within frontiers may continue even after the areas have ceased to be frontiers. The idea that a culture, once evoked in response to a particular ecology, can have a life of its own is important for many theories of culture (Chiu et al., 2010; Cohen, 2001; Zou et al., 2009).

One form of evidence for the frontier hypothesis comes from a study of the northern island of Japan (Hokkaido), which was the destination for many voluntary migrants in the late nineteenth century. Findings from a series of studies suggested stronger individualism among Japanese living in Hokkaido compared to those living outside of the island (Kitayama et al., 2006a). Similarly, another study found (a) stronger endorsement of individualistic values in Western than in Eastern regions in the United States, and (b) newborns receiving popular names less frequently in Western regions in the United States and Canada and also in world regions settled by Europeans (e.g., Australia, New Zealand) in comparison to European countries (Varnum and Kitayama, 2011).

Residential Mobility

Although the frontier hypothesis stresses the effects of historical migration patterns, research on residential mobility has examined psychological effects of moving using a variety of methodologies, including experiments (Oishi, 2010; Oishi et al., 2015). Results from these studies suggest that moving is associated with individualistic psychology. For example, one study found that American college students who had moved often in childhood rated their personal selves to be more central to their self-concepts, whereas the collective self was more central among the non-movers (Oishi et al., 2007). Similarly, movers were more likely to feel happier when their personal self was accurately perceived in a social interaction compared to non-movers who felt happier when their collective self was accurately perceived (Oishi et al., 2007). An association between mobility and individualistic psychology has been reported in a number of other studies (Oishi, 2010; Oishi et al., 2015).

Agriculture

Talhelm et al. (2014) argued that collectivism has emerged in Chinese regions that farm rice, whereas individualism has emerged in regions that farm wheat. According to this theory, rice farming gives rise to collectivistic culture, as farming rice is highly labor intensive and also necessitates the coordination of labor to build and maintain an elaborate irrigation system, as well as to plant and harvest rice within a short window of time. These labor practices gave rise to a culture that emphasizes cooperation and the avoidance of conflict. In contrast, wheat farming does not require as elaborate a system of irrigation or as rigid a coordination of labor, which gives rise to individualistic culture. Importantly, this theory maintains that the history of wheat/rice farming exerts its influence by shaping contemporary culture which affects even non-farming residents. Support for this theory was obtained in that participants from rice-growing southern Chinese provinces were more collectivistic compared with those from wheat-growing provinces. This pattern was found independently of differences in affluence. Hence, this theory suggests a continuing collectivism in historical rice-growing regions of China, despite transformative social and economic changes and their effects on rising individualism (Cai et al., 2011; Hamamura and Xu, 2015; Xu and Hamamura, 2014). Relevant to this theory is the work demonstrating that individuals living in farming, fishing, and herding communities are individualistic in their psychological tendencies. Presumably, compared to herding, farming and fishing require more systematic and elaborated cooperation, which may promote collectivism (Uskul et al., 2008; Uskul and Over, 2014; see also Witkin and Berry, 1975, for a precursor to the current work in this area).

Pathogens

Another theory of contemporary cross-cultural differences in individualism–collectivism is a historical prevalence of disease-causing pathogens (Fincher and Thornhill, 2012; Schaller and Murray, 2008). This theory maintains that, in ecologies characterized by a high historical prevalence of infectious diseases, norms of contagion-minimizing behaviors, such as restrained sexual behavior and xenophobia are strongly adhered (Fincher and Thornhill, 2012; Schaller and Murray, 2008). This theory argues that one set of norms which developed to mitigate the pathogen threats was collectivism, because it provides an effective defense by limiting interactions with members of outgroups, discouraging individuals from deviating from social and cultural traditions, and emphasizing obedience in child-rearing practices (Cashdan and Steele, 2013; Fincher et al., 2008; Murray et al., 2011). The association between historical pathogen prevalence and individualism–collectivism has been found independently of economic development (Fincher et al., 2008). Recent research suggests that this association can be explained by population frequencies of a genotype: a short allele on the promoter region polymorphism (5-HTTLPR) of the serotonin transporter gene (Chiao and Blizinsky, 2009; Kim and Sasaki, 2014). This finding provides evidence that collectivism as an adaptation to pathogen prevalence created environments that influence the processes of gene selection (Chiao and Blizinsky, 2009; Kim and Sasaki, 2014).

Sources of Cultural Differences in Individualism–Collectivism: Section Summary

Available evidence clearly indicates that social ecological attributes of economic prosperity – such as being urban, affluent, and technologically advanced – are associated with individualism–collectivism. This association has been found in comparisons of societies around the world, regions and individuals within a society, as well as across the same society at different time periods. However, a number of factors other than economic prosperity have also been proposed and empirical evidence is available for each of these factors. In fact, the role of these factors has been shown even when adjusting for developmental differences, suggesting that these are independent contributions. As summarized in this section, the question of where contemporary cultural differences in individualism–collectivism come from, arguably one of the most central questions in the social sciences, has attracted a great deal of empirical interest.

WHAT ARE THE PSYCHOLOGICAL PROCESSES ASSOCIATED WITH INDIVIDUALISM–COLLECTIVISM?

Research that uses the individualism–collectivism dimension has been highly successful in illuminating a large number of psychological processes affected by this dimension. Many studies have examined psychological differences between individualistic and collectivistic cultures. As the above discussion suggests, many of these findings were obtained from comparisons between different countries, most frequently these comparisons were between societies in East Asia (e.g., China, Korea, Japan) and those in North America or Europe (e.g., Canada, the United States, the United Kingdom). In recent years, an increasing number of studies have examined these differences in other contexts, such as comparing regions and individuals within the same society or the same culture in different time periods. This section provides a brief overview of the recent research findings in this area.

Self-Concept

One way in which psychological processes differ across cultures is through different ways of understanding the self (Cross et al., 2010; Markus and Kitayama, 1991). According to Markus and Kitayama (1991), a prevalent way to understand the self in individualistic societies is to see it as an autonomous and socially independent entity that carries a stable set of attributes across situations. These attributes are associated with tendencies to experience certain emotions, beliefs, and behaviors that are enacted appropriately in different situations. This model of the self is called an *independent self*. In collectivistic societies, Markus and Kitayama argued that a prevalent way to understand the self is to see it as relational in nature as informed by one's roles in a society and relationships with close others. As such, the self is seen as being highly situational – different social roles and relationships exert their influence on the self in different situations. Emotions, beliefs, and behaviors that are associated with this relational being are enacted flexibly to suit the needs of particular situations. This model of self is called an *interdependent self*.

The difference between independence and interdependence has been found in many studies. One classic study administered the Twenty Statement Test (TST) to university students in Japan and the United States and asked the participants to write 20 sentences that start with 'I am ... ' (Cousins, 1989). In this study, the self-descriptions provided by the American participants more often mentioned attributes that are dispositional and consistent across situations (e.g., 'shy', 'outgoing', 'honest') compared with the Japanese participants who provided descriptions that more often mentioned attributes that are based on social roles and confined to specific contexts (e.g., 'a college student', 'a daughter'). Interestingly, the Japanese participants provided more dispositional traits when a specific context was provided. Some studies used the TST to examine differences in independence–interdependence in other comparative contexts. For example, one study administered the TST to four samples in Kenya (students and workers in Nairobi and Maasai and Samburu Kenyans) and American undergraduates (Ma and Schoeneman, 1997). This study found that students in both countries were more likely to use self-descriptions associated with independence compared to participants from traditional communities in Kenya, who were more likely to use interdependent self-descriptions. A recent question in this area includes the definitiveness of TST as a measure of self-concept (del Prado et al., 2007).

Measurements of culturally shaped self-concepts have been a thorny issue. Although a number of measures that solicit participants' ratings on Likert-type scales have been developed, a meta-analysis of the findings obtained from these measures revealed a pattern that appears inconsistent with the theory of individualism–collectivism (Oyserman et al., 2002). Researchers have argued that this pattern indicates a limitation of self-report-based assessments in measuring culturally shaped selfhood due to response style issues (Hamamura et al., 2008; Heine et al., 2002; Schimmack et al., 2005) or a limitation of the existing measures in capturing the original theory (Brewer and Chen, 2007; Vignoles et al., 2016). In particular, Brewer and colleagues (Brewer and Chen, 2007; Brewer and Yuki, 2007) have drawn a distinction between collective and relational self and argued that 'collectivism' may be a misnomer because it conflates these two distinct elements of the self-representations. This issue is elaborated in the section 'Interpersonal Relationships and Group Processes'.

Markus and Kitayama's (1991) theory of culturally shaped self has had implications for personality theories (Church, 2016; Heine and Buchtel, 2009). It has been argued that '[…] personality (most broadly defined as the qualities and characteristics of being a person) is completely interdependent with the meanings and practices of particular sociocultural contexts' (Markus and Kitayama, 1998, p. 66). One way in which this argument has been examined is by observing cross-situational consistency of personality traits. Church and colleagues reported evidence for cross-situational consistency in personality traits among samples drawn from multiple individualistic and collectivistic societies (Church et al., 2008a, 2008b). At the same time, these studies also found that the association between personality traits and indices of relevant behaviors and psychological adjustments was lower in Asian (but not necessarily in other collectivistic countries such as Mexico) samples relative to Western samples, presumably reflecting a stronger emphasis on cross-situational consistency in individualistic societies relative to East Asian cultures (Church et al., 2008a, 2008b; Oishi et al., 2004).

Emotion

Markus and Kitayama (1991) delineated consequences of the culturally shaped self in the areas of emotion, motivation, and cognitive processes. With respect to emotional processes, the evidence is available that emotions facilitate individuals' pursuit of the culturally shaped self. For example, Kitayama et al. (2006b) maintain that the interdependent self is associated with a tendency to experience socially engaging emotions (e.g., friendly feelings, guilt), whereas independent self is associated with a pervasive tendency to experience socially disengaging emotions (e.g., pride, anger). Moreover, experiences of these emotions are predictive of subjective well-being.

The notion that emotions facilitate the pursuit of the culturally shaped self has also led to interesting cross-cultural findings concerning anger. Findings from multiple studies suggest that anger is more frequently experienced in individualistic cultures due to its emphasis on personal goals and agendas – failing to achieve these goals results in frustration and anger (Boiger et al., 2013; Park et al., 2013). Moreover, the association between anger and markers of biological health risk appears to be stronger among American participants compared to Japanese participants (Kitayama et al., 2015).

The influence of culture on emotional processes has also been examined in terms of ideal affect, or the affective states that individuals prefer to feel (Tsai, 2007).

Tsai et al. (2006) showed that, compared with East Asians, North Americans more strongly preferred to feel *high-arousal positive* states (e.g., excited, elated). In contrast, East Asians more strongly preferred to feel *low-arousal positive* states (e.g., calm, peaceful). Presumably, people in individualistic cultures may use their high-arousal positive states in order to influence others in an effort to satisfy their personal needs. People in collectivistic cultures, in contrast, tend to emphasize accommodating oneself to the welfare of others, which may involve a commitment to suppress one's personal needs. This commitment is supported by low-arousal positive states (Tsai et al., 2006). Within a culture, ideal affective states are socialized through its artifacts. An analysis of cultural products is a suitable research method for examining this issue (Morling and Lamoreaux, 2008). For example, one analysis identified that popular children's storybooks in Taiwan portray their main characters with more calm than excited smiles whereas characters in popular North American storybooks tended to have more excited rather than calm smiles (Tsai et al., 2007a). A similar finding was obtained in an analysis of religious texts (Tsai et al., 2007b).

The differential focus of selfhood in individualistic and collectivistic cultures influences cultural standards of right and wrong, and therefore emotional responses of approval and disapproval. In particular, although morality in individualistic cultures is mainly concerned with the protection of individual autonomy and integrity, morality in collectivistic cultures concerns a broader array of values also encompassing loyalty, respect for authority, and the avoidance of disgusting acts to preserve purity (Haidt, 2001, 2007; Haidt and Bjorklund, 2008; Rozin et al., 1999). Haidt and colleagues have found support for the idea that people's moral judgments are the results of quick emotional 'gut' feelings (often outside of consciousness), called *moral intuitions*, which signal whether perceived actions are right or wrong. These moral intuitions are derived 'from innate psychological mechanisms that co-evolved with cultural institutions and practices' (p. 1030; Graham et al., 2009). As such, different moral norms across cultures should result in the activation of this gut feeling in a culturally variable way (Haidt, 2001, 2007; Haidt and Bjorklund, 2008; Wheatley and Haidt, 2005).

Motivation

The idea of a culturally shaped self has led to several lines of inquiries on motivation. First, it has led to a re-examination of autonomy and its effect on motivation. One influential study (Iyengar and Lepper, 1999) instructed Asian- and European-American children to solve an educational puzzle. Half of the children worked on the puzzle they chose whereas the other half worked on the puzzle that was chosen by others, either close others (e.g., their mother, classmates) or more distant others. The findings indicated that European-American children were most strongly motivated when they solved a puzzle that they chose. The self-selected puzzle was also more enjoyable and their performance was better. This is consistent with the robust positive effect of autonomous motivation in Western contexts. In contrast, Asian-American children were motivated most strongly when they solved a puzzle that was chosen by a close other. The other-selected puzzle was also perceived as more enjoyable and better performance was recorded. This finding inspired research examining the conception of autonomy in different cultural contexts (Rudy et al., 2007). An emerging view is that, in collectivistic contexts, doing something that is expected of the self is not at odds with one's autonomy; rather it co-occurs and provides support to it (Markus, 2016).

Accumulated findings also suggest the independent self's motivation for uniqueness and the interdependent self's motivation for social harmony. This difference has been illuminated in a number of ways (Kim and

Markus, 1999; Savani et al., 2010; Snibbe and Markus, 2005; Yamagishi et al., 2008). One such experiment presented a set of five pens consisting of two colors (e.g., two blue and three red pens) to travelers at the San Francisco International Airport as a gift for the short survey that they completed (Kim and Markus, 1999). Participants' choice varied systematically as a function of their cultural upbringing: European-American participants tended to pick a pen of an uncommon color, whereas Asian participants were much less likely to do so. It is relevant to note that a meta-analysis of Asch's classic conformity paradigm found a smaller conformity effect size in individualistic relative to collectivistic societies (Bond and Smith, 1996). The same analysis also found that the conformity effect size has decreased over time in the United States (Bond and Smith, 1996), consistent with other findings of rising individualism in the United States reviewed earlier. It is important to note that these findings do not indicate that motivation for social harmony stems from superficial compliance or social pressures. Rather, the motivation for social harmony in collectivism stems from motivations to perform 'good' actions, where 'good' is construed in terms of fulfilling role-based duties and obligations – again, tuning of the self to others co-occurs with individual autonomy (Markus, 2016).

Cross-cultural research has also examined motivation to maintain a positive self-view in a few different ways. One is in terms of the motivation for positive self-esteem. Heine et al. (1999) have maintained that the strong emphasis on positive self-esteem in Western cultures may not emerge in East Asian cultures. Rather, the emphasis placed on the cultivation of positive self-esteem in East Asian cultures may be relatively weaker because the priorities for the selfhood revolve around ideals of social harmony. This theory is supported by many findings. In fact, a meta-analysis of this literature suggests not only the pervasive cultural differences in self-esteem but also the presence of self-criticism among those from East Asian cultures (Heine and Hamamura, 2007; Heine et al., 2007). Interestingly, available evidence suggests that this cultural difference may be widening with the strengthening norm of positive self-esteem in the United States (Twenge and Campbell, 2001) and the strengthening norm of self-criticism in Japan, as indicated by decreasing self-esteem (Ogihara et al., 2015; Oshio et al., 2014).

Another way in which the motivation to maintain positive self-views has been examined is the dissonance reduction paradigm. Given that dissonance reduction reflects one's concern for perceived competence and efficacy in domains that are important to the self, the theory of culturally shaped selfhood suggests that the domains in which the dissonance reduction is evident may vary across cultures (Heine and Lehman, 1997; Hoshino-Browne et al., 2005; Kitayama et al., 2004). Evidence in support of this idea has been obtained. For example, in one experiment, European-Canadian and Asian-Canadian participants were asked to justify choices (e.g., selecting a dish from a menu) they made for themselves and for a friend. The European-Canadian participants showed a larger spread of alternatives for the choice made for the self than the Asian-Canadian participants. In contrast, a larger spread of alternatives for the choice made for a friend was found for the Asian-Canadian participants (Hoshino-Browne et al., 2005).

Cognition

Individualism–collectivism has also been associated with basic processes of cognition. Nisbett et al. (2001) articulated that the system of thought prevalent in Western individualistic societies is an analytic system, such that it focuses on the attributes of an object that is decontextualized from the environment and uses them as the basis for explaining behaviors. In contrast, the theory proposed that the system of thought that is prevalent in East Asian collectivistic societies is holistic, such that it focuses on the relationships between the object and its context and uses these relationships as the basis for explaining behaviors.

In explaining social behavior, many individuals in Western societies exhibit a tendency to overly focus on internal characteristics relative to environmental characteristics (Ross, 1977). This style of attribution is congruent with a lay belief of social behavior that is prevalent in individualistic societies that decontextualize a person from the situation in trying to understand their behavior (Nisbett et al., 2001). In contrast, in collectivistic societies, a belief that social behavior reflects a complex range of situational factors is prevalent (Nisbett et al., 2001). To test this idea, American and Chinese high school students were shown cartoons of a group of fish swimming in a lake in which one fish is a different color (blue) from the others (green; Morris and Peng, 1994). Students were asked to respond to questions concerning the extent to which the blue fish's movement reflected internal factors ('To what extent do the blue fish's movements seem influenced by internal factors?') and external factors ('To what extent do the blue fish's movements seem influenced by the other fish?'). American students were more likely to say the movements of the fish were influenced by the internal factors rather than the external factors. In contrast, the Chinese participants were more likely to say that the movements of the fish were influenced by the external factors rather than the internal factors. A similar difference in attribution style has been found in comparisons between American and Indian students (Miller, 1984), between Japanese living in Hokkaido and outside Hokkaido (Kitayama et al., 2006a), and between Americans from middle-class and working-class backgrounds (Kraus et al., 2009). Cultural differences in systems of thought have also been examined in experiments. One study recruited university students in Hong Kong and randomly assigned them to view either symbols of American culture (e.g., national flag, Marilyn Monroe, Superman, the White House) or Chinese culture (e.g., national flag, a Chinese opera singer, Stone monkey, the Great Wall; Hong et al., 2000). The participants assigned to the American culture condition were more likely to make internal attributions for explaining a social behavior compared to those assigned to the Chinese culture condition.

Analytic and holistic thinkers also differ in their systems of attention and perception. In one experiment, participants in Japan and the United States were presented with several underwater scenes containing a multitude of background and foreground objects (Masuda and Nisbett, 2001). In recalling the scenes, Japanese participants remembered more background objects compared with European-Americans. Research has also examined the difference in categorization processes. In one study, American and Chinese students were instructed to categorize a list of words. As predicted, Chinese participants were more likely to categorize objects relationally whereas European-American participants were more likely to categorize taxonomically (Ji et al., 2004). For example, when presented with a list of words such as *carrot–rabbit–eggplant,* Chinese participants were more likely to group carrot and rabbit together, whereas American participants were more likely to group carrot and eggplant together. This task was used in a recent study which revealed a greater likelihood of relational classification among Chinese participants from rice-growing regions compared to those from wheat-growing regions (Talhelm et al., 2014).

Another interesting cultural effect on cognition is dialectical thinking, prevalent in East Asia and stemming from a lay belief that the world is inherently contradictory and in constant flux (Peng and Nisbett, 1999; Spencer-Rodgers et al., 2010b). One well-examined issue concerns the experience of mixed emotions (i.e., the co-occurrence of positive and negative emotions). Support has been found for the idea that mixed emotions are more prevalent among dialectical thinkers, reflecting their greater tolerance for conflicting emotional states (Hui et al., 2009; Lu et al., 2017; Miyamoto et al., 2010; Shiota et al., 2010; Spencer-Rodgers et al., 2010a).

Interpersonal Relationships and Group Processes

Independent and interdependent self–other relations, as delineated in the theory of the culturally shaped self, have also led to questions about the processes of close interpersonal relationships and group membership.

In the realm of interpersonal relationships, a key postulate has been that people in collectivistic societies tend to maintain a close-knit social network with others who are connected through social roles, whereas people in individualistic societies tend to have social networks that are less tightly knit and less inwardly focused. This consideration has led to research findings that counter a lay belief of collectivism that expects interpersonal harmony across all forms of social relationships. For instance, in a series of studies, Adams and colleagues (Adams, 2005; Adams and Plaut, 2003) compared attitudes toward friends and enemies among Americans and Ghanaians. These studies found that American participants tended to have a positive view toward friendship and tended to view having an enemy, and being a target of an enemy, as abnormal and something to be avoided. In contrast, Ghanaian participants tended to have more ambivalent attitudes toward friends and were more tolerant of having an enemy. Adams and colleagues argued that, in individualistic societies, a social network is constructed in accordance with one's needs and interests – a friend is chosen for shared interests and emotional support, and unpleasant social relations are terminated. In contrast, people in collectivistic societies tend to accommodate to established social networks. As such, a friend may not share your interests, and terminating social relations – even ones that are dreadful – is more difficult. This idea has led to cultural examinations of strategies used to establish and maintain social ties (Schug et al., 2009, 2010), interpersonal risk taking (Li et al., 2014, 2015), and psychological consequences of social exclusion (Uskul and Over, 2014). Another relevant research finding is that generalized trust of others – or willingness for social exchange with others in general – is more prevalent in individualistic societies (Gheorghiu et al., 2009; Hamamura, 2012; Yamagishi and Yamagishi, 1994).

Findings also suggest that a cultural norm of interpersonal harmony can become a burden. For example, Chinese participants have been found to be more reluctant than Canadian participants to accept a gift from an acquaintance in order not to be indebted (Shen et al., 2011). Cross-cultural research on social support seeking has identified a conceptually similar pattern. Studies in this area suggest that, although receiving social support is beneficial for various physical health outcomes across cultures, social support is sought more actively in Western cultures than in Asian cultures. This difference has been linked with collectivistic concerns regarding the disruption of social harmony. Instead, studies indicate that collectivists tend to draw more on implicit social support seeking and derive emotional benefits by thinking about close relationships (Kim et al., 2006, 2008; Taylor et al., 2004, 2007).

In the realm of group process and intergroup relations, cross-cultural research has led to a refinement of the individualism–collectivism dimension. In particular, Brewer and colleagues (Brewer and Chen, 2007; Brewer and Yuki, 2007; see also Cross et al., 2010; Kashima et al., 1995) have argued that collectivism may be a misnomer because collectivism implies individuals' affiliation with broader social groups and little research has examined this issue cross-culturally, unlike relationalism where the accumulated findings have clearly indicated cultural differences, as reviewed in the previous paragraphs. This conceptual refinement led to a novel theory of cultural differences in group processes (Brewer and Yuki, 2007; Yuki, 2003). According to this theory, individuals in Western societies tend to represent large social groups as a depersonalized entity, and their group membership is represented abstractly as an attachment to such entities and informed by comparisons with other social groups. In contrast, people in East Asian societies represent large social groups as consisting of a network of interpersonal ties, and individuals' group membership is represented in terms of these interpersonal ties.

This theory has been used in a number of cross-cultural studies. For example, one study used the theory to examine the importance of group membership for trust (Yuki et al., 2005). This study found that the American participants were more likely to trust a stranger if the person shared the same group membership (e.g., attending the same university), whereas Japanese participants were more likely to trust a stranger who shared a common interpersonal tie. In other words, this finding suggests that the conception of outgroup may differ across cultures, as individuals not belonging in the same group versus not belonging in the same social network. Implications of this theory for intergroup processes have also been examined. First, findings indicate that intergroup comparison is relatively more important for American participants than Japanese participants (Takemura et al., 2010). Presumably, this pattern reflects the importance of intergroup comparison in deriving social identity when individuals' membership to a social group is represented as an attachment to a depersonalized entity (Brewer and Yuki, 2007; Hamamura, 2016; Yuki, 2003). The observation of cultural differences in intergroup comparison, in turn, has been used to examine and confirm cross-cultural differences in self-stereotyping, a process that engages the intergroup comparison to inform one's self-concept (Guimond, 2008; Hamamura, 2011b). Findings from these studies indicate a stronger self-stereotyping effect, as evident in larger gender differences in self-rated personality traits and mathematic test performance (Guimond, 2008; Hamamura, 2011b).

Psychological Processes of Individualism–Collectivism: Section Summary

A large number of studies have examined cultural differences in psychological processes, especially during the last three decades. Many of these studies used the individualism–collectivism dimension or theories derived from this dimension to make specific predictions about cultural influence, particularly in the areas of self-concept, emotion, motivation, cognition, interpersonal processes, and intergroup processes. Our review provides only a snapshot of this vast literature and interested readers are recommended to consult reviews cited above for specific topics.

One significant trend in this literature is a greater diversity of methodologies and comparative contexts. Whereas earlier studies predominantly focused on comparisons between participants recruited in North America and East Asia using self-reported measures, studies conducted in recent years use a diverse range of research methods, including experimental designs, analyses of cultural products, and physiological and neurological assessments. As for the comparative contexts, an increasing number of studies have compared regions and individuals within a society, and compared the same society across different points in time.

CONCLUSION

Our observation is that many researchers in the field of cultural and cross-cultural psychology have a love–hate relationship with the individualism–collectivism dimension. On the one hand, there is a widely shared acknowledgment of the influence that the individualism–collectivism dimension has had on the conceptual and empirical development of cross-cultural psychology. The present reviews provided a brief and recent overview of these findings. On the other hand, there is also a widely shared agreement about the dimension's limitations because the results concerning cross-cultural differences have also illuminated nuances and complexities that were not a part of the original formulation of individualism–collectivism. Influential attempts to address this limitation (Brewer and Chen, 2007; Cross et al., 2010) have also been incorporated in the present review to project how this area of research may unfold in the coming years.

REFERENCES

Adams, G. (2005). The cultural grounding of personal relationship: Enemyship in North American and West African worlds. *Journal of Personality and Social Psychology*, 88, 948–968.

Adams, G., & Plaut, V. C. (2003). The cultural grounding of personal relationship: Friendship in North American and West African worlds. *Personal Relationships*, 10, 333–347.

Bianchi, E. C. (2016). American individualism rises and falls with the economy: Cross-temporal evidence that individualism declines when the economy falters. *Journal of Personality and Social Psychology*, 111, 567–584.

Boiger, M., Mesquita, B., Uchida, Y., & Feldman Barrett, L. (2013). Condoned or condemned: The situational affordance of anger and shame in the United States and Japan. *Personality and Social Psychology Bulletin*, 39, 540–553.

Bond, R., & Smith, P. B. (1996). Culture and conformity: A meta-analysis of studies using Asch's (1952b, 1956) line judgment task. *Psychological Bulletin*, 119, 111–137.

Brewer, M. B., & Chen, Y.-R. (2007). Where (who) are collectives in collectivism? Toward conceptual clarification of individualism and collectivism. *Psychological Review*, 114, 133–151.

Brewer, M. B., & Yuki, M. (2007). Culture and social identity. In S. Kitayama & D. Cohen (Eds.), *Handbook of cultural psychology* (pp. 307–322). New York, NY: Guilford.

Cai, H., Kwan, V. S. Y., & Sedikides, C. (2011). A sociocultural approach to narcissism: The case of modern China. *European Journal of Personality*, 26, 529–535.

Cashdan, E., & Steele, M. (2013). Pathogen prevalence, group bias, and collectivism in the standard cross-cultural sample. *Human Nature*, 24, 59–75.

Chiao, J. Y., & Blizinsky, K. D. (2009). Culture–gene coevolution of individualism–collectivism and the serotonin transporter gene. *Proceedings of the Royal Society, Series B: Biological Sciences*, 277, 529–537.

Chiu, C. Y., Gelfand, M. J., Yamagishi, T., Shteynberg, G., & Wan, C. (2010). Intersubjective culture: The role of intersubjective perceptions in cross-cultural research. *Perspectives on Psychological Science*, 5, 482–493.

Church, A. T. (2016). Personality traits across cultures. *Current Opinion in Psychology*, 8, 22–30.

Church, A. T., Anderson-Harumi, C. A., Del Prado, A. M., Curtis, G. J., Tanaka-Matsumi, J., Valdez Medina, J. L., ... Katigbak, M. S. (2008a). Culture, cross-role consistency, and adjustment: Testing trait and cultural psychology perspectives. *Journal of Personality and Social Psychology*, 95, 739–755.

Church, A. T., Katigbak, M. S., Reyes, J. A. S., Salanga, M. G. C., Miramontes, L. A., & Adams, N. B. (2008b). Prediction and cross-situational consistency of daily behavior across cultures: Testing trait and cultural psychology perspectives. *Journal of Research in Personality*, 42, 1199–1215.

Cohen, D. (2001). Cultural variation: Considerations and implications. *Psychological Bulletin*, 127, 451–471.

Cousins, S. (1989). Culture and self-perception in Japan and the United States. *Journal of Personality and Social Psychology*, 56, 124–131.

Cross, S. E., Hardin, E. E., & Gercek-Swing, B. (2010). The what, how, why, and where of self-construal. *Personality and Social Psychology Review*, 15, 142–179.

del Prado, A. M., Church, A. T., Katigbak, M. S., Miramontes, L. G., Whitty, M., Curtis, G. J., ... Reyes, J. A. S. (2007). Culture, method, and the content of self-concepts: Testing trait, individual-self-primacy, and cultural psychology perspectives. *Journal of Research in Personality*, *41*, 1119–1160.

Fincher, C. L., & Thornhill, R. (2012). Parasite-stress promotes in-group assortative sociality: The cases of strong family ties and heightened religiosity. *Behavioral and Brain Sciences*, *35*, 61–79.

Fincher, C., Thornhill, R., Murray, D. R., & Schaller, M. (2008). Pathogen prevalence predicts human cross-cultural variability in individualism/collectivism. *Proceedings of the Royal Society, Series B: Biological Sciences*, *275*, 1279–1285.

Gentile, B., Twenge, J. M., & Campbell, W. K. (2010). Birth cohort differences in self-esteem, 1988–2008: A cross-temporal meta-analysis. *Review of General Psychology*, *14*, 261–268.

Gheorghiu, M., Vignoles, V., & Smith, P. (2009). Beyond the United States and Japan: Testing Yamagishi's emancipation theory of trust across 31 nations. *Social Psychology Quarterly*, *72*, 365–383.

Graham, J., Haidt, J., & Nosek, B. A. (2009). Liberals and conservatives rely on different sets of moral foundations. *Journal of Personality and Social Psychology*, *96*, 1029–1046.

Greenfield, P. M. (2009). Linking social change and developmental change: Shifting pathways of human development. *Developmental Psychology*, *45*, 401–418.

Greenfield, P. M. (2013). The changing psychology of culture from 1800 through 2000. *Psychological Science*, *24*, 1722–1731.

Greenfield, P. M. (2015). Social change, cultural evolution, and human development. *Current Opinion in Psychology*, *8*, 84–92.

Grossmann, I., & Varnum, M. E. (2010). Social class, culture, and cognition. *Social Psychological and Personality Science*, *2*, 81–89.

Grossmann, I., & Varnum, M. E. (2015). Social structure, infectious diseases, disasters, secularism, and cultural change in America. *Psychological Science*, *26*, 311–324.

Guimond, S. (2008). Psychological similarities and differences between women and men across cultures. *Social and Personality Psychology Compass*, *2*, 494–510.

Haidt, J. (2001). The emotional dog and its rational tail: A social intuitionist approach to moral judgment. *Psychological Review*, *108*, 814–834.

Haidt, J. (2007). The new synthesis in moral psychology. *Science*, *316*, 998–1002.

Haidt, J., & Bjorklund, F. (2008). Social intuitionists answer six questions about morality. In W. Sinnott-Armstrong (Ed.), *Moral psychology (Vol 2). The cognitive science of morality: Intuition and diversity* (pp. 181–217). Cambridge, MA: MIT Press.

Hamamura, T. (2011a). Are cultures becoming individualistic? A cross-temporal comparison of individualism–collectivism in the United States and Japan. *Personality and Social Psychology Review*, *16*, 3–24.

Hamamura, T. (2011b). Power distance predicts gender differences in math performance across societies. *Social Psychological and Personality Science*, *3*, 545–548.

Hamamura, T. (2012). Social class predicts generalized trust but only in wealthy societies. *Journal of Cross-Cultural Psychology*, *43*, 498–509.

Hamamura, T. (2016). Social identity and attitudes toward cultural diversity: A cultural psychological analysis. *Journal of Cross-Cultural Psychology*, *48*, 184–194.

Hamamura, T., Heine, S., & Paulhus, D. (2008). Cultural differences in response styles: The role of dialectical thinking. *Personality and Individual Differences*, *44*, 932–942.

Hamamura, T., & Septarini, G. B (2017). Culture and self-esteem over time: A cross-temporal meta-analysis among Australians, 1978–2014. *Social Psychological and Personality Science*, 904–909.

Hamamura, T., Xu, Q., & Du, Y. (2013). Culture, social class, and independence–interdependence: The case of Chinese adolescents. *International Journal of Psychology*, *48*, 344–351.

Hamamura, T., & Xu, Y. (2015). Changes in Chinese culture as examined through changes in personal pronoun usage. *Journal of Cross-Cultural Psychology*, *46*, 930–941.

Heine, S. J. (2008). *Cultural psychology*. New York, NY: Norton.

Heine, S. J., & Buchtel, E. (2009). Personality: The universal and the culturally specific. *Annual Review of Psychology*, *60*, 369–394.

Heine, S. J., & Hamamura, T. (2007). In search of East Asian self-enhancement. *Personality and Social Psychology Review*, *11*, 4–27.

Heine, S. J., Kitayama, S., & Hamamura, T. (2007). Inclusion of additional studies yields different conclusions: Comment on Sedikides, Gaertner, & Vevea. *Asian Journal of Social Psychology, 10*, 49–58.

Heine, S. J., & Lehman, D. (1997). Culture, dissonance, and self-affirmation. *Personality and Social Psychology Bulletin, 23*, 389–400.

Heine, S. J., Lehman, D., Markus, H. R., & Kitayama, S. (1999). Is there a universal need for positive self-regard? *Psychological Review, 106*, 766–794.

Heine, S. J., Lehman, D. R., Peng, K., & Greenholtz, J. (2002). What's wrong with cross-cultural comparisons of subjective Likert scales? The reference-group effect. *Journal of Personality and Social Psychology, 82*, 903–918.

Henrich, J., Heine, S. J., & Norenzayan, A. (2010). The weirdest people in the world? *Behavioral and Brain Sciences, 33*, 61–83.

Hofstede, G. (1980). Culture and organizations. *International Studies of Management and Organization, 10*, 15–41.

Hong, Y.-Y., Morris, M. W., Chiu, C.-Y., & Benet-Martínez, V. (2000). Multicultural minds: A dynamic constructivist approach to culture and cognition. *American Psychologist, 55*, 709–720.

Hoshino-Browne, E., Zanna, A. S., Spencer, S. J., Zanna, M. P., Kitayama, S., & Lackenbauer, S. (2005). On the cultural guises of cognitive dissonance: The case of easterners and westerners. *Journal of Personality and Social Psychology, 89*, 294–310.

Hui, C. M., Fok, H. K., & Bond, M. H. (2009). Who feels more ambivalence? Linking dialectical thinking to mixed emotions. *Personality and Individual Differences, 46*, 493–498.

Inglehart, R., & Baker, W. (2000). Modernization, cultural change, and the persistence of traditional values. *American Sociological Review, 65*, 19–51.

Inkeles, A. (1975). Becoming modern. *Ethos, 3*, 323–342.

Inoguchi, T. (2000). Social capital in Japan. *Japanese Journal of Political Science, 1*, 73–112.

Iyengar, S., & Lepper, M. (1999). Rethinking the value of choice: A cultural perspective on intrinsic motivation. *Journal of Personality and Social Psychology, 76*, 349–366.

Ji, L. J., Zhang, Z., & Nisbett, R. E. (2004). Is it culture or is it language? Examination of language effects in cross-cultural research on categorization. *Journal of Personality and Social Psychology, 87*, 57–65.

Kashima, Y., Yamaguchi, S., Kim, U., Choi, S. C., Gelfand, M. J., & Yuki, M. (1995). Culture, gender, and self: A perspective from individualism–collectivism research. *Journal of Personality and Social Psychology, 69*, 925–937.

Kim, H. S., & Markus, H. R. (1999). Deviance or uniqueness, harmony or conformity? A cultural analysis. *Journal of Personality and Social Psychology, 77*, 785–800.

Kim, H. S., & Sasaki, J. Y. (2014). Cultural neuroscience: Biology of the mind in cultural contexts. *Annual Review of Psychology, 65*, 487–514.

Kim, H. S., Sherman, D. K., Ko, D., & Taylor, S. E. S. (2006). Pursuit of comfort and pursuit of harmony: Culture, relationships, and social support seeking. *Personality and Social Psychology Bulletin, 32*, 1595–1607.

Kim, H. S., Sherman, D., & Taylor, S. E. S. (2008). Culture and social support. *American Psychologist, 63*, 518–526.

Kitayama, S., & Cohen, D. (2010). *Handbook of cultural psychology*. New York, NY: Guilford Press.

Kitayama, S., Ishii, K., Imada, T., Takemura, K., & Ramaswamy, J. (2006a). Voluntary settlement and the spirit of independence: Evidence from Japan's 'northern frontier'. *Journal of Personality and Social Psychology, 91*, 369–384.

Kitayama, S., Mesquita, B., & Karasawa, M. (2006b). Cultural affordances and emotional experience: Socially engaging and disengaging emotions in Japan and the United States. *Journal of Personality and Social Psychology, 91*, 890–903.

Kitayama, S., Park, J., Boylan, J. M., Miyamoto, Y., Levine, C. S., Markus, H. R., ... Ryff, C. D. (2015). Expression of anger and ill health in two cultures: An examination of inflammation and cardiovascular risk. *Psychological Science, 26*, 211–220.

Kitayama, S., Snibbe, A. C., Markus, H. R., & Suzuki, T. (2004). Is there any "free" choice? Self and dissonance in two cultures. *Psychological Science, 15*, 527–533.

Kraus, M. W., Piff, P. K., & Keltner, D. (2009). Social class, sense of control, and social explanation. *Journal of Personality and Social Psychology, 97*, 992–1004.

Li, L. M. W., Adams, G., Kurtiş, T., & Hamamura, T. (2014). Beware of friends: The cultural psychology of relational mobility and cautious intimacy. *Asian Journal of Social Psychology*, *18*, 124–133.

Li, L. M. W., Hamamura, T., & Adams, G. (2015). Relational mobility increases social (but not other) risk propensity. *Journal of Behavioral Decision Making*, *29*, 481–488.

Liu, D., & Xin, Z. (2015). Birth cohort and age changes in the self-esteem of Chinese adolescents: A cross-temporal meta-analysis, 1996–2009. *Journal of Research on Adolescence*, *25*, 366–376.

Lu, M., Hamamura, T., Doosje, B., Suzuki, S., & Takemura, K. (2017). Culture and group-based emotions: Could group-based emotions be dialectical? *Cognition and Emotion*, *31*, 937–949.

Ma, V., & Schoeneman, T. J. (1997). Individualism versus collectivism: A comparison of Kenyan and American self-concepts. *Basic and Applied Social Psychology*, *19*, 261–273.

Markus, H. R. (2016). What moves people to action? Culture and motivation. *Current Opinion in Psychology*, *8*, 161–166.

Markus, H. R., & Kitayama, S. (1991). Culture and the self: Implications for cognition, emotion, and motivation. *Psychological Review*, *98*, 224–253.

Markus, H. R., & Kitayama, S. (1998). The cultural psychology of personality. *Journal of Cross-Cultural Psychology*, *29*, 63–87.

Masuda, T., & Nisbett, R. E. (2001). Attending holistically versus analytically: Comparing the context sensitivity of Japanese and Americans. *Journal of Personality and Social Psychology*, *81*, 922–934.

Miller, J. G. (1984). Culture and the development of everyday social explanation. *Journal of Personality and Social Psychology*, *46*, 961–978.

Miyamoto, Y. (2013). Culture and analytic versus holistic cognition: Toward multilevel analyses of cultural influences. *Advances in Experimental Social Psychology*, *47*, 131–188.

Miyamoto, Y., Uchida, Y., & Ellsworth, P. C. (2010). Culture and mixed emotions: Co-occurrence of positive and negative emotions in Japan and the United States. *Emotion*, *10*, 404–415.

Morling, B., & Lamoreaux, M. (2008). Measuring culture outside the head: A meta-analysis of Individualism–Collectivism in cultural products. *Personality and Social Psychology Review*, *12*, 199–221.

Morris, M. W., & Peng, K. (1994). Culture and cause: American and Chinese attributions for social and physical events. *Journal of Personality and Social Psychology*, *67*, 949–971.

Murray, D. R., Trudeau, R., & Schaller, M. (2011). On the origins of cultural differences in conformity: Four tests of the pathogen prevalence hypothesis. *Personality and Social Psychology Bulletin*, *37*, 318–329.

Nisbett, R. E., Peng, K., Choi, I., & Norenzayan, A. (2001). Culture and systems of thought: Holistic versus analytic cognition. *Psychological Review*, *108*, 291–310.

Ogihara, Y., Fujita, H., Tominaga, H., Ishigaki, S., Kashimoto, T., Takahashi, A., ... Uchida, Y. (2015). Are common names becoming less common? The rise in uniqueness and individualism in Japan. *Frontiers in Psychology*, *6*, 1490.

Oishi, S. (2010). The psychology of residential mobility implications for the self, social relationships, and well-being. *Perspectives on Psychological Science*, *5*, 5–21.

Oishi, S., Diener, E., Napa Scollon, C., & Biswas-Diener, R. (2004). Cross-situational consistency of affective experiences across cultures. *Journal of Personality and Social Psychology*, *86*, 460–472.

Oishi, S., Lun, J., & Sherman, G. D. (2007). Residential mobility, self-concept, and positive affect in social interactions. *Journal of Personality and Social Psychology*, *93*, 131–141.

Oishi, S., Schug, J., Yuki, M., & Axt, J. (2015). The psychology of residential and relational mobilities. In M. J. Gelfand, C. Y. Chiu, & Y. Y. Hong (Eds.), *Handbook of advances in culture and psychology* (Vol. 5, pp. 221–272). Oxford: Oxford University Press.

Oshio, A., Okada, R., Mogaki, M., Namikawa, T., & Wakita, T. (2014). Age and survey-year effects on self-esteem in Japan. *Japanese Journal of Educational Psychology*, *62*, 273–282.

Oyserman, D., Coon, H. M., & Kemmelmeier, M. (2002). Rethinking individualism and collectivism: Evaluation of theoretical assumptions and meta-analyses. *Psychological Bulletin*, *128*, 3–72.

Park, H., Twenge, J. M., & Greenfield, P. M. (2014). The Great Recession implications for adolescent values and behavior. *Social Psychological and Personality Science*, *5*, 310–318.

Park, J., Kitayama, S., Markus, H. R., Coe, C. L., Miyamoto, Y., Karasawa, M., ... Ryff, C. D. (2013). Social status and anger expression: The cultural moderation hypothesis. *Emotion, 13*, 1122–1131.

Peng, K., & Nisbett, R. E. (1999). Culture, dialectics, and reasoning about contradiction. *American Psychologist, 54*, 741–754.

Piff, P. K. (2014). Wealth and the inflated self: Class, entitlement, and narcissism. *Personality and Social Psychology Bulletin, 40*, 34–43.

Putnam, R. D. (2001). *Bowling alone: The collapse and revival of American community*. New York, NY: Simon and Schuster.

Ross, L. (1977). The intuitive psychologist and his shortcomings: Distortions in the attribution process. *Advances in Experimental Social Psychology, 10*, 173–220.

Rozin, P., Lowery, L., Imada, S., & Haidt, J. (1999). The CAD triad hypothesis: A mapping between three moral emotions (contempt, anger, disgust) and three moral codes (community, autonomy, divinity). *Journal of Personality and Social Psychology, 76*, 574–586.

Rudy, D., Sheldon, K. M., Awong, T., & Tan, H. H. (2007). Autonomy, culture, and well-being: The benefits of inclusive autonomy. *Journal of Research in Personality, 41*, 983–1007.

Savani, K., Markus, H. R., Naidu, N., Kumar, S., & Berlia, N. (2010). What counts as a Choice?: U.S. Americans are more likely than Indians to construe actions as choices. *Psychological Science, 21*, 391–398.

Schaller, M., & Murray, D. R. (2008). Pathogens, personality, and culture: Disease prevalence predicts worldwide variability in sociosexuality, extraversion, and openness to experience. *Journal of Personality and Social Psychology, 95*, 212–221.

Schimmack, U., Oishi, S., & Diener, E. (2005). Individualism: A valid and important dimension of cultural differences between nations. *Personality and Social Psychology Review, 9*, 17–31.

Schug, J., Yuki, M., Horikawa, H., & Takemura, K. (2009). Similarity attraction and actually selecting similar others: How cross-societal differences in relational mobility affect interpersonal similarity in Japan and the USA. *Asian Journal of Social Psychology, 12*, 95–103.

Schug, J., Yuki, M., & Maddux, W. (2010). Relational mobility explains between- and within-culture differences in self-disclosure to close friends. *Psychological Science, 21*, 1471–1478.

Shen, H., Wan, F., & Wyers, R. S. (2011). Cross-cultural differences in the refusal to accept a small gift: The differential influence of reciprocity norms on Asians and North Americans. *Journal of Personality and Social Psychology, 100*, 271–281.

Shiota, M. N., Campos, B., Gonzaga, G. C., Keltner, D., & Peng, K. (2010). I love you but...: Cultural differences in complexity of emotional experience during interaction with a romantic partner. *Cognition and Emotion, 24*, 786–799.

Snibbe, A. C., & Markus, H. R. (2005). You can't get always get what you want: Educational attainment, agency, and choice. *Journal of Personality and Social Psychology, 88*, 703–720.

Spencer-Rodgers, J., Peng, K., & Wang, L. (2010a). Dialecticism and the co-occurrence of positive and negative emotions across cultures. *Journal of Cross-Cultural Psychology, 41*, 109–115.

Spencer-Rodgers, J., Williams, M. J., & Peng, K. (2010b). Cultural differences in expectations of change and tolerance for contradiction: A decade of empirical research. *Personality and Social Psychology Review, 14*, 296–312.

Takemura, K., Hamamura, T., Guan, Y., & Suzuki, S. (2016). Contextual effect of wealth on independence: An examination through regional differences in China. *Frontiers in Psychology, 7*, 384.

Takemura, K., Yuki, M., & Ohtsubo, Y. (2010). Attending inside or outside: A Japanese–US comparison of spontaneous memory of group information. *Asian Journal of Social Psychology, 13*, 303–307.

Talhelm, T., Zhang, X., Oishi, S., Shimin, C., Duan, D., Lan, X., & Kitayama, S. (2014). Large-scale psychological differences within China explained by rice versus wheat agriculture. *Science, 344*, 603–608.

Taylor, S. E. S., Sherman, D. K., Kim, H. S., Jarcho, J., Takagi, K., & Dunagan, M. S. (2004). Culture and social support: Who seeks it and why? *Journal of Personality and Social Psychology, 87*, 354–362.

Taylor, S. E. S., Welch, W., Kim, H. S., & Sherman, D. (2007). Cultural differences in the impact of social support on psychological and biological stress responses. *Psychological Science, 18*, 831–837.

Torpe, L. (2003). Social capital in Denmark: A deviant case? *Scandinavian Political Studies*, 26, 27–48.

Triandis, H. C. (1995). *Individualism and collectivism*. Boulder, CO: Westview Press.

Tsai, J. L. (2007). Ideal affect: Cultural causes and behavioral consequences. *Perspectives on Psychological Science*, 2, 242–259.

Tsai, J. L., Knutson, B., & Fung, H. H. (2006). Cultural variation in affect valuation. *Journal of Personality and Social Psychology*, 90, 288–307.

Tsai, J. L., Louie, J. Y., Chen, E. E., & Uchida, Y. (2007a). Learning what feelings to desire: Socialization of ideal affect through children's storybooks. *Personality and Social Psychology Bulletin*, 33, 17–30.

Tsai, J. L., Miao, F. F., & Seppala, E. (2007b). Good feelings in Christianity and Buddhism: Religious differences in ideal affect. *Personality and Social Psychology Bulletin*, 33, 409–421.

Twenge, J. M., Abebe, E. M., & Campbell, W. K. (2010). Fitting in or standing out: Trends in American parents' choices for children's names, 1880–2007. *Social Psychological and Personality Science*, 1, 19–25.

Twenge, J. M., & Campbell, W. (2001). Age and birth cohort differences in self-esteem: A cross-temporal meta-analysis. *Personality and Social Psychology Review*, 5, 321–344.

Twenge, J. M., Campbell, W. K., & Gentile, B. (2012a). Generational increases in agentic self-evaluations among American college students, 1966–2009. *Self and Identity*, 11, 409–427.

Twenge, J. M., Campbell, W. K., & Gentile, B. (2012b). Increases in individualistic words and phrases in American books, 1960–2008. *PLoS ONE*, 7, e40181.

Twenge, J. M., Konrath, S., Foster, J. D., Campbell, W. K., & Bushman, B. J. (2008). Egos inflating over time: A cross-temporal meta-analysis of the Narcissistic Personality Inventory. *Journal of Personality*, 76, 875–902.

Twenge, J. M., Zhang, L., & Im, C. (2004). It's beyond my control: A cross-temporal meta-analysis of increasing externality in locus of control, 1960–2002. *Personality and Social Psychology Review*, 8, 308–319.

Uskul, A. K., Kitayama, S., & Nisbett, R. E. (2008). Ecocultural basis of cognition: Farmers and fishermen are more holistic than herders. *Proceedings of the National Academy of Sciences*, 105, 8552–8556.

Uskul, A. K., & Over, H. (2014). Responses to social exclusion in cultural context: Evidence from farming and herding communities. *Journal of Personality and Social Psychology*, 106, 752–771.

Vandello, J. A., & Cohen, D. (1999). Patterns of individualism and collectivism across the United States. *Journal of Personality and Social Psychology*, 77, 279–292.

Varnum, M. E., & Kitayama, S. (2011). What's in a name? Popular names are less common on frontiers. *Psychological Science*, 22, 176–183.

Vignoles, V. L., Owe, E., Becker, M., Smith, P. B., Easterbrook, M. J., Brown, R., ... Cadena, M. P. (2016). Beyond the 'East–West' dichotomy: Global variation in cultural models of selfhood. *Journal of Experimental Psychology: General*, 145, 966–1000.

Wheatley, T., & Haidt, J. (2005). Hypnotic disgust makes moral judgments more severe. *Psychological Science*, 16, 780–784.

Witkin, H. A., & Berry, J. W. (1975). Psychological differentiation in cross-cultural perspective. *Journal of Cross-Cultural Psychology*, 6, 4–87.

Xu, Y., & Hamamura, T. (2014). Folk beliefs of cultural changes in China. *Frontiers in Psychology*, 5, 1066.

Yamagishi, T., Hashimoto, H., & Schug, J. (2008). Preferences versus strategies as explanations for culture-specific behavior. *Psychological Science*, 19, 579–584.

Yamagishi, T., & Yamagishi, M. (1994). Trust and commitment in the United States and Japan. *Motivation and Emotion*, 18, 129–166.

Yamawaki, N. (2012). Within-culture variations of collectivism in Japan. *Journal of Cross-Cultural Psychology*, 43, 1191–1204.

Yuki, M. (2003). Intergroup comparison versus intragroup relationships: A cross-cultural examination of social identity theory in North American and East Asian cultural contexts. *Social Psychology Quarterly*, 66, 166–183.

Yuki, M., Maddux, W. W., Brewer, M. B., & Takemura, K. (2005). Cross-cultural differences in relationship- and group-based trust. *Personality and Social Psychology Bulletin*, 31, 48–62.

Zou, X., Tam, K. P., Morris, M. W., Lee, S. L., Lau, I. Y. M., & Chiu, C. Y. (2009). Culture as common sense: Perceived consensus versus personal beliefs as mechanisms of cultural influence. *Journal of Personality and Social Psychology*, 97, 579–597.

Exploring Potential Causes of Individual Differences in the Expression of Neonatal Imitation

Siobhan Kennedy-Costantini
and Mark Nielsen

Human beings are social animals, with the importance we place on social connection being integral to our success as a species (Heerey, 2015; Lakin et al., 2003; Simpson et al., 2016). We learn many of our social and cognitive abilities by observing and copying what others do (Legare and Nielsen, 2015). As such, imitation plays a huge part in the way we learn, communicate, and engage with others in our social world. Indeed, some argue that the ability to imitate is present from birth (Meltzoff, 2007; Simpson et al., 2014). Yet, the evidence for neonatal imitation remains unconvincing (Oostenbroek et al., 2016). Although some researchers report observing imitation in the first weeks of life (e.g., Meltzoff and Moore, 1977, 1983; Reissland, 1988), these reports may be a result of statistical and/or methodological artifacts. Alternatively, they could also represent a small subset of infants who have learned to engage in such a way. Although there remains no direct evidence that the capacity for imitation is inborn, there is much evidence to demonstrate that humans learn to imitate in the context of social interaction (Catmur et al., 2009; Ray and Heyes, 2011). In this chapter, we discuss the role of individual differences by exploring the imitation literature to date, the genetic evidence regarding its expression, how infants might learn to imitate, and by presenting two studies that investigate the underlying cause of these differences.

THE ELUSIVE CASE OF NEONATAL IMITATION

Whether newborns have an ability to imitate has been the focus of considerable research effort over the past four decades. Dozens of studies have attempted to document the phenomenon, using a range of gestures (e.g., index protrusion, blinking, head movements) presented to infants of different ages. Despite the enthusiasm with which this topic has been approached, evidence for neonatal imitation remains elusive, with studies producing both positive (e.g., Field et al., 1982, 1983; Meltzoff and Moore, 1989, 1992; Reissland, 1988; Vinter, 1986) and negative results (e.g., Hayes and Watson, 1981; Koepke et al., 1983; McKenzie and Over, 1983; Oostenbroek et al., 2016). Regardless of the inability to conclusively identify its existence, several authors are adamant that their studies demonstrate evidence of newborns' imitative behaviors (Field, 1982; Heimann et al., 1989). However, in a recent large-scale longitudinal study, Oostenbroek et al. (2016) charted the developmental trajectory of neonatal imitation. Testing 106 infants across four different time points (one, three, six, and nine weeks of age), they found no evidence of imitation at the group level or of intra-individual consistency in imitative responses across the neonatal period. This leaves the most liberal interpretation of neonatal imitation being that if it is indeed a phenomenon, it is at the least one that is both weak and fragile (Heimann, 2002). This variability in infants' responses through the course of early infancy could point to environmental factors playing a role in 'imitative' expression. Specifically, these differences may develop throughout early infancy as a result of early parent–infant interaction. Although there is no clear evidence for individual differences in imitation or an association between parental interaction and imitation, it is time these are more thoroughly investigated. If any such evidence is uncovered, it could be informative regarding later social-cognitive maturation and development.

GENETIC EVIDENCE?

Proponents of neonatal imitation favor the view that infants have an innate ability to compare the sensory information of a visually perceived expression (e.g., an adult producing facial gestures) with the proprioceptive feedback of the motor movements involved in matching that expression. However, if infants are born with the capacity to imitate, why do not all infants demonstrate it? A possible explanation is that there are individual differences in the degree to which infants imitate, and these differences are underpinned by environmental influences. It is implausible to conclude that imitation is a function of genetic influence alone, yet this does not presuppose that there exists no genetic influence on its development. Instead, imitation may be a result of underlying predispositions that are 'activated' or influenced by social interaction with caregivers (Heyes, 2016b). McEwen et al. (2007) explored this by looking at the imitation and 'socially insightful behavior' of a large community-based twin sample. After testing 5,206 two-year-old twin pairs, they found that 30% of the variance could be attributed to genetic factors; although, the authors caution that this could easily be accounted for by more basic perceptual or motivational factors. Meanwhile, the largest amount of variance (42%) was accounted for by environment influences. This demonstrates that, although there may not be a genetically inherited neurocognitive mechanism for imitation, there is another avenue through which we might 'inherit' our imitative skills. Imitation is often used by parents as a way to socially interact with their infants (Jones and Yoshida, 2011), and both infants and parents who are socially motivated may be more likely to use imitation during these interactions in the first place (McEwen et al., 2007).

ASSOCIATIVE SEQUENCE LEARNING

An avenue through which infants may learn to imitate is described by the

Associative Sequence Learning (ASL) model, which suggests that the underlying capacity for imitation is not a specific or innate mechanism but instead part of a general process of associative learning (Catmur et al., 2009; Heyes, 2016a; Ray and Heyes, 2011). The ASL model offers three key components in support of this perspective. First, infants' accuracy of imitation and range of imitative gestures improves over time as they gain more experience observing and executing the same actions (e.g., Abravanel et al., 1976; Jones, 2007; Killen and Uzgiris, 2006). Second, the types of actions that infants perform first are the ones they are more likely to have had the most experience of both seeing and doing (e.g., Kaye and Marcus, 1978; Piaget, 1945). Finally, individual variation in the development of imitation depends on imitation experience and the quality of the reciprocal 'seeing–doing' social interactions that infants have received (e.g., Field et al., 2005; McEwen et al., 2007).

It is common for parents to enthusiastically engage in imitative interactions, and parents regularly react with effusive positivity when their infant's behavior matches their own (Ray and Heyes, 2011). For example, Pawlby (1977) found that mothers reacted to infant 'imitation' (real or imagined) with delight, smiles, and a sense of encouragement. Catmur et al. (2009) argue that responding with encouragement and enthusiasm to imitation and imitative-like behaviors increases the frequency of infants' behavioral matching by fostering the learning of matching associations between sensory and motor information. As infants develop, the frequency and range of the imitative behaviors increase, and mothers take this opportunity to also increase the rate at which they imitate their infants (Flynn et al., 2004; Uzgiris et al., 1989). According to the ASL model, although reward is not necessary to create sensory and motor associations, it dramatically enhances the rate of learning.

Potential Explanations for Individual Differences in Infant Imitation

Despite the theorized importance of imitation (Meltzoff, 2007; Meltzoff and Decety, 2003), the origins of individual differences in imitation have not, so far, been a focus of research (Flynn et al., 2004). The aim of the studies presented in this chapter is to investigate individual differences in infant imitation and examine their potential correlates. The first study sought to examine individual differences in relation to breastfeeding. Given that oral gestures are more likely to be imitated by newborn infants than any other gesture (Anisfeld, 1991; Anisfeld et al., 2001; Heimann et al., 1989; Streri et al., 2012), what makes these special? To effectively feed, infants must latch properly onto their mother's breast, requiring the effective positioning of the mouth and tongue. Consequently, it has been suggested that variance in infants' imitation of oral gestures may be related to breastfeeding (Jacobson, 1979).

The second study investigated an alternative explanation that the variation in infants' imitative responses may instead develop within the context of the parent–infant relationship. Bjorklund (1987) has proposed that neonatal imitation is used by infants to socially engage with their caregiver until the infant can participate in more sophisticated social interactions. From the parent perspective, a newborn appearing to copy their actions can be viewed as responsive and communicative, thereby prompting parents to create opportunities for their infant to imitate. Interpreting their newborn's behavior as imitative may also lead to increased feelings of affection, such that imitative exchanges might encourage parental engagement (Locke, 2006) and foster an increased sense of understanding, manifesting in strengthened bonds and feelings of parental efficacy. Neither of the above theories have ever been empirically tested. Here, we examine whether breastfeeding and/or bonding either cause or predict individual differences in infants' imitative responses.

STUDY 1: BREASTFEEDING AS AN EXPLANATION FOR INDIVIDUAL VARIATION IN ORAL GESTURE IMITATION

Previous research has suggested that oral gestures are more likely to be imitated by newborn infants than any other (Heimann et al., 1989). Additionally, great individual variance has been reported regarding the rate to which infants imitate these (e.g., Heimann, 2002; Heimann et al., 1989). When investigating explanations for underlying causes of this variance, we must consider the development of the motor movements required to produce these oral gestures. Feeding is an activity in which all infants engage and relies on the successfully articulated movements of the mouth and tongue (Wallace and Clarke, 2006). Infants who are better feeders often have more control over their tongue and mouth, and this may, in turn, influence their rates of facial imitation. Conversely, oral imitation may offer a means for infants who have immature sucking and/or swallowing mechanisms to practice and refine their motor skills, thereby improving the maturation of the aerodigestive tract (Keven and Akins, 2017). Successful latching and suckling is of critical importance to infant survival, involving highly complex motor sequences in which the tongue is an integral component (Edmunds et al., 2011; Geddes et al., 2008).

The ASL model explains that the types of actions that infants perform first are the ones with which they are more likely to have had the most experience of both seeing and doing (Kaye and Marcus, 1978; Ray and Heyes, 2011). Oral gestures, specifically tongue protrusion, are gestures which newborn infants have vast experience producing.

To date, only one published study has examined the relationship between imitation and breastfeeding. Jacobson (1979) presented 24 full-term infants at six, ten, and 14 weeks of age with five stimuli in an effort to elicit tongue protrusion responses: adult tongue protrusions, hand opening and closing, a white ball and black pen slowly moving towards and then away from the infant's face, and an orange plastic ring on a string dangled above the infant's head. Jacobson reported that infants who were breastfed had a tendency to exhibit more 'long' (lasting more than .50 seconds) but not 'short' (lasting less than .50 seconds) tongue protrusions in response to the experimental stimuli at all time points. Based on these findings, Jacobson concluded that tongue-protrusion responses may serve an adaptive function related to feeding. An alternative interpretation is that breastfeeding may shape and influence the development of imitation.

As such, the study reported here aimed to explore this notion that differences in infants' imitative responses may be influenced by breastfeeding. As successful breastfeeding may be associated with greater motor control over tongue and mouth movements, we hypothesized that infants' imitation of oral gestures would be positively associated with mothers' self-reported confidence in breastfeeding abilities and negatively associated with mothers' self-reported difficulty establishing breastfeeding.

Method

Participants

Thirty-six infants ($n = 25$ female, $n = 11$ male) were tested on an imitation task at one week of age ($M = 8.31$ days, $SD = 1.74$). The majority were Caucasian ($n = 34$ Caucasian, $n = 2$ Asian), of normal birth weight (≥ 2500 g, $M = 3612.92$ g, $SD = 0.42$) and gestational age (≥ 37 weeks, $M = 39.96$ weeks, $SD = 1.08$). Thirty-five infants were breastfed, with one infant bottle-fed at the time of testing.

Measures

Breastfeeding Self-Efficacy Scale (Short Form). An adapted version of the Breastfeeding Self-Efficacy Scale, Short Form (BSES-SF; Dennis, 2003) was used to evaluate participants' breastfeeding experiences. The BSES-SF is a well-established scale and the adapted version had good internal consistency ($\alpha = .88$). The adapted version had 16 of the original 33 items that were preceded by the phrase 'I can always' (e.g., 'I can always determine that my baby is getting enough milk'). Responses were anchored using scales ranging from 1 (*not at all confident*) and 5 (*always confident*). The items used in the adapted scale were selected as they focused on the mother–infant dynamic during feeding as opposed to external factors. Mothers' responses were computed into a single index of breastfeeding efficacy. In addition to the BSES-SF items, a further 12 qualitative items were generated to directly address the research questions of this study. Of these 12 qualitative items, five were individually analyzed for this study. Three of these items were related to breastfeeding specifically: 'On a scale of 1 (no trouble at all) to 5 (very difficult), how easy was it for you to get your baby to latch?', 'On a scale of 1 to 5, how hard was it to get breastfeeding established in the first days and weeks of your baby's life?', and 'When breastfeeding, does your baby appear to have trouble sucking and swallowing?' Two additional questions were included after testing had begun to further examine the role oral gesture modeling might play. Twenty-two mothers were asked: 'Do you ever open your mouth or poke your tongue out at your baby to help with latching/breastfeeding?' and 'Do you ever open your mouth or poke your tongue out at your baby to engage or communicate with your baby?'

Imitation task

Infant imitation was assessed at one week of age. The first author tested each infant in the family home when infants were in a quiet, alert state. During testing, infants were placed on the experimenter's lap with their heads supported by her hand. A video camera recorded the infant's face, torso, and hands and a second camera recorded the experimenter's modeled gestures. With fussy infants, either a break in testing was allowed or the imitation task was rescheduled for another day. Four gestures were presented within a four-minute framework. These were: (1) tongue protrusion (TP); (2) mouth opening (MO); (3) the end of a wooden spoon protruding through a tube (TUBE); and (4) opening and shutting of a small box (BOX). The TUBE and BOX gestures were included as non-social approximations of the social gestures. These two non-social stimuli were included to address the reflex hypothesis (see Anisfeld, 1991, 1996) and arousal hypothesis (see Jones, 1996, 2006). Presentation of the gestures was counterbalanced and arranged to alternate between the mouth and tongue (i.e., TP and BOX, and MO and TUBE were presented in alternating pairs).

When presenting the TP gesture, the experimenter protruded her tongue such that it came between, and then extended beyond, her lips. The experimenter's MO gesture began with a closed mouth that opened with an abrupt jaw drop, opened wide and then closed. When presenting the TUBE gesture, a cardboard tube with a length of 10 cm and a diameter of 4 cm was held by the experimenter as she moved the wooden spoon through the tube, whereby the spoon's handle extended approximately 10 cm past the end of the tube. The BOX gesture was modeled by opening the lid of a red box approximately 45 degrees and then closing. The box measured 15 cm long, 10 cm wide, and 8 cm high, as seen in Figure 21.1.

Each gesture was modeled five times at three-second intervals, followed by a 15-second passive interval. Passive intervals for the social gestures consisted of the experimenter presenting a neutral and still face. For the non-social gestures, the experimenter held the BOX still, and closed, and held the

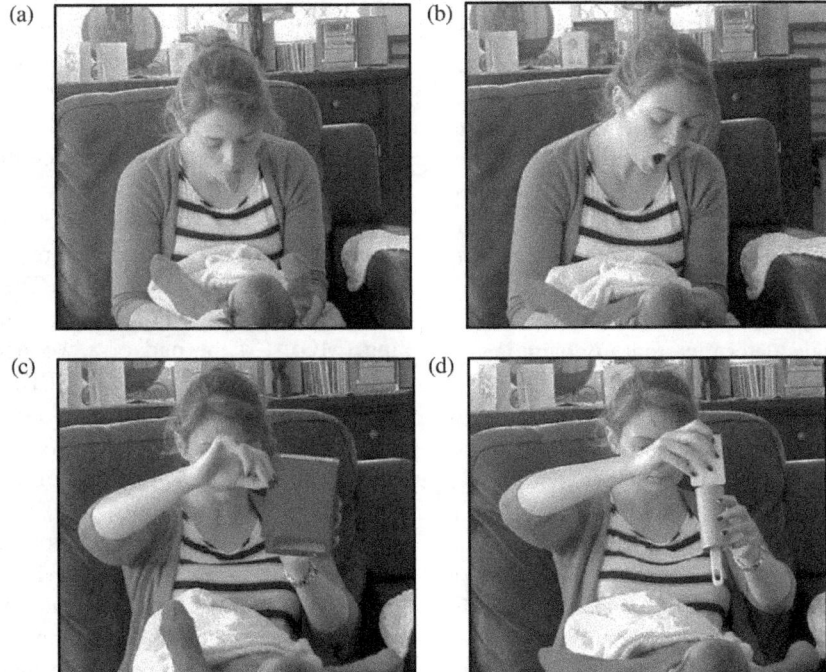

Figure 21.1 The four social and non-social gestures, as modeled by experimenter: (a) tongue protrusion; (b) mouth opening; (c) box; (d) tube

TUBE still, and without the spoon extended. Each gesture and passive interval was presented twice, resulting in a total of 30 seconds of modeling with an additional 30 seconds of the passive display. This follows the same burst–pause procedure as described by Meltzoff and Moore (1983), which has been suggested to be the most effective method to elicit imitation in newborns.

Coding

Imitation responses were coded from video by the first author. As the footage consisted of close-up images of the infant's face and torso, with no record of the experimenter's facial display, the coder was blind to the gestures modeled. Moreover, all video footage was de-identified at the time of coding, and all footage was coded several months after collection, rendering it unlikely that the specific infant would be recalled. For each infant, performance of both target behaviors (MO and TP) was noted by recording the time at which the onset of the behavior occurred. Then, using the corresponding experimenter footage, blocks of the modeled gestures and passive intervals for each infant were identified to determine which gesture the infant was viewing and to match infant responses to gestures modeled by the experimenter. Given the immaturity of motor skills at one week of age, the coding scheme did not distinguish between complete and partial responses. Following Meltzoff and Moore (1983), an infant's tongue protrusion was operationally defined as a clear forward thrust of the tongue, such that the tongue tip came between the lips or beyond. A mouth opening was defined as a closed or semi-open mouth that opened with an abrupt jaw drop and then closed, or attempted to close, with the height of the open mouth being greater than the width of the mouth. Target behaviors were not coded if the infants had their hands, fingers, or toes in their mouth or if they accompanied yawns, sneezes, crying, or fussing. Target actions were only coded when the infant was looking at the model with full attention. A two-second leeway was given, such that if the infant looked away from the model but returned their gaze within two seconds, the action was coded. Across the 36 observations, infant state was coded using the Brazelton Neonatal Behavioural Assessment Scale (Brazelton and Nugent, 1995). The majority of infants were deemed to be Alert (68.30%), with the rest of the infants coded as either Drowsy (18.40%) or Active/Agitated (13.30%). No differences in imitative responses were observed as a function of infant state. A second judge, blind to the aims and hypotheses of the study, coded a randomly selected subset of nine (25%) infant videos to assess reliability. Intraclass correlation coefficients (Shrout and Fleiss, 1979) indicated that inter-rater reliability was high for both TP responses, $r = .91$, $p < .001$, and MO responses, $r = .90$, $p < .001$. Mean frequencies of infants' responses were calculated by averaging responses across trials, with each gesture comprising four trials (i.e., TP, neutral face, TP, neutral face). For example, if an infant produced one TP when the TP gesture was being modeled, their mean frequency per trial would be .25 (i.e., 1/4 = .25). This method was employed to allow for the fact that some infants ($n = 7$ out of 36 observations) did not receive all trials of each gesture.

Results

Imitation

Means and standard deviations are presented in Table 21.1. First, to explore whether there was any evidence of *selective* imitation, infant TP responses to both the TP and MO models were compared. There was no significant difference between infants' production of TPs whether they viewed the experimenter modeling TP or MO gestures ($n = 36$, $Z = -.34$, $p = .73$). Additionally, there was no significant difference between infants' production of MOs whether they viewed the experimenter modeling MO or TP gestures ($n = 36$, $Z = -.73$, $p = .47$). Infant responses to non-social gestures (i.e., TUBE and BOX) were also assessed. Infants did not produce significantly more TPs to the TP model than the TUBE model ($n = 36$, $Z = -.56$, $p = .58$), nor did they produce significantly more MOs to the MO model than the BOX model ($n = 35$, $Z = -.01$, $p = .99$).

Individual differences in TP and MO responses

In this study, we observed a similar pattern of results to Heimann et al. (1989) whose responses could be divided into thirds. Here, 38.89% of infants produced more TPs to the TP model than to the MO model (i.e., matching responses). A quarter (25%) of the sample produced the same number of TPs to both the TP models and MO models (i.e., equal responses) and 36.11% of infants produced

Table 21.1 Infant behavior as a function of gesture modeled

	Infant behavior			
	Tongue protrusion		Mouth opening	
Gesture modeled	M	SD	M	SD
TP	0.52	0.85	0.20	0.27
MO	0.45	0.60	0.26	0.30
TUBE	0.36	0.54	0.19	0.30
BOX	0.57	0.81	0.93	4.20

Note: TP: tongue protrusion; MO: mouth opening; TUBE: spoon protruding through tube; BOX: box opening and closing. Infant behavior is presented as the frequency of responses divided by the number of gesture trials. The majority of infants received four trials per gesture (i.e., if an infant produced two TPs during the four TP trials, their response frequency = .50).

more TPs when viewing the MO model than when viewing the TP model (i.e., mismatched responses). With the MO responses, we observed a slight increase in matching responses such that 44% of the sample produced more MOs to the MO model than the TP model. However, the rest of the sample was evenly split between equal responses and mismatched responses, with 27.78% of infants producing just as many MOs to the TP model as the MO model and a further 27.78% producing more MOs to the TP model than the MO model. None of these differences were statistically significant and, instead, are reports of raw numbers. Given that there are three possible outcomes (i.e., an infant produces more, produces fewer, or produces the same number of responses to a stimuli), the observed pattern of results is likely attributable to chance. By calculating when infants produced more or fewer responses of a particular gesture to a particular model, we are simply reporting a pattern of results rather than taking into account the specificity of the response. When we evaluate the specificity of the response (i.e., *selective* imitation; see Nagy et al., 2013), we observe no evidence of imitation.

BSES-SF responses

Breastfeeding efficacy items were preceded by the phrase 'I can always...' and anchored with 1 (*not at all confident*) and 5 (*always confident*). For Questions 1–7, 9, 12, and 13 the mothers' responses ranged from 1 to 5. Questions 8, 11, and 15 had responses ranging from 2 to 5, and for Questions 10, 14, and 16, responses ranged from 3 to 5. Means and standard deviations of responses are presented in Table 21.2. An aggregate score of breastfeeding efficacy was calculated by adding together mothers' responses to 16 individual items pertaining to breastfeeding confidence. Breastfeeding efficacy ratings ranged from 28 to 80 ($M = 68.39$, $SD = 10.53$), with higher scores indicating greater levels of confidence and efficacy during the breastfeeding experience.

Five qualitative items were individually analyzed to specifically address the aims and hypotheses of this study. Three items were related to breastfeeding and evaluated how confident mothers were that they could secure a successful latch, how difficult it was to establish breastfeeding, and whether their infant had any issues sucking or swallowing while feeding. High ratings of how easy it was to secure a successful latch ($M = 4.00$, $SD = 1.10$) and low ratings of difficulty ($M = 2.03$, $SD = 1.08$) were reported; also, two mothers reported that their infant had issues with sucking and/or swallowing while feeding ($M = .05$, $SD = .23$). Two additional items examined whether mothers engaged in oral gesture modeling during interactions with their infants and if they were employed to assist with latching or for social/communicative purposes. Just over half the sample (52.27%) said they modeled oral gestures to their infant, with 27.27% saying they modeled these gestures to assist with latching and 68.18% stating that it was for social/communicative reasons.

Imitation and BSES-SF correlations

Sample size, means, standard deviations, and intercorrelations pertaining to imitation and breastfeeding variables are presented in Tables 21.3 and 21.4. It was hypothesized that infants' imitation of oral gestures would be positively associated with mothers' self-reported confidence in breastfeeding abilities and negatively associated with mothers' self-reported difficulty establishing breastfeeding. To test this hypothesis, eight non-parametric correlations between infant oral matching frequencies and breastfeeding items were conducted. Non-parametric correlations were used as neither imitation nor breastfeeding data were normally distributed.

Correlations between the aggregated score of breastfeeding efficacy and oral gesture matching (combined TP and MO matching responses) were computed. There were no significant correlations found between breastfeeding efficacy and oral

Table 21.2 Mean and standard deviations of maternal responses to BF-SF items

Item	M	SD
1. Determine that baby is getting enough	3.72	1.03
2. Successfully cope	4.14	0.96
3. Breastfeed without formula	4.19	1.33
4. Properly latched	4.00	1.10
5. Manage breastfeeding to satisfaction	3.83	1.00
6. Manage if baby is crying	4.06	1.01
7. Keep wanting to breastfeed	4.72	0.74
8. Feed with family members present	4.56	0.77
9. Satisfied with breastfeeding experience	4.28	0.97
10. Deal with the fact that time-consuming	4.50	0.65
11. Finish on one breast before switching	4.17	0.81
12. Breastfeed for every feeding	4.58	0.81
13. Keep up with demands	4.50	0.85
14. Tell when baby is finished	4.25	0.73
15. Recognize a good latch	4.44	0.73
16. Baby sucking properly	4.44	0.65
Breastfeeding efficacy (total)	**68.39**	**10.53**

Note: all statements are preceded by the phrase 'I can always…' and rated on a scale of 1 (*not at all confident*) to 5 (*always confident*).

gesture matching ($r_s = -.05$, $p = .77$), suggesting that imitation frequency was not related to how confident mothers were in their overall breastfeeding skills and abilities. Correlations were also calculated between oral gesture matching and three items of interest. No relationship was uncovered between responses to 'How easy was it for you to get your baby to latch?' and infants' frequency of oral gesture matching ($r_s = .14$, $p = .42$), demonstrating that imitation was not related to the ease with which their babies were able to latch onto the breast during feeding. Mothers' reports of difficulty in establishing breastfeeding were not related to their infants' oral matching behavior ($r_s = .21$, $p = .20$), indicating that neonatal imitation is unlikely to be associated with mothers' experiences with initiating breastfeeding.

Table 21.3 Intercorrelations between matching frequency and individual items

	M (SD)	Oral matching	Efficacy	Latch	Sucking, swallowing	Establish
Oral matching	.78 (.96)	—				
Efficacy	68.39 (10.53)	−.05	—			
Latch	4.00 (1.10)	.14	.48**	—		
Sucking, swallowing	.05 (23)	.36*	−.20	−.03	—	
Establish	2.03 (1.08)	.21	−.68**	.315	.25	—

Note: intercorrelations for frequency scores of oral gestures ($n = 36$) and correlates of interest are presented in the above table. Oral matching: combined tongue protrusion and mouth opening matching responses; efficacy: ratings of breastfeeding efficacy; latch: rating of ease of latching; sucking, swallowing: ratings of whether infant displays problems sucking and swallowing while breastfeeding; establish: ratings of how difficult it was to establish breastfeeding.
*$p < .05$, **$p < .01$.

Table 21.4 Intercorrelations between matching frequency and reasons for modeling

	M (SD)	Oral matching	Assist latch	Communication
Oral matching	.26 (.30)	—		
Assist latch	.27 (.46)	−.15	—	
Communication	.68 (.48)	−.02	.42	—

Note: intercorrelations for frequency scores of oral gestures (n = 36) and correlates of interest are presented in the above table. Oral matching: combined tongue protrusion and mouth opening matching responses; assist latch: Do you ever open your mouth or poke your tongue out at your baby to help with latching/breastfeeding?; communication: Do you ever open your mouth or poke your tongue out at your baby to engage or communicate with your baby?

Additionally, when we calculated correlations between BSES-SF scores and infants' individual differences in imitation responses (i.e., matching, equal, or mismatched responses), we found no relationship. Correlations between maternal reports of gesture modeling and infant imitation frequency were also calculated. Maternal modeling of oral gestures to assist with latch was not related to infants' oral matching frequencies ($r_s = -.15$, $p = .35$), nor was infant matching related to modeling oral gestures for communicative purposes ($r_s = -.02$, $p = 1.00$). Lastly, it is notable that two mothers reported their infants had trouble sucking and swallowing during breastfeeding and that these infants had high levels of oral matching behavior, such that they produced, on average, 12 matches per minute to modeled TP and MO gestures, six times higher than infants who had no difficulties. This likely explains the significant correlation between oral matching scores and ratings of sucking/swallowing difficulties ($r_s = .36$, $p = .03$). However, as only two mothers had infants with these difficulties, this finding must be treated with caution.

Discussion

This study tested the hypothesis that individual differences in the imitation of oral gestures are related to breastfeeding. It was expected that infants who had more success with breastfeeding would have better motor control over their mouth and tongue movements, allowing them to engage in higher rates of neonatal imitation. It was thus hypothesized that infants' imitation of oral gestures would be positively associated with mothers' self-reported confidence in breastfeeding abilities and negatively associated with mothers' self-reported difficulty establishing breastfeeding. These hypotheses were not supported.

Although failing to reject the null hypothesis, as is the case here, does not imply that it is accurate, the observed pattern of results in this study suggests there simply is no link between breastfeeding and neonatal imitation. Breastfeeding is a complex and mechanical process (Edmunds et al., 2011), with many factors determining whether or not mother and baby work well enough together to ensure it is consistently successful. Any contribution of the feedback cycle potentially started through the baby copying the mother, and the mother feeding back modeling opportunities might not therefore be sufficiently valuable so as to have any impact. In this context, Jacobson's (1979) proposal is invalid. Alternatively, there may indeed be a link between imitation of oral gestures and breastfeeding that has not been identified here. There are a number of reasons why this may be so. One reason is that the participants in this study did not, as a cohort, show evidence of imitation. That is, infant TP responses when TP was the model were compared to TP responses when MO was the model. Infants produced a similar number of tongue protrusions, regardless of the gesture modeled. Similarly, MO responses, when the experimenter modeled MO and when she modeled TP, were compared. Again, no significant difference was observed in infant MO responses when viewing the two models. This failure to find evidence of selective imitation is consistent with previous research (Anisfeld et al., 2001; Koepke et al., 1983; McKenzie and Over, 1983; Oostenbroek et al., 2016).

Neonatal imitation research continues to be a field of research in which much debate is generated, with fundamental characteristics of this phenomenon, such as the prevalence, scope, and time course, being poorly defined (Suddendorf et al., 2013). Although some researchers claim to demonstrate evidence of imitation (Field et al., 1982; Fontaine, 1984; Nagy et al., 2005) many studies, including this one, have attempted and failed to replicate Meltzoff and Moore's (1977) original study (e.g., Hayes and Watson, 1981; Koepke et al., 1983; McKenzie and Over, 1983; Oostenbroek et al., 2016). Specifically, through parental engagement, parental tongue protrusion modeling might assist breastfeeding, but only for babies who are particularly immature in their digestive development. This suggestion requires further research. Conversely, the phenomenon of neonatal imitation and breastfeeding may not be related at all. This study found no evidence of any such relationship, and rather than neonatal imitation being related to breastfeeding, it may instead develop alongside the parent–infant bond.

STUDY 2: EXPLORING INDIVIDUAL DIFFERENCES IN NEONATAL IMITATION WITHIN THE CONTEXT OF THE MOTHER–BABY RELATIONSHIP

Human babies enter the world with biases to attend to socially relevant stimuli (Machluf and Bjorklund, 2015). This neurobiological preparedness enables neonates to interact with their caregivers in coherent and rhythmic ways (Trevarthen and Aitken, 2001). Mothers and infants are not only sensitive to each other's presence but affect one another in complex, bidirectional ways (Field et al., 2004; Widmayer and Field, 1980). Given the multifaceted effects mother–infant interaction can have on development, we sought to determine whether maternal–infant bonding could help to explain variation in newborn imitation. To date, only one published study has explored imitation within the context of the mother–baby relationship: Heimann (1989) reported that eye-contact between the mother and the infant at three months of age was greatest when infants had shown more frequent imitation in the neonatal period. To successfully imitate their parents' facial gestures, infants must keenly observe their caregivers' actions. Subsequently, imitation exchanges often involve prolonged eye-contact. Additionally, mother–infant gaze has been linked with increased levels of maternal oxytocin (Kim et al., 2014), which in turn, promotes bonding.

The aim of the study reported here was to explore the hypothesis that imitation varies as a function of maternal ratings of bonding and efficacy. To test this, 36 mother–infant pairs participated in directed engagement, such that they either engaged in face-to-face (FTF) interactions with, or modeled tongue protrusions (TP) to, their infants for ten minutes per day for a fortnight. A control group received no special instructions. Imitation, maternal efficacy, and bonding were assessed both before and after two weeks of parental interaction. It was hypothesized that infants in the TP modeling group would have higher rates of matching post-modeling and significantly more than infants in the FTF or control conditions. It was further hypothesized that matching behavior would be positively associated with maternal ratings of bonding and efficacy.

Method

Participants

Thirty-six infants ($n = 21$ female, $n = 15$ male) and their mothers participated in this study. Infants were tested on a neonatal imitation task at approximately one week of age ($M = 9.86$ days, $SD = 2.75$). The majority of infants were Caucasian ($n = 31$ Caucasian, $n = 3$ Asian, $n = 2$ Hispanic) and delivered vaginally ($n = 29$ vaginal deliveries, $n = 7$ caesarean births). All infants were of normal birth weight (≥ 2500 g, $M = 3427.75$ g, $SD = 416.29$) and gestational age (≥ 37 weeks, $M = 39.61$ weeks, $SD = 1.12$). Thirty-two of the infants were exclusively breastfed at the time of imitation testing.

Imitation task

The first author tested each infant on the same imitation task as described earlier in Study 1 when they were one week of age. Again, the same four gestures (i.e., tongue protrusion, mouth opening, tube, and box) were presented in the same way as in Study 1 (see Figure 21.1).

Maternal Experience questionnaire

The Maternal Experience questionnaire comprised a Maternal Efficacy questionnaire (Teti and Gelfand, 1991) and a Maternal Bonding scale (Taylor et al., 2005). Teti and Gelfand's (1991) Maternal Efficacy questionnaire includes ten items measuring mothers' confidence in performing maternal tasks, and based on their sample of 86 mothers, the scale was found to have good internal reliability ($\alpha = .86$). Responses to these items are recorded on a four-point Likert scale, ranging from 1 (*not good at all*) to 4 (*very good*). In order to make the scale more appropriate for mothers of newborn infants, two items were removed (i.e., 'How good were you at making your baby understand what you wanted him/her to do?' and 'How good were you at getting your baby to show off for visitors?'). The second section of the questionnaire contained the Maternal Bonding scale, which listed eight maternal feelings that could have been experienced during the first few weeks of their infant's life, including *loving, resentful, neutral, joyful, dislike, protective, disappointed,* and *aggressive*. Each of these adjectives was rated as being felt 'very much', 'a lot', 'a little', or 'not at all'. The Maternal Bonding scale was validated by Taylor et al. (2005) with a sample of 162 mothers and was found to have reasonable internal reliability ($\alpha = .71$).

Coding

Imitation Scoring. Infants' responses were coded from video footage by the first author in the same manner as described in Study 1. Across the 36 observations, infant state was coded using the Brazelton Neonatal Behavioural Assessment Scale (Brazelton and Nugent, 1995). The majority of infants were deemed to be Alert (65.30%), with the rest of the infants coded as either Drowsy (19.40%) or Active/Agitated (15.30%). No differences in imitative responses were observed as a function of infant state.

As in Study 1, in this study a second judge, blind to the aims and hypotheses of the study, coded a randomly selected subset of nine (25%) infant videos to assess reliability. Intraclass correlation coefficients (Shrout and Fleiss, 1979) indicated that inter-rater reliability was high for both TP responses, $r = .93$, $p < .001$ and MO responses, $r = .92, p < .001$. Again, to assist with analyses, mean frequencies of infants' responses were calculated and derived in the same manner as described for Study 1. This method was employed to allow for the fact that some infants ($n = 7$ out of 72 observations) did not receive all trials of each gesture.

Maternal Experience and Bonding. The eight items of the Maternal Efficacy scale were added together to form a single index of *Maternal Efficacy*. Additionally, the eight items from the Maternal Bonding scale were added together to form an index measuring overall *Maternal Bonding*, after five of the eight items had been reverse-scored (resentful, neutral, disappointed, dislike, aggressive). In Taylor et al.'s (2005) original scoring method, 0 translated to 'very much', where 3 indicated 'not at all' for positive items and the reverse for negative items (e.g., resentful). In the current study, we modified this coding scheme to assist with interpretation, such that higher scores would refer to high ratings of maternal bonding (i.e., 'very much' = 4), and low scores to low ratings (i.e., 'not at all' = 1).

Results

Imitation

To investigate evidence of neonatal imitation, a series of one-tailed Wilcoxon Signed Ranks tests was conducted, comparing frequencies of TP and MO responding. Means and standard deviations are presented in Table 21.5. First, to explore whether there was any evidence of *selective* imitation, infant TP responses to both the TP model and MO model were compared. Infants did not produce significantly more TPs when viewing the TP model than the MO model ($n = 36$, $Z = -.45$, $p = .33$) or more TPs when viewing the TP than the TUBE model ($n = 36$, $Z = -.38$, $p = .35$). Likewise, to establish MO imitation, infant MO responses to both the TP and MO models were compared. Infants did not produce significantly more MOs when viewing the MO model than the TP model ($n = 36$, $Z = -1.23$, $p = .11$) or more MOs when viewing the MO than the BOX model ($n = 36$, $Z = -1.60$, $p = .06$).

Individual differences in TP and MO responses

In this study, we observed a similar pattern of results as in Study 1, with responses in this sample roughly divided into thirds. Here, 30.56% of infants produced more TPs to the TP model than the MO model (i.e., matching responses). An additional 33.33% of infants produced the same number of TPs to both the TP model and MO models (i.e., equal responses), and a final 36.11% of infants produced more TPs when viewing the MO model than when viewing the TP model (i.e., mismatched responses). Again, as in Study 1, with MO responses, we observed a slight increase in matching responses, such that 41.67% of the sample produced more MOs to the MO model than the TP model. The rest of the sample consisted of 36.11% of infants who had 'equal' responses, producing the same number of MOs to both the TP and MO models and 22.22% of infants who had mismatched responses, producing more MOs to the TP model than the MO model. Again, as in Study 1, none of these differences were statistically significant and instead are reports of raw numbers. As mentioned above, there are only three possible outcomes of infant responses: an infant produces more, produces fewer, or produces the same number of responses to a stimuli. The observation division of responses into thirds suggests the observed pattern of results is likely

Table 21.5 **Infant behavior as a function of gesture modeled**

	Infant behavior			
	Tongue protrusion		Mouth opening	
Gesture modeled	M	SD	M	SD
TP	0.52	0.69	0.28	0.34
MO	0.49	0.59	0.39	0.46
TUBE	0.48	0.72	0.22	0.34
BOX	0.44	0.66	0.22	0.31

Note: $n = 36$; TP: tongue protrusion; MO: mouth opening; TUBE: spoon protruding through tube; BOX: box opening and closing.

attributable to chance. By calculating when infants produced more, or less, of a particular gesture to a particular model, we are simply reporting a pattern of results, rather than taking into account the specificity of the response. When we evaluate the specificity of infants' responses (see Nagy et al., 2013), we do not observe evidence of imitation.

Maternal bonding and efficacy

Mothers reported high ratings of their *Maternal Efficacy*, with a third of the sample (33.30%) rating themselves as 'very good' mothers and the majority of the mothers reporting that they were 'good enough' (58.30%). The combined index of *Maternal Efficacy* had a possible range of 8–32; the mothers in this sample had values ranging from 13–32 and a mean of 24.91, where higher scores indicated a greater amount of self-reported efficacy. For the *Maternal Bonding* measure, mothers reported overall high levels of positive emotions (e.g., protective, joy) and lower levels of negative emotions (e.g., resentment, disappointment) towards their infant. Of a possible range of 8–32 on this scale, mothers' responses ranged from 6–32 (one mother chose to omit two questions, resulting in a score of 6). This mother was, by far, the exception, as the next lowest score a mother had on the *Maternal Bonding* scale was 26.50. Despite this, on average mothers in this sample reported high ratings of bonding, with a mean score of 29.76.

In order to establish whether individual differences in infants' imitation scores were related to *Maternal Bonding* or *Maternal Efficacy*, we correlated these scales with infants' oral matching scores. No significant correlations were observed between oral matching and ratings of efficacy ($r_s = .07$, $p = .67$) or bonding ($r_s = .19$, $p = .27$). These correlations are presented in Table 21.6.

Discussion

This study aimed to evaluate the way imitative responses influence caregivers by exploring the hypothesis that neonatal imitation relates to early mother–infant bonds and that this, in turn, is related to an increased sense of maternal efficacy. Specifically, we hypothesized that neonatal imitation would be positively related to maternal bonding and efficacy. We tested infant imitation at one week and found no evidence of selective imitation. Moreover, we did not demonstrate any evidence of a relationship between imitation and maternal ratings of efficacy or bonding. As such, this study provided no evidence in support of this hypothesis, as no correlations between either of the TP or MO matching behaviors and maternal bonding or efficacy scores were significant. No conclusions pertaining to a potential social or communicative function of neonatal imitation can be drawn, except that such a relationship may not exist.

Nonetheless, as with Study 1, failing to reject the null hypothesis does not allow obvious conclusions. Yet, it is possible that there simply is no link between maternal bonding, maternal efficacy, and neonatal imitation. The process of bonding is highly complex and dependent on a multitude of

Table 21.6 Intercorrelations between matching frequency and individual items

	M (SD)	Oral matching	Maternal efficacy	Maternal bonding
Oral matching	.91 (.98)	—		
Maternal efficacy	27.96 (4.38)	.07	—	
Maternal bonding	24.92 (3.87)	.19	.34*	—

Note: intercorrelations for frequency scores of oral gestures ($n = 36$) and correlates of interest are presented in the above table. Oral matching: combined tongue protrusion and mouth opening matching responses; efficacy: ratings of maternal efficacy; bonding: ratings of maternal bonding.
*$p < .05$.

dynamic components. It is possible that each individual parent's specific set of biological and psychological factors functions in social, societal, and cultural contexts to form the bond. A principal limitation of this study was the bonding and efficacy measure used, specifically the issue of using this scale with a non-clinical sample. The measures were chosen because they had previously been established as reliable and well-validated scales (Taylor et al., 2005; Teti and Gelfand, 1991). However, this was not apparent with the current samples for the bonding measure. Although the measures of efficacy demonstrated good internal consistency ($\alpha = .87$), the bonding measures demonstrated much lower reliability ($\alpha = .55$), limiting our confidence that we effectively measured constructs of maternal bonding. This limitation may be partially accounted for by the restriction of variance in our study (Field, 2009).

More extensive measures of bonding and efficacy, particularly those suited to non-clinical samples – such as semi-structured interviews – would allow for a more detailed and qualitative overview of the mother–infant bond. Using these methods may capture the wide range of experiences in the developing bonding experience, thereby improving our chances of detecting an effect, if one exists. Furthermore, the participants in this experiment were not representative of the range of mother–infant dyads that exist in the broader population. All participants were healthy, well-resourced mothers who were pleased with their situation of just having given birth. Consequently, it is feasible that our samples were genuinely approaching a ceiling on the bonding and efficacy measures, thereby restricting the variance in our results. If early bonding and efficacy does influence the development of neonatal imitation, it is likely to be a subtle effect given the vast number of biochemical, physiological and cultural variables that influence its expression. In order to uncover the potential effect, a much larger, more representative sample is needed. Finally, there is the distinct possibility that our results were due to the fact that experiences of bonding and efficacy in no way influence the development of neonatal imitation. It is worth noting that both sampling bias and a lack of power might have substantially impacted this study.

CONCLUSION: WHAT CAN THESE STUDIES TELL US?

Imitation is just one of the many ways parents socially interact with their infants (Jones and Yoshida, 2011). For the last four decades, researchers have argued that, from birth, infants use imitation to engage with others in their social world (Meltzoff, 2007; Meltzoff and Moore, 1977, 1992). However, the research supporting this claim remains far from compelling (Anisfeld et al., 1979; Heyes, 2016b; Oostenbroek et al., 2016). Although there is no direct evidence that the capacity for imitation is inborn, there is much evidence to demonstrate that humans learn to imitate in the context of social interaction (Catmur et al., 2009; Ray and Heyes, 2011). The studies presented in this chapter sought to investigate whether individual differences in infants' imitative responses might be driven by a subset of infants who have learned to engage in such a way. Specifically, we sought to determine whether the development of imitation is influenced by environmental influences such as breastfeeding experience and/or interactions that occur within the context of the mother–infant relationship. No evidence was found to support the existence of imitation in our samples or either of the above hypotheses. Although imitation has been reported in previous studies, our failure to observe any evidence of this behavior emphasizes that, if neonatal imitation exists, it is a weak and fragile phenomenon (Heimann, 2002), or perhaps not a legitimate phenomenon at all.

In both of these studies, like other studies before them (Heimann, 1989;

Heimann et al., 1989), we observed evidence of individual differences across infants' responses to viewing oral gestures. Yet, these differences reflect patterns that could be expected by chance; as such, it is unlikely that these differences are in any way meaningful. The evidence presented in this chapter does not uncover any information to help determine what might underlie, predict, or establish the meaningfulness of these differences. Given we identified no foundation for these apparent differences, the possibility remains that these individual differences are a statistical artifact and demonstrate no considerable difference in the way infants respond to modeled oral gestures. It may be the case that we are simply seeing a phenomenon where none exists. Meta-analyses may be a way forward to systematically investigate whether reported effects of imitation are true and sound effects or if they are more likely due to methodological and statistical error. Insofar as neonatal imitation is a phenomenon of infancy that humans are born to do, there remains no evidence to support this claim and much evidence to indicate the opposite (Anisfeld, 1996; Anisfeld et al., 1979, 2001; Hayes and Watson, 1981; Oostenbroek et al., 2016). We explored two environmental inputs that might be related to its development but found nothing. Additionally, in both studies, we find no evidence that that neonatal imitation is a legitimate phenomenon of infancy.

REFERENCES

Abravanel, E., Levan-Goldschmidt, E., & Stevenson, M. B. (1976). Action imitation: The early phase of infancy. *Child Development*, *47*(4), 1032–1044. https://doi.org/10.2307/1128440

Anisfeld, M. (1991). Neonatal imitation. *Developmental Review*, *11*, 60–97.

Anisfeld, M. (1996). Only tongue protrusion modeling is matched by neonates. *Developmental Review*, *16*, 149–161.

Anisfeld, M., Masters, J., Jacobson, S. W., Kagan, J., Meltzoff, A. N., & Moore, M. K. (1979). Interpreting 'imitative' responses in early infancy. *Science*, *205*, 214–219.

Anisfeld, M., Turkewitz, G., Rose, S. A., Rosenberg, F. R., Sheiber, F. J., Couturier-Fagan, D. A., ... Sommer, I. (2001). No compelling evidence that newborns imitate oral gestures. *Infancy*, *2*, 111–122.

Bjorklund, D. F. (1987). A note on neonatal imitation. *Developmental Review*, *7*(1), 86–92. https://doi.org/10.1016/0273-2297(87)90006-2

Brazelton, T. B., & Nugent, J. K. (1995). *Neonatal behavioral assessment scale* (3rd ed.). London: MacKeith Press.

Catmur, C., Walsh, V., & Heyes, C. (2009). Associative sequence learning: The role of experience in the development of imitation and the mirror system. *Philosophical Transactions: Biological Sciences*, *364*, 2369–2380.

Dennis, C. (2003). The breastfeeding self-efficacy scale: Psychometric assessment of the short form. *Journal of Obstetric, Gynecologic, and Neonatal Nursing*, *32*, 734–744.

Edmunds, J., Miles, S. C., & Fulbrook, P. (2011). Tongue-tie and breastfeeding: A review of the literature. *Breastfeeding Review: Professional Publication of the Nursing Mothers' Association of Australia*, *19*, 19–26.

Field, A. (2009). *Discovering statistics using SPSS* (3rd ed.). London: Sage.

Field, T. M. (1982). Individual differences in the expressivity of neonates and young infants. In R. Feldman (Ed.), *Development of nonverbal behavior in children* (pp. 279–298). New York, NY: Springer-Verlag.

Field, T. M., Diego, M., Hernandez-Reif, M., Vera, Y., Gil, K., Shanberg, S., ... Gonzalez-Garcia, A. (2004). Prenatal maternal biochemistry predicts neonatal biochemistry. *International Journal of Neuroscience*, *114*, 933–945.

Field, T. M., Hernandez-Reif, M., Vera, Y., Gil, K., Diego, M., Bendell, D., & Yando, R. (2005). Anxiety and anger effects on depressed mother–infant spontaneous and imitative interactions. *Infant Behavior and Development*, *28*(1), 1–9. https://doi.org/10.1016/j.infbeh.2004.06.003

Field, T. M., Woodson, R., Cohen, D., Greenberg, R., Garcia, R., & Collins, K. (1983). Discrimination and imitation of facial expressions by term and preterm neonates. *Infant Behavior and Development, 6*, 485–489.

Field, T. M., Woodson, R., Greenberg, R., & Cohen, D. (1982). Discrimination and imitation of facial expressions by neonates. *Science, 218*, 179–181.

Flynn, V., Masur, E. F., & Eichorst, D. L. (2004). Opportunity versus disposition as predictors of infants' and mothers' verbal and action imitation. *Infant Behavior and Development, 27*, 303–314.

Fontaine, R. (1984). Imitative skills between birth and six months. *Infant Behavior and Development, 7*, 323–333.

Geddes, D. T., Kent, J. C., Mitoulas, L. R., & Hartmann, P. E. (2008). Tongue movement and intra-oral vacuum in breastfeeding infants. *Early Human Development, 84*, 471–477.

Hayes, L. A., & Watson, J. S. (1981). Neonatal imitation: Fact or artifact? *Developmental Psychology, 17*, 655–660.

Heerey, E. A. (2015). Decoding the dyad: Challenges in the study of individual differences in social behavior. *Current Directions in Psychological Science, 24*, 285–291.

Heimann, M. (1989). Neonatal imitation, gaze aversion, and mother–infant interaction. *Infant Behavior and Development, 12*, 495–505.

Heimann, M. (2002). Notes on individual differences and the assumed elusiveness of neonatal imitation. In A. Meltzoff & W. Prinz (Eds.), *The imitative mind* (pp. 74–85). New York, NY: Cambridge University Press.

Heimann, M., Nelson, K. E., & Schaller, J. (1989). Neonatal imitation of tongue protrusion and mouth opening: Methodological aspects and evidence of early individual differences. *Scandinavian Journal of Psychology, 30*, 90–101.

Heyes, C. (2016a). Homo imitans? Seven reasons why imitation couldn't possibly be associative. *Philosophical Transactions of the Royal Society, B: Biological Sciences, 371*, 20150069.

Heyes, C. (2016b). Imitation: Not in our genes. *Current Biology, 26*, R412–R414.

Jacobson, S. W. (1979). Matching behavior in the young infant. *Child Development, 50*, 425–430.

Jones, S. S. (1996). Imitation or exploration? Young infants' matching of adults' oral gestures. *Child Development, 67*, 1952–1969.

Jones, S. S. (2006). Exploration or imitation? The effect of music on 4-week-old infants' tongue protrusions. *Infant Behavior and Development, 29*, 126–130.

Jones, S. S. (2007). Imitation in infancy: The development of mimicry. *Psychological Science, 18*, 593–599.

Jones, S. S., & Yoshida, H. (2011). Imitation in infancy and the acquisition of body knowledge. In V. Slaughter & C. Brownell (Eds.), *Early development of body representations* (pp. 207–226). Cambridge: Cambridge University Press.

Kaye, K., & Marcus, J. (1978). Imitation over a series of trials without feedback: Age six months. *Infant Behavior and Development, 1*(1), 141–155. https://doi.org/10.1016/S0163-6383(78)80025-3

Keven, N., & Akins, K. (2017). Neonatal imitation in context: Sensory-motor development in the perinatal period. *Behavioral and Brain Sciences*, 1–107. doi: 10.1017/S0140525X16000911.

Killen, M., & Uzgiris, I. C. (2006). Imitation of actions with objects: The role of social meaning. *Journal of Chemical Information and Modeling, 138*, 219–229. https://doi.org/10.1017/CBO9781107415324.004

Kim, S., Fonagy, P., Koos, O., Dorsett, K., & Strathearn, L. (2014). Maternal oxytocin response predicts mother-to-infant gaze. *Brain Research, 1580*, 133–142.

Koepke, J. E., Hamm, M., Legerstee, M., & Russell, M. (1983). Neonatal imitation: Two failures to replicate. *Infant Behavior and Development, 6*, 97–102.

Lakin, J. L., Jefferis, V. E., Cheng, C. M., & Chartrand, T. L. (2003). The chameleon effect as social glue: Evidence for the evolutionary significance of nonconscious mimicry. *Journal of Nonverbal Behavior, 27*, 145–161.

Legare, C. H., & Nielsen, M. (2015). Imitation and innovation: The dual engines of cultural learning. *Trends in Cognitive Science, 19*, 688–699.

Locke, J. L. (2006). Parental selection of vocal behavior: Crying, cooing, babbling, and the evolution of language. *Human Nature, 17*(2), 155–168. https://doi.org/10.1007/s12110-006-1015-x

Machluf, K., & Bjorklund, D. F. (2015). Social cognitive development from an evolutionary perspective. In V. Zeigler-Hill, L. L. M. Welling, & T. K. Shackelford (Eds.), *Evolutionary perspectives on social psychology* (pp. 27–38). New York, NY: Springer.

McEwen, F., Happé, F., Bolton, P., Rijsdijk, F., Ronald, A., Dworzynski, K., & Plomin, R. (2007). Origins of individual differences in imitation: Links with language, pretend play, and socially insightful behavior in two-year-old twins. *Child Development, 78*, 474–492.

McKenzie, B., & Over, R. (1983). Young infants fail to imitate facial and manual gestures. *Infant Behavior and Development, 6*, 85–95.

Meltzoff, A. N. (2007). 'Like me': A foundation for social cognition. *Developmental Science, 10*, 126–134.

Meltzoff, A. N., & Decety, J. (2003). What imitation tells us about social cognition: A rapprochement between developmental psychology and cognitive neuroscience. *Philosophical Transactions of the Royal Society, B: Biological Sciences, 358*, 491–500.

Meltzoff, A. N., & Moore, M. K. (1977). Imitation of facial and manual gestures by human neonates. *Science, 198*, 75–78.

Meltzoff, A. N., & Moore, M. K. (1983). Newborn infants imitate adult facial gestures. *Child Development, 54*, 702–709.

Meltzoff, A. N., & Moore, M. K. (1989). Imitation in newborn infants: Exploring the range of gestures imitated and the underlying mechanisms. *Developmental Psychology, 25*, 954–962.

Meltzoff, A. N., & Moore, M. K. (1992). Early imitation within a functional framework: The importance of person identity, movement, and development. *Infant Behavior and Development, 15*, 479–505.

Nagy, E., Compagne, H., Orvos, H., Pal, A., Molnar, P., Janszky, I., ... Bardos, G. (2005). Index finger movement imitation by human neonates: Motivation, learning, and left-hand preference. *Pediatric Research, 58*, 749–753.

Nagy, E., Pilling, K., Orvos, H., & Molnar, P. (2013). Imitation of tongue protrusion in human neonates: Specificity of the response in a large sample. *Developmental Psychology, 49*, 1628–1638.

Oostenbroek, J., Suddendorf, T., Nielsen, M., Redshaw, J., Kennedy-Costantini, S., Davis, J., ... Slaughter, V. (2016). Comprehensive longitudinal study challenges the existence of neonatal imitation in humans. *Current Biology, 26*, 1334–1338.

Pawlby, S. (1977). Imitative interaction. In H. R. Schaffer (Ed.), *Studies in mother–infant interaction* (pp. 203–223). London: Academic Press.

Piaget, J. (1945). *Play, dreams and imitation in childhood*. New York: Norton.

Ray, E., & Heyes, C. (2011). Imitation in infancy: The wealth of the stimulus. *Developmental Science, 14*, 92–105.

Reissland, N. (1988). Neonatal imitation in the first hour of life: Observations in rural Nepal. *Developmental Psychology, 24*, 464–469.

Shrout, P. E., & Fleiss, J. L. (1979). Intraclass correlations: Uses in assessing rater reliability. *Psychological Bulletin, 86*, 420–428.

Simpson, E. A., Miller, G. M., Ferrari, P. F., Suomi, S. J., & Paukner, A. (2016). Neonatal imitation and early social experience predict gaze following abilities in infant macaques. *Scientific Reports, 6*, 20233.

Simpson, E. A., Murray, L., Paukner, A., & Ferrari, P. F. (2014). The mirror neuron system as revealed through neonatal imitation: Presence from birth, predictive power and evidence of plasticity. *Philosophical Transactions of the Royal Society of London, B: Biological Sciences, 369*, 20130289.

Streri, A., Coulon, M., & Guellai, B. (2012). The foundations of social cognition: Studies on face/voice integration in newborn infants. *International Journal of Behavioral Development, 37*, 79–83. https://doi.org/10.1177/0165025412465361

Suddendorf, T., Oostenbroek, J., Nielsen, M., & Slaughter, V. (2013). Is newborn imitation developmentally homologous to later social-cognitive skills? *Developmental Psychobiology, 55*, 52–58.

Taylor, A., Atkins, R., Kumar, R., Adams, D., & Glover, V. (2005). A new mother-to-infant bonding scale: Links with early maternal mood. *Archives of Women's Mental Health, 8*, 45–51.

Teti, D. M., & Gelfand, D. M. (1991). Behavioral competence among mothers of infants in the first year: The mediational role of maternal self-efficacy. *Child Development, 62*, 918–929.

Trevarthen, C., & Aitken, K. J. (2001). Infant intersubjectivity: Research, theory, and clinical applications. *The Journal of Child Psychology and Psychiatry and Allied Disciplines, 42,* 3–48.

Uzgiris, I. C., Benson, J. B., Kruper, J. C., & Vasek, M. E. (1989). Contextual influences on imitative interactions between mothers and infants. In J. Lockman & N. Hazen (Eds.), *Action in social context: Perspectives on early development* (pp. 103–127). New York: Plenum Press.

Vinter, A. (1986). The role of movement in eliciting early imitations. *Child Development, 57,* 66–71.

Wallace, H., & Clarke, S. (2006). Tongue tie division in infants with breast feeding difficulties. *International Journal of Pediatric Otorhinolaryngology, 70,* 1257–1261.

Widmayer, S. M., & Field, T. M. (1980). Effects of Brazelton demonstrations on early interactions of preterm infants and their teenage mothers. *Infant Behavior and Development, 3,* 79–89.

Individual Differences and Romantic Relationships: Bidirectional Influences on Self and Relational Processes

Brent A. Mattingly, Kevin P. McIntyre and Dylan Faulkner Selterman

Individuals shape, and are shaped by, their close relationships, and so it is not surprising that these relationships are central to individuals' lives. Intimacy and relatedness are fundamental psychological needs that are satisfied through the formation and maintenance of close relationships (e.g., Baumeister and Leary, 1995; Bowlby, 1969/1982, 1973; Erikson, 1968; Maslow, 1968). For example, self-determination theory identifies relatedness as one of three basic needs (Deci and Ryan, 2000), and Maslow (1968) identified the need for love and belongingness as more fundamental than even feelings of self-worth. Failure to form relationships with others results in feelings of social exclusion which, in turn, carry a plethora of negative physical and psychological consequences (Baumeister and Leary, 1995; Williams, 2007).

Though there are many different types of close relationships that help satisfy these fundamental needs of belongingness (e.g., parent–child, sibling, friendships; cf. DePaulo and Morris, 2005), one specific type that has garnered ample attention is that of romantic relationships. Romantic relationships strongly impact both psychological well-being (Kamp Dush and Amato, 2005; Lucas and Dyrenforth, 2006) and physical and emotional health (Agnew and South, 2014; Loving and Slatcher, 2013). In this chapter, we posit and provide support for bidirectional links between romantic relationship functioning and personality and individual differences, such that individual differences both influence and are influenced by relational processes.

For this chapter, we focus on the self-concept as a quintessential individual difference, as it contains dynamic and static idiosyncratic properties regarding how individuals think about themselves and others (Cervone, 2004; Kernis and Goldman, 2003; Markus and Wurf, 1987; Swann, 1990). The self-concept can be construed at an individual (i.e., personal), interpersonal (i.e., relational), or group (i.e., collective) level (Brewer and Gardner, 1996; Sedikides and Brewer, 2001), and for this chapter, we focus on the individual and relational self (also see Andersen and Chen, 2002). Specifically, we examine how the self affects relational functioning, as well as how relational processes modify the self (Figure 22.1). Our conceptualization of the self as an individual difference is still quite broad, as it encompasses a wide range of psychological factors such as orientations (e.g., attachment, interdependent self-construal), beliefs and ideals (e.g., ideal standards, growth and destiny beliefs), personality traits (e.g., Big Five, narcissism), motivations (e.g., need to belong, approach and avoidance), and content and organizational structures (e.g., self-expansion, self-concept clarity).

We have structured this chapter into two main sections. In Part 1, we illustrate how pre-existing (static) aspects of the self-concept – or, simply put, the individual differences we bring with us into our relationships – affect romantic relationship functioning. In Part 2, we focus on how relational processes in turn affect the (dynamic) self-concept – or, more simply, how relationships change us. Within each part, we organize our discussion to parallel the traditional development of a romantic relationship, beginning with attraction and relationship initiation, moving to relationship functioning and maintenance, and concluding with relationship dissolution.

PART 1: INDIVIDUAL DIFFERENCES TO RELATIONSHIPS

In Part 1, we review research demonstrating how individual differences, namely the self, affect relational processes. We further divide Part 1 into three main subsections which parallel large relationship phases, specifically: (a) attraction and initiation; (b) relationship functioning and maintenance; and (c) relationship dissolution.

Attraction and Initiation

Attachment
Attachment theory (Bowlby, 1969/1982; see Mikulincer et al., 2003) is a framework for

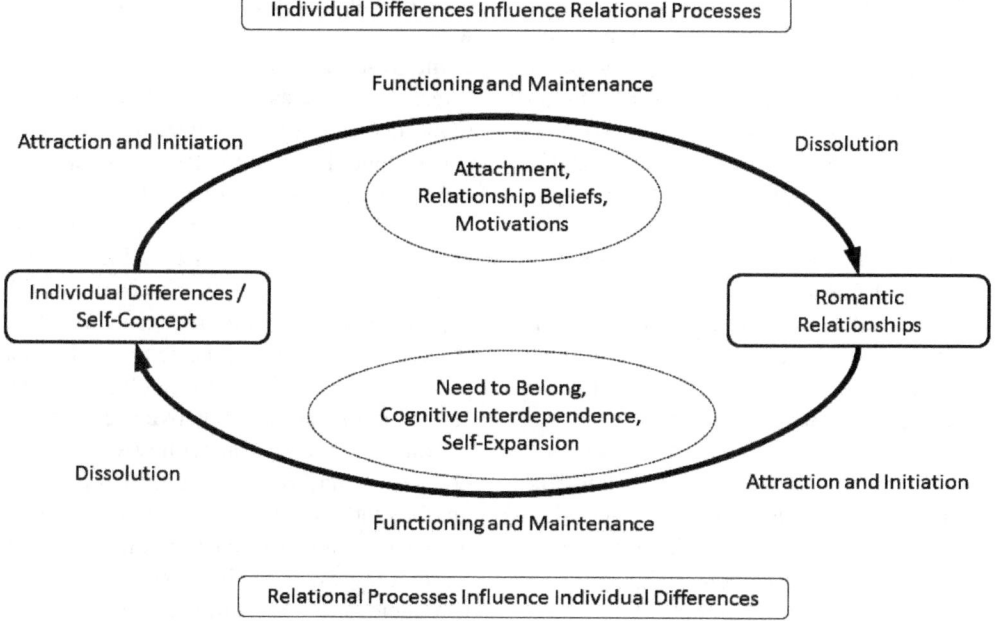

Figure 22.1 Bidirectional association of individual differences and relational processes

understanding intimate relationships from a developmental and individual-differences perspective. The theory suggests that cognitive representations of interpersonal relationships develop early in infancy, typically through interactions with the infant's primary caregiver(s). These mental representations manifest as *scripts* (Waters et al., 1998; Waters and Waters, 2006) and are relatively stable across time (Waters et al., 2000b). These representations are then applied – implicitly and explicitly – to other relationships throughout adulthood, including romantic partnerships (Hazan and Shaver, 1987). Thus, stable individual differences in *attachment styles* are linked with behaviors in romantic relationships. Most individuals have attachments marked by security, avoidance, or anxiety. Secure individuals trust romantic partners, expect positive outcomes in relationships, are comfortable with closeness, and are confident that their partners will support them. Avoidant individuals mistrust others, expect negative outcomes, resist intimacy, and engage in distancing behavior in times of stress. Anxious individuals possess a fearful approach to relationships: they crave intimacy but are (like avoidant individuals) distrustful of partners, often worry about abandonment, and exhibit excessive assurance seeking to confirm that their partners will not betray them (Mikulincer et al., 2003).

Several competing theories offer explanations for how attachment plays a role in romantic attraction, including *basic security* (attraction to secure partners regardless of one's own attachment style), *self-similarity* (attraction to partners who have similar attachment styles), *complementarity* (attraction to partners who confirm self-views), and *ideal-self similarity* (attraction to similar partners but only when those similar characteristics are highly valued). There is convergent evidence for the basic security hypothesis, such that attraction to a potential partner linearly increases with the partner's attachment security (Klohnen and Luo, 2003). Similarly, people are attracted to traits indicative of security, such as reliability and dependability, more than to generalized goodness traits such as warmth and kindness (Koleva, 2011). Moreover, secure individuals are more likely to date regularly, have follow-up dates with the same person, and begin new relationships (Poulsen et al., 2013). Thus, attachment security is an attractive trait.

There is also evidence for self-similarity, mainly among insecure people. Specifically, highly anxious individuals are more attracted to other anxious people, compared to highly avoidant individuals who are less attracted to anxious partners (Klohnen and Luo, 2003). There is less consistent support for complementarity and ideal-self similarity. Insecure individuals may feel the need to compensate for their insecurities that are less attractive than secure qualities, such as through flattery, social status, and physical beauty. For example, in one study, men (but not women) prioritized beauty over attachment security, and high status made potential partners more attractive to women (Brumbaugh et al., 2014).

Although support for the basic-security hypothesis suggests that security is most attractive, there are mixed findings regarding which type of insecurity is more attractive. Some research shows that avoidant characteristics such as minimization and emotional distance are attractive, but only when experimentally manipulated (Birnbaum and Reis, 2012), whereas other studies suggest that anxious characteristics are more desirable than avoidant (Klohnen and Luo, 2003). This inconsistency in the findings may be explained by several mechanisms. First, attachment anxiety may be comprised of both positive (i.e., desiring love, closeness, and care from others) and negative (i.e., preoccupation with abandonment) motivational facets. Lemay and Spongberg (2015) posit that anxious individuals' positive motivations are associated with desirable relational outcomes, which may explain why anxious attachment tendencies are more attractive than avoidant tendencies. Second, traditional gender roles – particularly in a heterosexual context – may result in avoidant (e.g., dismissive) tendencies being viewed as more attractive in men compared to women. Indeed, women find responsiveness less sexually appealing than do men (Birnbaum and Reis, 2012). Third, most research on attraction focuses on hypothetical partner characteristics; in live-attraction settings (e.g., speed dating), attachment styles appear to matter less than other characteristics, such as physical beauty, in predicting romantic interest (Luo and Zhang, 2009).

Beyond physical attraction, attachment styles are linked with preferences for different types of sexual and romantic relationships. For instance, both secure and anxiously attached individuals are attracted to emotionally deep relationships. However, anxious individuals crave extreme levels of closeness, often wanting to 'merge' with their romantic partners, which in turn scares away potential partners (Hazan and Shaver, 1987). By contrast, avoidant individuals are more attracted to sexual encounters with low levels of intimacy (Simpson et al., 2004), have more positive attitudes toward casual sex (Gentzler and Kerns, 2004), and desire consensually non-monogamous relationships (Moors et al., 2015), yet their actual relationships often lack these aspects (Mikluincer and Shaver, 2007; Moors et al., 2015).

Relational self-construal

As attachment theory provides a broad cognitive framework that grounds attraction and relationship initiation in early life experiences, models of self-construal propose that attraction and initiation are linked with self-relevant cognitive structures in which the self relates to others. An *independent self-construal* involves cognitions regarding one's distinctness and independence from others, whereas an *interdependent self-construal* involves cognitions regarding one's connections with and dependence on others (Markus and Kitayama, 1991). Though independent and interdependent self-construals are fostered by broad cultural contexts and focus more on group memberships and social roles (Cross and Madson, 1997; Markus and Kitayama, 1991), others have proposed an individual difference in the degree to which self-concepts are defined in terms of close relationships, termed *relational-interdependent self-construal* (RISC; Cross et al., 2000). Individuals high in RISC exhibit strong and diverse cognitive patterns indicating the centrality of relational constructs to the self-concept (Cross et al., 2002).

Notably, individuals high in RISC show cognitive, motivational, and behavioral patterns that facilitate relationship development. High RISC individuals show enhanced abilities to predict a new acquaintance's values and tend to perceive the acquaintance as feeling greater relational closeness (Cross and Morris, 2003). Additionally, high RISC individuals perceive greater similarity with close others (Cross et al., 2002). Consequently, high RISC individuals engage in more self-disclosure with new relational partners (Cross et al., 2000), which in turn enhances relationship quality (Gore et al., 2006). Therefore, high RISC fosters stronger self–other connections and promotes self-disclosure that is crucial for relationship development.

Beliefs about partners and relationships

In addition to their orientation toward relationships, individuals enter into relationships with pre-formed beliefs about what their ideal partners should be like – beliefs that affect how individuals evaluate potential mates and characteristics they find attractive. According to the Ideal Standards Model (ISM; Fletcher et al., 1999; Simpson et al., 2001), people seek out partners who possess three core features: warmth/trustworthiness, vitality/attractiveness, and status/resources. Of course, not all potential partners possess all of these features, so individuals must assess the extent to which potential (or current) partners meet or are discrepant from these ideal standards. When this discrepancy is perceived to be high, it forebodes an unsatisfactory relationship, especially to the degree that individuals hold ideal standards that are fixed rather than flexible (Campbell et al., 2001). Notably, individuals tend to be accurate in their predilection to avoid forming relationships with others who are discrepant from their ideal standards, as relationships characterized by larger partner-ideal discrepancies are less satisfying (Fletcher et al., 1999) and more likely to dissolve (Fletcher et al., 2000).

Individuals also enter into relationships with beliefs about the characteristics of ideal relationships, called implicit theories of relationships (ITRs; Knee, 1998; Knee et al., 2003). Two common implicit theories reflect whether individuals view relationships as relatively static and unchanging, called destiny beliefs, or relatively dynamic and malleable, called growth beliefs (Knee, 1998). When individuals hold destiny beliefs, they believe that they and their partners are meant to be together, are unlikely to change, and anticipate having longer relationships when initial satisfaction is high versus low (Knee, 1998). However, conflicts occurring early in a relationship lead individuals holding destiny beliefs to use this information diagnostically. They may view these conflicts as indicating that they are not meant to be together, and therefore abandon pursuing the relationship rather than working through their problems (Knee, 1998).

In contrast, when individuals hold growth beliefs, they view relationship problems as opportunities to grow closer together as they overcome these problems (Knee et al., 2003); therefore, individuals with growth beliefs may continue to pursue the relationship in spite of relational strife. Supportive of this notion, individuals with growth beliefs are less likely to engage in one-night stands and more likely to allow a relationship time to flourish (Knee, 1998).

Personality traits

Whether people decide to initiate a romantic relationship is also a function of their personality traits. Over the past decade, the study of how personality traits affect perceptions of attractiveness and relationship initiation have benefited greatly from advances in methodology (Finkel et al., 2007). Whereas many previous studies relied on participants' self-reports of the characteristics that they deem desirable or retrospective accounts of what individuals in relationships found attractive in their current partners (both of which may be subject to reporting biases), more recent methods have revealed surprising and informative results using speed-dating techniques, during which participants briefly meet several potential partners and indicate which ones they are interested in dating. Among the several advantages of this approach, one is that it allows researchers to examine the discrepancies between the characteristics people claim they are attracted to and the choices that they actually make while speed dating (Finkel and Eastwick, 2008; Luo and Zhang, 2009). Using this paradigm, Luo and Zhang (2009) found lower neuroticism and greater extraversion, agreeableness, and conscientiousness were associated with males' attraction toward females; conversely, none of the Big Five traits predicted females' attraction toward males. Similarly, in speed-dating sessions, extraversion and agreeableness predicted positive affective presence (i.e., being talkative, friendly, and energetic; Berrios et al., 2015).

In addition to how the personality characteristics that people bring with them into a relationship affect whether a relationship is initiated, the level of similarity in personality traits between partners may be equally as important in determining whether a relationship is formed. In particular, the similarity between partners is thought to be one of the most robust predictors of attraction (Montoya and Horton, 2013). Married couples, for example, have happier marriages when the couple have more similar personality traits (Caspi and Herbener, 1990).

Research on the similarity-attraction hypothesis reveals that actual and perceived similarity of traits can have differential impacts on attraction and relationship quality. Here, *actual similarity* reflects the degree to which partners' personality traits are (statistically) correlated, whereas *perceived similarity* reflects the degree to which partners believe that they are similar to each other. Research examining this distinction reveals that actual similarity significantly predicts attraction prior to initial interactions (Montoya et al., 2008), perhaps because actual similarity creates an expectation for liking and enjoyment (Sprecher, 2014). However, only perceived similarity predicts relationship interest following getting-acquainted interactions (Sprecher, 2014) and speed-dating interactions (Tidwell et al., 2013).

Approach and avoidance motivation

In addition to containing traits and inter- and intrapersonal cognitive structures, the self also consists of motivational aspects that direct and guide behavior. One fundamental motivational mechanism is the hedonic principle (Elliot, 2008; Higgins, 1998), which states that individuals are motivated to maximize pleasure and rewards while minimizing pain and threat. As such, individuals possess two distinct motivational systems: approach (i.e., directing behavior toward positive outcomes) and avoidance (i.e., directing behavior away from negative outcomes; Gray, 1987). Though a plethora of human behavior can be understood in terms of approach and avoidance motivation (see Elliot, 2008), most relevant to the current chapter is that of relational behavior.

Gable's (2006) approach–avoidance model of social motivation proposes that individuals' relational behavior may be directed by approach or avoidance goals (see also Gable and Impett, 2012). Specific to relationship initiation, Gable (2006) found that approach-motivated individuals seek relationships in order to affiliate with others, whereas avoidance-motivated individuals seek relationships to avoid loneliness. Moreover, approach-motivated individuals seek relationships that provide opportunities for self-concept growth and find others who may potentially inhibit self-growth particularly undesirable (Mattingly et al., 2012). Avoidance-motivated individuals, on the other hand, focus on negative information in social interactions (Strachman and Gable, 2006) and tend to be generally dissatisfied with the quality of their social interactions (Gable, 2006). Together, these motivational systems direct individuals toward pursuing potentially rewarding and avoiding potentially costly relationships.

Self-esteem

Global evaluations of the self, in particular self-esteem, also have the capacity to affect relationship initiation. Studies examining speed-dating interactions have found that men are more attracted to women who possess higher levels of self-esteem, but this pattern was not significant for the preferences of women (Luo and Zhang, 2009). Moreover, Zeigler-Hill and colleagues have suggested that self-esteem not only serves a status-tracking function (i.e., sociometer) but also a status-signaling function that indicates an individual's level of social status. In support of this, people are more romantically attracted to others who are high in self-esteem (Zeigler-Hill and Myers, 2011) and are more likely to attribute unrelated positive traits (e.g., extraversion) to high self-esteem in others (Zeigler-Hill et al., 2013).

One reason why people high in self-esteem may be perceived as more attractive by potential partners is that they are willing to take more interpersonal risks compared to low self-esteem individuals (Stinson et al., 2015a, 2015b). In general, initiating relationships carries the possibility of social rewards (e.g., forming new relationships with attractive partners), as well as social risks, such as rejection (Murray et al., 2006). For those social situations that carry some risk of rejection, high self-esteem individuals are less likely to exhibit distancing behaviors (i.e., inhibition, caution, passivity) relative to low self-esteem individuals (Stinson et al., 2015a). Similarly, in risky social situations, low (relative to high) self-esteem individuals are less sensitive to acceptance cues (Stinson et al., 2015b), more sensitive to rejection cues

(Dandeneau and Baldwin, 2004), and have more negative expectations for the outcomes of their social interactions (Back et al., 2011), each of which serves to inhibit the formation of a relationship.

Functioning and Maintenance

After people enter into romantic partnerships, individual differences continue to exert an influence on ongoing relational processes. We now turn our attention to the ways in which these individual differences associated with the self may impact relationship functioning and maintenance.

Attachment

As with relationship attraction, research suggests that attachment security is generally linked to adaptive relational functioning. Because attachment security fosters interpersonal trust (Mikulincer, 1998a), effective communication and smoother conflict resolution with less hostility (Pietromonaco et al., 2004; Simpson et al., 1996), and an ability to manage stress effectively (Simpson et al., 1992), individuals high in attachment security experience greater relationship satisfaction, interdependence, and positive emotions (Simpson, 1990). This is likely due to secure individuals' script-like expectations for supportive, nurturing behaviors in their partners, and communal approaches to relationships (Bartz and Lydon, 2006). Insecure individuals, by contrast, exhibit greater distress and less supportive behaviors with their partners (Campbell et al., 2005; Collins and Feeney, 2000; Simpson et al., 1992, 1996). These general patterns of attachment are consistent across cultures and demographics such as sexual orientation (Mohr et al., 2013).

Secure individuals also have more positive views toward themselves and intimacy, and this is evident in their sexual behaviors within the relationship. Attachment security is associated with safer and more pleasurable sexual behaviors, whereas attachment insecurity is linked with unsafe sex, lower likelihood of orgasm, and pain during intercourse (Birnbaum et al., 2006; Bogaert and Sadava, 2002; Mikulincer and Shaver, 2007). Moreover, avoidant attachment is linked with an unrestricted sociosexual orientation, which is a tendency to view love and sex as distinct and exhibit a preference for non-committed sexual encounters (Simpson et al., 2004).

Whereas attachment security is associated with positive relational functioning, insecurity is associated with greater relational strife. Specifically, insecure individuals are more likely to have conflicts, dysfunction, and negative emotion in their romantic relationships, which is due, in part, to their lack of confidence in their partners and their unhealthy perceptions of close relationships (Mikulincer et al., 2003). Both attachment avoidance and anxiety are linked with jealousy in relationships (Buunk, 1997; Sharpsteen and Kirkpatrick, 1997), whereas felt security is linked with less jealousy (Selterman and Maier, 2013).

Anxious attachment is linked with a heightened sensitivity to betrayal, specifically an increased likelihood to view romantic behaviors as cheating (Kruger et al., 2013) or immoral (Selterman and Koleva, 2015). Because anxiously attached individuals are preoccupied with partner betrayal and abandonment, they are more empathically accurate when inferring their partners' thoughts and feelings during relationship-threatening situations (e.g., when their partner views pictures of alternatives), which in turn is linked with greater distress and less closeness (Simpson et al., 1999, 2011).

Avoidant individuals are less skilled than secure individuals at managing relationship stress because their 'deactivation' strategies (e.g., internalization and thought suppression) often backfire (Mikulincer et al., 2003, 2004). Avoidant people seek greater distance from their romantic partners in an effort to prevent being hurt, but this can be distressing in the context of relationships because they cannot effectively utilize their partners as a secure base (Mikulincer et al., 2009; Simpson et al., 1992, 1996). The tendencies that insecure and secure individuals have (especially regarding their perceptions of availability and responsiveness in romantic partners) even manifest subconsciously in their dream content (Mikulincer et al., 2009, 2011; Selterman and Drigotas, 2009; Selterman et al., 2012, 2014).

Relational self-construal

Just as RISC promotes relationship initiation, it also facilitates adaptive relationship functioning and maintenance. Because individuals high in RISC tend to think in ways that promote mutuality with relational partners (Gore and Cross, 2011), they also tend to behave in constructive, pro-relational ways. For example, high RISC individuals are more likely to routinely provide relational partners with positivity (e.g., expressing thanks, being cheerful) and supportiveness (e.g., acceptance, assurances), which is partially due to stronger communal ties with the partner (Mattingly et al., 2011). When relational partners behave negatively, high RISC individuals are more likely to remain loyal to them (Sinclair and Fehr, 2005) and prefer constructive responses over destructive ones (Mattingly et al., 2011). High RISC individuals also show a greater willingness to sacrifice self-interests due to their focus on communal bonds (Mattingly et al., 2011). Cognitively, high RISC individuals are more likely to include a romantic partner into their own self-concept (Linardatos and Lydon, 2011). Because such pro-relationship behaviors and cognitions strengthen relational functioning (e.g., Arriaga, 2013), individuals high in RISC report experiencing greater need fulfillment and stronger relationship quality (Morry and Kito, 2009).

Beliefs about partners and relationships

Relationship functioning is also influenced by the pre-existing ideal-partner standards (Fletcher et al., 1999) and implicit theories of relationships (Knee et al., 2003) that individuals hold, and these standards and beliefs interact to predict relationship quality. That is, ideal standards and partners' discrepancies from those standards may be more important in determining individuals' levels of relationship satisfaction when individuals hold low versus high growth beliefs. In particular, Knee and colleagues found that, when individuals hold low growth beliefs, they tend to be less satisfied with their relationship if they have more negative views of their partner, whereas when individuals hold high growth beliefs, they tend to be satisfied regardless of whether their perception of their partner is positive or negative (Knee et al., 2001).

Beliefs about relationships extend to social networks as well. When family and friends approve (or disapprove) of a relationship, this may affect partners' perceptions of their relationship. Parents and friends tend to have more negative perceptions of a relationship's quality, relative to those in the relationship (MacDonald and Ross, 1999), and (in heterosexual couples) the female partner's friends tend to be more accurate at predicting the outcome of the relationship than the male partner's friends (Agnew et al., 2001). Perhaps the most famous research in this area is the so-called *Romeo and Juliet effect*, which purports to show that parental disapproval of a relationship increases perceptions of romantic love between relationship partners (Driscoll et al., 1972). However, recent replication studies have revealed the opposite effect, such that social network disapproval of a relationship predicts lower relationship quality (Sinclair et al., 2014).

Personality traits

Although personality traits play a notable role in attraction and relationship initiation, research paints a less clear picture regarding the role of the Big Five traits in relationship functioning and maintenance. For example, whereas neuroticism is negatively associated with relationship satisfaction (Donnellan et al., 2004; Gattis et al., 2004; Karney and Bradbury, 1995, 1997) and agreeableness is associated with fewer negative interactions and greater relationship quality (Donnellan et al., 2004), extraversion, openness, and conscientiousness exhibit weak and inconsistent associations with relational outcomes (Donnellan et al., 2004). Additionally, actual similarity in personality traits between partners is unrelated to relationship quality over the duration of a relationship (Montoya et al., 2008), and instead, only perceived similarity predicts long-term relationship quality for established relationships (Montoya et al., 2008).

However, an additional personality trait shows distinct and robust associations with various relational outcomes. Specifically, because romantic relationships often lead individuals to place a partner's needs ahead of personal desires (e.g., Arriaga, 2013), individuals who are strongly individualistic, selfish, and who have inflated self-beliefs (i.e., narcissists) should have trouble successfully navigating romantic relationships. Beyond desiring partners that enhance their own self-views (Campbell, 1999; Tanchotsrinon et al., 2007), narcissists exhibit cognitive and behavioral patterns that result in poorer quality relationships. Specifically, romantically involved narcissists perceive themselves to have more attractive alternatives to their current partner and pay greater attention to these alternatives (Campbell and Foster, 2002). Narcissists are less likely to forgive others' transgressions (Exline et al., 2004) and are more hostile and angry following rejection (Besser and Priel, 2009). Consequently, narcissists are less committed to their romantic partners than non-narcissists (Campbell and Foster, 2002; Foster et al., 2006), which reduces their likelihood of engaging in relationship maintenance behaviors (Campbell and Foster, 2002). However, when narcissists are made mindful of communal thoughts or motives, they show heightened levels of commitment (Finkel et al., 2009), suggesting that thinking communally may buffer against the deleterious effects of narcissism.

Approach and avoidance motivation

Relationship functioning is impacted by individuals' approach and avoidance motivational systems. When individuals possess approach-motivated goals in their relationships, they tend to experience greater relationship quality, whereas those who possess avoidance-motivated goals tend to experience poorer relationship quality (Impett et al., 2010). Additionally, those whose commitment to a romantic partner is primarily approach-motivated (e.g., feeling attached to and identifying with the partner) tend to experience greater relationship satisfaction over time relative to those whose commitment is primarily avoidance-motivated (e.g., feeling obligated to remain in the relationship and fearing a disruption to one's life if the relationship dissolved; Frank and Brandstätter, 2002).

Though certain relational behaviors may be primarily motivated by one system (Mattingly et al., 2012), considerable research has examined how both motivational systems affect relational behavior. For example, in day-to-day functioning in ongoing relationships, romantic partners regularly encounter situations in which their goals conflict with one another and, as a result, one partner may choose to sacrifice his or her self-interests (Van Lange et al., 1997). Though willingness to sacrifice is generally associated with greater relationship quality (Wieselquist et al., 1999) and can predict marital satisfaction long-term (Stanley et al., 2006), the motivation driving the sacrifice is critical. Specifically, individuals who make approach-motivated sacrifices tend to experience greater relationship quality over time (as well as more positive affect and satisfaction with life), whereas those who make avoidance-motivated sacrifices tend to experience reduced relationship quality (Impett et al., 2005). Notably, recipients of approach-motivated sacrifices also experience heightened relationship quality (Impett et al., 2014). Approach-motivated sacrifices are beneficial because they are perceived to be more genuine and authentic, whereas avoidance-motivated sacrifices feel disingenuous and less authentic (Impett et al., 2013a), though these negative effects are mitigated when individuals possess an interdependent self-construal (Impett et al., 2013b). Perhaps not surprisingly, insecure attachment influences the types of sacrifices individuals make. Specifically, avoidantly attached individuals make primarily avoidance-motivated sacrifices, whereas anxiously attached individuals make sacrifices for both approach- and avoidance-motivated reasons (Mattingly and Clark, 2012). Interestingly, though anxious individuals tend to experience lower relationship quality (e.g., Feeney et al., 1998) – partially due to making avoidance-motivated sacrifices (Mattingly and Clark, 2012) – their simultaneous enacting of approach-motivated sacrifices partially (and temporarily) offsets these impairments in relational functioning (Mattingly and Clark, 2012).

Additionally, sexual behavior is dually motivated. Similar to sacrificing, individuals who possess approach-motivated sexual goals (e.g., engaging in sexual activity to promote intimacy or to express love toward the partner) tend to experience greater relationship satisfaction, increased closeness, greater sexual satisfaction, and less relational conflict, whereas those who possess avoidance-motivated sexual goals (e.g., engaging in sexual activity to prevent the romantic partner from losing interest) tend to experience poorer relationship quality, less closeness, lower sexual satisfaction, and increased relational conflict (Impett et al., 2005; Muise et al., 2013). Moreover, approach-motivated sexual goals buffer against declines in sexual desire over time (Impett et al., 2008; Muise et al., 2013).

Structure of the self-concept

Given that broad orientations, cognitive representations, personality traits, and motivational states directly impact relationship functioning, it is not surprising that structural aspects of the self-concept also play a role in shaping relationships. Self-concept clarity, for example, describes the degree to which an individual maintains a clearly defined, cohesive, and stable self-concept (Campbell et al., 1996). When individuals hold clear self-concepts, they may act in more consistent and predictable ways, allowing their partners to also hold clear mental representations of them (Gurung et al., 2001), which should enable them to develop closer and more satisfying relationships (Lewandowksi et al., 2010). Self-concept clarity is also associated with self-esteem, and having low clarity is associated with a variety of mental health issues (Richman et al., 2016). Overall, research reveals that self-concept clarity is positively associated with measures of relationship closeness and quality (Lewandowski et al., 2010), in part because high self-concept clarity enables partners to more accurately perceive their personalities and make predictions about their behaviors (Lewandowski and Nardone, 2012). Not surprisingly, then, the degree to which a person views a partner's self-concept as clear predicts one's own level of relationship satisfaction (Gurung et al., 2001).

Relatedly, people also differ in their self-complexity, which is the degree to which individuals have numerous and non-redundant self-concept traits (Linville, 1985, 1987). Self-complexity is associated with the degree to which individuals maintain complex representations of their relationships (Kim, 2006) and close relationship partners (Brown et al., 2009). For example, individuals with high self-complexity tend to possess a larger number of differentiated relationship roles and attributes (i.e., relationship complexity), which in turn buffers against relationship-relevant negative emotions (Kim, 2006).

Dissolution

Attachment

Whereas attachment plays a vital role in relationship initiation, functioning, and maintenance, attachment security at the individual level is surprisingly not a strong predictor of relationship dissolution (Le et al., 2010). However, the interplay of attachment styles at the dyadic level does matter. Couples with two secure partners have the most stable romantic relationships (Mikulincer and Shaver, 2007) and, on average, are more likely to enjoy relationship longevity, even if they endure significant life stress (Treboux et al., 2004). Comparatively, couples with one secure and one insecure partner are more vulnerable to dissolution (Mikulincer et al., 2009). Secure people are often able to detect when a relationship is not working properly, based on their implicit knowledge of the secure base script (Mikulincer et al., 2009), and sense when their partners' insecurity is causing difficulties (e.g., when an avoidant partner resists emotional intimacy).

As for couples with two insecure partners, those relationships are surprisingly stable over time (Kirkpatrick and Davis, 1994), even though their relationships often contain significantly more conflict than those for secure couples (Mikulincer and Shaver, 2007). An explanation for this stability is that insecure romantic partners begin their relationship with maladaptive beliefs, attitudes, and behaviors, which are then reinforced by each other's insecure tendencies. Thus, insecure couples may believe their dysfunction is inevitable. Another explanation lies in gender roles, as pairs of avoidant men and anxious women are common and higher in longevity compared to pairs of anxious men and avoidant women (Kirkpatrick and Davis, 1994).

Beliefs about relationships

Relationship stability and dissolution are also associated with individuals' implicit beliefs about relationships (Knee et al., 2003). Individuals who hold strong destiny beliefs – that is, beliefs that romantic relationships are either meant to be or are destined for failure – are especially prone to relationship dissolution under certain conditions. Specifically, individuals with strong destiny beliefs are less likely to remain in a relationship to the extent that their initial relationship satisfaction was low (Knee, 1998). Similarly, destiny beliefs predict dissolution when individuals perceive that their partner is not their soulmate (Franiuk et al., 2002). In fact, a recent meta-analysis revealed that destiny beliefs reliably predict non-marital relationship dissolution (Le et al., 2010). One reason for this is that individuals with strong destiny beliefs disengage from negative relational events (Knee, 1998) and ultimately use relational information diagnostically to determine whether the partner and relationship is a proper fit (Franiuk et al., 2002; Knee et al., 2003).

Conversely, individuals with growth beliefs engage in more constructive coping strategies in the face of negative relationship events (Knee, 1998). They also make more sacrifices for, and are less violent toward, romantic partners (Cobb et al., 2013). Consequently, individuals high in growth beliefs may enact relationship behaviors to protect their relationships from dissolution.

Personality factors

Personality characteristics may directly contribute to relationship dissolution or may lay the groundwork for dissolution to become more likely through their impact on marital interactions (Donnellan et al., 2004). Neuroticism, in particular, seems to have pernicious consequences for close relationships (Karney and Bradbury, 1997). One study, for example, tracked couples from their time of engagement in the 1930s until the 1980s and found that the largest mean difference between still-married and divorced participants was their initial level of neuroticism (Kelly and Conley, 1987). One reason why neuroticism is particularly problematic in long-term relationships is that it is associated with increased negative communication patterns, especially with respect to negative affective communication, which undermines relationship satisfaction (Caughlin et al., 2000; Donnellan et al., 2004). Although the evidence suggests that neuroticism is an especially important predictor of divorce, a meta-analysis by Le et al. (2010) found that only agreeableness is significantly associated (negatively) with *non-marital* relationship dissolution. In contrast to the role of neuroticism in predicting marital dissolution, and agreeableness in predicting non-marital dissolution, conscientiousness, extraversion, and openness do not seem to predict breakup (e.g., Karney and Bradbury, 1995).

PART 2: RELATIONSHIPS TO INDIVIDUAL DIFFERENCES

In addition to individual differences and self-concepts affecting relational processes, there is a reciprocal link in which relationships impact and change the self. In Part 2, we review research demonstrating how relational processes affect individual differences and the self across the same relationship phases as in Part 1, namely: (a) attraction and initiation; (b) relational functioning and maintenance; and (c) relationship dissolution.

Attraction and Initiation

Attachment
There is evidence that romantic partners from present or past relationships can affect the way people perceive and interact with new partners, through a process referred to as *transference* (Andersen and Chen, 2002). Through this process, people view new others through the lens of existing/past partners, if the relevant schema for those partners is active during the new interaction. Past-partner schematic information is often more accessible and has a stronger influence on social perception than schemas of non-significant others, stereotypes, or personality traits (Andersen and Cole, 1990). This can lead to biases in social perception that are triggered by past partners, including false-positive memories, such that people misremember a new person as having attributes consistent with the schema of a significant other (Andersen and Baum, 1994). People may also transfer the affect associated with the significant other to the new person (Chen et al., 2013). In these ways, a past/current romantic partner changes the way people perceive new others, cognitively and emotionally. This process is automatic and occurs implicitly (Andersen et al., 1995; Chen et al., 2013).

Additionally, attachment transference manifests itself behaviorally (Chen et al., 2013). When interacting with a new partner, individuals may rely upon past-partner schematic information to guide the interaction. For example, when John meets someone new (Amy), his schema for a positively regarded romantic partner (Mary) is active. Consequently, three outcomes will result. First, John will exhibit transference, viewing Amy as similar to Mary and regarding her more positively. Second, John will view himself through the lens of his relationship with Mary, such that his relational self will shift toward behavior that he would typically display while interacting with Mary. Third, Amy's behavior will change, as John elicits her positive, Mary-like qualities through behavioral confirmation (Berk and Andersen, 2000).

Need to belong
One way to appreciate the impact of social relationships on the self-concept is to examine what happens when individuals lack sufficiently intimate relationships. Whether due to the possession of traits such as introversion and shyness, fear of rejection (Leary et al., 2013), or as a result of ostracism (Williams, 2007), individuals who lack quality relationships experience a heightened need to belong (see Baumeister and

Leary, 1995). This need is associated with neuroticism (Leary et al., 2013), social anxiety (Nichols and Webster, 2013), decreased satisfaction with personal relationships (Mellor et al., 2008), and the experience of life regrets (Morrison et al., 2012) among other undesirable outcomes (Baumeister and Leary, 1995).

Baumeister and Leary (1995) suggest that individuals respond to a heightened need to belong by experiencing an increased desire to initiate close relationships and, as a consequence, should engage in behaviors designed to attract potential partners (see also DeWall and Richman, 2011; Maner et al., 2007). Indeed, research reveals that individuals high (vs. low) in the need to belong (measured as an individual difference) are better at identifying facial expressions and vocal tones (Pickett et al., 2004), have better memories for social events (Gardner et al., 2000), and are more motivated to listen to emotional disclosures (Hackenbracht and Gasper, 2013). Similarly, excluded and rejected individuals engage in more prosocial behaviors (Maner et al., 2007), exhibit greater conformity (Williams et al., 2000), and are better at perceiving Duchenne versus non-Duchenne smiles (Bernstein et al., 2008), compared to accepted individuals. Thus, engaging in belongingness-seeking behaviors and forming intimate relationships with others directly impacts individuals' core need for relatedness.

Self-expansion

Just as individuals have a motivation for belongingness, they also have a motivation to efficaciously navigate their physical and social environments (Deci and Ryan, 2000), and one way they can increase their sense of self-efficacy and agency is by cognitively restructuring the self-concept through a process of self-expansion (Aron et al., 2013). The self-expansion model posits that, when individuals acquire new or augment existing resources, perspectives, identities, and capabilities, they cognitively expand and restructure the self-concept, which increases their ability to accomplish goals (Aron et al., 2001a, 2013). A primary way individuals accomplish self-expansion is through the formation of romantic relationships (Aron, 2003; cf. Mattingly and Lewandowski, 2014). Self-expansion within relationships occurs when couples jointly engage in novel, exciting, and challenging experiences (e.g., Aron et al., 2000, 2001b) or when individuals incorporate aspects of a romantic partner into their self-concept (e.g., Aron et al., 1991), such as after mutual self-disclosure (Aron et al., 1997; Sprecher et al., 2013). However, even prior to the early stages of relationship development, individuals merely interested in forming a relationship with a potential partner may spontaneously alter their self-concepts to include aspects of the potential partner (Slotter and Gardner, 2009), even if the attributes are negative (Slotter and Gardner, 2012a). Individuals high in attachment anxiety are especially prone to engage in this anticipatory self-other inclusion (Slotter and Gardner, 2012b), whereas those who possess low self–concept clarity are less likely to include a potential partner's attributes (Emery et al., 2015).

Functioning and Maintenance

The dynamics of ongoing romantic relationships have transformative effects on individuals' self-concepts. Individuals' self-views are directly shaped and actively modified by relational processes, which in turn impact relationship quality and functioning. Next, we provide an overview of how relationships result in self-concept malleability.

Attachment

The felt security (or lack thereof) that individuals experience in romantic relationships is largely a function of previous experiences – especially early childhood experiences with caregivers (Mikulincer and Shaver, 2007; Waters et al., 2000a). Attachment security is relatively stable across different relationships and across time, indicating trait-like tendencies in the way people navigate intimate relationships (Fraley et al., 2011). However, trait-like attachment styles can also change based on treatment by romantic partners, and events that occur in those relationships. For example, attachment-related anxiety and avoidance can decrease over time as a function of goal-validation and trust in romantic relationships (Arriaga et al., 2014). Moreover, those high in attachment anxiety have negative models of self (Collins, 1996; Mikulincer, 1998a, 1998b), which can become more positive over time (thus, more secure) if they perceive that their partner displays confidence in goal achievement. Conversely, those high in attachment avoidance have negative models of other (Collins, 1996; Mikulincer, 1998a), and if their relationships lead to them to feel that their partners can be trusted, they may become less prone to dismissing and withdrawing tendencies.

Landmark relationship events (e.g., marriage) can also result in changes in attachment. For example, though most engaged couples transitioning to marriage keep their initial attachment status, some become more secure over time (Crowell et al., 2002). Notably, one's partner does not need to be secure in order for this change to occur, leading Crowell and colleagues to conclude that 'a committed, devoted, but insecure partner can be as effective as a secure partner in fostering growth and change in the individual' (Crowell et al., 2002, p. 476). However, it should be noted that not all studies have found evidence for significant attachment-style change based on life events such as marriage (see Mikulincer and Shaver, 2007).

Such change in attachment style over time is conceptually similar to *earned security*, in which an individual with an initially insecure attachment style is able to develop a new, more secure attachment (Roisman et al., 2002). Though earned security is well documented in the developmental and clinical literatures (e.g., Odgers, 2014), less is known about how romantic partners foster earned security in their significant others. Some studies suggest that people can have secure attachments in their romantic relationships despite insecure attachments to their parents (Treboux et al., 2004). Romantic partners can make a person feel greater attachment security under conditions of low stress; however, this process is constrained under conditions of high stress (Treboux et al., 2004). This suggests that people are capable of forming attachment mental representations in their current relationships that differ in security from those formed in childhood.

Relationships are capable of altering individuals' attachment styles through the formation of a relationship-specific secure base and safe haven (Collins and Feeney, 2000; Feeney, 2004). When partners are available, provide encouragement, and refrain from undermining a partner's confidence and concentration, a secure base is developed (Feeney and Thrush, 2010; Feeney and Van Vleet, 2010). In this sense, a secure base relationship in marital couples is not fundamentally different from a secure base relationship between a parent and child (Bowlby, 1969/1982, 1988; Waters and Cummings, 2000). This secure base then helps partners mutually thrive in various ways, such as by providing affirmation, acceptance, perceptual assistance, and capitalization (see Feeney and Collins, 2015, for a review). Consequently, when romantic partners provide a secure base, individuals can more confidently and effectively explore the environment. In turn, people's emotional well-being, autonomy, physical health, goal pursuits, self-esteem, happiness, achievement, and other outcomes are driven, in part, by having a stable secure base throughout adult life (Feeney, 2006; Feeney and Collins, 2015).

Cognitive interdependence

Once a relationship forms, individuals begin developing emotional attachments with partners and long-term orientations toward the relationship, which are manifested in individuals' commitment level. Ample research supporting the Investment Model of Commitment (Le and Agnew, 2003; Rusbult, 1980, 1983) indicates that individuals' commitment is predicted by three primary factors: higher satisfaction level (i.e., the global evaluation of the general positivity or negativity of the relationship, which is determined by a comparison of subjective rewards and costs), greater investment level (i.e., the subjective perception of the tangible or intangible resources that would be lost if the relationship were to end, even if these resources are merely planned; Goodfriend and Agnew, 2008), and lower quality of alternatives (i.e., the subjective attractiveness of perceived alternatives to the relationship, such as other potential relationships or time alone). Higher commitment levels predict intentions to remain in the relationship, which in turn, predict relationship stability (VanderDrift et al., 2009), and commitment is one of the strongest known predictors of relationship persistence (Le and Agnew, 2003; Le et al., 2010).

Of particular importance to how relationships affect individuals' self-concepts, one consequence of heightened commitment is that individuals develop a sense of cognitive interdependence with romantic partners (Agnew et al., 1998). Individuals high (vs. low) in cognitive interdependence perceive greater inclusion of other in the self and spontaneously generate and use more plural pronouns (Agnew et al., 1998, 2004; Aron et al., 1991). Moreover, cognitively interdependent individuals perceive greater self–other similarity (Murray et al., 1996), which in turn, maintains relationship quality.

Cognitively interdependent individuals treat the partner's outcomes as their own (Aron et al., 1991; Gardner et al., 2002; Thai and Lockwood, 2015) and experience a transformation of motivation in which the needs of the relationship are placed ahead of personal desires (Arriaga, 2013; Van Lange et al., 1997; Yovetich and Rusbult, 1994). Consequently, cognitively interdependent individuals are more likely to enact behaviors that maintain the relationship (Arriaga, 2013; Ledbetter et al., 2013; Van Lange et al., 1997; Wieselquist et al., 1999), thereby maintaining self–other integration.

Relational self-change

As individuals become cognitively interdependent, they also experience a restructuring of the self-concept. Individuals who have recently fallen in love, for example, experience an increase in the amount and diversity of self-concept content (Aron et al., 1995). According to the self-expansion model, these changes to the self-concept occur through two primary means. Individuals gain dimensions of the self-concept when they: (1) incorporate their partners' traits, identities, resources, and perspectives into their own sense of self; and (2) complete shared novel and challenging activities as a result of the relationship (Aron et al., 2013). For example, Aron et al. (2000) randomly assigned couples to perform either novel and challenging activities, such as completing an obstacle course with their wrists and ankles bound to each other, or relatively mundane activities, such as crawling on the ground individually and unbound to their partner. Couples in the novel and challenging condition reported greater relationship quality than those in the mundane condition. Research employing an experience sampling approach (Graham, 2008) similarly found that performing shared exciting and activating activities led couples to experience greater feelings of relationship satisfaction.

Extending the self-expansion model to incorporate other types of self-concept changes, the Two-Dimensional Model of Relationship-Induced Self-Concept Change (TDM; Mattingly et al., 2014; McIntyre et al., 2015) proposes that romantic relationships affect both the direction and valence of self-concept content (Figure 22.2). In particular, relationships can increase or decrease the size of the self-concept (changes along the direction dimension), and modified self-concept content can be perceived as positive or negative in nature (changes along the valence dimension; Mattingly et al., 2014; McIntyre et al., 2015). These two independent dimensions combine to form four different types of self-concept change: self-expansion (increase in positive content), self-contraction (decrease in positive content), self-adulteration (increase in negative content), and self-pruning (decrease in negative content).

Considerable evidence supports each of the four self-change processes identified by the TDM. For example, Slotter and Gardner (2012a) found that individuals are willing to take on the negative trait of a potential partner (i.e., self-adulteration), especially when possession of that trait might make them more appealing to the potential partner. Research on the Michelangelo Phenomenon (e.g., DiDonato and Krueger, 2010; Drigotas et al., 1999) reveals that individuals can help their partners remove unwanted aspects of the self-concept via a process of interpersonal affirmation, akin to self-pruning. Additionally, self-change processes that improve the self-concept (i.e., self-expansion and self-pruning) enhance perceptions of relationship satisfaction, commitment, passionate love, and companionate love (Mattingly et al., 2014), whereas self-change processes that degrade the self-concept (i.e., self-contraction and self-adulteration) are associated with increased infidelity (Mattingly et al., 2014), attention to alternatives, and dissolution considerations (McIntyre et al., 2015). This model implies that relationships have the capability of altering the self-concept, and these self-concept changes have implications for relational outcomes (Mattingly et al., 2014; McIntyre et al., 2015).

Dissolution

Attachment

Romantic relationship dissolution impacts individuals for many reasons, one of which is the fact that individuals can no longer count on their ex-partner as an attachment

Figure 22.2 Two-dimensional model of relationship-induced self-concept change

figure. It is common for people after dissolution to struggle because they continue to desire their ex-partner for attachment-related needs, such as support and security (Fagundes, 2012; Perilloux and Buss, 2008; Sbarra and Emery, 2005).

Secure individuals tend to experience less distress after a romantic relationship ends (Gilbert and Sifers, 2011). Secure attachment is linked with less apprehension about contact with the former partner, less blame toward the ex-partner, and readiness to pursue a new relationship (Madey and Jilek, 2012). Security is also linked with more positivity toward the ex-partner, including having an amicable breakup, willingness to repair the relationship, or to remain friends (Madey and Jilek, 2012). However, other research has shown that continued attachment to a former spouse is associated with greater distress (Berman, 1988), and reducing both positive and negative attachments to ex-partners is essential to post-divorce adjustment (Tschann et al., 1989). 'Rebound' relationships, while commonly believed to be maladaptive, are actually linked with more beneficial mental and relationship health outcomes (Brumbaugh and Fraley, 2015) and may be especially beneficial for individuals high in anxious attachment for effectively letting go of their ex-partners (Spielmann et al., 2009). Other work shows that anxious attachment is linked with more breakup distress while avoidant attachment is linked with less breakup distress (Sprecher et al., 1998). Somewhat paradoxically, anxious individuals may have *hyperactive* breakup distress such that they experience more personal growth after a breakup compared to avoidant individuals who inhibit their own personal growth by *deactivating* post-relationship distress (Marshall et al., 2013). As with avoidant patterns in current close relationships, when avoidant individuals internalize stress and minimize emotional experiences, these tendencies backfire (Birnbaum et al., 1997; Mikulincer et al., 2004).

Beyond emotional distress due to the loss of an attachment figure, relationship dissolution can lead to a decrease in attachment security. Longitudinal research has shown that approximately 50% of secure individuals who experience dissolution retain their secure status over a four-year period, whereas approximately 90% of secure individuals retain their status if no breakup is experienced (Kirkpatrick and Hazan, 1994). However, this decrease in security may not be permanent and not all studies have shown evidence for such change (see Mikulincer and Shaver, 2007).

Self-contraction and post-dissolution growth

Relationship dissolution is particularly problematic to individuals' self-concept content. During the formation and maintenance of the relationship, individuals' self-concepts increase in size and diversity (Aron et al., 1995), which results in self–other confusion, such that individuals find it more difficult to identify traits that are self- but not partner-indicative than traits that are both self- and partner-indicative (Aron et al., 1991). Relationship dissolution consequently places individuals at risk of self-concept uncertainty regarding which aspects are their own rather than those of an ex-partner. Accordingly, upon dissolution, individuals exhibit impaired self-concepts, such that they report fewer and less diverse self-concept attributes (Lewandowski et al., 2006; Slotter et al., 2010). Effectively, individuals experience self-contraction as their working self-concepts shrink in size (Lewandowski et al., 2006; Mattingly et al., 2014). Self-contracted individuals are less clear about their self-concept content both short- and long-term, and this loss of self-concept clarity predicts emotional distress (Mason et al., 2012; Slotter et al., 2010).

However, not all individuals experience the deleterious effects of self-contraction upon relationship dissolution. For example, physiological evidence indicates that individuals who exert greater (vs. less) self-regulatory effort while coping with dissolution report less self-concept impairment (Mason et al., 2012; Sbarra and Borelli, 2013). Additionally, individuals who engage in cognitive reappraisals of the dissolved relationship (e.g., seeking meaning, identifying positive aspects of the relationship) experience less emotional distress over time, whereas those who do not cognitively reappraise show stable levels of emotional distress (Slotter and Ward, 2015).

There are cases, though, in which individuals' self-concepts actually *improve* post-dissolution. For example, individuals whose relationships inhibited self-expansion show self-concept growth following dissolution, largely due to individuals rediscovering aspects of their self-concepts that were neglected during the relationship (Lewandowski and Bizzoco, 2007). Additionally, individuals tend to have larger self-concepts, to the extent that they have had more previous romantic relationships, suggesting that self-contraction upon dissolution does not fully negate self-expansion experienced during the relationship (Carpenter and Spottswood, 2013). In this way, individuals' self-concepts cumulatively grow through a process of expansion and partial contraction, resulting in residual self-expansion.

Self-Esteem

The level of distress that individuals experience (e.g., reduced self-esteem, experience of negative affect) following relationship dissolution is critically affected by the manner in which the relationship ended. For example, initiating a breakup is less distressing than having one's partner initiate a breakup (Sprecher et al., 1998), and relationship dissolution is less distressing when it is mutual versus non-mutual (Sprecher, 1994). Continuing to love one's ex-partner also predicts greater decreases in self-esteem following breakup (Mason et al., 2012) compared to those who move on. Additionally, dissolution is particularly distressing for individuals whose self-esteem is contingent upon being in a romantic relationship (Park et al., 2011). Nevertheless, the overall impact of relationship dissolution on self-esteem is relatively modest. A meta-analysis of research examining the impact of real-world social rejection (including romantic rejection) found the effect size of rejection on self-esteem to be small to medium (Blackhart et al., 2009).

CONCLUDING THOUGHTS AND FUTURE DIRECTIONS

This chapter presents an integrative overview of the associations between individual differences and romantic relationship processes, with a specific focus on the motivational, organizational, and structural components of the self. We conceptualize these associations as bidirectional; the self directly influences relational processes and relational processes directly influence the self (see Figure 22.1). Specifically, we illustrate how central individual differences such as attachment, self-construal, personality, and motivation are linked to relationship processes such as satisfaction, commitment, communication, relationship maintenance, and closeness across the trajectory of relationship development, beginning at attraction and concluding with dissolution.

In many ways, the self and relational processes are fundamentally interconnected; however, researchers historically have approached these associations through a unidirectional lens. In contrast, we believe that to fully understand the nuanced – yet core – connections between individual differences and relationships, one must consider bidirectionality. Take, for example, attachment, which we discuss in both Parts 1 and 2 of the chapter and at each relationship phase. Ample research on attachment shows that these mental representations of others, formed early in life and which manifest themselves in adult relationships, both directly impact relational functioning yet are capable of being altered as a result of relational experiences.

Yet, it is important to recognize that the quantity of information examined above regarding what people bring to a romantic relationship (i.e., individual differences affecting relational processes) is more abundant than the amount of information regarding how romantic relationships change people (i.e., relational processes affecting individual differences). This may simply reflect the amount of research on each topic, as opposed to the validity of the bidirectional approach.

To reduce this disparity in the literature, we suggest that future research further explores a number of ways in which relational processes impact individual differences and the self. First, though it is logistically more difficult to study *in vivo*, there is much still to be learned regarding how dissolution impacts individuals' self-concepts, motivations, attachment orientations, and manifestations of personality traits. Second, future research should address the mixed findings regarding the question of whether changes in attachment security are relatively permanent, temporary, or non-existent, and under what circumstances people are most likely to experience changes in felt security. Third, future research should recognize that relational processes are often dyadic, and as a result, the bidirectional paths may operate distinctly for the specific partners in the relationship.

For example, Partner A's attachment security may lead to more regular maintenance behaviors enacted toward Partner B, which makes Partner B more satisfied and committed. In turn, Partner B's enhanced cognitive interdependence leads to greater trust of Partner A, which ultimately strengthens and reinforces Partner A's attachment security.

In closing, we hope that researchers continue to explore the complex dynamics of self and relationships. The scientific study of bidirectional and dyadic mechanisms between the self and close relationships can yield fruitful programmatic research, not just within the realm of personality psychology but in social, developmental, clinical, biological, and other areas of psychology as well. In sum, a full understanding of individual differences requires a sophisticated understanding of romantic relationship processes.

REFERENCES

Agnew, C. R., Loving, T. J., & Drigotas, S. M. (2001). Substituting the forest for the trees: Social networks and the prediction of romantic relationship state and fate. *Journal of Personality and Social Psychology*, 81, 1042–1057.

Agnew, C. R., Loving, T. J., Le, B., & Goodfriend, W. (2004). Thinking close: Measuring relational closeness as perceived self–other inclusion. In D. J. Mashek & A. Aron (Eds.), *Handbook of closeness and intimacy* (pp. 103–115). Mahwah, NJ: Lawrence Erlbaum.

Agnew, C. R., & South, S. C. (2014). *Interpersonal relationships and health: Social and clinical psychological mechanisms.* New York, NY: Oxford University Press.

Agnew, C. R., Van Lange, P. A. M., Rusbult, C. E., & Langston, C. A. (1998). Cognitive interdependence: Commitment and the mental representation of close relationships. *Journal of Personality and Social Psychology*, 74, 939–954.

Andersen, S. M., & Baum, A. (1994). Transference in interpersonal relations: Inferences and affect based on significant-other representations. *Journal of Personality*, 62, 459–497.

Andersen, S. M., & Chen, S. (2002). The relational self: An interpersonal social-cognitive theory. *Psychological Review*, 109, 619–645.

Andersen, S. M., & Cole, S. W. (1990). 'Do I know you?': The role of significant others in general social perception. *Journal of Personality and Social Psychology*, 59, 384–399.

Andersen, S. M., Glassman, N. S., Chen, S., & Cole, S. W. (1995). Transference in social perception: The role of chronic accessibility in significant-other representations. *Journal of Personality and Social Psychology*, 69, 41–57.

Aron, A. (2003). Self and close relationships. In M. R. Leary & J. P. Tangney (Eds.), *Handbook of self and identity* (pp. 442–461). New York, NY: Guilford Press.

Aron, A., Aron, E. N., & Norman, C. (2001a). Self-expansion model of motivation and cognition in close relationships and beyond. In M. Clark & G. Fletcher (Eds.), *Blackwell handbook of social psychology, Vol. 2: Interpersonal processes* (pp. 478–501). Oxford, UK: Blackwell.

Aron, A., Aron, E. N., Tudor, M., & Nelson, G. (1991). Close relationships as including other in the self. *Journal of Personality and Social Psychology*, 60, 241–253.

Aron, A., Lewandowski, G. W., Jr., Mashek, D., & Aron, E. N. (2013). The self-expansion model of motivation and cognition in close relationships. In J. A. Simpson & L. Campbell (Eds.), *The Oxford handbook of close relationships* (pp. 90–105). New York, NY: Oxford University Press.

Aron, A., Melinat, E., Aron, E. N., Vallone, R. D., & Bator, R. J. (1997). The experimental generation of interpersonal closeness: A procedure and some preliminary findings. *Personality and Social Psychology Bulletin*, 23, 363–377.

Aron, A., Norman, C. C., & Aron, E. (2001b). Shared self-expanding activities as a means of maintaining and enhancing close romantic relationships. In J. Harvey & A. Wenzel (Eds.), *Close romantic relationships: Maintenance and enhancement* (pp. 47–66). Mahwah, NJ: Lawrence Erlbaum.

Aron, A., Norman, C. C., Aron, E. N., McKenna, C., & Heyman, R. E. (2000). Couples' shared participation in novel and arousing activities and experienced relationship quality. *Journal of Personality and Social Psychology*, *78*, 273–284.

Aron, A., Paris, M., & Aron, E. N. (1995). Falling in love: Prospective studies of self-concept change. *Journal of Personality and Social Psychology*, *69*, 1102–1112.

Arriaga, X. B. (2013). An interdependence theory analysis of close relationships. In J. A. Simpson & L. Campbell (Eds.), *The Oxford handbook of close relationships* (pp. 39–65). New York, NY: Oxford University Press.

Arriaga, X. B., Kumashiro, M., Finkel, E. J., VanderDrift, L. E., & Luchies, L. B. (2014). Filling the void: Bolstering attachment security in committed relationships. *Social Psychological and Personality Science*, *5*, 398–406.

Back, M. D., Schmukle, S. C., & Egloff, B. (2011). A closer look at first sight: Social relations lens model analysis of personality and interpersonal attraction at zero acquaintance. *European Journal of Personality*, *25*, 225–238.

Bartz, J. A., & Lydon, J. E. (2006). Navigating the interdependence dilemma: Attachment goals and the use of communal norms with potential close others. *Journal of Personality and Social Psychology*, *91*, 77–96.

Baumeister, R. F., & Leary, M. R. (1995). The need to belong: Desire for interpersonal attachments as a fundamental human motivation. *Psychological Bulletin*, *117*, 497–529.

Berk, M. S., & Andersen, S. M. (2000). The impact of past relationships on interpersonal behavior: Behavioral confirmation in the social-cognitive process of transference. *Journal of Personality and Social Psychology*, *79*, 546–562.

Berman, W. H. (1988). The attachment bond as a unique aspect of divorce. *Journal of Family Psychology*, *1*, 333–336.

Bernstein, M. J., Young, S. G., Brown, C. M., Sacco, D. F., & Claypool, H. M. (2008). Adaptive responses to social exclusion: Social rejection improves detection of real and fake smiles. *Psychological Science*, *19*, 981–983.

Berrios, R., Totterdell, P., & Niven, K. (2015). Why do you make us feel good? Correlates and interpersonal consequences of affective presence in speed-dating. *European Journal of Personality*, *29*, 72–82.

Besser, A., & Priel, B. (2009). Emotional responses to a romantic partner's imaginary rejection: The roles of attachment anxiety, covert narcissism, and self-evaluation. *Journal of Personality*, *77*, 287–325.

Birnbaum, G. E., Orr, I., Mikulincer, M., & Florian, V. (1997). When marriage breaks up: Does attachment style contribute to coping and mental health? *Journal of Social and Personal Relationships*, *14*, 643–654.

Birnbaum, G. E., & Reis, H. T. (2012). When does responsiveness pique sexual interest? Attachment and sexual desire in initial acquaintanceships. *Personality and Social Psychology Bulletin*, *38*, 946–958.

Birnbaum, G. E., Reis, H. T., Mikulincer, M., Gillath, O., & Orpaz, A. (2006). When sex is more than just sex: Attachment orientations, sexual experience, and relationship quality. *Journal of Personality and Social Psychology*, *91*, 929–943.

Blackhart, G. C., Nelson, B. C., Knowles, M. L., & Baumeister, R. F. (2009). Rejection elicits emotional reactions but neither causes immediate distress nor lowers self-esteem: A meta-analytic review of 192 studies on social exclusion. *Personality and Social Psychology Review*, *13*, 269–309.

Bogaert, A. F., & Sadava, S. (2002). Adult attachment and sexual behavior. *Personal Relationships*, *9*, 191–204.

Bowlby, J. (1969/1982). *Attachment and loss: Vol. 1. Attachment*. New York, NY: Basic Books.

Bowlby, J. (1973). *Attachment and loss: Vol. 2. Separation anxiety and anger*. New York, NY: Basic Books.

Bowlby, J. (1988). *A secure base*. New York, NY: Basic Books.

Brewer, M. B., & Gardner, W. (1996). Who is this 'we'? Levels of collective identity and self representations. *Journal of Personality and Social Psychology*, *71*, 83–93.

Brown, C. M., Young, S. G., & McConnell, A. R. (2009). Seeing close others as we see ourselves: One's own self-complexity is reflected in perceptions of meaningful others. *Journal of Experimental Social Psychology*, *45*, 515–523.

Brumbaugh, C. C., Baren, A., & Agishtein, P. (2014). Attraction to attachment insecurity:

Flattery, appearance, and status's role in mate preferences. *Personal Relationships, 21*, 288–308.

Brumbaugh, C. C., & Fraley, R. C. (2015). Too fast, too soon? An empirical investigation into rebound relationships. *Journal of Social and Personal Relationships, 32*, 99–118.

Buunk, B. P. (1997). Personality, birth order and attachment styles as related to various types of jealousy. *Personality and Individual Differences, 23*, 997–1006.

Campbell, J. D., Trapnell, P. D., Heine, S. J., Katz, I. M., Lavallee, L. F., & Lehman, D. R. (1996). Self-concept clarity: Measurement, personality correlates, and cultural boundaries. *Journal of Personality and Social Psychology, 70*, 141–156.

Campbell, L., Simpson, J. A., Boldry, J., & Kashy, D. A. (2005). Perceptions of conflict and support in romantic relationships: The role of attachment anxiety. *Journal of Personality and Social Psychology, 88*, 510–531.

Campbell, L., Simpson, J. A., Kashy, D. A., & Fletcher, G. J. (2001). Ideal standards, the self, and flexibility of ideals in close relationships. *Personality and Social Psychology Bulletin, 27*, 447–462.

Campbell, W. K. (1999). Narcissism and romantic attraction. *Journal of Personality and Social Psychology, 77*, 1254–1270.

Campbell, W. K., & Foster, C. A. (2002). Narcissism and commitment in romantic relationships: An investment model analysis. *Personality and Social Psychology Bulletin, 28*, 484–495.

Carpenter, C. J., & Spottswood, E. L. (2013). Exploring romantic relationships on social networking sites using the self-expansion model. *Computers in Human Behavior, 29*, 1531–1537.

Caspi, A., & Herbener, E. S. (1990). Continuity and change: Assortative marriage and the consistency of personality in adulthood. *Journal of Personality and Social Psychology, 58*, 250–258.

Caughlin, J. P., Huston, T. L., & Houts, R. M. (2000). How does personality matter in marriage? An examination of trait anxiety, interpersonal negativity, and marital satisfaction. *Journal of Personality and Social Psychology, 78*, 326–336.

Cervone, D. (2004). The architecture of personality. *Psychological Review, 111*, 183–204.

Chen, S., Boucher, H. C., Andersen, S. M., & Saribay, S. A. (2013). Transference and the relational self. In J. A. Simpson & L. Campbell (Eds.), *The Oxford handbook of close relationships* (pp. 281–305). New York, NY: Oxford University Press.

Cobb, R. A., DeWall, C. N., Lambert, N. M., & Fincham, F. D. (2013). Implicit theories of relationships and close relationship violence: Does believing your relationship can grow relate to lower perpetration of violence? *Personality and Social Psychology Bulletin, 39*, 279–290.

Collins, N. L. (1996). Working models of attachment: Implications for explanation, emotion, and behavior. *Journal of Personality and Social Psychology, 71*, 810–832.

Collins, N. L., & Feeney, B. C. (2000). A safe haven: An attachment theory perspective on support seeking and caregiving in intimate relationships. *Journal of Personality and Social Psychology, 78*, 1053–1073.

Cross, S. E., Bacon, P. L., & Morris, M. L. (2000). The relational-interdependent self-construal and relationships. *Journal of Personality and Social Psychology, 78*, 791–808.

Cross, S. E., & Madson, L. (1997). Models of the self: Self-construals and gender. *Psychological Bulletin, 122*, 5–37.

Cross, S. E., & Morris, M. L. (2003). Getting to know you: The relational self-construal, relational cognition, and well-being. *Personality and Social Psychology Bulletin, 29*, 512–523.

Cross, S. E., Morris, M. L., & Gore, J. S. (2002). Thinking about oneself and others: The relational-interdependent self-construal and social cognition. *Journal of Personality and Social Psychology, 82*, 399–418.

Crowell, J. A., Treboux, D., & Waters, E. (2002). Stability of attachment representations: The transition to marriage. *Developmental Psychology, 38*, 467–479.

Dandeneau, S. D., & Baldwin, M. W. (2004). The inhibition of socially rejecting information among people with high versus low self-esteem: The role of attentional bias and the effects of bias reduction training. *Journal of Social and Clinical Psychology, 23*, 584–603.

Deci, E. L., & Ryan, R. M. (2000). The 'what' and 'why' of goal pursuits: Human needs and the self-determination of behavior. *Psychological Inquiry, 11*, 227–268.

DePaulo, B. M., & Morris, W. L. (2005). Singles in society and science. *Psychological Inquiry, 16*, 57–83.

DeWall, C. N., & Richman, S. B. (2011). Social exclusion and the desire to reconnect. *Social and Personality Psychology Compass, 5*, 919–932.

DiDonato, T. E., & Krueger, J. I. (2010). Interpersonal affirmation and self-authenticity: A test of Rogers's self-growth hypothesis. *Self and Identity, 9*, 322–336.

Donnellan, M. B., Conger, R. D., & Bryant, C. M. (2004). The Big Five and enduring marriages. *Journal of Research in Personality, 38*, 481–504.

Drigotas, S. M., Rusbult, C. E., Wiselquist, J., & Whitton, S. W. (1999). Close partner as sculptor of the ideal self: Behavioral affirmation and the Michelangelo phenomenon. *Journal of Personality and Social Psychology, 77*, 293–323.

Driscoll, R., Davis, K. E., & Lipetz, M. E. (1972). Parental interference and romantic love: The Romeo and Juliet effect. *Journal of Personality and Social Psychology, 24*, 1–10.

Elliot, A. J. (2008). *Handbook of approach and avoidance motivation*. New York, NY: Psychology Press.

Emery, L. F., Walsh, C., & Slotter, E. B. (2015). Knowing who you are and adding to it: Reduced self-concept clarity predicts reduced self-expansion. *Social Psychological and Personality Science, 6*, 259–266.

Erikson, E. H. (1968). *Identity: Youth and crisis*. Oxford, UK: Norton.

Exline, J. J., Baumeister, R. F., Bushman, B. J., Campbell, W. K., & Finkel, E. J. (2004). Too proud to let go: Narcissistic entitlement as a barrier to forgiveness. *Journal of Personality and Social Psychology, 87*, 894–912.

Fagundes, C. P. (2012). Getting over you: Contributions of attachment theory for post-breakup emotional adjustment. *Personal Relationships, 19*, 37–50.

Feeney, B. C. (2004). A secure base: Responsive support of goal strivings and exploration in adult intimate relationships. *Journal of Personality and Social Psychology, 87*, 631–648.

Feeney, B. C. (2006). An attachment theory perspective on the interplay between intrapersonal and interpersonal processes. In K. D. Vohs & E. J. Finkel (Eds.), *Self and relationships: Connecting intrapersonal and interpersonal processes* (pp. 133–159). New York, NY: Guilford Press.

Feeney, B. C., & Collins, N. L. (2015). A new look at social support: A theoretical perspective on thriving through relationships. *Personality and Social Psychology Review, 19*, 113–147.

Feeney, B. C., & Thrush, R. L. (2010). Relationship influences on exploration in adulthood: The characteristics and function of a secure base. *Journal of Personality and Social Psychology, 98*, 57–76.

Feeney, B. C., & Van Vleet, M. (2010). Growing through attachment: The interplay of attachment and exploration in adulthood. *Journal of Social and Personal Relationships, 27*, 226–234.

Feeney, J. A., Noller, P., & Roberts, N. (1998). Emotion, attachment, and satisfaction in close relationships. In P. A. Anderson & L. K. Guerrero (Eds.), *Handbook of communication and emotion: Research, theory, applications, and contexts* (pp. 473–505). San Diego, CA: Academic Press.

Finkel, E. J., Campbell, W. K., Buffardi, L. E., Kumashiro, M., & Rusbult, C. E. (2009). The metamorphosis of Narcissus: Communal activation promotes relationship commitment among narcissists. *Personality and Social Psychology Bulletin, 35*, 1271–1284.

Finkel, E. J., & Eastwick, P. W. (2008). Speed-dating. *Current Directions in Psychological Science, 17*, 193–197.

Finkel, E. J., Eastwick, P. W., & Matthews, J. (2007). Speed-dating as an invaluable tool for studying romantic attraction: A methodological primer. *Personal Relationships, 14*, 149–166.

Fletcher, G. J., Simpson, J. A., & Thomas, G. (2000). Ideals, perceptions, and evaluations in early relationship development. *Journal of Personality and Social Psychology, 79*, 933–940.

Fletcher, G. J., Simpson, J. A., Thomas, G., & Giles, L. (1999). Ideals in intimate relationships. *Journal of Personality and Social Psychology, 76*, 72–89.

Foster, J. D., Shrira, I., & Campbell, W. K. (2006). Theoretical models of narcissism, sexuality, and relationship commitment. *Journal of Social and Personal Relationships, 23*, 367–386.

Fraley, R. C., Vicary, A. M., Brumbaugh, C. C., & Roisman, G. I. (2011). Patterns of stability in adult attachment: An empirical test of two models of continuity and change. *Journal of Personality and Social Psychology, 101*, 974–992.

Franiuk, R., Cohen, D., & Pomerantz, E. M. (2002). Implicit theories of relationships: Implications for relationship satisfaction and longevity. *Personal Relationships, 9*, 345–367.

Frank, E., & Brandstätter, V. (2002). Approach versus avoidance: Different types of commitment in intimate relationships. *Journal of Personality and Social Psychology, 82*, 208–221.

Gable, S. L. (2006). Approach and avoidance social motives and goals. *Journal of Personality, 71*, 175–222.

Gable, S. L., & Impett, E. A. (2012). Approach and avoidance motives and close relationships. *Social and Personality Psychology Compass, 6*, 95–108.

Gardner, W. L., Gabriel, S., & Hochschild, L. (2002). When you and I are 'we' you are not threatening: The role of self-expansion in social comparison. *Journal of Personality and Social Psychology, 82*, 239–251.

Gardner, W. L., Pickett, C. L., & Brewer, M. B. (2000). Social exclusion and selective memory: How the need to belong influences memory for social events. *Personality and Social Psychology Bulletin, 26*, 486–496.

Gattis, K. S., Berns, S., Simpson, L. E., & Christensen, A. (2004). Birds of a feather or strange birds? Ties among personality dimensions, similarity, and marital quality. *Journal of Family Psychology, 18*, 567–574.

Gentzler, A. L., & Kerns, K. A. (2004). Associations between insecure attachment and sexual experiences. *Personal Relationships, 11*, 249–265.

Gilbert, S. P., & Sifers, S. K. (2011). Bouncing back from a breakup: Attachment, time perspective, mental health, and romantic loss. *Journal of College Student Psychotherapy, 25*, 295–310.

Goodfriend, W., & Agnew, C. R. (2008). Sunken costs and desired plans: Examining different types of investments in close relationships. *Personality and Social Psychology Bulletin, 34*, 1639–1652.

Gore, J. S., & Cross, S. E. (2011). Conflicts of interest: Relational self-construal and decision making in interpersonal contexts. *Self and Identity, 10*, 185–202.

Gore, J. S., Cross, S. E., & Morris, M. L. (2006). Let's be friends: Relational self-construal and the development of intimacy. *Personal Relationships, 13*, 83–102.

Graham, J. M. (2008). Self-expansion and flow in couples' momentary experiences: An experience sampling study. *Journal of Personality and Social Psychology, 95*, 679–694.

Gray, J. A. (1987). *The psychology of fear and stress*. Cambridge, UK: Cambridge University Press.

Gurung, R. A. R., Sarason, B. R., & Sarason, I. G. (2001). Predicting relationship quality and emotional reactions to stress from significant-other-concept clarity. *Personality and Social Psychology Bulletin, 27*, 1267–1276.

Hackenbracht, J., & Gasper, K. (2013). I'm all ears: The need to belong motivates listening to emotional disclosure. *Journal of Experimental Social Psychology, 49*, 915–921.

Hazan, C., & Shaver, P. (1987). Romantic love conceptualized as an attachment process. *Journal of Personality and Social Psychology, 52*, 511–524.

Higgins, E. T. (1998). Promotion and prevention: Regulatory focus as a motivational principle. *Advances in Social Psychology, 30*, 1–46.

Impett, E. A., Gere, J., Kogan, A., Gordon, A. M., & Keltner, D. (2014). How sacrifice impacts the giver and the recipient: Insights from approach–avoidance motivational theory. *Journal of Personality, 82*, 390–401.

Impett, E. A., Gordon, A. M., Kogan, A., Oveis, C., Gable, S. L., & Keltner, D. (2010). Moving toward more perfect unions: Daily and long-term consequences of approach and avoidance goals in romantic relationships. *Journal of Personality and Social Psychology, 99*, 948–963.

Impett, E. A., Javam, L., Le, B. M., Asyabi-Eshghi, B., & Kogan, A. (2013a). The joys of genuine giving: Approach and avoidance sacrifice motivation and authenticity. *Personal Relationships, 20*, 740–754.

Impett, E. A., Le, B. M., Asyabi-Eshghi, B., Day, L. C., & Kogan, A. (2013b). To give or not to give? Sacrificing for avoidance goals is not costly for the highly interdependent. *Social Psychological and Personality Science, 4*, 649–657.

Impett, E. A., Peplau, L. A., & Gable, S. L. (2005). Approach and avoidance sexual motives: Implications for personal and interpersonal well-being. *Personal Relationships, 12*, 465–482.

Impett, E. A., Strachman, A., Finkel, E. J., & Gable, S. L. (2008). Maintaining sexual desire in intimate relationships: The importance of approach goals. *Journal of Personality and Social Psychology, 94*, 808–823.

Kamp Dush, C. M., & Amato, P. R. (2005). Consequences of relationship status and quality for subjective well-being. *Journal of Social and Personal Relationships, 22*, 602–627.

Karney, B., & Bradbury, T. N. (1995). The longitudinal course of marital quality and stability: A review of theory, methods, and research. *Psychological Bulletin, 118*, 3–34.

Karney, B., & Bradbury, T. N. (1997). Neuroticism, marital interaction, and the trajectory of marital satisfaction. *Journal of Personality and Social Psychology, 72*, 1075–1092.

Kelly, E. L., & Conley, J. J. (1987). Personality and compatibility: A prospective analysis of marital stability and marital satisfaction. *Journal of Personality and Social Psychology, 52*, 27–40.

Kernis, M. H., & Goldman, B. M. (2003). Stability and variability in self-concept and self-esteem. In M. R. Leary & J. P. Tangney (Eds.), *Handbook of self and identity* (pp. 218–238). New York, NY: Guilford Press.

Kim, Y. (2006). Cognitive concepts of the self and romantic relationships. *Basic and Applied Social Psychology, 28*, 169–175.

Kirkpatrick, L. A., & Davis, K. E. (1994). Attachment style, gender, and relationship stability: A longitudinal analysis. *Journal of Personality and Social Psychology, 66*, 502–512.

Kirkpatrick, L. A., & Hazan, C. (1994). Attachment styles and close relationships: A four-year prospective study. *Personal Relationships, 1*, 123–142.

Klohnen, E. C., & Luo, S. (2003). Interpersonal attraction and personality: What is attractive – self similarity, ideal similarity, complementarity or attachment security? *Journal of Personality and Social Psychology, 85*, 709–722.

Knee, C. R. (1998). Implicit theories of relationships: Assessment and prediction of romantic relationship initiation, coping, and longevity. *Journal of Personality and Social Psychology, 74*, 360–370.

Knee, C. R., Nanayakkara, A., Vietor, N. A., Neighbors, C., & Patrick, H. (2001). Implicit theories of relationships: Who cares if romantic partners are less than ideal? *Personality and Social Psychology Bulletin, 27*, 808–819.

Knee, C. R., Patrick, H., & Lonsbary, C. (2003). Implicit theories of relationships: Orientations toward evaluation and cultivation. *Personality and Social Psychology Review, 7*, 41–55.

Koleva, S. P. (2011). *Birds of a moral feather: The role of morality in romantic attraction and relationship satisfaction* (Doctoral dissertation). University of California Irvine, Irvine, CA.

Kruger, D. J., Fisher, M. L., Edelstein, R. S., Chopik, W. J., Fitzgerald, C. J., & Strout, S. L. (2013). Was that cheating? Perceptions vary by sex, attachment anxiety, and behavior. *Evolutionary Psychology, 11*, 159–171.

Le, B., & Agnew, C. R. (2003). Commitment and its theorized determinants: A meta-analysis of the Investment Model. *Personal Relationships, 10*, 37–57.

Le, B., Dove, N. L., Agnew, C. R., Korn, M. S., & Mutso, A. A. (2010). Predicting nonmarital romantic relationship dissolution: A meta-analytic synthesis. *Personal Relationships, 17*, 377–390.

Leary, M. R., Kelly, K. M., Cottrell, C. A., & Schreindorfer, L. S. (2013). Construct validity of the need to belong scale: Mapping the nomological network. *Journal of Personality Assessment, 95*, 610–624.

Ledbetter, A. M., Stassen-Ferrara, H. M., & Dowd, M. M. (2013). Comparing equity and self-expansion theory approaches to relational maintenance. *Personal Relationships, 20*, 38–51.

Lemay, E. J., & Spongberg, K. (2015). Perceiving and wanting to be valued by others: Implications for cognition, motivation, and behavior in romantic relationships. *Journal of Personality, 83,* 464–478.

Lewandowski, G. W., Jr., Aron, A., Bassis, S., & Kunak, J. (2006). Losing a self-expanding relationship: Implications for the self-concept. *Personal Relationships, 13,* 317–331.

Lewandowski, G. W., Jr., & Bizzoco, N. M. (2007). Addition through subtraction: Growth following the dissolution of a low quality relationship. *Journal of Positive Psychology, 2,* 40–54.

Lewandowski, G. W., Jr., & Nardone, N. (2012). Self-concept clarity's role in self–other agreement and the accuracy of behavioral prediction. *Self and Identity, 11,* 71–89.

Lewandowski, G. W., Jr., Nardone, N., & Raines, A. J. (2010). The role of self-concept clarity in relationship quality. *Self and Identity, 9,* 416–433.

Linardatos, L., & Lydon, J. E. (2011). Relationship-specific identification and spontaneous relationship maintenance processes. *Journal of Personality and Social Psychology, 101,* 737–753.

Linville, P. W. (1985). Self-complexity and affective extremity: Don't put all of your eggs in one cognitive basket. *Social Cognition, 3,* 94–120.

Linville, P. W. (1987). Self-complexity as a cognitive buffer against stress-related illness and depression. *Journal of Personality and Social Psychology, 52,* 663–675.

Loving, T. J., & Slatcher, R. (2013). Romantic relationships and health. In J. A. Simpson & L. Campbell (Eds.), *The Oxford handbook of close relationships* (pp. 617–637). New York, NY: Oxford University Press.

Lucas, R. E., & Dyrenforth, P. S. (2006). Does the existence of social relationships matter for subjective well-being? In K. D. Vohs & E. J. Finkel (Eds.), *Self and relationships: Connecting intrapersonal and interpersonal processes* (pp. 254–273). New York, NY: Guilford Press.

Luo, S., & Zhang, G. (2009). What leads to romantic attraction: Similarity, reciprocity, security, or beauty? Evidence from a speed-dating study. *Journal of Personality, 77,* 933–964.

MacDonald, T. K., & Ross, M. (1999). Assessing the accuracy of predictions about dating relationships: How and why do lovers' predictions differ from those made by observers? *Personality and Social Psychology Bulletin, 25,* 1417–1429.

Madey, S. F., & Jilek, L. (2012). Attachment style and dissolution of romantic relationships: Breaking up is hard to do, or is it? *Individual Differences Research, 10,* 202–210.

Maner, J. K., DeWall, C. N., Baumeister, R. F., & Schaller, M. (2007). Does social exclusion motivate interpersonal reconnection? Resolving the 'porcupine problem.' *Journal of Personality and Social Psychology, 92,* 42–55.

Markus, H. R., & Kitayama, S. (1991). Culture and the self: Implications for cognitions, emotion, and motivation. *Psychological Review, 98,* 224–253.

Markus, H., & Wurf, E. (1987). The dynamic self-concept: A social psychological perspective. *Annual Review of Psychology, 38,* 299–337.

Marshall, T. C., Bejanyan, K., & Ferenczi, N. (2013). Attachment styles and personal growth following romantic breakups: The mediating roles of distress, rumination, and tendency to rebound. *PLoS ONE, 8(9),* e75161.

Maslow, A. H. (1968). *Toward a psychology of being.* New York, NY: Van Nostrand.

Mason, A. E., Law, R. W., Bryan, A. E. B., Portley, R. M., & Sbarra, D. A. (2012). Facing a breakup: Electromyographic responses moderate self-concept recovery following a romantic separation. *Personal Relationships, 19,* 551–568.

Mattingly, B. A., & Clark, E. M. (2012). Weakening relationships we try to preserve: Motivated sacrifice, attachment, and relationship quality. *Journal of Applied Social Psychology, 42,* 373–386.

Mattingly, B. A., & Lewandowski, G. W., Jr. (2014). Broadening horizons: Self-expansion in relational and non-relational contexts. *Social and Personality Psychology Compass, 8,* 30–40.

Mattingly, B. A., Lewandowski, G. W., Jr., & McIntyre, K. P. (2014). 'You make me a better/worse person': A two-dimensional model of relationship self-change. *Personal Relationships, 21,* 176–190.

Mattingly, B. A., McIntyre, K. P., & Lewandowski, G. W., Jr. (2012). Approach motivation and the expansion of self in close relationships. *Personal Relationships, 19,* 113–127.

Mattingly, B. A., Oswald, D. L., & Clark, E. M. (2011). An examination of relational–interdependent self-construal, communal strength, and pro-relationship behaviors in friendships. *Personality and Individual Differences, 50*, 1243–1248.

McIntyre, K. P., Mattingly, B. A., & Lewandowski, G. W., Jr. (2015). When 'we' changes 'me': The two-dimensional model of relational self-change and relationship outcomes. *Journal of Social and Personal Relationships, 32*, 857–878.

Mellor, D., Stokes, M., Firth, L., Hayashi, Y., & Cummins, R. (2008). Need for belonging, relationship satisfaction, loneliness, and life satisfaction. *Personality and Individual Differences, 45*, 213–218.

Mikulincer, M. (1998a). Attachment working models and the sense of trust: An exploration of interaction goals and affect regulation. *Journal of Personality and Social Psychology, 74*, 1209–1224.

Mikulincer, M. (1998b). Adult attachment style and affect regulation: Strategic variations in self-appraisals. *Journal of Personality and Social Psychology, 75*, 420–435.

Mikulincer, M., Dolev, T., & Shaver, P. R. (2004). Attachment-related strategies during thought suppression: Ironic rebounds and vulnerable self-representations. *Journal of Personality and Social Psychology, 87*, 940–956.

Mikulincer, M., & Shaver, P. R. (2007). *Attachment in adulthood: Structure, dynamics, and change*. New York, NY: Guilford Press.

Mikulincer, M., Shaver, P. R., & Avihou-Kanza, N. (2011). Individual differences in adult attachment are systematically related to dream narratives. *Attachment and Human Development, 13*, 105–123.

Mikulincer, M., Shaver, P. R., & Pereg, D. (2003). Attachment theory and affect regulation: The dynamics, development, and cognitive consequences of attachment-related strategies. *Motivation and Emotion, 27*, 77–102.

Mikulincer, M., Shaver, P. R., Sapir-Lavid, Y., & Avihou-Kanza, N. (2009). What's inside the minds of securely and insecurely attached people? The secure-base script and its associations with attachment-style dimensions. *Journal of Personality and Social Psychology, 97*, 615–633.

Mohr, J. J., Selterman, D., & Fassinger, R. E. (2013). Romantic attachment and relationship functioning in same-sex couples. *Journal of Counseling Psychology, 60*, 72–82.

Montoya, R. M., & Horton, R. S. (2013). A meta-analytic investigation of the processes underlying the similarity-attraction effect. *Journal of Social and Personal Relationships, 30*, 64–94.

Montoya, R. M., Horton, R. S., & Kirchner, J. (2008). Is actual similarity necessary for attraction? A meta-analysis of actual and perceived similarity. *Journal of Social and Personal Relationships, 25*, 889–922.

Moors, A. C., Conley, T. D., Edelstein, R. S., & Chopik, W. J. (2015). Attached to monogamy? Avoidance predicts willingness to engage (but not actual engagement) in consensual non-monogamy. *Journal of Social and Personal Relationships, 32*, 222–240.

Morrison, M., Epstude, K., & Roese, N. J. (2012). Life regrets and the need to belong. *Social Psychological and Personality Science, 3*, 675–681.

Morry, M. M., & Kito, M. (2009). Relational–interdependent self-construal as a predictor of relationship quality: The mediating role of one's own behaviors and perceptions of the fulfillment of friendship functions. *Journal of Social Psychology, 149*, 205–222.

Muise, A., Impett, E. A., & Desmarais, S. (2013). Getting it on versus getting it over with: Sexual motivation, desire, and satisfaction in intimate bonds. *Personality and Social Psychology Bulletin, 39*, 1320–1332.

Murray, S. L., Holmes, J. G., & Collins, N. L. (2006). Optimizing assurance: The risk regulation system in relationships. *Psychological Bulletin, 132*, 641–666.

Murray, S. L., Holmes, J. G., & Griffin, D. W. (1996). The benefits of positive illusions: Idealization and the construction of satisfaction in close relationships. *Journal of Personality and Social Psychology, 70*, 79–98.

Nichols, A. L., & Webster, G. D. (2013). The single-item need to belong scale. *Personality and Individual Differences, 55*, 189–192.

Odgers, A. (2014). *From broken attachments to earned security: The role of empathy in therapeutic change*. London, England: Karnac Books.

Park, L. E., Sanchez, D. T., & Brynildsen, K. (2011). Maladaptive responses to relationship dissolution: The role of relationship contingent self-worth. *Journal of Applied Social Psychology*, *41*, 1749–1773.

Perilloux, C., & Buss, D. M. (2008). Breaking up romantic relationships: Costs experienced and coping strategies deployed. *Evolutionary Psychology*, *6*, 164–181.

Pickett, C. L., Gardner, W. L., & Knowles, M. (2004). Getting a cue: The need to belong and enhanced sensitivity to social cues. *Personality and Social Psychology Bulletin*, *30*, 1095–1107.

Pietromonaco, P. R., Greenwood, D., & Barrett, L. F. (2004). Conflict in adult close relationships: An attachment perspective. In W. S. Rholes & J. A. Simpson (Eds.), *Adult attachment: Theory, research, and clinical implications* (pp. 267–299). New York, NY: Guilford.

Poulsen, F. O., Holman, T. B., Busby, D. M., & Carroll, J. S. (2013). Physical attraction, attachment styles, and dating development. *Journal of Social and Personal Relationships*, *30*, 301–319.

Richman, S. B., Pond, R. S., Jr., DeWall, C. N., Kumashiro, M., Slotter, E. B., & Luchies, L. B. (2016). An unclear self leads to poor mental health: Self-concept confusion mediates the association of loneliness with depression. *Journal of Social and Clinical Psychology*, *35*, 525–550.

Roisman, G. I., Padrón, E., Sroufe, L. A., & Egeland, B. (2002). Earned-secure attachment status in retrospect and prospect. *Child Development*, *73*, 1204–1219.

Rusbult, C. E. (1980). Commitment and satisfaction in romantic associations: A test of the Investment Model. *Journal of Experimental Social Psychology*, *16*, 172–186.

Rusbult, C. E. (1983). A longitudinal test of the Investment Model: The development (and deterioration) of satisfaction and commitment in heterosexual involvements. *Journal of Personality and Social Psychology*, *45*, 101–117.

Sbarra, D. A., & Borelli, J. L. (2013). Heart rate variability moderates the association between attachment avoidance and self-concept reorganization following marital separation. *International Journal of Psychophysiology*, *88*, 253–260.

Sbarra, D. A., & Emery, R. E. (2005). The emotional sequelae of nonmarital relationship dissolution: Analysis of change and intraindividual variability over time. *Personal Relationships*, *12*, 213–232.

Sedikides, C., & Brewer, M. B. (2001). *Individual self, relational self, collective self*. New York, NY: Routledge.

Selterman, D. F., Apetroaia, A. I., Riela, S., & Aron, A. (2014). Dreaming of you: Behavior and emotion in dreams of significant others predict subsequent relational behavior. *Social Psychological and Personality Science*, *5*, 111–118.

Selterman, D., Apetroaia, A., & Waters, E. (2012). Script-like attachment representations in dreams containing current romantic partners. *Attachment & Human Development*, *14*, 501–515.

Selterman, D., & Drigotas, S. (2009). Attachment styles and emotional content, stress, and conflict in dreams of romantic partners. *Dreaming*, *19*, 135–151.

Selterman, D., & Koleva, S. (2015). Moral judgment of close relationship behaviors. *Journal of Social and Personal Relationships*, *32*, 922–945.

Selterman, D. F., & Maier, M. A. (2013). Secure attachment and material reward both attenuate romantic jealousy. *Motivation and Emotion*, *37*, 765–775.

Sharpsteen, D. J., & Kirkpatrick, L. A. (1997). Romantic jealousy and adult romantic attachment. *Journal of Personality and Social Psychology*, *72*, 627–640.

Simpson, J. A. (1990). Influence of attachment styles on romantic relationships. *Journal of Personality and Social Psychology*, *59*, 971–980.

Simpson, J. A., Fletcher, G. J. O., & Campbell, L. (2001). The structure and function of ideal standards in close relationships. In G. J. O. Fletcher & M. S. Clark (Eds.), *Blackwell handbook of social psychology: Interpersonal processes* (pp. 86–106). Oxford, UK: Blackwell.

Simpson, J. A., Ickes, W., & Grich, J. (1999). When accuracy hurts: Reactions of anxious–ambivalent dating partners to a relationship-threatening situation. *Journal of Personality and Social Psychology*, *76*, 754–769.

Simpson, J. A., Kim, J. S., Fillo, J., Ickes, W., Rholes, W. S., Oriña, M. M., & Winterheld, H. A. (2011). Attachment and the management of empathic accuracy in relationship-threatening situations. *Personality and Social Psychology Bulletin*, *37*, 242–254.

Simpson, J. A., Rholes, W. S., & Nelligan, J. S. (1992). Support seeking and support giving within couples in an anxiety-provoking situation: The role of attachment styles. *Journal of Personality and Social Psychology*, 62, 434–446.

Simpson, J. A., Rholes, W. S., & Phillips, D. (1996). Conflict in close relationships: An attachment perspective. *Journal of Personality and Social Psychology*, 71, 899–914.

Simpson, J. A., Wilson, C. L., & Winterheld, H. A. (2004). Sociosexuality and romantic relationships. In J. H. Harvey, A. Wenzel, & S. Sprecher (Eds.), *The handbook of sexuality in close relationships* (pp. 87–112). Mahwah, NJ: Lawrence Erlbaum.

Sinclair, H. C., Hood, K. B., & Wright, B. L. (2014). Revisiting the Romeo and Juliet effect (Driscoll, Davis, & Lipetz, 1972). *Social Psychology*, 45, 170–178.

Sinclair, L., & Fehr, B. (2005). Voice versus loyalty: Self-construals and responses to dissatisfaction in romantic relationships. *Journal of Experimental Social Psychology*, 41, 298–304.

Slotter, E. B., & Gardner, W. L. (2009). Where do you end and I begin? Evidence for anticipatory, motivated self–other integration between relationship partners. *Journal of Personality and Social Psychology*, 96, 1137–1151.

Slotter, E. B., & Gardner, W. L. (2012a). The dangers of dating the 'bad boy' (or girl): When does romantic desire encourage us to take on the negative qualities of potential partners? *Journal of Experimental Social Psychology*, 48, 1173–1178.

Slotter, E. B., & Gardner, W. L. (2012b). How needing you changes me: The influence of attachment anxiety on self-concept malleability in romantic relationships. *Self and Identity*, 11, 386–408.

Slotter, E. B., Gardner, W. L., & Finkel, E. J. (2010). Who am I without you? The influence of romantic breakup on the self-concept. *Personality and Social Psychology Bulletin*, 36, 147–160.

Slotter, E. B., & Ward, D. E. (2015). Finding the silver lining: The relative roles of redemptive narratives and cognitive reappraisal in individuals' emotional distress after the end of a romantic relationship. *Journal of Social and Personal Relationships*, 32, 737–756.

Spielmann, S. S., MacDonald, G., & Wilson, A. E. (2009). On the rebound: Focusing on someone new helps anxiously attached individuals let go of ex-partners. *Personality and Social Psychology Bulletin*, 35, 1382–1394.

Sprecher, S. (1994). Two sides to the breakup of dating relationships. *Personal Relationships*, 1, 199–222.

Sprecher, S. (2014). Effects of actual (manipulated) and perceived similarity on liking in get-acquainted interactions: The role of communication. *Communication Monographs*, 81, 4–27.

Sprecher, S., Felmlee, D., Metts, S., Fehr, B., & Vanni, D. (1998). Factors associated with distress following the breakup of a close relationship. *Journal of Social and Personal Relationships*, 15, 791–809.

Sprecher, S., Treger, S., Wondra, J. D., Hilaire, N., & Wallpe, K. (2013). Taking turns: Reciprocal self-disclosure promotes liking in initial interactions. *Journal of Experimental Social Psychology*, 49, 860–866.

Stanley, S. M., Whitton, S. W., Sadberry, S. L., Clements, M. L., & Markman, H. J. (2006). Sacrifice as a predictor of marital outcomes. *Family Process*, 45, 289–303.

Stinson, D. A., Cameron, J. J., Hoplock, L. B., & Hole, C. (2015a). Warming up and cooling down: Self-esteem and behavioral responses to social threat during relationship initiation. *Self and Identity*, 14, 189–213.

Stinson, D. A., Cameron, J. J., & Robinson, K. J. (2015b). The good, the bad, and the risky: Self-esteem, rewards and costs, and interpersonal risk regulation during relationship initiation. *Journal of Social and Personal Relationships*, 32, 1109–1136.

Strachman, A., & Gable, S. L. (2006). What you want (and do not want) affects what you see (and do not see): Avoidance social goals and social events. *Personality and Social Psychology Bulletin*, 32, 1446–1458.

Swann, W. B., Jr. (1990). To be adored or to be known? The interplay of self-enhancement and self-verification. In E. T. Higgins & R. M. Sorrentino (Eds.), *Handbook of motivation and cognition* (Vol. 2; pp. 408–448). New York, NY: Guilford Press.

Tanchotsrinon, P., Maneesri, K., & Campbell, W. K. (2007). Narcissism and romantic attraction: Evidence from a collectivistic culture.

Journal of Research in Personality, *41*, 723–730.

Thai, S., & Lockwood, P. (2015). Comparing you = comparing me: Social comparisons of the expanded self. *Personality and Social Psychology Bulletin*, *41*, 989–1004.

Tidwell, N. D., Eastwick, P. W., & Finkel, E. J. (2013). Perceived, not actual, similarity predicts initial attraction in a live romantic context: Evidence from the speed-dating paradigm. *Personal Relationships*, *20*, 199–215.

Treboux, D., Crowell, J. A., & Waters, E. (2004). When 'new' meets 'old': Configurations of adult attachment representations and their implications for marital functioning. *Developmental Psychology*, *40*, 295–314.

Tschann, J. M., Johnston, J. R., Kline, M., & Wallerstein, J. S. (1989). Family process and children's functioning during divorce. *Journal of Marriage and the Family*, *51*, 431–444.

Van Lange, P. A. M., Rusbult, C. E., Drigotas, S. M., Arriaga, X. M., Witcher, B. S., & Cox, C. L. (1997). Willingness to sacrifice in close relationships. *Journal of Personality and Social Psychology*, *72*, 1373–1395.

VanderDrift, L. E., Agnew, C. R., & Wilson, J. E. (2009). Nonmarital romantic relationship commitment and leave behavior: The mediating role of dissolution consideration. *Personality and Social Psychology Bulletin*, *35*, 1220–1232.

Waters, E., & Cummings, E. M. (2000). A secure base from which to explore close relationships. *Child Development*, *71*, 164–172.

Waters, E., Hamilton, C. E., & Weinfield, N. S. (2000a). The stability of attachment security from infancy to adolescence and early adulthood: General introduction. *Child Development*, *71*, 678–683.

Waters, E., Merrick, S., Treboux, D., Crowell, J., & Albersheim, L. (2000b). Attachment security in infancy and early adulthood: A twenty-year longitudinal study. *Child Development*, *71*, 684–689.

Waters, H. S., Rodrigues, L. M., & Ridgeway, D. (1998). Cognitive underpinnings of narrative attachment assessment. *Journal of Experimental Child Psychology*, *71*, 211–234.

Waters, H. S., & Waters, E. (2006). The attachment working models concept: Among other things, we build script-like representations of secure base experiences. *Attachment and Human Development*, *8*, 185–197.

Wieselquist, J., Rusbult, C. E., Foster, C. A., & Agnew, C. R. (1999). Commitment, pro-relationship behavior, and trust in close relationships. *Journal of Personality and Social Psychology*, *77*, 942–966.

Williams, K. D. (2007). Ostracism. *Annual Review of Psychology*, *58*, 425–452.

Williams, K. D., Cheung, C. K., & Choi, W. (2000). Cyberostracism: Effects of being ignored over the Internet. *Journal of Personality and Social Psychology*, *79*, 748–762.

Yovetich, N. A., & Rusbult, C. E. (1994). Accommodative behavior in close relationships: Exploring transformation of motivation. *Journal of Experimental Social Psychology*, *30*, 138–164.

Zeigler-Hill, V., Besser, A., Myers, E. M., Southard, A. C., & Malkin, M. L. (2013). The status-signaling property of self-esteem: The role of self-reported self-esteem and perceived self-esteem in personality judgments. *Journal of Personality*, *81*, 209–220.

Zeigler-Hill, V., & Myers, E. M. (2011). An implicit theory of self-esteem: The consequences of perceived self-esteem for romantic desirability. *Evolutionary Psychology*, *9*, 147–180.

The Gender Similarities Hypothesis

Jennifer L. Petersen

The study of gender differences in psychology has a long history, with researchers debating whether men and women are very similar to each other or quite different. Some researchers contend that gender differences are significant and meaningful (e.g., Benbow and Stanley, 1980; Ceci and Williams, 2011), whereas others contend that gender similarities prevail and small differences are insignificant (e.g., Hyde, 2005). The gender similarities hypothesis, proposed by Hyde (2005), suggests 'that males and females are similar on most, but not all, psychological variables' (p. 581). Hyde supported this hypothesis by reviewing the results of 46 meta-analyses on gender differences in psychology. These meta-analyses spanned a variety of domains, including gender differences in cognitive abilities, communication, social and personality variables, psychological well-being, motor performance, and a few miscellaneous topics. The results indicated that 78% of the effect sizes were small (i.e., $d = 0.35$ or smaller). Therefore, with few exceptions, gender similarities prevail in the psychology of gender.

Zell et al. (2015) later tested the gender similarities hypothesis, as proposed by Hyde (2005), by using a technique called meta-synthesis on 106 meta-analyses, yielding 386 effect sizes. Meta-synthesis is a statistical tool that combines data across meta-analyses, providing for the analysis of gender differences across psychological domains. Results of the meta-synthesis indicated that 85% of the effect sizes examined were in the small (46%) or very small (39%) range, thus supporting the gender similarities hypothesis.

THEORIES OF GENDER SIMILARITIES AND DIFFERENCES

Numerous psychological theories lay the foundation for gender similarities in psychological constructs and attempt to explain why gender differences exist. A complete review of all theories that address the psychology of gender is beyond the scope of this chapter. Instead, we will focus on three specific theories that are often applied to the theoretical foundation of psychological gender differences. Below, we provide a brief description of evolutionary theory, social structural theory, and cognitive social learning theory and how these theories explain gender differences in psychology. Although these theories typically explain gender differences and not gender similarities, Hyde (2014) has provided an explanation of how these theories can be adapted to explain gender similarities as well.

Evolutionary Theory

Evolutionary theory examines how all living organisms, including humans, evolved adaptations through natural or sexual selection. Evolutionary psychology explains that gender differences are expected only in those specific domains in which males and females have recurrently confronted different adaptive problems that threatened survival or reproduction. One such domain in which men and women differ is the investment in their offspring (Buss, 2014; Trivers, 1972). Women must invest a great deal in their offspring. At the very least women must provide an egg, a long gestational period, and provide for the nourishment of their offspring even after birth. In comparison, men have much less obligatory investment. Evolutionary psychology proposes that individuals with a greater parental investment are more likely to want to ensure the survival of those offspring than individuals who have less parental investment. Therefore, greater female parental investment might explain why women are more likely to be involved in childcare than men are and why women might avoid challenging careers that might keep them away from their children, such as careers in math, science, and technology.

The same principles of adaptation and natural selection are used to explain why men and women are similar. For example, both men and women have a shared evolutionary human history and, therefore, have likely evolved similar adaptations (Buss, 2014; Hyde, 2014).

Social Structural Theory

Social structural theory suggests that gender differences are a result of men's and women's differing roles in society (Eagly and Wood, 1999; Wood and Eagly, 2012). Social structural theory suggests that biological sex differences produce different roles for men and women in society. For example, because women have the ability to gestate and nurse children, they have adopted the social role of caring for children, which results in stereotypes of women being more nurturing and kind than men. Men, who have greater size and strength than women, have adopted the social role of breadwinner and protector. These male roles are more powerful, and often more coveted, than the female roles, and thus men have typically assumed more power in societies, in which they adopt the role of protector and provider. According to this theory, men are more represented in positions of power such as business executives and CEOs because society is more accepting of men in roles of power, whereas society is more accepting of women in the role of homemaker and teacher because these roles involve interactions with children.

Social structural theory differs from evolutionary theory in that this theory does not assume that gender differences are universal. Evolutionary psychology relies on the assumption that all humans have a shared evolutionary origin, and thus gender differences resulting from adaptive behaviors are universal (Buss and Schmitt, 1993). Social structural theory acknowledges that men and women play different roles in different societies, and thus gender differences in one society may be very different in another.

Research using cross-national datasets supports this conclusion. Using the United Nations Gender Empowerment Index, Eagly and Wood (1999) found that the magnitude of gender differences in mate preferences is strongly correlated with the magnitude of the power differential between men and women in each nation. Nations with large gender differences in power also had a large gender difference in mate selection.

Although social structural theory has largely focused on gender differences, the theory could also be adapted to focus on gender similarities across society. As societies become increasingly egalitarian, with women taking on more substantial roles in the workplace and men increasing their childcare responsibilities, society may adapt by being more accepting of men and women in counter-stereotypical roles (Hyde, 2014). As a result, gender differences that are created by social roles may be reduced. For example, as society becomes more accepting of men taking on increased childcare responsibilities, men may adopt more of a nurturing role. Similarly, if society becomes more accepting of women in leadership roles, then the gender gap in leadership skills, such as assertiveness and power, should be reduced.

Cognitive Social Learning Theory

Cognitive social learning theory suggests that humans are likely to imitate behaviors that they have seen (Bussey and Bandura, 1999). For example, both humans and nonhumans often imitate behaviors for which others have been rewarded, and avoid behaviors for which others have been punished. Since society often rewards gender-consistent behavior and punishes gender-inconsistent behavior, girls and women are more likely to imitate the behaviors of other girls and women, whereas boys and men are more likely to imitate the behaviors of other boys and men. For example, even very young girls may notice that other girls are rewarded for nurturing behaviors and physical beauty, whereas boys may notice that other boys are rewarded for academic success and physical strength. Therefore, boys and girls may learn at a young age to conform to gender-consistent stereotypes, which may perpetuate gender differences in society.

Cognitive social learning theory also acknowledges the cognitive and decision-making component of imitation. For example, in order for a child to imitate a behavior, he or she must be paying attention to the behavior and believe that he or she is capable of reproducing it. Self-efficacy, or the belief that one is capable of accomplishing a task, plays a large role in gender differences in math. Although boys and girls perform equally well on math assessment tests, girls have lower self-efficacy for math than boys do (Else-Quest et al., 2010). This lower self-efficacy likely plays a role in the reluctance of girls to take challenging math courses, thus widening the gender gap in math-related careers.

Gender similarities may also be explained through cognitive social learning theory (Hyde, 2014). As society becomes more egalitarian, behaviors that were once considered gender-inconsistent may be rewarded. For example, as society increasingly sees the advantages of encouraging girls in science and math careers, more opportunities are becoming available for girls in the fields of math and science (e.g., math camps directed toward girls). These changes in rewarded behaviors may reduce the gender gap in science and math careers such as engineering.

IMPORTANCE OF META-ANALYSIS

Numerous empirical studies have been conducted to provide evidence for or against the theories of gender differences and similarities described briefly above. Summarizing each of these individual studies in a narrative review would be a monumental task and the limitations of these studies, such as small sample sizes, would be compounded. Instead, the gender similarities hypothesis relies largely on meta-analyses. Meta-analyses are particularly useful for describing the magnitude of gender differences in various areas of psychology because they combine empirical results from existing studies, creating a database of information from various populations and with a sample size exceedingly larger than any individual study.

Relying on opinions or a single study about the significance of gender differences is problematic because it may lead to alpha or beta bias. Alpha bias refers to the exaggeration of gender differences, whereas beta bias refers to the minimization of gender differences (Hare-Mustin and Marecek, 1988). Alpha bias can lead to sex discrimination if researchers or policy makers use it as justification for differential treatment for men and women. Beta bias may be problematic because it can be dismissive of important gender differences that deserve attention, such as gender differences in employee payment. A systematic review of empirical research through the quantitative process of meta-analysis can help to resolve differences in opinion and reduce bias by determining how large gender differences really are in any population.

Meta-Analysis Methodology

In contrast to traditional, narrative reviews, meta-analyses use quantitative methods to combine data from multiple empirical studies to determine the size of an effect between two groups. Many meta-analyses focus on gender because it is a category in which two groups are easily identified and empirical studies often report gender effects. Meta-analyses typically proceed in several steps, beginning with a computerized search that locates empirical studies to be included in the study. Once researchers have established a representative sample of the studies on the topic of interest, studies are then coded for information that will be included in statistical analyses. This information typically includes mean values for men and for women, standard deviations for each gender, and any additional information to be included as moderators (e.g., race/ethnicity, quality of the study, study design characteristics). This information is used to compute standardized statistics for each study. Once researchers have computed the effect size for each study, they then determine whether there is heterogeneity among the studies and compute an overall effect size to summarize the size of the effect across all studies.

Effect sizes can be calculated from a variety of different information, such as means and standard deviations, correlations, and binary data (Borenstein et al., 2009). Meta-analyses on gender difference typically focus on effect sizes of mean differences. This effect size, d, is calculated by subtracting the mean of one group from the mean of another and dividing by the pooled within-gender standard deviation:

$$d = (X_{male} - X_{female}) / s_p$$

In the above equation, the mean value for females (X_{female}) is subtracted from the mean value for males (X_{male}), but the order of groups is statistically irrelevant as long as the researcher is consistent across studies and he or she considers the order in interpretation. For example, if the mean value for females is subtracted from the mean value for males, then a negative effect size would indicate that females had higher means than males and vice versa. In this chapter, all negative effect sizes indicate a female advantage and all positive effect sizes indicate a male advantage. Note that the pooled within-gender standard deviation (s_p) in the denominator includes not only variability of each sample, but also includes sample size, thus standardizing the metric of d. This statistic also recognizes that men and women are not homogeneous by including a measure of within-gender variability.

When means and standard deviations are not available, d may also be calculated with t-values or F-values.

Once the effect size is calculated for all studies in the meta-analysis, homogeneity analyses may be conducted to determine the variation among studies. If heterogeneity exists, then moderator analyses may be conducted to determine which factors predict variation in the effect sizes. Moderator analyses may be conducted with either categorical factors, such as country of origin or ethnicity, or they may be conducted with continuous predictors, such as age of participants or the United Nations gender empowerment index for each nation (Petersen and Hyde, 2010).

Advantages of Meta-Analysis

Meta-analyses have many advantages over traditional, narrative reviews. Meta-analyses are very useful for the study of gender differences because they can determine the exact size of a gender effect. Narrative reviews may fall short because they do not always take into account sample size, study characteristics, and variability. In essence, narrative reviews may make conclusions about gender differences based on statistically significant results, without taking into account the size of the effect.

Both meta-analyses and narrative studies may use large studies from diverse populations, but meta-analyses also consider the sample size and power of each study. Meta-analyses can also use population characteristics such as age, ethnicity, or country of origin to determine whether effect sizes differ across populations. In addition, the sample size of the overall effect size is essentially the combined sample size for all studies included in the model. Therefore, the meta-analysis sample is exceedingly larger and more generalizable to diverse populations than any individual study, which results in increased levels of both external validity and construct validity.

Because d is standardized, studies with different designs and measures may all be included in the same analysis. For example, there are many scales that measure depression, and different scales might be used depending on the developmental level of the participants. Meta-analyses standardize these scales so that the effect size for gender differences in depression can be evaluated regardless of the scales used. Researchers who are interested in determining whether the scales affect the effect size can code for the different measures or the quality of the study design and use moderator analyses to determine whether the scale or type of study influence the effect size.

Narrative reviews often focus on the statistical significance of each study, sometimes even using a count of studies that indicated significant results in comparison to those studies without significant results. Meta-analyses, in contrast, focus on the size of the effect and compute statistical significance for the overall summary effect. Statistical significance is largely affected by sample size, such that studies with fewer participants are less likely to detect a significant difference, even when a medium or large effect is present. Meta-analyses may significantly increase power (Borenstein et al., 2009), thus providing a much more effective means for testing the null hypothesis. In addition, meta-analyses move beyond the dichotomy of significant and non-significant effects to provide a better description of the size of the effect.

Methodological Concerns

Despite the advantages of meta-analyses, there are several methodological concerns researchers must consider in their analyses. Fortunately, a conscientious researcher can easily mitigate these concerns by using systematic reviews and statistical procedures described below. In the case of both narrative reviews and meta-analysis, the authors must choose a sample of studies to include in the analysis. Reviews are only as good as their sample of studies, and studies that are selectively included or excluded in the analyses may produce biased results. When conducting searches for relevant studies, researchers must be careful to use terms that are broad enough to include all relevant results. For example, when conducting a meta-analysis on gender differences in depression, researchers will find more relevant results when conducting a search with the search term 'depression' than with the terms 'gender and depression'. The latter search will only result in studies that use the term 'gender' in the title, keywords, or abstract. Many studies about depression will include separate averages for males and females even when the study is not focused on gender differences. Including the term 'gender' in the search may bias the results to studies that find a significant gender difference and not gender similarities. Therefore, it is advisable to use search terms for the topic and not use terms such as 'gender' or 'sex'.

Even when the sample of studies is chosen with care using broad search terms, publication bias raises concerns about the sample of studies. Published studies are more likely to present significant results than unpublished studies, resulting in a bias toward gender differences over gender similarities (i.e., larger values of d). Researchers may combat this problem by including unpublished dissertations and large national datasets in addition to published studies.

Funnel plots may be used to determine whether a meta-analysis has a publication bias. In a funnel plot, the effect size is plotted along the x-axis of the graph and the sample size along the y-axis. Smaller studies should spread out further along the bottom of the graph because of their increased sampling error, whereas larger studies tend to cluster around the mean effect size at the top, resulting in a plot that looks like a funnel. Publication bias is evident when the distribution of studies is symmetrical at the top, some studies missing in the middle, and more studies missing at the bottom (Borenstein et al., 2009).

Since a review can only be as good as the studies that it includes, it is important to consider the quality of the studies included in a meta-analysis. Although the study design does not matter statistically because d is standardized, the theoretical meaning of different study designs may be meaningful. For example, measurement scales that are not generalizable or poorly designed studies will affect the quality of the overall meta-analysis. Moderator analyses may be used to code for the quality or type of study to determine whether study design affects the overall effect size. This procedure also helps to isolate the effect size for only high-quality studies.

The effect size, d, is standardized. However, like a z-score, there is no upward or lower limit to d. Interpretation of an effect as large or small is a concern because it may be somewhat subjective. Cohen has established guidelines for interpreting d. According to these criteria $d = 0.80$ indicates a large effect, $d = 0.50$ is a medium effect, and $d = 0.30$ is a small effect (Cohen, 1988). Hyde (2005) uses similar criteria by stating that effect sizes <0.35 are small or very small and that studies that meet this criteria support the gender similarities hypothesis. Effect sizes may also be interpreted in comparison to other effect sizes in a similar field. For example, researchers might compare the effect size for gender differences in math ability to the effect size for gender differences in verbal ability.

Criticisms of Meta-Analysis and the Gender Similarities Hypothesis

Zuriff (2015) contends that the gender similarities hypothesis is not testable because it does not provide criteria for importance and relevance of the studies included. For example, Zuriff (2015) criticizes Zell et al. (2015) for combining meta-analyses across disparate topics such as the masculinity scale and judgment of time duration. In Hyde's (2005) description of the gender similarities hypothesis, she is careful to discuss meta-analyses within relevant topics. For example, Hyde (2005) includes meta-analyses from topics such as communication, cognition, and social and personality variables.

Ball et al. (2013) note that meta-analyses used to test the gender similarities hypothesis often rely on tests of mean differences such as t-tests. These statistical tests, although prevalent in psychology, test for whether a mean difference is present, but do not test for gender similarities. The authors propose a test of equivalence instead of a t-test in order to test for gender equivalence. They employed the equivalence test on the Scholastic Aptitude Test–Math (SAT–M) and results indicated equivalent math scores for boys and girls for every year tested from 1996 to 2009. These results are consistent with other meta-analyses of gender differences in math (Lindberg et al., 2010) and consistent with the gender similarities hypothesis.

CURRENT META-ANALYSES SUPPORTING THE GENDER SIMILARITIES HYPOTHESIS

With only a few exceptions described later in this chapter, the majority of meta-analyses examining gender differences support the gender similarities hypothesis. According to Hyde (2005), effect sizes lower than $d = 0.35$ are small and support the idea that men and women are more alike than different. Effect sizes meeting these criteria have been found in the areas of cognitive performance, occupations and interests, social behavior, and psychological well-being.

Gender Similarities in Cognitive Performance

Stereotypes about gender differences in cognitive performance can lead to discrimination in the school or workplace and affect an individual's confidence in their academic abilities. However, if gender differences do exist in cognitive performance, then it is important to identify these areas so that individuals may receive additional support or identify the context in which they can excel. Meta-analysis is an excellent use of existing empirical data to determine whether the existing data suggest gender differences or similarities in cognitive and academic performance.

Verbal abilities

Traditional gender stereotypes would suggest that verbal ability is stronger in women than in men. Hyde and Linn's (1988) meta-analysis of 120 individual studies indicated a small female advantage in overall verbal ability, $d = -0.11$. However, when the overall effect size is broken down into different types of verbal ability, the results became more complex. Although girls performed somewhat better than boys at verbal fluency tasks, $d = -0.33$, there was no gender difference for vocabulary ($d = -0.02$), reading comprehension ($d = -0.03$), or essay writing ($d = -0.09$).

In order to more fully understand the small effect sizes from the Hyde and Linn (1988) meta-analysis, Hedges and Nowell (1995) conducted another meta-analysis on gender differences in vocabulary and reading comprehension. Similar to the previous meta-analysis, the results reported by Hedges and Nowell (1995) favored females, but were small. For reading comprehension, effect sizes ranged from −0.18 to +0.002. For vocabulary, effect sizes ranged from −0.06 to +0.25.

Large, international datasets are also helpful for determining whether effect sizes change across nations or international contexts. In an analysis of the Program for International Students Assessment (PISA) data, girls had higher reading achievement, $d = -0.44$, but variability in effect sizes was accounted for by the gender equality in participating nations (Reilly, 2012). Nations with greater gender equality had smaller effect sizes, indicating that social and cultural factors likely play a role in the magnitude of gender differences in verbal ability.

Another recent study of the Kaufman Assessment Battery for Children (KTEAS-II) examined gender differences in reading ability and writing (Reynolds et al., 2015). Results indicated that gender differences in reading comprehension and word recognition were very small and favored girls (ds ranged from −0.06 to −0.16). However, gender differences in writing were medium and favored girls (ds ranged from −0.44 to −0.46). The authors suggest that writing could be an exception to the gender similarities hypothesis.

Mathematics performance

Despite gender stereotypes about boys' superior performance in math, meta-analyses suggest that gender differences in math performance are trivial. In a recent assessment of state-standardized math tests representing over seven million students in the United States, effect sizes for math assessments were quite small, ranging from −0.02 in seventh grade to 0.06 in 11th grade (Hyde et al., 2008). Gender differences in math performance were trivial at all grade levels. Although there was greater variability in boys' math performance, the variability was small.

Another meta-analysis of 242 existing studies published between 1990 and 2007 found similar results indicating small gender differences in math performance (Lindberg et al., 2010). The overall effect size for all studies, including studies of adults, was $d = 0.05$. Some researchers have claimed that boys might perform better than girls in complex mathematical problem solving, which is not assessed on traditional computations math tests. However, this meta-analysis found an effect size of $d = 0.16$ for complex problem solving, indicating that gender differences in math performance remain small even for complex problems.

Math motivation and attitudes

Although gender differences in general math ability are trivial, gender differences continue to exist in math motivation. In particular, motivation factors such as expectancy for success and interest in mathematics are important for students pursuing advanced coursework and careers in mathematics and science. A meta-analysis indicated that boys had somewhat higher levels of math self-confidence when compared with girls, $d = 0.27$, and girls had slightly higher levels of math anxiety in comparison to boys, $d = -0.23$ (Else-Quest et al., 2010). Even when girls perform just as well as boys on mathematics assessments, girls were more likely than boys to underestimate their math ability, although the difference was small (Eccles et al., 1998). Girls who had higher levels of self-efficacy and self-perceived math ability were more likely to pursue careers in math and science than girls who had low levels of self-efficacy (Eccles, 1994).

Gender Similarities in Occupations

Although small gender differences in career interests and preferences may exist, gender similarities largely prevail in leadership effectiveness.

Job attribute preferences

A meta-analysis examined gender differences in job attribute preferences, such as the potential for high earnings, good work hours, challenges, and leadership opportunities (Konrad et al., 2000). The authors suggested that, according to gender stereotypes, men would prefer financial incentives and leadership opportunities in their careers, whereas women would prefer jobs that allow for flexibility and nurturance. Of the 40 preferences, 33 exhibited significant effects of gender, but the majority of the effect sizes were small. For example, men were only slightly more likely than women to report that earnings ($d = 0.12$) and leadership opportunities ($d = 0.14$) were important, whereas women were somewhat more likely to prefer working with people ($d = -0.35$) and having opportunities to help others ($d = -0.36$). Some of the job preferences displayed results contrary to gender stereotypes. For example, women were slightly more likely than men to prefer some stereotypically masculine roles, such as a feeling of accomplishment ($d = -0.14$) and good benefits ($d = -0.09$). In general, gender differences were smaller for masculine job attributes, but were larger for feminine job attributes. Women were more likely to endorse both masculine and feminine job attributes, wanting both a high salary and family flexibility for example, whereas men endorsed only masculine job attributes (Weisgram et al., 2010).

Although the majority of job attribute preferences showed significant differences, the differences were generally small (Konrad et al., 2000). The authors noted that the small gender differences may be due to few studies including homemakers in their sample. Homemakers are likely to hold the most traditional gender-role beliefs and traditional job attribute preferences, but they were missing from many of the samples.

Evidence suggests that, over time, women have become increasingly free to adopt masculine characteristics, but that men have not been eager to adopt feminine characteristics (Twenge, 1997). Job attributes traditionally associated with masculine careers became more important to women between the 1970s and 1980s, but became less important from 1980 to 1990 (Konrad et al., 2000). Traditionally feminine job attributes followed a similar trend (Konrad et al., 2000). Perhaps some changes from the feminist movement in the 1970s have leveled off.

Leadership

A meta-analysis examined data on gender differences in leadership effectiveness (Eagly et al., 1995; Paustian-Underdahl et al., 2014). Overall, there was no gender difference in leadership effectiveness, $d = -0.05$. Moderator analyses indicated that, when self-reports were used, men reported themselves as more effective leaders than women did, $d = 0.21$, but women were reported as more effective leaders when others' ratings were used, $d = -0.12$ (Paustian-Underdahl et al., 2014). Women may have lower confidence in their leadership ability than men do, despite others reporting them as being just as effective as men.

Men and women may also differ in their leadership style. Eagly et al. (2003) identified three different leadership styles: a transformational leader, a transactional leader, and a laissez-faire leader. A transformational leader attempts to gain the trust of others by serving as a role model. A transactional leader uses rewards and punishments to shape the behavior of her followers. A laissez-faire leader is hands-off and uninvolved with her followers. The meta-analysis indicated a trivial gender difference favoring females in transformational leadership, $d = -0.10$, and transactional leadership, $d = -0.13$. However, women were more likely to use reward-based systems, whereas men were somewhat more likely to use punishments when problems arose, $d = 0.27$. Men were also somewhat more likely to engage in laissez-faire leadership, $d = 0.16$. Overall, the gender differences for leadership effectiveness and style are small, despite gender stereotypes to the contrary.

Gender Similarities in Social Behavior

Popular opinion might suggest that men and women have very different social behaviors in areas such as aggression and communication. Meta-analyses suggest that gender differences in most social behaviors are trivial.

Helping

Eagly and Crowley (1986; see also Eagly, 2009) conducted a meta-analysis of research on gender differences in helping behavior. This meta-analysis yielded an overall $d = 0.34$, which is a small effect indicating that males help more. Moderator analyses indicated that some helping behaviors were more common among men, such as stopping to help a motorist with a flat tire, but that other types of helping were more common among women, such as helping a distressed child. The authors argued that women are more likely to engage in relational helping behavior and men are more likely to initiate agentic helping and prosocial behaviors that require strength because these actions are consistent with social gender roles.

Temperament

A meta-analysis examined gender differences in three broad dimensions of temperament, including effortful control, negativity, and surgency (Else-Quest et al., 2006). Dimensions of effortful control included attention regulation, inhibitory control, and perceptual sensitivity. Girls scored higher on all measures of effortful control than boys did (ds ranged from -0.31 to 0.09) but the differences were small. These results are consistent with findings that boys are more likely to display externalizing behaviors. Negativity included dimensions such as anger, frustration, and emotional intensity. The majority of the dimensions in negativity showed no gender differences or small gender differences (ds ranged from -0.12 to 0.10). Surgency – which is similar to extraversion – was represented by factors including smiling, laughing, and high-intensity pleasure. Boys had slightly higher levels of surgency than girls did, but the effect was small (d range from -0.11 to 0.30).

Communication

Stereotypes concerning gender differences in communication abound (e.g., Tannen, 1991). In particular, it has been said that women use more tentative speech than men do, as indicated by greater use of tag questions (e.g., 'He is correct, isn't he?') and hedge statements (e.g., 'I'm not an expert, but I will do my best'). These communication patterns are important because the use of tag questions and hedge statements convey a lack of self-confidence in one's ability. According to a meta-analysis of studies of tentative speech, however, the gender differences are small for tag questions, $d = -0.23$, and for hedges, $d = -0.15$ (Leaper and Robnett, 2011). Women used tag questions and hedges only slightly more often than men did. Importantly, the size of the effect depended on context, with larger gender differences in lab studies ($d = -0.28$) and smaller gender differences in naturalistic observation ($d = -0.09$).

Gender Similarities in Psychological Well-Being

Research concerning gender differences in psychological well-being may be subject to bias given assumptions about higher levels of depression and lower self-esteem among women in comparison to men. Meta-analyses are an excellent tool for synthesizing empirical results in order to obtain a more accurate representation of gender and psychological well-being.

Self-esteem

A meta-analysis examining gender differences in self-esteem found a small overall gender difference favoring boys and men, $d = 0.21$ (Kling et al., 1999). The effect size increased from 0.16 in elementary school to 0.23 in middle school and 0.33 in high school, but then declined to 0.18 among college students and 0.10 among adults between the ages of 23 and 59. The effect size was not large in any age group, and it decreased among adults. Sociocultural explanations may help explain gender differences in self-esteem because these differences may vary based on the context of self-esteem. A different meta-analysis examined studies that measured domain-specific self-esteem or self-concept (Gentile et al., 2009). Males scored higher than females on self-esteem domains concerning physical appearance ($d = 0.35$), athleticism ($d = 0.41$), and self-satisfaction ($d = 0.33$), whereas females scored higher on self-esteem domains concerning behavioral conduct ($d = -0.17$) and morality ($d = -0.38$). For all other domains, gender similarities were found such that effect sizes were close to zero for academic, social, and family self-esteem.

Depression

The Children's Depression Index is a commonly used scale that measures depression among children between the ages of eight and 16. A meta-analysis of 310 samples of children who completed the depression scale revealed a very small gender difference favoring girls ($d = -0.02$; Twenge and Nolen-Hoeksema, 2002). Further analyses indicated that there were no gender differences between ages eight and 12, but between the ages of 13 and 16 the effect size grew and favored girls more ($d = 0.16$).

According to Response Style Theory, women are more likely to ruminate on negative events, which may lead to higher rates of depression (Johnson and Whisman, 2013). A meta-analysis including 59 studies on gender differences in rumination concluded that women were slightly more likely to ruminate than were men ($d = -0.24$; Johnson and Whisman, 2013). In particular, women spent more time than men brooding ($d = -0.19$) and reflecting ($d = -0.17$). Although these effect sizes are significant, they are small and there are many other factors that might explain gender differences in depression. By exaggerating gender differences in depression, the public provides more support for girls and women who suffer and may ignore boys and men who often suffer depressive symptoms in silence. Understanding that gender similarities prevail in the experience of depression should lead to more support for boys and men to be correctly diagnosed and treated.

EXCEPTIONS TO THE GENDER SIMILARITIES HYPOTHESIS

The gender similarities hypothesis does not propose that gender differences in *all* psychological dimensions are small. In fact, Hyde (2005) was careful to note a few exceptions to the gender similarities hypothesis, notably gender differences in motor performance, sexuality, and aggression. Other research indicates that gender differences in spatial performance and career interests are moderate, or even large.

Gender Differences in Motor Performance

Gender differences in motor performance show some of the largest and most consistent gender differences. For example, a meta-analysis of gender differences in motor performance showed a large gender difference favoring males for throwing velocity, $d = 2.18$, and throwing distance, $d = 1.98$ (Thomas and French, 1985). However, in some areas of motor performance, such as balance, $d = 0.09$, and vertical jump, $d = 0.18$, gender differences were small. Developmental trends moderated gender differences in motor performance for many of the tasks. For example, gender differences for the majority of the motor tasks, including throwing velocity, balance, and grip strength, increased after puberty. The authors suggested that gender differences prior to puberty may be influenced more by environmental factors, whereas gender differences after puberty were more likely to be due to biological differences.

Gender Differences in Sexual Attitudes and Behavior

Gender differences in sexual behaviors are some of the largest gender differences in the psychology of gender, but research suggests that they are becoming smaller over time. This line of research benefits from two meta-analyses that use the same procedures, but analyzed data from separate time periods (Oliver and Hyde, 1993; Petersen and Hyde,

2010). Taken together, these meta-analyses describe temporal trends in gender differences in sexual attitudes and behavior.

Men were somewhat more likely to engage in heterosexual intercourse than women were, but the gender difference was small and decreasing. Oliver and Hyde (1993) found an effect size of $d = 0.33$ and Petersen and Hyde (2010) found an effect size of $d = 0.16$ for incidence of heterosexual intercourse. Both Oliver and Hyde (1993; $d = 0.25$) and Petersen and Hyde (2010; $d = 0.36$) found a small gender difference in number of sex partners, with men reporting somewhat more sex partners than women did. Petersen and Hyde (2010) found a gender difference in extramarital sex in which men reported more extramarital sexual behavior than women did ($d = 0.33$). This gender difference did not differ depending on the age of the sample, the year of publication, or the gender equality of the nation. Petersen and Hyde (2010) found a substantial gender difference in which men were more likely than women to report using erotic materials such as magazines, videos, and/or the internet ($d = 0.63$). This was the largest gender difference in any of the sexual attitudes and behaviors included in this meta-analysis.

Although researchers often examine gender differences in specific sexual attitudes, in some research a general scale of sexual permissiveness is used. An example is the Sexual Attitudes Scale (Hendrick et al., 2006), which examines sexual attitudes, including attitudes toward casual sex and attitudes toward contraception. Oliver and Hyde (1993) reviewed gender differences in these general sexual permissiveness scales and found a medium-sized effect in which men were more sexually permissive than women were ($d = 0.57$), but Petersen and Hyde (2010) found a small gender difference ($d = 0.21$). Both Oliver and Hyde (1993; $d = 0.37$) and Petersen and Hyde (2010; $d = 0.17$) found gender differences in attitudes toward premarital sex, indicating that men reported somewhat more permissive attitudes than women did. Women were more likely than men to feel negative emotions in response to sexual behavior, such as guilt or anxiety ($d = -0.35$ from Oliver and Hyde, 1993; $d = -0.19$ from Petersen and Hyde, 2010). Petersen and Hyde (2010) indicated that women had slightly more accepting attitudes toward gay men ($d = -0.18$) but that there was no gender difference in attitudes toward lesbian women ($d = -0.02$).

Overall, some sexual behaviors, such as pornography use, are significantly different for men and women, whereas other aspects of sexuality, such as incidence of intercourse, extramarital sex, number of sex partners, and sexual attitudes showed gender similarities. Moreover, gender differences in sexuality appear to be decreasing as society becomes more accepting of female sexuality.

Gender Differences in Aggression

A meta-analysis of gender differences in aggression indicated that, overall, males were more likely to be aggressive than were females, $d = 0.48$ (Hyde, 1984). Approximately 5% of the variation in aggression could be explained by gender. Gender differences in aggression were larger in correlational studies than in experimental studies. Studies in which aggression was observed, or peers reported the aggression, produced larger gender differences favoring men than studies in which aggression was self-reported. A subsequent meta-analysis using more advanced moderator procedures determined that gender differences in physical aggression, $d = 0.91$, were larger than gender differences in verbal aggression, $d = 0.46$, (Knight et al., 1996).

Gender differences in impulsivity could help in understanding the gender difference in aggression. A meta-analysis of gender differences in impulsivity indicated no gender difference in general impulsivity, $d = 0.08$ (Cross et al., 2011). One of the largest gender differences in specific types of impulsivity came from sensation seeking, $d = 0.39$, with men being somewhat more likely to report sensation seeking than women were. Perhaps gender differences in aggression are explained more by sensation seeking than by general impulsivity.

Gender Differences in Spatial Performance

One way to assess spatial performance is through 3D mental rotation tasks. In a 3D mental rotation task, individuals view a 3D object and then must visualize what it will look like after it is rotated. An older meta-analysis concerning 3D mental rotation suggested that boys performed better on these tasks than girls did, $d = 0.73$ (Linn and Petersen, 1985). A more modern meta-analysis indicated a smaller effect of 3D mental rotation, $d = 0.56$, but the effect was still significant and favored boys (Voyer et al., 1995). However, the majority of 3D mental rotation tasks are timed and may be a function of strict time limits as much as the actual spatial performance required. In fact, the gender difference in 3D mental rotation was large when studies had strict time limits ($d = 1.03$), but the effect size was only moderate when no time limits were used ($d = 0.51$; Voyer, 2011; see also Maeda and Yoon, 2013).

In most schools, there is rarely any formal spatial training. Spatial training is more likely to occur in informal settings, such as in sports and video games. Boys are more likely than girls to engage in these forms of information spatial training (Rideout et al., 2010), which might give them an edge over girls in the 3D mental rotation tasks. For example, in one study, boys and girls were given ten hours of training on a video game (Feng, 2007). After this training, gender differences in a 3D mental rotation task were not significant. A meta-analysis considering the effects of training on spatial ability indicated that spatial ability is quite malleable (Uttal et al., 2013). This analysis indicated that both men and women benefitted from training, but most spatial training studies did not close the gender gap.

Gender Differences in Career Interests

Meta-analytic results suggest that men and women may differ slightly in their career interests. Su and colleagues (2009) indicated that gender differences in career interests can be summarized as 'Men and Things, Women and People'. That is, women preferred jobs that required person-to-person interaction, whereas men preferred jobs that required working with physical objects, $d = 0.93$. In particular, men preferred careers in realistic ($d = 0.84$) and investigative fields ($d = 0.26$), whereas women were more interested in artistic ($d = -.35$), social ($d = -.68$), and conventional careers ($d = -.33$). One of the largest gender differences in career interests was in engineering ($d = 1.11$), with men preferring engineering careers more often than women did.

It is important to remember, however, that there are many counter-examples of the 'Men and Things, Women and People' dimension. For example, the world of business and politics, typically male-dominated fields, require a great deal of person-to-person interaction, whereas dental hygienists and librarians are female-dominated careers that require the employee to work with things. In addition, the gender differences in this meta-analysis were generally small, indicating great overlap in the distributions of scores for males and females. By implication, there are many individuals who are interested in counter-stereotypical careers. Assuming that girls are not interested in engineering, for example, or that boys are not interested in teaching may limit career aspirations and may lead to sex discrimination in the workplace. It is also important to recognize that these gender differences in career interests are not innate or immutable. Gender differences in interest among high school students, for example, are likely largely influenced by years of gender socialization that shape girls toward nurturance and people-oriented interests and boys toward athletics and mechanical toys such as trucks.

GENDER SIMILARITIES AND DIFFERENCES IN VARIABILITY

Effect sizes capture gender differences in average performance, but do not consider gender differences or similarities in variability. In 1894, Havelock Ellis proposed that males had greater variability in cognitive performance than females, thus explaining why men were more likely to be found in the tail ends of the normal distribution of intelligence (Shields, 1975). Similar to the effect size, d, the statistic to account for gender differences in variability is the variance ratio (VR). A variance ratio of one suggests equal variance for males and females. A $VR > 1$ indicates greater male variance and a $VR < 1$ indicates greater female variance.

The meta-analyses examining math performance (Lindberg et al., 2010) and verbal performance (Hedges and Nowell, 1995) calculated variance ratios. These studies indicated that males had slightly more variability than females on these dimensions. For mathematical performance, variability ratios ranged from 1.05 to 1.20, and for verbal ability, variance ratios ranged from 1.03 to 1.16. Although these variance ratios slightly favored males, they were not far from a variance ratio of one, which would indicate equal variability across genders. For example, in a distribution with $d = 0.01$ and $VR = 1.05$, there would be 111 boys for every 100 girls in the 95th percentile (Hedges and Friedman, 1993).

GENDER SIMILARITY AND INTERSECTIONALITY

Gender is only one of many social categories that play a role in psychological processes. The concept of intersectionality acknowledges that people belong to multiple social categories that work together to affect identity and social inequality, such as gender, sexual orientation, ethnicity, and ability (Cole, 2009). This concept acknowledges that many people, such as women of color, may be marginalized based on their identification with more than one group.

Intersectionality is a concept that is typically considered by qualitative research in fields such as sociology and anthropology (Else-Quest and Hyde, 2016a, 2016b). However, some meta-analyses examining gender differences on psychological variables have also examined the magnitude of the gender effect separately by other social categories such as race or sexual orientation. For example, although gender differences in self-esteem were small for all racial categories, the gender difference was larger among white individuals, $d = 0.20$, than among black individuals, $d = -0.04$ (Kling et al., 1999). Similarly, gender differences in mathematical performance may be more pronounced for white individuals, $d = 0.13$, than for black individuals, $d = -0.02$, Latinos, $d = 0.00$, and Asian Americans, $d = -0.09$ (Hyde et al., 1990).

Although ethnicity is more commonly used as a moderator of gender differences in meta-analysis, other social categories, such as sexual orientation and social class, may also be used. One meta-analysis indicated that sexual minorities are at increased risk of sexual abuse. However, male sexual minorities were at 4.9 times greater risk than heterosexual males, whereas female sexual minorities were at 1.5 times greater risk compared to heterosexual females (Friedman et al., 2011). Other meta-analytic research on handedness and sexual orientation found that homosexual participants had 39% greater odds of being non-right handed than heterosexual participants, but that this connection between sexual orientation and handedness was stronger for women than it was for men (Lalumier et al., 2000). Socio-economic status (SES) may also moderate the gender differences that are observed for some psychological variables. For example, the participants with higher SES tend to have greater life satisfaction, but this correlation was stronger for male samples than it was for female samples (Pinquart and Sorensen, 2000). This relationship can be explained by income and education, which were more strongly correlated with happiness among men than women.

There are many challenges to the analysis of intersectionality in meta-analytic research. First, race, sexual orientation, social class, and other social categories are often not included in published studies, despite the American Psychological Association's guideline suggestion for reporting them. Published articles that focus on gender often ignore other categories, or provide statistics separated by gender but not separately for other social categories. Second, even when ethnicity, social class, and sexual orientation are reported, the majority of published studies include samples of primarily white, upper-middle class, heterosexuals. If researchers intend to take intersectionality and generalizability seriously, they must seek out samples that are representative of the entire population. Convenience samples of university undergraduates often do not provide a representative sample of the United States. Finally, the intersectionality of ethnicity is complicated by international samples. Ethnic groups vary across countries and meta-analyses that use ethnicity as a moderator of gender differences must often restrict their analyses to samples from the United States in order to account for different ethnic groups in other countries (e.g., Petersen and Hyde, 2010).

CONCLUSION

The gender similarities hypothesis suggests that men and women are similar on most, but not all, psychological constructs (Hyde, 2005). Evolutionary theory, social structural theory, and cognitive social learning theory indicate that men and women have a shared evolutionary history and shared social environment, thus providing a theoretical foundation for the notion that men and women are more alike than they are different. The gender similarities hypothesis is largely supported by meta-analytic results (Hyde, 2005). Meta-analyses provide an opportunity to combine results from large numbers of participants across published and unpublished studies, leading to empirical evidence that is more generalizable and representative than any single study. The majority of meta-analytic results concerning psychological variables support the gender similarities hypothesis. In particular, gender similarities prevail in the areas of verbal ability, mathematics performance, job preferences, helping behavior, temperament, communication, leadership effectiveness, self-esteem, and depression.

Some exceptions to the gender similarities hypothesis include motor performance, some aspects of sexual behavior, some forms of aggression, spatial ability, and career interests. However, these exceptions are acknowledged by the gender similarities hypothesis (Hyde, 2005), and there are fewer gender differences in psychological constructs than there are similarities. Gender socialization from birth may explain why men and women differ in these categories. For example, aggression is likely to be larger among boys, who are encouraged to play with toys such as violent video games and superheros, than among girls, who are often encouraged to play with more cooperative toys.

This review acknowledges the importance of context in the psychology of gender. For example, the emerging field of intersectionality, which acknowledges that individuals often belong to multiple social categories and marginalized groups, should be an emphasis in future research. However, in order for this field to grow, researchers must focus on representative samples and report statistics separately for gender, race, social class, and sexual orientation. For too long, the field of psychology has used convenience samples of university undergraduates, who are disproportionately white and upper-middle class. Representative samples are imperative for generalizability and a shared understanding of the psychology of all people.

Finally, at the crux of the gender similarities hypothesis is the notion that gender similarities are just as important as gender differences. Journal editors and publishers should acknowledge the importance of null results and the cost of overemphasizing gender differences. For example, the emphasis on gender differences in depression may lead to less research concerning depression in men, with the result being that men may suffer silently with fewer opportunities for diagnosis and treatment. Similarly, emphasis on gender differences in cognitive performance, such as mathematics and spatial performance, seems to be affecting girls' math self-efficacy, which is likely one of the leading causes of women's underrepresentation in careers involving math and science (Else-Quest et al., 2010). Even when gender differences do appear consistently, it is important to question why these gender differences exist and whether they are important. For example, the gender difference in 3D mental rotation is one of the largest gender differences reviewed here and certainly has implications for gender differences in careers that require spatial reasoning, such as engineering. However, additional research suggests that these gender differences in 3D mental rotation can be minimized by simple training tasks (Feng, 2007) which may provide girls with more self-confidence in spatial tasks and may have the potential to reduce the gender gap in engineering careers. Future research in the psychology of gender should focus on identifying causes of gender differences and whether minimizing these differences may lead to more opportunities for both men and women.

An emphasis on gender differences over gender similarities is not only a distortion of the existing psychological data, but it may also have an effect on the marginalization of men and women. Gender stereotypes are restricting. They limit opportunities for both men and women who may otherwise be attracted to counter-stereotypical behaviors. The variability within each gender is often larger than the differences between the genders. Emphasizing gender similarities frees both men and women to seek opportunities consistent with their individuality, regardless of their gender.

REFERENCES

Ball, L. C., Bribbie, R. A., & Steele, J. R. (2013). Beyond gender differences: Using tests of equivalence to evaluate gender similarities. *Psychology of Women Quarterly, 37,* 147–154.

Benbow, C., & Stanley, J. (1980). Sex differences in mathematical ability: Fact or artifact. *Science, 210,* 1262–1264.

Borenstein, M., Hedges, L. V., Higgins, J. P. T., & Rothstein, H. R. (2009). *Introduction to meta-analysis*. West Sussex, UK: Wiley.

Buss, D. (2014). *Evolutionary psychology.* New York, NY: Routledge.

Buss, D., & Schmitt, D. (1993). Sexual strategies theory: An evolutionary perspective on human mating. *Psychology Review, 100,* 204–232.

Bussey, K., & Bandura, A. (1999). Social cognitive theory of gender development and differentiation. *Psychology Review, 100,* 204–232.

Ceci, S. J., & Williams, W. M. (2011). Understanding current causes of women's underrepresentation in science. *Proceedings of the National Academy of Sciences, 108,* 3157–3162.

Cohen, J. (1988). *Statistical power analysis for the behavioral sciences* (2nd ed.). Mahwah, NJ: Erlbaum.

Cole, E. R. (2009). Intersectionaility and research in psychology. *American Psychologist, 64,* 170–180.

Cross, C. P., Copping, L. T., & Campbell, A. (2011). Sex differences in impulsivity: A meta-analysis. *Psychological Bulletin, 137,* 97–130.

Eagly, A. (2009). The his and hers of prosocial behavior: An examination of the social psychology of gender. *The American Psychologist, 64,* 644–658.

Eagly, A. H., & Crowley, M. (1986). Gender and helping behavior: A meta-analytic review of the social psychological literature. *Psychological Bulletin, 100,* 283–308.

Eagly, A. H., Johannesen-Schmidt, M. C., & van Engen, M. L. (2003). Transformational, transactional, and laissez-faire leadership styles: A meta-analysis comparing women and men. *Psychological Bulletin, 129,* 569–591.

Eagly, A. H., Karau, S., & Makhijani, M. (1995). Gender and the effectiveness of leaders: A meta-analysis. *Psychological Bulletin, 117,* 125–145.

Eagly, A. H., & Wood, W. (1999). The origins of sex differences in human behavior: Evolved dispositions versus social roles. *American Psychologist, 54,* 408–423.

Eccles, J. S. (1994). Understanding women's educational and occupational goals. *Psychology of Women Quarterly, 18,* 585–609.

Eccles, J. S., Wigfield, A., & Schiefele, U. (1998). Motivation to succeed. In W. Damon & N. Eisenberg (Eds.), *Handbook of child psychology* (5th ed.; pp. 1017–1095) New York, NY: Wiley.

Else-Quest, N. M., & Hyde, J. S. (2016a). Intersectionality in quantitative psychological research II: Method & technique. *Psychology of Women Quarterly, 40,* 319–336.

Else-Quest, N. M., & Hyde, J. S. (2016b). Intersectionality in quantitative psychological research I: Theoretical and epistemilogical issues. *Psychology of Women Quarterly, 40,* 155–170.

Else-Quest, N., Hyde, J. S., Goldsmith, H. H., & Van Hulle, C. A. (2006). Gender differences in temperament: A meta-analysis. *Psychological Bulletin, 132,* 33–72.

Else-Quest, N. M., Hyde, J. S., & Linn, M. C. (2010). Cross-national patterns of gender differences in mathematics: A meta-analysis. *Psychological Bulletin, 136,* 103–127.

Feng, J. (2007). Playing an action video game reduces gender differences in spatial cognition. *Psychological Science, 18,* 850–855.

Friedman, M. S., Marshal, M. P., Guadamusz, T. E., Wei, C., Fong, C. F., Saewyc, E. M., & Stall, R. (2011). A meta-analysis of disparities in childhood sexual abuse, parental physical abuse, and peer victimization among sexual minority and sexual nonminority individuals. *American Journal of Public Health, 101,* 1481–1494.

Gentile, B., Grabe, S., Dolan-Pascoe, B., Twenge, J. M., Wells, B. E., & Maitino, A. (2009). Gender differences in domain-specific self-esteem: A meta-analysis. *Review of General Psychology, 13,* 34–45.

Hare-Mustin, R. T., & Marecek, J. (1988). The meaning of difference: Gender, theory, postmodernism, and psychology. *American Psychologist, 43,* 455–464.

Hedges, L. V., & Friedman, L. (1993). Gender differences in variability in intellectual abilities: A reanalysis of Feingold's results. *Review of Educational Research, 63,* 94–105.

Hedges, L. V., & Nowell, A. (1995). Sex differences in mental test scores, variability, and numbers of high-scoring individuals. *Science, 269,* 41–45.

Hendrick, C., Hendrick, S. S., & Reich, D. A. (2006). The brief sexual attitudes scale. *Journal of Sex Research, 43,* 76–86.

Hyde, J. S. (1984). How large are gender differences in aggression: A developmental meta-analysis. *Developmental Psychology, 20,* 722–736.

Hyde, J. S. (2005). The gender similarities hypothesis. *American Psychologist, 60,* 581–592.

Hyde, J. S. (2014). Gender similarities and differences. *Annual Review of Psychology, 65,* 373–398.

Hyde, J., Fennema, E., Lamon, S., & Appelbaum, M. I. (1990). Differences in mathematics performance: A meta-analysis. *Psychological Bulletin, 107,* 139–155.

Hyde, J. S., Lindberg, S. M., Linn, M. C., Ellis, A., & Williams, C. (2008). Gender similarities characterize math performance. *Science, 321,* 494–495.

Hyde, J. S., & Linn, M. C. (1988). Gender differences in verbal ability: A meta-analysis. *Psychological Bulletin, 104,* 53–69.

Johnson, D. P., & Whisman, M. A. (2013). Gender differences in rumination: A meta-analysis. *Personality and Individual Differences, 55*, 367–374.

Kling, K. C., Hyde, J. S., Showers, C. J., & Buswell, B. N. (1999). Gender differences in self-esteem: A meta-analysis. *Psychological Bulletin, 125*, 470–500.

Knight, G. P., Fabes, R. A., & Higgins, D. A. (1996). Concerns about drawing causal influences from meta-analyses: An example in the study of gender differences in aggression. *Psychological Bulletin, 119*, 410–421.

Konrad, A. M., Ritchie, E., Lieb, P., & Corrigall, E. (2000). Sex differences and similarities in job attribute pereferences: A meta-analysis. *Psychological Bulletin, 126*, 593–641.

Lalumier, M. L., Blanchard, R., & Zucker, K. J. (2000). Sexual orientation and handedness in men and women: A meta-analysis. *Psychological Bulletin, 126*, 575–592.

Leaper, C., & Robnett, R. D. (2011). Women are more likely than men to use tentative language, aren't they? A meta-analysis testing for gender differences and moderators. *Psychology of Women Quarterly, 35*, 129–142.

Lindberg, S. M., Hyde, J. S., Petersen, J., & Linn, M. C. (2010). New trends in gender and mathematics performance: A meta-analysis. *Psychological Bulletin, 136*, 1123–1135.

Linn, M. C., & Petersen, A. C. (1985). Emergence and characterization of sex differences in spatial ability: A meta-analysis. *Child Development, 56*, 1479–1498.

Maeda, Y., & Yoon, S. Y. (2013). A meta-analysis on gender differences in mental rotation ability measured by the Purdue Spatial Visualization Tests: Visualization of rotations (PSVT:R). *Educational Psychology Review, 25*, 69–94.

Oliver, M. B., & Hyde, J. S. (1993). Gender differences in sexuality: A meta-analysis. *Psychological Bulletin, 114*, 29–51.

Paustian-Underdahl, S. C., Walker, L. S., & Woehr, D. (2014). Gender and perceptions of leadership effectiveness: A meta-analysis of contextual moderator. *Journal of Applied Psychology, 99*, 1129–1145.

Petersen, J. L., & Hyde, J. S. (2010). A meta-analytic review of research on gender differences in sexuality: 1993–2007. *Psychological Bulletin, 136*, 21–38.

Pinquart, M., & Sorensen, S. (2000). Influences of socioeconomic status, social network, and competence on subjective well-being in later life: A meta-analysis. *Psychology and Aging, 15*, 187–224.

Reilly, D. (2012). Gender, culture, and sex-typed cognitive abilities. *PLoS ONE, 7*, e39904.

Reynolds, M. R., Scheiber, C., Hajovsky, D. B., Schwartz, B., & Kaufman, A. S. (2015). Gender differences in academic achievement: Is writing an exception to the gender similarities hypothesis? *Journal of Genetic Psychology, 176*, 211–234.

Rideout, V. J., Foehr, U. G., & Roberts, D. F. (2010). *Generation M^2: Media in the lives of 8- to 18-year-olds*. Menlo Park, CA: Kaiser Family Foundation.

Shields, S. (1975). Functionalism, Darwinism, and the psychology of women. *American Psychologist, 30*, 739–754.

Su, R., Rounds, J., & Armstrong, P. (2009). Men and things, women and people: A meta-analysis of sex differences in interests. *Psychological Bulletin, 135*, 859–884.

Tannen, D. (1991). *You just don't understand: Women and men in conversation*. New York, NY: Ballantine.

Thomas, J. R., & French, K. (1985). Gender differences across age in motor performance: A meta-analysis. *Psychological Bulletin, 98*, 260–282.

Trivers, R. L. (1972). Parental investment and sexual selection. In B. Campbell (Ed.), *Sexual selection and the descent of man, 1871–1971* (pp. 136–179). Chicago, IL: Aldine.

Twenge, J. M. (1997). Changes in masculine and feminine traits over time. A meta-analysis. *Sex Roles, 36*, 305–325.

Twenge, J. M., & Nolen-Hoeksema, S. (2002). Age, gender, race, socio-economic status, and birth cohort differences on the Children's Depression Inventory: A meta-analysis. *Journal of Abnormal Behavior, 111*, 578–588.

Uttal, D. H., Meadow, N. G., Tipton, E., Hand, L. L., Alden, A. R., Warren, C., & Newcombe, N. S. (2013). The malleability of spatial skills: A meta-analysis of training studies. *Psychological Bulletin, 139*, 352–402.

Voyer, D. (2011). Time limits and gender differences on paper-and-pencil tests of mental rotation: A meta-analysis. *Psychological Bulletin Review, 18*, 267–277.

Voyer, D., Voyer, S., & Bryden, M. P. (1995). Magnitude of sex differences in spatial abilities: A meta-analysis and consideration of critical variables. *Psychological Bulletin, 117,* 250–270.

Weisgram, E., Bigler, R., & Liben, L. (2010). Gender, values, and occupational interests among children, adolescents, and adults. *Child Development, 81,* 778–796.

Wood, W., & Eagly, A. (2012). Biosocial construction of sex difference and similarities in behavior. *Advanced Experimental Psychology, 46,* 55–123.

Zell, E., Krizan, Z., & Tetter, S. R. (2015). Evaluating gender similarities using meta-synthesis. *American Psychologist, 70,* 10–20.

Zuriff, G. E. (2015). The gender similarities hypothesis is untestable as formulated. *American Psychologist, 70,* 663–664.

Positive Personality Change Following Adversity

Eranda Jayawickreme and Corinne E. Zachry

> Everything struggles to live. Look at that tree growing up there out of that grating. It gets no sun, and water only when it rains. It's growing out of sour earth. And it's strong because its hard struggle to live is making it strong. – Betty Smith, *A Tree Grows in Brooklyn*

The resounding impact of the idea that adversity promotes character is often reflected in, and promoted by, popular culture and, more broadly, in the narratives most people relate about their lives. Unsurprisingly, the prevalence and pervasiveness of this perception have informed recent psychological research examining the apparent ubiquity of lasting positive life changes resulting from the experience of traumatic life events. Some researchers have labeled this change *posttraumatic growth* (PTG), a term coined by Tedeschi and Calhoun (2004) after they recognized that their patients were reporting positive life changes – including better relationships with others and greater appreciation for simple aspects of daily life – following stressful, challenging, and traumatic events (Calhoun and Tedeschi, 1990). Prominent PTG theories have claimed that these changes represent substantive changes in personality:

> The individual has not only survived, but has experienced changes that are viewed as important, and that go beyond what was the previous status quo. PTG is not simply a return to baseline – it is an experience of improvement that for some persons is deeply profound. (Tedeschi and Calhoun, 2004, p. 4)

Tedeschi and Calhoun (2004) identified five domains in which they perceive positive life changes: improvement in relationships with others, identification of new possibilities for one's life, increased perception of personal strength, spiritual growth, and enhanced appreciation of life. There has been a considerable line of research examining these dimensions of PTG and their relationship with physical and mental health (Park, 2004). Such positive life changes have been reported by as many as 70% of trauma survivors in at least one of the aforementioned domains (Linley and Joseph, 2004).

As we have noted elsewhere (Jayawickreme and Blackie, 2014), these reported changes should be of great interest to personality psychologists. In particular, the methodological approaches employed by personality psychology can be especially useful in examining the mechanisms behind positive personality change following trauma, and the extent to which those changes occur and endure. Moreover, recent work highlighting the malleable nature of personality over time (e.g., Caspi et al., 2005; Edmonds et al., 2008; see also Blackie et al., 2014; Fleeson and Jayawickreme, 2015) and the possibilities for both intentional personality change (Hudson and Fraley, 2015) and personality change following the experience of life events (Lüdtke et al., 2011) bolster the view that research on PTG can provide further insight into the mechanics of personality itself.

However, controversy exists over the research literature on PTG (Frazier et al., 2009, 2014; Jayawickreme and Blackie, 2014, 2016; Tennen and Affleck, 2009). Specifically, there is a lack of clarity in both definition and measurement of the construct, as there is not a consensus on what the oft-used retrospective self-reports of PTG in fact reflect. Although theories of PTG are reliant on consequential positive changes in an individual's thoughts, feelings, and behaviors – that is to say, meaningful personality changes – the retrospective self-report measures by which PTG has been previously researched serve to instead obstruct the evaluation of the true nature and predictors of growth. Given that the concerns about the validity of this method of PTG research have a history (e.g., Tennen and Affleck, 2002), and methodology used to examine this construct has been largely resistant to these concerns (Tedeschi et al., 2014), it is imperative that the weaknesses of existing research on positive personality change following adversity are acknowledged and overcome in order to further promote its meaningful study. In this chapter, we summarize current theoretical perspectives on positive personality change following adversity and extend the discussion of Jayawickreme and Blackie (2014) in offering some recommendations for new directions for research on a fascinating, yet challenging, topic.

CONCEPTUALIZATIONS OF POSITIVE PERSONALITY CHANGE FOLLOWING ADVERSITY

As noted earlier, the concept of PTG lacks definitional clarity, and consensus among researchers has not yet been reached regarding how the phenomenon should be conceptualized (Jayawickreme and Blackie, 2016). This lack of agreement is evidenced by a number of different names that have been used to allude to the same construct, such as *benefit finding* (Tomich and Helgeson, 2004), *stress-related growth* (Park et al., 1996), and *positive illusions* (Taylor and Armor, 1996). For this reason, it is beneficial to outline the most prominent existing theoretical conceptualizations of PTG. The present discussion focuses on four primary theoretical perspectives – Tedeschi and Calhoun's (2004) five-domain model of change in PTG, Joseph and Linley's (2008) account of PTG as eudaimonic well-being, Pals and McAdams' (2004) model of cognitively restructuring personal life narratives, and the 'action-focused growth' theory of Hobfoll and colleagues (Hobfoll et al., 2007), which conceptualizes PTG as an increase in both social and psychological resources.

TEDESCHI AND CALHOUN'S ACCOUNT OF PTG

The model of PTG posited by Tedeschi and Calhoun (2004) defines PTG as positive psychological changes resulting from struggling with highly challenging life circumstances. This account is distinctive due to its conceptualization of PTG as both a positive process *and* outcome, as the coping process and identification of positive life changes are also posited to lead to greater long-term satisfaction with one's life as well as increased resilience. One theorized additional benefit is the development of a greater sense of wisdom over time through the course of coming to terms with the traumatic experience. Thus, this model of PTG highlights long-term effects, even in the potential absence of short-term benefits.

JOSEPH AND LINLEY'S ACCOUNT OF PSYCHOLOGICAL WELL-BEING CHANGE FOLLOWING ADVERSITY

Joseph and Linley (2005) emphasize the similarities between Tedeschi and Calhoun's (2004) five domains of PTG and Ryff's (1989) conceptualization of psychological well-being. That is not to say that Joseph and Linley (2005) suggest that adversity is necessary in order for an individual to experience increases in psychological well-being. Instead, the researchers theorize PTG as a process that can facilitate well-being in the five domains specified by Ryff (1989): self-acceptance, purpose in life, environmental mastery, autonomy, and positive relations with others. The distinction between subjective well-being and eudaimonic (psychological) well-being is essential to Joseph and Linley's model of PTG. Subjective well-being includes affective states and global life satisfaction (Jayawickreme et al., 2012), whereas eudaimonic well-being takes this a step further, positing that constructs such as purpose, meaning, and autonomy comprise psychological well-being (Jayawickreme et al., 2012). Joseph and Linley (2005) suggest that, although an experience of trauma may be associated with an increase in depression, it may also yield a greater appreciation for, and commitment to, an individual's life and values.

MCADAMS' NARRATIVES OF REDEMPTION

A prevalent conceptualization of PTG existing in the narrative tradition in personality psychology involves narrating one's life in terms of *stories of redemption*. McAdams (1994) has defined personality as consisting of three levels: dispositional traits, personal concerns (this level includes an individual's priorities and goals), and personal narratives. Further, McAdams (1994) explains that these three levels differ in their stability across the individual's life, with dispositional traits being posited to be the most stable whereas personal concerns are often situationally contingent, and that those changes due to situational factors prompt the evolution of the life narrative. Pals and McAdams (2004) conceive of positive personality change as a process by which individuals alter their life narrative as a means of adapting to the trauma (see also Park, 2010). This revision in narrative serves as a catalyst for the benefits of PTG – namely, positive cognitive and behavioral changes. Thus, an individual's understanding of the ways in which they have changed since experiencing a traumatic event informs the ways in which the life narrative is revised.

An increased propensity toward positive personality change is associated with certain types of narratives that have been revised in response to changes in an individual's life. These specific kinds of narratives have been studied through life narrative interviews, in which individuals are asked to reflect on moments or 'scenes' in their lives (McAdams et al., 2001). The scenes involved in life narrative research include positive scenes, negative scenes, and experiences which are perceived to alter the trajectory of an individual's life, known as 'turning points' (Jayawickreme et al., 2017; Pillemer, 1998; Sutin et al., 2010). Characterization of life narratives depends on the transitions between positive and negative scenes, and the turning points that serve as stimuli for those transitions. For example, a narrative is described as 'redemptive' when an individual transitions from a negative life scene to a positive life scene (specifically, the negative life scene has to either change into a positive situation or lead to at least one positive psychological outcome), whereas the opposite (i.e., an individual's transition from a positive life scene to a negative life scene) is described as a 'contamination' narrative. Redemptive narrative revisions are often propelled by turning points (McAdams and Bowman, 2001), therefore, PTG can be understood through the lens of life narrative research as an expression of a redemptive narrative brought about by a traumatic turning point. Individuals high in generativity, high in self-esteem, and low in depressive symptoms are more likely to express such narratives (McAdams and de St. Aubin, 1992). One implication of this view is that personality change may not happen at the 'level' of the trait, but at that of the narrative (Kandler and Specht, 2014).

HOBFOLL'S MODEL OF BEHAVIORAL GROWTH FOLLOWING DISTRESS

Hobfoll and colleagues' (2007) 'action-focused growth' model aims to differentiate between actual and perceived PTG through the examination of behavioral changes. This view depicts the psychological distress that individuals experience following traumatic events as resulting from a strain on available psychosocial resources such as social support, health, and self-esteem, and characterizes 'actual' PTG as a genuine positive personality change, which is then reflected in growth-related behaviors and further in the reduction of distress. This model expands on the meaning-making and cognitive restructuring theories by requiring that individuals express those benefits as growth-related behaviors in order to experience true PTG. Although this theory recognizes that there may be immediate coping benefits associated with self-perceived PTG, it proposes that only growth expressed through action will lead to lasting positive personality change. Jayawickreme and Blackie's (2014) focus on behavioral change in their reconceptualization of PTG was, in part, influenced by this view (see also Seery et al., 2010).

WHAT CAUSES POSITIVE PERSONALITY CHANGE FOLLOWING ADVERSITY?

A number of psychological and social mechanisms have been purported to promote (or obstruct) positive personality change. Although these theories differ in many ways, one aspect that remains uniform across many of them is that additional factors beyond the mere experience of trauma are necessary for the facilitation of growth (Joseph and Linley, 2005; Park, 2010; Tedeschi and Calhoun, 2004). Specifically, they assume that individuals make assumptions about the predictability and safety of the world when interpreting, planning, and navigating the social world (Janoff-Bulman, 1992; Parkes, 1971). Traumatic experiences are inconsistent with these assumptions, often providing a challenge to this worldview with which an individual must contend. Individuals who have experienced trauma adapt their schemas to accommodate these experiences, making way for new beliefs and identities. As trauma is incorporated into the individual's new worldview, the adaptation of the schema promotes PTG (Park, 2010).

Changing one's beliefs about the world is central to PTG, as simply reconciling the traumatic experience with preexisting worldviews is not sufficient for PTG to occur (Tedeschi and Calhoun, 2004). Another expectation of PTG is that the traumatic experience will not be incorporated into the individual's new worldview in a negative way, as people who do so often exhibit vulnerability to negative mental health outcomes, such as the depression and hopelessness associated with post-traumatic stress disorder (Joseph and Linley, 2008). These principles have served as the basis for the identification of mechanisms for facilitating PTG by Tedeschi and Calhoun (2004; Cann et al., 2010). Namely, their comprehensive model has specified that deliberative rumination, gaining meaning, and the presence of social support are central to promoting PTG.

Deliberative rumination and meaning-making – two of the processes identified by Tedeschi and Calhoun's model (2004) – are each posited to be integral to positive schema change after trauma, as they allow the individual to move on from his or her previous worldview and adapt to the new circumstances. Rumination can be highly distressing in itself when an individual considers how and why the traumatic experience occurred, and reflecting upon that trauma is associated with intrusive thoughts and memories, as well as counter-factual thinking. However, when deliberative rumination is combined with meaning-making processes, such as contemplating what knowledge can be gained from the experience, an individual may experience some of the positive life changes associated with PTG. Additionally, Tedeschi and Calhoun (2004) have highlighted the association between social support and meaning-making processes, such that self-disclosure to trusted and empathetic others promotes an individual's ability to derive meaning from a traumatic experience. Through self-disclosure, a survivor of a traumatic experience can seek help from those who have had similar experiences, aiding in the meaning-making process and the construction of new self-narratives about positive change after adversity.

Tennen and Affleck (1998) further note that PTG is likely not experienced consistently across individuals. Specifically, they hypothesize that personality change will be consistent with pre-trauma personality traits and dispositions. Cognitive complexity, self-efficacy, and dispositional hope have also been posited to be associated with increased reports of growth following trauma (Tedeschi and Calhoun, 1995; Tennen and Affleck, 1998). These accounts do complicate the view that PTG is distinct from resilience (Tedeschi and Calhoun, 2004), given that, on this account, people who grow following adversity are those who have more psychological and social resources on which to capitalize pre-trauma – in other words, those who were more resilient (see also Seery et al., 2010).

Relatedly, certain personality traits have been found to be correlated with self-reports of PTG. Tedeschi and Calhoun (1996) found positive relationships between PTG and the traits of openness to experience, extraversion, and optimism. However, the evidence for correlations between openness to experience, extraversion and positive personality change is reliant on a small number of cross-sectional studies which only measured PTG retrospectively (Bostock et al., 2009; Linley and Joseph, 2004; Prati and Pietrantoni, 2009). It should be noted that the results connecting PTG with optimism were confounded due to two items intended to measure optimism on the original version of the Life Orientation Test (LOT; Scheier and Carver, 1985), which bore strong similarities to the measures of growth used in the study. Affleck and Tennen (1996) conducted an additional analysis of the data, omitting the confounding items, and found that there was no correlation between optimism and growth once these two items had been removed.

CURRENT ASSESSMENTS OF POSITIVE PERSONALITY CHANGE FOLLOWING ADVERSITY

Researchers have typically recruited study participants based on self-reports of trauma exposure (e.g., Shakespeare-Finch and Enders, 2008; Tedeschi and Calhoun, 1996) collected through clinical life event checklists that retrospectively address experiences over a specified time period (e.g., Gray et al., 2004; Norris, 1990). This method of participant recruitment typically leaves no opportunity for a comparison group, as individuals who have not experienced trauma are excluded from the sample. These event checklists focus specifically on discrete and non-normative life events that threaten the integrity of the individual or someone close to them (Gray et al., 2004). In the context of medical populations, PTG research often focuses on recruiting individuals who have had similar experiences of a particular type of trauma (e.g., cancer diagnosis and treatment; Helgeson et al., 2006).

Tedeschi and Calhoun's Posttraumatic Growth Inventory (PTGI; Tedeschi and Calhoun, 1996) is the most frequently used measure to assess PTG. The PTGI asks participants to reflect upon their lives before the traumatic event, and then asks them to identify how much they feel that they have changed in these areas since experiencing this event, and how much of that change is due specifically to the experience of trauma. This procedure is complicated, as it requires participants to complete the following steps for each possible area of change outlined in the PTGI (Ford et al., 2008): (1) deduce their current standing on the dimension, (2) recall their prior standing on the dimension before the traumatic or adverse event had occurred, (3) compare these two standings, (4) calculate the degree of change, and finally, (5) evaluate how much of the change was due to the traumatic event. Given the cognitively taxing nature of this procedure, it is not surprising that the few longitudinal studies examining the relationship between prospectively assessed growth and retrospectively perceived growth have only found small correlations (around 0.2 in Frazier et al., 2009). Asking participants to reflect upon this change in the context of a research study also has the potential to influence the responses themselves, further complicating the use of the PTGI as a measurement for true PTG.

Studies utilizing measures such as the PTGI have observed high rates of self-perceived personality change, with 58–83% of survivors of adversity and trauma reporting positive change in at least one life domain (Jayawickreme and Blackie, 2016). From these data, it would thus seem that positive personality change following adversity is ubiquitous. However, the greatest challenge with assessing change in this manner is the retrospective nature of these measures (Jayawickreme and Blackie, 2014; Tennen and Affleck, 2009). These scales rely heavily on the assumption that respondents are able to recall prior trait levels accurately. However, this assumption is inconsistent with research by personality psychologists who have examined the relationship between self-reports of change and 'real' change, finding that self-reports of perceived change are typically not indicative of the ways in which an individual has truly changed (Henry et al., 1994; Herbst et al., 2000; Robins et al., 2005).

Moreover, these measures ask participants to attribute a cause for their personality change (i.e., the amount of change they experienced *because of the traumatic event*). As Nisbett and Wilson (1977) have persuasively demonstrated, individuals likely have little or no direct introspective access to higher-order cognitive processes, meaning that they do not really know the causes for their behavioral change. Their attribution of self-perceived retrospective positive personality change from this view can be best explained as a form of cognitive dissonance, when benefits are reported after the fact to justify the experience, given that they have been primed by the questions to think specifically about change and growth in these contexts (Aronson and Mills, 1959). As traumatic experiences are unlikely to yield only positive changes, the PTGI is prone to positive response bias (Tomich and Helgeson, 2004) and overrepresentation of positive change (Park and Lechner, 2006). From this view, perhaps the most valid description for these measures may be *benefit-finding*, a form of secondary control where an individual changes the way they view the situation to see it as less threatening (Frazier et al., 2014; Rothbaum et al., 1982). Jayawickreme and Blackie (2014) have outlined four alternative explanations for retrospective reports of personality change: self-enhancement explanations invoking motivations to reaffirm important aspects of one's self-concept to feel good and confident about oneself, active coping efforts with differential effects across individuals, violation of post-event recovery expectations, and cultural scripts that promote growth following adversity.

Due to the nature of the phenomenon, research on positive personality change faces unique obstacles. The process of recruiting research participants who have experienced trauma is typically more difficult and resource-intensive than recruiting participants for studies examining other phenomena. Beyond recruitment of samples, the actual measurement of positive personality change itself faces a number of challenges, as noted above.

WHAT DO WE KNOW ABOUT POSITIVE PERSONALITY CHANGE FOLLOWING ADVERSITY?

Although we have acknowledged methodological limitations involved in existing PTG research, there are several facts that can be gleaned from current literature regarding PTG. The first of these facts is that when people are directly asked to consider the ways in which they have changed after a traumatic experience, they will often report PTG (Joseph and Linley, 2004). The extant research highlights the prevalence with which individuals perceive that they have grown as a result of adversity. Although the research does not, in our view, show evidence for normative positive personality change following adversity, the frequency of peoples' beliefs that they have changed warrants further empirical investigation of PTG.

That said, a longitudinal study by Frazier et al. (2009) was able to find empirical support for actual growth in a small number of the study's participants. However, this was not the case for the majority of the sample, although perceived growth, as assessed by the PTGI, was found to be associated with positive changes in adaptive coping strategies (Frazier et al., 2009). One possibility is that there is an antecedent relationship between the development of adaptive coping strategies after trauma and eventual true positive personality change, but the current literature has not adequately examined this possible association. This leads to the next question: what are the questions personality researchers should consider when studying the likelihood of positive personality change following adversity?

FUTURE DIRECTIONS FOR RESEARCH ON POSITIVE PERSONALITY CHANGE FOLLOWING ADVERSITY

Our review suggests that the extant literature provides a number of theoretical perspectives but little evidence for positive personality change following adversity, given the methodological limitations in much of the research. Nevertheless, this means that many unexplored questions on positive personality change following adversity remain. In this section, we outline some questions that we believe researchers should focus on:

Move Away from Retrospective Measures of Positive Personality Change

Given the limitations of retrospective self-report measures that we have described, we recommend a progression away from studies using such measures, like the PTGI, as the primary means of assessing PTG. Instead, research in the field would benefit from the use of prospective longitudinal studies to address theory-driven questions. This proposal echoes the suggestions of other researchers (e.g., Tennen and Affleck, 2009), who have emphasized the need for validated measures of self-reported PTG. The only objective way to assess actual positive personality change – that is, a change that represents improvement beyond baseline – is to collect pre-trauma baseline data and compare it to the same measures post-trauma (Jayawickreme and Blackie, 2014).

Use Alternative Methods to Global Self-Reports for Assessing Positive Personality Change

For situations where researchers are unable to collect baseline data, Helgeson's (2010) recommendation of using informant or acquaintance reports to substantiate self-reports is a practical suggestion. Personality psychologists have asserted that, in situations where researchers were not able to assess baseline levels, informant reports provide an accurate representation of an individual's behaviors and a viable alternative method of study (Furr, 2009). By corroborating self-reports of growth with acquaintance reports of growth-relevant behaviors, researchers address the limitation by which it is difficult to empirically distinguish between an individual's perceived and actual positive change. However, whereas past research has found evidence for the corroboration of PTG reports, evidence for the strength of agreement and the specific domains for which PTG is corroborated are inconsistent in the existing literature. The earliest PTG research using acquaintance reports found a small relationship ($r = .21$) between the self- and informant reports (Park et al., 1996). The strength of this agreement increased (to $r = .31$) when the researchers accounted for the closeness of the relationship between the target and the informant (Park et al., 1996). Subsequent research has found stronger agreements ($r = .40$ to $r = .69$) between self- and informant-reported PTG (McMillen and Cook, 2003; Shakespeare-Finch and Enders, 2008). These studies which found stronger agreement differed from the research by Park et al. (1996) in that the stronger relationship was found when the researchers classified traumatic experiences using clinical criteria, rather than more broadly to incorporate a wider set of adverse life events.

However, Helgeson (2010) did not find evidence of corroboration between survivors of breast cancer and their nominated informants ten years after diagnosis when using the standard and well-established PTGI. In our own work, we similarly found corroboration only for self-reported negative personality change (Blackie et al., 2015). However, we have used profile analysis procedures (Furr, 2008) to determine the degree to which participants and informants agree on which domains have relatively higher scores in the target's profile and which have relatively lower scores. These analyses found participant–informant agreement on domains of change that had relatively higher scores in the target's profile and those that had relatively lower scores. In other words, informants observed that targets had changed and were sensitive to the idiosyncratic ways in which these changes had manifested in targets' behavior, and were able to discriminate between domains of PTG in making their judgments.

Although it is undoubtedly the case that current measures of PTG are seriously flawed, we provide two reasons why we should see evidence of agreement between participants and informants as casting doubt upon the claim that self-perceived post-traumatic change is *completely* illusory (Blackie et al., 2015). First, given the likelihood that informants arrive at the same conclusions when judging the target participants, despite their own biases and prejudices, this would imply a greater likelihood that there is something objective to observe in the targets' behavior (Allport, 1937; Blackie et al., 2015). Second, showing evidence of agreement across different judges demonstrates the behavioral stability of PTG, as the positive changes are thus shown to manifest in different situations with different people (Blackie et al., 2015; Helzer et al., 2014). Showing agreement therefore provides support for the view that self-perceived post-traumatic change is not solely a reflection of the target's illusory beliefs. Informant reports can therefore be a useful tool for answering this question (Kenny and West, 2010; Vazire and Carlson, 2010).

This does not mean that using informant reports of measures such as the PTGI will completely solve matters, however. For one, PTG might manifest only as internal states (e.g., thoughts and feelings) that are less visible to informants. Also, some informants may be susceptible to shared biases stemming from their close relationship with the target participants (Frazier et al., 2014; Leising et al., 2010). For example, informants may simply be sharing stories about targets' behaviors that had been relayed to them, as opposed to actually witnessing them. In addition, participants and informants may both have a 'positivity bias', driven by a shared desire to believe that the target is coping well in the aftermath of adversity. Such a bias may artificially inflate levels of agreement between targets and informants. However, it should be noted that these forms of evaluative processes produce artificial agreement only if each pair of raters shares the same bias with each other, and this bias is moreover different from the bias shared by a different pair of raters about their own target (Blackie et al., 2015; Helzer et al., 2014; Jayawickreme and Blackie, 2016).

Another useful way to understand PTG would be through examining growth-relevant beliefs, emotions, and behaviors at the daily level. Fleeson (2014) argues that actual positive personality change manifests in state-level behaviors, necessitating the assessment of experiences as they are happening. Although Maercker and Zoellner (2004) suggest that trait reports of PTG may reflect an overall perception that an individual has changed, they emphasize that these summary claims may not be representative of actual day-to-day thoughts, emotions, and behaviors. This recommendation gets at an important challenge for developing interventions to facilitate PTG in that the intervention should, in order to contribute to actual positive personality change, impact thoughts, feelings, and behaviors relevant to domains of positive personality change, rather than trait self-reports of growth.

By employing experience sampling methodology (ESM; Conner et al., 2009; Fleeson, 2007b), researchers may be able to effectively capture participants' growth-relevant characteristics in the moment. ESM research involves asking participants to use a smartphone to complete multiple questionnaires per day for a period of several days in order to collect data about their daily processes – including their thoughts, feelings, and behaviors. Although experience sampling is another form of self-report measure, research has found that it has several advantages over trait-level self-reports, including greater ecological validity (Furr, 2009; Scollon et al., 2009) and avoidance of the memory biases common to retrospective assessment (Shiffman et al., 2008). By employing such methods, researchers can gain a broader understanding of PTG and related constructs through observable daily behaviors.

ESM can also be used to investigate the dynamic processes integral to personality change (DeYoung, 2015; Fleeson and Jayawickreme, 2015). Psychologists often conceptualize personality as a summation of general tendencies in thoughts, emotions, and behaviors – that is, people's personalities are understood by their typical dispositions. Although there are many advantages to this approach, including descriptive and predictive values (Jayawickreme et al., 2014), the density distribution of states approach may be more appropriate to reflect and predict personality (Fleeson, 2001). Additional research by Fleeson (2001, 2004, 2007a) has addressed the broad within-person variability in thoughts, feelings, and behaviors that manifests over the course of an experience sampling study.

Our lab has developed a daily measure of PTG (Blackie et al., 2017), with state items for each of the five PTG dimensions. In examining whether participants have experienced high levels of personal strength, for example, our lab tracked the frequency and duration of thoughts and feelings associated with successful coping with daily stressors (for example, 'I stayed calm' and 'I felt overwhelmed and unable to cope'). Our research found that the trait PTGI dimensions were not associated with daily PTGI (with the single exception of spirituality), casting doubt on the validity of the PTGI as a valid assessment of positive personality change in daily life (Fleeson, 2014).

Increase the Number of Longitudinal Studies Examining Positive Personality Change

Ultimately, we will not be able to draw firm conclusions on the nature and ubiquity of positive personality change following adversity without longitudinal data. Much of the confusion and controversy over the phenomenon of PTG has, in part, stemmed from inconsistent findings stemming from cross-sectional and non-longitudinal research designs. The extant longitudinal research on personality change and life events does not provide much evidence for normative positive personality change following the experience of adversity. Specht et al. (2011) did find evidence for increases in agreeableness and conscientiousness following divorce among both men and women during a four-year period, but this finding has been countered by others showing decreases in extraversion over a longer time frame (12 years; Allemand et al., 2015).

This points to another important point – identifying positive personality change following adversity may involve designs incorporating more than two waves of measurement (Bleidorn et al., 2016). Although longitudinal studies that include two waves of assessment can only be analyzed through linear change models, nonlinear or discontinuous change models – which require more than three waves of data – may be the best fit for describing how personality changes in response to adversity and other life events (Luhmann et al., 2014). Among other important questions, such designs could assess the important question of the impact of multiple life stressors on personality, and whether subsequent stressors are more or less impactful than the initial event (Bleidorn et al., 2016).

Longitudinal designs can also provide greater clarity on how adversity can lead to positive personality change. Moderators of positive personality change need to be subject to empirical verification through longitudinal design. Attachment style, social support, cognitive ability, socio-economic status, and pre-trauma adjustment are key moderators that should be tested in future research (Damian and Roberts, 2014; Fraley and Bonanno, 2004; Jayawickreme and Blackie, 2016). More knowledge is needed on the short-term processes associated with the experience of adversity and how this subsequently translates into personality change. A number of theoretical approaches have proposed frameworks for explaining how this change occurs. For example, Fleeson and Jayawickreme (2015) focus on how trait-relevant behavior is a result of expectations, goals, and other social-cognitive mechanisms triggering thoughts, feelings, and behaviors (or personality 'states') in relevant situations. In the short term, the experience of adversity will cause a shifting in personality 'states' to cope with the demands of the situation. However, depending on the nature of the adversity (i.e., whether the event impacts core beliefs and goals), the event can lead to a shifting in social-cognitive mechanisms and long-term changes in the trait. Wrzus and Roberts (2017) similarly have proposed that long-term personality development is a function of repeated short-term sequences of triggering situations, expectancies, states, and reactions. Future longitudinal work should attempt to identify the short-term processes that occur during the experience of adversity and their effect on personality (Bleidorn et al., 2016).

Broaden the Definition of Adversity Beyond Trauma, and to Other Dimensions of Personality

A review of the extant evidence should make it clear that no reliable evidence exists for the 'shattered assumptions' claim behind Tedeschi and Calhoun's theory of PTG (Jayawickreme and Blackie, 2014). Moreover, Seery and Kondrak (2014) note that traumatic events are best conceptualized as severe stressors that are, nevertheless, not qualitatively distinct from more 'everyday' adversity. Furthermore, personality researchers should broaden their focus to examine a wide range of life events that clinical researchers typically do not study. Additionally, researchers should employ a subjective criterion to distinguish adversity from other forms of life events.

Personality researchers should also consider examining traits other than those examined by PTG researchers. Although the dimensions of PTG do arguably map onto the Big Five (particularly openness and extraversion; Kandler and Specht, 2014), other traits, such as creativity (Damian and Roberts, 2014; Forgeard, 2013) may be important as well. It also may be that we do not, in fact, see positive personality change at the trait level following adversity, but instead at another layer of personality, such as in individuals' narratives (McAdams and Bowman, 2001). It is also possible that adversity may not typically lead to mean-level or rank-order positive personality change (that is, personality change at the population level) but does lead to changes in the configuration of personality changes within the individual (ipsative personality change; Bleidorn et al., 2016; Jayawickreme and Blackie, 2014).

Finally, if positive personality change following adversity in fact occurred at the narrative level of personality (Kandler and Specht, 2014), more research on identifying the value of this narrative development for well-being and adjustment is needed (Adler et al., 2016). We note, however, that were such narrative development to result in meaningful benefits for well-being and adjustment, such positive personality changes will also be seen at the trait level (Fleeson and Jayawickreme, 2015).

CONCLUSION

The field of positive personality change following adversity has been hampered by substantive measurement challenges. However, there are many exciting and appealing questions to be tested and replicated. We hope that this review inspires new and high-quality research that sheds light on whether, for whom, and how personality does change for the better following the experience of adversity.

ACKNOWLEDGMENTS

This publication discusses ideas first presented in Jayawickreme and Blackie (2014, 2016), and was supported by a grant from the John Templeton Foundation (grant #60699 to Frank Infurna and Eranda Jayawickreme). The opinions expressed in this publication are those of the authors and do not necessarily reflect the views of the John Templeton Foundation.

REFERENCES

Adler, J. M., Lodi-Smith, J., Philippe, F. L., & Houle, I. (2016). The incremental validity of narrative identity in predicting well-being: A review of the field and recommendations for the future. *Personality and Social Psychology Review, 20*, 142–175.

Affleck, G., & Tennen, H. (1996). Construing benefits from adversity: Adaptational significance and dispositional underpinnings. *Journal of Personality, 64*, 899–922.

Allemand, M., Hill, P. L., & Lehmann, R. (2015). Divorce and personality development across middle adulthood. *Personal Relationships, 22*, 122–137.

Allport, G. W. (1937). *Personality: A psychological interpretation*. Oxford, England: Holt.

Aronson, E., & Mills, J. (1959). The effect of severity of initiation on liking for a group. *Journal of Abnormal and Social Psychology, 59*, 177–181.

Blackie, L. E. R., Jayawickreme, E., Helzer, E. G., Forgeard, M. J. C., & Roepke, A. M. (2015). Investigating the veracity of self-perceived posttraumatic growth. *Social Psychological and Personality Science, 6*, 788–796.

Blackie, L. E. R., Jayawickreme, E., Tsukayama, E., Forgeard, M. J. C., Roepke, A. M., & Fleeson, W. (2017). Post-traumatic growth as positive personality change: Developing a measure to assess within-person variability. *Journal of Research in Personality, 69*, 22–32.

Blackie, L. E. R., Roepke, A. M., Forgeard, M. J. C., Jayawickreme, E., & Fleeson, W. (2014). Act well to be well: The promise of changing personality states to promote well-being. In A. C. Parks (Ed.), *Handbook of positive psychological interventions* (pp. 462–474). Oxford: Wiley-Blackwell.

Bleidorn, W., Hopwood, C. J., & Lucas, R. E. (2016). Life events and personality trait change. *Journal of Personality*. Advance online publication. doi: 10.1111/jopy.12286.

Bostock, L., Sheikh, A. I., & Barton, S. (2009). Posttraumatic growth and optimism in health-related trauma: A systematic review. *Journal of Clinical Psychology in Medical Settings, 16*, 281–296.

Calhoun, L. G., & Tedeschi, R. G. (1990). Positive aspects of critical life problems: Recollections of grief. *OMEGA – Journal of Death and Dying, 20*, 265–272.

Cann, A., Calhoun, L. G., Tedeschi, R. G., Taku, K., Vishnevsky, T., Triplett, K. N., & Danhauer, S. C. (2010). A short form of the Posttraumatic Growth Inventory. *Anxiety, Stress, & Coping, 23*, 127–137.

Caspi, A., Roberts, B. W., & Shiner, R. L. (2005). Personality development: Stability and change. *Annual Review of Psychology, 56*, 453–484.

Conner, T. S., Tennen, H., Fleeson, W., & Barrett, L. F. (2009). Experience sampling methods: A modern idiographic approach to personality research. *Social and Personality Psychology Compass, 3*, 292–313.

Damian, R. I., & Roberts, B. W. (2014). Integrating post-traumatic growth into a broader model of life experiences and personality change. *European Journal of Personality, 28*, 334–336.

DeYoung, C. G. (2015). Cybernetic big five theory. *Journal of Research in Personality, 56*, 33–58.

Edmonds, G. W., Jackson, J. J., Fayard, J. V., & Roberts, B. W. (2008). Is character fate, or is there hope to change my personality yet? *Social and Personality Psychology Compass, 2*, 399–413.

Fleeson, W. (2001). Toward a structure- and process-integrated view of personality: Traits as density distributions of states. *Journal of Personality and Social Psychology, 80*, 1011–1027.

Fleeson, W. (2004). Moving personality beyond the person–situation debate. The challenge and the opportunity of within-person variability. *Current Directions in Psychological Science, 13*, 83–87.

Fleeson, W. (2007a). Studying personality processes: Explaining change in between-persons longitudinal and within-person multilevel models. In R. W. Robins, C. R. Fraley, & R. F. Krueger (Eds.), *Handbook of research methods in personality psychology* (pp. 523–542). New York, NY: Guilford Press.

Fleeson, W. (2007b). Situation-based contingencies underlying trait-content manifestation in behavior. *Journal of Personality, 75*, 825–862.

Fleeson, W. (2014). Four ways of (not) being real and whether they are essential for post-traumatic growth. *European Journal of Personality*, *28*(4), 336–337.

Fleeson, W., & Jayawickreme, E. (2015). Whole trait theory. *Journal of Research in Personality*, *56*, 82–92.

Ford, J. D., Tennen, H., & Albert, D. (2008). A contrarian view of growth following adversity. In S. Joseph, & P. A. Linley (Eds.), *Trauma, recovery, and growth: Positive psychological perspectives on posttraumatic stress* (pp. 297–324). Hoboken, NJ: John Wiley & Sons, Inc.

Forgeard, M. J. C. (2013). Perceiving benefits after adversity: The relationship between self-reported posttraumatic growth and creativity. *Psychology of Aesthetics, Creativity, and the Arts*, *7*, 245–264.

Fraley, R. C., & Bonanno, G. A. (2004). Attachment and loss: A test of three competing models on the association between attachment-related avoidance and adaptation to bereavement. *Personality and Social Psychology Bulletin*, *30*, 878–890.

Frazier, P., Coyne, J., & Tennen, H. (2014). Post-traumatic growth: A call for less, but better, research. *European Journal of Personality*, *28*, 337–338.

Frazier, P., Tennen, H., Gavian, M., Park, C., Tomich, P., & Tashiro, T. (2009). Does self-reported posttraumatic growth reflect genuine positive change? *Psychological Science*, *20*, 912–919.

Frazier, P., Tennen, H., & Meredith, L. (2016). Three generations of research on perceived control. In John W. Reich and Frank J. Infurna (Eds.), *Perceived control: Theory, research, and practice in the first* (pp. 171–199). New York, NY: Oxford University Press.

Furr, R. M. (2008). A contrast analysis approach to change. *Educational Research and Evaluation*, *14*, 335–362.

Furr, R. M. (2009). Personality psychology as a truly behavioural science. *European Journal of Personality*, *23*, 369–401.

Gray, M. J., Litz, B. T., Hsu, J. L., & Lombardo, T. W. (2004). Psychometric properties of the life events checklist. *Assessment*, *11*, 330–341.

Helgeson, V. (2010). Corroboration of growth following breast cancer: Ten years later. *Journal Of Social And Clinical Psychology*, *29*(5), 546–574.

Helgeson, V. S., Reynolds, K. A., & Tomich, P. L. (2006). A meta-analytic review of benefit finding and growth. *Journal of Consulting and Clinical Psychology*, *74*, 797–816.

Helzer, E. G., Furr, R. M., Hawkins, A., Barranti, M., Blackie, L. E. R., & Fleeson, W. (2014). Agreement on the perception of moral character. *Personality and Social Psychology Bulletin*, *40*, 1698–1710.

Henry, B., Moffitt, T. E., Caspi, A., Langley, J., & Silva, P. A. (1994). On the 'remembrance of things past': A longitudinal evaluation of the retrospective method. *Psychological Assessment*, *6*, 92–101.

Herbst, J. H., McCrae, R. R., Costa, P. T. J., Feaganes, J. R., & Siegler, I. C. (2000). Self-perceptions of stability and change in personality at midlife: The UNC Alumni Heart Study. *Assessment*, *7*, 379–388.

Hobfoll, S. E., Hall, B. J., Canetti-Nisim, D., Galea, S., Johnson, R. J., & Palmieri, P. A. (2007). Refining our understanding of traumatic growth in the face of terrorism: Moving from meaning cognitions to doing what is meaningful. *Applied Psychology: An International Review*, *56*, 345–366.

Hudson, N. W., & Fraley, R. C. (2015). Volitional personality trait change: Can people choose to change their personality traits? *Journal of Personality and Social Psychology*, *109*, 490–507.

Janoff-Bulman, R. (1992). *Shattered assumptions: Towards a new psychology of trauma*. New York, NY: Free Press.

Jayawickreme, E., & Blackie, L. E. R. (2014). Post-traumatic growth as positive personality change: Evidence, controversies and future directions. *European Journal of Personality*, *28*, 312–331.

Jayawickreme, E., & Blackie, L. E. R. (2016). *Exploring the psychological benefits of hardship: A critical reassessment of posttraumatic growth*. Switzerland: Springer.

Jayawickreme, E., Brocato, N. W., & Blackie, L. E. R. (2017). Wisdom gained? Assessing relationships between adversity, personality and well-being among a late adolescent sample. *Journal of Youth and Adolescence*, *46*, 1179–1199.

Jayawickreme, E., Forgeard, M. J. C., & Seligman, M. E. P. (2012). The engine of well-being. *Review of General Psychology*, *16*, 327–342.

Joseph, S., & Linley, P. A. (2008). Psychological assessment of growth following adversity: A review. In S. Joseph & P. A. Linley (Eds.), *Trauma, recovery, and growth* (pp. 21–36). Hoboken, NJ: John Wiley & Sons.

Kandler, C., & Specht, J. (2014). Unravelling the post-traumatic growth paradox: Can negative experiences drive positive personality maturation? *European Journal of Personality, 28*, 341–342.

Kenny, D. A., & West, T. V. (2010). Similarity and agreement in self-and other perception: A meta-analysis. *Personality and Social Psychology Review, 14*, 196–213.

Leising, D., Erbs, J., & Fritz, U. (2010). The letter of recommendation effect in informant ratings of personality. *Journal of Personality and Social Psychology, 98*, 668–682.

Linley, P. A., & Joseph, S. (2004). Positive change following trauma and trauma: A review. *Journal of Traumatic Stress, 17*, 11–21.

Lüdtke, O., Roberts, B. W., Trautwein, U., & Nagy, G. (2011). A random walk down university avenue: Life paths, life events, and personality trait change at the transition to university life. *Journal of Personality and Social Psychology, 101*, 620–637.

Luhmann, M., Orth, U., Specht, J., Kandler, C., & Lucas, R. E. (2014). Studying changes in life circumstances and personality: It's about time. *European Journal of Personality, 28*, 256–266.

Maercker, A., & Zoellner, T. (2004). The Janus face of self-perceived growth: Toward a two-component model of posttraumatic growth. *Psychological Inquiry, 15*, 41–48.

McAdams, D. P. (1994). Can personality change? Levels of stability and growth in personality across the life span. In T. F. Heatherton, & J. L. Weinberger (Eds.), *Can personality change?* (pp. 299–313). Washington, DC: American Psychological Association.

McAdams, D. P., & Bowman, P. J. (2001). Narrating life's turning points: Redemption and contamination. In D. P. McAdams, R. Josselson, & A. Lieblich (Eds.), *Turns in the road: Narrative studies of lives in transition* (pp. 3–34). Washington, DC: American Psychological Association.

McAdams, D. P., & de St. Aubin, E. (1992). A theory of generativity and its assessment through self-report, behavioral acts, and narrative themes in autobiography. *Journal of Personality and Social Psychology, 62*, 1003–1015.

McAdams, D. P., Reynolds, J., Lewis, M., Patten, A. H., & Bowman, P. J. (2001). When bad things turn good and good things turn bad: Sequences of redemption and contamination in life narrative and their relation to psychosocial adaptation in midlife adults and in students. *Personality and Social Psychology Bulletin, 27*, 474–485.

McMillen, J. C., & Cook, C. L. (2003). The positive by-products of spinal cord injury and their correlates. *Rehabilitation Psychology, 48*, 77–85.

Nisbett, R. E., & Wilson, T. D. (1977). Telling more than we can know: Verbal reports on mental processes. *Psychological Review, 84*, 231–259.

Norris, F. H. (1990). Screening for traumatic stress: A scale for use in the general population. *Journal of Applied Social Psychology, 20*, 1704–1715.

Pals, J. L., & McAdams, D. P. (2004). The transformed self: A narrative understanding of posttraumatic growth. *Psychological Inquiry, 15*, 65–69.

Park, C. L. (2004). The notion of growth following stressful life experiences: Problems and prospects. *Psychological Inquiry, 15*, 69–76.

Park, C. L. (2010). Making sense of the meaning literature: An integrative review of meaning making and its effects on adjustment to stressful life events. *Psychological Bulletin, 136*, 257–301.

Park, C. L., Cohen, L. H., & Murch, R. L. (1996). Assessment and prediction of stress-related growth. *Journal of Personality, 64*, 71–105.

Park, C. L., & Lechner, S. C. (2006). Measurement issues in assessing growth following stressful life experiences. In L. G, Calhoun, & R. G. Tedeschi (Eds.), *Handbook of posttraumatic growth: Research and practice* (pp. 47–67). Mahwah, NJ: Lawrence Erlbaum.

Parkes, C. M. (1971). Psycho-social transitions: A field for study. *Social Science and Medicine, 5*, 101–115.

Pillemer, D. B. (1998). *Momentous events, vivid memories*. Cambridge, MA: Harvard University Press.

Prati, G., & Pietrantoni, L. (2009). Optimism, social support, and coping strategies as factors contributing to posttraumatic growth: A meta-analysis. *Journal of Loss and Trauma, 14*, 364–388.

Robins, R. W., Noftle, E. E., Trzesniewski, K. H., & Roberts, B. W. (2005). Do people know how their personality has changed? Correlates of perceived and actual personality change in young adulthood. *Journal of Personality, 73*, 489–521.

Rothbaum, F., Weisz, J. R., & Snyder, S. S. (1982). Changing the world and changing the self: A two-process model of perceived control. *Journal of Personality and Social Psychology, 42*, 5–37.

Ryff, C. D. (1989). Happiness is everything, or is it? Explorations on the meaning of psychological well-being. *Journal of Personality and Social Psychology, 57*, 1069–1081.

Scheier, M. F., & Carver, C. S. (1985). Optimism, coping, and health: Assessment and implications of generalized outcome expectancies. *Health Psychology, 4*, 219–247.

Scollon, C., Prieto, C. K., & Diener, E. (2009). Experience sampling: Promises and pitfalls, strength and weaknesses. In E. Diener (Ed.), *Assessing well-being: The collected works of Ed Diener* (pp. 157–180). New York, NY: Springer Science + Business Media.

Seery, M. D., Holman, E. A., & Silver, R. C. (2010). Whatever does not kill us: Cumulative lifetime trauma, vulnerability, and resilience. *Journal of Personality and Social Psychology, 99*, 1025–1041.

Seery, M. D., & Kondrak, C. L. (2014). Does trauma lead to 'special' growth? *European Journal of Personality, 28*, 348–350.

Shakespeare-Finch, J., & Enders, T. (2008). Corroborating evidence of posttraumatic growth. *Journal of Traumatic Stress, 21*, 421–424.

Shiffman, S., Stone, A. A., & Hufford, M. R. (2008). Ecological momentary assessment. *Annual Review of Clinical Psychology, 4*, 1–32.

Smith, B. (1992). *A tree grows in Brooklyn*. New York, NY: Random House.

Specht, J., Egloff, B., & Schmukle, S. C. (2011). Stability and change of personality across the life course: The impact of age and major life events on mean-level and rank-order stability of the Big Five. *Journal of Personality and Social Psychology, 101*, 862–882.

Sutin, A. R., Costa, P. T., Wethington, E., & Eaton, W. W. (2010). Turning points and lessons learned: Stressful life events and personality trait development across middle adulthood. *Psychology and Aging, 25*, 524–533.

Taylor, S. E., & Armor, D. A. (1996). Positive illusions and coping with trauma. *Journal of Personality, 64*, 873–898.

Tedeschi, R. G., Addington, E., Cann, A., & Calhoun, L. G. (2014). Post-traumatic growth: Some needed corrections and reminders. *European Journal of Personality, 28*, 350–351.

Tedeschi, R. G., & Calhoun, L. G. (1995). *Trauma and transformation: Growing in the aftermath of suffering*. Thousand Oaks, CA: Sage.

Tedeschi, R. G., & Calhoun, L. G. (1996). The Posttraumatic Growth Inventory: Measuring the positive legacy of trauma. *Journal of Traumatic Stress, 9*, 455–471.

Tedeschi, R. G., & Calhoun, L. G. (2004). Posttraumatic growth: Conceptual foundations and empirical evidence. *Psychological Inquiry, 15*, 1–18.

Tennen, H., & Affleck, G. (1998). Personality and transformation in the face of adversity. In R. G. Tedeschi, C. Park, & L. G. Calhoun (Eds.), *Posttraumatic growth: Positive changes in the aftermath of crisis* (pp. 65–98). Mahwah: NJ: Lawrence Erlbaum.

Tennen, H., & Affleck, G. (2002). Benefit-finding and benefit-reminding. In C. R. Snyder, & S. J. Lopez (Eds.), *Handbook of positive psychology*. (pp. 584–597). New York, NY: Oxford University Press.

Tennen, H., & Affleck, G. (2009). Assessing positive life change: In search of meticulous methods. In C. L. Park, S. C. Lechner, M. H. Antoni, & A. L. Stanton (Eds.), *Medical illness and positive life change: Can crisis lead to personal transformation?* (pp. 31–49). Washington, DC: American Psychological Association.

Tomich, P. L., & Helgeson, V. S. (2004). Is finding something good in the bad always good? Benefit finding among women with breast cancer. *Health Psychology, 23*, 16–23.

Vazire, S., & Carlson, E. N. (2010). Self-knowledge of personality: Do people know themselves? *Social and Personality Psychology Compass, 4*, 605–620.

Wrzus, C., & Roberts, B. W. (2017). Processes of personality development in adulthood: The TESSERA framework. *Personality and Social Psychology Review, 21*, 253–277.

Self-Sacrifice for a Cause: A Review and an Integrative Model

Jocelyn J. Bélanger, Birga M. Schumpe, Bhavna Menon, Joanna Conde Ng and Noëmie Nociti

'He who has a why to live for can bear almost any how'. – Friedrich Nietzsche

For thousands of years, theologians, philosophers, and dramatists have attempted to offer consolation for the inevitable tragedy that awaits us all: death. Some believe in an afterlife; others prefer to enjoy life while it lasts – but regardless of how we cope with the truth, at some level, we are all preoccupied by the coming of death, the moment when the matter that constitutes our bodies stops functioning. Suicide bombers unsettle this firmly established belief by trampling on the fundamental notion of self-preservation. But how do they willingly walk into the jaws of death? Surely, something must be wrong with them.

In reality, self-sacrifice is commonplace among living organisms. Even at the cellular level, bacteria are known to self-destruct when attacked by a bacteriophage to prevent parasite transmission to nearby relatives (a process also known as 'abortive infection'; Fineran et al., 2009; O'Connor et al., 1999; Refardt et al., 2013). The practice even extends to the insect world, where many species of ants and termites have perfected the gruesome art of blowing themselves up – long before terrorist groups such as Al-Qaeda and ISIS even existed. In a process known as 'autothysis' (Maschwitz and Maschwitz, 1974), minor worker ants in the *Camponotus cylindricus complex* can violently contract their abdomens until their body walls split open and compounds from the mandibular gland are ejected onto the body and limbs of the predator (Davidson et al., 2009, 2012; Jones et al., 2004). Worker ants display this behavior when defending their territory (Davidson et al., 2012; Jones et al., 2004), and termite species also use similar processes for tunnel defense during raids (Bordereau et al., 1997). Similarly, in a phenomenon called 'sting autotomy', workers in many honeybee and wasp species subject themselves to a slow death by pricking the skin of predators with a well-developed barbed sting lancet. When a honeybee worker stings a predator, the apparatus remains firmly fixed in the skin tissue of the victim with these barbs (Sakagami and Akahira, 1960). Other self-sacrificing behaviors observed among birds and mammals (e.g., squirrels, monkeys, and macaques) include alarm calling, which attracts the attention of the predator to the caller, reducing its own chances of survival while allowing others a quick escape (Cheney and Seyfarth, 1985; Dunford, 1977; Hollen and Radford, 2009). Although the modes and mechanisms of self-sacrifice are diverse, there is one common pattern that underlies all – the sacrificing organism is attempting to defend, protect, or empower its group to ensure its survival.

Without a shadow of doubt, under remarkable circumstances, humans can also muster the requisite will to engage in self-sacrificial behavior to protect a band of brothers, a nation, or a cause in peril. However, there are many reasons to believe that self-sacrifice at the human level is far more intricate than for many other organisms. First, people can choose from a wide range of self-sacrificial behaviors to support a cause of their liking. All exact some sort of cost, but some are clearly more mundane than others, and few are life-threatening decisions. Consequently, the study of self-sacrifice cannot be limited to understanding the small number of men and women who spectacularly obliterate themselves for different political or religious motives; our analysis must be less granular and more inclusive so that we may fully comprehend these acts. Furthermore, unlike any other species, humans are selective about the groups with which they identify, and their proclivity for a particular group may drastically change over time, reflecting our social and cognitive complexity and the fact that the willingness to die for a specific group is reversible. As such, there are many psychological forces at play that compel individuals to engage in cost-bearing behaviors. This brings the question of the psychological process that enables people to engage in self-sacrificial behavior of varying intensities into the forefront: what are the characteristics of these groups and ideologies for which individuals are willing to risk life and limb?

THE PRESENT CHAPTER

In this chapter, we review recent progress related to the psychology of self-sacrifice. This chapter begins by defining what self-sacrifice is as an object of study and how it is conceptualized and measured as an individual difference. The notion of self-sacrifice will then be situated among other related constructs to emphasize its unique contribution to psychological science. Once its nomological network has been delimited, we discuss several motivational components relevant to self-sacrifice using the 3N model of radicalization (Kruglanski et al., 2014b; Webber and Kruglanski, 2016) as an integrative framework. Finally, we review research on the interpersonal dimension of self-sacrifice and discuss potential research questions that can be fruitfully probed in the future.

DEFINING SELF-SACRIFICE

Self-sacrifice is defined as the psychological readiness to suffer and die for a cause (Bélanger et al., 2014). A breakdown of this definition indicates that self-sacrifice has a motivational component (i.e., readiness), it involves a cost (e.g., suffering, death), and it has an ideological component (e.g., a cause). The construct of self-sacrifice is thus an individual difference, a trait relatively stable across time (Bélanger et al., 2014), which – like most psychological constructs – can momentarily fluctuate following short-lived experimental inductions (Dugas et al., 2016; see also Kruglanski and Sheveland, 2012). It is also important to underscore that the willingness to self-sacrifice does not equate wanting to die; it rather reflects people's disposition to do so if necessary. Because the willingness to self-sacrifice can be situationally induced and is not associated with psychological distress, we posit that self-sacrifice is not a construct that is in the realm of abnormal psychology. Given this definition, self-sacrifice and the concept of martyrdom are considered functionally equivalent and interchangeable.

SELF-SACRIFICE AS COUNTERFINALITY

The study of human motivation is facilitated by mapping out people's mental representation of goals and their respective means of attainment. One approach that is particularly useful for this exercise is goal-systems theory (Kruglanski et al., 2002), which posits that goals are knowledge structures organized into associative networks (see also Anderson, 1983; Anderson et al., 2004). From this vantage point, the theory proposes three means–goal configurations that have unique psychological properties and implications for goal pursuit: (1) means that serve a single purpose (unifinal means), (2) means that concomitantly serve multiple goals (multifinal means), and (3) means that serve a single goal but are detrimental to alternative goals (counterfinal means; for a review, see Kruglanski et al., 2015a). In line with this nomenclature, engaging in self-sacrifice is quintessentially counterfinal, as it entails engaging in an activity (e.g., detonating a bomb belt) to attain a focal goal (e.g., furthering one's ideological cause) at the expense of an alternative goal (e.g., one's life). The same can be said about less extreme forms of self-sacrifice, such as going on a hunger strike, breaking the law, or donating money to an organization, if these behaviors are pursued in the furtherance of an ideological cause.

Why would anyone choose to perform an activity knowing that it would undermine the pursuit of other goals? The research has revealed that part of the answer lies in the fact that the costs associated with counterfinal means give them the appearance of being particularly effective or instrumental in attaining the focal goal they purportedly serve (Bélanger et al., 2016). In a series of experiments, Schumpe et al. (2017) demonstrated that the greater the perceived sacrifice is (e.g., pain, cost, effort), the greater the perceived means' instrumentality is for the goal. This 'no pain, no gain' type of heuristic was demonstrated to be stronger for individuals who are highly committed to both the focal and alternative goal. The implications of these findings for political activism are particularly interesting. For example, by studying a group of environmentalists, Schumpe and Bélanger (2017) revealed that extreme forms of activism – such as risky or illegal activities – were perceived as more effective in advancing the environmental cause because they were perceived as detrimental to the pursuit of other goals (e.g., avoiding being in harm's way).

Because counterfinal means appear to maximize the expectancy of goal achievement, sacrificing important life domains becomes particularly alluring when a goal appears out of reach. Bélanger et al. (2016) found support for this proposition by having participants evaluate the effectiveness of different means related to the pursuit of academic and romantic goals. Counterfinal means – such as neglecting sleep to study or neglecting one's friends to spend time with one's partner – were consistently shown to be preferred over other types of means for goal pursuit when participants were uncertain about reaching their focal goal. Hence, as the saying goes, sometimes the 'end justifies the means', and people willingly sacrifice objects of value to reach a goal that is considered important. Consistent with this perspective, Schumpe and Bélanger (2017) surveyed hundreds of environmentalists to gauge their willingness to self-sacrifice to protect the environment: the more they believed their cause was unlikely to succeed, the greater their motivation was to jump into the fray and risk life and limb for the cause. Further experiments revealed that making sacrifices increased people's commitment toward the cause; this observation is consistent with Bem's (1972) self-perception theory, which stipulates that 'individuals come to "know" their own attitudes, emotions, and other internal states partially by inferring them from observations of their own overt behavior and/or the circumstances in which this behavior occurs' (p. 1). In that regard, when the sacrifice is costlier, the commitment toward the cause and the intention of engaging in further sacrifice is stronger. Although preliminary in nature, these findings are indicative of a possible self-reinforcing cycle that can spiral out of control and ultimately produce detrimental outcomes.

DISTINGUISHING CONCEPTS

The concept of self-sacrifice bears some resemblance to many other psychological constructs. Thus, it is worth positioning this construct to underscore its unique properties. Again, a goal-systemic analysis appears to be useful in drawing these distinctions.

Goal Commitment

Self-sacrifice is intimately related to goal commitment, which is commonly defined as 'one's attachment to or determination to reach a goal' (Locke et al., 1988, p. 24). Indeed, it would be troubling to find individuals contemplating death for a cause without attributing considerable importance to it. However, goal commitment is relatively non-specific about concrete behavior (i.e., means) and generally involves persistence and the extension of effort (Wright et al., 1994).

Conversely, martyrdom is more specific, as it uniquely relates to sacrificial behaviors (i.e., means neglecting alternative goals) and is performed with the intention of advancing a cause.

Altruism

Another construct with which self-sacrifice shares similarities is that of altruism. The concept of altruism has long been discussed across almost all known fields, from theology to biology (Post et al., 2002), and there is still much debate related to its definition. We consider two definitions taken from the psychological literature and cover them in turn. The first is from Bar-Tal and Raviv (1982): the authors define altruism as a 'voluntary and intentional behavior carried out for its own end to benefit a person, as a result of moral conviction in justice, and without expectations for external rewards' (p. 199). The concept of self-sacrifice herein described contrasts with this definition in that self-sacrifice can be pursued for convictions unrelated to justice and with the expectation of reward such as praise and group recognition. The second definition is from Krebs and Miller (1985), who argue that genuine altruism 'involves the capacity in humans to behave in a manner that enhances the net welfare of another at some net cost to themselves' (p. 2). This is connected to the idea that altruism is strongly related to prosocial behavior (e.g., Batson and Shaw, 1991). However, this is not necessarily the case with sacrifice as it can promote peaceful or harmful behavior equally.

Furthermore, we note that, in psychology, altruism tends to be defined as a personality trait affecting a large spectrum of helping behaviors (Batson, 1987; Eisenberg, 1986; Rushton et al., 1981; for a discussion, see Carlo et al., 1991). Both altruism and self-sacrifice are conceptually related to notions of self-effacement and action on behalf of others; however, self-sacrifice promotes self-effacement for a specific cause. Notice also that altruism does not necessarily entail relinquishing objects of high value (e.g., well-being, wealth), whereas this is part and parcel of our self-sacrifice definition.

Egalitarianism

Self-sacrifice also bears some similarities with the concept of egalitarianism. Egalitarianism is the belief that all individuals have the right to equal opportunities and treatment (Monteith and Walters, 1998), such that an egalitarian is defined as 'anyone who cares at all about equality over and above the extent it promotes other ideals' (Temkin, 1993, p. 7). Accordingly, someone genuinely concerned about equality may make important sacrifices to help others in need, such as foregoing privileges and neglecting important life domains to foster equality. Self-sacrifice, as we have defined it here, is not always pursued to attain equality. In fact, self-sacrifice is often a means to benefit one's group over another to make it more competitive. Even in relation to one's own group, self-sacrifice could result in the person becoming disadvantaged compared to his or her counterparts.

MEASURING SELF-SACRIFICE

The scientific examination of any construct requires proper operationalization and measurement. Self-sacrifice is no exception; below, we offer a selective review of methods that have been used in prior works to measure self-sacrifice.

Explicit Measure: The Self-Sacrifice Scale

The Self-Sacrifice Scale (Bélanger et al., 2014) is a self-report measure designed to measure individuals' disposition to forfeit objects of high value (e.g., wealth, relationships, life) to support an ideological cause. The participants are first prompted to write down a cause that is important to them. The participants then respond to the ten items on the scale, five of which are reverse-scored. Sample items include statements such as, 'I would be prepared to endure intense suffering if it meant defending an important cause' and 'I would be ready to give my life for a cause that is extremely dear to me'. The participants rate each item on a seven-point scale ranging from 1 (*Do not agree at all*) to 7 (*Very strongly agree*). The Self-Sacrifice Scale has been translated in numerous languages (Arabic, French, Hebrew, Italian, Spanish, Tagalog, and Tamil), and its psychometric properties have been validated with samples of terrorists (i.e., Tamil Tigers and jihadists), activists (e.g., the Black Lives Matter movement, feminists, environmentalists), and ordinary people, making the Self-Sacrifice Scale uniquely positioned to empirically examine a vast repertoire of cognitive, emotional, and behavioral phenomena.

Using the Self-Sacrifice Scale, researchers (Bélanger et al., 2014) have recently made significant progress in mapping the nomological network of self-sacrifice. Consistent with our conceptual analysis, self-sacrifice and altruism have been found to be positively correlated, albeit weakly ($r = 0.20$), supporting the notion that both constructs are distinct. Believing in God also tends to be positively related to self-sacrifice, which is not surprising given that the vast majority of religious participants we have surveyed adhered to an Abrahamic religion (i.e., Christianity, Islam, Judaism), where the theme of self-sacrifice is recurrent (e.g., Jesus Christ on the cross, shahid, *kedoshim*).

The Self-Sacrifice Scale has also been useful in drawing important theoretical insights. For example, one of the strongest predictors of self-sacrifice is the extent to which an individual believes that a cause is *important* to them (Bélanger et al., 2014). Although this result is unsurprising, it is worth noting that having a positive attitude toward a given cause was found to be insufficient in predicting self-sacrifice for a cause. The latter finding fits well with recent motivation theories on the distinction between *liking* and *wanting* in goal pursuit (Kruglanski et al., 2015c). However, more fundamentally, this finding provides some evidence that self-sacrifice is related to the internalization of a cause in people's identities, which may explain why identity-related concepts such as harmonious and obsessive passion (Bélanger et al., 2013a, 2013b; Vallerand et al., 2003) are both positively associated with self-sacrifice (Bélanger et al., 2014). Understanding the process through which the ideological cause becomes deep-seated in the self is a critical question we address at a later stage.

Another meaningful piece of information taken from this research is the absence of correlation between the Self-Sacrifice Scale and different criteria of psychopathology, such as depression, suicide ideation, and psychopathy (Bélanger et al., 2014). Indeed, one perennial question in terrorism studies is the connection between mental illness and violent extremism (e.g., Weatherston and Moran, 2003). For many years, a common view was that to commit these gruesome acts of the lowest nature, violent extremists had to be deranged lunatics. This jaundiced view of a terrorist's psyche has drastically changed over the years, and most scholars today would admit that suicide terrorism bears no systematic relationship to psychopathology (e.g., Atran, 2003; Merari, 2010; Post et al., 2009; cf. Lankford, 2014). Data collected using the Self-Sacrifice Scale support this perspective. Furthermore, in addressing the notion of a 'terrorist's profile' – which is another major question in terrorism studies – no zero-order correlations were found between the Self-Sacrifice Scale and the Big Five personality traits (Bélanger et al., 2014). If anything, our data suggest that, in some samples, men tend to report greater willingness to self-sacrifice for a cause. Preliminary evidence also suggests that the relationship between gender and self-sacrifice is mediated by sensation-seeking (Bélanger and Schumpe, 2017).

One's place on the Self-Sacrifice Scale also influences a range of interpersonal and moral decisions by dictating who is right and wrong on certain issues. For example, self-sacrifice also predicts the extent to which people are prone to feel angry and lack sympathy toward people who do not respect their cause. Moreover, a positive relationship was found between one's readiness to self-sacrifice and perceiving other people self-sacrificing for the same cause as righteous and heroic. This finding resonates well with prior findings that people who share similar goals and values (e.g., in-group members) are perceived as more moral than individuals espousing different goals and values (e.g., Brewer and Campbell, 1976; Leach et al., 2007; Levine and Campbell, 1972).

Last, in samples of terrorists (Tamil Tigers) and environmental activists, people's readiness to self-sacrifice was demonstrated to positively predict their willingness to engage in illegal means to further their respective cause (Bélanger et al., 2014). In the case of the Tamil Tigers, this included support for suicide bombing as a means of furthering their ethnonationalist agenda. For environmentalists, this included physically harming people and sabotaging polluting industries. However, we should be careful in interpreting these results as saying that self-sacrifice unconditionally predicts violence. As discussed later in this chapter, ideological beliefs play a critical role in shaping one's proclivity toward peaceful or destructive means to further one's cause.

Implicit Measure: The Boom Task

Although self-report measures represent one of the most important tools in social psychology, there are several caveats associated with their use. A classic issue tends to be social desirability (i.e., the need of participants to 'obtain approval by responding in a culturally appropriate and acceptable manner'; Crowne and Marlowe, 1960, p. 353). Paulhus and John (1998) have posited the existence of two distinct, socially desirable responses: self-deceptive enhancement and impression management. The former refers to the tendency to cast oneself in a positive light due to an overly confident self-image (Paulhus and John, 1998), whereas the latter refers to 'a deliberate attempt to distort one's responses in order to create a favorable impression with others' (Barrick and Mount, 1996, p. 262). Bélanger and colleagues (2014) evinced that self-sacrifice was not correlated with self-deceptive enhancement and only weakly correlated ($r = 0.09$) with impression management. Therefore, social desirability does not have a strong influence on participants' responses to the Self-Sacrifice Scale.

Another foreseeable issue with the self-report measure is participants' unwillingness to report their genuine attitudes, fearing that this could create trouble with law enforcement agencies. This could indeed be a real problem if an inmate attains an extremely high score on the Self-Sacrifice Scale (e.g., dying for Daesh's ideology); jailers could use this information as an excuse for severe punishments. To circumvent these caveats, social psychologists have developed implicit measures that preclude participants from controlling their responses and relying on introspection. The participants' reaction times to experimental stimuli are measured in milliseconds and are compared to neutral, baseline stimuli. Such measures exist for a wide range of psychological attitudes (e.g., self-esteem, stereotypes), and self-sacrifice is no exception. Furthermore, the interpretation of these results requires relatively sophisticated data analytical skills; therefore, the risk associated with these measures (e.g., if they were intercepted by uninvited third parties) is greatly reduced from an ethical standpoint.

The implicit measure of self-sacrifice, the 'Boom Task' (Bélanger et al., 2014), involves participants playing a science-fiction computer game. The storyline is purposely unrealistic to prevent participants' ideological adherences from interfering with the task. Specifically, the participants play the role of a space traveler whose spaceship is invaded by aliens who aim to destroy humanity. The participants' mission, should they choose to accept it, is to save the human race by neutralizing the enemy using a bomb belt, which is presumably strapped to their chest. During the task, the participants explore the spaceship in search of the alien threat and are exposed to different stimuli. The participants are instructed to press the 'A' key when they see an alien, to blow themselves up and neutralize the threat, or press the 'L' key to holster their bomb when presented with a neutral image. The participants are instructed to respond as quickly and accurately as possible to the images. Prior to playing the game, the participants are shown all stimuli: four neutral images (a chair, a computer, a lamp, and a table) and one target image (alien). These images are randomly shown except for the alien image, which always comes last. The purpose of showing the alien image last is that it would not be logical for participants to detonate their bomb belts repeatedly. The participants' response latencies (measured in milliseconds) to the neutral images are compared to the alien image – quicker responses to the latter compared to the former indicate a greater proclivity to self-sacrifice. Research using this paradigm has demonstrated that the Self-Sacrifice Scale predicts how quickly participants press the detonator versus how quickly they holster their bomb (Bélanger et al., 2014). Reaction times to the Boom Task can be altered using different motivational inductions in the laboratory.

Decision-Making and Behavioral Measures

Psychologists have also relied on numerous decision-making and behavioral paradigms to measure people's willingness to self-sacrifice. One method is the use of a vignette-like scenario, also referred to as the 'trolley problem' (see Foot, 1967; Greene et al., 2001, 2009). There are several variations of this paradigm, but most involve telling the participants that a train hurtling down the tracks will kill several people if nothing is done to stop it. Whether the people being saved are in-group or out-group members can be altered to present a different version of this dilemma. Ultimately, participants are given the fictitious choice of either jumping on the tracks to stop the train (and save the people's lives) or passively watch the macabre spectacle. This paradigm has been successfully used in prior research (Orehek et al., 2014; Swann et al., 2014), and our own results indicate that participants' decision to stop the train is also positively correlated with their responses to the Self-Sacrifice Scale. Although the task is easy to administer, a sacrificial dilemma such as the trolley problem has recently been heavily criticized by several authors, such as Bauman and colleagues (2014). Their critique is threefold: '(1) they are amusing rather than sobering, (2) they are unrealistic and unrepresentative of the moral situations people encounter in the real world, and (3) they do not elicit the same psychological processes as other moral situations' (p. 536). The authors contend that the participants are extremely familiar with this paradigm, and as a result, the task is likely to elicit rehearsed responses. Supporting this view, Chandler et al. (2013) have reported that Mechanical Turk workers' familiarity with the task can range from 30% up to 85%, depending on their percentile of activity on this online platform. Considering these findings, it may be advantageous from a methodological and theoretical standpoint for researchers to study self-sacrifice using more realistic paradigms. In other words, the participants can talk the talk, but do they walk the walk when it comes to supporting the cause they presumably cherish? To answer this question, Bélanger et al. (2014; Study 4) had participants partake in a pain study, whereby they were told that, for each teaspoon of hot sauce they ate (i.e., tabasco sauce), the experimenter would give $1 to a charity of their choice. The task is endless, and people are allowed to eat as much hot sauce as they can or want. Typically, the participants eat three teaspoons of sauce, but there is significant variation (from zero to 30 teaspoons). In principle, the number of teaspoons of hot sauce that the participants eat reflects their willingness to self-sacrifice for this cause and, indeed, there is a positive correlation between the participants' placement on the Self-Sacrifice Scale and the number of teaspoons of hot sauce they eat (Bélanger et al., 2014).

Another method of studying self-sacrifice is through a donation paradigm, whereby participants are given the choice of giving (or not) real money to a charity associated with their cause. This approach measures two dimensions: (1) people's choice to engage in a cost-bearing behavior and, if so, (2) the magnitude of such a sacrifice (i.e., the amount of money donated to the cause). Using this paradigm with a sample of Christian participants, the ratings on the Self-Sacrifice Scale predicted how much money they donated to an organization whose mission was to protect Christians persecuted in the Middle East (Bélanger et al., 2014). Self-sacrifice was unrelated to giving money to a cause different from their own, attesting to the notion that self-sacrifice is associated with ideologically specific behavior.

THE 3N APPROACH TO SELF-SACRIFICE

The foregoing discussion gives us the lay of the land on self-sacrifice to tackle some of the biggest questions in this line of research, including the nature of (1) the motivational forces that compel individuals to engage in personally cost-bearing behavior, (2) the group and ideological features that make people more apt to sacrifice for the causes, and (3) the psychological processes through which people become devoted martyrs. In the present section, we review evidence collected both in the field and from lab experiments around the world to elucidate these questions and present the 3N theory of radicalization (Kruglanski et al., 2014b; Webber and Kruglanski, 2016) to integrate these findings into a comprehensive theoretical framework. However, we first turn to the concept of radicalization, which is interwoven with the concept of self-sacrifice. Understanding how both are connected will be useful to our analysis.

Radicalization is commonly defined as 'the social and psychological process of incrementally experienced commitment to extremist political or religious ideology' (Horgan, 2009, p. 152). Radicalization is not specific to any political or religious ideology, nor does it entail engaging in violence. According to Kruglanski and colleagues (2014b), radicalization may be experienced through different degrees of increasing intensity, whereby higher levels of radicalization represent greater 'imbalance between the focal goal served by the extreme behavior and other common ends that people have' (p. 71). At the lower end of the spectrum, people may simply agree with the group's ideology (passive support). At higher intensity levels, the individual becomes directly engaged in behaviors to further the cause (participation). Ultimately, when an individual is radicalized at the highest level, that person becomes ready to sacrifice everything, including his or her life, for the ideology. How, then, does the journey of radicalization begin?

THEORETICAL PRINCIPLES

The 3N theory postulates that radicalization occurs as a result of the confluence of three elements: Needs, Network, and Narrative.

Rather than being a list of additive factors that contribute to people's willingness to self-sacrifice, the theory also attempts to explicate the process of radicalization through these components. The Need element pertains to individuals' quest for personal significance, the desire to matter and to have respect in one's own eyes and those of others who are important (Kruglanski et al., 2009, 2013, 2014b, 2015b). Personal significance loss can be induced by any personal experience that injures an individual's sense of self-worth, including humiliation, stigmatization, or being afflicted by a sense of injustice (Dugas et al., 2016). Individuals seeking significance are likely to turn to group ideologies and collectivistic goals to restore their lost significance: group membership tends to be rewarded with prestige, status, resources, and a sense of belonging (e.g., Tajfel and Turner, 1979). This propensity to turn to groups when in need of significance is called a *collectivistic shift* (Kruglanski and Orehek, 2011; Kruglanski et al., 2013). The second N is the social Network in which individuals are embedded, which dictates how one should behave to gain status and recognition from the group. Embedded in such groups is an ideological component – the third N of the theory, the Narrative – in which the norms and values of comrades progressively permeate the person's identity and serve as a moral compass. The ideological narrative prescribes what is acceptable and what is worth defending at all costs. Some narratives may encourage building peace and equality through justice and conciliation, whereas others may glorify extreme aggression against the enemies of one's group and push individuals toward violent extremism.

THE EMPIRICAL EVIDENCE

A burgeoning body of empirical evidence supports the 3N model of radicalization.

It includes surveys and experiments performed in laboratory and field settings in a variety of locations and conflict zones. Research on the Need component of the 3N theory has been particularly substantial. For example, in a sample of Iraqi and Palestinian refugees, Dugas et al. (2016) found a negative relationship between feeling significant and willingness to self-sacrifice. Different ways of manipulating the feeling of significance have been utilized by the same authors, such as recalling a time when one felt socially rejected, falling short of accomplishing something meaningful, or having a low score on an IQ test. In all cases, these conceptually similar manipulations rendered the participants more prone to self-sacrifice for a cause. Dugas and colleagues also found that the relationship between significance loss and willingness to self-sacrifice for a cause was mediated by people's search for meaning in life. Furthermore, people recalling a time when they self-sacrificed for a cause (vs. recalling a positive memory) increased their personal significance. The latter results suggest that making sacrifices in the name of a cause is a more effective means to achieve a sense of significance than the pursuit of pleasurable activities – a set of findings that resonate well with the principles of existential and humanistic psychology, which connects self-transcendence (detachment from self-interest in the pursuit of a cause) and meaning in life (Frankl, 2000; Maslow, 1966; May, 1953).

Could this search for meaning also explain why people embrace unspeakable atrocities? In an attempt to answer this question, Bélanger and colleagues (2017) recently surveyed almost a thousand Canadians and measured how socially alienated they felt (a proxy for insignificance) with items such as 'I feel that Canadian society despises who I am' and 'I no longer support the way the Canadian government administers the country'. Consistent with our expectations, the participants' social alienation positively predicted support for violence against civilians and infrastructure and support for radical groups engaging in these various forms of violent activism. Similar patterns of results were obtained with a terrorist sample of 241 members of the LTTE (Liberation Tigers of Tamil Eelam), such that personal insignificance (i.e., feeling small, worthless, and hopeless) positively predicted their willingness to self-sacrifice for their group, which in turn predicted their support for the armed struggle to establish a separate state (Bélanger, 2013).

Other researchers from different theoretical perspectives have also theorized and adduced evidence in support of the Need component discussed in the 3N model of radicalization. For example, Terror Management Theory (TMT; see Burke et al., 2010, for a review) posits that humans are subject to existential anxiety. To counteract the fear of meaninglessness (existential angst), individuals ascribe great importance to cultural worldviews that provide a framework for understanding the universe in which they live by defining the beliefs, practices, and aspirations that are worth attaining. As a result, those who adhere to different cultural practices are often derogated. Among the lines of evidence marshaled in support of this thesis is TMT's demonstration that individuals who are reminded of their own mortality (the ultimate threat to one's significance) defend their cultural worldviews with great fervor (e.g., Greenberg et al., 1990). For example, Christian students reminded of their own mortality (vs. not reminded about their mortality) evaluated a Christian more positively and a Jew more negatively. In relation to self-sacrifice, inducing mortality salience in a sample of Iranian students resulted in increased positive attitudes toward someone wanting to die as a suicide bomber attacking the United States and greater willingness to join this cause (Pyszczynski et al., 2006). In the control condition, the participants had a more pacifistic stance and reported more favorable attitudes toward someone who spoke against martyrdom attacks and greater willingness to join a cause that did not support suicide bombings. Similarly, Routledge and Arndt (2008) evinced that mortality salience (vs. a control group) made British participants more prone to self-sacrifice for England. However, mortality salience only had this sort of impact when the group was described as transient. When the group was described as immortal, the participants who were subjected to the mortality salience condition did not report greater willingness to die for the sake of the group. Altogether, these results suggest that self-sacrifice is a means to feel significant when one's significance is under threat. By being registered in the collective memory of one's group, individuals can psychologically transcend death and live on in the memories of others (Elster, 2005).

As mentioned earlier, the Need and Network components are intimately related in that, once the significance quest is awakened, people are inclined to join a group to quench their thirst for meaning and recognition. This propensity to turn to groups is often referred to as a *collectivistic shift* (Kruglanski and Orehek, 2011; Kruglanski et al., 2013), and evidence related to this principle abounds. For example, in a survey distributed across 12 Arab nations, less life success (i.e., insignificance) was positively correlated with people's tendency to self-identify as members of a collectivity (e.g., their nation or their religion) rather than as individuals (Kruglanski et al., 2012). Similarly, experimental inductions of personal uncertainty have also been demonstrated to increase identification with cohesive groups (Hogg et al., 2007; Reid and Hogg, 2005).

At a certain point, it is said that a person's identity fuses with that of the group – that is, 'their personal self (characteristics of individuals that make them unique) joins with a social self (characteristics of individuals that align them with groups)' (Buhrmester and Swann, 2015, p. 1), and they come to experience a sense of 'oneness' with other group members. When this transformation occurs, individuals become empowered (strength in numbers), and they gradually become devoted to the defense of their group, even at the expense of their own lives (Atran et al., 2014; Kruglanski et al., 2013; Sheikh et al., 2016). In their systematic investigation of the psychological changes that occur when individuals define themselves as group members, Orehek and colleagues (2014) demonstrated that

> interdependent self-construals, compared to independent self-construals, attenuate death anxiety, reduce the avoidance of death, increase the approach to death-related stimuli, induce a greater willingness to become a martyr, and induce a greater willingness to sacrifice the self for other members of important groups. (p. 265)

In summary, when one's identity fuses with the identity of the group, that individual may be more willing to engage in cost-bearing behavior to support the group.

How does this process of fusion operate exactly? In a series of experiments, Swann et al. (2014) found that when 'fused' participants were made to believe that they shared core characteristics (e.g., genes, values) with other group members, their willingness to sacrifice themselves for the group was magnified. Furthermore, identity fusion with the group, coupled with beliefs in shared characteristics, led fused individuals to project familial ties on its members, which in turn made them more prone to self-sacrifice for the group, regardless of whether these characteristics were positive or negative.

Note that there is a connection between the concept of identity fusion, familial ties, and terrorism. One of the landmark findings in terrorism studies is the role of social networks in the process of radicalization. Specifically, one of the most robust risk factors associated with joining a violent extremist group is knowing someone who belongs to a radical organization. For example, Sageman (2008) reports that, for Al-Qaeda, 'about two-thirds of the people in the sample were friends with other people who joined together or already had some connection to terrorism' (p. 66). Similar findings were also reported by Della Porta (1988) with members of the Brigate Rosse, in which 69% of Italian left-wing militants who joined the group had been friends with at least one member before joining. In other words, it appears that people may be inclined to join radical movements because they already have strong affinities and common experiences with some of their members, which facilitates the projection of familial ties onto them. These ties are not only imagined but are often real. Terrorism often runs in families, as can be attested by the number of siblings who engage in violence: the Tsarnaev brothers (Boston bombings), the Kouachi brothers (Charlie Hebdo attacks), and the Bakraoui brothers (Brussels attacks) are a few examples.

We now turn to the last N of our model, the (ideological) Narrative to which individuals are exposed through the group. Here, we define ideologies as ideas and beliefs that influence people's decision-making and goal-related behavior – 'prepackaged units of interpretation that spread because of basic human motives to understand the world, avoid existential threats and maintain valued interpersonal relationships' (Jost et al., 2008, p. 1). As mentioned earlier, ideological narratives dictate how the person ought to behave to gain significance. Indeed, making sacrifices at the behest of these ideological imperatives can elevate one to a legendary status, an incentive rarely matched elsewhere. However, not all ideologies are created equal. Put simply, some ideas appear more worthy of sacrifice than others. In keeping with this view, scholars have recently introduced the notion of *sacred values* to refer to ideologies that have the necessary psychological hook to imbue their adepts with extraordinary determination to defend them. Formally, sacred values are defined as 'nonnegotiable preferences whose defense compels actions beyond…calculable costs and consequences' (Atran, 2016, p. 2; see also Ginges et al., 2007). Sacred values include religious (e.g., Islam, Christianity, ancestral land) and secular beliefs (e.g., human rights, democracy). Those who adhere to these sacred values are referred to as 'devoted actors' (Atran 2016; Atran et al., 2007), who behave based on what feels morally 'right' as opposed to what is rational (i.e., cost–benefit analysis). Devoted actors are immune to the temptation of materialistic concessions. In fact, such a proposition (e.g., trading ancestral land for cash) may foment moral outrage and violent actions (Dehghani et al., 2010; Ginges et al., 2007). Similar reactions would also be expected if the existence of the group holding the values was threatened in some way. In line with the devoted actor's model, Sheikh and colleagues (2016) demonstrated that Moroccans who hold sharia as a sacred value reported a greater willingness to die for sharia and support a militant jihad in comparison to those who did not believe in such a value (Sheikh et al., 2016). This effect was even stronger for individuals whose identity was fused with a kin-like group of friends. In a subsequent study, the interaction between sacred values and group-identity fusion was stronger for individuals whose democratic values were considered to be under threat (e.g., Spaniards considering the imposition of sharia in Spain).

In summary, the 3N model of radicalization appears particularly useful for understanding the psychological underpinnings of martyrs by integrating various theoretical perspectives into a unified framework. Although we discussed them separately, the three factors discussed in this chapter – Need, Network, and Narrative – operate in concert rather than in isolation from one another. To summarize, individuals transition from wanting significance to joining a powerful group to which they become fused, which in turn leads them to project familial ties and adhere to sacred values. When these values are imperiled, fighting against its detractors becomes a moral obligation, and those willing to answer the call of duty are bestowed with significance and glory.

INFLUENCE OF SELF-SACRIFICE ON OTHERS

In the previous sections of this chapter, we discussed various psychological forces that compel one to defend an idea or a group of like-minded individuals, regardless of the personal cost. Although all sacrifices involve a personal cost (e.g., enduring pain, losing one's life), most have far-reaching social implications. Indeed, people commonly neglect others (e.g., friends and family) to achieve their ideological ambitions. Much of what we know about the interpersonal consequences of self-sacrifice has not emerged from the confines of terrorism studies but from industrial-organizational psychology and, more specifically, from its vast literature on leadership. This may appear paradoxical because people commonly assume that, in the competitive world of organizations, successful leaders are 'snakes in suits' (Babiak and Hare, 2006) – ruthless, if not psychopathic, individuals who are incapable of empathy and who would not hesitate to throw people under the bus to rise to the top. Stated differently (and perhaps more nicely), sacrificing oneself for an organization appears at odds with the harsh and cruel corporate environment in which sacrificing employees (i.e., issuing a pink slip) is acceptable, if not desirable, in the name of profitability. However, history is rife with fully dedicated industry and military leaders who are willing to forego all for their organization in times of hardship. One classic example is American automobile executive Lee Iacocca, who sacrificed his own annual salary – down to US $1 – in a (successful) attempt to turn Chrysler around (Iacocca and Novak, 1984). One explanation for this outstanding volte-face is Iacocca's ability to convince his employees of the 'need for sacrifice and extra effort' (Bass, 1985, p. 15). It appears that, under certain circumstances, leaders' sacrifices can be contagious, providing their troops with an iron will to achieve specific organizational objectives. In fact, several authors have argued that this could be one of the reasons why revolutionary movements, such as Daesh (also referred to as ISIS, the Islamic State of Iraq and Syria), have been able to triumph, or at least resist against all odds, over more potent foes (e.g., Arreguin-Toft, 2001; Atran and Ginges, 2012).

Who are these people who are capable of inspiring such unwavering commitment? According to Conger and Kanungo (1994), they are charismatic leaders, people with the remarkable ability to 'formulate and articulate an inspirational vision' (Conger and Kanungo, 1994, p. 442) and to 'transform the follower's individual needs to the common need for the organization' (Choi and Mai-Dalton, 1998, p. 492). These are the type of leaders who galvanize their followers with an inspirational ideology to which they become faithful, respectful, and emotionally attached. How do charismatic leaders achieve such a feat? By and large, they pursue their vision by sacrificing objects of value for the organization. In other words, they engage in sacrificial (i.e., counterfinal) behaviors that display unequivocally to group members that they have skin in the game, that they are committed to the organization.

According to Choi and Mai-Dalton's (1998) analytical model of leadership, leaders can display self-sacrifice in three major organizational areas: (1) division of labor, (2) distribution of rewards, and (3) distribution of power. In the *division of labor*, leaders can engage voluntarily in more 'risky and/or arduous actions, tasks, turns, or segments of work in organizational settings' (Choi and Mai-Dalton, 1998, p. 478). At this level, the leader 'takes one for the team' and assumes all responsibility for negative outcomes. In the *distribution of rewards*, leaders can forego or postpone their share of organizational rewards, such as salaries, promotions, and benefits. A leader may resort to such behavior during an organizational crisis to signal the severity of the situation and demonstrate his or her dedication to the success of the organization. Last, in the *distribution of power*, leaders may forego exercising their privileges, such as abstaining from exercising their power in their positions despite having the right to do so.

Choi and Mai-Dalton (1999) evinced that leaders who self-sacrifice for the organization can have three major types of impact on their followers. First, leaders who make sacrifices tend to be perceived as more charismatic than leaders who do not; they inspire admiration, trust, and loyalty (Conger, 1989; Conger and Kanungo, 1987; House and Shamir, 1993; Yukl, 1994). Second, sacrificial leaders are perceived as more legitimate; they are viewed as having the proper status to lead and exert influence over others. Third, leaders play an important role in shaping the culture of their organizations. Because they are perceived as the epitome of virtue, self-sacrificial leaders build a norm of reciprocity. In line with their organizational role, followers are expected to adhere to the group norms and sacrifice for the organization. As a result, the practice of self-sacrifice is fostered and reinforced across the organization.

The latter mechanism is clearly apparent in Japan, where workers' devotion and sacrifice for the organization is practically unmatched. Herbig and Palumbo (1994) note that the amount of time expended at one's workplace is a symbolic statement of submission to the organization and leaders. Although overtime work statistics are severely underestimated due to unpaid and unlogged extracurricular work, on average, Japanese white-collar workers typically work 60–70 hours a week (Herbig and Palumbo, 1994). According to Tugawa (1991), of the paid holidays to which Japanese workers are entitled, more than 50% are not taken (Tugawa, 1991). However, to what extent and at what cost are Japanese workers willing to demonstrate such devotion to their companies? How can this bear any resemblance to the extreme forms of martyrdom we have discussed previously? The answer to both questions is an extreme form of workaholism – Karoshi, or death from overwork.

Karoshi is described as a 'fatal condition in which the living rhythm of a human being is collapsed due to excessive fatigue and the life maintenance function is ruined' (Kanai, 2009, p. 1). Victims of Karoshi characteristically sacrifice themselves for approximately 3,000–3,500 hours a year, working 14-hour days and seven days a week, resulting in their death at an average age of 40 years (Herbig and Palumbo, 1994). As Herbig and Palumbo (1994) stated, 'the economic ants are literally working themselves to death for the betterment of the colony' (p. 12). Although there are no official statistics, the National Defense Counsel for Victims of Karoshi (2017) estimates that the number of Karoshi victims reaches up to 10,000 deaths a year. In comparison, Japan recorded 4,411 traffic-related deaths in 2012 (*Japan Times*, 2013). Although it may appear that Karoshi is on the extreme end of cases, it is nevertheless a real phenomenon that demonstrates the ends to which individuals are willing to go to sacrifice for their organization. It displays the extent of workers' willingness to give, quite literally, their all – their personal interests, well-being, and health – for their organization.

CONCLUDING REMARKS

The study of self-sacrifice has generated a fascinating empirical literature at the intersection of anthropology, biology, criminology, social cognition, and political science. As the present chapter attests, there is a notable dialectic between field work and experimental research conducted in this area. As a result of this multidisciplinary and cross-cultural work, the study of self-sacrifice has matured tremendously over a short period. Additionally, it is relatively clear now that attitudes such as the willingness to die for a cause, once thought to be an irregularity of the mind, are in fact swayed profoundly by powerful social forces. If anything, being dedicated to a cause to the point at which one's self-interest is entirely subjugated by a higher cause is not irrational but, rather, a principled element of group survival. However, as we have seen through the lens of the 3N model of radicalization, self-sacrifice is not entirely a selfless act. Someone who fights tooth and nail for an ideal transforms from being a 'speck of dust in an uncaring universe' (Arie Kruglanski, personal communication, February 14, 2017) to a glorious hero who is remembered eternally in the collective memory of his or her group (e.g., Dugas et al., 2016; Elster, 2005; Kruglanski et al., 2009). As Kruglanski et al. (2009) note, 'paradoxically, *the willingness to die in an act of suicidal terrorism may be motivated by the desire to live forever*' (p. 336).

Arguably, one of psychology's most important goals is to reduce people's suffering and find ways to foster harmony in intergroup relations. The importance of this mission is conspicuous: we live in an increasingly splintered, yet fundamentally interdependent, world. Therefore, at this juncture, we believe that one of the most important challenges facing psychologists today is to find ways to temper zealotry and excessive commitment to groups. Although 'living passionately' is often touted as the ultimate maxim for success in life, when pursued obsessively (see Bélanger et al., 2015; Lafrenière et al., 2011; Vallerand et al., 2003), passions may abrogate one's moral bind to the law (Gousse-Lessard et al., 2013), promote moral disengagement (see Bandura, 1999), and result in the justification of violence. This echoes Descartes' (1649/1972) idea that passions can be ecstatic and helpful as long as they are somewhat constrained by reason. Thus, inoculating young members of our society against the lure of radical forces and rechanneling their motivation for significance toward peaceful groups and ideologies appear key to reducing violent extremism. These are pressing concerns because it is generally recognized that the problem of terrorism is not diminishing and, indeed, constitutes a serious threat to world security and stability. Critically, as noted by some of the leading experts in the field, 'our understanding of the causal processes of disengagement from terrorism remains theoretical or speculative' (Gill et al., 2015, p. 245). This is due to a general lack of evaluation in the field of counter-radicalization (Rabasa et al., 2010) and a complete absence of randomized controlled trials – the gold standard of scientific testing (Shadish et al., 2002) – to examine the impact of intervention methods on violent extremists (Gielen, 2015). Koehler (2016) notes that deradicalization 'remains one of the most under researched fields, which is even more surprising, as the connection to successful counter-terrorism, peacekeeping, and counter-radicalization policies is obvious' (p. 290).

We would like to conclude on a positive note by pointing out that researchers have recently made encouraging progress in helping people leave terrorism behind. Preliminary evidence for the effectiveness of the 3N model on deradicalization comes from a recent field study by Kruglanski and colleagues (2014a). This research was conducted with 1,906 members of the Liberation Tigers of Tamil Eelam (LTTE) who were detained in various deradicalization centers across Sri Lanka. The program aimed to address the detainees' 3Ns by having a group of detainees engage in a series of programs (e.g., educational, vocational, psychosocial, and creative therapies). The control group in this study did not have access to such opportunities. Psychological surveys were administered twice over a nine-month period. The results indicated that the Tamil Tigers' support for armed struggle significantly declined in the rehabilitation group but not in the control condition. These results provide partial support for the notion that addressing people's needs, narratives, and networks can be useful for promoting sustained deradicalization. However, a full understanding of how the 3Ns can be utilized to promote deradicalization requires careful attention to the cognitive and emotional processes underlying these effects. Clearly, a great deal of research is necessary before the 'art of deradicalization' can be mastered such that individuals may avoid ideologies legitimizing violence. Hopefully, this chapter will help stimulate further interest in this fascinating area of inquiry.

REFERENCES

Anderson, J. R. (1983). *The architecture of cognition*. Cambridge, MA: Harvard University Press.

Anderson, J. R., Bothell, D., Byrne, M. D., Douglass, S., Lebiere, C., & Qin, Y. (2004). An integrated theory of the mind. *Psychological Review, 111*, 1036–1060.

Arreguin-Toft, I. (2001). How the weak win wars: A theory of asymmetric conflict. *International Security, 26*, 93–128.

Atran, S. (2003). Genesis of suicide terrorism. *Science, 299*, 1534–1539.

Atran, S. (2016). The devoted actor: Unconditional commitment and intractable conflict across cultures. *Current Anthropology, 57*, S192–S203.

Atran, S., Axelrod, R., & Davis, R. (2007). Sacred barriers to conflict resolution. *Science, 317*, 1039–1040.

Atran, S., & Ginges, J. (2012). Religious and sacred imperatives in human conflict. *Science, 336*, 855–857.

Atran, S., Sheikh, H., & Gomez, A. (2014). Devoted actors sacrifice for close comrades and sacred cause. *Proceedings of the National Academy of Sciences, 111*, 17702–17703.

Babiak, P., & Hare, R. D. (2006). *Snakes in suits: When psychopaths go to work*. New York, NY: Regan Books.

Bandura, A. (1999). Moral disengagement in the perpetration of inhumanities. *Personality and Social Psychology Review, 3*, 193–209.

Barrick, M. R., & Mount, M. K. (1996). Effects of impression management and self-deception on the predictive validity of personality constructs. *Journal of Applied Psychology, 81*, 261–272.

Bar-Tal, D., & Raviv, A. (1982). A cognitive-learning model of helping behavior development: Possible implications and applications. In N. Eisenberg (Ed.), *The development of prosocial behavior* (pp. 199–217). New York, NY: Academic Press.

Bass, B. M. (1985). *Leadership and performance beyond expectations*. New York, NY: Collier Macmillan.

Batson, C. D. (1987). Prosocial motivation: Is it ever truly altruistic? *Advances in Experimental Social Psychology, 20*, 65–122.

Batson, C. D., & Shaw, L. L. (1991). Evidence for altruism: Toward a pluralism of prosocial motives. *Psychological Inquiry, 2*, 107–122.

Bauman, C. W., McGraw, A. P., Bartels, D. M., & Warren, C. (2014). Revisiting external validity: Concerns about trolley problems and other sacrificial dilemmas in moral psychology. *Social and Personality Psychology Compass, 8*, 536–554.

Bélanger, J. (2013). *The psychology of martyrdom* (Doctoral dissertation). Retrieved from the Digital Repository at the University of Maryland. (2013-06-28T06:25:42Z)

Bélanger, J. J., Caouette, J., Sharvit, K., & Dugas, M. (2014). The psychology of martyrdom: Making the ultimate sacrifice in the name of a cause. *Journal of Personality and Social Psychology, 107*, 494–515.

Bélanger, J. J., Lafrenière, M. A. K., Vallerand, R. J., & Kruglanski, A. W. (2013a). Driven by fear: The effect of success and failure information on passionate individuals' performance. *Journal of Personality and Social Psychology, 104*, 180–195.

Bélanger, J. J., Lafreniere, M. A. K., Vallerand, R. J., & Kruglanski, A. W. (2013b). When passion makes the heart grow colder: The role of passion in alternative goal suppression. *Journal of Personality and Social Psychology, 104*, 126–147.

Bélanger, J. J., McCaffery, P., Richardson, L., Lafrenière, M.-A. K., & Framand, K. (2017). *Support for extremist groups: Construct validity and psychometric properties of the Social Alienation and the Normative Beliefs Toward Political Violence Scales*. Unpublished manuscript.

Bélanger, J. J., Pierro, A., Kruglanski, A. W., Vallerand, R. J., De Carlo, N., & Falco, A. (2015). On feeling good at work: The role of regulatory mode and passion in psychological adjustment. *Journal of Applied Social Psychology, 45*, 319–329.

Bélanger, J. J., & Schumpe, B. M. (2017). *Gender and self-sacrifice: The role of sensation-seeking*. Unpublished manuscript.

Bélanger, J. J., Schumpe, B., Lafrenière, M.-A. K., Giacomantonio, M., Brizi, A., & Kruglanski, A. W. (2016). Beyond goal-commitment: How expectancy shapes means evaluation. *Motivation Science, 2*, 67–84.

Bem, D. J. (1972). Self-perception theory. *Advances in Experimental Social Psychology, 6*, 1–62.

Bordereau, C., Robert, A., Van Tuyen, V., & Peppuy, A. (1997). Suicidal defensive behaviour by frontal gland dehiscence in *Globitermes sulphureus* Haviland soldiers (Isoptera). *Insectes Sociaux, 44*, 289–297.

Brewer, M. B., & Campbell, D. T. (1976). *Ethnocentrism and intergroup attitudes: East African evidence*. Beverly Hills, CA: Sage.

Buhrmester, M. D., & Swann, W. B. (2015). Identity Fusion. *Emerging Trends in the Social and Behavioral Sciences: An Interdisciplinary, Searchable, and Linkable Resource*.

Burke, B. L., Martens, A., & Faucher, E. H. (2010). Two decades of terror management theory: A meta-analysis of mortality salience research. *Personality and Social Psychology Review, 14*, 155–195.

Carlo, G., Eisenberg, N., Troyer, D., Switzer, G., & Speer, A. L. (1991). The altruistic personality: In what contexts is it apparent? *Journal of Personality and Social Psychology, 61*, 450–458.

Chandler, J., Mueller, P., & Paolacci, G. (2013). Nonnaïveté among Amazon Mechanical Turk workers: Consequences and solutions for behavioral researchers. *Behavioral Research Methods, 46*, 112–130.

Cheney, D. L., & Seyfarth, R. M. (1985). Social and non-social knowledge in vervet monkeys. *Philosophical Transactions of the Royal Society of London, B: Biological Sciences, 308*, 187–201.

Choi, Y., & Mai-Dalton, R. R. (1998). On the leadership function of self-sacrifice. *The Leadership Quarterly, 9*, 475–501.

Choi, Y., & Mai-Dalton, R. R. (1999). The model of followers' responses to self-sacrificial leadership: An empirical test. *The Leadership Quarterly, 10*, 397–421.

Conger, J. A. (1989). *The charismatic leader: Behind the mystique of exceptional leadership*. San Francisco, CA: Jossey-Bass.

Conger, J. A., & Kanungo, R. N. (1987). Toward a behavioral theory of charismatic leadership in organizational settings. *Academy of Management Review, 12*, 637–647.

Conger, J. A., & Kanungo, R. N. (1994). Charismatic leadership in organizations: Perceived behavioral attributes and their measurement. *Journal of Organizational Behavior, 15*, 439–452.

Crowne, D. P., & Marlowe, D. (1960). A new scale of social desirability independent of psychopathology. *Journal of Consulting Psychology, 24*, 349–354.

Davidson, D. W., Anderson, N. F., Cook, S. C., Bernau, C. R., Jones, T. H., Kamariah, A. S., ... & Clark, D. A. (2009). An experimental study of microbial nest associates of Borneo's exploding ants (Camponotus [Colobopsis] species). *Journal of Hymenoptera Research, 18*, 341–360.

Davidson, D. W., Salim, K. A., & Billen, J. (2012). Histology of structures used in territorial combat by Borneo's 'exploding ants'. *Acta Zoologica, 93*, 487–491.

Dehghani, M., Atran, S., Iliev, R., Sachdeva, S., Medin, D., & Ginges, J. (2010). Sacred values and conflict over Iran's nuclear program. *Judgment and Decision Making, 5*, 540–546.

Della Porta, D. (1988). Recruitment processes in clandestine political organizations: Italian left-wing terrorism. *International Social Movement Research, 1*, 155–169.

Descartes, R. (1972). Les passions de l'âme [The passions of the soul]. In E. S. Haldane & G. Ross (Trans.), *The philosophical works of Descartes*. Cambridge, MA: Cambridge University Press. (Original work published 1649.)

Dugas, M., Bélanger, J. J., Moyano, M., Schumpe, B. M., Kruglanski, A. W., Gelfand, M. J., & Nociti, N. (2016). The quest for significance motivates self-sacrifice. *Motivation Science, 2*, 15–32.

Dunford, C. (1977). Kin selection for ground squirrel alarm calls. *The American Naturalist, 111*, 782–785.

Eisenberg, N. (1986). *Altruistic cognition, emotion, and behavior*. Hillsdale, NJ: Erlbaum.

Elster, J. (2005). Motivations and beliefs in suicide missions. In D. Gambetta (Ed.), *Making sense of suicide missions* (pp. 233–258). New York, NY: Oxford University Press.

Fineran, P. C., Blower, T. R., Foulds, I. J., Humphreys, D. P., Lilley, K. S., & Salmond, G. P. (2009). The phage abortive infection system, ToxIN, functions as a protein–RNA toxin–antitoxin pair. *Proceedings of the National Academy of Sciences, 106*, 894–899.

Foot, P. (1967). The problem of abortion and the doctrine of double effect. *Oxford Review, 5*, 5–15.

Frankl, V. E. (2000). *Man's search for ultimate meaning*. New York, NY: Basic Books.

Gielen, A. J. (2015). Supporting families of foreign fighters. A realistic approach for measuring the effectiveness. *Journal for Deradicalization, 2*, 21–48.

Gill, P., Bouhana, N., & Morrison, J. (2015). Individual disengagement from terrorism. In C. KennedyPipe, G. Clubb, & S. Mabon (Eds.), *Terrorism and political violence* (pp. 243–257). London: Sage.

Ginges, J., Atran, S., Medin, D., & Shikaki, K. (2007). Sacred bounds on rational resolution of violent political conflict. *Proceedings of the National Academy of Sciences, 104*, 7357–7360.

Gousse-Lessard, A. S., Vallerand, R. J., Carbonneau, N., & Lafrenière, M. A. K. (2013). The role of passion in mainstream and radical behaviors: A look at environmental activism. *Journal of Environmental Psychology, 35*, 18–29.

Greenberg, J., Pyszczynski, T., Solomon, S., Rosenblatt, A., Veeder, M., Kirkland, S., & Lyon, D. (1990). Evidence for terror management theory II: The effects of mortality salience on reactions to those who threaten or bolster the cultural worldview. *Journal of Personality and Social Psychology, 58*, 308–318.

Greene, J. D., Cushman, F. A., Stewart, L. E., Lowenberg, K., Nystrom, L. E., & Cohen, J. D. (2009). Pushing moral buttons: The interaction between personal force and intention in moral judgment. *Cognition, 111*, 364–371.

Greene, J. D., Sommerville, R. B., Nystrom, L. E., Darley, J. M., & Cohen, J. D. (2001). An fMRI investigation of emotional engagement in moral judgment. *Science, 293*, 2105–2108.

Herbig, P. A., & Palumbo, F. (1994). The effect of culture on the adoption process: a comparison of Japanese and American behavior. *Technological Forecasting and Social Change, 46*, 71–101.

Hogg, M. A., Sherman, D. K., Dierselhuis, J., Maitner, A. T., & Moffitt, G. (2007). Uncertainty, entitativity, and group identification. *Journal of Experimental Social Psychology, 43*, 135–142.

Hollen, L. I., & Radford, A. N. (2009). The development of alarm call behaviour in mammals and birds. *Animal Behaviour, 78*, 791–800.

Horgan, J. (2009). *Walking away from terrorism: Accounts of disengagement from radical and extremist movements*. London: Routledge.

House, R. J., & Shamir, B. (1993). Towards the integration of transformational, charismatic, and visionary theories. In M. M. Chemers & R. Ayman (Eds.), *Leadership theory and research: Perspectives and directions*. San Diego, CA: Academic Press.

Iacocca, L. A. & Novak, W. (1984). *Iacocca: An autobiography*. New York, NY: Bantam Books.

Fewest traffic deaths seen since '51. (2013, January 5). *The Japan Times*. Retrieved from http://www.japantimes.co.jp/news/2013/01/05/news/fewest-traffic-deaths-seen-since-51/#.WKFTWG996Uk

Jones, T. H., Clark, D. A., Edwards, A. A., Davidson, D. W., Spande, T. F., & Snelling, R. R. (2004). The chemistry of exploding ants, *Camponotus* spp.(*cylindricus* complex). *Journal of Chemical Ecology, 30*, 1479–1492.

Jost, J. T., Ledgerwood, A., & Hardin, C. D. (2008). Shared reality, system justification, and the relational basis of ideological beliefs. *Social and Personality Psychology Compass, 2*, 171–186.

Kanai, A. (2009). 'Karoshi (work to death)' in Japan. *Journal of Business Ethics, 84*, 209–216.

Koehler, D. (2016). *Understanding deradicalization: Methods, tools and programs for countering violent extremism*. London: Routledge.

Krebs, D. L., & Miller, D. T. (1985). Altruism and aggression. In G. Lindzey & E. Aronson (Eds.), *The handbook of social psychology* (3rd ed.). New York: Random House.

Kruglanski, A. W., Bélanger, J. J., Gelfand, M., Gunaratna, R., Hettiarachchi, M., Reinares,

F., & Sharvit, K. (2013). Terrorism: A (self) love story. *American Psychologist, 68,* 559–575.

Kruglanski, A. W., Chen, X., Dechesne, M., Fishman, S., & Orehek, E. (2009). Fully committed: Suicide bombers' motivation and the quest for personal significance. *Political Psychology, 30,* 331–357.

Kruglanski, A. W., Chernikova, M., Babush, M., Dugas, M., & Schumpe, B. M. (2015a). The architecture of goal systems: Multifinality, equifinality, and counterfinality in means–end relations. *Advances in Motivation Science, 2,* 69–98.

Kruglanski, A. W., Gelfand, M. J., Bélanger, J. J., Gunaratna, R., & Hetiarachchi, M. (2014a). Deradicalizing the Liberation Tigers of Tamil Eelam (LTTE): Some preliminary findings. In A. Silke (Ed.), *Prisons, terrorism and extremism: Critical issues in management, radicalization and reform* (pp. 183–196). London: Routledge.

Kruglanski, A. W., Gelfand, M. J., Bélanger, J. J., Hetiarachchi, M., & Gunaratna, R. (2015b). Significance quest theory as the driver of radicalization towards terrorism. In J. Jerard & S. M. Nasi (Eds.), *Resilience and resolve: Communities against terrorism* (pp. 17–30). London: Imperial College Press.

Kruglanski, A. W., Gelfand, M. J., Bélanger, J. J., Sheveland, A., Hetiarachchi, M., & Gunaratna, R. (2014b). The psychology of radicalization and deradicalization: How significance quest impacts violent extremism. *Political Psychology, 35,* 69–93.

Kruglanski, A. W., Gelfand, M. J., & Gunaratna, R. (2012). Terrorism as means to an end: How political violence bestows significance. In P. R. Shaver & M. Mikulincer (Eds.), *Meaning, mortality, and choice: The social psychology of existential concerns* (pp. 203–212). Washington, DC: American Psychological Association.

Kruglanski, A. W., Jasko, K., Chernikova, M., Milyavsky, M., Babush, M., Baldner, C., & Pierro, A. (2015c). The rocky road from attitudes to behaviors: Charting the goal systemic course of actions. *Psychological Review, 122,* 598–620.

Kruglanski, A. W., & Orehek, E. (2011). The role of quest for significance in motivating terrorism. In J. Forgas, A. Kruglanski, & K. Williams (Eds.), *Social conflict and aggression* (pp. 153–164). New York, NY: Psychology Press.

Kruglanski, A. W., Shah, J. Y., Fishbach, A., Friedman, R., Chun, W. Y., & Sleeth-Keppler, D. (2002). A theory of goal-systems. *Advances in Experimental Social Psychology, 34,* 311–378.

Kruglanski, A. W., & Sheveland, A. (2012). Thinkers' personalities: On individual differences in the processes of sense making. In S. T. Fiske and C. N. Macrae (Eds.), *Sage handbook of social cognition* (pp. 474–494). Thousand Oaks, CA: Sage.

Lafrenière, M. A. K., Bélanger, J. J., Sedikides, C., & Vallerand, R. J. (2011). Self-esteem and passion for activities. *Personality and Individual Differences, 51,* 541–544.

Lankford, A. (2014). Précis of the myth of martyrdom: What really drives suicide bombers, rampage shooters, and other self-destructive killers. *Behavioral and Brain Sciences, 37,* 351–362.

Leach, C. W., Ellemers, N., & Barreto, M. (2007). Group virtue: The importance of morality (vs. competence and sociability) in the positive evaluation of in-groups. *Journal of Personality and Social Psychology, 93,* 234–249.

Levine, R. A., & Campbell, D. T. (1972). *Ethnocentrism: Theories of conflict, ethnic attitudes, and group behavior.* New York, NY: Wiley.

Locke, E. A., Latham, G. P., & Erez, M. (1988). The determinants of goal commitment. *Academy of Management Review, 13,* 23–39.

Maschwitz, U., & Maschwitz, E. (1974). Platzende Arbeiterinnen: Eine neue Art der Feindabwehr bei sozialen Hautflüglern. *Oecologia, 14,* 289–294.

Maslow, A. (1966). Comments on Dr. Frankl's paper. *Journal of Humanistic Psychology, 6,* 107–112.

May, R. (1953). *Man's search for himself.* New York, NY: Norton.

Merari, A. (2010). *Driven to death: Psychological and social aspects of suicide terrorism.* Oxford: Oxford University Press.

Monteith, M. J., & Walters, G. L. (1998). Egalitarianism, moral obligation, and prejudice-related personal standards. *Personality and Social Psychology Bulletin, 24,* 186–199.

National Defense Counsel for Victims of Karoshi (2017, January 30). Retrieved from http://karoshi.jp/english/overwork1.html

O'Connor, L., Tangney, M., & Fitzgerald, G. F. (1999). Expression, regulation, and mode of action of the AbiG abortive infection system of Lactococcus lactis subsp. cremoris UC653. *Applied and Environmental Microbiology, 65*, 330–335.

Orehek, E., Sasota, J. A., Kruglanski, A. W., Dechesne, M., & Ridgeway, L. (2014). Interdependent self-construals mitigate the fear of death and augment the willingness to become a martyr. *Journal of Personality and Social Psychology, 107*, 265–275.

Paulhus, D. L., & John, O. P. (1998). Egoistic and moralistic biases in self-perception: The interplay of self-deceptive styles with basic traits and motives. *Journal of Personality, 66*, 1025–1060.

Post, J. M., Ali, F., Henderson, S. W., Shanfield, S., Victoroff, J., & Weine, S. (2009). The psychology of suicide terrorism. *Psychiatry: Interpersonal and Biological Processes, 72*, 13–31.

Post, S. G., Underwood, L. G., Schloss, J. P., & Hurlbut, W. B. (2002). *Altruism and altruistic love: Science, philosophy, and religion in dialogue*. Oxford: Oxford University Press.

Pyszczynski, T., Abdollahi, A., Solomon, S., Greenberg, J., Cohen, F., & Weise, D. (2006). Mortality salience, martyrdom, and military might: The great Satan versus the axis of evil. *Personality and Social Psychology Bulletin, 32*, 525–537.

Rabasa, A., Pettyjohn, S. L., Ghez, J. J., & Boucek, C. (2010). *Deradicalizing Islamist extremists*. Santa Monica, CA: Rand.

Refardt, D., Bergmiller, T., & Kümmerli, R. (2013). Altruism can evolve when relatedness is low: Evidence from bacteria committing suicide upon phage infection. *Proceedings of the Royal Society of London, Series B: Biological Sciences, 280*, 20123035.

Reid, S. A., & Hogg, M. A. (2005). Uncertainty reduction, self-enhancement, and ingroup identification. *Personality and Social Psychology Bulletin, 31*, 804–817.

Routledge, C., & Arndt, J. (2008). Self-sacrifice as self-defence: Mortality salience increases efforts to affirm a symbolic immortal self at the expense of the physical self. *European Journal of Social Psychology, 38*, 531–541.

Rushton, J. P., Chrisjohn, R. D., & Fekken, G. C. (1981). The altruistic personality and the self-report altruism scale. *Personality and Individual Differences, 2*, 293–302.

Sageman, M. (2008). A strategy for fighting international Islamist terrorists. *The ANNALS of the American Academy of Political and Social Science, 618*, 223–231.

Sakagami, S. F., & Akahira, Y. (1960). Studies on the Japanese honeybee, Apis cerana Fabricisu. VIII. Two opposing adaptations in the post-stinging behavior of honeybees. *Evolution, 14*, 29–40.

Schumpe, B. M., & Bélanger, J. J. (2017). *No pain, no political gain: The role of counterfinality in activism*. Unpublished manuscript.

Schumpe, B. M., Bélanger, J. J., Dugas, M., Erb, H.-P., & Kruglanski, A. W. (2017). *Counterfinality: On the increased perceived instrumentality of a means to a goal*. Unpublished manuscript.

Shadish, W. R., Cook, T. D., & Campbell, D. T. (2002). *Experimental and quasi-experimental designs for generalized causal inference*. Boston, MA: Houghton Mifflin.

Sheikh, H., Gómez, Á., & Atran, S. (2016). Empirical evidence for the devoted actor model. *Current Anthropology, 57*, S204–S209.

Swann, W. B., Jr., Gómez, Á., Buhrmester, M. D., López-Rodríguez, L., Jiménez, J., & Vázquez, A. (2014). Contemplating the ultimate sacrifice: Identity fusion channels pro-group affect, cognition, and moral decision making. *Journal of Personality and Social Psychology, 106*, 713–727.

Tajfel, H., & Turner, J. C. (1979). An integrative theory of intergroup conflict. In W. Austin & S. Worchel (Eds.), *The social psychology of intergroup relations* (pp. 33–48). Pacific Grove, CA: Brooks/Cole.

Temkin, L. S. (1993). *Inequality*. Oxford: Oxford University Press.

Tugawa, S. (1991). Workers call the tune as labor shortage intensifies. *Japan Economic Almanac, 1991*, 41–43.

Vallerand, R. J., Blanchard, C., Mageau, G. A., Koestner, R., Ratelle, C., Léonard, M., ... & Marsolais, J. (2003). Les passions de l'âme: On obsessive and harmonious passion. *Journal of Personality and Social Psychology, 85*, 756–767.

Weatherston, D., & Moran, J. (2003). Terrorism and mental illness: Is there a relationship? *International Journal of Offender Therapy and Comparative Criminology, 47*, 698–713.

Webber, D., & Kruglanski, A. W. (2016). Psychological factors in radicalization: A '3 N' approach. In G. LaFree and J. D. Freilich (Eds.), *The Handbook of the Criminology of Terrorism* (pp. 33–46). West Sussex, UK: Wiley-Blackwell.

Wright, P. M., O'Leary-Kelly, A. M., Cortina, J. M., Klein, H. J., & Hollenbeck, J. R. (1994). On the meaning and measurement of goal commitment. *Journal of Applied Psychology, 79*, 795–803.

Yukl, G. (1994). *Instructor's manual with test questions: Leadership in organizations*. Upper Saddle River, NJ: Prentice Hall.

Index

Note: page numbers in *italics* refer to figures and tables.

3N approach (model) 472–6
5-HT2C (serotonin 2C receptor) 28
5-HTTLPR (Serotonin Transporter Polymorphism) 21, 71, 72, 73, 369
    childhood and adolescence 28–30
    infants 23–8
25KDa (SNAP25) 31

abortion (birth control) 356, 358
abstract concepts 306
abuse 120, 156
academic abilities (achievements) 139, 191, 437
acculturation 168, 307
actions, target 389
activity levels 13, 23, 32, 33, 185
actors, devoted 476
Adams, G. 375
adaptability 23, 28–9, 210, 213
adaptations 117, 206–8, 235
Adler, Alfred 149–50
adolescence 96–7, 148, 263
    biological origins 51, 79
    peers 166, 173, 175
    social environment 245, 247
adultery (infidelity) 285, 408
adulthood (adults) 100, 101, 153, 167, 175
    character change 292–4
adversity 460
    see also trauma
Affect Intensity 325
affection 122, 385
affiliation 14, 292, 328, 331–5, 407
Affleck, G. 454
agency 101, 102, 231, 292
agreeableness 53
aggregation 221, 281
aggression
    biological origins 14, 28, 32, 41–2, 79
    developmental origins 115–16, 120, 137, 147, 172, 191
    environmental origins 352, 439, 442–3
aging 78, 325
agreeableness 45, 133, 172, 249, 292–3, 459
    adolescence 184, 189, 191, 193–4
    adulthood 263, 267
    cross-cultural perspectives 313
    cross-cultural perspectives 311

    families 148, 152, 154–5
    infectious disease 326–328, 334
    romantic relationships 406, 410
agriculture 368–9
Ainsworth, M. D. S. 153
Ainsworth's Strange Situation 27
alcoholism 6, 54, 72, 100–1, 102
Alexander, N. 73
Allport, G. W. 220, 261, 305, 314
Al-Shawaf, L. 337
Alternative Five-Factor Model 53
altruism 468, 469
American Psychiatric Association 156
American South 356–7
amygdala activity 72
Anderson, R. C. 104
androgen 351
anger 32, 117, 233, 371, 440, 470
Angst, J. 150
animals (studies) 14
anogenital distance (AGD) 40
Anthropology from a Pragmatic Point of View 20
Anusic, I. 184
anxiety 132, 157, 173, 442
    adolescence 185, 188, 191
    biological origins 10, 14, 23, 27–8, 32, 34
    evolution and survival 207, 212
    psychopathic traits 114, 117, 120, 124
    romantic relationships 404, 408, 414
apolipoprotein E (APOE) 32
approach-withdrawal 28
Arbelle, S. 29, 33
area-under-the-curve (AUC) 6
arginine vasopressin 13
Arndt, J. 475
Aron, A. 416
arrays, genotyping 77–8
Asendorpf, J. B. 247, 249
Asperger Syndrome (ASJ) 44
assertiveness 154, 185, 433
assessment
    gender (sex) 6–8
    hormones 5–8
Associated Sequence Learning (ASL) 384–5
assumptions, psychometric 287
ASTMA model 242–3

attachment 102–4, 338, 459
    biological origins 10, 12, 14
    developmental origins 152–6, 166, 211, 292
    romantic relationships 408–9, 412, 414–15, 417–18
attachment theory 174, 403–4
attention 30, 31
Attention Deficit Hyperactivity Disorder (ADHD) 23, 71
attitudes 325, 326
attraction and initiation 403–5, 413
attractiveness 243, 335
attribution styles 286
attrition 243
Austin, E. J. 45
Australia 33, 311, 367, 368
autism spectrum disorder (ASD) 44
autobiographical reasoning 99–101
autonomy 137
autothysis 465
Auwerx, J. 83
avoidance 9, 404, 408
awakening responses 10

Babiak, P. 122
Baby Boomers 133
Bachman, J. G. 136
Baker, J. H. 69
Bakweri (Cameroon) 355
Balbo, N. 169
Ball, L. C. 437
Barban, N. 169
Barona, M. 44
Bar-Tal, D. 468
Battaglia, M. 29
Bauman, C. W. 472
Baumeister, R. F. 173, 414
BBC Internet Study 43, 44, 45
Beguines 356
behavior 21, 171, 218, 230–234, 326, 389, 408
    antisocial 72, 73, 112, 148, 171
behavioral immune system (BIS) 321–2, 327
behavior genetics
    environment and heritability 69–70
    personality traits 70–1
Bélanger, J. J. 467, 472, 474
Belgium 185
Belief in a Dangerous World (BDW) 325
beliefs 367–8, 476
    change following adversity 453, 456, 458
    destiny 406, 412
    moral character 286, 288–9
    romantic relationships 405–6, 409, 412
belonging, need for 413–14, 473
Belsky, J. 147, 208, 212
Bem, D. J. 468
Benedict, R. 312
Benet-Martinez, V. 222
Benjamin, J. 71

Bernstein, D. 97
biases 104, 126, 413, 455–6, 458
    gender similarities 434, 436, 440
Big Five (personality traits) 81, 135, 247–9, 326, 460, 470
    adolescence 181–4, 187–9
    adulthood 261, 263–5, 267
    behavioral signature 221, 233
    biological origins 45, 53
    cross-cultural perspectives 306, 310
    moral character 283–5, 293
    romantic relationships 406, 409
Big Five Inventory (BFI) 45, 310, 328
Binet, A. 303
biofeedback 126
biological sensitivity to context (theory) 250
biomarkers 82
bipolar disorder 72
birds (study) 335
birth cohort 134
birth intervals 349
birth order 149–50
birth trauma 115, 120
birth weights 56, 207, 351
Blackie, L. E. R. 453, 456
Blair, R. J. R. 115
blame (blaming others) 282, 417
Bleidorn, W. 187, 191, 283
Block, J. 192, 193, 226
Block, J. H. 192, 226
blood spots (method of assaying) 7
body shape 336
Bohn, A. 97
boldness 118–19, 123, 125
Bollich, K. L. 281
bonding 393
bonds 409
Boom Task (measure) 470–1
Boosma, D. 69
Booth, A. 9
Borderline Personality Disorder (BPD) 13, 99, 102, 157
boredom susceptibility 45
Bowlby, J. 152, 153, 155
Boyce, W. T. 207, 208, 209, 212
brains, human 68, 115
    activity levels 308–9
    functioning 117–21, 124, 126
brains, non-human primates 204
Braly, K. 313
Brannick, M. T. 76
Bratko, D. 70
Brazelton Neonatal Behavioural Assessment Scale 389
breastfeeding 385
breastfeeding (study)
    discussion 392–3
    method 386–7
    results 389–92
    task 387–9

Breastfeeding Self Efficacy Scale, Short Form (BSES-SF) 387
responses 390
Brennan, K. A. 153
Brewer, M. B. 371, 375
Brewer, W. F. 103
bride prices (bride wealth payments) 355
brides 359
Brigate Rosse 476
Briley, D. A. 184, 187
Buss, D. M. 335
Buunk, B. P. 45

Calhoun, L. G. 450, 452
California Adult Q-Sort (CAQ) 229
callous-unemotional (CU) traits 112–13
Campbell, A. 13
Campbell, W. K. 136
Canada 311, 368, 375
candidate genes (study design) 21, 23, *24–7*
candidate gene studies 71–2
 additive and epistatic genetic effects 72–3
 epigenetics 74
 gene-environment interaction 73–4
capital, embodied 56
CAPTION model 228
career interests 443
caregivers
 developmental origins 97–8, 100, 152, 155
 environmental origins 384–5, 404, 414
caring 331, 349, 351, 352
Cashdan, E. 12
Caspi, A. 73, 171
catechol-*O*-methyltransferase (COMT) 29, 31
categorization (cognition) 374
Catmur, C. 385
Cattell, R. B. 220, 261, 303
causal-motivational coherence 96–7, 98
Chai, X. J. 43
Chandler, J. 472
change, personality in adulthood 261–266
changes, normative 293
Changing Lives (study) 134, 136
character, moral *see* moral character
character, national 312–15
character change 292–4
characteristic adaptations 235
cheating 285
see also fairness
Chen, C. H. 82
child abuse 74
see also maltreatment
child-care 30
childhood
 developmental origins 125–6, 166, 183, 204, 206
 environmental origins 359, 414
child rearing *see* nurturing

children 7, 40, 51, 432–3
 developmental origins 96–7, 113, 119, 137, 150, 204
Children's Depression Index 441
China (Chinese) 45, 175, 293
 environmental origins 358–9, 367, 368–9, 375
Choi, Y. 477–8
Christofou, A. 81
chronology coherence 96
chronotype 51, 52
Chrysler 477
circadian rhythms 5–6, 51
 master clock 52
Circadian Type Questionnaire (CTQ) 52
Circumplex Model 45–6
class assignment 195
cleanliness 334
Cleckley, H. 116, 118, 123
climates 329
clocks, internal *see* circadian rhythms
closeness 154, 166, 408
closure 101
coding 388–389, 394
cognition 21, 282, 373–5, 437
cognitive abilities 53
cognitive-affective processing system (CAPS) 230–1
cognitive interdependence 415–16
cognitive performance 437–8, 459
cognitive processes 371
cognitive social learning theory (gender) 433
Cohen, J. 436
Cohen, P. 156
Cohen, T. R. 280, 288, 289, 291
cohorts, definition 133
Coleman, E. 355
collaboration, in families 150
Collear, M. 44
collectivism 305, 331–3
 see also individualism-collectivism
collectivistic shift 473, 475
colonization 355, 356–7
commitment (commitment investment) 350, 416, 468
communication 157, 413, 437, 439, 440
communion 101, 102, 292
communities 124, 292
compassion 122, 279, 281
competition, intrasexual 348–9, 350, 351–3
competitiveness 32, 41, 42, 59
compliance 249, 373
concern for others 288, 289
concrete concepts 306
condescension 282
Conduct Disorder 112
confidence 154
configural invariance 135
confirmatory factor analysis (CFA) 134–5
conflict 150, 245, 248, 408, 412

conformity 13, 332, 333, 373
congenital adrenal hyperplasia (CAH) 40
Conger, J. A. 477
Conley, D. 68
conscience 114, 116
conscientiousness
    adolescence 182, 184–186, 189–191, 193–194
    adulthood 263, 267
    biological origins 53, 73
    cross-cultural perspectives 311, 313
    environmental origins 406, 410, 413, 459
    families 148, 150
    infectious disease 326–7
    neonatal imitation 285, 290, 292–3
    peers 172
    personal narrative 98, 102
    self-esteem and narcissism 133, 135
    social environment 247–8, 252
conservation 263
conservatism 333
consistency 220, 279–80, 281, 282, 284
consistency, cross-situational 218–20
    person as consistency 220–4
    person x situation interaction 230–4
    reflections and future directions 234–6
    situation as variability 224–30
contamination 101, 326
context 43, 46, 168, 323, 326
context (coherence) 96
context, sensitivity to 208
continuity, heterotypic 182
continuous variation 232
control 33, 148, 246, 367, 440
conviction, moral 291
Coolican, J. 43
cooperation 41, 59, 331
Coopersmith Self-Esteem Inventory 136
coping 253, 456
coreid bugs (study) 347
correlates (personality trait development) 186–91
corresponsive principle 243
Corticotropin-Releasing Hormone (CRH) 33
cortisol 5, 6, 9–11, 41, 59, 60, 73
cortisol awakening responses (CAR) 52
cortisol stress activity 72
Costa, P. T. 306
CpG islands 74
creativity 333, 460
criminal behavior (crime) 42–3, 359
Cronbach, L. J. 235
cross-cultural perspectives 303
    dimensions 304–6
    geography 309–12
    linking personality and culture 306–8
    national character 312–15
    relativism and universalism 308–9
cross-temporal meta-analysis 135

Crowley, M. 439
cues 414
cultures 56, 140, 187, 329
    artifacts 367, 368, 372
    change 332
    dimensions 304–6
    diversity 175
cumulative continuity principle 183
Curtis, V. 324
customs 304, 368

dandelions (children) 208, 210
dark traits 117
Dark Triad 53, 285
Darwin, C 308, 346
data collection 175, 218, 291, 310
    adolescence 183, 195–6
    biological origins 6, 23, 31
    self-esteem and narcissism 135–6, 141
daughters 355
decision-making, behavioral measures 471–2
defeat 9, 11
De Fruyt, F. 185
de Haan, A. D. 185, 194
Delayed Gratification Inventory (DGI) 58
delinquency 79, 148, 175, 191, 213
Della Porta, D. 476
De Luca, A. 28
de Moor, M. H. 69
Denissen, J. J. A. 185, 267, 283
Denmark 312, 367
depression
    adolescence 185, 191
    adulthood 270
    change following adversity 452–4
    evolution and survival 210
    families 152, 157
    gender similarities 440–1
    infectious disease 326
    molecular basis 72–3, 81
    molecular genetic studies 23, 28, 34
    morningness-eveningness 53
    psychopathic traits 120
    self-esteem and narcissism 136–7
    self-sacrifice 470
    social environment 244, 251
deprivation 114
destabilization 350
destiny beliefs 406, 412
detachment 119
    emotional 116, 122, 123
development, human 204–5
developmental adaptations 206–8
developmental systems 205–11, 266
developmental systems theory 205
deviant behavior 172
Deviation from Balanced Time Perspective (DBTP) 58

Diagnostic and Statistical Manuel of Mental Disorders -5th edition (DSM-5) 112
DIAMONDS (model) 229
diathesis-stress model 211, 250
Dick, D. M. 74
differences, individual
    attraction and initiation 403–8
    dissolution 412–13
    functioning and maintenance 408–11
differences, inter-individual 265–6
differential change 264
differential susceptibility hypothesis 250
digit ratio 46–7
    aggression 41–2
    challenge situations 41
    criminal behavior 42–3
    domination (dominance) 41–2, 43
    personality dimensions 45–6
    prenatal testosterone (PT) 40–1
    spatial ability 43–4
    systemizing/empathizing 44–5
dirtiness 334
disabilities 325, 330
disciplinary strategies 114, 156, 245
disconnectedness 9
discriminant validity 268
discrimination 175, 443
diseases, infectious 251, 321–2
    disgust 323–4
    future directions 337–9
    individual differences 322–3
    motives as framework 328–37
    pathogen threat 324–8
disgust 323–4
Disgust Sensitivity Scale 325
disinhibition 45, 118–19
disorders, psychiatric 14
dissolution 412–13, 417–19
dissonance reduction 373
distress 23, 114, 173, 323, 408, 417
Diurnal Type Scale (DTS) 52
divorce 252, 350, 459
DNA sequencing 35
domains 290
dominance 154, 247, 338
    biological origins 8–9, 11, 41–3, 71, 79
donations, charity 472
Donnellan, M. B. 137, 139
Dooling, D. J. 103
dopamine 212
dowries 355
DRD2 (dopamine receptor D2) 60
DRD4 (Dopamine Receptor D4) 21, 60
    childhood and adolescence 28–30
    infants 23–8
dreams 409
Dreber, A. 60

Drislane, L. E. 119
drug abuse 72
    see also substance abuse
dual-hormone hypothesis 10–11
DuBois, C. 312
Dugas, M. 474
Duncan, L. A. 324–5
Dunlop, W. L. 101
Dutton, K. 124
dyadic state of consciousness (DSC) 151

Eaglt, A. H. 433, 439
Ebstein, R. P. 23, 71
ecologies 329, 335, 338, 368
economies 355, 356, 366, 367
Edelstein, R. S. 12, 137
education (schools) 53, 309, 366
    developmental origins 124, 168, 190
    gender similarities 437, 443
    sex ratio 356, 359
effect sizes 434–5, 436
efficacy 366, 393
egalitarianism 469
ego-control 192
ego-resiliency 192
egotism 139
Eisenberg, D. T. 60
Eisenberg, N. 151, 158
Ellis, B. J. 150, 207, 208, 212
Ellis, H. 443
Ellis, L. 42
embodied capital 56
Emde, R. N. 151
Emlen, S. T. 346
emotional detachment 116, 122, 123
emotional instability 53
emotional intelligence 14
emotionality 23, 30, 31, 34, 116, 327
    positive 32
emotional reactivity 13, 120
emotional regulation 151–2
emotional stability 137, 148–9, 152, 267
    adolescence 184–5, 189, 191, 193
emotional state, mothers' 31
emotions 115, 122, 124, 212
    biological origins 45
    environmental origins 371–2, 374–5, 408
empathy 8, 13, 41, 44–5, 157, 477
    moral character 282, 285, 289, 293
    psychopathic traits 112, 114, 116, 119, 122
empathy quotient (EQ) 44
employees (Chinese study) 294–5
employment 359
endurance 13
enemies 375
entitlement 140
entrepreneurs 359

environmentalists 467–8
environments 43, 148–9, 170, 224–5, 323, 384
    adolescence 184, 187
    cross-cultural perspectives 306, 309
    evolution and survival 205, 207–8, 210–11, 213
    molecular basis 68, 70, 74
    molecular genetic studies 29–30, 34
    morningness-eveningness 52, 54–5, 56
    psychopathic traits 114–15, 117, 122
    self-esteem and narcissism 134, 140–1
epidemics 330
epistasis 71, 79
Epstein, S. 221
Equal Environment Assumption (EEA) 68
equality 304, 366, 469
equality matching 165–6, 171, 174
equifinality 193
Erikson, E. H. 184, 188
Ernst, C. 150
estradiol 7, 11, 12–13
estrogen 13
ethics 471
ethnicity 137, 139, 141, 165, 308–9, 444–5
Europe 358
eveningness 51–54, 56–9, 61
Event-Related potential (ERP) 29
evolutionary adaptive differences 203
    developmental systems 205–11
    human development 204–5
    life history theory 211–14
evolutionary developmental psychology 205–11
    theory 206
evolutionary theory (gender) 432
excitement 307
exercise 42
expectations 456
experience sampling methods (ESM) 458
exploitativeness 137
extraversion
    adolescence 185, 187, 189, 190–1, 193
    adulthood 263
    change following adversity 454
    cross-cultural perspectives 307, 311, 313
    digit ratio 45
    families 148, 150, 152–4
    gender similarities 440
    hormonal influences 10
    infectious disease 327–8, 333
    molecular basis 76, 79
    molecular genetic studies 30
    morningness-eveningness 53, 59
    peers 172
    personal narrative 98
    romantic relationships 406, 410, 413
    self-esteem and narcissism 132
    self-sacrifice 459
    social environment 247

extreme male brain (EMB) 44
extremism, violent 470, 473, 479
eye-contact 393
Eysenck Personality Questionnaire (EPQ) 53, 75, 77, 310

face-to-face (FTF), interactions 393
facets 222, 268, 285, 313
facial expressions (study) 308, 414
facial imitation 32, 386
facial symmetry 336
fairness 279, 281, 293
faith 292
Faith in Intuition 325
Falter, C. 43
families 115, 146–7, 157–8, 248
    attachment 152–6
    birth order 149–50
    emotional regulation 151–2
    environmental origins 338, 357, 409, 476
    parental personality 147–9
    personality disorders 156–7
    support from 190
farming 368–9
fathers 157, 349, 354, 357
fear (fearfulness) 23, 29, 207, 246, 338
fearlessness 119, 124
fecundity 348–350
Felson, J. 69
femininity 305
feminism 355, 356, 439
fertility 350, 351, 357
Festinger, L. 313
fidelity 351
fight-or-flight response 7
Fincher, C. L. 330, 332, 333, 338, 339
Fink, B. 43, 45
Finkel, D. 78
Finland 312
fish (studies) 347, 348
fish, colored (study) 374
Fiske, A. P. 165
Five Factor Model (FFM) 72, 153, 306, 310
five factor theory (FFT) 186
Fivush, R. 98
Fleeson, W. 221–224, 227, 232, 234, 458–9
food choices 329–30
foods 334
Foster, J. D. 140
Founier, M. A. 231
Fraley, R. C. 265, 293
Frazier, P. 456
friends (friendship) 11, 375
    see also peers
frontiers 368
frustration 23, 152, 245–6, 371, 440
functional flexibility principle 323
functional magnetic resonance imaging (fMRI) 4, 126

function and maintenance (romantic relationships)
    attachment 408–9
    beliefs 409
    motivation, approach and avoidance 410–11
    personality traits 409–10
    relational self-construal 409
    self-concept, structure 411
Fundamental Motives Theory 229
funnel plots 436

Gable, S. L. 407
Gallardo-Pujol, D. 252
Galton, F. 149, 303
games 59, 471
Gangestad, S. W. 335
gender (sex) 98, 139, 165, 336–7, 366, 470
    hormonal influences 6, 11–13
    molecular basis 73, 79
    molecular genetic studies 31
    morningness-eveningness 51
    ratios (fish) 205
gender similarities 445–446
    current meta-analysis 437–41
    exceptions 441–4
    intersectionality 444–5
    meta-analysis 433–7
    theories 431–3
    variability 444
gene effects 78–80
gene-environment correlations (rGEs) 69–70, 79
gene-environment interactions (GxEs) 69–70
gene methylation 74
Gene Ontology (GO) Consortium 80
generalizability 235
General Mixture Modeling 194
generations 133
generativity 101, 292, 453
generosity 13, 352
genes 306, 323, 336
gene set enrichment analysis (GSEA) 80
genetic imaging 78
Genetics of Personality Consortium (GPC) 76
Genome Project 78
Genome-Wide Association 35
Genome-Wide Association Studies (GWAS) 74–7, 80
Gentile, B. 136
geography 309–12, 329
Georgia 357
Germany 45, 136, 249
    Bavaria 350
Germ Aversion (GA) 324–5, 330
gestures 385, 387
    see also neonatal imitation
gifts 375
girls 31, 185, 356
Gladstone, W. E. 308
global coherence 97
Gluckman, P. 208

goals 328, 414, 468
    adulthood 262–5, 267
    individualism-collectivism 368, 371
    self-sacrifice 467, 470
Gottesman, I. I. 78
Graesser, A. C. 103–4
gratitude 282, 289
Great Recession 367
Greenberg, M. S. 104
Greenfield, P. M. 367
Grijalva, E. 139
Gross, J. J. 151
group-identity fusion 476
group membership 376, 405
group socialization theory 168, 170–1
growth (growth beliefs) 406, 409, 412, 453, 455, 456
guilt 280, 289, 442
    psychopathic traits 112, 114, 120, 122
Gunawardane, K. G. C. 57
Gunderson, J. G. 157
Guttentag, M. 354, 356
G x E (study type) 29, 30, 34

habits 367
Haenisch, B. 78
Haidt, J. 372
Ham, M. 169
Hamamura, T. 368
Hamilton, W. D. 335
handedness 444–5
Hanson, M. 208
hardiness 10
Hare, R. D. 122
harm avoidance 14, 28, 32–3
Harris, J. 170
Hayden, E. P. 29, 30, 34
Healey, M. D. 150
health 69, 101, 136, 335, 359, 371
    evolution and survival 207, 209–10
    infectious disease 325
    mental 249, 252, 454
    mental-health model 211
    morningness-eveningness 57
    peers 171, 175
    romantic relationships 411, 417
Hedges, L. V. 437
Heimann, M. 389, 393
Heine, S. J. 373
Helgeson, V. S. 457
Helzer, E. G. 280, 282
Hennecke, M. 294
Henri, V. 303
Herbig, P. A. 478
heritability 68, 184, 306, 335, 384
    missing 187
    sample size, additive and non-additive gene effects 78–80
    variants 77–8

Herlihy, D. 355
heroism 124
HEXACO (personality model) 45, 285–6, 328
history, human 354–9
Hobfoll, S. E. 453
Hoffman, P. D. 157
Hofstede, G. 305, 307, 365
Hokkaido (Japan) 368
homemakers 439
homophily 165
honesty 279, 280, 281, 293
hope 454
hopelessness 10, 454
hormones, influences of 9, 14–15
    circadian rhythms 5–6
    gender (sex) 11–12
    measurements 4–5
    steroids 3–4
Hoskin, A. W. 42
hostility 148
Hudson, N. W. 293
Hyde, J. S. 431, 436, 437, 442
hyperactive immune activity 323
hyperactivity 33
hypersensitivity 137
hypochondria 325
hypothalamic–pituitary–adrenal (HPA) axis 9–10, 60, 73, 207, 212
hypothalamic–pituitary–gonadal (HPG) axis 60
hypothalamus 5

Iacocca, L. 477
Iceland 312
Ideal Standard Model (ISM) 405
Ideker, T. 82
identity 157, 170, 315, 376, 444, 453
    adolescence 184, 188–9
    group 171, 473, 475–6
    moral 288–92
    moral character 286, 288–9, 291
    narrative 98, 195, 261
    personal 99–101, 184
    personal narrative 99, 102
    self-sacrifice 470, 475
ideologies 288
if-then 232, 294
illiteracy *see* literacy
illness (sickness) 82, 99, 331
    mental 470
    see also health, mental
illusions, visual 308–9
imagination 150
imitation 393, 433
    BSES-SF correlations 390–2
    neonatal *see* neonatal imitation
    results 389
    task 387–8, 394
immigration 354, 358

immunity 323
Implicit Association test (IAT) 325
implicit theories of relationships (ITRs) 406
impression management (self) 471
impulsivity (impulsiveness) 115–17, 123, 154, 207, 442–3
    morningness-eveningness 53, 58–9, 60
inadequacy, personal 120
Inbar, Y. 334
incarceration 102, 118, 252
income 69
individualism 139, 305, 331–3
    see also individualism-collectivism
individualism-collectivism 365–366, 376–7
    cultural differences 366–370
    psychological processes 370–6
individual-level change 185–6
industrialization 356
inequality, social 444
infants 206, 245, 404
    see also neonatal imitation
infection, abortive 465
influences, non-additive genetic 70–1
informant reports 457–8
Ingenuity Pathway Analysis (IPA) 80
inhibitions 60, 148
    behavioral 29, 30, 33
Inkeles, A. 366
innovation 333
integrative life stories 235
intelligence (IQ) 81, 82, 222, 310, 335, 349
    verbal 53
interactionism, doctrine of 219
interdependency 408
inter-individual differences 265–6
internal clocks *see* circadian rhythms
internal working models (IWM) 152, 154
Internet 310
intersectionality 444–5
intervals, passive 387
intimacy 12–13, 404, 408
intraclass correlation (ICC) 219
intra-individual change 265–6
introspection 99–100
intrusiveness 148
intuitions 282, 287
investment 349, 350
    parental 212, 338, 351–3, 432
Investment Model of Commitment 416
Iran 293
irritability 28, 120, 245
Italy 57
Item-Response Theory (IRT) 76
Ivorra, J. L. 27, 31

Jackson, J. J. 56, 224
Jacobs, L. F. 43
Jacobson, S. W. 386, 392

Jaffee, S. R. 79
Jankowski, K. S. 58
Japan 188, 366, 367–8, 370, 371, 478
Jayawickreme, E. 234, 281, 453, 456, 459
jealousy (jealous) 150, 408
job preferences 438–9
John, O. P. 182, 471
Johnson, W. 68, 69
Jorm, A. F. 28, 30, 33
Joseph, S. 452
Josephs, R. A. 10
Journal of Cross-Cultural Psychology 309

Kanazawa, S. 53, 54, 57
Kant, I. 20, 303
Kanungo, R. N. 477
Karoshi 478
Karpman, B. 116, 122
Katz, D. 313
Kelly, D. 324
Kelly, J. 147
Keltikangas-Järvinen, L. 33, 34
Kendler, K. S. 69
Kenya 370–1
Kim, H. M. 81
kindness 349, 352
Kirkpatrick, L. A. 56
Kitano, H. 82
Kitayama, S. 368, 370, 371
Klein, D. N. 73
Klimstra, T. A. 185, 192
Klinefelter syndrome 41
Knee, C. R. 409
Koehler, D. 479
Koffka, K. 309
Kondrak, C. L. 460
Konner, M. 204, 207
Krebs, D. L. 468
Kruglanski, A. W. 473, 479
Kyllonen, P. C. 53

labor (workforce), entering 269
Laceulle, O. M. 252
Lance, C. E. 134
language (words) 306, 367
Larson, R. 169
Latent Class Growth 194
Latent Profile Analysis 195
latent trajectory classes 265–6
latitude 52
laughter 32
law, single-child 358
law enforcement 471
    see also criminal behavior (crime)
layperson-derived situations 227
Le, B. 413
leadership 10, 139–40, 477–8
    gender similarities 433, 439

moral character 288, 294–5
psychopathic traits 117, 123
learning *see* education (schools)
Leary, M. R. 173, 414
LeBlanc, M. 193
Lee, A. J. 336
Lee, H. J. 29
Lee, S. W. 334
Lehnart, J. 172, 248
Lesch, K. P. 71, 72
LeVine, R. A. 304
Levi-Strauss, C. 308
lexicon-derived situations 227, 228
LiberationTigers of Tamil Eelam (LTTE) 470, 479
Lieberman, D. 329
life events 167, 244
    adulthood 263–4, 266, 268–9
    change following adversity 451, 455, 457, 460
    molecular basis 69, 73, 79–80
life experiences 168, 247
life history strategies 54–5
life history theory (LHT) 54–8, 61, 205, 211–214,
    338–9, 351
life narratives 286, 291, 452
Life Orientation Test (LOT) 454
life outcomes 222, 249–53
life phases 174
lifespans (life spans) 173, 184, 265
life stories, integrative 235
Linley, P. A. 452
Linn, M. C. 437
Lippa, R. 45
liquid chromatography/tandem mass spectrometry
    (LC/MS-MS) 7
literacy 308, 309, 310, 355, 356
literature 79, 251, 373
    behavioral signature 219, 222, 233–4
    change following adversity 451, 456
    moral character 289, 292
    peers 170, 173–4
Little Six 182
living arrangements 168
Lodi-Smith, J. 98
loneliness 9, 82, 137, 167, 407
longevity 249, 252, 355
    relationships 412
Louisiana Purchase 309
love, courtly 355
loving 352
Luo, S. 406
Luria, A. 309
Luxen, M. F. 45
Lykken, D. T. 117, 119, 120, 124
Lysaker, J. T. 99
Lysaker, P. H. 99

McAdams, D. P. 188, 452
McAdams, T. A. 79

McCrae, R. R. 306, 307
Machiavellianism 53, 59, 285
Maercker, A. 458
Maestripieri, D. 59, 60
Magnus, K. 248
Magnusson, D. 226
Mai-Dalton, R. R. 477–8
Major Depressive Disorder (MDD) 78
maltreatment 73, 114
manipulation 243
Manning, J. T. 40, 43, 44, 45
maps, personality 310
Marcia, J. E. 184
markers, biological 52, 82
Markus, H. R. 370, 371
marriage 350, 355, 356, 358, 359
martyrdom 467, 476
Marvel-Coen, J. 59, 60
masculinity 305
Maternal Bonding Scale 394
Maternal Efficacy questionnaire 394
math 437
mathematical performance 438
mating 55–6, 58–9, 328
    selectivity 335–6
    sociosexuality 336–7
    see also reproduction
maturity 248, 263
    personality 191
    principle 184–5, 193
    trends toward/away from *see* change
Mayan (community) 367
Mazur, A. 9
meaningful environment 225
meaninglessness 474
meaning making 101–2, 454, 474
mean-level change 184–5
meanness 118–19, 120, 122, 123
Meany, M. J. 212–13
measurement invariance 134, 139, 182–3
measurements 193–4, 222, 253, 261, 265
    biological origins 6, 35, 52
    change following adversity 459
    cross-cultural perspectives 308, 313–14
    individualism-collectivism 371, 376
    IRM-NS 218
    moral character 288
    positive personality change 456–57
media (magazines) 357, 366, 442
Mehl, M. R. 247
Mehta, P. H. 10
Meindl, P. 281
melatonin 52
Meltzoff, A. N. 388, 393
memory 81
    collective 475
    reconstruction 102–5
    working 53

men 10, 57, 335
mental-health model 211
mental rotation ability (MRT) 43
mental vitality 32
meta-analysis 433–4
    advantages 435
    cognitive performance and gender 437–8
    criticisms 436–7
    methodological concerns 435–6
    methodology 434–5
    occupations and gender 438–9
    social behavior and gender 439–40
    well-being and gender 440–41
metric invariance 135
Michelangelo Phenomenon 417
Middeldorp, C. 248
Middle Ages, Late 355–6
migration 357, 368
military service 168
Millennials 133
Miller, D. T. 468
Milton Index of Personality Styles 53
mind perception 289
Mischel, W. 230
mismatch effect 8
mobility 168, 269, 366, 368
models (modeling techniques)
    adolescence 182
    behavioral signature 219
    change following adversity 459
    families 147
    molecular basis 70, 82
    multilevel 232
    neonatal imitation 387
    peers 168
    personal narrative 105
    person-environment transactions 242–4, 249–50
    self-esteem and narcissism 135, 141
    social environment 253
molecular basis
    behavior genetics 67–71
    candidate gene studies 71–2
    convergence 83
    gene networks 80–1
    Genome-Wide Association Studies (GWAS) 74–7
    missing heritability 77–80
    systems biology 81–3
molecular genetics 20–3, 34–5
    DRD4, 5-HTTLPR and infants 23–8
    DRD4, 5-HTTLPR, childhood and adolescence 28–30
    other variants, childhood and adolescence 32–4
    other variants and infants 30–2
Møller, A. P. 335
Monitoring the Future (MTF) 136
Monoamine Oxidase A (MAOA) 27, 29, 31
Moore, M. K. 388, 393
moral behavior 279

moral character 278–9, 295–6
    change and improvement in adulthood 292–4
    defined and defended 279–80
    direct evidence 281–2
    functionalist approach 287–90
    indirect evidence 280–1
    moral exceptionalism 290–2
    traits 284–7
    transmission 294–5
    variability and character traits 283–4
moral cognition 282
moral conviction 291
moral disgust 324, 326, 337
moral exceptionalism 294
Moral Foundations Theory (MFT) 288–9
moral identity 288–9, 291
Moral Identity Centrality (MIC) 288
moral intuitions 282, 372
morality 372
moral judgments 41, 334
moral purity 326
morbidity-mortality 212
Morizot, J. 193
morningness 51–4, 56–9, 61
Morningness–Eveningness Questionnaire (MEQ) 52
Morse, L. 288, 289, 291
mortality 55, 204, 212, 338, 354, 474
mortality rates 321, 350, 351, 352, 359
    chimpanzees 349
Moskowitz, D. S. 45, 221, 228
mother-baby relationship (study) 393
    discussion 396–7
    method 394–5
    results 395–6
mothers 157, 351
motivation 174, 263, 328, 384, 416, 456
    approach and avoidance 407, 410–11
    biological origins 12, 60
    individualism-collectivism 371–3
    math 438
    moral character 286, 292, 294
    self-sacrifice 472, 479
motives 267
motor activity 32
motor organization 23
motor skills (performance) 386, 388, 392, 441
Mueller, A. 73
Mullins-Nelson, J. L. 120
Mund, M. 172
Munich Chronotype Questionnaire (MCTQ) 52
Murdock, G. P. 304
Murray, D. R. 327, 332, 333, 336
Murray, H. A. 225, 261

Nader-Grosbois, N. 152
Nakamura, G. V. 103
narcissism 9, 10, 53, 132–3, 285, 367, 410
    future directions 140–1

generational differences 137–40
study methods 134–6
terminology and change 133–4
Narcissistic Personality Disorder (NPD) 140
Narcissistic Personality Inventory (NPI) 134, 139, 140
Narcissistic Admiration and Rivalry Questionnaire 140
narrative coherence 96–9
Narrative Coherence Coding Scheme (NaCCs) 96
narrative identity 195–6, 261
narrative reviews 435
narratives 452, 460, 473
narrators 96, 97
national character 312–15
National Defense Counsel for Victims of Karoshi 478
national identity (character) 312–15
nationality 140
natural selection 204, 206, 323, 332, 432
Need for Structure 325
negative affect 28
neglect 120, 477
    see also abuse; maltreatment
neonatal imitation 383–4, 397–8
    ASL 384–5
    bonding study 393–7
    breastfeeding study 386–93
    explanations for individual differences 385–6
    genetic evidence 384
neuroticism 102, 172, 264, 326–7
    adolescence 185, 189
    biological origins 45, 72, 75–6, 79, 81
    cross-cultural perspectives 311, 313
    families 148–9, 154, 156
    romantic relationships 410, 412, 414
    self-esteem and narcissism 132, 135
    social environment 248, 251–2
neurotransmitters 4, 21
newborns see neonatal imitation
New England 356
New York 357
New Zealand 311, 368
Neyer, F. J. 172, 247, 248, 249
Nisbett, R. E. 373, 455
Noble, E. P. 28, 32
Noftle, E. E. 154, 222, 223, 285
normative changes 293
norms
    peer groups 170–1, 174
    peers 187
Norway 312
novelty seeking 307, 328–9, 335
    biological origins 9–10, 14, 28–9, 32–3, 53–4, 71
Nowell, A. 437
nuances 194, 222, 269
null-hypothesis 232
nurturing 149, 292, 369, 408, 433
nutrition 207

Obsessive Compulsive Disorder 326–7
occupations 438–9
Odbert, H. S. 305
Okbay, A. 77
Oliver, M. B. 442
O'Malley, P. M. 136
ontogeny 203, 205
Oostenbroek, J. 384
openness 248–249, 263, 285, 454
    adolescence 185, 187, 189
    biological origins 45, 53, 79, 81
    cross-cultural perspectives 307, 310–11, 313
    families 150, 154–5
    infectious disease 326–8, 330, 333–4
    personal narrative 98, 101
    romantic relationships 410, 413
Operational Sex Ratio (OSR) 346
Oppositional Defiant Disorder 112
oppositionality 79
optimism 53, 454
orchids (children) 208, 210
Orehek, E. 475
orientation 23, 43, 305
Oring, L. W. 346
Orth, U. 136
others 288–289, 291, 292, 468
Oud, J. H. 254
outgroups (ingroups) 330, 369, 376, 470
Overcontrollers 192–3, 195
oxytocin 7, 13–14, 212
    maternal 393
Ozer, D. J. 222

Pace, V. L. 76
pain study (hot sauce) 472
Pals, J. L. 452
Palumbo, F. 478
panic disorder 33
Papageorgiou, K. A. 21
parasites (study) 327, 332, 337
parental behavior 210
parental contribution 348
parental efficacy 385
parental investment 212, 352–3
parent-infant interaction 384
parenting 97–8, 117, 122, 156, 190, 210, 245
    biological origins 29–30, 34, 79
    environmental origins 328, 336, 359
    personality of 147–9
    social environment 251
parents' reports 183
Park, C. L. 457
Parrigon, S. 228
participants 5–6, 11
    breastfeeding (study) 386
    German students 57, 58
    New Zealand students 58
    Polish students 58

partnerships 269
Pasupathi, M. 100
paternal investment 351
pathogen prevalence 335
pathogen resistance 335
pathogens 332, 369
    disgust 324, 326, 333, 337
    historical 332
    threat 324–6
pathogen stress 336, 338, 354
Pathological Narcissism Inventory 140
Patrick, C. J. 118, 120, 122, 123
Patterns of Culture 312
Patterson, G. R. 148
Paulhus, D. L. 150, 471
Pawlby, S. 385
peers 29, 164, 173–6, 245, 280
    characteristics 165–6
    effects 170–3
    functions 166–7
    group and relationship 167–70, 174
    integration 169–70
    underlying mechanisms 170–3
pens (study) 373
Perceived Infectability (PI) 324–5
perceived vulnerability to disease (PVD) 324–6, 327–8, 330, 337
perception, mind 289
Pereda, N. 252
Perina, K. 53, 54, 57
persistence 29
PERSOC (framework) 168–9
person (concept) 219
    conceptualization of traits 220–2
    theory of traits 222–4
personality
    disorders 156–7, 222, 304–6
    factors 412–13
    maps 310
    traits 235, 406–7, 409–10, 419
personality development 181–2
    correlates 186–91
    future directions 194–6
    mechanisms in rank order stability 184–6
    personality traits 182–3
    person-centered approach 191–4
personality development, adulthood 260, 270–1
    concepts 260–1
    forms and findings 261–6
    questions and future directions 268–70
    theoretical accounts 266–8
personal narratives 95, 105–6
    autobiographical reasoning 99–101
    meaning making 101–2
    memory reconstruction 102–5
    narrative coherence 96–9
person-centered approach (personality development) 191–4

person-environment transactions
    evidence 244–7
    life outcomes 250–3
person x situation interaction 230–4
perspectives 13, 269–70, 289
Pervin, L. 225
Peters, M. 43, 44
Petersen, C. 285
Petersen, J. L. 442
Philibert, R. 74
philopatry 330
phobic anxiety disorder 33
phylogeny 203, 205
physiological immune system 321, 323
Pichert, J. W. 104
picture recall 43
Piffer, D. 53, 56, 57
pituitary gland 5, 13
Pizzaro, D. 334
plasticity 204–5, 207, 208, 266
    phenotypic 213
Plomin, R. 70–1
Pluess, M. 28
pollution 324
polygenic scores 35
polygyny 353–4
Ponzi, D. 57, 58–9
positive affect 10, 31
positive personality change 450
    causes 453–4
    current knowledge 456
    current assessment 454–6
    future research 456–60
    theories 451–3
posterior pituitary 13
posttraumatic growth (PTG) 450
    Hobfoll 453
    Joseph and Linley 452
    McAdams 452–3
    Tedeschi and Calhoun 451–2
Posttraumatic Growth Inventory (PTGI) 455, 459
posttraumatic stress disorder 454
Poulin, M. 43
power 11, 123, 247, 305, 337, 432
    sex ratio 353, 355
Power, R. A. 79
Preckel, F. 53
prediction 220
predictive adaptive responses 208
preference 13
pregnancy 13, 28, 31–2, 147, 207, 331
    teenage 350
prejudice 330–1, 334
prenatal *see* pregnancy
prenatal estrogen (PE) 40
prenatal testosterone (PT) 40
press (media) 13

presses 225
prestige 123, 337–8, 473
Price, T. S. 79
primates, non-human (studies) 348
proactivity 53
problem-solving 53
processes, relational
    attraction and initiation 413–14
    dissolution 417–19
    function and maintenance 414–17
profiles 191–2, 195
    psychopathic traits 120–4
progesterone 13
Program for International Students Assessment (PISA) 437
promiscuity 333, 350
prosperity, economic 367
prostitution 357, 358
protein-coding genes 32
psychiatric disorders 14
psychopathic traits 112, 124–5
    aggression 115–16
    bad profiles 120
    conceptualizations 116–19
    developmental pathways 114–15
    good profiles 120–4
    overview 113–14
    snake profiles 120–3
    treatments and prevention 125–6
psychopathology 72, 99, 101, 190, 211, 249
psychopathy 113, 116–17
    families 147
    infectious disease 326
    issues 118
    molecular basis 72
    moral character 285
    morningness-eveningness 53
    self-sacrifice 470
    successful and unsuccessful 117–18
    triarchic conceptualization 118–19
Psychopathy Checklist-Revised (PCL-R) 113
psychotherapy 102
puberty 208, 212, 441
public recognition 291
public speaking, ability in 139
Puts, D. A. 44

Queensland Institute of Medical Research (QIMR) 76–7
questionnaires 394
questions 222–3, 440
Quinlan, R. J. 339

radicalization 473–4, 479–80
Raffield, B. 358
railroads 357, 358
Randler, C. 58, 59, 60

rank order stability 183, 264–5
    mechanisms explaining change 184–6
Rauthmann, J. F. 228
Raviv, A. 468
reaction times 471
reactivity 13, 31, 120
Read, S. J. 233
rebelliousness 150
reciprocity 478
redemption 101, 452
Reece, E. 96
reflection, lack of 154
regulation (of personal state) 23, 31, 155
Reitz, A. K. 173
rejection 117, 410
relational-interdependent self-construal (RISC) 405, 409
relationship dissolution
    attachment 412
    beliefs 412
    personality factors 412–13
relationships 188, 251, 270, 325, 366, 413–14
    interpersonal 137, 190, 375–6
    parent-infant 385
    parent-infant (study) 393–7
    peers 168–9, 175
    romantic 190, 248, 349
relationships, romantic 402, 419–20
    individual differences 403–13
    relational processes 413–19
relativism 308–9
reliability 52, 389
    assessment 6
reliable change index (RCI) 261
religion (religiosity) 310, 333, 334, 356, 469, 476
relocation 167
    see also mobility
reminiscence (reminiscing) 97–8, 100
replication (research) 34, 72, 195, 234
reports
    parents 183
    retrospective 455–6
    see also self-reports
reproduction 54–5, 169, 326, 432
    evolution and survival 204–5, 212
    sex ratio 349, 354
    see also mating
research, genetic 210–11
researchers 227, 287, 289
research questions 456
resilience 53, 124, 125, 292, 454
Resilients 192–193, 195
resources 54, 55, 208
    environmental origins 323, 338, 349, 358
resource substitution hypothesis 250
respect 352, 473
respiratory sinus arrhythmia (RSA) 209
responses 208, 389–90, 395–6

Response Style Theory 441
responsivity 32
reverse causation hypothesis 307
Revised NEO Personality Inventory 310
rewards 60, 385, 468
    dependence 9, 28, 32–3
    systems 126, 439
Reynolds, C. A. 78
Rhesus macaques 348
    study 208–9, *210*
risk taking 41, 154, 307, 354, 375, 407
    evolution and survival 207, 213
    morningness-eveningness 53–4, 59–60
Rivers, W. H. R. 308
Riverside Situational Q-Sort (RSQ) 229, 254
Roberts, B. W. 137, 171, 265, 460
    behavioral signature 222–4, 228
    social environment 243, 247
Roberts, R. D. 53
Robinson, O. C. 293
roles 186, 188, 283
    gender 404, 412
    models 439
    social 244, 266–7, 432
Romeo and Juliet effect 409
Ronald, A. 21
Rosenberg Self-Esteem Scale (RSE) 136, 141
Rotter, J. B. 225, 227
Routledge, C. 475
Rozin, P. 324
Rueda, M. R. 30
rule-breaking 8, 41
rumination 454
Ryckmans, J. 43
Ryff, C. D. 452

sacrifice 410
    see also self-sacrifice
Sageman, M. 475
saliva 5, 7
sample sizes 78–80
sanctions 439, 471
Sanders, g. 43
Santucci, A. K. 151
Saudino, K. J. 79
savings, household 359
Sawyer, J. 304
scalar invariance 135
scar model 244
Schaal, S. 60
Schaller, M. 327, 333, 336
schemas, cognitive 102–3, 105
Schimmack, U. 184
schizophrenia 99, 102
Schofield, T. J. 148
Scholastic Aptitude Test-Math (SAT-M) 437
Schultheiss, O. C. 11, 12

Schumpe, B. M. 467
Schwartz, S. H. 263
Schwarz, N. 334
Schwerdtfeger, A. 42
Science 314
scorpionflies (study) 347–8
scripts 102–3, 104–5, 404, 456
search terms 436
seasons (seasonal variation) 6, 52
Secord, P. F. 354, 356
security 404, 408, 415, 417
Seery, M. D. 460
selection 243
selectivity 335–6
self 103, 152, 288, 370
self-categorization theory 170–1
self-change, relational 416–17
self-complexity 411
self-concept 261, 370–1, 411
self-concept, romantic relationships
    attraction and initiation 403–8
    dissolution 412–13
    function and maintenance 408–11
self-confidence 185, 440
self-construal, relational 405, 409
self-contraction 418
self-control 53, 58, 115, 175, 292
self-criticism 373
self-deception 471
Self-Determination Theory 229
self-discipline 148, 185
self-disclosure 454
self-efficacy 433, 438
self-enhancement 139, 263
self-esteem 10, 101–2, 132–3, 310, 440–1, 453
    adolescence 188–9
    adulthood 261, 264–5
    future directions 140–1
    generational differences 136–7
    individualism-collectivism 367, 373
    peers 166, 172–3, 175
    romantic relationships 407–8, 411
    study methods 134–6
    terminology and change 133–4
self-expansion 413–14
self-interest 279
self-preservation 465
self-protection 325, 328, 329
self-regulation 174, 252–3, 267, 288, 289–90, 292
self-reports 270, 282, 439, 455, 469, 470–1
    positive personality change 457–9
self-sacrifice 465–6, 478–80
    3N approach 472–6
    as counterfinality 467–8
    definition 466–7
    distinguishing concepts 468–9

    influence on others 477–8
    measuring 469–72
Self-Sacrifice Scale 469–70
self-similarity 404
self-transcendence 263
self-understanding 99
self-worth 366, 473
Seligman, M. E. P. 285
sensation seeking 29–30, 45, 53–4, 59, 443, 470
sensitivity to context 208
sex ratio 346–7, 359–60
    animal kingdom 347–9
    female bias 350–1
    human history 354–9
    humans 349–54
    male bias 351–3
sexual arousal 60
sexual attitude 58
Sexual Attitude Scale 442
sexual behavior 55, 58, 213, 334, 408, 411
    gender (sex) 441–2
sexual desire 58, 60
sexual disgust 324, 326, 333
sexual experience 59
sexual function 60
sexuality 350, 359, 442
    women's 353
sexual orientation 444–5
sexual selection 55
shallow affect 112
shame 120, 289
Shanahan, M. J. 252
Shaver, P. R. 153, 154
Shaw, Z. A. 45
Sheese, B. E. 29, 31
Sheikh, H. 476
Sherman, R. A. 228
Shifman, S. 75
Shoda, Y. 230, 232–3, 235
shyness 10, 28, 29, 172
siblings 44, 75, 149–50, 168, 310, 476
significance, personal 473
significance, personal (insignificance) 474, 479
similarity 223
    in partners 406–7
Simpson, J. A. 104
Sinderman, C. 45
single parent families 351, 358
situation, the (concept) 219, 224
    conceptualization of situations 225–6
    search for taxonomy 226–30
situational construal model (SCM) 254
Situational Eight DIAMONDS 229
situationism, doctrine of 219
skills, interpersonal 122, 123
Slagt, M. 210

person-environment transactions
    evidence 244–7
    life outcomes 250–3
person x situation interaction 230–4
perspectives 13, 269–70, 289
Pervin, L. 225
Peters, M. 43, 44
Petersen, C. 285
Petersen, J. L. 442
Philibert, R. 74
philopatry 330
phobic anxiety disorder 33
phylogeny 203, 205
physiological immune system 321, 323
Pichert, J. W. 104
picture recall 43
Piffer, D. 53, 56, 57
pituitary gland 5, 13
Pizzaro, D. 334
plasticity 204–5, 207, 208, 266
    phenotypic 213
Plomin, R. 70–1
Pluess, M. 28
pollution 324
polygenic scores 35
polygyny 353–4
Ponzi, D. 57, 58–9
positive affect 10, 31
positive personality change 450
    causes 453–4
    current knowledge 456
    current assessment 454–6
    future research 456–60
    theories 451–3
posterior pituitary 13
posttraumatic growth (PTG) 450
    Hobfoll 453
    Joseph and Linley 452
    McAdams 452–3
    Tedeschi and Calhoun 451–2
Posttraumatic Growth Inventory (PTGI) 455, 459
posttraumatic stress disorder 454
Poulin, M. 43
power 11, 123, 247, 305, 337, 432
    sex ratio 353, 355
Power, R. A. 79
Preckel, F. 53
prediction 220
predictive adaptive responses 208
preference 13
pregnancy 13, 28, 31–2, 147, 207, 331
    teenage 350
prejudice 330–1, 334
prenatal see pregnancy
prenatal estrogen (PE) 40
prenatal testosterone (PT) 40
press (media) 13

presses 225
prestige 123, 337–8, 473
Price, T. S. 79
primates, non-human (studies) 348
proactivity 53
problem-solving 53
processes, relational
    attraction and initiation 413–14
    dissolution 417–19
    function and maintenance 414–17
profiles 191–2, 195
    psychopathic traits 120–4
progesterone 13
Program for International Students Assessment (PISA) 437
promiscuity 333, 350
prosperity, economic 367
prostitution 357, 358
protein-coding genes 32
psychiatric disorders 14
psychopathic traits 112, 124–5
    aggression 115–16
    bad profiles 120
    conceptualizations 116–19
    developmental pathways 114–15
    good profiles 120–4
    overview 113–14
    snake profiles 120–3
    treatments and prevention 125–6
psychopathology 72, 99, 101, 190, 211, 249
psychopathy 113, 116–17
    families 147
    infectious disease 326
    issues 118
    molecular basis 72
    moral character 285
    morningness-eveningness 53
    self-sacrifice 470
    successful and unsuccessful 117–'
    triarchic conceptualization 118–19
Psychopathy Checklist-Revised (PCL-R) 13
psychotherapy 102
puberty 208, 212, 441
public recognition 291
public speaking, ability in 139
Puts, D. A. 44

Queensland Institute of Medical Research (QIMR) 76–7
questionnaires 394
questions 222–3, 440
Quinlan, R. J. 339

radicalization 473–4, 479–80
Raffield, B. 358
railroads 357, 358
Randler, C. 58, 59, 60

Obsessive Compulsive Disorder 326–7
occupations 438–9
Odbert, H. S. 305
Okbay, A. 77
Oliver, M. B. 442
O'Malley, P. M. 136
ontogeny 203, 205
Oostenbroek, J. 384
openness 248–249, 263, 285, 454
    adolescence 185, 187, 189
    biological origins 45, 53, 79, 81
    cross-cultural perspectives 307, 310–11, 313
    families 150, 154–5
    infectious disease 326–8, 330, 333–4
    personal narrative 98, 101
    romantic relationships 410, 413
Operational Sex Ratio (OSR) 346
Oppositional Defiant Disorder 112
oppositionality 79
optimism 53, 454
orchids (children) 208, 210
Orehek, E. 475
orientation 23, 43, 305
Oring, L. W. 346
Orth, U. 136
others 288–289, 291, 292, 468
Oud, J. H. 254
outgroups (ingroups) 330, 369, 376, 470
Overcontrollers 192–3, 195
oxytocin 7, 13–14, 212
    maternal 393
Ozer, D. J. 222

Pace, V. L. 76
pain study (hot sauce) 472
Pals, J. L. 452
Palumbo, F. 478
panic disorder 33
Papageorgiou, K. A. 21
parasites (study) 327, 332, 337
parental behavior 210
parental contribution 348
parental efficacy 385
parental investment 212, 352–3
parent-infant interaction 384
parenting 97–8, 117, 122, 156, 190, 210, 245
    biological origins 29–30, 34, 79
    environmental origins 328, 336, 359
    personality of 147–9
    social environment 251
parents' reports 183
Park, C. L. 457
Parrigon, S. 228
participants 5–6, 11
    breastfeeding (study) 386
    German students 57, 58
    New Zealand students 58
    Polish students 58

partnerships 269
Pasupathi, M. 100
paternal investment 351
pathogen prevalence 335
pathogen resistance 335
pathogens 332, 369
    disgust 324, 326, 333, 337
    historical 332
    threat 324–6
pathogen stress 336, 338, 354
Pathological Narcissism Inventory 140
Patrick, C. J. 118, 120, 122, 123
Patterns of Culture 312
Patterson, G. R. 148
Paulhus, D. L. 150, 471
Pawlby, S. 385
peers 29, 164, 173–6, 245, 280
    characteristics 165–6
    effects 170–3
    functions 166–7
    group and relationship 167–70, 174
    integration 169–70
    underlying mechanisms 170–3
pens (study) 373
Perceived Infectability (PI) 324–5
perceived vulnerability to disease (PVD) 324–6, 327–8, 330, 337
perception, mind 289
Pereda, N. 252
Perina, K. 53, 54, 57
persistence 29
PERSOC (framework) 168–9
person (concept) 219
    conceptualization of traits 220–2
    theory of traits 222–4
personality
    disorders 156–7, 222, 304–6
    factors 412–13
    maps 310
    traits 235, 406–7, 409–10, 419
personality development 181–2
    correlates 186–91
    future directions 194–6
    mechanisms in rank order stability 184–6
    personality traits 182–3
    person-centered approach 191–4
personality development, adulthood 260, 270–1
    concepts 260–1
    forms and findings 261–6
    questions and future directions 268–70
    theoretical accounts 266–8
personal narratives 95, 105–6
    autobiographical reasoning 99–101
    meaning making 101–2
    memory reconstruction 102–5
    narrative coherence 96–9
person-centered approach (personality development) 191–4

rank order stability 183, 264–5
    mechanisms explaining change 184–6
Rauthmann, J. F. 228
Raviv, A. 468
reaction times 471
reactivity 13, 31, 120
Read, S. J. 233
rebelliousness 150
reciprocity 478
redemption 101, 452
Reece, E. 96
reflection, lack of 154
regulation (of personal state) 23, 31, 155
Reitz, A. K. 173
rejection 117, 410
relational-interdependent self-construal (RISC) 405, 409
relationship dissolution
    attachment 412
    beliefs 412
    personality factors 412–13
relationships 188, 251, 270, 325, 366, 413–14
    interpersonal 137, 190, 375–6
    parent-infant 385
    parent-infant (study) 393–7
    peers 168–9, 175
    romantic 190, 248, 349
relationships, romantic 402, 419–20
    individual differences 403–13
    relational processes 413–19
relativism 308–9
reliability 52, 389
    assessment 6
reliable change index (RCI) 261
religion (religiosity) 310, 333, 334, 356, 469, 476
relocation 167
    see also mobility
reminiscence (reminiscing) 97–8, 100
replication (research) 34, 72, 195, 234
reports
    parents 183
    retrospective 455–6
    see also self-reports
reproduction 54–5, 169, 326, 432
    evolution and survival 204–5, 212
    sex ratio 349, 354
    see also mating
research, genetic 210–11
researchers 227, 287, 289
research questions 456
resilience 53, 124, 125, 292, 454
Resilients 192–193, 195
resources 54, 55, 208
    environmental origins 323, 338, 349, 358
resource substitution hypothesis 250
respect 352, 473
respiratory sinus arrhythmia (RSA) 209
responses 208, 389–90, 395–6

Response Style Theory 441
responsivity 32
reverse causation hypothesis 307
Revised NEO Personality Inventory 310
rewards 60, 385, 468
    dependence 9, 28, 32–3
    systems 126, 439
Reynolds, C. A. 78
Rhesus macaques 348
    study 208–9, *210*
risk taking 41, 154, 307, 354, 375, 407
    evolution and survival 207, 213
    morningness-eveningness 53–4, 59–60
Rivers, W. H. R. 308
Riverside Situational Q-Sort (RSQ) 229, 254
Roberts, B. W. 137, 171, 265, 460
    behavioral signature 222–4, 228
    social environment 243, 247
Roberts, R. D. 53
Robinson, O. C. 293
roles 186, 188, 283
    gender 404, 412
    models 439
    social 244, 266–7, 432
Romeo and Juliet effect 409
Ronald, A. 21
Rosenberg Self-Esteem Scale (RSE) 136, 141
Rotter, J. B. 225, 227
Routledge, C. 475
Rozin, P. 324
Rueda, M. R. 30
rule-breaking 8, 41
rumination 454
Ryckmans, J. 43
Ryff, C. D. 452

sacrifice 410
    see also self-sacrifice
Sageman, M. 475
saliva 5, 7
sample sizes 78–80
sanctions 439, 471
Sanders, g. 43
Santucci, A. K. 151
Saudino, K. J. 79
savings, household 359
Sawyer, J. 304
scalar invariance 135
scar model 244
Schaal, S. 60
Schaller, M. 327, 333, 336
schemas, cognitive 102–3, 105
Schimmack, U. 184
schizophrenia 99, 102
Schofield, T. J. 148
Scholastic Aptitude Test-Math (SAT-M) 437
Schultheiss, O. C. 11, 12

Schumpe, B. M. 467
Schwartz, S. H. 263
Schwarz, N. 334
Schwerdtfeger, A. 42
Science 314
scorpionflies (study) 347–8
scripts 102–3, 104–5, 404, 456
search terms 436
seasons (seasonal variation) 6, 52
Secord, P. F. 354, 356
security 404, 408, 415, 417
Seery, M. D. 460
selection 243
selectivity 335–6
self 103, 152, 288, 370
self-categorization theory 170–1
self-change, relational 416–17
self-complexity 411
self-concept 261, 370–1, 411
self-concept, romantic relationships
    attraction and initiation 403–8
    dissolution 412–13
    function and maintenance 408–11
self-confidence 185, 440
self-construal, relational 405, 409
self-contraction 418
self-control 53, 58, 115, 175, 292
self-criticism 373
self-deception 471
Self-Determination Theory 229
self-discipline 148, 185
self-disclosure 454
self-efficacy 433, 438
self-enhancement 139, 263
self-esteem 10, 101–2, 132–3, 310, 440–1, 453
    adolescence 188–9
    adulthood 261, 264–5
    future directions 140–1
    generational differences 136–7
    individualism-collectivism 367, 373
    peers 166, 172–3, 175
    romantic relationships 407–8, 411
    study methods 134–6
    terminology and change 133–4
self-expansion 413–14
self-interest 279
self-preservation 465
self-protection 325, 328, 329
self-regulation 174, 252–3, 267, 288, 289–90, 292
self-reports 270, 282, 439, 455, 469, 470–1
    positive personality change 457–9
self-sacrifice 465–6, 478–80
    3N approach 472–6
    as counterfinality 467–8
    definition 466–7
    distinguishing concepts 468–9

    influence on others 477–8
    measuring 469–72
Self-Sacrifice Scale 469–70
self-similarity 404
self-transcendence 263
self-understanding 99
self-worth 366, 473
Seligman, M. E. P. 285
sensation seeking 29–30, 45, 53–4, 59, 443, 470
sensitivity to context 208
sex ratio 346–7, 359–60
    animal kingdom 347–9
    female bias 350–1
    human history 354–9
    humans 349–54
    male bias 351–3
sexual arousal 60
sexual attitude 58
Sexual Attitude Scale 442
sexual behavior 55, 58, 213, 334, 408, 411
    gender (sex) 441–2
sexual desire 58, 60
sexual disgust 324, 326, 333
sexual experience 59
sexual function 60
sexuality 350, 359, 442
    women's 353
sexual orientation 444–5
sexual selection 55
shallow affect 112
shame 120, 289
Shanahan, M. J. 252
Shaver, P. R. 153, 154
Shaw, Z. A. 45
Sheese, B. E. 29, 31
Sheikh, H. 476
Sherman, R. A. 228
Shifman, S. 75
Shoda, Y. 230, 232–3, 235
shyness 10, 28, 29, 172
siblings 44, 75, 149–50, 168, 310, 476
significance, personal 473
significance, personal (insignificance) 474, 479
similarity 223
    in partners 406–7
Simpson, J. A. 104
Sinderman, C. 45
single parent families 351, 358
situation, the (concept) 219, 224
    conceptualization of situations 225–6
    search for taxonomy 226–30
situational construal model (SCM) 254
Situational Eight DIAMONDS 229
situationism, doctrine of 219
skills, interpersonal 122, 123
Slagt, M. 210

sleep (sleeping) 6, 30, 51–3, 57
smartphones 195, 458
Smith, D. J. 76
smoking 54, 72
Smoller, J. W. 33
sociability 32, 150
social alienation 474
social anxiety 10
social axioms 305
social behavior 374
    gender similarities 439–40
social-brain hypothesis 204
social communication 45
social connectedness 122
social convoy theory 166
social deprivation 173
social desirability 263, 471
Social Dominance Orientation (SDO) 325
social effects 14
social efficacy 125
social engagement 385
social environments 124, 249–50
social exclusion 375
social experience, idiosyncratic 244, *245*
social harmony 372–3
social influences 294, 338
social investment framework 171
    attachment theory 171–2
    sociometer theory 172–3
social investment model 243–4
social investment principle 186, 188, 266–7
socialization 307
    gender (sex) 443
socialization model 243–4
social jetlag 53
social learning 338
social networks 473, 475
social relationships 266, 268
social responsibility 292
social roles 244, 266–7
Social Role Theory 228
social structure 11
social support 247, 375, 454, 459
    biological origins 13–14, 29, 73, 79
sociocultural environments 134, 140–1
socio-economic status (SES) 10, 210, 222
    environmental origins 350–1, 366–7, 444–5, 459
socioemotional selectivity theory 167
Sociogenomic Model of Personality 223
sociometer theory 174
sociosexuality 54–57, 58–61, 333, 336–7
Sociosexual Orientation Inventory (SOI) 325, 336
software 218
sons 355, 359
Soto, C. J. 182, 185, 187
spatial ability (performance) 43–4, 443

Spearman, C. 304
Specht, J. 247–8, 249, 459
speed dating 404, 406
spoilage 329
sports 42
Sri Lanka 57
stability 10, 280–1, 282, 293, 306
    individual 261–2
    mean-level 262–4
    rank order 264–5
Stanley, J. H. 120
Stanton, S. J. 12
statements, hedge 440
state of consciousness (SOC) 151
status 118, 407
    biological origins 8–11, 59
    infectious disease 328, 335, 337–8
    peers 171, 174–5
    self-sacrifice 473, 478
    sex ratio 352, 357
status, socioeconomic 165, 222
    see also socio-economic status (SES)
stereotypes 313–15, 330–1, 432
stimuli 42, 126
    emotional 72
strangers, interaction with 27
stress 31–2, 60, 101, 212–13, 232
    hormonal influences 6–7, 9–10, 13–14
    maternal 207–9
    molecular basis 69, 73, 81
    psychopathic traits 113, 115, 125
    romantic relationships 404, 415
    social environment 249, 251, 253
Stressful Life Events (SLEs) 73
stressors 459
stress-vulnerability model 250
strict invariance 135
strife 406
structural stability 182–183
students 102, 293
studies, longitudinal 459
study designs 436, 459
styles, attribution of 286
Su, R. 443
substance abuse 72, 157, 171, 175, 191, 252
success (successful) 120, 122, 124, 136, 338
    academic 211
    professional 117
Suffragettes 356
suicide 72, 157, 470
Sulin, R. A. 103
Sulloway, F. J. 150
suprachiasmatic nucleus (SCN) 51
supremacy 150
survival (survivorship) 54, 206, 432, 466
    see also self-protection

susceptibility, differential 211–14
Swann, W. B. 475
Sweden 312
sympathizing quotient (SQ) 44
sympathy 470
systemizing 44–5

Tackett, J. L. 187
Taiwan 359
Talhelm, T. 368
TaqIA (A1+, A1-) 31
Tasai, J. L. 372
taxonomies 70, 268, 307
    behavioral signature 223, 225–30, 233, 235–6
Taylor, A. 394–5
Taylor, R. P. 43, 44
Taylor, S. E. 7
team players 59, 123
technologies 195, 357
Tedeschi, R. G. 450, 452
temperament 245–7, 440
temperamental activity 13
Temperament and Character Inventory 53
temporal (local) coherence 97
temporal coherence 96
temporal stability 281
tend-and/or-befriend response 7, 13
Tennen, H. 454
Terracciano, A. 75
Terrizzi, J. A. 333
terrorism 470, 475, 476, 479
Terror Management Theory (TMT) 474
TESSERA framework 267–8
testosterone 6, 7, 8–9, 13, 41, 59, 60
texts (storybooks) 372
thematic coherence 96–7, 98
theory-derived situations 227, 228
Thomas Theorem 234
Thornhill, R. 327, 330, 332, 333, 338, 339
threat 114, 120
Three Domains of Disgust Scale (TDDS) 326, 327–8, 337
Tilipoulos, N. 120
timescales (time limits) 294, 328, 393, 443
    fertility 348–9
tobacco 31, 33
    see also smoking
Torres Straits Expedition 308–9
Tracy, J. L. 101
trade-offs 211, 336, 351
traits 6, 234, 254, 267, 306, 325
    conceptualization 220–2
    core 268
    doctrine of 219
    dynamic 261
    moral character 284–6
    personality 235

    theory 222–4
    see also trait by name
transactionism 266
transactions, personality and social environment 241, 254–5
    Big Five 247–9
    consequences 249
    evidence 244–7
    future directions 253–4
    life outcomes, evidence 250–3
    models 242–4
    models and life outcomes 249–50
transference 413
transformation 243
transgressions 100, 334, 410
trauma 114, 117, 120, 450–1, 453
Treyens, J. C. 103
Triandis, H. C. 365
Triarchic Psychopathy Measure (TriPM) 118, 119, 125
Trier Social Stress Test (TSST) 74
trolley problem 472
Tronick, E. Z. 151
Trull, T. J. 157
Trumbetta, S. L. 78
trust 13, 41, 367, 375, 376, 408, 478
Trzesniewski, K. H. 136, 139
Tsimanes 310
Tucker-Drob, E. M. 184, 187
Tugawa, S. 478
Turkheimer, E. 67–8
turning points 453
    see also life events
Twenge, J. M. 136, 137
Twenty Statement Test (TST) 370–1
twins 68–9
Two-Dimensional Model of Relationship-Induced Self-Concept Change (TDM) 416, *417*
Tyber, J. M. 324, 326, 329, 333

UK (Great Britain) 311
UK Biobank 76–7, 293
uncertainty avoidance 45, 305, 307
unconditional means model 219
unconventionality 53
Undercontrollers 192–3, 195
understanding 349, 385
uniqueness 366, 372
United Nations Gender Empowerment Index 433
universalism 308–9
USA (America) 333, 354, 366, 367, 370, 371

validity 268, 435, 457, 458
    discriminant 268
values 288, 305, 367–8, 452, 470
    adulthood 263–5, 267
    sacred 476

Values in Action Scale 285
Vandenberg, R. J. 134
van den Oord, E. J. 75
van der Meij, L. 43
vanity 140
Van Mechelen, I. 233
Vansteelandt, K. 233
variability 218–20, 459
    character traits 283–4
    gender (sex) 444
    person as consistency 220–4
    person x situation interaction 230–4
    reflections and future directions 234–6
    situation 224–30
variation, seasonal 6
venturesomeness 119, 125
verbal abilities 437–8
verbal intelligence 53
verifiability 308
Verweij, K. J. H. 80
victimization 251–2
victory 9, 11
Viking raids 358
Vinkhuyzen, A. A. E. 78
violence 113, 352, 359, 470, 473, 474
Virginia 357
virtual reality (VR) environments 43
virtue ethics 291
visual illusions 308–9
vitality, mental 32
vocal tones 414
Voelkle, M. C. 254
Vukasovic, T. 70
vulnerability 326

Wai, M. 120
waking 6, 51
Walsh, A. 156
Wang, K. 80
washing, hands 334
Waters, T. E. A. 101, 105
Wediko Children's Services 227, 230

Wei, W. -H. 79
well-being 99, 101, 102, 249, 452, 460
West Africa 355
Western, Educated, Industrialized, Rich, and Democratic (WEIRD) 309
Western Roman Empire, fall of 355
Wetzel, E. 139, 141
Whole Trait Theory 224, 234
Wiebe, S. A. 33
Wilcoxon Signed Ranks tests 395
willfulness 137
Williams, E. G. 83
Wilson, T. D. 455
Winsper, C. 157
within-person variation 232
women 6–7, 10–11, 52, 57–8, 248
    sex ratio 335–7, 356–7, 359
    sexuality 353
Wood, W. 433
Woodworth, R. 309
workplaces 122, 125, 478
World Ethnographic Sample 304
World Value Survey (WVS) 312, 332, 338
Wright, J. C. 230
Wrzus, C. 247, 460
Wu, H. 156

Yamamoto, S. 83

Zeigler-Hill, V. 407
Zeitsch, B. P. 336
Zell, E. 436
Zeollner, T. 458
Zhang, G 406
Zhang, M. 31
Zhao, M. 82
Zhu, W. 294
Zimbardo Time Perspective Inventory (ZTPI) 57–8
Zimmerman, J. 248
Zion, I. B. 60
Zuk, M. 335
Zuriff, G. E. 436